DISPUTES AND DILEMMAS
IN HEALTH LAW

DISPUTES AND DILEMMAS
IN HEALTH LAW

Editors

Ian Freckelton

Kerry Petersen

THE FEDERATION PRESS

2006

Published in Sydney by:
  The Federation Press
  PO Box 45, Annandale, NSW, 2038
  71 John St, Leichhardt, NSW, 2040
  Ph (02) 9552 2200 Fax (02) 9552 1681
  E-mail: info@federationpress.com.au
  Website: http://www.federationpress.com.au

National Library of Australia
Cataloguing-in-Publication entry

  Disputes and dilemmas in health law.

  Bibliography.
  Includes index.
  ISBN 1 86287 553 7 (*from January 2007*: 978 1 86287 553 1).

  1.Medical laws and legislation – Australia, 2. Medical care – Law
  and legislation – Australia. 3. Health planning – Law and legislation
  – Australia. I. Freckelton, Ian R. II. Petersen, Kerry.

344.9404

Typeset by The Federation Press, Leichhardt, NSW.
  Printed by Ligare Pty Ltd, Sydney, NSW.

CONTENTS

PREFACE

A multi-authored work such as *Disputes and Dilemmas in Health Law* with 36 contributors only comes into being through the generosity of many busy people. We have called in favours from a large number of busy and high profile legal and medical practitioners. We would like to record our gratitude to all of them. Some have made huge efforts in personally and professionally trying circumstances to provide us with thoughtful and innovative analyses about difficult issues. They have also endured any number of edits and requests for different and sometimes better details. We hope that they will be pleased with the results.

We would also like to take the opportunity to mark the death of Danny Sandor (19 October 1960– 21 February 2006), who was a contributor to *Controversies in Health Law*, the predecessor in concept to this volume. He was a committed and a fine scholar with a special gift for legal writing and analysis, especially in the children's, family and human rights law areas. As well, he was a compassionate and courageous human being who lived life to the full for the whole of his too few 45 years. He was much loved and is mourned by many people from diverse walks of life.

We would also like to acknowledge the support over many years from Chris Holt and Federation Press who are a delight to publish with. In particular too we would like to thank our editors Clare Moss and Lynne Smith who have shepherded the volume through its journey and dealt with any number of infelicities and inelegancies that we have generated. They have been very tolerant, flexible and professional.

Ian would like to apologise for his distractedness and obsessionality to his remarkable children Leo, Julia and Lloyd. He particularly hopes that Julia will find some of the chapters in this volume stimulating. He would like to record his appreciation too to Dr Molloy for her inspiration and support. She makes every endeavour in law and medicine feel as though it has value and introduces passion and fun into even the most earnest of tasks. He hopes that the chapter on regulation will bring back happy memories for her of our time together on the Medical Practitioners Board of Victoria.

Kerry would like to pay a very special tribute to her mother for her understanding, encouragement and love. Sadly, she died last year and is greatly missed by her family, relatives and dear friends. Kerry would like to thank her friends in Australia and Britain for their support and kindness which is always greatly appreciated, but particularly last year. She would also like to thank the Law School, La Trobe University, for giving her leave to visit Cambridge University and conduct research for this book. As ever, she remains inspired by "four little Australians" Laura, Alexander, Lawrence and Isabella who are all forging ahead and embracing their individual life paths with vitality and gusto.

Ian Freckelton and Kerry Petersen
June 2006

For Julia Freckelton
IF

For Alexander Petersen
KP

CONTRIBUTORS

Michael Ashby

Michael Ashby commenced as Director of the Centre for Palliative Care in February 2005. From 1995 until 2004 he was Professor and Director of Palliative Care at McCulloch House, Monash Medical Centre and Monash University, Clayton, Victoria. He graduated from St Bartholomew's Hospital, London University in 1979, and trained in medicine, radiation and clinical oncology at Addenbrooke's Hospital (Cambridge), the Royal Marsden Hospital (London), Institut Curie (Paris) and Peter MacCallum Cancer Institute (Melbourne). In 1989 he was appointed as the first director of palliative care at the Royal Adelaide Hospital and Mary Potter Hospice, Calvary Hospital Adelaide. He is past President of the Australia and New Zealand Society for Palliative Medicine (ANZSPM) and current Chairman of the Chapter of Palliative Medicine at the Royal Australasian College of Physicians.

Belinda Bennett

Belinda Bennett is an Associate Professor at the Faculty of Law, University of Sydney. She teaches a number of health law courses at undergraduate and postgraduate level and is Director of the Faculty's Centre for Health Governance, Law and Ethics. She is a Board Member of the Australian and New Zealand Institute of Health Law and Ethics (ANZIHLE). She is co-editor (with George Tomossy) of *Globalization and Health: Challenges for Health Law and Bioethics* (Springer, 2006), and editor of *Health, Rights and Globalisation* (Ashgate, 2006) and *Abortion* (Ashgate, 2004).

Don Chalmers

Professor Donald Chalmers is Dean and Professor of the Law School, University of Tasmania. He is Chair of the Gene Technology Ethics Committee, Chair of the Australian Red Cross Ethics Committee, Deputy Chair of the NHMRC Embryo Licensing Committee. He was appointed to the Human Genetics Advisory Committee in 2006. He was Chair of the Australian Health Ethics Committee from 1994 to 2000. He was Law Reform Commissioner in Tasmania from 1991 to 1997 and member of the earlier Law Reform Commission from 1985 – 1989. He has been a consultant to the National Bioethics Advisory Commission, USA (2001), WHO (1998) and ALRC (2003) on the genetic privacy report.

His major research interests are law reform and health law and ethics. He is Director of the Centre for Law and Genetics, based in the Universities of Melbourne and Tasmania.

Georgina Clark

Dr Georgina C Clark is a medical practitioner and research academic with the Centre for Values, Ethics and the Law in Medicine at the University of Sydney. Prior to entering medicine, she completed graduate and undergraduate studies in history of philosophy, and biology at Stanford University. Her research interests focus primarily on ethical issues around the use of gene and tissue banks in medical research.

Rosalind Croucher

Rosalind Croucher (formerly "Atherton") was appointed Professor and Dean of Law at Macquarie University in November 1999. Her principal research interests are in the fields of inheritance and property law, with a particular focus on legal history. Her recent publications have also included a focus on management and administrative law issues. In 1993 she was elected to the International Academy of Estate and Trust Law; in 1999 she was elected a Fellow of the Royal Society of Arts; in 2004 she was awarded an Honorary Fellowship of the Australian College of Legal Medicine, elected to the Academy of Forensic Sciences and appointed a Foundation Fellow of the Australian Academy of Law.

John Devereux

John Devereux is Professor of Common Law and Academic Director of the TC Beirne School of Law at the University of Queensland. A former Rhodes Scholar, John has served as a Law Reform Commissioner for Queensland and a member of the Social Security Appeals Tribunal. John has a special interest in medical law, most notably in the areas of competency to consent to medical treatment and in epilepsy and the law.

Kate Diesfeld

Kate Diesfeld received her Bachelor's degree from Colgate University, New York, her Juris Doctorate from the University of San Diego. She is a member of the State Bar of California and represented people with developmental disabilities for Protection and Advocacy Inc in Los Angeles for three years. She was the Legal Supervisor of the Kent Law Clinic (Mental Health and Learning Disability) at the University of Kent at Canterbury from 1992 to 2000. She also represented patients before the Mental Health Review Tribunal for seven years in England. She is the Director of the National Centre for Health and Social Ethics at Auckland University of Technology in New Zealand. Kate's research focus is mental health, disability and medical law. She has a particular interest in the development of legal services for disabled people.

Thomas Faunce

Dr Thomas Faunce was associate to Justice LK Murphy of the High Court of Australia in 1983. He practised law with Mallesons (Canberra) and Freehills (Sydney) for five years before completing medicine at Newcastle University. He trained to senior registrar level in Intensive Care. His PhD on normative intersections in the doctor-patient relationship was awarded the Crawford Prize in 2001. He is currently senior lecturer in both the ANU College of Law and School of Medicine. He is Project Director of a three-year ARC grant investigating the impact of international trade agreements on medicines policy in Australia. Tom serves on numerous clinical and research ethics committees. He is a board member of the Australian and New Zealand Institute of Health Law and Ethics and is on the editorial board for the *Globalization and Health Journal*. He has served with UNESCO as an expert consultant on bioethics and health law.

Kim Forrester

Kim Forrester is a senior lecturer in Law, Medical Ethics and Professional Practice in the School of Medicine, Griffith University. She is a Registered Nurse with many years of experience working in intensive and coronary care units. She has post-basic qualifications in Intensive Care Nursing and established the Master in Emergency Nursing Program at Griffith University. She is admitted as a Barrister-at-Law in the Supreme Courts in New South Wales and Queensland. Her research interests include professional regulation, fitness to practise and professional misconduct. Kim has published extensively in a number of internationally refereed journals, is the editor of the Nursing Issues Column in the *Journal of Law and Medicine* and is the co-author of the text, *Essentials of Law for Health Professionals*.

Ian Freckelton

Ian Freckelton is a barrister in full-time practice in Melbourne since 1988, specialising at both trial and appellate level in administrative law, medico-legal cases and criminal law. Interweaved among his practice at the Bar, Ian has been a lawyer member of Victoria's Victorian Mental Health Review Board since 1996, Medical Practitioners Board since 2000 and Psychologists Registration Board since 1999.

Ian is an Adjunct Professor of the School of Law and Legal Studies at La Trobe University; an Honorary Professor of Law, Forensic Psychology and Forensic Medicine at Monash University; and an honorary Professor of Law at Deakin University.

He is the Vice-President of the International Academy of Forensic Studies, an international board member and the Australasian Vice-President of the International Association of Law and Mental Health, a board member of the International Network of Therapeutic Jurisprudence, a board member of the Public Health Law Centre, a board member of the Australia and New Zealand Institute of Health, Law and Ethics and was the President of the Australian and New Zealand Association of Psychiatry, Psychology and Law between 1991 and 1997. He was made a life member of the Association in 1997 and is currently the President-elect of the Victorian branch.

Ian is the founding editor of the *Journal of Law and Medicine* and is the Editor-in-Chief of the journal, *Psychiatry, Psychology and Law*. Ian is the author and editor of some 30 books on mental health law, therapeutic jurisprudence, medical law, criminal injuries compensation, coronial law, policing, criminal law, sentencing, expert evidence, and causation.

Reg Graycar

Reg Graycar is Professor of Law at the University of Sydney, and in 2005 was a Visiting Professor at Cornell Law School, USA. She has also visited and taught at law schools in South Africa (University of Cape Town), Canada (University of British Columbia), England (Keele University), Italy (European University Institute) and France (Université de Paris-1: Panthéon-Sorbonne). She is co-author, with Jenny Morgan, of the *Hidden Gender of Law* (Federation Press, 2nd edn, 2002) and has published extensively on a wide range of legal issues including tort law, feminist legal theory and law reform. From 1998 to 2002, she was full time Commissioner with the NSW Law Reform Commission and has also served as a part-time Commissioner with the Australian Law Reform Commission. She has been a member of the Family Law Council, a Hearing Commissioner with the Human Rights and Equal Opportunity Commission, and a legal member of the Social Security Appeals Tribunal.

Livia Iacovino

Livia Iacovino is an Honorary Senior Research Fellow in the Faculty of Information Technology at Monash University. Her research is focused on archival science, law and ethics, in particular ownership, access and privacy of networked electronic records. She has collaborated internationally as a Co-Chair of the Policy Research Group, International Research on Permanent Authentic Records in Electronic Systems (InterPARES) Project, and as a consultant with the International Records Management Trust. With her co-authors and Bernadette McSherry, she has been a Chief Investigator for Electronic Health Records: Achieving an Effective and Ethical Legal and Recordkeeping Framework, an Australian Research Council Discovery Grant. Livia's awards include the Australian Society of Archivists Mander Jones Award 1999 and the Monash University Mollie Holman Medal of Excellence 2003 for her PhD thesis in press (2006) as, *Recordkeeping, Ethics and Law: Regulatory Models, Participant Relationships and Rights and Responsibilities in the Online World.*

Louise Johnson

Louise Johnson was appointed as Chief Executive Officer for the Infertility Treatment Authority (ITA), Victoria in early 2005. She holds an honours degree in microbiology and postgraduate qualifications in management and education. She has worked in management and public education positions in not-for-profit organisations in the health sector for the past 20 years. Prior to joining the ITA, Louise worked as the Executive Director for OT AUSTRALIA (Victoria) representing the interests of occupational therapists. Her work in the health sector has encompassed the fields of occupational rehabilitation; occupational health and safety; cancer prevention and smoking cessation. Louise has developed health promotion and marketing campaigns incorporating printed and audiovisual resource materials for health professionals, teachers, primary and secondary students and the general public.

Chris Jordens

Chris Jordens is a part-time lecturer at the Centre for Values, Ethics and the Law in Medicine (VELIM). He has been involved in the development of the new bioethics program since 2003, and has primary responsibility for the Biomedicine and Society unit (BETH 5103).

Chris has broad-ranging interests in social and ethical issues relating to health and medicine, and he specialises in qualitative and linguistic methods of inquiry. Recent research interests include direct-to-consumer advertising of prescription drugs, advance care planning and patient experience of bone marrow transplantation and advanced ovarian cancer. As well as working at VELIM, Chris works part time as Clinical Research Fellow in an NHMRC Centre for Clinical Research Excellence that focuses on infection control and bioethical issues in haematological malignancies.

Chris has an honours degree in philosophy, a masters degree in public health, and a PhD which forms part of VELIM's ongoing research program. He has taught quantitative research methods to students in the Faculty of Medicine and at Yooroang Garang Centre for Indigenous Health Studies, and he has also taught in the Master of Professional Communications program in the English Department. He has worked as an interdisciplinary researcher at VELIM since 1997, and is currently co-editor of the new *Journal of Bioethical Inquiry*.

Ian Kerridge

Ian Kerridge trained in medicine at the University of Newcastle, philosophy at the Universities of Sydney, Newcastle and Cambridge, and haematopoietic stem cell transplantation at the Royal Free Hospital, London. He is Director and Associate Professor in Bioethics at the Centre for Values, Ethics and the Law in Medicine at the University of Sydney and Staff Haematologist/Bone Marrow Transplant physician at Westmead Hospital, Sydney. Ian was previously Director of the Clinical Unit in Ethics and Health Law at the University of Newcastle. He has published widely in ethics and medicine/haematology and is the author of over eighty papers in peer-reviewed journals and three textbooks of ethics, most recently *Ethics and Law for the Health Professions* (Federation Press, 2005). He is Vice-President of the Australasian Bioethics Association, a member of the NSW Health Department's Clinical Ethics Advisory Panel and a member of the Editorial Boards of the *Journal of Medical Ethics*, and the *Journal of Bioethical Inquiry*. His current research interests in ethics include the philosophy of medicine, stem cells and tissue engineering, end-of-life care, the experience of illness and survival following bone marrow transplantation, public health ethics, donor issues in transplantation, moral psychology, advance care planning and the pharmaceutical industry.

Marilyn McMahon

Marilyn McMahon graduated in psychology and law from the University of Melbourne. She has postgraduate qualifications in forensic psychology and is currently completing a doctorate in law. She teaches in the School of Law at La Trobe

University. Marilyn is currently a member of both the Mental Health Review Board and the Intellectual Disability Review Panel and is a past-chairperson of the ethics committee of the Australian Psychological Society. Her main teaching responsibilities are in psychology and the law, criminal law, and torts; her current research investigates the relationship between mental disorder and criminal defences.

John McPhee

John McPhee is an Honorary Associate with the Centre for Values, Ethics and the Law in Medicine at the University of Sydney and is a conjoint senior lecturer in the School of Medicine and Public Health at the University of Newcastle. He is co-author of *Ethics and Law for the Health Professions*, (Federation Press, 2nd edn, 2005).

Roger Magnusson

Roger Magnusson is Associate Professor in the Faculty of Law at the University of Sydney. He teaches and writes in the areas of health law and public health law. He is a member of the Board of the Australian & New Zealand Institute of Health Law & Ethics (ANZIHLE), and a member of the NHMRC Special Expert Committee on Transmissible Spongiform Encephalopathies (SECTSE), which advises Commonwealth Government agencies on Creutzfeldt Jakob disease (CJD) and variant CJD (the human equivalent of mad cow disease).

Danuta Mendelson

Danuta Mendelson, BA(Hon), MA, PhD, LLB(Hon) and LLM from Monash University, is an Associate Professor at the School of Law, Deakin University, Melbourne. Danuta has authored books on *Metaphor in IE Babel's Short Stories* (Ardis, 1982); *Interfaces of Medicine and Law: The History of the Liability for Negligently Caused Psychiatric Injury (Nervous Shock)*, (Ashgate, 1998); and *Torts Companion*, (Butterworths, 3rd edn, 2002). Her book on the *New Law of Torts*, (Oxford University Press) is forthcoming (September 2006). She has edited with Ian Freckelton *Causation in Law and Medicine*, (Ashgate, 2002), and is joint Editor (Legal Issues) for the *Journal of Law and Medicine*. She has published numerous book chapters and over 60 peer-reviewed articles on medico-legal issues, torts, and history of law and medicine.

Lexi Neame

Lexi Neame is the Senior Research and Policy Officer with the Infertility Treatment Authority, the statutory body responsible for regulating the provision of assisted reproductive technology services in Victoria, Australia. Before joining the ITA's staff, she was Research Officer for the Australian Centre for the Study of Sexual Assault, at the Australian Institute of Family Studies. She has recently completed a Master of Philosophy in Political Theory at the University of Queensland; her research focused on non-specialist representations of genetics and reprogenetic technologies.

Dianne Nicol

Dianne Nicol is a senior lecturer in the Law Faculty at the University of Tasmania and a senior research fellow in the Centre for Law and Genetics (CLG). Dianne has a PhD in cell biology and a LLM in intellectual property law. She has broad research interests in law, ethics, science and policy. At present she is involved in two research projects funded by the Australian Research Council. The first focuses on regulation of genetic databanking in Australia, in collaboration with other members of the CLG. The second involves an assessment of co-operative strategies for managing intellectual property in the Australian biotechnology industry, in collaboration with Janet Hope and John Braithwaite from the Australian National University. Dianne has also recently completed an empirical research project on biotechnology patents and patent licensing in collaboration with Jane Nielsen.

Brian Opeskin

Brian Opeskin has been a full-time Commissioner at the Australian Law Reform Commission since 2000 and its Deputy President since December 2005. He led the Commission's inquiries into the judicial power of the Commonwealth and the sentencing of federal offenders; and jointly led the inquiries into the protection of human genetic information, and gene patenting and human health. Brian was previously an Associate Professor at Sydney University Law School, where he taught in the fields of constitutional law, federal courts, international law and conflict of laws. He is the author of several books and many articles in these fields. Brian will be taking up a position as Professor of Law and Head of the Law School of the University of the South Pacific, in Vanuatu, in October 2006.

Margaret Otlowski

Margaret Otlowski is a Professor at the Faculty of Law, University of Tasmania and the Deputy Director of the Centre for Law and Genetics. Margaret has long-standing experience in health law and bioethics, having published extensively in the field, worked as consultant for Commonwealth and State bodies including the former National Bioethics Consultative Committee and the Australian Law Reform Commission (in connection with its inquiry in the protection of human genetic information), and served on various Committees and Tribunals, including the Tasmanian Anti-Discrimination Tribunal and Chair of the University of Tasmania and later the State HREC. She has recently been appointed to the NHMRC Human Genetics Advisory Committee Working Group on Industry and Commercialisation.

She has been involved as Chief Investigator on a number of ARC funded collaborative research projects that have been run through the Centre for Law and Genetics where her work has focused on issues of regulation, privacy and discrimination. She currently leads a multi-disciplinary research project investigating the nature and extent of genetic discrimination in Australia.

Angela Palombo

Angela Palombo is the Legal and Policy Officer at the Office of the Health Services Commissioner, Victoria. She has worked as a solicitor both in private practice and in community legal centres, including six years at the Fitzroy Legal Service. After that she operated a private practice in Fitzroy for 6 years, representing clients in diverse areas such as victims' compensation, equal opportunity and civil litigation. Her practice involved acting for clients with HIV in criminal proceedings and civil litigation, as well as clients with Hepatitis C in a number of areas of law. She also acted for organisations whose counselling records for victims of crime were subpoenaed to courts in criminal trials. Acting for victims of sexual abuse led her to having regular contact with psychologists and developing her interest in health law. Her position at the Health Services Commissioner mainly involves administering the *Health Records Act 2001* (Vic).

Malcolm Parker

Malcolm Parker has worked in general practice for 30 years, and is Associate Professor of Medical Ethics in the School of Medicine at the University of Queensland, where he introduced and continues to co-ordinate teaching and assessment in the domain of Ethics & Professional Practice in the MBBS program.

He has qualifications in medicine, philosophy and health law, and has published nationally and internationally in the philosophy of medicine, bioethics, medical ethics and health law, and medical education.

He is a committee member of the Australasian Bioethics Association and a board member of the Australian & New Zealand Institute of Health, Law and Ethics. He is chair of the University of Queensland's Human Experimentation Ethical Review Committee, a member of the Queensland Health Ethics Advisory Committee, a board member of the Postgraduate Medical Education Council of Queensland, and a member of the AMA (Qld) Ethics committee.

Moira Paterson

Moira Paterson is a senior lecturer in the Monash Law Faculty and has written and published extensively on privacy related topics. Her 1995 book, *Freedom of Information and Privacy in Australia: Government and Information Access,* was published by LexisNexis/Butterworths. She also teaches two privacy subjects in the Monash Law postgraduate program. Moira and her co-authors (together with Professor Bernadette McSherry) were joint recipients of an ARC Discovery grant for a research project titled "Electronic Health Records: Achieving an Effective and Ethical Legal and Recordkeeping Framework".

Moira is currently an FOI Editor for the *Australian Administrative Law Service* and was a member of an Expert Advisory Committee on Privacy to the Victorian Law Reform Commission.

Kerry Petersen

Kerry Petersen is an Associate Professor in the Law School at La Trobe University, Australia. Her main research interest is in the area of law and medicine exploring human rights and policy issues. She has published widely in the field of human reproduction law and in 2002 co-edited "Regulating Reproductive Technologies" a Special Issue of the *Journal of Law and Medicine*. In 2005, she visited the Centre for Family Research, University of Cambridge, United Kingdom, as an Australian Bicentennial Fellow examining current developments in the field of assisted reproductive technologies within a comparative framework.

Kerry and her colleague, infertility specialist, Professor Gordon Baker (Royal Women's Hospital), received a grant from the Fertility Society of Australia in 2005 to conduct research into the ethical and legal aspects of ARTs.

David Ranson

David Ranson is a medical practitioner with qualifications in both medicine and law. He is currently employed as the Deputy Director of the Victorian Institute of Forensic Medicine and heads the specialist death investigation unit at the Institute investigating deaths occurring in the setting of health care. He is also the Director of the National Coroners Information System based at the Institute. David is an honorary Associate Professor in the Department of Forensic Medicine at Monash University, an Associate in the Faculty of Law at Monash University, an Associate in the Department of Pathology at the University of Melbourne, and a Senior Fellow in the Dental School at the University of Melbourne. He is a member of a number of national and international medical and medico-legal associations and colleges, including the Australasian Coroners' Society. He has published widely in the field of forensic medicine and medical law and is the author and editor of a variety of texts in this area. He has produced medico-legal policy and research reports for government and private agencies and has given evidence to parliamentary and Senate inquiries on matters relating to forensic medicine and the coroners jurisdiction. With Ian Freckelton, he is the author of *Death Investigation and the Coroner's Inquest* (Oxford University Press, 2006).

Anne Rees

Anne Rees is an Associate Professor at the School of Law at the University of Newcastle where she teaches Health Law, Competition Law and Policy and Intellectual Property. She is also a former Dean of Law at the University of Newcastle. Associate Professor Rees was a Commissioner of the Australian Law Reform Commission from 2001 to 2004 (as Anne Finlay) and was a lead Commissioner on the Gene Patenting and Human Health reference. She is a legal member of the NSW Mental Health Review Tribunal and has previously reviewed health legislation in the Pacific island nation of Niue for the World Health Organisation.

Chris Reynolds

Chris Reynolds teaches law at Flinders University and was also a Co-Director at the National Centre for Public Health Law at La Trobe University. He has taught and researched public health law for the past 30 years. During that time he has also been involved in advising and implementing legislative reform in areas of communicable and non-communicable disease and environmental health. His most recent book in this field, *Public Health Law and Regulation* was published by Federation Press in 2004.

Peter Saul

Peter Saul graduated first in politics then in medicine from Cambridge University, England. He completed his medical training in London, Boston and Sydney, and now works in intensive care units at the John Hunter Hospital in Newcastle, and Newcastle Private Hospital. He works with the NSW Health Department on issues of medical ethics, particularly about end-of-life decision-making. Dr Saul currently has a major Commonwealth Government grant to promote the involvement of patients in their care plans, particularly for those with chronic or terminal illnesses.

John Seymour

Until the end of 1998, a Reader in the Faculty of Law, Australian National University, John is currently an Adjunct Professor in the ANU College of Law. His books and reports include: *Child Welfare* (Australian Law Reform Commission, 1981), *Dealing with Young Offenders* (1988), *Fetal Welfare and the Law* (1995) and *Childbirth and the Law* (2000).

In addition, he has published numerous journal articles on juvenile justice, child protection, children and the law and medico-legal topics. He is a member of The Canberra Hospital Clinical Ethics Committee. His research interests include children and parents' rights, the role of the state in protecting children, the legal status of the foetus, the law on the medical treatment of children, and the operation of medical malpractice law, particularly in the fields of obstetrics and midwifery.

Loane Skene

Loane Skene is a Professor of Law in the Law and Medical Faculties at the University of Melbourne. She is President of the Academic Board and a Pro Vice-Chancellor of the University. She has served on many federal and state medico-legal committees; written two books and numerous chapters and articles. The second edition of her book, *Law and Medical Practice* was published in 2004. She is Associate Editor of *The Journal of Medical Ethics* (UK) and was a Scholar in Residence at the Australian Law Reform Commission in its project on Genetic Privacy. She is Deputy Director of the Centre of Law and Genetics (University of Tasmania and University of Melbourne) and Program Director, Medical Ethics, at the Centre for Applied Philosophy and Public Ethics (CAPPE) (Charles Sturt University and University of Melbourne). In 2003, she was awarded a Centenary Medal for "Service to Australian Society through the Exploration of Legal and Ethical Issues of Health Care".

Cameron Stewart

Cameron Stewart is an Associate Professor of Law at Macquarie University. He has experience in commercial law, Supreme Court equity practice, and in policy formulation. He is also a Board Member of the Australian Institute of Health Law and Ethics. Cameron has published widely on end-of-life decision-making, and the law of advance care planning. He has also been involved in the NSW Health policy formulation of the Guidelines on End-Of-Life Decision-Making and the policy on Using Advance Care Directives. He is also a Foundational Member of the Clinical Ethics Advisory Committee, NSW Health Department (formed 2003). He is currently researching Australian guardianship law and practice, writing a book on end-of-life decision-making and the law, and publishing the *Australian Medico-Legal Handbook* for Elsevier (with Ian Kerridge and Mal Parker).

Helen Szoke

Helen Szoke is the Chief Executive Officer and Chief Conciliator of the Equal Opportunity Commission of Victoria. Previously, Helen was the Chief Executive Officer of the Infertility Treatment Authority in Melbourne since 1996.

Helen is currently a member of the National Health and Medical Research Licensing Committee and Past Chairperson of Women's Health Victoria. She has served as a committee member and Chairperson of the Ethics Committee of the Royal Women's Hospital, a member of the Victorian Family Therapy Association Ethics Committee, a member of the School Council of Melbourne High School, an executive member of the Victorian Council of Social Services and an inaugural executive member of the Consumers Health Forum of Australia. She also served one term as a city councillor in the Preston City Council.

George Tomossy

George Tomossy is a barrister and solicitor at the Bar of Ontario (Canada). He is also Executive Director of the International Academy of Law and Mental Health. George's principal area of research interest is the multidisciplinary field of health law (particularly human research ethics and drug regulation, ageing and mental health). A lecturer at the Division of Law, Macquarie University, he is presently involved in various editorial and publication projects, including an edited collection on "Medicine and Industry" to be completed later this year.

Beth Wilson

On 1 May 1997 Beth Wilson became Victoria's Health Services Commissioner. She is a lawyer by training, rather than by inclination, and has worked mainly in administrative law. Beth has had a long-standing interest in medico/legal and ethical issues. Before becoming Health Services Commissioner, Beth was the President of the Mental Health Review Board and a Senior Legal Member of the Social Security Appeals Board and the WorkCare Appeals Board.

Beth regularly conducts seminars, lectures and classes for consumers, health service providers and others. She is a past President of the Victorian Branch of ANZAPPL (the Australian and New Zealand Association of Psychiatry, Psychology and Law). In October 2002, Beth was awarded Monash University's Distinguished Alumni Award for her outstanding professional achievements and inspirational leadership. In April 2003, Beth was awarded the Centenary Medal for her services to health, and in May 2004 Beth was awarded an Honorary Doctorate from RMIT for her contributions to health education.

Penny Weller

Penny Weller is a lecturer in the School of Law at Victoria University. Her primary research interest is human rights in public health and public health law. She has contributed a socio-legal perspective to research and publications in public health and public health law including research ethics for young people, young people in the criminal justice system, national prevention policy for drug-related harm, and public health emergency powers. Penny is currently appointed to the Health Services Review Council.

TABLE OF CASES

TABLE OF STATUTES

TABLE OF STATUTES

PART I

INTRODUCTION

1

Disputes and dilemmas in health law: An overview

Ian Freckelton and Kerry Petersen

Health law is an increasingly recognised area of legal practice and discourse. However, it is fluid and diverse. Just as health knowledge and interventions are changing fundamentally with advances such as the Human Genome Project, so too is health law in order to impose regulation and constraint upon quickly evolving clinical developments. While it is subject to a combination of diverse local and international influences, health law is subject to many (sometimes conflicting) requirements. It needs to be adaptable and able to comply with human rights; to facilitate ethical practice by health practitioners; to satisfy the requirements of vested interests; to meet the challenges of fast-moving medical technologies; to address social policy developments and principles of governance and regulation; as well as to enable resolution of disputes in a way that satisfies community expectations of fairness and justice.

However, questions remain, especially in Australia, about the legitimacy and coherence of health law, given that it spans at least tort law, contract law, equitable principles, commercial and taxation law, administrative law, family law, child protection law, intellectual property law, international law and, of course, criminal law. Consistency, conformity with ethical principles, relevance and conceptual rigour are important qualities to which health law must aspire if it is to attain recognition as a major legitimate discipline, rather than merely a descriptor of different areas of jurisprudence which have an impact upon health interests.

This collection of chapters from lawyers, health professionals and policy-makers teases out the parameters and modern directions in health law. It analyses trends and developments across a wide range of theory and practice. Some chapters are theoretical in orientation but most are sharply focused upon difficult questions that are posing dilemmas for the provision of clinical treatment in the early stages of the 21st century.

A common concern that underlies the chapters in this volume is the future: how we should establish legal frameworks governing clinical and research practices as well as the application of technologies for the benefit of Australian citizens as members of a global community?[1] We have asked authors of chapters to

---

1   See further Bennett, B and Tomossy, GF (ed), *Globalization and Health: Challenges for Health Law and Bioethics*, Springer, Dordrecht, 2006.

reflect upon current debates in their area and to consider the ways in which those debates are likely to be constructed and even resolved in the years ahead. The result, we hope, is that the volume is lively and fresh, not mired in the orthodoxies and assumptions of the past but, building upon past experience and controversies,[2] and grappling with the dilemmas and disputes of today and tomorrow. Accordingly, our aspiration is that it be of use and interest to a wide readership amongst those with a focus on how the legal system intersects with the health professions and how it is likely to do so in the future.

Ethical frameworks

The ethics of health care are not static. They are fluid and the relationships of particular ethical principles one to another at any given time are controversial.[3] Fundamental to any conceptually rigorous discourse about health law is a clear enunciation of competing ethical values. Accordingly, we have structured this volume so as to commence with a discussion of pertinent issues that should underlie the provision of all health services and the development of laws to regulate them (Kerridge, McPhee, Jordens and Clark: Chapter 2). Then we move to contexts in which the balance is posing social and jurisprudential dilemmas.

Current ethical approaches tend to give primacy to patients' and consumers' autonomy and rights of choice. The move from paternalism to patient-centred decision-making was at the heart of the High Court decisions in *Rogers v Whitaker*,[4] *Rosenberg v Percival*[5] and *Breen v Williams*.[6] It has not been disturbed in post-Ipp Committee[7] legislation about obligations on the part of health practitioners to disclose risk but has been adjusted in respect of the yardsticks for compensability (see Bennett and Freckelton: Chapter 20). Access to records legislation now applies throughout Australia, New Zealand and the United Kingdom (see Palombo: Chapter 30) and provides patients with the opportunity to read the records generated about them by their medical practitioners.

However, the more traditional preoccupations on the part of health practitioners with beneficence and non-maleficence have an abiding significance for those who seek both to heal and to ensure that the outcomes of legal involvement are pro-therapeutic. In addition, justice, access to health services, dignity, and privacy have a vital role to play. The question in any given ethical dilemma in the health context is how an appropriate balance can be orchestrated amongst the

---

2   See, for example, Freckelton, I and Petersen, K (ed), *Controversies in Health Law*, Federation Press, Sydney, 1999.

3   See, for example, Kerridge, I, Lowe, M and McPhee, J, *Ethics and Law for the Professions*, 2nd edn, Federation Press, Sydney, 2005.

4   (1992) 175 CLR 479.

5   (2001) 205 CLR 434.

6   (1996) 186 CLR 71.

7   Panel of Eminent Persons to Review the Law of Negligence (the Ipp Committee), *Review of the Law of Negligence*, Second Report, Canberra, October 2002, <http://revofneg.treasury. gov.au/content/review2.asp> (accessed 20 April 2006).

different ethical considerations. Core issues in health law such as competence (Devereux and Parker: Chapter 4), the potential for advance decision-making (Stewart: Chapter 3) and reproductive interests and freedoms (Petersen: Chapter 11; Szoke, Neame and Johnston: Chapter 11) raise these questions acutely.

Human rights

Human rights are an integral aspect of justice considerations in respect of health.[8] Rights language is consolidating a place in legal discourse in relation to health issues. An example is the judgment of Lord Steyn in the 2004 House of Lords decision of *Chester v Afshar*[9] in which he emphasised that:

> Individuals have a right to make important medical decisions affecting their lives for themselves: they have the right to make decisions which doctors regard as ill advised. ... In modern law medical paternalism no longer rules and a patient has a prima facie right to be informed by a surgeon of a small, but well established, risk of serious injury as a result of surgery.

Likewise in *Royal Women's Hospital v Medical Practitioners Board of Victoria*[10] Maxwell P, President of the Victorian Court of Appeal, made a particular point of stating that:

1. The court will encourage practitioners to develop human rights-based arguments where relevant to a question in the proceeding.
2. Practitioners should be alert to the availability of such arguments and should not be hesitant to advance them where relevant.
3. Since the development of an Australian jurisprudence drawing on international human rights law is in its early stages, further progress will necessarily involve judges and practitioners working together to develop a common expertise.

Rights discourse is likely to assume an increasingly significant profile in a health care environment of limited resources and commercially competing providers – for instance in the areas of cosmetic surgery and laser eye interventions (see Wilson: Chapter 25). There is a need for policy-makers, judges and legislators to take rights considerations into account when seeking a reconciliation between individual rights and community or global interests (Reynolds: Chapter 7). The 2005–2006 Victorian litigation[11] in respect of the wish by the Medical Practitioners Board to gain access to patients' records to facilitate its investigations as against the rights of a patient to health privacy is an example of this tension. It led Justice Maxwell to observe that provisions in international treaties can be relevant to statutory interpretation; as a guide in developing the common law; and as an indication of the value placed by

---

8   See, for example, Bennett B (ed), *Health Rights and Globalisation*, Ashgate, Dartmouth, 2006.
9   [2004] UKHL 41 at [14]–[16].
10 [2006] VSCA 85 at [71].
11 Ibid.

Australia on the rights provided for in a convention to which Australia is a party and, therefore, indicative of contemporary values.[12]

The therapeutic relationship, the bedrock of early scholarship in health law, was encapsulated in Kennedy's pioneering book *Treat Me Right*.[13] This work, as well as the important analyses by Larry Gostin,[14] triggered an international dialogue in hospitals, universities and courts on patients' rights. It commenced in the 1990s and extends to the present. In turn, these concerns have led to a broader discourse on the relevance of human rights to health law issues as the courts increasingly invoke the right to self-determination as a framework for resolving consent and refusal disputes.[15]

However, the context within which human rights discourse takes place throughout the Australian federation is affected by particular considerations. Australia is increasingly isolated in terms of developments in health law jurisprudence by reason of not being part of confederations such as the European Union. This is only partially offset by charters of patient rights such as that existing in Queensland[16] and moves toward some limited human rights legislation in jurisdictions such as the Australian Capital Territory[17] and Victoria.[18] In addition, Australia is one of the few liberal democracies without a human rights charter.[19] This engenders fragmentation of approach and militates against coherent formulations of entitlements and obligations across different areas of law which have resonances for health service provision. Another important, and related, phenomenon is that Australia is increasingly taking its own path in relation to health law issues, unconstrained by the obligations that today drive developments in countries such as the United Kingdom. While this can result in developments that are diffuse and dependent upon particular decisions of judges – often on appeal from context-dependent specific scenarios – it does leave scope for judicial creativity.[20] Judicial decisions, particularly those from other common law jurisdictions such as Britain, New Zealand and Canada which have human rights charters, have only a modest influence on Australian courts, legal writing and legislative developments. If anything, the influence is waning.

However, as a countervailing influence, health service practice is not constrained by countries' boundaries. Advances in technology and knowledge pose

---

12 Ibid, at [75-77].

13 Kennedy, I, *Treat Me Right: Essays in Medical Law and Ethics*, Clarendon Press, Oxford, 1991.

14 See, for example, Gostin, L, *Public Health Law: Power, Duty, Restraint*, University of California Press and the Milbank Memorial Fund, 2000; Gostin, L *Public Health Law and Ethics: A Reader*, University of California Press and the Milbank Memorial Fund, 2002.

15 See latterly *Chester v Afshar* [2004] UKHL 41.

16 Queensland Health Public Patients Charter, <www.health.qld.gov.au/qhppc/documents/QHPPCbooklet.pdf> (accessed 14 April 2006).

17 See, for example, *Human Rights Act 2004* (ACT).

18 See Charter of Human Rights and Responsibilities Bill 2006 (Vic); Freckelton, I, "Human rights and Health Law: New Statutory Developments" (2006) 14(1) *Journal of Law and Medicine* 5.

19 See Freckelton, I and Loff, B, "Health Law and Human Rights" in Kinley, D (ed), *Human Rights in Australian Law*, Federation Press, Sydney, 1998.

20 See, for example, *Gardner; Re BWV* [2003] VCAT 121; [2003] VSC 173.

dilemmas that are international and ubiquitous. In addition, health law of its very essence is cross-disciplinary and global. A consequence is that health law has many international aspects and there cannot but be cross-pollination from one country to another, especially by reference to increasingly globally acknowledged human rights principles.[21] This is particularly exemplified in mental health law (Diesfeld and Freckelton: Chapter 6) and public health law (Weller: Chapter 5).

Public health law influences

An important contributor to health law discourse is modern public health law which has emerged from its early "Cinderella" status to be a significant voice in some of the most pressing contemporary health debates – particularly those with international ramifications such as trade agreements, environmental threats and disease control.

In this volume, Reynolds (Chapter 7) calls for a broad legal vision to deal more effectively with public health harms. He argues for a new set of powers to deal with public health emergencies, communicable diseases, non-communicable diseases (such as "lifestyle" diseases) and the complex challenges of environmental health. Faunce's approach (Chapter 9) is consistent with this. He examines the effect of multilateral trade agreements from a health perspective and stresses the need for public health professionals and organisations to participate actively in negotiations and dispute settlement processes involving decisions about entering into (and compliance with) international trade agreements. He argues for the development of policies which give public health considerations a high priority and recommends that a public health impact assessment should be prepared and subjected to rigorous scrutiny and debate before international trade deals are entered into.

Magnusson (Chapter 8) considers further dimensions of this issue in relation to public health policies developed for controlling transmissible spongiform encephalopathies (TSEs) such as Creutzfeldt-Jakob disease (CJD). He emphasises that health authorities and governments have an ethical obligation to balance public interests with the potential harms to individuals when developing precautionary strategies and public health policies. He adds that although national policies on the containment of serious transmissible diseases are naturally influenced by the responses and experiences of other nations, in Australia as elsewhere, the risks deemed appropriate for each society to bear are ultimately a political function.

Therapeutic jurisprudence

An increasingly influential strand in contemporary scholarship and research in health law is therapeutic jurisprudence.[22] It has application to the content,

---

21   See Bennett and Tomossy (2006) op cit.
22   See, for example, Wexler, D and Winick, B (eds), *Law in a Therapeutic Key*, Carolina Academic Press, Durham, 1996; Diesfeld, K and Freckelton, I (eds), *Involuntary Detention and Therapeutic Jurisprudence: International Perspectives on Civil Commitment*, Ashgate, Aldershot, 2003; Winick, B, *Civil Commitment: A Therapeutic Jurisprudence Model*, Carolina Academic Press, Durham, 2005.

interpretation and application of the law and offers a potential for thematic coherence within health law.[23] As Diesfeld and Freckelton (Chapter 6) point out though, it is not without its detractors. What therapeutic jurisprudence does do is to assert that the impact upon community and individual health of laws and legal decision-making should be a separate and valued consideration.

Diesfeld and Freckelton argue that the application of therapeutic juris-prudence to mental health law highlights the importance of minimising counter-therapeutic outcomes from decision-making about persons with disabilities. They contend too that the ultimate impact of Australia's diverse legislative provisions about imposition of involuntary status on mentally ill patients,[24] the interpretation of such provisions and the way in which litigation with a potentially adverse impact upon health is conducted, should factor in predictable health outcomes as a relevant consideration.

Self-determination dilemmas

As already observed, the value of patients' autonomy has received significant acknowledgment in Australian courts and even legislation. In *Secretary, Department of Health and Community Services v JWB and SMB (Marion's Case)*,[25] one of the few High Court decisions concerning the application of human rights in a health law context, leave was granted to the Human Rights and Equal Opportunity Commis-sion to intervene in the proceedings. The majority judgments drew heavily on a human rights analysis, particularly the right to self-determination in the context of consent to medical treatment and the assessment of competence – thus setting a judicial milestone in Australia for the application of human rights to the thera-peutic relationship. The High Court's decision imposed limitations on medical autonomy and thereby enhanced the autonomy rights of patients – particularly where disabled people, children and ageing adults are involved (Devereux and Parker: Chapter 4).

Claims to self-determination in the context of human reproduction have also been fashioned through negligence law. In *CES v Superclinics (Australia) Pty Ltd*,[26] for instance, the New South Wales Court of Appeal held that doctors had negligently misdiagnosed the plaintiff's pregnancy until such an advanced stage that she had lost the opportunity to have an abortion. As a result she gave birth to a healthy child. Graycar (Chapter 21) observes that Kirby J was the only member of the court to make

---

23 See too, Schopp, RF, *Competence, Condemnation and Commitment*, American Psychological Association, Washington DC, 2001.

24 In relation to NSW and analyses of a number of different Australian provisions, see Howard, D and Westmore, B, *Crime and Mental Health Law in New South Wales*, LexisNexis Butterworths, Sydney, 2005. See recently too, Slobogin, S, *Minding Justice*, Harvard Univer-sity Press, Cambridge, Massachusetts, 2006.

25 (1992) 175 CLR 218. See too McSherry, B, "Amici Curiae and the Public Interest in Medical Law Cases" (2003) 11 *Journal of Law and Medicine* 5.

26 (1995) 38 NSWLR 47.

the point that wrongful birth cases involving the birth of an unplanned child disproportionately affect women. The contentious question of damages for the cost of the child's upkeep in the *CES* case was taken to the High Court but settled before a judgment was entered. The High Court subsequently went a step further in *Cattanach v Melchior*[27] and controversially awarded damages for the upkeep of a healthy child born after a negligent sterilisation procedure. However, subsequent tort reforms in some jurisdictions have undermined this common law initiative, as well as the value attributed to reproductive choice (Graycar: Chapter 21).

The right to self-determination underpins the right to refuse treatment and assumes another dimension when people make advance directives in order to prevent being given potentially life-saving treatment such as blood transfusions for religious reasons or being forced to live a life they do not consider worth living (see Stewart: Chapter 3). Competent people have a degree of control over their treatment options, and courts and legislatures are gradually recognising that advance directives can enhance the rights of incompetent people also to have their wishes respected. This reflects the adoption of policies in secular societies which emphasise autonomy rights and increasingly turn to the law rather than religious institutions to resolve disputes.[28] As a result, courts have an important role in shaping ethical debates about medical care and decision-making at the end of life. Mendelson and Ashby (Chapter 19) argue that a greater acknowledgment of the reality of death and the dying process is necessary when difficult choices have to be made in such stressful circumstances. Whether or not an advance directive can be instrumental in forcing a doctor to provide or withdraw treatment presents an interesting dilemma between medical autonomy and a patient's rights. Stewart (Chapter 3) takes the view that, if an Australian court were presented with this issue, clinical judgment would be prioritised over the patient's wishes.

Liability and the courts

Developments under the common law in relation to liability for negligent provision of health services have now intersected with legislative changes in Australia. Much continues to depend upon evaluation of expert evidence, especially from medical practitioners[29] and psychologists.[30] Freckelton (Chapter 20) discusses the

---

27   [2003] HCA 38.

28   See also the decision of Morris J in *Gardner; Re BWV* [2003] VSC 173; Mendelson, D and Ashby, M, "The Medical Provision of Hydration and Nutrition: Two Very Different Outcomes in Victoria and Florida" (2004) 11 *Journal of Law and Medicine* 282; Rothschild, A, "Gardner; Re BWV: Resolved and Unresolved Issues at the End of Life" (2004) 11 *Journal of Law and Medicine* 292; Freckelton, I, "Withdrawal of Artificial Life Support" (2004) 11 *Journal of Law and Medicine* 265.

29   See the Medico-Legal Guidelines promulgated in 2006 by the Medical Practitioners Board of Victoria (http://medicalboardvic.org.au/pdf/Medico_Legal_Guidelines.pdf> (accessed 20 April 2006).

30   See the useful recent publication: Young, G, Kane, AW and Nicholson, K (ed), *Psychological Knowledge in Court*, Springer, 2006; see too Gold, AG, *Expert Evidence in Criminal Law: The Scientific Approach*, Irwin Law, Ontario, 2003; Freckelton, I and Selby, H, *Expert Evidence: Law, Practice, Procedure and Advocacy*, LBC, Sydney, 2005.

calls for changes to how medical evidence is adduced before the courts and argues that recent law reform recommendations are appropriate in encouraging an improved culture of forensic objectivity for experts. He expresses concern about what he identifies as the "naïve notion" that straightforward, dichotomous answers can regularly be provided by a single expert regime to resolve issues in dispute in litigation.

In the 1990s personal injury and medical negligence litigation increased (Seymour: Chapter 22), placing pressure on governments from various vested interests to limit the entitlements of plaintiff victims. A consequence of the Ipp Committee report has been a sequence of statutory tort reforms throughout Australia which have adjusted plaintiffs' entitlements (Bennett and Freckelton: Chapter 19).

An important aspect of the changes has been a modification of the liability of health professionals by virtue of the introduction of threshold requirements for litigation; a modified *Bolam* test; complex changes to causation law; restrictions on recovery for psychiatric harm; limits on awards of damages for wrongful birth; new mechanisms for calculating non-pecuniary losses; and statutory recognition of apologies. However, the changes are not uniform. An issue that emerges from them is the ongoing reconceptualisation of the health practitioner–patient relationship. Increasingly, it is regarded as a partnership[31] in which each participant has responsibilities that have an impact upon those litigation rights that remain.

A net effect of the post-Ipp Committee changes is that there will be fewer civil claims against a number of categories of health professionals. This may increase the role of health registration boards as mechanisms for accountability. Although patients do not gain financially from disciplinary decisions, there is the potential for more streamlined oversight of health practitioner conduct – with collateral advantages for the quality of health care provision. However, the situation differs from jurisdiction to jurisdiction in Australia and New Zealand (see Freckelton: Chapter 24). By contrast, as the role and professional activities of nurses have expanded, Forrester (Chapter 23) points out that their exposure to litigation has increased – at least in principle. Complex issues arise also for obstetricians and midwives (see Seymour: Chapter 22).

It is premature as yet to evaluate the overall impact of Australia's tort reforms. Their effect on aggrieved patients may never be a public statistic and much remains to be seen about whether the limitations upon capacity to obtain compensatory redress prove acceptable for those who suffer adverse consequences from health service provision.

---

31   See, for example, the European Federation of Internal Medicine, the American College of Physicians, the American Society of Internal Medicine and the American Board of Internal Medicine "Medical Professionalism Project", <www.abimfoundation.org/mpp2003/index. htm> (accessed 10 March 2006).

Governance and accountability

There is no controversy in principle as to the importance of health practitioners being accountable for their conduct or for health researchers to comply with ethical requirements. However, governance of health practitioners is in the process of fundamental transition with an increasing recognition that the traditional preoccupation with regulation of conduct should give way to acknowledgment of the various aetiologies of unsatisfactory outcomes for patients (Freckelton: Chapter 24). These comprehend phenomena such as the increased corporatisation of health services (Wilson: Chapter 25) and the entrepreneurialism which attends a variety of commercially attractive health procedures.

Merry and McCall-Smith emphasised a significant issue in our blame-dominated culture when in 2001 they argued for fair identification of the complex and often multifactorial causes of adverse outcomes so that our responses are founded on firm moral and scientific grounds: "The inadequacies of the system, the specific circumstances of the case, the nature of human psychology itself, and sheer chance may have combined to produce a result in which the doctor's contribution is either relatively or completely blameless".[32] It is vital that awareness of systemic factors inform governance over the delivery of health services because matters such as the profit motive can result in unacceptable pressures upon resources and practitioners. Similarly, the need for the law to respond to the problems posed by the commercialisation of research, such as the power imbalance between the subject and investigator, is a growing problem for research ethics governance in Australia (Tomossy: Chapter 26).

In addition, there is a need to evaluate effectively: the competencies of international medical graduates who may move from one jurisdiction to another; the ongoing skills and competencies of practitioners; and the potential for health conditions to erode performance. These issues raise the dilemma of the overall feasibility of rigorous accreditation of health practitioners by way of mechanisms such as revalidation.

End-of-life issues

An area of health law that has not received the level of attention that it deserves is the sequelae of death. In this volume Freckelton and Ranson (see Chapter 15) question in the aftermath of the Patel scandal[33] whether the ancient institution of coronership can effectively satisfy contemporary needs for death investigation. Croucher (Chapter 16) scrutinises rights and interests in the disposal of remains, identifying a series of sensitivities that attach to what at first might appear to be

---

32 Merry, A and McCall-Smith, A, *Errors, Medicine and the Law*, Cambridge University Press, Cambridge, 2001.

33 See Bundaberg Hospital Commission of Inquiry, <www.bhci.qld.gov.au/> (accessed 17 April 2006); Harvey, K and Faunce, T, "A Critical Analysis of Overseas Trained Doctor Factors in the Bundaberg Base Hospital Inquiry" (2006) *Law in Context* (in press).

questions of property and equity. Another aspect of death is the community interest in availing itself of the scarce resource of organs that can be transplanted (see Saul, McPhee and Kerridge: Chapter 17).

Finally, issues in relation to euthanasia and termination of life remain tense and unresolved (Mendelson and Ashby: Chapter 18) in the aftermath of the Commonwealth's overturning of the *Rights of the Terminally Ill Act 1995* (NT).[34] In Australia the work of Magnusson[35] and Otlowski[36] has highlighted the discrepancies and anomalies in both practice and theory within the area. In this volume Mendelson and Ashby (Chapter 18) seek to forge a path from a palliative care and legal perspective through the emotive rhetoric. They argue that courts have a duty to ensure that the rights and entitlements of individuals, including their lives, are protected, but acknowledge that it is also essential that the realities of death and the dying process are not forgotten. They contend that this can best be achieved by enhanced and informed cross-disciplinary understanding of death and its incidents when determining the difficult balance of contradictory ethical, medical and legal principles.

Information privacy and confidentiality

Information about health conditions has traditionally been regarded as confidential. However, new paradigms in provision of services have fundamentally eroded the extent of health service provider–patient confidentiality (McMahon: Chapter 27). As well, steps toward integrated record compilation and practitioner access to others' documentation have the potential to make problematic inroads on the traditional characteristics of especially the doctor–patient relationship (Iacovino, Mendelson and Patterson: Chapter 28). Likewise, entitlements of access to health records by patients (Palombo: Chapter 30) have changed both the nature of the documentation generated by practitioners and the relationship between practitioners and patients. Challenges such as the European Committee-funded 5th Framework Programme "Privacy in Medical Research and Law" (PRIVIREAL), which has brought together experts from across Europe, provides a baseline for contemporary analysis of many pressing issues.[37] In an environment of shared and increasingly regulated health care, traditional expectations of health privacy and confidentiality are taking on important new complexions. It is important that underlying values inform or at least influence the avalanche of statutory and practice changes.

---

34 See, for example, Mendelson, D, "The Northern Territory's Euthanasia Legislation in Historical Perspective" (1995) 3 *Journal of Law and Medicine* 136.

35 Magnusson, R, *Angels of Death: Exploring the Euthanasia Underground*, Melbourne University Press, Melbourne, 2002.

36 Otlowski, M, *Voluntary Euthanasia and the Common Law*, Oxford University Press, Oxford, 2000.

37 See Beyleveld D, Townend, D, Rouillé-Mirza, S and Wright, J, *The Data Protection Directive and Medical Research Across Europe*, Ashgate, Aldershot, 2004.

Reproductive technologies: Ethical and legal frameworks

The world's first two babies to be created with the assistance of in vitro fertilization (IVF) were born in Britain in 1978 and Australia in 1980. In 1996 Dolly the sheep was cloned from a somatic (non-germ) cell taken from an adult sheep and transferred from an enucleated sheep egg at the Roslyn Institute, Scotland. There have been numerous developments since these early days. A general consensus on the need to regulate human embryo research because of the serious ethical questions accompanying this relatively scientific activity has led to uniform controls over embryo research in Australia. Chalmers (Chapter 12) discusses the background and content of these laws and explores the difficulty of striking an ethical balance between the protection to be afforded to the human embryo and the social benefits to be gleaned from embryo research.

By contrast, uniform controls over assisted reproductive technologies (ARTs) used for treatment have not been achieved in Australia. This disunity suggests there is far less agreement concerning questions about fertilisation treatment and associated clinical practices. Much of the discussion in the late 20th century concerned the challenges ARTs presented to fundamental norms and institutions such as family structures and parenthood. Szoke, Neame and Johnson (Chapter 10) take the debate further and identify some new challenges such as equality, justice and most importantly, the nature of personhood. They also recognise the broad range of influences underlying policy decisions and regulatory initiatives and suggest that the timing of reform processes is critical to the process of legal reform. Petersen (Chapter 11) examines the ethical and regulatory frameworks governing the application of reproductive genetic technologies and argues the case for developing sound, principle-based regulatory processes. She warns that it is not appropriate for either professional or statutory regulation to be based on opinion polls, misinformation or political manipulation.

Genetic research and developments

The issue of competing interests surfaces again in the context of genetic research and development. Australian legislation governing genetic information in the modern health system is designed to safeguard privacy and anti-discrimination laws to protect genetic information from wrongful use when in the hands of third parties. Skene and Otlowski (Chapter 29) argue that current privacy safeguards are too restrictive and that broader familial interests in genetic information need more recognition and consideration. They also recommend more accountability and transparency in the insurance sector as a means of balancing the interests of consumers with those of the insurance sector to protect the viability of the industry.

The research and development of genetic technologies challenge legal traditions underpinning intellectual property laws and have generated new conflicts for public sector researchers and organisations functioning in commercial environments. Similarly, as government funding for research in universities and hospitals contracts, commercial imperatives generate new policies and challenges. The application of patent law to the new era of genetic materials and technology is perplexing. This is an area in which old systems are attempting to adapt to a new epoch and patent examiners, for example, are addressing an overwhelming array of problems which include novelty, pace of technology, the volume of inventions and the essentially different and specialised nature of genetic science and technology. Rees and Opeskin (Chapter 14) examine these questions and conclude that scientists, health professionals and public institutions have to come to terms with the strengths and limitations of patent law and utilise existing mechanisms provided by the law and the market place to ensure that genetic inventions serve the best interests of the community. Examining commercial and legal issues relevant to research practices in the biotechnical industry, Nicol (Chapter 13) concludes that an assessment of new policies as well as reforms to current laws and policies are needed.

Conclusion

In 1995 Furrow et al argued that, as health care was consuming approximately one-seventh of gross domestic product in the United States, the study of health law was "justified in part by the size and influence of the industry".[38] A similar claim might be made in respect of Australia in excess of a decade later. However, there is another consideration. Matters which have an impact upon the regulation of the beginning, end and quality of life are truly fundamental to all of us. So too is the quality of healthcare that is dispensed and the consequences that follow when it is unacceptably poor. We hope that this volume will inform, provoke and stimulate reflection upon a wide array of such issues and perhaps lay the groundwork for informed policy development and judicial and statutory law-making.

---

38 Furrow, BR, Greaney, TL, Johnson, SH, Jost, TS and Schwartz, RL, *Health Law*, West Publishing, St Paul, Minnesota, 1995, p v.

PART II

ETHICAL FRAMEWORKS
AND DILEMMAS

2

Moral frameworks in health care: An introduction to ethics

Ian Kerridge, John McPhee,
Chris Jordens, and Georgina C Clark

Introduction

Health professionals are often reluctant to analyse moral issues in health care as critically as they would epidemiological data or clinical pathology reports. They often seem more concerned about their legal rights or obligations than the morality or the ethical "correctness" of decisions. This may be because they regard ethics as "unscientific", as entirely subjective or as a matter for personal conscience; or it may be because they believe that it is impossible to resolve ethical issues. Nevertheless, health professionals inevitably confront difficult ethical issues in their practice, and making "ethically laden" decisions is therefore unavoidable. It follows from this that we should think of ethics not as the "application" of an academic discipline *to* the practice of health care, but rather, as an integral aspect *of* the practice of health care.

It is notoriously difficult to define ethics in a way that does not instantly give rise to dispute. The *Concise Oxford Dictionary* defines "ethics" as "relating to morals, treating of moral questions". This definition only shifts the question to the meaning of "moral", however. Some people maintain that there is a distinction between ethics and morals, but both of these words (along with their Greek and Latin roots, *ethikos* and *morales*) have been and still are used to refer to questions of character, patterns of behaviour, custom, legal sanction and/or the distinction between "right" and "wrong". Thus there is no firm ground for clearly differentiating the meaning of these terms either on historical grounds, or on the basis of current usage.

Instead of appealing to definitions, some people try to define ethics by distinguishing it from other human activities or capacities, such as the appreciation of beauty (aesthetics), or the ability to experience emotion. Others try to clarify what ethics is by differentiating it from things it is *not*, but with which it is said to be frequently confused. Peter Singer, for example, has suggested that it helps if we at least understand that ethics is neither law, nor professional opinion, religious belief, public opinion, empirical data, professional etiquette, intuition or hospital policy.[1]

Others have attempted to define ethics by identifying what the major moral philosophies and major religious beliefs have in common. While there is disagreement as to what these commonalities are, it has been suggested that on this basis, ethics (at least as an academic discipline of philosophy) can be understood in terms of the following generalisations:

- Ethics seeks principles of *overriding importance* – that is, principles that underpin legal systems, and transcend pragmatic considerations of politics and self-interest.

- Ethics seeks principles, moral concepts, and guides to action which are *universal* – that is, which could be applied to all persons equally.

- Ethics is broadly concerned with *human well-being* and the maintenance of a peaceful society in which all may benefit and flourish.

- Ethics is a *rational approach to morality* – that is, it seeks to base arguments and recommendations about what we ought or ought not to do on reason, or at least moral justification that is to some degree systematic.

- Ethics is *prescriptive* – that is, it refers more to what we *should* do than what we *can* do.

If there is any certainty about ethics, one is surely that is attracts a great deal of disagreement. Notwithstanding this important observation, we must begin somewhere if we are to give positive content to notion of ethics, and it is to this task that we now turn.

Disciplinary diversity, methodological heterogeneity and the ethical space

Ethics is, at the very least, concerned with behavioural norms and questions that concern *how we should live in relation to others*. Given this point of departure, we need to identify methods that allow us to reflect critically on human behaviour. While it is often assumed that ethics is a disciplinary domain of philosophy and can be understood only through apprenticeship into philosophical theory or logic, we would argue that philosophy offers only one means for understanding ethical concerns because other disciplinary perspectives, such as sociology, linguistics and law, also illuminate important aspects of human behaviour.

---

1   Singer, P, *Practical Ethics*, Cambridge University Press, Cambridge, 1979.

It follows that we should not think of ethics as having a single method, nor as being the domain of any one discipline. It would be better characterised as a *space* (a turbulent one, no doubt) whose contents and limits are defined according to how one responds to the question: *How should we live in relation to others?*

Given that "ethical space" is defined by a question, it must be accessible to any number of disciplines or perspectives, and furthermore, it can be explored – if only partially – by means of a method of inquiry that is peculiar to each discipline or perspective. Thus philosophy, for example, allows us to explore "ethical space" by means of logic or normative theories of ethics; bioethics allows us to explore it using ethical principles, law by means of legal reasoning, linguistics by means of discourse analysis, economics by means of cost–benefit analysis, and sociology by means of stakeholder analysis. We may explore "ethical space" as members of the lay public through our intuitions or "gut feelings". As adherents to a religious tradition we may become explorers by studying theological dogma or through personal revelation. As nurses we may explore with reference to an ethic of care or by undertaking phenomenological studies of clinical encounters. In each case the perspective defines the boundaries and contents of ethical space by the way in which it addresses the question: *How should we live in relation to others*?

No matter which discipline or perspective one adopts when responding to this question, there is a very basic decision or (more usually) assumption that one has to make, and that is to define the "other". The "other" may be defined narrowly in terms of one's own family, tribe, nation or race; or the "other" may be defined more widely so as to include all human beings. And it may be defined more broadly still, so as to include non-human animals, or even all forms of life. Indeed the "other" sometimes encompasses the non-living environment or the entire cosmos, as is the case in some Eastern philosophies or indigenous belief systems.

As well as attending to the question of who or what "others" are, we should attend closely to the terms of the basic question: *How should we live in relation to them?* Importantly, "should" does not refer us to actions or states of affairs as they are, but as they ought to be. This is a basic meaning in many human languages. As in English, it can be said in different ways (for example, "ought", "must"), but it cannot be simplified further. When we use "should", we usually do so not to *describe* but to *prescribe* and to *proscribe*, that is, to issue directives about what one should do (for example, "always give pain relief") and to issue prohibitions about what one should not do (for example, "do not kill"). "Should" also implies obligations: there is always an entity – an "I", "you", "we", "one" or "they" – on whom there is an *onus* to do (or not do) something. Furthermore, this "something" must be specified in terms that are never entirely innocent or ethically neutral. "Living" with others entails a multitude of different activities and processes, and it matters, for example, whether we ask "Should we kill him?", "Should we withdraw treatment?" or "Should we help him commit suicide?"

The overriding point here is that ethics is inescapably concerned with meanings, and with systems of meanings, because how we should live in relation to others is something that is regulated *symbolically* – that is, by meanings and symbols among which "should" is absolutely central. Another central meaning is the distinction between "good" and "bad" (or "right" and "wrong" when applied to behaviour).

This distinction may be understood dichotomously (good as the absence of bad, and vice versa), or good and bad may be understood as different qualities. The meanings are usually gradable (that is, our languages usually allow us to assign degrees of good and bad to people and actions), and they are elaborated in a bewildering variety of different ways that depend on situational, institutional and cultural contexts. These elaborations are usually called *value systems*, because they furnish the terms in which we make *value judgments* of people, behaviours and states of affairs. These value judgments are in turn part of the vast symbolic economy that regulates human behaviour.

By conceiving of ethics as a space defined by a question, we have opened ethics up to a range of disciplines and perspectives. This does not commit us to a "relativist" position: it does not lead us to conclude that all disciplines and perspectives are equally right. Rather, it provides us with a way of asking structured questions about them. Who or what figures within the ethical space (who counts as "others")? On whom do obligations fall in relation to these others? How is the nature of the obligation represented? What value systems are brought into play for the purpose of making value judgments?

Asking structured questions about different disciplines and perspectives helps us get comparable answers. This in turn puts us in a better position to test their relative value and limitations as ways of understanding and guiding human behaviour when it comes to answering what we take to be the central, defining question of ethics generally. This question is not a theoretical one, furthermore, but one which concerns us all in our daily lives: *How should we live in relation to others?* The question is no less relevant to the practice of health care than to everyday life. One of the things that makes it more relevant (as we suggested at the outset of our discussion) is that health professionals inevitably confront difficult ethical issues in their practice. Dealing with these is therefore an integral aspect of the practice of health care, and it follows that developing one's competence to do so is an integral aspect of the job. This is precisely the rationale for studying ethics.

Normative ethics

A number of terms have been used to describe the domain of philosophical ethics (moral philosophy). "Normative ethics" represents an attempt to develop moral principles and frameworks to guide actions and evaluate behaviour whereas "meta-ethics" is concerned with moral claims, with the distinction between normative theories of ethics, and with the meaning of terms such as "right", "good", "virtue", and "justice". "Practical ethics" refers to the implications that questions arising from ethics have in specific contexts. "Bioethics" may be understood as one type of practical ethics as it refers to ethics applied to anything in the bio realm. "Medical ethics", "nursing ethics", and "psychological ethics" are all parts of bioethics. "Clinical ethics" refers specifically to the ethical aspects of the clinical encounter between patient and therapists.

Deontology

Deontological theory, from the Greek *deon* meaning "binding duty", represents one of the major schools of moral philosophy. Deontology is also known as *intrinsicalism* because it embodies the notion that things or actions are right or wrong in and of themselves. The central theoretical focus of deontological theories is on doing one's duty, which may be expressed by certain universal statements or action-guides, including laws such as "do not kill", principles such as respect for human life, institutions such as the legal system and "relational laws" such as respect for one's parents. In order to determine what action is required in a particular circumstance, the deontological approach to moral reasoning involves the simple application of the appropriate universal statement to the specific situation. An example of such reasoning would be: killing is wrong; withdrawing treatment from this patient is killing, therefore, this action is wrong.

Four major types of justifications of moral rules have been presented: *theological* arguments justify rules by appeal to divine revelation, suggesting that the proper moral rules are those which God wills us to follow. Although attractive to many, the great problem with this argument is that there is so much conflict about the existence of God, about what actually *is* God's will, that theological arguments do not resolve many difficult moral problems. Another approach involves a *societal* justification whereby the correct moral rules are those believed in by most members of society. Unfortunately this is also inadequate as consensus is not always achievable, is not necessarily an adequate moral guide, and may indeed justify what we would normally regard as morally repugnant actions. A third approach favoured by some philosophers is known as the *intuitionist* approach. This suggests that morality is actually an intrinsic feature of the world and that the proper moral rules or actions are those which possess the intrinsic property of "rightness", a property which we can all perceive through our special faculty of moral intuition. While attractive to some, intuitionism is characterised by definitional vagueness and is not susceptible to proof or disproof.

The most influential proponent of rule-based morality was Immanuel Kant (1724–1804). Kant sought to establish the ultimate basis for valid moral rules in a fourth approach – that of *pure reason*. Kant emphasised a number of central concepts. First, he argued that the ideal moral life consisted of submission to a certain will or command expressed in universal moral imperatives (*categorical imperatives*), which always remain absolute and binding. Secondly, he suggested that people themselves have an absolute, inalienable, irreducible and unconditional value which derives from the fact that they are rational beings who are self-legislating and have personal dignity. Thus, to act morally is to respect each individual's dignity. According to Kant, this dignity is violated whenever a person is treated merely as an end. Following from this, Kant stressed the importance of liberal values such as autonomy, freedom, dignity, self-respect and individual rights.

The value of deontological theory is that it reminds us of the importance of rationality in moral judgment and of moral standards independent of consequences. It has tremendous appeal for those who seek certainties in life and for institutions (such as the church or government) who have a need to bind together groups of people under some identifiable moral code.

However, deontological theory has also been criticised because the rules or principles it espouses are often vague, difficult to define and open to debate. For instance, even if it is accepted that it is wrong to kill, it is still not clear whether this means that killing is always wrong, including in self-defence.

This gives rise to the major objection to deontological theory – the problem of *conflicting morals*. The basic difficulty lies in whether all rules or prohibitions are equal when two or more moral rules come into conflict. If they are equal, then there is no way to resolve moral conflict. If they are not equal, then this implies that rules are able to be overruled in some situations, or that there is a hierarchy of rules of differing urgency. Unfortunately, it has proven impossible for those who support deontological theory to provide an exception-free and conflict-free hierarchy of rules.

Consequentialist theories

The difficulties found with rule-based morality, have led many contemporary philosophers towards *consequentialist* or *teleological* theories instead. The basic tenet of consequentialism is that the rightness or wrongness of an action is based solely on the consequences of performing it. For a consequentialist, actions are neither intrinsically right nor wrong; rather, the moral value of any action is dependent upon the consequences of that action.

There are many variants of consequentialist theory but they share a common rational process of moral reasoning. To decide if an action is moral or not, a consequentialist will attempt to consider all the feasible alternative actions in a given situation, and calculate *all* the possible consequences for the parties involved. They will then choose the action that will result in the best outcome.

The most prominent consequentialist theory is *utilitarianism*. Utilitarianism is a normative moral theory that states that the single fundamental principle of ethics should be the "principle of utility" – that the morally right action is the action that produces the best possible outcome as determined from a perspective that gives equal weighting to the interests of each party.

The classical utilitarians, Jeremy Bentham (1748–1832) and John Stuart Mill (1806–1873) conceived utility entirely in terms of happiness or pleasure and they maintained that pleasure alone is intrinsically good, and pain (or the absence of pleasure) is intrinsically evil. This is known as *value hedonism*. Another approach to utilitarianism, favoured by philosophers such as Richard Hare[2] and Peter Singer,[3] is based upon maximising individual preferences or desires.

Controversy has also arisen over whether the principle of utility pertains to *acts* in specific contexts or, instead, to *rules* that determine the rightness or wrongness of actions. According to *act utilitarianism*, individuals should act in each situation using rules only as rules of thumb and each action should be judged independently to bring about the greatest balance of good over evil.

Rule utilitarianism has been proposed as a defence against the objection that utilitarianism may lead to morally indefensible conclusions. Like deontology, rule utilitarianism emphasises the centrality of rules in morality but, unlike deontology, it states that these rules should be formulated by reference to the principle of utility. Thus, the morality of actions is determined by reference to a system of moral rules formulated by society or individuals that are based on their ability to produce the best possible consequences.

Criticisms of consequentialist theories fall into several main groups. One group involves questions about the validity of the claim that consequentialism provides us with a simple, rational process of moral reasoning. Such critics consider consequentialism as fundamentally flawed because of methodological difficulties in assigning values to outcomes.

These methodological difficulties are basically threefold. The first methodological weakness is that the concept of utility or happiness is so unclear as to make it practically unworkable and that making comparisons between quantitative and qualitative outcomes themselves or assessing such outcomes for individuals and between individuals seems difficult if not impossible. The second weakness is that it is often unclear as to who are the parties involved in any moral action and what moral significance each of their interests should have. The third methodological weakness of consequentialism is that one cannot decide, on the basis of consequences alone (many of which may be unpredictable or unquantifiable), what moral action to follow.

Another criticism of consequentialism is that it does not account for certain aspects of ordinary moral thinking such as the importance of individual rights or basic convictions about justice and injustice in deciding moral issues.

The final argument against consequentialism is that it clashes with a broad range of considered beliefs and can lead to morally unacceptable conclusions. Utilitarianism may permit actions that are incommensurable with common

2   Hare, RM, *The Language of Morals*, Oxford University Press, Oxford, 1964.
3   Singer (1979) op cit.

morality, such as killing or torture, if these actions result in the best net balance of good over evil.

Consequentialists have adopted several arguments that attempt to meet these criticisms. Hard-line utilitarians suggest that if consequentialism does not accord with traditional morality this is because common morality is the result of incorrect moral reflection which should be rejected in favour of consequentialism. More commonly, consequentialists accept that there are significant difficulties with absolute utilitarianism, but argue that the natural solution is to expand consequentialist principles to make them more reconcilable with existing moral beliefs, rather than to abandon consequentialism altogether. This group proposes that distributive concerns, special obligations and individual rights can all be accommodated within a consequentialist framework if one accepts that they each have important consequences and thus need to be included in any evaluation of moral actions. Another strategy to answer criticism of consequentialism has been the elucidation of rule-utilitarianism whereby the *rightness* of a particular action lies in its conformity with a proper moral rule. Such moral rules are in turn based upon the value of their consequences. Rule-utilitarianism has thus been viewed by some critics as an attempt to occupy the philosophical "middle ground" and thus obtain the benefits of both consequentialism and non-consequentialism. Unfortunately rule utilitarianism appears to be liable to the same criticisms as act utilitarianism.

Virtue theory

Virtue ethics contains the notion that the rightness or wrongness of an action is derived not from the action itself or its consequences but from the underlying *motive* of the person making that action. "Virtue" here refers to competence in the pursuit of moral excellence and character traits that are morally valuable such as wisdom, compassion, fidelity, love, honesty, gentleness, integrity and discernment. By understanding moral behaviours as action that proceeds from virtue, one obviates the need for thinking of morality as "rule following".

The concept of moral virtue derives from the ancient philosophical traditions of Plato, Aristotle and Aquinas. In recent times, however, virtue ethics has been further developed by a number of contemporary philosophers including Philippa Foot, Alasdair MacIntyre, Martha Nussbaum, Bernadette Tobin and Justin Oakley, and has attracted considerable interest from physicians and nurse ethicists both in the United States and Australia.

Unfortunately, although virtues are clearly an integral aspect of "ethical" decision-making, it is not at all clear that virtues are a *sufficient* basis for determining the moral basis of behaviour. Virtue theory ignores the importance of rights, duties and responsibilities and appears to be too simplistic and imprecise to adequately explain the rightness or wrongness of actions. These normative failings are amplified by the difficulty that many virtue theories have had in defining and systematising the "essential" moral virtues and in defining moral goodness or virtue without circular argumentation. (The morally right is that which a virtuous person would do and the virtuous person is one who would do the morally right.) By emphasising the importance of professional virtues and the moral significance of "practical wisdom" whilst de-emphasising the importance of actions, rights and duties, virtue ethics also runs the risk of basing ethics on the beliefs and judgments of health professionals and giving moral sanction to unacceptable paternalism.

While virtue ethics appears to be deficient in several ways, the upsurge of interest in contemporary virtue ethics reminds us that when considering ethical issues in health care, these issues cannot be separated from either the moral characteristics of the individuals involved or the process of moral reasoning that forms the basis of their decisions.

Liberalism and communitarianism

Health professionals often frame arguments about contentious ethical issues in terms of conflicting rights. In this context "rights" refer to justifiable claims that individuals or groups can make upon society or upon other individuals. These may be expressed as *positive* rights or *negative* rights. A positive right is a right to be provided with a particular good or service by others whereas a negative right constrains others from interfering with an individual's exercise of that right. Thus, the language of rights also entails definite but often ill-defined notions of correlative obligations. For example – if one person possesses a right to life this imposes an obligation upon others not to deprive that person of life. The extent of this obligation is defined by contextual features and, as such, what is required is an exploration of the moral basis of rights and the contextual features that determine its correlative obligations.

Despite the fact that rights language has been critical to the development of ethics and civil law, the question of what role rights should play in defining law, morality and political organisation remains controversial. The notions that rights should provide the basis for an understanding of morality, that individual liberty or autonomy has moral primacy, and that the interests and liberties of individuals should be respected and protected by the state (except where there is a subsequent harm to another individual), form the normative basis of the philosophical liberalism of philosophers such as Mill, Dworkin and Charlesworth.

Although liberalism has become increasingly popular in recent years and is particularly compatible with secular politics and medical models of critical analysis, it has been criticised by a number of philosophers on the grounds that it overemphasises the significance of autonomy and individual liberty and fails to appreciate the role of the community and social relationships in determining, shaping and sustaining social and moral rules. *Communitarian* theories that emphasise communal values, cooperative virtues and social relationships and emphasise community standards of the "common good", are frequently advanced as the socio-political and philosophical alternative to liberalism.

But neither rights-based theories nor communitarian theories provide a comprehensive understanding or morality. In many ways, however, the distinction between community and liberty creates a false dichotomy as the two may in fact be politically compatible and philosophically complementary. Individuals are simultaneously members of many different communities including families, hospitals, cultures and nations from which they "inherit" a range of different and not always compatible social roles and communal obligations. The communities in turn are shaped by the values, perspectives and actions of their members. Respect for rights and individual liberty not only has independent moral value but allows individuals to prosper in community, promotes social cohesion and enables peaceful co-existence between individuals with divergent cultural, moral, religious or political beliefs.

Feminist moral philosophy and the ethics of care

Over the past 20 years contemporary feminist philosophers have challenged the rationality, practicality, and inherent sexism of Western moral philosophy. They contend that male-dominant western philosophical and medical traditions have failed to provide a coherent or universal moral philosophy that incorporates either the needs of women or the substantial philosophical contributions women have made regarding the relative importance of *care, interpersonal relationships* and *communitarianism*. There is of course no single feminist ethics or feminist moral theory. Feminist ethics are extraordinarily diverse with considerable variability among feminists in terms of methodology, ideology and interpretation of controversies in health care.[4]

The development of feminist bioethics is often described historically as a succession of "waves".[5] The "first wave" feminists shared an optimistic view of technology as a value-neutral means for women to liberate themselves from the biological tyranny of pregnancy, childbirth and mothering.[6] In the 1970s and 1980s the "second wave" feminists adopted a more critical and pessimistic attitude to technology whereby it was viewed as a means for the continued oppression of women.[7] "Third wave" feminists embody a diverse range of perspectives that reflect the growth, vitality and philosophical maturity of feminism but tend to share the belief that technology is not value-neutral but, can be used by women, for women, to end oppression.

---

4   Wolf, SM (ed), *Feminism and Bioethics: Beyond Reproduction*, Oxford University Press, New York, 1996.

5   Charlesworth, M, *Bioethics in a Liberal Society*, Cambridge University Press, 1993, Cambridge, pp 88–106.

6   Firestone, S, *The Dialectic of Sex*, Jonathan Cape, London, 1971.

7   Overall, C, *Ethics and human reproduction*, Allen & Unwin, London, 1983.

Despite significant differences, most feminist theories share a number of characteristics. In general, feminist philosophies:

- reject the overemphasis on individual rights, autonomy and rationality in bioethics;

- deny the requirement for value-neutral philosophies or abstract ethical principles;

- reject the adversarial nature of moral conflict as a means for resolving ethical issues in clinical practice;

- stress the significance of values such as empathy, interdependence and caring, and the importance of the shared responsibility that all members of society have to each other; and

- emphasise the importance of context and the relevance of politics and power to understanding ethics and health care.

In recent times, what has become known as an *ethics of care* (sometimes called feminine ethics) has been developed from within nursing ethics and contemporary feminist philosophy and has had a major impact on the concepts of health care and professional roles. The "ethics of care" derives largely from the work of developmental psychologist Carol Gilligan and her thesis that the primary moral orientation of girls and women is an ethic of "care" and that this may be contrasted with the "justice" orientation of men and boys that has dominated health care and bioethics.[8] Supporters of the "ethics of care", including feminist writers such as Nel Noddings and Sara Ruddick, reject the philosophical emphasis on universal moral rules, impartiality, individual rights, law, objectivity and autonomy, and instead emphasise the importance of personal responsibility, love, trust and caring.[9] Critics of an ethics of care[10] point out both that an emphasis on caring as an exclusively feminine virtue may serve simply to reinforce the sexual status quo and that an emphasis on care without consideration of autonomy, justice or rights is of limited value at the social and institutional levels.[11]

The importance of feminist ethics, gender attentive research and the "ethics of care" are that they have helped refocus our attention both on the importance of caring, relationships, emotion, tolerance and humanity and on the moral significance of power, gender and authority in specific clinical and cultural contexts.

---

8 Gilligan, C, *In a Different Voice: Psychological Theory and Women's Development*, Harvard University Press, Cambridge MA, 1982.

9 Baier, A, "Trust and Antitrust" (1986) 96 *Ethics* 248.

10 Sherwin, S, *No Longer Patient: Feminist Ethics and Health Care*, Temple University Press, Philadelphia, 1992.

11 Van der Broek, K, "A Critical Look at the Ethics of Care" in Shotton L (ed) *Health Care Law and Ethics*, Social Science Press, New South Wales, 1997.

Principle-based ethics

Principle-based approaches to moral reasoning are derived from the idea that it may be possible to specify a number of rules or "principles" to guide moral actions. The most notable example of this type of approach in bioethics is the "four principles" approach developed by Beauchamp and Childress in their book *The Principles of Biomedical Ethics*.[12]

Beauchamp and Childress recognise four moral principles – "autonomy", "beneficence", "non-maleficence" and "justice". Each principle is said to be *"prima facie"*, meaning that in particular situations it can be overridden by other principles or by more important considerations. Each principle also needs to be balanced with other principles, as obligations that are derived from one principle may conflict with those derived from another. There is no predetermined hierarchy of the principles as each is essentially of equal importance and may be given different priority by different individuals in different situations. Principle-based ethics does not provide an entirely value-free approach to solving ethical problems. On the other hand, principle-based ethics is not so content-filled that it provides an automatic answer to moral questions either. Indeed, it has been criticised because it does not precisely specify what health care workers should or should not do in every specific clinical context.[13]

However, for many, the great strengths of a principle-based approach is that it emphasises moral justification and the balancing of *prima facie* principles in specific contexts, and that it implicitly recognises that conflict, uncertainty and dialogue are unavoidable aspects of health care. While it is true that a principle-based approach does not provide a moral hierarchy for explicit decision-making, it does provide a moral language and analytical framework for bioethics that can be incorporated within many peoples' individual moral, religious, political and philosophical perspectives.[14] If used as a moral language, a principle-based approach to ethics allows for consideration of moral virtue, culture and gender-specific issues, care and compassion, and the social and clinical contextual features that determine how ethical problems are viewed.

Continental philosophy and discourse ethics

Contemporary bioethics has, without question, been dominated by Anglo-American philosophical traditions, most notably by analytical philosophy. In recent years, however, alternative perspectives drawn from "continental" (European) traditions have become popular. These perspectives, which include those of Hegel, Kierkegaard, Marx, Nietzsche, Heidegger, Gadamer, Merleau-Ponty,

---

12 Beauchamp, TL and Childress, JF, *Principles of Biomedical Ethics*, 5th edn, Oxford University Press, New York, 2001.

13 Clouser, KD and Gert, B, "A Critique of Principlism" (1990) 15 *Journal of Medicine & Philosophy* 219.

14 Gillon, R, "Defending the 'Four Principles' Approach to Biomedical Ethics" (1995) 21 *Journal of Medical Ethics* 323.

Sartre, Adorno, Habermas, Derrida, Levi-Strauss and Foucault, are extraordinarily diverse and share many of the preoccupations of postmodernism. They do, however, offer insights very different from those derived from traditional normative approaches to ethics and remind us of the need to be critical, the importance of historical and cultural particularity, the power of language, and the central relevance of the lived human experience.

Continental approaches to ethics which emphasise process or communication have recently had a major impact on the field of bioethics, none more so than *discourse ethics*. This approach to ethics owes much to the work of the German philosopher and social theorist, Jurgen Habermas. It argues that effective discourse between individuals can occur only when they respect each other and recognise the importance of rules of communication, such as the need to set aside power or self-interest. While discourse ethics may seem naïve and does not offer an adequate framework for the moral interaction between individuals or groups, it does remind us that ethics is primarily a social and communicative activity and that the resolution of moral conflict is only likely to result from genuine and mutually respectful engagement.

Postmodern ethics: Not one view but many

In recent years the traditional subjects, processes and ideologies of Western philosophy have increasingly been abandoned in favour of a postmodern approach to ethics. While the term postmodernism has entered into popular culture, there is very little agreement about what it actually means. Although postmodernism may be correctly defined as a philosophical movement that developed in France in the 1960s, it is more helpful to think of it in terms of its method(s) and project.

Postmodernism in ethics is not an identifiable school or body of thought – rather it promotes diversity of perspective and a discourse of reflective equilibrium. While postmodern ethics is extraordinarily diverse, it is possible to make some generalisations about postmodern approaches to ethics. Most importantly, they are generally characterised by a rejection of the need for a unifying normative theory or the belief that "truth" can be gained through human reason or the scientific method independent of the sociocultural context. Instead they argue that moral insights can be gained through a diverse range of perspectives, languages and methods.

In some ways, therefore, postmodern approaches to ethics are both "pragmatic" and deeply contextual, and, indeed, draw heavily on the genre of empirical research in ethics. This "new pragmatism"[15] appears to have arisen partly out of frustration with ethical analysis that is remote from the empirical realities of patients and disease and the tendency for bioethics to emphasise

---

15   Wolf, S, "Shifting Paradigms in Bioethics and Health Law: The Rise of a New Pragmatism" (1994) 20 *American Journal of Law & Medicine* 395.

autonomy and abstract reasoning but to ignore issues of race, gender and ethnicity. Thus the pragmatism of postmodernism is characterised by the recognition of the importance of such diverse areas as feminist moral philosophy, Marxism, psychology, phenomenology, sociology, and social anthropology.

Although such currents have broadened and deepened our understanding of ethics in health care, there exists the danger ethics may at times be seen purely in descriptive terms with little *critical* analysis of cultural relativism, liberalism, meta-ethics or the contribution of moral philosophy to ethical reasoning.

Ethics in health care institutions:
Discourse between moral acquaintances

When we consider the variety of different ways of viewing ethics and morality, it seems unlikely that two people can ever agree. Yet within the clinical setting, ethics is an integral aspect of health care and ethical decisions need to be made on a daily basis. How then is this possible?

Tristram Engelhardt addressed just this question in his book, *The Foundation of Bioethics*. Engelhardt argues that we can divide society into communities of "moral friends" and "moral strangers". Between moral friends it is possible to form a content-rich ethical consensus. For example, within a feminist group, it is likely that the issue of abortion will be approached in terms of a woman's right to control her body. Members of the group – ethical friends – will be able to debate this subject, learn from each other's views, and reach consensus. However, when one member of this group attempts to have an ethical discourse with a member of another group (such as members of the Catholic Church) they may find themselves to be ethical strangers – and be totally unable to form a consensus or to respond adequately to each other's views.

When we think about the health care system, the question then becomes whether health care professionals form a community of moral friends or a society of moral strangers. Members of the health care team are clearly not complete moral strangers. Many difficult ethical decisions are reached within the health care system with minimum conflict and despite the fact that individuals may approach different problems in different ways. Exactly why this occurs is uncertain – it may be because health professionals are a highly select group, because there are strong socialising forces within the health care system, because health workers minimise their differences by not holding strong beliefs, or because health workers generally hold the altruistic goal of providing care as "superior" to their own values or beliefs.

And yet health professionals are not moral friends either. Health professionals come from many religious, cultural and moral backgrounds and rarely share a complete, content-full morality. Indeed given that we live in a multicultural society characterised by cultural, racial, religious and moral pluralism, it is inevitable that the decisions health professionals make will not always accord with those of their peers, or their patients.

Perhaps, then, the best way to view the health care community is as a group of "moral acquaintances" who share sufficient moral beliefs or processes that agreement can be reached, and the health care institution as a sociomoral framework that tolerates pluralism but shapes it in a way that enables social cooperation and effective health care. This means that ethics, or at least the resolution of ethical concerns, is ultimately a matter of public discourse and political engagement. It also means that social and legal institutions must be an important feature of the moral landscape as they create the structures by which freedoms can be guaranteed, communicative structures established and agreed moral norms enforced.

Ethics and law

One of the questions often raised by health professionals when discussing moral issues is "What does the law say about this?". This question is often asked as if the answer to this question would resolve the moral issue and/or provide clear guidance for action or behaviour in all circumstances. It must be said plainly that *the law is not the same as ethics.* The law may be influenced by moral considerations, may reflect sociomoral consensus, may allow some degree of independent moral judgment and may share similar processes of reasoning to moral philosophy, but in the end the law is only of limited assistance in the discussion of moral issues.

What then is the law? It is perhaps trite to say that, as with the term "ethics", the word "law" means different things to different people and is used in many different contexts. Just as there are multiple normative theories of ethics, there are a number of schools of thought with views concerning the meaning of "law" including those of "natural law", "positivism", "sociological jurisprudence", "critical legal studies" and "feminist jurisprudence".

As a starting point law might be regarded as "a system of rules and principles, formally created, which govern specified areas of human activity".[16]

The practical approach to the issue of "what does the law say?" is to examine the sources of law. In the Anglo-Australian legal system there are principally two sources of law – the legislature and the courts. When attempting to identify what "the law" is on a particular issue we can look to the statutes passed by parliaments or the decisions of judges in the various court systems. In the Australian federation, it must be remembered that there are generally different statutes in different jurisdictions (States and Territories) as well as Commonwealth statutes (as limited by the Constitution). There may

---

16   Bates, P, Blackwood J, Boersig J, Mackie K, McPhee J. *The Australian Social Worker and the Law*, 4th edn, Lawbook Co, Sydney, 1996, p 1.

also be different interpretations of the common law by superior courts in the various jurisdictions.

Whilst rules and general principles may be referred to by a court when reaching a conclusion about a particular dispute, these rules and principles must be considered in the context of the case to be decided. This leaves generous scope for judges to interpret the rules and principles in such a way that is affected by their own views on the best outcome. The law as considered by the courts has a practical focus. The court is asked to resolve a dispute, a conclusion must be reached and reached according to statutes passed by the legislature or in accordance with rules or principles espoused by previous (authoritative) courts (that is, the system of precedent). If a party or the parties to the dispute consider that an error of law has been made or an injustice has occurred there is generally an avenue of appeal open to a higher court (except for the High Court of Australia). If the community is unhappy with the result, the legislature can pass a statute to remedy this fault (of course, it will be up to the courts to interpret this remedy).

For example, the High Court considered a "wrongful birth" case in *Cattanach v Melchior*.[17] The parents of a healthy child sued a doctor for negligence that caused them to have a child they had not planned on having. The question before the High Court was whether the costs of raising a healthy child could form part of the damages recoverable in a negligence action. By a majority of four to three, the court held that the parents could recover the cost of raising that child until he turned 18 years of age. One of the reasons given for the majority holding was that to deny recovery would be logically inconsistent with the existing and uncontested heads of recovery for the hospital and medical costs of the birth and for the attendant pain and suffering associated with it. The court's decision was followed by significant public comment. Perhaps not surprisingly, that public commentary essentially focused on the emotive and cultural issues raised by the appeal rather than on the extent to which the majority's conclusion was compelled and informed by a process of logical legal reasoning. Following this public reaction New South Wales and Queensland quickly passed legislation that prevents a court from awarding damages for the costs ordinarily associated with rearing or maintaining a child.

The important point is that the courts must resolve the dispute and decide the issue before them according to rules and principles which have been set out in statutes or developed by the courts. There is no general inquiry as to what is the "right" solution to the problem by reference to normative moral standards. It is only at the higher appellate level that courts have some degree of freedom to adapt or develop new legal principles.[18] A year after the *Cattanach* case the New South Wales Supreme Court of Appeal handed down its decision in a "wrongful

---

17   (2003) 215 CLR 1.

18   See, for example, *Secretary, Department of Health and Community Services v JWB and SMB* (1992) 175 CLR 218; *Airedale NHS Trust v Bland* [1993] AC 789.

life" case – *Harriton (by her tutor) v Stephens; Waller (by his tutor) v James; Waller (by his tutor) v Hoolahan.*[19] The appellants, Alexia Harriton and Keeden Waller, were each born with a disability. The damage that they were claiming was the harm suffered by being born in their disabled condition. They claimed that if the respondent doctors had properly diagnosed the particular circumstances that brought about them being born disabled they would not have been forced to endure the suffering that each has to endure and the consequent costs they will have to incur.

The trial judge, Studdert J, held that there was no duty on the respondents to provide the mothers of Alexia and Keeden with the necessary information to allow them to decide whether to terminate their pregnancy.

In the Court of Appeal, Spigelman CJ held that cases such as this, which involved a novel category of liability, require attention to the ethical foundation of the relevant legal principles. He held that a duty in negligence must reflect community values generally and that in these cases this was not so. Ipp JA held that not all harm caused by negligence is recoverable in law and not all negligence gives rise to recoverable harm. As the claims required a consideration of the comparison of being born with a disability and non-existence, it was not capable of being calculated and so policy would not support a move to allow such claims. He held that the law already gives a remedy for the parents to recover for the cost of raising and maintaining a child born following negligence and the interests of the disabled child are not such to require the protection of the law.

In a strong dissenting judgment Mason P held that there is no conceptual difference between the critical event that generates parents' "wrongful birth" claims and the child's claim for "wrongful life". The fact that the quantification of damages may be difficult should not prevent compensation when a negligent act has occurred.

Consider also the New South Wales Supreme Court decision of *Woods v Lowns.*[20] The plaintiff claimed that the medical practitioner had breached his duty of care to a 14-year-old boy (Patrick Woods) by not responding to a request to leave his surgery, go to the boy's nearby house and treat him when he was suffering an epileptic seizure. The boy was not, and had never been, a patient of Dr Lowns. The trial judge found that Dr Lowns owed the boy a duty of care and was in breach of this duty by not going to him. The doctor appealed to the New South Wales Court of Appeal. The majority of the Court of Appeal (Kirby P and Cole JA) found against the doctor on the issue.

Mahoney JA, in dissent, said:

> The issue – and in the end, the only issue – is whether the Court should impose on him [Dr Lowns] a legal obligation which did not previously exist and, by doing so, require him to pay $3 million and more. I think we should not do so. My

---

19 [2004] NSWCA 93; affirmed by High Court [2006] HCA 15.
20 (1995) 36 NSWLR 344.

colleagues think we should. What I say will not alter the result. Therefore I shall state my reasoning dogmatically, believing that my propositions could, if there were time, be justified.

Oversimplified, the position is: (a) the Court must determine whether there is a legal obligation upon a general practitioner to attend a person with whom he has no relationship; (b) before this case, he had no legal obligation to do so; (c) the courts can impose – and on occasion have imposed – a legal obligation where none previously existed; (d) in principle, it should not do so in this case; and (e) the imposition of such an obligation is not required by the way in which the trial was conducted.

(a) the issue in this case:
It is important to emphasise that we are not concerned with obligations in morals or charity, with professional obligations, or with statutory obligations. Dr Lowns is not liable because (if he did) he had a moral or a professional obligation to go to the child in this case.

Assuming the facts to be as found against him, a doctor may have had a moral obligation. Any decent person would help a child in trouble if he could: at least, if special cases be put aside. It may be that charity required that he go.

But moral obligations are not legal obligations. The two must not be confused. A great deal of the time of the legislature is taken up in deciding whether moral obligations should become legal obligations, under what circumstances, and with what qualifications and exceptions. Law, as an instrument of social control, is a blunt instrument. It is often inappropriate to the qualifications and exceptions to which, if made law, a moral obligation should be subject. But the imposition of a legal obligation produces consequences which often make it inappropriate as a means of enforcing moral obligations. We are concerned with whether the moral obligations to which (as I assume) the doctor was subject should be a legal obligation.[21]

"Dogmatically" and without attempting to fully justify his position, Mahoney J spent another 1800 words outlining his reasons (with references to earlier court judgments) for reaching the conclusion that Dr Lowns did not owe Patrick Woods a duty of care. Since Mahoney J was in the minority on this issue his views are not binding on other courts but they illustrate the nature of the legal inquiry as distinct from the moral inquiry.

The reference to *Woods v Lowns* and Mahoney JA's dissenting judgment illustrates how lawyers approach issues. They ascertain if a statute (or regulations) or a decision of a court may be applied to the factual issue before them. If there is no authority directly on point they will tend to reason by analogy in order to determine the likely outcome of any resort to the courts to resolve a dispute or determine liability (whether criminal or civil, or both). Although not binding, lawyers may also look to the way that courts have approached an issue in similar jurisdictions. Whilst some reference may be made to "morality" in arriving at a point of view in a court case, the judge (or judges) do not generally rely entirely on this to justify their position. The inquiry, however, is always to authority. Legislatures are not generally bound by previous court decisions or legislation

---

21   *Lowns v Woods* [1996] Aust Torts Reports ¶81-376 at 63,165–63,166.

(except where there may be limits imposed by the Constitution). Parliament may consider issues of morality when debating and drafting laws but legislators will also be influenced by pragmatic criteria such as political compromise and expediency.

Although appeal to authority and precedent represents an important distinction between ethics and law, both share a logical process of inquiry and an emphasis on rationality and argumentation. It is also the case that the law allows some flexibility for independent moral judgment and for consideration of contextual features both in the language of law and the process of judicial discretion.

Courts are generally reluctant to deal with issues that are not part of the factual context of the case before them. In the English case of *R (on the application of Burke) v General Medical Council*[22] Munby J was asked to consider the legality of the General Medical Council (GMC) guidelines on end-of-life decision-making – *Withholding and Withdrawing Life-prolonging Treatment: Good Practice and Decision Making*. The central issue of the case dealt with the circumstances in which artificial nutrition and hydration (AN&H) can be withdrawn from a patient. Mr Burke suffered from a congenital degenerative brain condition. He was concerned that at some future time he may need AN&H but that it would be denied to him by his doctors. Such a decision being supported by the GMC guidelines. Munby J declared that parts of the GMC guidelines were unlawful.

The GMC appealed to the Court of Appeal.[23] The court unanimously upheld the appeal. The court found that there were no grounds for thinking that those caring for Mr Burke would be entitled to or would take a decision to withhold or withdraw AN&H. The court also found that:

> [T]he manner and circumstances in which these proceedings were commenced suggest that [Mr Burke] was persuaded to advance a claim for judicial review by persons who wished to challenge aspects of the GMC Guidance which had no relevance to a man in [his] position.

The Court of Appeal noted:

> There are great dangers in a court grappling with issues such as those that Munby J has addressed when these are divorced from factual context that requires their determination. The court should not be used as a general advice centre. The danger is that the court will enunciate propositions of principle without full appreciation of the implications that these will have in practice, throwing into confusion those who feel obliged to attempt to apply those principles in practice. This danger is particularly acute where the issues raised involve ethical questions that any court should be reluctant to address, unless driven to do so by the need to resolve a practical problem that requires the court's intervention.

---

22   *R (on the application of Burke) v General Medical Council* [2004] EWHC 1879 (Admin).
23   [2005] EWCA Civ 1003.

When detailing the rules or principles which govern the decision they have reached in health care-related matters courts do, however, usually state them in a general way which will allow a large degree of flexibility in their application to specific incidents. For example, in the High Court decision in *Rogers v Whitaker*,[24] the court had to determine how much information had to be given to a patient when they are asked to consent to a procedure. The High Court upheld the lower court decisions that Dr Rogers had not adequately informed Mrs Whitaker of the material risks associated with the procedure undertaken. As guidance for other courts the majority (Mason CJ, Brennan, Dawson, Toohey and McHugh JJ) stated the general principle in the following way:

> The law should recognize that a doctor has a duty to warn a patient of a material risk inherent in the proposed treatment; a risk is material if, in the circumstances of the particular case, a reasonable person in the patient's position, if warned of the risk, would be likely to attach significance to it or if the medical practitioner is or should reasonably be aware that the particular patient, if warned of the risk, would be likely to attach significance to it. This duty is subject to the therapeutic privilege.[25]

Although such judgments may be criticised for being insufficiently directive or for providing medical practitioners with too much freedom – it is clear that they do allow for consideration of the therapeutic dyad, for independent moral judgments and for the process of discourse between "moral acquaintances". Importantly, such judgments also suggest that decisions about clinical practice should occur after consideration of both ethics *and* the application of law in the clinical context.

The inquiry as to "what does the law say about the issue" is a narrower question than the ethical inquiry about what one should do. The inquiry as to the correct ethical conduct may be informed and assisted by the legal position, but that is not the totality of the inquiry.

Conclusion

The failure of two millennia of moral philosophy to provide a single, universally acceptable normative moral theory has provided an impetus to the developments of postmodern ethics and led to more recent criticism of the very nature and relevance of ethics to health care. Whilst it is tempting to suggest that the inadequacy of available moral philosophy has negated its contribution to applied ethics, it is probably more correct to argue that a fuller understanding of bioethical issues is only gained where one accepts that many perspectives may illuminate ethical concerns and that no single perspective can give a complete account of ethics. While moral philosophy has made a valuable contribution to our under-standing of the way in which we should live in relation to others, other disciplinary perspectives, including law, linguistics, sociology, history, literature,

---

24   (1992) 175 CLR 479.
25   Ibid at 490.

art, economics, politics and theology, provide different accounts of ethics, adding substance, richness, content and complexity.

Ethics is integral to health care and good health care is impossible without good ethics. If the tensions between different approaches to the *ethical space* have taught us anything it is that there is enormous benefit to be derived from moral discourse and from political engagement. And just as this discourse has been enhanced and defined by perspectives traditionally excluded from practical and academic dialogue (such as those of patients/clients, women and members of non-Western cultures), so it can only gain from the participation of health professionals cognisant of the impact of ethics and law on their own judgments and behaviour, and those of others.

3

Advance directives:
Disputes and dilemmas

Cameron Stewart[1]

Introduction

"Advance directives" are decisions made by patients about what medical treatments they would like in the future, if at some point, they cannot make decisions for themselves. When thought of in these broad terms, advance directives can be seen as an existing part of everyday medical practice, particularly surgical procedures, where patients consent to treatments many days, even weeks, before they are sedated for their operation. Most academic and legal discussion of advance directives focuses particularly on those decisions about withholding or withdrawing treatments at the end of life. These directives (sometimes referred to as "living wills") usually record decisions about refusing life-sustaining treatments, but they can also contain the patient's preferences and desires about a whole range of treatment matters.

In Australia, the right to make an advance directive is enshrined in legislation in most States and Territories (as detailed below) but it is also sourced in the common law, in the fundamental right of self-determination.

In this chapter I will briefly review the background of laws relating to advance directives. I will first outline the position at common law, and then I will review the legislative regimes that exist in Australia. Thirdly, I examine some recent problematic cases, which highlight the inadequacies of advance directives. I conclude with the observation that the potential benefits of advance directives will only be realised when a wider culture of advance care planning is adopted by both the health and medical professions.

Common law advance directives

The common law supports a right to self-determination, which in the current context, allows competent adults to refuse any medical intervention, on any

---

1   Associate Professor Division of Law, Macquarie University.

ground. Even those choices considered as poor by the health professions, must be respected.[2] Lord Donaldson MR has stated that:

> This right of choice is not limited to decisions which others might regard as sensible. It exists notwithstanding that the reasons for making the choice are rational, irrational, unknown or even non-existent.[3]

Decisions regarding treatment can be made contemporaneously, or they can be made with the intention that they will come into effect in the future. To that extent advance directives are merely a logical extension of the right to self-determination.[4] Without this logical extension, the right to self-determination would become a nonsense. A doctor would only have to wait for a patient to fall into unconsciousness before they could proceed with treatments which had been refused by the patient. Conversely a doctor could cease to provide agreed upon treatments as soon as the patient became incompetent.

There are four questions that need to be answered before an advance directives becomes binding:

Was the decision-maker competent when they made the directive?

Obviously, the person must have been competent to make the directive at the time it was made.[5] The starting point in cases where capacity is an issue is that "every adult is presumed to have ... capacity, but it is a presumption which can be rebutted".[6] The test for capacity rests on the question of whether the patient understood the nature and purpose of the treatment when they made the decision to refuse it.[7] Capacity is presumed in adults, but it is a presumption that can be rebutted.

This is illustrated by the case of *NHS Trust v T*.[8] In this case a 37-year-old woman with borderline personality disorder had made an advance directive to

---

2   *Re PVM* [2000] QGAAT 1; *Re C (Adult: Refusal of Medical Treatment)* [1994] 1 WLR 290; *Nancy B v Hotel-Dieu de Quebec* (1992) 86 DLR (4th) 385; *Smith v Auckland Hospital* [1965] NZLR 191; *Re B (Adult: refusal of medical treatment)* [2002] EWHC 429 (Admin).

3   *Re T (An Adult) (Consent to Medical Treatment)* [1992] 2 Fam 458 at 460 per Lord Donaldson MR. See also similar comments by Butler-Sloss LJ (at 474), and Straughton LJ (at 478). In the United States it has been said that "the law protects [the patient's] right to make [his or] her decision to accept or reject treatment, whether that decision is wise or unwise": *Lane v Candura* 376 NE 2d 1232 at 1236 (Mass, 1978).

4   *Airedale NHS Trust v Bland* [1993] 2 WLR 316 at 367 per Lord Goff.

5   For a review of the law of competence and refusals of medical treatment see, Stewart, C and Biegler, P, "A Primer on the Law of Competence to Refuse Medical Treatment" (2004) 78 *ALJ* 325.

6   *Re T* [1992] 2 Fam 458 at 470 per Lord Donaldson MR. See Biegler, P and Stewart, C, "Assessing Competence to Refuse Medical Treatment" (2001) 174 *MJA* 522.

7   In *Re F (Sterilization: Mental Patient)* [1989] 2 Fam 376 at 419–20, Lord Brandon said that incapacity arises where an adult cannot understand the nature or purpose of an operation or other treatment. See also *Gillick v West Norfolk and Wisbech AHA* [1986] AC 112 and *Re C (Adult: Refusal of Medical Treatment)* [1994] 1 WLR 290.

8   [2004] EWHC 1279 (Fam).

refuse blood products on the grounds that she believed her blood to be evil. She had a history of repeated blood-letting, causing chronic anaemia, and leading on this occasion to emergency admission to hospital. Charles J was asked to make an interim order allowing a blood transfusion, prior to final hearing. Charles J began with the presumption that Ms T was competent, but felt the evidence was compelling enough to suggest that Ms T was suffering from a misperception of reality. This was enough for the judge to override the advance directive and allow blood transfusions until final hearing.

A useful point of contrast to *NHS Trust v T* is *In re W*.[9] This case concerned a prisoner who was suffering from a severe psychiatric disorder but who had been returned to the normal prison population after some treatment. To protest his conditions, the prisoner had cut open his shin and repeatedly inserted objects and rubbed faeces into the wound, with the intention of causing blood poisoning. He had also inserted two tap fittings into his anus. He had made an advance directive to refuse all treatment. The prison authorities sought an order authorising treatment. Butler-Sloss P refused the application as there was no evidence of a lack of competence on the prisoner's part. Even though he had a disorder, he was still able to receive and understand information, weigh it and communicate a decision. To that extent he was able to refuse or accept treatment, including future resuscitation.

Was the advance directive intended to cover the circumstances that have arisen?

After capacity has been established, the tribunal of fact needs to confirm the true scope and basis of the decision. Basically, this requires the advance directive to have been intended to apply to the circumstances which have arisen.[10]

Much of this question is answered by interpretive analysis of the patient's language and the meaning of particular words and phrases employed. Weight is also accorded to the remoteness, consistency and thoughtfulness of the statements or documents.[11] Evidence of a decision which consists of remote, general, spontaneous or casual comments will not support the claim of an advance directive.[12] However, evidence of cogent and serious decision-making which consists of written evidence or eye-witness accounts is usually strong enough to support the existence of an advance directive.[13] Evidence of oral directions can, by

---

9   [2002] EWHC 901 (Fam).

10   *Re T* [1992] 2 Fam 458 at 473 per Lord Donaldson. See Biegler, P, Stewart, C, Savulescu, J and Skene, L, "Determining the Validity of Advance Directives" (2000) 172 *MJA* 545.

11   *Matter of Conroy* 486 A 2d 1209 at 1230 (NJ, 1985); *Matter of Jobes* 529 A 2d 434 at 443 (NJ, 1987); *Matter of Welfare of Colyer*, 660 P 2d 738 at 748 (Wash, 1983).

12   *Matter of Jobes*, 529 A 2d 434, 443 (NJ, 1987).

13   In *Matter of Peter* 529 A 2d 419 (NJ, 1987) evidence was led of a medical power of attorney and a verbal direction to refuse treatment which was attested by nine reliable witnesses.

itself, support the finding of a valid advance directive[14] but, of course, a written directive has an evidential advantage given it is a more concrete record of the patient's decision.

Courts will often have regard to issues concerning whether the patient changed their mind after making the directive. In *HE v A Hospital NHS Trust*[15] a 24-year-old female Jehovah's Witness had signed an advance directive, but two years later had promised to convert to Islam after becoming engaged to a Muslim. She had been raised as a Muslim but had become a Jehovah's Witness after her parents separated and her mother joined the faith. An application was brought by her father after the woman became seriously ill following an operation. A blood transfusion was deemed necessary by medical staff but the woman's mother was adamant that the directive be followed. Munby J found the woman's promise to convert back to Islam to be an "essential and compelling aspect" for finding that the advance directive was no longer intended to apply.

Was the decision-maker unduly influenced?

The decision to refuse treatment must be free from the undue influence of others. Undue influence may impair the decision-making process of the person and invalidate the decision. In *Re T (An Adult) (Consent to Medical Treatment)*[16] a woman (whose mother was a Jehovah's Witness) had decided to refuse blood products after she was injured in a car accident. The court found that the woman's mother had exerted undue pressure on the woman to make her refuse the treatment prior to her becoming incapacitated. The woman's decision was therefore invalid and treatment could be provided by the doctors according to the patient's best interests. The court stated that when examining undue influence, one must inquire as to both the strength of will of the patient and the relationship of the patient with the persuader.[17] Given that the patient was in extreme pain and under the influence of drugs, and given that she had changed her mind about blood transfusions after being persuaded to do so by her mother, the court did not feel that there was enough evidence to support the directive.

What standard of evidence is appropriate?

The courts in the United States have required a higher standard of proof than the balance of probabilities in satisfying themselves of the veracity of anticipatory decisions to refuse treatment. The highest standard of evidence that can be required in civil proceedings in the United States is referred to as the "clear and

---

14   *Re Chad Swan*, 569 A 2d 1202 (Me, 1990); *Leach v Akron General Medical Center*, 426 NE 2d 809 (Ohio Comm Pl, 1980); *Matter of Eichner*, 420 NE 2d 64 (NY, 1981); *Re Martin*, 504 NW 2d 917 at 923 (Mich App, 1993).
15   [2003] EWHC 1017 (Fam).
16   [1992] 2 Fam 458.
17   See Stewart, C and Lynch, A, "Undue Influence, Consent and Medical Treatment" (2003) 96 *Journal of the Royal Society of Medicine* 598.

convincing standard" or the "clear, strong and cogent" standard.[18] A similar standard has been adopted in the United Kingdom. In the case of *HE v A Hospital NHS Trust*,[19] to which reference was previously made, Munby J found that the appropriate standard was "convincing and inherently reliable evidence".[20]

In Australia, best interests assessment in the context of family law has also been said to require clear and convincing evidence.[21] Additionally, in civil cases concerning serious claims of professional misconduct or in civil cases involving claims of criminality, Australian courts are to have regard to the *Briginshaw* standard which allows the court to consider:

> The seriousness of an allegation made, the inherent unlikelihood of an occurrence of a given description, or the gravity of the consequences flowing from a particular finding.[22]

Assessing the validity of an advance directive is a very serious task. Most often it involves matters of life and death. In many circumstances, the trier of fact is being asked to make a decision in an expedited forum where time limits may have prevented evidence from being properly prepared. There is, therefore, a real danger that a decision might be made erroneously. It is, therefore, submitted that the court should apply the *Briginshaw* test in its assessment of evidence concerning the above factors.

Statutory recognition of advance directives in Australia

In Australia, three States and two Territories have enacted legislation which secures the right of patients to make anticipatory decisions regarding health care.[23] Generally these statutes preserve any common law rights to refuse treatment and work as parallel schemes.[24]

---

18   *Cruzan v Director, Missouri Health Department* 497 US 261 (1990).

19   [2003] EWHC 1017 (Fam).

20   Ibid [23]–[25].

21   *Re Jane* (1988) 12 Fam LR 669.

22   *Briginshaw v Briginshaw* (1938) 60 CLR 336 at 362 Dixon J.

23   *Powers of Attorney Act 1998* (Qld) Pt 3; *Consent to Medical Treatment and Palliative Care Act 1995* (SA) Pt 2, Div 2; *Medical Treatment Act 1988* (Vic) Pt 2; *Medical Treatment Act 1994* (ACT) Pt II; *Natural Death Act 1988* (NT). It should be noted that the *Guardianship Act 1987* (NSW) provides for a "quasi-advance directive" in the form of an instrument to appoint an enduring guardian. The instrument appoints a proxy decision-maker but it can also contain directions to the guardian which presumably might include advance directives concerning medical treatment. Those directives are binding on the enduring guardian but not on the Guardianship Tribunal. However, given the uncertainty of the operation of these provisions, the Act is more aptly dealt with in the discussion of health care attorneys which is outside this paper.

24   *Powers of Attorney Act 1998* (Qld) s 39; *Medical Treatment Act 1988* (Vic) s 4. No such provision exists in the *Consent to Medical Treatment and Palliative Care Act 1995* (SA); *Medical Treatment Act 1994* (ACT) s 5; *Natural Death Act 1988* (NT) s 5.

Who can make a statutory directive and what types of treatment do they cover?

Statutory rights to make advance directives tend to be limited to people over the age of 18.[25] Directives to refuse treatment can relate to refusal of treatment generally, or of a particular kind of treatment.[26] However, in some jurisdictions a patient is prevented from refusing palliative care.[27]

In Victoria the patient can only refuse treatment which is related to a "current condition".[28] Unfortunately the meaning of "current condition" is not defined, but presumably it relates to treatment for a medical condition which is being suffered by the patient at the time the advance directive is completed. This means that these statutory directives are not available to people who would refuse treatment for conditions which they have not yet suffered, for example, strokes, or physical injuries which sustain blood loss. This is quite a severe limitation on the scope of statutory directives.

In the Northern Territory, the direction can be made at any time but only becomes effective when the patient is suffering from a "terminal illness", which is defined as an illness, injury or degeneration leading to an imminent death and from which there is no reasonable prospect of temporary or permanent recovery.[29]

South Australia has similar restrictions. The direction only becomes operative when the patient is in a terminal phase of a terminal illness, and is no longer competent.[30]

In Queensland the directive generally becomes effective on incapacity[31] but a direction to withhold life-sustaining treatment will not operate unless:

(a) the principal is terminally ill and is not expected to live more than a year, or is in a persistent vegetative state, or is permanently unconscious, or has a severe illness with no reasonable prospect of being able to live without the continued application of life-sustaining measures; and

(b) (if the direction concerns artificial hydration or nutrition) the life sustaining measure would be inconsistent with good medical practice; and

---

25 *Consent to Medical Treatment and Palliative Care Act 1995* (SA) s 7; *Medical Treatment Act 1988* (Vic) s 5(1)(d); *Medical Treatment Act 1994* (ACT) s 6; *Natural Death Act 1988* (NT) s 4(1).

26 *Medical Treatment Act 1988* (Vic) s 5(1)(a); *Medical Treatment Act 1994* (ACT) s 6. Queensland the patient can refuse or consent to future health care and require the withdrawal of life sustaining treatment, as well as authorise the use of force: *Powers of Attorney Act 1998* (Qld) s 35.

27 *Medical Treatment Act 1988* (Vic) s 5(2) (defined as the provision of reasonable medical procedures for the relief of pain, suffering and discomfort; or the reasonable provision of food and water); *Medical Treatment Act 1994* (ACT) s 4(2).

28 *Medical Treatment Act 1988* (Vic) s 5(1)(a).

29 *Natural Death Act 1988* (NT) s 3.

30 *Consent to Medical Treatment and Palliative Care Act 1995* (SA) s 7(1).

31 *Powers of Attorney Act 1998* (Qld) s 36(1)(a).

(c) the patient has no reasonable prospect of regaining capacity for health matters.[32]

What forms can the statutory directives take?

Statutory directives (like common law ones) can be created orally or in writing.[33] If a directive is made by means other than writing, some statutes require that it be witnessed by two health professionals.[34]

Written directives must take a prescribed form and are referred to as "refusal of treatment certificates"[35] or "advance health directives"[36] or "directions".[37] They must be signed, but if the patient is unable to do so, some Acts allow for another person to sign in the presence of the patient at their direction.[38]

Written directions must be witnessed.[39] Some statutes require one[40] or two witnesses to the directive, neither of whom needs to be medically qualified.[41]

Other statutes require witnessing by both a registered medical practitioner and an "other person" (who need not be a medical practitioner).[42] In Victoria, both witnesses must sign the certificate and be satisfied that the patient was of sound mind, was over 18 years, had made a voluntary decision, had been informed about there medical condition, and had understood the information about their medical treatment.[43]

Queensland requires the witness and a doctor to certify that the patient had the capacity to make the decision at the time it was made.[44]

---

32 Ibid s 36(2).

33 *Powers of Attorney Act 1998* (Qld) s 35; *Medical Treatment Act 1988* (Vic) s 5(3); *Medical Treatment Act 1994* (ACT) s 6; *Natural Death Act 1988* (NT) s 4(1). In the *Consent to Medical Treatment and Palliative Care Act 1995* (SA) s 7, directions can only be made in writing.

34 *Medical Treatment Act 1994* (ACT) s 8.

35 *Medical Treatment Act 1988* (Vic) s 5.

36 *Powers of Attorney Act 1998* (Qld) ss 35, 44.

37 *Consent to Medical Treatment and Palliative Care Act 1995* (SA) s 7(1); *Medical Treatment Act 1994* (ACT).

38 *Powers of Attorney Act 1998* (Qld) s 44(3)(a)(ii); *Medical Treatment Act 1994* (ACT) s 7(b).

39 *Powers of Attorney Act 1998* (Qld) ss 35, 44(3)(b); *Consent to Medical Treatment and Palliative Care Act 1995* (SA) s 7; *Medical Treatment Act 1988* (Vic) s 5; *Medical Treatment Act 1994* (ACT) s 7.

40 *Consent to Medical Treatment and Palliative Care Act 1995* (SA) s 7(2)(b).

41 *Medical Treatment Act 1994* (ACT) s 7(c), (d); *Natural Death Act 1988* (NT) s 4(2) (witnesses need to be at least 18 years and cannot be a practitioner responsible for the treatment of the patient).

42 *Medical Treatment Act 1988* (Vic) s 5.

43 Ibid s 5.

44 *Powers of Attorney Act 1998* (Qld) s 44(4), (5), (6). "Capacity" is defined in s 42 to be an understanding of the nature and effects of each direction, and an understanding of how the directive works, including the power of the principal to revoke the directive.

Some scheduled certificates provide a space for the patient to sign the certificate but they do not have to sign it in all jurisdictions for it to be valid.[45]

Can statutory directives be revoked or become ineffective?

A patient can cancel a directive (whether made orally or in writing) by clearly expressing or indicating their wish to a registered medical practitioner or another patient.[46] Space is provided on some certificates for the patients to record their wish for it to be cancelled.[47] However, it is not necessary for them to do so. In Queensland, where directives can only be made in writing, the "principal" can revoke the directive in writing.[48]

In the Australian Capital Territory a directive will cease to operate if the medical condition of the patient changes to such an extent that it no longer reflects the condition recorded in the directive.[49]

Disputes and dilemmas arising from the use of advance directives

Lack of remedies for patients whose advance directives are ignored

One of the main problems with advance directives is that remedies are hard to provide in cases where directives have been dishonoured. The legal system's ordinary response to medical treatment without consent is in trespass, specifically the tort of battery. A battery is an intentional, direct and non-consensual touching of a person's body.[50] Battery can be established not only in those cases where actual bodily harm is the result but where there is merely offensive touching.[51] However, unlike negligence actions, trespass are actionable per se.

The leading case concerning battery and advance directives is *Malette v Schulman*[52] where a doctor was held liable in battery when he ignored a Jehovah's Witness's advance directive to refuse blood products. The woman had presented in an unconscious state to the hospital after a serious car accident and was found to possess a card outlining her religious beliefs. The card stated that the patient refused blood transfusions under any circumstances. In upholding the card as a

---

45 *Medical Treatment Act 1988* (Vic) Sch 1.
46 *Medical Treatment Act 1988* (Vic) s 7(1); *Medical Treatment Act 1994* (ACT) s 9.
47 *Medical Treatment Act 1988* (Vic) Sch 1.
48 *Powers of Attorney Act 1998* (Qld) ss 48, 49(2).
49 *Medical Treatment Act 1994* (ACT) s 10.
50 Balkin, R and Davis, J, *Law of Torts*, 2nd edn, Butterworths, Sydney, 1996; Fleming, J, *The Law of Torts*, 9th edn, Lawbook Co, Sydney, 1998.
51 *Collins v Wilcock* [1984] 3 All ER 374.
52 (1990) 67 DLR (4th) 321.

valid advance directive the court stated that: "A doctor is not free to disregard a patient's advance instructions any more than he would be free to disregard instructions given at the time of the emergency".[53]

At trial and on appeal the plaintiff was awarded $20,000. The court stated the sum was appropriate given the patient's mental and emotional suffering.[54] The judgment therefore suggests that even in the absence of substantial physical harm a patient wrongly given life-sustaining treatment should be able to claim damages beyond the nominal, because non-consensual touching is considered to be a very serious infringement even where it causes no physical harm.

However, not all courts have been happy to award damages for breaching an advance directive, even in those cases where the patient appears to have suffered a consequential physical injury.[55] In *Anderson v St Francis – St George Hospital*[56] a patient commenced a claim for being resuscitated, despite having consented to a "do not resuscitate" order being placed on his chart. The day following the resuscitation he had a stroke and remained partially paralysed until his death two years after his resuscitation. The claim was continued by his estate. The claim was framed in both negligence and battery. It was said to be a claim for the "wrongful administration of life-prolonging treatment" or "wrongful living".[57]

The first problem for the court in this case was the issue of whether continued life was a harm suffered by the patient. On this issue the court found that life was not a compensable injury as the court could not weigh the relative benefits of being versus non-being and nor could a jury place a price tag on the benefits of life.[58] Furthermore, it was said that there are some mistakes and technical assaults for which there should be no monetary compensation.[59]

The court also refused to find that the continuation of the patient's life was the cause of his stroke. The mere fact that the patient continued to live did not mean that further injuries sustained by the patient were caused by his life.[60]

---

53 Ibid at 330.

54 Ibid at 338–339.

55 In addition to the cases below see *Benoy v Simons* 831 P 2d 167 (1992); *Allore v Flower Hospital* 699 NE 2d 560 (1997); *Estate of Taylor v Muncie Medical Investors LP* 727 NE 2d 466 (2000); *Furlong v Catholic Healthcare West* (unreported, Cal App, LEXIS 11667, 2004).

56 77 Ohio St 3d 82; 671 NE 2d 225 (1996).

57 Ibid at 83; Oddi, S, "The Tort of Interference with the Right to Die: the Wrongful Living Cause of Action" (1986) 75 *Georgetown Law Journal* 625; Knapp, W and Hamilton, F, "Wrongful Living: Resuscitation as Tortious Interference with a Patient's Right to Give Informed Refusal" (1992) 19 *NKy LR* 253; Kackelman, TJ, "Violation of an Individual's Right to Die: The Need for a Wrongful Living Cause of Action" (1996) 64 *University of Cincinnati Law Review* 1355; Malloy, SEW, "Beyond Misguided Paternalism: Resuscitating the Right to Refuse Medical Treatment" (1998) 33 *Wake Forest Law Review* 1035; Milani, A, "Better off Dead than Disabled? Should Courts Recognize a 'Wrongful Living' Cause of Action When Doctors Fail to Honor Patients" Advance Directives?" (1997) 54 *Washington & Lee Law Review* 149.

58 *Anderson v St Francis – St George Hospital* 77 Ohio St 3d 82 at 85; 671 NE 2d 225 (1996).

59 Ibid at 86.

60 Ibid at 86.

On pure battery grounds the patient had not suffered any physical harm (no tissue burns or broken skin nor, presumably, emotional distress). No consequential damages were therefore available and only nominal damages could be awarded.

What we can gauge from these debates is that advance directives will be difficult to enforce using traditional tort actions if a narrow view is taken of the damages suffered by the patient. Anderson's case exhibits a particularly narrow view of harm and causation, and it reflects a policy bias in favour of the sanctity of life ethic, similar to that shown in cases concerning the tort of wrongful life.[61] By stating that the life of the patient was not a recognisable harm, the judgment has the effect of filing down the teeth of the tort of battery, by leaving no option for enforcing the patient's own choice about how he valued his own life. The judgment ignores the fact that Mr Anderson did view his continued life as a harm and that, in all other aspects, the legal system recognised his right to make that choice. Even if one accepts the policy arguments against claims for wrongful life, those arguments are easy to distinguish from claims of wrongful resuscitation for one simple reason: claims for wrongful life are largely problematic because the foetus is unable to make and to voice choices about existence. In claims for wrongful resuscitation, the patient is able to make a choice and has communicated that choice effectively.

Further problems with the use of tortious enforcement mechanisms arise in those Australian jurisdictions where non-economic, aggravated and exemplary damages have been severely curtailed or removed.[62] In some jurisdictions statutory penalties apply and provide a realistic alternative, such as the statutory offence of medical trespass in Victoria.[63] But it is difficult to assess the effectiveness of this criminal law enforcement tool, because there is no record of anyone ever being prosecuted. In any event the general thrust of the statutory regimes is to provide immunities and protections to health professionals rather than penalties for non-compliance.[64] Given the lack of civil and criminal responses to breaches of advance directives, it could be argued that there is a real danger that the right to make an advance directive will become a right without a remedy.

---

61 See the discussion of Ipp JA in *Harriton v Stephens; Waller v James; Waller v Hoolahan* (2004) 59 NSWLR 694 at 731; affirmed by High Court [2006] HCA 15.

62 See, for example, *Civil Liability Act 2002* (NSW).

63 *Medical Treatment Act 1988* (Vic) s 6.

64 General immunities are provided in most regimes: *Powers of Attorney 1998* (Qld) ss 99–104; *Consent to Medical Treatment and Palliative Care Act 1995* (SA) s 16; *Medical Treatment Act 1988* (Vic) s 9(1); *Medical Treatment Act 1994* (ACT) s 22. Criminal and civil liability is abrogated in some jurisdictions by sections which state that the withdrawal or withholding of treatment in accordance with a statute is not the cause of death: *Consent to Medical Treatment and Palliative Care Act 1995* (SA) s 17(3)(b); *Natural Death Act 1988* (NT) s 6.

Institutional resistance to advance directives

Perhaps more worrying than the lack of effective enforcement regimes, is the institutional resistance that people face when they seek to employ advance directives in their health care.

This problem is without a doubt related to general ignorance about advance directives and their legal status. The Australian evidence indicates that advance directives are not generally known about, understood or commonly employed.[65] In a Queensland study it was found that a high proportion (more than 73 per cent) of the health professionals surveyed, including doctors, nurses and social workers, had heard of advance directives, but only 25 per cent of community members had heard of them.[66] Fewer than half of all the groups surveyed knew that the directives were accepted at law: such knowledge was reported by 48 per cent of doctors, 35 per cent of nurses, 45 per cent of social workers, and only 10 per cent of community members. Not surprisingly, this study also found that all groups said that lack of knowledge about advance directives was a major barrier to their adoption.

Research from the United States shows that there is general resistance on the part of health professionals to the use of advance directives, and to patient choice generally. The federal *Patient Self Determination Act 1990* required health care institutions to provide written information to each patient which outlined their rights to make advance directives and yet it has manifestly failed to raise the level of knowledge of or support for advance directives in health professionals.[67]

Similarly, the famously well-funded SUPPORT trial (Study to Understand Prognosis and Risks of Treatment) was also a failure.[68] SUPPORT sought to improve end-of-life decision-making and reduce the frequency of prolonged dying caused by mechanical intervention by increasing the level of patient-family involvement in decision-making. Nurse facilitators were used to provide advice and information as well as document patient and family preferences. At the end of five years, there was no noticeable improvement in the control of patients over their treatment.

---

65 See Nair, B, Kerridge, I, Dobson, A, McPhee, J and Saul, P, "Advance Care Planning in Residential Care" (2000) 30 *Australian & New Zealand Journal of Medicine* 339; Taylor, D, McD, Ugoni, AM, Cameron, PA and McNeill, JJ, "Advance Directives and Emergency Department Patients: Ownership Rates and Perceptions of Use" (2003) 33 *Internal Medicine Journal* 586.

66 Cartwright, AM, Williams, GM, Steinberg, MA and Najman, GM, *Community and Heath/ Allied Health Professionals' Attitudes to Euthanasia: What are the Driving Forces?* Report to the NHMRC, 2002.

67 For a discussion of the history of the *Patient Self Determination Act 1990*, see Rich, B, *Strange Bedfellows: How Medical Jurisprudence Has Influenced Medical Ethics and Medical Practice*, Kluwer Academic, New York, 2001, Ch 5.

68 SUPPORT Principle Investigators, "A controlled trial to improve care for seriously ill hospitalized patients – The Study to Understand Prognoses and Preferences for Outcomes and Risks of Treatment (SUPPORT)" (1995) 274 *Journal of the American Medical Association* 1591.

In Australia, there is also evidence that parts of the legal system are resistant to respecting patient choices via the use of advance directives, particularly at the level of guardianship bodies. For example in *Qumsieh v Guardianship and Administration Board*,[69] a female Jehovah's Witness had made a common law advance directive prior to giving birth in which she outlined her objection to blood products. She also had the hospital make notes of her objections. She haemorrhaged after giving birth and lapsed into unconsciousness. The hospital convinced her husband to ignore her wishes and both parties approached the Guardianship Board (now the Victorian Civil and Administration Tribunal) to have the husband appointed guardian for the purpose of giving consent to the transfusion. The board was not told of the woman's advance directive. Nor was the woman represented. After recovering, the woman sought judicial review of the decision to appoint a guardian. The trial judge dismissed the application and did not give reasons. She appealed that decision to the Victorian Court of Appeal. Again the woman's claims were dismissed. It was said that the issue was moot and that the court should not encourage further disagreement between the woman and her husband. As I have argued elsewhere, the entire episode represented a series of failures of the legal system to seriously deal with the obvious issues of Mrs Qumsieh's rights to refuse treatment and her rights to procedural fairness.[70]

More recent, but equally disturbing, is the case of *In AB (Application for Consent to Medical Treatment)*.[71] In this case, consent was given by the New South Wales Guardianship Tribunal for blood transfusions to be given to a man who had suffered a cerebellar haemorrhage. The man had converted to the Jehovah's Witness faith around 1995 to 1996 and had completed "no transfusion" cards every year since then up to 2003. The tribunal was shown a card completed in 2001 and the tribunal accepted that one had been signed in 2003. The patient's family were all Catholics and in favour of transfusion. The tribunal authorised a transfusion in spite of the valid advance directives.

The reasons provided by the tribunal are, with respect, rather strange and hard to reconcile with the established legal tests regarding competence and applicability of advance directives which are discussed above. A number of seemingly spurious or irrelevant factors were relied upon for questioning the seriousness of AB's advance directive. One factor considered by the tribunal was evidence that AB had drunk to excess on occasion, and for that reason there was "not the degree of close linkage with the Church and its teachings over a long period of time". Similarly strange was the acceptance of evidence that AB had

---

69 (1998) 14 VAR 46.
70 Stewart, C, "Advance Directives, the Right to Die and the Common Law: Recent Problems with Blood Transfusions" (1999) 23 *Melbourne University Law Review* 161; Stewart, C, "Qumsieh's case, Civil Liabilities and the Right to Refuse Medical Treatment" (2000) 8 *JLM* 56.
71 Unreported, NSWGT, 2004/1867, 6 April 2004.

not objected to his grandchildren being baptised as Catholics. Finally, the tribunal took into account that the patient had already been given blood products by the treating doctor prior to the doctor being informed that AB was a Jehovah's Witness. The tribunal accepted that AB's fellow church members viewed further transfusions as a continued violation of his rights, but the tribunal seemed to view the strength of the family's position in favour of transfusion as an overriding reason for giving the order to transfuse.

Importantly, the patient had given some conflicting evidence as to whether he was consenting to blood transfusions by nodding. This is clearly important information in the assessment of whether the patient was now consenting to the treatment, and disavowing the directive. However, the tribunal appeared to accept that AB was not competent at the time he nodded, so it is difficult to understand how this evidence was weighed against the existence of a valid advance directive.

Throughout the decision the tribunal made reference to how it was for the tribunal to assess facts and take matters into account. It was stated that the "Tribunal does not go into all the details but simply indicates in a broad brush way the nature of the evidence". With respect, this is completely unacceptable. If the tribunal is unsure or unable to assess facts in a matter of substantial human rights, it should have immediately referred the decision to the New South Wales Supreme Court, which has the resources and experience to deal with evidential concerns.

One of the most disturbing features of the case is how the tribunal completely failed to treat the validity of the advance directive as a threshold issue relating to its jurisdiction. Arguably the tribunal had no jurisdiction to deal with the matter at all because Pt 5 of the *Guardianship Act* only applies to patients who cannot consent to treatment.[72] Mr AB had clearly refused treatment when competent on several occasions, as evidenced in his "no transfusions" cards. To that extent it could be argued that a decision had been made by a competent patient, leaving no room for the Guardianship Tribunal to step in. Unfortunately, instead of examining the validity of the advance directive, the entire matter was dealt with on the best interests model, which is a model normally employed in the absence of an advance directive.

Both *AB* and *Qumsieh* raise real questions about the ability of some guardianship tribunals to deal with the human rights issues raised by advance directives. Moreover they show that these systems have the potential to resist the use of advance directives in ways which do not accord with long-established legal principles.

---

72   *Guardianship Act 1987* (NSW) s 34(1)(b).

Can advance directives force doctors to provide treatment?

Recently, the common law of advance directives was considered in the context of the British *Human Rights Act 1998* (UK) in *R (on the application of Burke) v General Medical Council*.[73] Mr Burke suffered from spino-cerebellar ataxia, a condition which would eventually require him to receive artificial nutrition and hydration (AN&H). Burke was seeking judicial review of the General Medical Council's policy, *Withholding and Withdrawing Life-prolonging Treatments: Good Practice in Decision-making*. Burke believed the policy breached human rights principles because it did not recognise a patient's rights to make an advance directive *requesting* AN&H to be provided when he was no longer competent. Instead the policy focused solely on the right of a patient to *refuse* treatment, and in the absence of advance directives, the right of doctors to *withdraw* treatment. Burke argued that the policy allowed a doctor to withdraw AN&H from him when he became incompetent, even though he wished for it to be continued during his incompetence.

At trial Munby J accepted Burke's arguments that he had a right to use an advance directive to require AN&H in the future, during the period where he would be sensate, although incompetent, and up to the point that he became insensate (comatose). This right was primarily built upon Burke's rights to personal dignity and autonomy (Article 8), the prohibition on torture (Article 3) and his right to life (Article 2), under the *Human Rights Act*. Munby J believed that these rights would be offended by the withdrawal of AN&H because Mr Burke would be exposed to acute mental and physical suffering. Once in a coma, AN&H could be considered as futile because it would not serve any purpose apart from the very short prolongation of life. In that situation it would not breach the afore-mentioned articles for it to be withdrawn presumably because he would be insensate and not able to feel distress or pain.

Munby J found that another argument supporting Burke concerned the "best interests" test. In the absence of an advance directive doctors would have made an assessment of Burke's best interests as to whether AN&H should be provided. Munby J stated that if a patient has an advance directive, the directive determines the best interests of the patient.[74] Burke's advance directive requiring treatment was therefore conclusive of the issue of whether AN&H was in his best interests.

Munby J's decision was unanimously overturned by the Court of Appeal. The Court of Appeal was critical of the way Munby J had taken up a number of wide-ranging questions which were not pertinent to the particular issue at bar. The court felt that the judgment was premature in many aspects because Mr Burke was

---

73   [2005] EWCA Civ 1003.
74   Ibid at [116].

competent and would remain so for some time, and there was no evidence that AN&H would be withdrawn from Mr Burke in the future.

The Court of Appeal did not accept a number of Munby J's findings. The most relevant to the current discussion was the notion that Mr Burke could demand AN&H be provided to him via an advance directive. The court dismissed this proposition saying that it would be contrary to common law principles and the *Mental Capacity Act 2005* (UK). The court stated that at common law the doctor's duty was to provide a range of treatment options. If the patient sought another treatment which the doctor believed was not clinically indicated he or she was not under a legal duty to provide it.[75]

Could a patient in Australia use an advance directive to force doctors to provide treatment? That would seem unlikely given that *Burke* quite clearly states a doctor's duty is to provide a range of treatment options based on his or her clinical judgment. In Australia (as in the United Kingdom) there are generally no positive rights which could force a doctor to provide a treatment which they did not believe was appropriate to provide. The only examples of where this has occurred are where the decision not to provide infertility treatment has breached anti-discrimination provisions (such as the *Sex Discrimination Act 1984* (Cth)[76]), or where an incorrect assessment has been made as to the patient's diagnosis and prognosis resulting in flawed conclusions about futility and the patient's best interests.[77]

Conclusion

The right to make an advance directive is firmly built on the bedrock of common law, and supported by numerous legislative frameworks. Advance directives should be understood as another tool for patients in the exercise of their autonomy. They are one of a number of existing mechanisms, which have the purpose of improving decision-making at the end-of-life.

Unfortunately, as this chapter has shown, there appears to be a number of barriers to their adoption, foremost of which appears to be a culture of ignorance in both the health and legal professions. Do we need further regulation to improve the efficacy of advance directives?

My own view is that further regulation is a necessary but not a sufficient condition for successful use of advance directives. The fact that a jurisdiction adopts a statutory form of advance directive is not a solution to the availability and enforceability of these decisions, as *Qumsieh's* case rightly shows. However, the absence of statutory mechanisms may account for the ignorance of the New

---

75   Ibid at [50]–[57].

76   *Pearce v South Australian Health Commission* (1996) 66 SASR 486; *McBain v State of Victoria* (2000) 99 FCR 116; *Re McBain; Ex parte Australian Catholic Bishops Conference* (2002) 209 CLR 372.

77   *Northridge v Central Sydney Area Health Service* [2000] NSWSC 1241.

South Wales Guardianship Tribunal in *AB's* case. In the end, the law can only provide a framework within which a culture of advance care directives can grow. No amount of regulatory mechanisms will work unless health professionals begin to see advance directives as part of the ordinary steps they take to ensure that the patient's wishes are carried out. Equally important is the education of the public so that they see advance directives as an ordinary part of their care. If this happens, the combination of a culture of planning ahead and solid enforcement controls should lead to more successful outcomes. It may prove that even in such a culture, advance directives are still not widely employed. But at the very least patients will know that if they do exercise their rights via an advance directive, those rights will be respected.

4

Competency issues for young persons and older persons

John Devereux and Malcolm Parker

Introduction

Competency is a key concept in both bioethics and law, and a matter of considerable controversy, particularly where the subjects of the competency determination are either the young or the elderly. This chapter explores some current issues involving competency. In the first section we examine competency's ethical and legal functions. In the second section we attempt to clarify some of the conceptual confusions involving competency, and we also scrutinise some recently proposed alternative models. In the final section of the chapter, we highlight on-going controversies involving children and the elderly.

We argue that the major competency issues in respect of children are legal definitional issues; that is, what the law requires for a young person to be competent. The major issues in respect of adults (especially elderly adults) are less definitional disputes than difficulties concerned with operationalising the legal definitions through the use of appropriate tests by health professionals.

Our aim is not to provide an exhaustive coverage of the area, and the chapter is no substitute for professional legal and medical advice in the event that particular competency issues arise in practice. However, the chapter provides an overview of the more prominent, currently debated issues.

Ethical and legal functions of competency

Role of competency

A study of the role something plays often betrays its nature. One of the roles of a teacher is to impart knowledge to students. The nature of a teacher is thus, in part, an information imparter. What is the role, and consequently the nature, of competency?

Broadly speaking, competency operates as a "gatekeeper". Competency tells us which bioethical principle, respect for autonomy or beneficence, should take precedence in any particular patient's case. Respect for autonomy is the idea that every rational person should be able to decide matters for him or herself. Thus respect for autonomy decrees that a person should be free to decide how to spend his or her own money (on clothes, on gambling or on a loved one). In medical settings, respect for autonomy means allowing patients to make their own choices whether to undergo certain treatments or not.

Beneficence, broadly speaking, is the principle of ensuring the optimal medical outcome for the patient – "doing what is best" in a medical sense.

Autonomy and beneficence often happily co-exist. If a patient consults a doctor, receives medical advice and decides to undergo the recommended treatment, the principles of respect for autonomy and beneficence operate in harmony. The doctor's preference for promoting the well-being of his or her patient (beneficence) does not conflict with the patient's free choice in adopting the treatment (autonomy). Problems may arise when a doctor prefers a certain treatment option in order to promote the health or well-being of a patient, whereas the patient prefers not to undergo treatment.

Competency solves the impasse. A competent patient will have his or her autonomy respected. Incompetent patients may have treatment, which is in their best interests, imposed upon them. As Lord Donaldson, Master of the Rolls, put it, "[t]he right to decide one's own fate presupposes a capacity to do so".[1] Incompetent patients will find that beneficence overrides respect for autonomy, unless, when competent, they had declared their wishes for future care by writing an advance health directive, appointed an attorney to speak on their behalf, or even discussed their general views concerning medical treatment under different circumstances with their loved ones. Competency and its consequent rights can thus be extended into the future.

Legal function of competency

At a legal level, competency again functions as a gatekeeper. It is trite learning to state that any person who has force applied to him or her by another, in circumstances where that first person has not given consent for such intervention, will have an action in battery. This applies equally in the case of bar brawls, unsolicited kisses or medical treatment. A valid consent will operate as a good defence to a battery. What then is a valid consent? A consent is valid if, and only if, it meets three criteria:[2]

(a) it must be given by someone of sufficient capacity;

(b) it must be given by someone who has been given sufficient information to make the decision; and

(c) the decision must be voluntary.

The third element is easily understood. A patient who is drugged when giving consent,[3] or who is forced to consent,[4] is not giving a voluntary consent.

---

1   *Re T* [1993] Fam 95 at 112 per Lord Donaldson.
2   Jones, M, *Medical Negligence*, Sweet & Maxwell, London, 1991 p 209.
3   *Beausoleil v Sisters of Charity* (1964) 53 DLR (2d) 65.
4   *Freeman v Home Office (No 2)* [1984] QB 524.

The next question which arises is, what type of information needs to be understood by a patient? What is required to be understood to be competent? Cases have established that the patient need only understand "in broad terms, the nature of any procedure proposed to be performed upon them".[5]

What then is the nature of the procedure? At the very minimum, it includes information about the physical contact which is likely to occur if the procedure is carried out. Ignorance of the general nature of what is to occur precludes consenting to it, so lack of general information is sufficient for battery. Is a knowledge of the risk attendant to the procedure also necessary before a patient can be said to have given a valid consent? Courts, both in Australia and in England, have answered this question in the negative.

In *Chatterton v Gerson*,[6] a woman suffered post-operative pain in the region of a scar. Her specialist advised her to undergo an intrathecal block, which would block the pain messages from the region. The procedure was competently performed, but the woman's pain became much worse – so much so that she could not bear anything but the lightest of fabrics in contact with the affected area. She sued her specialist in battery and negligence. In relation to the battery allegation, Mrs Chatterton argued that, because her specialist had not informed her of the risks of the procedure, she had not given a valid consent to what otherwise amounted to a battery.

In rejecting Mrs Chatterton's claim for battery, Bristow J said that once a patient was informed in broad terms of the nature of the procedure, and gave her consent, then the patient could not complain that a battery had been committed. Any allegation that the patient should have been informed of the risks of a procedure went to a question of negligence, and not battery. This view was followed by the High Court of Australia in *Rogers v Whitaker*.[7] It follows that a patient need not be informed of (nor understand) the risks of a procedure, in order to give valid consent to treatment.

Although the risks inherent in a procedure are not, then, relevant to the validity of consent, the concept of risks may be relevant in another way. Sometimes in the literature, the term "risk" refers to the outcome of making a "correct" or "incorrect" treatment decision. So, if a patient were to decline treatment, and a risk of death follows – the treatment decision is said to be more risky than where there is no risk of death following an "incorrect" treatment decision. There have been arguments that the more serious the decision to be undertaken, the higher the degree of competency required. This is referred to as a sliding-scale of competency. The debate as to whether competency is a sliding-scale or a threshold question will explored more fully in the next section.

---

5   *Rogers v Whitaker* (1993) 175 CLR 479 at 484.
6   [1981] QB 432.
7   (1992) 175 CLR 479.

Definitions, distractions and debates

Traditional concepts

The terms competency and capacity are frequently used interchangeably by both health and legal professionals. Strictly speaking, competency refers to the legal concept, while decision-making capacity is assessed by health professionals, with these assessments forming the basis of medical advice and recommendations concerning legal competency.[8]

The legal notion of competency has developed consistently in the direction of a functional concept, by which a person's understanding, in relation to the task at hand, is preferred to either a status approach[9] or a focus on the outcome of decisions.[10] This reflects the law's support for individual self-determination and flexibility,[11] rather than rigidly distinguishing the competent from the incompetent according to age, diagnostic status (for example, presence of mental illness), or conformity with some objective standard of medical best interests.

Nevertheless, it could also be said that, in practice, a positive, quasi-status approach operates through the presumption of competency, also strongly supported in law.[12] The presumption of competency maximises freedom and self-determination, and also increases efficiency, since it obviates the need to perform competency assessments on most patients, who are clearly "alert and oriented".[13] A more explicit recognition that the presumption of competency amounts to an initial status approach could provide a better balance between preventing false positive attributions of competency and protecting individual freedom,[14] by

---

8 Collier, B, Coyne, C and Sullivan, K (eds), *Mental Capacity: Powers of Attorney and Advance Health Directives*, Federation Press, Sydney, 2005, p 165.

9 Kennedy, I and Grubb, A, *Medical Law: Text with Materials*, 2nd edn, Butterworths, London, 1994, p 107.

10 United Kingdom Law Reform Commission, *Mental Incapacity*, Report No 231, 1995, para 3.4.

11 Kennedy and Grubb (1994) op cit.

12 Both the common law and numerous statutes explicitly presume the capacity of adults. For example, in *Re C (Refusal of Medical Treatment)* [1994] 1 FLR 31 at 35, Thorpe J said: "Prima Facie every adult has the right and capacity to decide whether or not he will accept medical treatment, even if a refusal may risk permanent injury to his health or even lead to premature death". In Queensland's *Mental Health Act 2000* (Qld) s 8(b) requires that "to the greatest extent practicable, a person is to be encouraged to take part in making decisions affecting the person's life, especially decisions about treatment; to the greatest extent practicable, in making a decision about a person, the person's views and the effect on his or her family or carers are to be taken into account; a person is presumed to have capacity to make decisions about the person's assessment, treatment and choosing of an allied person. Queensland's *Powers of Attorney Act 1998* (Qld) and *Guardianship and Adminis-tration Act 2000* (Qld) subject a number of their provisions to the following statement in their schedules; namely "An adult is presumed to have capacity for a matter": Sch 1, Pt 1.1 in both Acts.

13 Wear, S, " Informed Consent" in Khushf, G (ed), *Handbook of Bioethics: Taking Stock of the Field from a Philosophical Perspective*, Kluwer Academic Publishers, Dordrecht 2004, p 276. Wong, JG, Clare, ICH, Gunn, MG and Holland, AJ, "Capacity to Make Health Care Decisions: its Importance in Clinical Practice" (1999) 29 *Psychological Medicine* 437 at 439.

14 Wear (2004) ibid p 277.

facilitating systematic approaches to what should *trigger* an assessment of competency on the one hand, and what should *constitute* the assessment, on the other.[15] A positive status approach is easily distinguished from the negative form (above), which the law has rejected.[16]

Once an assessment is appropriately triggered, the functional approach, which aims to determine whether the patient understands, in broad terms, the nature of the proposed treatment, is generally strongly supported. There has been some discussion, however, as to whether understanding refers to actual understanding or the ability to understand. The ability formulation arguably protects those whose doctors may provide insufficient information for decision-making, and who may be judged, because of that, to be incompetent. The ability formulation rightly emphasises that competency is located *within* the patient. However, given adequate disclosure, the two formulations are equivalent. While it is important to explicitly distinguish the notions of competency and disclosure (see below), actual understanding is to be preferred, if we accept that competency is task-specific. Stewart and Biegler have also pointed out that, although some case law supports the ability formulation, there is stronger support in the cases for a test of actual understanding, and that the ability formulation amounts to a minimal competency standard which could operate similarly to a negative status approach, and define some people who have adequate understanding in a specific context as incompetent.[17]

Conceptual confusions

The consensus on the actual understanding formulation may be the source of some confusion, due to the separate though overlapping and related elements which constitute it. The following abilities are generally agreed to be required for competency: (a) receive, understand, retain and recall relevant information; (b) integrate the information received and relate it to one's situation; (c) evaluate benefits and risks in terms of personal values; (d) rationally manipulate the information in order to select an option, and give cogent reasons for the choice; (e) communicate one's choice to others; and (f) persevere with the choice until the decision is acted upon.[18]

The *concept* of capacity is sometimes taken to include the provision or existence of adequate information, rather than the information being a *requirement* for adequate deliberation in the particular context. Absent sufficient information, I cannot decide properly, and this is interpreted as incapacity. Competency can also

15 Ibid p 280. Cockerill, J, Collier, B and Maxwell, K, "Legal Requirements and Current Practices" in Collier, Coyne and Sullivan (2005) op cit pp 39–41.

16 Stewart, C and Biegler, P, "A Primer on the Law of Competence to Refuse Medical Treatment" (2004) 78 *ALJ* 325 at 326.

17 Ibid at 328–329.

18 Wong et al, (1999) op cit at 440. See also Kerridge, I, Lowe, M and McPhee, J, *Ethics and Law for the Health Professions*, 2nd edn, Federation Press, Sydney, 2005, pp 175–176.

be conflated with voluntariness of decision-making. Again, a distinct requirement for legally valid decision-making – voluntariness – is taken to be an element of another requirement – competency. This error has even been included in legislation. For example, Queensland's *Powers of Attorney Act 1998* and *Guardianship and Administration Act 2000* both define capacity (for a person for a matter) as meaning that the person is capable of: (a) understanding the nature and effect of decisions about the matter; (b) freely and voluntarily making decisions about the matter; and (c) communicating the decision in some way.[19] It is, however, understandable that competency and voluntariness are sometimes treated together, since checking for evidence that an individual is competent will sometimes raise questions about whether the person was coerced.[20]

The mere expression of a choice, while necessary for a judgment of competency, is certainly not sufficient,[21] since it may be an impulsive or ill-considered expression. On the other hand, the inclusion of communication in the concept of competency may sometimes result in an excessively rigid interpretation, such as in cases where unusual and unfamiliar forms of expression result from physical limitations. Later in this chapter we discuss a Queensland case where medical specialists came to different conclusions regarding a patient's competency, and where this was partly explained by unfamiliarity with his mode of communication.

Some of these examples may appear to be unimportant. However, we suggest that unless the fundamental concept of competency is clarified and delimited, appropriate roles may be misunderstood, and people may either be put at risk of abandonment to a false competency, or be prevented from exercising a genuine one.

Threshold or degree?

It is intuitively appealing to think of decision-making capacity as occurring in degrees, given that in everyday life, we rank different people's skills at common tasks, and rank one person's skills on the same task at different times. It is natural to think that different people will also have different capabilities in relation to a given decision-task, and that a person's capacity in relation to a given decision-task will vary according to circumstances. The degree concept also seems to be consistent with different tests of competency (see below). Now, even if a degree concept is coherent, it must somehow be translated into a threshold judgment when a court decides whether a person is competent *or not*.[22] However, we consider that the notion of degrees of competency is itself incoherent.

---

19 *Powers of Attorney Act 1998* (Qld) Sch 3; *Guardianship and Administration Act 2000* (Qld) Sch 4, <www.legislation.qld.gov.au/legisltn/current/p/powersofatta98.pdf> (accessed 20 August 2005) and <www.legislation.qld.gov.au/legisltn/current/g/GuardAdminA00.pdf> (accessed 20 August 2005).

20 Stewart and Biegler (2004) op cit at 335.

21 Wong et al (1999) op cit at 440.

22 Sullivan, K, "Measuring Mental Capacity: Models, Methods and Tests", in Collier, Coyne and Sullivan (2005) op cit pp 109–110.

Some writers have suggested the need for subcategories of competence such as "adequate", "marginal" and "inadequate",[23] "borderline-competent" or "competent in area x".[24] The idea of being competent in one area but not in another seems straightforward, but just what can be made of ideas like marginal or borderline competency?

White defines a marginally competent person as someone who "can usually, with on-going assistance, come to a conclusion that will (probably) promote her well-being",[25] where the assistance includes reminders of information, identification and organisation of information, indications of the importance of information in order to understand it, help in correlating information to values, and where the person is unlikely to be able to project him or herself into the future, and to weigh burdens or benefits. Given that White defines competency in similar terms to the sequence of abilities given at p 6, this account of marginal competency surely collapses into one of incompetence. This is not to say that people whose competency is in question cannot be assisted to understand information and deliberate about it. (The clearest case here is treatment of an illness which is causing the person to temporarily lack capacity.) But once a person is rendered competent, White's various kinds of assistance become redundant.

Furthermore, the degree concept demands the insertion of thresholds to be of any use – in practice, the degree concept will look like the threshold concept, since someone must eventually decide what degree of understanding is sufficient for competency. But even this idea is problematic. It is certainly the case that a higher degree of understanding will be required to assess and decide about a *complex* procedure, (ie competence is decision-relative,[26]) such that some people will be competent and others incompetent in relation to it. However, this does not amount to saying that competency is a matter of degree. In relation to a particular procedure, we agree with Stewart and Biegler that people will either be competent or incompetent.[27]

Competency in relation to outcome risk

The difference between decision-relativity and a degree or sliding scale approach to competency is illustrated in the controversy concerning the risk-related standard of competency attribution. According to supporters of a risk-related standard, patients should be held to a higher standard of competency in cases where the risks of, say, refusing a treatment, are high, sometimes including death.[28] It is not

23   White, BC, *Competence to Consent*, Georgetown University Press, Washington, 1994.
24   Sullivan (2005) op cit p 110.
25   White (1994) op cit p 155.
26   Berghmans, R, Dickenson, D and Ter Meulen, R, "Mental Capacity: In Search of Alternative Perspectives" (2004) 12(4) *Health Care Analysis* 251 at 253.
27   Stewart and Biegler (2004) op cit at 333.
28   Roth, L, Meisel, A and Lidz, C, "Tests of Competency to Consent to Treatment" (1977) 134 *American Journal of Psychiatry* 279.

surprising that health professionals, who must "attempt to balance the competing principles of autonomy and beneficence",[29] are attracted to an outcome risk-related standard.[30] Bioethicists, too, such as Alan Buchanan and Dan Brock, initially through their influential text *Deciding for Others: The Ethics of Surrogate Decision Making*,[31] have supported an outcome risk-related standard. The standard has been attacked by Wicclair,[32] on the grounds that it implies that a prior assessment of justified paternalism *constitutes* part of the competency determination, whereas these things are clearly independent, and that the standard implies an incoherent asymmetry in competency, whereby a person could be held competent to *consent* to beneficial, life-saving treatment, but incompetent to *refuse* it. Standards of understanding and reasoning would arguably be set at unreasonably high levels by those who were motivated by a belief in justified paternalism in high-risk situations, and this is certainly borne out by paternalistic claims like the following:

> It is reasonable for persons to want their self-determination respected when there is little or no harm that will come to them from others doing so, but it is also reasonable to place limits on the sacrifice in their own well-being that they will accept in order to have their own impaired choice accepted.[33]

Other criticisms point out that the outcome risk-related standard conflates the determination of competency and the normative evaluation of outcome.[34] These criticisms appear to be consistent with the law's insistence on a procedural rather than a substantive standard for competency determination. For example, Butler-Sloss P stated in *Re B (Adult: refusal of medical treatment)*:

> If there are difficulties in deciding whether the patient has sufficient mental capacity, particularly if the refusal may have grave consequences for the patient, it is most important that those considering the issue should not confuse the question of mental capacity with the nature of the decision made by the patient, however grave the consequences. The view of the patient may reflect a difference in values rather than an absence of competence and the assessment of capacity should be approached with this firmly in mind. The doctors must not allow their emotional reaction to or strong disagreement with the decision of the patient to cloud their judgment in answering the primary question whether the patient has the mental capacity to make the decision.[35]

---

29 Youngner, S, "Bureaucratizing Suicide" (2000) 6 *Psychology, Public Policy and Law* 402.

30 Strang, D, Molloy, DW and Harrison, C, "Capacity to Choose Place of Residence: Autonomy vs Beneficence?" (1998) 14 *Journal of Palliative Care* 25. Werth, JL, "Requests for Physician-Assisted Death: Guidelines for Assessing Mental Capacity and Impaired Judgment" (2000) 6 *Psychology, Public Policy and Law* 348.

31 Buchanan, AE and Brock, DW, *Deciding for Others: The Ethics of Surrogate Decision-Making*, Cambridge University Press, Cambridge, 1989.

32 Wicclair, M, "Patient Decision-Making Capacity and Risk" (1991) 5 *Bioethics* 91.

33 Brock, DW, "Decision-Making Competence and Risk" (1991) 5 *Bioethics* 105 at 112.

34 Cale, G, "Continuing the Debate Over Risk-Related Standards of Competence" (1999) 13 *Bioethics* 131. Checkland, D, "On Risk and Decisional Capacity" (2001) 26 *Journal of Medicine & Philosophy* 35

35 [2002] 2 All ER 449 at 474.

However, we suggest that distinguishing between doctors' and patients' values does not explicitly rule out the outcome risk-related standard; and previous judgments, for example Lord Donaldson's following statement, appear to support the standard:

> What matters is that the doctors should consider whether at [the relevant time] he [the patient] had a capacity which was commensurate with the gravity of the decision which he purported to make. The more serious the decision, the greater the capacity required.[36]

Lord Donaldson's statements have been interpreted to mean that in life-threatening conditions, greater *scrutiny* of the presence of capacity should be undertaken.[37] But however much we might wish to interpret it this way, the wording explicitly refers to capacity itself, and we suggest this reflects a common understanding between the law and clinical practice about the required relation between competency and outcome risk. We further suggest that if the belief in what amounts to an incoherent notion[38] is maintained in both clinical practice and the law, the effect may well be to declare some competent people incompetent, due to a less than scrupulous concern to positively demonstrate incompetence.[39]

Cognitive-rational or hermeneutic-narrative?

A recent challenge to "mainstream" conceptualisations of competency and its assessment supports an enrichment of theory and practice through considering the contributions of hermeneutics, narrative and feminist philosophical traditions.[40] This development accords with recent departures from the perceived dominance of an autonomy-rationality model in Western bioethics, seeing it as paying insufficient attention to context, motivation and meaning, and as unnecessarily confined to cognition. One of the motivations for this development of alternative conceptions is that a narrowly cognitive approach may tend to discriminate against those

---

36 *Re T (Adult: Refusal of Treatment)* [1993] Fam 95 at 113 per Lord Donaldson. Lord Donaldson also stated (at 115–116):

> Doctors faced with a refusal of consent have to give very careful and detailed consideration to what was the patient's capacity to decide at the time when the decision was made. It may not be a case of capacity or no capacity. It may be a case of reduced capacity. What matters is whether at that time the patient's capacity was reduced below the level needed in the case of a refusal of that importance, for refusals can vary in importance. Some may involve a risk to life or of irreparable damage to health. Others may not.

This strongly suggests a sliding scale of capacity in proportion to the risk of refusal of treatment.

37 Stewart and Biegler (2004) op cit at 333.

38 In addition to the arguments against the degree concepts of capacity in the previous section, see Parker, M, "Judging Capacity: Paternalism and the Risk-Related Standard" (2004) 11 *Journal of Law and Medicine* 482. The author argues against degree and risk-related concepts in terms of the constitutive and overlapping elements of competency attribution, the distinction between risk level and complexity, and the problem of deciding under variable conditions of ignorance.

39 This point is also applied in subsequent sections.

40 Berghmans, Dickenson and Ter Meulen (2004) op cit at 252.

whose lives are cognitively affected, such as those with neurodegenerative diseases and mental illnesses.[41] It is also claimed that a rationalist model of decision-making is not consistent with the way in which we make decisions from day to day, because we decide and act according to a range of emotions, intuitions and values, which are often not conscious.[42] Consistency and rationality are necessary, but far from sufficient components of competency, on this view, and proponents of a broader conception urge research into personal constructs and values, biographical, social and contextual factors, and how these may be evaluated "as objectively as possible".[43]

Hermeneutics allegedly helps us to reach a different appreciation of competency. Benaroyo and Widdershoven suggest that it is "not primarily a matter of being able to reason, but of being able to interpret the world and respond to it".[44] Accordingly, people are competent if they can understand the world, give meaning to the situation, find their way round in the world, and orient themselves in order to know what to do.[45] When this is not the case, it should not be a matter of measuring incompetence, but of helping people to develop or regain it:

> From a hermeneutic perspective, assessing this patient's capacity entails then a personal and institutional commitment to identifying and establishing conditions that encourage him to face the adversity and threats to self inevitable as a result of the disability and illness. Assessing his capacity requires attending to those things with which he can truly and significantly identify, even when identification is difficult to assess. Patients frequently respond, albeit minimally and in deficient ways, to direct contact with caregivers and others.[46]

These newer, broader approaches have not yet been developed at a level sufficient for application.[47] But we also question whether they could ever fulfil the promise claimed by their supporters. The fact that we act on the basis of emotions, intuitions, values, and biographical, social and contextual factors, does not make it the case that when we are faced with important decisions, such as those affecting our health, we do not step back and at least attempt to rationally deliberate about what we want to do, and here we understand rationality to mean the employment of good reasons. The model of rational decision-making which has attracted considerable "mainstream" consensus includes the appreciation of *relevant* information, relating the information to *one's situation*, and the evaluation of risks and benefits *in*

---

41   Ibid at 257–258.
42   Breden, TM and Vollmann, J, "The Cognitive Based Approach of Capacity Assessment in Psychiatry: A Philosophical Critique of the MacCAT-T" (2004) 12 *Health Care Analysis* 273 at 276–277.
43   Ibid at 280–281.
44   Benaroyo, L and Widdershoven, G, "Competence in Mental Health Care: A Hermeneutic Perspective" (2004) 12 *Health Care Analysis* 295 at 298.
45   Ibid.
46   Ibid at 303.
47   Nys, H, Welie, S, Garanis-Papadatos, T and Ploumpidis, D, "Patient Capacity in Mental Health Care: Legal Overview" (2004) 12 *Health Care Analysis* 329 at 336.

terms of personal values. This would seem to accommodate a considerable range of those things which supporters of these newer approaches claim are missing from the mainstream view. We suggest that attention would be better paid to educating clinicians to take into account a comprehensive definition of competency in their assessments, such as the one above, than to developing an ostensibly different understanding.

Stipulations that our focus should be on helping people to develop or regain competence rather than measuring or assessing it, miss the point, because assessing and restoring competence are important and related, but distinguishable tasks. Indeed, if these issues are not distinguished, and acted upon as distinct obligations, we may fail to fully protect some vulnerable people, by thinking that our efforts to enhance competence have established it. We can only promote or restore a person's competency *after* we have judged that it is in question. If emotional and psychological maturity are seen as necessary for competency,[48] we require an account of how far they take us beyond the conventional "cognitive" account, and what judging a person incompetent on a basis which explicitly includes them, would amount to. Finally, how are values, biographical factors, social and contextual factors, to be evaluated *objectively*, so as to make distinctions between those who are competent, and who consequently must be respected as independent decision-makers, and those who are not?

These difficulties do not rule out the emotions as crucial elements in competency. The emotions are an important part of people's responses, operating to reveal the significance and meaning of situations, and to develop and modify their preferences.[49] The emotions feed into the background of values against which we deliberate and decide things, and as such they are legitimate factors in ratio-cination. Again, however, if the emotions do play a role in the selection of information and the evaluative appraisal of situations, this means that they help constitute rational manipulation, rather than call it into question as an excessively narrow process.

Continuing issues for children and adults

Children and competency

Disputes between children and their parents about how best to proceed in life are far from new. As the law moves away from status-based approaches to functional ones, the cutting edge of the debate has been the child–parent interaction. Parents are, understandably, concerned to ensure that their children are protected from the consequences of rash decision-making in life-changing circumstances. Adolescents,

---

48 Berghmans, Dickenson and Ter Meulen (2004) op cit at 261.

49 Van Leeuwen, E and Vellinga, A, "Knowing Well Or Living Well: Is Competence Relevant to Moral Experience and Capacity in Clinical Decision-Making?" in Thomasma, D and Weisstub, D (eds), *The Variables of Moral Capacity*, Kluwer, Dordrecht, 2004, pp 196–197.

on the other hand, are concerned to exercise their right to make decisions about their own body, and about pursuing their own interests.

Given the inevitability of the conflict, it is surprising that the law on children's competency remains considerably uncertain. The uncertainty has only been partly ameliorated by the development of some "woolly" common law formulations of what amounts to child competency. Much remains difficult.

The question of consent to medical treatment for a child has been the subject of 1996 and 2004 Law Reform Commission Reports.[50] In all States except New South Wales and South Australia, the law regulating competency is common law (that is, judge-made law). In New South Wales and South Australia, statutes govern the question.

Competency at common law

The High Court of Australia in *Secretary, Department of Health and Community Services v JWB and SMB (Marion's* case)[51] considered the law in Australia in a case where the parents of a 14-year-old girl with severe intellectual and physical disabilities sought authorisation for a sterilisation operation to be performed on her. The court was concerned with the question of whether the girl's parents could give consent for a sterilisation procedure, or whether only a court could give such an authorisation. The High Court noted:

> The common law in Australia has been uncertain as to whether minors under sixteen can consent to medical treatment in any circumstances. However, the recent House of Lords decision in *Gillick v West Norfolk AHA* is of persuasive authority. The proposition endorsed by the majority in that case was that parental power to consent to medical treatment on behalf of a child diminishes gradually as the child's capacities and maturities grow and that this rate of development depends on the individual child ... A minor is, according to this principle, capable of giving informed consent when he or she "achieves a sufficient understanding and intelligence to enable him or her to understand fully what is proposed". This approach, though lacking the certainty of a fixed age rule, accords with experience and with psychology. It should be followed in this country as part of the common law.[52]

There are some procedures which the High Court regarded as being so serious that even the parent(s) could not validly consent to them. These were procedures which involved:

(a) Invasive, irreversible and major surgery where there is a significant risk of making the wrong decision, either as to the child's present or future capacity to consent or about what are the best interests of a child who cannot consent and

(b) where the consequences of a wrong decision are particularly grave.

---

50   New South Wales Law Reform Commission, *Minor's Consent to Medical Treatment*, Issues Paper No 24, NSWLRC, 2004; Queensland Law Reform Commission, *Consent to Medical Treatment of Young People*, Report No 51, QLRC, 1996.

51   (1992) 175 CLR 218.

52   Ibid at 237.

Such procedures include abortions,[53] sterilisations, the removal of life support, the removal of organs for transplants, gender re-assignment[54] and bone marrow harvest.[55] It should be remembered, however, that the focus of *Re Marion* was on incompetent minors, and that the court was recognising the ability of competent, or "mature" minors, to make their own decisions.

Remaining confusions and uncertainties in respect of the common law and children

The first difficulty in this area relates to the definition of child competency as requiring "understanding fully" the nature and consequences of treatment. Understanding fully is quite different from the adult test – "understanding in broad terms". As Nicholson CJ notes in *Re Alex*:

> It is one thing for a child or young person to have a general understanding of what is proposed and its effect but it is quite another to conclude that he or she has sufficient maturity to full understand the grave nature and effects of the proposed treatment.[56]

Why does the law not simply apply the same tests of competence as that which is used for adults? It is not clear precisely what amounts to sufficient intelligence and maturity – the threshold a child must reach before he or she can consent to his or her own treatment. Does it, for example, include complex moral and family issues associated with some treatments, as suggested by one of the Law Lords in *Gillick's* case?

More troublesome is the question of whether the child's competency to consent includes the competency to refuse treatment.

The English Court of Appeal, in two cases, *Re R*[57] and *Re W*,[58] thought not. The court in those cases held that no child has the power to refuse health care so as to override a consent given by someone with parental responsibility or a court. In the former case, the patient in question was a ward of the local authority, suffering from recurring psychotic states. While in a calm state, she convinced a social worker from the local authority that she no longer wished to take her medication. In the latter case, the patient who was in the care of the local authority, suffered from anorexia and did not want treatment that was indicated for her. Only McHugh J of the High Court addressed the question of refusal of treatment in *Re Marion*.[59] His Honour suggested that *Re R* should not be followed. In the recent

---

53   Ibid at 317 per McHugh J.
54   See *Re Alex* (2004) 31 Fam LR 503. The Queensland Law Reform Commission suggested this procedure, plus the two proceeding it: see Queensland Law Reform Commission (1996) op cit p 61.
55   *Re GWW and GMW* (1997) FLC ¶92-747; 21 Fam LR 612.
56   *Re Alex* (2004) 31 Fam LR 503 at 531.
57   [1992] Fam 11.
58   [1993] Fam 64.
59   *Re Marion* (1992) 175 CLR 218 at 316–317.

Family Court decision of *Re Alex*,[60] Nicholson CJ, without deciding the issue, also cast doubt on the advisability of applying *Re R* and *Re W*.

Whether competency to consent includes competency to refuse is an important conceptual issue. If a child, however competent, may not validly refuse consent to treatment, then what has competency given the child?

Suppose a parent sits her child down and tells her "we think that you are sufficiently mature and responsible to make your own decisions. You may choose to stay out after 2 am if you wish". If the child chooses to come home before 2 am, would we think it rational that the parents get upset when she does so – and force her to stay out until after 2 am? Or, in a medical context, if a competent 15 year-old is pregnant but does not want an abortion, should that refusal to consent to the abortion be able to be overruled by her parents?

The cases, *Re R* and *Re W* involve difficult areas – anti-psychotic medication and anorexia. It is a well-known maxim of the law that hard cases make bad law. The words of Nicholson CJ seem apposite: "the circumstances in which a child or young person has the right to make his or her decisions as to medical treatment are far from precise".[61] In hard cases where the outcome risks for young people are high, it is arguable that the courts have tried to steer a middle course between a purely rational/technical competency and a more dispositional and reflective kind – one which young people have simply not had the life-experience to have developed.[62]

Transgender issues and the law

Australian courts have recently had to wrestle with another difficult fact situation – the question of adolescents who wish to undergo gender re-assignment treatment. The issues have been thoroughly considered by Scheuber and Parlett.[63]

In *Re A*,[64] the patient concerned was a genetic female with an extreme degree of masculinisation as a result of congenital adrenal hyperplasia. She had previously undergone genital reconstruction surgery and hormone therapy to make her appear more feminine. The medical treatment proved unsuccessful. A's mother brought an action in the Family Court seeking to have gender re-assignment surgery performed.

The Family Court, following *Marion*, noted that although A understood the problem and, in general, the proposed resolution to the problem, he did not have "sufficient capacity and maturity to fully appreciate the matter and to assess the options available to him".[65]

---

60   *Re Alex* (2004) 31 Fam LR 503 at 532.
61   Ibid at 529.
62   *Minister for Health v AS* [2004] WASC 286.
63   Scheuber, KM and Parlett, K, "Consent to Treatment for Transgender and Intersex Children" (2004) 9 (2) *Deakin Law Review* 375.
64   (1996) 16 Fam LR 715.
65   Ibid at 719.

Additionally, because the consequences of making the wrong decision for A were sufficiently grave, it followed that A's parents did not have capacity to consent to treatment. It followed that only the court had the authority to approve the procedure. In approving the procedure, the court focussed upon the extreme psychological harm which would occur to A if he did not have the procedure. It decided that the procedure was in A's best interests.

In *Re Alex*,[66] the challenge facing the court was somewhat different. Alex did not have "abnormal" sexual organs – rather she experienced gender identity dysphoria – a strong and persistent cross-gender identification. Alex's guardian made an application to the Family Court for approval of certain treatment which would have an irreversible effect on Alex's ovarian function and fertility, and would give Alex a masculine appearance. The treatment was not surgical in nature, but involved the prescription of hormonal treatment.

In considering whether Alex was competent to consent to treatment, the court noted that she understood in broad terms what was proposed, but that this was not the same as "sufficient maturity to fully understand the grave nature and effects of the proposed treatment". It followed that Alex was not competent.

In considering whether Alex's guardian could consent to treatment, the court noted that the High Court in *Re Marion* had referred to treatment for "malfunction or disease". The Family Court was not of the opinion that the treatment proposed for Alex did not fall within this rubric. Nonetheless, the nature of the treatment was such that it required court approval. The court was not persuaded that court authorisation was limited to circumstances where what was proposed was surgical intervention. The court decided to approve the application for consent to treatment, noting it was in Alex's best interests.

Questions remain. Scheuber and Parlett suggest that a reading of the court's decision in *Re Alex* "evidences more of a concern with the appropriateness of a thirteen-year-old being responsible for such a serious decision than a true inquiry into Alex's capacity to consent to medical treatment".[67] This seems to be a question of risk-outcome assessment which, it has been earlier argued, should not be relevant to competency determination. Alternatively, the common law in these cases could again be seen to have been attempting to hold the young people to a comprehensive definition of competency, in preference to "mere" understanding.

Statutory changes to the law

Competency of children in South Australia and New South Wales

The law on child consent to treatment in New South Wales is governed by s 49F of the *Minors (Property and Contracts) Act 1970* (NSW). Under that provision, a person who gives medical or dental treatment to a person under the age of 16 is protected from liability if a parent or guardian has consented. A practitioner who performs

---

66   (2004) 180 FLR 89.
67   Scheuber and Parlett (2004) op cit, at 387.

medical or dental treatment on a person 14 years' or older with the consent of that person is similarly protected from liability.

In South Australia, the *Consent to Medical Treatment and Palliative Care Act 1995* (SA) governs child consent to treatment. Section 6 of that Act provides that a person 16 years of age or older may make decisions about their own medical treatment as validly and effectively as an adult. Section 12 provides that treatment may be provided to a child if the parent or guardian consents or, if the child consents and:

(a) the medical practitioner is of the opinion that the child is capable of understanding the nature, consequences and risks of the treatment and that the treatment is in the best interests of the child's health and well being; and

(b) that opinion is supported by the written opinion of another medical practitioner who has examined the child.

There is obviously a lack of uniformity in the law governing the rights of young people to consent to medical treatment across Australia, and there would be clear benefits from a uniform national approach. This would not be easy, especially if the asymmetry between consent and refusal, based on outcome assessment and which we have argued against in the case of adults, were to be recognised at least in grave cases.

Competency and confidentiality

Whether a child patient is competent or not has sometimes been suggested to be irrelevant to the existence of an obligation of confidence owed by the practitioner to the patient. "The right to confidentiality exists independently of the competence to consent to treatment".[68] An alternative view links the obligation of confidentiality to the person being competent to participate in medical decision-making. In 1996, the Queensland Law Reform Commission endorsed the view that once a young person's competency is accepted, his or her confidentiality ought to be respected, on pain of inhibiting young people from seeking appropriate medical treatment.[69] The commission nevertheless declined to recommend specific legislative changes regarding confidentiality, on the grounds that any review of confidentiality should not be limited by age, and that restricting confidentiality to competent young people could disadvantage incompetent people inquiring about health care.[70]

Most recently it has become a possibility in Queensland that even competent children's rights to confidentiality may be threatened. A recent amendment to the *Health Services Act 1991* (Qld) (s 62C(b), (c) & (d)) allows disclosure of information relating to a child in *any* of three circumstances:

---

68 Larcher, V, "Consent, Competence and Confidentiality" (2005) *British Medical Journal* 353 at 354.

69 Queensland Law Reform Commission (1996) op cit p 147.

70 Ibid pp 346–347.

(1) If the child is judged by the health professional to be capable of understanding the nature of consenting to the disclosure, and the child consents to the disclosure;

(2) If the child is judged by the health professional to be incapable of understanding the nature of consenting to the disclosure, and the child's parent or guardian consents to the disclosure;

(3) If the health practitioner reasonably believes that disclosure is in the best interests of the child.

The apparent protection afforded in (1) is weakened, or even nullified, by the unconditional discretion given doctors in (3).[71] This change is motivated by the understandable difficulties parents encounter when, confronted by serious health problems affecting their children, they are prevented by the rules of confidentiality from participating fully in their care. Nevertheless, the proposal leaves open the possibility that idiosyncratic versions of young people's best interests may be used to rationalise disclosure. Interestingly, as the Act only covers public provision of health care, the uncertainty at common law would persist in respect of the private provision of medical treatment.

There is much to be clarified in respect of children, confidentiality and competency – mostly in the area of the legal definition of competency. In the next section, on-going issues in respect of adults will be discussed. The major issues in respect of adults (particularly elderly adults) are not so much in clarifying the legal definitions, but in terms of operationalising them.

Assessing the capacity of adults

Our ageing populations present not only logistic challenges for health and legal professionals in the area of competency assessment, but also moral challenges, given that assessment has substantial implications for individual self-determination and family and social dynamics. A significant proportion of patients admitted to hospital lack decision-making capacity, but there is evidence that the identification of incapacity by clinicians and relatives is inadequate.[72] In the case of clinicians, this may be partly due to the fact that many patients, incompetent or competent, trust doctors and do not question proposed treatments, so the issue of competency does not arise in the doctor's mind. Social and legal changes are demanding that clinicians become more aware of the place of competency in the clinical-ethical-legal setting, that they make the assessment of competency more routine, and that they are prepared to revise their estimations of competency in response to clinical changes.[73]

---

71   Parker, M, "Changes to Confidentiality for Young People" (2004) *Doctor Q* 30.

72   Raymont, V, Bingley, W, Buchanan, A, David, AS, Hayward, P, Wessely, S and Hotopf, M, "Prevalence of Mental Incapacity in Medical Inpatients and Associated Risk-factors: Cross-sectional Study" (2004) 364 *Lancet* 1421.

73   Cain, JM and Hammes, BJ, "Ethics and Pain Management: Respecting Patient Wishes" (1994) 9(3) *Journal of Pain & Symptom Management* 160. Brady, LS and Kirschner, KL, "Ethical Issues for Persons with Aphasia and their Families" (1995) 2 (3) *Topics in Stroke Rehabilitation* 76.

Statute law and the cases have never specified procedural requirements for assessing competency, or who should assess it, but have confined themselves to broad definitional guidance.[74] During the last decade, increased efforts have been made to develop structured methods of assessing competency, in response to evidence of the unreliability of clinical assessments and the lack of agreement between clinical and psychometric assessments,[75] and the existing and further predicted growth in demand for assessments in areas such as advance care planning and mental health.[76]

How would the combined "positive status" and/or actual understanding model of decision-making capacity be best operationalised?

Triggering a competence assessment

If we value maximal freedom and efficiency, through the prima facie presumption of competency, we also must be alert to those conditions which should trigger an assessment of competency, and while we should avoid substantive judgments when assessing it, there is surely room for something like a reasonable person standard in *raising the question* as to the presence of competency.[77] A refusal of treatment which has serious possible consequences should always be explored, in order to distinguish between possible incompetence and a stable decision. Organic brain syndromes associated with trauma, drugs, alcohol, infection, dementia, and so on, should also be regarded as potentially extinguishing competency, as should mental states characterised by fear, anxiety, and depression, whether or not these are associated with mental illness.[78] Nevertheless, it is crucial to accept that the mere presence of mental illness, or any of the other medical conditions mentioned, do not, ipso facto, imply incompetence.[79]

Facilitating and maximising the expression of competence

Having argued above that hermeneutic, narrative and feminist philosophical considerations have insufficiently distinguished between assessing competency and helping people to develop or regain it, we nevertheless strongly support procedures which address the potential barriers to recognising genuine competency and to its expression. In a number of cases, of course, the medical treatment of a condition will restore competency by removing the pathological influence which temporarily extinguished it. This may be as straightforward as treating a urinary

---

74 Cockerill, Collier and Maxwell (2005) op cit p 46.

75 Sullivan (2005) op cit pp 102–108, 122–123.

76 Ibid pp 96–97.

77 Skene, L, "Risk-Related Standard Inevitable in Assessing Competence" (1991) 5 *Bioethics* 113.

78 Stewart and Biegler (2004) op cit at 339.

79 Sullivan, D, "How can Valid Informed Consent be Obtained from a Psychotic Patient for Research into Psychosis? Three Perspectives (III)" (2003) 22(4) *Monash Bioethics Review* 69 at 70. Cockerill, Collier and Maxwell (2005) op cit pp 40–41.

infection in an elderly person who has become delirious. While the concept of competency is sometimes incorrectly taken to include the provision of information, adequate explanations and time for deliberation are clearly required, and failure to provide them may result in the appearance of incompetence. Careful explanations including simplifications,[80] visual aids and family involvement,[81] are all legitimate means of facilitating and maximising the recognition of competency, but it is important to remember that this is in the sense of reducing the number of false negative attributions of competency; that is, increasing the accuracy of competency assessment, and that assessment is the focus of the exercise.

Clinical testing, formal psychometric testing and "legal" testing

Once a competency assessment is triggered, how is it best undertaken, bearing in mind that we are interested in the person's ability to make a particular decision, and assuming that he or she is adequately informed, is not being coerced, and that steps have been taken to reduce the chance of a false attribution of incompetence?

Assessing competency is not the same thing as diagnosing a medical condition, but where the medical condition primarily affects cognition and other mental phenomena, we find overlaps. For example, the Mini-Mental State Examination (MMSE) is a test of cognitive function, often used in diagnostic work-up of conditions such as Alzheimer's and other dementias,[82] and the cognitive domains evaluated in the examination include orientation, registration, attention, recall, language and constructional praxis.[83] Clearly, some of these domains are also relevant to the assessment of competency. But the MMSE has been criticised in the clinical setting because it fails to take into account educational levels and other factors,[84] and it has a relatively high measurement error, leading to poor tracking of cognitive decline.[85] Other neuropsychological tests have been found wanting in terms of focussing on one or a few areas relevant to competency and omitting others, failing to test decision-making capacity specifically, and so on.[86] As a

---

80 Sullivan (2005) op cit pp 137–138. Tulskey, JA, Fischer, GS, Rose, MR and Arnold, RM, "Opening the Black Box: How do Physicians Communicate about Advance Directives?" (1998) 129 *Annals of Internal Medicine* 441. Ryan, S, "Competence and the Elderly Patient with Cognitive Impairments" (1996) 30 *Australian & New Zealand Journal of Psychiatry* 769.

81 Stewart and Biegler (2004) op cit at 339.

82 Meade, CE and Bowden, SC, "Diagnosing Dementia: Mental Status Testing and Beyond" (2005) 28 *Australian Prescriber* 11.

83 Folstein, MF, Folstein, SE and McHugh, PR, "Mini-mental State. A Practical Method for Grading the Cognitive State of Patients for the Clinician" (1975) 12 *Journal of Psychiatric Research* 189, <www.minimental.com/article.html> (accessed 12 September 2005).

84 Kerridge, Lowe and McPhee (2005) op cit p 177.

85 Clark, CM, Sheppard, L, Fillenbaum, GG, Galasko, D Morris, JC, Koss, E, Mohs, R, Heyman, A, "Variability in Annual Mini-mental State Examination Score in Patients with Probable Alzheimer Disease: a Clinical Perspective of Data from the Consortium to Establish a Registry for Alzheimer Disease" (1999) 56 *Archives of Neurology* 857.

86 Sullivan (2005) op cit pp 19–122.

consequence of these problems, and of the poor reliability of purely clinical assess-ment of competency, specific tests of competency, as distinct from diagnostic tests of cognition, have been developed over recent years. Sullivan divides these into competency tests (structured or semi-structured patient interviews), question sets and vignette-based interviews.[87] Of the competency tests, the MacArthur Com-petence Assessment Tool for Treatment (MacCAT-T) has been described as the gold-standard.[88] It deliberately tests for the abilities which the law requires – namely understanding, appreciation, deliberation and expression of a choice – but it does so in terms of the specific problem facing the patient; that is, the particular decision is "inserted" into the test template. Even so, the results are not taken to be directly translatable into a judgment about competency. It is designed to be taken into account along with other factors, including clinical assessment, mental status and psychiatric background, if applicable.

While tests such as the MacCAT-T have focused on the elements which legal judgments have isolated as being crucial for competency, and hence might appear to show the greatest promise for adequate assessment of competency, they too have been criticised as being too narrowly cognitive, and of omitting emotional and other elements.[89] We reiterate here the gist of our response concerning emo-tions above – if the emotions are an important element of deliberation, and if the generally accepted definition of competence includes understanding, appraisal, recall, integration, evaluation, and manipulation of information, and justification and communication of one's choice, then the emotions are integral to the constitution and demonstration of competency. There is no further fact which needs to be adduced to broaden the notion of competency, and its assessment.

Sullivan advances a two-step model of decision-making capacity which involves a core of cognitive abilities, together with knowledge specific to the decision being contemplated.[90] The core cognitive abilities would continue to be assessed by comprehensive neuropsychological testing, while the specific aspects would be tested by one of the more recent competency tests such as the MacCAT-T. Sullivan considers the specific tests to be insufficient for reasons of recency and inadequate validation, but also because the general tests can yield information which helps explain incompetence and could point to remediation processes. Nevertheless, it should be noted that the semi-structured interview format is congruent with legal requirements and will be generalisable to core cognition in many cases, since it is only *made* specific by the provision of knowledge specific to the particular decision. The distinction between the two steps should therefore not be over-stated. As relatively time-efficient, the semi-structured competency tests should also prove to be a practical means by which clinicians can be encouraged to

---

87   Ibid at 122–130.
88   Breden and Vollmann (2004) op cit at 274.
89   Charland, LC, "Appreciation and Emotion: Theoretical Reflections on the MacArthur Treatment Competence Study" (1998) 8 *Kennedy Institute of Ethics Journal* 359.
90   Sullivan (2005) op cit pp 131–132.

assess competency more routinely and less intuitively, and hence to reduce their rates of error in these assessments.

Competence and psychiatry

Jeffrey Spike reports that it has become common for United States physicians to call a psychiatrist to determine a patient's competency when this is in doubt.[91] It is certainly generally believed that psychiatrists have the greatest expertise for the task of assessing competency. Yet Spike also contends that the "undoing of the damage of a psychiatric consultation is one of the most common sources of requests for ethics consultation", and that "psychiatry in hospitals often practises an unreasonable and unnecessary 'sanism'".[92] Spike describes a case in which the consultant psychiatrist scored the patient 10 out of 30 on an MMSE but failed to pay sufficient attention to the consistency between her current and lifelong wishes, and suggests that the views of relatives may often be more accurate than the abstract determinations of psychiatrists. This does not constitute an evidence-based indictment of psychiatrists' abilities to determine competency compared with others, but the question remains whether psychiatrists are the natural and obvious choice for these assessments.

When the Northern Territory's *Rights of the Terminally Ill Act 1995* was in force, a psychiatrist was required to assess the competency of a patient who requested active assistance to die under that Act,[93] and psychiatrists are sometimes asked for an assessment of competency when patients refuse treatment, especially life-sustaining treatment. Psychiatrists are experts in the phenomena of the mind, both normal and abnormal, so it is natural to call on them when the stakes are high.

The stakes were high in a Queensland case in 2000, involving a tetraplegic patient who wanted life-sustaining treatment withdrawn. He could communicate only by shaking or nodding his head. Three psychiatrists argued that he was not competent, one being unable to convince him or herself that the patient was competent to make a life-death decision regarding life-sustaining treatment, others because it was not possible to ascertain his wishes about his current treatments and whether he required further ventilation, because he was giving inconsistent responses, and because he was unable to comprehend the questions given and unable to clearly indicate his wishes. In contrast, his intensive care specialists, experienced in communicating with such patients and in continuous contact with the man, were *convinced* of his competence, and it was their opinion which the Guardianship and Administration Tribunal favoured.[94]

---

91 Spike, J "Capacity is Not in Your Head: Why it Can be a Mistake to Request a Psychiatric Consultation to Determine Capacity" in Thomasma and Weisstub (2004) op cit pp 113–119.

92 Ibid at 113.

93 Section 7(1)(c).

94 Re *PVM* [2000] QGAAT 1, <www.austlii.edu.au/au/cases/qld/QGAAT/2000/1.html> (accessed 15 September 2005). See also Parker, M, "Judging Capacity: Paternalism and the Risk-Related Standard" (2004) 11 *Journal of Law and Medicine* 482.

Would psychiatrists *tend* to assess people as incompetent more frequently than other health professionals? The empirical work to answer this question is yet to be done, but arguments have been made which suggest that it should be.

One line of thought links (a) medicine's and psychiatry's tendency to conceptualise active euthanasia more readily than treatment withdrawal as suicide, (b) psychiatry's role in preventing suicide, and (c) the strong empirical connection between suicide and mental disorder, with the assumption in favour of mandatory psychiatric assessment of anyone who would request assistance in dying.[95] Set against the traditional moral distinction between actions and omissions, psychiatry may tend to search for explanations for requests for assistance to die which can be responded to medically, so that the idea of a rational request will be downgraded. One of the present authors has suggested:

> That psychiatrists are not *required* to evaluate treatment refusals reflects a presumption in these cases in favour of patient competence, a cornerstone of law in western jurisdictions, whereas the requirement for psychiatric assessment of requests for assistance to die reflects a presumption of incompetence for which there is neither empirical evidence nor moral justification.[96]

Thus, in the light of strong historical, cultural and professional traditions and assumptions, there may be a tendency amongst some psychiatrists, to *rule out* as incompetent any request for active assistance to die,[97] and to at least *raise the bar* in relation to the level of competency required in relation to the withdrawal of life-sustaining treatment. If, as we have suggested, degree conceptualisations of competency, as applied in the form of risk-related standards, are incoherent, psychiatric assessments of competency in cases of treatment withdrawal, let alone requests for active assistance to die, may tend to produce false negative competency judgments.

Finally, false positive attributions must also be guarded against, particularly in research settings, where competency "enhancement" for patients with mental disorders may be motivated by desires for research funding and results. As Sullivan points out, "it is important not to equate improved participation rates with improved competence: psychosis does not preclude rational refusal!"[98]

---

95   Parker, M, "Medicine, Psychiatry and Euthanasia: an Argument Against Mandatory Psychiatric Review" (2000) 34 *Australian & New Zealand Journal of Psychiatry* 318.

96   Ibid at 322 (emphasis not in original).

97   Consider the following statements. "Clinicians need to recognise the hopelessness hidden beneath a rationally presented desire to die. While intellectually each one of us might conceive of a rational suicide, in clinical practice, making explicit the reasons that underpin this choice reveals a different narrative with complex circumstances": Kissane, D, Clarke, D and Street, A, "Demoralization Syndrome – a Relevant Psychiatric Diagnosis for Palliative Care" (2000) 17 *Journal of Palliative Care* 12. "Rational suicide is an intellectual notion ... A request for euthanasia is invariably a cry for help": Kissane, D, "How to Treat Existential Distress in Palliative Care" *Australian Doctor* 27 September 2002, Sup I–VIII.

98   Sullivan (2005) op cit pp 70–71.

Conclusion

In this chapter, we have shown that the link between attributions of competency and rights to self-determination continues to be questioned in both theory and practice. The link is certainly more widely recognised than in previous years, both in young people yet to achieve legal majority, where a status approach has been rejected, and in older people who are able to project their competent wishes into the future through new legal instruments. However, theoretical questions remain, such as whether or not competency is a matter of degree, whether outcome risk should influence the level of competency required for decision-making, whether the idea of different levels of competency is itself coherent, and whether the symmetry between consent and refusal of treatment vouchsafed adults should also pertain to apparently competent minors. We have argued that a traditional but comprehensive conception of competency may assist in tackling these difficult questions.

Good practice depends on clear and distinct ideas. Specific areas such as psychiatry illustrate the need for constant vigilance concerning the way in which our values and interests may distort our objective scientific assessments. In practice, specific tests of competency and better education of clinicians in both theoretical considerations and practical application should produce improvements in the accuracy of assessments, thereby securing greater protection for vulnerable patients and greater liberty for the competent.

PART III

HUMAN RIGHTS AND THERAPEUTIC JURISPRUDENCE

5

Human rights, health rights and the jurisprudence of public health law

Penny Weller[1]

Introduction

The natural affinity between public health and human rights dictates the application of human rights principles in health and public health contexts.[2] Yet the concerns of individualised medical care influenced by the language of rights, and the human rights frame in public health are not reconciled. Rights debates have enjoyed prominence in health and public health over the last four decades. The achievement of rights, however, has proved elusive. Apparent successes seem hollow, irrelevant or unsubstantiated, while additional instability is engendered by a broader debate that questions the transformative capacity of individual rights strategies. One response to the rights "dilemma" in the health sector is to engraft a bourgeoning human rights ethic upon the individual rights campaign that has characterised earlier decades of rights activism in Australia. Appeals to human rights law as an authoritative body of legal principle have appeared, mirroring the international emergence of the "human rights movement" in public health.[3] In the following discussion I will argue that while the human rights approach holds the potential to reconcile the fissures in rights debates and strategies, there remain areas of contestation concerning the relevance of rights strategies, the status of individual rights in health, their connection to human rights and the universality of human rights principles in public health. These issues drive the development of the jurisprudence of public health law. The critical contribution of this field of jurisprudence is the identification of categories of evidence that will properly inform consideration of issues or scenarios that posit the necessity of subordinating individual rights and interests to the public good. This positioning of public health law logically follows the expansive definition of health as a state of optimal well-being. Importantly, it claims for public health law a field that extends well beyond the traditional boundaries of its content and concern.

---

1   I am grateful to Kerry Petersen for her helpful comments on earlier drafts of this chapter.

2   Mann, J, Gruskin, S, Grodin, M and Annas, G (eds), *Health and Human Rights: A Reader*, Routledge, New York, 2001, p 1.

3   The "Human Rights Movement" refers the application of human rights principles to public health. See Burris, S, Lazzarini, Z and Gostin, L, "Taking Rights Seriously in Health", (2002) 30 *Journal of Law, Medicine & Ethics* 490.

Individual rights and health care

In Australia the grass roots consumer movements of the late 1960s and early 1970s identified the traditional principle of medical beneficence as a ruse of power. Challenges to authoritarianism and paternalism in the delivery of health care were spearheaded by the women's movement, principally in the campaign to secure the right to control reproductive capacity.[4] The explicit resistance to medical dominance articulated by women's rights advocates rapidly expanded into a proliferation of challenges to the organisation and culture of the medical system. Active consumer rights organisations also sought improved delivery of health care services and systems, demanded expansion of primary care and preventive medicine, promoted the value and efficacy of alternate therapies, challenged traditional patient–professional relationships, and drew attention to the social determinants of health.[5]

Consumer advocacy in health included a specific agenda of "patient rights". The movement sought to articulate the legal and ethical principles that should properly bind the relationship between practitioner and patient.[6] Rights advocacy was also mobilised to directly improve the quality of the clinical encounter. The circulation of consumer rights information aimed to transform the nature of the interactions between patient and practitioner by actively engaging consumers in the assertion of rights, particularly in terms of facilitating access to health information and health services.[7]

While there is some debate about the measure and quality of social change that might be directly attributable to rights activism, the pursuit of individual rights in health contexts marks a unique phase of legal engagement in the health field. This engagement is characterised by the enactment of legislation that addresses the changed public expectations about the delivery of health care.

The program of legislative reform that developed against the backdrop of rights advocacy privileges the notion of patient autonomy. In Victoria, for example, several related statutory schemes provide procedural entitlement to health care consumers. The reforms include substantial review of mental health

---

4   See Boston Women's Health Collective, *Our Bodies, Our Selves – A Book by and for Women*, Simon & Schuster, New York, 1976; Ehrenreich, B and English, D, *For Her Own Good: 150 Years of the Experts' Advice to Women*, Anchor, New York, 1978; Broom, D, *Damned if We Do: Contradictions in Women's Health Care*, Allen & Unwin Sydney, 1991; Annandale, E, *The Sociology of Health and Medicine*, Polity Press, Cambridge, 1998.

5   Baldry, E, *The Development of the Health Consumer Movement and its Effect on Value Changes and Health Policy in Australia*, University of New South Wales Press, Sydney, 1992.

6   Darvall, LW, *Medicine, Law and Social Change: The Impact of Bioethics, Feminism and Rights Movement on Medical Decision-making*, Dartmouth, Aldershot, 1993.

7   See *The Choice Handbook of Your Health Rights: The Essential Guide for Every Australian*, Australasian Publishing, Sydney, 1998; Skene, L, *You, Your Doctor and the Law*, Oxford University Press, Melbourne, 1990; Australian Consumers' Association, *Your Health Rights*, Random House, Sydney, 1992.

provisions especially as they relate to involuntary commitment,[8] (limited) rights to access ones own medical records,[9] the establishment of a formal health services complaints system[10] and the introduction of "living wills".[11] These provisions are further reinforced by the subsequent introduction of privacy legislation[12] and the ability to access records in the private sector.[13] Their express consumer focus is complemented by the requirement that health institutions adopt risk management and quality assurance processes,[14] and by the establishment of National Health and Medical Research Committee (NHMRC) ethics committees to oversee the proper conduct of medical research.[15] Similar innovations throughout Australian jurisdictions have arguably transformed the context of health care delivery.

Despite this contribution, rights advocacy in the domestic health field is muted. The numerous changes in the administration and funding of the health care system appear in a rhetorical environment that equates the notions of autonomy and self-determination with the more limited concept of "consumer choice".

The medical indemnity insurance crisis created a hostile response to patient-initiated litigation, while the elaboration of risk management strategies provides an opportunity to understand complaints processes as merely a valuable contribution to quality assurance mechanisms.[16] Recent events in Queensland illustrate that health delivery remains characterised by a complex interplay of system, authority, personality and interpersonal relationships.[17] Furthermore, at the level of bioethical debate, the tendency for individual rights claims to pose end-of-life, beginning-of-life and access to biotechnology issues in terms of rights claims and counter-claims has diminished the prescience of an individual rights approach.[18]

---

8   *Mental Health Act 1986* (Vic).

9   *Freedom of Information Act 1982* (Cth); *Freedom of Information Act 1982* (Vic).

10 The *Health Services (Conciliation and Review) Act 1987* establishes the Office of the Health Services Commissioner in Victoria.

11 *Medical Treatment Act 1988* (Vic) with the *Medical Treatment (Enduring Power of Attorney) Act 1990* (Vic).

12 *Privacy Act 1988* (Cth); *Information Privacy Act 2000* (Vic).

13 *Information Privacy Act 2000* (Vic).

14 *Health Services Act 1988* (Vic).

15 The *National Health and Medical Research Council Act 1992* established the National Health and Medical Research Council.

16 Carter, M, "Patients Rights" unpublished conference paper, Medicine and Law Conference, 3–5 May, Melbourne, 2001.

17 Insight, "Inquiry into the Alleged Misconduct of Dr Patel", *The Age*, 28 May 2005, p 1.

18 For example, the right of women to reproductive control is pitted against the right of the foetus to life. The right to access fertility treatment is pitted against the potential child's right to a socially preferred social environment. See, McLean, S, *Contemporary Issues in Law, Medicine and Ethics*, Dartmouth Publishing, Aldershot, England, 1996.

Health strategies that explicitly frame individual rights approaches in human rights principles have similarly struggled to maintain a lasting impact. For example, the National HIV/AIDS Strategy in Australia drew upon the international health and human rights movement to successfully champion the notion that protection of the rights of people living with HIV and AIDS is an essential component of the effective management of HIV/AIDS.[19]

The cooperative interaction between government, the health sector and community organisations that characterised the Australian public health approach to HIV/AIDS is regarded internationally as an exemplar of innovative health management.[20] The perception that the HIV/AIDS crisis has passed in the developed world, however, has tended to dissipate active support for the realisation of individual rights for people living with HIV and AIDS.[21]

The social and legal complexity engendered by health policy that is embedded in human rights principles is also illustrated by the National Mental Health Policy released by the Commonwealth Government in 1992. The policy endorses human rights principles for the protection of persons with mental illness as expressed in the United Nations Declaration on the Rights of Persons with Mental Illness of 1991. The Burdekin report released shortly after in 1993, noted that the legislative regimes in a number of Australian jurisdictions failed to adequately protect the rights and freedoms of people with mental illness.[22] While the report prompted some pertinent legislative amendments in State jurisdictions, its central observation that rights injunctions have little relevance in the absence of effective or adequate service provision remains a salient criticism of health service delivery in Australia.

The effect of the development of "rights" approaches in Australian medical law is also limited. The body of law that has developed around negligence, nuisance, and trespass to the person has acknowledged the importance of individual autonomy, particularly in relation to the provision of information about medical procedures.[23] The High Court of Australia's consideration of these issues, however, remains centred upon the interaction between an individual patient and their health care provider. This leaves the law, at its current point of development, ill versed in the legal ambiguities that arise in public health contexts. For example, public health authorities remain charged with the task of monitoring the HIV/AIDS epidemic. The preferred strategy in Australia, New

---

19 Department of Community Services and Health, *National HIV/AIDS Strategy*, AGPS, Canberra, 1989.

20 Kirby, J, "Foreword" in Gostin, LO, *The AIDS Pandemic: Complacency, Injustice, and Unfulfilled Expectations*, University of North Carolina Press, Chapel Hill, 2003.

21 Ibid.

22 *Report of the National Inquiry into the Rights of People with a Mental Illness*, AGPS, 1993 (Burdekin Report); see Freckelton, I and Loff, B, "Health Law and Human Rights" in Kinley, D, *Human Rights in Australian Law: Principles, Practice and Potential*, Federation Press, Sydney, 1998.

23 See full discussion in Freckelton and Loff (1998) op cit.

Zealand and the United Kingdom is "unlinked" or "blind" monitoring".[24] Blood collected for specified laboratory testing with patient consent is subsequently tested anonymously, without the patient's knowledge, for HIV antibodies. This system evolved in deference to express cautions against the utility of rights infringements associated with universal or compulsory screening. The blind sampling and testing procedure ensures anonymity and is designed so that it is impossible to identify (or notify) a person who may have provided a positive sample. The sampling system operates on the assumption that it complements an effective medical system that is capable of identifying and treating individual cases of HIV/AIDS. This capacity ultimately rests upon the quality of clinical services. While Australia boasts a high standard of medical care, in practice, HIV/AIDS testing tends to be recommended for persons who are deemed to be "at risk". Patients who present a "risky" profile are actively counselled toward testing. The efficacy of this arrangement ultimately rests upon the capacity of individuals to recognise and report behaviour that might alert medical staff to the need for testing, and upon medical staff to elicit, and appreciate, pertinent clinical histories. As community-wide focus on HIV/AIDS diminishes, the likelihood that some patients may not be recognised, or recognise themselves, as being "at risk" increases the chance of the system failing to diagnose individual cases of HIV infection. Potential litigation arising from this hypothetical fact situation would of necessity prompt further development in Australian medical law by requiring consideration of how the competing interests of the individual (to receive proper medical advice) and the community (to benefit from epidemiological surveillance) might be reconciled.[25]

The imperative that the law develop principles with which to reconcile the competing interests of individual patients with the requirement of sound community or public health policies is anticipated in public health debates about the relevance of international covenants and statements.[26] In recent years the health community has demonstrated an increased familiarity with the work of the international community. International injunctions and covenants are more commonly invoked in support of rights claims and human rights principles are alluded to in health and public health contexts.[27] While human rights principles

---

24 Johnson, L, "Particular Issues of Public Health: Infectious Diseases" in Martin, R and Johnson, L, *Law and the Public Dimension of Health*, Cavendish Publishing, London, 2001.

25 In North American case law "State interests" have been recognised as modifying the right of self-determination particularly in relation to end-of-life decisions. See Stewart, C, *Public Interests and the Right to Die: Compelling Reasons for Overriding the Right to Self-determination*, Issues Paper 14, Australian Institute of Health Law and Ethics, 2001.

26 See the Universal Declaration of Human Rights (1948); the International Covenant on Economic, Social and Cultural Rights (1966); the International Covenant on Civil and Political Rights (1966).

27 See, for example, International Convention on the Elimination of All Forms of Racial Discrimination (1969); Convention on the Elimination of All Forms of Discrimination Against Women (1979); Convention on the Rights of the Child (1989); United Nations HIV/AIDS and Human Rights International Guidelines (September 1996); United Nations Declaration on the Rights of Persons with Mental Illness (1991).

hold a significant normative influence in policy development and public health practice, they are yet to crystallise into a strongly articulated rights approach in Australian law.[28] The blurring of conceptual boundaries between civil rights and human rights, and between health and public health, that accompanies contemporary shifts in public health discourse further complicates the articulation of legal principle in health and public health contexts. These conceptual difficulties sharpen the necessary orientation of public health law toward a jurisprudence that addresses the competing interests that arise in public health contexts in terms of human rights.[29]

Human rights and public health

The human rights approach in public health is attributed to the work of the late Jonathan Mann.[30] Mann argued that the natural affinity between public health and human rights dictates the application of human rights principles in health and public health contexts because both public health and human rights are societal mechanisms committed to securing the conditions necessary for promoting the health and well-being of the population.[31] Mann, with others, identifies three points of relationship or linkage between human rights and public health. The first linkage recognises that as public health programs are promulgated, implemented and enforced by the state, the impact of public health policies on human rights must be assessed. The second linkage identifies the direct and indirect health burden of human rights violations. The third linkage posits a fundamental connection between human rights and public health such that human rights considerations augment the socioeconomic analysis of the health gradient to elucidate a deeper analysis of poverty, marginalisation and unequal relationships of power.[32]

As the apparent resurgence of infectious disease threatens to erupt, the experience of the outbreak of Severe Acute Respiratory Syndrome (SARS) has refocused attention upon the legitimacy of coercion in public health policy.[33] In the context of infectious disease the maxim, developed in recognition of the rights approach to the management of HIV/AIDS, that the protection of individual rights

---

28 Freckelton and Loff (1998) op cit at note 22.

29 The emerging health focus in domestic and international systems of governance, and in human rights law, is a phenomenon of interest that lies beyond the scope of the present discussion. see Burris, S, "Governance, Microgovernance and Health", Conference on SARS and the Global Governance of Public Health, Temple University Beasley School of Law, 2004.

30 Editorial note, "Symposium: Health, Law and Human Rights: Exploring the Connections" (2002) 30 *Journal of Law, Medicine & Ethics* 4.

31 Mann et al (2001) op cit.

32 Mann, J, Gostin, LO, Gruskin S, Brennan T, Lazzarini Z, and Fineberg, H, "Health and Human Rights" (1994) 1 *Health & Human Rights* 1 at 12.

33 Gostin, LO, Bayer, R, and Fairchild A, "Ethical and Legal Challenges Posed by Severe Acute Respiratory Syndrome: Implications for the Control of Severe Infectious Disease Threats" (2003) 290 *JAMA* 24 at 9.

will necessarily accord with the securement of the public good, underestimates the ambiguities and contradictions that arise when public health strategies are advanced within a human rights frame. Consideration of the nature of these contradictions has informed recent developments in the jurisprudence of public health law.[34]

The international community has long recognised that circumstance will sometimes warrant legitimate limitation of human rights principles. In 1985, the United Nations Economic and Social Council (ECOSOC), the body then charged with implementation of the International Covenant on Civil and Political Rights (ICCPR) adopted the Siracusa Principles as a guide to assess whether or not derogations from the principles of the ICCPR were acceptable. The principles provide that restrictions may be acceptable if they are:

- provided for and implemented in accordance with the law;
- directed toward a legitimate objective of general interest;
- do not impair the democratic functioning of society;
- are not imposed in an arbitrary or discriminatory manner; and
- utilise the last restrictive means available to reach the stated goal.[35]

Applying theses principles to public health law Gostin identifies four key criteria that must be satisfied in order for a restriction of individual liberty to be considered an acceptable derogation of human rights.[36] These are:

1   The precautionary principle, described as the obligation of governments in Western liberal democracies to protect populations against reasonably foreseeable threats provided that the obligation is bound with safeguards to individual rights.

2   The principle of adopting the least intrusive or restrictive alternative which dictates that interventions are balanced by the recognised imperatives of privacy, freedom of association and liberty.

3   The principle of justice that requires the benefits and burdens of public health action to be fairly distributed, with protection actively extended to socially vulnerable populations.

4   The principle of transparency which requires that decisions are made openly and accountably, with the full participation of affected communities.[37]

---

34   Gostin, LO, "Law and Ethics in Population Health", unpublished paper, Conference in Law and Population Health, Melbourne, National Centre for Public Health Law, 2003.

35   ECOSOC, "The Siracusa Principles on the Limitation and Derogation Provision in the International Covenant on Civil and Political Rights" Geneva, 1985.

36   Gostin et al (2003) op cit at note 33.

37   Gostin et al (2003) op cit; Gruskin and Loff also interpret the criterion as outlining acceptable derogation of human rights principles in public health contexts provided that the objectives for the restriction are clear, they acknowledge the principles of non-discrimination and equality, and pursue genuine participation of affected communities. Gruskin, S and Loff, B, "Do Human Rights Have a Role in Public Health Work?" (2002) 360 *Lancet* 1880.

In terms of their application to the management of infectious disease Gostin seeks to reconcile the contradiction between rights and public health principles by imposing strict procedural safeguards that limit the use of coercive public health powers. He contends that the ultimate effect of these processes is the adoption of voluntary mechanisms for disease control with individual restriction used only as a measure of last resort and in accordance with human rights principles.

The success of this approach, however, is highly dependent upon the quality of debate that is generated in relation to a given situation. Pitched at a high level of abstraction the principles necessarily require elaboration. The content of policy derived from them will depend on the character of the disease or incident in question, the type of danger, and which communities are wholly or partly affected. As was demonstrated in the early phase of the HIV/AIDS epidemic the effort to construct disease containment strategies compatible with human rights principles rested on the capacity of the public health community to devise responses that were cognisant of the socio-legal environment and sensitive to different modes of transmission, virulence, infectivity and preventative possibilities.

As the preceding discussion suggests, the fundamental strength of Gostin's principles lie with the requirement of community consultation. In Western contexts the human rights model in public health represents a "grass roots" approach that is predicated on rights advocacy and engagement with an identified community. The development of a rights response to HIV/AIDS was fundamentally dependent upon the mobilisation and engagement of the gay community. In offering a model of universal application, however, rights approaches have been criticised for failing to take account of the unique conditions generated in each public health context. Cock and colleagues argue that in Africa, approaches to the prevention and control of HIV/AIDS that are heavily based upon experiences and policies from industrialised countries are poorly suited to tackling the African epidemic and that the epidemic in Africa ought to be understood and responded to as a public health emergency. This shift in classification is a strategy to trigger a different range of public health responses, and provides an opportunity to reconsider the efficacy of rights strategies. In support of their argument the authors note that in 2001, the region hosted two-thirds of the world's 40 million HIV sufferers, had 77 per cent of AIDS deaths, accounted for 90 per cent of orphans and children infected with HIV and counted the prevalence amongst pregnant women to be greater than 40 per cent in Botswana, Zimbabwe and Swaziland. They further argue that a crisis of this dimension demands a re-evaluation of strategies that have proved effective in other contexts but seem to inhibit progress in this instance. For example, they see the emphasis placed on anonymity for HIV-infected people as promoting, rather than breaking, a destructive silence around HIV/AIDS. Cock and colleagues recommend that in high prevalence settings universal and mandatory testing should be considered, with every citizen encouraged to know their HIV status.[38] Similar criticism has arisen in relation to the promotion of condom use in Africa where health education programs were informed by the assumption that if women were appraised of the values of condoms in preventing disease they would protect themselves from HIV/AIDS infection.[39] Johnson argues that the failure of these programs illustrates the importance of recognising that local attitudes to sex, procreation and bodily fluids cannot be divorced from economic and social conditions. While HIV/AIDS must be recognised as a global issue, assumptions about sexuality and society derived from a Western perspective, have presented barriers to effective containment measures. Albeit developed as a "grass roots" response to the HIV/AIDS epidemic in Western liberal democracies, the model of individual rights and its associated method of empowerment has not provided an effective local strategy in its new context. As Cock and colleagues acknowledge, the reorientation of rights strategies and principles toward effective disease containment in Africa will require an open debate about the ethical and socio-legal rationales that underpin practice in the field.[40]

The latter point echoes the implicit requirement for open debate suggested by Gostin. Gostin's principles presuppose the generation of detailed and sustained debate about the acceptable limits of public health strategies. They also require a process of consultation with affected communities. This criterion reflects recognition of the fundamental principle that policy responses must be grounded in the knowledge and experience of affected persons. The experience of HIV/AIDS in Africa illustrates that a deep engagement with local conditions is required to render a salient and workable human rights response to public health threats in any given location or instance.

Public health and the public good

Although beyond the traditional scope of public health law, the definition of public health as concerned with the well-being of populations invites the public health sector, including public health law practitioners, to engage in broader thematic debates. Foremost amongst these is debate about the legitimacy of general policies that sanction infringements of individual health and well-being on the grounds that such impositions further the public good or protect the health and well-being of the general population.

In 2005, two Australian academics suggested that torture should be considered a legitimate strategy provided it is directed at eliciting information that will save multiple lives.[41] These comments flowed from the current debate in

---

38   Cock, K, Mbori-Bgacha D, and Marum E, "Shadow on the Continent: Public Health and HIV/AIDS in Africa in the 21st Century" (2002) 360 *Lancet* 67 at 70–72.

39   See Johnson (2001) op cit at 253.

40   Cock et al (2002) at 72.

41   *The Age*, 17 May 2005, p 1.

America about the legality of interrogation procedures implemented in the Abu Ghraib Prison and Guantanamo Bay Army Base.[42] They were posed in terms of a challenge to the current absolute prohibition against torture in international law[43] and employed analytic tools from moral philosophy to establish the logical and moral validity of derogating from that prohibition.[44] It is the invocation of the hypothetical "ticking bomb" scenario, and the argument that one person's life or well-being must be balanced against the lives and well-being of many people, that places this debate in a public health context, and dictates the engagement of the public health sector.[45]

In response to a perspective that privileges the goal of absolute security above competing considerations, human rights approaches elicit consideration of the societal impact of policies posed for the "public's good". As they are derived from the Siracusa principles, Gostin's approach gives rise to an initial question about the status of the right to bodily inviolability. The recognition that this principle underpins both international and domestic law suggests that the prohibition against torture represents a more fundamental principle than critics of rights approaches allow.

The High Court of Australia explicitly considered the significance of rights as they relate to the concept of bodily integrity in the landmark case *Secretary, Department of Health and Community Services v JWB and SMB (Marion's case)*.[46] This case dealt with an appeal from a decision of the Full Court of the Family Court of Australia regarding the question of consent to the sterilisation of a mentally incompetent child.[47] In *Marion's* case, Mason CJ, with Dawson, Toohey, and Gaudron JJ found that in the case of an intellectually disabled minor, the authorisation of the court was required for invasive, irreversible surgery to

---

42   Annas, G, "Unspeakably Cruel – Torture, Medical Ethics and the Law" (2005) 352 *New England Journal of Medicine* 20.

43   The rights to be free from torture or cruel, inhuman or degrading treatment is found in Article 7 of the International Covenant on Civil and Political Rights reflecting Article 15 of Universal Declaration of Human Rights. Bateup, C, "Reproductive Rights" (2000) *Australian Journal of Human Rights* 3 at 5.

44   Australian statutory prohibitions against torture are generally found in the State and Territory Crimes Acts. The *Crimes (Torture) Act 1988* (Cth), with offshore operation, gives effect to commitments relating to "certain provisions of the Convention Against Torture and Other Cruel, Inhuman or Degrading Treatment or Punishment". The Convention Against Torture and Other Cruel, Inhuman or Degrading Treatment or Punishment is included as a Schedule to the Act.

45   Wendel, B, "Legal Ethics and the Separation of Law and Morals", *Cornell Law School Legal Studies Research Paper Series*, Cornell Law School, New York, 2004. <http://ssrn.com/abstract=687804> (accessed 16 July 2005).

46   *Secretary, Department of Health and Community Services v JWB and SMB (Marion's case)* (1992) 175 CLR 218.

47   *Re Marion* (1990) 14 Fam LR 427. In *Re Marion*, Nicholson CJ found that there exists in the common law a fundamental right to reproduce which is independent of the right to personal inviolability. The majority in *Marion's Case* explicitly rejected this conclusion, (1992) 175 CLR 218 at [81] per Mason, Dawson, Toohey, Gaudron JJ.

proceed.[48] Their Honours expressly based their finding upon the fundamental right to personal inviolability.

> As we have indicated the conclusion relies on a fundamental right to personal inviolability existing in the common law, a right which underscores the principles of assault, both criminal and civil, as well as on the practical exigencies accompanying this kind of decision.[49]

The recognition of the right to bodily inviolability as a fundamental human right existing at common law, secures its validity as a foundational principle in Australian law.[50] This recognition poses a considerable barrier for those who advocate a departure from the current expression of international law.

Brennan J, in a separate opinion, similarly recognised the significance of human rights in Australian law. He considered human dignity to be a core human value in common law, as indicated by the international instruments relating to human rights.[51] Brennan J expressed the scope of the concept in the following passage:

> Human dignity requires that the whole personality be respected: the right to physical integrity is a condition of human dignity but the gravity of any invasion of physical integrity depends on its effect not only on the body but also upon the mind and on self-perception.[52]

The majority formulation in Marion's case supports the argument that torture should remain prohibited in Australian law because acceptance of torture would contravene fundamental principles. Importantly, Brennan J's focus on human dignity explicitly extends the principle beyond the concept of physical integrity to include its psychological, emotional and perhaps spiritual dimensions. This expansion of principle is significant because it opens the possibility that the effects of torture beyond mere physical harm may be recognised in law. It also opens the possibility that effects of torture may be recognised as adhering beyond the individual torture victim, attaching to the community or society in which torture victims reside. Brennan J comments in Marion's case, therefore, begin to lead judicial reasoning in Australia toward a human rights approach that has the capacity to reconcile the competing claims between individual well-being and community safety that are encapsulated in the "ticking bomb" scenario.

---

48 The consideration of rights in Marion's case is also noteworthy because the Human Rights and Equal Opportunity Commission intervened in the proceedings pursuant to s 11(1)(o) of the Human Rights and Equal Opportunity Commission Act 1986 (Cth).

49 (1992) 175 CLR 218 at [55] per Mason, Dawson, Toohey, Gaudron JJ.

50 Charlesworth, H, "The High Court and Human Rights" in Cane, P (ed), Centenary Essays for the High Court of Australia, LexisNexis Butterworths, Australia, 2004.

51 Brennan J cites the United Nations Charter; the International Covenant on Civil and Political Rights (Article 9); the Universal Declaration of Human Rights, the International Covenant on Economic, Social and Cultural Rights; and the Convention on the Rights of the Child; United Nations Declaration on the Rights of Mentally Retarded Persons.

52 (1992) 174 CLR 218 at 317 per Brennan J.

Pre-empting the direction of Brennan J's rationale, Gostin's framework is also capable of guiding a pertinent jurisprudential response by providing a process through which a reconciliation of human rights and public health goals might proceed. Beyond the threshold issue of lawfulness, the framework primarily requires consideration of the validity of the assumptions embedded in the proposed "trade off" between the well-being of the individual and the well-being of the community. First, the principles bring forward the considerable public health literature concerning the mental and physical impact of torture as evidence that will underpin legal debate. Second, the principles provide for the participation of survivors of torture or their representatives in debate and decision-making. Third, the principles allow consideration of the individual, public health and human rights implications of sanctioning torture. A public health response, embedded in a jurisprudence of public health law, offers a coherent challenge to the conclusion that torture might be permissible in some circumstances. It shows the circularity of logic in the arguments offered by pro-torture advocates, and reiterates through evidence and reasoning, the fundamental principles that support the maintenance of an absolute prohibition against torture. As the example of the torture debate illustrates, public health law principles stand as an effective tool to evaluate policy arguments posed in terms of "the public good".

Conclusion

Public health law derives its scope and content from the intersection of public health and law. As public health embraces a broader conception of health, new capacities are generated for legal jurisprudence. Approaching public health issues from a legal perspective creates new fields of public health inquiry. Similarly, the elaboration of principles that further develop the human rights frame in public health law reflects the construction of a reflexive jurisprudence that has the capacity to recognise the interplay of legal principle and bodily experience as they arise in different public health events, and to incorporate these into effective public health policy. As the intersections between public health and law, and health and society are more widely recognised, public health law is steered towards new areas of interest. Following these trajectories, public health law finds itself engaged at the multiple points of interaction between the individual, community, society and state. In public health law, human rights approaches reconcile the dual imperatives of security and liberty that lie at the core of the debate about the conflict between individual and public good.[53] The different points of inquiry required of a reflexive jurisprudence of public health law are directed by the epidemiological profile and the socio-political contexts in which new public health threats arise.

---

53   Gruskin and Loff (2002) op cit at 33.

6

Mental health law and therapeutic jurisprudence

Kate Diesfeld and Ian Freckelton

Introduction

Mental health law constitutes a continuing point of tension between those inclined toward paternalism in decision-making and those with a propensity toward concern for the individual's rights in respect of persons alleged to have disabilities.[1] Therapeutic jurisprudence has sought to achieve a reconciliation of the two extremes and to provide a constructive framework for mental health law reform. Three discrete areas of therapeutic jurisprudence scholarship have provided an important focus for discourse amongst those with contrasting perspectives in a number of jurisdictions:

- the criteria for involuntary status – both legislated and non-legislated;
- the emergence of involuntary outpatient treatment as a means of coercing mandatory treatment in the community for those with mental illnesses; and
- review tribunal decision-making.

This chapter reviews current issues in each of these areas. It explores how therapeutic jurisprudence analyses have facilitated better understanding by both clinicians and lawyers about the potential for pro-therapeutic outcomes for patients and the importance of minimising the likelihood of counter-therapeutic outcomes.

Therapeutic jurisprudence as an approach to health law

Therapeutic jurisprudence is a lens through which the effects of the law can be viewed and analysed.[2] It inquires whether the law is, or could be, employed for pro-therapeutic ends. It is of relevance to the content of the law, interpretation of

---

1   See, for example, Slobogin, C, *Minding Justice: Laws that Deprive People with Mental Disability of Life and Liberty*, Norton, New York, 2006; Winick, BJ *Civil Commitment: A Therapeutic Jurisprudence Model*, Carolina Academic Press, Durham, 2005; Diesfeld, K and Freckelton, I (eds), *Involuntary Detention and Therapeutic Jurisprudence: International Perspectives on Civil Commitment*, Ashgate, Aldershot, 2003; Schopp, RF, *Competence, Condemnation and Commitment*, APA, Washington DC, 2001.

2   See Winick (2005) op cit, pp 6–8.

the law and practical application of the law, such as in court and tribunal procedures. It particularly identifies the propensity of the law in its terms and its procedures to have counter-therapeutic consequences. It enables a focus upon the impact of the law at a macro-level as a means of facilitating public health and safeguarding the community in the face of risk and upon the impact of the law upon a particularly vulnerable set of individuals, such as those with mental illnesses.

The originators of therapeutic jurisprudence, David Wexler and Bruce Winick,[3] emphasise that legal processes have an impact upon the psychological and physical well-being of all participants. Their approach has been described as "the use of social science to study the extent to which a legal rule or practice promotes the psychological and physical well-being of the people it affects".[4]

The perspective of Wexler and Winick is informed by experience as mental health advocates and legal academics during a period of social, political and legal reforms in the United States, in particular the time surrounding the controversies of persons with mental illnesses said to be "dying with their rights on".[5] They argue that legal processes and systems can be reconfigured to be more therapeutic if freed of some of the traditional constraints that have fettered courts and tribunals. This is not to say that achieving less damaging consequences for litigants and others is a transcending consideration. Rather, they acknowledge that the primary objective of litigation and decision-making by bodies such as tribunals must be rigour, correctness and fairness. However, they contend that it is important that the multi-faceted consequences for participants in the legal process be acknowledged as one of a number of relevant factors in matters such as statutory interpretation, policy development and the conduct of hearings.

One of the characteristics of therapeutic jurisprudence has been the fillip it has given to international and interdisciplinary research, especially in the mental health law area. It has attracted support because Winick and Wexler have articulated concerns that have been recognised, although not so often described, by many clinicians and legal representatives about the dysfunctional effects of the legal system. Their impetus for reform began with consideration of the destructive impact of the law upon vulnerable people with a mental illness or a mental disability.[6] Based upon their experiences within mental health law, they inquired whether the law could be used to minimise counter-therapeutic outcomes and to maximise consequences which actively promote good health. As Winick put it in 2005:

---

3   See, for example, Wexler, D and Winick, B (eds), *Law in a Therapeutic Key*, Carolina Academic Press, Durham, 1996.

4   Slobogin, C, "Therapeutic Jurisprudence: Five Dilemmas to Ponder" in Wexler and Winick (1996) op cit, pp 763–794, esp p 769.

5   See Appelbaum, P, *Almost a Revolution: Mental Health Law and the Limits of Change*, Oxford University Press, New York, 1994.

6   See, for example, Winick, BJ, "Coercion and Mental Health Treatment" (1997) 74 *Denver Law Journal* 1145.

Therapeutic jurisprudence suggests that law should value psychological health, should strive to avoid imposing anti-therapeutic consequences whenever possible, and when consistent with other values served by law, should attempt to bring about healing and wellness. Unlike the medical model, it does not privilege therapeutic values over others. Rather, it seeks to ascertain whether the law's anti-therapeutic effects can be reduced and its therapeutic effects enhanced without subordinating due process and other justice values.[7]

A particular focus in this regard was reduction in levels of alienation and disempowerment within the legal process for litigants such as those with mental illnesses, brain injuries and intellectual disabilities. Aside from the fact that such marginalisation is offensive in terms of human rights,[8] it may obstruct tribunals of fact from obtaining information that otherwise might be available for better informed decision-making. This information is more likely to emerge if key players, such as those with disabilities, feel better able to participate.[9] There is also another consideration. Persons with mental illnesses have conditions which involve a substantial adjustment in cognition and lifestyle. In part, "recovery" involves taking back control and seeing oneself as more than a stigmatising label. Minimisation of coercive procedures and orders by clinicians, tribunals and courts reduces the dynamic of imposed passivity and encourages people to regain autonomy by active decision-making about management of their illness or condition. A series of therapeutic jurisprudence studies has established that marginalisation and a sense of unfairness are lessened when proceedings are more participatory and when authoritarian and coercive measures are kept to a minimum.[10]

Controversies and therapeutic jurisprudence

After a little more than one and half decades of life, therapeutic jurisprudence remains controversial,[11] although increasingly mainstream. Many mental health law academics and practitioners have considered the merits of this fresh

---

7   Winick (2005) op cit, pp 6–7.

8   See, for example, Minkowitz, T *No Force Advocacy by Users and Survivors of Psychiatry*, Mental Health Commission of New Zealand, Wellington, 2006; Slobogin, S *Minding Justice: Laws that Deprive People with Mental Disability of Life and Liberty*, Harvard University Press, Cambridge, Mass, 2006, p 122.

9   See, for example, Freckelton, I, "Involuntary Detention Decision-making, Criteria and Hearing Procedures: An Opportunity for Therapeutic Jurisprudence in Action" in Diesfeld and Freckelton (2003) op cit.

10   See, for example, Tyler, TR, "The Psychological Consequences of Judicial Procedures: Implications for Civil Commitment Hearings" (1992) 46 *Southern Methodist University Law Review* 433. See also Freckelton, I, "Civil Commitment: Due Process, Procedural Fairness and the Quality of Decision-making" (2001) 8(1) *Psychiatry, Psychology & Law* 105.

11   See, for example, Arrigo, B, "The Ethics of Therapeutic Jurisprudence: A Critical and Theoretical Inquiry of Law, Psychology and Crime" (2004) 11 *Psychiatry, Psychology & Law* 23; Eastman, N and Peay, J (eds) *Law Without Enforcement: Integrating Mental Health and Justice*, Hart Publishing, Oxford, 1999; Nolan, J *Justifying Government at Century's End*, New York University Press, New York, 1998; Petrila, J, "Paternalism and the Unrealized Promise of Essays in TJ" in Wexler and Winick (1996) op cit, pp 685–705.

perspective on the workings of the legal system[12] and procedures and courts implementing the tenets of therapeutic jurisprudence have proliferated. The diversity and volume of research devoted to the subject demonstrates its prominence in contemporary medico-legal debates.[13]

The following offers a snapshot, but not an exhaustive list, of recent scholarship on therapeutic jurisprudence. It has been used to analyse specialist courts,[14] including mental health courts,[15] drug courts,[16] and teen courts.[17]

The philosophy has also offered a foundation for analysis of broader health law issues. For example, Stolle considered the prophylactic potential of a therapeutic jurisprudence approach for HIV-positive clients[18] while Brookbanks considered its role in developing narrative medical competence.[19] Also, the pro-therapeutic perspective has been applied to wider scopes of professional legal practice including family law,[20] tort litigation,[21] malpractice law,[22] professional

---

12   See Wexler and Winick (1996) op cit; Diesfeld and Freckelton (2003)op cit; Winick (2005) op cit.

13   The therapeutic jurisprudence website is located at <www.therapeuticjurisprudence.org> (accessed 20 April 2006).

14   See, for example, Rottman, D, "Does Effective Therapeutic Jurisprudence Require Specialized Courts (and Do Specialized Courts Imply Specialized Judges?)" (2000) 37 *Court Review* 22.

15   See, for example, Kondo, L, "Advocacy of the Establishment of Mental Health Speciality Courts in the Provision of Therapeutic Justice for Mentally Ill Offenders" (2000) 24 *Seattle University Law Review* 373; Slate, R, "From the Jailhouse to Capitol Hill: Impacting Mental Health Court Legislation and Defining What Constitutes a Mental Health Court" (2003) 49 *Crime & Delinquency* 6; Steadman, H, Redlich, A, Griffin, P, Petrila, J and Monahan, J, "From Referral to Disposition: Case Processing in Seven Mental Health Courts" (2005) 23 *Behavioral Sciences & the Law* 215; Trupin, E and Richards, H, "Seattle's Mental Health Courts: Early Indicators of Effectiveness" (2003) 26 *International Journal of Law & Psychiatry* 1 at 33.

16   Brown, A, "Drug Courts Help Keep Families Together" (15 September 2001) 1 *Florida Bar News;* Hora, P, Schma, W, and Rosenthal, J, "Therapeutic Jurisprudence and the Drug Treatment Court Movement: Revolutionizing the Criminal Justice System's Response to Drug Abuse and Crime in America" (1999) 74 *Notre Dame Law Review* 439; Hora, P, "A Dozen Years of Drug Treatment Courts: Uncovering Our Theoretical Foundations and the Construction of the Mainstream Paradigm" in Harrison, L, Scarpitti, F, Amir, F and Einstein, S (eds) *Drug Courts: Current Issues and Future Perspectives,* Office of International Criminal Justice Publishers, 2002.

17   See, for example, Weisz, V, "A Teen Court Evaluation with a Therapeutic Jurisprudence Perspective" (2002) 20 *Behavioral Sciences & the Law* 381.

18   Stolle, D, "Advance Directives, AIDS and Mental Health: TJ Preventive Law for the HIV-positive Client" (1998) 4 *Psychology, Public Policy & Law* 854.

19   Brookbanks, W, "Narrative Medical Competence and Therapeutic Jurisprudence: Moving Towards a Synthesis" (2003) 20 *Law in Context* 2.

20   Alfred, A, "The Past, Present and Future of Mental Health Law: A Therapeutic Jurisprudence Analysis" (2003) 20 *Law in Context* 2; Armstrong, M, "Therapeutic Justice: An Interdisciplinary Approach to Family Law Cases" (1999) 3 *Maricopa Lawyer* 1 (July); Babb, B and Moran, J, "Substance Abuse, Families and Unified Family Courts: The Creation of a Caring Justice System" (1999) 3 *Journal of Health Care Law & Policy* 1.

21   Conaghan, J, "Tort Litigation in the Context of Intra-Familial Abuse" (1998) 61 *Modern Law Review* 132.

22   Daver, EA, "A Therapeutic Jurisprudence Perspective on Legal Responses to Medical Error" (2003) 24 *Journal of Legal Medicine* 37.

regulation,[23] nursing,[24] workers' compensation,[25] criminal law,[26] coronial law,[27] elder law,[28] international law,[29] and indigenous people's rights,[30] to name but a selection of areas.

However, fundamental reservations about therapeutic jurisprudence have been voiced by a number of scholars. The tension has been characterised as follows:

> [T]he recent argument, represented by the "therapeutic jurisprudence" movement, that all law should be designed towards therapeutic advantage, clearly implies that mental health law should be seen as equivalent to a clinical tool. The obvious counter view, characteristically represented by lawyers rather than clinicians, is that although English and Welsh mental health law does indeed have a therapeutic purpose, much of it is properly concerned with the protections of patients' civil rights against unjustified therapy or deprivation of their civil liberty. The juxtaposition of these two approaches to mental health law describes a core public policy tension in the field between the pursuit of paternalistic welfare and autonomy derived justice.[31]

Likewise, Petrila[32] has identified a number of criticisms. First, many academics and others (including former patients) may dispute the assertion that therapeutic aims should play a dominant role in judicial decision-making. Secondly, the assertion that therapeutic jurisprudence offers a novel approach to disability law may be overstated. Thirdly, therapeutic jurisprudence fails to identify who will decide whether an initiative is "therapeutic". Petrila has questioned whether therapeutic

---

23   See, for example, Freckelton, I and Flynn, J, "Paths Toward Reclamation: Therapeutic Jurisprudence and the Regulation of Medical Practitioners" (2004) 12 *Journal of Law and Medicine* 91; Freckelton I and List, D, "The Transformation of Regulation of Psychologists by Therapeutic Jurisprudence" (2004) 11(2) *Psychiatry, Psychology & Law* 296.

24   See, for example, Kjervik, D, "TJ and Nursing" (2000) 8 *Journal of Nursing Law* 4 at 19–22.

25   See, for example, Lippel, K, "Therapeutic and Anti-therapeutic Consequences of Workers' Compensation" (1999) 22 *International Journal of Law & Psychiatry* 521; Wilkinson, W, "Therapeutic Jurisprudence and Workers' Compensation" (1994) 30 *Arizona Attorney* 28.

26   See, for example, McGuire, J, "Can the Criminal Law Ever be Therapeutic?" (2000) 18(4) *Behavioral Sciences & the Law* 413.

27   See, for example, Freckelton, I and Ranson, D, *Death Investigation and the Coroner's Inquest*, Oxford University Press, Melbourne, 2006.

28   Stolle, D, "Professional Responsibility in Elder Law: A Synthesis of Preventive Law and Therapeutic Jurisprudence" (1996) 14 *Behavioral Sciences & the Law* 459.

29   See, for example, Aponte, T and Roberto, P, "Sanity in International Relations: An Experience in Therapeutic Jurisprudence" (2000) 30 *University of Miami Inter-American Law Review* 659.

30   See, for example, Anaya, S, "The United States Supreme Court and Indigenous Peoples: Still a Long Way to Go Toward a Therapeutic Role" (2000) 24 *Seattle University Law Review* 229.

31   Eastman, N and Peay, J (eds), *Law Without Enforcement: Integrating Mental Health and Justice*, Hart Publishing, Oxford, 1999, Preface.

32   Eastman and Peay (1999) op cit, p 693.

jurisprudence rejuvenates health law "because it does nothing to challenge professional domination of mental disability law and treatment".[33]

Nolan[34] has offered a sociological critique of therapeutic jurisprudence, observing that the emergence of a pro-therapeutic ethos is part of the political trend by the United States government to justify its own control through a "therapeutic" rationale. He is concerned that the new language of therapeutic jurisprudence justifies the expansion of the coercive powers of the state under a "therapeutic canopy". The broad acceptance of vague therapeutic goals paves the route for the state's comprehensive and diffuse powers. In his view, the pervasive "therapeutic code of moral understanding" is derivative of both the "modern 'scientific' discipline of psychology and is quasi-religious in nature".[35] One danger is that the practitioners of "the therapeutic orientation do not see the institutional applications of the therapeutic model as coercive or as in any way violative of individual liberties".[36] Accordingly, the state applies therapeutic codes and symbols as tools for its expansion further into citizens' private lives. He identified diverse examples of health, educational, and legal initiatives that were created by government under the guise of benevolent "therapeutic" measures.

Therapeutic jurisprudence is one of Nolan's examples. He observed that many government programs are purportedly founded on therapeutic principles and portrayed as benevolent, personal, humane and sensitive to the individual needs of citizens. However, he warned that "it may not be so easy to dismiss the state's adoption of the therapeutic ethos as a benign, linguistically neutral development".[37] Convincingly, he observed: "The therapeutic orientation provides a personalized remedy to a highly impersonal, rationalized bureaucratic system, but without fundamentally altering the system".[38]

Like Nolan, Arrigo argued that a central flaw in the therapeutic philosophy has been its failure to reform the system. He also offered a more radical critique, contending that "therapeutic jurisprudence wrongly assumes law's legitimacy, neglects (or dismisses) the ideology imbedded within legal texts, promotes a unitary model subject in law, and fosters a false consciousness among citizens". His critique drew upon critical legal studies, feminist jurisprudence, anarchy theory, and post-modern psychoanalysis.

Arrigo posed the following questions: "Are there any conditions under which formal law can be defined as healthy for people? To what extent, if at all, is the informal legal decision-making process a veiled expression of hierarchy,

---

33   Ibid, p 693.
34   Ibid, p 19.
35   Ibid, p 19.
36   Ibid, p 394.
37   Ibid, p 291.
38   Ibid, p 20.

centralisation, and authority?" He expressed deep concerns about the question: "Can the law function therapeutically?".

However, while there can be little doubt that therapeutic jurisprudence has not fundamentally overthrown the injustices of the legal system, or even a preponderance of imbalances within mental health law, it has prompted considerable amounts of reflection amongst clinicians, practising lawyers, decision-makers and law reformers. This has resulted in not just greater sensitivity but a number of subtle shifts in both the content and practice of modern mental health law.[39]

The next sections identify issues of therapeutic jurisprudence relevance in the legislative criteria for involuntary status of patients in Australia and New Zealand while explaining how therapeutic jurisprudence has been used as an analytic tool in the areas of involuntary mandated community treatment and tribunal decision-making.

Involuntary treatment criteria

The criteria for involuntary status vary across Australia and New Zealand both as to the definitions of the prerequisite mental condition and also as to the criteria for involuntariness. It is apparent firstly that there is an extraordinary diversity in the criteria and also the extent to which the criteria facilitate recovery by those with mental illnesses that is participatory and has not been coerced. The specific provisions are listed in an appendix to this chapter.

What stands out from the various legislative provisions is the diversity of approaches within Australia and New Zealand based on the basic terminology which defines the criteria for imposition of involuntariness. A therapeutic jurisprudence critique might well observe that many of the provisions have blurred and that there are uncertain criteria for serious intrusion into patients' liberties. Core requirements include the existence of a condition (or in some jurisdictions the appearance of a condition) and the risk to the person or others. However, the roads to such general propositions regarding the basis for compulsory care are diversely cobbled.

For example, in Australia the qualifying threshold for these two requirements varies from "serious harm" (New South Wales and Australian Capital Territory), to "significant risk of harm" (Tasmania), to "imminent harm" (Queensland and Northern Territory), to the lower threshold of risk to "health and safety" (South Australia, Victoria and Western Australia). Variations also include "substantial danger to the general community" (Northern Territory) and "to prevent serious damage to any property" (Western Australia).

Likewise, the person's inability to consent to treatment or a refusal by them as to the provision of treatment features as a criterion in some but not all jurisdictions (Queensland, Victoria, Western Australia and Northern Territory).

---

39   See, for example, Winick (2005) op cit.

Also, the majority of jurisdictions require consideration of whether compulsory care provides the least restrictive option (Queensland, Victoria, Western Australia, Australian Capital Territory, Northern Territory and New Zealand). Problematically, some jurisdictions require that there be appropriate services available (Queensland and Northern Territory) and in Tasmania that the "approved hospital" is properly staffed for the person's care and treatment (Tasmania). Interestingly, this shifts the focus from the person's qualifying condition to the availability of services, an issue that warrants critique. Arguably, this criterion creates positive pressure to develop services but it may also create a lacuna for people who are unwell but neglected under the legislation due to the absence of services.

This brief review highlights the essential ambiguities of involuntariness for psychiatrically unwell patients. There are significant differences of legislative approach within Australia and New Zealand, as well as in many other places, as to the triggering condition for imposition of involuntary status. For instance, a disorder of volition or orientation (see Western Australia) is sufficient in some jurisdictions but not in others. An actual condition within the meaning of the World Health Organisation's *International Classification of Diseases* or the American Psychiatric Association's *Diagnostic and Statistical Manual of Mental Disorders* is necessary in some jurisdictions but not in others. There must be a mental illness, mental disorder, mental condition, mental dysfunction or abnormal state of mind (for example, New South Wales, Queensland, South Australia, Tasmania, Western Australia, Australian Capital Territory, Northern Territory and New Zealand) but in Victoria there need only be the appearance of mental illness.

There are also major differences as to the nature of the risk. Risk of deterioration in mental or physical health is central in some, but not all jurisdictions. In certain jurisdictions, such as Western Australia, there is a specific provision enabling imposition of involuntariness where the risk is not physical but in terms of damage to property, finances, relationships and reputation.[40]

The differences are not just superficial. They are illustrative of contrasting approaches toward the imposition of involuntary status and of the thresholds for clinical and review body decision-making. If the focus of legislative provisions is upon the potential for worsening of symptomatology, in the short, medium or long-term (generally, this is not specified[41]), there is significant scope for unarticulated ideological orientations toward paternalism or civil libertarianism to be the driving force in decision-making.

Comparable risks have been identified in respect of extra-legislative matters such as "insight", "compliance", "sexual promiscuity", "substance dependence"

---

40 See further Freckelton, I, "Bipolar Disorders and the Law" (2005) 13 *Journal of Law and Medicine* 153 at 159–160.

41 Compare *Mental Health Act 2000* (Qld) s 14.

and "absconding".[42] An important therapeutic jurisprudence contribution to understanding about the "real-world" criteria applied by clinicians and review bodies alike to decision-making about involuntary status has been provided by Michael Perlin.[43] He has identified the phenomena of "sanism" and "pretextuality" in such decision-making whereby extra-legislative, unarticulated values and considerations often covertly impact upon both ultimate decisions and the rhetoric formally employed in arriving at them.

Another contribution by therapeutic jurisprudence has been the paring away of assumptions, expressions and appearances in relation to legislative direction underpinning decision-making about involuntary status for those with mental illnesses. An important challenge that remains is the construction of tests, criteria and indicia which give guidance to decision-makers and make clear which factors should and should not be taken into account in relation to coerced compulsory care. Although this is an intellectual dilemma, it is also legally and ethically difficult because it requires the balancing of considerations that are inevitably dependent on context, culture and resources.

Therapeutic jurisprudence frames the following observations. First, we might inquire whether the lower threshold for entrance into compulsion is more health-promoting. Arguably, more people will enter treatment with a lower threshold, but at the expense of their liberty. Secondly, although the emphasis on the availability of services is beneficial if it provides the impetus to create responsive services, it also excludes people who warrant treatment and would otherwise obtain it but for the absence of resources. It is problematic to have criteria based on resource availability with no obvious resolution or therapeutic remedy for the unwell person. Thirdly, the focus on the least restrictive alternative mirrors the therapeutic jurisprudence objective that liberty should not be reduced unnecessarily. Fourthly, it is debatable whether in any meaningful sense it can be asserted that persons with a demonstrable need for treatment have an enforceable right to obtain the treatment they require.

Mandated outpatient orders

Mandated outpatient treatment, often known as "community treatment orders" (CTOs), offers an alternative to inpatient hospitalisation for people with disabilities to obtain treatment and support. CTOs escalate patients' priority for scarce resources in the form of treatment following hospitalisation. In Australia and New

---

42 See Freckelton, I, "Ideological Divarication and Civil Commitment Decision-making" (2003) 10(2) *Psychiatry, Psychology & Law* 390; Freckelton, I, "Distractors and Distressors in Involuntary Status Decision-making" (2005) 12(1) *Psychiatry, Psychology & Law* 88; Diesfeld, K and McKenna, B, *Insight and Other Puzzles in the Decisions of New Zealand Mental Health Review Tribunal*, Mental Health Commission of New Zealand, Wellington, 2005; Diesfeld, K and Sjostrom, S, "Interpretive Flexibility: Why Doesn't Insight Incite Controversy in Mental Health Law?" (2006) 24 *Behavioral Sciences & Law* 1.

43 Perlin, M, *Mental Disability Law: Civil and Criminal*, 2nd edn, Michie Publishing, Charlottesville, 1998.

Zealand they have constituted the most utilised form of compulsory treatment for patients with mental illness for many years.[44]

However, mandated outpatient treatment has attracted criticism because it extends the state's powers by intrusion into peoples' civil liberties,[45] with potential for ongoing stigmatisation.[46] The portrayal of its invasive and coercive impact has created vigorous debates about whether using leverage to coerce treatment can be justified on moral grounds.[47] Opponents argue it may deter people from voluntarily seeking treatment thereafter[48] particularly if they are threatened with the sanction of involuntary hospitalisation. Based on this controversy, Monahan has observed that: "Mandating adherence to mental health treatment in the community is the single most contested human rights issue in mental health law and policy at the beginning of the twenty first century".[49]

One argument for mandatory outpatient treatment draws upon the principles of beneficence and paternalism, asserting that vulnerable individuals who are incapable of making medical decisions in their own interests should be protected and treated until their decision-making capacity is restored. Doing so in the community is less intrusive than doing so via lengthy stays in hospital. Also, there are potentially wider benefits if harm to others is prevented through the person's treatment. Some have reframed the procedure as benevolent "assisted treatment" that should be an option for anyone with a "severe psychiatric disorder who has impaired awareness of his or her illness and is at risk of becoming homeless, incarcerated, or violent or of committing suicide".[50] In their view, involuntary community-based treatment frees people from their illnesses and restores their dignity and ability to exercise their liberty. Supporters argue that mandatory community treatment is less restrictive of liberty, less stigmatising, and less coercive than inpatient detention. In an environment where institutions which provided insufficient community services were closed (deinstitutionalisation), it offered an alternative form of supervision and care, thereby increasing the likelihood that people would have sustained engagement with mental health services. It may be preferred to hospital detention (or abandonment) because it provides maintenance where ongoing care may not otherwise occur, thereby reducing the revolving door dilemma.

---

44 See McKenna, BG, Simpson, AIF and Coverdale, JH, "Outpatient Commitment and Coercion in New Zealand: A Matched Comparison Study" (2006) 29 *International Journal of Psychiatry & Law* 145.

45 See, for example, Torrey, EF and Zdanowicz, M, "Outpatient Commitment: What, Why, and for Whom?" (2001) 52 *Psychiatric Services* 337–341.

46 See, for example, Diesfeld and Freckelton (2003) op cit.

47 See, for example, Monahan, J, "Mandated Community Treatment: The Potential Role of Violence Risk Assessment" in Diesfeld and Freckelton (2003) op cit, pp 455–468.

48 See, for example, Hiday, V, "Coerced Community Treatment: International Trends and Outcomes" in Diesfeld and Freckelton (2003) op cit, pp 435–453.

49 See Monahan, J, "Mandated Community Treatment: The Potential Role of Violence Risk Assessment" in Diesfeld and Freckelton (2003) op cit, p 205.

50 See Torrey and Zdanowicz (2001) op cit, at 337.

A number of academics and practitioners have structured their analysis of outpatient involuntary treatment either explicitly, or implicitly, by reference to the question of whether involuntary outpatient treatment can function thera-peutically. For example, Simpson asked: "How best can I relieve this person's suffering, and enhance their ability to lead as successful and autonomous a life as possible?"[51] Hiday's research in the United States[52] indicated that "coerced com-munity treatment" may obtain positive outcomes. The results of the Duke Mental Health Study reflected the earlier findings that people experienced reduced hospitalisation, increased compliance, higher maintenance voluntarily in com-munity treatment and better adjustment in the community. However, Hiday (and Simpson) noted that the positive effects of such processes only occurred in conjunction with appropriate services and that a treatment order was insufficient in isolation to achieve positive results. She also questioned whether provision can be made for severely mentally ill persons who seem not to want treatment *without* invocation of the law.[53]

In New Zealand, research indicated that many people who are subject to such orders do not find them overly coercive.[54] Dawson and colleagues found that "the majority of patients were generally supportive of the community treatment order, especially if the alternative was hospital"; only a minority strongly opposed its use in their cases.[55] The patients had a generally positive opinion of mandatory outpatient treatment because they compared their expe-rience favourably with their prior negative experiences in institutions. They reported that the option offered greater freedom and control than hospitalisation. Also, many people valued the services and security that accompanied an order and attributed their restored health to it. The majority of patients viewed the order as a "helpful step towards stability" in the community.

The summary of the 42 patients' attitudes to the community treatment order was: 19 per cent were wholly favourable; 46 per cent were generally favourable but noted disadvantages; 21 per cent were equally for and against; 7 per cent were generally opposed but noted advantages and 7 per cent were totally opposed.[56] However, some people also reported that restrictions on their choice of medication, residence, and travel were detrimental. Accordingly, a minority was strongly opposed to the order, "but for most the restrictions did not unduly hinder them".[57] The patients expressed a range of perspectives. Some

---

51   Simpson, AIF, "A Clinical Perspective on Involuntary Outpatient Treatment" in Diesfeld and Freckelton (2003) op cit, p 471.

52   Diesfeld and Freckelton (2003) op cit, p 435.

53   Ibid, p 451.

54   Gibbs, A, Dawson, J, Ansley, C and Mullen, R, "How Patients in New Zealand View Community Treatment Orders" (2005) 14 *Journal of Mental Health* 357.

55   Ibid, at 357.

56   Ibid, at 362.

57   Ibid, at 357.

patients said the orders had saved their lives,[58] another person reported the medication "dragged her down",[59] and another reported that the order was "like a prison sentence".[60] Importantly, some people felt that they would never be discharged and did not know what the health professionals expected as a basis for discharge from the order. For example, Sasha asked: "What level of wellness do they want the patient to be before they come off?"[61] Significantly, of course, such a study focuses upon the needs and interests of individuals; the balancing consideration of community interests (however they be framed) is the background against which such matters needs to be framed.

Similarly, other researchers have extended the inquiry to patients' experience of involuntary inpatient admission in New Zealand. The study of McKenna and colleagues in 2001[62] inquired whether an enhanced experience of procedural justice would reduce patients' perceptions of coercion and ultimately increase the therapeutic benefits.[63] The researchers assessed patients' experiences of involuntary and voluntary admission processes based on principles of fairness and justice, transparent and bias-free processes, representation, clear decisions, and appeal processes. The findings suggested that approximately half of the involuntary patients did not experience a "voice" or "validation" during the admission process and cited problems with communication, listening, and constructive dialogue.[64] These results could be construed as furthering the therapeutic jurisprudence inquiry because they scrutinised whether the admission process functioned pro-therapeutically.

Although the research studies on mandated outpatient treatment and admission processes referred to above did not explicitly apply a therapeutic jurisprudence analysis, they did explore whether the law functioned therapeutically by examining whether patients experienced beneficial results from the coercive procedures. Given the importance of patients' perceptions of fairness and of keeping to a minimum their perceptions of coercion, a number of important issues remain for the development of mandated outpatient treatment regimes. Prominent amongst them is what is necessary to preclude CTOs being rolled over semi-automatically so that patients have unnecessarily long-term experiences of being subjected to mandated treatment. Experience in both Australia and New Zealand suggests that there is a common phenomenon of patients being retained for lengthy periods on outpatient orders with relatively

---

58   Ibid, at 362.

59   Ibid, at 363.

60   Ibid, at 363.

61   Ibid, at 364.

62   McKenna, B Simpson, AIF, Coverdale, J and Laidlaw, T, "An Analysis of Procedural Justice During Psychiatric Hospital Admission" (2001) 24 *International Journal of Law & Psychiatry* 573.

63   See also, McKenna , Simpson and Coverdale (2006) op cit.

64   Ibid.

little consideration appearing to be given to practical measures promoting their resumption of responsibility for treatment. In short, CTOs can become a habit.

Integral to the potency and workings of mandated outpatient orders are resource issues. In Australia this is emerging as increasingly problematic. The public mental health system is strained to its limits. Morale is low. Case loads are very heavy. Mobility of key staff is high. Patients regularly bemoan that they hardly see their allotted psychiatrist and that their case managers keep changing. This precludes the development of rapport and the creation of effective therapeutic relationships between patients and community clinicians. It substantially undercuts the asserted justification for the mandatory community treatment.

Also, there is the risk that review bodies, such as mental health review tribunals and boards, will not effectively discharge their responsibilities to evaluate in a real sense on each occasion whether such mandated regimes continue to be necessary. Patients often lose faith in the utility of attending hearings, reports from clinicians read much as they have previously, and there can be a sense of sameness about yearly hearings regarding CTOs. However, in fact, it is important that regardless of clinicians' and patients' expectations active measures are taken to facilitate patients' resumption of voluntary status with the responsibilities and risks that such status entails.

Another important issue for review processes is when and where they take place. Review bodies differ as to when hearings into CTOs first occur and then how often, if the patient does not lodge a formal appeal against clinicians' decisions. In addition, the extent of participation in such hearings by clinicians and case managers differs. Such practical issues have important ramifications for the quality of review decision-making and for the energy which in reality is taken in the overall review process.

In Victoria, a new initiative is the requirement for the Mental Health Review Board to review patients' treatment plans. This is an attempt to impose an additional level of scrutiny in relation to the measures adopted clinically to address individuals' reintegration and rehabilitation needs. It is particularly important for people on mandated outpatient treatment orders.

In preparing, reviewing and revising a treatment plan for a patient, authorised psychiatrists in Victoria are obliged to take into account:

(a) the wishes of the patient, as far as they can be ascertained; and

(b) unless the patient objects, the wishes of any guardian, family member or primary carer who is involved in providing ongoing care or support to the patient; and

(c) whether the treatment to be carried out is only to promote and maintain the patient's health or well-being; and

(d) any beneficial alternative treatments available; and

(e) the nature and degree of any significant risks associated with the treatment or any alternative treatment; and

(f) any prescribed matters.[65]

As yet there are no "prescribed matters". The obligation appears on its face to impose important obligations on clinicians while requiring that the Mental Health Review Board scrutinise all treatment plans of patients who appear before it.

However, the reality is otherwise. Importantly, the role of the Board is very limited. It must review the treatment plans:

[T]o determine whether (a) the authorised psychiatrist has complied with section 19A [quoted above] in making, reviewing or revising the plan (as the case may be); and (b) the plan is capable of being implemented by the approved mental health service.

The consequence thus far is that the majority of treatment plans are short and significantly "pro forma", containing little indication of sophisticated and individualised planning to address patients' needs, and the Mental Health Review Board has limited scope for addressing the deficits. Again, this constitutes a problem. There is a disjunction between the legislative intent and the reality of its application for those on mandatory community treatment regimes.

There is a need for further high quality, therapeutic jurisprudence-influenced, empirical research into the strengths and weakness of mandated community treatment regimes in Australia and New Zealand. Such research needs to go beyond individual reports of satisfaction or dissatisfaction and inquire whether objectives of CTOs are being met, whether services required by patients are being adequately dispensed and whether patients' capacity to manage their mental illnesses is effectively being enhanced by the innovation of mandatory treatment in the community – in short is coercion achieving its public health objectives?

Review tribunal decision-making

The ethos surrounding therapeutic jurisprudence has the potential to lead to better ways to administer the mental health legislation within hearings by emphasising pro-therapeutic approaches. In the past two decades increasing attention has been directed at the decisions and reasoning by mental health review bodies. The seminal studies in England were conducted by Peay in 1989[66] and Perkins in 2000.[67] Both concluded that there was a lack of clarity in the

---

65   *Mental Health Act 1986* (Vic) s 19A.

66   Peay, J *Tribunals on Trial,* Clarendon Press, Oxford, 1989.

67   Perkins, E, Arthur, S and Nazroo, I, *Decision-making in Mental Health Review Tribunals,* University of Liverpool Health and Community Care Research Unit, 2000; Perkins, E, *Decision-making in Mental Health Review Tribunals,* Central Books, London, 2002.

application of United Kingdom involuntary detention legislation to patients' individual circumstances. More recently, Perkins reflected upon the significance of therapeutic jurisprudence for tribunals' decision-making[68] and this was complemented by Ferencz's research with consumers regarding their (often adverse) experience of tribunal proceedings.[69]

Therapeutic jurisprudence has offered a foundation for analysis of tribunals' processes by asking whether review systems function therapeutically. Ferencz stressed the need for consumer-driven research based on the following perspectives: "Well, I thought the judge was really over-powering";[70] "I didn't get my say. [The Tribunal members] wouldn't let me talk, let me tell my side of the story. They were listening to all the others first";[71] "Yes you can get confused at a tribunal because they talk amongst themselves. It is like a trial really".[72] These findings give an important insight into whether tribunal proceedings are functioning therapeutically or counter-therapeutically.

Suggestions about how review tribunal hearings could enhance detained persons' well-being include: creating a patient-centred hearing; reducing perceptions of bias; striking the appropriate balance between formality and informality; and conducting sensitive and dignified questioning.[73] Part of this includes reducing the impact of insensitive or indifferent advocacy during proceedings and the use of language that is prone to later misconstruction in tribunal decisions.[74]

These critical perspectives have informed recent research on New Zealand written decisions by review tribunals.[75] A further critique of Australian mental health review processes recommended specific reforms to establish and enforce legal rights because this would not only serve the interests of justice "but the increasingly recognised objectives of therapeutic jurisprudence".[76]

---

68 Perkins, E, "Mental Health Review Tribunals" in Diesfeld and Freckelton (2003) op cit.

69 Ferencz, N, "Patients' Views of the Mental Health Review Tribunal in England" in Diesfeld and Freckelton (2003) op cit.

70 Ibid, p 246.

71 Ibid, p 246.

72 Ibid, p 246.

73 Du Fresne, S, "Therapeutic Potential in Review of Involuntary Detention" in Diesfeld and Freckelton (2003) op cit; Freckelton, I, "Involuntary Detention Decision-making, Criteria and Hearing Procedures: An Opportunity for Therapeutic Jurisprudence in Action" in Diesfeld and Freckelton (2003) op cit; Freckelton, I, "Decision-making About Involuntary Psychiatric Treatment: An Analysis of the Principles Behind Victorian Practice" (1998) 5 *Psychiatry, Psychology & Law* 249.

74 Freckelton, I, "Distractors and Distressors in Decision-making: Therapeutic Jurisprudence in Action" (2005) 12 *Psychiatry, Psychology & Law* 88.

75 Diesfeld, K and McKenna, B (2005) op cit.

76 Delaney, S, "An Optimally Rights Recognising Mental Health Tribunal" (2003) 10 *Psychiatry, Psychology & Law* 71 at 81.

Another strand of tribunal research has focused upon the relationships between consumers, staff and clinicians. A review tribunal hearing may be an opportunity to reduce the person's experience of coercion.[77] In fact, the New Zealand Mental Health Review Tribunal has formally signalled that its intention is for its decision-making to be influenced by pro-therapeutic intentions.[78] The Southern Tribunal reported in 2001:

> [T]he procedures adopted try and avoid any unnecessary confrontation between an applicant and his/her responsible clinician or care giving team. Therapeutic alliances should not be shattered, but where possible, encouraged.[79]

Furthermore, the tribunal recorded that in the majority of cases its decisions are contrary to the outcome sought by patients so "an effort is made to provide the applicant with constructive and positive comment by way of support and encouragement" with an attempt "to conduct hearings in such a way as to enhance rather than damage therapeutic relationships".[80] However, the extent to which these intentions are translated into outcomes requires further analysis – specifically, how those therapeutic intentions are manifested in the written decisions, and their impact upon consumers and the process.

In summary, thoughtful and fair review processes may have a positive influence upon the participants. By extension, applying therapeutic jurisprudence considerations to decision-making may improve the process. Those who have conducted research on tribunal processes encourage participants to pay closer attention to the impact of process upon all involved, particularly those subject to involuntary status. Related research on procedural justice indicates that people may experience the review process as just, although they do not secure the outcome to which they aspire. It is likely that Mental Health Review Tribunal research will now routinely incorporate a therapeutic jurisprudence framework.

Arguably, research on decision-making would have occurred anyway. For example, Peay's research occurred prior to the emergence of therapeutic jurisprudence. But it is significant that a substantial amount of more recent research on tribunal processes has incorporated therapeutic jurisprudence perspectives.[81] Many consumers, academics and practitioners who have reviewed mental health law practices have found a resonance in the principles of therapeutic jurisprudence.

---

77   See Feencz (2003) op cit; Freckelton (2003) op cit.

78   See Diesfeld, K and McKenna, B, "The Therapeutic Intent of the New Zealand Mental Health Review Tribunal" (2006) 13(1) *Psychiatry, Psychology & Law* (in press).

79   New Zealand Mental Health Review Tribunal *Annual Report of Southern Tribunal 2001*, New Zealand Mental Health Review Tribunal, Wellington, 2001, p 6.

80   Ibid, p 10.

81   See, for example, Perkins (2000) op cit, and Perkins (2003) op cit; Delaney (2003) op cit; Freckelton (2003) op cit, and Freckelton (2005) op cit; Ferencz (2003) op cit; Diesfeld and McKenna (2005) op cit.

Conclusion

Therapeutic jurisprudence has provided an international and inter-disciplinary framework for evaluating mental health laws and, in particular, it has fostered a consumer-focused critique. However, there have been important criticisms that it sacrifices liberty interests and lacks a coherent and distinctive philosophical foundation. Although it has attracted controversy, it has helpfully generated debate about the existing, and potential, philosophical underpinnings of matters such as imposition of involuntary status. Also, therapeutic jurisprudence has fostered an environment in which researchers share perspectives on areas such as mental health law. It has created a platform where people from diverse specialties and jurisdictions are conducting innovative, comparative, and often collaborative, research on mental health law issues.[82] One of its attributes is its "interpretive flexibility"[83] to examine the broad powers of law (for example, in relation to outpatient treatment) and more discrete processes (for example, the dynamics and reasoning of mental health proceedings which often involve closeted deliberations by review tribunals).

As of the early phase of the 21st century, discussions about mental health law reform are likely to include consideration of the principles of therapeutic jurisprudence. Consequent research could contribute to an international laboratory of mental health law; by contemplating different approaches to mental health law, we could observe approaches that would be impossible within our jurisdictions (due to constitutional or other constraints).[84] Therefore, as the debates in mental health law continue, we predict they will increasingly incorporate dimensions of therapeutic jurisprudence.

What is necessary, though, is that debates about threshold issues in the mental health law area proceed now beyond dichotomous debates about paternalism and civil liberties. Therapeutic jurisprudence has gone a long way toward ensuring that health outcomes are recognised, at least in mental health law, as commanding a legitimate place on the agenda – that they are a relevant factor in the framing of involuntary status legislation, in the evolution of mandated outpatient treatment, and in the conduct of review tribunal hearings and formulation of written reasons. The next phase of analysis needs to focus upon:

- the fair-minded balancing between different ideological positions in terms of the formulation of definitions of core concepts such as mental illness and the criteria for involuntary status;

- the resourcing and other exigencies of a public mental health system in which mandated outpatient treatment has a prospect of securing its stated objectives;

---

82 See, for example, Diesfeld and Freckelton (2003) op cit; Diesfeld and McKenna (2005) op cit; Diesfeld and McKenna (2006) op cit (in press).

83 See, for example, Diesfeld and Sjostrom (2006) op cit.

84 See, Wexler and Winick (1996) op cit.

- rights to adequate treatment within an environment of limited mental health care resources;
- the provision of services for people who otherwise qualify for compulsory care but the legislative criteria for "available services" have not been met;
- incorporation and enforcement of the principle of reciprocity whereby adequate treatment is provided when liberty is reduced on the basis of the person's mental condition; and
- the attributes of both review hearings and decision-making which are fair, rigorous and such as effectively to yield a combination of correct results and perceptions of fairness and minimal authoritarianism and coercion.

Appendix: Criteria for Compulsory Mental Health Care in Australia and New Zealand

New South Wales. In New South Wales "mental illness" is defined as "a condition which seriously impairs, either temporarily or permanently, the mental functioning of a person and is characterised by the presence in the person of any one or more of the following symptoms:

(a)   delusions;

(b)   hallucinations;

(c)   serious disorder of thought form;

(d)   a severe disturbance of mood;

(e)   sustained or repeated irrational behaviour indicating the presence of any one or more of the symptoms referred to in paragraphs (a)-(d)".[1]

Considerable latitude and subjectivity attaches to the notion of "irrational behaviour". In general, a person can only be compulsorily detained as an involuntary patient if classified as a "mentally ill person" or "mentally disordered person".

A person is defined to be "a mentally ill person" if they are suffering from mental illness and, owing to that illness, there are reasonable grounds for believing that care, treatment or control of the person is necessary:

(a)   for the person's own protection from serious harm; or

(b)   for the protection of others from serious harm.

In considering whether a person is a mentally ill person, the continuing condition of the person, including any likely deterioration in the person's condition and the likely effects of any such deterioration, are to be taken into account.[2]

In general, a person can only be compulsorily detained as an involuntary patient, subject to orders by the Mental Health Tribunal, if classified as a "mentally ill person" or "a mentally disordered person". A person (whether or not they are suffering from mental illness) is defined to be "a mentally disordered person" if the person's behaviour for the time being is so irrational as to justify a conclusion on reasonable grounds that temporary care, treatment or control of the person is necessary:

(a)   for the person's own protection from serious physical harm, or

(b)   for the protection of others from serious physical harm.[3]

Queensland. In Queensland a "mental illness" is defined as "a condition characterised by a clinically significant disturbance of thought, mood, perception or memory".[4] (1) The treatment criteria for a person, all of which must be complied with, are that:

(a)   the person has a mental illness;

(b)   the person's illness requires immediate treatment;

(c)   the proposed treatment is available at an authorised mental health service;

(d)   because of the person's illness –

(i)   there is an imminent risk that the person may cause harm to himself or herself or someone else; or

(ii)   the person is likely to suffer serious mental or physical deterioration;

(e) there is no less restrictive way of ensuring the person receives appropriate treatment for the illness;

(f) the person –

   (i) lacks the capacity to consent to be treated for the illness; or

   (ii) has unreasonably refused proposed treatment for the illness.[5]

An involuntary treatment order[6] is subject to review by the Mental Health Review Tribunal.

South Australia. In South Australia a "mental illness" is defined as "any illness or disorder of the mind".[7] Involuntary status is subject to review by the Guardianship Board. If it is satisfied (a) that a person who is being detained in an approved treatment centre still has a mental illness that requires treatment; and (b) that the person should be further detained in an approved treatment centre in the interests of his or her own health and safety or for the protection of other persons, it may order that the person be detained in that centre or some other centre for a further period, not exceeding 12 months.[8]

Tasmania. In Tasmania a "mental illness" is defined as "a mental condition resulting in:

(a) serious distortion of perception or thought; or

(b) serious impairment or disturbance of the capacity for rational thought; or

(c) serious mood disorder; or

(d) involuntary behaviour or serious impairment of the capacity to control behaviour".[9]

A person may be detained as an involuntary patient in an approved hospital if:

(a) the person appears to have a mental illness; and

(b) there is, in consequence, a significant risk of harm to the person or others; and

(c) the detention of the person as an involuntary patient is necessary to protect the person or others; and

(d) the approved hospital is properly equipped and staffed for the care or treatment of the person.[10]

Such a status is subject to review by the Mental Health Review Tribunal.

Victoria. In Victoria a person is regarded as "mentally ill" if he or she has a mental illness, defined as "a medical condition that is characterised by a significant disturbance of thought, mood, perception or memory".[11]

The criteria for involuntary treatment of a person are that –

(a) the person appears to be mentally ill; and

(b) the person's mental illness requires immediate treatment and that treatment can be obtained by the person being subject to an involuntary treatment order; and

(c) because of the person's mental illness, involuntary treatment of the person is necessary for his or her health or safety (whether to prevent a deterioration in the person's physical or mental condition or otherwise) or for the protection of members of the public; and

(d) the person has refused or is unable to consent to the necessary treatment for the mental illness; and

(e)   the person cannot receive adequate treatment for the mental illness in a manner less restrictive of his or her freedom of decision and action.[12]

Treatment is broadly defined to mean "things done in the course of the exercise of professional skills to (a) remedy the mental disorder; or (b) lessen its ill effects or the pain and suffering which it causes".[13]

Clinical decisions concerning imposition of involuntariness are subject to review by the Mental Health Review Board.

Western Australia. In Western Australia a person is defined to have a mental illness if "the person suffers from a disturbance of thought, mood, volition, perception, orientation or memory that impairs judgment or behaviour to a significant extent".[14]

A person can only be designated an "involuntary patient" if:

(a)   the person has a mental illness requiring treatment;

(b)   the treatment can be provided through detention in an authorised hospital or through a community treatment order and is required to be so provided in order:

   (i)   to protect the health or safety of that person or any other person;

   (ii)   to protect the person from self-inflicted harm of a kind described in subsection (2); or

   (iii)   to prevent the person doing serious damage to any property;

(c)   the person has refused or, due to the nature of the mental illness, is unable to consent to the treatment; and

(d)   the treatment cannot be adequately provided in a way that would involve less restriction of the freedom of choice and movement of the person than would result from the person being an involuntary patient.[15]

The kinds of self-inflicted harm from which a person may be protected by making the person an involuntary patient are:

(a)   serious financial harm;

(b)   lasting or irreparable harm to any important personal relationship resulting from damage to the reputation of the person among those with whom the person has such relationships; and

(c)   serious damage to the reputation of the person.

Australian Capital Territory. In the Australian Capital Territory a person must be mentally dysfunctional[16] or mentally ill to be made involuntary. A mental illness is defined as "a condition that seriously impairs (either temporarily or permanently) the mental functioning of a person and is characterised by the presence in the person of any of the following symptoms:

(a)   delusions;

(b)   hallucinations;

(c)   serious disorder of thought form;

(d)   a severe disturbance of mood;

(e)   sustained or repeated irrational behaviour indicating the presence of the symptoms referred to in paragraph (a), (b), (c) or (d)".[17]

As in most jurisdictions, a series of factors such as the person's sexual orientation, promiscuity, political beliefs, religious beliefs and practices, substance dependency, as well as the fact that they may have engaged in antisocial conduct, are stipulated not alone to permit of the inference of mental dysfunction.[18]

The Mental Health Review Tribunal of the Australian Capital Territory may make a psychiatric treatment order in relation to a person if:

(a)   the person has a mental illness; and

(b)   the tribunal has reasonable grounds for believing that, because of the illness, the person is likely to:

   (i)   do serious harm to himself, herself or someone else; or

   (ii)   suffer serious mental or physical deterioration;

unless subject to involuntary psychiatric treatment; and

(c)   the tribunal is satisfied that psychiatric treatment is likely to reduce the harm or deterioration (or the likelihood of harm or deterioration) mentioned in paragraph (b) and result in an improvement in the person's psychiatric condition; and

(d)   the treatment cannot be adequately provided in a way that would involve less restriction of the freedom of choice and movement of the person than would result from the person being an involuntary patient.

Northern Territory. In the Northern Territory "mental illness" is defined to mean "a condition that seriously impairs, either temporarily or permanently, the mental functioning of a person in one or more of the areas of thought, mood, volition, perception, orientation or memory and is characterised –

(a)   by the presence of at least one of the following symptoms:

   (i)   delusions;

   (ii)   hallucinations;

   (iii)   serious disorders of the stream of thought;

   (iv)   serious disorders of thought form;

   (v)   serious disturbances of mood; or

(b)   by sustained or repeated irrational behaviour that may be taken to indicate the presence of at least one of the symptoms referred to in paragraph (a)".[19]

The criteria for the involuntary admission of a person on the grounds of mental illness are that –

(a)   the person has a mental illness;

(b)   as a result of the mental illness –

   (i)   the person requires treatment that is available at an approved treatment facility;

   (ii)   the person –

     (A) is likely to cause imminent harm to himself or herself, a particular person or any other person; or

     (B) is likely to suffer serious mental or physical deterioration, unless he or she receives the treatment; and

    (iii)   the person is not capable of giving informed consent to the treatment or has unreasonably refused to consent to the treatment; and

(c)   there is no less restrictive means of ensuring that the person receives the treatment.[20]

The criteria for the involuntary admission of a person on the grounds of mental disturbance are that:

(a)   the person does not fulfil the criteria for involuntary admission on the grounds of mental illness;

(b)   the person's behaviour is, or within the immediately preceding 48 hours has been, so irrational as to lead to the conclusion that:

    (i)   the person is experiencing or exhibiting a severe impairment of or deviation from his or her customary or everyday ability to reason and function in a socially acceptable and culturally appropriate manner; and

    (ii)   the person is behaving in an abnormally aggressive manner or is engaging in seriously irresponsible conduct that justify a determination that the person requires psychiatric assessment, treatment or therapeutic care that is available at an approved treatment facility;

(c)   unless the person receives treatment or care at an approved treatment facility, he or she:

    (i)   is likely to cause imminent harm to himself or herself, to a particular person or to any other person;

    (ii)   will represent a substantial danger to the general community; or

    (iii)   is likely to suffer serious mental or physical deterioration;

(d)   the person is not capable of giving informed consent to the treatment or care or has unreasonably refused to consent to the treatment or care; and

(e)   there is no less restrictive means of ensuring that the person receives the treatment or care.[21]

Such orders are subject to the jurisdiction of the Mental Health Review Tribunal.

New Zealand. In New Zealand "mental disorder", in relation to any person, means an abnormal state of mind (whether of a continuous or an intermittent nature), characterised by delusions, or by disorders of mood or perception or volition or cognition, of such a degree that it:

(a)   poses a serious danger to the health or safety of that person or of others; or

(b)   seriously diminishes the capacity of that person to take care of himself or herself.[22]

Application for a compulsory treatment order and an application to extend an order must be heard by a Family Court judge or District Court judge.[23] The patient must be reviewed when an initial application has been made by the patient (or any other person specified in s 10(4)(a)) during the first period of assessment and treatment by a District Court judge.[24] The Mental Health Review Tribunal is a second tier of review.[25] Appeal against a review tribunal's decision to the District Court provides a further level of review.[26]

Appendix notes

1   *Mental Health Act 1990* (NSW) Sch 1.
2   Ibid, s 9.
3   Ibid, s 10.
4   *Mental Health Act 2000* (Qld) s 12.
5   Ibid, s 14.
6   Ibid, s 108.
7   *Mental Health Act 1993* (SA) s 3.
8   Ibid, s 13.
9   *Mental Health Act 1996* (Tas) s 4.
10   Ibid, s 24.
11   *Mental Health Act 1986* (Vic) s 8(1A).
12   Ibid, s 8(1).
13   Ibid, s 3.
14   *Mental Health Act 1996* (WA) s 4.
15   Ibid, s 26.
16   "Mentally dysfunctional or mentally ill offender" means a person who has been ordered by a court, under the *Crimes Act 1900* (ACT), Pt 13 or the *Children and Young People Act 1999* Pt 6.2 (which is about dealing with young offenders within the Australian Capital Territory), to submit to the jurisdiction of the tribunal to enable the tribunal to make a mental health order in respect of the person.
17   *Mental Health (Treatment and Care) Act 1994* (ACT), Dictionary.
18   Ibid, s 5.
19   *Mental Health and Related Services Act 1998* (NT) s 6.
20   Ibid, s 14.
21   Ibid, s 15.
22   *Mental Health (Compulsory Assessment and Treatment) Act 1992* (NZ) s 2.
23   Ibid, s 17(1) and (2).
24   Ibid, s 88.
25   Ibid, s 76(7).
26   Ibid, s 83(1).

PART IV

PUBLIC HEALTH

7

New directions in public health law

Chris Reynolds[1]

Introduction

Public health law *as a body of law and legislation* is to be found in an assortment of statutes, regulations and bylaws. Most obviously it covers the environmental health issues resulting from poor sanitation and unhealthy conditions. This is in keeping with its historical focus on the 19th century urban environment formed by the Industrial Revolution. But the discipline also covers the laws relating to food quality, the control of disease and drugs and, more recently, tobacco. These are all important issues that can and do affect the health of so many. Yet public health law has often been neglected, left unreformed for decades to occupy the dusty nooks and crannies of the statute books in ancient legislation or forgotten by laws.

Public health law *as a critical discipline* in many respects remains to be fully discovered. There are few texts that cover the field and few articles in the Australian journals: the number of articles devoted to *Rogers v Whitaker*[2] appear to well outnumber the total articles written in the field of public health law: a search of the Australian databases yielded 35 articles on public health law as opposed to 179 on *Rogers v Whitaker*.[3] Yet its significance is great. Perhaps our most important common law case *Donoghue v Stevenson*,[4] the snail in the ginger beer bottle, is a commentary on food preparation and a public health issue.

Public health law has long risked "being taken for granted" as effective prevention and public health more generally often is so. More immediate crises in the hospital system tend to overshadow and delay legislative reform. Yet there has been increased interest in the discipline driven by public health practitioners, federal, State and Territory Departments of Health and the National Public Health Partnership. Most importantly advocates for public health law have emerged among practitioners and a body of scholarship, both in Australia and overseas has allowed the creation of a systematic approach to the discipline that can describe

---

1   Chris Reynolds teaches law at Flinders University. He is the author of two texts on public health law and was the Director (Research) at the National Centre for Public Health Law between 2002-2005.

2   (1992) 175 CLR 479 (HCA).

3   The search was done in January 2005 via the AGIS (Law) and APAIS databases entering the terms "public health law" and "Rogers v Whitaker" respectively. Both covered the same period from 1992 onwards.

4   [1932] AC 562.

and coordinate its components and predict future directions. This chapter seeks to do just that. It provides a survey of the main currents in the development of public health law in Australasia and then offers some ideas for its future directions. In all cases, it will be argued that the role of law in this field is to support the public health process and, if it were to be distilled into one key idea, to do the things that are necessary to help people to live longer and healthier lives.

The three periods of public health law

While the current period of active public health law reform will be the main theme of this chapter, it is important to place this in a wider context. It is the third period to have occurred over the span of the past 150 years.

The first period was in the mid-19th century when the first recognisably modern public health laws were drafted. These established responsibilities for public health, vested in both local and national government. They instituted the power to order the removal of a statutory "nuisance" (insanitary or unhealthy conditions as defined) and provided a system of reporting and accounting for ongoing standards of public health.[5] These Acts joined other legislation that strengthened the powers of local government and were part of a sweeping series of reforms. Collectively they were public responses to what the social reformers and the medical reformers were loudly telling people – that there was a crisis in the new urban landscape of Industrial Britain.[6] The reform program gathered pace; by 1875 when the great consolidating *Public Health Act* was passed, there were some 29 separate pieces of public health law that were swept up into it. It is interesting that the main structure and the remedies provided by these first mid-19th century Acts have endured and remain a feature of current public health legislation in much of Australia and New Zealand. Indeed, were he to be summoned from his grave, John Snow could quite happily work with and apply the existing public health laws in most Australian States and New Zealand, so similar are they to their 19th century predecessors.

The second period of activity, perhaps less well known but also very significant, was around the beginning of the past century, a little over 100 years ago. During that period we saw food and drug regulation, alcohol laws in the control of "inebriates" and the rudiments of tobacco laws prohibiting sales to children. We also saw the bringing together of communicable disease and sanitary reform in single pieces of legislation. While a number of things might have contributed to this flurry of public health reform, a powerful reason was the fear (both in Australia and Britain) of national deterioration, of social and racial decay and

---

5 *Public Health Act 1848* (Eng) and *Nuisance Removal and Disease Prevention Act 1848* (Eng).

6 See Chadwick, E, *Report on the Sanitary Condition of the Labouring Population of Great Britain*, 1842; and the publications of the Health of Towns Association listed in Wohl A, *Endangered Lives: Public Health in Victorian Britain*, University Press, London, 1983, p 417 and also Wohl more generally.

decline of the birth-rate. There was some basis for this fear; by some accounts the population of Britain (and logically other urbanised communities) was becoming very unfit. According to one historian, Anthony Wohl, in 1901 one assessment concluded that less than 10 per cent of volunteers were considered fit enough to be sent to South Africa to fight in the Boer War.[7] A colonial war was one thing; the ever-present prospect of wide-scale European conflict made this issue a great deal more alarming. As a result a Committee on National Deterioration was established in Britain and a series of public health reforms were recommended, some of which required legislation. In Australia fears about the decline of the birth-rate and the corresponding threat from the "Asian hordes" also made social and legislative reform a serious issue.[8] It also spurred town planning reforms. It was said that the threats of "racial decay" lurked in the slums (together with the Chinese opium dens): by contrast the well-planned and airy environments of the garden suburb allowed for the flourishing of "better human machines" and a "virile race of White Australians".[9]

The third period of public health reform in Australia was from around 1985 to the present, a period during which reforms have been made in the control of non-communicable disease (or "lifestyle" disease), communicable disease and the health problems caused by pollution and poor environments. The process gathered pace by the late 1990s and those involved in it were thinking at a far more sophisticated level about the role of law and most importantly legislation in public health. Most significantly current public health reformers are aware of the need to remap the traditional boundaries of their discipline and to make it fit the public health demands of a new century. Over this third period there have been a number of strands of activity shaped by our recognition of the nature and demands of newly emerging public health problems.

The first strand was the focus on non-communicable disease, often known as the lifestyle disease or diseases of over-consumption, manifesting themselves in cardiovascular problems and a range of cancers. This was a different public health issue to sanitation or the regulation of communicable disease and it led to a different legislative response. In particular, tobacco consumption was seen as a major cause of preventable sickness and mortality and in response, we saw the development of tobacco laws that increasingly grew more stringent in their rest-rictions on advertising and sponsorship. The first tentative responses of the 1980s were strengthened into comprehensive State and Territory legislation and in 1992, national control was set in place through the Commonwealth's *Tobacco Advertising Prohibition Act*. The overall effect of these controls was to phase out direct tobacco advertising and sponsorship messages (indirect advertising) and to regulate

---

7   Wohl (1983) op cit p 332. Even less extreme assessments were damning, another being that only half the "manpower of the nation" was sufficiently fit for military service at all.

8   See generally Hicks, N, *This Sin and Scandal*, ANU Press, Canberra, 1978.

9   Freestone, R, *Model Communities: The Garden City Movement in Australia*, Nelson, Melbourne, 1989, p 84.

promotions and point of sale advertising. These laws were very important for their direct impact on tobacco consumption. They were also important for the lessons it offered public health generally. First, there was recognition that law was one aspect of the public health response and that it could join and support other elements such as health promotion. Secondly, officers involved in developing and implementing public health law came together at a national level with the States learning from each other's experience and moving towards a common national framework for tobacco control within a federal system. Finally, the tobacco laws also gave policy-makers the opportunity to rethink the role of law in lifestyle areas; that is, how much control and regulation was justifiable with regard to a product whose supply and use still remained legal. There was also the opportunity to translate this debate into other areas of lifestyle regulation, into nutrition for example – where there were both similarities and differences with tobacco.

The second strand involved a rethink of our communicable disease controls and for this the obvious driver was the HIV/AIDS crisis which first emerged as a prominent issue in Australia in the mid to late 1980s. Here was an unwelcome reminder of the problems of an earlier period in our public health, a period that antibiotics and medical advances had meant to have eliminated. In dealing with HIV/AIDS we were thrown back on the old public health coercive options of quarantine, compulsory examination and penalties for those infecting others. Worryingly, the responses and the fears that were spreading about HIV/AIDS were in so many cases the latest expressions of a tradition of fears. As the Jews were said to have spread the Black Death in medieval Europe by poisoning wells; as the Chinese were said to have introduced and then spread small pox and plague through 19th century Sydney; so now that other stigmatised minority, homosexuals, were said to be spreading HIV and – as lepers were always believed to have been doing – were taking pleasure in infecting others.[10] So HIV/AIDS told us a lot about how tied to the past we were. It also prompted the first national review of public health law undertaken by the HIV/AIDS Legal Working Party (established by the Intergovernmental Committee on AIDS). This provided the opportunity to rethink all of our public health laws relating to communicable disease and in November 1992 the Legal Working Party released a report that focused on a range of issues including rights and responsibilities, the use of coercive powers such as examination and detention and the application of criminal liability for those infecting others. Some of these recommendations have been implemented but, in other jurisdictions, public health laws in this area are many decades behind.

The third strand by comparison to the other two was less active. For the most part environmental health controls in Australia and New Zealand remained as they were when first drafted with the nuisance or insanitary conditions remedy remaining as the basic response. While other far more detailed and more impressive regulatory systems grew around the environmental health powers, notably

---

10   Reynolds, C, *Plagues and Prejudice: Boundaries Outsiders and Public Health,* unpublished doctoral thesis, University of Adelaide, 1992.

those offered by environment protection legislation, no Australasian jurisdiction (with the exception of the Australian Capital Territory and to some extent Tasmania) by 2000 had given any serious thought to the upgrading of their environmental health controls.

New directions in public health law reform

This takes us to the present and our need to respond to new issues and problems in public health. During the period from 1995, far more planning and thinking about public health law occurred than had ever occurred previously. The work done by a number of government-sponsored bodies and academic institutions including the National Public Health Partnership, the Environmental Health Council, the Australian Institute of Health law and Ethics, and the National Centre for Public Health Law, has mapped and described public health law and explored the ways that it might support the work of public health practitioners in meeting new and emerging public health threats. This chapter now considers the main directions that this work has gone in.

Public health emergencies

The first of these, though not strictly new, are the problems of epidemic disease and bioterrorism following on from the SARS scares of 2003 and 2004, the continuing (as of 2006) threat of "bird flu", the anxieties post-September 11, and the public health catastrophes following on from the Indian Ocean Tsunami of Boxing day 2004. Much of this is speculation and fear. Yet, underlying it is the need for effective responses to large-scale and urgent crises in public health. To date our laws do not deal well with this area: when the major reviews of the disease controls were being undertaken in the 1990s the powers to respond to a major epidemic were not carefully considered, largely because HIV/AIDS did not present that kind of problem. As a result, the laws that we do have in place are not so well adapted to deal with a major public health crisis. What is needed is a broad set of powers to do the things necessary in emergencies to secure public health. These centre on the need to contain infection and other public health risks and should include the powers to examine, isolate and quarantine, to order the evacuation from a specified area or restrict entry to an area, to require that persons undertake medical treatment or vaccination, and to seize or destroy any property or article where necessary to deal with the emergency.

Such sweeping powers need to take account of human rights (an issue which few Public Health Acts currently address) and sweeping powers to respond in emergencies must exist within a framework that confines the response by ideas of proportionality. In other words the capacity of the legislation to have an impact on persons' lives should be proportionate to the public health needs. The controls must be subject to overriding principles such as the following:

- the overriding principle that the liberty and rights of persons be respected at all times;

- these should be infringed, only when the interest in protecting public health is compelling and then only to the minimum extent necessary to secure this end;

- consistent with the interest to protect public health *the least intrusive power* is always to be used.

The United States[11] has developed draft emergency public health laws to deal with the public health demands of future crises. A *Model State Emergency Health Powers Act* (prepared October 2001 in the midst of the "anthrax crisis")[12] provides for the public health surveillance provisions of tracking, the declaration of states of emergency and special powers to control people and things (which includes compulsory examinations and detention). The Model Act is premised on the idea that governments have a duty to safeguard public health, especially in emergencies when extraordinary measures may be required but that "it is the duty of the State to act with fairness and tolerance towards individuals and groups"; and the rights of people to liberty, bodily integrity and privacy must be respected to the fullest extent possible, consistent with the overriding importance of the public's health and security.[13]

Non-communicable disease

Over the past decades new lifestyle diseases continue to emerge as serious public health problems. We have mentioned tobacco, which has been the subject of public health legislation but perhaps the most compelling emerging issue is the diseases linked with obesity. As a population we are becoming heavier and the proportion of overweight and obese members of the community is increasing steadily. With that comes a range of weight-related diseases including cardiovascular disease and diabetes, burdening to their victims while adding substantially to the health budget.

Increasing levels of obesity are a feature of both developed and many developing countries. In Australia, it has been estimated that "around seven

---

11 Specifically the Center for Law and the Public's Health (Georgetown and Johns Hopkins Universities), which prepared a model for States to implement. This was prepared for the United States Centers for Disease Control and Prevention (CDC) in collaboration with the National Governors Association, 23 October 2001, <www.publichealthlaw.net> (accessed 21 April 2005).

12 Though very worrying to a community shaken by the 11 September attacks, the anthrax outbreak was restricted to about 22 cases up to December 2001 (most of which were not fatal): *CDC Update: Investigation of Bioterrorism-Related Anthrax*, <www.cdc.gov/mmwr/preview/mmwrhtml/mm5048a1.htm> (accessed 21 April 2005); see also UCLA's Department of Epidemiology <www.ph.ucla.edu/epi/bioter/bioterrorism.html> (accessed 21 April 2005).

13 Section 102 legislative findings of the Model Act. See also the discussion in Matei, L, "Quarantine Revision and the Model State Emergency Health Powers Act: "Laws for the Common Good'" (2002) 18 *Santa Clara Computer & High Tech L J* 433.

million Australians are either overweight or obese". Estimates taken in 2000 suggest that, while more men are overweight than women (67 per cent compared to 52 per cent), obesity is more prevalent among women (22 per cent) than men (18 per cent). At this rate, it is thought that about 75 per cent of the Australian population will be overweight or obese by 2020".[14] Children's weight also increased dramatically with "about 23% of Australian children and adolescents being overweight with 6% being obese.[15] These are said to be conservative estimates and they point to a very worrying trend and a future epidemic with huge individual and collective health costs. Indigenous Australians are more obese than non-indigenous Australians, contributing to the very high burdens of indigenous illness. It is also known more generally that obesity correlates with poverty which is ironic given its association with abundance rather than deprivation.[16]

The dramatic increase in overweight and obese Australians is not surprising; there have been two major environmental changes over the past few decades. First, food, especially high energy convenience foods have become far more available, are extensively promoted and are relatively cheap, packaged to eat whenever their consumers have the inclination or the opportunity. Secondly, work and travel now demands less physical energy of participants as jobs have become more sedentary and people travel to work, shops or school by cars (this is discussed below under the heading "New issues and sustainability").

Considering how we might respond to the first change, current food laws in Australia provide little regulation of promotion or advertising. Rather they aim to protect against the traditional issues of food-borne illness and adulteration by creating offences for the sale of dangerous (unsafe) food and call upon the food standards agreed to nationally by the Food Standards Australia New Zealand arrangements. Standards that relate to labelling and packaging and nutritional and energy contents of foods are in many cases required by law. However, there are

---

14   Department of Human Services Victoria <www.betterhealth.vic.gov.au/bhcv2/bhcarticles. nsf/pages/Obesity?open> (accessed 13 February 2006). See also Australian Institute of Health and Welfare, *Bulletin: A growing problem: Trends and patterns in overweight and obesity among adults in Australia, 1980 to 2001*, AIHW, Canberra, 2003, p 1, <www.aihw.gov.au> (accessed 13 February2006). See also Cameron, A, Welborn, T, Zimmet, P, et al "Overweight and obesity in Australia: the 1999–2000 Australian Diabetes, Obesity and Lifestyle Study (AusDiab)" (2003) 178 *Medical Journal of Australia* 427.

15   Waters, E and Baur, L, "Childhood Obesity: Modernity's Scourge" (2003) 178(9) *Medical Journal of Australia* 422. See also Australian Institute of Health and Welfare, *Australia's Health 2002*, AIHS, Canberra, 2002, p 178, <www.aihw.gov.au> (accessed 13 February 2006).

16   Australian Institute of Health and Welfare, *The Health and Welfare of Australia's Aboriginal and Torres Strait Islander Peoples 2003*, AIHW, Canberra, 2003, p 171, <www.aihw.gov.au/ publications/ihw/hwaatsip03/index.html> (accessed 13 February 2006). The report (p 206) indicates that among Indigenous Australians:

Approximately 25% of adult Indigenous males and 29% of adult Indigenous females were classified as obese compared to about 19% of both other Australian adult males and adult females.

See also O'Dea, J, "Differences in Overweight and Obesity Among Australian School-children of Low and Middle/high Socioeconomic Status" (2003) 179(1) *Medical Journal of Australia* 63

still some foods that the requirements do not apply to, notably unpackaged or "take away" food and this is where some of the sustained criticism about high energy food often comes from.[17] Labelling could also be clearer, perhaps stating the proportion of daily nutritional needs the food contains or the energy expenditure necessary to burn off the food.

Serving sizes can add to the problem, having increased dramatically in some cases over the past decades. Some snack foods can contain as much as 20 to 25 per cent of a person's daily nutritional needs, yet are packaged as one serving. Furthermore, "large" options are typically available in take-away restaurants and are better value than "standard" options, with the result that individuals take in more calories in one sitting.[18]

The most controversial and problematic component of an obesity strategy would be restrictions on advertising and promotion of foods and, if imposed, the extent of those restrictions. For example, a ban on the advertising of "undesirable" food would be difficult to define and enforce. Yet, difficult as it may be, there is a case to develop some controls, since, as with tobacco, the advertising budget of the food industry will vastly overshadow the budgets of health agencies trying to put a counter message.[19] There are also examples of advertising aimed blatantly at children. This could suggest a partial regulation or ban that could focus on representations aimed obviously at children. Another option would be to prevent food advertisements from focusing on toys that come with the food or that can be collected during a visit to a restaurant since they are also aimed particularly at children and distort nutritional choices. It might also be possible to prevent the promotion of certain types of food at certain times, for example during children's television periods.

Sponsorship can be read as a benevolent action, an industry giving back something to a community or activity that supports it. But it also allows for loosely disguised advertising and promotion. Sponsorship in schools is of particular concern, though arrangements vary. Sponsorship of a school soccer team by the local supermarket is different to a national sponsorship run by a fast-food company. Another problem of sponsorship in the education environment is that they can "capture" schools offering a much-needed source of revenue for many schools, masking legitimate concerns about the longer-term adverse impact on students.

---

17 Current requirements for labelling are provided by Standard 1.2.8 of the *Food Standards Code* (Nutritional Information requirements), <www.foodstandards.gov.au/foodstandards code/> (accessed 21 April 2005).

18 Critser, G, *Fat Land: How Americans became the Fattest People in the World*, Penguin, London, 2003; Critser claims, for example, that a serving of McDonalds chips has increased from 200 calories (1960) to 610 calories (2002): p 28.

19 Critser (2003) op cit, claims that in the United States, the advertising budget of the soft drink industry is US$600 million annually. By comparison, the National Cancer Institute has a budget of US$1 million to promote healthy eating of fruit and vegetables: p 173. See also position in Britain where it is said that "less than £2m was being spent to encourage children to eat and drink healthy products, compared with £600m on commercial food". Wintour, P, "Ad Agency Apologises over 'Pester Mum' Commercial", *Guardian Weekly*, 20–26 November 2003.

This is particularly serious since "education", rather than bans or restrictions, is often offered as a way of helping children make sensible nutritional choices.[20]

How formal should our approach be? Self-regulation is commonly offered as an alternative to regulation. But self-regulation such as "codes of conduct" are often not sustained by any real penalties and are expressed in broad general terms which allow for technical interpretation and nitpicking exclusions when the need arises. Often they are "policed" by bodies that have close association with the industry. Significantly, self-regulation is often proposed by an industry facing the real prospect of actual regulation, and may well be an attempt to forestall government action, offered and policed by an industry which has the understandable goal of selling of much of its product as possible to as many people as possible.

To summarise, as with tobacco, legislation can change the environment in which certain types of food are presented and marketed. This is not imposing requirements or coercions on the community. Rather it is seeking to level the playing field, to create an environment within which the pressures of marketing and advertising are eased in order to facilitate free and informed choice. While the opponents of these kinds of controls can paint them as coercive and interventionist, an example of the "nanny state" at work, and roll out their ideological arguments about the value of minimal regulation and freedom to be informed, it is more cogently the impact on corporate profits that concerns them. Freedom of choice is in fact enhanced where the playing field is as level as governments can make it. It is diminished where there is no check on the amounts or content of the advertising. Levelling the playing field in this and other lifestyle areas also helps to encourage a key idea from the Ottawa Charter on Health Promotion (1986) that "healthy choices should be easy choices": logically, they are easier when not made against a barrage of counter-advertising.

There is another interesting issue that has emerged from the non-communicable disease area. This relates to private litigation, of which *Donoghue v Stevenson* was possibly the first celebrated example. While public health law is generally the product of statutes and the possibilities canvassed above would be introduced by legislation, there is another dimension to public health enforcement that is offered by the courts. More particularly, if governments refuse to regulate in this area, they may implicitly be opting for civil actions that will fill the regulatory vacuum. To date, civil actions have been prominent responses to outbreaks of food poisoning. The damages and costs that come with them also provide substantial incentives for companies to improve their performance, more so than prosecution. A well-publicised case of peanut paste contamination occurred in 1997. If the manufacturer, had been prosecuted it might – if found guilty – have risked a fine of less than $10,000 under the food laws existing at the time. The costs associated with settling the various civil claims brought against it were reportedly many

---

20   See Nestle, M, *Food Politics: How the Industry Influences Nutrition and Health*, University of California Press, Berkeley, 2002, Ch 9; Critser (2003) op cit p 170; and Schlosser, E, *Fast Food Nation*, Penguin, London, 2002, pp 51–57.

millions of dollars. In terms of financial risk-management, civil litigation was of far greater concern.[21]

Civil actions and the threat of them can also change marketing practices. In July 2003, Kraft Foods announced that it was proposing to reduce its serving sizes and discontinue its marketing in schools. It also announced that it was considering expanding its nutritional information to include the value of the food in a packet as a proportion of a person's daily calorific needs and how much physical activity is required to burn off those calories.[22] This new policy happened in the wake of a short-lived case against the company in respect of its failure to list the "trans fat" content of its Oreo biscuits.[23] Litigation has also been brought against fast-food companies in respect of their products contributing to obesity among child customers. While these cases are very difficult to prove (since obesity is multi-causal) and they attract criticism from many quarters, they do make the point that companies are liable for their products and that there is often scope for a healthier version and more nutritional information.[24]

In short, civil proceedings can fill a void that the public health regulations may have chosen not to occupy. However recent changes to Australian tort law have limited the rights of plaintiffs and implicitly weakened these alternative public health sanctions. In the United States, some regulators have sought to limit the food industry's risk of litigation by specifically protecting it from obesity-related claims.[25]

New issues in environmental health

The "core" public health laws (the Health Acts and the Public Health Acts) developed from their 19th century origins and with little real change continue to offer the same general remedy which operates on complaint. A person who is the "victim" of a nuisance or insanitary condition as defined can ask the local council to order its removal. This was the prime public health remedy and it was also, for much of the past 100 years, the prime environmental remedy. The Public Health Acts were the closest we had to Environmental Protection Acts.[26] This was also consistent with the

---

21   Radio National Transcripts: *The Law Report*, 3 June 1997 (class actions) <www.abc.net.au/rn/talks/8.30/lawrpt/lstories/lr970603.htm/> (accessed 27 July 2005).

22   See <www.kraft.com/obesity/responses.html> (accessed 21 April 2005).

23   These are hydrogenated oils, which raise "bad" cholesterols. See Reynolds, C, *Public Health Law and Regulation*, Federation Press, Sydney, 2004, p 204; and Severson, K, "Lawsuit Seeks to Ban Sale of Oreos to Children in California", *San Francisco Chronicle*, 12 May 2003, <http://sfgate.com/cgi-bin/article.cgi?f=/c/a/2003/05/12/OREO.TMP> (accessed 27 July 2005).

24   "Kraft plans to cut snack sizes", *BBC News*, 2 July 2003 <www.bbc.co.uk/food/features/news.shtml> (accessed 21 April 2005).

25   See the proposed United States federal *Personal Responsibility in Food Consumption Act 2003*, Colorado legislation 2004 HR339 IH; and also 2004 Colorado Senate Bill 04-020, cited in Reynolds, C, "Law and Public Health: Addressing Obesity" (2004) 29 *Alternative Law Journal* 162 at 165.

26   The *Environment Protection Act 1970* (Vic) was the first comprehensive legislation; other States and Territories moved towards consolidated pollution control laws through the 1980s and 1990s.

way that the causes of disease were seen: the remedial power applied to "things of an offensive nature or likely to be prejudicial to health". These were the environmental eyesores, conditions that were noticeably unpleasant and offensive (generally evidenced by their smells). This merging of health and environmental concerns was an expression of the prevailing idea about the way disease was spread. It was thought that offensive conditions were unhealthy on account of the "miasmas" or "effluvia" or exudation emitted by them. The visual and the malodorous became a telltale sign of the source of infections and things that were offensive were by their nature also prejudicial to health; thus the public health pursuit of pollution control. Today, it is more comprehensively regulated through Environment Protection Acts. Indeed, these Acts carry greater penalties and offer their administering agencies a more flexible and versatile series of options. The upshot is that many issues, such as water pollution, noise, contaminated land or air pollution, can be characterised equally as a public health issue and as an environment protection issue, with the latter offering a modern and much more comprehensive series of remedies. Given this, is there a future for environmental health as a distinct and separate form of administrative and legislative response?

It has been argued by the National Public Health Partnership and others (see below) that a new approach to public health is required, based on the idea of "risk to health" and that this should be the single organising idea around which new legislation is structured. At the outset we should also state that there is a case for maintaining a public health gaze on environmental issues. There is value in continuing to characterise problems as "public health problems" rather than redefining them as environmental protection or consumer affairs problems.

The argument for the public health approach is that it has great historical depth, concerned at each point with the well-being of individuals. The ideals of its present-day practitioners are the descendants of the ideals of the 19th century social reformers who realised the value and legitimacy of state intervention. The public health approach also has a great breadth; it recognises the value of other interests and regulatory systems and that the social determinants of health, which are many and complex, take the discipline a long way beyond its sanitary origins. Indeed, this view is a key point within the Ottawa Charter. Many disciplines contribute to public health policy and for all of these reasons, public health, its supporters can argue, has richness and depth and the ability to see the comp-lexities of particular problems that draw on the lessons of history and the contribution of a wide range of perspectives. To take an obvious example, a public health approach to indigenous health would say that it was more than the practical issues of service delivery. It would say that past histories are also significant and that issues such as discrimination and social status are important and must be recognised if the appalling levels of indigenous ill-health are ever to be addressed.

If a case for maintaining a public health approach can be made, this needs to be supported by legislation which is sufficiently versatile to sustain responses. Contemporary thinking about public health law has been to replace the specific remedies of "nuisance" or "insanitary condition" with a general duty. This idea was first explored by the National Public Health Partnership in 2000 and it was envisaged that the duty might be expressed as follows:

> A person must not undertake any activity that may result in harm to health unless the person takes all reasonable and practical measures to eliminate the possibility of that harm occurring.[27]

It was argued that a statutory duty might apply to a range of situations beyond the scope of nuisance as traditionally defined. These are particularly new and emerging problems. Some we know about such as new age "therapeutic" procedures that are not regulated elsewhere. Others are yet to emerge and the duty would apply to a range of unknown future problems its scope "unfolding" to meet new challenges as they occur.

Another issue with environmental health legislation is its lack of serious offences. This is always a controversial area and the "command and control" approach implicit in penalties has its critics. Certainly, the test of good and effective legislation should not be judged just by the size of the penalty. Rather the extent to which people comply with the Act is the better measure of its effectiveness. But penalties are significant since they are part of the mechanisms to ensure compliance and in particular cases, the community will also expect serious punishments to be available when necessary so that the "penalty can fit the crime". For example, following on from the 1995 Garibaldi mettwurst poisonings in South Australia (which led to the death of a child and serious injury to many others) there was great public concern that the penalties then in the *Food Act 1985* were far too inadequate to deal with the seriousness of the offence. More particularly, environmental health or public health offences are usually very modest by comparison with environmental protection offences; the latter having terms of imprisonment for up to seven years for the most serious breaches of these Acts.[28]

As a result, a number of jurisdictions are considering the creation of an offence which is committed where a person causes a "risk to health". As with the general duty, the potential scope of the offence is wide. The discussion paper on the review of the Victorian *Health Act 1958* considered that it might apply in a range of possibilities including the following:

- allowing a drain to overflow, with the possibility of transmission of diseases;
- operating a public swimming pool in breach of the guidelines for chlorination;

---

27 National Public Health Partnership, *The Application of Risk Management Principles in Public Health Legislation*, NPHP, Melbourne, 2000, <www.nphp.gov.au/publications/legislation/riskmgtrep.pdf>, Pt 6.3 (accessed 21 April 2005). Statutory duties already exist in legislation. For example, s 25(1) of the *Environment Protection Act 1993* (SA) provides that:

> A person must not undertake an activity that pollutes, or might pollute, the environment unless the person takes all reasonable and practicable measures to prevent or minimise any resulting environmental harm.

28 *Protection of the Environment Operations Act 1997* (NSW) s 119 relating to environmental harm; *Environment Protection Act 1970* (Vic) s 59E relating to serious environmental damage.

- operating a tattooing parlour in such a way as to risk the spread of disease to clients;
- a person infected with a sexually transmitted disease who engages in unsafe sex;
- a person with active tuberculosis who obtains a job in a child care centre.

These examples reflect the traditional dimensions of public health legislation, where its abiding concerns for environmental health and the containment of disease are self-evident.[29]

But there are other examples where the use of the offence would not be so clear. For example, persons who expose their children to tobacco smoke in the home or in a vehicle are causing a risk to health, but should they be prosecuted? There may be other ways of addressing this issue and this emphasises the point that prosecutions are never automatic, there is always discretion on whether or how to act and prosecutors will need to be satisfied that it is in the "public interest" to bring a case. Some activities are very risky but socially acceptable (riding a motor cycle with a pillion passenger, for example) and would not be the subject of prosecution. In other cases where there is a risk to health, such as where a factory emits carcinogens and other chemicals into the atmosphere or where there is a breach of food safety procedures leading to cases of salmonella infection it is preferable to prosecute under other Acts (in this case the environment protection and the food laws). But, as with the general duty there are also new and unfolding risks to health and the strength of a generic approach is that a prosecution can be brought in novel situations. Two "real life" examples are:

- a diving shop attaching unreliable dials to air tanks; and
- the sale of "safe" (in fact hazardous) glasses to watch a solar eclipse.[30]

Overall the approach canvassed here strengthens the public health approach by making it more versatile and more significant in terms of the options available. But some problems remain, notably that of distinguishing between a public (or environmental) health problem and an environment protection problem. Poor air quality can, for example, be seen both as a risk to health and a case of atmospheric pollution. These overlapping interests are best resolved by discussions between the relevant regulatory agencies with the delineation of responsibilities agreed beforehand.

---

29 Department of Human Services, Victoria, *Review of the Health Act 1958: A new legislative framework for public health in Victoria*, Discussion Paper, August 2004. <www.health. vic.gov.au/healthactreview> (accessed 21 April 2005). In July 2005, the Western Australian Government released its Discussion Paper of the *Health Act 1911* (WA): *A New Health Act for Western Australia*, which took a similar approach to Victoria: <www.health.gov.wa.au> (accessed 27 July 2005).

30 The author was involved in preparing this material for the August 2004 Victorian Discussion Paper.

New issues and sustainability

The 21st century will see a continuing of the public health problems we know about and have canvassed in this chapter. Potentially it will also see very significant problems emerging from new issues, perhaps the most important being the environmental and human health issues caused by climatic events and the cumulative problems of our unsustainable lifestyle. These new issues are likely to present our greatest public health challenges over the coming century. How will public health legislation respond? At the outset it demands that we recognise that the problems of climate change and the challenges of sustainability are, on account of their dire impacts on humans, public health issues. In doing so, we will dramatically and very significantly change the focus and priorities of public health law. We must argue that sustainability is a public health issue (as it is also an environmental issue) and that public health laws should support sustainability policy. In particular, public policy should recognise the links between public health and environmental issues and allow both areas of concern to support each other.

But how is this to be done in practice? One important way is to allow public health concerns to influence wider land-use policies through a process of health impact assessment which requires health to be considered as an issue in proposed developments or planning initiatives. This will give a public health voice in many areas of the built and natural environment that impact on sustainability and on the quality of life generally. While much work has been done on how health impacts are to be assessed, there remains the question of how it will be integrated into the formal assessment process and how widely it can be applied. For example, environmental impact assessment (a process related to health impact assessment and into which health concerns might be integrated) applies only for major developments – generally those that governments are eager to have go ahead. But it could apply more generally to the range of planning decisions that have an impact on public health (new subdivisions on the urban fringe, the siting of factories or new transport corridors) through referrals by planning authorities to public health agencies or officers or within local councils.

Health impact assessment and its links with the urban environment is often seen as a new direction for public health, yet it is not; it offers the opportunity to rediscover links that early town planners made with public health. The planning visionaries of a century ago saw their work as closely linked with human betterment; a well-planned community was a healthier community, whose parks and gardens provided opportunities for children to exercise and whose pleasant streetscapes gave its residents a sense of worth. Indeed, the 1918 Town Planning Conference in Brisbane made infant health a focus.[31] For them the link between healthy babies and the work of town planners was obvious. Current planning has lost those explicit connections. Now, it is more a technical component of a land-use

---

31   Fraser, H, *The Federation House*, New Holland Publishers, Sydney, 2002, p 12.

control system rather than a visionary and reforming enterprise. Health impact assessment allows us to rediscover those links.

Another link with the environment lies in the work currently being undertaken in the development and implementation of sustainability policy. At the time of writing the most substantial work in this area has occurred in Western Australia where the essence of sustainability has been defined in *Hope for the Future: WA Sustainability Strategy* which offered the view that:

> [S]ustainability ... demands that we act together, providing an integrated and mutually reinforcing approach to issues that in the past have been treated more in isolation.[32]

This idea, which calls for intersectoral cooperation, resonates with the Ottawa Charter on Health Promotion.[33] It invites us to consider how public health legislation might support sustainability principles and be broad enough to allow new and imaginative uses of public health law.

The Western Australian Sustainability Bill imposes a set of reporting and accountability requirements on the public sector. Its definition of sustainability is broad, going beyond the traditional environmental questions and incorporating social issues such as the quality of life, community and a sense of place.[34] This resonates with the wider definition of health provided in the WHO Constitution.[35] The Bill provides a charter for public health policy to pursue sustainability outcomes (and therefore public health outcomes) at both local and State government levels. Most importantly it provides the opportunity to identify the common interests of public health and environmental sustainability. These links are extremely important: too often sustainability is presented as a trade-off between the environment *or* development, one is enhanced to the detriment of the other. We don't so often consider how policies operating in the same area can be mutually supporting. The following illustrate this point.

Example 1 – commuting patterns: Our commuting pattern (largely by private vehicles) has many well-recognised environmental costs, including increased greenhouse production and adverse affects on the urban environment. By comparison, active commuting, by foot, bicycle or public transport is a more sustainable option, one that is worth pursuing for environmental reasons. Active commuting by foot, bicycle and public transport (which involves walking to and from bus stops and train stations) provides the crucial "built in" opportunities for regular exercise. It therefore supports population health strategies. By contrast, our

---

32 "What Sustainability Means" in *Western Australia: Hope for the Future, WA Sustainability Strategy*, Department of the Premier and Cabinet, 2003, p 24 <www.sustainability.dpc.wa. gov.au/docs/Final%20Strategy/SSSFinal.pdf> (accessed 27 July 2005)

33 Ottawa Charter for Health Promotion, 1986 <www.who.int/hpr/NPH/docs/ottawa_charter _hp.pdf> (accessed 27 July 2005).

34 See Sustainability Bill 2004 (WA) Sch 1.

35 "Health is a state of complete physical, mental and social well-being and not merely the absence of disease or infirmity", Preamble to the Constitution of the World Health Organisation, 1947 (set out in Sch 1 to the *World Health Organisation Act 1947* (Cth)).

dependence on private vehicle use is a major cause of inactivity, leading to obesity, a major health issue. This example provides an obvious synergy between sustainability policy and population health policy. Initiatives that help change commuting patterns (taxing car parking, increased priority for buses on roads, the provision of safe routes to school through reduced speed limits in suburban streets, the creation of liveable neighbourhoods that are pedestrian friendly, and so on) and also at a Commonwealth level (stopping salary sacrificing of vehicles, taxing fuel and vehicles, and so on) can contribute both to good environmental and good population health outcomes.

Example 2 – nutrition policy – minimising energy inputs: Food produced and then consumed locally generally involves less energy inputs than packaged foods transported long distances from factories interstate or overseas. Where the locally produced food is fruit and vegetables (as it often is) it provides a healthier alternative to packaged or highly refined food. Thus a strategy that encourages local production and consumption of fresh food is desirable environmentally and also for public health. Strategies to encourage local production of fresh food and to identify barriers to it (such as land-use policies) further both interests.

To conclude, the issues raised in this part have not usually been seen as high priorities for public health policy yet they will provide some of its most significant public health challenges. They will take public health away from its sanitary origins and towards a more holistic view of the discipline, a view that seeks to implement some key ideas in the Ottawa Charter and contributes to the bigger pictures of sustainability and a healthy society.

Conclusion

Public health law has led a "Cinderella-like" existence for much of the past 100 years – shabby, undervalued and slow to be reformed. Its traditional areas of regulation were often left to atrophy, with remedies so ancient that they offered an approach that was derived from a world that existed before bacteria were known about. Until recently there was never a serious vision for the discipline. Rather interest in it was fuelled by crises and immediate issues, with the Acts being patched and repatched as the need arose. Yet we know that the "public health approach" can achieve much and it deserves legislation that can intelligently and usefully contribute to the potentially very great human health issues of the 21st century. This vision now sustains the reforms in public health law that are being undertaken in many Australian jurisdictions. Indeed, the future for public health law and policy looks promising. There is a growing consensus both in Australia and New Zealand that an extensive rethink of the traditional directions of public health law needs to occur. This rethink should lead to legislation that:

- builds on the traditions and values of public health as a reforming enterprise;
- does not lose sight of established issues and concerns, but which can respond to them in a more generic and imaginative way, bringing with it the ability to respond also to new and emerging public health issues;
- can make a distinct and useful contribution to the wider environmental and land-use process, ensuring that in this process public health concerns and health impacts are effectively identified and assessed; and
- can respond to significant future public health needs – both the acute needs brought on by emergencies and the more gradual issues caused by climate change and our unhealthy and unsustainable lifestyles.

But change in this area never comes easily and effective public health laws will always be controversial and they will challenge vested interests, as public health laws often have done in the past. For this reason and also for the urgency of the problems we face, public health needs defenders and those who are interested in public regulation and who aware of the existing and potential threats to human health to argue the case for public health law whenever the opportunity exists.

8

Mad cows and prions: Legal, ethical and operational challenges in responding to Creutzfeldt-Jakob Disease (CJD) and variant CJD

Roger S Magnusson[1]

Introduction

Creutzfeldt-Jakob disease (CJD) is a rare and fatal neurodegenerative disease that causes rapidly progressive dementia. The average age of onset of symptoms is 60 years, with 90 per cent of patients dying mute, immobile, and incontinent within 12 months (median four to five months).[2] First described in the 1920s, it is the best-known human form of a class of diseases known as transmissible spongiform encephalopathies (TSEs) that includes scrapie in sheep and goats, chronic wasting disease in deer and elk, and bovine spongiform encephalopathy (or BSE) – popularly known as "mad cow disease" – in cattle. There are several lesser-known human TSEs. These include kuru (a disease affecting the Fore tribe in Papua New Guinea,

---

1   Associate Professor, Faculty of Law, University of Sydney. The author is a member of the Special Expert Committee on Transmissible Spongiform Encephalopathies (SECTSE), a committee of the National Health and Medical Research Council (NHMRC). The views expressed in this paper are personal views, not the views of the NHMRC or SECTSE. I am grateful to the following for their helpful comments: Professor Graeme Ryan, Chair, SECTSE; Professor Richard Smallwood, Chair, National Blood Authority Board; Associate Professor Steven Collins, Co-Director, Australian National CJD Registry, Department of Pathology, Faculty of Medicine, Dentistry and Health Sciences, University of Melbourne; Dr David Adams, Senior Principal Research Scientist, Office of the Chief Veterinary Officer, Commonwealth Department of Agriculture, Fisheries and Forestry; Professor Colin Masters, Laureate Professor, Department of Pathology, Faculty of Medicine, Dentistry and Health Sciences, University of Melbourne; and Dr Anthony Keller, National Donor & Product Safety Manager, Australian Red Cross Blood Bank. Any errors are mine.

2   Collins, S, Lawson, V and Masters, C, "Transmissible Spongiform Encephalopathies" (2004) 363 *Lancet* 51 at 54. This description refers to the majority of cases of CJD that are classified as "sporadic", meaning that there is no known, specific cause of the disease. A minority of cases are classified as "inherited", and cases of acquired infection have also been documented following certain medical procedures.

unwittingly transmitted by eating the brains of relatives in ritualistic mourning ceremonies); Gerstmann-Sträussler-Scheinker disease (a hereditary disorder marked by progressive lack of coordination, prior to dementia); and fatal familial insomnia (a hereditary disorder marked by sleeping problems, followed by dementia).

Although rare, CJD has generated significant concern in the community. In 1996, a variant form of CJD (vCJD) was identified, transmitted by eating beef and beef products infected with "mad cow disease".[3] Besides demonstrating that BSE can jump the species barrier, vCJD focused attention on "intra-species recycling": the industry practice of feeding cattle with meat and bone meal, derived from the carcasses of other cattle, as a protein supplement. This practice – analogous to the cannibalism of the Fore – is now recognised to be responsible for BSE transmission among cattle.[4] In contrast to the classical form of CJD, the average age of onset of vCJD is much younger (late 20s), while the duration of illness is longer (median 14 months). Psychiatric symptoms – including depression, anxiety, withdrawal, and personality disturbance – affect 60 per cent of cases.[5] Some patients develop psychotic features, while pain and neurological symptoms (tremor, gait and speech disturbances) also occur. As with classical CJD, patients lose awareness of their surroundings, become bedridden, require artificial feeding and constant care, before slipping into coma.[6]

CJD, vCJD and other TSEs are known as "prion diseases" because they are caused by a rogue form of a naturally occurring cellular protein: the prion protein.[7] The emerging consensus is that TSEs are caused by a structurally aberrant ("misfolded") form of the prion that acts as a trigger or template for production of other misfolded proteins.[8] In its misfolded form, the prion protein is relatively

---

3   Will, R, Ironside, J, Zeidler, M et al, "A New Variant of Creutzfeldt-Jakob Disease in the United Kingdom" (1996) 347 *Lancet* 921; Bruce, M, Will, R, Ironside, J et al, "Transmissions to Mice Indicate that 'New Variant' CJD is Caused by the BSE Agent" (1997) 389 *Nature* 498.

4   Masters, C, "The Emerging European Epidemic of Variant Creutzfeldt-Jakob Disease and Bovine Spongiform Encephalopathy: Lessons for Australia" (2001) 174 *Medical Journal of Australia* 160; Goldwater, P, "Bovine Spongiform Encephalopathy and Variant Creutzfeldt-Jakob Disease: Implications for Australia" (2001) 175 *Medical Journal of Australia* 154. Intra-species recycling continues to occur in the pork and poultry industries.

5   Collins et al (2004) above note 2 at 56. See also Spencer, M, Knight R, Will, R, "First Hundred Cases of Variant Creutzfeldt-Jakob Disease: Retrospective Case Note Review of Early Psychiatric and Neurological Features" (2002) 324 *British Medical Journal* 1479.

6   See Commonwealth Department of Health and Ageing, Communicable Diseases and Health Protection Branch, *A Family Support Plan for Variant Creutzfeldt-Jakob Disease* (confidential draft). For an illustrative case description, see Wiersma, Set al, "Probable Variant Creutzfeldt-Jakob Disease in a U.S. Residence – Florida, 2002" (2002) 51(41) *MMWR* 927.

7   Collins et al (2004) op cit. The word "prion" is short for "*prion*aceous *in*fectious *un*it"; however, the term is misleading because the prion protein (PrP^c) occurs naturally in the brain, spinal cord and central nervous system tissue of healthy humans and it is only the structurally misfolded form (PrP^{Sc}) that causes disease.

8   The "protein only" hypothesis of prion disease, advocated by Nobel laureate Stanley Prusiner of the University of California, San Francisco, is that TSEs are not caused by viruses and that prions require no genetic content in order to spread. Consistent with this hypothesis, a University of California team recently created a "synthetic prion" that resulted in vacuolation and BSE-like symptoms when injected into mouse brains: see Legname, G, Baskakov, I, Nguyen H-O et al, "Synthetic Mammalian Prions" (2004) 305 *Science* 673; "Rogue Protein Link to Mad Cow's Disease" *Sydney Morning Herald*, 31 July–1 August 2004, p 20. Recent thinking is also that different strains of TSE may be caused by different forms of twisting or misfolding of the prion protein.

protease-resistant. In other words, it is resistant to enzymes that would ordinarily break it down, with the result that prion accumulates in the brain as deposits and plaques, and disrupts normal cell function. "Spongiform encephalopathy" describes the microscopic holes ("vacuoles") that destroy the brains of those affected with the disease. The mechanism behind prion diseases may share similarities with other neurodegenerative diseases including Alzheimer's disease, which is thought to be caused by the misfolding of the beta amyloid protein.

Human TSEs present complex and uniquely challenging infection control scenarios for public health authorities. Five factors deserve emphasis. First, although not contagious, TSEs are infectious. A number of clinical procedures pose a transmission risk, due to the presence of prion in organs and tissues. In classical CJD, prion infectivity is largely confined to brain and central nervous system tissue; in vCJD, infectivity is also present in lymphoreticular tissue (tonsils, appendix, spleen). Recent reports also suggest that, unlike classical CJD, vCJD is transmissible to recipients of blood and blood products.[9] This has placed further pressure on the Australian Red Cross Blood Service (ARCBS) since currently TSE transmission risk can only be minimised by geographically-based donor deferral measures.

Secondly, in the minority of TSE cases that are hereditary, genetic testing is available to confirm diagnosis. Predictive and carrier testing is also available for genetic relatives, although the psychosocial issues here rival those of other fatal, late-onset, neurodegenerative diseases such as Huntington's disease. For the majority of non-familial cases, however, there is currently no practical or effective screening test to determine the presence of pre-clinical infection. Diagnosis has hitherto depended on clinical signs, with definitive diagnosis requiring a brain biopsy or autopsy.[10] There are several auxiliary diagnostic methods including EEG, and more recently magnetic resonance imaging (MRI) scans, surrogate markers in cerebrospinal fluid, and (for vCJD) tonsil biopsy.[11] The absence of a screening test, however, creates risks of secondary transmission when pre-clinical carriers undergo surgery and other procedures, or (in the case of vCJD) when they donate blood. Thirdly, these transmission risks are exacerbated by the long period of pre-symptomatic infection, which varies for different forms of TSE but can span several decades.

---

9   Llewelyn, C, Hewitt, P, Knight, R et al, "Possible Transmission of Variant Creutzfeldt-Jakob Disease by Blood Transfusion" (2004) 363 *Lancet* 417; Peden, A, Head, M, Ritchie, D et al, "Preclinical vCJD After Blood Transfusion in a PRNP Codon 129 Heterozygous Patient" (2004) 364 *Lancet* 527.

10 Commonwealth Department of Health and Ageing, *Infection Control Guidelines for the Prevention of Transmission of Infectious Diseases in the Health Care Setting* (January 2004), §31.9.2. The guidelines were prepared by the Communicable Diseases Network Australia, a subcommittee of the National Public Health Partnership (hereafter "CDNA Guidelines"). They are currently under review.

11 Glatzel, M, Stoeck, K Seeger, H et al, "Human Prion Diseases: Molecular and Clinical Aspects" (2005) 62 *Archives of Neurology* 545 at 547.

Fourthly, risks of secondary transmission are further complicated by the fact that prion is uniquely resistant to deactivation by conventional sterilisation methods.[12] In circumstances where health care institutions have advance warning of a patient's at-risk status, complex protocols are applied that take into account the patient's risk category, the procedure and tissues involved, and instruments used. In most cases, however, knowledge about a patient's diagnosis or exposure risk will come after the event. Hospitals must then decide whether to conduct a look-back and to notify patients who underwent procedures *after* the clinical case (using the same potentially contaminated instruments) of their exposure risk. Now that vCJD is thought to be blood-transmissible, look-back issues also arise when donors of blood and blood products later develop symptoms. Finally, as noted above, TSEs are invariably fatal and there are no proven treatments or vaccines.[13]

This chapter provides an introduction to some of the operational, legal and ethical challenges that accompany public health efforts to control TSE transmission risk. The second section expands upon the risks posed by, and some institutional responses to, CJD and vCJD in Australia. These themes are then discussed more specifically in the following three sections. The third section explores the policy challenges raised by efforts to secure the safety of blood and blood products in the face of vCJD risk. The fourth section explores issues raised by look-backs and patient notifications carried out in response to exposure to classical CJD in health care contexts, taking an incident that occurred at the Royal Melbourne Hospital in December 2004 as a case study. The fifth section identifies some of the key issues for consideration if a screening test for vCJD becomes available.

The risks of TSE transmission raise issues that have biological, clinical, legal and ethical components. One feature of public policy-making that this chapter aims to highlight, however, is that neither biological knowledge about prion behaviour, nor statistical assessments of transmission risk, nor opinions about legal liability, nor ethical perspectives on fairness and justice, provide definitive guidance on what should be done. Ultimately, the task of deciding what risks are appropriate for society to bear is a political function.[14] While public policy decisions must be based on best assessments of transmission risk, in an environment characterised by uncertainty and guesswork, there are benefits in adopting a

---

12 Currently recommended methods involving steam autoclaving at high temperatures may destroy medical devices containing plastic, joints or electronic components, while chemical sterilisation using sodium hypochlorite solution has a corrosive effect on some metals. There are a variety of instruments (such as flexible endoscopes) that cannot be adequately cleaned using current methods: see CDNA Guidelines, §§ 31.8.2, 31.14; Fichet, G, Comoy, E and Duval, C, "Novel Methods for Disinfection of Prion-Contaminated Medical Devices" (2004) 364 *Lancet* 521.

13 One recent report suggests that pentosan polysulphate, a drug used for urinary tract infections, was effective in reversing the progression of disease in one patient, "Drug Battles Human Form of Mad Cow Disease", <www.macleans.ca/topstories/health/article.jsp?content=20050202_101720_3872> (accessed 31 August 2005). Experimental treatments do not, however, reverse existing brain damage.

14 See European Commission, *Communication from the Commission on the Precautionary Principle*, Brussels, 2 February 2000, COM(2000) p 1.

precautionary, yet cross-disciplinary approach that seeks to avoid policy paralysis and to move forward by broad consensus.[15]

Epidemiological features of TSEs and their implications for infection control

Human TSE cases can be categorised as inherited, acquired, or sporadic diseases. Around 12 to 14 per cent of TSEs, including the familial form of CJD, are *hereditary*. Various mutations to the PRNP gene (which encode for the prion protein and are inherited in an autosomal dominant pattern), create a susceptibility to production of misfolded forms of prion.[16] The majority of *acquired* TSEs have arisen from grafts of contaminated tissue or treatment with human derived pituitary hormones (see below), although there are some older cases of transmission through EEG electrodes and neurosurgical instruments.[17] Overall, the majority of cases are classified as sporadic, meaning that there is no known cause.[18] Regardless of its origin, both classical and variant forms of Creutzfeldt-Jakob disease are infectious.

Classical Creutzfeldt-Jakob disease

The classical form of CJD is a rare disease with a relatively stable incidence in Australia of between one and 1.5 cases per million per year. To 31 December 2004, the Australian National CJD Registry (ANCJDR) had recorded 476 definite or probable CJD cases.[19] Of these, over 90 per cent were classified as sporadic cases; eight per cent were familial cases involving inherited forms of the PRNP gene, and nine cases involved iatrogenic (health care-related) transmission.

The iatrogenic cases deserve further mention. In classical CJD, the disease-associated form of the prion protein accumulates primarily in the central nervous

---

15   This approach to policy development is evident in the contribution the NHMRC has made to TSE risk, as reflected in SECTSE, which (through the NHMRC) advises Commonwealth agencies, and in the consensus conference concept that the NHMRC and other agencies have used as a way of working through and developing agreement on particular issues.

16   Collins (2004) op cit at 55. An autosome is a chromosome other than the sex chromosome and the term "autosomal dominant" means that a genetic mutation inherited from only one parent is sufficient to develop the symptoms of the disease. The genetic susceptibility caused by mutations to the PRNP gene is also thought to increase the likelihood of iatrogenic transmission after an exposure event.

17   See Will, R, "Acquired Prion Disease: Iatrogenic CJD, Variant CJD, Kuru" (2003) 66 *British Medical Bulletin* 255. All of these reports are at least 25 years old.

18   Sporadic cases are thought to arise because the PRNP gene in cells expressing the prion protein either spontaneously mutates or cells otherwise lose their capacity to eliminate the misfolded form of prion.

19   The ANCJDR, located at the Department of Pathology, University of Melbourne, investigates and classifies cases of TSE reported to it as definite, probable, possible or incomplete, according to internationally recognised case definitions. Of the 479 definite/probable cases to 31 December 2004, 434 cases were sporadic, 36 were familial and nine were iatrogenic. Twenty-five definite/probable cases were recorded during 2004. Data drawn from the ANCJDR Semi-Annual Report, December 2004, used with permission.

system. High infectivity tissues include the brain, spinal cord, eye (posterior tissues: optic nerve and retina), pituitary and dura mater. Neurosurgery, ophthalmic surgery, lumbar punctures and laboratory procedures involving manipulation of brain tissue therefore represent the highest risk of iatrogenic transmission.[20] Other procedures, such as endoscopy (for example, colonoscopy), or dental surgery, involve a theoretical risk of transmission, and this has created considerable uncertainty.[21] As noted above, these uncertainties are compounded by the difficulty of removing prion from contaminated instruments using conventional sterilisation methods. The higher temperatures and pressures required for clearance can also destroy expensive medical equipment.[22]

Iatrogenic transmission cases in Australia have arisen from pituitary hormone therapy and dura mater transplants. From 1967 to 1985, nearly 2,100 Australians were supplied with cadaver-derived human pituitary hormones manufactured by the Commonwealth Serum Laboratories (now CSL Ltd) as treatment for growth hormone deficiency, and for infertility, respectively. The Australian Human Pituitary Hormone Program (AHPHP) was discontinued in 1985, following reports of deaths from CJD in overseas recipients. Four female recipients of human pituitary gonadotrophin died during the period 1988 to 1991, following an average symptom-free incubation period of 15 years. A mass notification exercise took place and recipients were told of their exposure. This caused enormous anxiety, and resulted in an independent inquiry into the AHPHP (the Allars Report).[23] The ANCJDR was originally set up in 1993 to assist in identifying any further cases (further deaths from this cause are now unlikely).

The remaining five iatrogenic cases of CJD in Australia are part of the 170 global cases relating to the use of dura mater grafts, mainly Lyodura, a commercially produced form of human cadaveric dura mater imported from Germany. Surveys indicate that from 1972 to 1987, some 2208 to 2478 sheets of Lyodura were used in Australia in neurosurgery and a broad range of other surgical procedures.[24]

---

20 CDNA Guidelines, §31.7.2.

21 See, for example, Bramble, M and Ironside J, "Creutzfeldt-Jakob Disease: Implications for Gastroenterology" (2002) 50 *Gut* 888; Smith, A, Dickson, J, Aitken, J et al, "Contaminated Dental Instruments" (2002) 51 *Journal of Hospital Infection* 233.

22 See CDNA Guidelines, §§31.8, 31.12, and 31.14. The CDNA Guidelines classify individuals into higher and lower risk categories, with different procedures applying to each. Instruments used in neurosurgery, neuroradiology or ophthalmic (posterior segment) surgery on all patients must either be destroyed, used for the particular patient only, placed in quarantine pending determination of risk status, or alternatively single-use instruments must be used. In other kinds of surgery, instruments used on higher risk patients may be reused if processed using certain heat or chemical sterilisation methods (one method requires autoclaving at 134° for 18 minutes). Dry heat is less effective in removing prion and some agents, including aldehydes, may have the effect of fixing prion onto surfaces. Instruments that cannot be adequately reprocessed include endoscopes, ultrasound transducers, and some kinds of ophthalmic equipment.

23 Allars, M, *Inquiry into the Use of Pituitary Derived Hormones in Australia and Creutzfeldt-Jakob Disease*, tabled in the House of Representatives, 28 June 1994.

24 Brooke, F, Boyd, A, Klug, G, et al, "Lyodura Use and the Risk of Iatrogenic Creutzfeldt-Jakob Disease in Australia" (2004) 180 *Medical Journal of Australia* 177. See also Cooke, J, "The Transplant Time Bomb", *Sydney Morning Herald*, 19 March 2001.

Although the last death occurred in 2001, incubation periods of up to 23 years have been documented in Lyodura cases, so further cases cannot be ruled out. In the meantime, the difficulty of identifying recipients of Lyodura raises the possibility of secondary transmission by infected, preclinical patients.

Variant Creutzfeldt-Jakob disease

At the time of writing, no cases of vCJD have been reported in Australia. Australia also remains free of BSE. Worldwide, 178 cases of vCJD had been reported to June 2005, including 156 in the United Kingdom, and 13 in France. Excluding Britain, five European countries have reported vCJD cases (France, Ireland, Italy, Netherlands, Portugal), as have Canada, the United States, Japan and Saudi Arabia.

BSE was first identified in cattle in the United Kingdom in 1986, with the first cases of vCJD following 10 years later.[25] While BSE was spread among cattle by contaminated meat and bone meal (MBM), vCJD transmission is thought to have resulted from human consumption of prion-contaminated bovine offal, and from the contamination of meat destined for human consumption with brain and central nervous system tissue of infected animals through the mechanical meat recovery process or the advanced meat recovery process.[26] One study estimates that two million cattle were infected with BSE in the United Kingdom, with rates of

---

25   Almond, J and Pattison, J, "Human BSE" (1997) 389 *Nature* 437. Key features of Britain's response to BSE and vCJD include a ban on the feeding of MBM to sheep and cattle (1988), the slaughter of all cattle showing signs (1988), making BSE notifiable (1988) and a ban on the use of specified offal in human food (1989). In 1989 the European Union banned the export of all United Kingdom cattle born before the ruminant feed ban (that is, July 1988), but this did not prevent the spread of the disease to Europe (beginning with Ireland in 1989; and France and Switzerland in 1991). The ban on MBM in sheep and cattle feeds was not entirely effective and an estimated 40,000 cases of BSE were reported in the United Kingdom following the ban. In March 1996, the United Kingdom's Spongiform Encephalopathy Advisory Committee (SEAC) announced the probable link between BSE and vCJD. As a result, the European Union again banned British beef. The United Kingdom introduced a ban on cattle over 30 months old from entering the human food chain (April 1996), and the existing ban on feeding mammalian protein to sheep and cattle was extended to all farmed animals. A similar ban on the use of MBM in foodstuffs for farmed animals was introduced throughout the European Union from 2001, together with a ban on all cattle over 30 months old from entering the human food chain unless a brain scan for the abnormal prion had been carried out. See further, Smith, P, "The Epidemics of Bovine Spongiform Encephalopathy and Variant Creutzfeldt-Jakob Disease: Current Status and Future Prospects" (2003) 81(2) *Bulletin of the World Health Organization* 123; Goldwater (2001) op cit at 155; Department of Health and Ageing, "Chronology of Events and Responses", <www.health.gov.au/internet/wcms/publishing.nsf/Content/phd-bse-chronology.htm-copy2> (accessed 31 August 2005).

26   "Mechanically recovered meat" (MRM) is a process used to recover residual meat adhering to bone after the prime cuts have been removed. Beef, pork or chicken bones are forced at high pressure through a sieve or similar device and removed meat forms a slurry that may include bone marrow and nervous system tissue: see, for example, <www.priondata.org/data/A_MRM.html> (accessed 31 August 2005). "Advanced meat recovery" (AMR) involves the extraction of muscle and meat trimmings by scraping, shaving or pressing bones, but without grinding or breaking them. MRM and AMR meat are both "at risk" products due to the possible presence of (infectious) dorsal root ganglia (nervous system tissue) in the product resulting from these processes.

infection peaking in 1992.[27] Critical features of the United Kingdom response to BSE include the ban on feeding MBM to sheep and cattle (1988), which was extended to all farmed animals in April 1996 when the link between BSE and vCJD became clear. Since 2001, all European Union countries require brain testing on cattle more than 30 months old, prior to human consumption. Despite this, the tail of the BSE epidemic continues. There were 256 reported cases of BSE in the United Kingdom in 2004.

Key features of Australia's response to BSE/vCJD include, from 1988, an import ban on live cattle originating from the United Kingdom and Ireland (since extended to cover beef and feed products from 30 countries with cases of BSE),[28] and from May 1996, a domestic ban on the feeding of ruminant-derived meat and bone meal to ruminants.[29] Despite this, it is likely that cases of vCJD will be identified in Australia, probably in persons who visited the United Kingdom and ate contaminated beef there during the peak period for exposure through the human food chain (1988 to 1993).[30] The risk of an endemic case of vCJD (or BSE) is thought to be very low.

---

27 Donnelly, C, Ferguson, N, Ghani, A, et al "Implications of BSE Infection Screening Data for the Scale of the British BSE Epidemic and Current European Infection Levels" (2002) 269 *Proceedings of the Royal Society of London: Biological Sciences* 2179.

28 Imported cattle that are still alive are under quarantine surveillance and are excluded from entering the human or animal food chain. The Australian Quarantine and Inspection Service (AQIS), on advice from Food Standards Australia and New Zealand (FSANZ), administers a certification system to ensure that all beef products imported into Australia are derived from animals free from BSE.

29 Animal Health Australia oversees Australia's TSE Freedom Assurance Program in accordance with the World Organisation for Animal Health. This program includes ruminant feeding restrictions, quarantine of imported cattle, and an inspection-based compliance program covering all parts of the livestock feed chain. The ruminant feed ban has a statutory basis in each State and Territory. Since 2002 it applies to "restricted animal material" (RAM) including meals derived from ruminants and other animals, including fish and birds: see *Stock Foods Regulation 1997* (NSW) s 9; *Stock Diseases (General) Regulation 2004* (NSW) s 59; *Stock Diseases Act 1923* (NSW) s 23FB; *Agricultural Standards Regulation 1997* (Qld) ss 42–43, 46(2); *Veterinary Preparations and Animal Feeding Stuffs Regulation 1998* (SA) ss 5, 8A; *Animal Health Regulations 1996* (Tas) ss 10A–10F; *Agricultural and Veterinary Chemicals (Control of Use) Act 1992* (Vic) s 25A; *Livestock Regulations 1998* (WA) ss 36, 41, 49; *Stock Act 1991* (ACT) ss 36A–36H; *Stock Diseases Regulations* ss 20A–20E (NT). In Victoria, the ruminant feed ban has been implemented by Executive Order: see Order Declaring a Control Area Relating to the Feeding of Restricted Animal Material made pursuant to *Livestock Diseases Control Act 1994* (Vic) s 29(5). See <www.animalhealth australia.com.au/aahc/programs/adsp/tsefap/feedban.cfm> (accessed 31 August 2005). At Commonwealth level, the *Quarantine Proclamation 1998* ss 32–33 prohibits the importation of animal foods into Australia without a permit. Stockfeed derived from animal material (other than from New Zealand) is prohibited, although an import permit may be granted following an import risk analysis in certain circumstances: see Biosecurity Australia, *Importation of Stockfeed and Stockfeed Ingredients – Finalised Risk Management Measures for Transmissible Spongiform Encephalopathies (TSEs)*, 13 March 2003, <www.affa.gov.au/content/publications.cfm?ObjectID=B9E32DC2-578D-456B-927A46F26FE2C070> (accessed 31 June 2005).

30 The ban on the feeding of MBM to cattle was introduced by the United Kingdom Government in 1988, but this was not completely effective: see above, note 25. The BSE incubation period averages five years, and clinical cases of BSE in the United Kingdom did not peak until 1992: see Donnelly et al (2002) op cit. Thus the period of maximum exposure to contaminated beef was 1988–1993.

The primary vCJD epidemic – those cases caused by oral consumption of contaminated meat – now appears to be in decline in the United Kingdom (there were nine cases in 2004, from a peak of 28 cases in 2000).[31] Recent modelling suggests that the primary epidemic will remain small, with a best estimate of 69 future cases caused by oral exposure developing over the period 2004 to 2080.[32] However, with a best estimate of 5,413 individuals who are thought to be asymptomatic carriers, the implications for the secondary epidemic remain uncertain.[33]

Uncertainty about the scale of the vCJD epidemic in the United Kingdom persists for several reasons. First, a recent study investigating the presence of the disease-associated form of prion in stored appendicectomy tissue suggests there may be a higher level of subclinical vCJD in the United Kingdom than previously assumed.[34] Together with recent case reports suggesting that vCJD infection may be transmissible by blood transfusion,[35] this raises the disturbing prospect that up to one in every 4,000 blood donors in the United Kingdom might be a subclinical carrier. A clearer picture is hampered by the lack of a sensitive screening test.

Secondly, until recently it was thought that, due to genetic factors, less than half of the United Kingdom population were susceptible to vCJD infection. This is because all cases of primary vCJD that have arisen through oral exposure have been in individuals who were methionine homozygous (MM) at codon 129 of PRNP. The PRNP gene, which encodes for the production of prion protein, contains a polymorphism at position 129 of the gene. Here, the gene codes for one of two amino acids: either methionine (M) or valine (V). Since individuals inherit a copy of the prion gene from each of their parents, each person will therefore be either "homozygous for methionine (129-MM), homozygous for valine (129-VV), or heterozygous (129-MV)".[36]

---

31   Mayor, S, "Only a Few More Deaths from vCJD Likely in UK" (2005) 330 *British Medical Journal* 164. To 1 July 2005 there were two further cases: see <www.cjd.ed.ac.United Kingdom/figures.htm> (accessed 31 August 2005).

32   Clarke, P and Ghani, A, "Projections of the Future Course of the Primary vCJD Epidemic in the UK: Inclusion of Subclinical Infection and the Possibility of Wider Genetic Susceptibility" (2005) *Journal of the Royal Society* (doi:10.1098/rsif.2004.0017) at 7.

33   Ibid at 7.

34   Hilton, D, Ghani, A Conyers, L et al, "Prevalence of Lymphoreticular Prion Protein Accumulation in UK Tissue Samples" (2004) 203 *Journal of Pathology* 733. Unlike classical CJD, in vCJD the disease-associated form of the prion protein is *not* largely confined to the central nervous system, but also accumulates in lymphoreticular tissues (tonsils, appendix, spleen). Hilton's study investigated stored tonsillectomy and appendicectomy specimens from across the United Kingdom. It revealed three infected tissues from a sample of 12,674, or a prevalence of 237 cases of infection per million. This may be an underestimate, however, given that the sensitivity of the test may be lower in respect of those early in the incubation period. See also Hawkes, N, "Britain Has Mad Cow Time Bomb", *Weekend Australian* 22 May 2004, p 13.

35   Llewelyn et al (2004) op cit; Peden et al (2004) op cit.

36   See Knight, R, "Background and Epidemiology of vCJD" in Blajchman, M, Goldman, M, Webert, K et al, "Proceedings of a Consensus Conference: the Screening of Blood Donors for Variant CJD" (2004) 18(2) *Transfusion Medicine Reviews* 73 at 76. Homozygous (MM) individuals comprise 38 per cent of the United Kingdom population, whereas 51 per cent of the population are heterozygous (methionine/valine), and 11 per cent are homozygous (valine).

Since those individuals who developed vCJD as a result of eating contaminated beef have hitherto all been methionine homozygous (MM) at codon 129, this genotype appears to be linked with susceptibility to vCJD. Doubt persists, however, over whether people who are valine homozygous (VV) or heterozygous (MV) are capable of being pre-clinical carriers (albeit with a longer incubation period than methionine homozygotes), or alternatively, are subclinical carriers who will never exhibit the disease in their lifetime. In July 2004, Peden and colleagues reported the case of a patient who had received a blood transfusion from a donor who subsequently developed vCJD. The recipient died from a non-neurological disorder, but showed evidence of vCJD infection at autopsy. Significantly, this recipient was heterozygous (MV) at codon 129, suggesting that secondary cases of the vCJD epidemic will *not* necessarily be limited to the 38 per cent of the United Kingdom population who are homozygous (MM).[37] Heterozygous (MV) individuals comprise roughly 50 per cent of the population. The doubling of the pool of asymptomatic people who are potentially capable of transmitting vCJD through blood and tissue donations, contaminating surgical instruments that come in contact with lymphoid tissues and thereby exposing downstream surgical patients, creates uncertainty and difficulty for infection control efforts. The full extent of the secondary vCJD epidemic in the United Kingdom, therefore, remains unclear.

In summary, the most important unknowns are the size of the epidemic in heterozygous (MV) and homozygous (VV) populations, and the number of pre-clinical individuals, particularly blood donors, capable of transmitting the disease.[38] An estimated 80,000 Australians were living in the United Kingdom during the period of the BSE outbreak in the mid-1980s.[39] The larger the pool of infections in the United Kingdom, therefore, the more likely it is that cases of vCJD will be imported into Australia.

---

37 Peden, A, Head, M, Ritchie, D et al, "Preclinical vCJD After Blood Transfusion in a PRNP Codon 129 Heterozygous Patient" (2004) 364 *Lancet* 527; Cooke, J, "BSE Experts Fear Second Disease Phase in Humans", *Sydney Morning Herald*, 24–25 July 2004, p 23. An earlier case of vCJD transmitted through blood was reported in February 2004: see Llewelyn et al (2004) op cit. The extent to which asymptomatic individuals may be natural reservoirs of infection remains unclear: see Collins, S, Lewis, V, Brazier, M et al, "Extended Period of Asymptomatic Prion Disease After Low Dose Inoculation: Assessment of Detection Methods and Implications for Infection Control" (2005) 20(2) *Neurobiology of Disease* 336-346.

38 While noting the downward trend in the primary vCJD epidemic, the authors of one recent study caution that "the high estimate of prevalence of infection, whether preclinical or subclinical, from [Hilton's survey of lymphoreticular tissues] could have important implications for the potential for future cases of vCJD arising via past exposure to infected blood" Clarke, P and Ghani, A, "Projections of the Future Course of the Primary vCJD Epidemic in the UK: Inclusion of Subclinical Infection and the Possibility of Wider Genetic Susceptibility" (2005) *Journal of the Royal Society* (doi:10.1098/rsif.2004.0017) at 10.

39 See Victorian Department of Human Services, Clinical Governance Unit, *Report of the Consensus Workshop: Creutzfeldt-Jakob Disease: Preventing Transmission in the Health Care Setting* (draft), March 2005, p 8.

TSE surveillance in Australia

As it is, the ANCJDR is likely to be underestimating the incidence of TSEs in Australia. Recognition depends on cooperation with treating health care workers and families of affected patients. As noted above, there is currently no pre-mortem diagnostic test for sub-clinical CJD or vCJD infection. Diagnosis is triggered by clinical symptoms and confirmed by neuropathological examination of brain tissue, usually at autopsy. However, rates of autopsy are falling in Australia due to occupational health and safety concerns, lack of resources and inadequate funding.[40] There has been no coordinated approach to post-mortem surveillance, either in the United Kingdom[41] or Australia.

On the other hand, on the recommendation of the Communicable Diseases Network Australia (CDNA), and the National Health and Medical Research Council's (NHMRC) Special Expert Committee on Transmissible Spongiform Encephalopathies (SECTSE), CJD is in the process of becoming a nationally notifiable disease.[42] The national surveillance function is carried out by the ANCJDR, a non-statutory register based at the University of Melbourne. Privacy and non-disclosure provisions that bind the health departments in each State and Territory present a possible barrier to the lawful on-disclosure of name-identifying information to the ANCJDR, potentially scuttling its specialist role in confirming diagnosis and ensuring accurate national surveillance.[43] TSE surveillance is just one

40   The need for an appropriate facility for conducting autopsies of suspected CJD cases in each State and Territory is the subject of continuing discussions between the Commonwealth and the Communicable Diseases Network Australia (CDNA). Not all States or Territories have this capability at the moment.

41   Bird, S, "Attributable testing for abnormal prion protein, database linkage, and bloodborne vCJD risks" (2004) 364 *Lancet* 1362 at 1363.

42   At the time of writing, notification is a legal requirement in New South Wales, Tasmania, Victoria and Western Australia: see *Public Health Act 1991* (NSW) s 14, Sch 1; *Human (Infectious Diseases) Regulations 2001* (Vic) s 6, Sch 3. In Western Australia, CJD is notifiable pursuant to *Health Act 1911* (WA) s 267 (as amended in 2005). For Tasmania, see *Guidelines for Notification of Notifiable Diseases, Human Pathogenic Organisms and Contaminants 2003* (Table 1) (pursuant to *Public Health Act 1997* (Tas) s 40). CDNA is currently attempting to broker a nationally applicable case definition that applies to the different types of TSE.

43   The legislative position in each State and Territory is complex: see Thomson, C, *The Regulation of Health Information Privacy in Australia*, NHMRC, 2004. In New South Wales, privacy legislation applies to the personal information of living individuals as well as those who have been dead less than 30 years. The Health Privacy Principles (HPPs) in the *Health Records and Information Privacy Act 2002* (NSW) would preclude the disclosure of identifying health information held by NSW Health to a non-statutory register unless one of the exceptions enumerated in HPP 11 applied. The exceptions include circumstances where disclosure is necessary to lessen or prevent "a serious threat to public health or public safety" (HPP(1)(c)(ii)), or where disclosure is in accordance with guidelines issued by the New South Wales Privacy Commissioner relating to research or the compilation or analysis of statistics: HPP(1)(c)(f). The Privacy Commissioner is also directly empowered to exempt agencies from a HPP in accordance with a written direction: s 62. A separate Act, the *Health Administration Act 1982*, s 22 contains a non-disclosure provision that applies to public sector-held information. However, the *Health Administration Regulation 2000*, s 13(2) authorises disclosure of epidemiological data with the authority of the Director-General. The relationship between privacy legislation, and the older health services provisions (such as s 22) is unclear. For further discussion of privacy legislation and the status of non-statutory registers, see Clarke, C and Magnusson, R, "Data Registers in Respiratory Medicine" (2002) 10 *Journal of Law and Medicine* 69.

of many examples illustrating how the growth and complexity of privacy law threatens a national approach to epidemiological surveillance.[44]

Against this background, then, it is clear that public health agencies and health care institutions face difficult risk assessments, based on complex and uncertain assumptions. The following section reviews some of the challenges that vCJD creates for the regulation of blood and blood products.

Variant CJD and the regulation of transmission risk through blood and blood products

Regulatory background

Voluntary donation is the foundation of Australia's blood supply. Human Tissue Acts in each State and Territory authorise voluntary blood donation with consent. In practice, this occurs at local collection centres staffed by the Australian Red Cross Blood Service (ARCBS).[45] Collection centres are required to meet licensing standards under the *Therapeutic Goods Act 1989* (Cth), including the *Australian Code of Good Manufacturing Practice – Human Blood and Tissues*.[46] The medical history of each donor is evaluated, and donors are required to sign a questionnaire that excludes a list of risk factors that have grown over time. Legislation in each State and Territory includes offences for the provision of false or misleading information by donors.[47]

Australia's blood supply comprises a complex set of relationships. Whole blood is collected by the ARCBS, separated into component products (red cells, platelets and fresh frozen plasma) and supplied to hospitals and health care providers. The ARCBS also collects plasma, which undergoes fractionation at CSL Ltd, which is now a private company, and also the world largest plasma fractionator. CSL produces plasma-derived products (immunoglobulin, albumin and clotting factors) that are returned to the ARCBS and distributed through its network. Australia also imports some plasma-derived products, and all recombinant products.[48]

---

44   See further Magnusson, R "Data Linkage, Health Research and Privacy: Regulating Data Flows in Australia's Health Information System" (2002) 24 *Sydney Law Review* 5.

45   Since 1996, the ARCBS has operated as a national service, jointly funded by the Commonwealth and State governments.

46   See, *Therapeutic Goods Act 1989* (Cth) s 36; Therapeutic Goods Administration, *Australian Code of Good Manufacturing Practice – Human Blood and Tissues*, 24 August 2000, <www.tga. gov.au/docs/pdf/gmpbltic.pdf> (accessed 31 August 2005).

47   *Human Tissue Act 1983* (NSW) ss 20D–20E; *Transplantation and Anatomy Act 1979* (Qld) s 48A; *Transplantation and Anatomy Act 1983* (SA) s 38A; *Blood Contaminants Act 1985* (SA) s 4; *Blood Transfusion (Limitation of Liability) Act 1986* (Tas) ss 4(1)(a), 7; *Health Act 1958* (Vic) ss 135–136; *Blood Donation (Limitation of Liability) Act 1985* (WA) s 12; *Criminal Code* (WA) s 170; *Blood Donation (Transmittable Diseases) Act 1985* (ACT) s 8; *Criminal Code* (ACT) ss 337–338; *Notifiable Diseases Act 1999* (NT) s 26E.

48   See generally, National Blood Authority, *Supply of Defined Blood Products: Future Arrangements*, Discussion Paper, 18 July 2005, <www.nba.gov.au> (accessed 31 August 2005).

Both the ARCBS and CSL Ltd are regulated by the Therapeutic Goods Administration (TGA) (an agency within the Commonwealth Department of Health and Ageing), which requires compliance with the *Australian Code of Good Manufacturing Practice – Human Blood and Tissues* and with Council of Europe requirements relating to the preparation, use and quality assurance of blood products.[49] The National Blood Authority (NBA), which was established in 2003 as an independent statutory body, coordinates demand and supply planning for blood and blood products on a national basis. The NBA also manages contracts for the supply of blood and blood products, and purchases products from suppliers.[50] Product safety, however, remains the responsibility of the TGA.

Legal risks of blood-borne transmission: Past experience with HIV/AIDS

The ARCBS is no stranger to controversy in its responses to new infections, as the epidemics of transfusion acquired HIV/AIDS[51] (and later, of hepatitis C[52]), demonstrate. Inevitably, infection risks create legal risks as well. In the early 1980s, several hundred people – many of them haemophiliacs – contracted transfusion-acquired HIV/AIDS before the introduction of HIV antibody testing in May 1985. This precipitated a wave of litigation against (what at the time were) State-based Red Cross blood banks, the Commonwealth Serum Laboratories (as manufacturer of plasma and plasma-derived products) and hospitals.[53] Most plaintiffs sued under the tort of negligence, for misleading conduct and implied warranties under the *Trade Practices Act 1974* (Cth),[54] and under Pt VA of the *Trade Practices Act*, which imposes strict liability for defective goods. A Victorian jury award of $870,000, followed by two later Victorian cases that were settled for $300,000 and

---

49 See Therapeutic Goods Order No 72 (21 April 2004) which also includes the additional requirement that all blood and blood products be manufactured from blood negative to HIV and HCV (Hepatitis C) using nucleic acid amplification testing. NAT detects viral genes rather than antibodies or antigens, dramatically reducing the "window period" for these infections. The Council of Europe's *Guide to the Preparation, Use and Quality Assurance of Blood Components*, 2005, is in its 11th edition, see <www.coe.int/T/E/Social_Cohesion/Health/Activities/Blood_transfusion/> (accessed 31 August 2005).

50 See *National Blood Authority Act 2003* (Cth) s 8; National Blood Authority, *Annual Report 2003-2004*, Part 2.

51 See Ballard, J, "Australia: Participation and Innovation in a Federal System" in Kirp, D and Bayer, R (eds), *AIDS in the Industrialized Democracies: Passions, Politics, and* Policies, Rutgers University Press, New Brunswick, 1992, pp 134–165, see pp 138–139; *E v Australian Red Cross Society* (1991) 31 FCR 299 at 308ff.

52 Commonwealth, Senate Community Affairs References Committee, *Hepatitis C and the Blood Supply in Australia*, June 2004, <www.aph.gov.au/senate/committee/clac_ctte/completed_inquiries/2002-04/hepc/report/index.htm> (accessed 31 August 2005).

53 In a number of associated claims, plaintiffs sought to discover the identity of donors so that they could subpoena donor medical records in order to prove that the donor was HIV-infected, an element of proof of causation in their own claims: see Magnusson, R, "Public Interest Immunity and the Confidentiality of Blood Donor Identity in AIDS Litigation" (1992) 8(3) *Australian Bar Review* 226.

54 See, for example, *Trade Practice Act 1974* (Cth) ss 55A, 71, 74.

$600,000, respectively, maintained pressure for the eventual settlement of these cases by State governments.[55] Blood shield legislation in the States and Territories now creates a defence for the ARCBS and hospitals that, in reliance upon the donor's certificate of suitability, inadvertently supply blood containing a "prescribed contaminant". These provisions provide a defence for the transmission of Hepatitis B and C, and HIV. vCJD is not, however, a prescribed contaminant.[56]

Claims based on the *Trade Practices Act* face the difficulty that the gratuitous provision of blood or blood products will not be "in trade or commerce" for the purposes of consumer protection provisions.[57] This is not only due to doubts about whether blood or plasma is "goods" for the purposes of *Trade Practices Act* provisions,[58] but because where blood or blood products are administered in a clinical context, the relevant contract will be one for the provision of medical and nursing services, rather than the provision of blood per se.[59]

There is no doubt, however, that the ARCBS and CSL Ltd owe recipients of blood and blood products a duty of care. In light of recent reports, the risk of vCJD transmission is also clearly foreseeable. In spelling out what the reasonable manufacturer or supplier would do in response to a foreseeable risk, courts have adopted a costs–benefits analysis that focuses on four variables: the probability and gravity of the risk, weighed against the practicability of any precautionary measures, and the justifiability of implementing them.[60] In the classic Australian formulation of standard of care, Mason J said:

> The perception of the reasonable man's response [to a foreseeable risk of injury to the plaintiff and the class he or she falls within] calls for a consideration of the magnitude of the risk and the degree of the probability of its occurrence, along with the expense, difficulty and inconvenience of taking alleviating action and any other conflicting responsibilities which the defendant may have. It is only when these matters are balanced out that the tribunal of fact can confidently assert what is the standard of response to be ascribed to the reasonable man placed in the defendant's position.[61]

---

55   Intergovernmental Committee on AIDS Legal Working Party, *Civil Liability for Transmission of HIV/AIDS*, Department of Health, Housing and Community Services, Canberra, 1992, pp 35–37.

56   See, for example, *Human Tissue Act 1983* (NSW) s 20F(4); *Human Tissue Regulation 2000* (NSW) s 5; Godwin, J, et al *Australian HIV/AIDS Legal Guide*, 2nd edn, Federation Press, Sydney, 1993, pp 435ff.

57   See *E v Australian Red Cross Society* (1991) 27 FCR 310 at 350 per Wilcox J. This conclusion is reinforced by the agreement of the Commonwealth and States, through the National Blood Agreement, to ensure that blood and blood products are supplied free of charge to patients on the basis of clinical need: National Blood Authority, *Annual Report 2003–2004*, § 2.1.3.

58   See Magnusson, R, "Proprietary Rights in Human Tissue" in Palmer, N and McKendrick, E (eds), *Interests in Goods*, 2nd edn, Lloyds of London Press, London, 1998, pp 25–62, see pp 46–48.

59   *E v Australian Red Cross Society* (1991) 31 FCR 299 at 306 per Lockhart J.

60   See Luntz, H and Hambly, D, *Torts: Cases and Commentary*, 5th edn, LexisNexis Butterworths, Sydney, 2002, pp 210ff. This approach has its origins in the formula expressed by Learned Hand J in *United States v Carroll Towing Co* 159 F 2d 169 (2d Cir 1947).

61   *Wyong Shire Council v Shirt* (1980) 146 CLR 40 at 47–48 per Mason J; compare *Koehler v Cerebos (Australia) Ltd* [2005] HCA 15 at [54]. These principles have been absorbed into legislation in some States: see eg *Civil Liability Act 2002* (NSW) s 5B; *Wrongs Act 1958* (Vic) s 48.

Personal injury claims arising from infection with a blood-borne disease require courts to balance each of these factors and to assess the defendant's conduct in responding to foreseeable risks of harm in the light of emerging knowledge. As the existence of risks becomes clearer, the failure to respond appropriately by or after a critical date may, in appropriate circumstances, be seen as evidence of the defendant's breach of duty of care. This, in turn, may create pressure to settle other claims in the class, depending on the period during which other claimants were exposed to the risk of harm.

In *E v Australian Red Cross Society*,[62] one of the HIV/AIDS blood transfusion cases, the plaintiff was transfused with plasma from an HIV-infected donor (D9), who had donated on 3 October 1984. HIV antibody tests were not available in Australia until May 1985. However, due to the proactive approach of the director of the New South Wales Red Cross at that time, Dr Archer, the New South Wales division introduced surrogate anti-HBc testing, which was phased in from 5 October. Due to limited capacity and teething problems with the test, priority was given to testing new donors. As a result, D9's donation on 3 October went untested, and the plaintiff was transfused with infected blood on 14 October. On all occasions, D9 signed the donor form excluding risks, despite the fact that D9's partner was an IV drug user.

The Full Court of the Federal Court of Australia dismissed the argument that the failure to introduce anti-HBc surrogate testing earlier than 5 October was a breach of duty. New South Wales was alone among the State divisions to have implemented surrogate testing. The court cautioned that perceptions of what was a reasonable response should not be clouded by hindsight.[63] Surrogate testing was controversial: anti-HBc testing was expected to lead to the loss of some 5 per cent of donations, the correlation between anti-HBc and HIV was less than 50 per cent, and some experts believed that such testing could attract unhealthy donors who wanted to discover their status (the so-called "magnet" problem).[64] Importantly, the court accepted that in determining what reasonable care required, it was proper to have regard to the impact of surrogate testing on the sufficiency of the blood supply.[65]

Legal risks of iatrogenic transmission: Past experience with CJD

As noted above, the exposure of nearly 2100 human pituitary hormone recipients to the risk of CJD has also resulted in litigation. In May 1993, claims were filed on

---

62   (1991) 31 FCR 299.

63   Ibid at 322, 329.

64   Ibid at 320–321, 325–327. Sheppard J points out that the hepatitis B core antigen (anti-HBc) test did not diagnose persons who were currently infectious with HBV, but those who had recovered from HBV, and whose blood was otherwise not an infection risk: ibid at 324–325.

65   Ibid at 321, 332, 333.

behalf of recipients who had died from CJD. The overwhelming majority, however, comprised the "worried well" who had been exposed to a transmission risk, and now faced a lifetime of uncertainty and anxiety. By April 1997, 133 claims had been filed against the Commonwealth and the Commonwealth Serum Laboratories in Victoria alone.[66] Unlike the personal injury claims illustrated by *E v Red Cross Society*,[67] these were claims that sought damages for psychiatric harm resulting from knowledge of future risk.

In *APQ v Commonwealth Serum Laboratories*,[68] a test case for this class, Harper J refused the defendants' application for summary judgment, stating that:

> [I]t seems to me that a person who suffers psychiatric illness when informed that medical treatment undergone by her may leave her with a horrible and terminal disease probably has a good cause of action against the manufacturer of a drug used in the plaintiff's treatment where its manufacture (and its subsequent distribution) was conducted negligently and where that negligence exposed the plaintiff to that risk.[69]

His Honour regarded the foreseeability of psychiatric harm in these circumstances as "beyond argument".[70] The judgment confirms that the failure to take reasonable care to avoid exposing a plaintiff to a risk of TSE transmission may state a cause of action for psychiatric harm regardless of whether actual transmission (and resulting physical harm) occurs. Since the number of individuals exposed to a risk of transmission is likely to greatly exceed those who actually acquire the disease, nervous shock claims present a far more significant *legal risk* to the ARCBS and other bodies making decisions about transmission risks, than traditional claims for personal injury.

The potential for psychiatric injury claims arising from the fear of acquiring CJD/vCJD, following an exposure event, is supported by the High Court's decisions in *Tame v New South Wales; Annetts v Australian Stations Pty Ltd*.[71] Here, the court confirmed that nervous shock claims do not necessarily require the plaintiff's injury to have been caused by a "sudden shock", or by the "direct perception" of a distressing event or its aftermath. The harm suffered by the plaintiff must, however, amount to a psychiatric illness, as distinct from mere anxiety or mental distress. Frivolous and manipulative claims of CJD transmission will not succeed.[72]

---

66 Commonwealth, Senate Community Affairs Committee, *Report on the CJD Settlement Offer*, October 1997, para 2.119, <www.aph.gov.au/senate/committee/clac_ctte/completed_inquiries/1996-99/cjd/report/contents.htm> (accessed 31 August 2005).

67 (1999) 31 FCR 299.

68 [1999] 3 VR 633.

69 Ibid at 635.

70 Ibid at 636. United Kingdom courts have taken a similar approach: see *The Creutzfeldt-Jakob Disease litigation; Group B; Plaintiffs v Medical Research Council* [2000] Lloyd's Rep Med 161. For further discussion, see also Hurley, A, "Prospects of Recovery in Negligence and Under Statute for Creutzfeld[t]-Jakob Disease Resulting from Human Pituitary Gland Derived Hormone Products" (1996) 4 *Torts Law Journal* 60.

71 See *Tame v New South Wales; Annetts v Australian Stations Pty Ltd* [2002] HCA 35 at [18], [51]–[52], [189]–[191], [208], [225], [277], [305]; compare at [366].

72 *Farrell v CSL Ltd* [2004] VSC 308.

In April 1997, the claims brought by APQ and other recipients of human pituitary hormones were settled on terms that included the Commonwealth agreeing to pay compensation if any members of the class contracted CJD. Members continued to receive benefits under a trust fund established in 1994 to provide counselling and other services.[73] In 1999, an ex gratia payment scheme was established for recipients who could prove psychiatric loss as a result of discovering their at-risk status.

Responding to vCJD transmission risks through blood and blood products

Past experience illustrates the need to closely monitor and respond to the transmission risks of emerging, communicable diseases. However, applying abstract legal principles about duty of care to the emerging understanding of vCJD is no easy task. There is no evidence that (classical) CJD is transmitted through blood or blood products.[74] Nevertheless, the ARCBS has taken a precautionary approach, excluding donors with a history of familial TSEs, and others whose risk of exposure arises as recipients of human pituitary hormones, dura mater grafts and corneal grafts.[75]

Since vCJD emerged in 1996 there have been suspicions that it may be blood transmissible, by analogy from demonstrated cases of BSE transmission in sheep, and of sheep scrapie.[76] While the causal connection is difficult to prove, there have been two putative case reports of vCJD transmitted through blood; one in a recipient showing only subclinical infection at the time of their death from other causes. As this chapter goes to press, a third case of "probable" vCJD has been diagnosed, in a patient who developed symptoms eight years after receiving a blood transfusion. The donor in question developed symptoms 20 months after donating blood.[77] These reports strengthen assumptions that vCJD may be transmitted through blood by pre-symptomatic donors.[78] As noted above, the second case was heterozygous (MV) at codon 129 of the prion gene, renewing uncertainty about the prevalence of pre-clinical vCJD among blood donors in the United Kingdom.

---

73 Commonwealth, Senate Community Affairs Committee, *Report on the CJD Settlement Offer*, October 1997, paras 2.117–2.122.

74 CDNA Guidelines, §31.7.1; Llewelyn et al (2004) op cit at 417.

75 CDNA Guidelines, §31.7.1; Commonwealth, Senate Community Affairs Committee, *Report on the CJD Settlement Offer*, October 1997, para 2.105ff.

76 Hunter, N, Foster, J, Chong, A et al, "Transmission of Diseases by Blood Transfusion" (2002) 83 *Journal of General Virology* 2897.

77 Department of Health (United Kingdom), Press Release, "New Case of Variant CJD Associated with Blood Transfusion", 9 February 2006.

78 Llewelyn et al (2004) op cit; Peden et al (2004) op cit; Cooke, J "BSE Experts Fear Second Disease Phase in Humans", *Sydney Morning Herald*, 24–25 July 2004, p 23.

There are strong financial incentives to develop prion reduction filters capable of reducing risks of blood infectivity.[79] In their absence, and in the absence of a screening test for prion in blood, donor exclusion criteria are the mainstay of blood safety. In December 2000, Australia introduced indefinite deferral of donors who had lived in the United Kingdom for a cumulative period of six months or more between 1980 and 1996.[80] These criteria assume a constant relationship between length of residency in the United Kingdom, and risk of exposure to vCJD through eating contaminated beef. Six months is a compromise figure that balances blood safety against blood sufficiency: it does not guarantee that individuals who visited the United Kingdom for a shorter time period were not exposed to vCJD. On the other hand, given the low prevalence of Australian blood donors exposed to the BSE agent during residence in Britain, close to 100 per cent of those excluded will pose no infection risk. Data from a survey of blood donors carried out by the ARCBS in 1998 indicated that the implementation of the six-month residence exclusion would result in the loss of 5.3 per cent of all donations.[81] Deferral criteria therefore have a significant impact on the blood supply. Only about 3 per cent of the Australian population are blood donors, regular donors are difficult to replace, and first-time donors are more likely to have risk factors (such as infectious viruses). Balanced against the impact of donor deferral on blood sufficiency is, of course, the gravity of harm if vCJD transmission occurs. In July 2003, in response to the consensus emerging from a vCJD donor deferral workshop hosted by SECTSE and the Department of Health and Ageing, deferral was further extended to anyone who had themselves received a blood transfusion or blood products in the United Kingdom from 1980 onwards. This led to a further estimated drop of 0.7 per cent of donors.

The spread of the vCJD epidemic beyond the United Kingdom, particularly to France (13 cases so far), indicates the need for ongoing monitoring of deferral criteria. More stringent responses to vCJD blood risk include the universal leuco-depletion of donated blood (that is, removal of infection-carrying white blood cells), which could potentially reduce overall TSE infectivity by up to 50 per cent, with the added advantages of reducing viral risk.[82] Other measures include

---

79 The Pall Corporation recently released a Leukotrap® Affinity Prion Reduction Filter that filters out leucocytes (white blood cells) and achieves a four log (99.99 per cent) reduction in infectivity, based on animal studies of blood infected in the laboratory: see "Novel Technology that Reduces Infectious Prions ... from Blood Unveiled at International Transfusion Meeting", <www.pall.com/news_articles_28122.asp> (accessed 31 August 2005).

80 The deferral period only extends until the end of 1996, since during 1996, the United Kingdom strengthened its ban on the feeding of MBM to all farmed animals, and excluded cattle over 30 months old from entering the food chain: see above, note 25.

81 Correll, P, Law, M, Seed, C, et al, "Variant Creutzfeldt-Jakob Disease in Australian Blood Donors: Estimation of Risk and the Impact of Deferral Strategies" (2001) 81 *Vox Sanguinis* 6. In fact, this turned out to be an underestimate.

82 At the time of writing there is no national policy on leucodepletion and practices vary from State to State. One study estimates that universal leucodepletion would reduce overall TSE blood infectivity by 42 per cent: Gregori, L, McCombie, N, Palmer, D, et al "Effectiveness of Leucoreduction for Removal of Infectivity of Transmissible Spongiform Encephalopathies From Blood" (2004) 364 *Lancet* 529.

shortening the United Kingdom residency criteria for donor deferral, and extending the residency exclusion to other countries, such as France, where vCJD cases have arisen following oral exposure.

Reynolds points out that risk assessment in public health goes beyond estimates of statistical likelihood to include qualitative issues: "public concerns about [blood safety]; the extent to which the risk will be treatable if it occurs and the costs of treating it; and the social or policy significance of it occurring".[83] To this might be added the possible political repercussions of infections in a sector that has previously faced criticism over HIV and hepatitis C. In social and political terms, blood safety is a cardinal public good, and past experience suggests that governments will invest significant sums in order to promote public confidence in the blood supply.

At the same time, a striking contrast can be drawn between the low risk of vCJD transmission, and the far higher risk of injury from the transfusion of incompatible blood and blood products. In the United Kingdom, the SHOT (serious hazards of transfusion) study provides ongoing surveillance of notifications of transfusion-related adverse events. The latest figures, for 2003, cover 85 per cent of all British hospitals. Forty-seven per cent of hospitals reported adverse events, including 33 ABO incompatible transfusions, 22 cases of unintended RhD incompatible transfusions and a further 22 cases of red cell antigen incompatible transfusions. There were 906 "near miss" reports during the period.[84]

These "human error" events contrast with two cases of transfusion-related HBV (Hepatitis B) one of HIV, and the first case of transfusion-acquired vCJD. Clearly, blood transfusions are far from being perfectly safe.[85] The risks are relative, however, and there is little public debate about the relative costs and priorities of managing different risks.[86] It is difficult for such a debate to occur in Australia since there is currently no national haemovigilance system and no single agency overseeing the blood transfusion "safety chain".[87]

---

83   Reynolds, C, *Public Health: Law and Regulation*, Federation Press, Sydney, 2004, p 146.

84   Serious Hazards of Transfusion Steering Group, *Serious Hazards of Transfusion: Annual Report 2003*, SHOT Office, Manchester, p 8. See further the SHOT website at <www.shot UnitedKingdom.org/>.

85   In Australia, a patient's risk of acquiring a blood-borne virus through a blood transfusion has been estimated as 1:7,000,000 (HIV), 1:3,000,000 (HCV), and 1:1,000,000 (HBV): Boyce, N and Brook, C, *Towards Better, Safer Blood Transfusion: A Report for the Australian Council for Safety and Quality in Health Care*, Consultation Draft, October 2004, p 9.

86   McClelland, B and Contreras, M "Appropriateness and Safety of Blood Transfusion" (2005) 330 *British Medical Journal* 104.

87   Boyce and Brook (2004) p 9. The urgent introduction of a national haemovigilance system was one recommendation made by the Senate Community Affairs References Committee inquiry into *Hepatitis C and the Blood Supply in Australia*, 2004. Boyce and Brook recommend the appointment of a "National Better, Safer Transfusion (BeST) Program" that would provide national leadership and would report to the Jurisdictional Blood Committee. The Jurisdictional Blood Committee represents Australian governments under the National Blood Agreement: see National Blood Authority, *Annual Report 2003-2004*, §§ 2.1.6, 2.3.1.

Notification following exposure through blood and blood products

While the risk of acquiring vCJD through the blood supply is very low, the benefits of a precautionary approach go beyond the absolute risk of transmission. Since there is no screening test for vCJD, "[p]eople who have received blood or blood products that are highly at risk for vCJD will now need to be managed as if vCJD had been diagnosed".[88] Such individuals will need to be notified of a potential life-long risk of developing vCJD, and appropriate infection control procedures must then be adopted when they subsequently undergo invasive clinical procedures. Bird notes that recipients will also be concerned about "the unquantified potential for possible maternal or sexual transmission, if any, of vCJD".[89]

In the United Kingdom, the Department of Health has introduced a range of measures aimed at preventing vCJD through the blood supply. Since 1997, all new diagnoses of vCJD trigger a search of National Blood Service donor records.[90] In November 1999, universal leucodepletion of donated blood was introduced, thereby removing an estimated 42 per cent of total infectivity.[91] In December 2002, the Department of Health purchased an independent United States plasma collector in order to ensure that plasma and fractionated products were all derived from non-United Kingdom donors.[92] Only since April 2004, however, have blood transfusion recipients themselves been excluded from donating blood.[93] In August 2004, this was extended to those who were unsure of whether they had ever been transfused, and to apheresis donors (who donate platelets).

The tracing of blood donors, and of recipients, and the process of notifying them of the risk of vCJD infection, can run in two directions. That is, blood donors can develop symptoms of vCJD, raising the possibility that vCJD was previously transmitted to blood recipients. Conversely, recipients of blood and blood products can develop vCJD, possibly due to infection from donors who for genetic or other reasons remain asymptomatic. In this second scenario, rapid tracing of possibly infectious donors is important in order to exclude them, and their blood, from the blood system.

Notification to blood recipients

As at January 2005, 17 United Kingdom blood donors were known to have developed vCJD, possibly infecting 50 recipients (ranging from 30 to 88 years of age), 18

88 Bird, S "Recipients of Blood or Blood Products 'at vCJD risk'" (2004) 328 *British Medical Journal* 118 at 118.

89 Ibid at 118.

90 Department of Health (United Kingdom), Press Release, "Update on Precautions to Protect Blood Supply", 22 July 2004.

91 Gregori et al (2004) op cit.

92 Pincock, S, "Patient's Death from vCJD May be Linked to Blood Transfusion" (2004) 363 *Lancet* 43.

93 Department of Health (United Kingdom), Press Release, "vCJD: Further Precautionary Measures Announced", 21 September 2004.

of whom are still alive.[94] As noted above, two of the recipients (now deceased) are thought to have acquired vCJD infection.[95] To September 2004, nine United Kingdom plasma donors were also known to have subsequently developed vCJD.[96] These donors made 23 blood donations that were added to 200 batches of various anti-clotting factors.

In September 2004, motivated by the two cases of transfusion-acquired vCJD infection and based on estimates of TSE transmission risk through blood in sheep, the Department of Health introduced a new and highly precautionary recipient notification program. Recipients of blood or implicated plasma products whose risk of exposure to vCJD infection was considered to be 1 per cent or greater than the background risk of the general population were contacted and advised that they were "at risk".[97] Due to the pooling of donations used in the manufacture of anti-clotting factors, an estimated 4000 people with haemophilia and other bleeding disorders fell into this category. All of Britain's estimated 6,000 haemophilia patients were sent letters inviting them to find out if they were at risk. Recipients of implicated batches of blood products were further divided into high, medium and low "at risk" categories, depending on the particular batches and kinds of product they received.[98] All "at risk" patients were asked not to donate blood or tissues and to inform public or private clinicians of their status so that appropriate infection control procedures could be taken for all future medical, surgical or dental treatment. The departmental booklet setting up these procedures envisages that clinicians responsible for determining a patient's "at risk" status will inform the patient's general practitioner, and that the patient's status will be recorded in primary care records and included in any letters of referral.[99] Patients are also asked to inform their families in case emergency surgery is required.

It is likely that some of the 4,000 persons exposed to vCJD through blood and blood products in the United Kingdom are now living in Australia. It is not yet clear if any steps will be taken to identify and exclude such individuals from

---

94   McClelland, B and Contreras, M, "Appropriateness and Safety of Blood Transfusion" (2005) 330 *British Medical Journal* 104; Donnellan, E, "A Blood Donor with vCJD Leads to Major Implications", *Irish Times*, 1 July 2005.

95   As noted above (note 77) a third case of "probable" transfusion acquired vCJD was announced by the UK Department of Health on 9 February 2006.

96   Health Protection Agency, "vCJD and Plasma Products – Clinical Information", 7 September 2004, <www.hpa.org.United Kingdom/infections/topics_az/cjd/menu.htm> (accessed 3 August 2005).

97   Ibid. The report that was the basis for risk assessment was carried out by Det Norske Veritas: *Risk Assessment of Exposure to vCJD Infectivity in Blood and Blood Products for Department of Health*, February 2003, <www.dnv.com/binaries/vCJD_Update_Report_tcm4-74414.pdf> (accessed 3 August 2005).

98   See Kmietowicz, Z, "Patients Informed of Increased Risk of vCJD Contact" (2004) 329 *British Medical Journal* 702. The Department of Health notes "It is likely that many patients with bleeding disorders will have been exposed to a potential additional risk of 1 per cent or greater. It is also likely that further batches of UK-sourced plasma products will be implicated in the future as more cases of vCJD arise": Health Protection Agency (2004) op cit p 6.

99   Health Protection Agency (2004) op cit pp 11–12.

Australia's blood donor pool, or to ensure that additional infection control safeguards are taken when they undergo procedures that require contact with at-risk tissue. Similar issues arise with Australian residents who were administered possibly-implicated plasma derivatives imported from the United Kingdom prior to the introduction of safety measures discussed above.

In March 2004, the United Kingdom's CJD Incident Panel published a "Framework Document" for managing exposure to TSEs through medical procedures.[100] The framework envisages that persons exposed to TSEs will be assessed for inclusion in a "contactable group" whose at-risk status would be notified both to them, and to relevant health care providers. As discussed above, recipients of blood and plasma (and in some cases, derivative products) sourced from donors who later developed vCJD, will fall into this group. Secondly, the framework proposes a confidential database comprising other "possibly exposed" people. Consistent with the argument that an exposure database is needed to monitor the fortunes of those exposed to iatrogenic TSE risks,[101] the database would be used for public health research and long-term follow up. In order not to unnecessarily alarm individuals, those individuals would be included on the register *without their consent*, although they could, if they wished, find out whether they were included in the database and why. This proposed database is still being debated.

Notification to blood donors

In July 2005, the Department of Health also undertook a reverse notification exercise. In this case, some 110 blood donors who, in 1993–1994, had donated blood to three recipients who later died from vCJD, were contacted and asked not to donate further blood or tissue as a precaution against the possibility that the recipients' infections were transmitted through blood.[102]

The discovery that vCJD is blood-transmissible, and its implications for the blood supply, underscore the importance of a precautionary approach, quite apart from considerations of legal risk and liability. As the self-described "canaries in the mineshaft",[103] those with haemophilia and bleeding disorders are particularly vulnerable, due to their frequent use of pooled donor products. In August 2004, in response to the Senate inquiry into hepatitis C and the blood supply, the

---

100 CJD Incidents Panel (United Kingdom), *Management of Possible Exposure to CJD through Medical Procedures: Framework Document*, 15 March 2004, p 43, <www.hpa.org.United Kingdom/infections/topics_az/cjd/framework%2015.3.04.pdf> (accessed 31 August 2005).

101 See Bird, S, "Attributable testing for abnormal prion protein, database linkage, and blood-borne vCJD risks" (2004) 364 *Lancet* 1362 at 1363.

102 Department of Health (United Kingdom), Press Release, "Notification Exercise Begins to Reduce Risk of vCJD Transmission", 20 July 2005; Lister, S, "You May Have vCJD, 100 Blood Donors Are Told", *Timesonline*, 21 July 2005, <www.timesonline.co.United Kingdom/article/0,,8122-1702287,00.html> (accessed 31 August 2005).

103 Haemophilia Foundation Australia, "The Impact of Hepatitis C Upon People with Haemophilia and Related Bleeding Disorders", submission to the Senate Community Affairs References Committee, *Hepatitis C and the Blood Supply in Australia*, 4 February 2004, p 5.

Commonwealth agreed to fund increased access to recombinant (that is, non-plasma derived) clotting factors in order to minimise risks of viral transmission.[104] While recombinant products will also avoid the risks of vCJD transmission, there is no recombinant product available for patients with von Willebrand's disease. As a result of recommendations from the NHMRC (following advice from SECTSE, its expert committee on TSEs) to the TGA, CSL Ltd has undertaken to produce Biostate® – a plasma-derived factor VIII product – entirely from plasma derived from donors who have not travelled outside Australia and New Zealand since 1980. This will take effect from April 2006.

Classical CJD, notification and look-backs after iatrogenic exposure

Even in the absence of vCJD, Australia faces similar challenges to those that have arisen in the United Kingdom following diagnosed cases of vCJD among blood and plasma donors. With about 20 new diagnoses of (classical) CJD each year, a number of incidents have occurred in which a newly-diagnosed patient is discovered to have previously undergone brain or spinal surgery, or retinal or posterior eye surgery that possibly contaminated instruments and exposed later patients who came in contact with those instruments to a risk of transmission. While this risk is highest when instruments are in direct contact with the CNS tissues,[105] difficult questions also arise when, for example, the patient who developed CJD previously underwent gastroscopy or colonoscopy.

What the duty of reasonable care requires, in response to such an exposure, is uncertain. The issue is not resolved by inferences about whether those exposed would want to be told of the risk.[106] As discussed above, the limits of legal liability require attention to the probability and gravity of transmission risk weighed against the practicability and justifiability of precautionary measures.[107] With only a few reported cases of iatrogenic CJD arising through contaminated instruments (and none for the past 25 years), the risk of acquiring CJD through contaminated instruments must be extraordinarily low.[108] On the other hand, CJD is a terrible disease and there is great community concern about it. To ignore the exposure and not to inform at-risk patients would mean that if a patient *had, in fact,* acquired CJD, no precautions would be taken to prevent the patient donating blood or tissue

---

104 The Hon Tony Abbott MHR, Minister for Health & Ageing, Media Releases, "Government Response to the Senate Inquiry into Hepatitis C and the Blood Supply", 30 August 2004.

105 CDNA Guidelines, §§31.7.3 and 31.12.3.

106 The issue here is what the duty of care requires in response to the exposure of a class of patients to a risk of transmission. This issue is conceptually separate from the duty to advise of material risks that arises prior to performing a clinical procedure, as recognised by the High Court in *Rogers v Whitaker* (1992) 175 CLR 479 at 490.

107 See above, notes 60–61.

108 Will (2003) op cit.

in future,[109] nor would extra precautions be taken when the patient subsequently underwent invasive procedures involving contact with contaminated tissue. If subsequent infections did occur as a result of an at-risk patient unknowingly infecting others, the decision not to notify might well be interpreted harshly, in the light of hindsight.

The alternative is to inform at-risk patients that they may or may not have been exposed to a fatal illness with a variable incubation period for which there is no diagnostic test, and no treatment available. Notification brings not only the burden of uncertainty, but also the risk of discrimination, especially in health care contexts. Anti-discrimination statutes in all States and Territories prohibit discrimination on the grounds of a person's "disability" or "impairment" in a range of areas, including the provision of services, which includes medical and clinical services.[110] However, the legislation provides some exemptions, including where discrimination is reasonably necessary to protect public health,[111] or where provision of the service at all, or on equal terms, would cause unjustifiable hardship.[112] For at-risk patients, the concern is that these provisions will be relied upon to deny them elective surgery or dentistry due to fear, lack of knowledge about how to deal with transmission risks, or due to the costs of quarantining or destroying otherwise re-usable instruments that cannot be cleaned appropriately (for example, flexible endoscopes).[113]

Case study: The Royal Melbourne Hospital incident

A recent example of the operational and ethical dilemmas that iatrogenic exposure can cause occurred in Melbourne in late 2004. The patient in question underwent surgery to remove melanomas from his frontal lobe in January, and again in November 2003. In April 2004, the patient began experiencing mood changes, fatigue, and he began seeing a psychiatrist. In late May the psychiatrist noted muscular twitching: this worsened and the next day the man was admitted to hospital with myoclonus and increased drowsiness. The neurologist suspected CJD, and the National CJD Incidents Panel was informed. The man died in June 2004 and CJD was confirmed by autopsy.

---

109 There is, however, no evidence of transfusion-acquired (classical) CJD: CDNA Guidelines, §31.7.1; Llewelyn et al (2004) at 417.

110 *Anti-Discrimination Act 1977* (NSW) s 49M; *Anti-Discrimination Act 1991* (Qld) ss 7, 46; *Equal Opportunity Act 1984* (SA) s 76; *Anti-Discrimination Act 1998* (Tas) ss 16(k), 22(1)(c); *Equal Opportunity Act 1995* (Vic) ss 6, 42; *Equal Opportunity Act 1984* (WA) ss 66A, 66K; *Discrimination Act 1991* (ACT) ss 7(j), 20; *Anti-Discrimination Act 1992* (NT) ss 19(j), 41. In New South Wales, "disability" is defined to include "the presence in a person's body of organisms causing or capable of causing disease or illness": s 4(1). Legislation in other jurisdictions is in similar terms.

111 For public health exceptions, see ibid. NSW: s 49PL; Qld: s 107; Tas: s 47; Vic: s 80; ACT: s 56; NT: s 55.

112 For unjustifiable hardship (or similarly worded exceptions), see above, note 108: NSW: s 49C; Qld: s 51; SA: s 76(3); Tas: s 48; Vic: s 46; WA: s 66K(2); ACT: s 47; NT: s 58.

113 See, for example, Cooke, J, "Hospitals Misreading CJD Risk" *Sydney Morning Herald*, 14 March 2005, p 5.

On the recommendation of the National CJD Incidents Panel, all 1056 neuro-surgery patients operated on at the hospital from the date of the January 2003 surgery were sent letters by courier advising them of the risk (albeit remote) of transmission.[114] A 1-800 hotline was set up and thousands of phone calls were taken. In addition, the hospital's entire stock of 15,000 neurosurgical instruments was placed in quarantine: replacement instruments needed for emergency surgery were provided by another hospital. These extraordinary measures were taken because during the 18-month period of possible exposure (January 2003 to June 2004) the hospital had no tracking system in place permitting individual instruments to be matched with individual patients. There was no way of excluding the possibility that instruments used on the index patient were subsequently used on each of the patients who subsequently underwent neurosurgery at the hospital.

Evaluating look-back and notification practices

The decision to carry out a look-back investigation and to notify previously exposed patients is a decision for each health care institution, in consultation with State health departments.[115] Given the prevailing ethic of patient self-determination, and hospitals' desire to avoid scandal and perceptions of a "cover-up", there are certain built-in incentives to adopt a policy of absolute transparency and to inform patients of any risk, however speculative. In this case, the transmission risk was low, but in quantitative terms, probably anyone's guess. In qualitative terms, the core ethical issue was whether the harm that would be caused by possible iatrogenic transmission (which exposed patients could possibly spread even further, if infected) outweighed the harm caused by plunging the exposed class into a potentially life-long state of uncertainty, stress, and even despair.

Several years earlier, a similar exposure event occurred at Melbourne's Royal Dental Hospital. In that case, however, the estimated 100 patients who underwent procedures after the index patient were *not* informed, due to the assessment that the transmission risk was "extraordinarily low and theoretical".[116] Clearly, the risk will depend on the nature of the procedure and the tissues with which instruments have come in contact. In the Royal Melbourne incident, however, what is surprising is that the decision to notify extended to patients who had been operated on more than three months after the index case. The risk of transmission via instruments is considered far less significant after 10 cycles of

---

114 Cooke, J, "The Unkindest Cut", *Sydney Morning Herald* 18–19 September 2004, p 30; Noble, T, "Health Alert as Hospital Warns of Brain Disease", *The Age*, 14 September 2004; Kaye, A, "Presentation: CJD: A Local Perspective" in Victorian Department of Human Services, Clinical Governance Unit (2005) op cit pp 31–32. The patients, who ranged from 10 to 99 years, were classified into three risk categories depending on whether the dura mater was pierced in the operation, and whether the patient was operated on within three months of the index case.

115 CDNA Guidelines, §31.16.2.

116 Noble (2004) op cit. It is worth adding that there have been no documented cases of CJD transmission through dentistry.

cleaning using standard instrument decontamination procedures,[117] and by *six weeks* the instruments from the Royal Melbourne Hospital had been through at least *12 cycles* of sterilisation.[118] In the United Kingdom, the CJD Incident Panel's Framework Document recommends notification only to the first six "downstream" patients following a high-risk procedure (CNS, retina, optic nerve procedures) carried out on an index patient with CJD.[119]

The risk of iatrogenic TSE transmission through procedures involving contact with high-risk tissues has created impetus for the use of disposable instruments and instrument parts (where financially viable), and for the centralisation of procedures involving higher-risk individuals at designated facilities where health care workers are familiar with infection control procedures. One recommendation from the consensus conference convened by the Victorian Department of Human Services to discuss issues raised by the Royal Melbourne Hospital incident was that hospitals performing procedures that involve contact with higher risk tissues should introduce procedures permitting individual instruments to be tracked to individual patients.[120] Another recommendation was that triage procedures should be implemented (based on questions relating to family history and other risk factors), in order to identify higher risk patients. Such screening procedures do, however, generate a high proportion of false negative results.[121] Nor will they identify sporadic cases who are in the pre-clinical phase. For this reason, it is likely that a "universal precautions" approach will ultimately evolve for all neuro-surgery, spinal surgery, surgery involving the piercing of the dura, pituitary surgery and posterior eye surgery. As with prion reduction filters for blood, there are strong commercial incentives for the development of effective prion decontamination agents for cleansing surgical instruments and scopes.[122]

---

117 Health Protection Agency (2004) above note 96 at p 13; CJD Incidents Panel (United Kingdom), Framework Document, above note 100 at para 2.65.

118 Victorian Department of Human Services, Clinical Governance Unit, (2005) above note 39 at p 31.

119 CJD Incidents Panel (UK), Framework Document, p 43.

120 See Victorian Department of Human Services, Clinical Governance Unit (2005) above note 39 at p 3.

121 Ibid p 3. The CDNA Guidelines make similar recommendations: see §31.12.1. It has been estimated that:

> [I]f a large hospital performs 15,000 non-neurosurgical procedures per year, even assuming that the CJD risk in hospitalised patients ... is 10 times greater than the general community, there would only be one new case of CJD every 10 years in that hospital population. One hundred and fifty thousand questionnaires would have been administered to find this case. If the false-positive rate per questionnaire is 1% there would be approximately 150 false positives per year (or 3 per week) during this time. All of those with positive questionnaires would have their procedure delayed and suffer some inconvenience.

> Victorian Department of Human Services, *Background Paper for the Consensus Workshop: Creutzfeldt-Jakob Disease: Preventing Transmission in the Health Care Setting*, December 2004, p 9.

122 See Jackson, G, McKintosh, E and Flechsig, E, "An Enzyme-Detergent Method for Effective Prion Decontamination of Surgical Steel" (2005) 86 *Journal of General Virology* 869.

The purpose of look-back and patient notification is to alert exposed individuals and to prevent further transmission. There is, however, no formal system in place to ensure that patients exposed to the risk of iatrogenic CJD transmission disclose their status when undergoing surgical or dental treatment in future. In accordance with current ARCBS screening procedures, such patients would be ineligible to donate blood. However, the ANCJDR is not an "exposures database", and in the absence of voluntary disclosure, there are no mechanisms that would automatically flag an at-risk patient's subsequent interactions with the health care system.

Whether or not it would be lawful to disclose a person's at-risk status to a health care provider without the patient's consent depends on the mix of privacy and non-disclosure legislation operating in each State or Territory.[123] Personal information within private health care institutions is governed by the National Privacy Principles, and Victoria, New South Wales and the Australian Capital Territory have introduced health privacy principles that apply to health information in both the public and private sectors. This legislation shares similar provisions that would permit non-consensual disclosure of a person's health information when it is necessary to lessen or prevent a "serious and imminent" threat to another's life, health or safety, or "a serious threat to public health and safety".[124] The key consideration, then, is in what circumstances the risk of iatrogenic TSE transmission represents a "serious threat" to public health and safety. Given that there have been no documented cases of CJD transmitted via contaminated instruments in Australia, and none for 25 years worldwide,[125] it is far from clear that this risk would qualify.[126]

Key issues raised by the likely future development of a vCJD screening test

Evidence that vCJD is transmissible through blood has increased the incentives for the development of a reliable screening test that can distinguish between the presence of normal and aberrant forms of the prion protein. There is a potentially enormous market for vCJD test kits, with estimates of up to 62 million tests per year.[127] In a perfect world, a screening test for TSEs would be 100 per cent *sensitive*,

123 See above, note 43.

124 *Privacy Act 1988* (Cth) Sch 3 (National Privacy Principles, NPP 2.1(e)); *Health Records and Information Privacy Act 2002* (NSW) Sch 1 (HPP 11(1)(c)); *Health Records Act 2001* (Vic) Sch 1 (HPP 2.2(h)); see also *Health Records (Privacy and Access) Act 1997* (ACT) s 5 (Privacy Principle 10.1(c)).

125 See above, note 17.

126 State legislation variously authorises disclosure in other circumstances, including with the consent of the Director-General of the New South Wales Health Department or the Victorian Minister: see *Health Administration Act 1982* (NSW) s 22(e) and *Health Administration Regulation 2000* (NSW) s 13(2); *Health Services Act 1988* (Vic) s 141(3)(h).

127 "Market for blood tests for CJD", <www.priondata.org/data/A_mktblood.html> (accessed 31 August 2005).

meaning that it would identify all individuals who truly carried the disease: there would be no false negatives. Such a test would also be 100 per cent *specific*: it would return a negative result for all who were not infected, and there would be no false positives. Given the difficulty of developing a test that meets these para-meters, current screening strategies that protect the blood supply usually depend on a screening test that is highly sensitive. Samples returning positive results are then re-tested using a highly specific confirmatory test. At present, there is no confirmatory test that reliably determines the presence of subclinical vCJD infection. This amplifies the disadvantages that a less than perfect vCJD screening test will present for policy-makers, assuming one becomes available.

The effectiveness of a vCJD screening test

The overall public benefit of introducing a vCJD screening test requires the improved level of safety of the blood supply resulting from the introduction of the test to be weighed against the psychosocial implications of screening for a devasta-ting, fatal disease in an asymptomatic population. At first glance, the experience with HIV and hepatitis C suggests that reasonable care would require the adoption of a screening test as soon as logistically possible. Bird advocates the development of a national protocol for vCJD counselling, as well as guaranteed access to the insurance terms the individual could have obtained prior to donating or receiving at-risk blood.[128] Assuming that a vCJD test were extremely sensitive and highly specific, it remains the case, however, that due to the low prevalence of vCJD in the general population, the vast majority of positive results from the vCJD screen will be false positives.[129] The same issue will arise if a screening test for classical CJD is ever developed. Basing estimates on a large metropolitan hospital that carries out 15,000 general surgical procedures a year, an incidence of CJD 10 times that of the general population, and a test with 100 per cent sensitivity and 95 per cent specifi-city, Johnson calculates:

> It would take an average of 10 years before a single case of CJD would be identi-fied. In this time, there would be 7,499 false positives (an average of 14 per week) that would have to be followed up, and you would have operated on 3 asym-ptomatic cases [of sporadic CJD] that you did not know about.[130]

In the absence of an *extremely specific* confirmatory test, the human cost of these putative diagnoses would be so devastating that no such screening test could ever be implemented. Not only is a "gold standard" confirmatory test necessary, as Vamvakas points out, in order to reliably estimate the specificity and sensitivity of

---

128 Bird, S, "Attributable testing for abnormal prion protein, database linkage, and blood-borne vCJD risks" (2004) 364 *Lancet* 1362.

129 Vamvakas, E, "Sensitivity, Specificity, and Predictive Value of Screening Tests" in Blajchman et al (2004) op cit p 83.

130 Johnson, P, "Presentation: A View from a Health Service" in Victorian Department of Human Services, Clinical Governance Unit (2005) op cit p 17.

the screening test,[131] but in its absence, the ARCBS might well be exposed to psychiatric injury claims for harm flowing from (what turned out to be) false positive diagnoses.[132]

The donor deferral criteria that currently operate in Australia lack specificity: most deferred donors are not infected with vCJD just because they spent six months or more in the United Kingdom. On the other hand, the risks of infection in the Australian donor population are low, and this risk is decreased significantly by current donor deferral criteria. The reasonableness of introducing a screening test would therefore require the superiority of the test in lowering the risks of infection, to be demonstrated. In the HIV and hepatitis C context, antibody screening tests were simply added on to screening questions that related to sexual behaviour and drug use. If a vCJD test were simply added to current deferral criteria, the marginal improvement in safety that might be expected to result would come at a very high cost to falsely diagnosed donors.

Given the problem of false positives, another strategy might be to test higher risk populations only. For example, the test could investigate the exclusion status of currently deferred donors, or those undergoing neurosurgery and other procedures involving a vCJD transmission risk. Such a strategy could serve the public interest not only by reducing the risk of iatrogenic transmission, but by restoring deferred donors to the blood donor pool.

Whatever screening strategy is implemented, there is no doubt that, given the psychosocial consequences of diagnosis, the risk of infection will be a "material risk" that donors and other test subjects should be made aware of prior to donation and relevant forms of surgery.[133] Far from the availability of a vCJD test being a "magnet" attracting higher risk donors to donate blood, as some feared when surrogate testing for HIV was introduced,[134] the likely scenario is that the risk of diagnosis with a fatal, irreversible disease will create powerful *disincentives* to voluntary donation by existing donors, reducing to that extent the sufficiency of the blood supply.

---

131 Vamvakas, E, "Sensitivity, Specificity, and Predictive Value in Screening Tests" in Blajchman et al (2004) op cit p 84.

132 Unlike *APQ v Commonwealth Serum Laboratories* [1999] 3 VR 633, discussed above, the claim here would be that the screening protocol itself, and the disclosure of a false diagnosis (as distinct from the administration of a TSE infected product) was a breach of duty of care causing psychiatric harm.

133 In *Rogers v Whitaker* (1992) 175 CLR 479 at 490, the High Court of Australia confirmed that health care workers owe a duty to tell patients about the "material risks" associated with a medical procedure. A risk is material if either: (i) a reasonable person in the patient's position would be likely to attach significance to the risk in the circumstances of the case, or if (ii) the medical practitioner is aware that *this particular patient*, if warned of the risk, would likely attach significance to it.

134 See *E v Australian Red Cross Society* (1999) 31 FCR 299 at 320–321, 325–327.

Psychosocial impact of vCJD screening

To understand the psychological impact of vCJD screening, prior to blood donation and certain forms of surgery, it is helpful to compare vCJD with Huntington's disease (HD), another fatal, neurodegenerative disease. HD is not infectious, and testing is carried out by registries in a non-directive, supportive context. Despite this, only 10 to 20 per cent of those at risk for HD request testing: those who do would appear to be a self-selected group best able to deal with the result, while those who decline testing are significantly more pessimistic and depressed.[135] The literature confirms that testing is an extremely stressful and confronting turning point in the lives of those who choose it, with profound implications for family functioning, as well as for those who inherit the relevant gene.[136] Despite this, there are several reasons why the experience with HD testing may significantly underestimate the impact of vCJD testing upon those who test positive. First, although HD is heritable, most TSEs are not. It follows that the wider family dysfunction that may accompany HD, as the family seeks to cope with or to externalise the common risk, may be absent for vCJD. On the other hand, with no family history of disease, those undergoing CJD testing will have no expectation of a positive result, with the consequence that vCJD diagnosis may even be more catastrophic in personal terms.

Secondly, while the element of coercion is absent in HD testing, it is likely to be present with vCJD screening. Donors might choose not to donate (to the detriment of the blood supply), but neurosurgery patients will have little choice. Those being tested will not be a self-selecting group best able to deal with the results. Prior to blood donation, in particular, testing is likely to take place in a swift and routine manner. Such pre-test counselling as there is will have little hope of preparing a donor for a positive result. The option of screening subjects for vCJD, but giving them the opportunity not to know the result, will almost certainly prove fanciful. The consequence of such a policy for blood donors would be that the ARCBS would be required to keep accepting donations from donors who might be known to be infected in order not to "tip them off" or interfere with their mental equilibrium. Accepting non-usable donations would waste resources, and could lead to unnecessary risks (for example, vCJD-implicated blood making its way into the blood supply in error). If an organisation withheld knowledge of an individual's vCJD infection, they might well be regarded as breaching their duty of care if that person (unaware of their status), did something that resulted in onward transmission.[137] Not

---

135 Meiser, B, "Psychological Effect of Genetic Testing for Huntington's Disease: An Update of the Literature" (2000) 69 *Journal of Neurology, Neurosurgery & Psychiatry* 574.

136 Sobel, S and Dowan, D, "Impact of Genetic Testing for Huntington Disease on the Family System" (2000) 90 *American Journal of Medical Genetics* 49; Taylor, C and Myers, R, "Long-Term Impact of Huntington Disease Linkage Testing" (1997) 70 *American Journal of Medical Genetics* 365; Rees, G, Fry, A and Cull, A, "A Family History of Breast Cancer: Women's Experiences from a Theoretical Perspective" (2001) 52 *Social Science & Medicine* 1433.

137 An analogy can be drawn here with cases in which the failure of a doctor to diagnose a sexually transmissible infection in their immediate patient (or to adequately counsel the patient to take an HIV test), amounted to a breach of the duty of care owed to the patient's sexual partner, to whom the immediate patient transmitted the infection: see *BT v Oei* [1999] NSWSC 1082.

surprisingly, the United Kingdom's National Blood Service recognises that if vCJD testing is introduced, patients will need to be informed of test results.[138]

The psychological implications of vCJD diagnosis raise a core issue about screening: diagnosis furthers the public interest, but almost certainly does great harm to all who test positive. Submitting to testing, in any context, is an altruistic act. The state has a reciprocal duty, I would argue, to ensure that there exists an adequate network of health care providers willing to provide services to those at risk of TSE transmission, actively countering the risks of discrimination they might otherwise face.[139]

Conclusion

The transmission risks posed by CJD and vCJD require public health authorities to monitor emerging evidence and to reassess operational responses and policies in the light of new developments. Decisions about risks to human health depend upon a complex body of biological and epidemiological information. This evolving body of knowledge feeds directly into the duties of care owed by the ARCBS, hospitals, and other health care providers to patients, blood recipients, those exposed to the risk of infection, and others whom they, in turn, may potentially infect. In the end, however, questions of judgment remain about the relative weight to assign to demonstrated and assumed risks. Responses to TSE transmission through the blood supply, and via surgical procedures, in particular, are influenced by political, as well as ethical and legal considerations.

With no cases of vCJD, so far, and about 20 new cases of sporadic CJD each year, TSEs present a real, but low-level public health threat to Australia. The containment of the TSE epidemic so far reflects the significant resources that Australia has devoted to it. There is an important ethical dimension to that response that is often obscured by the more immediate biological and epidemiological issues. Ultimately, the value of a precautionary approach to TSE transmission risks must itself be balanced against the need to protect the sufficiency of Australia's blood supply, and against the benefits of protecting exposed individuals whose chance of developing symptoms is speculative or unknown from the psychological harm this knowledge may cause. The development of a standard, "universal precautions" approach to certain kinds of surgery, together with prion reduction filters and screening tests for TSEs, may significantly alter the shape of public health responses in the future. At the same time, there is still much to learn about prion diseases, including the extent to which individuals may act as reservoirs of infection, perhaps never developing symptoms in their lifetime, while remaining capable of transmitting disease to others.

---

138 Hewitt, P, "Donor Perceptions and Ethical Aspects of an Eventual Testing and Notification Program" in Blajchman et al (2004) op cit pp 87–88.

139 I am indebted to Professor Michael Alpers, a member of the NHMRC's SECTSE committee, for his helpful elaboration of this point.

9

International trade agreements and the practice of medicine

Thomas Alured Faunce[1]

Introduction: Challenges for trade and health

The practice of medicine, variably from the perspectives of policy-makers, the community and the profession, has traditionally been regulated within the confines of three great normative traditions: bioethics, health law and, more recently, international human rights. This chapter, however, makes the case that major structural and attitudinal changes in the practice of medicine are being orchestrated, often deleteriously for the global and domestic burden of illness, by the business plans of corporate globalisation enforced through the dispute settlement mechanisms of multilateral and bilateral trade agreements. This could be described as a controversial thesis. It confronts traditional and widely held assumptions about parliamentary sovereignty and the rule of law, as well as the regulatory role of medical ethics. Yet, the evidence and support for many of its implicit understandings is substantial.[2] I hope to demonstrate that consideration of its impact should be a priority for medical regulators and educators.

The two multilateral trade agreements I particularly wish to discuss in this context are the World Trade Organisation's (WTO) General Agreement on Trade in Services (GATS) and the Agreement on Trade-Related Aspects of Intellectual Property Rights (TRIPS).[3] The chief bilateral agreement evaluated will be the

1   Dr Thomas Faunce, BA LLB(Hons) B Med. PhD Senior lecturer, College of Law and Medical School, Project Director Globalisation and Health, Centre for Governance of Knowledge and Development, Australian National University. Statement of competing interests: Nil. This research was funded by Australian Research Council Discovery Grant DP0556635.

2   Farmer, P, *Pathologies of Power: Health, Human Rights and the New War on the Poor*, University of California Press, Berkeley, 2003; Shaffer, ER and Brenner, JE, "International Trade Agreements: Hazards to Health?" (2004) 34(3) *International Journal of Health Services* 467; Hilary, J, *The Wrong Model: GATS, Trade Liberalization and Children's Right to Health*, Save the Children, London, 2001; Angell, M, *The Truth About Drug Companies: How They Deceive Us and What to Do About it?* Random House, New York, 2005; Kassirer, JP, *On the Take: How Medicine's Complicity with Big Business can Endanger Your Health*, Oxford University Press, New York, 2004.

3   Marrakech Agreement Establishing the World Trade Organisation [1995] Australian Treaty Series 8, Annex 1C, pt2, s 5 (TRIPS).

Australia–United States Free Trade Agreement (AUSFTA). Other deals are also likely to become relevant, such as the China–Australia Free Trade Agreement (China-AusFTA), regional bilateral agreements with Singapore, Thailand, Malaysia and the 1983 Closer Economic Relations Agreement with New Zealand, as well as other multilateral international arrangements promoting trade and investment to which Australia is a party.

Medical practice in the Australasian region will soon face significant regulatory challenges from the higher proportion of elderly persons more reliant for duration and quality of life on policies promoting universal access to health services, affordable medications, safe food, clean air, and water and environmental conditions.[4] These citizens will be less able to assimilate adverse changes in these areas if trade agreements remove or alter respective protective regulations as "unnecessarily restrictive non-tariff barriers to trade".[5] Regional change in climate, travel, security and agricultural practices are also likely to expose the Australian population to greater risks of pandemic influenza or bioterrorist attack.[6] Trade agreement intellectual property provisions, like those considered here in relation to the AUSFTA, may controversially restrict government capacity to stockpile and compulsorily licence vaccines in such public health emergencies.[7]

Much medical practice in contemporary Australia is organised around primary, secondary and tertiary prevention of health problems created by alcohol and tobacco consumption.[8] A survey of 42 countries from 1970 to 1995, showed that international trade agreements, by removing import restrictions and weakening the capacity for government regulation over price, advertising and anti-competitive practices, have commonly led to an increase in tobacco and alcohol consumption.[9] Yet, tobacco smoking and alcohol are set to be included in a Pacific Island Countries Trade Agreement (PICTA), which Australia can apply to join after eight years.[10] The

4   Andrews, K, *National Strategy for an Ageing Australia*, Department of Health and Ageing, Canberra, 2002.

5   Shaffer, E, Waitzkin, H, Brenner, J and Jasso-Aguilar, R, "Global Trade and Public Health" (2005) 95(1) *American Journal of Public Health* 23.

6   World Health Organisation, *WHO Consultation on Priority Public Health Interventions Before and During an Influenza Pandemic*, WHO, Geneva, 2004.

7   A government's capacity to stockpile generic medicines prior to brand name patent expiry was held, for example, to be contrary to TRIPS in *Canada-Patent Protection of Pharmaceutical Products-Compliant by the European Communities* WT/DS114/R (17 March 2000).

8   Mathers, CD, Vos, ET, Stevenson, CE and Begg, SJ, "The Australian Burden of Disease Study: Measuring the Loss of Health from Diseases, Injuries and Risk Factors" (2000) 172 *Medical Journal of Australia* 592.

9   Taylor, A, Chaloupka, FJ, Guindon, E and Corbett, M, "The Impact of Trade Liberalization on Tobacco Consumption" in Jha, P and Chaloupka, FJ (eds), *Tobacco Control in Developing Countries*, Oxford University Press, Oxford, 2000.

10   Secretariat of the Pacific Community, *Public Health Programme, Tobacco and Alcohol in the Pacific Island Countries Trade Agreement*, Noumea, New Caledonia, 2005. Article 8(13) of PICTA states that the obligation to reduce and eliminate tariffs under Article 7 shall not apply to tobacco or alcoholic beverages. However within two years of PICTA entering into force (13 April 2005) the parties must consider appropriate rules to govern trade in tobacco and alcohol and insert those into PICTA as a new annex.

Pacific Agreement on Closer Economic Relations (PACER) which entered into force on 3 October 2002, amongst other things, guarantees Australia and New Zealand the right to negotiate with Pacific Island countries to establish reciprocal free trade agreements without necessitating prior public health impact statements.[11]

The chapter begins by briefly describing some disputes and dilemmas set to be occasioned for the regulation of the Australian medical practice by the TRIPS agreement and GATS. Some of these include structural shifts to private enterprise models, the patenting of medically important knowledge, restrictions on universal access to basic health care and limitations on the capacity for local professional standard-setting in both qualifications of practitioners and clinical research.

The emphasis thereafter shifts to the AUSFTA. Potential controversies for medical practice here include whether the decision of a three-person panel of trade lawyers, in a bilateral forum chosen by the dominant disputing party, should have practical authority to decide whether Australian public health policy will continue to support essential medicines made universally affordable by government reimbursement based on objectively demonstrated therapeutic significance. It looks at counterbalancing constitutional and trade strategies. The chapter concludes by discussing some relevant implications for education in bioethics, health law and human rights, particularly concerning professional responsibility and the ethos of medical practice.

TRIPS: The impact of information feudalism on medical practice

Intellectual property provisions in international trade agreements are set to create many controversies for the practice of medicine globally and in Australia. These include disputes concerning the impact of patents on affordable patient access to essential pharmaceuticals and the use of trade marks, secrets and industrial designs to control institutional access to medical equipment. The WTO TRIPS agreement creates primary obligations on signatory member states, enforceable by threat of rule-based trade sanctions, to pass legislation for expanded minimum levels of patent protection over intellectual property (20 years under Article 28) for products and processes (particularly pharmaceuticals) that, under Article 27, are new, involve an "inventive step" and are "capable of industrial application".[12]

The driving force behind the TRIPS agreement was an Intellectual Property Committee, whose members comprised key executives from the multinational corporations Bristol Myers, DuPont, General Electric, Hewlett Packard, IBM,

---

11 Pacific Agreement on Closer Economic Relations, opened for signature on 18 August 2001, [2004] ATS 10 (entered into force 3 October 2002).

12 Gervais, D, *The TRIPS Agreement: Drafting History and Analysis*, 2nd edn, Sweet & Maxwell, London, 2003.

Johnson & Johnson, Merck, Monsanto, Pfizer, Rockwell and Warner.[13] TRIPS was designed to ensure intellectual property in areas such as health care remained a private, monopolistic rent-making right (in reality, of well-resourced transnational corporations), not something generated, for example, in the intellectual commons for collective good by university medical schools or the profession.[14] It arguably permits the modern-day metaphoric corporate barons of medically-relevant knowledge to shape the direction of research, as well as government expenditure in areas such as pharmaceuticals, and through them, the structure and ethos of clinical practice.[15] The countervailing argument is that strong intellectual property protection, by attracting investment and encouraging technological innovation, is in the interest of all countries, regardless of their economic circumstances.[16]

Minor concessions to TRIPS obligations were allowed, after intense lobbying by developing nations. These permitted limited exceptions to pharmaceutical patents (Article 30) and compulsory licensing for medicines production (after payment of reasonable compensation) for public health reasons (Article 31), as well as staggered implementation dates.[17] Despite frequently utilising compulsory licences (for example during the anthrax bioterrorist crisis), the United States has since been actively lobbying to restrict other nations access to even these modest restrictions. The United States has also been using bilateral trade agreements such as the AUSFTA to circumvent the social justice clarification of intellectual property rights over pharmaceuticals enunciated in the Doha Declaration on TRIPS and Public Health.[18] This instrument requires that "trade agreements should be interpreted and implemented to protect public health and promote universal access to medicines".[19] Section 2101(b)(4)(C) of the *Trade Promotion Authority Act 2002* (US) requires United States negotiators ensure that their trade agreements uphold it.

---

13 Drahos, P, "The TNC Bias in TRIPS" in Drahos, P (ed), *Intellectual Property*, Ashgate, Aldershot, 1999, pp 158–161.

14 See generally: Sell, SK, *Private Power, Public Law. The Globalisation of Intellectual Property Rights*, Cambridge University Press, Cambridge, 2003; Faunce TA, (2005) "Global Intellectual Property Protection for Innovative iPharmaceuticals: Challenges for Bioethics and Health Law" in Bennett, B and Tomossy, GF (eds), *Globalisation and Health: Challenges for health law and Bioethics*, Springer, Dordrecht.

15 Drahos, P and Braithwaite, J, *Information Feudalism. Who Owns the Knowledge Economy?*, New Press, New York, 2003.

16 Industry Functional Advisory Committee on Intellectual Property Rights for Trade Policy Matters (IFAC-3), *Report to the President, Congress and the US Trade Representative on the US–Australia Free Trade Agreement*, Washington, 2004, pp 2–6.

17 Article 65(4) allowed developing nations to have a delayed implementation phase, but Article 70(8) allowed patent applications in the interim to be stored in what was termed a "mailbox".

18 Gathii, JT, "The Legal Status of the Doha Declaration on TRIPS and Public Health Under the Vienna Convention on the Law of Treaties" (2002) 15(2) *Harvard J Law & Technology* 291.

19 World Trade Organisation, Doha Declaration on the TRIPS Agreement and Public Health, WT/MIN/(01)/Dec/W/2, 2001.

Assume a dispute arises concerning national legislation providing cheap generic medicines. The TRIPS dispute settlement mechanism potentially grants ultimate determination in such a case (unless the disputant chooses a bilateral forum), not to a WTO member nation's constitutional court, but a panel of three trade lawyers appointed under that multilateral agreement. In the WTO *Canada-Patent Protection of Pharmaceuticals Case*, for instance, the European Community (unsuccessfully) challenged Canadian legislation permitting generic pharmaceutical manufacturers to apply for quality and safety approval before the relevant brand name patent expires (the "*Bolar* exemption"). They were permitted to impugn the legislation as not a "limited" enough exception to fall within Article 30 of TRIPS, or for being "discriminatory" as to "field of technology" under Article 27.[20] A Canadian statute permitting stockpiling of generic drugs in expectation of brand name patent expiry, however, was held to be contrary to these TRIPS provisions. That government then risked the threat of trade sanctions if the offending statute was not repealed or amended.[21] Such a case indicates that legislation, for example by a future Australian government, limited to regulating pharmaceutical products, or whose adverse effects or objective indications of purpose were deemed by such a panel to be limited to the pharmaceutical industry, would similarly subject that domestic administration to what, in an era of globalisation, is the almost insurmountable threat of massive trade penalties.[22]

The "intellectual property ratchet" refers to a process whereby so-called "TRIPS-plus" provisions in bilateral trade deals such as the AUSFTA (generally facilitated by the less equal bargaining power than that present in multilateral agreements) may subsequently be able, through the "most favoured nation" provision in Article 4 of TRIPS, to increase the levels of intellectual property protection available to all WTO members.[23] This process, by increasing pharmaceutical patent protection and restricting the capacity of governments to regulate its adverse effects on access to medicines, as well as through the opportunity cost of increased government expenditure in this area, may lead to major structural changes in the practice of medicine.

GATS: Restrictions on universal access to health services and professional licensing standards

Considerable evidence supports the cost-effectiveness of taxpayer-funded schemes providing universal free access to basic health services, particularly in

---

20 This was despite Australia joining with Argentina, Hungary and Israel in creating such "*Bolar*" exemptions allowing "springboarding" of generics upon brand name patent expiry.

21 Canada-Patent Protection of Pharmaceutical Products-Compliant by the European Communities WT/DS114/R, 17 March 2000.

22 Ibid at 174.

23 Drahos, P, "BITS and BIPS: Bilateralism in Intellectual Property" (2001) 4 *Journal of Intellectual Property* 791.

emergencies.[24] This policy has been a distinguishing, well-respected egalitarian feature of medical practice in Australia through Medicare, as it has in the United Kingdom under the National Health Service.[25] The Doctors Reform Society (DRS) formed in 1973 to support Australia's Medibank (now Medicare system), believes, however, the latter is seriously threatened by market-driven principles underlying international trade agreements such as GATS.[26]

GATS is a WTO agreement setting rules for the "liberalisation" or "free market access" of global trade in services by private transnational corporations. The influential United States Coalition of Service Industries (CSI), has stated that its GATS objectives are to obtain, through successive rounds of negotiations and Mutual Recognition Agreements (MRAs):

(a) globally transparent licensing of health care professionals and facilities (under Article IV.4 GATS "not more burdensome than necessary");

(b) market access and national treatment commitments for all health care services cross border;

(c) majority foreign ownership of health care facilities; and

(d) inclusion of health care in WTO government procurement disciplines.[27]

Australia currently has GATS commitments to liberalise dentistry, veterinary services, podiatry, chiropody and health insurance. In the 2004 GATS round, Australia made requests to liberalise services in the private health sector of 16 WTO members and one member made an offer in this sector.[28] A future privatisation-minded Australian government may renegotiate with the states for federal control over public hospitals. Having achieved this goal, the federal executive, without recourse to Parliament, may elect, as have many OECD countries and the United States, to place "hospital services" on its "schedule of commitments" to be covered by the "bottom up" rules of GATS, including "modes" of service delivery (direct foreign investment, across borders, use by foreign travellers or immigrating workers). This may re-organise ownership, management and operation by contract of hospitals on a "for fee" basis, creating a brief influx of foreign capital into the

---

24 Blendon RJ, Schoen C, DesRoches CM, Osborn R, Scoles KL and Zapert K, "Inequities In Health Care: A Five-Country Survey' (2002) 21 *Health Affairs* 182. Goldberg MA and White, J, "The Relation between Universal Health Insurance and Cost Control' I(1995) 332 (11) *New England Journal of Medicine* 742.

25 Chernichovsky D, "Health System Reforms in Industrialised Democracies: An Emerging Paradigm" (1995) 73(3) *Milbank Quarterly* 339.

26 Schrader, T, *Health Implications of the Proposed Free Trade Agreement between Australia and the United States,* submission to the Department of Foreign Affairs and Trade by the Doctors Reform Society, 2003; Schrader, T, *Health and GATS,* submission to DFAT by the Doctors Reform Society, 2002.

27 Coalition of Service Industries (CSI), *Submission to United States Trade Representative* (USTR), 1998.

28 Department of Foreign Affairs and Trade, WTO's *General Agreement on Trade in Services (GATS): Current State of Play,* Discussion Paper, June 2004 <www.dfat.gov.au/trade/negotiations/services/gats_discussion_paper_2004.html> (accessed 8 February 2006).

sector. Under the "market access" requirement, however, subsequent governments will be unable to legislate or otherwise regulate the total number, value of hospital or health care services or suppliers (for example, by an economic means test or numerical quotas) and cannot limit the percentage of foreign ownership in that sector.[29]

The GATS rule of "national treatment" in relation to such commitments would similarly require that an Australian government could not provide, even unintentionally, more favourable conditions to domestic health care companies than to foreign corporations. The most-favoured nation (MFN) rule would obligate the same administration to ensure that the most favourable treatment in terms of trade granted to any foreign company was extended to all foreign companies wishing to enter this "liberalised" sector. The "domestic regulation" rule would likewise make domestic laws and regulations, including those which protect the public's health and safety, subject to challenge and possible elimination if they are determined to be "unnecessary barriers" to trade, or more "burdensome than necessary" to assure the quality of a service.[30]

GATS has encouraged Australian State and federal governments to continue economic rationalist approaches to health care with a significant emphasis on contract-based privatisation.[31] This can take the form of co-location of private with public hospitals, or contracting out infrastructure services of public hospitals.[32] Public hospitals may also pay for capital works through loans raised in the private sector.[33] Health Care Australia (HCA) is Australia's largest private health care manager.[34] The United States multinational HealthSouth and domestic corporation Mayne Nickless have also been major players in the Australian health care sector. In late 2003, Mayne sold all of its hospitals to a group of venture capitalists dominated by a Citigroup subsidiary.

Through successive rounds of negotiations, WTO member nations continually add to a growing list of services that will be opened up to trade by private, foreign corporations. These are extremely difficult (expensive) to remove once agreed to. Negotiations on specific commitments by countries to open up trade in services on a sector-by-sector basis are conducted bilaterally (nation-to-nation) through a "request-offer" process. Powerful groups in the United States have been lobbying at the WTO for international trade "liberalisation" of Australian hospital

---

29 GATS Article XVI.2.

30 Wallach, L and Sforza, M, *The WTO: Five Years of Reasons to Resist Corporate Globalization*, Seven Stories Press, New York, 1999.

31 "More Public Hospitals To Be Run Privately", *Sydney Morning Herald*, 21 March 1997.

32 "Mayne Player Plans Hospital Spree", *Australian Financial Review*, 18 October 1997; "Under Doctors Orders", *The Australian*, 9 January 1998.

33 Pollock, AM, Shaoul, J, and Vickers, J, "Private Finance and 'Value For Money' in NHS Hospitals: A Policy in Search of a Rationale?" (2002) 324 *British Medical Journal* 1205.

34 "Health Care Growing Pool for Big Fish, Says Giant", *Courier Mail*, 8 September 1997.

services.[35] United States insurance companies have signalled the need for governments such as Australia to commit to GATS obligations "relaxing" licensing of health care professionals, as well as privacy and confidentiality regulations, while undertaking not to impose unnecessarily stringent regulations and laws in the future.[36]

The Australian medical profession's capacity to maintain adequate skills levels in a workforce increasingly reliant on "area-of-need" overseas-trained staff, may be significantly influenced by such GATS obligations.[37] This may also have deleterious consequences on the skills bases in developing nations.[38] Other key structural aspects of medical practice similarly affected include industry funding for key regulatory institutions, such as the Pharmaceutical Benefits Advisory Committee (PBAC) and the Australian Drug Evaluation Committee (ADEC). This could lead to their services being categorised as delivered on a commercial basis and so not subject to the "governmental authority" exemption to the GATS "national treatment" rule. Another important area involves GATS-promoted and increasingly under-regulated multinational corporate influence in the health services sector (through lobbying, gifts, sponsored medical education and publishing) on the fundamental professional virtues and principles, by which those studying or practising medicine choose to organise their careers and life narratives.[39]

Australian medical practice and the AUSFTA

As an item of public health policy, Australia's Pharmaceutical Benefits Scheme (PBS) has unquestioned democratic legitimacy. Commencing as a formulary of essential drugs under the Curtin and Chifley administrations after the Second World War, it had to survive two High Court challenges and required a successful

---

35   Public Health Association of Australia (PHAA), revised by Prof Abelin, Policy Committee of the WFPHA, 19 April 2004, <www.apha.org/wfpha/2004_trade.htm> (accessed 4 October 2005).

36   United States Coalition of Services Industries, recommendations to the Office of the United States Trade Representative on priorities for trade negotiations for health care, 27 November 2000.

37   In 2005, the Productivity Commission was requested by the Council of Australian Governments (COAG) under the *Productivity Commission Act 1998* (Cth), to undertake a research study to examine issues impacting on the health workforce including the supply of, and demand for, health workforce professionals. The Australian National Council on Drugs (ANCD), appointed by the Australian Prime Minister to advise him, the Ministerial Council on Drugs (MCDS) and COAG in drug matters, has an Asia-Pacific Issues Sub-Committee interested in this issue. Productivity Commission Health Workforce Inquiry, <www.pc.gov.au/study/healthworkforce/tor.html> (accessed 13 May 2005).

38   Editorial, "Migration of Health Workers: An Unmitigated Crisis" (2005) 365 *Lancet* 1825.

39   In the United Kingdom, most postgraduate medical education is now corporate funded. United Kingdom House of Commons, Health Committee, *The Influence of the Pharmaceutical Industry*, Stationery Office Ltd, London, 2005, <www.publications.parliament.uk/pa/cm200405/cmselect/cmhealth/42/4202.htm> (accessed 20 April 2005). See also: Ferner RE, "The Influence of Big Pharma" (2005) 330 *British Medical Journal* 855; Smith, R, "Medical Journals are an Extension of the Marketing Arm of Pharmaceutical Companies" (2005) 2(5) *PLoS Medicine* 100.

constitutional referendum, before being supported by Prime Minister Menzies in the *National Health Act 1953* (Cth) and enhanced by each subsequent government.[40]

The *National Health Act 1953* (Cth) Pt VII, s 85, states that the relevant Minister may declare a medicine listed on the PBS and so subject to government reimbursement. This listing is required to only occur, however, after ADEC has approved the relevant pharmaceutical's safety and efficacy and, under s 101(4), after the PBAC has evaluated and approved its cost-effectiveness against therapies in a comparative class. Once a decision is made to list the drug, the Pharmaceutical Benefits Pricing Authority (PBPA) then evaluates the requested price against an international benchmark price for drugs in that class. Under the PBS, the members of the PBAC use pharmaco-economic analysis and reference pricing to determine the community value of a new drug against an agreed comparator therapy, while the monopoly bargaining power of the PBPA is used to counter the increasingly prolonged and wide potential for monopoly rents accorded to brand name pharmaceutical patent holders.[41] The relative fiscal and public health success of the PBS scientific comparative cost-effectiveness evaluations for government reimbursement is highlighted in the Productivity Commission's 2001 research report *International Pharmaceutical Price Differences*.[42]

The AUSFTA's PBS provisions, however, were viewed by United States pharmaceutical corporations as a crucial initial phase in the global dismantling of government controls over medicine prices.[43] Their argument was that distributive justice and public health mechanisms such as the PBS, allow foreign nations to "free ride" on United States research and development and so promote high domestic United States drug prices.[44] The *Medicare Prescription Drug Improvement and Modernisation Act 2003* (US), passed just before negotiations on the AUSFTA concluded, prohibited the United States Federal Government from instituting PBS-type cost-effectiveness evaluation for reimbursement systems and required a study be performed on similar price controls imposed on pharmaceuticals in OECD countries such as France, Germany, Australia, Japan, the United Kingdom and

---

40 Sloan, CA, *History of the Pharmaceutical Benefits Scheme 1947–1992*, Department of Human Services and Health, Canberra, 1995.

41 Harvey, K and Murray, M, "Medicinal Drug Policy", in Gardner, H (ed), *The Politics of Health: The Australian Experience*, 2nd edn, Churchill Livingstone, Melbourne, 1995.

42 Australian Productivity Commission, *International Pharmaceutical Price Differences Research Report*, AusInfo, Canberra, 2001.

43 Pharmaceutical Research and Manufacturers of America, "PhRMA 'Special 301'" submission to the Office of the United States Trade Representative: Australia, Pharmaceutical Research and Manufacturers of America, 2003, <www.cptech.org/ip/health/c/australia/phrma-au-2003.html> (accessed 8 February 2006).

44 Senator Kyl, Chairman of the Subcommittee on Health Care, Joint Hearing by the Subcommittees on Health Care and International Trade of the United States Senate Committee on Finance, 27 April 2004, <http://finance.senate.gov/hearings/statements/042704k.pdf> (accessed 5 October 2004).

Canada (reviewing their impact on American consumers, and on innovation in medicine).[45]

The United States AUSFTA negotiators were required by legislation to seek through such international trade agreements (and this one in particular), the "elimination" of medicines reference pricing systems.[46] In January 2003, the United States Pharmaceutical Research and Manufacturers Association (PhRMA), through its representatives on an industry committee called IFAC3, began working closely with United States trade negotiators to insert articles beneficial to their members and to this Congressional agenda, in the AUSFTA.[47] The Coalition of Service Industries (CSI) also viewed the AUSFTA "negative list", as creating opportunities for health industry suppliers in telecommunications, insurance, professional services and all sectors not specifically exempted.[48]

The 1000 page AUSFTA contains approximately 50 provisions in seven areas of concern regarding the PBS. Four are detailed in Annex 2C (Pharmaceuticals), the fifth is contained in a side-letter between Trade Minister Vaile and United States Ambassador Zoellick, the sixth resides in Chapter 17 (IP Rights) and the seventh is in Chapter 21 (Dispute Resolution Procedures).[49] PhRMA gained much with the AUSFTA PBS provisions, but not necessarily all it wished. It did however create a series of negotiating or lobbying points by which pressure for regulatory change conformable to corporate pharmaceutical interests potentially could be brought to bear on the Australian government and its relevant regulatory officials.

Annex 2C pharmaceutical interpretive principles, transparency and DTCA

The principles in Annex 2C.1(a)–(d) emphasise the need for the respective governments to recognise, to a greater extent "innovation" and "research and development" in pharmaceuticals. To say such principles have no binding legal force misunderstands their intended use by United States' interests (side letters and careful wording appear to indicate they are chiefly designed to apply to Australia). They arguably represent a de-facto normative tradition created by corporate interests to covertly (through lobbying activities) subvert contrary norms

45 *Medicare Prescription Drug Improvement and Modernization Act 2003* (US) s 1123. US Department of Commerce, Pharmaceutical Price Controls in OECD Countries, Implications for US Consumers, Prices, R&D and Innovation. <http://www.ita.doc.gov/drugpricingstudy> (accessed 8 February 2006), Testimony of Grant D Aldonas, Under Secretary for International Trade, US Department of Commerce Before the Committee on Health, Education, Labor and Pensions US Senate Washington, DC, 17 February 2005 <http://www.ita.doc.gov/media/Speeches/0205/aldonas_021705.html> (accessed 8 February 2006).

46 *Trade Act 2002* (US), 107–210 §2102 (b) (8) (D).

47 Becker, E and Pear, R, "Trade Pact May Undercut Inexpensive Drug Imports", *New York Times*, 12 July 2004.

48 <www.uscsi.org/publications/papers/05-18-04.htm> (accessed 8 February 2006).

49 Department of Foreign Affairs and Trade, Australia–United States Free Trade Agreement, 2004, <www.dfat.gov.au/trade/negotiations/us.html> (accessed 8 February 2006).

arising from democratically legitimate normative processes involved with the rule of law. This interpretation is supported, as will be explained, by their linkage to a non-violation nullification of benefits clause.[50]

Importantly for the possible survival of Australia's PBS cost-effectiveness pricing system in an AUSFTA dispute panel hearing, the principles emphasising recognition of "innovation" and "research and development", are set out as non-exhaustive subsidiary components of the overarching primary commitment to "facilitating high quality health care and continued improvements in public health for their nationals".[51]

Annex 2C.1(c) thus indicates, for example, that it is the legitimate expectation of both parties that "innovative" drugs will be evaluated for their "affordability" and extent to which they lead to "continued improvements in public health" for Australian nationals. This approach of setting "innovation" within a social context is supported by a developing literature which arguably is relevant to interpretation of this aspect of the text under Article 32 of the Vienna Convention on the Law of Treaties (incorporated by Article 21.9.2 of the AUSFTA).[52]

Further supportive of the proposition that "innovation" in Annex 2C.1 must be proven to have a community benefit is subparagraph (d) which links the requirement to recognise a pharmaceutical's "innovation" to the operation of "competitive markets", or its "objectively demonstrated therapeutic significance". The latter is a distinct concept from "quality, safety and efficacy" as appears in subparagraph (c) and is likely to refer to a process resembling (though not necessarily identical with) the PBS comparative cost-effectiveness evaluations. In the absence of reimbursement set by such a scientific process, the marketing offices of pharmaceutical companies would have relatively free reign in setting prices in a market heavily characterised by information asymmetries, poor knowledge flows and actors (governments, patients and doctors) with decreasing regulatory strength. Nonetheless, the subparagraph (d) reference to "competitive markets" appears to open the door for evaluation of pharmaceutical "innovation" changes

---

50   AUSFTA Article 21.2.(c).

51   Department of Foreign Affairs and Trade, Australia–United States Free Trade Agreement, 2004, <www.dfat.gov.au/trade/negotiations/us.html> (accessed 8 February 2006):

> The Parties are committed to facilitating high quality health care and continued improvements in public health for their nationals. In pursuing these objectives, the Parties are committed to the following principles [emphasis added]: a) the important role played by innovative pharmaceutical products in delivering high quality health care b) the importance of research and development in the pharmaceutical industry and of appropriate government support, including through intellectual property protection and other policies c) the need to promote timely and affordable access to innovative pharmaceuticals through transparent, expeditious, and accountable procedures, without impeding a Party's ability to apply appropriate standards of quality, safety, and efficacy; and d) The need to recognize the value of innovative pharmaceuticals through the operation of competitive markets or by adopting or maintaining procedures that appropriately value the objectively demonstrated therapeutic significance of a pharmaceutical.

52   Abraham, J and Reed, T, "Progress, Innovation and Regulatory Science in Drug Development. The Politics of International Standard Setting" (2002) 32(3) *Social Studies of Science* 337.

brought about under the AUSFTA, by the Australian Competition and Consumer Commission under the *Trade Practices Act 1974* (Cth).

One possible dispute looming about the "recognition of innovation" principles in Annex 2C.1 may arise from brand name pharmaceutical company lobbyists encouraging the Australian government to drive down the reimbursement prices of generic competitors. These corporations may then seek to dismantle the link that comparative cost-effectiveness evaluation by the pharmaco-economic experts of the PBAC Economic Sub Committee (ESC) provides between their new brand name medicines sponsored for PBS listing, and generic competitors in the same therapeutic class. As a worst case, PhRMA (through the United States Trade Representative) (USTR) might store data on PBAC refusals to list on the PBS list, to later initiate a Chapter 21 dispute. They would then ask the panel to require repeal of s 101(3) of the *National Health Act 1953* (Cth) because the mechanism it promotes does not adequately recognise pharmaceutical innovation. Alternatively, PhRMA and the USTR could challenge PBAC choice of comparator, lobby for loosening of price premium considerations for innovations over therapeutic competitors (improved effectiveness, better adverse event profile or delivery system), tighten commercial-in-confidence data protections and ensure "agreed price-for agreed volume of sales" agreements are not enforceable. They may also controversially prevent legislative or regulatory changes permitting the PBAC to ask the pharmaceutical manufacturer for additional information, or being given legal power to compel its production, even if not covered by commercial-in-confidence protections.

The fact that Annex 2C.1(c) of these initial interpretive principles emphasises "timely and affordable access to innovative pharmaceuticals" through "transparent, expeditious, and accountable procedures" creates a bargaining position with which pharmaceutical companies can seek to lobby governments to remove regulatory obstacles to "fast-track" marketing of their products. Subparagraph (f) of Annex 2C.2 allows United States pharmaceutical applicants to ask for an "independent review process" of a PBAC recommendation or determination. A mechanism for this process has been worked out by the Australian government, that does not involve overturning a PBAC decision. When the PBAC refused a few applications early in 2005, the pharmaceutical company decided not to dispute it through the review process.

Annex 2C.3 establishes a Medicines Working Group between health officials from each country. The Medicines Working Group is prohibited by Annex 2C.4. from discussing "making innovative medical products more quickly available". The Medicines Working Group also appears to be not authorised under the AUSFTA, to explore elements of the cost-effectiveness system established by judicial decision.[53] Similarly, it appears restricted from discussing comparison of the product proposed for marketing approval against non-pharmaceutical

---

53   *Pfizer v Birkett* [2002] FCA 303.

alternatives.[54] The Medicines Working Group met in Washington for the first time, in January 2006. Not only was the removal of Australia's so-called "anti-evergreening" amendments on the table, but so was the industry lobbying principle of pharmaceutical "innovation," despite academic pleas that it needed to be more thoroughly tested by democratic processes before it could be allowed to drive public health policy in this country.[55]

Annex 2C.4 requires the Australian Therapeutic Goods Administration (TGA), a now wholly industry-funded body responsible for evaluating pharmaceutical quality, safety and efficacy to liaise with the similarly funded United States Food and Drug Administration (FDA) concerning "fast-tracking"; that is, "making innovative medical products more quickly available to their nationals". Annex 2C.5 permits a pharmaceutical manufacturer to disseminate pharmaceutical information via the Internet (for example via links on sites frequently used by Australian patients). This raised concerns it might facilitate direct-to-consumer advertising (DTCA) in Australia. DTCA is legal in the United States, but not in Australia. It has been associated with a substantial increase in usage of the products which are often not in accord with clinical best practice.[56]

DTCA, "fast-track" regulatory approval, and pharmaceutical lobbying of the profession, all played large parts in the public health scandal surrounding the proven but tardily announced significant heart attack risks arising from the billion dollar sales "blockbuster" anti-arthritis medication Vioxx.[57] It is unclear how these dilemmas will resolve in the context of the mooted (but stalled) Trans-Tasman Therapeutic Products Agency, that combines the TGA with its New Zealand counterpart. Perhaps the New Zealanders will "carve out" the Annex 2C.4 and article 17.10.4 AUSFTA obligations on Australia's TGA, to create bargaining chips to achieve their own FTA with the US.[58]

---

54   *GlaxoSmithKline Australia v Anderson* [2003] FCA 617.

55   Faunce TA and Henry D, "Drug Lobby Preparing a Bitter Pill", *The Age*, 13 January 2006 <http://www.theage.com.au/news/opinion/durg-lobby-preparing-a-bitter-pill/2006/01/12/1136956298032.html> (accessed 8 February 2006).

56   Mintzes B, Barer ML, Kazanjan A, Bassett K, Evans RG, Morgan S, "An Assessment of the Health System Impacts of Direct-to-Consumer Advertising of Prescription Medicines (DTCA)", Centre for Health Services and Policy research, University of British Columbia, Vancouver, BC, Canada, 2002, <www.chspr.ubc.ca/hpru/pdf/dtca-v1-execsum.pdf> (accessed 27 April 2006).

57   Kaufman, M, "Merck CEO Resigns as Drug Probe Continues", *Washington Post*, 6 May 2005. Congressional investigators in the United States House Committee on Government Reform have released documents detailing how Merck directed its 3,000 sales representatives to avoid discussions with doctors about Vioxx's five-fold increased risks of coronary and cerebral occlusion (identified as killing 55,000 patients by major clinical trials and causing 140,000 acute myocardial infarctions and strokes). The company apparently also attempted to "neutralise" doctors who had concerns about Vioxx's safety, by paying them to take part in clinical trials and offering grants and consultancies.

58   Trans-Tasman Therapeutic products Agency Project website <www.tgamedsafe.org/> (accessed 31 May 2005); Faunce TA and Johnston K, "Impact of the AUSFTA on Medicines Policy in Australia, New Zealand and their Region" *Wellington University Law Review* (in press).

Patent protection, parallel importation, compulsory licensing and evergreening

Article 17.9.8 of the AUSFTA locks the parties into "TRIPS-plus" patent terms (up to five more years than the 20 years required by Article 28 of TRIPS) where there have been unreasonable delays in issuing patent approval. This will increase the period in which Australian patients will have to pay higher prices for necessary drugs. It controversially creates the impression that patients or doctors "own" a medicine they purchase, when what they really do is pay ever increasing rent for the knowledge that allows chemical compounds to be developed and marketed in a particular therapeutic way.

Article 17.9.6 prohibits Australia from exporting drugs in accord with Article 31(f) of TRIPS and the Doha Declaration to help a neighbouring country without pharmaceutical manufacturing capacity fulfil a compulsory licence issued for a public health crises (for example, with HIV/AIDS) by neighbouring countries. Article 17.9.7(b) is "TRIPS-plus" (though it could equally be termed "TRIPS-negative" if TRIPS rights are truly read in accordance with the Doha Declaration) in restricting compulsory licences to "national emergency, or other circumstances of extreme urgency".[59]

Article 17.9.14 requires a "harmonisation" of intellectual property law and practice between the two countries. This could also create a dispute or dilemma given that Australia is strongly interested in continuing or developing in a formal sense the university research or experimental use patent exemption that was recently specifically denied by the authoritative United States patent court.[60] This decision was unsuccessfully appealed to the United States Supreme Court where its deleterious effect on medical research, particularly for the so-called "neglected" unprofitable diseases of developing nations, was mentioned in amicus curiae submissions by the Association of American Medical Colleges and the Association of American Universities.[61]

Article 17.9.4 prevents Australia from taking competitive advantage of the low prices its PBS reference reimbursement system has produced, to export (or parallel import) medicines back to the United States to the benefit of United States patients and the Australian economy. This is "TRIPS-plus" (or "TRIPS-negative" if TRIPS rights are interpreted primarily as facilitating competition) because the Doha Declaration had confirmed that each WTO member may establish its own regime of exhaustion of intellectual property rights.[62]

---

59   Abbott, FM, "The TRIPS-legality of Measures Taken to Address Public Health Crises: Responding to USTR-State-industry Positions that Undermine the WTO" in Kennedy, DL and Southwick, JD (eds), *The Political Economy of International Trade Law*, Cambridge University Press, Cambridge, 2002, pp 311–348.

60   *Madey v Duke University*, 307 F3d 1351 (Fed Cir, 2002).

61   *Duke University v Madey*, No 02-1007, cert denied US (27 June 2003).

62   t'Hoen, E, "TRIPS, Pharmaceutical Patents and Access to Essential Medicines: A Long Way from Seattle to Doha" (2002) 3 *Chi J Int'l L* 27.

Article 17.10.4 sets the scene for one of the likely disputes over medicines under the AUSFTA. It pursues PhRMA's global agenda (repeatedly stated on the USTR Trade Watch List) of ensuring pharmaceutical marketing approval (usually a question of establishing a generic product's bio-equivalence and safety) is linked with manifest, notified patent validity.[63] Canada was made to implement a similar provision in its *Patented Medicines (Notice of Compliance) Regulations* in 1993 after entering the North American Free Trade Agreement (NAFTA). This linkage has lead to anti-competitive "evergreening" of soon-to-expire brand name patents against cheaper, high quality generic medicines.

The new ss 26C and 26D in the *Therapeutic Goods Act 1989* (Cth) added by the AUSFTA implementing legislation, were designed by the Australian government to prevent such "evergreening" under Article 17.10.4.[64] Narrow profit margins, cross-ownership by larger multinationals and lack of a legislated incentive (period of market exclusivity for the first generic entrant) make it unlikely that any Australian-based generic company will use these provisions to litigate.[65]

Of crucial importance, however, might be interpretive implication behind the capacity of the Commonwealth Attorney-General to claim damages where an injunction issued to support a "claimed" brand name patent, has caused additional costs under the PBS.[66] Under Article 32 of the Vienna Convention on the Law of Treaties (Article 21.9.2 of the AUSFTA) this amendment to the AUSFTA implementing legislation could allow Australia to claim before an AUSFTA dispute panel that its actionable legitimate expectation (under Article 21.2(c)) was specifically that Article 17.10.4 or any support it gave to the patent claims of "innovative" medicines, would not increase the cost of government reimbursement under the PBS. Delayed market entry of generic drugs, from "evergreening-type" tactics, is highly likely, they could claim, to raise the prices of pharmaceuticals on the PBS, purchased by private and public hospitals and for over-the-counter medicines not covered by government safety nets. The end result is likely to be higher pharmaceutical costs for the Commonwealth and State governments, as well as for consumers, which could result in decreased access and increased morbidity and mortality.

---

63 Office of the United States Trade Representative, Trade Watch List, <www.ustr.gov/Document_Library/Press_Releases/2005/April/Special_301_Report_Finds_Progress_Need_for_Significant_Improvements.html> (accessed 19 May 2005).

64 *United States Free Trade Agreement Implementation Act 2004* (Cth) Sch 7.

65 Faunce T, Doran E, Henry D, Drahos P, Searles P, Pekarsky B, Neville, W, "Assessing the Impact of the Australia-United States Free Trade Agreement of Australian and Global Medicines Policy" (2005) 1 *Globalisation and Health* 1-15.

66 The cost to the PBS and Australian taxpayers of a 24-month delay to generic competition has been estimated to be $1.1 billion over four years for just five PBS medications coming off patent.

Dispute resolution, cross-retaliation and non-violation nullification of benefits

Under AUSFTA Chapter 21 on dispute resolution, an unelected panel of three nominated trade lawyers[67] will have the power to interpret compliance with obligations in the AUSFTA. Perhaps of greatest concern for the PBS and Australian medical practice is Article 21.2 (c). This is what is known in international trade law as a "non-violation nullification of benefits" clause. It allows a damages claim, for example, where a "benefit" that the United States had a legitimate expectation might accrue through, inter alia the AUSFTA Annex 2C or Chapter 17 on intellectual property, is not realised, even though no specific provision has been breached. Such provisions are really a supercharged mechanism of commercially-focused treaty interpretation. Developing countries have placed a moratorium on their use under TRIPS.[68] The upshot of this is that PBAC decisions not to "list" allegedly "innovative" new United States drugs (because they were not cost-effective) will be made in the shadow not only of possible consumer pressure under AUSFTA-facilitated DTCA, but possible United States trade cross-retaliation in important areas such as manufacturing and agriculture.[69] The USTR has already signalled an impending dispute over the Australian anti-evergreening amendments, claiming they are contrary to Article 27.1 of TRIPS as discriminating against a field of technology.[70] The *Canada-Patent Protection of Pharmaceuticals* case decided, however, that Article 27.1 of TRIPS did not foreclose countries from providing reasonable and bona fide public interest exceptions to intellectual property protection problems that, like "evergreening," only exist in certain product areas.[71]

The impact of the AUSFTA on the practice of medicine in Australia is not a foregone conclusion. It may be that, as the result of AUSFTA changes to evaluative structures and processes, communication between industry and regulators is improved and more medicines are listed for Federal Government reimbursement on the PBS, for a wider range of indications and at a faster rate. Pharmaceutical companies, further, making claims that the high cost of "innovative" products will be offset by health gains through reduction in the burden of illness will be locked

---

67 AUSFTA Article 21.7.

68 Trachtman, JP, "The Domain of WTO Dispute Resolution" (1999) 40 *Harvard International Law Journal* 333.

69 Late in September 2004 eight major public health organisations and many of Australia's most eminent public health experts signed an open letter to the leaders of both major federal political parties. It called for Australia to place on record at the time of ratifying the AUSFTA a unilateral interpretive declaration over those ambiguities in its text most likely to adversely effect the PBS and over which there was a clear difference of opinion between United States and Australian authorities: "Open Letter to Prime Minister and Leader of the Opposition: Leading Health Experts Say Ambiguities in Trade Deal Put PBS at Risk", 27 September 2004 <www.phaa.net.au/Media_Releases/OpenLetteronPBSandFTA.pdf> (accessed 6 October 2004).

70 "Australia Poised to Pass US FTA with Controversial Drug Amendments" (2004) 22(33) *Inside US Trade* 12.

71 Faunce TA and Lokuge, B, "Strange Article Lurking at Back of FTA Could Bring Nasty Surprise" *Canberra Times*, 29 September 2004.

in to periodic reviews of the estimates so given. If they do not eventuate, the reimbursement price can be reduced.

Whether, despite this, the Australian community ends up getting more health outcome value for the money it spends on medicines, may depend on the outcome of the broader community, government and regulator debates that the AUSFTA engenders. Crucial here will be how pharmaceutical "innovation", as mentioned in AUSFTA Annex 2C, is defined by key regulators and with what scientific rigor it is evaluated by them for reimbursement purposes. The prices of medicinal drugs in Australia, for example, may be very different if generic manufacturers are permitted to make a case to Australian pricing evaluators that pharmaceutical innovation is not exclusively tied to concepts of intellectual property in the AUSFTA and that their capacity to market high quality medicines at a lower marginal cost of production involves an element of innovation deserving recognition.

The limited data on the actual cost of producing allegedly "innovative" drugs will need to be expanded and made more readily available to regulators.[72] Pharmaceutical companies, for example, to justify claims of genuine innovation will need to produce data for an individual product confirming they do not spend at least two to three times more on related marketing, administration and lobbying, than on its research and development, and that there is a socially useful reason why any community should tolerate their profits being approximately twice costs.[73] The Australian Productivity Commission has confirmed that the largest medicines price differences between Australia and the United States are not for new, "innovative" compounds, but for aggressively marketed "me-too" pharmaceuticals involving small molecular variations and little improved community benefit.[74]

One scenario is that the Australian PBS may end up paying more for what are represented by the industry to be "innovative" drugs than would previously have been justified economically under its existing evaluation strategies. This may result in adverse health outcomes (for example, scripts forgone and increased emergency department visits).[75] Another is that the PBS is strengthened and improved as larger economies, such as China, attempt to emulate its success.

---

72 National Science Foundation, *Research and Development in Industry 2000*, NSF, Division of Science Resources Statistics, 2003.

73 Families USA Foundation, *Profiting from Pain: Where Prescription Drug Dollars Go*, Publication No 02-10, Families USA, 2002.

74 Productivity Commission, *International Pharmaceutical Price Differences: Research Report*, Productivity Commission, Melbourne 2001, <www.pc.gov.au/study/pbsprices/finalreport/pbsprices.pdf> (accessed 8 February 2006).

75 Following the PBS co-payment rise that took effect on 1 January 2005, for example, over two million fewer PBS prescriptions were filled during the first quarter of 2005, than the equivalent period in 2004: Health Insurance Commission (HIC) database (accessed 26 April 2005).

Trade Agreements, medical education and future prospects

The increasingly important role of international trade agreements such as TRIPS and the GATS in shaping the architecture of medical practice will necessitate medical students and postgraduate vocational trainees learning to understand a changed terminology and regulatory focus.[76] Medicare subsidies, or the system of government reimbursement for medicines prices provided by the PBS, for example, may be described by the corporate proponents of such trade deals as "non-tariff barriers to trade" or "market distorting practices". In this world, patients become "revenue raising units" and "transparency" means relying on "commercial-in-confidence" to protect your own data while obtaining that of regulators. "Innovation", similarly, is a meta (industry lobbying) principle purportedly overriding other more democratically legitimate public health goals, that requires additional government reward (a subsidy or extended monopoly) outside that substantial amount already granted it through the patent system, without needing to produce credible evidence of its community benefit. Students attempting to make countervailing distributive justice arguments will need to be aware of the relevant public health exclusions to GATS, the Doha Declaration on TRIPS and Public Health and obligations arising from commitments flowing from the international right to health, as expressed in instruments such as the International Covenant on Economic, Social and Cultural Rights (ICESCR) to which Australia is a party.[77] Students should also be taught to consider whether the overemphasis on invariably positively reported, carefully constructed, drug company-sponsored randomised control trials is likely to erode some value from the ubiquitous diagnostic and therapeutic doctrine of "evidence-based-medicine".[78]

The China–AusFTA is an international trade agreement that may have an even greater effect on the Australian practice of medicine than the AUSFTA. In 2001, the sales income of China's (mostly generic) pharmaceutical industry totalled US$21 billion. China's pharmaceutical market has averaged 18–20 per cent growth over the last 20 years, significantly higher than United States and European growth over the same period; by 2020 it will be the world's largest.[79]

---

76 Faunce TA and Gatenby P, "Flexner's Ethical Oversight Reprised? Contemporary Medical Education and the Health Impacts of Corporate Globalization" (2005) 39(10) *Medical Education* 1066-74.

77 Faunce TA, "Health Legislation: Interpretation Coherent with Conscience and International Human Rights" in S Corcoran and S Bottomley (eds) *Interpreting Statutes*, Federation Press, Sydney, 2005.

78 Faunce TA, "Nurturing Personal and Professional Conscience in an Age of Corporate Globalisation: Bill Viola's The Passions" (2005) 183(11/12) *Medical Journal of Australia* 599-601.

79 China currently produces over 1350 medicines in 24 classes. In recent years, China has patented only two "innovative" drugs (arteannuin and sodium dimercaptosuccinate) that have received international marketing approval. Yet, China's pharmaceutical production capacity ranks second only to the United States and it has strong ambitions to move into "innovative" pharmaceutical production.

One of the most common models for pharmaceutical development in China involves joint ventures with local partners facilitating regulatory approval and market share. Creation of an evidence base to inform government and industry decision-making is a crucial precondition, however, for the establishment of an innovative pharmaceutical industry. It is also vitally important for instituting and maintaining the type of pharmaceutical reference pricing and reimbursement systems present in China and in Australia with the PBS.

A specific Annex in the China–AusFTA could establish a Medicines Pricing and Regulation Committee facilitating regulatory harmonisation, research collaborations, clustering, networking and partnership arrangements between pharmaceutical regulators, researchers and managers of the two countries.[80] In particular, Australian PBS and Chinese medicines price regulators could discuss how best to enhance comparative cost-effectiveness pricing, exchange relevant information and signal the marginal cost of production internationally. Focused state incentives for "innovation", outside profit-driven intellectual property protection, the reduction of development costs for "innovative" drugs, global marketing strategies for generic medicines and the human rights of workers in this industry would be other particularly beneficial topics of discussion. Such an initiative, not in any way contrary to the TRIPS agreement, would build on previous government efforts to spur the growth of an Australian pharmaceutical industry.[81]

Australia can boast world's best practice expertise in pharmaceutical regulation through the TGA, PBAC and its economic and pricing subcommittees. Australia also has excellent capability in critical new knowledge areas and platform technologies: genomics, bio-informatics fast screening and world's best practice ethical supervision. Also significant is the medical research capacity building achieved by government through the National Health and Medical Research Council (NHMRC) and the Australian Department of Industry, Tourism and Resources $300 million Pharmaceutical Industry Investment Program and Pharmaceuticals Partnerships Program.[82] The current Australian pharmaceutical manufacturing industry is small by global standards, predominantly generic and characterised by much cross-ownership and licensing arrangements with large

---

80   Faunce TA, "Cashing in on our Pharmaceutical Expertise" [on a Medicines Working Committee in the China-Australia Free Trade Agreement] *Canberra Times*, 11 April 2005.

81   In May 2001, the then Minister of Industry, Tourism and Resources announced a Pharmaceuticals Industry Action Agenda. Its objectives were to: "promote increased investment in pharmaceutical goods and services" (action 2); "identify opportunities and facilitate growth in the export of pharmaceuticals" (action 7); "promote two-way movement between industry and academia" (action 11); and "align industry activity with the National Innovation Awareness Strategy" (action 14). Despite this, the Foreign Affairs, Defence and Trade References Committee Report "Opportunities and Challenges: Australia's Relationship with China" (Senate, Canberra, November 2005) made no references to pharmaceuticals at all.

82   Department of Industry, Tourism and Resources, *Pharmaceutical Industry Investment Program*, Department of Industry, Tourism and Resources, 2004, <www.industry.gov.au/content/sitemap.cfm?objectid=48A506B0-20E0-68D8-ED81D261FE5594> (accessed 8 February 2006).

multinationals. It might rapidly expand, however, if Australian manufacturers were accorded access to the vast Chinese market through the China–AusFTA.

Conclusion

For the practice of medicine to continue reflecting its traditional ethos of beneficent, egalitarianism, in an era of globalisation, public health professionals and organisations need to participate not only in the negotiation but make submissions to the dispute settlement process involved with international trade agreements. Certain features of international trade agreements, such as dispute settlement investor state provisions, should never be agreed to by an Australian government conscious of its public health responsibilities. If Australia had been privy to an international trade agreement with such a provision at the time, universalistic health care schemes such as Medicare and the PBS would never have eventuated.[83] In the interests of ensuring maximum access by Australian citizens to safe medical practice, obligations should be created for the Australian executive to prepare a public health impact assessment before commencing to negotiate international trade deals, to have them subjected to parliamentary vote beyond that necessary to pass implementing legislation and to allow relevant public health organisations and key regulators and academics to make submissions to any associated dispute settlement process.[84]

---

83 Chapter 11 of NAFTA contains investor/state dispute settlement procedures. These allows foreign companies to make claims for compensation for nationalisation or expropriation of their services directly to the relevant national government.

84 The World Federation of Public Health Associations (WFPHA) has asked the WHO to develop and promulgate a policy requiring national health impact assessments and developing nation technical assistance for any proposed trade agreement (whether multilateral or bilateral). It also urged the WHO to seek participatory status at WTO Tribunal and Appellate body hearings in order to represent the health interests of populations in countries with disputes before these bodies: WFPHA, *Resolution on Health and the Liberalisation of Trade in Services Brighton*, United Kingdom, 19 April 2004, <www.phaa.net.au/policy/wfpha.htm> (accessed 18 May 2005).

PART V

REPRODUCTIVE TECHNOLOGIES

10

Old technologies and new challenges: Assisted reproduction and its regulation

Helen Szoke, Lexi Neame and Louise Johnson[1]

Reproductive technology is now officially one generation old, with the marriage of the first IVF baby, Louise Brown, in the United Kingdom in 2004. Her marriage was covered with much media fanfare and, like a hapless royal princess, the world will wait to see if she can produce a child naturally, or whether the technology that resulted in her birth will be called upon to assist her. During the lives of the first generation of children born as a result of reproductive technologies, we have seen the passage of many of the first generation of regulatory regimes, as they respond to the new challenges posed by the rapid development of the technologies.

Internationally, the development of the technology for deriving embryonic stem cells from human embryos has captured the limelight. Whilst a significant number of jurisdictions have moved quickly to prohibit reproductive cloning,[2] and attempts continue to introduce an international ban through the United Nations,[3] there has been a more fragmented response to the issue of embryonic stem cell (ES cell) research, as countries grapple with the implications of the moral weighting given to embryos used for this purpose.[4] In Australia, the simultaneous threat and

---

1   Dr Helen Szoke is Chief Conciliator/CEO of the Equal Opportunity Commission, and past CEO of the Infertility Treatment Authority. Ms Lexi Neame is Senior Research and Policy Officer for the Infertility Treatment Authority and Ms Louise Johnson is the CEO of the Infertility Treatment Authority. Those aspects of this manuscript which are opinion or an evaluation are not the opinion or the evaluation express or implied of the Victorian Infertility Treatment Authority.

2   Annas, GJ Andrews, LB and Isasi, RM, "Protecting the Endangered Human: Toward an International Treaty Prohibiting Cloning and Inheritable Alterations" (2002) 28(2–3) *American Journal of Law & Medicine* 151 (Appendix "Legislation in Force Related to Human Species Protection").

3   Walters, L, "The United Nations and Human Cloning: a Debate on Hold" (2004) 34 *The Hastings Center Report* 5; Mayor, S, "Claim of Human Reproductive Cloning Provokes Calls for International Ban" (2004) 328 *BMJ* 185; Tauer, C, "International Policy Failures: Cloning and Stem-cell Research" (2004) 364 (9429) *Lancet* 209.

4   Russo, E, "Follow the Money – the Politics of Embryonic Stem Cell Research" (2005) 3(7) *PLoS Biology* 234; Isasi, RM, Knoppers, BM, Singer, PA and Daar, AS, "Legal and Ethical Approaches to Stem Cell Cloning and Research: A Comparative Analysis of Policies in Latin America, Asia, and Africa" (2004) 32(4) *Journal of Law, Medicine & Ethics* 626; Sandel, MJ, "Embryo Ethics – The Moral Logic of Stem-Cell Research" (2004) 351(3) *New England Journal of Medicine* 207; McHugh, PR, "Zygote and 'Clonote' – The Ethical Use of Embryonic Stem-Cells" (2004) 351(3) *New England Journal of Medicine* 209; Harding, A, "The Politics of Science" (2005) 19(2) *Scientist* 37.

promise embodied in ES cells resulted in the Prime Minister calling on the Council of Australian Governments to agree to the passage of legislation which would nationally regulate the use of embryos for research, and allow ES cells to be derived from excess assisted reproductive technology (ART) embryos.[5] The *Research Involving Human Embryos Act 2002* (Cth) and the *Prohibition of Human Cloning Act 2002* (Cth) are rare examples of State and federal cooperation in the passage of legislation, and are indicative of both the ethical controversy and commercial imperatives which attend research in this area.

As the emphasis of regulation has begun to shift from treatment to research, and with these technologies promising to deliver applications in broader areas of medicine and biotechnology, along with expanded commercial opportunities, it is timely to examine the development of regulatory responses to ARTs in Australia, and how these fit with the global context of regulation in this area.

What is different about reproductive technologies?

Reproductive technologies have always been considered exceptional, and their use contentious, because they involve the start of new life under assisted circumstances and the creation and use (including the discarding or destruction) of human embryos. The value ascribed to a naturalised conception of the family, and the moral weight given to the embryo, will determine how reproductive technologies are perceived.

The changes in reproductive technologies since the birth of the first in vitro fertilisation (IVF) baby in 1978 have been rapid, with many developments posing ethical and social challenges. In 1999, scientists announced that it was possible to freeze ovarian tissue for patients undergoing chemotherapy, and by 2004, a viable human embryo had been formed from frozen-thawed ovarian tissue. Preimplantation genetic diagnosis (PGD), the earliest form of genetic screening carried out on an ART embryo, has moved from experimental to clinical practice. By 1995, PGD had shifted from genetic testing to avoid severe genetic conditions to a predominance of aneuploidy screening[6] to increase the efficiency of infertility treatment.[7] By 2000, genetic testing had expanded to include a number of novel applications,

---

5   *Research Involving Human Embryos Act 2002* (Cth).

6   Where the embryos of IVF patients with a poor prognosis undergo PGD using fluorescence in situ hybridisation (FISH) as an additional intervention to select embryos for transfer that have the correct number of chromosomes. Aneuploidy screening has been applied primarily to women with one of three indicators for infertility: advanced maternal age, recurrent implantation failure and recurrent miscarriage. The use of PGD for aneuploidy screening was first reported in 1995, but has developed rapidly, particularly as more extensive screening has become feasible. In fact, aneuploidy screening has become the most widely used application of PGD, due to both the relative ease of the technique and the large potential group of patients who are already undertaking IVF due to infertility.

7   Verlinsky, Y et al, "Over a Decade of Experience with Preimplantation Genetic Diagnosis: A Multicenter Report" (2004) 82(2) *Fertility and Sterility* 292.

including: screening for genetic mutations that increase the risk of cancer;[8] sex selection to lower the risk of conditions like autism;[9] and exclusion testing for prospective parents at risk of autosomal dominant conditions.[10] Particularly controversial has been the combination of PGD with human leukocyte antigens (HLA) tissue typing to select embryos for transfer that will be both free of a genetic condition and a suitable cord-blood or bone marrow donor for an existing affected child.[11] HLA typing has also been performed without PGD of a causative gene, where the existing child suffers from a sporadic rather than inherited disease, and the sole purpose of PGD is to produce a tissue-matched offspring, rather than to prevent the transmission of a genetic condition.[12] Also coinciding with the expansion of PGD has been the completion of the human genome sequence, a decade sooner than was projected at the commencement of the Human Genome Project. This has generated significant, albeit extremely speculative, concern about whether reprogenetic technologies may lead to the creation of "designer babies".[13]

The potential of embryonic stem cells to create "breakthrough" advances in numerous aspects of medicine has also been a key factor in the development of research priorities within the field of reproductive technology. Stem cell lines have been grown and a stem cell line has been derived from a human embryo. Indeed, Australia has recently produced its first ES cell lines.[14] In the past 25 years we have gone from one IVF birth to an expansion of the technology into broader areas of medical science. Robert Edwards, one of the pioneers of IVF technology, predicted this in 1980:

> One day all of the secrets of this early development may be known and those same secrets may help us to repair the ravages and defects in the tissues of sick and ageing men and women.[15]

In addition to the challenges posed by the expansion of ART into reproductive and genetic technologies (reprogenetics) and its evolving importance to medical research and biotechnology, concerns remain about the safety of reproductive technologies, both for users and children born as a result of their use. It is estimated that nearly two million babies have been born as a result of IVF since the

8   Rechitsky, S, Verlinsky O, and Chistokhina A, "Preimplantation Genetic Diagnosis for Cancer Predisposition" (2002) 5(2) *Reprod Biomed Online* 148.

9   Infertility Treatment Authority, *Annual Report*, 2004, p 11.

10   Braude, PR, et al, "Non-disclosure Preimplantation Genetic Diagnosis for Huntington's Disease: Practical and Ethical Dilemmas" (1998) 18(13) *Prenatal Diagnosis* 1422.

11   Wolf, SM, Kahn, JP and Wagner, JE, "Using Preimplantation Genetic Diagnosis to Create a Stem Cell Donor: Issues, Guidelines and Limits" (2003) 31(3) *Journal of Law, Medicine & Ethics* 327.

12   Verlinsky, Y et al, "Preimplantation HLA testing" (2004) 291(17) *JAMA* 2079..

13   Gosden, R, *Designer Babies: The Brave New World of Reproductive Technology*, Phoenix, London, 2000.

14   National Health and Medical Research Council (NHMRC), "NHMRC Licensing Committee Issues Seventh Licence" (2004) 1(2) *NHMRC Licensing Committee Bulletin* 1.

15   Edwards, R and Steptoe, P, *A Matter of Life: The Story of a Medical Breakthrough*, Sphere, London, 1980, p 97.

first birth in 1978.[16] Over this time many studies have been undertaken to evaluate the safety or otherwise of the procedures, and many still remain inconclusive. In the United States, a panel of experts was convened to review all of the available data on the health of children conceived through ARTs.[17] The panel included experts from the fields of paediatrics, obstetrics and epidemiology, and conducted reviews of studies published in the medical literature that reported on neonatal outcomes, malformations and genetic anomalies, paediatric cancer, psychosocial and developmental outcomes, and health outcomes beyond one year.

Overall, the findings concluded that the technologies were relatively safe in terms of these criteria. There were, however, findings of a higher incidence of extremely rare syndromes such as Beckwith-Wiedemann syndrome.[18] The evidence of the review also indicated that reproductive technologies were associated with some adverse neonatal outcomes such as low birth weight, perinatal mortality and premature birth:

> Singleton babies born through IVF are about twice as likely to be premature and to die within a week of birth compared with children not conceived through IVF, and IVF babies are 2.7 times more likely than naturally conceived children to be underweight.[19]

Clearly more research needs to be undertaken, including on the outcomes for children and the effect on treatment success of lowering the numbers of embryos transferred per treatment cycle.[20]

Apart from research into the long-term safety of reproductive technologies, the regulation of treatment needs to be reviewed. Most regulatory regimes include some component of self-regulation, where the profession identifies clinical and technical standards for the provision of treatment, in addition to laws that identify the moral boundaries of treatment. Furthermore, where significant commercial interests are involved, the legal parameters relating to the provision of some treatment services, and particularly the potential for over-servicing, may need to be reviewed.

Various distinct phases can be identified in the development of reproductive technologies. Once the technology emerged and began to consistently produce results between 1978 and 1984, the demand for reproductive technology was established,

---

16 Hampton, T, "Panel Reviews Health Effects Data for Assisted Reproductive Technologies" (2004) 292(24) *JAMA* 2961.

17 Ibid.

18 Beckwith-Wiedemann syndrome is a treatable condition where certain parts of the body, such as the tongue, grow larger than normal and which can increase the risk of certain cancers.

19 Dr Kathy Hudson, Director of the Genetics and Public Policy Center at the John Hopkins University, in Washington DC, as quoted in Hampton (2004) op cit, at 2962.

20 Thurin, A et al, "Elective Single-Embryo Transfer versus Double-Embryo Transfer in In Vitro Fertilization" (2004) 351(23) *New England Journal of Medicine* 2392; Davis, OK, "Elective Single-Embryo Transfer – Has its Time Arrived?" (2004) 351(23) *New England Journal of Medicine* 2440.

with a focus primarily on IVF as a cure for infertility.[21] Between 1984 and 1987, the feminist critique became vocal, while hundreds of small clinics opened up with private funding in the United Kingdom, the United States and Australia. The huge investment from drug companies and the medical profession during this phase clearly indicated the perceived commercial value of reproductive services.[22] The next phase until 1991 saw the growing acceptance of the routinely used technologies.

Since this time, public acceptance of the "standard" image of infertility treatment (IVF for married couples using their own gametes) has been consistently high, at around 80 per cent acceptance according to a number of surveys.[23]

Also during this period, a number of States began to regulate the provision of reproductive services, and this provided some level of endorsement of the technologies. Male infertility became the focus in the mid-1990s, with the introduction of intracytoplasmic sperm injection (ICSI), and renewed concerns about inherited abnormalities as a result of the increased invasiveness of new procedures.[24]

The late 1990s saw the focus of these procedures broaden significantly with the birth of the cloned sheep Dolly, and the possibilities anticipated for ES cell research and the extension of the use of cloning techniques for therapeutic purposes.[25] More recently the embryo has provided ES cells, which may be used for cell replacement for various degenerative conditions.[26]

The development of the technology attracted a particular response at each of these phases from the public, institutions and government. The relationship between technological and regulatory developments is shown in Figure 10.1.

The spectre of cloning for reproductive and therapeutic purposes[27] has launched the debate about regulation and the social control of science more

---

21　Szoke, H, "Social Regulation, Reproductive Technology and the Public Interest: Policy and Process in Pioneering Jurisdictions", unpublished doctoral dissertation, University of Melbourne, 2004.

22　Van Dyck, J, *Manufacturing Babies and Public Consent*, Macmillan, Basingstoke, 1995.

23　Szoke (2004) op cit, pp 89–98.

24　Bonduelle, M et al, "Seven Years of Intracytoplasmic Sperm Injection and Follow-up of 1987 Subsequent Children" (1999) 14(Suppl 1) *Human Reproduction* 2339.

25　See, for example, Australian Health Ethics Committee, *Scientific, Ethical and Regulatory considerations Relevant to Cloning of Human Beings*, NHMRC, December 1998; Human Genetics Advisory Commission and Human Fertilisation and Embryology Authority, *Cloning Issues in Reproduction, Science and Medicine*, December 1998.

26　Ibid; House of Representatives, Standing Committee on Legal and Constitutional Affairs, *Human Cloning: Scientific, Ethical and Regulatory Aspects of Human Cloning and Stem Cell Research*, Commonwealth Parliament, August 2001.

27　Cloning is defined in the *Prohibition of Human Cloning Act 2002* (Cth) s 8 as the creation of a human embryo that is a genetic copy of another living or dead human, but does not include a human embryo created by the fertilisation of a human egg by a human sperm. Reproductive cloning would involve the transfer of a cloned embryo to the body of a woman in an attempt to achieve a pregnancy that results in a live birth. Therapeutic cloning, in contrast, would involve the attempt to derive stem-cells from an embryo that is genetically identical to an existing person for use in medical treatment that would avoid an immune response and possible rejection by the recipient. Embryos cloned for therapeutic purposes would not be allowed to develop for long, and would certainly not be placed in the body of a woman.

Figure 10.1: Timeline for technological and regulatory developments

Technological advance	Year	The Australian response
1st IVF baby – UK	1978	*Medical Journal of Australia* calls for legislation to regulate IVF
1st Australian IVF baby – Vic	1980	
	1981	Roman Catholic Archbishop telegrams PM – stops grants to embryo research
1st donor egg baby; embryo freezing	1982	State inquiries into IVF; NHMRC Statement on Human Experimentation Supplementary Note 4; Fertility Society of Australia (FSA) formed
Request to biopsy embryo – Vic	1984	*Infertility (Medical Procedures) Act* (Vic) Senate Select Committee (Cth)
	1986	Embryo experimentation Bill not passed (Cth)
	1987	Amendment to Victorian legislation; Reproductive Technology Accreditation Committee (RTAC) formed, begins accreditations
1st IVF surrogacy	1988	*Reproductive Technology Act* (SA); *Surrogate Parenthood Act* (Qld); National Bioethics Consultative Committee disbanded after recommending surrogacy to be permitted
	1990	Changes to proposed Victorian legislation
	1991	*Human Reproductive Technology Act* (WA)
ICSI and PGD introduced	1992	
	1994	*Substitute Parent Agreement* Act (ACT)
PGD for aneuploidy screening	1995	*Infertility Treatment Act* (Vic); *Surrogacy Contracts Act* (Tas)
	1996	NHMRC Ethical guidelines in Assisted Reproductive Technology; Review of *Human Tissue Act* commenced (NSW); Legal challenge to marriage requirement – State Act, SA
Dolly cloned	1997	Amendment to Victorian legislation
	1998	National Committee – Therapeutic Cloning
	1999	Review of WA legislation
Embryonic stem cells	2000	House of Representatives Committee – Therapeutic Cloning; Legal challenge to marriage requirement – State Act, Vic
PGD with HLA tissue typing	2001	Amendment to Victorian legislation; Council of Australian Governments meeting – ES cells
Claims of 1st human clone	2002	*Research Involving Human Embryos Act* (Cth); *Prohibition of Human Cloning Act* (Cth); Victorian Law Reform Commission reviews eligibility criteria
	2003	*Infertility Treatment Act* (Vic) amended October; ART draft exposure Bill – Assisted Reproductive Technology Bill (NSW)
1st live birth from transplanted/thawed ovarian tissue; preimplantation HLA tissue typing	2004	Human Reproductive Technology Amendment Act (WA); NHMRC Ethical guidelines on the use of assisted reproductive technology in clinical practice and research
	2005	Revised RTAC Guidelines; Federal review of embryo experimentation and prohibition of human cloning legislation
Proposed 1st clinical trials for therapeutic purposes – ES cells	2006	Lockhart Review Reports released December 2005

generally into a global context. Much of the world is working towards consensus that reproductive cloning will be prohibited.[28] Therapeutic cloning generates many competing views and broadens the debate to include general medical research, given the possibilities of ES cell lines derived from cloned embryos.[29] ES cell research and the claims of significant medical advances have had the dual effect of globalising the views about this area of research and galvanising governments into legislative action. For example, in Australia the impediment to national legislation, that infertility treatment regulation is a matter of State jurisdiction, was overcome when the Prime Minister gained agreement from all States and Territories to pass national legislation.[30] The United Kingdom extended its jurisdiction through enabling regulations to allow the development of ES cells as one possible use of embryos for the purposes of research.[31] Bonnicksen has argued that ES cell research "has generated a different political context, with considerably more support for investigations than during earlier rounds of policy deliberations in the 1970s and 1980s".[32]

As ES cell research extends its offerings to other areas of medicine, inevitably other interests come into play. The prospect of significant advances in medical treatment has further important implications for the pharmaceutical industry and biotechnology companies, as it promises the next great medical breakthrough and commercial bonanza. Where the advances occur will be influenced by the presence or absence of regulatory structures, as well as where medical research infrastructure is strongest and capital investment readily available. According to commentators such as Francis Fukuyama,[33] countries such as Singapore, China and South Korea have strong market incentives to compete in these areas, and are rapidly developing the necessary research structure to encourage this to happen. In addition, it has been suggested that "China has a cultural environment with fewer moral objections to the use of ES cells than many Western countries",[34] and while remaining firmly opposed to reproductive cloning, therapeutic cloning is legally permitted. It is no coincidence that the first cloned human embryos have been produced by South Korean scientists.

28   Annas et al (2002) op cit.

29   Bonnicksen, A, "Human Embryonic Stem Cell Research: the Role of Private Policy" in Healy, DL, Kovacs, GT, McLachlan, R, Rodriguez-Armas, O (eds) *Reproductive Medicine in the Twenty-first Century*, Parthenon, New York, 2002, pp 21–29.

30   *Research Involving Human Embryos Act 2002* (Cth); *Prohibition of Human Cloning Act 2002* (Cth).

31   *Human Fertilisation and Embryology (Research Purposes) Regulations 2000* (UK); see Szoke (2004) op cit, pp 244–245.

32   Bonnicksen (2002) op cit, p 21.

33   Fukuyama, F, *Our Posthuman Future: Consequences of the Biotechnology Revolution*, Farrar, Straus & Giroux, New York, 2002, p 193.

34   Yang, X, "An Embryonic Nation" (2004) 428 *Nature* 210.

Reproductive technology and regulation in the international context

Notwithstanding the high level of public interest in these technologies and their developments, governments have historically not rushed to pass laws to regulate their use in treatment. The exceptions are few, and include Victoria in Australia, Sweden and Austria – the first jurisdictions to pass laws in the 1980s. Interestingly, the laws passed by these jurisdictions had far-reaching provisions about protecting the rights of children born as a result of donor treatment to access identifying information about their donor origins. Two decades later, this issue has once again become central to debates about the regulation of reproductive technologies, as regulators feel the impact of the first generation of donor-conceived children beginning to seek information about their biological origins.

Generally, in those jurisdictions where ART legislation has been passed, there has been a significant time-lag between the initial conduct of an inquiry about the need for formal regulation of ART and the actual passing of statutes. In the United Kingdom, for example, the Warnock Committee was established in 1982 and reported in 1984, but the *Human Fertilisation and Embryology Act* was not passed until 1990.

In Europe in 2002, seven out of the 15 countries that were then members of the European Union had legislation dealing primarily with reproductive technologies.[35] Italy passed highly restrictive legislation in 2003, which has since been retained after a referendum in June 2005, aiming to relax some of the provisions, but failed to achieve the minimum required voter turnout. Of the 10 additional countries which joined the European Union in 2004, only a small number passed legislation regulating reproductive technologies.

Of the 52 countries in Asia, reproductive technologies are offered as a form of treatment in about half (25 countries). Regulation is present in one form or another in 19 of these jurisdictions (see Figure 10.2). Perceptions of reproductive technologies in Asia are also influenced by spiritual or religious considerations that promote "human and natural creation into a single seamless cosmos".[36] The concern about the protections which must be placed on the human embryo are not as great as in many Western contexts, although different religious and cultural traditions will have an impact on views about surrogacy, donor treatment procedures, sex selection and even human cloning.

---

35 Pattinson, S, "Current Legislation in Europe" in Gunning, J and Szoke, H (eds), *The Regulation of Assisted Reproductive Technology*, Ashgate, Aldershot, 2003. Since that time, other countries have joined the European Union including Hungary, the Czech Republic, Slovenia, Slovak Republic, Poland, Lithuania and Estonia. Wilson, P, "Europe's Suffering From Growing Pains", *Weekend Australian*, 1-2 May 2004, p 14.

36 Fukuyama (2002) op cit, p 192.

Figure 10.2: Regulation of ARTs in Asia

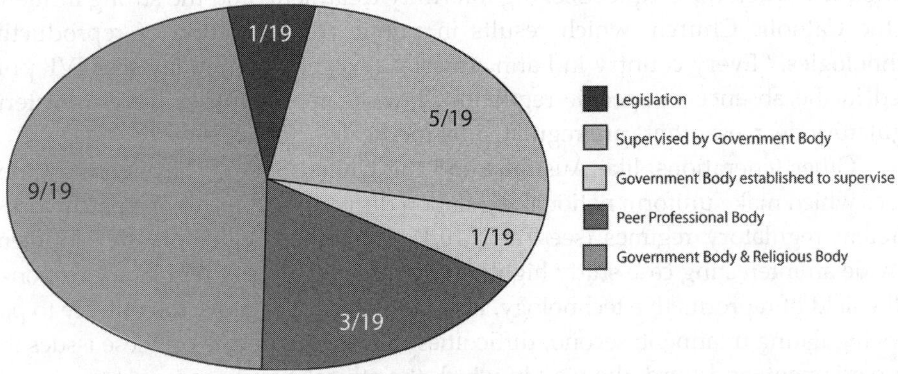

Figure 10.3 below adapts Fukuyama's continuum of regulatory regimes around the world.[37] The countries of continental Europe and Germany in particular, have a traumatic history of human medical research, experimentation and eugenics arising from the middle of the 20th century. The legacy of this is a strong suspicion of and opposition to biotechnology, which affects legislation on some aspects of reproductive technologies, particularly genetic testing via PGD.[38] These countries have varying restrictions on embryo research, genetic testing, and donor treatment procedures, reflecting caution and a desire for constraint and control.

Figure 10.3: Continuum of regulatory regimes

Most restrictive			Least restrictive
Prohibitive or restrictive legislation	Religious or spiritual considerations in the absence of legislation	Facilitative regulation	No legislation; professional guidelines
Continental Europe	Consideration	UK	China
Italy	Middle East	USA	South Korea
Germany	Latin America	Canada	
Austria		NZ	
		Australia	
		SE ASIA	

37   Szoke, H, "Lessons from the Law – the Regulation of ARTs", poster presentation, IFFS Montreal, 2004.

38   Feichtinger, W, "Preimplantation Genetic Diagnosis (PGD) – A European Clinician's Point of View" (2004) 21(1) *Journal of Assisted Reproduction & Genetics* 15.

The countries of Latin America do not have laws. Zegers-Hochschild[39] attributes this to two key factors: the low priority given to infertility, which is not seen as a disease and consequently does not receive public health funding, creating a heavy economic burden for couples seeking infertility treatment; and the strong influence of the Catholic Church, which results in public condemnation of reproductive technologies. "Every country in Latin America (except Cuba) today sees IVF practiced in the absence of specific regulatory laws (some countries have ministerial regulatory decrees, others are regulated by medical societies)".[40]

Other federations, like Australia and the United States,[41] have constitutional issues which make uniform national regulation difficult, and result in a patchwork of different regulatory regimes (see Table 10.1). Australian regulatory developments provide an interesting case study highlighting three features of regulatory responses in the field of reproductive technology. First, a reluctance to move too quickly to pass laws regulating treatment; second, difficulties in bringing debate on these issues into the parliament; and third, the way in which the ethical significance and commercial prospects of ES cell research can force the introduction of legislation.

National regulation in Australia

When the world's third IVF baby was born in Melbourne, there were a number of attempts at a national level to pass laws restricting the use of reproductive technologies.[42] These attempts did not result in national regulation. However, the Fertility Society of Australia (FSA) developed an accreditation scheme, and established the Reproductive Technology Accreditation Committee (RTAC)[43] to monitor compliance. RTAC is responsible for producing guidelines which define the standards of clinical, scientific and technical practice in treatment and research provided by infertility clinics in Australia.[44] This is an important self-regulatory mechanism which ensures that the standard of treatment provided by Australian clinics is the responsibility of the professionals providing that treatment. There is also a significant financial incentive for clinics to receive this accreditation, as the Health Insurance Commission approval of fertility drugs is linked to the accreditation: "Without such accreditation, the patients would bear the full cost of their expensive fertility drugs, a significant additional financial burden on their treatment".[45]

---

39 Zegers-Hochschild, F, "Key Health Policy Issues in Newly Industrialized Countries – Latin America", in Lunenfeld, B and Van Steirteghem, A, *Conclusions of 2nd Global Conference*, 18-19 November 2002, *Infertility in the Third Millennium. Implications for the Individual, Family and Society*, Bertarelli Foundation, 2002, p 38.

40 Ibid, p 43.

41 Katayama, AC, "US ART Practitioners Soon to Begin Their Forced March into a Regulated Future" (2003) 20(7) *Journal of Assisted Reproduction & Genetics* 265.

42 Szoke, H, "Regulation of Assisted Reproductive Technology: The State of Play in Australia" in Freckelton, I and Petersen, K (eds), *Controversies in Health Law*, Federation Press, Sydney, 1999.

43 Ibid, p 244.

44 Currently, RTAC, *Code of Practice for Assisted Reproductive Technology Units*, February 2005.

45 Ibid.

In addition to industry self-regulation of professional and laboratory standards through the RTAC guidelines, the National Health and Medical Research Council's (NHMRC) Australian Health Ethics Committee (AHEC) has produced ethical guidelines for assisted reproductive technologies. These have developed in three stages, in part reflecting the development of reproductive technologies and changing attitudes towards their use. In October 1982, the NHMRC issued guidelines on the ethical aspects of research related to the use of assisted reproductive technology as Supplementary Note 4 (SN4) to the *Statement on Human Experimentation*. When the *National Health and Medical Research Council Act 1992* (Cth) was passed, all guidelines remained in force *with the specific exception of SN4*. The exclusion of SN4, and the requirement that the NHMRC issue revised guidelines pertaining to ART, reflects that by 1992 it was no longer appropriate that reproductive technologies be regarded as human experimentation.

After two rounds of public consultation by the Reproductive Technology Working Group, the NHMRC released its *Ethical Guidelines on Assisted Reproductive Technology* (1996). These guidelines noted that the development of ART raised complex "social and political issues" relating to eligibility for treatment and practices such as surrogacy, consent for posthumous use, as well as genetic diagnosis and selection. However, at that time the guidelines described these issues as "beyond the remit of AHEC in relation to medical research",[46] and consequently did not offer guidance on such practices. Instead, they issued a strong call for comprehensive and uniform (or at least complementary) legislation in all States and Territories in order to address the social and ethical challenges posed by developments in reproductive technologies.[47]

In September 2004, the 1996 guidelines were replaced with a significantly more comprehensive document which addresses many of the ethical implications of treatment and research previously considered "beyond the remit" of the AHEC.[48] These changes include guidelines on the use of PGD[49] and a prohibition on social sex selection,[50] and a significant strengthening of the requirements relating to the recording of information about donor procedures, which explicitly ties these requirements to a child's "right to knowledge of genetic parents and siblings".[51] These changes may well be because the NHRMC's advice in the 1996 guidelines that reproductive technologies should be regulated by statute in each State went unheeded. Another factor is that since 1996, PGD and the consequences of donor procedures for children have been two of the most important issues addressed by States with legislation.

---

46   NHMRC, *Ethical Guidelines on Assisted Reproductive Technology*, AGPS, Canberra, 1996, p v.
47   Ibid, pp iv–v.
48   NHMRC, *Ethical Guidelines on the Use of Assisted Reproductive Technology in Clinical Practice and Research*, NHMRC, Canberra, 2004.
49   Ibid, pp 40–41.
50   Ibid, pp 39.
51   Ibid, pp 16–17.

The new guidelines also integrate the requirements of the *Prohibition of Human Cloning Act 2002* (Cth) and the *Research Involving Human Embryos Act 2002* (Cth). Where the 1996 guidelines specified that "embryo experimentation should normally be limited to therapeutic procedures which leave the embryo ... with an expectation of implantation and development",[52] the current guidelines deal extensively with research involving excess embryos, "which may involve harming or destroying the embryo".[53] Additionally, both the RTAC and NHMRC guidelines have taken on greater power with the passage of the *Research Involving Human Embryos Act 2002* (Cth) and the *Prohibition of Human Cloning Act 2002* (Cth).

The *Research Involving Human Embryos Act 2002* (Cth) outlines the provisions in relation to the use of excess ART embryos for the purposes of research. The legislation is quite explicit about the definitions of an embryo,[54] an excess ART embryo,[55] and how proper consent is to be given to the declaration that an ART embryo is in excess.[56] Significantly, the legislation contains a provision that only embryos formed before 5 April 2002 can be used for destructive embryo research.[57] However, the Act also contains a sunset clause, stipulating that the requirement to utilise embryos formed before that date no longer applies after the 5 April 2005.[58] From this date, until the legislation is reviewed and amended, any excess embryos can be donated to and used in research.

The NHMRC Licensing Committee was established by the *Research Involving Human Embryos Act 2002* (Cth) to consider applications for the licensing of embryo research and to conduct monitoring and inspection of licensed centres where research is undertaken. The committee contains representation which requires the agreement of State, Territory and federal governments. This process of approving members to the Licensing Committee is indicative of the sensitive nature of embryo research and the difficulty of working across different levels of government. Since its formation in 2003, the NHMRC Licensing Committee has issued nine licences, four of which have been related to embryonic stem cell research: to develop ES cell lines for research in the treatment of diabetes; to develop improved culture conditions for establishing ES cell lines; and another two to derive stem cells for medical research. Five other licences have related to the development of genetic tests to improve IVF success rates, research to enhance understanding of embryo metabolism, and training for practitioners. All licences have been issued to locations in Melbourne and Sydney, where the main centres of research are located.[59]

---

52   NHMRC (1996) guidelines op cit, p 10.
53   NHMRC (2004) guidelines op cit, p 49.
54   *Research Involving Human Embryos Act 2002* (Cth) s 7(1).
55   Ibid, s 9.
56   Ibid, s 8.
57   Ibid, s 24(3).
58   Ibid, s 46.
59   NHMRC, "NHMRC Licensing Committee Issues Seventh Licence" (2004) 1(2) *NHMRC Licensing Committee Bulletin* 1.

The *Prohibition of Human Cloning Act 2002* (Cth) also contains a range of prohibitions which relate to various uses of embryos. These prohibitions include the creation of a cloned human embryo[60] (defined as "a human embryo that is a genetic copy of another living or dead human, but does not include a human embryo created by the fertilization of a human egg by a human sperm"[61]), as well as placing such an embryo in the body of a human or animal, and the import or export of cloned human embryos. The *Prohibition of Human Cloning Act 2002* (Cth) also bans the creation of a human embryo *other than by fertilisation*,[62] and for a purpose *other than achieving pregnancy in a woman*,[63] thus specifically preventing therapeutic as well as reproductive cloning. At the time of writing, both Acts are being reviewed, with the responsible committee (Legislation Review Committee) due to report to the Commonwealth Parliament by December 2005.[64] The review will canvass a range of matters including whether amendments should be made to allow the use of therapeutic cloning, how the current regulatory regime has operated, whether there should be a national ES cell bank established in Australia, and whether the legislation should be made more restrictive or facilitative.[65]

The passage of the Commonwealth statutes is significant for two reasons. In the first instance, they require that embryos to be used for research must be formed at a place accredited under the RTAC Guidelines.[66] This provides an important model for how self-regulatory mechanisms can be combined with laws to achieve best practice in an area. The second aspect of significance is the weighting given to the NHMRC ethical guidelines: in deciding whether to issue a licence, the Licensing Committee must have regard to any relevant guidelines issued by the NHMRC.[67] This in effect gives much greater enforcement powers to guidelines and accreditation schemes without enshrining these provisions in law. Given the nature of reproductive technology, the pace at which it develops, and the tendency of technologies to expand into novel and unanticipated applications, a disadvantage of highly prescriptive legislation is that very rapidly it may unintentionally permit or prohibit a practice which was simply not conceptualised when the legislation was created. For this reason, legislation which creates enforcement mechanisms for the guidelines from RTAC and the NHMRC reduces the need for legislative amendment, thus providing greater regulatory flexibility while retaining processes for public oversight. This model may provide an important basis for future regulation in Australia in the area of biotechnology.

---

60 *Prohibition of Human Cloning Act 2002* (Cth) s 9.
61 Ibid, s 8.
62 Ibid, s 13.
63 Ibid, s 14.
64 Australian Government (2005). Legislation Review: Prohibition of Human Cloning Act 2002 and the Research Involving Human Embryos Act 2002, Reports, Canberra, December 2005. Available at <www.lockhartreview.com.au>.
65 Ibid, s 25.
66 Fertility Society of Australia, RTAC Committee, *Code of Practice for Assisted Reproductive Technology Units*, revised February 2005.
67 *Research Involving Human Embryos Act 2002* (Cth), s 21(4)(c).

State laws and regulatory models

The Australian States responded differently to the emergence of reproductive technologies, with a number of States choosing to legislate specifically on ART, and others relying on the professional accreditation process. These various responses have resulted in different standards and guidelines in operation throughout Australia, with the associated issues of State variations. In some cases, original legislation has been reviewed and replaced. In some States without legislation, reviews have commenced afresh. Many important and controversial issues remain subject to different State standards.

South Australia and Western Australia[68]

Western Australia and South Australia passed laws regulating the use of reproductive technologies in the late 1980s and early 1990s.[69] There are still clear requirements in both States enshrined in the legislation stipulating who may receive treatment. In South Australia (as in Victoria) the marriage requirement was rendered inoperative by the Supreme Count of South Australia on the grounds that it conflicted with the federal Sex Discrimination Act 1984.[70] Although the wording of the Act remains unchanged, since 1996 single and lesbian women have been able to access ART services, although the requirement for medical infertility or risk of transmitting a genetic disease remains.

The details of what is regulated by these laws are outlined in Table 10.1. These jurisdictions have opted for the definition of principles enshrined in legislation and have delegated the task of implementation to codes or directions.[71] These codes are periodically amended and then endorsed by the parliament or the parliamentary representative through the bureaucratic head of the relevant government department. This model of statutory regulation captures the public interest through the articulation of principles, but allows a certain amount of flexibility in relation to its implementation. This model also reflects the government's understanding of community acceptance of clinical and research procedures in the contentious field of reproductive technologies. Notwithstanding the clear articulation of principles, it becomes possible to check and monitor the community's response to the imposition of a statutory structure. Legislation which provides regulatory powers or the development of codes to enhance its operation is more likely to be flexible and responsive than legislation which requires statutory amendment to reflect its intent.

Review and consultation in this area is important and is usually undertaken prior to the amendment of any legislation. In South Australia in particular,

---

68 Generally, residents of the Northern Territory seek treatment from clinics in South Australia because of the lack of facilities in the Northern Territory.

69 *Reproductive Technology (Clinical Practices Act) 1988* (SA); *Human Reproductive Technology Act 1991* (WA).

70 *Pearce v South Australian Health Commission* (1996) 66 SASR 486.

71 *Reproductive Technology Council (Code of Ethical Clinical Practice) Regulations 1995* (SA); *Human Reproductive Technology Act 1991* (WA); Directions, *West Australian Government Gazette*, Perth, Tuesday, 30 November 2004, No 201.

community consultation has been undertaken around issues associated with donor record-keeping, statutory requirements determining who is fit to parent, and the use of preimplantation genetic diagnosis procedures.[72] In Western Australia an extensive review of the State human reproductive technology legislation was undertaken by a Legislative Assembly Select Committee in the 1990s. The committee visited national and international jurisdictions to review other regulatory regimes and produced a report to the parliament in 1999 outlining a range of recommendations for changes to the Western Australian legislation. In particular, it recommended that "the *Human Reproductive Technology Act* 1991 be amended to allow preimplantation genetic diagnosis to occur under restrictions determined by the Reproductive Technology Council".[73] This and most other significant recommendations in the report were incorporated into amending legislation.[74]

Changes to human reproductive technology statutes are often avoided by the political process due to the highly controversial and potentially divisive nature of the issues. Historically, amendments to legislation have followed immense public lobbying or the need for change imposed by the requirements of federal legislative compliance. In Western Australia, for example, amendment to the Act was expedited by the passage of national legislation regulating embryo research, which required State "mirror" legislation to be passed. At that time, the *Human Reproductive Technology Amendment Act 2004* (WA) and the *Acts Amendment (Prohibition of Human Cloning and Other Practices) Act 2004* (WA) were introduced into the parliament and additional matters were included which addressed the use of PGD for the purpose of preventing the transmission of genetic disease or abnormality. Before the *Human Reproductive Technology Amendment Act 2004* (WA) was passed, diagnostic procedures were limited to those instances where the proposed procedure was intended to be therapeutic for the egg or embryo.[75] Consequently, the Western Australian Reproductive Technology Council could not license PGD for therapeutic purposes. However, this provision has been repealed and council may now approve PGD where the diagnostic procedure is for the genetic testing of the embryo where "there is a significant risk of a serious genetic abnormality or disease being present in the embryo".[76]

The Western Australian Parliament has also passed other laws which have an impact on the use of reproductive technologies. As part of its Gay and Lesbian Law Reform Package, the *Acts Amendment (Lesbian and Gay Law Reform) Act 2002*, all gender-specific references have been removed from the *Artificial Conception Act 1985* and the *Human Reproductive Technology Act 1991*. Where a woman in a de facto relationship with another woman undergoes an artificial conception procedure with

---

72 South Australian Council on Reproductive Technology, "Donor Conception in South Australia" (2000) (15) *SACRT Quarterly Bulletin* 5.

73 Parliament of Western Australia, *Select Committee on the Human Reproductive Technology Act 1991 (WA)*, Report No 97, 1999.

74 *Human Reproductive Technology Amendment Act 2004* (WA).

75 *Human Reproductive Technology Act 1991* (WA) s 14(2) (repealed).

76 Ibid, s 14(2B).

the consent of her partner, and becomes pregnant, the partner will be legally recognised as a parent of any child born as a result.[77] This is a significant recognition of alternative family structures, which will affect future amendments of the *Human Reproductive Technology Act 1991* in that State. As well, these amendments also allow single women or women in a same sex relationship, where they are infertile or at risk of transmitting a genetic abnormality or disease, to access IVF procedures. They also clarify some uncertainty that previously existed about the legal status of gamete or embryo donors where the husband or de facto partner of a woman undergoing an artificial fertilisation procedure had not given consent to the procedure.[78]

Victoria

Victoria, in contrast, has implemented a statutory regime where both the principles and the "rules of conduct" are expressed in the comprehensive *Infertility Treatment Act 1995* which delegates administrative power to the Infertility Treatment Authority. In the Act, principles are clearly defined in descending order of importance. The interests of the person to be born are paramount, while the interests of the infertile couple are incorporated, but are not of equal status.[79] The Act contains comprehensive details about who may access treatment, where the treatment should be provided, who should provide the treatment, how consent and information must be given and specific provisions relating to the recording of information about donor treatment procedures and birth origin information.[80] Since its proclamation in 1998, the Act has undergone three amendments.[81] The comprehensive detail of the primary legislation, and the consequent difficulty of resolving matters of interpretation, is evident in the number of legal opinions sought by the Infertility Treatment Authority on aspects of the Act's application – 32 during the five years of the Authority's operation.[82]

---

77   *Acts Amendment (Lesbian and Gay Law Reform) Act 2002* (WA).

78   The authors wish to acknowledge the contribution made by staff at the Western Australian Reproductive Technology Council to our understanding of the history of ART legislation in Western Australia.

79   Infertility Treatment Act 1995 (Vic) s 5:

> It is the Parliament's intention that the following principles will be given effect in administering this Act, carrying out functions under this Act, and in the carrying out of activities regulated by this Act – (a) the welfare and interests of any person born or to be born as a result of a treatment procedure are paramount; (b) human life should be preserved and protected; (c) the interests of the family should be considered; (d) infertile couples should be assisted in fulfilling their desire to have children.

> The Act requires that the principles must be applied in the descending order of importance as written in the Act.

80   See Table 10.1: Guidelines and legislation – ART in Australia.

81   *Infertility Treatment (Amendment) Act 1997* (Vic); *Infertility Treatment (Amendment) Act 2001* (Vic) and *Health Legislation (Research Involving Human Embryos and Prohibition of Human Cloning) Act 2003* (Vic).

82   Infertility Treatment Authority, Submission to Victorian Law Reform Commission, *Assisted Reproductive Technology and Adoption: Should the Current Eligibility Criteria in Victoria be Changed?*, Consultation Paper, 2004.

The most significant change to the Act occurred when the Federal Court of Australia struck down the statutory marriage requirement in *McBain v Victoria*.[83] Victorian legislation had excluded single women from access to reproductive treatment by its definition of who may receive treatment. The ruling in the *McBain* case determined that the "marriage requirement" contained in s 8(3)(a) of the Act was in breach of the *Sex Discrimination Act 1984* (Cth), and therefore inoperative. Following the decision, the Infertility Treatment Authority sought legal advice about eligibility under the Act, and ruled that although the marriage requirement was inoperative, the requirement for infertility remained.[84] Ultimately, the Victorian Government referred the matter of access to infertility treatment and adoption services, as well as the issue of surrogacy, to the Victorian Law Reform Commission (VLRC) for consideration. At the time of writing, the VLRC had produced a consultation paper, three expert papers and three position papers following targeted and public consultation on the issue.[85] It is anticipated that the VLRC's final report will be presented to the Victorian Attorney-General by the end of 2006. The *McBain* case demonstrates that while the courts cannot resolve the policy issues underlying contentious areas such as reproductive technologies and their use, they can play a role in bringing such issues to the government's attention.

New South Wales

Although the New South Wales Parliament has passed mirror legislation in accordance with the *Research Involving Human Embryos Act 2002* (Cth) and the *Prohibition of Human Cloning Act 2002* (Cth),[86] legislation to regulate infertility services has never been enacted. A 1996 review of the *Human Tissue Act 1983* (NSW) proposed a regulatory framework that would have a "light touch", requiring the licensing of places where infertility treatment would be provided, and certain provisions around the recording of birth origin information.[87] In response to the review, the Assisted Reproductive Technology Bill was presented to parliament in 2003. The aim of the proposed legislation is to prevent the commercialisation of human reproduction and to protect the interests of people affected by infertility treatment procedures. If passed, the legislation would: require ART providers to be registered by the Director-General of the Department of Health; make counselling mandatory; establish a

---

83 *McBain v Victoria* [2000] FCA 1009.

84 Gavan Griffith QC, *In the matter of Infertility Treatment Act 1995 and Sex Discrimination Act 1984, Section 22*, 4 August 2000, <www.ita.org.au/_documents/policies/Legal%20Opinion. pdf> (accessed 27 January 2006).

85 VLRC, *Assisted Reproduction and Adoption: Should the Current Eligibility Criteria in Victoria be Changed? A Consultation Paper*, VLRC, 2003; VLRC, *Assisted Reproductive Technology and Adoption, Position Paper 1 – Access*, July 2005; VLRC, *Assisted Reproductive Technology and Adoption, Position Paper Two – Parentage*, VLRC, July 2005; VLRC, Assisted Reproductive Technology and Adoption, Position Paper Three – Surrogacy, November 2005.

86 *Human Cloning and Other Prohibited Practices Act 2003* (NSW); *Research Involving Human Embryos Act 2003* (NSW).

87 NSW Health, *Review of the Human Tissue Act 1983*, Discussion Paper, Assisted Reproductive Technologies, 1999.

central ART register to facilitate the exchange of information between people involved in donor procedures; and prohibit commercial surrogacy and make all surrogacy agreements void. At the time of writing, the Bill is again being revised following consultation on the exposure draft.

Given the absence of legislation, the RTAC and NHMRC guidelines assume a far greater importance in the regulation of infertility services in New South Wales. The recent expansion of these guidelines to provide directives on ethical issues, such as non-medical sex selection, surrogacy, limits to the number of families formed with donor gametes, and the collection of information about donor treatment procedures, has had particular impact in New South Wales. While there are other States where infertility treatment is not regulated by statute, New South Wales's ART industry is large and well established, and has offered types of treatment which may not be available in smaller unregulated States. For instance, both of the two clinics in Australia which offer social sex selection procedures via PGD are in Sydney. These services are no longer available to patients in New South Wales due to the 2004 NHMRC guidelines.[88] This demonstrates the potential efficacy of guidelines in regulating the social aspects of reproductive technologies, in addition to technical and professional standards. Regulation in the absence of legislation may initially appear to lack an enforcement mechanism; however, adherence to the NHMRC guidelines has been achieved by an RTAC requirement to abide by them,[89] alongside the financial incentives for clinics to have RTAC accreditation. Another layer of compliance has been added by the *Research Involving Human Embryos Act 2002* (Cth), and the requirement that excess embryos to be used for research conducted under that Act must have been formed at an RTAC-accredited facility. An interconnected web of regulations is developing that is proving capable of capturing even those States which have eschewed regulation via statute. Whether the extension of regulation into such areas reflects the strong public interest in the social and ethical challenges posed by ART, or constitutes an infringement on the autonomy of patients, clinicians and business, is a matter of heated debate.

Queensland, Tasmania and the Australian Capital Territory

Although Queensland, Tasmania and the Australian Capital Territory have not passed specific ART statutes, all have passed miscellaneous laws including surrogacy and status of children statues.[90] These jurisdictions have also passed legislation to give effect to the requirements of the *Research Involving Human Embryos Act 2002* (Cth) and the *Prohibition of Human Cloning Act 2002* (Cth).[91]

---

88 NHMRC (2004) guidelines op cit, p 39; Robotham, J, "Banned: choosing a baby's sex", *Sydney Morning Herald*, 25 March 2005.

89 Guideline 1(18) of the Fertility Society of Australia, RTAC Committee, *Code of Practice for Assisted Reproductive Technology Units*, revised February 2005.

90 *Surrogate Parenthood Act 1988* (Qld); *Surrogacy Contracts Act 1993* (Tas); *Substitute Parent Agreement Act 1994* (ACT); *Parentage Act 2004* (ACT).

91 *Research Involving Human Embryos and Prohibition of Human Cloning Act 2003* (Qld); *Human Embryonic Research Regulation Act 2003* (Tas).

While the Australian Capital Territory has undertaken a number of reviews in relation to proposing a regulatory scheme for infertility treatment in that jurisdiction, legislation has not eventuated. The Australian Capital Territory has, however, enacted groundbreaking legislation in the area of surrogacy regulation, with the passage of the first Australian law to define the legal parentage for a child born as a result of a surrogacy arrangement.[92] The *Substitute Parent Agreement Act 1994* (ACT) has been repealed and replaced with the *Parentage Act 2004* (ACT), which also incorporates the provisions of the *Artificial Conception Act 1985* (ACT) and the *Birth (Equality of Status) Act 1988* (ACT). The purpose of the new statute is to clarify legal recognition of parentage and family relationships. The Act is certainly not facilitative of surrogacy: commercial surrogacy is prohibited,[93] surrogacy agreements are not accorded any legal validity and, indeed, are discouraged by the provisions of the Act (the woman who gives birth to a child is always presumed to be the mother, and her domestic partner, if she has one, the father).

However, the Act does establish the circumstances under which some altruistic surrogacy agreements can be given effect through a court order transferring the parentage of a child from the birth parents to the commissioning parents. Such a parentage order can only be granted where at least one of the commissioning people provides the gametes used in the pregnancy and neither the surrogate nor her domestic partner contributes gametes; in other words, where the child is not genetically related to the birth mother or her domestic partner, and is genetically related to at least one of the commissioning parents. It must be emphasised that a parentage order is not the outcome of a surrogacy agreement, nor does it represent enforcement of such an agreement: before issuing a parentage order the Supreme Court must be satisfied that it is in the best interests of the child and that both birth parents, who are the legal parents under the Act, are fully informed and agree freely to the making of the parentage order. This Act is significant, as surrogacy is very difficult to access in most States in Australia, and even in those States where it occurs, such as New South Wales, the legal issues associated with the parentage of the child have not been clarified.[94]

The *Parentage Act 2004* (ACT) is also intended to remove discrimination relating to sexuality and parentage, thus enabling same sex couples to be recognised as parents of a child. Where a woman with a same sex domestic partner undertakes an artificial reproductive procedure with the consent of her partner, then the domestic partner, regardless of their sex, is presumed to be the parent of the child.

---

92   *Substitute Parent Agreement Act 1994* (ACT) Pt 4.

93   *Parentage Act 2004* (ACT).

94   The jurisdictions in Australia with statutes which directly address surrogacy are Queensland, Tasmania, Victoria and the ACT: *Surrogate Parenthood Act 1988* (Qld); *Surrogacy Contracts Act 1993* (Tas); *Infertility Treatment Act 1995* (Vic); *Parentage Act 2004* (ACT).

Conclusion

There is increasing worldwide pressure on governments to respond to the use of these technologies and the demand for regulation. At least with regard to human reproductive cloning, therapeutic cloning and ES cell research, this pressure makes it highly likely that government intervention in the field of reproductive techno-logies will increase in the future. Not all governments in the past have succeeded in regulating by statute,[95] even though numerous committees and commissions have been established. Despite the difficulties of instituting statutory regulation in the field of ART, governments are the bodies that must facilitate public dialogue about the use of reproductive technologies and ensure that communities are kept abreast of developments.

Government intervention is problematic and controversial in this area. There are two main philosophical critiques of ART legislation. One is that it encroaches on reproductive freedom, professional autonomy and the personal ethics of treatment providers.[96] The second is that legislation cannot hope to resolve con-flicts over contentious social and ethical issues (such as who should have access to the technology, and how applications like PGD, sex selection and surrogacy should be used) and that governments should therefore refrain from legislating at all.

A brief response to these claims might be that, although governments are of course subject to political imperatives, there is nevertheless at least the potential for them to constitute an independent player in this arena, and assist in resolving conflicts and formalising an expression of the public interest. Of course, such a resolution will not satisfy all parties, as the conflict is often based on incom-mensurable moral values, and we live in a pluralistic society. However, it should be emphasised that in refraining from intervention, governments implicitly sanc-tion the resolution of such ethical conflicts according to a medical model which is highly individualistic, and prioritises the choices of free-market actors above other considerations. In the absence of regulation, the interests which predominate are those of practitioners and clinics (as significant business entities) and patients (as consumers of services). There are other parties with strong claims to a legitimate interest in the ways in which reproductive technologies are used. These include the children born as a result of ARTs; those who contribute their gametes for use in donor treatment procedures; those with strong views about the beginning of life and the status of human embryos; and those living with disabilities which may be increasingly targeted for prevention via PGD.

Beyond these specific actors, it may be argued that society as a whole has an interest in ART, because of the challenges these technologies pose to fundamental norms and institutions. For the first quarter century of IVF, this has predominantly

---

95 Lee, RG, and Morgan, D, *Human Fertilisation and Embryology. Regulating the Reproductive Revolution*, Blackstone, London, 2001 p 6; Pattinson (2003) op cit.

96 Petersen, K, Baker, HW, Pitts, M and Thorpe, R, "Assisted Reproductive Technologies: Professional and Legal Restrictions in Australian Clinics" (2005) 12(3) *Journal of Law and Medicine* 373.

meant challenges to the traditional family structure. Laws and cultural institutions exist which define the family and the organisation of the family unit, and these laws and institutions will change over time. Indeed, the family, both in practice and in law, has already been modified through the opportunities generated by reproductive technologies. Additionally, ART legislation, which many have claimed discriminates against women and children in alternative family structures, has been subject to challenge, with some provisions rendered inoperable, and others currently under review. However, as ART finds new areas of application like genetic testing or sex selection, and expands into broader areas of medicine, norms other than the family may be challenged by technology. Such norms could include equality, justice and, in the case of reproductive cloning, the very nature of personhood. In such a complex and dynamic field, the government's role is to manage this process of change; to regulate with a view to protecting fundamental interests; to engage the community in ongoing dialogue about what such interests are; and to ensure that science remains accountable to the society within which it is embedded.

A more practical objection is that professional regulation through bodies such as RTAC is highly effective and that legislation, particularly in a federation such as Australia, is unnecessarily cumbersome and costly. The authors would certainly not contest the importance of a regulatory mechanism such as RTAC. Indeed, we regard legislation which devolves the proscriptive regulations governing practice and implementation to guidelines, directives or codes as a promising model for the regulation of ART in Australia in the future. However, the fact remains that without legislation there exists no watertight enforcement mechanism for such codes; adherence to the RTAC Code of Practice (and through that, compliance with the NHMRC ethical guidelines) is currently facilitated by financial incentive. Although it is unlikely, there is little apart from economic constraint to prevent a clinic from forgoing RTAC accreditation, along with its financial benefits, and offering applications of the technology prohibited by RTAC or the NHMRC, should the market exist.

The federal legislation on embryo research, which effectively creates an enforcement mechanism for RTAC and NHMRC guidelines, is an example of an innovative potential model for regulation. Under this model, statutes build on self-regulatory mechanisms developed by the professions, and ethical guidelines that are able to be reviewed and changed within the context of law. Such a model would allow responsiveness to technological developments and flexibility to monitor and adapt to changing community attitudes, while also providing an effective means for enforcement.

Despite the promise of this new model, the regulation of infertility treatment still remains in a state of flux. Victoria awaits the review of the access requirements and surrogacy provisions contained in its legislation; Western Australia has only just begun to implement its newly amended Act; proposed amendments to the

South Australian Act are stalled without resources or political will; and another round of redrafting is in progress on the New South Wales Exposure Bill.[97]

It is unlikely that a push to achieve national regulation of infertility treatment will emerge similar to that which precipitated federal legislation on embryo research and human cloning. In the latter case, the financial prospects of ES cell research and the threat of human reproductive cloning provided the incentive to regulate. Where embryo research and human cloning are regulated separately from infertility treatment, and as the public becomes more accepting of reproductive technologies and alternative family structures, the impetus for national regulation will be lessened.

However, a number of important considerations remain in terms of the current national regulatory situation. Access provisions vary between States, which results in reproductive tourism to circumvent the requirements. As Petersen and colleagues point out, this enables women with sufficient economic resources to exercise reproductive choices which are denied to others.[98] The legal status of children born as a result of surrogacy is unresolved in all jurisdictions with the exception of the Australian Capital Territory, and jurisdictions with legislation that does not prohibit altruistic surrogacy may have access requirements which are inconsistent and lead to inequitable outcomes. Victoria remains the only State where the right of children born as a result of donor treatment procedures to access identifying information about their biological parents is enforceable (the effect of the new NHMRC and RTAC guidelines on this issue remains to be seen in other States). That said, the Victorian experience is demonstrating the complexities of creating and administering such a right, in a context where there is no guarantee that children will be told of their donor origins by their parents. Some consistency in these matters would enhance the protection of children's rights and the interests of people accessing infertility treatment, as well as recognising the importance of these technologies to the wider community.

Yet the international experience shows us that reform of existing laws and the introduction of new legislation does not happen easily and time is needed to ensure that the political climate is appropriate for the conduct of debate and community discussion.

---

97   Assisted Reproductive Technology Bill 2003 (NSW).

98   Petersen, Baker, Pitts and Thorpe (2005) op cit, p 384.

Table 10.1: Guidelines and legislation – ART in Australia (current at April 2005)

Legislation and / or Guidelines	Cth	NHMRC	NSW	QLD	SA	TAS	VIC	WA	ACT	NT	RTAC
Specific legislation or guidelines	Research Involving Human Embryos Act 2002 and Prohibition of Human Cloning Act 2002	Ethical Guidelines on the Use of Assisted Reproductive Technology in Clinical Practice & Research 2004	Nil; Artificial Conception Act 1984; Assisted Reproductive Technology Bill 2003. Draft currently under consultation	Nil; Surrogate Parenthood Act 1988	Reproductive Technology (Clinical Practices) Act 1988	Nil; Surrogacy Contracts Act 1993	Infertility Treatment Act 1995, previously – Infertility (Medical procedures) Act 1984	Human Reproductive Technology Amendment Act 2004. This Act is silent on donor insemination	Nil; Parentage Act 2004	Nil; guided by South Australian legislation	Code of Practice for Assisted Reproductive Technology Units. Applies to all IVF clinics in Australia & NZ
Access to services	N/A	None specified	Ethics committee decision. Access by de facto couples and legally married couples. Some examples of services to single women and same sex couples	De facto and legally married couples. Individual clinic decision whether to treat single or lesbian women	Act specifies legally married and heterosexual de facto cohabiting for 5 years. However, Supreme Court ruled the marital status requirement invalid as inconsistent with the federal Sex Discrimination Act	Clinic decision	Act specifies legally married & heterosexual de facto. However, McBain case means marriage requirement cannot be applied. Single women who are infertile or at risk of transmitting a genetic condition are eligible	Heterosexual de facto and legally married couples. Single women or lesbian women can access DI which is not within regulatory reach of Act	Clinic decision	SA legislation	None specified

Legislation and / or Guidelines	Cth	NHMRC	NSW	QLD	SA	TAS	VIC	WA	ACT	NT	RTAC
Access to services (cont)					Since 1996 single women who are infertile or at risk of transmitting a genetic condition can access services						
Selection criteria for access to services	N/A	None specified	None specified	None specified	Medical infertility; or prevention of a genetic defect being transferred to child; and requirements of parenting code to be met	None specified	Evidence that a woman is unlikely to become pregnant other than by a treatment procedure; or to prevent the transfer of a genetic abnormality or disease	Infertile or prevent risk of transfer of genetic abnormality	None specified	SA legislation	None specified
Time limit for storage of gametes and embryos	N/A	Embryos: 5 years, with option to renew consent for a further 5 years. Gametes: Time limit specified by person; clinics also must have policy	NHMRC guidelines; RTAC guidelines	NHMRC guidelines; RTAC guidelines	Ten-year limit for embryos; no provision for extension; requirement to contact couples every 12 months	NHMRC guidelines RTAC guidelines	Gametes 10-year limit; embryos 5-year limit; can apply for extension of storage period	Maximum period of storage 10 years, except with extension granted by council under special circumstances	NHMRC guidelines RTAC guidelines	SA legislation	Embryos: 5 years, with option to renew consent for a further 5 years Gametes: Time limit specified by person; clinics also must have policy

Legislation and / or Guidelines	Cth	NHMRC	NSW	QLD	SA	TAS	VIC	WA	ACT	NT	RTAC
Donor limit	N/A	Unspecified. Emphasises importance of limiting number of genetic relatives for both donors and offspring	RTAC guidelines	RTAC guidelines	10 offspring	RTAC guidelines	10 families	5 families, except with RTC approval in exceptional circumstances	RTAC guidelines	SA legislation	10 families
Record-keeping for donor offspring	N/A	Requirement to uphold the right to knowledge of genetic parents and siblings	Bill proposes register to be kept; not retrospective	No specific provisions – no records required to be made accessible. Clinic decision. RTAC and NHMRC guidelines	Licensee to maintain records of donors. Access to non-identifying information is available for offspring	Clinic decision	Central register established to record information about donors and offspring. Offspring have a right to access identifying information; other parties may access with consent. Voluntary register established to address needs of offspring and donors not covered by legislation	Register to be kept by the Commissioner of Health. Records to be kept by licensees. Record the identity of offspring and donor, and identity of parents of the child. Confidentiality of information assured. Voluntary register established 2003	Clinic decision	SA legislation	No disclosure of patient or donor identifying information, except with the person's written consent. But also stresses child's right to know their genetic parents

Legislation and/or Guidelines	Cth	NHMRC	NSW	QLD	SA	TAS	VIC	WA	ACT	NT	RTAC
Legislative definition of "parentage" in donor procedures	Family Law Act 1975	N/A	Artificial Conception Act 1984		Family Relationships Amendment Act 1984 Ibid	Status of Children Act – Amendment 1985	Status of Children Amendment Act 1984 Ibid	Artificial Conception Act 1985 Ibid	Parentage Act 2004	Status of Children Amendment Act 1985	N/A
Informed decision-making	N/A	Specific provisions, eg consent in writing, medical practitioners' responsibility, adequate information, providing for counselling	RTAC and NHMRC guidelines	RTAC and NHMRC guidelines	Specific provisions in relation to consent and consent forms. Information Statement Standards specified – written information that must be distributed	RTAC and NHMRC guidelines	Specific requirements for consent outlined in ITAs. Conditions for Licence and in the Act. Prescribed matters to be covered in counselling specified in regulations. Counselling mandatory	Specific requirements outlined in the Act. Guidelines in relation to information, consent and counselling. Differentiate information giving, counselling and consent	RTAC and NHMRC guidelines	SA legislation	Mandatory for patients to be fully and comprehensively informed, both verbally and in writing of all aspects of their specific treatment. Mandatory for ART units to have a consent process
Research	Research Involving Human Embryos Act 2002 and Prohibition of Human Cloning Act 2002 – apply to all of Australia and over-ride State legislation	Part C of 2004 ART ethical guidelines	Human Cloning and Other Prohibited Practices Act 2003; Research Involving Human Embryos (New South Wales) Act 2003	Research Involving Human Embryos and Prohibition of Human Cloning Act 2003	Research Involving Human Embryos Act 2003 (SA); Prohibition of Human Cloning Act 2003 (SA)	Human Embryonic Research Regulation Act 2003	Health Legislation (Research involving Human Embryos and Prohibition of Human Cloning) Act 2003	Human Reproductive Technology Amendment Act 2004; Acts Amendment (Prohibition of Human Cloning and Other Practices) Act 2004	Human Cloning and Embryo Research Act 2004	Common-wealth legislation	N/A

Legislation and / or Guidelines	Cth	NHMRC	NSW	QLD	SA	TAS	VIC	WA	ACT	NT	RTAC
Preimplantation genetic diagnosis (PGD)	N/A	Advises serious consideration; prohibits selection in favour of genetic defect or disability; limits tissue matching to be for the benefit of siblings only; requires specialist genetics counselling	NHMRC guidelines	NHMRC guidelines	Permitted since 1991 within research protocols with ethics committee approval, monitoring, and licensing by SA Council on Reproductive Technology. Moving towards recognition of current uses as clinical practice	NHMRC guidelines	Permitted where a socialist geneticist is satisfied that a genetic abnormality or a disease may be transmitted to a child. Cannot be used to select in favour of disability. ITA policy specifies various requirements for different applications	Can be licensed by the Reproductive Technology Council where "there is a significant risk of a serious genetic abnormality or disease being present in the embryo"	NHMRC guidelines	SA	None specified. Compliance with NHMRC guidelines required for accreditation
Sex selection	N/A	Must not be undertaken by any means except to reduce the risk of transmission of a serious genetic condition	NHMRC guidelines	NHMRC guidelines	No prohibition specified in legislation; however, compliance with NHMRC guidelines required for a licence, therefore prohibited		Illegal to sex select except to avoid transmission of a genetic abnormality or a disease	Not permitted	NHMRC guidelines	SA	No prohibition specified. ART units required to abide by NHMRC ART ethical guidelines, which prohibit non-medical sex selection

213

Legislation and / or Guidelines	Cth	NHMRC	NSW	QLD	SA	TAS	VIC	WA	ACT	NT	RTAC
Posthumous use of gametes and embryos	N/A	Clearly expressed and witnessed directions consenting to posthumous use by the deceased; counselling; consideration by clinical ethics committee.	NHMRC guidelines	NHMRC guidelines	No blanket prohibition. Sperm can be used if both husband and wife have consented to the use of the sperm in the event of the death of the husband. In such cases, the woman must be medically infertile to be eligible for treatment as a single woman	NHMRC guidelines	Embryos may be transferred after death of husband. Husband's consent to post-humous use is required to form embryos and woman must be eligible for treatment as a single woman. Counselling and written consent of donors and recipients required for post-humous use of donated gametes. Insemination of a woman with sperm from a man known to be dead prohibited	Use of gametes from a person know to be deceased prohibited	NHMRC guidelines	SA	None specified. Compliance with NHMRC guidelines required for accreditation

Legislation and / or Guidelines	Cth	NHMRC	NSW	QLD	SA	TAS	VIC	WA	ACT	NT	RTAC
Surrogacy	NA	Prohibits commercial surrogacy. In States where altruistic surrogacy is not prohibited, clinics must ensure information and counselling. Clinicians must not advertise a service to facilitate surrogacy nor receive a fee for services to facilitate surrogacy arrangements	No explicit laws but: birth parents registered as parents; adoption – do not facilitate adoption in surrogacy – refer the matter to the Family Court	*Surrogate Parenthood Act 1988*. Offence to make or seek surrogacy arrangement. Surrogacy agreements unenforceable	Contracts non-legal and void, but no penalties imposed. Rely on *Family Relationships Act 1975* to define parentage of children which poses an impediment	*Surrogacy Contracts Act 1993*. Offence to make or seek surrogacy arrangement. Surrogacy agreements unenforceable Offence to offer support or assistance for such an arrangement	Surrogacy agreements void. Illegal to advertise or receive payment for surrogacy arrangement. Birth parents registered as parents, commis–sioning couple regarded as donors under ITA. Surrogate (and partner) must be eligible for treatment including meeting eligibility requirement for donor treatment	No specific legislation. Rely on common law provisions. Also view that surrogacy is against public policy and therefore any contracts are void	*Parentage Act 2004*. Surrogacy agreements unenforceable, but can form the basis for the Supreme Court to issue a Parentage Order transferring parentage from the birth parents to the commissioning parents. Child must not be genetically related to the surrogate or her partner, and must be genetically related to at least one of the commis–sioning parents	SA	None specified. Compliance with NHMRC guidelines required for accreditation

11

Genetic technologies and ART: Ethical values, legal regulation and informal regulation

Kerry Petersen[1]

Introduction

The world's first two babies created with the assistance of in vitro fertilisation (IVF) technologies were born in Britain in the 1970s (1978 and 1979) and the third in Australia in 1980. It is estimated that in Britain 1 per cent of all children are conceived though IVF,[2] and in Australia the figure is 2.7 per cent.[3] In the early days, many feared the potential of the "reproductive revolution".[4] However, some assisted reproductive technologies (ARTs) have become accepted by both society and the medical profession over the last few decades, and are now regarded more as routine clinical procedures[5] with broadly standardised scientific and clinical methodology. Nevertheless, ARTs raise issues concerned with both individual freedoms and the status of the human embryo, both of which continue to be contentious.

1   I would like to thank the Menzies Centre for Australian Studies for awarding me an Australian Bicentennial Fellowship and the Fertility Society of Australia for a research grant enabling me to visit the Centre for Family Research, University of Cambridge and conduct research on ART developments. I would also like to thank Professors Martin Johnson and Martin Richards for assistance with research in the United Kingdom, Dennis Warren, Law Librarian, La Trobe University for library support and Lexi Neame, Senior Research and Policy Officer of the Victorian Infertility Treatment Authority, for help with some aspects of this chapter.

2   United Kingdom, House of Commons, Science and Technology Committee, *Human Reproductive Technologies and the Law*, Fifth Report of Session 2004–2005, Written Evidence, Memorandum from British Fertility Society, para 3(b) (2004).

3   See Bryant, J, Sullivan, EA and Dean, JH, *Assisted reproductive technology in Australian and New Zealand 2002*, AIHW National Perinatal Statistics Unit, 2004, <www.npsu.unsw.edu.au/art8high.htm> (accessed 13 February 2006).

4   This term was coined in the 1980s by Singer and Wells. See, Singer P and Wells, D, *The Reproductive Revolution*, Oxford University Press, Oxford, 1984.

5   United Kingdom, House of Commons, Science and Technology Committee *Human Reproductive Technologies and the Law*, Fifth Report of Session 2004–2005, Vol 1, para 391 (hereafter the United Kingdom Science and Technology Committee (2004–2005); HMSO *Government Response to the Report from the House of Commons Science and Technology Committee: Human Reproductive Technologies and the Law*, Cm6641, 2005, para 4 (hereinafter United Kingdom Government Response (2005)).

Many of the early fears and social concerns about ART have been realised as these technologies have contributed to changing views of parenthood and new patterns of family formation.[6] Laws and clinical practices restricting access to infertility treatment to married heterosexual couples have been eased due to discrimination laws[7] and changing social attitudes. However, while this has facilitated greater acceptance of non-conventional families, it has also posed further legal problems.[8]

In this chapter, I review the informal and formal regulatory controls that have been placed upon ART, particularly genetic technologies, in Australia and consider the relationship between ethical principles and legal and informal regulation. An examination of this relationship is central because although informal regulatory instruments such as codes of practice and ethical guidelines are highly appropriate tools for the control of professional activities for a host of reasons, they are not legal instruments and not subject to the same controls.

In the recent case, *YZ v Infertility Treatment Authority*[9] Morris J emphasised that the National Health and Medical Research Council (NHMRC) ART Guidelines[10] "do not have the same status as a statute; and should not be interpreted or applied like a statute". He added: "The guidelines are intended to be just that – guidelines".[11]

These dicta raise some critical issues for the control of ART practice because informal regulatory instruments play an integral and significant role in Australia. As both formal and informal regulation can have serious consequences for human rights, freedoms and interests in ART practice, ways of incorporating and enforcing process requirements such as accountability and transparency into all areas of ART regulation need to be given a high priority.

From IVF to genetic technologies

By the 1990s, the concept of parental choice took on a new dimension as the science of IVF developed to the stage where clinicians could screen and select embryos on the basis of the genetic information obtained from biopsied embryonic cells. The information obtained from pre-implantation genetic diagnosis (PGD) provides an alternative to prenatal testing for those at risk of transmitting a genetic condition. The public response to PGD has been mixed and much of the controversy is generated by the fear that it will be used to create so-called

6   Johnson, M, "A Biomedical Perspective on Parenthood" in Bainham, A Sclater, SD and M Richards *What is a Parent? A Socio-Legal Analysis*, Hart Publishing, Oxford, 1999, p 49.
7   *McBain v Victoria* (2000) 99 FCR 116.
8   See Victorian Law Reform Commission, *Assisted Reproductive Technology & Adoption: Parentage*, Position Paper No 2, p 17; *Re Patrick* [2002] FLC 93-096.
9   [2005] VCAT 2655.
10   NHMRC, *Ethical Guidelines on the Use of Assisted Reproductive Technology in Clinical Practice and Research*, NHMRC, Canberra, 2004.
11   [2005] VCAT 2655 at [68].

"designer babies". Nevertheless, individuals and families at risk of transmitting genetic disorders are considering this option more frequently. In 2004, a Westpoll survey, published in *The West Australian* reported that 88 per cent of the respondents supported genetic testing and only 9 per cent supported banning it in all circumstances. The survey also found that "young people and men (rather than women)" were more likely to believe that screening should not be subject to restrictions. Additionally, people living in the country were more likely to be opposed to all screening than those living in the metropolitan area.[12] In the 2004 Annual Report of the Victorian Infertility Treatment Authority (ITA), it was noted that applications for PGD were increasing as "the capacity to identify specific single gene defects in embryos develops".[13] There are no national figures in Australia about the incidence of PGD, but it is gradually increasing.[14]

Before embryo screening and selection became available, options for individuals and families suffering from serious genetic disorders were limited. They could decide not to have a family, adopt a child, have a child by donation or take their chances. Alternatively, they could undertake prenatal diagnosis during pregnancy and decide whether or not to terminate the pregnancy in the event of an adverse diagnosis. This can be a particularly burdensome path for both partners, but particularly for a woman who may undergo more than one abortion before conceiving a healthy foetus. This path is also predicated on the availability of lawful and affordable abortion.

Furthermore, as Bennett reminds us, terminating an unwanted pregnancy can be hard enough for many women, but to terminate a wanted pregnancy is much more difficult and the grieving process even more painful.[15] The Australian fertility clinic, Monash IVF, introduced PGD into all its clinics in 2001 and it was noted that, "[c]ouples choose PGD for many reasons including objections to the termination of pregnancy, previous pregnancy terminations or loss of a child from the diseases".[16] As PGD is an alternative to the other choices previously mentioned, it seems ethically questionable not to present this avenue to the people concerned for their consideration. Nevertheless, it must be recognised

---

12 Cited in the Western Australia Reproductive Technology Council, *Annual Report* 2004, p 28.

13 Infertility Treatment Authority, Victoria, *Genetic Testing and the Requirements of the Infertility Treatment Act 1995: Policy in Relation to the Use of Preimplantation Genetic Diagnosis for Genetic Testing*, ITA, 2004.

14 The Victorian ITA reported that in 2003 the total number of cycles where PGD was performed for known genetic risk was 39 and for IVF and pregnancy failure 142; and in 2004 the total number of cycles where PGD was performed for known genetic risk was 45 and for IVF and pregnancy failure 1188 in 2004. The United Kingdom Human Fertilisation and Embryology Authority (HFEA) reported about 200 PGD treatments per year in the United Kingdom see, HFEA *Choices & Boundaries*, 2005, p 7.

15 Bennett, B, "Prenatal Diagnosis, Genetics and Reproductive Decision-making" (2001) 9 *Journal of Law and Medicine* 28 at 38. See also Rothman, BK *The Tentative Pregnancy: Amniocentesis and the Sexual Politics of Motherhood*, Pandora, London, 1988.

16 Monash IVF, Fact Sheet, <www.monashivf.edu.au/library/vicfertility/fertility-7.html> (accessed 13 February 2006).

that PGD is a long and complex process, which may fail at all stages. Pregnancy rates are low and there is no guarantee that the embryos selected will not carry diseases.[17] Although there is relatively little evidence about the safety of PGD, particularly in the long term, it has been found that "the incidence of birth abnormalities is not significantly higher in children born by these techniques than the general population".[18] It is therefore important that people considering this option are offered genetic counselling and medical information so they can make a fully informed decision after all the risks and possible outcomes of the procedure has been thoroughly considered.[19]

Reasons for screening and selecting embryos

There are four main reasons for undertaking pre-implantation genetic diagnosis (PGD) and these reasons reflect the trajectory of a technique that has been developed to prevent and cure heritable diseases and can now be applied for a range of broader purposes.[20]

The first reason is to select an embryo which is unaffected by an inherited disease. This involves creating several embryos in order to screen them for serious genetic conditions and selecting those that are unaffected for implantation. The information obtained from PGD permits people with known heritable genetic conditions in their families to have the chance of a healthy child and avoid the risk of the condition being transmitted to the next generation.

The second reason is to select an embryo that is more likely to implant and develop in the uterus. The purpose of pre-implantation genetic screening (PGS) is to screen the embryos for aneuploidy (abnormal number of chromosomes) and to select those embryos for implantation which appear relatively unaffected so as to reduce the risk of miscarriage and enhance the chances of a successful term pregnancy.

PGS is generally used when there is a higher risk than average of the woman conceiving abnormal embryos or miscarrying and is generally sought by women over 35 years or where there is a history of a multiple miscarriages.

The third reason for embryo typing and selection is to identify an embryo that is a tissue match for an existing sick person. The purpose of pre-implantation tissue typing (PTT) is to test for histocompatibility leukocyte antigen (HLA) (sometimes in conjunction with PGD where there is also a genetic risk factor). This is so that the embryo, when developed to a child (the so-called

---

17   United Kingdom, Human Genetics Commission, *Making Babies: Reproductive Decisions and Genetic Technologies*, 2006.

18   Ibid, para 4.13.

19   Pennings, G, Schots, R, and Liebaers, I, "Ethical Considerations on Preimplantation Genetic Diagnosis for HLA Typing to Match a Future Child as a Donor of Haematopoietic Stem Cells to a Sibling" (2002) 17 (3) *Human Reproduction* 534 at 536.

20   United Kingdom Science and Technology Committee (2004–2005) op cit, para 120.

saviour sibling)[21] can supply a source of stem cells from the cord blood, and potentially from the bone marrow to assist a person, usually a sibling, who is suffering from a serious medical condition.

The fourth reason is to select an embryo with a desired biological or physical characteristic. The purpose here would be to determine the sex, physical characteristics or possibly the intelligence of a born child.

Increasingly, PGD/PGS is being used to avoid the transmission of a heritable gene for serious disorders or to improve the chances of a successful pregnancy. Testing and excluding embryos with lower and variant penetrance medical conditions, where not everyone with the faulty gene will develop the condition and/or where the symptoms may not become manifest until adulthood, is being considered by more and more people, even though discarding embryos in these circumstances is ethically contentious.[22] Selecting embryos for the benefit of another, albeit a seriously ill person and selecting embryos for non-therapeutic reasons, are highly controversial practices because the embryo is being used as a means to an end and reawakens fears of a *Brave New World* society.[23]

Genetic technologies: Social and ethical background

State intervention in the area of human reproduction is controversial and it is unlikely that there will ever be consensus on the role of the state in reproductive decision-making or the level of protection to be given to the embryo. Drawing on a range of Western philosophies and jurisprudence, the Warnock Committee supported claims to reproductive freedoms and distinguished the issue of infertility treatment and establishing a family from the issue of human embryo research, on the ground that the former belongs to the private domain and the latter to the public domain. It was stated that:

> In the case of treating infertility, or of establishing a family, there was a fairly strong view that the freedom of the individual to take what steps he could ought to be respected. ... In the case of research, on the other hand, there was general agreement that the issue of individual liberty did not arise.[24]

The freedom to establish a family

Ethical values, such as the freedom to establish a family, underpin support for using PGD as it can be argued that establishing a *healthy* family is a logical

---

21   This unfortunate term has now become commonplace and is borrowed from Spriggs, M and Savulescu, J, "Saviour Siblings" (2002) 28 *Journal Medical Ethics* 289.

22   See HFEA (2005) op cit.

23   See also the chilling futuristic depiction of women and motherhood in Margaret Atwood's *The Handmaid's Tale*, Virago, London, 1985.

24   HMSO, A *Question of Life: The Warnock Report on Human Fertilisation and Embryology*, 1984, Introduction, p xiv (hereinafter Warnock Report).

extension to that freedom. However, this freedom is not a right per se; rather it is an interest, which constrains society from interfering with the exercise of reproductive choice without justification.[25] The more benefits that are attached to an activity, the more necessary it is for protagonists to demonstrate widely accepted and established ethical objections in order to justify restrictions. This demonstration requires evidence that the alleged harms to society outweigh individual or social benefits.[26] A distinction is often drawn between therapeutic and non-therapeutic justifications. Thus, the justification for constraining reproductive freedom is harder to demonstrate if PGD is used for therapeutic purposes, as medical harms and benefits are generally more identifiable and quantifiable than social ones. However, prioritising medical benefits over social benefits is not necessarily the better or even an acceptable approach, and the distinction between the two is not always clear. For example, would it be ethical to support the use of PGD to screen for genes connected to depression or obesity or homosexuality or even infertility – remembering that infertility was once regarded as a social problem?

While it is generally accepted that society must justify an intrusion on personal liberties belonging to the private domain, the principles underlying the onus and burden of proof are undefined and unclear. The House of Commons Science and Technology Committee has recommended that the onus should be on prohibitionists to provide evidence of harm. The committee stated that the regulation of "reproductive and research freedoms must be balanced against the interests of society but the alleged harms to society too, should be based on evidence".[27] Adding that justification for interference with liberties should proceed under the precautionary principle prevalent in scientific research and clinical practice, requiring "that alleged harms to society or to patients [should] be demonstrated before forward progress is unduly impeded".[28] The *Government Response to the Report from the House of Commons Science and Technology Committee*[29] was more restrictive and interpreted the precautionary principle as requiring harms to society to include consideration of potential harms to future offspring.[30] The Government Response is generally more in line with various regulatory mandates which promote the welfare of children born as a result of assisted reproduction. The burden of proving potential harm to future people in these circumstances is based on conjecture, albeit usually expert conjecture, and therefore a seriously onerous hurdle.

---

25   *Secretary, Department of Health and Community services v JWB and SMB* (1992) 175 CLR 218 (*Marion's* case).

26   The House of Common Science and Technology Committee recommended that claims of alleged harms to society "should be based on evidence" see United Kingdom Science and Technology Committee (2004–2005) op cit, para 46.

27   Ibid.

28   Ibid, para 47.

29   United Kingdom Government Response (2005) op cit.

30   Ibid, paras 5–6.

While it may be risky to "wait and see" what harms, if any may eventuate, this must be balanced against the risks attached to imposing a constraint on the reproductive freedom of existing people to make choice, when there is no evidence of harm.

The protection to be afforded an embryo

Debate on the status of the human embryo, and the protection it should be afforded at different stages of development, was an issue for the Warnock Committee in the early 1980s and remains one for contemporary regulators. In spite of considerable opposition from "absolutists", the gradualist or developmental approach articulated by the Warnock Committee has dominated ethical debate and underscored regulation in Australia and Britain. The Warnock Committee was not prepared to confer full human rights on an embryo nor was it prepared to treat the embryo as a collection of cells with human potential. Instead it viewed the development of personhood as a gradual process, which conferred some protection on the embryo, and stated that "unlike a full human being, [the embryo] may be legitimately used as a means to an end that was good for other humans, both now and in the future".[31]

Two decades later, the House of Commons Science and Technology Committee endorsed the gradualist approach and stated that:

> While this gradualist approach to the status of the embryo may cause difficulties in the drafting of legislation, we believe that it represents the most ethically sound and pragmatic solution and one which permits in vitro fertilisation and embryo research within certain constraints set out in legislation.[32]

The Australian Senate of the Community Affairs Legislative Committee chose a "third way" between the denial of any moral status to the embryo and the full conferral of human rights on the embryo.[33] This is similar to the gradualist approach and is reflected in the *Research Involving Human Embryos Act 2002* (Cth). Most of this debate has taken place in the context of embryo research but it is also relevant to the debate on PGD.

The debate over the protection to be afforded to the embryo and the issue of discarding embryos for eugenic reasons are major arguments against using PGD. Those who absolutely oppose the creation and destruction of embryos in ART programs, as well as those who hold less entrenched views but are particularly concerned about eugenic issues, oppose PGD on these grounds. As Robertson says, "PGD is ethically controversial because it involves the screening and likely

---

31 Warnock Report (1984) op cit, Introduction p xv.
32 United Kingdom Science and Technology Committee (2004–2005) op cit, Recommendation 1.
33 Parliament of Australia, Report of the Senate Committee Affairs Legislation Committee, *Provisions of the Research Involving Embryos and Prohibition of Human Embryo Cloning Bill 2002*, ch 3.

destruction of embryos, and the selection of offspring on the basis of expected traits".[34] The "gradualist" approach, which gives some protection to the embryo, is reflected in the procedures that have been developed by Australian regulators and the Human Fertilisation and Embryology Authority (HFEA) governing PGD practices.

Applications: PGD and PTT

The potential benefits of reducing the risk of transmitting a heritable genetic disease for individuals, families and society are particularly high and long-term harm is as yet unknown.[35] PGD (including PGS) is therefore accepted as ethical if used for the benefit of the born child. Beyond this, however, there are other very real concerns about an embryo being used as a means to an end, the potential for embryos to be seen as "products" or "commodities", the potential for selection to be based on "trivial" characteristics, and for reproductive discrimination on disability grounds.[36]

The debate over PTT is complex because the procedure is not undertaken for the benefit of the born child, but is used to meet the needs of an existing, albeit seriously ill person, who is usually a sibling. Much of the public debate is based on compassion for the sick person. However, those who support using PTT argue that the born child will belong to a family and all family members will collectively benefit if the sick member becomes healthy. Some would use this argument to support people who want to implant an embryo with a genetic disorder, such as deafness, for the benefit of a deaf family on the grounds that the justification for interfering with reproductive choice in this case is similar to that for PTT, because it is prima facie unethical to create an embryo for the benefit of another (or others). However, others may adopt a different tack and argue that intentionally creating an unhealthy embryo for the collective benefit of a family is quite different from creating a healthy embryo for the collective benefit because of the strong ethical imperative requiring a doctor not to harm a patient. Nevertheless, views on these questions are diverse and it can also be argued that PTT is possibly and potentially harmful. The assessment of harm is difficult in the case of PTT because the effects on the child born in these circumstances are impossible to assess. And who is speaking on behalf of the existing sick child? In Britain and Australia, this procedure is restricted to seriously ill siblings and not allowed for purposes of treating other seriously ill family members.

Fear of the "slippery slope" is less relevant to PGD and PTT because the impact of PGD, unlike IVF, is likely to be quite restricted while there are few

---

34   Robertson, J, "Extending Preimplantation Genetic Diagnosis: Medical and Non-medical Uses" (2003) 29 *Journal of Medical Ethics* 213.

35   Rhodes, R, "Ethical Issues in Selecting Embryos" (2001) *Annals of the New York Academy of Sciences* 360.

36   Department of Health, *Review of the Human Fertilisation and Embryology Act: A Public Consultation*, 2005, chap 5.

diseases for which single gene predispositions are known.[37] In addition, relatively few parents will have to decide whether or not to conceive another child in order to provide an existing sibling with matched stem cells. As the Human Genetics Commission pointed out:

> The anxiety that PGD lies at the top of the slippery slope leading to the possibility of a wide range of potential enhancements, such as intelligence and beauty is misplaced. While we are still far from a full understanding of how such characteristics are transmitted to children, it is clear that very many genes are likely to be involved and there will be complex interactions between these and other developmental factors. Even if all the genes to be involved were identified, prediction of the required characteristics would remain uncertain and the limited supply of embryos available for selection would make the finding of particular gene variant combinations very unlikely.[38]

In the United Kingdom, the debate over PTT has been more public and volatile than in Australia with litigation over the application of reproductive genetic technologies and public disquiet about the "gate-keeping" role of the HFEA. The practice of PGD is not expressly included in the *Human Fertilisation and Embryology Act 1990* (UK) but it is licensed by the HFEA and the Code of Practice (sixth edition) imposes conditions on its use.[39] In July 2004, the HFEA agreed to grant licences for tissue typing[40] and the House of Lords has confirmed that the HFEA has power to determine fundamental ethical issues about the use of PGD and to license PGD in combination with tissue typing for the benefit of a seriously ill sibling within the meaning of para (1)(d) of Sch 2 of the HFE Act.[41]

Applications:
Sex and other characteristics

Using PGD for sex selection is usually accepted as ethical in cases where there are sex-linked disorders, because the procedure is being used for the benefit of the embryo. However, using genetic technologies to choose the sex of children according to the personal preference of the parent is highly controversial because it is argued the choice is made to gratify parental wishes rather than for the benefit of the born child.[42] The desire of parents to choose the sex of children is not new and traditional

---

37   Robertson (2003) op cit.

38   United Kingdom, Human Genetics Commission, *Making Babies: Reproductive Decisions and Genetic Technologies*, 2006, para 31.

39   *Human Fertilisation and Embryology Act 1990* (UK) ss 3(1), 11, 13 and Sch 2 para 1.1(d).

40   HFEA, <www.hfea.gov.United Kingdom/PressOffice/archive/1090427358> (accessed 30 January 2006).

41   *Quintavalle v Human Fertilisation and Embryology Authority* [2005] UKHL 28.

42   For further discussion on the reasons for opposing sex selection on social grounds see Williamson, S, "Sex (ist) Selection" (2004) *Medical Law International* 185; Dickens, B, "Can Sex Selection be Ethically Tolerated? (2002) 28 *Journal of Medical Ethics* 335; Savulescu, J and Dahl, E 'Sex Selection and Preimplantation Diagnosis (2000) (15) 9 *Human Reproduction* 1879.

techniques have been practised for centuries and did not attract regulation – probably because there was no proof that the techniques worked.[43] Societal attitudes towards prenatal sex selection testing have been ambivalent because once the woman has the information, she (and her partner) can choose whether or not to continue with the pregnancy.[44] The use of PGD offers people the opportunity to choose the sex of their future child from the outset and avoid abortion. There are mixed views on the issue[45] and the literature is extensive. For the purposes of this chapter I would like to make a few brief observations only. New reproductive technologies continue to trigger fears of the unknown as well as concerns about the potential for "unnatural, harmful outcomes, social disruption, and destruction of conventional families".[46] Even though attempts to select the sex of offspring are not new, it is probable that now it can be done public attitudes are influenced by a fear of the possibilities. For example, it is common for people to oppose social sex selection because of the apprehension that it will distort the natural sex ratio and lead to a severe gender imbalance. Sex selection policies in China and India are often cited as illustrations of "demographic disasters" because people overwhelmingly choose sons if the opportunity arises. However, this overlooks cultural differences and the research which has found that people in Western countries generally want a child of a particular sex for "family balancing" reasons.[47] Authoritative empirical studies have not been undertaken in Australia and sex selection is now banned by the NHMRC ART Guidelines (2004). It has been reported that prior to the ban, there was some interest in seeking the procedure but there was no evidence that male children were the preferred choice. It was stated that:

> [T]he number of parents using PGD for sex selection has increased four-fold in three years. More than 250 couples have had sex selection done at Sydney IVF since 1995, with 120 of them in 2002. About one third resulted in a pregnancy. ... Despite fears that parents would choose only boys, the Director of PGD at Sydney IVF, Dr Kylie de Boer, says that 64% wanted a girl and when only one parent wanted to select the sex, it was nearly always a mother who wanted a daughter.[48]

---

43   Traditional sex selection techniques such as herbal medicines, sexual positions and the timing of sexual intercourse have been commonly used for centuries. See, Williamson (2004) op cit.

44   For a discussion of abortion law in Australia in the context of prenatal diagnosis see, Bennett B, "Prenatal Diagnosis, Genetics and Reproductive Decision-making" (2001) 9 *Journal of Law and Medicine* 28.

45   In 2003, the HFEA ruled against sex selection for non-medical reasons after conducting a consultation which found an 80 per cent public disapproval rate, see HFEA *Sex Selection: Options for Regulation*, A Report of the HFEA's 2002–2003 Review of Sex Selection Including a Discussion of Legislative and Regulatory Options, HFEA, 2003.

46   Dickens, B, "Can Sex Selection be Ethically Tolerated? (2002) 28 *Journal of Medical Ethics* 335.

47   Dahl, E, Beutel, M, Brosig, B and Hinsch, KD, "Preconception Sex Selection for Non-medical Reasons: a Representative Survey from Germany" (2003) 18 (7) *Human Reproduction* 1368; Savulescu, J, "Sex Selection: the case for" (1999) 171 *MJA* 373.

48   Report from *Daily Telegraph* and cited in the Western Australia Reproductive Technology Council, *Annual Report*, 2004, p 28.

There has not been any significant public debate on social sex selection in Australia. However, in Britain the issue is very controversial.[49] The House of Commons, Science and Technology Committee recommended that the current evidence on family balancing should be examined carefully and the onus placed on those who oppose sex selection for social reasons using PGD to demonstrate harm from its use. The committee suggested that there should be more research into the matter and concluded that, "On balance we find no adequate justification for prohibiting the use of sex selection for family balancing".[50] The Government Response seeks to maintain the current prohibitions but to search for further information about sex selection for family balancing reasons.[51]

As people have increasingly sought the benefits offered by medicine and science to make reproductive choices about whether or not to have children, to limit family size, to overcome infertility and to prevent the transmission of heritable disease, the expectation of being able to control reproductive decision-making has increased and it is no longer plausible to claim that admission to life is unconditional. Prohibiting parents from choosing the sex of their children for social reasons is a constraint on the exercise of reproductive choice. However, as the procedure is used primarily for the parents and there are no overall social benefits, it can be argued that to discard embryos not of the desired sex in order to choose embryos of a particular sex is tantamount to treating an embryo as a commodity and thus restrictions are justifiable. But it can also be argued that it is similar to PTT insofar as the choice is made for the benefit of the family as a whole – particularly, as there is evidence that most people seek to use this technique to balance their families. Furthermore, it is different from intentionally creating a born child with a genetic disorder, as no harm is intended. Using PGD to select an embryo on the basis of physical and intellectual characteristics or biological advantage is highly contentious because it is has the potential for born children to be treated as a means of parental self-expression rather than human beings in their own right. Therefore it is easier to justify constraints being imposed. Nevertheless, this is a less practicable application of the technologies and is more remote as the genetic basis for many of these desirable characteristics is not well understood and involves multiple genes. The Human Genetics Committee noted that "for practical reasons, the number of conditions for which PGD can be offered is limited and few tests can be done on the DNA extracted from a single cell taken from an embryo".[52] The non-therapeutic uses of PGD,

---

49   After conducting a review of sex selection the HFEA found that people in Britain were opposed to sex selection for social reasons and recommended that sex selection should not be permitted. See, HFEA *Sex Selection: Options for Regulation*, A Report of the HFEA's 2002–2003 Review of Sex Selection Including a Discussion of Legislative and Regulatory Options, HFEA, 2003.

50   United Kingdom Science and Technology Committee (2004–2005) op cit, para 142.

51   United Kingdom Government Response (2005) op cit, para 45.

52   United Kingdom, Human Genetics Commission, *Making Babies: Reproductive Decisions and Genetic Technologies*, 2006, para 31.

other than for sex selection, are not likely "to be practically feasible for at least a decade or more".[53] As the House of Common Science and Technology Committee has pointed out, the debate is largely an academic and philosophic one at this stage.[54]

Australia: Regulatory overview[55]

In Australia, control over ART was removed from the privacy of the therapeutic relationship relatively early and clinical practice and research have been subject to regulation for some time – unlike most other areas of medicine. ART regulation is a maze of interlocking professional, bureaucratic, ethical and legal controls.[56] Informal regulation such as professional accreditation, licensing and ethical guidelines, play an important role in the national framework. The Fertility Society of Australia (FSA) through its Reproductive Technology Accreditation Committee (RTAC) is responsible for the accreditation of ART units; and the NHMRC through its principal committee, the Australian Health Ethics Committee (AHEC), provides ethical guidelines for clinics and research centres. The pattern of legal regulation is a product of federalism. The Commonwealth has passed laws prohibiting human cloning and permitting embryo stem cell research, but infertility treatment is left to the six States and two Territories.

The States of Victoria, South Australia and Western Australia have passed ART statutes. The Victorian *Infertility Treatment Act 1995* is administered by the ITA which is an "arms length" statutory body. In contrast, legislation in South Australia and Western Australia is complemented by codes of practice and directions. In South Australia, the *Reproductive Technology (Clinical Practices) Act 1988* (SA) is administered jointly by the South Australia Council on Reproductive Technology (SACRT) and the Department of Human Services.[57] In Western Australia, the Commissioner of Health sets the standards of practice under the *Human Reproductive Technology Act 1991* (WA) on the advice of the Western Australian Reproductive Technology Council (WARTC). The remaining States and Territories regulate through miscellaneous laws and professional controls.[58] It is not clear why only three States have passed ART statutes, but legal diversity is a

---

53 Ibid.

54 United Kingdom Science and Technology Committee (2004–2005) op cit, para 143.

55 For further discussion on the regulatory framework see, Petersen, K, Pitts, M, Baker, HW and Thorpe, R, "Assisted Reproductive technologies: Professional and Legal Restrictions in Australian Clinics" (2005) 12 *Journal of Law and Medicine* 366.

56 Chalmers, D, "Professional Self-regulation and Guidelines in Assisted Reproduction" (2002) 9 *Journal of Law and Medicine* 414.

57 See <www.dh.sa.gov.au/reproductive-technology/legislation.asp> (accessed 20 January 2006).

58 In 2002, the Commonwealth Parliament introduced federal laws prohibiting human cloning and permitting embryo stem cell research in restricted circumstances. *Prohibition of Human Cloning Act 2002* (Cth); *Research Involving Human Embryos Act 2002* (Cth). Subsequently, the State and Territories have passed parallel laws further to a Council of Australian Governments (CoAG) agreement.

feature of federalism and it is not uncommon for States to have different laws on similar topics. This incoherent legal framework could be symptomatic of concerns about biotechnology, although it is more likely that it is an indication of the lack of consensus in the community about some of the ethical issues – particularly where the embryo is concerned. The NHMRC suggests that differences in "national, state and territory legislation reflects the variation of opinion and lack of consensus on many of these issues".[59]

Professional regulation

FSA Code of Practice

Since the 1980s the FSA through the RTAC has been involved in establishing and monitoring a system of self-regulation for ART clinics designed to regulate safety and promote high standards of health care in clinics through a code of practice. Non-compliance with the RTAC Code of Practice can lead to a review and possible suspension of a unit's accreditation.[60]

If there are differences between the RTAC Code of Practice and other legal and professional controls, the general rule is that national legislation overrides State legislation, and legislation overrides regulation. As part of the integrated system of informal regulation, the RTAC Code of Practice requires ART units to comply with relevant legal regulation and the NHMRC ART Guidelines (2004).[61]

NHMRC ART Guidelines (2004)

In 1996, the NHMRC through the AHEC issued the first ethical guidelines on ART and in 2004 these were replaced by the current guidelines.[62] The AHEC consists of a chairperson and members with expertise relevant to the functions of the committee who are nominated by representative organisations such as peak religious bodies and public health bodies. The members are appointed by the Commonwealth Minister of Health and Ageing after consultation with the Health Minister of each State and Territory. Members of the AHEC advise the NHMRC, and the NHMRC is accountable to the Commonwealth Minister of Health. This process is not transparent and there are no means of challenging provisions in the Guidelines.

In the 1996 ART Ethical Guidelines, the NHMRC recommended that New South Wales, Queensland and Tasmania as well as the Australian Capital

---

59 NHMRC ART Guidelines (2004) op cit, Appendix C: C1.

60 Fertility Society of Australia, Reproductive Technology Accreditation Committee, *Code of Practice for Assisted Reproductive Technology Units*, revised February 2005, pp 15, 21.

61 Ibid, 1.17, 1.18.

62 NHMRC, *Ethical Guidelines on Assisted Reproductive Technology*, NHMRC, 1996; NHMRC ART Guidelines (2004) op cit.

Territory and Northern Territory[63] should pass ART legislation. As the NHMRC viewed "surrogacy, eligibility, consent for posthumous use, preimplantation diagnosis and sex selection" as social and political issues beyond its remit at that time, the clinics were able to adopt their own ethical standards subject to relevant State legislation, that is, until the most recent NHMRC ART Guidelines were issued in 2004.[64] As already noted, only three States have passed ART statutes in Australia.

In the NHMRC ART Guidelines (2004), the NHMRC has adopted a different approach to some of the issues which it had previously regarded as beyond its remit. In particular, the NHMRC earmarked genetic technology associated with ART and sex selection for non-medical reasons[65] for special consideration because "[e]ach of these practices affects people other than the person who has decided to use the technology. Each is properly a matter for community debate and discussion".[66]

The NHMRC ART Guidelines (2004) state that sex selection must not be undertaken pending further community discussion except to reduce the risk of transmission of a serious genetic condition. Accordingly, Australian clinicians are no longer permitted to offer this service and the justification for this restriction is that "admission to life should not be conditional upon a child being a particular sex".[67] On the other hand, admission to life may be conditional if tests on an embryo indicate that a born child will have a serious genetic condition and parents and doctors choose to use PGD, or in some cases, if there is a seriously ill existing child in the family.

The guidelines permit the use of PGD to detect serious genetic conditions and to improve ART outcomes. PGD and PTT may also be used to select an embryo with compatible tissue for a sibling with a life-threatening illness if there are no medical alternatives and the parents wish to have another child not just a source of tissue.[68] ART clinics must ensure that people seeking PGD testing have access to both clinical geneticists and genetic counsellors[69] and they are given up-to-date, objective, accurate information and provided with readily accessible services from accredited counsellors.[70] It is not clear if applications for inherited cancer conditions, which may not manifest until adulthood when treatment may be available, such as familial adenomatous polyposis (FAP) and some inherited

---

63 In the Northern Territory, South Australian clinicians provide ART services pursuant to guidelines mostly consistent with South Australian legislation.

64 For discussion about the differences between clinical practices in New South Wales and Victoria see Petersen et al (2005) op cit.

65 Surrogacy has also been included but is not being considered in this chapter.

66 NHMRC ART Guidelines (2004) op cit, Appendix C:C1.

67 NHMRC ART Guidelines (2004) op cit, para 11.1; see <www.sydneyivf.com/pages/pgd/sexselect.cfm> (accessed 20 January 2006).

68 NHMRC ART Guidelines (2004) op cit, para 12.

69 NHMRC ART Guidelines (2004) op cit, para 12.5.

70 NHMRC ART Guidelines (2004) op cit, paras 9, 12.

breast and ovarian cancers, qualify under these guidelines. The NHMRC has avoided ruling on applications for the more ethically controversial diseases describing them as "on the horizon".[71]

As the FSA Code of Practice requires ART clinics to comply with the NHMRC ART Guidelines, the NHMRC ART Guidelines recognise the FSA RTAC as the accreditation body for ART units and require clinics to comply with the standards contained in the code of practice.[72]

Legal regulation

Reproductive genetic technologies have been included in ART regulatory frameworks in countries such as Britain and Australia because these procedures are an extension of IVF and involve the embryo. There is minimal case law on ART in Australia and most of the litigation has been concerned with discriminatory eligibility provisions and post-mortem insemination. Unlike Britain, there have been no cases providing judicial guidance in the area of genetic technologies.[73] Clinical practice is regulated by the NHMRC ART Guidelines (2004) in jurisdictions where ART statutes have not been passed.

Victoria

Victoria set the precedent for regulating genetic technologies when the now repealed *Infertility (Medical Procedures) Act 1984* restricted IVF to infertile married couples except in cases where natural conception for fertile couples would cause "an undesirable hereditary disorder" to be "transmitted to a child born as a result of the pregnancy".[74] This exception laid the foundation for the uncontroversial passage of s 8(3)(b) in the substitute legislation, the *Infertility Treatment Act 1995* (Vic), which permits people to use PGD when a doctor with specialist qualifications in human genetics is satisfied that "a genetic abnormality or a disease might be transmitted to a person born as a result of the pregnancy".[75]

---

71 In the United Kingdom, the HFEA issued a licence for inherited colon cancer on 1 November 2005, <www.hfea.gov.United Kingdom/PressOffice/Archive/1099321195> (accessed 3 February 2006).

72 NHMRC ART Guidelines (2004) op cit, paras 1.5, 3.3.

73 *Quintavalle, R (on the application of) v Human Fertilisation and Embryology Authority* [2003] EWCA Civ 667; *Quintavalle v Human Fertilisation and Embryology Authority* [2005] UKHL 28.

74 *Infertility (Medical Procedures) Act 1984* (Vic) s 13(3)(d)(ii) (repealed).

75 Since the decision in *McBain v Victoria* (2000) 99 FCR 116, eligibility for infertility treatment is now based on clinical infertility or the genetic ground in s 8(3)(b) of the *Infertility Treatment Act 1995* (Vic). This would suggest that a single woman who is a carrier of a serious medical condition would be eligible for treatment even though the subsection refers to a woman or her husband. See VLRC, *Assisted Reproductive Technology & Adoption: Should the Current eligibility Criteria in Victoria be Changed?* Consultation Paper, 2004, paras 355–326.

The utilisation of embryo screening and selection procedures in Victoria has been greatly facilitated by the provision in the original Act which permitted access to IVF where natural conception for fertile couples could result in the transmission of a genetic disorder. The basic requirement that PGD cannot be offered unless the reason is to prevent transmitting a "genetic abnormality or disease" prevents PGD from being used for a "biological advantage" (for example intelligence) in Victoria. In addition, sex selection is prohibited for non-medical reasons but allowed if it is necessary to avoid the risk of transmitting a genetic abnormality or disease.[76]

Policies have been developed by the ITA in accordance with the four guiding principles, which are listed in descending order of importance as follows:

- the welfare and interest of the person born or to be born are paramount;
- human life should be preserved and protected;
- the interests of the family should be considered; and
- infertile couples should be assisted in fulfilling their desire to have children.[77]

The ITA will not authorise screening for affected embryos such as genetic deafness or dwarfism where the intention is to use the affected embryos. It has ruled that using PGD for conditions or abnormalities which will significant adversely affect the health of a person is not consistent the intention of the Act.[78]

In Victoria, applicants may utilise PGD, PGS and PTT procedures if they comply with the consent and counselling conditions and satisfy the eligibility requirements required for IVF. To be eligible, a woman (or heterosexual couple) must be "clinically infertile" or establish that the treatment is necessary in order to avoid the transmission of a genetic abnormality or disease.[79] As there is no legislative definition of the words "genetic abnormality or disease", the ITA takes the view that the Act vests responsibility for assessing the risk of transmission in a doctor who has specialist qualifications in human genetics.[80] If applicants are not "genetic carriers", they may be eligible on the "clinical infertility" ground if the purpose of genetic testing is to identify chromosomal abnormalities which may contribute to infertility. The Infertility Treatment Authority permits PGS and PGD to be used without special notification for

---

76   *Infertility Treatment Act 1995* (Vic) s 50.

77   Ibid, s 5; Peterson, K, "The Regulation of Assisted Reproductive Technology: A Comparative Study of Permissive and Prescriptive Laws and Policies" (2002) 9 *Journal of Law and Medicine* 483.

78   ITA, *Genetic Testing and the Requirements of the Infertility Treatment Act 1995: Policy in Relation to the Use of Preimplantation Genetic Diagnosis for Genetic Testing*, 2004, <www.ita.org.au> (accessed 20 January 2006).

79   *Infertility Treatment Act 1995* (Vic) s 8(3)(a) and (b). See also ITA, *Conditions for Licence: Applications for Licences by Hospitals and Day Procedure Centres*, 2002, para 2.2.1.

80   ITA, *Genetic Testing and the Requirements of the Infertility Treatment Act 1995: Policy in Relation to the Use of Preimplantation Genetic Diagnosis for Genetic Testing*, 2004, <www.ita.org.au> (accessed 20 January 2006).

medical indications set out in Lists A and B. List A sets out the cases where PGD can be used to detect chromosomal disorders and List B sets out cases where an embryo can be excluded because of sex-linked disorders, known chromosome re-arrangements, and single gene disorders of autosomes. Disorders such as Huntington's Disease, BRAC1, FAP and Fragile X are included. List C sets out cases where approval is required on a case-by-case basis for conditions.[81]

The Authority has ruled that PGD and PTT may be utilised where embryos are tissue-type matched and intended for a sibling who has a genetic condition which is severe or life-threatening and where all other treatment possibilities have been exhausted. Approval from the ethics committee at the institution where the procedure is to be undertaken must be obtained.[82] However, the Authority cannot license PTT per se because there is no legal pathway for fertile people, who are not at risk of transmitting a genetic disease unless they can qualify as clinically infertile under the licence conditions.[83] This has occurred because the legislation was drafted before histocompatibility leukocyte antigen-typing was even conceptualised and demonstrates how hard it is for the law to keep abreast with science particularly when the legislation is not flexible enough to accommodate technological change. Significantly, fertile people in these circumstances are denied the choice of having another child who could provide stem cells for an affected sibling.

South Australia

In South Australia, PGD is licensed by the SACRT under the Reproductive Technology (Clinical Practices) Act 1988 (SA),[84] which permits access to PGD treatment for the purpose of identifying chromosomal abnormalities which may contribute to infertility, or where there is a risk that a genetic defect would be transmitted to a child conceived naturally.[85] The term "genetic defect" has no legal definition, and the SACRT interprets it as "a single gene or chromosome disorder the likely effect of which is to seriously impair a person who inherits the disorder from one or both parents".[86] The applicants must receive counselling

---

81 The ITA Approved Genetic Testing January 2006. List A, B and C.

82 ITA, Tissue Typing in Conjunction with Preimplantation Genetic Diagnosis, 2004, <www.ita.org.au> (accessed 20 January 2006).

83 See ITA *Conditions for Licence: Applications for Licences By Hospitals and Day Procedure Centres*, 2002, para 2.2.1.

84 *Pearce v South Australian Health Commission* (1996) 66 SASR 486; *McBain v Victoria* (2000) 99 FCR 116.

85 See, *Reproductive Technology (Clinical Practices) Act 1988* (SA) s 13(3)(b)(i) and (ii) as interpreted by the SACRT *Annual Report for 2004*, Appendix 2, Memorandum 1. The term "genetic defect" is defined as a "single gene disorder or chromosome disorder already affecting one parent or carried by both parents, the likely effect of which is to seriously impair a person who inherits this disorder". Note also counselling and "fitness for parenting" conditions.

86 SACRT *Annual Report for 2004*, Memorandum 12.

from a clinical geneticist who is responsible for confirming the risk of them transmitting a genetic defect if a child is conceived naturally and that accurate testing for the genetic defect is available.[87] Reflecting the relatively flexible nature of the South Australian ART statute, the SACRT has the authority to take into account legal and medical developments, and it may impose further requirements in the absence of legislative direction.[88] The legislation does not explicitly refer to sex selection and PTT. However, sex selection to avoid the transmission of a sex-linked genetic defect clearly comes within the purpose of the Act.[89] The NHMRC ART Guidelines (2004) would cover social sex selection and PTT.[90]

Western Australia

Before 2004, it was an offence to perform a diagnostic procedure on an embryo in Western Australia.[91] However, as a result of amendments to the *Human Repro-ductive Technology Act 1991* (WA),[92] the WARTC may approve genetic testing of embryos if the applicants consent and are eligible to receive IVF treatment under s 23 of the Act. To be eligible for IVF, a woman or a couple (heterosexual or same sex and in a stable relationship) must be unable to conceive a child for medical reasons (they are infertile); or it is known that the child, if born, would be affected by a genetic abnormality or disease. All PGD procedures must have the prior approval of the Western Australian Council.[93] The approval must be based on existing scientific and medical knowledge which indicates that the diagnostic procedure is unlikely to leave the embryo unfit for implantation and there is a significant risk of a serious genetic abnormality or disease being present in the embryo.[94] The council may not approve the use of PGD for sex selection unless it is for a serious sex-linked genetic disease.[95] As there is no legislative or regulative direction on using PTT, it is likely that provisions of the NHMRC ART Guidelines (2004) will be applied.[96]

---

87 Ibid.

88 Ibid, Appendix 1, Memoranda 1 and 12.

89 *Reproductive Technology (Clinical Practices) Act 1988* (SA) s 13(3)(b)(ii).

90 NHMRC ART Guidelines (2004) op cit, paras 11, 12.2, 12.3.

91 *Human Reproductive Technology Act 1991* (WA) s 7(1)(b).

92 Ibid, as amended by the *Acts Amendment (Lesbian and Gay Law Reform) Act 2002* (WA) and the *Human Reproductive Technology Amendment Act 2004* (WA).

93 *Human Reproductive Technology Act 1991* (WA) s 7(1)(b). Testing may be conducted by licensed places for genetic screening PGS (aneuploidy screening) and single gene defects and translocation (PGD).

94 *Human Reproductive Technology Act 1991* (WA) s 14(2)(b)(i) and (ii).

95 Ibid, s 14(2)(b)(ii). See WARCT *Annual Report*, 2004, p 21.

96 NHMRC ART Guidelines (2004) op cit, paras 12.3.

Conclusions

The task of developing sound principle-based regulation which simultaneously protects human rights and liberties and minimises harm, while also providing scope for scientific advances and innovation, is a complicated process. Caulfield and colleagues observe that the many challenges to responsible regulation in the field of reproductive genetics are exacerbated by the complexity of the relevant scientific information and also because policy is being made in a context which often engages strongly held moral values. This results in numerous political dilemmas which frequently frustrate attempts to generate balanced debate on many of the most central issues.[97]

As society wrestles with these issues, the current benefits offered to individuals, families and society by reproductive genetic technologies seem, on the whole, to outweigh the harms. As well, potential harms can be minimised by legal and professional controls and information obtained from clinical studies and research. Caulfield and colleagues oppose prohibition as a means of control and argue that the challenges associated with reproductive genetics will endure and regulatory regimes must work within the scientific reality. They state:

> Steps must be taken now to move towards a flexible regulatory scheme that promotes ongoing public and professional dialogue, sets limits which respect ethical commitments we hold as a society, and fosters a climate which will promote valid scientific and clinical endeavour. Prohibitory bans seem to be the least appropriate tool in this context.[98]

The FSA RTAC Code of Practice and the NHMRC ART Guidelines (2004) do not have the force of law, but they play an important role in professional self-regulation. For ART clinics they constitute a key element in accreditation processes and non-compliance can have serious financial and professional consequences; however, unlike health registration boards little information about enforcement measures is on the public record. As far as patients are concerned, the licensing system and ethical guidelines are relied upon to promote high standards of medicine and ethical practice. However, some of the provisions in the NHMRC ART Guidelines (2004) impose restrictions on reproductive freedoms through a decision-making process which is not transparent and legally unchallengeable. Notably, in Appendix C of the NHMRC ART Guidelines (2004), *Issues for further community discussion*, the relevance of reproductive freedoms and liberties to the debate on genetic technologies associated with ART is not a significant consideration, rather sympathy and compassion appear to be the driving concerns. As well, the NHMRC claims that "[c]ommunity regulation [for PGD and social sex selection] may be necessary, but the justification for such intervention will need to

---

97   Caulfield, T, Knowles, L, and Meslin, EM, "Law and Policy in an Era of Reproductive Genetics" (2004) 30 *Journal of Medical Ethics* 414.

98   Ibid.

be decided for each issue based on such community debate and discussion". What is "community regulation"?

Informed public debate is a very important part of the regulatory decision-making process. The Lockhart Report notes that: "where benefits are not yet established, or where there is wide spread and deeply held community objection, the total prohibition through the legal system may be justified".[99] As social attitudes and technological developments drive much of the debate in the area, more needs to be done by the scientific community to educate the public about the science of ART. It is not appropriate for either professional or legal regulation to be based on opinion polls, misinformation and political manipulation.

99 Australian Government, Legislation Review of Australia's *Prohibition of Human Cloning Act 2002* and the *Research Involving Human Embryos Act 2002*, Canberra, December 2005, p xiv, <www.lockhartreview.com.au/index.aspx> (accessed 23 April 2006) (Lockhart Review).

12

The regulation of cloning and stem cell research

Donald Chalmers[1]

Introduction

The joint announcement in June 2000 of the first published draft of the entire DNA sequence of the human genome marked the start of what Francis Collins, Director of the National Human Genome Research Institute, has described as the Genome Era of science.[2] But, it was an event a few years before that attracted the greatest world attention. In 1996, at the Roslyn Institute in Edinburgh, Scotland, a company called PPL Therapeutics created Dolly the sheep from a somatic (non-germ) cell taken from an adult sheep and transferred into an enucleated sheep egg. The world's first cloned animal was created by somatic cell nuclear transfer ((SCNT) sometimes referred to as cell nuclear replacement (CNR)) and also created an extraordinary international reaction – frenzy would be more accurate. The Dolly announcement generated this reaction because the technology had the potential for application in humans, as well as animals.[3] If this technology could be applied to humans, could the old escape death by cloning themselves? Could the dead child be recreated by cloning? Could armies of clones be the new military option? These and other fanciful scenarios were debated in the media and, even the academic literature.[4] It seemed that cloning of individuals might allow *homo sapiens* to become *homo proteus* by genetic intervention.[5]

1   Professor Chalmers wishes to thank the Australian Research Council for support and Professor Ryuichi Ida and the Graduate School of Law, University of Kyoto, the Japanese Ministry of Education, Culture, Sport, Science and Technology and the delegates to the Dialogue on Asian Bioethics held in Seoul, Korea, December 2002 and Kyoto, Japan, September, 2003.

2   *Australian Biotechnology News*, 4 July 2003, p 8.

3   See Australian Academy of Science Symposium on *Therapeutic Cloning for Tissue Repair*, Canberra, 16 September 1999; and National Bioethics Advisory Commission (USA) *Cloning Human Beings*, Report 1998; Childress, J, "The Challenges of Public Ethics: Reflections on NBAC's Report" (1997) 27 *Hastings Centre Report* 9 and Callahan, D, "Cloning: The Work not Done" (1997) 27 *Hastings Centre Report* 18.

4   Cohen, JR, "In God's Garden Creation and Cloning in Jewish Thought" (1999) 29 *Hastings Center Report* 7; Harris, J, "Cloning and Human Dignity" (1998) 7 *Cambridge Quarterly of Health Care Ethics* 163; Harris, J, "Goodbye Dolly" (1997) 23 *Journal of Medical Ethics* 353.

5   See Silver, L, *Re-making Eden*, Weidenfeld & Nicholson, London, 1998; see also, Kitcher, P, "Creating Perfect People" in Burley, J, and Harris, J, *A Companion to Genethics*, Blackwell Publishing, London, 2004, pp 229–242.

As the debate matured, the ethical and legal issues were clarified.[6] Gradually, a distinction was drawn between cloning for "reproductive" purposes, which was generally opposed and cloning for "therapeutic" purposes, which might be acceptable.[7] This chapter examines both the current prohibitions on human cloning and the restrictive regulatory regime for stem cell research.[8]

Human cloning

What is cloning?

The technology for cloning animals was first developed in the 1950s with major advances in the 1970s and 1980s.[9] Until Dolly, cloning had meant the creation of genetically duplicated organisms *rather than genetically duplicated individuals*. Much of the modern DNA technology is premised on the ability to create clone libraries of fragments of DNA. Clone libraries which exist around the world for the entire human genome are invaluable research tools for locating individual genes by the process of hybridisation. Under this process a cloned fragment attaches to a complementary sequence of bases on a single strand of DNA after it has been separated from its pair. Once the gene has been located, it can be sequenced and it can itself be cloned. Once the gene is sequenced and cloned, the development of a genetic test for the gene may be developed.

Human cloning now more commonly refers to the creation of genetically duplicated individuals. Cloning in this sense can occur naturally when identical twins are born. Theoretically, this may be done through asexual reproduction, by stimulating a single egg cell to commence cell division. Cloning has also been achieved by splitting an embryo. However, Dolly was created via SCNT, a technology that aroused international concern.

In can be seen, therefore that the term "cloning" is imprecise. When used in the sense of "making a copy" cloning is not a precise term and has developed a "social" meaning referring to the cloning of genetically identical human beings.[10] The term *clone*, therefore has a number of meanings:

- an exact copy or replica;

---

6   Thomson, J, "Legal and Ethical Problems of Human Cloning" (2000) 8 *Journal of Law and Medicine* 31.

7   This is the distinction made by Japan with legislation banning cloning (*Law for the Prohibition of Reproductive Cloning 2000*) and regulation for stem cells (*Guidelines for the Derivation and Utilisation of Human Embryonic Stem Cells 2001*)

8   On stem cells and regulation see Chalmers, D and Nicol, D, "Embryonic Stem Cell Research: Can the Law Balance Ethical, Scientific and Economic Values?" Parts 1 and 2 (2003) 18 *Law and the Human Genome Review* 43 and 91; Chalmers, D, Nicol, D and Gogarty, B, "Regulating Biomedical Advances: Embryonic Stem Cell Research" (2002) 2 *Macquarie Law Journal* 31.

9   Sun, FZ and Moor, RM, "Nuclear Transplantation in Mammalian Eggs and Embryos" (1995) 10 *Current Topics in Developmental Biology* 147.

10 Like the cloned copies of Hitler in the film "Boys from Brazil".

- a group of genetically identical cells descended from a single common ancestor; or

- a recombinant DNA molecule containing a gene or other DNA sequence of interest.

Major reports on human cloning

The debate about the appropriate boundaries to be drawn in regulation between unacceptable cloning procedures and "therapeutic" applications began at the time of the Dolly announcement[11] and set off a chain of national inquiries into the public policy and regulatory response to this event.[12] Cloning of a genetically duplicated individual ("reproductive cloning") has been outlawed universally. The UNESCO Declaration on the Human Genome and Human Rights was an early example and stated in Article 11: "Practices which are contrary to human dignity,[13] such as reproductive cloning of human beings shall not be permitted".[14] Although not a binding international convention, it was followed by the Council of Europe's Protocol on Prohibition on Cloning of Human Beings and the Convention on Human Rights and Dignity with regard to the application of Biology in Medicine that also prohibited: "[a]ny intervention seeking to create a human being genetically identical to another human being, whether living or dead".[15] This protocol was incorporated in legislation prohibiting cloning in many European countries.[16] In the United States, the National Bioethics Advisory Commission Report, *Cloning Human Beings* (NBAC Report) recommended legislation banning human cloning combined with a moratorium.[17] Most recently, the United Nations passed a

---

11   Robertson, J, "Human Cloning and the Challenge of Regulation" (1998) 339 *New England Journal of Medicine* 119; Annas, G, "Why We Should Ban Human Cloning" (1998) 339 (2) *New England Journal of Medicine* 122.

12   See Macklin, R, "Cloning and Public Policy" in Burley, J and Harris, J, *A Companion to Genetics*, Blackwell Publishing, London, 2004, pp 206–215.

13   On the vagueness of this term see Harris, J, "Goodbye Dolly? The Ethics of Human Cloning" (1997) 23 *Journal of Medical Ethics* 353.

14   The Declaration was proclaimed at the 29th Session of the General Conference of UNESCO on 11 November 1997. Article 11 provides:

      Practices which are contrary to human dignity, such as reproductive cloning of human beings, shall not be permitted. States and competent international organisations are invited to cooperate in identifying such practices and in determining, nationally or internationally, appropriate measures to be taken to ensure that the principles set out in this Declaration are respected.

15   The Convention for the Protection of Human Rights and Dignity with regard to the application of biology and medicine was approved by the Council of Europe in November 1996 and has been signed by 20 of the 40 member states. The Additional Protocol on the Prohibition of Cloning Beings was adopted by the Parliamentary Assembly of the Council of Europe on 22 September 1997.

16   For example, Denmark: Act No 503 on the *Scientific Ethical Committee System and the Handling of Biomedical Research Projects 1992*; Act No 4060 *Medically Assisted Procreation 1997*; Germany: *Federal Embryo Protection Act 1990*; Norway: Law No 56 *Medical Use of Biotechnology 1994*; Slovakia: *Health Care Law 1994*; Spain: Law No 35 *Assisted Reproduction Procedures 1988*; Sweden: Law No 115, 1991.

17   See National Bioethics Advisory Commission, *Cloning Human Beings*, June 1997, Recommendation II (NBAC Report 1997) <www.georgetown.edu/research/nrcbl/nbac/pubs.html> (accessed 7 July 2005).

non-declaration to ban reproductive cloning after some two years of debate, in which agreement could not be reached on a form of words that would have an impact on stem cell work in member nations.[18]

Australia has had a long record of regulating assisted reproductive techno-logy (ART) since the world's first legislation, the *Infertility (Medical Procedures) Act* was introduced in 1984 in the State of Victoria.[19] The issue of human cloning was referred to the Australian Health Ethics Committee (AHEC) that produced a *Report on Scientific, Ethical and Regulatory Considerations Relevant to Cloning of Human Beings*[20] (AHEC Report) recommending that the Commonwealth endorse the UNESCO Declaration on the Human Genome and Human Rights prohibiting reproductive cloning. This AHEC Report was presented to the Minister for Health and Aged Care who referred it to the Australian House of Representatives Standing Committee on Constitutional and Legal Affairs. This committee appointed Kevin Andrews to chair a formal inquiry that took extensive public submissions. The subsequent report entitled *Human Cloning: Scientific, Ethical and Regulatory Aspects of Human Cloning and Stem Cell Research* (Andrews Report) was tabled in the House of Representatives on 17 September 2001. It included a unanimous view that repro-ductive human cloning was entirely unacceptable.

Prohibition of Human Cloning Act 2002 (Cth)

The Andrews Report was followed by the introduction of the Research Involving Embryos and Prohibition of Human Cloning Bill into the Commonwealth Parlia-ment in 2002. This Bill was split into two separate Bills: the Research Involving Embryos Bill 2002 (Cth) and the Prohibition of Human Cloning Bill 2002 (Cth). There was unanimous support for the prohibition on human cloning but controversy over research involving embryos that could be the source of human stem cells. In the Senate, one speech summarised the reasons for banning human cloning, noting:

- considerable uncertainty surrounding the long-term well-being of potential subjects;

- danger that unregulated human cloning will provide fertile ground for enthu-siasts of selective breeding/eugenics (such as the well-publicised Dr Antinori);

- concerns over allocating scarce resources to the imprecise science of cloning;

---

18   See, Mayor, S, "UN Committee Approves Declaration on Human Cloning" (2005) 330 *BMJ* 496; and "UN Calls for Ban on All Forms of Human Cloning" (2005) 149 *BioEdge* at 3–5.

19   On ART regulation in Australia, see Chalmers, D, "Professional Self-Regulation and Guidelines in Assisted Reproduction" (2002) 9 *Journal of Law and Medicine* 414. Law No 1140 of 20 December 1984 was also passed in Sweden at the end of 1984, but only applied to artificial insemination.

20   Australian Health Ethics Committee, *Scientific, Ethical and Regulatory Considerations Relevant to Cloning of Human Beings*, report to the Commonwealth Minister for Health and Aged Care, 16 December 1998; Professor D Chalmers was Chair of AHEC and Chair of the working party of AHEC on Human Cloning during the time of this report.

- implications for public safety; and
- threats posed to notions of identity and individual autonomy.[21]

The *Prohibition of Human Cloning Act 2002* (Cth) created a long menu of prohibited practices overseen by statutory inspectors and each carrying heavy criminal penalties. These offences are: creating an embryo other than by fertilisation[22] or other than for a pregnancy;[23] mixing the genetic material of more than two people;[24] developing an embryo outside the body of a woman for more than 14 days;[25] using precursor cells from an embryo to create an embryo;[26] creating heritable alterations to a genome;[27] removing a viable embryo from a woman;[28] creating a chimeric embryo (created by combining human embryos and animal cells)[29] or placing an embryo in an animal.[30] In addition, there are offences in relation to the import and export of "prohibited embryos"[31] and commercial trading in human eggs, sperm and embryos.[32] These offences carry a maximum penalty of 10 years' imprisonment, which may be supplemented with a monetary penalty.

Future directions

Imprecision in language usually reflects imprecision in the scientific or moral idea. Early in the cloning debate a distinction was drawn between "reproductive" cloning and "therapeutic" applications of this procedure. These terms were originally coined in a United Kingdom report, which described them as misleading.[33] The terms employed are still imprecise. However, the term "therapeutic cloning" is generally used as a synonym for stem cell research and the term "reproductive cloning" refers to "cloning of a human being" that is prohibited generally around the world.

As the therapeutic applications of the science develops, the law may have to be reviewed to accommodate procedures that are prohibited currently under legislation. Two cases, neither at this stage established beyond experimental procedures, illustrate the potential divergence between current regulation and the

---

21 Commonwealth, Senate, *Parliamentary Debates* (Hansard), 11 November 2002, p 5820 per Senator Chris Evans.
22 *Prohibition of Human Cloning Act 2002* (Cth) s 13.
23 Ibid, s 14.
24 Ibid, s 15.
25 Ibid, s 16.
26 Ibid, s 17.
27 Ibid, s 18.
28 Ibid, s 18.
29 Ibid, s 20.
30 Ibid, s 21.
31 Ibid, s 22.
32 Ibid, s 23.
33 See, the joint report of the Human Genetics Advisory Commission and the Human Fertilisation and Embryology Authority, *Cloning Issues in Reproduction, Science and Medicine* (1998).

developing science. First, there are expectations that it may be possible to create customised autologous stem cells by placing an individual's own somatic cells inside an enucleated human egg. The Nuffield Council recognised this procedure as early as 2002.[34] Technically this procedure is in breach of current legislation yet it may be a procedure with the potential to produce a supply of personalised genetically altered, and therapeutically improved, cells for an individual. A first step towards this procedure was claimed in 2004, when a Korean team announced that they had created the world's first such cloned human stem cell line from an SCNT embryo.[35] In this scenario, there would be no intention whatsoever to develop this embryoid[36] body into a "whole human being".[37] The second case involved Chinese researchers who reported efforts to develop autologous stem cells, not by transfer of somatic cells to a human egg but to that of a rabbit. The mixing of human and animal cells is an offence under ss 21 and 22 of the *Prohibition of Human Cloning Act 2002* (Cth) and equivalent legislation in other countries. Interestingly, there is one national exception to this uniform prohibition on the mixing of human and animal material. The Korean *Bio-ethics and Bio-safety Act 2004*[38] prohibits the transfer of a human embryo into the uterus of an animal and vice versa the transfer of an animal embryo in a human uterus. However, Article 12 excludes from this prohibition "the act of transferring a human somatic cell nucleus into an animal egg cell". This partial permission for inter-species transfer was included in the original terms of the Act and, therefore, preceded the announcement of the Chinese rabbit–human experiment.

As the research develops and practices are improved and perfected in some jurisdictions, the strict prohibitions in cloning legislation may require some reconsideration, particularly if it can be demonstrated according to accepted scientific standards that the benefit overrides the harm.

---

34 Nuffield Council on Bioethics, *Stem Cell Therapy: the Ethical Issues*, Discussion Paper, 2000 (updated July 2004).

35 See, (2005) 291 *BioNews* (10 January 2005) at 17–19. Charges of misconduct and data fabrication were upheld by Seoul University and Dr Hwang retracted his lead articles in *Science* (*Science* 303 (5664) 1669-1674; 508 (5729) 1777-1783). See *Science* 311 (5759) 335b.

36 An embryo-like body that may have the potential to develop to a foetus.

37 Another imprecise and rather misleading expression, used in the AHEC Report and which was actually included in the interim anti-cloning legislation. See *Gene Technology Act 2002* (Cth) ss 192B, 192C and 192D repealed by Sch 1 to the *Prohibition of Human Cloning Act 2002* (Cth).

38 Statute No 750 was proclaimed in January 2004 but did not come into force until 1 January 2005.

Embryo research and stem cell technology[39]

The reports referred to earlier were unanimous in their condemnation of human cloning. Most were also unanimous in their agreement about the potential therapeutic benefits of stem cells. Notably, these reports cautioned against the introduction of regulation that might stifle this line of research.[40] In the United States, the NBAC Report noted, "any regulatory or legislative actions undertaken should be carefully written so as not to interfere with other important areas of scientific research" (Recommendation III). These "other important areas" in the NBAC Report included stem cell technology with its potential to provide autologous cells for transplantation[41] and other therapies. Similarly, a United Kingdom Department of Health Report[42] and the AHEC Report acknowledged the therapeutic potentialities of stem cell technology. The United Kingdom report specifically noted that the Human Embryology and Fertilisation Authority be allowed to license research to investigate the potential benefits of these techniques to mitochondrial diseases and damaged tissues and organs.[43] Both reports advised that human embryos were a source of stem cells.[44] As such, stem cells derived from this source re-ignited the ethical and moral controversies in the embryo research debate.[45] This was acknowledged in the Andrews Report that recorded a six to four disagreement over embryo research but agreement on the possible benefits of embryonic stem cell technology.

---

39 On stem cells and regulation see, Chalmers, D and Nicol, D, "Embryonic Stem Cell Research: Can the Law Balance Ethical, Scientific and Economic Values?" Parts 1 and 2 (2003) 18 *Law and the Human Genome Review* 43 and 91; Chalmers, D Nicol, D and Gogarty, D, "Regulating Biomedical Advances: Embryonic Stem Cell Research" (2002) 2 *Macquarie Law Journal* 31.

40 See Harris, J, "The Ethical Use of Human Embryonic Stem Cells in Research and Therapy" in Burley, J and Harris, J, *A Companion to Genethics*, Blackwell Publishing, London, 2004, pp 158–174.

41 Reported in Cibelli, JB, Kiessling, AA, Cunniff, K, Richards, C, Lanza RP and West, MD, "Somatic Cell Nuclear Transfer in Humans: Pronuclear and Early Embryonic Development" (2001) 2 *Journal of Regenerative Medicine* 25.

42 See Department of Health United Kingdom, *Stem Cell Research: Medical Progress with Responsibility*, June 2000 (report from the Chief Medical Officer's Expert Group Reviewing the Potential of Developments in Stem Cell Research and Cell Nuclear Replacement to Benefit Human Health) and *Government Response to the Recommendations Made in the Chief Medical Officer's Expert Group Report*, Cmnd 4833, August 2000.

43 Trouson, A and Gillam, L, "What Does Cloning Offer Human Medicine?" (1999) 11 (2) *Today's Life Science* 12.

44 Stem cells may be derived from embryos as well as from adult cells. Bone marrow and foetal cord blood have been sources of these cells.

45 Holm, S, "Going to the Roots of the Stem Cell Controversy" (2002) 16 *Bioethics* 493; Green, R, "Benefiting from Evil: an Incipient Moral Problem in Stem Cell Research" (2002) 16 *Bioethics* 544.

The promise of stem cells

Both the science and the ethics of stem cell technology have been endlessly debated since the Dolly announcement.[46] Stem cell technology involves the extraction of cells from the developing blastocyst or other "adult" cells, which have the required quality of self-reproducing pluripotency. Stem cell technology relies on the regenerative qualities of these cells.[47] The AHEC Report noted that these cells have "prolonged proliferation with retention of their undifferentiated form ... together with a stable developmental potential to give rise to derivative cells".[48] The regenerative characteristics of stem cells are not unique and are manifested in bone marrow, cord blood, skin, and foetal tissue as key examples. These are referred to as "adult" stem cells. Human stem cell work is based on earlier animal studies.[49] However, stem cells derived from human embryos (referred to as human embryonic stem cells (ES cells)) have attracted the most attention – both ethical and scientific. The ethical attention concentrates on the status of the embryo; the scientific attention focuses on the potential of ES cells to produce new therapies and to generate commercial development opportunities.

The promise of stem cells is considerable. There are shortages of organs for transplants in most developed countries and stem cell technology is seen as a potential source of compatible organs for transplantation. Stem cells may produce tissue to replace damaged nerve, muscle, liver, pancreas and heart cells. This technology is being promoted as a potential treatment for disorders such as Parkinson's disease and Alzheimer's disease. There are promises of stem cells providing a source of safe blood and blood products. This optimistic promise was reflected in submissions to the Andrews Inquiry where stem cell research was described as "the greatest and most exciting medical breakthrough" and "one of the biggest breakthroughs in human medicine", promising "very great potential benefits".[50] The United States National Academies Committee on the Biological and

---

46 See, Jaenisch, R, "Human cloning: The Science and Ethics of Nuclear Transplantation" (2004) 351 *New England Journal of Medicine* 27: 2787-2791.

47 The first human tissue used as source material for therapies was bone marrow. The first controversial tissue use involved aborted foetal tissue. For a gruesome fictional account of the belief in regenerative young tissue see Hayder, M, *Tokyo,* Bantam Press Ltd, New York, 2004.

48 See Australian Health Ethics Committee, *Scientific, Ethical and Regulatory Considerations Relevant to Cloning of Human Beings: A Report to the Commonwealth Minister,* 16 December 1998, para 2.17. See generally Chapter 2 on the Background Science to the Cloning of Human Beings in General and Stem Cell Technology in Particular. See also the *Government Response to the Recommendations Made in the Chief Medical Officer's Expert Group Report: Stem Cell Research: Medical Progress with Responsibility,* Cmd 4833, 2000.

49 The isolation of embryonic stem cells from mouse embryos was reported as early as 1981. Martin, G, "Isolation of a Pluripotent Cell Line from Early Mouse Embryos Cultured in Medium Condition by Teratocarcinoma Stem Cells" (1981) 78 *Proceedings of the National Academy of Science* 7634; Evans, M, Kaufman, M, "Establishment and Culture of Pluripotential Cells from Mouse Embryos" (1981) 292 *Nature* 154.

50 See generally the House of Representatives Standing Committee on Legal and Constitutional Affairs, *Human Cloning: Scientific, Ethical and Regulatory Aspects of Human Cloning and Stem Cell Research,* AGPS, 2001, paras 3.23–3.34.

Biomedical Application of Stem Cell Research expressed the view that: "[s]tem cell research offers unprecedented opportunities for developing new medical therapies for debilitating diseases and a new way to explore fundamental questions of biology".[51]

However, some of these expressions of optimism may prove to be overstated. In spite of the considerable public investment in this research,[52] embryonic stem cell technology is at a preliminary research stage and announcements about its potential may be premature. The reported breakthroughs have been modest to say the least with few trials and no clinical applications as yet. There have been a handful of reports of instances of the use of stem cells in clinical therapy with some success. Heart disease has been a major target for research effort. Interestingly, however, the cells used for this procedure were not derived from embryos but from adult cells. There has also been a reported use of stem cells, again adult cells, in China to treat spinal cord injury, which is another major target. The late Christopher Reeve, who suffered quadriplegia after a riding accident, was a major advocate for stem cell research, not only in the United States but also in Europe and Australia. He believed that stem cells promised an avenue for spinal cord injury repair. The therapeutic application of human stem cell technology is still at a very *early stage* of development.

Background to regulation of embryo research

The development of clinical applications of in vitro fertilisation (IVF) prompted discussion about the need for regulation and also wide discussions on the biological, ethical and legal status of the human embryo.[53] As noted, Victoria passed the first statute, the *Infertility (Medical Procedures) Act 1984*. At the Commonwealth level, a private member's Bill, the Human Embryo Experimentation Bill was introduced in the Senate in 1985. This Bill was not passed but was referred to a Senate Select Committee. The Select Committee Report *Human Embryo Experimentation in Australia* (Tate Report) recommended regulation at the Commonwealth level, with the cooperation of the States and the Northern Territory.[54] The Tate Report also recommended a national body issuing research licences for experimentation on human embryos.[55]

Australia developed a State-based ART regulatory system with considerable differences among the jurisdictions. The legislation in Victoria, South

---

51 National Academies Committee on the Biological and Biomedical Application of Stem Cell Research, *Stem Cells and the Future of Regenerative Medicine*, National Academies Press, Washington DC, 2001, p 1.

52 The Australian Government allocated $42 million to the National Stem Cell Centre and the California State legislature has promised some $3 billion for research in this area.

53 See, Chalmers, D, "Professional Self-Regulation and Guidelines in Assisted Reproduction" (2002) 9 *Journal of Law and Medicine* 414.

54 Senate Select Committee on the Human Embryo Experimentation Bill 1985, *Human Embryo Experimentation in Australia*, AGPS, 1986 (the Tate Report).

55 Ibid, ch 4, para. 4.25.

Australia and Western Australia dealing with ART included provisions regulating research on embryos. The *Infertility Treatment Act 1995* (Vic) did not prohibit research but had a very "restrictive tilt".[56] Any embryo in Victoria used for the purposes of re-implantation or "approved research"[57] had to retain the capacity of that embryo to be re-implanted into a woman.[58] This effectively barred the extraction of stem cells from an embryo. This "restrictive tilt" applied in Western Australia and South Australia also. Both jurisdictions required approval from their councils to carry out any embryo research and that research had to demonstrate protection for the embryo and ensure later re-implantation into the woman.[59] In South Australia, the approved research was not to be "detrimental" to the embryo,[60] and, in Western Australia research had to be "therapeutic for that ... embryo" with "existing scientific and medical knowledge indicat[ing] that no detrimental effect on the well-being of [it] is likely thereby to occur".[61] Both States required that research could only be undertaken within a period not exceeding 14 days from fertilisation.[62] In the non-legislative States and Territories, the NHMRC *Guidelines on Assisted Reproductive Technology*[63] required:

> [T]he recognition that any experimentation and research involved in these technologies should be limited in ways which reflect the human nature of the embryo, acknowledging that there is a diversity of views on what constitutes the moral status of a human embryo, particularly in its early stages of development.[64]

---

56   Brownsword, R, "Regulating Human Genetics: New Dilemmas for a New Millennium" (2004) 12 *Medical Law Review* 14.

57   *Infertility Treatment Act 1995* (Vic) ss 49 and 22.

58   Ibid, s 24.

59   The *Reproductive Technology (Clinical Practices) Act 1988* (SA) s 10(2) states that:
> The welfare of any child to be born in consequence of an artificial fertilisation procedure must be treated as of paramount importance, and accepted as a fundamental principle, in the formulation of the code of ethical practice.

Prior to the *Human Reproductive Technology Amendment Act 2004* (WA) the long title of the *Human Reproductive Technology Act 1991* (WA) stated inter alia that:
> Parliament considers ... this legislation should respect the life created by this process by giving an egg in the process of fertilisation or an embryo all reasonable opportunities for implanting ... [Parliament] does not approve the creation of a human egg in the process of fertilisation or an embryo for a purpose other than the implantation in the body of a woman.

However, this statement has been altered by the 2004 amending legislation so that preimplantation genetic diagnostic procedures can be practised lawfully in Western Australia.

60   *Reproductive Technology (Clinical Practices) Act 1988* (SA) s 14(b); see also SACRT *Annual Report 2004*, Appendix 1, Memoranda 1 and 12.

61   *Human Reproductive Technology Act 1991* (WA) s 14(2). However, this has now been repealed and substituted by s 14(2), (2A) and (2B) thus making provision for research on excess embryo and diagnostic procedures. See *Human Reproductive Technology Amendment Act 2004* (WA) s 11.

62   *Reproductive Technology (Code of Ethical Research Practice) Regulations 1995* (SA) reg 4; *Human Reproductive Technology Act 1991* (WA) s 14(1)(d).

63   NHMRC, *Guidelines on Assisted Reproductive Technology*, NHMRC, Canberra, 1996 (revised and replaced in 2004).

64   NHMRC Guideline 6.

The 1996 guidelines also limited embryo experimentation to "therapeutic procedures, which leave the embryo, or embryos, with an expectation of implantation and development" [65] except in "exceptional circumstances". [66] Approval was required from a Human Research Ethics Committee, which had to be satisfied about:

- evidence of a likelihood of significant advance in knowledge or improvement in technologies for treatment as a result of the proposed research;
- the use of a restricted number of embryos; and
- consent to the specific form of research on the part of the gamete providers and their spouses or partners.[67]

These provisions have now been superseded by the embryo research licensing scheme introduced by the *Research Involving Human Embryos Act 2002* (Cth) and the consent provisions in the Ethical Guidelines in the use of assisted reproductive technology in clinical practice and research (NHMRC, 2004).

Andrews Report recommendations: Towards a national approach

The Andrews Inquiry included a term of reference to report on the issue of the need for national legislation. The Andrews Report proposed a national licensing scheme for research on human embryos. Licences were to apply to "surplus" embryos from ART programs, subject to requirements[68] and the consent of all relevant persons.[69] The Andrews Report recommended an end to the mixed State and Territory regulatory system, concluding that "questions raised by human cloning and research involving the use of embryos are complex social and ethical questions and should not be left to individual ethics committees to decide. Nor should the answer to such fundamental questions depend on geography or source of funding". [70] This nationally consistent regime would apply to the public and private sector and should display the features of accountability, enforceability, responsiveness, flexibility, practicality and consistency.[71]

In July 2000, Australian Health Ministers agreed to develop a national framework "to prevent the exploitation of human cloning". Subsequently, in June 2001, the Council of Heads of Australian Governments (COAG) meeting agreed to

---

65   Ibid, 6.2.
66   Ibid, 6.4.
67   These conditions were repeated in s 24(1)(a)–(c) of the *Research Involving Human Embryos Act 2002* (Cth).
68   Andrews Report, paras 12.41–12.44.
69   Ibid, paras 12.69–12.78.
70   Ibid, para 9.50.
71   Ibid, para 11.63.

develop nationally consistent legislation to prohibit human cloning.[72] There was general agreement that the cloning of a whole human being should be banned.[73] At the COAG meeting on 5 April 2002 agreement was also reached that the use of embryos *surplus* to ART requirements for embryonic stem cell research should be allowed, but only in limited circumstances and subject to strict regulation.

Parliamentary debates on the human embryo research and human cloning legislation

The Research Involving Embryos and Prohibition of Human Cloning Bill was introduced into the Commonwealth Parliament in 2002 following the COAG agreement. The Prime Minister introduced the Bill and explained that the object of the Bill was to ban human cloning and other unacceptable practices associated with reproductive technology and to regulate research involving the use of excess human embryos created by ART.[74] This Bill was later split into two separate Bills: one dealing with research, the Research Involving Embryos Bill 2002 (Cth) and one dealing with cloning,[75] the Prohibition of Human Cloning Bill 2002 (Cth). The Prohibition of Human Cloning Bill received unanimous support and was passed very quickly with reference to the fact that cloning was an affront to human dignity. The Research Involving Embryos Bill provided the longest ever debate in the history of the Parliament – debate that was long, passionate, difficult and highly emotional. The Bill was enacted under the title of *Research Involving Human Embryos Act 2002* (Cth). The arguments raised in the debates are summarised below[76] and can be divided into eight themes:

---

72 Ibid, para 11.38.

73 This inelegant expression was derived from the AHEC Report. This same expression was later used in the ban on human cloning introduced on an interim basis in the *Gene Technology Act 2000* (Cth) ss 191A–191D.

74 Commonwealth, House of Representatives, *Debates* (Hansard), 27 June 2002, p 4541.

75 Commonwealth, House of Representatives, *Debates* (Hansard), 29 August 2002, pp 6115–6116. On the same day, the Prohibition of Human Cloning Bill 2002 was read a second and third time and passed (p 6167) 16 September; Research Involving Embryos Bill 2002 supported and read a second time (Commonwealth, House of Representatives, *Debates* (Hansard), 16 September 2002 pp 6291–6292). Debate continued on the 24 and 25 with the Bill read a third time and passed (Ayes 99 with Noes 33 Commonwealth, House of Representatives, *Debates* (Hansard), 25 September 2002, pp 7233–7234). Commonwealth, Senate, *Debates* (Hansard), 18 September 2002, p 4421. 15 October: Research Involving Embryos Bill 2002 read a first and second time (Commonwealth, Senate, *Debates* (Hansard), 15 October 2002, p 5142) with debate on 11, 12, 13 and 14 November. The Prohibition of Human Cloning Bill 2002 was read a third time and passed on November 14 (Commonwealth, Senate, *Debates* (Hansard), 14 November 2002, p 6342). The Research Involving Embryos Bill 2002 debate continued on 2, 3, 4 and 5 December: and read a third time and passed (Ayes 45 with Noes 26).

76 For a fuller discussion of these arguments see Chalmers, D and Nicol, D, "Embryonic Stem Cell Research: Can the Law Balance Ethical, Scientific and Economic Values, Part Two" (2003) 18 *Law and the Human Genome Review* 95.

1. *Potential therapeutic benefits* of embryonic stem cell research.

2. *Use of surplus embryos* for research purposes provided they were surplus to the requirements of those participating in the ART program. There was no support for the *creation* of embryos for such research.

3. *Moral status of the embryo* was a major theme of speeches with a range of views expressed that the moral status of the embryo was equal to an adult human being; that the embryo had no moral status; and that the embryo had moral status but less than that of an adult human being.

4. *Adult stem cell research as a preferable alternative* and that there had not been sufficient investigation of the possibilities of adult stem cells to produce cells with similar constituencies.

5. *Commercial exploitation* concerns were expressed about the biotechnology industry and the commodification of embryos without due ethical regard.

6. *The slippery slope to more contentious research* argument proposed that any successful embryonic stem cell research would lead to the development of tissue banks and mass production of human eggs, and even the cloning of human embryos.

7. *Economic benefits and scientific implications for Australia.*

8. There was unanimity in the debate that comprehensive *national legislation was essential*.

Research on human embryos:
The national regulatory framework

The *Research Involving Human Embryos Act 2002* (Cth) was passed with a comfortable majority. The Act creates a Licensing Committee within the National Health Medical Research Council that administers a national licensing scheme for embryo research in the private *and* public sectors. The Act allows the use of "*excess* ART (IVF) embryos" to carry out approved research. Criminal offences apply when excess ART embryos are used *without* a valid licence. The regulatory scheme has many features – giving it a "restrictive tilt"[77] and *not* a permissive one.

Features of the licensing scheme[78]
Approval by the applicant's Human Research Ethics Committee

At the first stage, an applicant for a research licence must present the research proposal to their Human Research Ethics Committee (HREC) in their institution. The HREC must be satisfied that:

---

77 Brownsword, R, "Regulating Human Genetics: New Dilemmas for a New Millennium" (2004) 12 *Medical Law Review* 14.

78 See Chalmers, D and Nicol, D, "Embryonic Stem Cell Research: Can the Law Balance Ethical, Scientific and Economic Values" (2003) 18 *Law and the Human Genome Review* 101.

- the embryos are excess to the needs of the couple in the ART program;
- that all the consents have been obtained; and
- that approval has been given for the activity and the project by the HREC.

If the HREC approves, the application can be referred to the National Licensing Committee for consideration.

Embryo research Licensing Committee

A Licensing Committee is set up within the National Health and Medical Research Council (NHMRC),[79] which has the principal task of granting licences to conduct research on excess human embryos in both the private and public sectors.[80] The Licensing Committee must first be satisfied[81] that all the required consents have been obtained and, secondly, that the applicant has obtained approval for the project by the properly constituted HREC.[82] Thirdly, the Licensing Committee is directed to have regard to the following matters in deciding whether to issue the licence:[83]

(a)   restricting the number of excess ART embryos to that likely to be necessary to achieve the goals of the activity or project proposed in the application;

(b)   the likelihood of significant advance in knowledge or improvement in technologies for treatment as a result of the use of excess ART embryos proposed in the application, which could not reasonably be achieved by other means;[84]

(c)   any relevant guidelines, or relevant parts of guidelines, issued by the NHMRC under the *National Health and Medical Research Council Act 1992* and prescribed by the regulations for the purposes of this paragraph;

(d)   the HREC assessment of the application mentioned in paragraph (3)(c);

(e)   such additional matters (if any) as are prescribed by the regulations.

In practice, the Licensing Committee's deliberations have concentrated on the first two issues, namely restricting the number of excess ART embryos and the likelihood of significant advancement in knowledge or improvement in technologies. The Licensing Committee has developed published guidance statements of its

---

79   *Research Involving Human Embryos Act 2002* (Cth) s 12.

80   Ibid, s 20.

81   Ibid, s 21(3).

82   Ibid, s 23(3)(c).

83   Ibid, s 21(4).

84   The purpose of research criterion is important. In Japan: basic research only is allowed with a ban on reproductive use of embryonic stem cells. In the United Kingdom: infertility, miscarriages, congenital diseases, contraception and gene/chromosome abnormalities were the original purposes to which were added development of embryos; knowledge of *serious* disease; treatment of *serious* diseases (*Human Fertilisation and Embryology Act (Research Purposes) Regulations 2001* (UK).

practice on the issue of "likelihood of significant advance".[85] In addition, the licences so far issued have included special and detailed conditions,[86] particularly about the numbers of embryos able to be used by a licence holder.

At the time of writing, the Licensing Committee had issued nine licences.

Excess embryos for licensed research

A key feature of the Act is that only "excess ART embryos" may be used. This follows the majority recommendation of the Andrews Report and the majority in the parliamentary debates. The Act provides that the couple in an ART program must declare their embryos to be surplus to their needs, and consent to the embryos being classified as excess under the terms of the Act. These embryos may then be used for research, in strictly limited circumstances. An embryo can only be "excess" if each responsible person[87] has authorised in writing the use of the embryo for a purpose other than the ART treatment of the woman concerned[88] or has determined in writing that the embryo is excess to their needs.[89] The legislation does not permit the creation of embryos for research purposes.

The Act originally distinguished between research that *damages or destroys* the embryo and non-destructive research.[90] There was a requirement that only "excess" embryos in storage prior to 5 April 2002 could be used for research that damages or destroys the embryo. This date represented the time of the decision to enact this legislation and a compromise between different views of the Council of Australian Governments. These sections were repealed and not continued.[91]

Consent of parties

The pivotal requirement for the issue of a licence is consent. In particular, s 24(1) provides that, before an excess ART embryo is used as authorised by the licence each *responsible person* (that is, all those involved in providing the egg or sperm for the creation of the embryo and any spouses) must consent. As such, not only must there be written authorisation or determination from the woman (and her spouse) that an embryo is an excess ART embryo,[92] there must also be consent from each of those people[93] that the embryo may be used for an approved research purpose. In effect, the legislation prescribes *two* separate consents. Consent forms in ART clinics had to be redrafted to reflect these two stages. The Licensing Committee has drafted

---

85   NHMRC Licensing Committee, *Report to the Parliament of Australia*, period 1 April to 30 September 2004, p 8.

86   *Research Involving Human Embryos Act 2002* (Cth) s 24.

87   Ibid, s 8.

88   Ibid, s 9(2)(a).

89   Ibid, s 9(2)(b).

90   Ibid, ss 21(3)(b), 24(1)(c) and 24(3).

91   See ibid, Pt 5, s 46.

92   Ibid, s 9(2).

93   Potentially, consent may be required from four people (if the egg and sperm are provided by donors) for the particular use of the embryo: s 24(1)(a).

a guidance statement on the consent requirements of the Act.[94] These requirements are different from the consent processes for an ART procedure. In essence, the legislation establishes a *two stage* consent process (consent that the embryo is excess *and* that the embryo may be used in research).

Monitoring and offences

The Act establishes an inspectorate and a system of monitoring not only of licensed research but also any possible breaches of the cloning legislation. The Act creates a series of criminal offences relating to the use of excess ART embryos without a licence.

International approaches

The regulatory scheme in Australia is in broad terms similar to schemes internationally. Some countries have maintained their ban on research, such as Austria, Ireland, Canada, Philippines and Germany. Interestingly, Germany bans embryo research but still allows stem cells to be imported.[95] However, those countries that have moved to approve stem cell research have generally introduced some form of licensing of the research with access to excess (surplus)[96] ART embryos. This is by far the most common regulatory model with a number of countries having introduced legislation such as the United Kingdom, Finland, Greece, Israel, The Netherlands, Singapore, Sweden, South Korea, the American States of California and New Jersey, and Australia.[97] Some other countries have also followed the surplus embryos approach but have preferred to use guidelines (China,[98] Spain and Japan[99]).

The legislation and guidelines include broadly similar provisions dealing with embryo research and establishing a generally "restrictive tilt",[100] including:

- Only surplus ART embryos allowed may be used (except in the United Kingdom).

---

94 NHMRC Licensing Committee, *Report to the Parliament of Australia*, period 1 April to 30 September 2004, p 7.

95 Heinemann, T and Honnefelder, L, "Principles in Ethical Decision-making" (2002) 16 *Bioethics* 530 at 541.

96 Halliday, S, "A Comparative Approach to the Regulation of Human Embryonic Stem Cell Research in Europe" (2004) 12 *Medical Law Review* 40, Halliday suggests there are different models but essentially there are bans or licensing.

97 See also Isasi, R et al, "Legal and Ethical Approaches to Stem Cell and Cloning Research: A Comparative Analysis of Policies in Latin America, Asia and Africa" (2004) 32 *Journal of Law & Medical Ethics* 626.

98 See "China and UK Could Lead World in Stem Cell Research" (2005) 292 *BioNews* (17 January 2005) at 15–17.

99 Japan has a mixed system with legislation banning cloning (*Law for the Prohibition of Reproductive Cloning 2000*) and regulation for stem cells (*Guidelines for the Derivation and Utilisation of Human Embryonic Stem Cells 2001*).

100 Brownsword, R, "Regulating Human Genetics: New Dilemmas for a New Millennium' (2004) 12 *Medical Law Review* 14.

- The consent of the parties creating the embryos is required at two stages – a consent that the embryos are no longer required for their IVF treatment and also consent to the research.

- The purposes of the research must be explained and mostly the research purposes are limited and require careful justification.

- The research purposes must be approved by an ethics review committee.

- The research is generally required to be reported and the research results published.

- National committees must license or approve the research and, in the case of licensing, have the power to impose conditions in the licence.

Restrictions in relation to the purpose of human embryo research are common. As yet, no country has allowed undefined research on embryos. In Australia, for example, the research licence applicant must demonstrate that there is a "likelihood of significant advancement of knowledge or improvement in technologies for treatment". Similarly in Japan, the researcher may only use embryonic stem cells for basic research and cannot use them reproductively. The United Kingdom originally set out research purposes which related principally to understanding the causes of infertility, miscarriages, genital diseases, contraception and chromosome abnormalities. These purposes were expanded to include research for the purposes of understanding the development of embryos, and increasing knowledge and treatment of serious disease.[101]

The United Kingdom has gone further and has introduced legislation allowing the actual creation of embryos, in very strict circumstances to obtain embryonic stem cells.[102] Licences have been issued by the Human Fertilisation and Embryology Authority to use the cell nuclear replacement technique to produce specific stem cells for the study of motor neuron disease.[103] This is a step beyond other European Union countries. However, it has not signed the Council of Europe Convention on Biomedicine.[104] Finally, there are some countries that, as yet, have not introduced specific legislation. The United States is also following an individual track and has not introduced legislation. Instead it has imposed restrictions on the use of public funds for such research. Public funds can only be used on the stem cell lines that were reported to the National Institutes of Health in 2002, in spite of the fact that many of these lines have not been able to be replicated. This has had the effect of development of stem cell work in the private institutions.[105]

---

101 *Human Fertilisation and Embryology Act (Research Purposes) Regulations 2001* (UK).

102 See Halliday, S, "A Comparative Approach to the Regulation of Human Embryonic Stem Cell Research in Europe" (2004) 12 *Medical Law Review* 40; see also, Isasi, R et al, (2004) op cit.

103 These licences were interestingly issued to the Roslyn Institute that cloned Dolly, (2005) 295 *BioNews* (7 February 2005) at 8–11.

104 Romeo-Casabona, C, "Embryonic Stem Cell Research and Therapy: The Need for a Common European Framework" (2002) 16 *Bioethics* 557.

105 Green, R, "Benefiting from Evil: an Incipient Moral Problem in Stem Cell Research" (2002) 16 *Bioethics* 544.

Future directions

Stem cell science is at a very early stage and is marked by rapid reporting of experimental results[106] rather than established procedures. Clearly, the time from research result to clinical trial, much less any clinical application, are many years apart. Of course, the vast majority of research results will never lead to any clinical application. The infancy of the science can be demonstrated in a number of ways. First, research aims to develop pure embryonic stem cell lines. Most current stem cell lines have been cultured on murine feeder cells and, therefore, are unsuitable for any clinical application on humans. Moreover, the *Stem Cells and Regenerative Medicine Report* noted that: "most of what is known about ES [cells] come from studies in the mouse, which ... cannot be presumed to provide definitive evidence of the capabilities of human cells".[107] Secondly, as yet there is no established standard for scientifically certifying whether an embryonic stem cell line is "established". During the United States debates on stem cells, the National Institutes of Health invited researchers in 2002 to register their stem cell lines. Some 64 stem cell lines from around the world were registered.[108] Within a few years, it was clear that the vast majority of these cell lines were not "established"; that is they did not have the capacity to continue replication. At the time of writing, researchers are trying to set standards for stem cell lines by reference to the number of times the lines should be able to be frozen, thawed and still demonstrate their capacity to replicate.[109] Standards for Good Manufacturing Practice are a necessary precondition to the use of embryonic stem cells in a clinical setting as part of "established" clinical practice.[110] Finally, the *Stem Cells and Regenerative Medicine Report* noted that stem cell lines may be unstable and exhibit genetic mutations[111] and the possibility of tumour development and stated "[m]ajor questions remain about the genetic or environmental factors ... that control the fate of ES [cells] and about the ... various stages of cell differentiation".[112]

Overall, the reports in the media tend toward substantial exaggeration of the state of the science; the researchers cannot be blamed for this over-optimistic

---

106 The scientific journals are deluged with such reports, for instance Kuehn, B, "Researchers Coax Human Stem Cells to Become Motor Neurons" (2005) 293 *JAMA* 1047.

107 National Academies Committee on the Biological and Biomedical Application of Stem Cell Research, *Stem Cells and the Future of Regenerative Medicine*, National Academies Press, Washington DC, 2001, p 22.

108 Green, R, "Benefiting from Evil: an Incipient Moral Problem in Stem Cell Research" (2002) 16 *Bioethics* 544 at 552.

109 The standards will include reference to a set of genetic tests to determine viability of the stem cells.

110 The quality and lack of contamination of existing stem cells is an acknowledged problem. See "Stem Cell Lines Available to US State Researchers Are Contaminated" (2005) 292 *BioNews* week (17 January 2005) at 8–12.

111 National Academies Committee on the Biological and Biomedical Application of Stem Cell Research, *Stem Cells and the Future of Regenerative Medicine*, National Academies Press, Washington DC, 2001, p 27.

112 Ibid, at 23.

reporting. Australian scientists are at the forefront of stem cell research but the bulk of their funding flows from the public sector. The private sector has seen the departure of some former research companies, of which BresaGen was the most prominent example.[113]

The stem cell debate, particularly in the United States, has revived discussion on the biological definition of a human embryo. One aspect of this discussion is whether it may be possible by SCNT to create a source of stem cells from an embryo-like (embryoid) body that could never develop to a later stage embryo and certainly not into a "whole human being". Various proposals emerged during 2004 and the United States President's Council on Bioethics considered a particular proposal[114] which was later scientifically criticised.[115] Other reports have been made about protein injection to human eggs to stimulate a parthenogenic blastocyst development that could produce a source of cells without creating an embryo.[116] If any of these proposals achieved their aim of producing stem cells without destroying human embryos, the moral objections to embryo research could be avoided. At this stage, the science is the primary driver of the debate.

Conclusions

The cloning and stem cell technology debates were followed fairly promptly by regulation. This was one of the rarer examples of a merging of the usually staggered scientific, ethical and legal timeframes.[117] The international science has been regulated at the national level but there are many common features in the legislation and guidelines within the permissive jurisdictions, although they contain some restrictive elements. Interestingly, although the Australian research legislation is commonly referred to as the "stem cell" Act, there is no mention whatsoever of stem cells in the wording of the Act.

A tension was apparent in the longest-ever debate by the Australian Parliament on the cloning and embryo research legislation between those who wanted to

---

113 BresaGen Ltd, based in Adelaide went into receivership at the end of 2003. Along with Monash University and the Monash Institute of Reproduction and Development in Victoria, BresaGen had been recognised as a leader in the field in the Andrews Report, paras 4.8–4.10.

114 Dr William Hurlbut, Stanford University proposed using DNA from a skin cell that had been treated to prevent the trophectoderm from developing into the outer layer of cells that form the placenta. In this way the SCNT entity could never become a viable embryo, yet be a source of stem cells. Hurlbut, W, "Stanford Bioethicist Closes Gap Between Ethics and Science of Embryo Stem Cells" (2004) 143 *Bioedge* 3.

115 Dr Charles Jennings of the Harvard Stem Cell Institute has argued the Cdx2 gene will not work on humans as on mice: Melton, D, Daley, G and Jennings, C, "Altered Nuclear Transfer in Stem Cells: A Flawed Proposal" (2004) 351 *New England Journal of Medicine* 2791 with reply from Hurlbut in (2005) 352 *New England Journal of Medicine* 1153.

116 See "Eggs Tricked into Becoming Embryos" (2004) 287 *BioNews* (29 November 2004) at 6–9.

117 Somerville, M, *The Ethical Canary: Science, Society and the Human Spirit*, Viking, Victoria, 2000.

promote freedom in research[118] and the national biotechnology strategy,[119] and those morally concerned over the status of the embryo and the permissible limits of research on embryos. The legislation was a compromise between these approaches but a compromise that only permitted the research subject to significant restrictions. A national regulatory scheme for embryo research on excess ART embryos was an essential precondition to the development of stem cell technology and its potential consistent with the commitments of the government to its biotechnology policy. In essence, the implementation of the recommendations of the Andrews Report in the *Research involving Human Embryos Act 2002* (Cth) also realised the recommendations of the reports of the Family Law Council and the Senate Select Committee some 20 years before and of the AHEC in 1998 calling for a uniform national approach to regulation.[120]

The tension between research and protection of the human embryo was recognised in the provisions of the legislation that included a requirement for an independent review of both *Research involving Human Embryos Act* and the *Prohibition of Human Cloning Act*. The review[121] examined not only the legislation but also the operation of the licensing scheme, including the monitoring and enforcement provisions as well as the alignment of the legislation with scientific developments. The review recommended that the regulatory regime continue (Recommendations 1, 14). The review also recommended that SCNT should be permitted, under licence, to create and use human embryo clones for research (Recommendations 23-27).

---

118 In this respect see Article 12 of the *Declaration of the Human Genome and Human Rights,* which states that "freedom of research, which is necessary for the progress of knowledge is part of freedom of thought. The applications of research ... shall seek to offer relief from suffering and improve the health of individuals and humans as a whole".

119 See *Australian Biotechnology: A National Strategy,* Commonwealth of Australia, Canberra, 2000.

120 See Chalmers, D and Nicol, D, "Embryonic Stem Cell Research: Can the Law Balance Ethical, Scientific and Economic Values" Parts 1 and 2 (2003) 18 *Law and the Human Genome Review* 43 and 91, particularly at 107–108.

121 See *Legislation Review,* Australian Government, December 2005 (Chair, the late Justice John Lockhart). At the time of writing there has been not formal government response.

PART VI

RESEARCH AND VULNERABILITY

13

Genetic research and commercialisation

Dianne Nicol

Introduction

The results of the Human Genome Project and other biomedical research are being used in the development of new drugs, diagnostics and therapies by the medical biotechnology industry in Australia and elsewhere.[1] Whilst the path from research to clinical practice is significantly longer and more tortuous than some media reports may have us believe, it is probably fair to say that the outcomes of this research are likely to play a significant role in alleviating human suffering caused by disease within the next decade or so. Hence, provided that equitable access to these new health care developments can be secured,[2] there are good social justifications for continuing to support this research drive and encouraging its dissemination into practice by industry. There are also sound economic reasons for supporting the development of an indigenous biotechnology industry. The Human Genome Project and parallel studies have played a pivotal role in the development of thriving biotechnology industries in many developed countries. At the same time, both the research and commercial components of human genetic technology raise some unique ethical, legal and social implications, which may become particularly acute where these two components intersect and overlap.

The consequences of this overlap between research and development are being subjected to some intensive scrutiny, along with the many other ethical, legal and social implications arising from developments in human genetic technology.[3] There are a host of concerns associated with the commercialisation of human genetic research, many of which were canvassed by the Australian Law Reform Commission in its inquiry into gene patenting and human health.[4] In this chapter,

---

1   For a history of the Human Genome Project and information on some of the current and future research programs in this area see: Genome Programs of the United States Department of Energy Office of Science <http://doegenomes.org/> (accessed 9 February 2006).

2   This, of course, is a significant issue in its own right. Although it is beyond the scope of this chapter to canvass access to health care in any depth, other chapters discuss this issue more fully. See particularly Chapter 30.

3   Many of these complex ethical, legal and social issues we canvassed in an inquiry jointly conducted by the Australian Law Reform Commission and Australian Health Ethics Committee, *Essentially Yours: the Protection of Human Genetic Information*, Report No 96, ALRC, Canberra, 2003, <www.austlii.edu.au/au/other/alrc/publications/reports/96/> (accessed 9 February 2006).

4   Australian Law Reform Commission, *Genes and Ingenuity: Gene Patenting and Human Health*, Report No 99, ALRC, Canberra, 2004, <www.austlii.edu.au/au/other/alrc/publications/reports/99/> (accessed 1 April 2005) (ALRC). See also the summary of the report in Chapter 22: Current issues in gene patenting.

the focus of inquiry is on the disputes and dilemmas that arise for public sector researchers and organisations in this new commercialised research environment. According to Sheldon Krimsky:

> In such a picture, university science becomes entangled with entrepreneurship; knowledge is pursued for monetary value; and expertise with a point of view can be purchased.[5]

Krimsky's premise is that the growing trend towards commercialisation of academic research inevitably leads to conflicts of interest. Whilst conflict of interest is a matter of genuine and increasing concern, it would be wrong simply to classify all commercialisation as "bad".[6] Commercialisation is important from both the economic and the social perspectives. In Australia, it is both necessary and desirable for research to be commercialised by Australian industry to benefit the national economy and to ensure that the products of commercialisation are made available to the Australian community. The benefits of commercialisation must be recognised, but at the same time the risks must be acknowledged and guarded against. In the first part of this chapter, the commercialisation imperative in human genetic research in Australia is discussed. Practical and other implications of this imperative on traditional research practices are then considered.

Policy considerations: The commercialisation imperative

One of the defining features of pharmaceutical and medical biotechnology industries throughout the world is their reliance on patents to recover the enormous costs of research into and development of new products. Pharmaceutical patents have been available for many years in most of the developed world. One of the significant changes that has occurred more recently is that patents are being claimed for inventions much higher up the road from basic research to commercial product. This is sometimes referred to as the patent gold rush.[7] It is marked by a shift in research culture into the commercial sphere and an increase in types and numbers of patent applications that are being filed.[8]

---

55 Krimsky, S, *Science in the Private Interest: Has the Lure of Profits Corrupted Biomedical Research?* Rowman & Littlefield, United States, 2003, p 1.

6   Nicol, D, "The Golden Path from the Ivory Tower of Academic Science" (2004) *Australian Review of Public Affairs*, 1 November 2004, <www.australianreview.net/> (accessed 9 February 2006), which reviews Krimsky, S, *Science in the Private Interest: Has the Lure of Profits Corrupted Biomedical Research?* Rowman & Littlefield, United States, 2003.

7   Nicol, D and Nielsen, J, "The Australian Medical Biotechnology Industry and Access to Intellectual Property: Issues for Patent Law Development" (2001) 23 *Sydney Law Review* 347 at 360–362. The United Kingdom-based Royal Society has referred to this as "a most unhealthy gold rush mentality": Royal Society, *Keeping Science Open: The Effects of Intellectual Property Policy on the Conduct of Science*, Royal Society, London, 2003, <www.royalsoc. ac.uk/document.asp?tip=0&id=1374> (accessed 9 February 2006).

8   See, for example, CHI Research Inc, *Inventing Our Future: the Link Between Australian Patenting and Basic Science*, AGPS, Canberra, 2000.

Patent policy

Patents give their owner the right to exclude all others from commercially exploi-ting the invention for a limited period (usually 20 years). They are granted for products and processes that provide a technical solution to a technical problem. Traditionally, a range of subject matter has been considered to be unpatentable, including such things as laws of nature, physical phenomena and abstract ideas, which can be thought of as discoveries rather than inventions.[9] As a consequence, patents can be seen as creatures of applied science, not basic science. However, there is extensive and ongoing debate as to the patentability of a wide range of subject matter at the "fuzzy line" between discovery and invention, including living organisms, gene sequences and other material found in the natural environ-ment.[10] In Australia, patents continue to be granted for products and processes that fall within this fuzzy line, including genetically modified living organisms, cells, proteins, genes and methods of medical treatment.[11] Although there is little in the way of clear statutory or judicial authority permitting such grants,[12] nor has there been any legislative or judicial intervention to prevent them.

As with most other developed countries, patent filing activity has increased sharply in Australia over the last decade. In genetic technology, aside from gene patents, there has been increased patent activity in relation to other research tools.[13] Some of these research tools are particularly important to the future development of the technology. As Arti Rai explains, these are the "fundamental research plat-forms that open up new and uncharted areas of investigation".[14] Notable patented research tools include recombinant DNA technology, the polymerase chain reaction, intron sequence analysis, human embryonic stem cell technology and many others.[15]

9 *Diamond v Chakrabarty* 447 US 303 (1980) at 309.

10 See, for example, Kevles, D and Berkowitz, A, "The Gene Patenting Controversy: a Con-vergence of Law, Economic Interests and Ethics" (2001) 67 *Brooklyn Law Review* 233 at 240–241; Burk, D, "Patenting Transgenic Human Embryos: A Nonuse Cost Perspective" (1993) 30 *Houston Law Review* 1597 at 1599.

11 IP Australia, *Australian Patents For: Biological Inventions*, IP Australia, Canberra, 2005. Note that *Diamond v Chakrabarty* 447 US 303 (1980), the leading United States case on patentability of living organisms, was referred to with approval by the High Court in *Grain Pool of Western Australia v Commonwealth* (2000) 46 IPR 515. See particularly paras [46] and [47] of the majority judgment and [134] of Kirby J's judgment. Paragraphs 46 and 47 of the majority judgment could be read as referring only to the applicability of *Chakrabarty* in United States law, or could be read more broadly, applying in Australian law as well. See Rimmer, M, "Franklin Barley: Patent Law and Plant Breeders Rights" (2003) 10(4) *Murdoch Electronic Law Journal* <www.murdoch.edu.au/elaw> (accessed 9 February 2006).

12 The case of *Bristol Myers Squibb v FH Faulding & Co Ltd* (2000) 46 IPR 553, which permits patenting of methods of medical treatment, is one notable exception.

13 Research tools can be defined as "resources used by scientists, where those resources have no immediate therapeutic or diagnostic value": ALRC (2004) op cit, p 301.

14 Rai, A, "Genome Patents: A Case Study in Patenting Research Tools" (2002) 77 *Academic Medicine* 1368 at 1369.

15 Details as to the nature of these and other research tools and ownership of the patents associated with them can be found in Nicol, D and Nielsen, J, *Patents and Medical Biotech-nology: An Empirical Analysis of Issues Facing the Australian Industry*, Centre for Law and Genetics, Occasional Paper No 6, 2003 pp 10–12 and 40–49 (Nicol–Nielsen study).

Australian governmental policy

Australia has a number of strengths in medical biotechnology, including world-class expertise in research, geographical advantages in terms of expanding regional markets and appropriate structures to promote close cooperation between the public and private sectors.[16] These strengths were recognised in the Wills Review, a major inquiry into health and medical research in Australia that was completed in 1999, citing figures that indicate that our research output is far in excess of what would be expected for the size of the Australian population.[17] However, the review also emphasised that commercialisation of this research output needs to be improved, and that this window of opportunity would close given the pace of change unless Australia acts immediately.[18]

The Federal Government has responded to the recommendations of the Wills and other reviews in a number of ways. In particular, it has established a program: Backing Australia's Ability to promote science and innovation.[19] The first phase of the program was introduced in 2001, with a commitment of $3 billion over five years, and a second phase added a further commitment of $5.3 billion over seven years in 2004. The stated aims of Backing Australia's Ability are the pursuit of excellence in research, science and technology through the generation of new ideas, the commercial application of ideas, and developing and retaining skills.[20] Additional funding of almost $60 million was provided to the Australian Stem Cell Centre through the Biotechnology Centre of Excellence program. Commercialisation is also a key objective of this funding program, which specifically refers to the need to foster creation of spin-offs, networks and clusters of commercial activity and to commercialise intellectual property to ensure maximum financial and investment benefit accrues to Australia.[21] The establishment of these programs by the Federal Government illustrates a clear policy of encouraging commercialisation of public sector research. This policy of merging of basic research and applied technology, particularly genetic technology, is common throughout the developed world.[22]

---

16 Health and Medical Research Strategic Review, *The Virtuous Cycle: Working Together for Health and Medical Research: Final Report*, AGPS, Canberra, 1999 p 1 (referred to as the Wills Review, after the Chair of the review committee, Mr Peter Wills).

17 Ibid.

18 Ibid. See also ALRC (2004) op cit, Ch 17.

19 For information about the Backing Australia's Ability program see: <http://backingaus. innovation.gov.au/> (accessed 9 February 2006).

20 Ibid.

21 See Department of Industry, Tourism and Resources, *Biotechnology Centre of Excellence, The Australian Stem Cell Centre Fact Sheet*, 2005, at: <www.industry.gov.au/intrinternet/cms content.cfm?objectID=09C86ED8-BA68-4C89-AE3B13AD3BC149C2> (accessed 9 February 2006).

22 See particularly, Eisenberg, R and Nelson, R, "Public vs Proprietary Science: a Fruitful Tension?" (2002) 77 *Academic Medicine* 1392; see also Chalmers, D and Nicol, D, "Commercialisation of Biotechnology: Public Trust and Research" (2004) 6 *International Journal of Biotechnology* 116.

In line with Australian government policy, technology-driven research is also favoured by funding agencies and institutions. For example, the *National Principles of Intellectual Property Management for Publicly Funded Research* state that "[r]esearch institutions, and where appropriate, individual researchers, *are expected* to consider the most appropriate way of exploiting the IP generated from publicly funded research".[23]

Social policy

Government policy of encouraging commercialisation and patenting of public sector research assumes that this is the optimal social strategy for Australia. There is some merit in this assumption, particularly if the claim that the patent system promotes indigenous innovation is correct.[24] However, it would perhaps be naïve to assume that the pursuit of this commercialisation imperative will always be in harmony with other social objectives. The impact of the commercialisation of genetic technology on the research, industry and health care sectors needs to thoroughly evaluated. It is beyond the scope of this chapter to explore these issues fully, but three key points are canvassed below.

First, patents may not always encourage innovation; those that claim broad rights over foundational research tools may be particularly problematic. There is debate internationally about the social consequences of granting such patents.[25] Owners of these broad patents could exercise significant control over whole areas of research and development. On the one hand, they could allow their patented technology to be used widely for minimal costs, particularly in the research sector. On the other hand, they could refuse to allow others to use the technology, or restrict access, or charge excessive prices for use, amounting to a constructive refusal to use. As such, in the right hands, these foundational patents could have a powerful positive impact on innovation, by encouraging further development of new technology. In the wrong hands, they could have a serious negative impact, particularly if basic researchers are denied access.

---

23 Working party comprising the Australian Research Council, the Australian Tertiary Institutions Commercial Companies Association, the Australian Vice-Chancellors' Committee, the Department of Education, Training and Youth Affairs, the Department of Industry, Science and Resources, IP Australia and the National Health and Medical Research Council, *National Principles of Intellectual Property Management for Publicly Funded Research, Australian Research Council,* 2001, p 6, <www.arc.gov.au/pdf/01_01.pdf> (accessed 9 February 2006). (Emphasis added.)

24 See, for example, the comments by Senator Robert Ray to this effect in the second reading speech to the Patents Bill 1990 in: Australia, Senate, *Debates* (Hansard), 29 May 1990, p 1271.

25 Although it is impossible to list all relevant sources, see particularly Heller, M and Eisenberg, R, "Can Patents Deter Innovation? The Anti-commons in Bio-medical Research" (1998) 280 *Science* 698. Other notable sources include: Nuffield Council on Bioethics, *The Ethics of Patenting DNA: A Discussion Paper,* Nuffield Council, London, 2002; National Research Council (NRC), *Intellectual Property Rights and Research Tools in Molecular Biology,* National Academy of Sciences, Washington DC, 1997; ALRC (2004) op cit, Ch 12. See Nicol–Nielsen study (2003) op cit, at 50–63 for further references.

A number of patents claiming rights over foundational research tools have been identified as being particularly likely to have an impact on future genetic research, because of their broad scope and because of the way in which they are being exploited.[26] Despite this, empirical evidence tends to suggest that working solutions are being found by the industry to ensure that the path from research to product development is not blocked.[27] In particular, most key technologies tend to be non-exclusive licensed for small fees, for the benefit of owners and users alike. For example, recombinant DNA technology has been described as "arguably the defining technique of modern molecular biology" and "the founding technology of the biotechnology industry".[28] At the same time, the patents claiming the technology, owned by Stanford University and widely licensed for modest fees, have been described as "the most successful patent[s] in university licensing" with returns of US$139 million by 1995.[29]

It should also be noted that although there are presently no restrictions on the grant of such patents in Australia, some of these problematic patents have not actually been granted here and hence the potential for a negative impact on innovation may be less here than in some other developed countries.[30] Nevertheless, that potential does exist. To guard against this, the ALRC has recommended that public funding agencies should develop principles and guidelines to ensure that commercial exploitation is balanced with wide dissemination of research tools.[31] The Centre for Law and Genetics agrees with this recommendation, and has noted that:

> Key features might include directions to engage in non-exclusive licensing in most instances and ensuring that the research community has access to fundamental research resources. However, the guidelines must also reflect commercial realities. For example, in some circumstances broad non-exclusive licensing will not be appropriate. The guidelines should be cast in terms that allow for the best technology transfer options to be pursued, based on all relevant considerations, including the broader public benefit.[32]

---

26   Listed in the Nicol–Nielsen study (2003) op cit, at 40–49.

27   See particularly Walsh, J, Arora, A and Cohen, W, "Effects of Research Tool Patenting and Licensing on Biomedical Innovation" in Cohen, WM and Merrill, SA (eds), *Patents in the Knowledge-Based Economy*, National Academies Press, Washington, 2003 p 287, <http://books.nap.edu/books/0309086361/html/285.html#pagetop> (accessed 9 February 2006); see also Walsh, J, Arora, A and Cohen, W, "Working Through the Patent Problem" (2003) 299 *Science* 1021 and a summary of their more recent study in: Walsh, JP, Cho, C and Cohen WM, "View from the Bench: Patents and Material Transfers" (2005) 309 *Science* 2002.

28   National Research Council, *Intellectual Property Rights and Research Tools in Molecular Biology*, summary of workshop at the National Academy of Sciences, 15–16 February 1996, <www.nap.edu/readingroom/books/property/> (accessed on 9 February 2006) Ch 5.

29   Ibid.

30   Nicol–Nielsen study (2003) op cit, at 40–49. The results of Nicol–Nielsen study on this point are closely aligned with those in the study by Walsh, Arora and Cohen (2003) op cit. See particularly the Nicol–Nielsen study (2003) op cit, at 254–257.

31   ALRC (2004) op cit, p 314.

32   This quotation from the Centre for Law and Genetics' submission to the ALRC inquiry, extracted by the ALRC (2004) op cit, p 315.

Secondly, the release of research results into the public domain can play equally as influential a role in commercialisation as patenting (if not more so). A report commissioned by the Australian Research Council (ARC) in 2003 on the return on investment from ARC-funded research concludes that there was a 10 per cent social rate of return based on building of the basic knowledge stock and only a 3 per cent return from generation of commercialisable intellectual property.[33] The report explains that basic knowledge delivers benefits through an indirect "route to use", usually through publication of research papers, and refers to other studies showing a heavy usage of publicly funded Australian science in Australian patenting.[34] It notes that:

> [R]elative to total research output, Australian-invented US patents are ten times more heavily reliant on Australian science than on global science. These findings highlight the crucial importance of publicly funded domestic science to Australian patent activity.[35]

Finally, although commercialisation of public sector research may be in the national interest, it may not provide sufficient rewards for individual research organisations. For example, the 2003 report commissioned by the ARC notes that commercialisation returns to universities are relatively small when compared with money spent on research.[36] Ann Monotti and Sam Ricketson also comment that the increased propensity to patent in the public sector has not been matched by increased output, even in the United States with the bulk of technology transfer revenue coming from a few successful inventions, the "big hits" or "block-busters".[37] Yochai Benkler provides further data, which shows that in the United States, revenues obtained from patent licensing provide an "insignificant portion of total university revenues".[38]

However, the 2003 ARC report notes that companies that have been specifically established to commercialise publicly funded research may be much more successful with regard to return on investment.[39] A report to the Prime Minister's Science, Engineering and Innovation Council in 2001 strongly supports the strategy of forming spin-off companies for the purpose of commercialising research, noting that:

> If we can grow 200–250 more Australian research-based companies ... over the next five years, the prize would be around AU$20 billion added to our annual

---

33 Allen Consulting Group, *A Wealth of Knowledge: The Return on Investment from ARC-funded research*, report to the Australian Research Council, 4 September 2003, <www.arc.gov.au/ publications/arc_publications.htm#2003> (accessed 9 February 2006), pp 44 and 49–50.

34 Ibid, pp 42–43.

35 Ibid.

36 Ibid, p 46.

37 Monotti, A and Ricketson, S, *Universities and Intellectual Property: Ownership and Exploitation*, Oxford University Press, Oxford, 2003, pp 446–451.

38 Benkler, Y, "Commons-based Strategies and the Problems of Patents" (2004) 305 *Science* 1110 at 1110–1111.

39 Allen Consulting Group (2003) op cit, p 49.

export earnings. Australia would be well on the way to reducing the national debt and the cost of servicing it.[40]

Although these reports both lend support to this commercialisation strategy, they fail to acknowledge that many biotechnology products, particularly drug-related products never make it to market. There may be some spectacular successes, as highlighted in the ARC report, but companies that are reliant on the success of single products have a high risk of failure. Monotti and Ricketson note that although there is no data on the survival rate of spin-offs, they are prone to failure for a number of reasons, including economies of scale, entering into inappropriate alliances and developing high-risk embryonic technologies.[41]

A need for reform?

It can be concluded that commercialisation of public sector research does seem to have a sound policy foundation from both the economic and social perspectives.[42] However, there will be instances where the national benefit may be better served by release of research results into the public domain. The ALRC recognises as much, and goes so far as to recommend that public funding agencies should be prepared to place conditions on grant funding, requiring, in exceptional circum-stances, that research results should either be placed in the public domain or, if patented, widely licensed.[43] The Centre for Law and Genetics has expressed support for this recommendation:

> We do not see that the implementation of this Proposal would in any way impinge on commercialisation in the normal course of events for "commercialisable" research. We see that the circumstances in which the NHMRC or ARC would impose such conditions as being strictly limited to foundational research disco-veries of the nature of the human genome project, the SNP project [Single Nucleotide Polymorphism (SNP) Project] and the HapMap project. In our view, these projects should be freed from the fetters of commercialisation.[44]

---

40 Prime Minister's Science, Engineering and Innovation Council, *Commercialisation of Public Sector Research*, working group report presented at the Council's Seventh Meeting, 28 June 2001, Commonwealth of Australia, Canberra, 2001) p 3, <www.dest.gov.au/science_innovation/publication-resources/profiles/commercialisation-research.htm> (accessed 9 February 2006).

41 Monotti and Ricketson (2003) op cit, pp 451–456. See also Department of Education, Science and Training, *Best Practice Processes for University Research Commercialisation*, DEST, Canberra, 2002, p 28; ALRC (2004) op cit, p 419.

42 Note, however, that the United Kingdom Royal Society has pointed out that the merits of universities obtaining intellectual property as opposed to disseminating knowledge have not been well documented and are worthy of further study: The Royal Society (2003) op cit, p v.

43 ALRC (2004) op cit, p 289.

44 This quotation is part of the Centre for Law and Genetics' submission to the ALRC inquiry, extracted by the ALRC (2004) op cit, p 285.

Practical considerations: Challenges to institutional practices

There has been some empirical analysis of the practical impact of commercialisation of public sector research and the views of researchers about the commercialisation process. For example, Monotti and Ricketson report on the results of a survey of academics from Monash University in 1997, which revealed that 68 per cent of respondents agreed or strongly agreed that academic staff should explore the commercial potential of their research and teaching materials.[45] The Centre for Law and Genetics has obtained data on this and related issues as part of a more comprehensive study on patenting and patent licensing in the Australian medical biotechnology industry in 2002–2003 (hereafter the Nicol–Nielsen study).[46] This study included surveys and interviews with participants across the industry, spanning the public research, private industry and diagnostics sectors. It highlights some of the practical considerations faced by public sector research institutions and researchers in the commercialised research environment. Key findings are summarised below.[47]

Research, commercialisation and technology transfer

The strengths in the biomedical research in Australia were widely acknowledged by many survey and interview respondents in the Nicol–Nielsen study. Public and private sector respondents alike confirmed that there are extensive research opportunities here. The survey and interview data also confirm that patenting is common in the Australian public sector and reveal extensive collaborative activity between the public and private sectors. For most researchers, commercialisation has become a reality, albeit an unwelcome one for some. For example, one technology transfer officer noted that:

> There are two types of researchers: those that always have their eye on further activities. For them, intellectual property is the currency. They know that it is an important part of their work. Others (generally older academics) find it really annoying. They find it difficult to understand corporate bodies, ownership of intellectual property and employment issues. But this culture is changing. We rarely come across problems now.

Perhaps surprisingly, some respondents commented that some public institutions may have actually become over-enthusiastic in their adoption of a pro-patenting stance, to such an extent that patents are taken out when there is little or no likelihood of commercial exploitation. It was noted that the quality of patent applications is sometimes poor because provisional applications are rushed through to allow research results to be published or presented at a conference. An intellectual property adviser noted that:

---

45   Monotti and Ricketson (2003) op cit, pp 433–434.
46   Nicol–Nielsen study (2003) op cit.
47   For detailed results, see Nicol–Nielsen study (2003) op cit, at 122–136. This component of the study was written by the author. To avoid excessive footnoting, individual page numbers are not referred to in the following summary.

Generally there will be no intellectual property strategy and the patent will have been filed at the last minute. The patent attorney will not have been given adequate advice about strategy. Fair basing will be a problem – it may be necessary to re-file unless claims are broad enough.

Problems also arise in transferring patented technology to the private sector. Various respondents confirmed that one of the biggest problems in Australia is naivety in bargaining and lack of consistency in intellectual property management strategies across institutions. Nevertheless, it was generally recognised that these strategies have greatly improved over the last decade or so. Some of the larger Australian institutions have their own technology transfer office, staffed by people with expertise in patent prosecution, deal negotiation and science. Other institutions may have a single technology transfer officer or business manager, but some still have no one at all, or have part-time assistants with a low level of expertise.

Respondents emphasised the importance of being flexible in technology transfer negotiations and utilising various strategies, including assignment, forming spin-off companies, licensing and collaborations. One of the most difficult issues in technology transfer negotiations is settling on the value of the technology. Respondents acknowledged that in the past Australian public sector organisations tended to under-value their intellectual property, giving it away too soon for too little. However, some noted that attitudes may now have swung too far the other way, with some organisations over-valuing their intellectual property. Part of the problem is in making the distinction between research outcomes and commercial products. As one company respondent put it: "We don't care what they have spent on it, the question is what it's worth to us". This quotation highlights the fundamental dilemma for public sector organisations noted earlier: they are being encouraged to follow a commercialisation path but it is questionable whether they can realistically hope to profit, or even recover the costs of managing patents and technology transfer.

Impact on publication

Many respondents in the Nicol–Nielsen study acknowledged that patenting is having an effect on traditional research practices.[48] One of the biggest challenges for public sector researchers is balancing the need to publish their research results in high quality peer-reviewed journals against the need for secrecy and limited disclosure to protect the patentability of inventions. Respondents indicated that patents and publications can be complementary if managed properly. The requirement to maintain secrecy is not necessarily a problem provided that this does not

---

48   For discussions on the impact of commercialisation on the traditional norms of science, as identified by Robert Merton in *The Sociology of Science*, University of Chicago Press, Chicago, 1973, see particularly: Eisenberg, R, "Proprietary Rights and the Norms of Science in Biotechnology Research" (1987) 97 *Yale University Law Journal* 177; Merges, R, "Property Rights and the Commons: the Case of Scientific Research" (1996) 13 *Social Philosophy & Policy* 145; Rai, A, "Regulating Scientific Research: Intellectual Property Rights and the Norms of Science" (1999) 94 *Northwestern University Law Review* 77.

unduly delay publication of research results. As Monotti and Ricketson put it: "it is not secrecy per se that is the problem: it is the length of the delay before information is publicly available".[49]

Nicol–Nielsen study respondents noted that most research institutions have a requirement that all publications have to be vetted and signed off either by the head of the research group or a technology transfer officer. Some have arrangements with industry that require that the industry partner inspects and approves all publications, which inevitably slows the publication process. However, the length of delay is extremely variable, from 24 hours to several months. Some mentioned that a 30-day period for review is usually provided for, but often turn around may be much more rapid.

The importance of publishing is widely recognised both in the public and private sectors. One company respondent said that his company recognises and respects the right to publish. Others agreed but noted that it is not always beneficial to put too much information into the public domain, particularly when research is only in the pre-commercial phase. One respondent noted that sometimes it would be better to keep information proprietary as secret know-how, but because of the publishing ethos it was necessary to file provisional patent applications instead. Granting agencies are also increasingly recognising patenting as a measure of academic excellence. However, this is not necessarily the case for the research institutions themselves. One university technology transfer officer said that academic promotions policy needed to be amended to reflect changes to publication practices.

Ownership and clean title

One of the most important aspects of intellectual property management is ensuring that there is no uncertainty about ownership. It is generally recognised that where intellectual property is created by an employee during the normal course of their employment then ownership vests in the employer, absent any agreement to the contrary. However, in the public sector the issue is complicated by a number of factors including, but not limited to, the following:

- uncertainty as to the "normal course of employment";
- involvement of students and visiting scholars in particular research projects generating intellectual property;
- funding arrangements;
- collaborative arrangements; and
- background intellectual property and know-how brought to particular projects by individual researchers.

---

49 Monotti and Ricketson (2003) op cit, p 42. Note that Australia now has a "grace period" meaning that publications by or with consent of the patentee within 12 months prior to filing the patent do not compromise the novelty of the invention. However, the fact that a number of other countries do not have provision for a grace period is problematic. For information on grace periods see: <www.ipaustralia.gov.au/patents/what_quiet_grace. shtml> (accessed 9 February 2006).

A report commissioned by the Commonwealth Department of Education, Science and Training provides a detailed analysis of the complex legal issues associated with patent ownership in the public sector.[50] It recommends that the Australian position should be further clarified in order to remove impediments to effective management and commercialisation of intellectual property in the public research sector. Its recommended position is that ownership vest in the institution by default.[51] The Nicol–Nielsen study indicates that most research institutions are already moving towards this position, with the notable exception of the University of Melbourne, where ownership is vested in the inventor.[52]

A need for reform?

Many of the practical commercialisation issues faced by Australian public sector organisations are being resolved. Researchers are becoming more willing to embark on the commercialisation and patenting process. Attempts are being made to manage ownership issues and the tension between the need for secrecy during the patent filing process and the need for rapid publication of research results. Nevertheless, there are huge challenges involved in the technology transfer process from the research sector to the industry sector. Major obstacles include finding partners, valuing the technology and acquiring appropriate negotiating skills. The process could be made far more efficient by education and consolidation of resources and knowledge bases both at the local and at the national level. The ALRC, in its inquiry on gene patenting and human health, also focused attention on these issues, emphasising the importance of clean ownership and control and good intellectual property management and technology transfer strategies.[53]

Other implications in playing the commercialisation game: Patent infringement and exemptions

Where a public sector organisation engages in commercial practices, it must expect to encounter intellectual property owned by others and must have strategies in place to mitigate the risk of exposure to patent infringement actions. The question addressed in this section is whether the organisation's research work is included in these commercial practices. It is often said that the use of patented inventions in non-commercial research does not amount to patent infringement, because such

---

50 Christie, A, D'Aloisio, S, Gaita, S, Howlett, M and Webster, E, *Analysis of the Legal Framework for Patent Ownership in Publicly Funded Research Institutions*, Commonwealth of Australia, Canberra, 2003.

51 Ibid, p 212.

52 The University of Melbourne is specifically referred to because a number of respondents drew attention to the University's unique arrangements regarding ownership. Christie et al (2003) op cit, also make specific reference to the ownership arrangements at the University of Melbourne.

53 See generally ALRC (2004) op cit.

use is exempt. However, if a so-called "research exemption" exists in Australia, its ambit is far from clear,[54] and the growth in private funding of research and other commercial arrangements in the public sector is increasing the fog of uncertainty that surrounds it. There is no express exemption for acts done for research purposes under existing Australian legislation and there has been no consideration of whether or not an exemption could be read into the legislation by Australian courts. However, patent law in other jurisdictions provides some assistance. In the United Kingdom, for example, an express exemption exists,[55] and in the United States, despite the lack of an express exemption, there is a line of authority providing that certain uses are exempt.[56] As a general rule, the exemption is recognised as having two limbs, the first encompassing non-commercial research and the second dealing with experimentation aimed at testing the efficacy of the invention or making improvements to it (sometimes referred to as *research on* the invention as opposed to *research with* it). In the United States, for example, in the old case of *Whittemore v Cutter* Story J stated:

> It could never have been the intention of the legislature to punish a man who constructed such a machine merely for philosophical experiments [the first limb] or for the purpose of ascertaining the sufficiency of the machine to produce its described effects [the second limb].[57]

Similarly, in the United Kingdom legislation there also two distinct limbs.[58]

The two components to the exemption can be justified on a number of grounds. In particular, the *research on* limb is justified because it is a logical extension of the disclosure requirement in patent law (people should be allowed to test the adequacy of the disclosure) and because it satisfies the primary purpose of the patent system to encourage innovation (people should be allowed to improve on the patented invention). The non-commercial research limb can be justified on the basis that the patent grant only allows the holder to exclude others from exploitation and it should not be used in a way that stifles non-commercial research, because this could negate the innovation goal of the patent system. This

---

54 For a review of exemption from infringement for non-profit research see Nottenbaum, C, Pardey, PG and Wright, BD, "Accessing Other People's Technology for Non-profit Research" (2002) 43 *Australian Journal of Agricultural & Resource Economics* 3. See also Rimmer, M, "The Freedom to Tinker: Patent Law and Experimental Use" (2005) 15 *Expert Opinion* 167.

55 *Patents Act 1977* (UK) s 60(5).

56 This line of authority starts with *Whittemore v Cutter* 1 Gall 429, 29 F Cas 1120 at 1121 (CCD Mass 1813), as cited in *Roche Products Inc v Bolar Pharmaceutical Co Inc* 733 F 2d 858 (1984) and extends to the recent decisions of *Madey v Duke University* 307 F 3d 1351 at 1360–1 (Fed Cir, 2002) and *Merck KgaA v Integra Lifesciences I, Ltd* No 03-1237 (SCt 2005). (Note, however, that the *Merck* case focused primarily on a statutory provision relating to pharmaceuticals).

57 1 Gall 429 29 F Cas 1120 (CCD Mass 1813).

58 The first, in s 60(5)(a) of the *Patents Act 1977* (UK), relates to private, non-commercial use of the invention, the second, in s 60(5)(b), relates to experimental use of the invention for purposes relating to the subject matter of the invention.

is most likely to arise in the non-commercial research context when the patent claims a fundamental research tool. It must, of course, be recognised that the patent system, by its very nature, allows for restrictions on access to patented inventions and that when a patent is granted for a research tool the patentee should, as a general rule, be able to enforce it. To make all uses of research tools exempt would effectively reduce the value of such patents to zero.

If the judges of the Federal Court of Australia and High Court of Australia were given the opportunity to decide these issues they may well read some sort of implied exemption into patent law. However, as with any matter based on judicial decision-making there can never be certainty as to the outcome. Hence, there may be some justification for creating an express exemption or exemptions in Aust-ralian patent law, but only if their scope can be defined clearly and if they do not limit protections that are presently accepted as appropriate in practice.

Current practice in Australia

Results from the Nicol–Nielsen study suggest that at the time that the study was undertaken there was a widespread belief in all sectors of the Australian biotech-nology industry that non-commercial research was or should be exempt from patent infringement.[59] A significant number of company respondents said that they would not seek licences from participants in the research institution sector because it was not a wise decision from a business perspective. One pharmaceutical company respondent explained that, even though intellectual property is the company's life-blood, there are benefits to be derived from encouraging research. He stated that his company would provide research materials to public sector researchers and that the starting premise is supply rather than denial. However, he added that if the research becomes commercially valuable the researcher has to come back to the company to renegotiate. Another respondent said that it would be ridiculous to contemplate chasing universities for infringement, in part because it would affect the company's reputation in the academic community and in part because damages would not be recovered in any event.

Research institution respondents generally confirmed that at that time that it was a rare thing for a patent to be enforced against them. One respondent said:

> Patents held by others are never a problem. I have never had an infringement letter, except one years ago relating to taq polymerase. We were making it. Roche wrote a letter to us. We wrote back saying that we were not infringing and would not pay anyway. That was the end of it.

As such, at the time the Nicol–Nielsen study was undertaken, it would seem that a general practice-based research exemption was operating in Australia, despite the lack of certainty in the law. Many patent holders either assumed that non-commercial use was exempt, thought that it should be, or considered that it would be inappropriate or impractical to pursue researchers using their patented

---

59   See generally Nicol–Nielsen study (2003) op cit, at 218–222.

inventions for non-commercial research purposes. Similarly, those respondents who used patented technology for non-commercial research purposes generally expressed the belief that their use was exempt, or that it should be, or that they didn't need to worry about it because of the low risk that they would be pursued for infringement.

Although the study did not explore fully the question of whether or not *research on* the patented invention was generally considered to be exempt by industry participants, some respondents did acknowledge that all research on patented inventions is exempt irrespective of whether it is done in the public sector or the private sector.

A need for reform?

Despite the findings in the Nicol–Nielsen study, it would be unwise for public research institutions to assume that they are, in fact, protected from patent infringement actions. The ALRC and the Advisory Council on Intellectual Property (ACIP) have both been conducting public inquiries on this issue over the past couple of years: the ALRC as part of its broader inquiry into gene patenting and human health,[60] and the ACIP through a specific reference from the Federal Government.[61] The drivers leading to these inquiries probably can be attributed to increasing concerns about the impact of patents on the research sector arising from a small number of enforcement actions relating to key research tool patents and the fear that such actions could have a detrimental effect on innovation[62] together with the influential decision of Untied States Court of Appeals for the Federal Circuit in *Madey v Duke University.*[63] The court in *Madey* followed a line of precedent limiting the exemption to actions performed for "amusement, to satisfy idle curiosity, or for strictly philosophical inquiry".[64] The court concluded that this does not include use that is in any way commercial in nature or conduct that is "in keeping with the alleged infringer's legitimate business, regardless of commercial implications".[65] Consequently, a public research institution may not be able to rely on the exemption when a researcher uses a patented invention in a research project because it furthers that institution's legitimate business objectives.[66]

Although the non-commercial research issue prompted the ALRC and ACIP inquiries, for the most part they both focused on the question of whether there should be a *research on* exemption. The ALRC, for example, has recommended that an exemption from patent infringement should be established for acts done to

---

60 ALRC (2004) op cit.

61 For further details see <www.acip.gov.au/reviews.htm#expuse> (accessed 9 February 2006).

62 See above, note 25 and associated text.

63 *Madey v Duke University* 307 F 3d 1351 at 1360–1 (Fed Cir, 2002).

64 Ibid, at 1362.

65 Ibid.

66 Ibid.

study or experiment on the subject matter of a patented invention,[67] but has concluded that arguments in favour of a non-commercial research exemption are not compelling.[68] The ACIP made similar recommendations in its final report, released on 9 November 2005.[69]

This is problematic, because whilst there is merit in exempting research on the invention from infringement, much non-commercial research making use of patented gene sequences and other patented research tools is unlikely to come within the ambit of such an exemption. It may be that no research using patented research tools should be protected by an exemption. Rebecca Eisenberg, a prominent United States commentator in the field, would seem to support this proposition. She has stated that there should be no exemption where research is the primary market for the patented invention.[70] However, this seems to be contrary to current Australian practice.

The question of how to distinguish between non-commercial research with a patented invention, which may be exempt, and commercial research, which is not, is by no means easy to answer, and this may be one of the reasons why there is reluctance to enter into the debate. There is some commentary that supports a non-commercial research exemption, most notably by Katherine Strandburg[71] and Rochelle Dreyfuss and others.[72] Dreyfuss proposes that researchers could have the option of self-defining as non-commercial users.[73] Public statements have already been made to this effect by various research groups, including, for example, the Human Genome Project through its Bermuda Declaration and the Single Nucleotide Polymorphism Project. Dreyfuss and others have suggested more formalised waiver mechanisms to enable reliance on a non-commercial research exemption, which would apply in the following circumstances:

- unwillingness or inability on the part of the patent holder to supply the patented materials on reasonable terms;

- agreement by the researcher to publish the work;

---

67 ALRC (2004) op cit, Recommendation 13-1.

68 ALRC (2004) p 340.

69 Advisory Council on Intellectual Property, *Patents and Experimental Use*, ACIP, Canberra, 2005. The discussion in this part of the chapter formed the basis of part of the author's contribution to the Centre for Law and Genetics' submission to the ALRC and ACIP inquiries.

70 Eisenberg, R, "Patents and the Progress of Science: Exclusive Rights and Experimental Use" (1989) 56 *University of Chicago Law Review* 1017.

71 Strandburg, K, "What Does the Public Get? Experimental Use and the Patent Bargain" (2004) *Wisconsin Law Review* 81.

72 Dreyfuss, RC, "Varying the Course in Patenting Genetic Material: A Counter-Proposal to Richard Epstein's Steady Course", Public Law Research Paper No 59, NYU Law School, 8 April 8 2003, <http://ssrn.com/abstract=394000> (accessed 9 February 2006). See also an unpublished article by Richard Nelson cited in Strandburg (2004) op cit, note 207 and the discussion at 136–137.

73 See Dreyfuss (2003) op cit, p 9.

- agreement by the researcher to refrain from patenting the results of the research, or to patent and non-exclusively license on reasonable terms.[74]

A self-defining option is attractive, but one problem with requiring non-commercial researchers to sign a formal waiver is that it would require them to conduct patent searches and approach relevant patent holders. Given that the patent landscape is becoming increasingly complex, these obligations may be quite onerous in some areas of research.

In the alternative, it may be sufficient for researchers to make undertakings in accordance with the second and third dot points above; that is, to publish their work and to refrain from patenting the results of their research. Dreyfuss also points out that given the nature of this type of research, it may be necessary to provide for a buy-out from the waiver to enable patenting and commercial development.[75] There is merit in this proposition, given the serendipitous nature of basic research.

Other options for dealing with patent issues for the research sector

The merging of basic and applied research and the increasing commercial influences in the public sector are making the distinction between non-commercial and commercial research increasingly difficult to draw. Indeed, it may be that attempts to draw this distinction are "misconceived".[76]

Ultimately, a non-commercial research exemption may provide only limited assistance in protecting the delicate balance between rewarding innovators through the patent system and advancing knowledge through research. Some of the potential problems associated with enforcing patents against public sector researchers could be ameliorated by ensuring that patent holders engage in sensible licensing practices, for example, by licensing patents for foundational research tools for research purposes on a non-exclusive basis for small fees using standard term contracts.[77]

Patent legislation also provides for use without the authorisation of the patent holder in particular circumstances, through compulsory licensing and government use.[78]

Other strategies are also being mooted as mechanisms that may assist in protecting the flow of basic scientific knowledge in the commercialised research

---

74 Strandburg has isolated these requirements from the work of Rochelle Dreyfuss (2003) op cit, and from Richard Nelson, in an unpublished article. See Strandburg (2004) op cit, at 137. See also Mueller, J, "No 'Dilettante Affair': Rethinking the Experimental Use Exception to Patent Infringement for Biomedical Research Tools" (2001) 76 *Washington Law Review* 1 at 54–66.

75 Dreyfuss (2003) op cit, at 11.

76 See ALRC (2004) op cit, p 330.

77 Some of these issues were canvassed by the ALRC (2004) op cit, Ch 17.

78 See ALRC (2004) op cit, chs 26 and 27 for detailed discussion on these points.

environment, including commons-based approaches, clearing house mechanisms and open licensing.[79] Given the complex policy and practical issues that are arising in this process of commercialising public sector research, the time is now ripe for detailed assessment of the efficacy of these approaches.

---

79 See, for example, Benkler (2004) op cit; Atkinson, R, Beachy, RN, Conway, G, Cordara, FA, Fox, MA, Holbrook, KA, Klessig, DF, McCormick, RL, McPherson, PM, Rawlings III, HR, Rapson R, Vanderhoef, LN, Wiley, JK and Young CE, "Public Sector Collaboration for Agricultural IP Management" (2003) 301 *Science* 174.

14

Current issues in gene patenting

Anne Rees and Brian Opeskin[1]

Introduction

When old machinery is required to do new work for which it was not designed, there are bound to be difficulties. So it is when a patent system, designed 400 years ago, comes face-to-face with the cutting edge of genetic science and technology. This chapter examines some emerging issues that arise from the patenting of genetic materials and technologies, with a particular focus on the implications of gene patents for human health.

Patent law reflects a complex and delicately balanced system, whose under-lying goals are fundamentally economic. Researchers, scientists, and policy-makers often misunderstand the system, or have unreasonably high expectations of its capacity to address a range of social and ethical concerns. To put these expecta-tions in perspective, this chapter begins by briefly outlining the nature of Australia's patent system and the sorts of concerns that have been raised about the patenting of genetic inventions. The chapter then examines a variety of special issues, focusing where possible on case studies that illustrate the difficulties and the manner in which the patent system has addressed those difficulties.

The patent system

A patent is an intellectual property right granted by the state to the inventor of a new, inventive and useful product or process. Patent law has been described as a "stressful if fertile union" between certain contradictory principles: self-interest and the common good; monopoly rights and liberty; and the ownership of ideas and public disclosure of knowledge.[2] This union results from the dual goals of patent law – to benefit society by encouraging the provision of new and useful goods, and to encourage and reward inventiveness.

---

1   The authors jointly led the Australian Law Reform Commission's inquiry into gene patenting and human health, which reported to the Australian Government in 2004. This chapter draws on the final report to that inquiry, but any opinions expressed are those of the authors, not the Commission.

2   Kass, L, "Patenting Life" (1981) 63 *Journal of the Patent Office Society* 570 at 580.

These goals are achieved by providing incentives for innovation and knowledge-sharing by granting monopoly rights, for a limited period, to "exploit" a new product or process.[3] Monopoly rights encourage investment by providing an opportunity to recoup the financial outlays involved in developing an invention. They also reward the inventor by allowing a return to be made on the time and resources expended on research and development.

The limited duration of the monopoly (20 years) means that the patented invention will eventually be available for free and unrestricted use when the patent term expires. In addition, patents promote knowledge-sharing during the term of the patent by requiring the patent holder to place the details of the invention in the public domain.[4]

A patent gives the inventor the right to stop others from exploiting the invention for a limited period, but it does not grant an absolute right to exploit an invention in any way the inventor may choose. A patent holder has to comply with the law of the land in exploiting the patented invention, including regulatory laws and criminal laws. Additionally, while patents are a form of intellectual property, they do not confer ownership in the physical material described in the patent claims: thus, a patent over a genetic sequence does not amount to ownership of the sequence itself.

A patent holder is not obliged to exploit a patented invention, but the failure to do so may have implications for the patent holder's rights. For example, the patent could be subjected to compulsory licensing or "Crown use", in circumstances discussed later in this chapter.

Although there is considerable variance in detail from one jurisdiction to another, most developed countries apply similar tests for patentability. Many of these requirements are established by the international obligations in the "TRIPS Agreement", to which Australia is a party.[5] In Australia, the requirements for patentability are that the invention: must be a "manner of manufacture" within the meaning of s 6 of the *Statute of Monopolies*; is novel (that is, new); involves an inventive or innovative step; is useful; and has not been used secretly within Australia prior to filing the patent application.[6]

Certain inventions may be expressly excluded from patentability. Australia has relatively few express exclusions, but they include inventions involving "human beings, and the biological processes for their generation", as well as inventions the use of which would be contrary to law.[7] Other jurisdictions recognise a

---

3   "Exploit" includes to make, hire, sell or otherwise dispose of the product, use or import it, or keep it for the purpose of doing any of those things: *Patents Act 1990* (Cth) s 13(1), Sch 1.

4   See, for example, *Integra Life Sciences v Merck KgaA* 307 F 3d 1351 (2002) (Newman J dissenting).

5   *Agreement on Trade-Related Aspects of Intellectual Property Rights*, Annex 1C of the *Marrakech Agreement Establishing the World Trade Organization*, [1995] ATS 8 (entered into force generally on 1 January 1995).

6   *Patents Act 1990* (Cth) s 18.

7   Ibid ss 18(2), 50(1)(a), 101B(2)(c), (d).

broader range of exceptions, including inventions involving diagnostic, therapeutic and surgical methods of treatment of humans and animals; and inventions whose commercial exploitation would be contrary to morality or public order.[8] Exclusions from patentability are also discussed later in this chapter.

Accommodating gene patents

The patent system has accommodated the arrival of many new technologies. Each new field of technology has brought with it new challenges for the patent system, as those responsible for processing patent applications seek to assess the novelty, inventiveness and usefulness of each new claimed invention, in the light of what has gone before.

In the past 20 years, inventions in the field of biotechnology have become a new focus of the patent system. Here the difficulties faced by the patent examiners have been compounded by the newness of the claims, the increasing pace of technological change, the global nature of scientific inquiry, the highly specialised nature of genetic science and technology, and the sheer volume of inventions.

Concerns about the application of patent law to genetic materials and technology fall into two classes: those relating to the law or practice of patenting genetic materials and technologies; and those relating to the manner in which gene patents are exploited in the marketplace. In the former category, gene patents have been criticised on the following grounds:

- Patent legislation fails to take sufficient account of ethical considerations, such as whether human genetic sequences are a proper subject matter for a statutory monopoly.

- Human genetic sequences should not be patentable because they are discoveries, not inventions.

- Patents granted over genetic materials and technologies are often too broad.

- Patents over genetic materials and technologies are too easily granted and patent examiners should be more highly skilled in assessing applications in this field.

In the latter category (manner of exploitation in the marketplace), gene patents have been criticised on the following grounds:

- Restrictive licensing practices limit access to medical genetic testing, and compromise the quality of such testing, to the detriment of public health.

- Gene patents drive up the cost of medical genetic testing beyond a fair and equitable level, to the detriment of public health.

---

8   See *Agreement on Trade-Related Aspects of Intellectual Property Rights*, Annex 1C of the *Marrakech Agreement Establishing the World Trade Organization*, [1995] ATS 8 (entered into force generally on 1 January 1995), art 27(2).

- Licensing practices restrict access to genetic materials and technologies for research purposes.

- The use of gene patents for experimentation or research should be exempt from claims of patent infringement, so as to facilitate research, not hinder it.

It remains to examine some of these claims in greater detail.

Patentability of genetic materials

Internationally, there has been criticism that many of the patents over genetic material are questionable. As one writer has noted, "the advent of biotechnology has posed significant challenges for patent law, and many argue that patent law is struggling to meet that challenge".[9] Broadly, there are three types of patents – product patents, process patents and use patents. It is product patents over gene sequences that generally raise the most concerns. One of the key issues involves the requirement of "inventiveness" and arguments that genetic material is a discovery not an invention and hence ought not be patentable; another concerns speculative patents – patents granted where the use for the patented material is unknown at the time of patenting; and a third concerns broad patents – patents that grant broad rights to the patent holder and may be seen as covering applications invented later by someone else.

Discoveries

Patent law has always drawn a distinction between mere discoveries, which are said to be non-patentable, and inventions. Until a controversial decision in 1980 of the United States Supreme Court in *Diamond v Chakrabarty*,[10] it was assumed that living organisms generally – being part of nature – were not patentable. The court allowed a patent to be granted for a recombinant bacterium. In so doing it drew a distinction between a "product of nature", which is not patentable, and a "non-naturally occurring composition of matter", which it said was patentable. This decision had profound ramifications for the patenting of DNA and, soon after, the United States Patent and Trademark Office (USPTO) began issuing patents on human genetic material.[11] In 1995 in Australia, the Deputy Commissioner of Patents allowed an application concerning the purified or isolated DNA sequence encoding the human protein erythropoietin[12] because the claims were "an artificially created state of affairs".[13] The distinction drawn by patent offices[14] between

---

9   Black, J, "Regulation as Facilitation: Negotiating the Genetic Revolution, (1998) 61 *Modern Law Review* 621 at 646.

10   447 US 303 (1980).

11   Demaine, L and Fellmeth, A, "Reinventing the Double Helix: A Novel and Nonobvious Reconceptualization of the Biotechnology Patent" (2002) 55 *Stanford Law Review* 303 at 319.

12   This sequence plays a major role in the formation of red blood cells.

13   *Kiren-Amgen Inc v Board of Regents of University of Washington* (1995) 33 IPR 557 at 569.

purified and isolated genetic materials and naturally occurring ones has been criticised on the basis that the two types are structurally similar or identical, and that the useful properties of the isolated sequences are naturally occurring.[15] Biotechnology patents have blurred the distinction between discoveries and inventions,[16] but as the Australian Law Reform Commission (ALRC) stated in its report, *Genes and Ingenuity*, "there are attractive arguments for the view that such [isolated and purified biological] materials should not have been treated as patentable subject matter. However, the time for taking this approach to the patenting of products and materials has long since passed".[17]

Inventive step

With the increasing use of computational techniques (bioinformatics), isolation and purification of genetic sequences may now be routine. This raises the issue of whether gene sequences, in particular, can be said to meet the requirement of an "inventive step" (called "non-obviousness" in the United States). It has been suggested that the need to demonstrate an inventive step may be a basis for limiting such patents in the future.[18] This already appears to be the case in Europe where the European Patent Office (EPO) has stated that applicants for patents over a genetic invention must "demonstrate that obtaining the sequence was in fact a technical achievement or that they have discovered a new or unexpected property associated with the gene".[19] This is not the approach in the United States where the Court of Appeals for the Federal Circuit has stated that the existence of a general method of isolating genetic sequences is "essentially irrelevant",[20] preferring to focus instead on whether, in the absence of relevant prior information, a person skilled in the relevant art could know the structure of that sequence without

---

14   All major patent offices recognise the distinction. In 1988, the USPTO, European Patent Office, and the Japanese Patent Office issued a joint statement stating that purified natural products were not products of nature and were therefore eligible for patenting: "Trilateral Co-operation of the US, European and Japanese Patent Offices" (1988) 7 *Biotechnology Law Review* 159 at 163 cited in Crespi, R, "Patenting and Ethics: A Dubious Connection" (2001/2002) 5 *Bio-Science Law Review* 71.

15   Nuffield Council on Bioethics, *The Ethics of Patenting DNA*, NCB, London, 2002, pp 27–28; Keays, D, "Patenting DNA and Amino Acid Sequences: An Australian Perspective" (1999) 7 *Health Law Journal* 69 at 76.

16   Danish Council of Ethics, *Patenting Human Genes and Stem Cells*, 2004, <www.etiskraad. dk/sw475.asp> (accessed 2 February 2006) Ch 10.

17   Australian Law Reform Commission, *Genes and Ingenuity: Gene Patenting and Human Health*, Report No 99, ALRC, Canberra, 2004, paras [6.51]–[6.52].

18   Cornish, W, Llewelyn, M and Adcock, M, *Intellectual Property Rights (IPRs) and Genetics*, Public Health Genetics Unit, University of Cambridge, 2003, p 32. See also Nuffield (2002) op cit, p 29.

19   United States National Research Council, *A Patent System for the 21st Century*, 2004, p 76 (prepublication copy).

20   *Re Dueul* 51 F 3d 1552 at 1559 (Fed Cir, 1995), citing *Re Bell* 991 F 2d 781 (Fed Cir, 1993). See ALRC (2004) op cit, para [6.115].

conducting appropriate experiments.[21] In Australia, a recent study concluded that Australian patent examiners generally do not consider that the "application of standard techniques and practice in the art to isolate and sequence a gene from the tissue of interest" constitutes an inventive step, unless "the isolated sequence possesses an unexpected property that provides an advantageous effect".[22]

Usefulness

A further debate has centred on whether isolated genetic materials meet the requirement that an invention be "useful" (known as "utility" in the United States). Concerns have particularly focused on claims involving snippets of genetic material: expressed sequence tags (ESTs) and single nucleotide polymorphisms (SNPs), which may be used in research as probes[23] to locate previously unknown genetic sequences or as place-markers on DNA sequences. There are concerns that granting such patents, on what are described as routine discoveries, may impede further research if they prevent the granting of later patents to those who determine the biological function or commercial application of genes since the presence of the patent over the EST would deprive the full-length gene of novelty.[24]

Gene patents have also been criticised on the basis that they allow claims over unproven or speculative uses. However, recent changes within patent offices may limit such claims. In 2001, the USPTO issued revised examination guidelines to require a patent applicant to demonstrate that the utility claims for an invention are "specific, substantial and credible".[25] Similarly, in 2003 the EPO issued guidelines that indicate the need for gene sequence patents to specify their function.[26] The ALRC recommended that the Patents Act 1990 (Cth) be amended to "provide that an invention will satisfy the requirement of 'usefulness' only if the patent application discloses a specific, substantial and credible use".[27]

---

21 *Re Dueul* 51 F 3d 1552 at 1558–1559 (Fed Cir, 1995), *Re Bell* 991 F 2d 781 at 784–785 (Fed Cir, 1993).

22 Howlett, M and Christie, A, *An Analysis of the Approaches of the Trilateral and Australian Patent Offices to Patenting Partial DNA Sequences (ESTs)*, 2003, p 16.

23 IP Australia states that if a claim defines a DNA sequence, it is insufficient to describe the sequence as being broadly useful as a "probe" and it must disclose a specific gene or specific use: IP Australia, *Patent Manual of Practice and Procedure*, Vol 2: National, 2002, para [8.4.2].

24 Howlett and Christie (2003) op cit p 3. Demaine and Fellmeth (2002) op cit, at 323.

25 United States Patent and Trademark Office, *Manual of Patent Examining Procedure*, 8th edn, 2003, para [2107] cl II(A).

26 European Patent Office, *Guidelines for Examination in the European Patent Office*, 2003, Pt C, IV.4.5.

27 ALRC (2004) op cit, rec 6.3. In 2000, the Intellectual Property Competition Review Committee endorsed the approach adopted by the USPTO and recommended that IP Australia should ensure that "the use described in the specification is specific, substantial and credible to a person skilled in the art", Intellectual Property and Competition Review Committee, *Review of Intellectual Property Legislation under the Competition Principles Agreement*, IP Australia, Canberra, 2000, p 154.

Broad patents

Allied to the issue of usefulness are concerns about the breadth of some gene patents – notably product patents over gene sequences – that may extend to applications invented later by someone else. All patents include claims that determine the scope of the patent. Gene sequence patents have potentially wide scope and may inhibit further research and product development because: there is a need to pay licence fees to the original inventor; or the patents cover all uses of the product (even those not envisaged by the inventor); or the patents cover a generally applicable research tool or technique. A patent over a gene or gene sequence may extend to all its uses even if the inventor was aware of only one of these.

Case study: CCR5 and the AIDS virus

A United States company, Human Genome Sciences Inc (HGS), was granted a United States patent in 2000 containing claims covering an isolated gene – later known as the CCR5 gene – and all its medical applications. Research by a different group of scientists found that the CCR5 gene makes a protein crucial for the entry of the HIV virus into human immune cells. HGS's patent application indicated that the utility of the CCR5 protein was as a cell-surface receptor for protein molecules termed "chemokines", which have a role in inflammatory diseases. CCR5's potential use in relation to HIV was not disclosed on the patent specification. However, HGS's patent claims were broad enough to allow it to assert rights over any use of the gene, including its use as a viral receptor, even though it had played no part in the research that led to that discovery. HGS agreed to license the use of the CCR5 receptor gene for research into new drugs, including for the development of AIDS therapies. However, the fact that it was able to assert rights over the use of CCR5 in AIDS research, when it had played no part in this work, was controversial.

The CCR5 patent is an example of the potential impact of broad patent claims and patent protection being granted for inventions involving genetic sequences where the applicant has an incomplete knowledge of the function of the gene. It has been argued that "identifying a target's role in one disease pathway should not necessarily give the patent owner plenary rights over all uses of the target".[28] However, the issue illustrated by the CCR5 gene may already be out of date. Most human genetic sequences are now in the public domain as a result of the Human Genome Project and hence it is likely that future gene patents will be granted only over new uses for human genetic sequences, rather than over the sequences themselves. But it is not clear that it would be easy to legislate against such patents. The ALRC concluded that reform to limit the rights granted to a patentee in this area ought not be recommended because it would be "a radical departure from the existing patent system [and] would involve treating gene

---

28   Rai, A, "Genome Patents: A Case Study in Patenting Research Tools" (2002) 77 *Academic Medicine* 1368 at 1369.

patents differently to patents over other technologies"[29] and would be likely to be contrary to Australia's treaty obligations.[30]

Exclusions from patentability for medical treatment

Aside from patents over genetic material, there are issues around whether methods of medical treatment should be patentable. This has implications for genetic testing and in the developing area of gene therapy. Internationally, there are several approaches to the issue of the patenting of methods of surgical or medical treatment of the human body. In Australia, there is nothing in the *Patents Act 1990* (Cth) that excludes methods of medical or surgical treatment from being patented and there is case law that provides that they are patentable.[31] By contrast, in the United Kingdom, the *Patents Act 1977* expressly provides that methods of medical treatment on the human body are not capable of "industrial application"[32] and are therefore not patentable. Methods of medical treatment are similarly excluded under the European Patent Convention[33] and in Canada and New Zealand. However, the scope of these exclusions is limited to treatment or diagnosis on the human body – and not to procedures carried out *in vitro*, or exclusively outside the body,[34] including tests performed on tissues or fluids that have been permanently removed from the body.[35] Given that most genetic testing is performed on DNA samples taken from the body, most diagnostic and predictive genetic tests are therefore not caught by the exclusion and are patentable if they otherwise meet the legislative criteria. However, the exclusion may become more relevant as gene therapies applied directly to the human body become more common. This may assist access to such therapies but arguably could impede the development of such therapies if they cannot be patented in many jurisdictions.

The United States adopts a different and so far novel approach to the issue. Although permitting diagnostic, therapeutic or surgical methods of treatment on the human body to be patented, the United States patents legislation grants a "medical practitioner" or a "related health care entity" a limited defence to infringement claims in connection with their performance of a "medical activity".[36] The scope of the defence is limited and probably does not apply to most medical

---

29   ALRC (2004) op cit, para [6.152].

30   Ibid, para [6.153].

31   *Anaesthetic Supplies Pty Ltd v Rescare Ltd* (1994) 50 FCR 1; *Bristol-Myers Squibb Co v FH Faulding & Co Ltd* (2000) 170 ALR 439.

32   See *Patents Act 1977* (UK) s 4(2).

33   European Patent Convention (entered into force generally on 7 October 1977), art 52(4).

34   Ontario Ministry of Health and Long-Term Care, *Genetics, Testing & Gene Patenting: Charting New Territory in Healthcare: Report to the Provinces and Territories*, 2002, p 51. United Kingdom Patent Office, *Manual of Patent Practice*, 5th edn, 2003.

35   United Kingdom Patent Office (2003) op cit.

36   This defence was introduced in 1996 and does not apply to any patent with an effective filing date before 30 September 1996: 35 USC s 287(c).

treatments involving gene patents because they generally take place outside the human body. Gene therapy directly on the human body is rare and still largely experimental. However the defence may take on more importance as gene therapy develops.

The introduction of a medical treatment defence specifically to address concerns raised by gene patents on health care has been considered by several countries. In Canada, an Ontario Government report recommended that its medical treatment exclusion be replaced with a medical treatment defence.[37] A report for the United Kingdom Department of Health noted strong calls to allow methods of medical treatment to be patented[38] but concluded that, if this were done, clinicians would require the benefit of a medical treatment defence.[39] However, the Organisation for Economic Cooperation and Development (OECD) has observed that there may be a difficulty distinguishing clinical use from commercial use.[40]

In Australia, the ALRC addressed the issue of whether there should be a medical treatment defence in Australian patent law. The ALRC noted that "there are genuine difficulties in framing the scope of any new medical treatment defence"[41] and did not recommend either a general medical treatment defence[42] or one specific to patented genetic materials. Difficulties noted by the ALRC included defining what medical activities the defence should cover, and defining the persons or organisations that should be able to invoke it. The ALRC suggested that these would be exacerbated if the defence were to apply only to patents on genetic materials and technologies. Problems noted included distinguishing genetic medical technology from other medical technology, especially in relation to *in vitro* diagnostics, and any distinctions required between commercial and non-commercial genetic testing. Any medical treatment defence limited to genetic materials and technologies may also be inconsistent with international obligations under the TRIPS Agreement,[43] which generally require patent law to be technologically neutral. The ALRC concluded that access issues would be better dealt with through appropriate measures to ensure fair exploitation of gene patents, including if necessary the use of Crown use provisions and compulsory licensing (see below).

---

37 Ontario Ministry of Health and Long-Term Care, *Genetics, Testing & Gene Patenting: Charting New Territory in Healthcare: Report to the Provinces and Territories*, 2002, rec 13(e), p 51. The recommendation said the defence should be extended to treatment and diagnosis.

38 Cornish, Llewelyn and Adcock (2003) op cit, p 23.

39 Ibid p 83.

40 Organisation for Economic Cooperation and Development, *Genetic Inventions, Intellectual Property Rights and Licensing Practices: Evidence and Policies*, 2002, p 73.

41 ALRC (2004) op cit, para [21.43].

42 On the basis that this was outside its terms of reference: ibid, para [21.43].

43 *Agreement on Trade-Related Aspects of Intellectual Property Rights*, Annex 1C of the *Marrakech Agreement Establishing the World Trade Organization*, [1995] ATS 8 (entered into force generally on 1 January 1995).

Research use of patented inventions

Researchers in many countries assume that their use of a patented invention is immune from claims of patent infringement. They view their research as altruistic and in the public interest, so how could it be unlawful? Yet the law does not necessarily conform to their assumptions.

Legal uncertainty and its consequences

Nowhere does the *Patents Act 1990* (Cth) contain an express defence for research use of a patented invention. Some people argue that a research use defence can be implied from the definition of "exploit" in the Act, and the commercial conduct (such as hiring and selling) that the term seems to imply.[44] Others rely on the occasional judicial decision that has supported the idea of a research use defence, but the authorities are usually old and foreign.[45] In short, the evidence that Australian law recognises a research use defence is, at best, equivocal.[46]

This uncertainty has implications for all the relevant actors. Researchers "self-define" the scope of their protected research activity. They often see the claimed exemption as extending to the boundaries of their own research, at least until they have commercial outcomes. And they seldom seek out patent holders to obtain licences to use the invention. On the other hand, patent holders often fail to pursue researchers for infringement. There are many reasons for this: the patent holder may be unaware of what goes on in laboratories behind closed doors; research can increase the value of a patent and so is not to be entirely discouraged; enforcing patents against academic institutions can be bad public relations; and the cost of enforcement proceedings can make it uneconomic to pursue infringers.

The consequence is that the system seems to work, in a kind of a fashion, on a "speak no infringement, see no infringement" basis. Yet, all the parties are forced to live with uncertainty and risk, which might have a chilling effect on research.

A legislative exemption?

In 2004 the ALRC recommended that the *Patents Act 1990* (Cth) should be amended to give the research use exemption a clear statutory basis. Underpinning this legislative solution is the view that the law should be clear so that researchers and patent holders can know the legal consequences of their actions (an aspect of the rule of law). It is also unrealistic to expect these issues to be resolved by the courts: patent decisions of higher courts are uncommon in Australia; and judicial outcomes are not always desirable from a policy perspective, as the United States experience shows.[47]

---

44 The argument is strained because the definition of "exploit" is not exhaustive, and in any case includes "use" of the invention.

45 See, for example, *Frearson v Loe* (1876) 9 ChD 48.

46 In some other jurisdictions the situation is somewhat clearer, with either judicial or legislative recognition of a research use exemption.

47 See *Madey v Duke University* 307 F 3d 1351 (Fed Cir, 2002), which is regarded as having substantially inhibited the use of patented inventions in research.

While there are benefits to be derived simply from the fact of clarifying this aspect of the law, many of the benefits will depend on the precise scope of the statutory exemption. Several European countries have a statutory exemption for research use, which is based on the Community Patents Convention.[48] However, the scope of protected research is quite narrow. Article 27(b) of the Convention grants protection only for "acts done for experimental purposes relating to the subject matter of the patented invention". The practical effect, supported in Australia by the ALRC, is that research is protected if it is research on the subject matter of the patented invention itself, but not if it is research that merely uses the patented invention for other purposes.

This limitation is important both in principle and in practice. To grant a researcher freedom from the operation of patent law simply because he or she is conducting "research" would be to carve a very big hole in the exclusive rights of the patent holder, particularly in relation to research tools. Of course, researchers who develop downstream products often require ready access to patented inventions, including research tools, for the purpose of producing those products. However, upstream patent holders may view the research tool as a valuable end product in itself. A research use exemption that is too broad may thus be one researcher's pill, but another's poison.

Case study: research use of non-coding DNA

The primary function of the human genome is to provide instructions for the manufacture of proteins within the body. Yet 98 per cent of the genome does not have this coding function. For a long time these non-coding regions were regarded as "junk" – the debris from millennia of evolutionary change. Today scientists believe that the non-coding DNA explains the sophistication of the human genome, permitting 30,000 genes to produce about 200,000 proteins.

Beginning in 1993, an Australian scientist, Dr Malcolm Simmons, patented the use of non-coding DNA in genetic analysis and gene mapping. These patents are now owned by an Australian company, Genetic Technologies Ltd (GTG), which has adopted an aggressive strategy toward the enforcement of its patent rights. GTG charges high fees for the commercial use of non-coding DNA (which is fundamental to many applications in genetic analysis, diagnostics and genomics), and has commenced legal proceedings against alleged infringers.

However, GTG has been willing to license the research use of the non-coding patents for modest sums – such as the USD$1,000 reported to have been paid by the University of Sydney for a non-exclusive licence in 2003.[49] This transaction raises many interesting issues: could the university have used the non-

---

48 *Council Agreement relating to Community Patents No 89/695/EEC*, 15 December 1989, OJ L 401/01. The convention must be ratified by all European Union member states before it takes effect.

49 Genetic Technologies Ltd, "GTG Grants First Research License", *Press Release*, 25 July 2003, <www.gtg.com.au/index_archivenews.asp?art_id=589&menuid=070.150.010> (accessed 8 February 2006).

coding DNA for research in the absence of a licence; what are the cumulative costs of obtaining licences for the research use of patented inventions; and what benefits accrue from avoiding "dirty intellectual property" by clarifying the legal basis of the research use?

Benefit sharing by research participants

Genetic research can involve the participation of hundreds of individuals whose family histories and tissue samples may help to identify particular genes and genetic mutations that are implicated in certain diseases. If patents are granted over the isolated genes and other genetic material, and that research is subsequently commercialised, issues may be raised as to whether those who took part in the research – individually or collectively – should have any rights, entitlements or expectations to exercise control over, or benefit from, the research results. Such benefit-sharing could take a number of forms, both financial (such as a share in any profits or royalties made from the patent), or in kind (such as access to free medical care, treatment or therapy derived from the research). Concerns are sometimes expressed that willingness to participate in research may be impeded if participants are aware that others may make large profits from the research. Two examples from the United States illustrate different approaches to the issue.

In one case – *Greenberg v Miami Children's Hospital Research Institute* – the Greenberg family (joined by other families and patient groups) instituted legal proceedings against the hospital and a scientist who identified and patented the gene associated with Canavan disease. The scientist undertook the research at the request of the Greenbergs, who had two children afflicted with disease. The family assisted him with money and tissue samples from their own children and others. The scientist identified the gene and developed a diagnostic genetic test for it. The hospital where the research was done patented the gene, and began charging a fee for the test. The Greenbergs sought a permanent injunction restraining the hospital and scientist from enforcing the patent rights.[50] The issue was not that they wished to share in the profits, rather that they considered they should have some rights of control and wished to see the test freely available.

In the other example, the parents of two children with a rare genetic disease[51] established a foundation, found 2,000 people with the disease to donate tissue for research, set up a repository to store the tissue samples, and raised money for research. They developed a practical solution to the issue by requiring

---

50 Nichols Hill, A, "One Man's Trash is Another Man's Treasure, Bioprospecting: Protecting the Rights and Interests of Human Donors of Genetic Material" (2002) 5 *Journal of Health Care Law & Policy* 259. The plaintiffs asserted the following causes of action: lack of informed consent, breach of fiduciary duty, unjust enrichment, fraudulent concealment, conversion and misappropriation of trade secrets. In May 2003, the court granted a motion to dismiss each of these counts except unjust enrichment: *Greenberg v Miami Children's Hospital Research Institute* (unreported, District Court for the Southern District of Florida, Moreno J, 29 May 2003).

51 Pseudoxanthoma elasticum (PXE), which causes mineralisation of elastic tissue.

researchers to enter into a contract that provided that the foundation would be named in any patent applications arising from the work, any profits or revenue from the discoveries would be shared with the foundation, and any genetic test would be made readily available to the foundation.[52]

Under Australian law, there are several barriers to research participants asserting a legal right to share in any financial benefits of gene patents, although there may be greater capacity to have a say in what is done with the research. The law is currently uncertain about the nature of property rights in human tissue[53] and there are prohibitions in the various state Human Tissue Acts[54] on the sale of human tissue. The *Patents Act 1990* (Cth) provides that a patent may be granted only to a limited category of persons, which does not specifically include research participants.[55] However, theoretically, research participants and researchers could enter into contractual arrangements providing some form of benefit in exchange for participation in the program.

An analogy is with those who participate in clinical trials for new drugs and who subsequently continue to have access to those drugs for little or no cost in exchange for their participation. Whether the fact that others may profit from genetic research will impede research participation is debateable. The ALRC concluded that the issues of control and benefit sharing were better addressed outside the patent system through the established system for ethical approval for research and through contractual arrangements between researchers and research participants.[56]

Access to health care

Given the link between patents and commercial exploitation, patents over genes raise issues about access to genetic tests and gene therapies. Genetic testing involving a sequence covered by a patent may constitute an infringement of the patent, unless a licence has been obtained from the patent holder or testing is conducted through another licensee. In Australia, the issue particularly concerns governments rather than individuals because most testing is conducted at public hospital laboratories at little or no charge to the person tested. However, licence fees and royalties have an impact on health budgets and clinical decisions. There

---

52 Kolata, G, "Sharing of Profits is Debated as the Value of Tissue Rises", *New York Times*, 15 May 2000.

53 See Australian Law Reform Commission and Australian Health Ethics Committee, *Essentially Yours: The Protection of Human Genetic Information in Australia*, Report No 96, ALRC, Canberra, 2003.

54 See, for example, s 32(1) and (5) of the *Human Tissue Act 1983* (NSW).

55 Patents may be granted to a person who is the inventor; would be entitled to have the patent assigned to him or her; derives title to the invention from the inventor or an assignee; or is the legal representative of a deceased person who falls within these categories: *Patents Act 1990* (Cth) s 15(1). In the PXE example, the work of the parents in collecting and managing the tissue samples allowed them to be included as inventors.

56 ALRC (2004) op cit, para [3.55].

are around 230 medical genetic tests available in Australia.[57] One study of Australian patents identified 60 medical genetic tests that are subject to patent rights.[58] Where licence fees are payable for testing, this raises costs and increases the constraints on who may have access to the tests. If testing is restricted for this reason, it may limit the potential for genetic testing to identify preventable or treatable diseases and limit its potential to lower health costs.

Monopoly control raises the further issue that a patent or licence holder could insist on all testing being carried out in its laboratory. This raises concerns that private laboratories may bypass best-practice guidelines in relation to testing and counselling; that there may be a loss of expertise from publicly funded laboratories; and that exclusive control may stifle further innovation and research. In Australia, the public sector laboratories that carry out most tests also provide genetic counselling services in association with the testing. There are concerns that "commercial testing might [dissociate] genetic testing from proper screening and genetic counselling"[59] and have consequences in relation to access to genetic counselling.[60] Whether this will occur may depend on having appropriate clinical guidelines and practices. It may be possible for a private laboratory to carry out the testing on behalf of the public sector, leaving the public clinical service to provide counselling and other patent liaison. There are also fears that patent laws and practices may direct the use of particular tests, constraining laboratories from choosing the most clinically appropriate test.[61] In the United States, some laboratories ceased providing a certain prenatal test for Down syndrome because the fees charged by a patentee of the relevant gene exceeded the Medicaid reimbursement.[62]

Case study: the BRCA1 and BRCA2 genes

The most notorious instance of a gene sequence patent holder seeking to enforce its rights in relation to medical genetic testing is that of the United States company, Myriad Genetics Inc (Myriad) in relation to breast cancer testing. In the United States and internationally, Myriad held patents over two genes that may indicate a predisposition to breast and ovarian cancer, BRCA1 and BRCA2.[63] Although the

57 Brasch, J, *DNA Diagnosis of Genetic Disorders in Australasia* (2000) Human Genetics Society of Australasia <www.hgsa.com.au/labs.html> (accessed 8 February 2006). Not all tests are available from all laboratories. The register does not include newborn screening laboratories.

58 ALRC (2004) op cit, para [20.16], citing a submission from Dr John Abbot.

59 See Rimmer, M, "Myriad Genetics: Patent Law and Genetic Testing" (2003) 25 *European Intellectual Property Review* 20 at 26.

60 The role and importance of genetic counselling is described in Australian Law Reform Commission and Australian Health Ethics Committee, *Essentially Yours: The Protection of Human Genetic Information in Australia*, Report No 96, ALRC, Canberra, 2003, Ch 23.

61 Merz, J, "Disease Gene Patents: Overcoming Unethical Constraints on Clinical Laboratory Medicine" (1999) 45 *Clinical Chemistry* 324 at 327.

62 Demaine and Fellmeth (2002) op cit, at 416.

63 Somewhere between 5 to 10 per cent of breast cancers are thought to have a genetic link.

research leading to its BRCA1 patents was the product of international collaboration, Myriad, in association with scientists from the University of Utah,
obtained the United States and international patents on BRCA1 on the basis of
being the first to complete its identification and sequencing.[64] This patent covered
methods and materials used to isolate and detect BRCA1. Myriad subsequently
obtained United States, but not United Kingdom, patents over a second isolated
gene, BRCA2.[65] Myriad's patents cover methods for predictive testing[66] and
products and processes involved in its breast and ovarian cancer predisposition
test, called "BRCAnalysis". Myriad is said to have a dominant patent position in
relation to BRCA1 because any technique for BRCA1 testing is likely to require use
of its patents. That is, it is not possible to develop alternative screening tests.

Concerns about the breadth of Myriad's patents and the manner of their
exploitation lead to calls for patent law reform in France and Canada.[67] In Europe,
a number of genetic organisations filed objections to the patents[68] and in October
2001, the European Parliament adopted a resolution opposing the patenting of the
BRCA genes on the basis of the principle of non-patentability of human genes or
cells "in their natural environment".[69] In the United States, Myriad threatened legal
action against laboratories that marketed or performed genetic predisposition tests
for breast cancer. Similarly, Myriad sought to require testing laboratories in Europe
to send DNA samples to Myriad's Utah laboratories for full sequencing. Myriad
also sought to enforce its patent rights against Canadian provincial health authorities. This caused one authority, British Columbia, to suspend all BRCA testing
for several months.[70] However, other provinces announced they would ignore
Myriad's demands. Generally there were concerns about the price proposed by
Myriad for the tests (up to three times those charged by laboratories in Europe and
Canada); the quality of the tests; the potential loss of research expertise and data;
and the separation of clinical services from research and counselling.

---

64   Genewatch United Kingdom, *Patenting Genes – Stifling Research and Jeopardising Healthcare*,
     <www.genewatch.org/PatentingReports/Patents.pdf> (accessed 6 December 2004) p 2.

65   The Institute of Cancer Research (ICR) holds the patent in the United Kingdom. Much of
     the research on BRCA2 was done by the Sanger Centre and ICR.

66   See Rimmer, M, "Myriad Genetics: Patent Law and Genetic Testing" (2003) 25 *European
     Intellectual Property Review* 20 at 21–23.

67   See Gold, R, "Gene Patents and Medical Access" (2000) 49 *Intellectual Property Forum* 20
     at 23.

68   Opponents included the Assistance Publique-Hôpitaux de Paris, the Paris public hospitals
     authority; the Institut Curie, the Institut Gustave-Roussy, the Belgian Society for Human
     Genetics and the Associazione Angela Serra per la Ricerca sul Cancro: European Patent
     Office, "'Myriad/Breast Cancer' Patent Revoked after Public Hearing", press release,
     Munich, 18 May 2004.

69   European Parliament, *Bulletin EU 10-2001 Human Rights (3/9): Parliament Resolution on the
     Patenting of BRCA1 and BRCA2 Genes*, 2001, <http://europa.eu.int/abc/doc/off/bull/en/
     200110/p102003.htm> (accessed 8 February 2006).

70   Gold, R, "Gene Patents and Medical Access" (2000) 49 *Intellectual Property Forum* 20 at 23;
     "British Columbia Government Decision to Ignore Myriad Patent", *CanWest News Service*,
     16 February 2003.

In May 2004, a panel of the EPO revoked one of Myriad's BRCA1 patents in Europe, on the basis that it did not satisfy the requirements for patentability, particularly in relation to inventive step.[71] In January 2005, the EPO amended two other of Myriad's patents on BRCA1. The amended patents now no longer include claims for diagnostic methods and, in one case, therapeutic methods.[72] At the heart of the opposition has been concern about the impact of Myriad's patents on health care provision and the conduct of genetic research. The effect of the EPO's decisions is that European research and health care institutions may develop other diagnostic tests associated with BRCA1.

In Australia, Myriad licensed its patents to an Australian company, GTG, which announced that it did not intend to enforce its rights in relation to the patents. Hence breast cancer predisposition testing has largely remained with the public sector laboratories and there has been no replication of the problems that arose overseas. To date, Myriad is something of an isolated example of the potential for patents to have a dramatic impact on the cost of, and access to, genetic tests. Nevertheless, concerns have remained within the health sector that other companies holding patents over genes associated with predictive and diagnostic testing will, in time, replicate the behaviour of Myriad.

Crown use and compulsory licensing

The Crown use provisions of the *Patents Act* are an important mechanism through which the governments and their agencies may address, in specific cases, concerns that gene patents hinder research or the provision of health care.

The Crown use provisions allow the Commonwealth or a State either to exploit a patented invention without infringement, or to authorise another person to do so. The Crown use provisions are similar in purpose to those relating to compulsory licensing in that they allow the exploitation of an invention without the consent of the patent holder – in effect creating a compulsory licence in favour of the Crown. Like compulsory licensing, the terms of remuneration or compensation are agreed or determined by a court. Unlike compulsory licensing, the Crown may invoke the Crown use provisions without first seeking agreement of the patent holder. Further, unlike compulsory licensing, there is no requirement to satisfy a court that the reasonable requirements of the public with respect to the patented invention have not been met.[73]

The Crown use provisions seem to be used only rarely in Australia, but their importance lies more in their potential for use. It has been said that the primary

71 European Patent Office, "'Myriad/Breast Cancer' Patent Revoked after Public Hearing", Press Release, Munich, 18 May 2004.

72 European Patent Office, "Patent on breast and ovarian cancer susceptibility gene amended after public hearing", press release, Munich, 21 January 2005 and "European patent on mutations in breast and ovarian cancer susceptibility gene amended after public hearing", press release, Munich, 25 January 2005.

73 See *Patents Act 1990* (Cth) s 133.

purpose of the Crown use provisions is "to force an unwilling licensor to the negotiating table" and that the "threat of resort to the Crown use provisions may assist in ensuring an acceptable result from those negotiations".[74] Nevertheless, even if used in this way, the provisions constitute an important safeguard in helping ensure that patent protection does not have an adverse impact on significant public interests.

The Crown use provisions involve significant interference with the rights that patent holders otherwise have under the patent system. It is arguable that the Crown use provisions should not be relied upon too readily and should be invoked only in exceptional circumstances if confidence in the patent system is to be preserved. For example, reliance upon the provision may be justifiable in the case of public health emergencies, such as those in which the United States and Canadian governments contemplated compulsory use of Bayer AG's patent on the ciprofloxacin antibiotic following bio-terror attacks using the anthrax organism in the United States.[75]

Even in these circumstances, Crown use of a patent may be controversial and this factor may act as a political constraint on the exercise of these provisions. Another constraint is that, where the provisions are invoked, adequate remuneration or compensation must still be paid to the patent holder.

The Crown use provisions are of broad potential application to the conduct of research and the provision of health care, but there are some legal uncertainties about the application of the provisions in these areas. These relate to whether particular bodies are "the Crown" and whether exploitation is "for the services of the Crown", as the legislation requires. For example, it is likely that use of a patented genetic test by a public hospital would be held to be "for the services of the State", but the changing mix of public/private health care provision may leave room for doubt in particular cases.

The ALRC's 2004 report demonstrated that some people in the Australian public health sector harbour genuine and serious concerns about the implications of gene patents for the quality of health care provision. One of the ALRC's proposed solutions was for health care providers and health care policy-makers to be proactive in responding to problems as they emerge. Thus, where particular gene patents have an adverse impact on the provision of health care, health departments at all levels of government should consider whether to exercise existing legal options to facilitate access to the inventions, including Crown use of the patent. In this way, patent holders will be put on notice that health authorities may take action if patent rights are exploited in a manner that threatens the public interest in cost-effective and high quality health care.

---

74 Cornish, Llewelyn and Adcock (2003) op cit, p 74.

75 Consumer Project on Technology, *Ciprofloxacin: The Dispute over Compulsory Licenses* (2002) <www.cptech.org/ip/health/cl/cipro> (accessed 9 December 2005).

Challenging patent rights

A final area of current controversy concerns the means by which patents may be challenged. Criticisms of existing mechanisms usually raise systemic questions about the operation of the patent system; however, gene patents provide a particular focus for these concerns.

Opportunities to object to the grant of patent rights exist at each stage of the patenting process: prior to acceptance of a standard patent application through intervention in the examination process;[76] after the Commissioner of Patents has accepted an application through opposition proceedings or re-examination;[77] and after a patent has been sealed through revocation proceedings.[78]

Each procedure has its own peculiarities, such as who may initiate the challenge; whether the procedure is adversarial or is conducted *ex parte*; the possible outcomes of the challenge; and whether the parties have a right to appeal against an adverse decision. There are also differences in the use that is made of different procedures in practice. For example, only a very small proportion of accepted applications – approximately 1.5 per cent – are subject to opposition proceedings, and this is true of biotechnology patents as well.

The principal difficulty with the mechanisms for challenging patent rights is not that they are insufficient in number or efficacy, but that the financial cost of pursuing them is often prohibitive, particularly for smaller organisations and individual public sector institutions. The effect of this may be that gene patents of questionable validity might go unchallenged. In this connection it is worth noting that there is no presumption in Australia that a granted patent is valid: the system relies on parties pursuing their individual interests to test a patent, including through the courts.

One possible solution is patent litigation insurance, which indemnifies the insured for the legal costs incurred in enforcing patent rights or in defending a claim of patent infringement. This protection does not come without its problems: it is expensive, not readily available in Australia, and is sometimes the source of bad publicity. However, where it has been obtained, patent litigation insurance may assist small and medium sized enterprises in enforcing their patent portfolios against, or defending allegations of patent infringement by, larger companies without having to settle or license to avoid escalating costs. For example, GTG – the holder of several patents over non-coding DNA – has indicated that patent litigation insurance is an important part of its licensing and enforcement strategy, and this has allowed the company to initiate proceedings against major biotechnology companies in the United States.[79]

---

76 *Patents Act 1990* (Cth) s 27.

77 Ibid ss 59, 97.

78 Ibid s 138.

79 Walker, J, "Patents Insurance Has Its Virtues", press release, 30 May 2002; ABC Television, "Patently a Problem", *Four Corners*, 11 August 2003, <www.abc.net.au/4corners/archive. htm> (accessed 9 December 2005).

Another possible solution is for health departments collectively to take a more active role in monitoring gene patents and intervening in the patent process where appropriate. Health departments and other public health organisations are directly affected by the patenting of genetic materials and technologies. As the main funders and users of these technologies, they have a major stake in the effects of the patent system on health care provision and medical research. There are overseas precedents for intervention by public sector authorities in patent processes, such as the revocation of Myriad's BRCA1 patents in Europe, which was discussed in a case study above. Oppositions to the patent were filed by a number of parties including the Assistance Publique-Hôpitaux de Paris, the Paris public hospitals authority.[80] The Belgian, Netherlands and Austrian Ministries for Health are among the bodies that have filed oppositions to another Myriad patent.[81]

Conclusion

The issues identified in this chapter suggest that we should always be open to improving the patent system to meet the challenges posed by new technologies, including genetic technologies. But it should also be remembered that the patent system is a generic system, which is intended to accommodate all new technologies as they arise. Thus, the patenting of genetic materials and technologies presents challenges not only for the patent system itself, but also for the scientists, health professionals and public institutions that are now compelled to engage with an unfamiliar system in ever increasing numbers. One of those challenges is to utilise existing mechanisms provided by the law and the marketplace to ensure that genetic inventions serve the fundamental goal of improving the well-being of society.

---

80   Other opponents included: the Institut Curie, the Institut Gustave-Roussy, the Belgian Society for Human Genetics and the Associazione Angela Serra per la Ricerca sul Cancro: European Patent Office, "'Myriad/Breast Cancer' Patent Revoked after Public Hearing", press release, Munich, 18 May 2004.

81   EPO705902. Institut Curie and Assistance Publique Hôpitaux de Paris and Institut Gustave-Roussy, *Against Myriad Genetics's Monopoly on Tests for Predisposition to Breast and Ovarian Cancer Associated with the BRCA1 Gene*, 2002, p 7.

PART VII

THE SEQUELAE OF
THE END OF LIFE

15

The evolving institution of coroner

Ian Freckelton and David Ranson

I'm the Coroner. I dish nothing out. I make findings about causes. Occasionally, just occasionally, I might recommend a prosecution.

Ian Callinan[1]

Introduction

The jurisdiction of the coroner dates back arguably to the ninth century in Anglo-Saxon England[2] but on any view to the 1194 Council of Eyre.[3] It made its way to Australia and New Zealand at settlement but has assumed a number of distinctive characteristics. While coroners' inquests constitute one of the oldest components of our legal system, coronership of the early 21st century is evolving in important new directions. Gone are the roles of the keeping of fines, the award of compensatory deodands to the relatives of those killed by dangerous acts, the taking of recognisances and the jurisdiction over shipwrecks. Responsibilities concerning Royal fish and treasure trove are no more. Dealing with abjuring of the realm and exigents is no longer necessary. Fining the local community via the "murdrum" when an unexplained murder has been committed is not a task for modern coroners.[4] Nor does the coroner any longer arrange the funerals of those who have committed suicide.[5]

An increasingly peripheral aspect of the jurisdiction of the modern coroner is the non-death investigation role. While in the 19th century the fire jurisdiction of coroners was a vital part of their responsibilities,[6] only in the Australian Capital

1   Callinan, I, *The Coroner's Conscience*, Central Queensland University Press, 1999, p 30.
2   See, for example, Vickers, RH, *The Powers and Duties of Police Officers and Coroners*, TH Flood, Chicago, 1889, pp 166–167; Waldo, FJ, "The Ancient Office of Coroner" (1910) 8 *Transactions of the Medico-Legal Society* 101.
3   See Holdsworth, W, *A History of English Law*, vol 1, 7th edn, Methuen & Co, London, 1956, p 82; McKeough, J, "The origins of the Coronial Jurisdiction" (1983) 6 *UNSWLJ* 191; Hunnisett, RF, *The Medieval Coroner*, Cambridge University Press, Cambridge, 1961.
4   See generally Freckelton I and Ranson, D, *Death Investigation and the Coroner's Inquest*, Oxford University Press, Melbourne, 2006, ch 1.
5   See Kadri, S, *The Trial: A History from Socrates to OJ Simpson*, Harper Collins, London, 2005, p 1178.
6   See Freckelton and Ranson (2006) op cit.

Territory,[7] New South Wales,[8] Tasmania[9] and Victoria[10] can coroners still investigate fires if there have not been fatalities. In New South Wales,[11] coroners can investigate explosions. In the Australian Capital Territory[12] and the Northern Territory[13] they can investigate "disasters".

What dominates the jurisdiction of Australian and New Zealand coroners at the start of the third millennium is investigation of death by inquiry and at open inquest – scrutinising manner and circumstances of death and its causes. Coroners' functions are inquisitorial and thus an anomaly on our courts' largely adversarial landscape. Coroners no longer preside over juries save in New South Wales. Nor in most jurisdictions can they commit for trial (again, save in New South Wales). Controversially, they are entitled still to append a modern version of riders to the inquisition – recommendations or comments arising out of their findings. This role has the potential to forge an ongoing relevance for coroners but raises many of the most difficult issues about the capacity of coroners to meet modern needs for death investigation.

This chapter reviews latter-day evaluations of the role and performance of the modern coroner, particularly focusing upon coronial investigation of iatrogenic and hospital environment deaths. It observes that the sacrosanct status of coronership outside the mainstream of critical legal scholarship has come toward its end and that coronership now has significant vulnerabilities. We identify an increasing body of commentators questioning whether coroners can fulfil their rhetoric of protecting the living by speaking for the dead. We pose fundamental questions about what changes need to be made to enable coroners to function as a linchpin in modern death investigation.

Changes to coroners' legislation

A characteristic of coroners over the past two decades is that their enabling legislation in Australia and New Zealand has been in a state of major evolution commencing with the *Coroners Act 1985* in Victoria. However, even this Act has been serially amended including in 1999 and in 2004 with the introduction of the concept of "reviewable deaths" to deal with multiple child deaths in the one family.[14] The Australian Capital Territory recast its coronial legislation with the *Coroners Act 1997* (ACT); the Northern Territory with the *Coroners Act 1993* (NT); Queensland with the *Coroners Act 2003* (Qld); South Australia with the

---

7   *Coroners Act 1997* (ACT) s 18.
8   *Coroners Act 1980* (NSW) s 15.
9   *Coroners Act 1995* (Tas) s 40.
10 *Coroners Act 1985* (Vic) s 31.
11 *Coroners Act 1980* (NSW) s 15.
12 *Coroners Act 1997* (ACT) s 19.
13 *Coroners Act 1993* (NT) s 28.
14 *Coroners (Amendment) Act 2004* (Vic).

Coroners Act 2003 (SA); Tasmania with the Coroners Act 1995 (Tas), and Western Australia with the Coroners Act 1996 (WA). New South Wales has enacted serial amendments to its Coroners Act 1980 (NSW). New Zealand has the Coroners Bill 2005 (NZ) before its Parliament, while Victoria has commenced the latest phase of coronial law reform by a thoroughgoing reference before the Law Reform Committee of the Parliament.[15] These legislative amendments have reflected changes in the way in which the community expects death to be investigated.

The coroner and medical treatment-related deaths

The investigation of deaths occurring in the setting of medical treatment is a good example of the dilemmas for coroners as modern death investigators to command community confidence. Deaths that occur in the setting of health care provision represent a large component of a coroner's work. Coroners' recommendations in relation to needed improvements to health service provision have the potential to save lives and reduce injuries associated with adverse medical treatment events.

Of course, the process of health care delivery carries inherent risks recognised particularly where the death is associated with a surgical procedure (perioperative) or occurs during an invasive diagnostic procedure. However, there are also risks that arise in the context of health care which are not necessarily related to complex or difficult medical procedures. A patient may slip on a wet floor in a hospital and sustain a fatal injury; someone may be allergic to a medication and suffer a fatal anaphylaxis; a person may develop a wound infection that leads to fatal septicaemia; or he or she may be given the wrong medication or an excessive dose of medication.

Medical treatment and diagnosis are not infallible. The simple fact that a person has died in hospital or following medical treatment is not of itself enough to raise community concern, or to attract the attention of the police or the coroner. Coroner's legislation with respect to the definition of reportable deaths is usually framed in such a way as to require deaths, which may have occurred as a result of an adverse medical treatment event, to be reported. Yet the linkage between the legislative definitions of reportable death and adverse medical treatment events is not always clear.

An "adverse medical treatment event" can be defined by reference to whether:

- the event occurred during health care management;
- the event had a negative impact on the patient; and
- the event was not attributable to the patient's underlying disease and its natural progression.

---

15   Law Reform Committee of the Parliament of Victoria, Coroners Act 1985, Discussion Paper, Victorian Government Printer, Melbourne, 2005.

Adverse treatment events are now considered to be a significant public health issue. Although the problem is not new,[16] it is only relatively recently that public policy interest has focused on this aspect of health care.[17] Various studies have shown that adverse treatment events are associated with both mortality and morbidity.[18] This, as well as recent evidence that simple strategies could reduce the incidence of such adverse events,[19] has prompted coroners to focus their investigations on factors relevant to public health.

Reviews of deaths and injuries associated with medical treatment have been undertaken in a number of jurisdictions. A leading example is the Quality in Australian Health Care Study commissioned by the Commonwealth Department of Human Services and Health in 1994 which sought to determine the proportion of hospital admissions in Australian hospitals associated with an "adverse event".[20] This study reviewed the medical records of over 1,400 admissions to 28 hospitals in New South Wales and South Australia and found that 16.6 per cent of hospital admissions were associated with an "adverse event". Fifty-one per cent of these adverse events were considered preventable and 13.7 per cent resulted in permanent disability. Of particular interest with respect to coroners' investigations is the fact that 4.9 per cent of patients suffering an "adverse event" died. This study built substantially upon the 1984 Harvard Medical Practice Study.[21] The Harvard study examined records of 3195 patients and identified 1,133 adverse events, 28 per cent of them resulting from negligent care.

---

16 Shimmel, EM, "The Hazards of Hospitalization" (1964) 60 *Annals of Internal Medicine* 100.

17 Barraclough, BH, "Safety and Quality in Australian Healthcare: Making Progress" (2001) 174 *Medical Journal of Australia* 616.

18 See Wilson, R, Runciman, WB, Gibberd, R et al, "The Quality in Australian Health Care Study" (1995) 163 *Medical Journal of Australia* 458; Wilson, R, Harrison, BT, Gibberd, R and Hamilton, J, "An Analysis of the Cause of Adverse Events from the Quality in Australian Health Care Study" (1999) 170 *Medical Journal of Australia* 411; O'Hara, DA and Carson, NJ, "Reporting of Adverse Events in Hospitals in Victoria 1994–1995" (1997) 166 *Medical Journal of Australia* 460; Brennan, TA, Leape, LL and Laird, NM, "Incidence of Adverse Events and Negligence in Hospitalized Patients: Results of the Harvard Medical Practice Study I" (1991) 324 *New England Journal of Medicine* 370; Thomas, EJ, Studdert, DM et al, "Incidence and Type of Adverse Events and Negligent Care in Utah and Colorado" (2000) 38(3) *Medical Care* 261; McNeil, JJ, Ogden, K et al, Improving Patient Safety in Victorian Hospitals, Report for the Victorian Department of Human Services, September 2000; Brennan, TA, Leape LL, Laird, NM et al, "The Nature of Adverse Events in Hospitalized Patients: Results of the Harvard Medical Practice Study II" (1991) 324(6) *New England Journal of Medicine* 377.

19 Vincent, C, Neale, G and Woloshynowych, M, "Adverse Events in British Hospitals: Preliminary Retrospective Record Review" (2001) 322 *British Medical Journal* 517; Wolff, A, "A Limited Adverse Occurrence Screening: A Medical Quality Control System for Medium Sized Hospitals" (1992) 156 *Medical Journal of Australia* 449; Wolff, A, "Limited Adverse Occurrence Screening: Using Medical Record Review to Reduce Hospital Adverse Patient Events" (1996) 164 *Medical Journal of Australia* 458.

20 Wilson R et al, "The Quality in Australian Health Care Study" (1995) 163 *Medical Journal of Australia* 458.

21 Leape LL et al, "The Nature of Adverse Events in Hospitalised Patients: Results of the Harvard Medical Practice Study II" (1991) 324 *New England Journal of Medicine* 377.

Subsequent to the study, a number of potentially alarmist articles appeared in the general press. Extrapolating from this study to inferences about deaths on a national basis led to suggestions that in Australia up to 14,000 patients a year died as a result of hospital treatment errors.

If this figure were amortised amongst Australian jurisdictions, approximately 3,000 of these deaths could be expected to have occurred, for example, in Victoria. In practice, however, the Victorian State Coroner's Office investigates only about 1,000 hospital deaths each year. This raises the somewhat difficult question as to why the other 2,000 deaths associated with an "adverse medical treatment event" were not reported to the coroner.

Confusion and lack of clarity in legislation often make identification of reportable deaths problematic. For example, the definition of "unexpected" or "unnatural" deaths is far from clear.[22] Phraseology that has technical legal definitions raises real problems for medical practitioners who are obliged to consider whether the death of their patients should be reported to a coroner.

By contrast, deaths occurring in a setting of an accident or injury are far more straightforward and nearly all of these are referred to coroners for investigation. As a result, these cases provide a useful model of how the coroner's process investigates deaths occurring in a medical treatment setting.

The coroner and
trauma-related deaths

In trauma-related deaths, coroners tend to focus on the nature of the accident and how it occurred, rather than on the subsequent medical treatment of the victim. Research into health care provision in trauma cases has shown substantial problems in medical treatment provided to victims. For instance, a 1986 study in San Diego in the United States of America[23] revealed that errors in medical diagnosis, judgment, or technique contributed significantly to the fatal outcome for people treated as a result of accidental trauma. The study involved a medical audit of 7,936 cases. 9.1 per cent of these patients suffered significant morbidity or received treatment that violated standard hospital protocols. Further, 7.6 per cent of deaths that occurred in non-trauma medical centres and 2 per cent of deaths at major trauma centres were considered to have been preventable.

Looking in more detail into deaths associated with road trauma has provided a useful model of the significance of adverse events in hospital treatment. A Victorian study of people who died following treatment for injuries sustained in

---

22   Must the death be unexpected by the coroner, unexpected by the deceased, unexpected by the treating doctor, or unexpected by the family of the deceased? Is a death from mesothelioma, caused by industrial exposure to asbestos 40 years before, a natural or unnatural death? See further Freckelton and Ranson (2006) op cit.

23   Shackford, SR et al, "Assuring Quality in a Trauma System – The Medical Audit Committee: Composition, Cost and Results" (1986) 27(8) *Journal of Trauma* 866.

road traffic accidents between 1992 and 1993[24] reviewed 137 deaths. All of the patients had survived for a period of time and had received some medical treatment, which varied from ambulance officer attention to long-term hospital care. For the 137 patients receiving treatment, 1,012 problems were identified in various areas of their medical care; 65 per cent of these were management errors and 21 per cent were systemic inadequacies. Medical technique areas, diagnostic delays and diagnostic errors together accounted for only 10 per cent of the problems.

The treatment of these patients was evaluated in the study by a broad-ranging team of medical practitioners, including surgical, anaesthetic and intensive care specialists, emergency department specialists, and pathologists. The medical team concluded that 470 of these problems contributed to the patient's death. Sixty-two per cent of the deaths were assessed as non preventable, 33 per cent as potentially preventable and 5 per cent as preventable.

Given that these medical evaluations were carried out retrospectively on a documentary review and that some of the deaths were regarded as having been preventable had the patient received appropriate medical management, one might expect that the coroner investigating the trauma death would have identified significant problems in medical care in a substantial percentage of these cases. In fact this did not occur. A 1998 study[25] of these cases showed that in only one coroner's finding were there comments on a potential inadequacy in the medical management.

All of these deaths, whether or not they involved an adverse event, were reported to the coroner simply by virtue of their being deaths associated with a motor vehicle fatality. However, the adverse events noted in the patients' medical treatment were not unique to motor vehicle trauma; they arose out of ordinary, everyday hospital practice. It follows that many other patients probably suffer the same sorts of adverse events. What we do not know is how many other deaths of patients in hospital occur without report to a coroner when their circumstances included dangerous treatment. This shines an uncomfortable light on the coroner system and raises questions about its effectiveness.

The failure to report reportable deaths

There are major issues in terms of the numbers and categories of deaths that are reported to coroners. To take Victoria as an example, each year some 500 deaths are reported to the coroner by the Registrar of Births, Deaths and Marriages. This occurs when the Registrar receives a medical certificate of death which on its face discloses causes which would make the death reportable.

24   McDermott, FT, Cordner, SM and Tremayne, AB, "Evaluation of the Medical Management and Preventability of Death in 137 Road Traffic Fatalities in Victoria, Australia: An Overview" (1996) 40(4) *Journal of Trauma: Injury, Infection & Critical Care* 520.

25   Ranson, DL, "How Effective? How Efficient? The Coroner's Role in Medical Treatment Related Deaths" (1998) 23 *Alternative Law Journal* 284.

In most of these cases the treating medical practitioner has provided a death certificate and not reported the case to the coroner. Review of such cases has shown that a substantial number are trauma-related deaths which would traditionally be thought to be easily identifiable as such by medical practitioners.

In a recent Victorian study of deaths occurring at two major public hospitals,[26] underreporting of reportable deaths varied between 10 per cent and 40 per cent. Why are such deaths not reported? Much depends upon the definition of what is "reportable" and the perceptions of those mandated to report the deaths – principally the medical staff involved.

There is a difficult issue that those most under the scrutiny of coroners in a hospital death – the doctors – are the ones who are legislatively mandated to report these deaths and therefore are the gatekeepers to investigation into their own conduct. Is the failure to report deaths to coroners a result of ignorance about the definition of "reportable deaths"? Or do doctors not report deaths associated with an adverse treatment event because they have something to hide?

There is little direct evidence of doctors deliberately concealing deaths from the coroner. Indeed, review of hospital procedures reveals that because there are a multitude of medical, paramedical and nursing staff involved in the care of patients, deliberately concealing a reportable death from a coroner would involve an extremely complex conspiracy of silence. Part of the answer may lie in long-time practice and culture within the medical profession together with an acknowledgment that many families are not keen to have coronial involvement or the spectre of an autopsy.

Failure of the coroner's investigation

It seems that where coroners investigate deaths following medical treatment, there is a high likelihood that the investigation will not uncover issues that a specialist medical panel would identify as significant in contributing to the death. Apart from brief initial medical witness statements of fact from treating medical staff, coroners rely on hospital pathologists, forensic pathologists, government medical officers and police to provide them with the basic information and analysis regarding a death in hospital. A reviewing forensic pathologist may not have been engaged in clinical medical practice for many years – indeed, the nature of contemporary sub-specialisation in medicine is such that a histopathologist may have little experience in modern intensive care unit procedures. This problem is not confined to non-clinical specialities. A gynaecological surgeon may not know about recent trends in neurosurgery and a neurosurgeon may not know what is current acceptable practice in nephrology.

Given this, it seems unlikely that one doctor from any particular specialty could be expected to identify all potential procedural errors in complex treatment

---

26   2005 personal communication with the Clinical Liaison Service of the Victorian Institute of Forensic Medicine.

regimes that cross medical disciplines. If an individual clinician may not be capable of correctly identifying all the issues of possible concern in situations involving complex medical management, why would we expect a police officer to be able to do so or, for that matter, a non-medically trained coroner?

The development by some coroner's jurisdictions of specialised clinical death investigation teams has the potential to go some way toward changing this. The inclusion of clinicians working together with pathologists in death investigation allows for a far wider scope of investigation.

In addition, communication between the coroner, the medical profession and health service providers can be enhanced, in turn increasing the likelihood that coroners' recommendations will be implemented by the healthcare sector.

Criticisms of the modern institution of coroner

By the early part of the 21st century telling criticisms have started to be directed towards the operation of the coronial system. Many relate to the extent to which coroners have responded to the needs of the general community in relation to avoidance of avoidable deaths and also to the distress and concerns of family members.

Perhaps mostly notably Dame Janet Smith in the United Kingdom Shipman Inquiry has pointed to what she termed "the poor quality of many coroners' decisions and the superficiality of investigation".[27] The following section analyses the bases upon which such criticisms have been directed.

Confused modern status of the coroner

The modern coroner is an entity shorn of most of its past functions. Not only this, but, as noted above, coroners rarely any longer sit with the democratising and populist input of juries. Most cannot commit for trial. They are generally precluded from framing findings in language suggestive of criminal or civil liability. In England and Wales their powers to impose riders have been removed and replaced by a behind-the-scenes function, rarely employed, of drawing dangerous practices to the attention of the appropriate arm of government. Elsewhere, to the extent that coroners have arrogated to themselves a public health and safety role, they have done so largely extra-legislatively – in other words, without clear parliamentary or community authorisation. Many legal practitioners and judicial officers are concerned about the phenomenon of coroners overreaching their role.[28]

Further, it has reached the point that the institution of coroner has been the subject of so many reforms over the past two centuries that its contemporary role is

---

27   Dame Janet Smith, *Third Report: Death Certification and the Investigation of Death by Coroners*, Cmnd 5834, 2003.

28   See, for example, Nathan, J, in *Harmsworth v State Coroner* [1989] VR 989.

unclear, both in theory and in practice. This has the potential to result in diverse and unpredictable investigation processes and decision-making.

Inconsistency of decision-making

Coroners' decisions comprise a disparate and inconsistent set of rulings, both across and within jurisdictions.[29] Some decisions are of the highest standard: legally rigorous, sensitive, informed by expert material, and transparent and lucid in their reasoning. However, significant numbers of inquest decisions are still undertaken in a relatively amateur, disjointed way by magistrates who only occasionally act as coroners and have little understanding of modern principles of risk management and occupational health and safety.

There is no formal or official legal reporting of coroners' decisions. Occasionally coroners' offices publish a few highly edited findings and recommendations in newsletters, or place extracts of selected cases on a website. Queensland has been an innovator in this regard.

A result of this inaccessibility of decisions has been that the notion of precedent, or perhaps more correctly consistency, has exercised relatively little impact upon decision-making or findings. To the extent that coroners traditionally have referred to one another's decisions, it has tended to be only within the same jurisdiction or by reference to well-known coroners' manuals. This has meant that little has been learnt from decisions even in other parts of the same country, and the use of international experience has been very limited, consisting mostly of Commonwealth countries referring to major English authorities. As a consequence, there has been a failure to develop an international corpus of law and practice.

A potential for improvement exists with the development of the National Coroners Information System (NCIS). However, the NCIS is still not publicly available or even accessible to legal practitioners engaged in work within the coroner's jurisdiction. Thus far the use of the NCIS by coroners themselves has been limited. For the NCIS to have a real impact on coronial practice the circumstances of each and every death investigated by a coroner need to be checked against the database to look for patterns and trends that might enable identification of significant causal factors. It is problematic, and arguably indicative of an old-fashioned culture among coroners, that such a rich database of information including autopsy reports, police reports, toxicology reports, and coroners' findings and recommendations, is still used so patchily, and has not been made publicly accessible in any form.

---

29   See, for example, *United Kingdom, Death Certification and Investigation in England, Wales and Northern Ireland: The Report of a Fundamental Review*, Cmnd 5831, 2003, ch 7 (Luce Report).

Inflexibility of inquest procedure

Although flexibility is often asserted to be an advantage of the inquisitorial process of inquests, in fact coroners have tended to be hesitant to move away from traditional adversarial processes in their courts. For instance, it has not been coroners' courts which have generated innovations in the adducing of expert evidence – rather, it has tended to be commercial courts in the civil jurisdiction.[30]

By contrast with procedures in Canada in relation to hospital inquests, coronial hearings in most countries continue to take place only in courts. Coroners, too, have tended to be reactive to notifications and reports, rather than taking pre-emptive investigative steps based on their own knowledge and skill as to what may be required in a particular death investigation. In spite of being free from the constraints of the adversary system, such as the technical rules of evidence and procedure, coroners have proved conservative and somewhat rigid in their processes.

The result is that coronial procedures often remain fixed in an adversarial model. This detracts substantially from the advantages which could accrue from the true inquisitorial model. This inflexible approach to procedure presents particular difficulties with respect to health care-related death investigations. The medical practice model of the "combined team" offers considerable advantages when dealing with complex medical problems and yet the coroner's inquest usually places one health care professional in the witness box at a time. The introduction of a "hot tub" procedure in an inquest could allow this combined team approach to the admission of oral testimony which with improvements for the capacity of coroners to investigate deaths associated with complex medical treatment.

Lack of rigour in decisions

The task of writing decisions in a narrative style, as is the practice of coroners in Australia and New Zealand, is demanding. In the past this was not an issue for coroners because arriving at verdicts was the role of coroners' jurors, who did not need to give reasons and tended to give relatively short (although occa-sionally idiosyncratic) verdicts. In general, coronial jurors were provided with pro forma potential verdicts and rarely departed very far from them.

However, the combination of coroners' juries falling into disuse in most places and the modern predilection of Australian coroners to provide a full narrative account of the circumstances and manner of death has changed the role of the modern coroner. A number of judges have lately suggested that coroners' analyses have lacked robustness and the hallmarks of sound legal reasoning. An example lies in the obligation, not always rigorously adhered to by coroners, to distinguish clearly between statutory findings and sub-findings of fact.

---

30   See New South Wales Law Reform Commission, *Expert Witnesses*, NSWLRC, Sydney, 2005.

Batt J in *Keown v Khan*[31] commented that while it is open to coroners to "discuss the evidence and explain their findings", he had the impression that "in more contentious inquests coroners' reports have of late tended to be prolix". He observed: "At least as a general rule, that is unnecessary".

Thus, the question is whether enough modern coroners are equipped with the skills to do what is the staple of intermediate and superior court judges, namely to compose lucid, legally correct and internally consistent written reasons for their findings. Dame Janet Smith has observed:

> [T]here are grounds for concern about the soundness of the decisions of some coroners and coroner's staff on jurisdiction. Although I have no doubt that many coroners understand and apply the correct statutory tests ... there is also evidence that some either do not understand the criteria or are influenced, deliberately or not, by extraneous matters. On occasions, it appears that decisions are taken for frankly improper reasons.[32]

It is likely that as coroners' findings and recommendations become available on the internet, from sources such as the NCIS, coroners' decisions will become subject to a level of scrutiny from which their anonymity and inaccessibility thus far have protected them.

This in turn has the potential either to bring the jurisdiction into disrepute or to improve the quality of decision-making.

A subsidiary, connected question relates to coroners' ability effectively to undertake the challenging public policy task of synthesising the vast amounts of material relevant to the making of recommendations, and formulating such recommendations in a way that is amenable to practical implementation. This requires non-judicial skills of the kind found within high levels of specialist bureaucracies, particularly those of senior research analysts and policy developers.

Uninformed recommendations

Another difficulty with coroners' decisions has been that a percentage of recommendations have been labelled as ill-informed and impractical.

For instance, following Coroner Barritt's recommendations after the first Chamberlain inquest,[33] his suggestions about safety were popularly denounced in the Northern Territory as "impossible to implement".

Such responses to coroners' recommendations have led to coroners' findings being dismissed as amateur "do-goodism": assertions that coroners' proposals are often insufficiently informed by knowledge of the relevant area, practicalities, and sensitivities to indirect consequences that would accompany implementation. A

---

31 [1999] 1 VR 69.

32 Dame Janet Smith, *Third Report: Death Certification and the Investigation of Death by Coroners*, Cmnd 5834, 2003, para 7.74.

33 See also Bryson, J, *Evil Angels*, Penguin Books, Melbourne, 1985, p 247.

number of reformists have advanced such criticisms, leading to calls for the removal of the rider power from coroners.[34]

Inconsistency of recommendations

A problem inherent in the ad hoc process of the formulation of riders or recommendations arising from findings is that they arise piecemeal, and inevitably in a way that is coloured by and responsive to the dilemmas posed by particular cases. What occurs in recommendations is that a coroner is persuaded to extrapolate from deficiencies highlighted in an individual death to propose reforms in comparable scenarios – to move from the specific to the more general. The challenge for coroners is to refrain from wide-scale recommendations where they lack sufficient information to appreciate the ramifications of their proposals for change, and yet to have the fortitude to advance constructive proposals where the information before them lays an appropriate groundwork.

Probably the worst scenario, though, is erroneous, impractical or ill-informed recommendations. Such proposals reduce the esteem in which coroners are held and detract from the force that better formulated recommendations would command.

Another risk is that for political reasons, an ill-conceived recommendation may be adopted and acted on without further consideration by a nervous agency. If the implementation of the ill-conceived recommendation actually leads to further injury and death, this would have the potential to prompt a major backlash against the role of the coroner.

Although recommendations are asserted to be one of the most powerful aspects of a coroner's findings with respect to achieving public good, it is remarkable how little this power is used. A recent study by the NCIS in Australia has demonstrated that it is rare for coronial recommendations to be made.[35] The study showed that of the 90,000 coroners' findings contained in the national database, only 0.05 per cent contained any clearly identified formal recommendations. Moreover, there was considerable variation among coroners as to the frequency with which they made recommendations. An examination of 21,000 completed coroners' case files from the State of Victoria revealed only 133 decisions that contained formal recommendations. Sixty-three per cent of these had

---

34 The Brodrick Committee was particularly strident in this regard: "Relative to the number of inquests held annually, animadversions are uncommon, but, because they may be extensively reported, they may harm reputations far more than the coroner ever intended. Comments on the morals, ethics or professional standards of those who have no opportunity to answer back made by someone who speaks from a position of privilege are reprehensible and we should like to see them discontinued".United Kingdom, Report of the Committee on Death Certification and Coroners, Cmnd 4810, 1971, para 16.54 (Brodrick Committee Report). See, too, United Kingdom, *Report of Home Office Departmental Committee on Coroners*, Cmnd 5070, 1936 (Wright Committee Report).

35 Bugeja, L and Ranson, D, "Coroners' Recommendations: a Lost Opportunity" (2005) 13 *Journal of Law and Medicine* 173.

been made by just three full-time coroners. If coroners are to establish themselves as 21st century public health officials, this is a problematically low exercise of a function contended by some to be a major rationale for the ongoing relevance of the institution of coroner.

Weakness of recommendations involving government

Another criticism that has been raised against the coroner's jurisdiction is that it has failed to deliver accountability in relation to state agencies and officials. Speaking of deaths of people, especially those of an Indigenous background, Hogan has launched perhaps the most searing critique of the effectiveness of contemporary Australian coroners:

> Almost uniformly, the inquests ... have been characterised by the lack of recommendations, the lack of critical attention to departmental powers and procedures, the lack of charges laid as a result of the coronial investigation and inquest, and the ineffectiveness of preventing similar deaths. The cases where such issues have been properly addressed are conspicuous by their rarity. The coronial system has shown itself to be insufficiently independent, impartial and effective.[36]

He has highlighted what at least in some places is the gap between, on the one hand, the rhetoric of the coronial jurisdiction as a mechanism to provide public protection and exposure of governmental and other dangerous conduct, and, on the other hand, the limitations imposed by available evidence, the proper legal parameters of the evidence, and the skills and experience of the coroner.

Under coronial legislation in Australia there is a dearth of clear statements expressing the objectives of the coronial process (in contrast to New Zealand). There is also an absence of statutory and bench book standards for the making and distribution of recommendations. While such matters are left to the unreviewable discretion of individual coroners, it is unlikely there will be a consistent and robust formulation of coroners' recommendations with respect to the investigation of the conduct of government agencies and services.

Poor utilisation of data and expertise

In 1907 William Brend[37] observed:

> [The] value of the statistics [of coroners] is diminished by absence of co-ordination. Hence we have the anomaly that while full inquiry is conducted into deaths from violence and unnatural causes, practically no subsequent use is made of the information for public health purposes.

Traditionally coroners' offices and even institutes of forensic medicine have not had persons on staff with strong quantitative backgrounds. Coroners have tended

---

36   Hogan, R, Brown, D and Hogg, R (eds) *Death in the Hands of the State*, Redfern Legal Centre Publishing, Sydney, 1988, pp 121–122.

37   Brend, W, "Bills of Mortality" (1907) 5 *Transactions of the Medico-Legal Society* 140.

to work closely with certain categories of experts in the modern era; however, epidemiologists and experts on occupational health and safety have tended to be conspicuous by their absence from coroners' staff in most jurisdictions. The availability of hard empirical or epidemiological data for coroners' investigations and recommendations at inquest has rarely been strong; instead such statistical analysis has been utilised on an ad hoc basis in a particular inquiry.

For the present, interrogation of the NCIS database tends to occur when a coroner has already identified issues of interest in a particular death type, the database searches being used to demonstrate the validity of the coroner's concern on the basis of the numerical frequency of cases of that type.

While this is a worthwhile use of the data in that it correctly demonstrates the seriousness of the issues relating to that death type by virtue of its frequency, sophisticated use of the data in the NCIS could enable much more. Unless specialists with skills in epidemiological analysis are employed by coroners' offices on a regular basis, it seems unlikely that the available data sets will be mined in the way that their potential would allow.

Limited implementation of coroners' recommendations

Coroners have no power to enforce compliance with their recommendations. In the Australian Capital Territory and the Northern Territory, there is a limited statutory obligation on some government departments to respond to a coroner's recommendations. However, this is rare. Most recommendations by coroners make their way into a void that risks relieving those to whom the recommendations were directed of the need to be responsive.[38] Given the costs of inquests and death investigations undertaken by coroners, this leaves a great deal to be desired.

In practice the only recourse available to a coroner, if a recommendation is not followed, is to wait until a similar death occurs and then comment adversely on the inactivity of the government department, agency, or private person or organisation that failed to take heed of the earlier recommendation. While such an approach may generate extensive media coverage and may lead eventually to compliance with the prior recommendation, the cost is ethically unacceptable: an unnecessary death.

Coroners generally do not report to parliament. Nor do they have compliance or monitoring divisions enabling evaluation of the impact of their recommendations. Scholarly studies, inside or outside coroners' offices, which assess the extent to which coroners' recommendations for public health and safety have been adopted (or ignored) by government or industry are almost unknown. If the much-vaunted facility to enhance community health and safety is to be a major

---

38 In respect of recommendation about deaths of persons with psychiatric illnesses, see Freckelton, I, "Untimely Death, Law and Suicidality" (2005) 12(2) *Psychiatry, Psychology & Law* 265.

reason for retention of coroners,[39] it is remarkable that no empirical base has been generated to enable objective measurement of the impact of coroners' work in this respect.

Anomalous culture of the coroners' courts

Coroners are usually appointed from the lower end of the judicial hierarchy or from among legal practitioners with little practical experience of judicial office or the conduct of inquisitorial investigations. As a consequence, the approaches taken by coroners often differ from those of senior judicial officials. In addition, when coroners' decisions are appealed, there can be considerable variation between judicial adversarial approaches and the inquisitorial culture of the coroner's jurisdiction.[40] The more junior legal status of coroners also affects their standing in the general, political and legal communities, reducing the likelihood that their findings and recommendations will have the authority that would be required in order for the recommendations to command respect.

Were the appointee pool for coroners to be more diverse or the role of coroners differently conceptualised, judicial status comparisons would be less likely to be made. There would be advantages in establishing an operational legal framework for coroners that is seen to be distinctive in nature and form from that of the remainder of the judiciary. This would in turn emphasise the difference between the legal process of the coroner's jurisdiction and that of the adversarial courts.[41]

Inadequate training for coroners

A key aspect of the coroner's jurisdiction and one that clearly distinguishes it from the adversarial jurisdiction of other courts is that the coroner is required to manage the practical aspects of the death investigation process as well as being the judicial head of that service, the trier of fact and the decider of law. Managing the coronial jurisdiction is a sophisticated administrative task engrafted upon the traditional legal decision-making responsibility. While raising the standards and skills of coroners in management would be beneficial, the mix of roles expected of modern coroners is diverse and demanding: directing complex medical and scientific investigations, managing an office dealing with often overwhelming amounts of data, and functioning as decision-makers in a continuing flow of complex cases.

---

39 See, for example, Johnstone, G, "Coroners' Recommendations" in Selby, H (ed), *The Aftermath of Death*, Federation Press, Sydney, 1999.

40 Compare though *R v Doogan* [2005] ACTSC 74.

41 McEwen has argued that while the coroners' jurisdiction is asserted to be free of the obligation to apply the rules of evidence, there is a greater inclination to apply such familiar rules than there should be: McEwen, J, *Evidence and the Adversarial Process – The Modern Law*, 2nd edn, Hart Publishing, Oxford, 1998, p 28.

Unsatisfactory legal guidance for coroners

A consequence of the unique nature of the coroner's jurisdiction is a relative lack of guidance for coroners as to how their enabling statutory provisions are to be interpreted. This lack of certainty has enabled creative evolution of the coroner's role by innovative coroners. However, such an approach has the potential to be disturbed by appellate intervention. The slowly rising status of the coroners' courts has generated an escalation of appellate litigation from coroners' findings and even from their recommendations. The results of these appeals have not disclosed uniform approaches by the higher courts, highlighting the difficulties attaching to the coroner's role as currently drawn by legislators who tinker continually with coroners' legislation but have failed fundamentally to redefine the place of the coroner in contemporary death investigation and prevention.

There has been little appreciation within the appellate levels of the litigation hierarchy of the complexity and uniqueness of the contemporary coroner's role. Training for coroners too remains limited. Bench books for coroners are only starting to be developed. In some jurisdictions there are some training programs and conferences dedicated to coroners' practice, but once more, this is a reasonably new phenomenon. For many coroners, especially those functioning in rural and remote areas, their work in that role is a part-time activity. This limits their ability to develop specialist skills and an appropriate knowledge base. There is still relatively little interaction among coroners at an international level, leaving systems to evolve separately but often along parallel lines in response to similar community pressures and dynamics. However, the Australasian Coroners' Society has become a lively forum and is now providing training and the opportunity for scholarly exchange, while the Victorian State Coroner, Graeme Johnstone, publishes an occasional journal, *In-Quest*.

Inadequate resources

Coroners need more than functional courthouses. There is as yet little apparent understanding by governments that coroners' courts are fundamentally different from magistrates' courts and cost considerably more if they are to meet modern objectives of risk prevention assessment and decision-making. Some are run on a shoestring, are understaffed in terms of coroners and administrative backup, are not properly supported by institutes of forensic medicine and science, do not have prompt access to basic litigation needs such as inquest transcription, and constantly need to curtail necessary investigative expenditures in order to remain within their budgets. Apart from generating low morale, such penny-pinching affects the quality of the investigative and adjudicative work able to be undertaken by coroners. It erodes what might otherwise be accomplished by innovative coroners' offices focused upon death prevention and high-quality multidisciplinary investigations.

Reliance on reporting of deaths

In spite of the independent nature of coroners' death investigations, a coroner currently has no power to proactively seek out or otherwise discover deaths that require medico-legal investigation. Instead the coroner usually relies on police officers and medical practitioners[42] to report deaths that require a coroner to be involved in the death investigation. Ironically, perhaps the most controversial of the deaths investigated by coroners are those deaths that are alleged to be associated with the activities of medical practitioners and police. There is a concern that the very people whose actions may be subject to coronial investigation and adverse comment are the same individuals who actually cause the deaths the coroner investigates. Medical practitioners and police officers are therefore the true gatekeepers who control the work of the coroner by determining which cases the coroner investigates, and in the case of police, how they are investigated. Not surprisingly, this has generated criticism, as has the role of police officers in assisting the coroner during inquest hearings when the officers are desultory or negligent in the discharge of their forensic duties.[43]

Dependency on delegation of investigations

As noted above, coroners delegate the practical aspects of death investigation to other specialists, such as medical practitioners and police officers. However, these are professional groups who come under particular scrutiny by coroners with respect to their contribution to deaths. Although the coroner in principle is an independent investigator, this independence is circumscribed by medical practitioners and police being the effective instruments of coronial investigation. A result is that in many coroners' cases, the investigation comes full circle with investigators investigating their own professional colleagues, a situation which does not enhance public confidence.[44] In 1986 the lawyers' organisation "Justice" in the United Kingdom published the results of a "committee of inquiry" into coroners' cases.[45] It endorsed an important recommendation of the Brodrick Report that police officers should be phased out of the coronial service and replaced by civilians, expressing the view that "it would go a long way to dispel suspicions aroused under present arrangements when deaths occur in police custody, and remove doubts about whether in any particular situation the officer was working for the Coroner and for the police".[46]

---

42 Most deaths are reported to a coroner by medical practitioners who were involved in the recent medical management of the deceased person or by police officers who have attended an unexpected or traumatic death. See Thomas, L, Friedman, F and Christian, L, *Inquests – A Practitioner's Guide*, Legal Action Group, London, 2002.

43 See Austin, M, "In Need of Physical Protection", in Hogan, Brown and Hogg (eds), (1988) op cit, p 22.

44 See Hogan, M, "Let Sleeping Watchdogs Lie: The NSW Coronial System and Deaths Involving State Agencies'", in Hogan, Brown, and Hogg (eds) (1988) op cit.

45 Justice (Chair: E Stone QC), *Coroners' Courts in England and Wales*, Justice, London, 1986 (Justice Report).

46 Ibid, paras 21–23.

Excessive resort to autopsies

The English lobby group INQUEST highlighted the distress caused to family members, especially those who are Jewish or Muslim, by the performance of autopsies. It has noted that 24 per cent of deaths were subject to autopsy in England and Wales in 2001, while the figure was approximately half that in Scotland and only 8 per cent in the United States. INQUEST has argued that the coroner's system in England and Wales relies excessively on autopsies to make up for poor investigation, particularly in relation to the scene and the history. Carpenter and colleagues in 2006[47] observed also that the numbers of full autopsies undertaken in Queensland may well exceed those that are required. They have argued for a reduction in internal autopsies, maintaining that adequate information can still frequently be gathered without compromising investigations into the cause and circumstances of death.

The move towards more flexible death investigation processes is growing in jurisdictions outside the United Kingdom, with the use of toxicology and radiological examinations such as CT scans in place of traditional body dissection in selected cases. These techniques, however, have not yet been fully validated in respect of death investigations without autopsy with the potential for difficulties in inquests and other court hearings in the future.

Undue focus on deaths

For the most part, aside from a jurisdiction existing in relation to the cause and origin of fires, and sometimes explosions, modern coroners are empowered to inquire only into certain categories of deaths. The difficulty in this regard is that deaths represent only a small subset of adverse incidents in which people's lives are put at risk and in the course of which serious injuries may have been sustained. The result is that the base for coroners' inquiries, findings and recommendations is skewed, not always fairly, in the direction of deaths, whereas conduct that causes only a small number of deaths may also be causing considerable numbers of serious injuries. The focus of coroners therefore may be on an unrepresentative sample of conduct that endangers the health and safety of the community.

Descent into the cult of personality

A concern has arisen about expert witnesses, especially well-known forensic pathologists and other leading medical practitioners, who solicit media attention and notoriety for the sake of it. The same concern from time to time is murmured about coroners whose names have become a byword by reason of the ongoing media publicity generated by their visits to scenes of crime, as well as their willingness to avail themselves of media opportunities. It is said of such coroners,

---

47 Carpenter, B et al, "Issues Surrounding the Reduction in the Internal Autopsy in the Coronial System" (2006) 14 *Journal of Law and Medicine* (in press).

whose goal seems to be securing a place in coronial history, that they devote too much energy to their public profile and insufficient attention to the core of their task, and that they exhibit inadequate sensitivity to the distress of family members. Another difficulty is that their high public profile can generate expectations unable to be satisfied by the inquests over which they preside.

Where personality plays an excessive role in coronership, continuity of purpose and philosophy is lost and reborn with a different emphasis as each coroner is replaced. What is needed is for there to be a transfer of the beneficial aspects of enlightened coronial practice away from the cult of personality and into modern legislation with a clear definition of the role of coroners and the purpose of inquests and coronial inquiries.

Delays in inquests

Another concern about coroners' inquests is that they often take place months or years after the death.[48] This reduces the immediacy of the coronial response, allows distress and anger to fester on the part of family and community members, and takes the sting out of recommendations by coroners for change, as these can be readily dismissed as dealing belatedly with different times and different factual scenarios than those obtaining by the time of the hearing. It is also very distressing for family members as delays in inquests preclude or delay emotional closure.

Inability to procure necessary evidence

In a number of jurisdictions the availability of the privilege against self-incrimination[49] thwarts coroners' attempts to obtain from crucial witnesses their accounts of what occurred around the time of the death of the deceased. The consequence can be an inability on the part of the coroner to make findings because he or she has not had the opportunity to test and thereby evaluate the assertions of those instrumentally responsible for a death.[50] The scenario has particularly arisen in the context of fatal shootings by police officers, who routinely (and understandably) avail themselves of the right to decline to answer questions. This has led some to despair as to the utility of inquests when the privilege so effectively precludes the coroner from obtaining the information that would be most pertinent to the findings he or she must make.

---

48 See Submissions of C Storm to Parliament of Victoria, Law Reform Committee, *Inquiry into the Coroners Act 1985*, <www.parliament.vic.gov.au/lawreform/Coroner/old%20 web/Submission%2028%20-%20Caroline%20Storm.pdf> (accessed 4 October 2005).

49 See Freckelton and Ranson (2006) op cit.

50 Northern Territory Law Reform Committee, *Report on Privilege Against Self-Incrimination*, Report No 23, 2001, p 7.

Dissatisfaction on the part of families

The English lobby group INQUEST in its 2002 submission to the government's *Fundamental Review of Coroner Services* maintained that there is a high level of dissatisfaction with the inquest system among bereaved people:

> [O]f those we surveyed 69% said their level of confidence in the inquest system decreased after their experience and for 83% this applied to the law in general and 87% for the criminal justice system.[51]

It found in its survey of 130 families who experienced sudden and unnatural deaths between January 1997 and December 2000, that only 26 per cent were given information about post-mortem examinations and what they involved. It endorsed the sentiments expressed by the Retained Organ Commission that while consent is not required for coroners' post-mortem examinations, distress is unnecessarily caused by the failure to provide information about the process.[52] A further issue it raised was the frequency with which full autopsies are conducted, a matter that can be distressing for family members.[53]

Families also reported discontent about the amount of time bodies were retained by the coroner. A quarter of the families surveyed reported waiting between a week and a month, while 10 per cent waited for over a month.[54] They also expressed dissatisfaction about not being informed of their right to have a second, independent post-mortem carried out on the body of their loved one.[55]

Another point of criticism for family members arises when inquests are booked in for unrealistically short periods of court time and have to be adjourned serially in order to complete examination-in-chief and cross-examination of witnesses and the drafting of submissions on behalf of interested parties. Again, the delays are counter-therapeutic and can be stressful. There is every reason to expect that many of these same criticisms could be levelled at Australian coroners' inquests.

Cultural insensitivity

The cultural insensitivity of the coroner's inquest system has also been lambasted by some in relation to Indigenous issues. It has been said that in many instances in

---

51 INQUEST, *How the Inquest System Fails Bereaved People*, INQUEST, London, 2002, p 3, <http://inquest.gn.apc.org/publications.html> (accessed 25 April 2006).

52 Retained Organ Commission, *Report of the Independent Investigation into Organ Retention at Central Manchester and Manchester Children's Hospital Trust*, London, July 2002.

53 See, for example, Carpenter, B, op cit, "Issues Surrounding the Reduction in the Internal Autopsy in the Coronial System" (2006) 14 *Journal of Law and Medicine* (in press).

54 INQUEST (2002) op cit, p 8.

55 The Luce Report acknowledged the legitimacy of the criticisms, noting that, especially in matters which do not proceed to inquest in England and Wales, family members receive a problematically low level of information about the death: See United Kingdom, *Death Certification and Investigation in England, Wales and Northern Ireland: The Report of a Fundamental Review*, Cmnd 5831, 2003, ch 7, p 75 (Luce Report).

New Zealand, Maori culture has not been respected[56] and in Australia that Aboriginal and Torres Strait Islander customs and religious beliefs have been ignored. For example, use of the dead person's name in proceedings is culturally offensive in many Cape York communities in the far north of Australia. Yet such names have been used on many occasions.[57]

Another complaint that has been made is that next of kin have not been adequately informed by coroners' offices of the progress of investigations and that they are allowed to play little role in the investigative or even hearing processes.

Coroners in many jurisdictions are appointed on a part-time or temporary basis. This has a number of consequences. There may not be continuity of the investigating coroner in respect of a long-running investigation. Further, coroners tend to carry high caseloads, meaning that unless they are well supplied in respect of administrative resources – and they often are not – communication by them or their investigators with family members is given a secondary priority. In addition, training is not always as sophisticated as it might be in relation to matters such as cultural sensitivities.

In some quarters, concern is also raised as to the extent to which the coroner is representative of the community. In New Zealand the absence of indigenous coroners has been remarked upon by the Law Commission.[58]

Undemocratic characteristics

The abolition of coroners' juries has been criticised as a regressive, undemocratic step, removing coroners' decision-making from its roots and placing it into the hands of lawyers. Justice in 1986 argued:

> The presence of a jury is to be justified not only in terms of the experience the individual jurors bring with them from their daily lives, but also (perhaps principally) in terms of their independent status within the inquiry. The presence of a jury in cases of public concern makes for greater openness, and gives better grounds for public confidence in the impartiality of proceedings.[59]

INQUEST too, in 2002 argued in favour of the use of juries, especially in cases involving the use of unreasonable force or gross negligence, as these involve questions of judgment particularly within the scope of jurors to evaluate in conformity with contemporary community standards.[60]

---

56 See Law Reform Commission of New Zealand, *Coroners*, Report No 62, 2000; see also Explanatory Memorandum to Coroners Bill 2004 (NZ).

57 INQUEST reported in 2002 that 16 per cent of the 130 families it surveyed felt that their cultural and religious needs had not been respected by coroners; only 44 per cent reported that these needs had been met: INQUEST (2002) op cit, p 8.

58 See Law Reform Commission of New Zealand (2000) op cit, para 44.

59 Justice Report (1986) op cit, para 36.

60 INQUEST (2002) op cit, p 31.

Moreover, when a jury is the decision-maker, this avoids the uncomfortable situation that arises if the coroner has made his or her own observations when visiting the scene of death. It separates the investigative and decision-making roles.

Inadequacy of funding for participation in inquests

Another crucial aspect of coroners' hearings is the expense involved in legal representation for family members. Often this precludes their active participation. Traditionally, there have been major constraints on the availability of legal aid for family members at inquests unless a public interest factor particularly distinguished the case.[61]

The Macpherson Inquiry into the death of Stephen Lawrence in England recommended in 1999 that consideration be given to the provision of legal aid to victims or the families of victims to cover representation in appropriate cases.[62] Justice has criticised the absence of legal aid for coroners' inquests and argued that it should routinely be available.[63]

INQUEST has gone further, acknowledging some improvement in the availability of legal funding for families at inquests,[64] but has argued that it should be routinely available and not means-tested.[65]

A trend towards death prevention

An identifiable international trend is for coroners to play an important role, alongside other agencies, in promoting public health and occupational health and safety. This is particularly pronounced in Australia and Canada, as well as in New Zealand, albeit somewhat less consistently.

The prophylactic and public health official function of coroners has the potential to revitalise the office and to give it a new sense of relevance,[66] but only if the function is scientifically, informedly and effectively discharged. The difficulty is that there are other public agencies outside the legal framework with the potential to undertake such a function.

Offices of Public Health and Safety, staffed by medical practitioners with public health and epidemiology experience, statisticians, occupational health and safety experts and risk management experts could readily enough be constituted with a specific mandate to work toward constructive objectives, informed by

---

61   See, for example, Levine, M and Pyke, J, *Levine on Coroners' Courts*, Sweet & Maxwell, London, 1999, p 149.

62   Macpherson, S *Stephen Lawrence Inquiry Report*, Cmnd 4262, HMSO, London, 1999.

63   Justice Report (1986) op cit, paras 38–44.

64   See Matthews, *Jervis on the Office and Duties of Coroners*, 12th edn, 2002, p 224.

65   INQUEST (2002) op cit, p 35.

66   See, for example, Bennett, RC, "The Changing Role of the Coroner" (1978) 118 *Canadian Medical Association Journal* 1133; also Law Commission of New Zealand, *Coroners*, Report No 62, NZLRC, Wellington, 2000, para 181.

known examples of serious injury and death caused by dangerous conduct. The question is whether the function best resides within coroners' inquests or coroners' offices.

The World Health Organisation has maintained that the important factor in preventing death is being able to break the lethal chain of events and begin treatment. From the standpoint of public health, the most effective form of intervention is elimination of the prime causes of risks. This has been the orientation of modern coroners' practice in Australia. However, with the increased focus upon prophylaxis comes a series of challenges for the office of coroner.

Most prominent among them is that the means for enabling the office to function as a vehicle for injury prevention is, ironically, the marginalised mechanism of riders. In the past, riders were not even a part of the coroner's inquisition. There are historical examples of pronouncements by coroners' juries, and, more recently, by coroners in the form of recommendations of steps to be taken to avoid deaths. However, they have always been a secondary component of the coroner's role, which is to establish who died, when, the circumstances or manner of death, and the cause of death. Legislative provision for riders has been incorporated in most (not all) coroner's jurisdictions[67] so that recommendations and suggestions arising from findings can be made – mostly now by coroners themselves.

However, inquests cannot be held for the purpose of making riders, save in New Zealand. The legislative focus tends to be upon coroners' obligation to find statutorily prescribed facts about the circumstances and aetiology of death. It follows that while some coroners are particularly attuned to the public health and safety implications of inquests and inquiries, together with the potential for use of the information to which they become privy, legislators have not yet officially sanctioned this shift in role. There is much to be said for the New Zealand model (in the current legislation and that in the Coroner's Bill 2005 (NZ)) under which there is explicit authorisation and delineation of the public health and safety role of coroners.

Another challenge lies in the fact that technically it is still the case that coroners' recommendations can be utterly ignored and rejected by those to whom they are directed. The Alberta practice whereby such recommendations are collated in the annual report of the Attorney-General, together with any implementation of the recommendations, is a constructive compromise.

The modern relevance of coroners arises from several factors, of which the following four are perhaps the most important with respect to death and injury prevention:

• the capacity of coroners to assuage public anxiety about deaths by open hearings and findings about matters of community concern;

• the coverage given by the media to their recommendations and findings;

---

67   See Freckelton and Ranson (2006) op cit, ch 18.

- the stature within the community of individual coroners; and
- the persuasiveness of particular recommendations.

Accordingly, some coroners have expended significant energy upon subtly fostering links with the media so as to optimise the chances of publicity for their recommendations. This constitutes a significant departure from the traditional role of judicial officers. In addition, some coroners (like pathologists) have become very prominent public figures. The consequence of this is that it becomes more difficult for government in particular to ignore or repudiate well-known and highly regarded coroners' proposals for reform and expenditure when they are overtly advanced to protect public safety.

However, technically, in most jurisdictions, the coroner is simply a magistrate with a specialist function. This is so even though a state or chief coroner has a myriad of demanding responsibilities and functions. There would be much to be said for recognising the reality of the requirements for administrative, investigative, public health and legal expertise in the modern chief coroner and attaching to the appointment intermediate judicial officer status.

The need for efficient death investigation mechanisms

At a straightforward level, modern society needs to know which of its members are alive and dead, as well as how and why they passed away. Much of our social administrative machinery (for example, licensing, taxation, probate, and social services) relies on this information. The criminal justice system needs information on deaths to ensure that homicides are correctly recognised, investigated and prosecuted. The commercial world, including insurance companies, needs details about deaths, as does the civil justice system in relation to wills and succession, and liability for dependency claims arising from negligent conduct causing death.

In addition to this rather pragmatic list of consumers of death investigation is the group which can easily be forgotten by scientific investigators: namely the family and friends of the deceased and the people who make up the same social group as the person who has died. We are all affected by the death of someone close to us. Such an event highlights our own vulnerability and reveals our own mortality. Further, the grief sequelae of unexpected, unnatural and avoidable deaths are significant from a public health perspective. An effective and efficient death investigative process has the potential to go a substantial way towards enabling closure for those who were close to the deceased, with attendant benefits in terms of their well-being and their productivity.[68]

---

68 Submissions of C Storm to Parliament of Victoria, Law Reform Committee, *Inquiry into the Coroners Act 1985*, <www.parliament.vic.gov.au/lawreform/Coroner/old%20web/Sub mission%2028%20-%20Caroline%20Storm.pdf> (accessed 4 October 2005).

The future of the coroner

The office of coroner has been distinguished historically by its shape-shifting capacity. Its ability to evolve has been apparent in its movement from being a collector of revenues, facilitator of funerals for those who have died by their own hand, and protector of those entering exile to a summoner of juries variously to investigate deaths, disasters, shipwrecks, and fires. It has proved able to adapt to changing community needs. Analysis of the strengths, weaknesses, and future potential of the institution of coroner, may enable its reshaping so as to build upon its past and facilitate its role as an effective part of society's investigation and response to deaths.

One of the difficulties for modern coroners and coroners' offices is that contemporary expectations of death investigation, and of those who make decisions about circumstances and causes of death, can be confused and even unrealistic. At one level the community expects a full and open, highly resourced investigation that will result in an outcome that reduces the incidence of risk and danger. Yet the scientific, medical and legal machinery, as well as the resources for achieving such objectives, are frequently woefully inadequate.

Ideally, a society's death investigation processes need to ensure that the right skills are employed at the right time to minimise community harm and to maximise community benefit. Coroners' legislation needs to be carefully restructured to meet individual government and community needs, with inclusion of specific provision for articulating and then implementing the intention and purpose of the contemporary role of the coroner. This should include explicitly specifying that a purpose of coroners' inquests is to enhance public health and safety, including by the making of recommendations to facilitate the prevention of deaths. The other aspect is that the practical phase of the death investigation needs to involve personnel with the appropriate technical skills who can extract the maximum community benefit from the process.

The front end of most current death investigation processes, where a single treating medical practitioner issues a death certificate, is usually managed by doctors, nurses, health administrators, and funeral directors. Police usually only become involved in death investigation processes when the death is reported to the coroner. The early stages of any death investigation involve addressing medical issues including liaising with the deceased person's medical practitioners, dealing with bereaved families, collecting sensitive medical and personal information, and physically moving and examining the body of the deceased. These are matters which in the case of most deaths are well managed by a broad medical team whose individual skills are well suited to various aspects of the work. If all of these deaths were to be reported to the coroner, the workload for coroners' offices would probably increase tenfold, to little useful end. In addition, families would have to deal with a larger group of non-medical personnel, including court staff and police.

While reporting all deaths to a coroner would have advantages in relation to the establishment of an independent death investigation process, it is hard to identify how the involvement of the coroner and the police and legal team would benefit a sufficient cross-section of investigations or be of advantage to families.

The reporting of all deaths to a central or regional non-coronial medical death investigation service, however, would have considerable benefits. The use of such a medical death investigation service would reduce the need for specific medical training of clerical and administrative staff whose background is in the area of courts and justice administration rather than health management. Experienced nurses, social support and medical administrative staff as well as forensic pathologists, clinicians, and medical, technical or scientific staff, clearly have more appropriate skills in this area and are better able to support families than traditional court staff.

Given that there are forensic pathologists and clinicians with administrative and even in some cases legal skills, many issues that might arise in the early stages of a medically based death investigation could be addressed.

At first glance it would seem impossible for enough suitably qualified medical staff to be found to review all death certificates issued by treating medical practitioners.

In reality, however, it is the ethos of the investigation rather than the exact qualifications of the participants that is important. Many medical procedures are carried out in a team setting, involving a range of medical and non-medical personnel who pool their skills and actions so as to provide a functional and cost-effective service. In this way protocols and policies could be established that structure work practices for the medical investigation of deaths. For example, a screening process with defined audit filters could be applied to death certificates and medical records by nursing staff. Deaths could be categorised into those with a low, medium or high risk of being associated with fraud, negligence or criminal activity, and then tailored investigation protocols could be applied to each category.

To validate and provide ongoing audit of this process, a quality management program could be introduced to review the working of the system. This could involve a random and selective audit whereby a proportion of cases designated low-risk are subject to formal review using the more intensive investigation protocols reserved for high-risk cases. This has the potential to address the Shipman phenomenon whereby strange patterns of deaths went undetected for many years.

This medicalisation of the early stages of a death investigation process (the early contact with family members and so on) would almost certainly provide a more "therapeutic" environment for grieving families. Speed of medical assessment would be improved by lack of duplication of effort by coroners and medical staff, and it would be possible to review a far wider range and greater number of deaths than those currently reported to the coroner.

The grief counselling service provided by some coroners' offices is an example of a specialist court providing direct medical and therapeutic services to the community. These social work and grief counselling staff are a valuable resource for coroners, court clerical staff, forensic pathologists, and the bereaved. Whether such a therapeutic service is best located in a court environment or a medical health service environment is debatable. Certainly the therapeutic benefits for the family would go beyond the provision of sympathetic communication, and would also include assessment of the immediate and medium-term physical and mental health needs of the grieving family. Today the identification of natural disease processes during a medical death investigation has important medical consequences for families. The discovery of the presence of infectious diseases or diseases involving a genetic susceptibility means that there needs to be rapid and appropriate communication of these matters to susceptible family members in a health care environment.

Modern forensic pathologists and forensic physicians, by virtue of having been exposed to public health issues in their medical training, are well aware of coroners' needs in respect of the identification of preventable factors in a death, arguably more so than many of the coroners' own administrative staff. As a result, making the entry point to the coroner's death investigation more medical is likely to enhance the coroner's effectiveness in preventing avoidable deaths.

The public health and safety aspect of a death investigation also involves the identification of risk factors that may exist in the community generally, or in specific areas such as the workplace, in relation to diseases and injury. Medical, scientific and technical specialists in these fields are able to provide practical advice and policy assistance in these areas. Such advice can enhance the work of the coroner, particularly where the coroner has little experience in these areas. As a result, there is a strong basis for concluding that the results of all death investigations should be considered by a multidisciplinary team, to ensure that the community gains the maximum benefit from information uncovered.

A death review unit in an institute of forensic medicine with a public health focus would be well positioned to draw together the lessons to be learnt from avoidable deaths and to enable measures to be taken in response to such lessons. It could monitor the implementation of coroners' recommendations and act as a focal point for data-based strategies for promoting health and safety measures that have been identified. Such a division of responsibilities would leave the coroner principally as a judicial officer and the manager of the process of inquest. The coroner's office should not be responsible for the "policing" roles of compliance monitoring or enforcement of recommendations. To the extent that such a role is undertaken, it should be performed by investigators in the death review unit, who can integrate this information into their investigations of any subsequent similar deaths.

There is merit in division of such functions by the creation of a director of investigations within coroners' officers, armed with the current significant powers of coroners. Different skills are required on the part of investigators, administrators and legal decision-makers. It is a rare person indeed who can combine them in a sophisticated way. A director of coronial investigations with necessary staff should have responsibility, like a director of public prosecutions, to receive reports of reportable deaths, to direct how investigations are conducted, and to liaise with the death review unit in the institute of forensic medicine, as well as with other relevant professionals. Then he or she should have responsibility for formally assembling a brief for a coroner to determine whether an inquest should be ordered. This would leave coroners uncontaminated by continuing involvement in the death investigation process, allowing them to make the sometimes difficult decision as to whether an inquest should take place and to evaluate the strengths and weaknesses of the evidence adduced during the inquisitorial processes of the inquest.

In summary, the current death investigation system by coroners should be adjusted so that all deaths are referred to a central medical death review unit based around a forensic medicine and pathology service, and ideally located in proximity to or operationally grouped with a central coroner's office. Coroners' legislation should be amended to provide for a clear statement explaining the purpose of the jurisdiction to guide coroners and appellate bodies. The focus of the coroner should shift toward a determination of factors that cause deaths and an identification of "opportunities for improvement" in the community, which, if implemented, could lessen the likelihood, or even prevent the occurrence, of such deaths in the future. The category of deaths reportable to a coroner should be maintained, but those deaths that are investigated should be scrutinised by a death review unit, with direct oversight by the coroner's director of death investigation. Death investigation should be subject to ongoing quality review processes, including random and selective audits of all stages of the investigation.

Epidemiological information concerning disease and injury into death investigation processes should be a standard part of death investigations, including data on the death certification practices of treating medical practitioners compared with the practice profiles of their peers. There should be a separation of the judicial role of the coroner from the administrative and operational aspects of investigations of reportable deaths through the establishment of a director of death investigation in the coroner's office. There should be a therapeutic focus on death investigation that takes into account the needs of the family as well as the needs of the community.

This cocktail of reforms would continue the evolution of the role of the coroner, enabling the jurisdiction to fulfil its modern objective more effectively – that of investigating and making findings about deaths, together with facilitating changes so that avoidable deaths are rendered less likely in the future.

16

Disposing of the dead:
Objectivity, subjectivity and identity

Rosalind F Croucher[1]

In 1993, during the Battle of Mogadishu in Somalia, American servicemen repeatedly risked their lives to rescue the bodies of their slain comrades ... This is an ancient military tradition, going back to the battle fought over the body of Patroklos on the plains of Troy. It is also a powerful illustration of the symbolic importance that the bodies of the dead have for the hearts and minds of the living.

Janicki v Hospital of St Raphael[2]

Introduction

This chapter focuses on disputes concerning disposing of the dead. The inclusion of this topic in a volume which addresses dilemmas in health law provides an opportunity to acknowledge that such dilemmas are not just "in health law". The identification of the fact of "dilemma" gives a chance to open the door to different perspectives on approaching the problem that provokes the dilemma. Disputes concerning the dead are underpinned by a layer which is fundamentally a public one: reflecting public health concerns and the utility of bodies and body parts for re-use for the living. But they are also profoundly private, in which the central concerns are ones of identity and relationship. Burials and funerals are resonant with both. They symbolise the passage from life to death – the hereafter – the endpoint of personhood and identity and the transition into reflected identity

---

1   Professor and Dean of Law, Macquarie University. Until 2004 the author wrote under the name of "Atherton".

2   744 A 2d 963 (1999) at [964] per Blue J. (The case involved dissection of a stillborn non-viable foetus (of gestational age of 19 weeks) against the express direction of the mother.) Patroclus was said to have saved the day in this battle, but he also died in the fight. The soldiers formed a circle around the corpse to protect it. The Greek soldiers, having fended off the Trojans, carried the body of Patroclus back to the Greek ships he had saved. In relation to the incident in Mogadishu, Blue J cites Bowden, B, *Black Hawk Down: A Story of Modern War*, Atlantic Monthly Press, 1999, pp 282–285. The episode was also portrayed in a movie of the same name.

through the memories of others. This is the "symbolic importance" of the body of the dead so acutely captured in the opening quote.

The central character in our narrative is the corpse, or the deceased.[3] The corpse itself is a matter of status – or stasis – of object-ness rather than subject-ness.[4] Being a "corpse" is a physical fact. The process of disposing of the dead in the funeral context is not, however, so much about a corpse; it is about "the deceased" – the deceased as the deceased *person*, the subject-ness of the corpse – as friend, comrade, relative, loved one.[5] It is a process of sanctifying death through rituals of celebration and commemoration expressive of personality – of family, kinship, connectedness. Burials and funerals are both religious and practical processes expressed around the corpse. They are expressions of the living in honour of the dead. The idea of remembering here is the flip side of dying in the context of the subjectivity of death.

There are many other issues surrounding the body, as corpse. A particularly lively area of concern is whether the body can be seen "as property". This is seen most acutely in the context of arguments about the accessibility of the body for therapeutic purposes.[6] Through the practical arguments about the utility of the body for the living is also interlaced the philosophical question of the nature and status of the corpse itself. These are intriguing, challenging questions, in which there is not necessarily one answer for all questions at the one time.[7] When the focus is on disputes among family members, the subjective, or subject-ness of the body, is the driving focus: the deceased person is seen as family, not as corpse. Managing "remembering" within the family is a key aspect of the legal framework in this context.

In this chapter I have singled out three concepts in play in the law and literature concerning disposal of the dead. Ideas of objectivity are seen most clearly in managing burial grounds, and, more recently, in contests regarding ashes. Subjectivity is evident in the law's reaction to these disputes through giving scope for kinship relationships in managing the disposal of the body itself. Identity is

---

3   Or "decedent" as known in the United States.

4   Of "thing-ness" rather than "person-ness", as I have referred to it before: Atherton, R, "Claims on the Deceased: The Corpse as Property" (2000) 7(4) *Journal of Legal Medicine* 361 at 362–363; Atherton, R, "Who Owns Your Body?" (2003) 77 *Australian Law Journal* 178 at 179.

5   The concept of "loved one" is one that sees the body as the reflection of the emotions of others. It was satirised heavily in the book of the same name by Evelyn Waugh first published in 1948.

6   See Chapter 17.

7   There is considerable academic debate in this area. An extended consideration of the arguments is provided in, for example, Davies, M and Naffine, N, *Are Persons Property? Legal Debates About Property and Personality*, Ashgate, Aldershot, 2001. See also, Skene, L, "Proprietary Rights in Human Bodies, Body Parts and Tissue: Regulatory Contexts and Proposals for New Laws" (2002) 22 *Legal Studies* 102; Skene, L, "Arguments Against People Legally 'Owning' their own Bodies, Body Parts and Tissue" (2002) 2 *Macquarie LJ* 165; Atherton, R, "Book Symposia – Commentary on Davies and Naffine, *Are Persons Property? Legal Debates About Property and Personality*, Ashgate 2001" (2003) 28 *Australian Journal of Law and Philosophy* 206.

seen in the balance between objectivity and subjectivity; and in the extent given to the deceased person, him or herself, in having a say as to what is, or is not, to happen on their own demise. Extending beyond the moment of death and disposal a further question concerns what is to happen to remains: this is both an objective and a subjective question with respect to place and person, expressed in terms of a right (or not) to remain undisturbed. The latter question has proven particularly acute in relation to the burial of indigenous peoples.[8]

A central issue to consider in the context of these disputes is the place for the subjective expressed in the voice of the testator: how far can a person control what is to happen after death. This is both an issue of the reach of the autonomous self (here, after death) in law; and how the law arbitrates amongst claims to the body. In focusing upon the idea of autonomy as the subjective, it also entails a consideration of the reach of the concept of autonomy itself: what Katherine O'Donovan and Roy Gilbar describe as the distinction "between autonomy within relationships and autonomy as individualism".[9] A notion of autonomy that includes family is described as "communitarian".[10] I have described it in terms of "surrogate autonomy", where decision-making is focused through others who have been chosen, or are related to, the relevant person.[11]

This chapter considers the legal framework for disposing of the dead. It does so principally through a focus on Australian law, but also through the larger matrix of the common law as played out in the United Kingdom and its former colonies, particularly the United States. The main disputes concerning disposing of the dead are arguments with a coroner or arguments amongst family members. Disputes with the coroner are considered in another chapter;[12] the principal concern of this chapter is therefore the arguments among family members.[13] This chapter will focus upon disposing of the dead through the topics of responsibility for burial; choices about burials; and arbitrating disputes about burials. "Burial" is

---

8   A distinctive feature is that in non-indigenous culture in Australia remembering and land are not connected. Once the body is decomposed, it merges with the land. The "appropriation" of land as the grave of the deceased is but a "temporary" one, the cemetery being rather "the common property of the living": *Gilbert v Buzzard* (1820) 2 Hagg Con 333 at 353 per Sir William Scott; 161 ER 761 (*The Iron Coffin* case). As Prue Vines has commented, "the body disappears both legally and literally, and the land becomes usable again as a commodity": "Bodily Remains in the Cemetery and the Burial Ground: A Comparative Anthropology of Law and Death *or* How Long Can I Stay?" in Manderson, D, (ed), *Courting Death – the Law of Mortality*, Pluto Press, London, 1999, p 118. Vines points out the different conception of land amongst indigenous Australians, where the land itself takes on a sacred character, where the individual is remembered as place. In this chapter it is the framework of the common law, and hence principally of non-indigenous people, that is the focus.

9   O'Donovan K and Gilbar R, "The Loved Ones: Families, Intimates and Patient Autonomy" (2003) 23 (2) *Legal Studies* 332 at 333.

10   Ibid, at 338-339.

11   Atherton (2003) op cit.

12   Disputes with the coroner are considered: see Chapter 15.

13   The authorisation of the coroner or any other relevant authority to dispose of the body is presumed throughout.

used here as a generic term, embracing all manner of disposals of the body. The coverage in the chapter is broadly of the common law tradition and references are made principally to the case law of the United Kingdom, the United States, Australia and Canada.

Responsibility for burial[14]

The law concerning burial and funerals in Australia derives from a mixture of inherited ecclesiastical law and common law. English ecclesiastical law managed matters of ritual and sacrament, and what the American writer, Percival Jackson, described in his comprehensive treatise on burial and burial places as "the sentimental and superstitious matters concerned with life and death";[15] the common law, on the other hand, dealt with matters such as property rights, crimes and torts.[16] The "sentimental and the superstitious" were expressed in terms of rights, or not, to be buried in the churchyard; when one could, or could not, be moved from a churchyard; and how grief could, or could not, be expressed on, for example, headstones.

Dealing with bodies immediately after death was, however, first and foremost, a matter of public health expressed in legal terms as duties to bury. This was very much an aspect of the objective fact of the body as decaying corpse. The obligations reflect the utilitarian concern of public health. These are concerns of the common law. But they also embody the principle of respect for the dignity of the person. Hence the notion of "duty" may reflect one or other, or both of these concerns. The articulation of such concerns through case law is marked by both the duty as a community requirement, but also a responsibility to the individual as person: the allowing of a dignified space on death.

The public health concerns are now expressed legislatively. Each Australian jurisdiction, for example, has legislation which governs the management of corpses from a public health point of view: the need for a coffin, the period of time before burial, the depth of the ground, and so on.[17] Once cremation became a lawful and

---

14 For a general overview on the subject see Hume, SG, "Dead Bodies" (1956) 2 *Sydney Law Review* 109; Conway, H, "Dead, But Not Buried: Bodies, Burial and Family Conflicts" (2003) 23(3) *Legal Studies* 423; White, S, "The Law Relating to Dealing with Dead Bodies" (2000) 4 *Medical Law International* 145; Griggs, L and Mackie, K, "Burial Rights: The Contemporary Australian Position" (2000) 7(4) *Journal of Law and Medicine* 404.

15 Jackson PE, *The Law of Cadavers*, 2nd edn, Prentice-Hall, New York, 1950, p lxxxv.

16 Ibid. Young J includes an excellent summary of the background to the jurisdiction in *Smith v Tamworth City Council* (1997) 41 NSWLR 680 at 685–688; and in *Beard v Baulkham Hills Shire Council* (1986) 7 NSWLR 273 at 276–277. Dr JM Bennett has also undertaken invaluable research on the "ecclesiastical jurisdiction" of the Supreme Court of New South Wales: "A Research Project on the Ecclesiastical Jurisdiction exercised in the Supreme Court of NSW 1824–1900", University of Sydney, Faculty of Law, 1967.

17 See "Public Health" (title 350), *Halsbury's Laws of Australia*, para [350]–[4100]. The relevant provisions are found in Acts and regulations on cemeteries and crematoria, public health, and local government.

accepted practice in common law countries in the 19th century, it also became the subject of regulation.[18]

The question of obligation, however, was another matter. Upon whom did the obligation fall to attend to the burial? This was a matter of the common law. And here, too, it is necessary to distinguish between a duty to pay for the burial and a duty to attend to it. The two are intertwined, but they are distinct.

In general terms it can be said that the obligation fell principally upon the executor, who was accorded a right to claim the body for the purpose of arranging for burial or other lawful disposal.[19] The executor was entitled to pursue this right to the body against others who held the body. So, for example, the gaoler who sought to retain the deceased prisoner's body (and so exercise a lien over it) until certain debts had been repaid to him for things supplied to the deceased, was compelled to hand the body over to the executor in two mid-19th century cases.[20] This position has been endorsed as Australian law.[21]

If there were no executor, then the responsibility was expressed in terms of rights to claim the body and/or an obligation to pay for the funeral.[22] While the estate of a deceased person has to bear the cost of funeral expenses as a principal liability,[23] where there is no estate the person who has to pick up the cost is also the one who, as a matter of principle, bears the responsibility for the task. In the event of someone else having undertaken it, that responsibility is expressed in terms of a liability to recoup the costs incurred.[24]

The duty to bury falls upon the near relatives: spouse, parents or children.[25] Where there is no identifiable relative then the common law placed the responsibility of attending to burial upon the householder in whose house a person died. It was an obligation to inter the body decently.[26] The common law required the

---

18 Some of the background of the introduction of cremation as a lawful practice is provided by Stephen White in "A Burial Ahead of its Time? The Crookenden burial case and the sanctioning of cremation in England and Wales" (2002) 7(2) *Mortality* 171.

19 *Williams v Williams* (1882) 20 Ch D 659 at 664 per Kay J. I have avoided using the term "possess" which is often used in this context. The term "claim" is neutral. Words of possession are anchored in the language of property law, hence I have chosen a term which defers neither to property nor the personal. In *Williams*, for instance, the claim to the body was acknowledged, but the notion that there was a right of property in the body was denied. The case is considered below.

20 *R v Fox* (1841) 2 QB 246; *R v Scott* (1842) 2 QB 248.

21 See, in particular, *Smith v Tamworth City Council* (1997) 41 NSWLR 680.

22 As Young J noted in *Smith*, it is important to distinguish the questions as to (a) who is responsible for burying a body; (b) who has the obligation to pay for the burial; and (c) who has the privilege of deciding where the body is to buried: at 692 (relying on Jackson (1950) op cit).

23 *Blackstone's Commentaries on the Laws of England* (1765-1769), vol 2, p 508.

24 See Hume (1956) op cit; *Smith v Tamworth City Council* (1997) 41 NSWLR 680 at 691–693.

25 *Smith v Tamworth City Council* (1997) 41 NSWLR 680 at 691–692.

26 *R v Stewart* (1840) 113 ER 1007. *Clark v London General Omnibus Co Ltd* [1906] 2 KB 648 at 778 per Lord Denman CJ: "[T]he individual under whose roof a poor person dies is bound to carry the body decently covered to the place of burial: he cannot keep him unburied, nor do anything which prevents Christian burial: he cannot therefore cast him out, so as to expose the body to violation, or to offend the feelings or endanger the health of the living".

householder to undertake certain duties in the interests of public health and morals – to carry the body to the churchyard, decently covered.[27] The obligation on the householder was a natural default position; "the product of dictates of health and morals", commented Jackson:

> The performance of the function cannot await the discovery of wills and their probate, nor the disposition of conflicts respecting the personnel of administrators … An executor may never qualify. Besides, ordinary proprieties usually defer even the opening of a will until after the funeral. So, as a practical matter, it must be the householder and not the executor upon whom must rest the primary and common law obligation to see that the body of a person dying in his home is properly disposed of, whether or not the deceased was indigent in life.[28]

The responsibility for arranging the disposal of the dead is now essentially a secular matter, with the ultimate responsibility defaulting to relevant local authorities, rather than the church, in the absence of next of kin who are able to pay for the expenses of burial.

Choices about burials

The right to make choices about disposing of the body – by which method (burial/cremation) and where – involves both a consideration of the extent to which the deceased him or herself may have a say and the principles developed for according priority to claimants to undertake the task.

The directions of the deceased

A person may wish to state what is, or is not, to happen to their body on death. The law in the common law context allows a person a limited right to intrude upon the post-mortem fate of their own body. Where a person does not wish to be cremated, this is made binding by force of statute.[29] The deceased may also appoint a representative, an executor. The deceased may authorise the use of his or her body for therapeutic purposes.[30] With respect to other wishes with respect to the body, however, they remain essentially only as requests in Anglo-Australian jurisprudence, without binding force. So, for example, a testator's own directions in a will as to the disposal of the body are regarded as merely declaratory.

---

27 Once buried the common law also provided some protection against the interference with the interred body itself: *R v Lynn* (1788) 2 TR 733; 100 ER 1389 – as a crime *contra bonos mores*: see Atherton (2003) op cit.

28 Jackson (1950) op cit, p 36.

29 For a summary of the legislation see *Halsbury's Laws of Australia* [350]–[4180] and Griggs and Mackie (2000) op cit, at 408. A testator's direction may be overridden by certain authorities for example in the interests of public health; conversely, a direction to cremate may also be overridden: [350]–[4180].

30 See Chapter 17.

The extent to which the law permits, or limits, the deceased to determine what is to be done with his or her body after death is an expression of the limit to the individual's autonomy. The individual was allowed to say what not to do, with respect to cremation, but no more than that. There was some space for an expression of the deceased's autonomy, but essentially in the negative, not the affirmative sense. With respect to cremation the fact that a person may prohibit cremation may also be considered not so much as a matter of autonomy, but rather the historical discomfort with cremation itself. Cremation ran counter to the "right to a Christian burial";[31] it ran counter to the practice of the Christian church, with its focus upon resurrection and, with it, a concept of the resurrection of the body.[32] So, while cremation was an early rite, it came to be regarded as improper and it was only through express permission of the deceased – and then only once it had been accepted as a lawful practice. *Williams v Williams*[33] sits at the centre of this. It tested the extent to which a testator could give binding directions with respect to his body, in the context of the doubtful legality of cremation in the United Kingdom at the time. The deceased, Henry Crookenden, had been buried by his widow. He was later exhumed and cremated, which he had wanted. Eliza Williams, the person who had followed his direction, with the assistance of the Cremation Society of England, sought to recover the expenses of doing so. She failed.[34]

Kay J held that the testator could not bind survivors to respect his wishes as to the disposition of his body: a consequence of the proposition that there was "no property in a body". This case is one of the leading cases in this area and it has been influential on Australia, Canadian and New Zealand law.[35] It established that a person has no control over what was to be done except through an expression of wish or to provide endorsement to the actions of the executor. It was the executor who was given authority under the common law.

The executor, as the chosen appointee of the deceased, is a reflection of the person of the deceased personally. By giving the executor precedence the logic of the common law is to give space to the deceased. To the extent that it gives any room to the deceased, I have argued that it may be seen as an expression of extended, or surrogate, autonomy.[36] It is limited to choosing an executor, trusting to the selected person to carry out the deceased's wishes with respect to burial or

---

31   *R v Stewart* (1840) 12 Ad & E 773; 113 ER 1007.

32   See discussion in Vines, P and Atherton, R, "Religion and Death in the Common Law" in Radan, P, Meyerson, D and Croucher, R *Law and Religion – God, the State and the Common Law*, Routledge, London, 2005, pp 308ff.

33   (1882) 20 Ch D 659.

34   The lawfulness of cremation as such was only considered finally in *R v Price* (1884) 12 QB 247, where it was held that cremation was not unlawful so long as it did not create a nuisance. Stephen White (2002) op cit, provides an excellent study of these cases which tested the limits of the law in this area.

35   See in particular *Smith v Tamworth City Council* (1997) 41 NSWLR 680. Young J provides a thorough analysis of existing case law and a summary of propositions arising out of it.

36   See in particular my introduction and development of this idea in Atherton (2003) op cit.

other disposal. The executor, in this trusted capacity, is the repository for the deceased's wishes with respect to his or her body.

While the Anglo-Australian common law asserts that the testator's directions merely have the force of request, American law allowed the testator more room to govern.[37] The executor in the American context is considered custodian of the deceased's wishes, which must be respected, unless they are unable to be fulfilled or are unreasonable.[38] One distinct consequence of the difference of approach is with respect to the room given under American law for the testator's own directions with respect to burial. These will be upheld against the objections of the next of kin.[39]

For example, in *Re Eichner's Estate*,[40] the testator requested his executors to have his body cremated and his ashes placed in a certain cemetery in close proximity to the graves of his parents. Some of the next of kin objected and the executors sought the court's advice. It was held that the direction contained in the will was reasonable, practical and capable of performance, and that if the executors violated the duty cast upon them by the will they might leave themselves open to criminal prosecution. However if the testator's directions are not considered reasonable the claim of the next of kin may take precedence. Hence in *Enos v Snyder*[41] the deceased's widow and daughter succeeded in claiming the deceased's body against the directions in the will in which the testator had given precedence to his de facto wife.

The American cases suggest that while the next of kin are considered as having a primary claim to the body, the testator, through the executor, can override this right.[42] The right includes choosing the place and rites of burial, and if appropriate, later re-interring of the remains. Any tortious interference with this right, such as unlawful autopsy, improper burial, or unauthorised re-interment, gives right to an action for damages in tort including damages for mental distress.[43]

---

37 For a summary see Atherton (2000) op cit; also see notes 34 and 35, Griggs and Mackie (2000) op cit.

38 An example is *In the Estate of Meksras* Pa D & C 2d 371 (1974). The testator wanted to be buried in her jewellery. This was not upheld on the basis that it would encourage grave-robbing.

39 *Holland v Metalious* 105 NH 290, 198 A2d 654, 7 ALR3d 742 (1964). the Supreme Court of New Hampshire held that although in the ordinary case the deceased's instructions, by will or otherwise, as to disposition of his or her body or funeral services, should be followed in preference to opposing wishes of survivors, nevertheless, there was no abuse of discretion in the denial of an injunction against funeral services in this case since the testamentary provision against funeral services was coupled with the testatrix's attempted donation of her body for scientific uses, and such primary purpose failed when the donees declined to accept the body. The court includes a discussion of many of the cases dealing with the rights and duties of survivors with respect to the disposition of the body of a deceased: at 745.

40 173 Misc 644, 18 NYS 2d 753 (1940).

41 131 Cal 68, 63 P 170, 53 LRA 221 (1900).

42 The executor is the one charged with the duty of fulfilling the testator's wish. And where the testator's wishes can no longer be met the executor might control the manner of burial where there is no surviving next of kin: Jackson (1950) op cit, p 49.

43 *Carney v Knollwood Cemetery Association* 33 Ohio App 3d 31, 35–37, 514 NE 2d 430, 434–435 (1986).

In addition, the surviving spouse or next of kin retains a claim of sorts in the place where the body is buried. Hence the spouse or next of kin retains an ongoing right to have the body remain undisturbed in the grave. While the Anglo-Australian rules are not as forceful in their expression as the American authorities, there are certain similarities of approach.[44] As between the subjective wish of the deceased and the rest of his or her family, the testator's wishes will rule (and the executor is the custodian of that wish), but the executor has no power of choice beyond that, and the kin have more say.[45]

Some have argued for greater force to be given to the testator's directions with respect to burial in English law. Heather Conway, for example, argues that burial instructions should be upheld as an aspect of respect for the autonomy of the person.[46] She recognises, however, that individual autonomy may, on occasion, need to be restricted, using the American approach as a guide. Conway rightly recognises that burial "is not merely about the deceased; it is also a process for the living".[47] And a principle which accords paramountcy to the wishes of the deceased will detract from the process for the living. There is a clash, therefore, between the idea of autonomy as an aspect of individualism (in this context, respecting the deceased's own wishes or as expressed through an agent or surrogate) and autonomy within relationships (recognising circumstances in which the individual's wish may be overridden in circumstances considered, for example, unreasonable in the context of family).[48]

Where the next of kin are given the paramount right, subject or not to the right of the testator to indicate what is to happen, the concept of autonomy is seen in the "within relationships" sense. While this has a certain theoretical consistency within the broader concept of autonomy, it may, however, break down in practical application, where the law's definition of next of kin is out of step with reality. Conway identified this as a problem in the United Kingdom with the limited recognition of the rights of a de facto spouse as next of kin at the time she was writing.[49] Australian jurisdictions have gone much further in this regard with de

---

44 Bray describes the American rules as "functionally similar" to the Anglo-Australian position while being "formally opposed" to it Bray, MB, "Personalizing Property: Toward a property Right in Human Bodies" (1990) 69 *Texas LR* 209 at 227.

45 The articulation of this position has been muddied up with "property" words. It has been said that in the United States the next of kin have a "quasi-property" right in the body to attend to its disposal: for example, *Pierce v Proprietors of Swan Point Cemetery* (1872) 10 RI 227; 14 Am Rep 667; *Whaley et al v County of Tuscola* 1995 Fed App 0205P (6th Cir) (Michigan). While using the language of property, even using the term "possession" regularly to describe the right to claim the body, it is singularly inappropriate language to describe the decaying body of the deceased. I have written elsewhere in terms of preferring the language of "custody" to that of "possession": Atherton (2000) op cit, at 375; Atherton (2003) op cit, at 184. Jackson (1950) op cit, p 46 drew attention to the "fallacious" nature of using property language in this context.

46 Conway (2003) op cit, at 432–433, 438.

47 Conway (2003) op cit, at 434.

48 See O'Donovan and Gilbar (2003) op cit.

49 Conway (2003) op cit, at 435.

facto partners and now also same sex partners included almost uniformly as next of kin. In theoretical terms the principle is, however, the same broad one. If next of kin (however defined) are given the principal claim, even according the deceased more force with respect to his or her instructions as to burial, this may still be seen as an expression of autonomy – either in the extended sense that I have expressed,[50] or in the O'Donovan–Gilbar sense of "autonomy within relationships".

The recognition of the will (in the sense of intentions) of the testator more broadly in the succession context can be urged as a reason for greater acknowledgment of the force of testamentary instructions with respect to the body, to give greater scope for autonomy as individualism. One of the hallmarks of wills law in Australia since 1975 has been a greater recognition of testamentary freedom through the introduction of so-called "dispensing powers" which have allowed for the admission to probate of documents which lack formality but which are otherwise considered as satisfying the relevant threshold of testamentary intentions.[51] Testamentary freedom enshrines notions of autonomy with respect to property, but it is more than this. It involves an expression of self, through property, but not necessarily limited to it. Allowing greater scope to the testator's wishes with respect to the disposal of her or his body would be consistent with the expanded role for testamentary freedom evident in these changes to wills legislation.

Arbitrating disputes

The symbolic importance of the bodies of the dead referred to in the opening quotation is sometimes manifested in fights amongst those for whom this importance is not only symbolic but also deeply personal, and in conflict. It is then that the court may become involved. In Australia there is virtually no legislative guidance with respect to how to manage competing claims to the body for burial. It is a matter of common law.[52] The cases also largely comprise decisions made in haste, having to manage the fact of a decaying body with little time to reflect on the issues.[53] The "unseemliness" of this context has been remarked upon.[54] Where disputes have arisen in the context of claims to ashes at least this imperative is removed. Ashes cases do not involve the public health issues of the decaying corpse. The principles can therefore be considered for their own sake, without the pressures of practicalities identified in the unburied bodies cases.[55]

---

50   Atherton (2003) op cit, at 188–189.

51   See Atherton, R and Vines P, *Succession – Families, Property and Death; Text and Cases,* 2nd edn, Butterworths, Sydney, 2003, para [8.13] ff.

52   Young J in *Smith v Tamworth City Council* referred to the "dearth of authority": at 685.

53   Ibid.

54   *Buchanan v Milton* [1999] 2 FLR 844 at 854 per Hale J; *Calma v Sesar* (1992) 106 FLR 446 at 452 per Martin J; *Murdoch v Rhind* [1945] NZLR 425 at 426 per Northcroft J; *Re Korda, Times,* 23 April 1958, Vaisey J ("all very sordid and unpleasant").

55   Cases which have considered claims with respect to ashes include: *Robertson v Pinegrove Memorial Park Ltd & Swann* (1986) ACLD 496; *Fessi v Whitmore* [1999] 1 FLR 767; *Leeburn v Derndorfer* [2004] VSC 172.

In *Smith v Tamworth City Council*[56] Young J made an exhaustive analysis of the available authorities and provided a summary of the law with respect to claims, and hence competing claims, to bodies on death.[57] The right of the executor was followed by "the person with the highest rank to take out administration", with the surviving spouse or de facto being preferred to the right of children. Where claims were regarded as "equally ranking", "the practicalities of burial without unreasonable delay will decide the issue". The propositions summarise the framework for dealing with both bodies and with cremated remains. They also capture the scattering of largely single instance decisions in which the issues have been played out. How has the law resolved the dilemma of arbitrating such disputes, and often amongst family members – the son, daughter, wife, husband, de facto partner, often challenging each other?

The right of the executor

Robertson v Pinegrove Memorial Park Ltd & Swann[58] concerned the vindication of the claims of the executor. As the executor was also fulfilling the wishes of the deceased, it is an example of the weight given to the instructions of the testator through the persona of the executor as his chosen agent. The deceased had appointed an executor and left instructions as to the disposal of his body. In this case the deceased had been cremated. Half had been given to the widow; the other half had been placed in a rose garden at Pinegrove Memorial Park pursuant to a contractual arrangement between Graham Swann, a son of the deceased, and the Memorial Park. The executor sought to recover the ashes from the Memorial Park. He intended to give them to the widow so that she could fulfil the deceased's request that they be scattered over a park near where he had lived in England before coming to Australia. Reasoning by analogy from the rule of the general law, that an executor has a right to claim the corpse of the deceased for the purpose of its lawful disposal by burial or cremation or otherwise, Waddell CJ in Equity concluded that an executor had a right to the ashes of a deceased who had been cremated that included a right to determine the manner of their final disposal.[59]

While the executor is not required to act in accordance with the testator's directions,[60] the executor's choice is not unlimited. In *Grandison v Nembhard*[61] Vinelott J commented, for example, that:

---

56   (1997) 41 NSWLR 680.

57   After a thorough consideration of relevant English, United States and Australian authorities, Young J stated the propositions to be drawn from them in numerical format of 15 propositions: at 693–694.

58   (1986) ACLD 496.

59   In *Leeburn v Derndorfer* [2004] VSC 172 it was commented that what enabled the discussion in *Robertson* to take place was that the ashes remained intact.

60   See, for example, *Meier v Bell* (1997) (unreported, VSC, Ashley J, 3 March 1997, BC9700457).

61   (1989) 4 BMLR 140.

The court will not interfere with the exercise of [the executor's discretion] unless is exercised in a way which shows that he has not properly weighed the factors which ought to have been taken into account in that it is wholly unreasonable.

What Vinelott J did was to open the door to a challenge to the executor analogous to the challenges that might be made to the exercise of a trustee's discretion. It was left rather formless and ill-defined. As he commented, "it would be surprising to find that the court had no power in any circumstances to interfere, save only where questions of expense are involved". This was expressed, in a similar vein, though from a slightly different perspective by Dr Tristram in the late 19th century in *In Re Dixon*,[62]

Can an executor, to gratify his own fancy, without the deceased's sanction, cremate the body of his testator, and so deprive it of being buried in the state and condition contemplated by [the] rule of law?[63]

While the executor has clearly been given the overriding right in Anglo-Australian law, what happens, for instance, when the executors themselves cannot agree? This was the issue in question in *Leeburn v Derndorfer*.[64] The executors, the three adult children of the deceased, were unable to agree as to the fate of the ashes of their father, John Leeburn. The deceased had been cremated pursuant to his wish expressed in his will, but he had said nothing else. His ashes had been retained by the funeral director pending an instruction from the executors. Two executors (the daughters, Sonia and Monica) wanted the ashes interred at Yan Yean Cemetery; another (the son, Paul) wanted them divided, so that each executor could dispose of "their third" as they pleased. This proposition was unacceptable to the other two executors.[65] They collected their father's ashes and had them interred in a sealed container (without their brother's knowledge or approval). Paul began proceedings seeking an order that the ashes, or part of them, be delivered to him.

Was this an issue of the authority of executors generally, or something else? The normal rule about acts of executors is that the act of any one of multiple executors with respect to estate property will bind the estate.[66] But here it was not a dealing "with respect to any property of the estate"; it was an entirely different matter:

[T]he question in this case is not a contest as to the validity of the executors' decision; it is a contest between the next-of-kin as to the mode of disposition of the remains of their father.[67]

---

62 [1892] P 386.
63 Ibid, at 393. The assistance of the court could be enlisted, however, where the executor was fulfilling the wishes of the deceased.
64 [2004] VSC 172. The case is considered in the note by Matthew Groves, "The Disposal of Human Ashes", in McSherry, B (ed), "Legal Issues", (2005) 12 *Journal of Law and Medicine* 267.
65 It was described as "disgusting and sacrilegious": [2004] VSC 172 at [9].
66 *Union Bank of Australia v Harrison, Jones and Devlin Ltd* (1910) 11 CLR 492 at 516–517 per Isaacs J. See Atherton and Vines (2003) op cit, paras [17.28]–[17.31].
67 [2004] VSC 172 at [15].

The fact that the body had been cremated and not simply buried gave the court an opportunity to consider the matter. In the case of the buried body, executors discharge their obligation by having the body buried; the body becomes part of the land in which it is buried. The executors have no further function to perform and no further interest in the remains. But, where ashes are still "intact", in some container as distinct from being scattered, they have some notional "identity" as "the deceased", or, in this case, "Dad".[68] Ultimately, however, Bryne J confronted the "practicalities", as identified by Young J in *Smith*. The ashes had been at Yan Yean for over four years; and two of the three executors had selected this location. So, "Dad" was left where he was.

No executor

In Young J's hierarchy in *Smith*, after the executor the next person with a claim to the deceased's body was the one entitled to take out administration. This is a conclusion based on an analogy to the executor's right. But is it a good one?

The authority of the executor is a direct expression of the will of the deceased: the person is his or her choice; the executor's decision about the deceased's body is then a surrogate extension of the deceased's own decisions. But the authority of the administrator is of an entirely different character. In an intestate estate the administrator will normally be the next of kin (including for this purpose the spouse within the contemporary concept of kin). But this is not necessarily the case. In the case of letters of administration with the will annexed (*cum testamento annexo*) the administrator will usually be the one with the largest interest – often the residuary beneficiary.[69] This is an expression not of kinship but of the need for the property of the deceased to be administered.

Why, then, should the administrator of the estate be accorded *ex officio* the same right as the executor with respect to the body of the deceased? This is not a property question. If the issue of dealing with the body of the deceased is considered within the context of autonomy, the right to the body of the deceased should

---

68 So what is the nature of the executors' interest in the ashes? Although their static quality lends itself to more of a property analysis, they are not part of the estate so that they pass under the will. Byrne J considered (at [27]) that so long as ashes were not dispersed or had otherwise lost their character as ashes they might be owned or possessed:

> To my mind, therefore, it is apt to characterise the legal status of the ashes similar to that of the preserved body in *Doodeward v Spence*. In this way the application of fire to the cremated body is to be seen as the application to it of work or skill which has transformed it from flesh and blood to ashes, from corruptible material to material which is less so ... Ashes which have in this way been preserved in specie are the subject of ordinary rights of property, subject to one possible qualification. The only qualification, which, if it exists, may require some working out, arises from the fact that the ashes are, after all, the remains of a human being and for that reason they should be treated with appropriate respect and reverence.

Another approach is to use that of Skene "Arguments Against People Legally 'Owning' their Own Bodies ..." (2002) op cit, where the property analysis only comes into play once strangers (third parties) are introduced.

69 *Estate of Slattery* (1909) 9 SR (NSW) 577.

follow the connection of kin, not property. The deceased in this context is seen as a family member and it is the family which expresses the extended autonomy of the deceased with respect to his or her body. In most cases the person entitled to a grant of letters of administration *will* be the next of kin and saying that that person has the right to determine the funeral is unobjectionable. But when you move away from the kin connection the basis of making the decision as to who will decide needs to be considered and understood appropriately. Hence I would argue that custody of the body for funeral arrangements ought to be given to a kin member and not the administrator. The administrator, *as* administrator, should not decide; the administrator *as* kin, should. Where the two are not the same, then the decision should follow the connection of kin, not property.[70]

An example can be seen in the South Australian case of *Jones v Dodd*.[71] Here the claimants to the body of the deceased were the deceased's father, Paddy Jones, and his former de facto spouse, Laurie Dodd. Paddy wished to have his son buried at Oodnadatta in accordance with Aboriginal law, so that the deceased's spirit could come back in animal form.[72] Laurie sought to have the body of the deceased buried at Port Augusta so that their children could visit the grave easily. There was no executor. There was no estate and no likelihood of a grant ever being sought.

Who had the highest rank to take out administration with respect to the deceased's estate? Although in South Australia the de facto spouse of the deceased would be entitled to seek a grant of administration, Laurie's status was not as de facto wife of the deceased when the deceased died; she was his former de facto wife. The children (10 and 11) were too young to claim administration of the estate, although Laurie, as their guardian, may have been able to seek a grant of letters of administration *durante minore aetate*. At first instance Debelle J held in favour of the father as the nearest in kin. The appeal was dismissed unanimously.[73]

What was particularly notable in the appellate judgment was the acknowledgment of the relevance of spiritual and cultural values. Perry J, delivering the judgment of the court, stated that spiritual or cultural values ought to be taken into account as part of the "proper respect and decency" necessary in resolving the dispute.[74] To do so, moreover, he considered was consistent with principles of international law – as expressed for example in the *International Covenant on Civil and Political Rights* (ICCPR) – 1976, ratified by Australia on 13 August 1980 – in its

---

70 While Young J's proposition four suggests that the right to administration leads to a right to the body, his earlier comment with respect to *Brown v Tullock* (1992) 7 BPR 15101, suggested that the claim of the de facto wife took precedence and not merely for the fact that she might become administrator. It was her position as de facto wife which led to her taking precedence over the deceased's brother, according to Young J: (1997) 41 NSWLR 680 at 689–690.

71 [1999] SASC 125.

72 Ibid, at [14].

73 This is one of the few decisions in this area that was considered by an appellate court.

74 Ibid, at [52] per Perry J. Perry J was here citing Martin J in *Calma v Sesar* (1992) 2 NTLR 37 at 42, who emphasised the need to resolve things practically, but "with all proper respect and decency".

endorsement of the "right to freedom of thought, conscience and religion" as a fundamental human right. Perry J also referred to the Draft Declaration on the Rights of Indigenous Peoples in which it was acknowledged that the "right to the repatriation of human remains" was inherent to the right "to manifest, practice ... their religious traditions, customs and ceremonies".[75]

What then of the application of such principles to the particular context – the dispute over the disposal of a body? Perry J stated:[76]

> [I]t seems to me that common considerations of decency and respect for human dignity should lead those responsible for the burial of a corpse to recognise, and where possible give effect to, the cultural, spiritual and religious beliefs, practices and traditions of the deceased. Furthermore, for similar reasons, an appropriate degree of sensitivity and respect should be accorded the feelings of the surviving members of the deceased's family.

Perry J concluded that, in all cases, consideration should be given to cultural, spiritual and religious factors, where such factors are present.[77] What conclusion did this suggest in the present case? Such factors were emphasised by the deceased's father. Perry J considered that the views of the father as, in this case, head of the family should prevail. His decision supported the conclusion of the judge at first instance, but for the reasons outlined above.

So does such a case indicate that cultural or religious values will necessarily play a role in resolving the claims to the body? It is, after all, left in somewhat general terms. Or can some other logic be found? Perry J considered that *Smith* provided a framework more by way of a summary of outcomes than a defining set of propositions for future judgment, so that, for example, the notion that the person entitled to a grant of administration should also be the one to deal with the body should not be regarded as a fixed principle.

My argument is that cultural or religious values may play a role within the logic of autonomy, but in a different sense than that evident in the space accorded the executor. When the deceased has made no choice, through the appointment of an executor, or the chosen person cannot execute the responsibility, then the decision should be left to another in a further surrogate sense – a second layer or second generation effect by seeing the deceased as part of a kin network - the "within relationships" sense of autonomy. The deceased's personhood finds expression as kin of others; and the kin may choose what is to happen with the body. And it is here that cultural or religious views may be particularly significant and relevant – as the expression of the wishes of kin. In this context, in my view, the decision in *Jones v Dodd* reaches the right result. Laurie had a claim to administer the estate as the guardian of her children (who were the next of kin), but the court allowed the grandfather to decide about the funeral as the nearest adult kin. But had Laurie been the de facto wife at the deceased's death, then her claim,

---

75 [1999] SASC 125 at [59].

76 Ibid, at [60].

77 Ibid, at [68].

as kin, should have prevailed, notwithstanding the cultural issues raised by the deceased's father.

The place of religious and cultural values has taken on a further dimension through international conventions such as those referred to by Perry J in *Jones v Dodd*. In the United Kingdom these have gained greater force through enactment into domestic law in the *Human Rights Act 1998*.[78] While articles in such conventions which refer to rights to freedom of thought and religion provide an additional channel through which to raise the kinds of questions as raised in *Jones*, the issue still remains as to the logic for finding the answers. Here, I would argue, identifying the rationale as an expression of defining the extent – and limit – to the autonomy of the deceased in both the primary and secondary senses provides the theoretical context for dealing with such matters. It will also help focus upon contests where the deceased and the surviving kin have contrasting views.

Claimants of equal standing

Continuing the statement of propositions in *Smith*, as between the surviving spouse[79] and children, the spouse is to be preferred; and where two or more persons "have an equally ranking privilege", the practicalities of burial "without unreasonable delay" will govern the situation.[80] Cases involving children illustrate the arbitration of those with competing claims. A number of the cases have involved a consideration of whether the claimants did, in fact, have competing rights. So, for example, it has been held that natural parents take precedence over foster parents;[81] and adoptive parents over the natural parents.[82] Three examples of claimants of equal standing are the Western Australian case of *Burrows v Cramley*[83] the United Kingdom case of *Fessi v Whitmore*[84] and the Northern Territory case of *Calma v Sesar*.[85]

In *Burrows v Cramley* the deceased, aged 17, died in a motor vehicle accident. His parents each sought to exercise the right of burial. Mrs Burrows (formerly

---

78   Conway (2003) at 442–449, includes a study of the intersection of the European Convention on Human Rights in the area of burial conflicts.

79   The spouse may include de facto and same sex partners, depending on the particular definitions of next of kin in the relevant jurisdiction.

80   *Smith v Tamworth City Council* (1997) 41 NSWLR 680 at 694, propositions five and six.

81   *Warner v Levitt* (unreported, NSWSC, Brownie J, 23 August 1994), following the English decision in *R v Gwynedd County Council; Ex parte B* [1992] 2 All ER 317.

82   *Buchanan v Milton* [1999] 2 FLR 844. This case also raised the matter of Aboriginal customs. The deceased was an Australian Aboriginal who had been adopted by an English family. The birth parents wanted him to be buried in Australia; the adoptive parents in England. The adoptive mother was entitled to letters of administration. Further discussion of the Australian position may be found in: Dickey, A, "Parental Rights and Duties upon the Death of a Child" (1992) 66 *Australian Law Journal* 35; Dickey, A, "More on Parental Rights to Bury a Child" (1993) 67 *Australian Law Journal* 149.

83   [2002] WASC 47.

84   [1999] 1 FLR 767.

85   (1992) 106 FLR 446.

Cramley) wanted to bury him in Perth; Mr Cramley in Sydney. When the Cramleys separated in 1987, Mr Cramley was granted custody of their son, Ross, the deceased, and the mother was granted reasonable access. Ross and his father then moved to Sydney. In 1998, when Ross was 14, he wanted to return to live with his mother and this was arranged, though he retained close contact with his father. In 2000, Ross returned to Sydney to live with his father and for the next two years he moved between Sydney and Perth. While each parent had a competing claim to administration of their son's estate, Pullin J was "driven back to a consideration of practicalities";[86] he opted for the burial in Perth.

Fessi v Whitmore[87] concerned the body of a 12-year old child, Mark Whitmore. After his parents' divorce Mark lived with his father. Just before his death he and his father had moved to Wales. His mother lived in the Nuneaton area – where both sides of the family still lived. The mother wanted Mark's ashes to be in Nuneaton; the father in Wales. The mother proposed in the alternative that the ashes be divided. As a child, there was no estate and therefore no legal personal representative. The idea of dividing the ashes was rejected and the ashes were allowed to be scattered at the Nuneaton crematorium.

In *Calma v Sesar*[88] the decision was essentially a practical one that the body was not permitted to be moved. Like *Fessi*, the case was one of the competing claims of both parents of the deceased (here an adult man), both equal next of kin to the deceased. Like *Jones v Dodd*[89] and *Buchanan v Milton*,[90] there were also issues of Aboriginal burial customs. The deceased had been killed in Darwin. The mother, who lived in Alice Springs, had made arrangements for a Roman Catholic burial in Darwin. The father had made arrangements for his son's body to be flown to Western Australia for burial at Port Hedland. The family was of Aboriginal descent and there were many relatives in both Darwin and Port Hedland. There were deep divisions between the members of the family as to the most appropriate place to inter the deceased's remains. The paternal grandfather, a member of the Bardi Aboriginal tribe, asserted that it was his culture that the dead should be buried in their homeland, and that the homeland was at South Hedland, where the family had a burial plot. He did not wish the deceased to be buried in Darwin as he believed it to be disrespectful to him to bury him in the same vicinity as the presence of his alleged killer.

There were two key elements to consider: equal claims of kin; and the claims of culture. On the facts, as the body of the deceased was in Darwin and proper arrangements had been made for burial there, Martin J considered that "there was no good reason in law why that should not be done and no good reason in law why the removal of the body from the Territory and burial in Western Australia

---

86   [2002] WASC 47 at [30].
87   [1999] 2 FLR 844.
88   (1992) 106 FLR 446, noted in (1993) 67 *Australian Law Journal* 149.
89   [1999] SASC 125.
90   [1999] 2 FLR 844.

was to be preferred".[91] So, at the end of the day, the cultural issues (which suggested that the body should be returned to the Bardi homeland in South Hedland) did not prevail. The claim of the next of kin was determinative – and, as between two equal claimants, the practicalities of the situation, in the estimation of the court, governed. Practicality in such situations is a way of resolving the impossible; or as Hale J commented in *Buchanan v Milton* in 1999, "[t]he law cannot establish a hierarchy in which one sort of feeling is accorded more respect than other equally deep and sincere feelings".[92] The situations are of a kind, according to McEvoy J of the Canadian Court in 1930, "where honest sentiment and honest religious conviction have brought about an intensely sad struggle between two factions of a family".[93]

Conclusion

Celia Hammond argues that the rules for arbitrating at common law are "akin to the priority rules developed to deal with competing property claims".[94] While there are certain similarities – as in the ordering of claims for certain purposes – the function is entirely different. The rules for determining who should be next of kin have nothing to do with priorities. The latter are rules developed for arbitrating who will take priority to property according to the principles of law and equity. These are principles for resolving proprietary rights. The rules for arbitrating claims to the body of the deceased are not about proprietary issues; not about property at all. They are reflective of an entirely different logic. They are hierarchical, necessarily, but reflect a different concept. As Jackson argued somewhat quaintly, they lie in the field of "domestic relations".[95] Heather Conway's argument that the executor's right is "an exception to the 'no property' rule", can also be contradicted in a similar vein: namely, that rather than being an "exception" to a rule, it has, in fact, nothing to do with property at all.

Death and the process of disposing of the dead involve an overlayering of objectives and subjectives. Burial is both the disposal of the body as object, but also the focus of the subjective through the grief and remembering of friends and family. A process or legal hierarchy which conflicts with the wishes of family necessarily intrudes upon their subjective. In arbitrating disputes about the body, the key issue for the future is resolving the extent to which the testator may govern what is to happen in the affirmative and not just the negative sense; and govern in his or her own words, not through the medium or choice of the executor as surrogate. Allowing greater space for the testator takes it back into the area of control

---

91   See also *Manktelow v Public Trustee* [2001] WASC 290.
92   [1999] 2 FLR 844, at 855.
93   *Hunter v Hunter* (1930) 65 OLR 586, at 587.
94   Hammond, C, "Property Rights in Human Corpses and Human Tissue: The Position in Western Australia" (2002) 4 *University of Notre Dame Australia Law Review* 97 at 105.
95   Jackson (1950) op cit, p 46.

of the testator – a post-mortem expression of autonomy with respect to the person/ body of the now deceased. This will define autonomy in the primary sense of individuality in the O'Donovan–Gilbar dichotomy.[96]

While some have found the decisions concerning claims to the body of the deceased to be inconsistent,[97] I would argue that there is an underlying logic expressed through gradations, extensions of an idea of autonomy, expressed first, through a surrogate, the executor, as the one chosen by the deceased, and secondly, through seeing the deceased as a member of a kin network.[98] This has similarities with the theoretical distinctions made by O'Donovan and Gilbar.[99] Such a logic suggests that, in the absence of an appointed executor, the claim of a person who is entitled to letters of administration should not rest on that fact alone, but rather the claim is one of kin. In the event that the person entitled to take out administration is not kin, the claim of kin should be the relevant one.[100] Such logic is also consistent with the framework applied in the American cases. The theoretical positioning is expressed somewhat differently, but the fundamental logic is the same, namely the importance of the kin connection – expressed not as concepts of property, but as concepts of relationship, of identity, in which ideas of autonomy are central.

---

96   O'Donovan and Gilbar (2003) op cit.
97   Hammond (2002) op cit, at 112.
98   Atherton (2003) op cit.
99   O'Donovan and Gilbar (2003) op cit.
100 Ibid.

17

Organ donation and transplantation in Australia

Peter Saul, John McPhee, and Ian Kerridge

Preamble

Jim, a 37-year-old blue-collar worker, collapsed at home with a sudden headache. He was taken to hospital, and admitted to intensive care where he was placed on a breathing machine (mechanical ventilator).

His wife, Narelle, and his teenage children were informed that he had had a cerebral haemorrhage, and that he may die. The next day, they were told that, though he appeared outwardly unchanged, he was certified to be dead according to clinical criteria. He was brain dead. Organ donation was requested by the Intensive Care Unit specialist.

Jim had not discussed this with his family, and there was no written record of his views.

Motivated by a desire to enable someone to live a better life, Narelle agreed, signed the consent form and went home.

Late that night, while Narelle lay sleepless at home, surgical teams arrived by helicopter. Jim, at this time still fully maintained on life support systems but legally a corpse, was taken to the operating theatre and his heart, lungs, liver, kidneys, pancreas and eyes were removed. These organs were subsequently transplanted successfully into several recipients in Australia, with the liver being transplanted into a New Zealand national.

Narelle subsequently received a letter from the Transplant Co-ordinator, describing in broad terms what had become of the organs, and was later delighted to receive an anonymous letter of thanks from the recipient of one of the kidneys, describing his joy at being free from dialysis for the first time in years.

This story is fictional, but portrays the story and time frame of a typical donor, based on the Australian and New Zealand Organ Donation Registry (ANZODR) 1996.[1] It is shorn of all the emotion and immediacy of the real

---

1   Australia and New Zealand Organ Donation Registry, *1997 Report*, Vol 1.

stories: the tragedy, the tears, the sleeplessness, the uncertainty and, at times, the bizarreness, all essential to a worthwhile understanding of the web of laws, guidelines and ethical debates surrounding the current practice of organ donation in Australia. As we explore these legal and ethical dilemmas, we invite the reader to return repeatedly to "Jim and Narelle's" experience, currently, in unique ways, occurring about 200 times a year in Australia.

Introduction

Organ transplantation is exemplary of the relationship between advances in medical technology and the legal and social framework within which these innovations have been accommodated. It has progressed in a predictable pattern, with initial, experimental and largely unsuccessful efforts, followed by a decade of sporadic success, recognition of the effectiveness of the technique in question, then logarithmic growth in its applications. Legal response to the challenge, of necessity, only began in the later stages, after the rapid expansion had occurred, and occurred largely as a reactive process. Institutional research ethics committees did not exist until most current forms of transplantation had become well established: transplantation, at that time seen as a "desperate remedy", created its own "lifeboat" ethics.[2] Consent as we now understand it was not at the forefront of *clinical* thinking, despite the fact that clearly defined legal and ethical parameters for medical science and research existed (in the Nuremburg Code and the Declaration of Helsinki). A more parentalistic approach based on the duty to save life dominated, as evidenced by first person accounts of this era.[3]

It was thus typical of medical progress that in 1954 the first renal transplant would create an enormous and essentially insatiable demand for transplantable tissues, challenge philosophers and lawyers to redefine the world for ordinary people (in this case to redefine the concept of death), and push the issue of consent to the forefront of medical ethics.

Supply, demand and allocation

The demand for transplantable tissue is unmet worldwide. This problem can be addressed, as will be discussed below, but it will not be solved. Transplantation is typical of medical technology in being supply-driven, demand being essentially inexhaustible. As yesterday's targets are met, broader indications for transplantation arise, experimental techniques are deemed no longer experimental, new opportunities for research emerge.[4]

---

2   Moore, FD, "Three Ethical Revolutions: Ancient Assumptions Remodelled under Pressure of Transplantation" (1988) 38(1) *Transplantation Proceedings* 1061.

3   Lovell, RRH, "Ethics Law and Resources at the Growing Edge of Medicine" (1990) 10(3) *Bioethics News* 7.

4   Cassell, EJ, "The Sorcerer's Broom – Medicine's Rampant Technology" (1993) 23(6) *Hastings Center Report* 32.

The process of allocation of transplantable tissue is enormously problematic. While technical advances and changes in availability of organs will shift the ground, issues of justice and equity will remain much the same.

Demand

Current types of non-regenerative human tissue used in transplantation (allo-grafting) are: cornea, kidney, liver, heart, lung (or heart/lung together) pancreas, islet cells (the insulin manufacturing cells of the pancreas), skin, bone, adrenal glands, peripheral nerves and dopaminergic brain tissue. Intestine has been transplanted, often as part of a "cluster" graft of visceral organs. This list is not exhaustive and is likely to grow. The general indications for transplantation can be summarised as complete or near-complete failure of an organ, in the case of vital organs likely to prove fatal within a predictable period of time. However, the exact reasons for putting patients on a waiting list for transplantation cannot be so easily summarised, relying on initial referral, assessment and acceptance. At each of these stages there is the potential for great increases in numbers. In addition, the ageing and expanding population of Australia will include increasing numbers of potential recipients of organs (but not of donors).

Demand for transplantable tissue outstrips supply for all types of tissue in Australia, despite an efficient use of donated tissue.[5] Twenty to 30 per cent of potential heart and liver recipients die while waiting.[6] The situation in the United States is claimed to be worse, presumably because of broader indications for transplantation and less governmental control over healthcare delivery.

Supply

Supply of transplantable tissue should be considered under the following headings:

- cadaveric beating-heart donors;
- cadaveric non-beating heart donors; and
- living donors.

Cadaveric beating heart donors are the dominant source of solid organs (kidney, heart, lungs and pancreas) in Australasia.[7] Australia has one of the lowest rates of donation of this type among developed nations, at 10.6 per million population, less than half that of the United States and certain European countries. The reasons for this are unknown, but may relate to a legal and organisational framework

---

5   ANZODR (1997) op cit, Vol 1.
6   National Health and Medical Research Council, Ethical Issues Raised by Allocation of Transplant Resources, Ethical Issues in Organ Donation, Discussion Paper No 3, AGPS, Canberra, 1997.
7   ANZODR (1997) op cit, Vol 1.

which strongly supports autonomy; altruism and voluntarism being the underlying principles.

Clear support for voluntarism as the guiding principle for cadaveric organ donation in Australasia can be found in the *Statement and Guidelines on Brain Death and Organ Donation* from the Australian and New Zealand Intensive Care Society.[8] This document stresses the principle of the duty of care to the patient, and goes on: "Ensuring fulfillment of the wishes of a person to donate their organs after death is consistent with that principle". A final paragraph speaks of the need to recognise potential recipients as vital but "secondary". This approach has met with strong support from the main Christian churches, members of which provide the overwhelming proportion of organs for donation.[9]

The altruism of this act emerges in the unique donor family study[10] which found that the commonest motive given by families who had actually signed consent for the donation of a relative's organs had been "to enable someone else to have a better life".

The low rate of organ donation in Australia compares unfavourably with that of other countries with voluntary systems such as Spain and the United States, and those with presumption of consent, such as Austria and Belgium. Simplistic comparisons are to be avoided, as cultural influences play an important part. However, Austria (with the world's highest rate of donation) has compulsory autopsy and presumed consent for donation, while Japan (with the lowest), has widespread support for organ donation in the community, but is still struggling with legislation about brain death and organ donation. Legislation clearly has some role in determining donation rates. In making these comparisons with other countries, it is important to recognise that organ transplantation has many elements, each of which has to be balanced and integrated to provide an ethical result.

Medical, legal and demographic factors could further lower the already low donor rate in Australia. Medical factors include the steady decrease in the incidence of conditions causing brain death (stroke and neurotrauma may be decreasing by 5–10 per cent each year) and the spread of hepatitis C, which may cause a sharp rise in demand for liver transplantation while reducing supply.[11] An ageing population, with many ethnic groups known not to favour organ donation, and possibly fickle public opinion, are just some examples of demographic problems.

Legal barriers to donation may include the interpretation of the legislation relating to Coroners. In Australia, 50 per cent of cadaveric, beating heart donors in

---

8   Australian and New Zealand Intensive Care Society, *Statement and Guidelines on Brain Death and Organ Donation – 1993*, a report of the ANZICS Working Party on Brain Death and Organ Donation, May 1993.

9   ANZODR (1997) op cit, Vol 1.

10   "Family Experiences of Organ Donation. The First Australian Study", (1996) 14 *ACCORD* (Newsletter of Australian Coordinating Committee on Organ Registries and Donation) July 1996.

11   Kerridge, I, Saul, P and Batey, R, "The Clinical and Ethical Implications of Hepatitis C for Organ Transplantation in Australia" (1996) 165 *Medical Journal of Australia* 282.

2004 were subject to coronial inquiry (in which the coroner has discretionary powers to allow or disallow organ donation), similar to 2003. In New Zealand, it was 43 per cent for 2004, compared to 53 per cent in 2003.[12] Evidence from overseas suggests that this may vary among jurisdictions and may limit the availability of organs for donation.[13]

Increasing supply of cadaveric beating-heart organ donors

A large increase (perhaps a doubling) in supply is unlikely without considerable changes to the current Australian system. However, commentators have argued that any changes which threaten the altruistic and voluntaristic basis of the current arrangements would not be supported by "the transplant lobby" in the United States or Australia, because of a perceived threat to public support for the present system.

Options to increase the rate of donation of organs from this source include:

- further legal redefinition of death to include more people as dead, and therefore potential cadaveric organ donors;

- major revision of the consent process toward a situation of "presumed consent";

- offering of financial incentives to individuals;

- life support for patients not expected to benefit themselves, but who may become suitable donors; and

- an attempt to work within current laws and guidelines, but to "normalise" the process from a sociological point of view and so increase rates of consent.

The legal redefinition of death, and revision of the concept of consent will be reviewed below.

Financial incentives, ranging from tax relief to cash payments have been canvassed, but s 32 of the *Human Tissue Act 1983* (NSW) expressly forbids the creation of any contract or arrangement for the "sale" of any tissue. In common law, a cadaver has been construed as "quasi-property", and family members, while having some rights, do not have rights to the body or its parts in a com-mercial sense. There is some commentary in this area,[14] and a Western Australian case[15] which dealt with the collection of tissue samples from deceased persons.

---

12 Australian and New Zealand Organ Donation Registry *2005 Report* (2004 figures).

13 Shafer, T, Schkade, LL, Warner, HE, Eakin, M, O'Connor, K, Springer J, Jankiewicz T, Reitsma W, Steele J, Keen-Denton, K, "Impact of Medical Examiner/Coroner Practices on Organ Recovery in the United States" (1994) 272(20) *Journal of the American Medical Association* 1607; Shafer, TJ, Schkade, LL, Evans, RW, O'Connor KJ and Reitsma, W, "Vital Role of Medical Examiners and Coroners in Organ Transplantation" (2004) 4(2) *Am J Transplant* 160.

14 Griggs, L, "The Ownership of Excised Body Parts: Does an Individual Have the Right to Sell?" (1994) 1 *Journal of Law and Medicine* 223; Childress, JF, "Organ and Tissue Procurement: Ethical and Legal Issues Regarding Cadavers" in Reich, WT (ed), *Encyclopedia of Bioethics*, rev edn, Simon & Schuster Macmillan, New York, 1995, p 1857.

15 *Roche v Douglas* [2000] WAR 331.

These difficulties, and the absence of proof that this would increase the availability of organs for donation, suggest there is no current support for "rewarded giving" in Australia.

Mechanical ventilation purely for the purposes of organ donation (that is, where there is no possibility of benefit to the patient) has been practised, but the legality of this has been questioned in the United Kingdom,[16] based on an inter-pretation of the House of Lords decision in *Airedale NHS Trust v Bland*.[17] While at first sight ethically questionable and possibly illegal (instituting a form of treatment with no prospect of benefit to the recipient fails the requirement of beneficence), there are pragmatic grounds for debating this further. In practice, such a judgment (that instituting life support is pointless) can be difficult, and, may depend more on the way in which the patient presents to the intensive care physician than the actual condition or its prognosis. Consequentialist arguments are then applied in defence of the practice (which continues in the United Kingdom despite its potential illega-lity). The debate is important, and highlights the frequent conflict between medical practice and the law caused by "distinctions without differences".[18] In Australia, there has as yet been no legal challenge to the practice of putting patients on life support purely for the purposes of organ donation.

Normalisation of the donation process is essentially a sociological concept, legally inoffensive. The intent of semi-autonomous organisations, such as Aust-ralians Donate (previously ACCORD) is to promote this[19] through advertisements, school projects and literature for the bereaved. Importantly, while there is some evidence that discussion of organ donation can be promoted in the community, there is currently no evidence that this has led to an increased permission rate for organ donation.

Brain death

An understanding of the history and legal implications of brain death is important to any discussion of cadaveric, beating-heart organ donation. As a concept, death of the brain through lack of blood flow has a history which goes back to Harvey Cushing in 1902, but was not medically relevant until mechanical ventilators were developed in the 1950s in response to the polio epidemics in Scandinavia at that time. Mechanical ventilation, along with other intensive forms of support, allowed health care workers to keep alive patients with no brain function (and therefore no ability to breathe for themselves). Patients without detectable brain function were

---

16   Riad, H and Nicholls, A, "An Ethical Debate: Elective Ventilation of Potential Organ Donors" (1995) 310 *BMJ* 714.

17   [1993] AC 789.

18   Hogffenberg, R, Lock, M, Tilney, N, Casabona, C, Daar, AS, Guttmann, RD, Kennedy, I, Mundy, S, Radcliffe-Richards, J, Sells, RA, "Should Organs from Patients in Permanent Vegetative State be Used for Transplantation?" (1997) 350 *Lancet* 1320.

19   (1997) 18 *ACCORD* (Newsletter of the Australian Coordinating Committee on Organ Registries and Donation) November 1997.

identified by French neurologists as having "coma depasse" – a coma from which there could be no return.

In a series of connected events, this diagnosis became well recognised, and simple bedside tests described which would accurately diagnose it.[20] None of this would have attracted much attention but for the parallel need for organ donors with preserved circulation, to provide kidneys for transplantation. It was this development which provoked the need for legislation, and brought this rare (about 0.5 per cent of all deaths) and obscure diagnosis into the public spotlight.

Organ transplantation from cadavers, after a stuttering start in the 1950s and modest success in the 1960s, was well established as a life-saving intervention by the time legislation was drafted in the 1970s and early 1980s. It was 1977 when the Australian Law Reform Commission (ALRC) recommended that all Australian States and Territories should pass uniform legislation regulating organ donation and tissue transplantation.[21] The ALRC expressed the view that removal of an organ from a living person, even with the consent of the person, could constitute an assault.[22] This view arose at a time when the medical need for organs, as at present, was from patients whose hearts were still beating. The inevitable conclusion, following the lead set by the United States, and echoed (but not in statutory form) in the United Kingdom, was that patients who had proven death of the brain should be legally regarded as dead. This would allow either unilateral discontinuation of treatment or organ donation, dependent on a prescribed form of consent. As Professor Lovell, a pioneer of renal transplantation in Australia, remarked: "The law did enter in a specific way later on, as the transplantation programme developed, because of the desire for a legal definition of death that was relevant to obtaining kidneys from cadavers".[23]

All Australian States and Territories passed laws, which despite certain variations in detail (see Tables 17.1, p 350, and 17.2, pp 351-353) defined two legal forms of death: one an irreversible cessation of circulation in the body as a whole, and the other, irreversible cessation of all brain function (known as "whole brain death"). Criteria for making this latter diagnosis of death were intentionally not spelled out in the Acts, the ALRC having suggested that "[f]lexibility to allow adoption of criteria to accord with the best current professional procedures is preferable to verbose legislation". However, the criteria in existence at the time and refined further since were (and are still) not strictly in accordance with "whole brain death".

20　Australian and New Zealand Intensive Care Society, *Statement and Guidelines on Brain Death and Organ Donation – 1993*, report of the ANZICS Working Party on Brain Death and Organ Donation, May 1993.

21　Dix, A, Errington, M, Nicholson, K and Powe, R, *Law for the Medical Profession*, 2nd edn, Butterworth Heinemann, Australia, 1996, Para [1202].

22　Bennett, B, *Law and Medicine*, Lawbook Co, Sydney, 1997, Ch 9; Australian Law Reform Commission, *Human Tissue Transplants*, AGPS, Canberra, 1977.

23　Lovell (1990) op cit.

Table 17.1: Human tissue legislation

Human Tissue Act 1983 (NSW)	Transplantation and Anatomy Act 1979 (Qld)
Transplantation and Anatomy Act 1983 (SA)	Human Tissue Act 1985 (Tas)
Human Tissue Act 1982 (Vic)	Human Tissue and Transplant Act 1982 (WA)
Transplantation and Anatomy Act 1978 (ACT)	Human Tissue Transplant Act 1979 (NT)

The chief medical concern is over the legal need to ascertain that the whole brain has died, even though the prescribed clinical tests are of the function of a limited part of the brain known as the brain stem. No "gold standard" test exists which incontrovertibly demonstrates death of the whole brain in the clinical setting of a beating-heart donor: even autopsy may fail to confirm this.[24] However, simple tests and criteria were developed which would establish beyond reasonable doubt that a crucial part of the brain, the brainstem, had died, and this rapidly became the surrogate for whole brain death. To quote Pallis, an originator and strong proponent of this surrogate diagnosis: "The destruction of a few cubic centimetres of tissue [in the brain stem] seems to be all that is needed to ensure irreversible loss both of the capacity for consciousness and of the capacity to breathe spontaneously, ie death".[25] The surrogate use of brainstem death for whole brain death has not, so far, been legally challenged in Australia. The tests of brainstem function, while widely supported by intensive care physicians[26] may not be beyond challenge, especially in defining brainstem death in infants.[27]

What of the other, more conventional form of death experienced by the remaining 99.5 per cent of us? While a failure of the heart to beat is obviously very bad, it becomes necessary to define at what point this can be deemed irreversible. The law does not dictate how physicians are to establish its irreversibility: consensus points to 10 minutes, but this may be challenged as the demand for transplantable tissue continues to rise.

As the ALRC in 1977 noted, "the recommended statutory definition of death is intended to have general application. It should not be limited in its legal effect to any particular kind of patient ... not to transplantation".[28] In practice, however, two forms of death produce two forms of corpse, which appear not to be treated equally under acts such as those relating to autopsy, where the disposition of removed tissues is subject to less restraint in the case of conventional death than in

---

24 Halevy, A and Brody, B, "Brain Death: Reconciling Definitions, Criteria, and Tests" (1993) 119(6) *Annals of Internal Medicine* 519.

25 Pallis, C, "Further Thoughts on Brainstem Death" (1995) 23(1) *Anaesthesia & Intensive Care* 20.

26 Pearson, IY and Zurynski, Y, "A Survey of Personal and Professional Attitudes of Intensivists to Organ Donation and Transplantation" (1995) 23(1) *Anaesthesia & Intensive Care* 68.

27 Farrell, MM and Levin, DL, "Brain Death in the Paediatric Patient: Historical, Sociological, Medical, Religious, Cultural, Legal, and Ethical Considerations" (1993) 21(12) *Critical Care Medicine* 1951.

28 Bennett (1997) op cit, ch 9.

Table 17.2: Variations between the jurisdictions

Issue	NSW	QLD	SA	TAS	VIC	WA	ACT	NT
ADULTS								
Written consent for removal of *regenerative tissue* by a person over the age of 18 years required	✓	✓ Must be signed in presence of designated officer	✓ Must NOT be signed in presence of donor's family	✓	✓	✓ Must NOT be signed in the presence of donor's family or friends	✓	✓
Written consent for removal of *non-regenerative tissue* and 24-hour waiting period	✓	✓	✓ Must NOT be given in the presence of family members	✓	✓	Must NOT be signed in the presence of donor's family or friends	✓	✓
Time of consent to be stated on the consent	✓ Day and time consent given must be recorded	✓	✗	✓	✓	✗	✓	✓
Medical certificate	✓	Obligatory	✗	✓	✓	✗	✓	✓

CHILDREN	NSW	QLD	SA	TAS	VIC	WA	ACT	NT
Parental consent for removal of regenerative tissue for the purpose of transplantation	✓	✓	✓	✓	✓	✓	✓	✗
Parent or sibling	✓	✓	✓ The SA legislation does not specify who may be a recipient, but approval from a ministerial committee is required before removal of tissue	✓	✓	✓		✗
Other relative	✗	✗	✓	✓	✗ May be removed where the child is too young to understand, only where it is necessary to save the life of the sibling	✓	✓	✗
Consent of the child required	✗ Consent is not required if the child is too young to understand the nature and effect of the proposed donation. Two doctors (one of whom is a paediatrician) must certify that there is minimal risk to the child and the sibling would be likely to die or suffer serious damage to health without the transplant	✗ Three medical practitioners certify that there is minimal risk to the child and sibling or parent would be likely to die without transplant	✓	✓		✓	✓	

CHILDREN	NSW	QLD	SA	TAS	VIC	WA	ACT	NT
Non-regenerative tissue may not be removed from a child	✓						✗ Only for a family member who is in danger of dying; consent of both parents (where available); medical practitioner may give a certificate; 24-hour waiting period; referral to ministerial committee.	✓

DEATH	NSW	QLD	SA	TAS	VIC	WA	ACT	NT
Death: Irreversible cessation of all brain function; or Irreversible cessation of blood circulation General application	✓	✓ Restricted to tissue donation and transplantation	✓ Death (Definition) Act 1983	✓	✓	✗ Irreversible and complete cessation of all brain function – transplantation only	✓	✓

those deemed "brain dead".[29] As a legal commentator in the United Kingdom remarked: "United States and Australian State statutes with dual, disjunctive concepts of death mislead and suggest, as many critics have argued, that death means different things in different contexts".[30] Some have even suggested that the "brain dead" heart-beating corpse should have a unique name, with "neomort" an early, but so far unaccepted offering.

The major philosophical debate has centred on the concept of brain death: how much brain, or, more specifically, which brain functions, have to die in order for somebody to be considered dead? Irreversible loss of all awareness can occur in other disorders of neurological function such as post-coma unresponsiveness (vegetative state (VS)) and anencephaly. Should this be considered death? The only pragmatic difference between the patient with brain death and another with post-coma unresponsiveness (VS) is that the former can live for several days or weeks only with the help of a mechanical ventilator (at which point he or she will probably die) where the post-coma unresponsiveness (VS) patient may live for an average of two to five years with the aid of tube feeds and occasional antibiotics.[31] Both are unaware and dying. Philosophically this difference appears small, yet one is considered dead and the other alive. However, there is a distinction here which may elude non-clinicians. Patients who are in a post-coma unresponsiveness (VS) state sleep and wake up, yawn and maintain all basic non-voluntary bodily systems. It would not be rational to attempt to pronounce such a person as dead, even though their situation is usually hopeless, and even though withdrawal of life-sustaining treatment may be justified.[32] Lack of awareness and a hopeless prognosis, although they are indicative of dying, do not constitute death, and this has not been legislated anywhere in the world. A more reasonable solution to the philosophical dilemma would be to abandon attempts to define death in terms of degrees of brain malfunction, and return to the cardiovascular definition.[33]

While it is tempting to wish to return to a single, whole body, definition of death, organ donation in its present form would essentially cease unless the fundamental objection to removal of organs from a "living" body, even with consent, could be overcome. The act of removal of organs would then be viewed as a form of justified killing, not currently accepted in Australia especially in the wake of the emotive euthanasia debate. It is interesting to note, however, that a small number of people who have agreed to donation of a loved one's organs, think that this is the reality of the current system,[34] and that surveys suggest a certain level of acceptance of other forms of euthanasia within the medical and lay community.

---

29   Royal College of Pathologists of Australasia, Position Statement, "Autopsy and the Use of Tissues Removed at Autopsy" (1994) 160 *MJA* 442.

30   Price, DPT, "Organ Transplant Initiatives: the Twilight Zone" (1997) 23 *Journal of Medical Ethics* 170.

31   The Multi-Society Task Force on PVS, "Medical Aspects of the Persistent Vegetative State" (First of Two Parts) (1994) 330(21) *New England Journal of Medicine* 1499.

32   See *Airedale NHS Trust v Bland* [1993] AC 789.

33   Truog, RD, "Is It Time to Abandon Brain Death?" (1997) 27(1) *Hastings Center Report* 29.

34   "Family Experiences of Organ Donation. The First Australian Study" (1996) 14 *ACCORD*.

There is another, essentially sociological critique of brain death, mounted not by sociologists but by a variety of intensive care specialists. In essence this critique is of the loss of ritual and meaning associated with a declaration of death which leaves the patient looking very much alive, and after which the "body" cannot immediately be claimed by the grieving family.[35]

One cannot help but feel for Dr R Kunin, who gave permission for his son to become an organ donor and wrote later: "We clung to him in our minds, seeking to keep him alive within ourselves. In part, this was because we didn't actually see him dead. And so we didn't really feel him dead".[36]

For a substantial minority, especially among ethnic and religious minorities, the perception that people who are "brain dead" are not really dead may be quite strong, and accompanied by a general distrust of doctors and high-tech Western medicine. This lack of faith in brain death has produced legislation in New Jersey, United States[37] which allows "opting out" of this legal concept on religious grounds, and in Singapore, where Muslims are exempted from presumed consent for organ donation. No such concessions have been canvassed in Australia, but the low rate of donation from some ethnic minorities speaks for itself.[38]

In summary, the legal and medical concept of brain death has produced the necessary conditions for beating-heart organ donation, and has, as intended, protected doctors from accusations of murder in this setting (unlike Japan, where the first heart transplant ended in a murder trial). The concept does have significant flaws: in having created two legal definitions of death with unforeseen consequences; in having a definition of death in legislation not matched by the criteria used to diagnose it; in engendering an unresolved philosophical debate about the true nature of death and personhood; and in having infringed some important ritual aspects of death.

To quote Professor Powner: "Defining lifelessness without a requirement for absent cardiovascular function may be a pause for convenience, but cannot yet suffice as the necessary prerequisite for society's current ritual recognising that death has been defined".[39]

Cadaveric (non-beating heart)

There is evidence that the general public may have some reservations about organ removal from beating heart donors. Unfortunately, organs (other than corneas and possibly kidneys) removed from people who have suffered a cardiovascular form

---

35 Powner, DJ, Ackerman, BM and Grenvik, A, "Medical Diagnosis of Death in Adults: Historical Contributions to Current Controversies" (1996) 348 *Lancet* 1219.

36 Iserson, KV, "Voluntary Organ Donation: Autonomy ... Tragedy" Letter (1993) 270(16) *Journal of the American Medical Association* 1930.

37 Olick, RS, "Brain Death, Religious Freedom, and Public Policy: New Jersey's Landmark Legislative Initiative" (1991) 1(4) *Kennedy Institute of Ethics Journal* 285.

38 ANZODR (1997) op cit, Vol 1.

39 Powner, Ackerman and Grenvik (1996) op cit.

of death (that is, heart not beating for more than 10 minutes) are generally not useful for transplantation. There were only two non-heart beating donors in Australia in 1996, four in 2004 and a total of 31 between 1989 and 2004.

To provide more tissues from this source would currently require some form of intervention to preserve the organs before enough time had elapsed for the patient to be truly dead. This violates beneficence/non-maleficence, and may not be acceptable even if valid consent could be obtained. It is interesting to speculate, however, if a form of organ preservation could be invented which could be applied to a *clearly dying* patient (who could be seen to be beyond benefit or harm) *without actually killing him or her*, then the option of a delayed removal of viable organs may be legally possible.

The transplantation service in Pittsburgh, United States, trialled a protocol where the organs are removed two minutes after the heart stops beating.[40] This is a clear attempt to provoke another new definition of death (that is, that absence of heartbeat is irreversible at two minutes), and is unlikely to gain wide support. The Maastricht protocol demands 10 minutes of absent heartbeat before removal of the kidneys, and is gaining popularity despite its dependence on a rather arbitrary definition of death. The definition of a non-heart-beating donor provided in the report of the Australian and New Zealand Organ Donation Registry is as follows:

> A non-heart-beating donor is defined as a patient who is certified dead using the criterion of irreversible cessation of circulation. As soon as cardiac death is confirmed the retrieval procedure is commenced in order to minimize warm ischaemia time.[41]

Living donors

Living donors of all types represent up to 40 per cent of kidney donations but only 14 per cent of all donations in Australia.[42] The majority of donors are close relatives (usually the mother), and the organ is usually a kidney, though parts of liver and lung can, and have been, transplanted elsewhere.

The giving of an anatomical gift is legally sanctioned in Australia, though there are restrictions for minors. Section 8 of the *Human Tissue Act 1983* (NSW) focuses largely on ensuring that consent has occurred, and mandates a 24-hour "cooling-off" period before donation can take place.

Living donation poses unique problems, as it is a surgical procedure in which the burdens fall almost entirely on the donor, while all the benefits (aside from the psychological) accrue to the recipient. How are these to be balanced? Also, at what point does the risk of harm to the donor (which is considerable, especially with lung and liver donation) make it inappropriate to allow the

---

40   Truog (1997) op cit.
41   ANZODR (1995) op cit.
42   Mathew T, Faull R and Snelling P, "The Shortage of Kidneys for Transplantation in Australia" (2005) 182(5) *MJA* 204.

donation to take place? The issue is hotly debated, with strong opposition coming even from pioneers of transplant surgery (such as Thomas Starzl).[43]

Living donation of non-regenerative tissue presents special problems when the donor is unrelated to the recipient. It appears that this extreme form of altruism raises suspicion in the minds of some legislators, to the point where it is essentially illegal in the United Kingdom. While not illegal in Australia, State governments have been very cautious in response to calls to enable unrelated living donation of solid organs and have proposed strict guidelines for the practice.[44]

Selling organs (such as a kidney) in life, has been documented to have occurred in a number of countries.[45] This act of "rewarded giving" has been made illegal in almost all countries with a regulated transplantation program, including Australia, even though it can be argued that such a transaction is not fundamentally unethical when judged by the criteria of principles-based ethics, and that the restriction of organ commerce in developing nations by industrialised nations may represent unjustifiable medical parentalism. It seems clear, however, that a trade in organs, once started, would be impossible to regulate, equity in allocation could not be preserved, and therefore that making such a trade illegal has considerable merit. It is noteworthy that 170 Japanese nationals have received legal transplants overseas – it is hard to imagine that these recipients were drawn randomly from the pool of potential recipients. This is an unusual example of a law governing medical activity arising very early, before the practice is already widespread. There are no publicised efforts to change this law at present.[46]

Alternative sources of transplantable tissue

An alternative source of organs is xenotransplantation, where the organs are transplanted from an animal into a human. This has famously been attempted in the United States (for instance, in the case of Baby Fae), and less famously on many other occasions, often much more successfully. By agreement, rather than by law, there is a widespread moratorium on this practice at present, but research in this area is feverish.

Only from animals could a truly huge increase in donor tissue be expected. Such an increase would be necessary for instance to support islet cell transplants to cure diabetes, a very common condition in the Western world.[47]

The major problem is rejection of the organ, but many approaches to this are being researched, including genetically manipulating the animal to "humanise" its

---

43   Starzl, T, "Organ Transplantation: A Practical Triumph and Epistemologic Collapse", (2003) 147(3) *Proc An Philos Soc* 226-45.

44   NSW Health guidelines, "*Kidney Donation by Live Donors*" NSW Health, Sydney, 2004.

45   See Griggs, L, "The Ownership of Excised Body Parts: Does an Individual Have the Right to Sell" (1994) 1 *Journal of Law and Medicine* 223.

46   See Kennedy, SE, Shen, Y, Charlesworth, JA, Mackie, JD, Mahony, JD, Kelly, JJP and Pussell, BA, "Outcome of Overseas Commercial Kidney Transplantation: an Australian Perspective" (2005) 182(5) *MJA* 224.

47   Mandel, TE, "Future Directions in Transplantation" (1993) 158 *MJA* 269.

organs. Although this sounds far-fetched, herds of such animals already exist in the United Kingdom with the approval of the Nuffield Trust and British Medical Association. The rapid advances in cloning technology, gene manipulation and gene therapy make the development of xenograft tissue banks a realistic prospect for the future.[48]

The complex issues relating to xenotransplantation have been the focus of inquiries by the National Health and Medical Research Council (NHMRC) over the past few years. At its 154th session in September 2004, the NHMRC considered the final report prepared by the Xenotransplantation Working Party. A communiqué reporting the outcome of this consideration was issued by the NHMRC on 20 September 2004. In addition, an updated report providing further details on the outcome of the council's deliberations was released by the CEO of the NHMRC, Professor Alan Pettigrew, in early October 2004. In brief, the council decided that there should be no clinical trials in animal-to-human whole organ transplants for a period of five years. It also requested more time to consider other animal-to-human transplantation therapies.

At the 155th session in Canberra on 9 December, the council considered further the issue of animal cellular therapies and animal external therapies, concluding that there should be no clinical trials in Australia using animal cellular therapies or animal external therapies for five years. The council also asked the Gene and Related Therapies Research Advisory Panel (GTRAP) of the NHMRC Research Committee to provide regular updates to the council during this period on new information that arises on the potential benefits and risks for animal-based human treatments.

Legal impediments to the use of animals for these purposes are complex. Clearly primates, especially the great apes, as well as being difficult to breed and adequately house, are a protected species. Apes are also not routinely bred and killed as a source of food, which may also restrain their sacrifice for transplantation. The hapless pig, however, may have no protection other than that accorded to other experimental animals (such as by the *Animal Research Act 1985* (NSW)).

Press speculation on the production of headless human clones as sources of transplantable tissue is evidence more of the newsworthiness of such ideas than their likelihood.[49]

Distribution and/or allocation

Given the continuing and unresolved shortage of donor organs, the question of how organs should be allocated emerges as a major concern. The allocation tissues for transplantation occurs at two distinct levels: "macro-allocation", where the government and its agencies control overall activity by legislation and (more potently funding), and "micro-allocation", which deals with who gets the organ.

---

48   Nicholson, RH, "This Little Pig Went to Market" (1996) 26(4) *Hastings Center Report* 3.
49   "Embryology. Problem with Cloning? Then Get Your Head Around This", Editorial, *Sydney Morning Herald*, 20 October 1997.

Macro-allocation is based on the perceived efficacy, effectiveness and cost-effectiveness of transplant programs. Federal and State governments determine transplant activity through funding administered by quasi-autonomous committees. When such a committee in the United States announced in 1983 that liver transplantation was an effective treatment (as opposed to an experiment) there was a rise in transplant rates (35-fold from 1981 to 1986) and each transplant was estimated at that time to cost $US230,000. Comparable Australian figures from 1992 were $A120,000 per transplant ($A12 million for 100 transplants).[50] The cost-effectiveness of renal transplantation reflects in large part the existence of an alternative, less effective and more expensive therapy for chronic renal failure – renal dialysis. Even with the costs of expensive drugs used indefinitely to suppress rejection, transplantation appears more cost-effective. In the case of liver, heart and lung transplants, the alternative to transplantation (by definition) is death. The calculation of effectiveness therefore must depend on consideration of complex parameters such as opportunity cost, the value of life and of symbolic gestures. If, on the other hand, an effective but fiercely expensive form of artificial liver were developed, liver transplantation would leap to the top of the list of cost-effective treatments. Transplantation offers a challenge to utilitarian ethicists to do the impossible: define *and measure* outcomes which are valid and comparable.

Comparison with what good could be done by such sums in a primary care setting (the opportunity cost) is irresistible, even to those responsible for the initiation of transplant programs. As Professor Lovell asks (but cannot answer): "How many gifts of primary health care equate with one heart transplant?".[51] While it is undeniable that the resources expended in any high-tech, high-cost intervention may be more ethically directed elsewhere, to Aboriginal health or to population control, the issues of opportunity cost, which have been generally ignored in medicine and in ethics, are too complex for us to more than simply acknowledge in this chapter.

Two issues emerge in micro-allocation: how is someone in need excluded from the waiting list for donation, and how is an organ allocated once donated?

Both issues are hard to analyse succinctly, since even the medical dimensions are multiple, often disputed and may, on reflection, be quasi-medical. Non-medical, "lifestyle" issues are also contributory to the decision-making process, as are the principles of equity and justice. A number of different processes of organ allocation have been proposed, including the equitable but impractical idea of a lottery. In Australia, best match of the organ to the patient's blood type and size is the most frequent criterion used in selecting a recipient, but many other criteria including age, co-morbidity, aetiology and compliance, are also used in an extremely complex way.[52]

---

50 Mitchell, SV, Smallwood, RA, Angus, PW and Lapsley, HM, "Can We Afford to Transplant?" (1993) 158 *MJA* 190.

51 Lovell, RRH, "Ethics law and resources at the growing edge of medicine" (1990) 10(3) *Bioethics News* 7.

52 National Health and Medical Research Council, *Ethical Issues Raised by Allocation of Transplant Resources, Ethical Issues in Organ Donation*, Discussion Paper No 3, AGPS, Canberra, 1997.

Committees have succeeded individual physicians as the arbiter of allocation, but the transparency of the process can be challenged.

Any system should meet the principles associated with justice; based on need (most imminent risk of death), equal shares (not very applicable since organs cannot be divided up), merit (a controversial area: when the famous baseball player, Mickey Mantle, needed a liver transplant, it became available within two days, provoking an outcry) or contribution (denying infants, children and the poor!).[53] Looking purely at outcomes is obviously post hoc, and individual good or community good would have to be debated. A fair procedure (a transparent process) rather than a fair outcome may constitute the only form of justice in this area at present.

An individual patient does not have a legal right to demand that an organ be made available. While some commentators are predicting the end of medical paternalism in the face of consumer pressure, and citing recent court judgments as supporting this view, there have been no legal challenges to the allocation of organs in Australia.[54] However, in the United States, where health expenditure is determined increasingly by insurers, refusal to pay for an expensive transplant procedure by an insurer was overruled in court. The implication may be that it is unwise to initiate any new and expensive form of transplantation without prior commitment of adequate resources to deal with the ensuing demand.

Consent

As already discussed, obtaining organs from living donors is largely a matter of consent. In drawing up the human tissue legislation in Australia (Tables 17.1 and 17.2), ensuring valid consent in this context was of paramount concern. The validity of consent here depends on the minimisation of coercion, careful selection of donors and recipients to reduce risks to both parties, and full disclosure of risk and benefits to the donor.[55]

For "cadaveric" ("brain dead") donors, consent relies at present on advance directives and surrogate decision-making, in the form of substituted judgment. In the context of organ donation such directives have been widely canvassed, through organ donor cards and a "tick box" section on drivers' licences. The validity of such a directive is implicitly questioned by the universal practice in Australia of asking for permission from the next of kin for donation even where such a document exists, and even where the Act does not demand this. This may be a recognition of the still low community understanding of brain death and organ donation.

The efficacy of the currently available forms of advance directives for organ donation is very low: in 1996, 75 per cent of all donors had no donor card or record

53 Gillam, L, "Resource Allocation: The Unavoidable Debate" (1992) 11(3) *Bioethics News* 49.
54 Nisselle, P, "Shifting Medicolegal Sands" (1995) 163 *MJA* 229.
55 Kramer, MR and Sprung, CL, "Living Related Donation in Lung Transplantation" (1995) 155 *Archives of Internal Medicine* 1734.

on their driver's licence.[56] Even in the few cases where a signed licence is available, the "next of kin" is invited to sign consent: a refusal to do so results in the donation not proceeding.

A surrogate decision (supposedly a substituted judgment) is thus the norm in gaining consent for organ donation. The human tissue legislation in most jurisdictions in Australia asks only for an absence of objection, but in practice a positive commitment in the form of a signature is demanded. Anticipating the possibility of family conflict, the human tissue legislation spells out who is the "senior available next of kin" for the purpose of giving consent.

In the absence of a prior directive from the deceased, evidence from the donor family study suggests that the "next of kin" makes a decision based on his or her own moral judgment, reflecting a belief in altruism rather than the perceived wishes of the deceased. This creates potential for some form of moral coercion to enter into the consent process, and for changes in public opinion to impact rapidly on consent rates for organ donation, which are indeed quite volatile in New South Wales. Despite the evidence to the contrary, it is necessary to see this process, as in the ANZICS Guidelines previously referred to, as "honouring the patient's wishes", even though these are not known, to avoid dispute about "ownership" of the organs of a dead person.

Alternatives to this fragile system of consent have been suggested and are in use elsewhere. The most common alternative is presumed consent (or "opting out"), where the body is deemed to be at the state's disposal (*res communitatis*) unless there is documentation of refusal by the person during life. In practice, most countries with this law (apart from Austria and Belgium) do seek permission from relatives, so the difference may be more apparent than real. A change to this system has, in the case of Belgium, increased donation rates, but there are grounds for fearing loss of community acceptance if the voluntaristic nature of the Australian system were changed in this way.[57]

Widely canvassed in the United States, which, like Australia has stayed with "opting in", is the suggestion of obliging all adults to make a decision about organ donation and record this in an accessible way (a forced advance directive or "required response"). This may be practical in Australia (as with compulsory voting), but would suffer all the caveats associated with advance directives: merely making it obligatory answers none of the fundamental questions about validity. It is noteworthy that in Belgium, which has a system which tries to encourage registration of views (by otherwise presuming consent), figures from 1990 show that only 1.8 per cent of the population had opted out, and 0.2 per cent had voluntarily opted in: 98 per cent of the population were, at that time, "don't knows".

---

56   ANZODR (1997) op cit, Vol 1.

57   Shann, FA, "Personal Comment: Whole Brain Death Versus Cortical Death" (1995) 23 *Anaesthesia & Intensive Care* 14; Organ Donation – Presumed Consent for Organ Donation, January 2005, BMA, <www.bma.org.uk/ap.nsf/Content/OrganDonationPresumedConsent> (accessed 3 April 2005); "AMA backs review of presumed consent on organ donations" *American Medical News*, 5 July 2004.

Having considered all the alternative forms of consent, it is likely that great efforts will be made to preserve the present system, recognising that a long-term investment in an altruistic system may ultimately produce a manageable, even if very inadequate, outcome. Most current efforts at increasing donor rates are local and essentially sociological, with "normalisation" and community acceptance of organ donation the hoped for result.

Conclusions

Two of the three major issues in organ donation and transplantation in Australia are addressed fully by the legislation known in most jurisdictions as the *Human Tissue Act*, namely a definition of death which permits removal of organs from people with beating hearts without killing them, and specific guidelines about the form of consent required. While honouring a widespread community desire for voluntarism, the legislation in these two areas has provoked considerable debate about the nature of death and the validity of consent. While every effort has been made to preserve the spirit of the current legislation, in the long term major changes may be required.

The third issue, that of distribution and allocation of transplantable tissue, while not addressed by systematic legislation, may come to drive the debate, with only the uncertain concept of "cost-effectiveness" to inform difficult decisions. The challenge to clinicians and policy-makers is to preserve the integrity and equity of the system. It would be immoral, for instance, to introduce a new system of consent which limits individual freedom unless the entire framework of transplantation were ready to deal with the increased load and ready to make transparent the changes to existing procedures. In the immediate term, the challenge is to encourage robust public debate and to press for transparency in the present arrangement for distribution of organs, to avoid panic and to hope for a technological advance to emerge from transplant immunology, molecular genetics, xenotransplantation and cloning, which may get us out of an undeniable crisis.

18

Arbitrating "end-of-life" decisions: Issues, processes, and the role of the law

Danuta Mendelson and Michael Ashby

Introduction

Since the early 1990s, there has been a steady flow of legal cases concerning decision-making relating to end-of-life treatment as well as legislation enabling appointment of medical agents, and creation of advance directives.[1] Nevertheless, recourse to the law for resolution of disputes about end-of-life treatment abatement[2] has hitherto been relatively uncommon, especially in countries other than the United States. The majority of these decisions have usually been made by the doctors and health care teams responsible for the care of the patient in question, without external adjudication or arbitration. Medical staff would usually do this in consultation with patients, if they are competent, and, as is more frequently the case, if not, with families; and in the minority of cases where the patient has appointed an agent or made an advance directive (or both), as directed by these instruments.

The trend to seek judicial intervention in end-of-life decisions may be explained by the ethical, religious, social and legal questions posed by the issue of death causation. It has been argued that there are widespread misconceptions amongst health care professionals and the public about what the law requires them to do; doctors often perceive that they are required to treat all patients with curative intent, regardless of the patient's condition and prognosis, or, sometimes even of their wishes. In fact, the balance of evidence from government reports, judgments and parliamentary committee proceedings shows that this is not the case, and, both palliative care and appropriate treatment abatement for dying persons, are broadly supported in law and public policy in many countries.[3]

---

1   Mendelson, D and Jost, TS, "A Comparative Study of the Law of Palliative Care and End-of-Life Treatment" (2003) 31(1) (Spring) *Journal of Law, Medicine & Ethics* 130.

2   This term encompasses both non-initiation and cessation of medical treatment. See Weir, RF, *Abating Treatment with Critically Ill Patients. Ethical and Legal Limits to the Prolongation of Life*, Oxford University Press, New York, 1989.

3   Ashby, M, "Natural causes? Palliative Care and Death Causation in Public Policy and the Law", unpublished MD Thesis, University of Adelaide, 2001; Mendelson D, Jost, TS and Ashby, M, "Legal Aspects of End of Life Treatment in Australia, Canada, the United States, the United Kingdom, Poland, France, Germany, Japan, and the Netherlands" in Dostrovsky, JO, Carr, DB and Koltzenburg, M, (eds) *Proceedings of the 10th World Congress on Pain. Progress in Pain Research & Management*, IASP Press, Seattle, 2003.

Moreover, in increasingly secular societies, which emphasise personal autonomy and rights-based approaches to the conduct of both public and private affairs, parties involved in end-of-life decisions now tend to turn more towards the law for arbitration of disputes, than to religious institutions. Statutory interpretation[4] or public uncertainty about the legality of stopping treatment, in situations where death will almost certainly ensue, have occasionally triggered a need for litigation. However, courts are reluctant to intervene in these essentially clinical decisions. Indeed in *Airedale NHS Trust v Bland*[5], Hoffmann LJ observed that:

> To argue from moral rather than purely legal principles is a somewhat unusual enterprise for a judge to undertake. It is not the function of judges to lay down systems of morals.

In this area of the law, courts are dealing with a profound moral fault-line in societies, between those who believe that human agency cannot be involved, and those who believe that, in certain circumstances, not only may it be, but it ought to be.[6]

A number of recent cases centre on insistence by families on the continuation of life-sustaining treatment in situations of overwhelming organ failure or brain injury, where physicians have advised that it would be preferable to let the dying process proceed without impediment. This reluctance to allow death to occur, despite the absence of any reasonable prospect of recovery due to permanent unconsciousness and/or multi-system failure, and refusal to accept the "futility" of further treatment often results in court challenges.[7] It has been suggested that a broad public health and public policy effort is required to restore some sense of the inevitability of natural death in developed societies, with which many seem to struggle.[8]

Decisions about nutrition and hydration have been the subject of a number of prominent cases. This chapter will review the case law to discern trends and common threads and attempt to identify and address the principal issues at stake. It will focus on issues that arise in cases where patients are incompetent, and life is being sustained by medically administered nutrition and hydration (MAN&H), but neither written instructions exist about their wishes regarding medical care, nor has an agent been appointed.

---

4 *Gardner; Re BWV* [2003] VSC 173. See Ashby, M and Mendelson, D, "*Gardner; Re BWV*: Victorian Supreme Court Makes Landmark Australian Ruling on Tube Feeding" (2004) 181(8) *MJA* 442, <www.mja.com.au/public/issues/181_08_181004/ash10074_fm.html> (accessed 26 March 2006).

5 [1993] AC 789.

6 Quill, TE and Battin, MP (eds), *Physician-Assisted Dying. The Case for Palliative Care and Choice*, The Johns Hopkins Press, Baltimore, 2004.

7 Dyer, O, "Judges Support Doctors' Decision to Stop Treating a Dying Man" (2005) 331 *BMJ* 536.

8 Ashby, M, Kellehear, A and Stoffell, B, "Resolving Conflict in End-of-Life Care" (2005) 183 *MJA* 230.

The authors suggest that greater recourse to justice is the result, at least in part, of a combination of the polarisation of societies on ethical and moral issues, as well as unrealistic expectations of the capacity of modern medicine to cure, heal, and prolong life.

Medically administered nutrition and hydration in the medico-legal context

Popular notions of death without MAN&H as being a cruel form of suffering in which the dying person "starves" to death, need to be dispelled through explanation of the normal process of dying, and the capacity of palliative care to adequately prevent any potential discomfort that may result from decreasing oral intake.

A gradual reduction, and eventual cessation, of oral intake is a normal part of the dying process. Clinical experience shows no basis for supposing that patients receiving palliative care are experiencing symptoms of starvation and dehydration, which would be lessened or eliminated by the routine provision of MAN&H through a nasogastric or percutaneous gastrostomy tube, or by intravenous feeding. Poor appetite and lack of energy are intrinsic effects of the underlying condition, and cannot be overcome by treatment. Inevitably as the disease progresses and death approaches, patients show biochemical and clinical evidence of dehydration, and profound loss of weight, anorexia and lassitude. There is no evidence, however, that correction of dehydration in the terminal phase is beneficial. For example, although assisted nutrition earlier in the cancer journey may improve outcomes and life quality; this is not the case in the later stages.

Consequently in palliative care units, all treatments which are not required for comfort are stopped when a person is dying. Food and drink as well as assistance with eating and drinking is always available to satisfy a patient's thirst and hunger, but MAN&H is not routinely used when oral intake ceases. MAN&H through subcutaneous fluid infusion, is only used for symptomatic thirst or hunger which cannot be adequately treated by other means.

Clinical decisions to abate MAN&H for patients who have reached the final stages of life and have no hope of recovery are made every day in palliative care units, intensive care wards, in general wards of public and private hospitals, private residences and nursing homes. Clearly, however, abatement of artificial sustenance involves sensitive issues, with ethical, cultural, social and religious dimensions that have generated public and health professional concern in many countries over recent years.[9]

In the vast majority of cases, MAN&H is withheld or stopped as part of non-controversial clinical care; however, there are generally three situations where the abatement tends to be considered by courts or tribunals. The first involves doctors

---

9   Cantor, NL "Twenty-Five Years after Quinlan: A Review of the Jurisprudence of Death and Dying" (2001) 29 *Journal of Law, Medicine & Ethics* 182.

and hospitals who are requested by relatives or legal guardians to terminate MAN&H. Since in almost all cases,[10] the result of termination of artificial nutrition and hydration is death, the courts have been asked to declare the abatement lawful. This was the case in the House of Lords' judgment in *Airedale NHS Trust v Bland*[11], and the Supreme Court of United States' decision in *Cruzan v Director, Mo Department of Health*[12]. The Supreme Court of Victoria in *Gardner; Re BWV*[13] and the Guardianship and Administration Tribunal in Queensland in *Re MC*[14] were also requested, essentially on behalf of medical personnel, to consider the lawfulness of the withdrawal of MAN&H under the relevant statutes.

The second reason for curial involvement relates to conflict between relatives and guardians in relation to the abatement of MAN&H. Perhaps the internationally best known example in this category was the case of *Schindler v Schiavo (Re Schiavo)*.[15] The third situation involves a conflict between the relatives or guardians of the patient and the medical personnel; this also happened in *Northridge v Central Sydney Area Health Service*.[16]

The advent of modern life-sustaining technology in the middle of the 20th century raised the legal question of the nature of "effectiveness of treatment" and the legal duty to treat incompetent patients who have no hope of becoming conscious.[17] Generally, doctors do not have a duty to continue ineffective treatment.[18] However, in many instances, the treatment, while ineffective in curing the condition, is effective in prolonging the patient's life. As the Massachusetts Court of Appeals[19] put it in 1978:

> "Prolongation of life" ... does not mean a mere suspension of the act of dying, but contemplates, at the very least, a remission of symptoms enabling a return towards a normal, functioning, integrated existence.

10   In *Rasmussen v Fleming* 154 Ariz 207 at 211; 741 P 2d 674 at 678 (1987), Mildred Rasmussen, at the age of 64 suffered three strokes in 1979. According to medical opinion provided in 1985, at least since 1983 she "existed in a profound vegetative state from which she would never recover", and was fed via nasogastric tube. After commencement of proceedings to authorise the abatement of MAN&H, Rasmussen's physician removed the nasogastric tube, and it transpired that once the nursing staff placed food in her mouth, she was able to swallow it. She died before the court determined that her guardian had the right to refuse MAN&H on her behalf.

11   [1999] AC 789.

12   110 S Ct 2841 (1990).

13   [2003] VSC 173.

14   [2003] QGAAT 13.

15   *Schindler v Schiavo (Re Schiavo)* 780 So 2d 176 at 176; 26 Fla L Weekly D305 (2001); *Bush v Schiavo* 885 So 2d 321 (Fla 2004); *Schiavo ex rel Schindler v Schiavo* No 8:05-CV-530-T-27TBM (MD Fla Mar 22, 2005) (slip opinion), rehearing denied 22 February 2001.

16   [2000] NSWSC 1241.

17   *In re Quinlan* 70 NJ 10, 355 A 2d 647, 665, cert denied, 429 US 922 (1976); *Cruzan v Director, Missouri Department of Health* 497 US 261 (1990); *Vacco v Quill* 521 US 793 (1997); *Washington v Glucksberg* 521 US 702 (1997); *Airedale NHS Trust v Bland* [1993] AC 789; *NHS Trust A v M; NHS Trust B v H* [2001] 1 All ER 801; [2001] 1 FCR 406; [2001] 2 WLR 942; [2001] 2 FLR 367.

18   *Barber v Superior Court* 147 Cal App 3d 1006; 195 Cal Reptr 484 (1983).

19   *Matter of Dinnerstein* 6 Mass App 466; 380 NE2d 134 at 138 (1978).

The chief function of MAN&H is to provide a fixed-term alternative to oral intake of food and water for the purpose of sustaining life and promoting recovery from disease or injury that has led to a temporary inability to do so by normal oral intake. Alternatively it may be used long-term where gut damage is the sole or major problem and such treatment restores a patient to an otherwise acceptable existence. At the same time, hydration and alimentation by means of a feeding tube inserted into the stomach via the nose (nasogastric tube) or stomach (gastrostomy or "PEG") may also for many years sustain the life of patients who have no prospect of ever returning to "a cognitive, sapient state".[20]

Generally, all common law and most civil law jurisdictions presume every adult to have the mental capacity to consent to or to refuse any medical intervention, including life-saving or life-sustaining treatment, unless and until that presumption is rebutted.[21] This means that in relation to competent persons, doctors are under a legal duty to continue life-sustaining measures unless and until the patient refuses further treatment.[22] In cases of severely incompetent (unaware of their environment) or unconscious patients, in the majority of cases both a valid consent to the initial treatment by MAN&H and an express refusal of its continuation, would be lacking.

Thus, in *Cruzan*, at the age of 24, Nancy Cruzan sustained severe injuries in an automobile collision. She was brought to the hospital unconscious, and initially, a feeding tube was inserted in the hope that her condition was reversible. Six years later, though her respiration and circulation were within the normal limits of a 30-year-old female, she was "oblivious to her environment except for reflexive responses to sound and perhaps painful stimuli" and had "no cognitive or reflexive ability to swallow food or water", with her daily essential needs maintained through PEG.[23]

Nancy Cruzan was diagnosed as being in a persistent vegetative state (PVS),[24] suffering:

> [A]noxia of the brain, resulting in a massive enlargement of the ventricles filling with cerebrospinal fluid in the area where the brain has degenerated and [her] cerebral cortical atrophy [was] irreversible, permanent, progressive and ongoing.[25]

---

20 *In re Quinlan* 70 NJ 10, 355 A2d 647 (1976).

21 Mendelson, D, Jost, TS and Ashby, M,, "Comparative Legal and Ethical Aspects of End of Life Treatment in Australia, Canada, the United Kingdom, France, Poland, Germany, the Netherlands, and Japan", in Dostrovsky, JO, Carr, DB and Koltzenburg, M (ed), *Proceedings of the 10th World Congress on Pain, Progress in Pain Research and Management*, IASP Press, Seattle, 2003, p 803. See also *Mental Capacity Act 2005* (UK) c 9, s 1(2).

22 *Airedale NHS Trust v Bland* [1993] AC 789; *Rodriguez v Attorney General of Canada* [1994] 2 LRC 136; *Vacco v Quill* 521 US 793 (1997) and *Washington v Glucksberg* 521 US 702 (1997); *Pretty v United Kingdom* (2002) 35 EHRR 1.

23 *Cruzan v Harmon* 760 SW 2d 408, 411 (Mo 1988).

24 Now known as "post-coma unresponsive state".

25 *Cruzan v Harmon* 760 SW 2d 408, 411 (Mo 1988) (en banc).

Likewise in *Bland*, the 17-year-old Anthony David Bland was one of the victims of the Hillsborough football ground disaster in April 1989. He sustained a severe crushed chest injury which caused catastrophic and irreversible damage to the higher functions of his brain. At the age of 21 he was diagnosed as being in a PVS and his life was supported through PEG.

In *Schiavo*, in 1990 Theresa Schiavo suffered cardiac arrest as a result of a potassium imbalance brought about by bulimia. In 2001, the court found that:

> [O]ver the span of this last decade, Theresa's brain has deteriorated because of the lack of oxygen it suffered at the time of the heart attack. By mid-1996, the CAT scans of her brain showed a severely abnormal structure. At this point [2001], much of her cerebral cortex is simply gone and has been replaced by cerebral spinal fluid. Medicine cannot cure this condition.[26]

Schiavo was fed and hydrated by tubes.

In *BWV*, a 69-year-old woman was a nursing home resident in the advanced stages of dementia, diagnosed clinically as Pick's Disease. Her husband had agreed to the PEG insertion in 1995 when she was still ambulant, but incompetent and unable to communicate with anyone apart from him. She subsequently progressed to a PVS and in 2002 her husband requested that feeding cease.[27]

The case of Mrs MC was very similar. Following a major stroke in 2000, Mrs MC, an 80-year-old nursing home resident with advanced dementia, was described as being in a "state of total incapacity". At this stage, her husband requested that Mrs MC be fed via PEG; however, though unconscious, she was experiencing reflux of food into her mouth and other discomforts.[28]

The case of *Northridge* was different.[29] On 2 March 2000, Mr Thompson at the age of 37 suffered a cardiac arrest as a result of an overdose of heroin, and was unconscious when admitted to hospital. On 7 March 2000, he was diagnosed as having a lung infection, irreversible brain damage, and being in a "chronic vegetative state". This led to the decision by the hospital on 8 March 2000 to discontinue antibiotic treatment and MAN&H, which was contested by Mr Thompson's family.

In each case, the body of the patient could breathe and react in a reflex manner to painful stimuli, but with the exception of Mr Thompson, none had an awareness of their environment, their own existence, sensations or thoughts. The

---

26 780 So 2d 176 at 177; 26 Fla L Weekly D305 (2001).

27 When the general practitioner and the nursing home management expressed concerns about the lawfulness of such an action in Victoria, the husband sought the assistance of the Public Advocate. The Public Advocate, having been appointed Mrs BWV's guardian, sought clarification from the Supreme Court of Victoria on the question of whether under the *Medical Treatment Act 1988* (Vic) feeding and hydration via a PEG tube constituted "medical treatment" (which agents and guardians of incompetent persons can refuse), or "palliative care" (which cannot be lawfully refused guardians and agents acting on behalf of incompetent patients). See Ashby, M and Mendelson D, "Natural Death in 2003: Are We Slipping Backwards?" (2003) 10 *Journal of Law and Medicine* 260.

28 In June 2003, Mrs MC's sons applied to the Queensland Guardianship and Administration Tribunal for consent to the withdrawal of artificial hydration and nutrition via the PEG.

29 See Freckelton, I, "Withdrawal of Life Support" (2004) 11 *Journal of Law and Medicine* 265.

MAN&H kept their bodies alive. To use the words of the Supreme Court of Arizona:

> Medical technology has effectively created a twilight zone of suspended animation where death commences while life, in some form, continues.[30]

Apart from *Northridge,* the cases came before the court when patients' guardians or family sought declaratory judgment to uphold their right to direct medical personnel to terminate artificial hydration and nutrition for the respective patients. In *Northridge,* Mr Thompson's sister, Mrs Northridge, who was appointed as tutor for her brother, obtained a court order to prevent the withdrawal of treatment and life support from the patient.

Decisions relating to withholding or abatement of MAN&H were once fairly straightforward. They are now often viewed as being amongst the most difficult that confront patients and their families, medical and other health personnel as well as the law. At a clinical level, decisions whether to withdraw or withhold life-sustaining treatment, though sometimes predicated by the level of available resources,[31] may be influenced by the individual physician's level of professional experience as well as his or her understanding of the ethics and legality of the proposed course of action.

The major questions relating to withholding or abatement of MAN&H in the legal context have been:

- What constitutes medical treatment in relation to life-sustaining measures?
- What is meant by the concept of "best interests"?
- Is it legally permissible to abate life-sustaining treatment, and if so, who should have the authority to direct it?[32]

This chapter will discuss each of these questions in turn.

What constitutes medical treatment in relation to life-sustaining measures?

Issues involved in the decision to withdraw or withhold life-sustaining treatment at the end-of life lie at the very core of medicine and of medical ethics. One example is the question of whether provision of hydration and nutrition should or should not be considered a medical treatment. In particular, should provision of hydration and nutrition be understood literally, as oral ("natural") intake of solids and liquids, or should it also include medical ("artificial") means of hydration and alimentation through intravenous drips, or insertion of a feeding tube into the stomach via the nose (nasogastric tube) or stomach (gastrostomy or PEG)? The

---

30 *Rasmussen v Fleming* 154 Ariz 207, 211, 741 P2d 674, 678 (1987) (en banc).
31 See *Messiha (by his tutor Magdy Messiha) v South East Health* [2004] NSWSC 1061 at [9].
32 *Barber v Superior Court* 147 Cal App 3d 1006; 195 Cal Reptr 484 (1983).

answer to these questions has legal ramifications in terms of the clinical decision to withhold or withdraw life-sustaining or life-saving treatment from incompetent patients who have no prospects of returning to conscious life on the one hand, and ethical and religious implications on the other.

Medicine and common law do not distinguish between palliative care and other aspects of medical treatment. It is a normal part of the dying process for there to be a gradual reduction and eventual cessation of oral intake. In palliative care units food and drink, and assistance with eating and drinking, is always available to satisfy a patient's thirst and hunger, but medical means are not routinely used when oral intake ceases. Clinical experience shows no basis for believing that patients receiving palliative care are experiencing symptoms of starvation and dehydration, which would be lessened or abolished by the routine provision by medical means of hydration and nutrition.[33] In *Airedale NHS Trust v Bland*, Hoffmann LJ commented that as a general rule it does not matter whether the administration of liquid food through a tube is called "medical treatment, nursing, care or anything else".[34]

The common law seems to accept the position of the Supreme Court of New Jersey in the *Matter of Quinlan*[35] that:

> [T]he focal point of [medical] decision should be the prognosis as to the reasonable possibility of return to cognitive and sapient life, as distinguished from the forced continuance of that biological vegetative existence.

In some jurisdictions, legislation[36] such as the *Medical Treatment Act 1994* (ACT) and the *Medical Treatment Act 1988* (Vic) have created a distinction between "medical treatment"[37] and "palliative care".[38] In Victoria, the *Medical Treatment Act 1988* excludes "palliative care" from the purview of the legislation. Under s 3 of the Act "palliative care" includes: "(a) the provision of reasonable medical procedures for the relief of pain, suffering and discomfort; or (b) the reasonable provision of food and water". In the same provision, "medical treatment" is defined as: (a) the carrying out of an operation; or (b) the administration of a drug or other like substance; or (c) any other medical procedure – but does not include palliative care".

---

33   For a rebuttal of the negative and cruel imagery sometimes used in this debate, and the inappropriateness of applying it to the non-feeding of dying persons, see Ahronheim, JC and Gasner, MR, "The Sloganism of Starvation" (1990) 335 *Lancet* 278.

34   *Airedale NHS Trust v Bland* [1993] AC 789 at 834 per Hoffmann LJ commenting on the judgment of Sir Stephen Brown P in the same case.

35   *In re Quinlan* 70 NJ 10, 355 A 2d 647 at 669 (1976).

36   The relevant statutes enable adults of sound mind to refuse medical treatment and appoint an agent or guardian with the power to refuse medical treatment once they become incompetent.

37   *Medical Treatment Act 1994* (ACT) s 3 defines "medical treatment" as: "(a) the carrying out of an operation; or (b) the administration of a drug; or (c) the carrying out of any other medical procedure".

38   *Medical Treatment Act 1994* (ACT) s 3 defines "palliative care" as: "(a) the provision of reasonable medical and nursing procedures for the relief of pain, suffering and discomfort; and (b) the reasonable provision of food and water".

This means that while competent patients are able to provide instructions concerning palliative treatment (but not refuse it outright), agents and guardians can only refuse medical treatment on behalf of an incompetent patient (they have no statutory powers in relation to palliative care).

In *BWV*, Morris J of the Supreme Court of Victoria interpreted the part of the statutory definition of palliative care relating to "reasonable provision of food and water" as reference to "ordinary feeding by mouth", carried out by the patient or non-medical personnel.[39]

His Honour determined[40] that "the use of a PEG for artificial nutrition and hydration, or for that matter any form of artificial feeding, is a 'medical' procedure" involving "protocols, skills and care which draw from, and depend upon, medical knowledge", and "inevitably require careful choice of and preparation of materials to be introduced into the body, close consideration to dosage rates, measures to prevent infection and regular cleaning of conduits". His Honour found[41] that the administration of artificial nutrition and hydration, via a PEG falls into the category of life-prolonging medical treatment rather than palliative care.[42] A similar conclusion regarding consent to abatement of medically administered nutrition and hydration was reached by the Queensland Guardianship and Administration Tribunal in the case of Mrs MC.[43]

What is meant by the concept of "best interests"

The decision regarding reasonable benefits of life-sustaining treatment "is essentially a medical one to be made at a time and on the basis of facts which will be unique to each case".[44] As a general rule, decisions to discontinue medication or MAN&H, to undertake terminal weaning from ventilation, or withhold cardiopulmonary resuscitation and mechanical ventilation from an incompetent patient, are determined on the basis of "best interests".

The concept of "best interests" has its origins in Hippocratic medicine. In the clinical setting, the patient's best interests will be determined by such objective criteria as the therapeutic efficacy of the proposed treatment, relief from suffering, the degree of bodily invasion required by the procedure, discomforts which may accompany administration of the substances, and the chances of preservation or

---

39 Morris J distinguished between medical procedures to sustain life and palliative case in the sense of measures to manage the dying process "so that it results in as little pain and suffering as possible": at [¶81]. See also Freckelton, I, "Withdrawal of Life Support" (2004) 11 *Journal of Law and Medicine* 265; Rothschild, A, "Gardner; Re BWV: Resolved and Unresolved Issues at End of Life" (2004) 11 *Journal of Law and Medicine* 292.

40 *Gardner; Re BWV* [2003] VSC 173 at [76] per Morris J.

41 Ibid, at [81].

42 Thus, under the *Medical Treatment Act 1988* (Vic), lawfully appointed agents and guardians have the power to refuse MAN&H on behalf Of incompetent patients.

43 Under the *Guardianship and Administration Act 2000*(Qld) s 82(1)(f).

44 *Barber v Superior Court* 147 Cal App 3d 1006; 195 Cal Reptr 484 (1983) per Compton AJ.

restoration of mental competence.[45] In *Barber v Superior Court*,[46] Compton AJ explained the best interests principle in terms of proportionality:

> A rational approach involves the determination of whether the proposed treatment is proportionate or disproportionate in terms of benefits to be gained versus burdens to be caused.
>
> Under this approach, proportionate treatment is that which, in the view of the patient, has at least a reasonable chance of providing benefits to the patient, which benefits outweigh the burdens attendant to the treatment. Thus, even if a proposed course of treatment might be extremely painful or intrusive, it would still be proportionate treatment if the prognosis was for complete cure or significant improvement in the patient's condition. On the other hand, a treatment course which is only minimally painful or intrusive may nonetheless be considered disproportionate to the potential benefits if the prognosis is virtually hopeless for any significant improvement in condition.

The characteristic feature of the best interest principle, common to both law and medicine, is that it focuses exclusively upon the incompetent patient and his or her best interests; other interests – including those of the family, community, and socioeconomic concerns – being subordinate to those of the incompetent person. In law, the best interest standard is the traditional test used by courts to determine whether guardians have acted in a way which would most effectively promote their ward's material interests as well as his or her physical and emotional welfare. In a medical setting, this legal test will also apply to medical personnel caring for an incompetent patient. Thus, in *Northridge v Central Sydney Area Health Service*[47] O'Keefe J stated (at [24]) that the court exercising common law *parens patriae* jurisdiction acts:

> [T]o protect the right of an unconscious person to receive ordinary reasonable and appropriate (as opposed to extraordinary, excessively burdensome, intrusive or futile) medical treatment, sustenance and support. ... The Court also has jurisdiction to prevent the withdrawal of such treatment, support and sustenance where the withdrawal may put in jeopardy the life, good health or welfare of such unconscious individual. What constitutes appropriate medical treatment in a given case is a medical matter in the first instance. However, where there is doubt or serious dispute in this regard the court has the power to act to protect the life and welfare of the unconscious person.[48]

The ethical concept of best interest has been re-interpreted in some countries in terms of personal autonomy that may or may not be in harmony with the religious and ethical beliefs of patients, medical practitioners and the legal system that governs them. Patients' requests prior to losing consciousness that transfusion of blood be withheld, or caesarean section be foregone where their life or the life of a

---

45   Meisel, *The Right to Die*, Wiley Law Publications, New York, 1989, p 266.
46   *Barber v Superior Court* 147 Cal App 3d 1006 at 1019; 195 Cal Reptr 484 at 491 (1983).
47   (2000) 50 NSWLR 549 at [24].
48   *Northridge v Central Sydney Area Health Service* [2000] NSWSC 1241 at [24].

viable foetus is at stake, are the starkest examples of the clash between medical and ethical values with profound legal implications.[49]

In most countries, the legal interpretation of what constitutes the patient's best interest will determine the nature and the scope of the medical duty to treat. In *Bland*, Lord Mustill explained that the provision of MAN&H, which he characterised as an intrusive treatment, to incompetent patients is, by definition, unconsensual. As long as there is hope of recovery, such life-sustaining treatment can be justified on the basis of necessity, for it is in the incompetent patient's best interests to keep him or her alive. However, once it becomes clear that the condition is irreversible, the patient:

> [H]as no further interest in being kept alive, the necessity to do so, created by his inability to make a choice, has gone; and the justification for the invasive care and treatment together with the duty to provide it have also gone. Absent a duty, the omission to perform what had previously been a duty will no longer be a breach of the criminal law.[50]

According to Lord Goff in the same case:

> [I]f the question is asked, as in my opinion it should be, whether it is in his best interests that treatment which has the effect of artificially prolonging his life should be continued, the question can sensibly be answered to the effect that his best interests no longer require that it should be.[51]

Presumably spurred by the euthanasia debate,[52] the British Parliament in the *Mental Capacity Act 2005* (UK) s 4(5) decreed that a decision-maker determining provision or abatement of life-sustaining treatment[53] for a person who lacks capacity "must not, in considering whether the treatment is in the best interests of the person concerned, be motivated by a desire to bring about his death".

The wording of this provision is rather opaque, and it appears to create a difficult distinction between the motive for and the intention of the determination to withhold or withdraw life-sustaining treatment. The implication, however, is that a decision, which is motivated by a desire to bring about the death of an incompetent patient, is incompatible with his or her best interests. As such, it reflects the approach in *Bland*. Conversely, a decision to withhold or withdraw MAN&H in order to "let the nature take its course" may, in appropriate circumstances, fall within the concept of best interests.

---

49 Mendelson D, "Historical Evolution and Modern Implications of the Concepts of Consent to, and Refusal of, Medical Treatment in the Context of the Law of Trespass" (1996) 17 *Journal of Legal Medicine* 1.

50 *Airedale NHS Trust v Bland* [1993] AC 789 at 896–897.

51 Ibid, at 869.

52 Assisted Dying for the Terminally Ill Bill (L) (failed Bill 2003/04 Session).

53 Defined in s 4(10) as: "treatment which in the view of a person providing health care for the person concerned is necessary to sustain life".

Best interests and substitute decision-making

Recasting the principle of best interests in terms of personal autonomy has led to the creation of the "substituted judgment" doctrine. Where the incompetent patient receiving life-sustaining treatment has left no written directives, it is now expected under both common law and under statute, that the person with power to make determination on behalf of such person should do so after considering – if known – the wishes, feelings, beliefs and values of the patient, when he or she was competent.[54] In other words, the substitute decision-maker (the next of kin, legal guardian, donee of enduring powers of attorney, and so on), is required to ask a hypothetical question, namely: what course of action would the patient have chosen in the present circumstances, had he or she been competent? Given that none of us can predict how we would react in a life-and-death situation, and that incompetent persons cannot convey their feelings, thoughts and wishes, the answer to this question is a mere guess. In the absence of a written statement or directive left by the unconscious patient, the accuracy of recollection of his or her supposed feelings, values and wishes is incapable of being tested. The inherent problem with substitute decision-making (or substituted judgment) is that despite the rhetoric of respect for the incompetent patient's personal autonomy, the actual determination is the product of the decision-maker's personal values, biases and interests. Thus Brennan J of the High Court of Australia observed that:

> [I]n the absence of legal rules or a hierarchy of values, the best interests approach depends upon the value system of the decision-maker. Absent any rule or guideline, that approach simply creates an unexaminable discretion in the repository of the power.[55]

The case of *Re Schiavo* can serve as an illustration of divergent values and interests that may underlie decisions relating to abatement of MAN&H.[56] Following Theresa Schiavo's cardiac arrest in 1990, Michael Schiavo sued her doctors in negligence, claiming that they misdiagnosed his wife's condition. In November 1992, he was awarded more than US$700,000 for Theresa's care, as well as US$300,000 in damages for pain and suffering. A "bitter dispute" ensued between Michael and Theresa's parents, the Schindlers, in relation to the money. If his wife died, Michael Schiavo would inherit the fund money under the Florida laws of intestacy.[57]

---

54 See, for example, *Mental Capacity Act 2005* (UK) c 9, s 4(6).

55 *Secretary, Department of Health & Community Services (NT) v JWB and SMB (Marion's Case)* (1992) 175 CLR 218 at 271 (Brennan J in dissent). The case involved a question of who has the power to determine whether a severely intellectually impaired minor should undergo a non-therapeutic sterilisation procedure.

56 See Mendelson, D and Ashby, M, "The Medical Provision of Hydration and Nutrition: Two Very Different Outcomes in Victoria and Florida" (2004) 11 *Journal of Law and Medicine* 282.

57 The Court of Appeals stated: "When a living will or other advance directive does not exist, the fact that a surrogate decision-maker may ultimately inherit from the patient should not automatically compel the appointment of a guardian; on the other hand there may be occasions when an inheritance could be a reason to question a surrogate's ability to make an objective decision": *Schindler v Schiavo (Re Schiavo)* 780 So 2d 176 (2001) at 178; review denied, 789 So 2d 348 (Fla 2001).

However, if he divorced Theresa (or was replaced as her guardian), the fund remaining at the end of Theresa's life would presumably go to the Schindler family.[58] In July 1993, the Schindlers unsuccessfully petitioned to have Michael Schiavo removed as Theresa's guardian.[59] One of the arguments involved their opposition to Michael's desire that MAN&H be withdrawn from Theresa.

Since Theresa did not execute a document expressing her wishes in case of incompetence, under Florida law, Michael Schiavo, as her husband and legal guardian became the surrogate decision-maker.[60] In 1998, Michael Schiavo invoked the Guardianship Court's jurisdiction to serve as the surrogate decision-maker on the question of whether artificial sustenance should be withdrawn from Theresa.[61] He argued that while competent, Theresa indicated a wish not to be kept alive through medical life-prolonging measures. The Schindlers, inter alia, claimed that as a devout Catholic Theresa would not have contemplated abatement of MAN&H. The Florida Guardianship Court accepted her husband's evidence regarding Theresa's wishes,[62] and ordered that bio-medical life-prolonging measures be removed. The Schindlers appealed, and the case eventually went through a number of guardianship and federal courts, and spawned legislation in Florida and the United States Congress.[63]

In Re Schiavo, both Michael Schiavo and the Schindlers professed to act in Theresa's best interests while advocating diametrically opposite courses of action. The documented background of financial wrangles and mutual hatred, and of obsessive parental love on the one hand and frustration at a life suspended in limbo on the other provides an insight into the complexity of factors and unarticulated personal considerations that influence the judgment of substitute decision-makers.

---

58 *Schindler v Schiavo (Re Schiavo)* 780 So 2d 176 (2001) at 178; review denied, 789 So 2d 348 (Fla 2001).

59 In the absence of a husband, the Schindlers, as Theresa's parents, would have been able to act as guardians and thus make a surrogate decision for their daughter: Fla Stat §765.401 (2000).

60 Fla Stat §765.401 (2000): where "an incapacitated patient … has not executed an advance directive, or designated a surrogate to execute an advance directive …, health care decisions may be made for the patient by … (a) the court appointed guardian; (b) the patient's spouse".

61 Fla Stat §765.101(10) defines a "life-prolonging procedure" as "any medical procedure, treatment, or intervention, including artificially provided sustenance and hydration, which sustains, restores, or supplants a spontaneous vital function. The term does not include the administration of medication or performance of medical procedure, when such medication or procedure is deemed necessary to provide comfort care or to alleviate pain". *Schindler v Schiavo (Re Schiavo)* 780 So 2d 176 (2001) at 178.

62 In the United States, there exists a constitutionally protected right of privacy, which encompasses the right to choose or refuse life-prolonging procedures. The right to privacy is not lost or diminished by the patient's later physical or mental incapacity (Florida *Constitution*, Art I, s 23). Florida courts have affirmed this right in *Re Guardianship of Browning* 568 So 2d 4 (1990).

63 In *Re Guardianship of Schiavo*, 800 So 2d 640 (Fla 2d Dist Ct App 2001); *Bush v Schiavo*, 885 So2d 321 (Fla 2004); *Schiavo ex rel Schindler v Schiavo*, No 8:05-CV-530-T-27TBM (MD Fla Mar 22, 2005) (slip opinion); President's statement on Terri Schiavo, 17 March 2005, <www.whitehouse.gov/news/releases/2005/03/20050317-7.html> (accessed 22 March 2005).

Who should decide the appropriateness of MAN&H?

In *Bland*, Lord Mustill declared that a decision on best interests is "ethical, not medical, and that there is no reason in logic why on such a decision the opinions of doctors should be decisive".[64] Depending on the jurisdiction, the power to direct withdrawal of MAN&H can be made by medical personnel, relatives, guardians or courts.[65]

It is arguable, however, that a determination made by an outside judicial tribunal, or an appointed guardian guided by objective criteria of the best interests of the incompetent person, is less open to abuse or subjective bias than a decision of persons who are intimately involved with the mentally incompetent patient, be it family or medical personnel. For, as the case of *Northridge* illustrates, doctors do sometimes make hasty diagnosis and treatment decisions. Made within five days of admission, a diagnosis of "chronic vegetative state" was clearly questionable, and the decision to discontinue antibiotic treatment and withdraw MAN&H was inappropriate in the circumstances as there had been inadequate time for this state to be firmly diagnosed. Following the diagnosis, the patient was transferred from intensive care to the transplant ward. The transfer was, as the court found, prompted by pressure on beds in a public hospital, but it gave an impression that the hospital had an ulterior motive in ordering the withdrawal of treatment. The timing of the decision to withdraw life-sustaining treatment would invariably depend on the patient's medical condition.

More recently, principles governing withdrawal of life-sustaining treatment were discussed in the case of *Messiha (by his tutor Magdy Messiha) v South East Health*,[66] in which Howie J of the Supreme Court of New South Wales refused the application brought by Mr Messiha's family that the court restrain the hospital staff from withdrawing artificial ventilation and MAN&H from him. Mr Messiha, aged 75 years, had a severe lung disease and a history of cardiac arrests. On 17 October 2004, he suffered an asystolic cardiac arrest whereby his heart had completely stopped beating depriving his body, including his brain, of the supply of oxygen for at least 25 minutes. As a result, he was unconscious and in a deep coma (an EEG scan taken of the patient's brain suggested there was no cortical activity).[67] His family claimed that: "they have observed purposive eye movements by the patient in recognition of those speaking to him and what was said".[68] However, Howie J found[69] that these claims were "inconsistent with the medical findings and tests conducted by hospital staff" and by Professor Lance, a neurologist not attached to the hospital, who conducted an examination of the

---

64 *Airedale NHS Trust v Bland* [1993] AC 789 at 897.
65 The *Mental Capacity Act 2005* (UK) Pt II establishes Pt 2: the Court of Protection and the office of Public Guardian.
66 [2004] NSWSC 1061.
67 Ibid, at [11].
68 Ibid, at [12].
69 Ibid, at [14].

patient on 27 October 2004 in the presence and at the request of members of the patient's family.[70]

Howie J acknowledged[71] that applications relating to life-prolonging medical treatments (be it MAN&H or artificial ventilation), "give rise to difficult moral and ethical questions upon which there can be very different views within both the medical profession and the general public". When such controversies arise, the court's jurisdiction may be invoked to determine the issue of abatement; and according to Howie J (drawing on O'Keefe J's judgment in *Northridge*), where the court "is concerned with the best interest of the health and welfare of the patient ... it is not bound to give effect to the medical opinion, even where ... it is unanimous".[72] His Honour, however, added that:

> [I]t would be an unusual case where the Court would act against what is unanimously held by medical experts as an appropriate treatment regime for the patient in order to preserve the life of a terminally ill patient in a deep coma where there is no real prospect of recovery to any significant degree. This is not to make any value judgment of the life of the patient in his present situation or to disregard the wishes of the family and the beliefs that they genuinely hold for his recovery. But it is simply an acceptance of the fact that the treatment of the patient, where ... the Court is satisfied that decision as to the appropriate treatment is being made in the welfare and interest of the patient, is principally a matter for the expertise of professional medical practitioners.[73]

Howie J concluded[74] that in the case at hand, the court's jurisdiction was not:

> [E]nlivened by the evidence ... from the family members. The Court is in no better position to make a determination of future treatment than are those who are principally under the duty to make such a decision. The withdrawal of treatment may put his [Mr Messiha's] life in jeopardy but only to the extent of bringing forward what I believe to be the inevitable in the short term. I am not satisfied that the withdrawal of his present treatment is not in the patient's best interest and welfare.

The examination of the case-law suggests that the courts are reluctant to arbitrate "end-of-life" decisions. Judges place great emphasis on objective evidence (signs and symptoms of the patient as documented by medical tests and expert testimony) before applying the best interest test to determine whether the court's jurisdiction should be invoked to resolve a conflict relating to abatement of life-sustaining treatment for patients whose life is nearing its last stage.

---

70 Ibid, at [28]. Howie J found that the treatment, which the Messiha family wished to prolong was futile in the sense that it could only extend "the patient's life for some relatively brief period", burdensome and potentially intrusive.

71 Ibid, at [24].

72 Ibid, at [25].

73 Ibid, at [24] where Howie J referred to *Northridge* [2000] NSWSC 1241.

74 Ibid, at [28].

Concluding remarks

There is a steady flow of cases coming before courts for arbitration on treatment that will determine the timing and mode of death for incompetent persons. Due to its emotive overtones, MAN&H tends to be the treatment in dispute. It is clear that there is ongoing international unease concerning this issue. "Right to life" activists and certain religious leaders are keen to see that abatement rarely if ever occur. However, it is essential for the dignity and comfort of persons that the inevitability of death be acknowledged, and appropriate and timely palliative care be deployed accordingly. Medicine and the law is being confronted, on the one hand, by those who insist that life-prolonging treatment be continued nearly always, and, on the other, by public pressure for the legalisation of euthanasia. Both law and medicine also have to contend with claims and requests that amount to a total misunderstanding of the capacity of modern medicine to cure and heal, and disregard the rights of the dying person to comfort and dignity. These requests are often based on the expectations and perceived entitlements of patients and families. Without laying "down systems of morals", the courts can, nevertheless, have a vital role in shaping the ethical debates about medical care and decision-making at the end of life. Courts have a duty to ensure that the rights and entitlements of individuals, indeed their lives, are protected, but together with medicine, it is also essential that the reality of death and the dying process are not forgotten. This can best be achieved by understanding the reality of death, and the dying process when determining the difficult balance of contradictory ethical, medical and legal principles that are inherent in abatement on MAN&H from incompetent patients in their final stages of life.

PART VIII

LITIGATION AND LIABILITY

19

Life after the Ipp reforms: Medical negligence law

Belinda Bennett and Ian Freckelton[1]

In 2002 the Australian Federal Government appointed a Panel of Eminent Persons to review the country's laws of negligence.[2] The terms of reference for the Review indicated that:

> The award of damages for personal injury has become unaffordable and unsustainable as the principle source of compensation for those injured through the fault of another. It is desirable to examine a method for the reform of the common law with the objective of limiting liability and quantum of damages arising from personal injury and death.[3]

The recommendations of what became known as the Ipp Committee played a key role in shaping the statutory reforms to tort law that have since been enacted in most States and Territories. While these reforms are of significance for tort law generally, many reforms have been particularly relevant to medical negligence actions, including the introduction of a modified form of the *Bolam* test; changes to the laws relating to causation; restrictions on recovery for psychiatric harm; limits on damages for personal injury; changes to compensability for wrongful birth;[4] and statutory recognition of apologies and expressions of regret.

Many of the changes are subtle and not all of the statutory amendments are nationally consistent. We chart the changes to the common law which have particular relevance to medical negligence litigation. Ultimately, we argue that the capacity for injured plaintiffs to sue their doctors and health care facilities has become more limited as a result of the statutory reforms.

---

1   The authors acknowledge with gratitude the helpful suggestions and comments of David Hirsch.

2   Panel of Eminent Persons to Review the Law of Negligence (the Ipp Committee), *Review of the Law of Negligence*, Second Report, Canberra, October 2002, <http://revofneg.treasury.gov.au/content/review2.asp> (accessed April 2006). For a discussion of the review see Cane, P, "Reforming Tort Law in Australia: A Personal Perspective" (2003) 27 *Melbourne University Law Review* 649; McDonald, B, "Legislative Intervention in the Law of Negligence: The Common Law, Statutory Interpretation and Tort Reform in Australia" (2005) 27 *Sydney Law Review* 443.

3   Ipp Committee, op cit, para 1.3.

4   See Chapter 21: "Judicial activism or 'traditional' negligence law".

Determining the standard of care: The *Bolam* test

The question of whether a doctor has breached his or her duty of care to a patient is determined by reference to the standard of care. In the 1957 United Kingdom case of *Bolam v Friern Hospital Management Committee*[5] it was held that the standard of care was determined by professional practices. As Lord Scarman noted in the case of *Sidaway v Governors of Bethlem Royal Hospital*:[6]

> The *Bolam* principle may be formulated as a rule that a doctor is not negligent if he acts in accordance with a practice accepted at the time as proper by a responsible body of medical opinion even though other doctors adopt a different practice. In short, the law imposes the duty of care: but the standard of care is a matter of medical judgment.

The *Bolam* test was moderated to some extent by the House of Lords in 1997 in *Bolitho v City and Hackney Health Authority*[7] where it was held that:

> [I]n cases of diagnosis and treatment there are cases where, despite a body of professional opinion sanctioning the defendant's conduct, the defendant can properly be held liable for negligence. ... In my judgment that is because, in some cases, it cannot be demonstrated to the judge's satisfaction that the body of opinion relied upon is reasonable or responsible.[8]

The High Court of Australia's decision of *Rogers v Whitaker*[9] marked an historically important rejection of the *Bolam* principle for Australian medical negligence law. In the context of a woman particularly anxious about the possible results of an operation upon her eye, the court rejected the United Kingdom *Bolam* test and in its place changed the yardstick for assessment of breach of the duty of care by health professionals. Substantially following North American authorities, it focused upon the needs of patients for information, rather than the practices and attitudes of the preponderance of health practitioners. The decision was in the context of the absence of advice to a patient who was blind in one eye about the risk of succumbing to a rare risk (1:14,000) of ophthalmic surgery (sympathetic ophthalmia), which could affect the patient's vision in the eye that had not been operated on. The patient had expressed anxiety about risks to her vision. Many surgeons at the time would not have warned of the risk of sympathetic ophthalmia.

The High Court held that the law imposes on a medical practitioner a duty to exercise reasonable care and skill in the provision of both professional advice and treatment. It classified the duty as a "single comprehensive duty covering all the ways in which a doctor is called upon to exercise his skill and judgment" and

---

5   [1957] 1 WLR 582.

6   [1985] AC 871 at 881, cited in *Rogers v Whitaker* (1992) 175 CLR 479 at 484.

7   [1997] UKHL 46; [1998] AC 232; [1997] 4 All ER 471; [1997] 3 WLR 1151.

8   [1998] AC 232 at 243.

9   (1992) 175 CLR 479.

held that the duty covered the examination, diagnosis and treatment of the patient, as well as the provision of information.[10] In *Rogers v Whitaker* the High Court rejected the application of the *Bolam* test. It drew a distinction between diagnosis and treatment where "the patient's contribution is limited to the narration of symptoms and relevant history; the medical practitioner provides diagnosis and treatment according to his or her level of skill" and the provision of information or advice where "except in cases of emergency or necessity, all medical treatment is preceded by the patient's choice to undergo it".[11] This distinction between diagnosis or treatment and the provision of information or advice is significant. While the court accepted that the question of "*Whether* a medical practitioner carries out a particular form of treatment in accordance with the appropriate standard of care is a question in the resolution of which responsible professional opinion will have an influential, often a decisive, role to play", the question of whether a patient had received all the information relevant to making a decision about a particular form of treatment was a question which did not generally depend on professional standards or practices.[12]

Importantly, the decision of whether the required standard of care had been met was a matter for the court, rather than professional practices, to determine. This is so regardless of whether the case concerns diagnosis, treatment or advice. This position was reinforced by Gleeson CJ in *Rosenberg v Percival*:

> In many cases, professional practice and opinion will be the primary, and in some cases it may be the only, basis upon which a court may reasonably act. But, in an action brought by a patient, the responsibility for deciding the content of the doctor's duty of care rests with the court, not with his or her professional colleagues.[13]

The Ipp Committee analysed the decisions in *Bolam, Bolitho* and a variety of other cases.[14] It concluded that:

> [T]he *Bolam* rule, when strictly applied, can give rise to results that would be unacceptable to the community. They show the main weakness of the *Bolam* rule to be that it allows small pockets of medical opinion to be arbiters of the requisite standard of medical treatment, even in instances where a substantial majority of medical opinion would take a different view. It is well-established that in many aspects of medical practice, different views will be held by bodies of practitioners of varying size and in different locations. This can result in the development of localised practices that are not regarded with approval widely throughout the profession. Thus, the *Bolam* rule is not a reliable guide to acceptable medical practice.[15]

---

10   Ibid, at 483. See, too, *Gover v South Australia* (1985) 39 SASR 543 at 551.
11   (1992) 175 CLR 479 at 489.
12   Ibid, at 489.
13   [2001] HCA 18 at [7]; 205 CLR 434 at 439.
14   In particular, also *Hucks v Cole* [1993] 4 Med LR 393.
15   Ipp Committee (2002) op cit, para 3.11.

The committee recommended implementation of the *Bolitho* approach and regarded it as giving medical practitioners:

> [A]s much protection as is desirable in the public interest, because the chance that an opinion which was widely held by a significant number of respected practitioners in the relevant field would be held irrational is very small indeed. But, if the expert opinion in the defendant's favour were held to be irrational, it seems right ... that the defendant should not be allowed to rely on it.[16]

It contended that the approach contained a series of advantages:

> [It] contains sufficient safeguards to satisfy the reasonable requirements of patients, medical practitioners and the wider community. It is hoped that the test will address the sense of confusion, and the perception of erratic decision-making, which (the Panel has been told) have contributed to the difficulty that medical practitioners face in obtaining reasonably priced indemnity cover and which have, in consequence, harmed the broader community.
>
> The recommended rule recognises, first, that there might be more than one opinion widely held by a significant number of respected practitioners in the field. It provides a defence for any medical practitioner whose treatment is supported by any such an opinion, provided the court does not consider it irrational. It would not be for the court to adjudicate between the opinions.
>
> Because there may be more than one opinion that meets the description in the recommended rule, it protects the practitioner who is at the cutting edge of medical practice provided that the procedure followed was in accordance with an opinion that meets that description.
>
> The "irrational treatment" proviso enables the community, through the court, to exercise control over the very exceptional cases where even the modified *Bolam* test does not provide adequate safeguards.[17]

As a result of the tort reforms that have been enacted in most parts of Australia, a modified form of the *Bolam* test has been introduced in some jurisdictions,[18] as recommended by the Ipp Committee. However, the situation is not uniform with Western Australia, the Australian Capital Territory and the Northern Territory being exceptions. In New South Wales s 50 of the *Civil Liability Act 2002* provides that:

> (1) A person practising a profession ("a professional") does not incur a liability in negligence arising from the provision of a professional service if it is established that the professional acted in a manner that (at the time the service was provided) was widely accepted in Australia by peer professional opinion as competent professional practice.
>
> (2) However, peer professional opinion cannot be relied on for the purposes of this section if the court considers that the opinion is irrational.

---

16   Ibid, para 3.18.
17   Ibid, paras 3.21–3.24.
18   *Civil Liability Act 2002* (NSW) s 50; *Civil Liability Act 2003* (Qld) s 22; *Civil Liability Act 1936* (SA) s 41; *Civil Liability Act 2002* (Tas) s 22; *Wrongs Act 1958* (Vic) s 59.

(3) The fact that there are differing peer professional opinions widely accepted in Australia concerning a matter does not prevent any one or more (or all) of those opinions being relied on for the purposes of this section.

(4) Peer professional opinion does not have to be universally accepted to be considered widely accepted.

In Victoria the equivalent provision in s 59 of the *Wrongs Act 1958* is expressed in similar terms but uses the term "unreasonable" instead of "irrational". Although s 50 of the NSW Act clearly introduces a modified form of the *Bolam* principle, this test does not apply to the duty to advise of risks of treatment. Section 5P of the Act expressly exempts the new provisions from "liability arising in connection with the giving of (or the failure to give) a warning, advice or other information in respect of the risk of death of or injury to a person associated with the provision by a professional of a professional service". Similar provisions exist in other States.[19]

These provisions clearly draw a distinction then between diagnosis and treatment, to which the statutory form of the *Bolam* test will apply, and the provision of information about risks of treatment, to which the statutory form of the *Bolam* test will not apply. What constitutes "widely accepted" practice in Australia will be a question of fact in each case – the delineation between eccentric forms of practice and respectable minorities of practice that can be said to be "widely accepted" will not always be easily identified.

Following the recommendation of the Ipp Committee,[20] the statutory reforms in some States also restate the law in relation to the standard of skill required of a professional. Section 58 of the *Wrongs Act 1958* (Vic) for example, provides that in an allegation of negligence against a person holding himself or herself out as possessing a particular skill:

> [T]he standard to be applied by a court in determining whether the defendant acted with due care is ... to be determined by reference to (a) what could reasonably be expected of a person possessing that skill; and (b) the relevant circumstances as at the date of the alleged negligence and not a later date.

A similar provision exists in South Australia,[21] while s 42 of the *Civil Law (Wrongs) Act 2002* (ACT) is not limited to those holding themselves out as having special skill and simply states that:

> For deciding whether a person (the defendant) was negligent, the standard of care required of the defendant is that of a reasonable person in the defendant's position who was in possession of all the information that the defendant either had, or ought reasonably to have had, at the time of the incident out of which the harm arose.

---

19   *Civil Liability Act 2003* (Qld) s 22(5); *Civil Liability Act 1936* (SA) s 41(5); *Civil Liability Act 2002* (Tas) s 22(5); *Wrongs Act 1958* (Vic) s 60.

20   Ipp Committee (2002) op cit, paras 3.32–3.34.

21   *Civil Liability Act 1936* (SA) s 40.

Duty to advise of material risks:
The common law

In *Rogers v Whitaker* the High Court defined "material risks" as follows:

[A] risk is material if, in the circumstances of the particular case, a reasonable person in the patient's position, if warned of the risk, would be likely to attach significance to it or if the medical practitioner is or should reasonably be aware that the particular patient, if warned of the risk, would be likely to attach significance to it.[22]

It expressed this responsibility to be subject to the doctrine of therapeutic privilege under which in certain limited circumstances doctors remain free to withhold information from patients on the basis of the significant counter-therapeutic effects that provision of the information would be likely to have.[23] The High Court agreed that the factors discussed in *F v R*[24] by King CJ needed to be taken into account by a doctor in deciding whether to tell a patient of a treatment-related risk.

These factors were: the nature of the matter to be disclosed; the patient's desire for information; the patient's health and temperament; and the general surrounding circumstances.[25]

Just under a decade after its decision in *Rogers v Whitaker*, the High Court in *Rosenberg v Percival*[26] was urged to reconsider its "material risks" test in light of the many criticisms that had been made of its ruling in *Rogers v Whitaker*.[27] It declined to do so, this time in the context of a dental negligence complaint in respect of a failure by a dentist to warn a patient of potential temporomandibular complications from an osteotomy procedure. The court emphatically endorsed its previous approach. Kirby J wrote the most extensive judgment. He held that reasons of both principle and policy supported the stringency of the *Rogers v Whitaker* approach:

[T]he rule is a recognition of individual autonomy that is to be viewed in the wider context of an emerging appreciation of basic human rights and human dignity. There is no reason to diminish the law's insistence, to the greatest extent possible, upon prior, informed agreement to invasive treatment, save for that which is required in an emergency or otherwise out of necessity.[28]

---

22   (1992) 175 CLR 479 at 490 per Mason CJ, Brennan, Dawson, Toohey, and McHugh JJ.
23   See generally Mulheron, L, "The Defence of Therapeutic Privilege in Australia" (2003) 11 *Journal of Law and Medicine* 201.
24   (1983) 33 SASR 189.
25   (1992) 175 CLR 479 at 488, 490.
26   [2001] HCA 18; 205 CLR 434.
27   For discussion of these arguments see Kirby J's judgment in *Rosenberg v Percival* [2001] HCA 18 at [143]; 205 CLR 434 at 478-79.
28   Ibid, at [145]; at 480.

He held that minimum legal obligations should be imposed "so that even those providers who are in a hurry, or who may have comparatively less skill or inclination for communication, are obliged to pause and provide warnings of the kind that *Rogers* mandates".[29]

He observed that the collateral advantages of such an approach include "redressing, to some small degree, the risks of conflicts of interest and duty which a provider may sometimes face in favouring one health care procedure over another" and may assist in redressing the "inherent inequality in power between the professional provider and a vulnerable patient".[30]

In *Rosenberg v Percival* Gummow J noted that the factors relevant to disclosure of treatment-related risks discussed by King CJ in *F v R*[31] are an adaptation of the calculus of negligence set out in *Wyong Shire Council v Shirt*[32] which weighs the magnitude of the risk and the probability of its occurrence against the expense, difficulty and inconvenience of avoiding the harm and any other conflicting duties owed by the defendant.[33]

In a case involving a doctor's failure to advise a patient of risks associated with treatment, the severity of the potential injury and the likelihood of it occurring are of significance. As Gummow J noted:

> A slight risk of serious harm might satisfy the test, while a greater risk of a small harm might not. It is also important to note that, in considering the severity of the potential injury, that severity is judged with reference to the plaintiff's position. ... The patient's need for the operation is important, as is the existence of reasonably available and satisfactory alternative treatments. A patient may be more likely to attach significance to a risk if the procedure is elective rather than life saving.[34]

Following the Ipp Committee's recommendation that the calculus of negligence be set out in legislation,[35] most Australian jurisdictions have now introduced a statutory form of the calculus of negligence.[36]

The risks that a patient must be warned of are not confined to common risks. A patient should be advised of all risks unless they are "'immaterial', in the sense of being unimportant or so rare that they can be safely ignored".[37] Some writers have suggested that a doctor's duty to advise a patient of alternative treatments

---

29 Ibid, at [145]; at 480.

30 Ibid, at [145]; at 480.

31 (1983) 33 SASR 189 at 196, 200, 202, 205.

32 (1980) 146 CLR 40 at 47–48.

33 [2001] HCA 18 at [76]; 205 CLR 434 at 458, per Gummow J.

34 Ibid, at [77]–[78]; at 458-59.

35 Ipp Committee (2002) op cit, para 7.17.

36 *Civil Liability Act 2002* (NSW) ss 5B, 5C; *Civil Liability Act 2003* (Qld) ss 9, 10; *Civil Liability Act 1936* (SA) s 32; *Civil Liability Act 2002* (Tas) s 11; *Wrongs Act 1958* (Vic) ss 48, 49; *Civil Liability Act 2002* (WA) s 5B; *Civil Law (Wrongs) Act 2002* (ACT) ss 43, 44.

37 *Rosenberg v Percival* [2001] HCA 18 at [149]; (2001) 205 CLR 434 at 482, per Kirby J.

may extend to discussion of alternative and complementary medicine[38] although to date there is no clear Australian authority on this.[39]

It is important to note that the test for "material risks" laid down by the High Court in *Rogers v Whitaker* contains both an objective limb and a subjective limb. The first part of the test is the objective limb, and uses the language of reasonableness that is familiar from tort law. In this limb a doctor has a duty to tell his or her patient of those risks that "a reasonable person in the patient's position ... would be likely to attach significance to". The second limb of the test is more subjective, although not totally so. This limb of the test focuses on the "particular patient" rather than the reasonable patient. This limb "recognises that the particular patient may not be a 'reasonable' one; he or she may have a number of 'unreasonable' fears or concerns".[40] It indicates that a doctor should advise his or her patient of risks of proposed treatment if the doctor knows or should know that this patient would be likely to attach significance to the risk. It is important to realise that the subjective nature of the focus on the particular patient is qualified somewhat by the words "if the medical practitioner is or should reasonably be aware". Without these words, the second limb would be a purely subjective one. The addition of these words ensures that there must be something more than the subjective views of the patient in order to satisfy the test of materiality. This need for "something more" may be satisfied for example, by an inquiry by the patient about the risks associated with the proposed procedure, or the patient's medical history may mean that the patient has a greater chance of the risk eventuating.[41] It is of course important to note that the test for causation in Australia is subjective, regardless of which limb of the test for material risks is relevant to a particular action.

The evolving position in the United Kingdom was pushed to the next step by the House of Lords in the specific context of failure to warn of risks in *Chester v Afshar*.[42] A surgeon had operated on a patient's back and did not warn her of the small (1–2 per cent) but unavoidable risk that the operation might have a seriously adverse result, known as cauda equina syndrome. This is what ensued for the patient, although it was in no way the result of procedural negligence by the surgeon. The patient sued for negligence, alleging not that she would never have had the operation if she had been given advice about the risks but that she would

---

38 Brophy, E, "Does a Doctor Have a Duty to Provide Information and Advice About Complementary and Alternative Medicine?" (2003) 10 *Journal of Law and Medicine* 271; Weir, M, "Obligation to Advise of Options for Treatment: Medical Doctors and Complementary and Alternative Medicine Practitioners" (2003) 10 *Journal of Law and Medicine* 296. For discussion of the duty to advise of alternative and complementary medicine see Skene, L, *Law and Medical Practice: Rights, Duties, Claims & Defences*, 2nd edn LexisNexis Butterworths, 2004, pp 187–188.

39 Skene (2004) op cit, p 188.

40 *Rosenberg v Percival* [2001] HCA 18 at [79]; 205 CLR 434 at 459, per Gummow J.

41 Addison, T, "Negligent Failure to Inform: Developments in the Law Since *Rogers v Whitaker*" (2003) 11 *Torts Law Journal* 165 at 181.

42 [2004] UKHL 41; [2005] 1 AC 134.

not have consented to the surgery on the day and would have consulted with others about whether to submit to the surgery.

The case divided the House of Lords three to two. At first instance the trial judge found the surgeon liable in damages and the Court of Appeal[43] upheld the decision. The House of Lords by a bare majority dismissed the appeal and maintained the trial judge's decision holding the surgeon responsible. In doing so all members emphasised the contemporary significance of warnings about risk. Many of the statements by the Law Lords are indicative of an increasing international convergence of judicial (and community views) about patient entitlements. It is significant too that much of the rhetoric from the Law Lords was in terms of patient "rights" and that they expressed themselves in unequivocal language.

Lord Bingham, for instance, stressed that the obligation of the surgeon to advise the patient of the risks of cauda equina syndrome "is not in doubt. Nor is its rationale: to enable adult patients of sound mind to make for themselves decisions intimately affecting their own lives and bodies".[44] Lord Steyn was more expansive, holding that what he termed "the correlative rights and duties of the patient and surgeon must be kept in mind".[45] Echoing Cardozo J's dicta in the early 20th century case *Schloendorff v Society of New York Hospital*[46] Lord Steyn stated:

> The starting point is that every individual of adult years and sound mind has a right to decide what may or may not be done with his or her body. Individuals have a right to make important medical decisions affecting their lives for themselves: they have the right to make decisions which doctors regard as ill advised. Surgery performed without the informed consent of the patient is unlawful.[47]

He emphasised that a "surgeon owes a legal duty to a patient to warn him or her in general terms of possible serious risks involved in the procedure", the only exception being where it would be contrary to the best interests of the patient.[48] He commented:

> In modern law medical paternalism no longer rules and a patient has a prima facie right to be informed by a surgeon of a small, but well established, risk of serious injury as a result of surgery.[49]

By way of rationale, Lord Steyn indicated that:

> [A] rule requiring a doctor to abstain from performing an operation without the informed consent of a patient serves two purposes: it tends to avoid the

---

43   *Chester v Afshar* [2002] EWCA Civ 724; [2003] QB 356.
44   [2004] UKHL 41 at [5]; [2005] 1 AC 134 at 140.
45   Ibid, at [14]; at 143.
46   211 NY 125 (1914).
47   [2004] UKHL 41 at [14]; [2005] 1 AC 134 at 143.
48   Ibid, at [16]; at 143.
49   Ibid, at [16]; at 143.

occurrence of the particular physical injury the risk of which a patient is not prepared to accept. It also ensures that due respect is given to the autonomy and dignity of each patient.[50]

Lord Hope observed that the duty of the surgeon was owed to the patient "so that she could make her own decision as to whether or not she should undergo the particular course of surgery" which the surgeon was proposing.[51] He noted that the patient had three possibilities:

> She might have agreed to go ahead with the operation despite the risks. Or she might have decided then and there not to have the operation then or at any time in the future. Or she might have decided not to have the operation then but to think the matter over and take further advice, leaving the possibility of having the operation open for the time being. The choice between these alternatives was for her to take, and for her alone. The function of the law is to protect the patient's right to choose.[52]

Statutory reform of the duty to warn of risks

Under the Ipp Committee-inspired statutory reforms a person does not owe a duty to another person to warn that person of an obvious risk.[53] The obviousness of a risk is also potentially relevant to determining the scope of a duty of care or a breach of duty.[54] For health professionals it will be important to realise the limits of the provisions. For example, although s 5H of the *Civil Liability Act 2002* (NSW) provides that there is no duty to warn of an obvious risk, the section expressly states that it does not apply if the plaintiff has asked the defendant for information about the risk, if the defendant is required by written law to warn the plaintiff of the risk or if the "defendant is a professional and the risk is a risk of the death or of personal injury to the plaintiff from the provision of a professional service by the defendant".[55] Similar provisions exist in South Australia and Tasmania.[56] Although s 5H states that it does not create a presumption of a duty to warn of an obvious risk,[57] it does mean that health professionals will not be able to rely on this provision as a defence in an action in which a patient alleges that there was a failure to warn of a risk of harm (which could be classed as an obvious risk) in proposed treatment.

---

50 Ibid, at [18]; at 144.

51 Ibid, at [55]; at 153.

52 Ibid, at [56]; at 153.

53 See, for example, *Civil Liability Act 2002* (NSW) s 5H(1); *Civil Liability Act 2003* (Qld) s 15; *Civil Liability Act 1936* (SA) s 38; *Civil Liability Act 2002* (Tas) s 17; *Wrongs Act 1958* (Vic) s 53; *Civil Liability Act 2002* (WA) s 50.

54 McDonald, op cit, at 469.

55 *Civil Liability Act 2002* (NSW) s 5H(2)(c)

56 *Civil Liability Act 1936* (SA) s 38; *Civil Liability Act 2002* (Tas) s 17.

57 *Civil Liability Act 2002* (NSW) s 5H(3); *Civil Liability Act 1936* (SA) s 38(3); *Civil Liability Act 2002* (Tas) s 17(3).

In Queensland s 21(1) of the *Civil Liability Act 2003* expressly provides that:

[A] doctor does not breach a duty owed to a patient to warn of risk, before the patient undergoes any medical treatment (or at the time of being given medical advice) that will involve a risk of personal injury to the patient, unless the doctor at that time fails to give or arrange to be given to the patient the following information about the risk:

(a) information that a reasonable person in the patient's position would, in the circumstances, require to enable the person to make a reasonably informed decision about whether to undergo the treatment or follow the advice;

(b) information that the doctor knows or ought reasonably to know the patient wants to be given before making the decision about whether to undergo the treatment or follow the advice.

The general tenor of the provisions is to extend to medical practitioners in particular some leeway in terms of treatment and diagnosis but to maintain the distinctive *Rogers v Whitaker* approach in terms of warning about risks, side-effects and options as to treatment.

Causation and advice on risks of treatment

In both *Chappel v Hart*[58] and *Rosenberg v Percival*[59] the High Court confirmed that the common law test for causation in Australia was subjective, with causation determined by reference to what the plaintiff would have done if he or she had been warned of the risk that eventuated. Since an action in negligence requires the plaintiff to establish that the defendant's breach of duty caused the plaintiff's damage, if the plaintiff would have had the procedure even if the warning had been given, then the plaintiff will fail to establish causation.

In the important decision of *Chappel v Hart*[60] the plaintiff alleged that the defendant had failed to warn her of the risk of damage to her voice from surgery on her oesophagus to correct a pharyngeal pouch. As in *Rogers v Whitaker*, the patient was concerned about the risks of the procedure. This meant that, like Mrs Whitaker, she fell into the second category of patients for the purpose of provision of information about "material risks". During the procedure the patient's oesophagus was perforated, and this was complicated by the development of an infection, known as mediastinitis, which caused damage to the patient's laryngeal nerve. Perforation of the oesophagus was a known, inherent risk of the procedure. Although the plaintiff had been warned of the risk of perforation, she was not warned of the risk of injury to her laryngeal nerve and the possible risk of damage to her voice.[61]

---

58   *Chappel v Hart* [1998] HCA 55; 195 CLR 232.
59   *Rosenberg v Percival* [2001] HCA 18; 205 CLR 434.
60   *Chappel v Hart* [1998] HCA 55; 195 CLR 232.
61   Ibid, at 254; at [59].

The plaintiff's condition was described as "relentlessly progressive" and, since her condition would worsen over time, it was clear that she would have had to have surgery at some stage.

> Mrs Hart swore that if she had been told by Dr Chappel of the risks to her voice she would not have gone ahead with the operation by him. She would have sought further advice. She would have wanted the operation performed by the most experienced person available.[62]

By a majority the High Court held for the plaintiff. Gaudron and Kirby JJ applied the Australian law that prima facie the harm is regarded as caused by a tortious act if the harm ensues in the immediate aftermath of the tortious act.[63] However, this leaves open arguments by health professionals that:

- the link between the breach of duty and the damage was simply temporal and purely coincidental;
- the damage was inevitable in that it probably would have occurred regardless of the breach of duty;
- the breach of duty was logically irrelevant to the damage;
- the event was the immediate result of the plaintiff's unreasonable action; and
- "the event was ineffective as a cause of the damage, given that the event which occurred would probably have occurred in the same way even had the breach not happened".[64]

The majority also were influenced by the fact that the plaintiff swore that had she been given the information about possible adverse outcomes she would have postponed the operation and sought a more experienced surgeon. Gaudron J raised the possibility that the doctor may owe a duty to a patient to advise on the experience of the surgeon:

> If the foreseeable risk to Mrs Hart was the loss of an opportunity to undergo surgery at the hands of a more experienced surgeon, the duty would have been a duty to inform her that there were more experienced surgeons practising in the field.[65]

Kirby J inclined to a similar effect, commenting that "intuition and common sense suggest that the greater the skill and more frequent the performance, the less the risk of perforation".[66] McHugh J rejected this position stating:

---

62 Ibid, at 267; at [91] per Kirby J.
63 *Chappel v Hart* (1998) 195 CLR 232 at 238–239 per Gaudron J, at 273 per Kirby J applying *Betts v Whittingslowe* (1945) 71 CLR 637 at 649.
64 *Chappel v Hart* (1998) 195 CLR 232 at 271; [1998] HCA 55 at [93] per Kirby J.
65 Ibid, at 239; at [10] per Gaudron J.
66 Ibid, at 277; at [97].

Nothing in the evidence suggested that there was available to the plaintiff the services of a surgeon of such skill that he or she would never perforate the oesophagus while performing this procedure ... The evidence was all one way that perforation of the oesophagus was an inherent risk of the procedure.[67]

Hayne J was similarly cautious stating that:

I agree with McHugh J that there is insufficient evidence in this case to say, on the balance of probabilities, that the appellant's failure to warn exposed the respondent to greater risk of injury. The respondent would have had the operation at some time. The operation has risks even if performed by the most skilled surgeon available.[68]

At one level the analysis of Gaudron J, in particular, has much to commend it in terms of obligating doctors to supply to patients a category of information likely to make a difference as to whether or not they provide consent to a surgical or other form of health intervention. The information required by a patient, after all, extends beyond just the actuarial risks applicable to a particular procedure. There are other factors that bear upon the predictable outcome. Included among these are the proficiency of the practitioner (including his or her experience in the procedure) and the conditions obtaining at the particular health care facility. However, it has been pointed out that there is also a significant downside to a common law or legislated obligation to provide information about levels of proficiency and experience which in potential could have an impact upon the risks run by a particular patient in submitting to the procedure at the hands of the particular practitioner.[69]

In *Rosenberg v Percival* the High Court grappled with the question of causation in one aspect of medical negligence litigation. The resolution was reasonably straightforward in that McHugh, Kirby and Gummow JJ specifically endorsed the "subjective approach" and found that the question to be asked is what the particular patient would have done in terms of treatment or a procedure if given the proper warning by the medical practitioner.

However, merely because it is the ostensible position of the plaintiff that he or she would not have had the procedure if warned of the risk that eventuated, it does not follow that the courts will accept it unquestioningly. For instance, in *Rosenberg v Percival* where a nurse with a doctoral qualification swore that had she been given information about the potential adverse consequences of a surgical procedure, she would not have had the surgery, her account was rejected by the trial judge. The High Court found no error to have been committed by the trial judge. Callinan J summarised the position of the High Court as follows:

---

67   Ibid, at 249–250; at [41].

68   Ibid, at 289-290; at [146].

69   See, Freckelton, I, "Materiality of Risk and Proficiency Assessment: The Onset of Health Care Report Cards?" (1999) 6 *Journal of Law and Medicine* 313.

In this case [the] concerns [of the respondent] are outweighed by the fact of the respondent's awareness, as a highly experienced practising and teaching nurse, of risks going beyond those of frequent or regular occurrence, her stressed desire for the "best result" before the surgery, the inherent undispelled improbability of a categorical denial that she would have had the operation, and the time and circumstances in which she made the denial that the primary judge rejected.[70]

It is likely that the statutory reforms introduced in some jurisdictions will have a significant, and potentially detrimental, effect on the ability of plaintiffs to establish causation in cases where the plaintiff alleges that there was a failure to advise him or her of a material risk of proposed medical treatment. The Ipp Report supported the retention of the subjective test of causation in Australia but recommended that for the purposes of determining causation "any statement by the plaintiff about what they would have done if the negligence had not occurred should be inadmissible".[71] This recommendation has been adopted by a number of Australian jurisdictions and introduced in statutory provisions relating to causation. In New South Wales, for example, s 5D(3) of the *Civil Liability Act 2002* states:

If it is relevant to the determination of factual causation to determine what the person who suffered harm would have done if the negligent person had not been negligent:

(a) the matter is to be determined subjectively in the light of all relevant circumstances, subject to paragraph (b), and

(b) any statement made by the person after suffering the harm about what he or she would have done is inadmissible except to the extent (if any) that the statement is against his or her interest.

Similar provisions have been enacted in Queensland, Western Australia and Tasmania,[72] although the wording of the West Australian provisions is more restrictive from a plaintiff's perspective as evidence about what the injured person would have done if the tortfeasor had not been negligent is inadmissible, and not simply inadmissible if the statement is against his or her interests.[73]

It is difficult to know what impact these statutory reforms will have in the long term on the subjective test for causation. It is difficult to see how a subjective test can remain if a plaintiff's evidence of what he or she would have done if warned of the risk is inadmissible.

---

70   *Rosenberg v Percival* [2001] HCA 18 at [223]; 205 CLR 434 at 505.

71   Ipp Committee (2002) op cit, para 7.40.

72   *Civil Liability Act 2003* (Qld) s 11(3); *Civil Liability Act 2002* (Tas) s 13(3); *Civil Liability Act 2003* (WA) s 5C(3).

73   Mendelson, D, "Australian Tort Law Reform: Statutory Principles of Causation and the Common Law" (2004) 11 *Journal of Law and Medicine* 492 at 508.

Causation and the scope of liability

A new statutory test for causation has replaced that which had evolved at common law. The post-Ipp amendments[74] provide a two-tier test:

- negligence must be a necessary condition of the occurrence of the harm (factual causation); and

- it must be appropriate for the scope of the negligent person's liability to extend to the harm so caused (scope of liability).

However, South Australia has a distinctive provision (dealing specially with asbestos cases where it is unclear which asbestos environment caused the ultimate lung disease in the plaintiff) whereby s 34(2) of the *Civil Liability Act 1936* (SA) provides that where a plaintiff has been negligently exposed to a similar risk of harm by a number of different defendants, and it is not possible to assign responsibility for causing the harm to any one or more of them, a "court may continue to apply the principle under which responsibility may be assigned to the defendants for causing the harm" but it "should consider the position of each defendant individually and state the reasons for bringing the defendant within the scope of liability".

Section 34(3) provides that "for the purpose of determining the scope of liability, the court is to consider (amongst other relevant things) whether or not and why responsibility for the harm should be imposed on the negligent party". Similar provisions exist in the Australian Capital Territory.[75]

Victoria's general legislation on causation is similar but s 51(2) of the *Wrongs Act 1958* (Vic) varies somewhat. It provides that in determining "in accordance with established principles whether negligence that cannot be established as a necessary condition of the occurrence of harm should be taken to establish factual causation", courts are obliged to "consider (amongst other relevant things) whether or not and why responsibility for the harm should be imposed on the negligent party". Section 51(3) provides that "if it is relevant to the determination of factual causation to determine what the person who suffered harm ... would have done if the negligent person had not been negligent, the matter is to be determined subjectively in the light of all the relevant circumstances". Section 51(4) provides that when determining the scope of liability, a court is obliged "to consider (amongst other relevant things) whether or not and why responsibility for the harm should be imposed on the negligent party". There are similar provisions in New South Wales, Queensland and Tasmania.[76]

---

74 *Civil Liability Act 1936* (SA) s 34(1). See also, *Civil Liability Act 2002* (NSW) s 5D(1); *Civil Liability Act 2003* (Qld) s 11(1); *Civil Liability Act 2002* (Tas) s 13(1); *Wrongs Act 1958* (Vic) s 51(1); *Civil Law (Wrongs) Act 2002* (ACT) s 45(1).

75 See also *Civil Law (Wrongs) Act 2002* (ACT) s 45(2), (3).

76 *Civil Liability Act 2002* (NSW) s 5D; *Civil Liability Act 2003* (Qld) s 11; *Civil Liability Act 2002* (Tas) s 13.

The impact of the new provisions is yet to be authoritatively determined. It is apparent that they contain an overt acceptance of the policy considerations that permeate causation evaluation under the common law. This is evident from two important recent decisions of the House of Lords. In *Fairchild v Glenhaven Funeral Services Ltd*[77] an employee had been employed at different times and for differing periods by more than one employer. He developed a condition of mesothelioma as a result of the inhalation of asbestos dust at work.

The question arose whether in the circumstances he was entitled to recover damages against either employer or both of them even though he was unable to prove, on the balance of probabilities, that his condition was the result of inhaling asbestos dust during his employment by one or other or both of his employers. The claims were dismissed in the Court of Appeal but were allowed by the House of Lords. The House of Lords decided that, in certain special circumstances, the court could depart from the usual *"but for"* test of causal connection and treat a lesser degree of causal connection as sufficient, namely that the defendant's breach of duty had materially contributed to causing the claimant's disease by materially increasing the risk of the disease being contracted. In the circumstances of that case the House of Lords thought it would be just, and in accordance with common sense, to treat the conduct of both employers, in exposing the employee to a risk to which he should not have been exposed, as making a material contribution to the employee contracting a condition against which it was the duty of both employers to protect. Any injustice that might be involved in imposing liability on a duty-breaking employer in such circumstances was heavily outweighed by the injustice of denying redress to the victim. Policy considerations therefore weighed in favour of allowing the employee to recover against both employers, and that conclusion followed even if one of them was not before the court.

Similarly in *Chester v Afshar*[78] the House of Lords by a majority held that causation was established as a matter of public policy in spite of the fact that the plaintiff had not proved that had it not been for the surgeon's failure to provide her with information about risks she would not have submitted to the operation.

Lord Hope observed that determining causation by an appeal to common sense can be valuable "in the right context" but commented that "out of its proper context, and without more, it may pull in two or more directions. ... On its own common sense, and without more guidance, is no more reliable as a guide to the right answer in this case than an appeal to the views of the traveller on the London Underground".[79] He held that "the issue of causation cannot be separated from issues about policy"[80] and started his analysis with "the proposition that the law which imposed the duty to warn on the doctor has at its heart the right of a patient to make an informed choice as to whether, and if so when and by whom, to be

---

77   [2002] UKHL 22; [2003] 1 AC 32.
78   [2004] UKHL 41; [2005] 1 AC 134.
79   Ibid, at [83]; at 161.
80   Ibid, at [85]; at 162.

operated on".[81] He held that in the factual circumstances of the case the injury ultimately sustained by the patient was:

> [I]intimately involved with the duty to warn. The duty was owed by the doctor who performed the surgery that Miss Chester consented to. It was the product of the very risk that she should have been warned about when she gave her consent. So I would hold that it can be regarded as having been caused, in the legal sense, by the breach of that duty.[82]

He explicitly adopted the reasoning of Kirby J in *Chappel v Hart*.

Thus, the somewhat unclear policy considerations articulated in Australia's post-Ipp reforms to a significant degree replicate the unclear policy-perfused decision-making on the subject in the United Kingdom courts.

Trespass or negligence

In *Rogers v Whitaker* the High Court confirmed that an action in which the plaintiff alleges that the defendant failed to advise the plaintiff of a material risk associated with medical treatment should be brought in negligence rather than trespass. Stating that "consent is relevant to actions framed in trespass, not in negligence"[83] the High Court noted that:

> Anglo-Australian law has rightly taken the view that an allegation that the risks inherent in a medical procedure have not been disclosed to the patient can only found an action in negligence not in trespass; the consent necessary to negative the offence of battery is satisfied by the patient being advised in broad terms of the nature of the procedure to be performed.[84]

It seems clear that, where a plaintiff alleges that a health professional failed to warn him or her of a material risk of proposed treatment, the action must be brought in negligence rather than trespass. If, however, the plaintiff receives different treatment from that which was consented to, trespass may be the appropriate action. Trespass actions have a number of advantages for plaintiffs including that trespass actions are actionable per se, namely without proof of damage. Furthermore, the limits that have been imposed on negligence actions, including significant limits on damages, by the Ipp reforms may not apply to trespass actions.[85] Cockburn and Madden have argued:

> Although it seems that the Ipp Review recommendations were not meant to apply to intentional torts to the person and were meant to be incorporated in uniform

---

81 Ibid, at [86]; at 162.

82 Ibid, at [87]; at 163.

83 (1992) 175 CLR 479 at 490.

84 Ibid, at 490.

85 Cockburn, T and Madden, B, "Intentional Torts Claims in Medical Cases" (2006) 13 *Journal of Law and Medicine* 311 at 334.

legislation across Australia, this has not happened. Intentional torts are exempted from the operation of the Civil Liability Acts to various degrees across Australia.[86]

Psychiatric harm

Significant liberalisation was implemented to the restrictive laws of recovery for "pure psychiatric injury" at common law by the High Court decisions in *Tame v New South Wales*[87] and *Annetts v Australian Stations Pty Ltd*.[88] In short, the High Court substantially realigned pure psychiatric injury law with recovery for physical injuries. It removed the requirement that there be "nervous shock" in the sense of a sudden affront to the senses, that the plaintiff be a person of ordinary fortitude, that in bystander cases there be a familial relationship between the deceased or injured person and the bystander, and that the plaintiff be actually present at the scene of an accident or shortly thereafter. It noted, however, that each of these considerations would continue to be relevant indicia to what it emphasised was the fundamental criterion for recovery: reasonable foreseeability. It mandated that the plaintiff suffer a recognised psychiatric illness, maintaining the position that recovery is precluded for "mere" psychological distress, trauma or upset.

The Ipp Committee recommended overturning parts of the High Court decision, in particular to bring back the "ordinary fortitude" rule.[89] Six jurisdictions have legislated to do so.[90] The committee also proposed that:

> In an action for damages for negligently-caused pure mental harm arising out of an incident in which a person was injured, killed or put in peril as a result of negligence of the defendant, any damages awarded shall be reduced by the same proportion as any damages recoverable from the defendant by the injured person (or his or her estate) would be reduced.[91]

The committee also recommended that a "panel of experts (including experts in forensic psychiatry and psychology) should be appointed to develop guidelines, for use in legal contexts, for assessing whether a person has suffered a recognised psychiatric illness".[92]

The six reforming jurisdictions have accepted the High Court's approach generally but have adopted the Ipp Committee proposals and reinstated the

---

86   Ibid, at 334.

87   [2002] HCA 35; 211 CLR 317

88   Ibid. See generally Handford, P, *Mullany and Handfords' Tort Liability for Psychiatric Injury*, 2nd edn, Thomson, Sydney, 2006.

89   Ipp Committee (2002) op cit, Recommendation 34.

90   *Civil Liability Act 2002* (NSW) s 32; *Civil Liability Act 1936* (SA) s 33; *Civil Liability Act 2002* (Tas) s 34; *Wrongs Act 1958* (Vic) s 72; *Civil Liability Act 2002* (WA) s 5s; *Civil Law (Wrongs) Act 2002* (ACT) s 34.

91   Ipp Committee (2002) op cit, Recommendation 36.

92   Ibid, Recommendation 33.

"normal fortitude" or "ordinary robustness rule". The Western Australian provision in s 5s(1) of the *Civil Liability Act 2002* (WA) is typical of the provisions:

> A person (the "defendant") does not owe a duty of care to another person (the "plaintiff") to take care not to cause the plaintiff mental harm unless the defendant ought to have foreseen that a person of normal fortitude might, in the circumstances of the case, suffer a recognised psychiatric illness if reasonable care were not taken.

For the purpose of the application of determining liability, in all jurisdictions (save Tasmania) the circumstances of the case are stipulated to include the following:

- whether or not the mental harm was suffered as the result of a sudden shock;
- whether the plaintiff witnessed, at the scene, a person being killed, injured or put in danger;
- the nature of the relationship between the plaintiff and any person killed, injured or put in danger;
- whether or not there was a pre-existing relationship between the plaintiff and the defendant.[93]

It appears that the four factors are not cumulative and that only one of them will need to be satisfied to satisfy the circumstances of the case.[94]

In Victoria, s 72 of the *Wrongs Act 1958* (Vic) is expressed differently but has the same fundamental reforming objective:

> (1) A person (the defendant) does not owe a duty to another person (the plaintiff) to take care not to cause the plaintiff pure mental harm unless the defendant foresaw or ought to have foreseen that a person of normal fortitude might, in the circumstances of the case, suffer a recognised psychiatric illness if reasonable care were not taken.
>
> (2) For the purposes of the application of this section, the circumstances of the case include the following –
>
> (a) whether or not the mental harm was suffered as the result of a sudden shock;
>
> (b) whether the plaintiff witnessed, at the scene, a person being killed, injured or put in danger;
>
> (c) the nature of the relationship between the plaintiff and any person killed, injured or put in danger;
>
> (d) whether or not there was a pre-existing relationship between the plaintiff and the defendant.
>
> (3) This section does not affect the duty of care of a person (the defendant) to another (the plaintiff) if the defendant knows, or ought to know, that the plaintiff is a person of less than normal fortitude.

---

93   See also *Civil Liability Act 2002* (NSW) s 32(2); *Civil Liability Act 1936* (SA) s 33(2); *Civil Liability Act 2002* (Tas) s 34(2); *Wrong) Act 1958* (Vic) s 72(2); *Civil Liability Act 2002* (WA) s 55(2); *Civil Law (Wrongs) Act 2002* (ACT) s 34(2).

94   Mendelson, D, "The Modern Australian Law of Mental harm: Parochialism Triumphant" (2005) 13 *Journal of Law and Medicine* 164 at 171.

Section 73(1) provides that:

> This section applies to the liability of a person (the defendant) for pure mental harm to a person (the plaintiff) arising wholly or partly from mental or nervous shock in connection with another person (the victim) being killed, injured or put in danger by the act or omission of the defendant.

The statutory test is based upon the potential for a defendant to foresee that a person in the plaintiff's position "might" suffer a recognised psychiatric illness. This has prompted Mendelson to comment:

> Whether by design or inadvertence, a statutory test for the imposition of a duty to take reasonable care based on a possibility or chance of mental harm is much more onerous on the defendant than the statutory test for the duty of care in general negligence, which grounds the duty on foreseeability of "not insignificant" risk.[95]

The phrase "normal fortitude" is not defined by the statutory reforms and will be interpreted in accordance with the general common law approach on the subject

New South Wales, Victoria and Tasmania impose additional threshold requirements for recovery for pure psychiatric injury. The reforming provisions preclude recovery for mental harm "arising wholly or partly from mental or nervous shock in connection with another person (the victim) being killed, injured or put in peril (danger, in Victoria) by the act or omission of the defendant" unless:

- the plaintiff witnessed at the scene the victim being killed, injured or put in peril/danger (or in Tasmania, the immediate aftermath); or
- the plaintiff is (or was, in Victoria) a close member of the family of the victim (or in Victoria, was in a close relationship with the victim).[96]

In South Australia, damages can only be awarded for mental harm if the plaintiff "was physically injured in the accident or was present at the scene of the accident when the accident occurred" or "is a parent, spouse or child or a person killed, injured or endangered in the accident".[97]

Thus, the changes impose an additional impediment in the way of actions for pure psychiatric injury. How much of an impact they have in their escalation of the "ordinary fortitude" indicium to the status of a rule remains to be seen. It may be that once again persons in the position of the *Annetts* parents will be precluded from being able to recover on the basis that while it could reasonably be foreseen that they would suffer grief and distress at the negligently caused death of their son, it would not be regarded as reasonably foreseeable that

---

95   Ibid at 170.

96   See *Civil Liability Act 2002* (NSW) s 30(2)(b); *Civil Liability Act 2002* (Tas) s 32(2); *Wrongs Act 1958* (Vic) s 73(2).

97   *Civil Liability Act 1936* (SA) s 53.

persons of ordinary fortitude might suffer a psychiatric disorder as a result of such a tragedy.

Limits on damages

There are three kinds of damages that can be awarded in principle under the common law: ordinary compensatory damages, aggravated compensatory damages and exemplary, vindictive or punitive damages. The tort reforms around Australia introduced significant changes to the recovery of compensatory damages for personal injury actions.[98]

In general these changes introduced thresholds for damages for non-economic loss,[99] caps on damages for loss of earning capacity;[100] an increase in the discount rate from 3 to 5 per cent[101] and limits on recovery of damages for gratuitous services.[102] Luntz has noted that the increase in the discount rate from 3 to 5 per cent:

> [H]as the most significant impact on the most severely injured since they are the ones whose future economic loss is greatest. Quadriplegics and brain-injured plaintiffs, whose needs for care extend far into the future are the people most likely to find that their damages will not stretch to meet those needs.[103]

In New South Wales damages for non-economic loss cannot be awarded "unless the severity of the non-economic loss is at least 15% of a most extreme case".[104] In Victoria a person is not entitled to recover damages for non-economic loss unless they have suffered a "significant injury", defined by reference to the level of impairment suffered under the American Medical Association's *Guides to Permanent Impairment*.[105]

Aggravated damages compensate a plaintiff for additional mental suffering or hurt that results from the way in which the defendant engaged in his or her

---

98 For discussion of the reform of damages see Luntz, H, "Damages in Medical Litigation in New South Wales" (2005) 12 *Journal of Law and Medicine* 280; Mullany, NJ, "Tort Reform and the Damages Dilemma" (2002) 25(3) *UNSWLJ* 876.

99 *Civil Liability Act 2002* (NSW) ss 16-17A; *Civil Liability Act 1936* (SA) s 52; *Civil Liability Act 2002* (WA) s 9; *Personal Injuries (Liabilities and Damages) Act 2003* (NT) ss 26–28.

100 *Civil Liability Act 2002* (NSW) s 12; *Civil Liability Act 2003* (Qld) s 54; *Civil Liability Act 1936* (SA) s 54; *Civil Liability Act 2002* (Tas), s 26; *Wrongs Act 1958* (Vic) s 28F; *Civil Liability Act 2002* (WA) s 11; *Civil Law (Wrongs) Act 2002* (ACT) s 98; *Personal Injuries (Liabilities and Damages) Act 2003* (NT) s 20.

101 *Civil Liability Act 2002* (NSW) s 14; *Civil Liability Act 2003* (Qld) s 57; *Civil Liability Act 2002* (Tas) s 28A; *Wrongs Act 1958* (Vic) s 28I; *Personal Injuries (Liabilities and Damages) Act 2003* (NT) s 22.

102 *Civil Liability Act 2002* (NSW) s 15; *Civil Liability Act 2003* (Qld) s 59; *Civil Liability Act 1936* (SA) s 58; *Civil Liability Act 2002* (Tas) s 28B; *Wrongs Act 1958* (Vic) s 28IA; *Civil Liability Act 2002* (WA) s 12; *Personal Injuries (Liabilities and Damages) Act 2003* (NT) s 23.

103 Luntz (2005) op cit, at 286.

104 *Civil Liability Act 2002* (NSW) s 16(1).

105 *Wrongs Act 1958* (Vic) ss 28LE-LF.

tortious behaviour.[106] The availability of aggravated damages for negligence under the common law was a subject of some controversy before the statutory reforms.[107] Exemplary, vindictive or punitive damages are awarded in order to deter others from engaging in comparable conduct, to punish the defendant and to mark the court's disapproval for such behaviour.[108] In medical negligence cases,[109] as in other areas of the law, they have been controversial and seldom awarded.[110]

A number of jurisdictions have partially or completely abolished aggravated or exemplary damages.

In Queensland,[111] for instance, a court cannot award exemplary, punitive or aggravated damages in relation to a claim for personal injury damages unless the act that caused the personal injury was an unlawful intentional act done with intent to cause personal injury; or an unlawful sexual assault or other unlawful sexual misconduct.

In New South Wales, the preclusion is even broader: in an action for the award of personal injury damages where the act or omission that caused the injury or death was negligence, a court cannot award exemplary or punitive damages or damages in the nature of aggravated damages.[112] The Northern Territory provides that a court "must not award aggravated damages or exemplary damages in respect of a personal injury".[113] The limited statutory changes appear to leave scope for aggravated and exemplary damages in medical negligence litigation in most jurisdictions although it is clear that the circumstances which would justify such awards are limited and need to be egregious.

Apologies

The role of apologies in resolving disputes between health professionals and patients has attracted significant discussion in the academic literature.[114] It has also figured diversely in the post-Ipp Committee reforms. Indeed, in Australia this is

---

106 Luntz (2005) op cit, at 281.

107 See *Hunter Area Health Service v Marchlewski* (2000) 51 NSWLR 268; [2000] NSWCA 294; *Tan v Benkovic* [2000] NSWCA 295l; 51 NSWLR 292.

108 Luntz, (2005)op cit, at 282.

109 See, for example, *Backwell v AAA* [1997] 1 VR 182; *A v Bottrill* [2003] 1 AC 449; [2002] UKPC 44.

110 See, for example, Mendelson, D, "The Case of Backwell v AAA: Negligence – A Compensatory Remedy or an Instrument of Vengeance?" (1996) 4 *Journal of Law and Medicine* 114; Freckelton, I, "Exemplary Damages in Medico-Legal Litigation" (1996) 4 *Journal of Law and Medicine* 103; Todd, A, "Outrageous Negligence" (2004) 12 *Tort Law Review* 8.

111 *Civil Liability Act 2003* (Qld) s 52.

112 *Civil Liability Act 2002* (NSW) s 21; however, it appears not to apply to intentional torts: see *New South Wales v Ibett* [2005] NSWCA 445. See further Luntz (2005) op cit.

113 *Personal Injuries (Liabilities and Damages) Act 2003* (NT) s 19.

114 For an excellent discussion see Vines, P, "Apologising to Avoid Liability: Cynical Civility or Practical Morality?" (2005) 27 *Sydney Law Review* 483.

one reform which "has been taken up by every jurisdiction except for the Commonwealth".[115]

There have been concerns that apologies or expressions of regret may be seen as amounting to an admission of liability, which could in turn have adverse consequences under an alleged wrongdoer's insurance policy.[116] Statutory reforms have included provisions relating to apologies to address these concerns, although several different models have been adopted.[117] South Australia has perhaps the simplest version of the reform, s 75 of the *Civil Liability Act 1936* (SA) stating:

> In proceedings in which damages are claimed for a tort, no admission of liability or fault is to be inferred from the fact that the defendant or a person for whose tort the defendant is liable expressed regret for the incident out of which the cause of action arose.

In New South Wales protection is given for "an apology" which is defined in s 68 of the *Civil Liability Act 2002* as:

> [A]n expression of sympathy or regret, or of a general sense of benevolence or compassion, in connection with any matter whether or not the apology admits or implies an admission of fault in connection with the matter.

In the Australian Capital Territory the definition is very similar.[118] The statutory definitions indicate that in New South Wales and the Australian Capital Territory an apology may include an admission of fault.[119]

This can be contrasted with the definitions of apology in Victoria, Queensland, Tasmania, Western Australia and the Northern Territory, which exclude an "acknowledgement of fault".[120] For example, in Tasmania,[121] an "apology" is defined as "an expression of sympathy or regret, or of a general sense of benevolence or compassion, in connection with any matter, which does not contain an admission of fault in connection with the matter". The equivalent provision in Victoria has similarly limited scope. An apology is defined to mean "an expression of sorrow, regret or sympathy but does not include a clear acknowledgment of fault".[122] Protections for apologies are therefore deprived of most of their potency in terms of encouraging genuine expressions of remorse by medical and other personnel who have made errors. This is unfortunate because anecdotal evidence

---

115 Ibid, at 483.

116 Ibid, at 486–487.

117 Ibid, at 487.

118 *Civil Law (Wrongs) Act 2002* (ACT) s 13.

119 Vines (2005) op cit, at 488.

120 *Civil Liability Act 2003* (Qld) s 71; *Civil Liability Act 2002* (Tas) s 7(3); *Wrongs Act 1958* (Vic) s 14I; *Civil Liability Act 2002* (WA) s 5AF; *Personal Injuries (Liabilities and Damages) Act 2003* (NT) s 12.

121 *Civil Liability Act 2002* (Tas) s 7(3).

122 *Wrongs Act 1958* (Vic) s 14I.

suggests that the desire for an apology is often the motivation for patients lodging complaints.[123]

There are significant differences between the States in the effect of an apology on the liability of the alleged wrongdoer. In New South Wales s 69 of the *Civil Liability Act 2002* provides that an apology has the following effect:

> (1) An apology made by or on behalf of a person in connection with any matter alleged to have been caused by the fault of the person:
>
>> (a) does not constitute an express or implied admission of fault or liability by the person in connection with that matter, and
>>
>> (b) is not relevant to the determination of fault or liability in connection with that matter.
>
> (2) Evidence of an apology made by or on behalf of a person in connection with any matter alleged to have been caused by the person is not admissible in any civil proceedings as evidence of the fault or liability of the person in connection with that matter.[124]

In Queensland, s 72 provides:

> An expression of regret made by an individual in relation to an incident alleged to give rise to an action for damages at any time before a civil proceeding is started in a court in relation to the incident is not admissible in the proceeding.

Tasmanian[125] and Western Australian[126] provisions stipulate that an apology made by or on behalf of a person in connection with any matter alleged to have been caused by the fault of the person:

- does not constitute an express or implied admission of fault or liability by the person in connection with that matter/incident; and

- is not relevant to the determination of fault or liability in connection with that matter/incident.

Furthermore, "evidence of an apology made by or on behalf of a person in connection with any matter alleged to have been caused by the fault of the person is not admissible in any civil proceedings as evidence of the fault or liability of the person in connection with that matter".[127] In Victoria s 14J(1) of the *Wrongs Act 1958* (Vic) provides:

> In a civil proceeding where the death or injury of a person is in issue or is relevant to an issue of fact or law, an apology does not constitute –
>
> (a) an admission of liability for the death or injury; or
>
> (b) an admission of unprofessional conduct, carelessness, incompetence, or unsatis-factory professional performance, however expressed, for the purposes of any Act regulating the practice or conduct of a profession or occupation.

---

123 Vines (2005) op cit, at 483.

124 See also *Civil Law (Wrongs) Act 2002* (ACT) s 14(2).

125 *Civil Liability Act 2002* (Tas) s 7(1).

126 *Civil Liability Act 2002* (WA) s 5AH(1).

127 *Civil Liability Act 2002* (Tas) s 7(2); *Civil Liability Act 2002* (WA) s 5AH.

In the Northern Territory, "[a]n expression of regret about a personal injury made at any time before the commencement of a proceeding in respect of that injury is not admissible as evidence in that proceeding".[128]

From the above it can be seen that while a number of jurisdictions provide that an apology does not amount to an admission of liability, the definitions of apology in some jurisdictions mean that there remains a powerful disincentive for health practitioners in those jurisdictions to do other than offer platitudinous expressions of regret without any form of admission of fault.

Overall impact of the reforming legislative provisions

The post-Ipp statutory reforms will exercise an important impact upon medical negligence actions in Australia. In general, the reforms have created additional barriers to smaller claims or constructed new restrictive mechanisms for calculating non-pecuniary losses. Generally these are not to the benefit of plaintiffs, when contrasted to the previous common law entitlements and practices. The changes to calculation of damages are likely to have a significant impact upon the most severely injured. Some aspects of the *Bolam* rule have been introduced to Australia. In addition, the capacity for plaintiffs to recover for pure psychiatric injuries is somewhat reduced by the escalation of the "ordinary fortitude" indicium to its erstwhile status as a rule. Whether, the social aims of the amending legislation coincide with community expectations or whether they unacceptably reduce the rights of persons harmed by poor quality health service provision awaits evaluation after the passage of a sufficient period of time.

---

128 *Personal Injuries (Liabilities and Damages) Act 2003* (NT) s 13.

20

Doctors and
forensic expertise

Ian Freckelton

Introduction

Medical practitioners have little option but to participate from time to time in the litigation system by writing reports, answering subpoenas and being called as witnesses. The forensic role is an incident of contemporary practice, in the same way that administrative responsibilities and other functions constitute part of the panoply of tasks that doctors are expected by their patients to perform.

There is a begrudged dependency by courts and tribunals in respect of expert opinions. The role of expert report writers and witnesses is fundamental to the resolution of many forms of civil litigation, compensation and medical negligence cases to name just two categories.

In the criminal jurisdiction, medical practitioners' evidence in sexual assault cases is fundamental, as is the evidence of pathologists in cause of death disputes and that of psychiatrists when criminal culpability or predictive issues such as dangerousness are in issue.

While the law needs the evidence of medical practitioners, doctors remain mistrusted guests at the legal table. Too often, they are perceived as obligatory but unwelcome invitees, possessed of an unethical propensity to tailor their views to the party which has brought them to the forensic banquet.

Doctors, for their part, for over a century have voiced their frustrations at the way that the adversary system dictates the drawing up of the guest list for the legal table.

In submissions to the New South Wales Law Reform Commission (NSWLRC)[1] once again in 2005 they complained about the pressures, both subtle and overt, exerted upon them even before their arrival at the gathering. They have long remonstrated about the "troubles" for their professional practice imposed by the legal system and about being kept waiting for intolerable periods

---

1   New South Wales Law Reform Commission *Expert Witnesses*, NSWLRC, Sydney, 2005.

of time when asked to give evidence.[2] Many have expressed themselves aggrieved about the manners and ethics that they have found at table – so
obnoxious, they have said, that many worthies amongst their number continue to
elect not to participate if given the choice.[3] In 2006 medical practitioners
succeeded in convincing Collins J in the English High Court that if doctors could
be subjected to disciplinary proceedings arising out of their forensic work, there
would be an intolerable dearth of paediatricians prepared to give evidence in the
criminal courts.[4]

Others from the medical profession have contended for upwards of one and
a half centuries that, if medical mores and proprieties are to be the subject of fact-
finding, they should be liberated from the shackles of the adversary-generated
selection system. Many would have as those doctors available to give expert
evidence practitioners from amongst an agreed panel of doctors, both general
practitioners and specialists, prepared to do forensic work. They would prefer too
to have complex issues determined by a jury of experts, a special jury of medical
personnel, rather than by persons ignorant in the ways of medicine. They argue
that such changes would enhance the quality of the fact-finding process and
promote respect within the medical sector, as well as within the community
generally, for the role of the law in adjudicating upon important interactions
between professional and medical service consumer.

Building upon the results of surveys of Australia's judges and magistrates
about expert evidence, and 2005 reports of the Australian, New South Wales and
Victorian Law Reform Commissions, this chapter re-evaluates the debates about
the role of medical practitioners as independent providers of opinion evidence
within the adversary system. It argues that although malcontent with the role of
expert witnesses, and medical experts in particular, is apparent in the views of
many judicial officers, it is not sufficiently thoroughgoing or irremediable
that radical surgery to the adversary system is necessary. Rather, the extensive
procedural changes being made by the courts and the encouragement being given

---

2 See the example cited by Crawford in a 1678 murder trial where a London physician
  testified that he had declined to attend an autopsy in the hope of avoiding attendance at
  court:

   [W]hen I came I found him dying, and seeing no hopes of his recovery, left him; I was desired to be
   present at the dissection, but because of the rumour of this business, I said it would be a troublesome matter, and therefore would purposely avoid it.

  Similarly she cites a London midwife at the trial of Elizabeth Canning for perjury in 1754
  saying on oath that she had been requested to examine a suspected rape victim but
  declining: "I never was before the face of a judge in the Old-Bailey in my life, and I did not
  care to be in dirty work": Crawford, C, "Legalizing Medicine: Early Modern Legal Systems
  and the Growth of Medico-Legal Knowledge" in Clarke, M and Crawford, C *Legal Medicine
  in History*, Cambridge University Press, Cambridge, 1994, pp 90–91.

3 Percival commented that medico-legal investigations were "generally painful, always
  inconvenient, and occasion[ed] an interruption to business of a nature not to be easily
  appreciated or compensated": Percival, T *Medical Jurisprudence; or a Code of Ethics and
  Institutes, Adapted to the Professions of Physic and Surgery*, Manchester, 1794, p 89.

4 *Meadow v General Medical Council* [2006] EWHC 146 (Admin).

to experts to abandon the culture of partiality are likely, in combination, to provide to the court system for the most part expert opinions of the quality upon which it needs to rely.

The exclusionary rules of expert evidence

One of the limiting factors, often misunderstood by doctors, is the way in which evidence that they would like to provide to courts and tribunals is circumscribed by the admissibility rules. These are constituted by the exclusionary rules of expert evidence that have been developed by the common law over the past one and a half centuries and are also to be found in another form in federal, New South Wales and Tasmanian legislation.

The common law

In general terms, evidence law provides that it is only expert witnesses who may give evidence in the form of opinions. Medical experts, for instance, may be called as witnesses to offer to the courts inferences drawn from data made available to them, such as about a patient's pre-operative medical condition, and so to opine whether a surgical intervention was a reasonable response to the patient's symptoms. Like lay witnesses, doctors may also give evidence of fact. For instance, medical practitioners may describe what they saw around a wound site, what the patient said, and what they did in response to a nurse's report. Philosophical debates may be constructed about the extent to which expert knowledge and evaluation colour any evidence of fact, particularly when it is provided by expert witnesses, but a meaningful distinction can usefully be drawn between evidence of fact and evidence which interprets or evaluates facts. However, this is not to downgrade evidence of fact which is often undervalued as a source of valuable information coming before courts and tribunals. In the case of medical practitioners trained in scientific method, such evidence has the potential to be detailed and informed by an understanding of what matters are pertinent in terms of observation in relation to a patient's condition, for instance, at a particular stage in the course of a progressive disease.

However, just because a person is an expert, or thinks that they are, this does not mean that they are (or should be) given free rein to proffer opinions at large to the courts or to invest "mere speculation" "with a spurious appearance of authority" – otherwise "legitimate processes of fact-finding may be subverted".[5] The potential influence of evidence from impressive, articulate and eminent experts carries a danger that it will command undeserved sway from decision-makers, particularly if they are jurors.[6] This risk is exacerbated if the evidence is especially complex or if thoroughgoing disagreements pervade evidence given by

---

5   *HG v R* (1999) 197 CLR 414; 73 ALJR 281; 160 ALR 554 at 563, 564.
6   Ibid.

experts from different schools of thought within their own or cognate disciplines. Another difficult factor can be where the performance of counsel in making such witnesses accountable in cross-examination is inadequate. The common law in Australia has generated five rules of expert evidence which can result in expert opinions being determined inadmissible and so not available to be put before the trier of fact:

- the expertise rule (that an expert must be an expert);

- the area of expertise rule (that expert evidence must emanate from an area of expertise);

- the common knowledge rule (that experts may not give evidence about matters of common knowledge about which the trier of fact does not need or would not be helped by expert opinion);

- the basis rule (that the bases of expert opinion must be proved by admissible evidence); and

- the ultimate issue rule (that expert may not give evidence on the ultimate issue).

In addition, a judge or magistrate has a discretion, especially in criminal matters, to exclude evidence that is more prejudicial than it is probative.[7] In Canada this has been described as itself a rule of expert evidence.[8]

The rules are of significance for the drafting of reports and the giving of oral evidence by medical practitioners because a failure to comply with them may render doctors' opinions inadmissible, or at least an evaluation that the opinions are of low probative value. The rules remain controversial and in flux, although in New South Wales, Tasmania and at the federal level they have been simplified by the substantial abolition of the common knowledge and ultimate issues rules and the omission from the legislation of the basis and area of expertise rules.[9] Much work in these jurisdictions in relation to sifting evidence fit to go before jurors from that which is determined unfit for such a purpose is left to be done by the statutorily enshrined discretions on the part of judges and magistrates to exclude unfair and prejudicial evidence.[10]

Looked at in historical perspective, the exclusionary rules of expert evidence and the discretion to exclude it been fashioned by judicial concerns about:

- the bias or partiality of expert witnesses;

- the selection process whereby experts unrepresentative of their discipline could appear to be representative;

---

7   See *Evidence Act 1995* (Cth) ss 135, 137; *Evidence Act 1995* (NSW) ss 135, 137; *Evidence Act 2001* (Tas) ss 135, 137.

8   *R v Mohan* (1994) 85 DLR (4th) 402.

9   *Evidence Act 1995* (Cth) s 80; *Evidence Act 1995* (NSW) s 80; *Evidence Act 2001* (Tas) s 80.

10 See Freckelton, I and Selby, H, *Expert Evidence: Law, Practice, Procedure and Advocacy*, 3rd edn, Thomson, Sydney, 2005.

- complexities in the language of experts;

- the poor quality of expert evidence, whose poverty may not be sufficiently exposed; and

- limitations in the capacity of the trier of fact, particularly the jury, to understand and adequately evaluate complex or conflicting expert evidence.[11]

For example, as long ago as 1849 Best noted that:

> There can be no doubt that testimony is daily received in our courts as "scientific evidence" to which it is almost profanation to apply the term; as being revolting to common sense, and inconsistent with the commonest honesty on the part of those by whom it is given.[12]

Even in 1873 Sir George Jessel, the Master of the Rolls, expressed a view which has since been frequently cited by judges facing a conflict of expert evidence:

> In matters of opinion I very much distrust expert evidence, for several reasons. In the first place, although the evidence was given upon oath, in point of fact the person knows that he cannot be indicted for perjury, because it is only evidence as to a matter of opinion ... but that is not all. Expert evidence of this kind is evidence of persons who sometimes live by their business, but in all cases are remunerated for their evidence. An expert is not like an ordinary witness, who hopes to get his expenses, but he is employed and paid in the sense of gain, being employed by the person who calls him. Now it is natural that his mind, however honest he may be, should be biased in favour of the person employing him, and accordingly we do find such bias ... Undoubtedly there is a natural bias to do something serviceable for those who employ you and adequately remunerate you.[13]

The unclear legal line between insufficient and sufficient expertise is apparent from a number of recent appellate decisions. Expertise is generally regarded as consisting of specialised knowledge arising from skill, training or experience, howsoever obtained. This does not mean that the test is laissez-faire, though. For instance, the Ontario Court of Appeal in *R v Millar*[14] subjected the evidence of a Dr M to the following analysis:

> The subject of child abuse is a speciality and clearly the training and experience of this witness fell considerably short of that of the other Crown witnesses on the subject. When I refer to the narrowness of Dr M's experience, I have regard to his evidence that in his practice as a family physician he had only one case of child abuse, which he described as "one of the most profound cases of child abuse in P County" and, since becoming regional coroner, he had been involved in "the investigation and evaluation of four deaths that have been believed to be associated with intent and [intentional?] child abuse".

---

11   See further Freckelton, I, "Judicial Attitudes Toward Scientific Evidence: the Antipodean Experience" (1997) 30(4) *University of California Davis Law Review* 1137.

12   Best, WM *A Treatise on the Law of Evidence*, Sweet, London, 1849.

13   *Lord Abinger v Ashton* (1873) 17 LR Eq 358 at 374; see also *Plimpton v Siller* (1877) 6 Ch D 412 at 416; *More v R* [1963] SCR 522 at 537–538.

14   (1989) 49 CCC 193 at 220.

The issue focused upon was whether the medical practitioner's clinical exposure to the area in question was sufficient to enable him properly to be regarded as an expert.

Similarly, in a key decision on expert evidence in 1995 the New South Wales Court of Appeal determined the evidence of a highly regarded Sydney paediatrician inadmissible on the subject of child victims' characteristic behaviour after they have been sexually assaulted.[15] The court held that the witness had not been shown to be "properly qualified to give evidence about matters within the expertise of a psychologist or psychiatrist". A little earlier, arguably Australia's then most eminent forensic psychiatrist had been permitted by a trial judge to give evidence about battered woman syndrome in the Victorian case of *J v The Queen*.[16] Brooking J on appeal, though, found that the witness had not demonstrated that he was qualified to give evidence about the subject, in spite of having been in practice as a forensic practitioner for some decades and being familiar with articles about the subject. It appears that more than mere acquaintance by an expert with a subset within his or her area of expertise by means of general reading is required. In addition, in *HG v R*[17] Gleeson CJ held evidence by an expert not to constitute expert opinion if it was properly to be classified as "speculation" and not as arising wholly or substantially from the expert's field of expertise.[18]

What is necessary for a medical practitioner to give admissible opinion evidence is that they should have specialised current knowledge about an area. This may exist because of recent specialisation in a particular area of clinical practice or because of especial interest and study. However, if the practitioner's alleged knowledge arises from an inadequate acquaintance with a particular condition or if their evidence is out-of-date or not based upon significant clinical or theoretical experience, the evidence may well be found inadmissible.

The relevant experience on the part of the practitioner must be such as to lead a court to conclude that the person has information of contemporary expertise. Mere possession of medical qualifications or even membership of a learned college in the era of sub-specialisation will not suffice. It is the sufficiency of the specialist knowledge possessed by the doctor held out as an expert which counts. For those with uncertain or emerging expertise, as they gain experience and authority in relation to an aspect of their work, the approach favoured by the courts appears to be one of caution – if in doubt, one should not hold oneself out as an expert.

Ongoing uncertainty exists about whether it is the representativeness of an expert's opinions within the context of his or her expert community or the

---

15   *F v The Queen* (1995) 83 A Crim R 502 at 509.
16   (1994) 75 A Crim R 522 at 532.
17   (1999) 197 CLR 414.
18   See Freckelton, I and Henning, T, "Speculation, Uncorroborated Opinions and Forensic Expertise in Child Sex Prosecutions" (1999) 6(1) *Psychiatry, Psychology & Law* 105.

reliability of an expert's views that determines whether they fall within the necessary "area of expertise". Australian decisions have repeatedly conflated the terminology of the United States *Frye*[19] "general acceptance test" and the notion of reliability which was subsequently adopted by the United States Supreme Court in *Daubert v Merrell Dow Pharmaceuticals*,[20] a case dealing with the teratogenic qualities of Bendectin as asserted by epidemiologists' re-analyses and by unpublished animal studies. The *Daubert* decision has subsequently been applied in the New Zealand High Court.[21]

Bernstein has correctly pointed out that Australia has had perhaps the most vociferous debate outside the United States[22] over the vexed issue of when experts should be able to give evidence about areas of substantial controversy. A series of disuniform judgments, on occasions determined in ignorance of key decisions, has suggested that an exclusionary condition precedent may form part of Australian law, save perhaps in Victoria,[23] in relation to whether expert evidence falls within an area of expertise. However, the issue has not been finally determined by the highest courts in Australia[24] or in New Zealand and it is especially unclear whether, if such a rule exists, its criterion is determined by the preponderance of

---

19   *Frye v United States* 293 F 1013 (1923).

20   501 Us 579; 113 S Ct 2786 (1993).

21   *R v Calder* (unreported, NZHC, 12 April 1985); *R v Brown* (unreported, NZHC, 19 September 1997). See Freckelton and Selby (2005) op cit.

22   Bernstein, D, "Junk Science in the United States and the Commonwealth" (1996) 21 *Yale Journal of International Law* 123; see further Freckelton, I *The Trial of the Expert*, Oxford University Press, Melbourne, 1987; Gerber, P, "Playing Dice with Expert Evidence: The Lessons to Emerge from *R v Chamberlain*" (1987) 147 *MJA* 243; Freckelton, I, "Novel Scientific Evidence: the Challenge of Tomorrow" (1987) 3 *Australian Bar Review* 243; Holdenson, OP, "The Admission of Expert Evidence of Opinion as to the Potential Unreliability of Evidence of Visual Identification" (1988) 16 *Melbourne University Law Review* 521; Giugni, P, "*Runjanjic v R*" (1992) 14 *Sydney University Law Review* 511; Freckelton, I, "Science and the Legal Culture" (1993) 2 *Expert Evidence* 107; Samuels, G, "Is This the Best We Can Do?" (1993) 25 *Australian Journal of Forensic Sciences* 3; Bourke, J, "Misapplied Science: Unreliability in Scientific Test Evidence (Pt 1)" (1993) 10 *Australian Bar Review* 123; Freckelton, I, "Expert Evidence and the Role of the Juries" (1994) 12(1) *Australian Bar Review* 73; Williams, CR, "Evidence and the Expert Witness" (1994) 26 *Australian Journal of Forensic Sciences* 3; Odgers, SJ and Richardson, J, "Keeping Bad Science out of the Courtroom – Changes in American and Australian Expert Evidence Law" (1995) 18 *UNSWLR* 108; Freckelton, I, "Judicial Attitudes Toward Scientific Evidence: An Antipodean Perspective" (1997) *University of California Davis Law Review* 1137; Edmond, G and Mercer, D, "Keeping 'Junk' History, Philosophy and Sociology of Science Out of the Courtroom: Problems with the Reception of *Daubert v Merrell Dow Pharmaceuticals Inc*" (1997) 20 *UNSWLJ* 48; Ligertwood, A, *Australian Evidence*, 3rd edn, Butterworths, Sydney, 1998, para 7.35; Edmond, G and Mercer, D, "The Secret Life of (Mass) Torts: The 'Bendectin Litigation' and the Construction of Law-Science Knowledges" (1997) 20(3) *UNSWLJ* 666; Aronson, M and Hunter, J, *Litigation - Evidence and Procedure*, LexisNexis, 6th edn, Sydney, 1998; Ligertwood, A, *Australian Evidence*, 4th edn, LexisNexis, Sydney, 2004; Freckelton, I and Selby, H, *Expert Evidence: Law Practice, Procedure and Advocacy*, 3rd edn, Thomson, Sydney, 2005.

23   See *J v The Queen* (1994) 75 A Crim R 522.

24   In *Osland v R* (1998) 197 CLR 316, the High Court expressly refrained from determining the status of *Daubert* under Australian law.

expert opinion or by resort to the criterion of reliability. The articulation of principle thus far has primarily been from single judges and has been very limited. There has been repeated mixing of concepts. For the present, it appears that if an expert's views are out-of-step with the preponderance of opinion within the intellectual marketplace, they may not be admissible. If they are unreliable, in the sense of the theories or methodologies underlying them being unfalsifiable, they will be accorded little value and may in time be determined to be inadmissible. This has ramifications for medical evidence that is iconoclastic or concerning techniques or methodologies that are under development or not generally regarded by peers as legitimate. Such evidence may well not be admitted. If it is, it will be open to being impugned in terms of its probative value on the same basis upon which its admissibility was open to be attacked.

The requirement that evidence by an expert relate to matters outside the common knowledge of lay triers of fact arises from a concern that such evidence may be invested, by jurors especially, with undue respect and may be given a deference which in fact it does not merit. Factors such as the specialist's aura of infallibility, the surgeon's commanding demeanour, and the professor of haematology's impression of esoteric insights have been regarded by judges as carrying with them the potential for jurors to be overwhelmed and by dint of that undiscriminating. The risk that has been identified is that in effect the expert will usurp the jury's role in fact-finding. This approach has confined psychiatrists and psychologists in particular to evidence concerning the mental processes of persons with mental illness or intellectual disability.

Important recent Australian decisions, however, have attenuated the harshness of this preclusion. For instance, courts have permitted counter-intuitive evidence about the factors that might lead women battered by their spouses to remain in a dangerous relationship;[25] evidence has been permitted about the capacity of a person of borderline intellectual disability to form the capacity to commit a crime[26] and to make a police confession;[27] and evidence has also been allowed about the propensity of persons with personality disorders to lie.[28] Increasingly, the focus is not so much upon whether information able to be provided by expert medical witnesses is or is not within the public domain but whether its provision may assist the decision-making processes by clarifying a focus or removing from potential decision-making processes a source of error. Another important issue is whether error in fact-finding is likely to occur if the expert evidence is not adduced.

Over the 1980s and 1990s it is probable that a rule emerged in Australia that, unless the expert's bases for opinion are proved, the opinion would itself be

---

25   *Runjanjic and Kontinnen v The Queen* (1993) 53 A Crim R 362.

26   *R v Schultz* (1981) 5 A Crim R 234; see also *R v Falconer* (1989) 46 A Crim R 83 at 94.

27   *Murphy v The Queen* (1989) 167 CLR 94.

28   *Farrell v The Queen* (1998) 194 CLR 286.

inadmissible. Continuing debate exists about the rule,[29] but it is undeniable that, if such bases are not proved, the evidence, even if admitted, will be accorded minimal probative value.[30] The reasons for this approach are sound and of particular relevance in the context of opinion evidence given by medical practitioners. A doctor's opinion about a patient's medical condition is frequently a product of their general skill and knowledge, but also their specific reading of portions of textbooks and learned articles, the history provided by a patient, the patient's prior medical records, observations from nurses, x-rays conducted by radiologists, the results of procedures such as blood and urine tests conducted by pathologists, information from family members of the patient, and opinions from other doctors. As Abadee J held in *R v Pantoja*,[31] "[a]n expert opinion is only as persuasive as the facts upon which it is based". If the data cannot be evaluated because those providing them are not called to give evidence, the value of the ultimate opinion cannot be assessed. The rule is not stringently applied in relation to evidence that is partly the product of general or even specific reading. Its application is to be found where, for instance, an orthopaedic surgeon's opinion is substantially formed by reference to CAT scans and MRIs which are not adduced in evidence. This existence of the basis rule highlights the need for practitioners to indicate clearly in any written report that they produce the information upon which they have relied and the steps they have undertaken in arriving at their opinions.

Finally, experts historically have not been permitted to trespass upon the ultimate domain for the court; that is, the actual decisions needing to be made, including the credibility of witnesses, whether a person charged with dishonesty has or has not acted honestly, whether a person lacked testamentary capacity, whether someone was insane, and whether a person's behaviour was negligent. Information enabling a decision-maker to arrive at such a conclusion can be provided but language encapsulating the conclusion has been precluded, especially if it utilises legal terminology. Again, this rule has been applied most strictly, although not exclusively, where juries have been used and has functioned to compel experts to step one pace back from the key decisions to be made by triers of fact. It is another manifestation of courts' concern about the excessive influence liable to be wielded by impressive experts, especially medical practitioners. In *Anasson v Koziol*, Miles CJ referred to the preclusion in the context of general comments about medical expertise in the courts:

---

29 See, for example, Australian Law Reform Commission, New South Wales Law Reform Commission and Victorian Law Reform Commission, *Uniform Evidence Law*, 2005, para 9.63.

30 The ALRC, NSWLRC and VLRC (2005) op cit, has contended that the "basis rule" acts as shorthand for two orthodox propositions: that (a) the lower the correlation between the facts proved and the facts assumed, the less weight can be given to the expert opinion evidence; and (b) where the facts proved and the facts assumed are substantially different, the point might be reached where the opinion evidence carries so little weight that it is not probative, and hence inadmissible.

31 (1996) 88 A Crim R 246 at 271.

The term "expert witness" is something of a misnomer: The expert witness is entitled to express an opinion in the appropriate field of knowledge and experience. The expert witness does not have to be skilled or experienced in giving evidence. Some experienced witnesses know how to avoid the use of language which strays outside the area of expertise and into the area of the function of the court. The use of such language does not assist the court in evaluating the evidence of the witness, but it does not necessarily rob it of all force.[32]

To similar effect, Gaudron J in *Naxakis v Western General Hospital*[33] commented that it was not for medical witnesses in a case about whether all necessary investigations had been undertaken "to say whether those steps were or were not reasonable. Much less was it for them to say, as they were frequently asked, whether, in their opinion, the hospital and Mr J were negligent in failing to take them".

Statutory law

However, statutory changes have intervened in important ways at Commonwealth level[34] and in New South Wales[35] and Tasmania[36]. Sections 79 and 80 of the "uniform evidence legislation" provide that:

79. If a person has specialised knowledge based on the person's training, study or experience, the opinion rule does not apply to evidence of an opinion of that person that is wholly or substantially based on that knowledge.

80. Evidence of an opinion is not inadmissible only because it is about:

(a) a fact in issue or an ultimate issue, or

(b) a matter of common knowledge.

Justice of Appeal Heydon[37] has maintained that the following elements of the common law have been enacted by s 79:

- it must be agreed or demonstrated that there is a field of "specialised knowledge";

- there must be an identified aspect of that field in which the witness demonstrates that by reason of specified training, study or experience, the witness has become an expert;

- the opinion proffered must be "wholly or substantially based on the witness' expert knowledge";

---

32 Unreported, ACTSC, 20 December 1996, p 17.

33 [1999] HCA 22 at [21].

34 *Evidence Act 1995* (Cth).

35 *Evidence Act 1995* (NSW).

36 *Evidence Act 2001* (Tas).

37 *Makita (Australia) Pty Ltd v Sprowles* (2001) 52 NSWLR 705 at [85]; see also *Sydneywide Distributors Pty Ltd v Red Bull Australia Pty Ltd* (2002) 55 IPR 354 at [8]; *Neowarra v Western Australia* (2003) 134 FCR 208 at [24].

- so far as the opinion is based on facts "observed" by the expert, they must be identified and admissibly proved in some other way;

- it must be established that the facts on which the opinion is based form a proper foundation for it;

- the opinion of an expert requires demonstration or examination of the scientific or other intellectual basis of the conclusions reached: that is, the expert's evidence must explain how the field of "specialised knowledge" in which the witness is expert by reason of "training, study or experience", and on which the opinion is "wholly or substantially based", applies to the facts assumed or observed so as to produce the opinion propounded".

Gaudron and Gummow JJ have expressed the view that s 79 does not give rise "to a test which is in any respect narrower or more restrictive than the position at common law".[38] The statutory formulation excluded a "field of expertise rule"[39] but scope probably remains for the *Daubert* indicia (falsifiability, existence of controls, peer reviews and general acceptance in the scientific community) to be applied as yardsticks for application of the prejudice–probative discretion. The statutory formulation does not explicitly include a "basis rule" and goes a substantial distance toward abolishing the common knowledge and ultimate issue rules. The substance of the exclusionary function under the statutory regimes at Commonwealth level and in New South Wales and Tasmania is undertaken by the discretionary provisions[40] which mandate a balancing of the probative and prejudicial impacts of expert opinion evidence. Thus far, the statutory regimes have not significantly changed the incidence and characteristics of judicial reception of expert evidence in Australia.

The role of expert evidence within the adversary system

It can be seen, therefore, that the courts and to a lesser degree recent legislation have imposed limitations upon the impact likely to be exerted by experts by setting substantial, and sometimes arbitrary, limits upon the evidence that they are permitted to give. This fundamentally affects the contribution that they can make to the resolution of disputes which may result in litigation. Medical practitioners, like all other experts, provide their opinions within the confines of the system within which they write their reports and give their evidence. Under the Anglo-Australian legal system, the quest is not for so elusive a concept as "truth". What is sought is a fair resolution of the differences between parties on the basis of the evidence made available, be the litigation between the Crown and an accused in a criminal trial, between a plaintiff and a defendant in a civil

---

38 *HG v The Queen* (1999) 197 CLR 414 at [58]; see also *Velevski v The Queen* [2002] HCA 4; 187 ALR 233.

39 See ALRC, NSWLRC and VLRC (2005) op cit.

40 Sections 135 and 137.

dispute, or between a husband and wife in a matrimonial contest. The standard of proof is borne by the party initiating proceedings and may vary between criminal and non-criminal proceedings, but the role of the judge remains primarily to be at a remove from the interstices of party–party conflict and to ensure that the conflict is fair and contested according to the rules. The judge is a ring-keeper[41] who traditionally only intrudes into the pugilism acted out at the bar table on behalf of the parties before him or her to prevent abuse of process or unfairness and to facilitate the decision-making process by a jury, if there is one. The question for the trier of fact, be it judge or jury, is whether the case for the Crown is proved beyond reasonable doubt or whether the case for the plaintiff or the applicant is proved on the balance of probabilities – on the evidence which is adduced.

The adducing of evidence is by and large under the version of the adversary system prevailing in Australia the province of the parties.[42] They make their own decisions about the evidence that is called, affected by tactical considerations, the extent of their lawyers' competence, and their financial resources – the depth of their pockets. It occurs from time to time that key witnesses are not called by either side to the litigation. This happens less often in criminal matters because of the duty of the Crown to call all relevant witnesses of truth, or at least to make them available, but it is by no means unknown in civil matters for important potential witnesses to be secreted or taken out-of-play by being commissioned by one side in order to make them less accessible for the party to whose position their views are thought likely to incline. In such situations, there is a theoretical possibility for the presiding judge to call a witness in criminal matters but it is scarcely ever done.[43] In civil matters, it has been held to be very dangerous for a judge to call a witness against the wishes of one of the parties.[44] Herein lies a fundamental difference between the adversarial and inquisitorial systems of justice. In the inquisitorial system, glimpsed in the Anglo-Australian tradition in the working of the coroners' courts,[45] the trier of fact also carries the responsibility of having all pertinent evidence made available for the court's considerations; under the adversary system, the role of calling evidence is almost exclusively that of the parties, the decision to call witnesses being dictated by an evaluation of the extent to which such evidence can be expected to advance the interests of the party contemplating calling them.

---

41 *R v Dora Harris* [1927] 2 KB 587 at 590.

42 See Malsch, M and Freckelton, I, "Expert Evidence in The Netherlands and Australia" (2005) 11(1) *Psychology, Public Policy & the Law* 42.

43 *R v Damic* [1982] 2 NSWLR 750; *Titheradge v The King* (1917) 24 CLR 107 at 116–117; *Whitehorn v The Queen* (1983) 49 ALR 448; *R v Apostilides* (1984) 53 ALR 445.

44 *Re Enoch and Zaretzky* [1910] 1 KB 327 at 333.

45 See Freckelton, I and Ranson, D *Death Investigation and the Coroner's Inquest*, Oxford University Press, Melbourne, 2006.

Court-appointment of expert witnesses

One means of addressing the potential for unrepresentative, uninformed or incomprehensible medical evidence to lead decision-makers into error would be for the courts themselves to call expert evidence where such a step is regarded as likely to advance the quality of fact-finding. However, this must be recognised as a significant qualification upon the traditional functioning of the Anglo-Australian adversary process. Such court-calling of expert witnesses has been little availed of under Australian, English and United States law, in spite of the fact that most judges technically have the power to initiate such a step. This said, it may be that changes to trial procedure (generated by intolerable delays and costs) will bring back into favour the option of courts appointing their own experts where the trier of fact needs non-partisan expert evidence not otherwise made available. The major impediments to this are cost and mechanisms for court selection of experts.

It may be that the adherence of Australia's judiciary to the traditional demarcation of parties' and presiding judges' roles is starting to change. In a survey of all Australian judges, conducted on behalf of the Australian Institute of Judicial Administration (AIJA), and published in 1999 a result comparable to results in a survey of United States judges was apparent. Many members of the Australian judiciary stated that they had not themselves appointed expert witnesses but saw merit in the procedure. They thought that it might well be of advantage for the fact-finding process.[46] The results from the survey bear further analysis as they are likely to add significantly to the lobby from medical practitioners that they be relieved from formal allegiance to parties to litigation and identified as witnesses of the court.

Judges were asked about their powers to call expert witnesses to assist them in the evaluation of expert evidence. Just over half of those answering the question indicated that they had such a power (52.97 per cent, n=116), a slightly smaller number indicating to the contrary (47.03 per cent, n=103).[47] Over-whelmingly, those possessed of such a power maintained that they had not exercised their power (81.88 per cent, n=122). Only a very small percentage of judges had appointed an expert witness themselves in the past five years. One in 20 answering the question (4.70 per cent, n=7) said that they had appointed an expert once in the last five years; 8.05 per cent (n=12) said that they had done so between once and five times, and 5.37 per cent (n=8) said that they had done so more than five times within that period. Judges were asked about why they had failed to appoint expert witnesses if they had the power to do so. The most common answer from those responding to the question (n=164) was that it had

46   See Freckelton, I, Reddy, P and Selby, H, *Australian Judicial Perspectives on Expert Evidence: An Empirical Study*, AIJA, Melbourne, 1999. See also Freckelton, I, Reddy, P and Selby, H, *Magistrates' Perspectives on Expert Evidence: An Empirical Study*, AIJA, Melbourne, 2001.

47   The survey instrument was sent to all 478 judges in Australia and yielded a response rate of 51 per cent. The response rate in fact was significantly higher because judges whose judicial experience was exclusively appellate were not eligible to respond.

not been "necessary" (41.46 per cent, n=68). Other answers included the response that no party had requested the judge to exercise the power (34.76 per cent, n=57). A smaller number of judges (10.66 per cent, n=26) maintained that they had declined to appoint an expert on the basis that such a measure would be contrary to the adversary process.

Significantly, of those who had appointed an expert, most judges found that the exercise had been "helpful" (69.23 per cent, n=27) or "very helpful" (28.21 per cent, n=11) to the fact-finding process. Only one judge, who apparently had had an adverse experience with the appointment of a court expert, indicated that the experience had been "unhelpful".

Judges were asked whether they were of the view that more use of court-appointed experts would be helpful to the fact-finding process. Nearly half of the judges answering the questionnaire expressed the opinion that it would be "helpful" (48.77 per cent, n=119), with about a third expressing the contrary view (30.33 per cent, n=74). About one fifth of judges either did not have a view (10.66 per cent, n=26) or did not respond to the question (10.25 per cent, n=25).

The questions in relation to court-appointed experts prompted a high volume of comments. One judge noted that in the Chelmsford Private Hospital litigation, dealing with the sequelae of the deep-sleep therapy in a private hospital, after consultation with the parties, the trial judge appointed a court expert in each of the 15 cases. The trial judge indicated that he had found considerable utility in this process, although he noted that the parties had either called their own experts in addition to the court-appointed expert or indicated that they proposed to do so before the matter being resolved by settlement.

Some judges indicated that they had never even contemplated trespassing into the arena of litigation to appoint an expert. The extent to which such a measure is inconsistent with the traditional role of the judge as ring-keeper under the adversary system is captured by the response of one judge: "It has never occurred to me to do so and I have no idea how I would go about it". Other judges were troubled by the practicalities of such a course, one commenting that it was more trouble than it was worth and another identifying as "problems: (i) Who will pay the expert?; (ii) What opportunity do the parties have to influence the court expert's advice to the judge?". Other judges noted that the procedure of the court appointing experts could have ramifications for courts' budgets unless parties are prevailed upon to pay, an option that will not always be feasible.

A number of judges noted that in certain compensation areas the court "has the benefit of Medical Panel certificates". By and large they indicated satisfaction with the process but in the same context one judge noted, "I believe I would have been assisted if I had exercised a power and called doctors in some instances".

Interestingly, the judicial comments were not characterised by a worry that court-appointed experts would exercise overmuch sway over the decision-making process, even if that task was the province of jurors. Such a concern has been expressed on occasions about involvement by judges in selecting and questioning witnesses but was rejected as a significant issue by researchers in 1991 who concluded that "fears that a court-appointed expert would overwhelm and unduly influence the jury are largely unsupported".[48]

The comments in relation to the utility of greater use of court-appointed experts provided something of a qualification upon the support otherwise given by the judges' answers to the survey instrument. A series of respondents supported the more frequent appointment of experts by courts provided that the process was carefully case-managed. One judge indicated that:

> The idea has a superficial appeal but: (1) The court-appointed expert acquires a status that is not warranted. (2) In cases of controversy between experts, it is usually because they come from different schools. Any court expert is likely also to come from one of the two "schools". (3) A court expert is not needed usually to identify flaws in the opinions of the experts called. It would be of value and save costs if parties do not have an expert and can agree on one to be appointed by the court. They would also have to agree on the briefing given to the expert.[49]

The results of the survey of Australian judges have many features in common with the results obtained by Cecil and Willging in their survey of United States Federal District Court judges.[50] In that study, of the 86 judges who had availed themselves of the power to appoint experts (20 per cent of the overall number), 255 appointments had been made. Fifty of the 86 judges who had made appointments replied that they perceived the appointment of court-appointed experts to be an extraordinary action:

> The importance of reserving appointment of experts for cases involving special needs was especially apparent in the responses of the judges who had made only a single appointment. Thirty-two of the forty-five judges who had appointed an expert on a single occasion indicated that they had not used the procedure more often because the unique circumstances in which they employed the expert had not arisen again. They simply had not found another suitable occasion in which to appoint an expert.

---

48   Brekke, NJ, Enko, PJ, Clavet, G and Seelau, E, "Of Juries and Court-Appointed Experts" (1991) 15 *Law & Human Behavior* 451 at 469–470.

49   The comment is reminiscent of the equivocal support for such a procedure given by Lord Denning MR in *Re Saxton* [1962] 1 WLR 968 at 972:

> It is said to be a rare thing for it to be done. I suppose that litigants realise that the court would attach great weight to the report of a court expert, and are reluctant thus to leave the decision of the case so much in his hands. If his report is against one side, that side will wish to call its own expert to contradict him, and then the other side will wish to call one too. So it would only mean that the parties would call their own experts as well. In the circumstances, the parties usually prefer to have the judge decide on the evidence of experts on either side, without resort to a court expert.

50   Cecil, JS and Willging, TE *Court-Appointed Experts: Defining the Role of Experts Appointed Under Federal Rule of Evidence*, Federal Judicial Center, Washington DC, 1993.

Similarly, in the Cecil and Willging study, 87 per cent of the judges indicated that court-appointed experts are likely to be helpful in at least some circumstances.[51] In other words, they manifested the same in-principle support for more extended use of court-appointed experts but shared with their Australian cousins a diffidence about exercising this aspect of their powers. Cecil and Willging concluded that this was attributable primarily to the difficulty of accommodating court-appointed experts in a legal system that values and generally anticipates adversarial presentation of evidence.[52]

However, it is apparent that pressures caused by the unavailability of legal aid, the high cost of litigation and the delays in cases being completed have generated an environment more amenable to fundamental change to litigation procedures than has previously existed. It may well be that the exclusive role of parties as the sole determiners of who will be called as expert witnesses will change in the foreseeable future.

Enhanced pre-trial communication

Another prominent feature of the qualitative data obtained by the judicial survey was the preparedness of many judges to contemplate procedures to bring experts together, generally pre-trial, to crystallise what matters they agree about and those upon which there is disagreement. This approach appears to be born of frustration at the unnecessary canvassing within court of expert opinions not fundamentally in dispute and a perception that such processes are engendering unsatisfactory trial delays, expense and obfuscation. Such an approach does not involve the imposition of arbitrary caps on the numbers of expert witnesses permitted to be called by parties but focuses upon enhancing the delineation of what is in dispute from what is not, and thereby factoring out sources of potential confusion and misunderstanding of the import of expert evidence.

Bias

The charge of "bias" or "partisanship" has been preferred against expert medical witnesses for the better part of two centuries. By the mid-19th century, the issue was one of considerable sensitivity. In the trial of William Palmer for strychnine poisoning, for instance, Lord Campbell savagely criticised medical experts adduced for the defence, in particular singling out a Dr Herepath of Bristol:

---

51 See also the small and inconclusive study on the subject by Champagne, A, Shuman, DW and Whitaker, E, "The Problem with Empirical Examination of the Use of Court-Appointed Experts: A Report of Non-findings" (1996) 14 *Behavioral Sciences & the Law* 361.

52 Cecil, JS and Willging, TE *Court-Appointed Experts: Defining the Role of Experts Appointed Under Federal Rule of Evidence*, Federal Judicial Center, Washington DC, 1993, p 5; see also Sink, JM, "The Unused Power of a Federal Judge to Call His Own Expert Witness" (1956) 29 *Southern California Law Review* 195.

[H]e has been prepared to come forward as a thoroughgoing partisan, advising the defence, suggesting question upon question on behalf of a man who he has again and again asserted he believed to be a poisoner. I abhor the traffic in testimony in which I regret to say men of science sometimes permit themselves to condescend.[53]

In a leading article in the 1897–1898 *Harvard Law Review* Foster J noted that:

This "bias", or inclination in favor of the party by whom the witness is employed, is probably the most frequent complaint of all against the expert witness; and the inclination of partiality is often characterized by terms indicating dishonesty and corruption.[54]

Ninety-nine years later, Lord Woolf's report into "Access to Justice" stressed the potential that experts may espouse the views of those who commission their reports and call them as witnesses.[55] He classified impartiality on the part of expert witnesses as "of paramount importance".[56] Many of his proposals for reform were developed expressly to break down the affiliation between experts and the commissioning parties with vested interests in the litigation.

In Australia a series of recent cases has identified expert bias as a phenomenon that has particularly troubled the courts in relation to evidence by medical practitioners, especially psychiatrists. In *Re W (Abuse Allegations: Expert Evidence)*,[57] for instance, Nicholson CJ and O'Ryan J (with whom Kay J agreed) warned of giving too much weight to expert evidence of a psychiatrist who had not seen the parties but had been prepared to proffer purportedly expert opinions. They warned: "there are grave dangers in reliance upon expert evidence given in such circumstances."[58] Much of the rejection of the psychiatrist's evidence arose from the view on the part of the appellate judges that he must have brought unconscious bias to his task. In *Re W (Sex Abuse: Standard of Proof)*[59] the Full Court of the Family Court affirmed that it was highly problematic for a first instance judge to accord significant weight to an expert medical witness if he or she has not seen all the parties, even if the witness is called by the court. It was a combination

---

53 Knott, DH (ed) *The Trial of William Palmer*, rev ER Watson, Notable British Trials Series, Hodges & Co, London, 1856.

54 Foster, WL, "Expert Testimony – Prevalent Complaints and Proposed Remedies" (1897–1898) 11 *Harvard Law Review* 169 at 171; see also Hand, L, "Historical and Practical Considerations Regarding Expert Testimony" (1901–1902) 15 *Harvard Law Review* 40 at 53.

55 Lord Woolf MR, *Access to Justice*, Final Report to the Lord Chancellor on the Civil Justice System in England and Wales, HMSO, London, 1996, p 143. He particularly noted the comment of the Court of Appeal in *Abbey National Mortgages Pty Ltd v Key Surveyors Nationwide Ltd* [1996] EGCS 23: "For whatever reason, and whether consciously or unconsciously, the fact is that expert witnesses instructed on behalf of parties to litigation often tend ... to espouse the cause of those instructing them to a greater or lesser extent, on occasions becoming more partisan than the parties".

56 Ibid, at 142.

57 (2001) FLC ¶93-085.

58 Ibid, at [147].

59 (2004) FLC ¶93-192; [2004] Fam CA 768.

of concerns about bias and methodology that generated the radical procedures now promulgated in the *Family Court Rules 2004* (Cth) which mandate single experts unless the need for further experts is established to the court.

Judges were asked in the AIJA survey whether they had encountered a number of problems that could impact upon the utility of expert evidence. Two-thirds of those who answered the question (68.10 per cent, n=158) reported that they "occasionally encountered" bias on the part of experts, while just over a quarter (27.59 per cent, n=64) reported that they encountered this phenomenon "often".

This latter statistic is in some ways the more significant. If bias is so prevalent that over a quarter of judges meet it often, this has ramifications for the functioning of the civil and criminal trial processes if it is not satisfactorily addressed. When asked about what quality they found most persuasive in an expert witness, judges also identified the absence of bias as very important – while 27.48 per cent of responses identified "clarity of explanation" as the most persuasive characteristic in an expert witness, 25.64 per cent identified "impartiality".

The questions about bias and partiality prompted a high incidence of commentary which particularly highlighted judges' views about the prevalence or lack of neutrality on the part of medical witnesses.

A number of judges cavilled at the term "bias", linking it with the notion of deliberate disingenuousness and locating the source of frequent disagreements amongst experts in other factors. One respondent commented that experts tend to favour the party calling them, but that to call this propensity "bias" was too strong a use of the term.

A similar view was expressed by another respondent: "I have never found an expert who has put forward a view which he/she does not genuinely hold, for the sake of merely supporting a case. Some views become untenable, but not because of 'bias' in the sense of a desire to further the case dishonestly". Another interpreted "bias" as a "dishonest attempt to support the party calling the expert".

However, other judges appeared to take it as a given that a large proportion of expert witnesses were partisan and variously opined that bias was particularly to be found in criminal pleas and in civil litigation in medical cases and in engineering cases.

The comments which lamented the incidence of the abandonment of neutrality particularly singled out medical witnesses, and a number focused upon the evidence given by psychiatrists. The comment of one judge seemed to sum up the views of many: "[Bias] is not unknown in other areas but is more entrenched in the medical profession". A number of cynical comments were notable: "I suspect that the expert says what she/he believes the party paying for the report/evidence wishes to read/hear"; "Bias is almost inevitable given that the expert is paid by one party and only called if his/her evidence helps the party's case"; "Experts seem to have a bias in favour of the party calling them. It may be an unconscious bias of course"; "The expert frequently slants his evidence in favour of the litigant on whose behalf his evidence is given"; "There are plaintiffs' doctors and defendants' doctors".

A number of responses indicated that bias became apparent in the proclivity of some experts to function as advocates. Others identified as a category of particularly biased experts those who made their living or a substantial part of their living out of providing forensic advice. Again, medical witnesses were particularly identified in this regard. One judge summed up the views of several: "Experts very readily fall into categories (Plaintiff or Defendant) when they develop an advising practice".

Some assumed that expert witnesses were not impartial but did not blame them: "Many experts are predictable in the sense of it is easy to know in advance what tack they will take. They are honest, but not necessarily objective".

The responses in relation to "bias" were significant, particularly the considerable proportion of the Australian judiciary reporting a pattern of finding partisanship on the part of specialist witnesses called before them. The definition of bias, that is to say whether the connotation of the word necessarily involves deliberate or unwitting lack of objectivity, is less important. What appears to concern judges is the product of the bias, namely the frequency with which reports and oral evidence end up inclining markedly toward one side in the litigation and lacking rigour and objectivity.

Selection processes for medical witnesses

As already noted, medical witnesses are not selected (in civil litigation especially) for their ability to assist the court in a search for truth. They are selected out of a perception that their opinions and the way in which they express them are likely to advance the cause of the party which commissions their report or seeks to have them give evidence. Pertinent knowledge is a prerequisite to their status as experts but considerations such as their capacity to convey their opinions lucidly, comprehensibly and memorably are just as important to those deciding whether to call them as their status as leaders in their professional field. These kinds of ability are what mark an expert within the Anglo-Australian legal system as a "forensic expert" likely to be in demand.

The adverse side of such an approach on the part of litigators is that it places a premium upon "performance" to the potential exclusion of "substance" in terms of their evidence. The positive side is that recognition of the importance of effective communication has the potential to bring witnesses before courts and tribunals who have the skills to impart esoteric information in a way likely to be effectively evaluated by decision-makers. Nonetheless, the reality of the dynamics and tactics that generate the process by which experts are selected under the current system to pen reports or to give oral evidence is that the best are sometimes passed over or at least apparently passed over.

The legal system has long been conscious of the potential unrepresentativeness of the information that comes before courts for the purposes of decision-making and that decisions can only be as sound as the information made available to form the bases of decisions. In the 19th century case of *Thorn v Worthing Skating Rink Co*, for instance, Lord Jessel commented:

> A man may go, and does sometimes, to half-a-dozen experts. I have known it in cases of valuation within my own experience at the Bar. He takes their honest opinions, he finds three in his favour and three against him; he says to the three in his favour, will you be kind enough to give evidence? and he pays the three against him their fees and leaves them alone; the other side does the same. It may not be three out of six, it may be three out of fifty. I was told in one case, where a person wanted a certain thing done, that they went to sixty-eight people before they found one.[60]

The adversary system depends upon many assumptions. Two in this context are particularly pertinent: (a) that each side in litigation has an opportunity to seek out experts who favour their contentions; and (b) that counsel's skills in making witnesses accountable in the course of cross-examination will expose biases, frauds and inadequacies. Unfortunately, inequalities in litigants' access to resources and the variability of solicitors' and barristers' skills mean that the dynamics which result in experts being selected to author reports and give evidence can result in evidence going before decision-makers which is not representative of the community of views within most areas of expert endeavour. This in turn has the potential to result in miscarriages of civil and criminal justice.

Therefore, it is not surprising that a lobby has long been undertaken on the part of medical practitioners that the adversary system be changed so that medical witnesses, especially in the civil area, only be able to be selected from a designated panel of experts chosen for their reputation and proficiency by the learned colleges. The advantage of such a system would be to remove from the litigation system the charlatans and the ground-breakers. Only those would give evidence as accredited medical experts whose views were representative of the community of opinions within their area of practice. The adverse side of such a system would be that the iconoclasts, the free-thinkers, and those outside the mainstream of the medical establishment would be frozen out of the courts and tribunals. There would be a complete tyranny of the majority medical opinion of the day. The legal system would become even more conservative than it currently is. The major losers would be plaintiffs.[61]

---

60 (1877) 6 Ch D 415.

61 Ironically, such a process would run counter to the spirit of the High Court approach in *Rogers v Whitaker* (1992) 175 CLR 479 to determine the existence of departure from acceptable standards of information provision to patients by reference to standards other than those current within the medical profession. It would impose the medical norm as the standard against which medical propriety must be judged, to the exclusion of dissentient and minority voices within and outside the profession.

In 2005, the New South Wales Law Reform Commission identified cons-tructive advantages in the development of accreditation processes for forensic experts but stopped short of recommending that they be mandatory:

> The Commission has no doubt that properly run schemes of accreditation, especially those involving forensic accreditation, have considerable potential to assist the system of justice by educating potential expert witnesses in their responsibilities, and helping them understand and work effectively within the justice system. Such schemes are likely to enhance the skills and understanding of those who participate in them, both as to the discipline and as to the role of the expert witness. Schemes of accreditation that advance an understanding of the role of the expert witness might have the effect of excluding or discouraging individuals who are, as stated in one submission, "malleable in their views and who do fall within the rubric of 'guns for hire'".[62]

Comprehensibility of evidence

If a decision-maker, be it a judge or a juror, is unable to comprehend medical evidence sufficiently to appreciate the distinctions in the terminology and opinions expressed by opposing witnesses, this too has the potential to generate a wrong result in litigation. The difficulty likely to be encountered by lay decision-makers such as jurors in understanding the subtle differences of opinion amongst medical witnesses, especially where the divergences are the subject of complex and conflicting testimony, has long been advanced as a ground for removing the calling and selection of doctors from the responsibility of the parties and investing it in the hands of courts and tribunals. It has also been argued to be a ground for removing decision-making in such matters from lay members of the public selected to be jurors.

The momentum to make such changes to the functioning of the adversary system can be identified in the mid-19th century when a series of initiatives was promoted as an improvement on the system obtaining at the time in England to remove decision-making in cases involving medical evidence from lay tribunals of fact to ones that were constituted by experts. The alternative mooted was the establishment of panels of experts from which courts could draw when needing authoritative opinion from members of the learned colleges.[63]

The problem of wrong decision-making generated by misunderstanding or failure to understand expert medical evidence is generally said to relate to trials conducted before juries. Relatively little sound scholarship, though, has been devoted to assessing the limitations upon jurors' ability to understand and evaluate complex medical evidence. A range of impediments under the Anglo-

---

62 New South Wales Law Reform Commission, *Expert Witnesses*, NSWLRC, Sydney, 2005, at para 9.59.

63 See Jones, CAG, *Expert Witnesses*, Clarendon Press, Oxford, 1994; Golan, T *Laws of Men and Laws of Nature*, Harvard University Press, Cambridge, MA, 2004.

Australian legal system stands in the way of approaching jurors to ask them about their impressions of their ability to cope with the intellectual rigours of civil and criminal trials.

Most of the research about levels of understanding and about the potential for prejudices and misunderstandings to infect the decision-making process in the face of complex and conflicting expert evidence has been derived from North American mock juror studies, suggesting diversely and without clear consistency that:

- jurors are more influenced by an expert's ability to convey technical information comprehensibly and to draw firm conclusions than by educational credentials;[64]

- jurors are impressed by an expert's reputation and educational credentials but clarity of presentation is the most important factor;[65]

- jurors want articulate experts, and to a lesser degree experts who draw firm conclusions;[66]

- jurors do not find experts who are very technical and complex particularly persuasive;[67]

- jurors with less management experience may be more suspicious of experts;[68]

- jurors are especially influenced by expert evidence given early in proceedings;[69]

- jurors may undervalue match probabilities;[70]

- jurors who are more educated may be less likely to accept the views of expert witnesses uncritically;[71]

- jurors who are more educated are more likely to participate actively in juror deliberations;[72]

---

64 Champagne, A, Shuman, D and Whitaker, E, "An Empirical Examination of the Use of Expert Witnesses in American Courts" (1991) 31 *Jurimetrics Journal* 375 at 388.

65 Shuman, DW, Champagne, A and Whitaker, E, "An Empirical Examination of the Use of Expert Witnesses in the Courts – Part II: A Three City Study" (1994) 34 *Jurimetrics Journal* 193.

66 Ibid.

67 Ibid.

68 Austin, AD, "Jury Perceptions on Advocacy: A Case Study" (1982) 8 *Litigation* 15.

69 Brekke, N and Borgida, E, "Expert Psychological Testimony in Rape Trials: A Social-Cognitive Analysis" (1988) 55 *Journal of Personality & Social Psychology* 372.

70 Faigman, DL and Baglioni, AJ, "Bayes' Theorem in the Trial Process: Instructing Jurors on the Value of Statistical Evidence" (1988) 12 *Law & Human Behavior* 1.

71 Saks, MJ and Wisler, RL, "Legal and Psychological Bases of Expert Testimony: Surveys of the Law and Jurors" (1984) 2 *Behavioral Sciences & the Law* 361 at 435.

72 Hastie, R, Penrod, SD and Pennington, N, *Inside the Jury*, Harvard University Press, Cambridge, 1983, pp 137–138.

- jurors who are younger find psychologists and psychiatrists more credible than do older jurors;[73]

- jurors who are older tend generally to believe expert witnesses more readily than do younger jurors;[74]

- while jurors are conscientious about their task, their enthusiasm and vigilance reduce in the course of the trial;[75]

- most jurors can understand and remember evidence from the trial where they were empanelled a short while before;[76]

- jurors rely on fluency, vocal inflection and appearance to evaluate witnesses generally;[77]

- jurors who find evidence unduly complex tend to turn to factors such as appearance and communication skills to evaluate its value;[78]

- jurors are suspicious of experts' impartiality if they learn that the experts have been paid by the lawyers representing the litigants;[79]

- male jurors tend to refer to abstract and rational concepts of fairness, whereas female jurors tend to refer to relationships and principles of affiliation and responsibility;[80]

- male jurors tend to approach decision-making in a more binary fashion (guilty/not guilty) than do female jurors;[81] and

- jurors who have previously functioned as jurors in criminal cases may be more prosecution-oriented[82] than first-time jurors.

---

73   Saks, RJ and Wisler, RL, "Legal and Psychological Bases of Expert Testimony: Surveys of the Law and Jurors" (1984) 2 *Behavioral Sciences & the Law* 361 at 445.

74   Ibid.

75   Stephenson, GM, *The Psychology of Criminal Justice*, Blackwell, Oxford, 1992.

76   Zander, M and Henderson, P, "The Crown Court Study. Royal Commission on Criminal Justice", Study No 19, Research Bulletin No 35, Home Office, Research and Statistics Department, 1994. However, there are doubts about whether this is a correct interpretation of the data: see Kapardis, A, *Psychology and Law*, Cambridge University Press, Cambridge, 2004, p 142.

77   Rosenthal, P, "Nature of Jury Response to the Expert Witness" (1983) 28 *Journal of Forensic Science* 528.

78   Ibid. See also Tanton, RL, "Jury Preconceptions and their Effect on Expert Scientific Testimony" (1979) 24 *Journal of Forensic Science* 681. However, the Shuman et al (1994) op cit, study and the Champagne et al (1991) op cit, studies found that pleasant personality and attractive appearance were the least important factors to jurors in determining the credibility of an expert.

79   See Shuman et al (1994) op cit; Champagne et al (1991) op cit.

80   Poulin, AB, "The Jury: the Criminal Justice System's Different Voice" (1994) 62 *University of Cincinnati Law Review* 1377.

81   Ibid, at 1396; see also Dooley, LG, "Sounds of Silence on the Civil Jury" (1991) 26 *Valparaiso University Law Review* 405.

82   Hastie, R, Penrod, SD and Pennington, N, *Inside the Jury*, Harvard University Press, Cambridge, 1983, p 143.

Many of these research findings are open to criticism in terms of their methodology, their selection procedures, and their cultural matrix. Nonetheless they cannot be dismissed out of hand. Researchers Shuman, Champagne and Whitaker summed up the state of empirical knowledge disturbingly:

> The typical juror forms impressions of experts stereotypically, based on the occupation of the experts, and superficially, based on the personal characteristics of the experts ... This image of jurors is troubling not only because it questions the capacity of the majority of the populace, but also because it flies in the face of 200 years of experience with the jury system. Our retention of the jury system with only minor tinkering over this time is an affirmation of our belief that the jury usually gets it right.[83]

In the AIJA survey, judges were asked about whether they, as opposed to jurors, had encountered evidence which they had not been able to evaluate adequately because of its complexity. Just over half (53.19 per cent, n=125) said that they had not had such an experience, while just under a half (45.11 per cent, n=106) said that they had occasionally met such a problem. Only four judges said that they encountered such a problem "often" (1.70 per cent). The numbers of judges sitting in the family and civil law jurisdictions who said that they had "never" been unable to understand expert evidence was higher than in the criminal law area.

A series of respondents made the point in comments that they had the power to rectify the situation by demanding clarification or obtaining explanations. How effective such measures had proved to be for the substantial percentage who had occasionally had problems in evaluating particularly complex expert evidence could not be evaluated from the answers provided.

Those judges who said that they had encountered such a problem were asked which discipline the witness had come from. Sixteen per cent indicated psychiatry, 13 per cent said psychology and just over 10.5 per cent said medicine and surgery.

While the figures indicating difficulty with evidence given by mental health professionals are pronounced, the combined figures for medical evidence are even more so (26.5 per cent), emphasising both the amount of such evidence and the difficulty that it is perceived to pose by many within Australia's judiciary.

Whether these difficulties, as identified by the judges, and as speculated about by many commentators, will generate any serious momentum toward change in trial procedures remains to be seen. Early indications, though, suggest that they may.

---

83 Shuman, DW, Champagne, A and Whitaker, E, "Juror Assessments of the Believability of Expert Witnesses: A Literature Review" (1996) 36 *Jurimetrics Journal* 371 at 382; see too Edmond, G and Mercer, D, "The Politics of Jury Competence" in Martin, B (ed), *Technology and Public Participation*, University of Wollongong, Wollongong, 1999.

Ethical duties of expert witnesses

It is not the case, as noted already, that debates about expert evidence and expert witnesses are new. The common law has responded by evolving little by little sets of ethical responsibilities to which experts are expected to conform. They were summarised by Cresswell J in The *Ikarian Reefer*[84]:

(1) Expert evidence presented to the court should be and seen to be the independent product of the expert uninfluenced as to form or content by the exigencies of litigation.

(2) An expert witness should provide independent assistance to the court by way of objective unbiased opinion in relation to matters within his expertise. An expert witness in the High Court should never assume the role of advocate.

(3) An expert witness should state the facts or assumptions on which his opinion is based. He should not omit to consider material facts which detract from his concluded opinions.

(4) An expert should make it clear when a particular question or issue falls outside his expertise.

(5) If an expert's opinion is not properly researched because he considers that insufficient data is available then this must be stated with an indication that the opinion is no more than a provisional one.

(6) If after exchange of reports, an expert witness changes his view on material matters, such change of view should be communicated to the other side without delay and when appropriate to the court.

Wall J in *Re AB (Child Abuse: Expert Witnesses)*[85] added the following:

Where that occurs, the jury will have to resolve the issue which is raised. Two points must be made. In my view, the expert who advances such a hypothesis owes a very heavy duty to explain to the court that what he is advancing is a hypothesis, that it is controversial (if it is) and placed before the court all material which contradicts the hypothesis. Secondly, he must make all his material available to the other experts in the case. It is the common experience of the courts that the better the experts the more limited their areas of disagreement, and in the forensic context of a contested case relating to children, the objective of the lawyers and the experts should always be to limit the ambit of disagreement on medical issues to the minimum.

In *Harris v The Queen*[86] the Court of Appeal held that the guidance given by both Cresswell J and Wall J "are very relevant to criminal proceedings and should be kept well in mind by both prosecution and defence".

In *Bowman v The Queen*[87] it was proposed too that reports provide:

---

84 [1993] 2 Lloyds Rep 68 at 81.
85 [1995] 1 FLR 181 at 192.
86 [2005] EWCA Crim 1980 at [273].
87 [2006] EWCA 417 at [177].

1. Details of the expert's academic and professional qualifications, experience and accreditation relevant to the opinions expressed in the report and the range and extent of the expertise and any limitations upon the expertise.

2. A statement setting out the substance of all the instructions received (with written or oral), questions upon which an opinion is sought, the materials provided and considered, and the documents, statements, evidence, information or assumptions which are material to the opinions expressed or upon which those opinions are based.

3. Information relating to who has carried out measurements, examinations, tests etc and the methodology used, and whether or not such measurements etc were carried out under the expert's supervision.

4. Where there is a range of opinion in the matters dealt with in the report a summary of the range of opinion and the reasons for the opinion given. In this connection any material facts or matters which detract from the expert's opinions and any points which should fairly be made against any opinions expressed should be set out.

5. Relevant extracts of literature or any other material which might assist the court.

6. A statement to the effect that the expert has complied with his/her duty to the court to provide independent assistance by way of objective unbiased opinion in relation to matters within his or her expertise and an acknowledgment that the expert will inform all parties and where appropriate the court in the event that his/her opinion changes on any material issues.

7. Where on an exchange of experts' reports matters arise which require a further or supplemental report the above guidelines should, of course, be complied with.

In short therefore the common law is in the process of enunciating stringent requirements for expert witness and report-writer conduct. These are of particular application to medical practitioners.

Reforms

Many changes have been recommended latterly or been implemented in Australia in relation to expert evidence. Already disclosure of medical reports is mandated in all jurisdictions for civil litigation. The Crown has to disclose reports of witnesses upon whom it intends to rely at trial in its depositions in criminal matters. Particularly onerous obligations to disclose material exist on the part of defendants in some jurisdictions in civil matters. For instance, in Victoria, where a personal injury claim is made by a plaintiff, a defendant is obliged to serve upon the plaintiff any medical report (very widely defined) in their possession, custody or power, even if the defendant does not intend to rely upon it at trial.[88]

---

88   *Supreme Court Rules* (Vic) O 33.07(3).

In 2005 the Australian, New South Wales and Victorian Law Reform Commissions[89] advanced recommendations in relation to evidentiary reform including expert evidence. The commissions recommended maintenance of the provisions in the Uniform Evidence Acts but suggested for clarification purposes a specific provision to stipulate the admissibility of expert opinion as counter-intuitive evidence in relation to child development and behaviour.

In 2005 the New South Wales Law Reform Commission[90] reported on proposed changes to reports and evidence by expert witnesses. Its recommendations too were very modest in extent. Aside from some technical proposals in relation to the *Supreme Court Rules* and *Code of Conduct for Expert Witnesses*, it suggested that there should be a provision, by rule or Federal Court Practice Direction, requiring that expert witnesses be informed of the sanctions relating to inappropriate or unethical conduct.[91] It found contingency arrangements for expert witnesses to be extremely rare and did not recommend they be banned outright.

In 1998 the Australian Federal Court promulgated an innovative practice direction, "Guidelines for Expert Witnesses in Proceedings in the Federal Court of Australia". It has since been substantially adopted throughout the Australian legal system[92] with the result that there is explicit prescription that an expert has an over-riding duty to assist the court on matters relevant to the expert's area of expertise. They stress that an expert witness is not an advocate for a party. They state explicitly that an expert witness' paramount duty is to the court and not to the person retaining the expert.

Expert witnesses are expected to qualify findings in their reports (where they believe their report may be incomplete or inaccurate without some qualification), and in a number of jurisdictions to give reasons for each opinion that they express. They must indicate what the material is upon which they rely for the purposes of their reports. Experts are also required to articulate any assumptions upon which they have acted in their expression of opinions. Expert witnesses are also mandated to disclose all instructions given to them which define the scope of their reports, and to disclose the facts, matters and assumptions upon which their report proceeds. Expert witnesses are obliged also to disclose if their opinions are not fully researched because they consider that insufficient data are available, and if a particular question or issue falls outside their field of expertise.

In another major change, court rules generally now provide that if expert witnesses retained by parties in a case meet at the direction of the court, it is

---

89   Ibid.

90   Ibid.

91   Recommendation 9.3.

92   See *Family Law Rules 2004* (Cth); *Uniform Civil Procedure Rules 2005* (NSW) Sch 7; *Uniform Civil Procedure Rules 1999* (Qld); Practice Direction 46 of the Supreme Court of South Australia; *Supreme Court Rules* (Tas) rr 515–517; *Supreme Court Rules* (Vic) O 44; *Supreme Court Rules* (WA) O 36A; Practice Direction No 3, 2000 of the Supreme Court of the Australian Capital Territory; *Supreme Court Rules* (NT) O 44.

improper conduct for an expert to be given or to accept instructions not to reach agreement in that meeting. If expert witnesses at such a meeting cannot reach agreement on matters of expert opinion, they must provide reasons for this to the court.

Under the Federal Court Guidelines, at the end of a report experts are expected to declare that:

> I [the expert] have made all the inquiries which the expert believes are desirable and appropriate and that no matters of significance which I [the expert] regard as relevant have, to my [the expert's] knowledge, been withheld from the court.

The initiatives within the Federal Court's Practice Direction and the various court rules that have adopted the substance of its procedures have as one of their purposes changing the culture that exists in some quarters of expert witness practice. They are aimed at crystallising issues in dispute and enabling parties more effectively to evaluate the strength of not just expert reports but of individual opinions within them. Most importantly, generally they mandate the provision of reasons for each and every opinion expressed, thereby facilitating a new level of evidentiary transparency. They represent a significant intrusion into the traditional style of medical reports, for instance, requiring reference to assumptions, material upon which reliance is placed and disclosure of reasoning processes employed. Moreover, they state in unequivocal terms the obligation for expert witnesses not to function as, or regarded themselves as being, advocates for parties to the litigation.

The most radical initiatives that have been promulgated in relation to the entitlements of parties to adduce expert evidence are in the Family Court, and in Queensland and the Australian Capital Territory in respect of civil litigation. In each of these jurisdictions, there is now a presumption that there will be a single expert on any given topic, although entitlements remain for the calling of more experts with leave of the court. Anxiety has been expressed in some quarters[93] that the new arrangements encroach unduly upon parties' litigation autonomy and excessively curtail legitimate differences of approach amongst experts. Whether the new rules operate in a draconian way cannot yet be evaluated. However, it is apparent that different judicial officers interpret the rules with varying levels of stringency.

Witness immunity

A curious but probably short-term anomaly has arisen in relation to the role of medical practitioners who undertake forensic work. There has long been a rule that expert witnesses are immune from civil action in respect of the opinions that they express in order to encourage experts to express views to the courts fearlessly and

---

93 See, for example, Freckelton, I, "Expert Evidence in the Family Court: the New Regime" (2005) 12 *Psychiatry, Psychology & Law* 234.

without favour.[94] In *Meadow v General Medical Council*,[95] Collins J ruled that the same justifications apply to the risk of disciplinary proceedings. He overturned a decision of a Fitness to Practise Panel of the General Medical Council, striking off the well-known paediatrician, Sir Roy Meadow, for unacceptable methodology in a forensic report and in oral evidence that he gave in a criminal trial. Collins J accepted the need for regulation of medical practitioners but concluded that they should only be at risk of disciplinary proceedings if referred (in extreme cases) by the courts to their regulatory body.

The decision of Collins J contains many problematic aspects[96] and was subject to further appeal at the time of the writing of this chapter. Most importantly, it places forensic work in a special category of sequestered immunity when it is a significant aspect of contemporary medical practice and can have devastating ramifications for those affected by expert reports and evidence. Further, there is little evidence that the potential for disciplinary action to be taken when egregiously poor reports are written or evidence given will have a freezing effect upon the availability of forensic expertise. In Australia where the Western Australian Court of Appeal[97] has not signalled any disinclination to hear an appeal from a disciplinary body concerning misuse of a forensic test in a civil action medical witnesses continue to be readily available. Finally, the notion that the entry-point to disciplinary regulation should be the courts rather than disciplinary bodies constituted for the purpose of investigating issues of unprofessional conduct is highly problematic.

While it is important that expert report writers and witnesses not be deterred in any way from discharging their functions without concern as to adverse consequences, this does not legitimise protecting them from professional regulation if their conduct is seriously substandard and foreseeably carries with it serious risks for others. It is unlikely that the decision of Collins J in respect of Sir Roy Meadow will be applied in Australia.

Expert report writing and testimony: The future

The role of the medical practitioner as a report-writer and as a forensic expert at the coal-face of litigation is controversial and will remain so. The sensitivity of different perspectives on the part of pathologists have latterly been particularly pronounced in the United Kingdom in relation to SIDS/suspected child

---

94   See, for example, *Stanton v Callaghan* [2000] 1 QB 75 at 109; *Darker v Chief Constable of Midlands Police* [2001] 1 AC 435 at 469.

95   [2006] EWHC 146 (Admin).

96   For a critique see Freckelton, I, "Immunity for Experts from Disciplinary Regulation" (2006) 13 *Journal of Law and Medicine* 393.

97   *Mustac v Medical Board of Western Australia* [2004] WASCA 156; Freckelton, I, "Regulating Forensic Deviance" (2004) 12 *JLM* 141.

abuse cases.[98] However, merely because different views are expressed by well-qualified experts is not necessarily sinister. To believe so constitutes indulging in both naïveté and the "fallacy of positivism" – the erroneous notion that there are definitive answers to all medical and scientific questions.

The AIJA survey of judges highlighted the degree of judicial concern in Australia about medical witness partiality and about the compromising of neutrality. The courts' procedural reforms are a major initiative on the part of Australia's judiciary to change expert culture so as to orchestrate the provision of high quality, transparent information to the courts from professionals not suborned by the adversary processes.

The courts' procedural reforms will not meet all of the concerns of medical practitioners. Reformers will continue to articulate consternation about the subtle effects of the dynamics inherent in the functioning of the adversary system. They will worry, too, about the capacity of lay triers of fact to comprehend and evaluate the subtleties of medical practitioners' differences of opinion. Many will call for more involvement by the judiciary in reducing party-engineered obfuscation of expert evidence and the calling of witnesses unrepresentative of the community of informed opinion within medicine. Ultimately, though, reliance for some time to come will continue to be placed in the hands of counsel and the vagaries of the adversary system to expose frauds, fringe dwellers and practitioners with impoverished theories and methodologies. It will only be by informed expectations and by the improved understanding by lawyers of medical practice and by medical practitioners of legal practice that the role of the medical expert will evolve into a genuinely effective component in resolving the problems posed by the litigation process.

Should the anxieties manifested in the AIJA studies about unreliability and bias in expert evidence, particularly on the part of medical witnesses, continue to escalate, the moderate reports from the New South Wales Law Reform Commission in relation to expert witnesses in 2005 and by the Australian, New South Wales and Victorian Law Reform Commissions in relation to evidentiary rules generally in 2005, will not hold back the tidewaters of ad hoc reform. There is a real risk that the initiatives of the Family Court and those in Queensland and the Australian Capital Territory will be emulated. That would be an unfortunate invitation to the tyranny of orthodoxy and would be detrimental to litigants seeking to ventilate legitimately alternative medical views in Australia's courts and tribunals.

---

98   See *R v Clark* [2002] EWCA Crim 54; *R v Clark* [2003] EWCA Crim 1020; *Cannings v The Queen* [2004] EWCA Crim 1; *R v Kai-Whitewind* [2005] EWCA Crim 1092; *Lu v LB* [2005] EWCA Civ 567.

21

Judicial activism or "traditional" negligence law? Conception, pregnancy and denial of reproductive choice

Reg Graycar[1]

In 2003, the High Court of Australia's first hearing of the year was the case of *Cattanach v Melchior*.[2] Significantly, this was the first case heard by an all male High Court in the 16 years since 1987 when Justice Mary Gaudron joined the bench.[3] The case involved a woman in her 40s with two children. She had sought to ensure that she not have any more. At the age of 44, she discovered that she was pregnant, even though she had undergone a surgical sterilisation procedure. She went on to give birth to a baby boy, Jordan. In a four to three decision, the High Court upheld an award of damages of just over $100,000 for the cost of Jordan's upkeep.[4]

In this chapter, I discuss what have come to be known as actions for wrongful birth, wrongful pregnancy or wrongful conception.[5] While these cover a range of phenomena, I will focus on the type of situation that has ended up being litigated by the highest courts of the United Kingdom and Australia in recent years. This situation is where due to the negligence of a medical practitioner a child has been born to parents who did not plan or choose to have that child

---

1   Professor of Law, University of Sydney; Visiting Professor, Cornell Law School. Thanks to Tiffany Hambley and Hilarie Lloyd for excellent research assistance, and to Tiffany Hambley, Isabel Karpin, Nicky Priaulx, Elizabeth Adjin-Tettey, Anita Bernstein and Harold Luntz for their extremely helpful comments on earlier drafts.

2   (2003) 215 CLR 1; [2003] HCA 38. Note that the references to the judgments will be by paragraph number of the medium neutral citation.

3   She served until early 2003 and was replaced by Justice Dyson Heydon.

4   *Cattanach v Melchior* (2003) 215 CLR 1; [2003] HCA 38. The majority judges were McHugh and Gummow JJ, Kirby J, and Callinan J; in dissent were Gleeson CJ, Hayne J and Heydon J. While some of the media discussions of this case were critical of the finding of negligence, by the time the matter reached the High Court negligence was no longer in issue; the only matter upon which the High Court gave leave was the assessment of damages for the costs of Jordan's upbringing: *Cattanach v Melchior* (unreported, HCA, Gaudron and Kirby JJ, 19 March 2002, Transcript of Special Leave to Appeal), <www.austlii.edu.au/cgi-bin/disp.pl/au/other/hca/transcripts/2001/B59/1.html?query=+%28%28cattanach%29+and+%28on%29%29> (accessed 17 August 2005).

5   The different uses of terminology will be discussed below.

(indeed, who may actively have planned *not* to have a child). I do not discuss here the conceptually separate, but somewhat related action known as "wrongful life" – an action brought not by the parent(s) but by the child (usually a child born with serious disability), alleging that but for the negligence of the defendant, the child would not have been born.[6] This action, at the time of writing due to be heard by the High Court of Australia for the first time,[7] raises separate and perhaps more philosophically difficult questions. However, the main focus of my discussion is the former situation, what Nicky Priaulx has termed "unsolicited parenthood".[8]

Within the United Kingdom and Australia, the issue that has raised most contention in such cases is whether, as an aspect of damages for what is clearly accepted by courts as negligence, the parents might receive compensation for the costs of raising the child.[9] Unlike in the United States, where some States have imposed statutory bars on those actions (though others allow them),[10] there has never been any suggestion that the negligence go completely unremedied, even in such cases as *Udale v Bloomsbury Area Health Authority*[11] (discussed below), which is widely cited in defence of denying this type of claim. So in one sense it might be said that this is a very narrow legal issue, confined as it is to the recovery of one head of damages.

In this discussion I will focus on an underlying theme and one that is rarely expressly articulated (but in my view underpins this debate): the issue of reproductive choice and in particular, the challenge to women's autonomy that denying recovery entails.[12] I argue that those who oppose the award of damages for this type of negligence are engaging in what conservative commentators tend to refer

---

6   The leading (English) case on this is *McKay v Essex Area Health Authority* [1982] QB 1166. The action is also excluded by the *Congenital Disabilities (Civil Liability) Act 1976* (UK) s 1(5). For a recent discussion that also canvasses the highly controversial decision of the French Cour de Cassation in *Perruche*, 17 November 2000, <www.courdecassation.fr/agenda/arrets/arrets/99-13701rap.htm> (accessed 12 February 2006), a decision overturned by legislation; see Morris, A and Saintier, S, "To Be or Not to Be: Is that the Question? Wrongful Life and Misconceptions" (2003) 11 *Medical Law Review* 167.

7   See *Harriton v Stephens* (2004) 59 NSWLR 694. These cases were granted leave to appeal to the High Court and judgment was handed down in May 2006. The High Court affirmed the decision of the Court of Appeal: *Harriton v Stephens* [2006] HCA 15.

8   See Priaulx, N, "That's One Heck of an 'Unruly Horse'! Riding Roughshod Over Autonomy in Wrongful Conception" (2004) 12 *Feminist Legal Studies* 317 at 317.

9   This is commonly expressed as the "costs of raising a healthy child".

10 See, for a State-by-State summary Annotation, "Recoverability of Cost of Raising Normal Healthy Child Born as result of Physician's Negligence or Breach or Contract or Warranty" 89 ALR 4th 632 and for one of a number of discussions, Strasser, M, "Misconceptions and Wrongful Births: A Call for a Principled Jurisprudence" (1999) 31 *Arizona State Law Journal* 161. United States law is discussed further below.

11 *Udale v Bloomsbury Area Health Authority* [1983] 2 All ER 522.

12 A striking exception to the silence about these issues is Baroness Hale's extra curial discussion of these cases: "The Value of Life and the Cost of Living – Damages for Wrongful Birth" (2001) 7 *British Actuarial Journal* 747. The commentary was originally presented as the annual Staple Inn Reading, an address delivered to the Institute of Actuaries, 28 June 2001.

to as "judicial activism"; that is, making decisions expressly on the basis of policy preferences, in this case, exhibiting a lack of respect or support for women's reproductive autonomy.[13] But first: a note on terminology.

Terminology

A number of commentators have attempted to separate out, and assign distinct meaning to, the range of terms used to describe legal claims about unsolicited parenthood. For example, United States law professor Mark Strasser has attempted to develop a typology of claims, while simultaneously recognising their commonality in that "in all of these ... a pregnancy and live birth occurred which would not have but for the negligence of a medical professional".[14] There are four terms most commonly used: wrongful conception, wrongful pregnancy, wrongful birth and wrongful life. In Strasser's view, the first two usually involve the birth of a healthy, though unplanned child; while in relation to the second two, he claims that each involves the birth of a child with some form of disability. He also refers to a decision of the Supreme Judicial Court of Massachusetts that has derided the use of the terms, pointing out that the wrongfulness "lies not in the life, the birth, the conception or the pregnancy, but in the negligence of the physician".[15] Similar sentiments have been expressed by a number of other judges, including Kirby J in the High Court in *Cattanach*;[16] and by McMurdo P in the Queensland Court of Appeal decision from which the appeal was taken.[17] Perhaps its clearest expression is in the joint judgment of McHugh and Gummow JJ:

---

13 I explore the notion of judicial activism below. I am aware that the notion of "reproductive autonomy" requires perhaps some more extensive elaboration, beyond the scope of this chapter. For present purposes, I mean simply the right of women to make independent decisions about their reproductive bodies.

14 Strasser, M, "Yes, Virginia, There Can Be Wrongful Life: On Consistency, Public Policy, and the Birth-Related Torts" (2003) 4 *Georgetown Journal of Gender & the Law* 821 at 823; see also, on terminology, Mason, JK, "Wrongful Pregnancy, Wrongful Birth and Wrongful Terminology" (2002) 6 *Edinburgh Law Review* 46.

15 *Viccaro v Milunsky* 551 NE2d 8 (Mass 1990) at 9. The court continued:

    The harm, if any, is not the birth itself but the effect of the defendant's negligence on the parents' physical, emotional, and financial well-being resulting from the denial to the parents of their right, as the case may be, to decide whether to bear a child or whether to bear a child with a genetic or other defect. We abstained from using any label in the *Burke v Rivo* 551 NE 2d 1 (Mass 1990) opinion, such as wrongful pregnancy, and shall similarly abstain in this case from using the labels "wrongful life" or "wrongful birth".

16 "In any event, it is not the birth of the child that constitutes the harm, injury or damage for which the parents sue. Instead, it is for the economic harm inflicted upon them by the injury they have suffered as a consequence of the negligence that they have proved": (2003) 215 CLR 1; [2003] HCA 38 at [148].

17 "What then is wrong with a parent or parents claiming damages for raising a child conceived because of medical negligence; this is no criticism of the blameless child but is a recognition of the parents' entitlement to economic loss suffered through the appellants' negligence": *Melchior v Cattanach* [2001] QCA 246 at [60] per McMurdo P. A different distinction is made by Baroness Hale who distinguishes wrongful conception (a child would not have been conceived but for the negligence) and wrongful birth (a child would not have been born but for the negligence, which might consist of failure to detect a *(cont)*

The unplanned child is not the harm for which recompense is sought in this action; it is the burden of the legal and moral responsibilities which arise by reason of the birth of the child that is in contention. The expression "wrongful birth" used in various authorities to which the Court was referred is misleading and directs attention away from the appropriate frame of legal discourse. What was wrongful in this case was not the birth of a third child to Mr and Mrs Melchior but the negligence of Dr Cattanach.[18]

As this paragraph makes clear, the phrase most commonly used in the Anglo-Australian jurisprudence to describe this type of claim is "wrongful birth", notwithstanding reservations about its use and Strasser's claim that (at least in the United States) this usually involves the birth of a child with serious disability. So for the purposes of this discussion, I will use that term, though acknowledging its limits.

A brief history of Anglo-Australian "wrongful birth" jurisprudence

The case law preceding the decision of the High Court in *Cattanach*, and of the House of Lords in *Rees v Darlington*,[19] is reasonably well known, yet it is worth revisiting some of the history here, and in particular, drawing attention to the theme that I have identified as the central issue; namely reproductive autonomy. While some might argue that the first of the English decisions, the 1983 case of *Udale v Bloomsbury Area Health Authority*,[20] sits somewhat uncomfortably with current attitudes and indeed, current law, I would suggest that the sentiments expressed by the trial judge there and the "policy" arguments he articulated still underpin many of the contemporary judicial responses to these issues, though they are not always discussed quite so overtly nor quite so polemically.[21]

In *Udale*, the plaintiff was the mother of four daughters. She and her husband decided not to have any more children and in October 1977 she

---

(cont)

    pregnancy or to screen for birth defects that might have prompted a decision not to continue with the pregnancy): see Hale (2001) op cit, at 750. Lax J, in the Ontario case, *Kealey v Berezowski* (1996) 136 DLR (4th) 708 at [40] drew a distinction between wrongful birth, wrongful life and wrongful pregnancy as follows:

> This is a case of "wrongful pregnancy". Unlike "wrongful birth" and "wrongful life" cases, the act here complained of is always pre-conception. The claimants are parents who allege that the defendant's negligence has caused an unwanted pregnancy and birth. The negligence occurs through a failed sterilization or through the preparation or dispensing of a contraceptive medication. The claim has been advanced for children born healthy and for those born unhealthy. In either case, the child is unplanned.

    And in *McFarlane v Tayside*, Lord Clyde preferred the term "wrongful conception": [2000] 2 AC 59 at 99.

18   *Cattanach v Melchior* (2003) 215 CLR 1; [2003] HCA 38 at [68] (footnotes omitted).

19   *Rees v Darlington* [2004] 1 AC 309.

20   *Udale v Bloomsbury Area Health Authority* [1983] 2 All ER 522.

21   This part of the discussion draws in part upon a 1996 article by Graycar, R and Morgan, J, "Unnatural Rejection of Womanhood and Motherhood: Pregnancy, Damages and the Law" (1996) 18 *Sydney Law Review* 323.

underwent a laparoscopic sterilisation. However, in November 1978 she gave birth to a baby boy. There was no dispute about the negligence of the doctor in performing the operation; the only issue was the question of damages.[22]

After the operation, Mrs Udale had complained of pain, particularly after intercourse, and inter-menstrual bleeding. She was referred to a psychiatrist and was also prescribed antibiotics and medication for blood pressure. Finally, in July 1978, she discovered she was 16 weeks pregnant. Mrs Udale stated that she was shattered by the news and was angry at having been deprived of the choice of bearing a child or terminating the pregnancy, since it was too late for the latter option. She was also worried about the possible effects on her baby of the medication, which she would not have taken had she known that she was pregnant.

In his judgment, Jupp J described Mrs Udale as "a motherly sort of woman, nice looking but rather overweight ... Psychologically, she gave the appearance of being healthy".[23] He continued:

> It did take ... some time for Mrs Udale to settle down to the idea of having a baby. But then things began to change. She is not only an experienced mother but, so far as I am able to judge, a good mother, who has all the proper maternal instincts which make her work long and hard to look after her offspring. ... Moreover, as she said in evidence, her husband had always wanted a boy and I think she must have wished one of her four children had been a boy.[24]

Jupp J said:

> Mrs Udale was grateful [David] was a boy, she felt it was her reward at the end of it all. Another girl, she said, would not have been welcome. ... Mrs Udale, to her credit, made no attempt to play down the fact that here was a son, David, who was happy, healthy and, as it turned out, much loved. One is inevitably reminded of the Gospel (John 16:21): "A woman when she is in travail hath sorrow, because her hour is come: but as soon as she is delivered of the child, she remembereth no more the anguish, for joy that a man is born into the world".[25]

---

22 It is worth noting that while in several of the cases, the argument is that the relevant negligence was a failure to warn of the possibility that the surgery would not be 100 per cent successful (see, for example, F v R (1983) 33 SASR 189; Thake v Maurice [1984] 2 All ER 513), in Udale, the surgery itself was negligently performed. During the operation metal clips (which were integral to the sterilisation procedure) were negligently placed. The right-hand side clip was never attached to Mrs Udale's fallopian tube, as should have occurred, but was instead affixed to a "nearby ligament": Udale v Bloomsbury Area Health Authority [1983] 2 All ER 522 at 523. Mrs Udale's symptoms post-surgery were extreme: she suffered hot flashes, often came close to fainting and was bed-ridden at times, stating that "her inside throbbed like an infected finger". She required both antibiotics and pain-killers and was tender whenever touched below her abdomen. The plaintiff also had to undergo two more surgeries after the baby's birth. The first, a re-sterilisation procedure carried out two to three days after her giving birth, must, said Jupp J, "of course, be included in the damages and ... is an operation in which she was, as I understand it, cut open in order for the re-sterilisation to be effected". The second operation was to remove a metal clip that had remained inside Mrs Udale's body: "the last vestiges of the useless operation". As Jupp J commented, "[s]he was ten days in hospital and her abdomen had to be cut open yet again to get rid of the clip": [1983] 2 All ER 522 at 526–527.

23 Ibid, at 526.

24 Ibid.

25 Ibid, at 527.

The defendants did not dispute that damages were payable for her loss of earnings, for the original operation, the shock and anxiety of an unwanted pregnancy, the symptoms of pregnancy which she thought attributable to illness or disease and which led to her taking unnecessary medication, and as Jupp J put it: "the very real fear, after the pregnancy was diagnosed, that the drugs may have harmed, even deformed, the child; she must have feared a mongol might be born".[26] However, Mrs Udale had also claimed damages for the extra costs involved in raising the child to age 16. On those matters, Jupp J concluded as follows:

> The considerations that particularly impress me are the following. (1) It is highly undesirable that any child should learn that a court has publicly declared his life or birth to be a mistake, a disaster even, and that he or she is unwanted or rejected. Such pronouncements would disrupt families and weaken the structure of society. (2) A plaintiff such as Mrs Udale would get little or no damages because her love and care for her child and her joy, ultimately, at his birth would be set off against and might cancel out the inconvenience and financial disadvantages which naturally accompany parenthood. By contrast, a plaintiff who nurtures bitterness in her heart and refuses to let her maternal instincts take over would be entitled to large damages. In short virtue would go unrewarded; unnatural rejection of womanhood and motherhood would be generously compensated. This, in my judgment, cannot be just. (3) Medical men would be under subconscious pressure to encourage abortions in order to avoid claims for medical negligence which would arise if the child were allowed to be born. (4) It has been the assumption of our culture from time immemorial that a child coming into the world, even if, as some say, "the world is a vale of tears", is a blessing and an occasion for rejoicing.
> I am reinforced in the second of these considerations by the fact that, if I had to award damages to Mrs Udale under the disputed heads, I would have to regard the financial disadvantages as offset by her gratitude for the gift of a boy after four girls. Accordingly ... the last three heads of damage are irrecoverable.[27]

Jupp J concluded that it was legitimate, "without detracting from the above principles of public policy, to have some regard to the disturbance to the family finances which an unexpected pregnancy causes".[28] In fact, he decided that increasing the award for "pain, suffering, inconvenience, anxiety and the like" could take some account of those factors "without regarding the child as unwanted" and awarded £8,000 under that head.

Following *Udale*, there were several other cases in the United Kingdom, though in none of them was the same approach taken. For example, in *Thake v Maurice*,[29] a case involving a failed vasectomy,[30] Peter Pain J in the English High

---

26 Ibid, at 527.

27 Ibid, at 531.

28 Ibid.

29 [1984] 2 All ER 513.

30 Baroness Hale shares my long-held curiosity about the different results in these two cases. As she put it: "I find it mildly interesting that the trial courts which first considered the public policy issues involved in wrongful conception claims, reached different conclusions according to whether it was the mother's or father's sterilisation which had failed": Hale (2001) op cit, at 751.

Court awarded damages, including for the costs of upkeep, and explicitly rejected the policy arguments put by Jupp J in *Udale*. Instead, he drew attention to issues of choice, and the community acceptance of family planning:

> I have to have regard to the policy of the state as it expresses itself in legislation and in social provision. I must consider this in light of modern developments. By 1975 family planning was generally practised. Abortion had been legalised over a wide field. Vasectomy was one of the methods of family planning which was not only legal but was available under the national health service. It seems to me to follow from this that it was generally recognised that the birth of a healthy baby is not always a blessing. ...
>
> The policy of the state, as I see it, is to provide the widest freedom of choice. It makes available to the public the means of planning their families or planning to have no family. If plans go awry, it provides for the possibility of abortion.[31]

He also dismissed the suggestion that an award of damages would lead the child to feel rejection.[32] The Court of Appeal rejected the claim based on breach of contract, but upheld the negligence finding and allowed a cross-appeal increasing the damages by £1500.[33]

In *Emeh v Kensington Area Health Authority*,[34] a child was born with a congenital abnormality (thereby needing extra care) to a plaintiff who had undergone a negligently performed sterilisation operation, and who did not discover that she was pregnant until she was 20 weeks pregnant.

The Court of Appeal allowed an appeal by the plaintiff, awarding her damages for loss of future earnings, the plaintiff's pain and suffering up to the time of the trial and future loss of amenity and pain and suffering, including the extra care that the child would require. Significantly, she was also awarded the costs of maintenance of the child to trial and in the future. After considering the decisions in *Udale* and *Thake*, all three members of the Court of Appeal expressed their preference for the approach in *Thake*.[35] Significantly, they also rejected the

---

31 *Thake v Maurice* [1984] 2 All ER 513 at 526.

32 Ibid, at 526 per Pain J:

> I do not think that if I award damages here it will lead little Samantha to feel rejection. She is surrounded by a happy, albeit somewhat poverty-stricken, family life. It is this that must make her feel wanted and not rejected. She may learn in years to come that her conception was unwanted. But there is nothing exceptional about this. What matters to a child is how it is received when it enters life. It so often happens that parents reconcile themselves to an unwelcome conception and accept the child with joy.

> Compare McHugh and Gummow JJ in *Cattanach v Melchior* (2003) 215 CLR 1; [2003] HCA 38 at [79], who stated:

> The perceived disruption to familial relationships by, for example, the Melchiors' third child later becoming aware of this litigation, is at best speculative. In the absence of any clear and accepted understanding of such matters, the common law should not justify preclusion of recovery on speculation as to possible psychological harm to children.

33 [1986] QB 644.

34 [1985] 1 QB 1012.

35 For another English decision following this approach, see *Allen v Bloomsbury* [1993] 1 All ER 651.

defendant's argument that the plaintiff should have had a late-term abortion rather than continue with the pregnancy.[36] I will return to the issue of mitigation below.

When the issue arose again in subsequent (first instance) cases, the matter was considered settled,[37] but in *McFarlane v Tayside*,[38] the House of Lords held that while compensation was available for the negligence involved in the McFarlanes having a child they did not plan to have, as a matter of policy, no damages were available for the costs involved in raising that child.[39]

Meanwhile the issue had arisen in Australia in 1996 with *CES v Superclinics*.[40] That case involved a 21-year-old woman, who, concerned that she might be pregnant, had made several visits to a medical centre. She claims that she advised the doctors she saw that she did not want to have a child and would terminate the pregnancy if it transpired that she was pregnant. Through a series of errors, including some false negative test results, her pregnancy was not finally diagnosed until she saw her family doctor at which time she was 19.5 weeks pregnant and it was decided that it would not be safe to terminate the pregnancy at that late stage. All the medical evidence adduced at the trial was to the effect that the doctors were negligent and the medical treatment she received was inadequate. The trial was heard before Newman J who said that if these were the only issues, he would have to agree that there had been a breach of duty.[41]

However, Newman J decided that the plaintiff was not entitled to damages since her case depended upon a claim that she had lost an opportunity to do something he determined was illegal (namely, have her pregnancy terminated) and therefore the law did not permit her to claim damages.[42] The Court of Appeal by majority (Kirby A-CJ, Priestley JA; Meagher JA dissenting), reversed this decision, but the majority could not agree on the appropriate approach to the

---

36 Counsel for the defendants had argued that the "plaintiff's refusal to have the abortion was so unreasonable as to eclipse the defendants' wrongdoing. ... Her refusal of the abortion was a *novus actus interveniens* which broke the chain of causation. Alternatively, there was a failure by her to mitigate her damage": *Emeh v Kensington Area Health Authority* [1986] QB 644 at 1014. This argument was accepted at first instance, but emphatically rejected by all members of the Court of Appeal.

37 *Gold v Haringey Health Authority* [1988] 1 QB 481; *Allen v Bloomsbury* [1993] 1 All ER 651.

38 [2002] 2 AC 59. For detailed discussions of the decision in McFarlane see Priaulx, N, "Joy to the World! A (Healthy) Child is Born! Reconceptualizing 'Harm' in Wrongful Conception" (2004) 13 *Social and Legal Studies* 5; and Hoyano, L, "Misconceptions about Wrongful Conception" (2002) 65 *Modern Law Review* 883.

39 For a discussion of the use of "policy" arguments, and attempts to distinguish between "legal policy" and "public policy" see Cane, P, "Another Failed Sterilisation" (2004) 120 *Law Quarterly Review* 189 and Cane, P, "The Doctor, the Stork and the Court: A Modern Morality Play" (2004) 120 *Law Quarterly Review* 23. Of the five law lords, only Lord Millett would have rejected the claim for all damages involving the birth, pain and suffering and so on. But despite that, he still argued that some award ought to be made to Mr and Mrs McFarlane for their loss of autonomy, and proposed the idea of a "conventional sum" of £5000, an idea taken up by the majority in *Rees v Darlington* [2004] 1 AC 309.

40 (1995) 38 NSWLR 47.

41 *CES v Superclinics* (unreported, NSWSC, Newman J, 18 April 1994).

42 For details of the availability of abortion in Australia, see below, note 98.

assessment of damages. This was because while Kirby A-CJ (as he then was) would have awarded damages for the costs of the child's maintenance, Priestley JA held that the plaintiff's choice to keep the child – that is, not to give her daughter up for adoption – constituted a *novus actus interveniens* (broke the chain of causation) and therefore damages could not be awarded after the birth.[43] So the majority position would have seen the plaintiff with no damages for the costs of upkeep, and this was the ground for the cross-appeal by the plaintiff, when the matter went to the High Court, where it settled before a judgment was entered.[44]

To complete the picture of the case law, it is necessary to return to England where the decision in *McFarlane* soon came to be tested. In *Parkinson v St James*,[45] the plaintiff had given birth to a child with severe disability and the Court of Appeal, by a majority, had decided that this case was distinguishable from *McFarlane* by reason of the child's disability. In *Rees v Darlington*,[46] while the child born as a result of the doctor's negligence was a healthy child, the mother was blind, and it was her disability that had led her to decide not to have children. She also was awarded damages for the costs of care of her child, a decision affirmed by a majority of the Court of Appeal.[47] It was this latter decision that was appealed to the House of Lords, which, while notionally affirming its view from *McFarlane* that no damages can be awarded for the costs of bringing up a healthy child, albeit one who would not have been born but for negligence, nonetheless decided that a "conventional sum" of £15,000 was to be awarded in such cases.[48]

---

43   At [29] per Priestley JA. Note that Meagher JA, who would have rejected the claim in any event, also found that no damages would be awarded if a claim were to be recognised, since, in his view, as part of her duty to mitigate, the plaintiff would have been considered unreasonable in keeping the child, rather than giving her up for adoption: *CES v Superclinics* (1995) 38 NSWLR 47 at [11] per Meagher JA.

44   See *Superclinics Australia Pty Ltd v CES* (unreported, HCA, Brennan CJ, Dawson, Toohey, Gaudron, McHugh, Gummow JJ, 11 September 1996, Transcript of Special Leave to Appeal) <www.austlii.edu.au/au/other/hca/transcripts/1996/S88/1.html> (accessed 12 August 2005) and *Superclinics Australia Pty Ltd v CES* (unreported, HCA, Brennan CJ, Dawson, Toohey, Gaudron, McHugh, Gummow JJ, 12 September 1996, Transcript of Special Leave to Appeal), <www.austlii.edu.au/au/other/hca/transcripts/1996/S88/2.html> (accessed 12 August 2005). See also Lamont, L, "Church prays for abortion ruling to go Higher", *Sydney Morning Herald*, 10 October 1996.

45   *Parkinson v St James and Seacroft University Hospital NHS Trust* [2002] QB 266.

46   *Rees v Darlington* [2003] QB 20.

47   Ibid. Hale and Walker LJJ allowed recovery, whilst the dissenting judge, Waller LJ, did not.

48   *Rees v Darlington* [2004] 1 AC 309 at [8]–[10] per Lord Bingham; at [19] per Lord Nicholls; at [125]–[126] per Lord Millett; and at [148] per Lord Scott. The idea of a "conventional sum", while not unprecedented, hardly fits within a compensatory framework of *restitutio in integrum*. The only other area in which such an approach is taken is in relation to damages for "loss of expectation of life" where the House of Lords, in what Harold Luntz describes as "an amazing bit of judicial legislation" set a nominal figure for this head: at the time, it was £200: see *Benham v Gambling* [1941] AC 157 (HL); and see Luntz H, *Assessment of Damages for Personal Injury and Death*, 4th edn, Butterworths, Sydney, 2002, para 3.4.2.

Why so contentious?

Immunity

Much ink has been spilt analysing and critiquing various aspects of the decision in *Cattanach v Melchior* and there is little point repeating these here in any detail.[49] Instead, I have chosen to focus on how the discomfort expressed by Jupp J in *Udale*, by a range of commentators, and by the dissenting judges in *Cattanach v Melchior*, manifests a lack of understanding of the importance of, or in some cases, outright hostility to, women's reproductive autonomy, and in particular, shows a failure to appreciate the negative impact on women of being deprived of that autonomy.

To place these decisions in a negligence law context, it is useful to follow the approach adopted by McHugh and Gummow JJ. In the absence of the articulation of the type of policy arguments set out at such length by Jupp J in *Udale* (and repeated, in various forms, in subsequent cases), general negligence principles would otherwise result in the award of damages once it was established that the defendant had breached a duty of care which caused damage. So those who disagree – the minority judges in *Cattanach*, and the members of the House of Lords – are effectively creating a new category of negligence immunity. As McHugh and Gummow JJ put it:

> Merely to repeat those propositions upon which the appellants [and minority judges] rely does not explain why the law should shield or immunise the appellants from what otherwise is a head of damages recoverable in negligence under general and unchallenged principles in respect of the breach of duty by Dr Cattanach.[50]

They go on to discuss the other categories of cases in which "immunity" from negligence liability has been conferred on various categories of people (perhaps most notoriously, barristers),[51] and discuss the various policy rationales that underpin such an immunity. They also point out that, unlike in those cases (for example, where immunity is conferred upon members of the armed forces in time

---

49 These include Golder, B, "From McFarlane to Melchior and Beyond: Love, Sex, Money and Commodification in the Anglo-Australian Law of Torts" (2004) 12 *Torts LJ* 128; Burns, K, "The Way the World is: Social Facts in High Court Negligence Cases" (2004) 12 *Torts LJ* 215; Vranken, M, "Damages for 'Wrongful Birth': Where to After Cattanach?" (2003) 24 *Adelaide Law Review* 243; Seymour, J, Case Note: "Cattanach v Melchior: Legal Principles and Public Policy" (2003) 11 *Torts LJ* 208; and Cane, P, "The Doctor, the Stork and the Court: A Modern Morality Play" (2004) 120 *Law Quarterly Review* 23; Dimopoulos, P and Bagaric, M, "Why Wrongful Birth Actions are Right" (2003) 11 *Journal of Law and Medicine* 230; Telford, P, "Assessing the Cost of Our Children: Case Note: Cattanach v Melchior" (2003) 19 *Australian Insurance Law Bulletin* 1; White, B, "Cattanach v Melchior: Babies, Blessings and Burdens" (2004) 24 *Queensland Lawyer* 296; Thomas, C, "Claims for Wrongful Pregnancy and Damages for the Upbringing of the Child" (2003) 26 *UNSWLJ* 125; and Seymour, J, "Cattanach v Melchior: Legal Principles and Public Policy" (2003) 11 *Torts LJ* 208.

50 *Cattanach v Melchior* (2003) 215 CLR 1; [2003] HCA 38 at [57].

51 *Giannarelli v Wraith* (1988) 165 CLR 543; and *D'Orta-Ekenaike v Victoria Legal Aid* [2005] HCA 12. However, note that the House of Lords in *Arthur JS Hall v Simons* [2002] 1 AC 615 had earlier reached a different conclusion as to advocates' immunity.

of war),[52] what is claimed here is not that public policy precludes a duty of care, but simply, that once duty breach and damage are made out (or conceded), one particular category of damages may not, for a variety of policy reasons, be awarded.[53]

Interestingly, the most vociferous dissenting judgment, and the one that most vigorously relies on arguments of policy, rather than traditional negligence principles, is that of Heydon J who, shortly before his appointment to the court, had spoken out very publicly against what he had called "judicial activism"[54] and criticised "[e]xcessive and self-indulgent surveys of the law and debates about the background to and future of particular rules".[55] He also said:

> When judges detect particular community values ... as supporting their reasoning, they may sometimes become confused between the values which they think the community *actually holds* and the values which they think the community *should hold*. ...
>
> [T]he soigné, fastidious, civilised, cultured and cultivated patricians of the progressive judiciary – our new philosopher-kings and enlightened despots – are in truth applying the values which they hold, and which they think the poor

---

52 *Shaw, Savill and Albion Co Ltd v Commonwealth* (1940) 66 CLR 344.

53 *Cattanach v Melchior* (2003) 215 CLR 1; [2003] HCA 38 at [69].

54 The term "judicial activism" is almost invariably employed by those who see themselves as conservative, and decry what they see as "creative" law-making by courts. The usage is not indigenous to Australia. In the United States the phrase is used as a term of abuse against judges seen as insufficiently conservative and has provoked the creation of a movement, "Justice Sunday", devoted to, according to its website, discussing "judicial activism and how we can stop it": see <www.justicesunday.com> (accessed 29 August 2005). That organisation's poster for the Second Justice Sunday event (August 2005) referred to "How activist judges subvert the family, undermine religious freedom and threaten our nation's future": <www.justicesunday.com/downloads/JS11.pdf> (accessed 29 August 2005). In a recent discussion, Paul Gewirtz and Chad Golder, having noted that "activist" is rarely defined, examined via an empirical study of United States Supreme Court decisions the frequency with which judges struck down Acts of Congress. By this scale, the most activist were Justice Thomas, Justice Kennedy, Justice Scalia and Chief Justice Rehnquist; the least activist was Justice Breyer, followed by Justice Ginsburg: see "So Who Are the Activists?", Opinion page, *New York Times*, 6 July 2005.

55 Heydon, D, "Judicial Activism and the Death of the Rule of Law" (2003) 47 *Quadrant* 9 at 15. This is a revised version of an address he gave to an annual Quadrant dinner on 30 October 2002, shortly before his appointment to the High Court of Australia was announced in December 2002. The (widely circulated) original text contained a number of quite personal disparaging comments about individual judges of whom the author disapproved; these were removed in the published version cited here. This speech was discussed in media reports of the time as an act that was "interpreted as being a job application" or "an application to fill the vacancy on the High Court left by Mary Gaudron". See Haslem, B, "Gaudron vacancy activates lobbying" *The Australian*, 4 December 2002 and Banham, C, "Woman should have got High Court Job, Say Critics", *Sydney Morning Herald*, 19 December 2002. Heydon J's speech has been published in a number of places, in addition to *Quadrant*: see "Judicial Activism and the Death of the Rule of Law" (2004) 10 *Otago Law Review* 493; "Judicial Activism and the Death of the Rule of Law" (2003) 14 *Australian Intellectual Property Journal* 78; "Judicial Activism and the Death of the Rule of Law" (2003) 23 *Australian Bar Review* 110. Abridged versions were also published as: "To Do Justice, Not Lay Down the Law", *Sydney Morning Herald*, 19 December 2002; "Judicial Activists Do No Favours for the Legal System", *The Age*, 19 December 2002; and "Precedent Must be Seen to Keep a Rein on Bench", *The Australian*, 19 December 2002.

simpletons of the vile multitude – the great beast, as Alexander Hamilton called it – ought to hold even though they do not.[56]

Despite this excoriation of judges' resort to policy and values, Heydon J's judgment is replete with exhortations to various values, for example, his critique of the Queensland Court of Appeal reasons in *Cattanach v Melchior* for taking "insufficient account of the law's assumptions about some key values in family life as reflected in the unenacted and enacted law".[57]

In her discussion of the use by courts of "social facts",[58] which she describes as "a continuum of assumptions about society, the world and human behaviour that courts, including the High Court, make in an appellate case",[59] Kylie Burns points out that of the 169 statements of what she identifies as "social fact" in the judgments in *Cattanach v Melchior*, no fewer than 79 of these were made by Heydon J. She lists these as including consideration of matters such as:

> [A]ssumptions about human life in families; the psychology of litigants, parents and children; a parent's moral duties even though these are not enforceable by the law; and the "disquieting possibilities" in relation to other much more ambitious claims of a type not before the court that might create an "odious spectacle".[60]

The judgments in *Cattanach* present us with a complete reversal of the more common argument made by Heydon J and others who share his views: that reliance on policy (whether legal policy or some other kind),[61] is something activist judges do, while those who aspire to "strict and complete legalism", to use Sir Owen Dixon's term, rely instead on principle or authority. As Kirby J put it in an extra curial comment about *Cattanach*, responding to Heydon J's widely publicised views about what he calls "judicial activism":

> The application of the basic common law principles of recovery for proved negligence favoured the claimants. ... [T]o cut damages off arbitrarily involved "judicial activism".[62]

He describes the case as "notable for the candid discussion ... of the issues of public and legal policy which the case was seen as presenting".[63] As he put it, the parents' argument "relied on strict judicial adherence to the general principles of negligence law", and the burden of persuasion lay on those "who sought a departure from such principles, the general refusal of the common law to accept

---

56 Heydon, D, "Judicial Activism and the Death of the Rule of Law" (2003) 47 *Quadrant* 9 at 21.

57 *Cattanach v Melchior* (2003) 215 CLR 1; [2003] HCA 38 at [322].

58 Burns, K, "The Way the World is: Social Facts in High Court Negligence Cases" (2004) 12 *Torts LJ* 1.

59 Ibid, at 12.

60 Stapleton, J, "The Golden Thread at the Heart of Tort Law" (2003) 24 *Australian Bar Review* 135 at 137, quoted in Burns (2004) op cit, at 29.

61 Compare Cane, P, "The Doctor, the Stork and the Court: A Modern Morality Play" (2004) 120 *Law Quarterly Review* 23 on this.

62 Justice Michael Kirby, "Beyond the Judicial Fairy Tales" (2004) 48 *Quadrant* 26 at 31.

63 Ibid, at 29.

zones of legal immunity for professional people, and the need to redress the particular burden which such an immunity would impose on women and mothers".[64]

Remarkably, given that this case involved pregnancy, childbirth and the responsibility for raising a child, at least for 18 years, of the High Court justices who dealt with this case, only Kirby J distinguished the mother from the formally gender-neutral parent referred to in the other judgments (though Heydon J did spend some considerable time referring to now obsolete but gender-specific family law rules giving fathers absolute rights to the custody of their infant children).[65]

Gender

As mentioned earlier, in a judgment that runs to 414 paragraphs, Kirby J was alone in drawing attention to the fact that cases involving negligent denial of reproductive choice resulting in the birth of an unplanned child disproportionately affect women. And it is not just bearing a child that is in issue: as the minority is so keen to remind us, a child is a little person, and little people require parents to raise, support, nurture and care for them until they become adults. It is no answer to suggest that the child could be adopted out as a means of mitigating the loss (Meagher JA's approach in *CES v Superclinics*),[66] nor has it ever been held that failure to terminate a pregnancy is a breach of the duty to mitigate.[67]

I noted at the outset that this was the first case heard by a High Court with no women among its members since 1987 when Justice Gaudron was appointed, and that the issue of damages for the costs of bringing up a child had been before the High Court once before in the context of an appeal from the New South Wales

---

64 Ibid.

65 *Cattanach v Melchior* (2003) 215 CLR 1; [2003] HCA 38 at [328]–[330]. On some of the ways in which "gender-neutrality" might mask what is a highly gendered situation, see Graycar, R, and Morgan, J, *The Hidden Gender of Law*, 2nd edn, Federation Press, Sydney, 2002.

66 In Meagher JA's words: "The law ordains that a plaintiff must mitigate her damages. In the present context, why does that not require the mother to put the child of which she vociferously complains out to adoption? Why should the law treat seriously her claim for the recovery of expenses which she does not need to incur?": *CES v Superclinics* (1995) 38 NSWLR 47 at [11]. A variant was the suggestion by counsel in the Superclinics hearing in the High Court that the plaintiff in that case give the child over to the father, who lived in Melbourne and saw her only a few times a year. Upon hearing counsel describe this course of action as "an opportunity to mitigate", Justice Gaudron responded, "That would be about the cruellest and most inhumane submission I have heard put in this Court since I have been here. I must say, it took my breath away when I read the judgments below suggesting that that was a proper form of mitigation". *Superclinics Australia Pty Ltd v CES* (unreported, HCA, Brennan CJ, Dawson, Toohey, Gaudron, McHugh, Gummow JJ, 11 September 1996, Transcript of Special Leave to Appeal), <www.austlii.edu.au/au/other/hca/transcripts/1996/S88/1.html> (accessed 12 August 2005).

67 This argument was put, and rejected, by all three members of the English Court of Appeal in *Emeh v Kensington, Chelsea and Westminster Area Health Authority* [1985] QB 1012 and has been specifically rejected by the House of Lords in *Rees v Darlington* [2004] 1 AC 309.

decision of *CES v Superclinics*.[68] That hearing took place over two days, and the High Court then adjourned to allow the interveners[69] to prepare submissions, but not long after the hearing, the case settled. In the course of the argument, Gaudron J commented:

> GAUDRON J: In realistic terms one knows that the birth of a child has, nine times out of ten, quite serious consequences for the employment and career opportunities available to women.
>
> MR GARLING: There is no question about that, your Honour, but if one was to look ...
>
> GAUDRON J: And that involves no question of valuing a human life or anything of those matters which everybody has found so difficult to deal with.[70]

Her comments have significant resonance with those of Baroness Hale who has discussed these issues in a published speech, delivered after the English Court of Appeal, of which she was a member until her appointment to the House of Lords in 2003, made two significant post-*McFarlane* decisions in *Parkinson*[71] and *Rees*.[72]

Speaking to an audience of actuaries, she started by noting that bringing up children has significant economic effects on women, and she provided detailed tables of what it costs women in life-time career earnings to take time out for parenting.[73] And the research she cited[74] also has counterparts in Australia; in 1988, Bruce Chapman and John Beggs published the first version of *The Foregone Earnings*

---

68   *Superclinics Australia Pty Ltd v CES* (unreported, HCA, Brennan CJ, Dawson, Toohey, Gaudron, McHugh, Gummow JJ, 11 September 1996, Transcript of Special Leave to Appeal), <www.austlii.edu.au/au/other/hca/transcripts/1996/S88/1.html> (accessed 12 August 2005) and *Superclinics Australia Pty Ltd v CES* (unreported, HCA, Brennan CJ, Dawson, Toohey, Gaudron, McHugh, Gummow JJ, 12 September 1996, Transcript of Special Leave to Appeal) <www.austlii.edu.au/au/other/hca/transcripts/1996/S88/2.html> (accessed 12 August 2005).

69   In a surprising decision, the Catholic Bishops Conference and the Catholic Health Care Provider's Federation were granted leave by the High Court to participate in the case as amicus curiae. The application for amicus curiae standing was itself contested: it was decided by a vote of three to three of the members of the High Court. There were only six members hearing the application as Kirby J did not sit: he had been a member of the New South Wales Court of Appeal when it considered the matter. When the application for leave to intervene was made, Chief Justice Brennan said: "I have asked the Senior Registrar to inform counsel that I know Father McKenna, a deponent to one of the affidavits in support of the application to intervene, or to appear amicus curiae, and a number of members of the Australian Catholic Bishop's Conference": Transcript of Proceedings, 11 September 1996, p 4. The Chief Justice then used his casting vote to grant them leave. Following that decision, the Abortion Providers Federation was also granted leave to participate.

70   *Superclinics v CES* (unreported, HCA, Brennan CJ, Dawson, Toohey, Gaudron, McHugh, Gummow JJ, 12 September 1996, Transcript of Special Leave to Appeal).

71   *Parkinson v St James and Seacroft University Hospital NHS Trust* [2002] QB 266.

72   *Rees v Darlington* [2003] QB 20.

73   Hale (2001) op cit, at 747–749.

74   Dr Katherine Rake (ed), *Cabinet Office Briefing: Women's Incomes over the Lifetime*, HMSO, 2000.

from Child-Rearing in Australia; of which a second edition published in 2001 showed that the impact of having children, while slightly diminished, was still dramatic.[75]

Significantly, Baroness Hale makes it clear that this is a highly gendered issue. For all the talk of "parents" in the judgments, she draws attention to the fact that it is women upon whom the burden falls most heavily. "I do wonder whether it is a question which men and women may look at rather differently".[76] "The one thing which inevitably distinguishes women from men is the experience of conception, pregnancy and childbirth".

> First, left to myself, I would not regard the upbringing of a child as pure economic loss, but loss which is consequential upon the invasion of bodily integrity and loss of personal autonomy involved in an unwanted pregnancy.
>
> ... Secondly, I would regard that loss of autonomy as consisting principally in the resulting duty to care for the child, rather than simply to pay for his keep.
>
> The point about pregnancy and childbirth is that it brings about profound and lasting changes in a woman's life. Those changes last for much longer than the pregnancy, birth and immediate aftermath. Whatever the outcome, happy or sad, a woman never gets over it. There are, of course, many men who never get over becoming a father, but the consequences may be rather different.[77]

Baroness Hale also has a response to the benefit/burden or, as she calls it, the "deemed equilibrium"[78] argument; that is, that the benefits from having a child cancel out the burden of the interference to reproductive autonomy. In her view, this "seems to assume that the one – usually the mother – who gets the trouble also gets the fun, whereas the father gets only the expense".[79] But this is contrary to the way in which women's and men's roles around childcare are perceived by courts in a range of legal contexts. From research I have undertaken into decisions around assessment of personal injury damages for pain and suffering and loss of amenities, it appears that, if one were to talk of social facts, the law's assumptions about children are that women care for them, while men play with them. So in case after case, courts referred to a woman's loss or impairment of her capacity to do the physical job of caring for children (and the household generally), while for men, it was their capacity to *play* with their children that was at issue.[80]

---

75 Beggs, J and Chapman, B, *The Foregone Earnings from Child-Rearing in Australia*, Discussion Paper No 190, ANU Centre for Economic Policy Research, commissioned for the AIFS, June 1988; Gray, M and Chapman, B, "Foregone Earnings from Child Rearing" (2001) 58 *Family Matters* 4.

76 Hale (2001) op cit, at 760.

77 Ibid, at 761.

78 Ibid, at 760.

79 Ibid, at 756.

80 See Graycar, R, "Sex, Golf and Stereotypes: Measuring, Valuing and Imagining the Body in Law" (2002) 10 *Torts LJ* 205 at 206–208. Compare, for example, the court's reference in *Ibrahim v GIO (NSW)* (unreported, NSWCA, Kirby P and Powell JA, 28 March 1995) to the female plaintiff's loss of ability to partake of "normal social activities" such as "gardening and housework", with the construction of a male plaintiff's loss of the ability to "play vigorously with his six-year-old son", in *Standing v NSW Insurance Ministerial Corporation* (unreported, NSWSC, Dunford J, 3 March 1994).

Baroness Hale graphically describes the irrevocable changes in women's lives that flow from having a child. These include: a "severe curtailment of personal freedom"; the almost certain interruption of paid employment; the physical and psychological changes that accompany pregnancy; and the responsibility for the life of another. She also discusses limits on the availability of legal abortion, and the moral dilemmas that accompany abortion decision-making. In any event, as she points out, no court would require a woman to terminate a pregnancy as a means of mitigating loss.[81]

And, as she goes on to remind us, the "invasion of the mother's personal autonomy does not stop once her body and mind have returned to their pre-pregnancy state".[82] Here Baroness Hale reminds us of some of the many legal consequences of parenthood, independent of the duty to pay for the care of the child. She concludes this discussion by demonstrating, convincingly, that birth is not a logical cutting off point for the attribution of legal responsibility and the duty to compensate for the negligence involved in a child being born who would not have been born but for negligence.

Some lessons from the United States[83]

If there was any doubt about the centrality (and indeed, fragility) of women's reproductive autonomy to these issues, one has only to look at the United States.[84]

---

81 Hale (2001) op cit, at 762. She points out that this was expressly ruled out by the House of Lords, confirming the earlier decision of the Court of Appeal in *Emeh*. Only in Australia has the argument been put that giving up the child for adoption was a relevant form of mitigation, though for Priestley JA the failure to do so broke the chain of causation: *CES v Superclinics* (1995) 38 NSWLR 47 at [31]–[34] per Priestley JA, but compare Meagher JA at [11] who treated it as a mitigation issue.

82 Hale (2001) op cit, at 762.

83 It is not my intention here to canvass at any length the United States law on these issues, other than to say that while it varies from State to State, most States do not award damages for the costs of rearing a child if they do recognise the action for wrongful conception. For a comprehensive account of the law governing wrongful conception across the States, see Annotation, "Recoverability of Cost of Raising Normal Healthy Child Born as result of Physician's Negligence or Breach or Contract or Warranty" 89 ALR 4th 632 (2004).

84 For some discussions that focus on the tension between reproductive autonomy and wrongful birth or wrongful conception actions, see Gold, S, "An Equality Approach to Wrongful Birth Statutes" (1996) 65 *Fordham Law Review* 1005; Note, "Wrongful Birth Actions: The Case Against Legislative Curtailment" (1987) 100 *Harvard Law Review* 2017; Podewils, LA, "Traditional Tort Principles and Wrongful Conception Child-Rearing Damages" (1993) 73 *Boston University Law Review* 407; Intromassi, C, "Reproductive Self-Determination in the Third Circuit: The Statutory Proscription of Wrongful Birth and Wrongful Life Claims as an Unconstitutional Violation of Planned Parenthood v Casey's Undue Burden Principle" (2003) 24 *Women's Rights Law Reporter* 101; Kowitz, JF, "Not Your Garden Variety Tort Reform: Statutes Barring Claims for Wrongful Life and Wrongful Birth are Unconstitutional Under the Purpose Prong of Planned Parenthood v Casey" (1995) 61 *Brooklyn Law Review* 235; Say, K, "Wrongful Birth: Preserving Justice for Women and their Families" (2003) 28 *Oklahoma City U L Rev* 251; Gantz, J, "State Statutory Preclusion of Wrongful Birth Relief: A Troubling Rewriting of a Woman's Right to Choose and the Doctor-Patient Relationship" (1997) 4 *Virginia Journal of Social Policy & the Law* 795; Pollard, D, "Wrongful Analysis in Wrongful Life Jurisprudence" (2004) 55 *Alabama Law Review* 327.

In that country, the anti-choice lobby has been instrumental in the increasing intervention of legislatures banning actions for wrongful birth or wrongful conception.[85] A common form of these statutes is:

> There shall be no cause of action on behalf of any person based on the claim that but for an act or omission, a person would not have been permitted to have been born alive but would have been aborted.[86]

Some of these bans have been challenged as being in contravention of the constitutionally protected right to reproductive autonomy based on *Roe v Wade* and its successors, but thus far, none of these challenges has succeeded.

In perhaps the best known of these, *Hickman v Group Health Plan Inc*, while the first instance Minnesota judge held that that State's statutory bar on wrongful birth actions did infringe the constitutional right to reproductive autonomy, first articulated in *Roe v Wade*, the appellate court reversed, holding first, that there was no "State action" involved and secondly, that there was no undue burden imposed by the statute on women's right to an abortion.[87] The majority drew an unconvincing analogy with wrongful death, suggesting that since at common law the death of a person did not constitute an injury, so also the common law did not recognise wrongful birth:

> Before addressing the Hickmans' constitutional challenges to subdivision 2, we find it helpful to discuss the legal basis of the wrongful birth cause of action. At common law, no cause of action existed for either wrongful birth or wrongful death.[88]

While it is true that wrongful death is a creature of statute, wrongful birth or wrongful conception actions involve no more than the application of general negligence principles; therefore, this analogy simply does not hold. Moreover, this was, in effect, conceded by the majority in a footnote as follows:

---

85 For example, Gold notes that a number of anti-abortion groups filed amicus briefs with the Supreme Court of Minnesota in support of wrongful birth statutes as part of the *Hickman* challenge: Americans United for Life Legal Defense Fund, the Catholic Health Association of the United States, the Catholic League for Religious and Civil Rights, and the National Right to Life Committee: Gold (1996) op cit, at note 68.

86 This is the version quoted in 100 *Harvard Law Review* 2017 as the model legislation proposed by "Americans United for Life Legal Defense Fund". The note goes on to discuss the various models (and slight variations) used by those State legislatures that have enacted such legislation. Some exclude all actions, others such as Minnesota and Idaho do not expressly preclude actions for wrongful conception, but nonetheless use formulations that might include it: for example, the Minnesota statute s 145.425 reads (in part):

> Subdivision 1. *Wrongful life action prohibited*. No person shall maintain a cause of action or receive an award of damages on behalf of that person based on the claim that but for the negligent conduct of another, the person would have been aborted.

> Subdivision 2. *Wrongful birth action prohibited*. No person shall maintain a cause of action or receive an award of damages on the claim that but for the negligent conduct of another, a child would have been aborted. (Minn Stat §145.424 (1984)).

87 *Hickman v Group Health Plan, Inc* 396 NW 2d 10 (1986).

88 Ibid, at para [1]. See, for example, *Baker v Bolton* 170 Eng Rep 1033 (N P 1808) (denying recovery for wrongful death); Keeton, W, Dobbs, D, Keeton, R & Owen, D, *Prosser and Keeton on the Law of Torts*, 5th edn, 1984, §§ 55, 125A.

> Technically, wrongful birth and life actions are a form of negligence while wrongful death is a separate tort based on intentional acts, negligence or strict liability.[89] The torts, however, involve strikingly similar policy considerations and have a similar history.[90]

Nor did this reasoning persuade the Chief Justice, who dissented from the majority appellate court decision, noting:

> The interest in protecting the health of the mother cannot be used to justify subdivision 2. I cannot accept as fact that physician negligence protects a woman's health. On the contrary, subdivision 2 would seem to endanger a woman's health by not discouraging the negligent withholding of medical information.[91]

It has been suggested that wrongful birth statutory bans constitute "covert abortion restraint".[92] Katherine Say argues that legislatures have resorted to "tort reform" "as a means to circumvent constitutional bans on restricting abortions".[93] Echoing Gold, she notes the overt involvement of anti-choice groups in the enactment of such statutes.[94]

Some courts have addressed these issues of reproductive autonomy directly. A clear example is the Connecticut decision in *Ochs v Borelli* where the five member Supreme Court described the argument put by the defendants (which they unanimously rejected) as follows:

> The defendants ask us to carve out an exception, grounded in public policy, to the normal duty of a tortfeasor to assume liability for all the damages that he has proximately caused. ... But public policy cannot support an exception to tort liability when the impact of such an exception would impair the exercise of a constitutionally protected right. It is now clearly established that parents have a constitutionally protected interest located "within the zone of privacy created by several fundamental constitutional guarantees",95 to employ contraceptive techniques to limit the size of their family. The defendants' general argument of public policy is therefore unpersuasive.[96]

These commentators and the occasional explicit references by courts, leave us in no doubt that this is a tort action infused with a range of deeply held and conflicting ideological positions. Failure to acknowledge this does not assist in understanding

---

89 Referring to Keeton et al (1984) op cit, §§ 55, 125A–26.

90 396 NW 2d 10 (1986) at footnote 3.

91 Ibid, at [20] per Amdahl CJ.

92 Say (2003) op cit, at 276.

93 Ibid.

94 "Pro-life organizations have launched heavy campaigns to promote wrongful birth legislation", ibid, at 286.

95 *Griswold v Connecticut* 381 US 479 (1965) at 485; *Roe v Wade* 410 US 113 at 153 (1973).

96 *Ochs v Borelli* 445 A 2d 883 (Conn, 1982) at 885. See also, *Marciniuk v Lundborg* 450 NW 2d 243 (1990), where the court rejected arguments that the damages for the cost of upkeep were too speculative; that a child would be harmed by learning that he or she was unwanted and so on. The court also expressly rejected the use of "offsetting", holding that the requirement in the Restatement (2d) of Torts, s 920 could not apply as the benefits of having a child was not "the same interest" as the interest harmed (for discussion of this point in the Australian context see *Cattanach v Melchior* (2003) 215 CLR 1; [2003] HCA 38 at [85]–[90] per McHugh and Gummow JJ.

the approaches taken by various courts, not only in the United States, but also in Canada and the United Kingdom.[97]

Some concluding thoughts

As Rosamund Scott has noted, a significant difference between the right to abortion in the United Kingdom (and Australia),[98] on the one hand, and the United States on the other, is the constitutional rights-based status of the latter.[99] Yet despite the lack of a clear constitutional right, there has been thus far less (or at least less effective) anti-choice activity in Australia compared to the United States.[100] The arguments used to deny recovery for the costs of upbringing for a child born as a result of a doctor's negligence are instead notionally based in tort law (with a number of explicit references to public policy). And they are not good arguments: each can be responded to very simply. Take, for example, the argument that a child will be harmed if damages are awarded for the cost of his or her upkeep if/when he or she finds out that he or she "was not wanted".[101] This might

97 English and Canadian commentators have also drawn these links between wrongful birth/conception actions and anti-choice sentiment. See, for example, Scott, R, "Prenatal Screening, Autonomy and Reasons: The Relationship between the Law of Abortion and Wrongful Birth" (2003) 11 *Medical Law Review* 265; Langevin, L, "The Compensation of Wrongful Pregnancy in Quebec Civil Law" (1999) 14 *Canadian Journal of Law & Society* 61.

98 Scott (2003) op cit, at 265–268. Under English law abortion is available to a woman if she meets one or more of the grounds specified in the *Abortion Act 1967* (UK). Similarly, for women in Australia, the availability of abortion is governed by a combination of statute and common law. These laws vary from State to State, but, like English law, the approach in Australia is not rights-based. Every State and Territory in Australia (except the Australian Capital Territory) continues to have some form of legislative limit on abortion in its criminal code or other statutes. As in the United Kingdom, then, abortion in Australia is permissible only subject to certain grounds being made out. See: *Crimes Act 1900* (NSW) ss 82, 83, and 84; *Criminal Code* (Qld) ss 224, 225 and 226; *Criminal Law Consolidation Act 1935* (SA) ss 81(1), 81(2), 82 and 82(2); *Criminal Code* (Tas) ss 134(1), 134(2), 135 and 164; *Crimes Act 1958* (Vic) ss 65 and 66; *Criminal Code* (WA) s 199; *Health Act Acts Amendment (Abortion) Act 1998* (WA); and *Criminal Code* (NT) ss 172, 173 and 174. In practice, Medicare pays for over 70,000 terminations of pregnancy per year.

99 Scott (2003) op cit, at 266–267.

100 This is not to deny the seriousness of various attacks on the availability of abortion, particularly those coming from Health Minister Tony Abbott. Note also that a doctor in New South Wales has been charged with unlawfully terminating a pregnancy, the first such prosecution in New South Wales for over 30 years: see Summers, A, "Future of Abortion Hangs on Landmark Hearing", *Sydney Morning Herald*, 9 August 2005.

101 Compare the treatment by McHugh and Gummow JJ at [79]ff; compare Hayne J at [204]. Heydon J's treatment of this issue is particularly interesting. He cites a range of United States decisions (of which, as noted above, there is a variety of views amongst the States) and refers to other dissenting judgments (such as the highly polemical judgment of Meagher JA in *CES v Superclinics*) as if they were authority, rather than expressions of (dissenting) opinion. And most notably, he brings to bear an analogy from adoption law, claiming that the secrecy that surrounds adoption is evidence of the harm to a child of learning that they were not wanted. However, his authority for this proposition is an article from the United States, published in 1965 in the *Utah Law Review*. It hardly describes the situation surrounding adoption in Australia, where the veil of secrecy has been increasingly lifted over recent decades: see [374]ff. Most ironically, it is Heydon J who has been most publicly critical of long and detailed footnotes and citations, yet he travels far and wide (though very selectively) in his search for authority to back his hunch about the harm that will flow to a child from the availability of child-rearing damages.

make some sense if there were some evidence-based research upon which this view was based, but those who make this assertion have thus far failed to provide any evidence for it. Moreover, if that really were the case, then, as McHugh and Gummow JJ noted:

> Logically, those persons like Lord Millett who would deny the cost of maintaining the child because of what they see as the immeasurable benefits gained from the birth of the child must deny the right of action itself. If the immeasurability of those benefits denies damages for the cost of maintaining the child, there must also be denied recovery for the hospital and medical costs of the birth and for the attendant pain and suffering associated with the birth. Yet, illogically as it seems to us, those persons permit the action and allow damages to be recovered in respect of these two heads of damage.[102]

Another argument often given against awarding damages for the costs of upkeep (and emphasised by the minority in *Cattanach*, most particularly by Heydon J), is that this commodifies human life, and turns children into things.[103] But the same could be said about the child support system. As one commentator put it some years ago:

> No court would be moved by the argument coming from a putative father that he should not be required to provide financial support for the child he has fathered on the grounds that he has bestowed on the mother a priceless blessing.[104]

Justice McMurdo, the President of the Queensland Court of Appeal, noted in the decision from which the appeal in *Cattanach* was taken:

> Whilst recognising that only the crustiest of curmudgeons is not warmed by the miracle of new life, I am far from persuaded that the blessing of parenthood should prohibit or even limit a claim for the modest reasonable costs of rearing to majority the baby conceived as a result of medical negligence following a failed sterilisation performed for socio-economic reasons.[105]

Another concern that has been raised is *how* do we calculate the costs of bringing up a child? In fact, there are many recognised methods of doing so, used by bodies

---

102 *Cattanach v Melchior* (2003) 215 CLR 1; [2003] HCA 38 at [91].

103 Some of these arguments have been previously published in Graycar, R, "A Loved Baby Can't Cancel Out a Clear Case of Medical Negligence", *Sydney Morning Herald*, 21 July 2003; and Graycar, R, "The value of a loved baby can't cancel out a clear case of medical negligence", *Online Opinion*, 25 July 2003 <www.onlineopinion.com.au/view.asp?article =573> (accessed 12 August 2005).

104 Bickenbach, JE, "Damages for Wrongful Conception: Doiron v Orr" (1980) 18 *University of Western Ontario Law Review* 493 at 498, cited by Reichman, A, "Damages in Tort for Wrongful Conception – Who Bears the Cost of Raising the Child?" (1985) 10 *Sydney Law Review* 568 at 575. Also cited by McMurdo, P in *Melchior v Cattanach* [2001] QCA 246 at note 94.

105 *Melchior v Cattanach* [2001] QCA 246 at [49]. This reference to sterilisations as performed for "socio-economic reasons" may be somewhat problematic. Some Canadian courts have expressed the view that damages may be awarded for the costs of upkeep if economic reasons were the motivating factor behind the sterilisation (see, for example, *Kealey v Berezowski* (1996) 136 DLR (4th) 708 (Ont HC)). But as Langevin points out, this imposes constraints on women's autonomy by suggesting that family planning choices are legitimately made solely for economic reasons: Langevin (1999) op cit, at 76.

such as the Child Support Agency (CSA), the Australian Institute of Family Studies (AIFS), and so on.[106] In Australia, Australian National University economist Bruce Chapman has calculated the earnings that women forgo by having and raising children.[107] Similar data available in England were referred to by Baroness Hale in her speech to the actuarial association.[108]

The law has methods of valuing all sorts of things that do not have obvious means of calculation. The clearest example is the award of damages for non-pecuniary losses, but there are other examples. Some years ago, footballer Andrew Ettingshausen was awarded around $100,000 (a very similar amount to what was awarded for bringing up Jordan Melchior) for defamation after a magazine published a (shadowy) photo of his genitalia.[109] "Reputation", the currency of defamation law, is a much less tangible item than working out how much it costs to feed and clothe a child.

There is no doubt that there are some very strong and conflicting views about the propriety of awarding damages for the costs of bringing up a child born as a result of negligence. One only has to recall the public debate, following the decision in *Cattanach v Melchior*, when the Deputy Prime Minister attacked the decision of the High Court (a critique in which many joined).[110] Both the New

---

106 The AIFS has produced a thoroughgoing publication called *A Guide to Calculating the Costs of Children* (AIFS, 2000). In compiling the guide, the AIFS, "invited researchers based at three eminent institutions to write fresh articles ... explaining how they thought the costs of children should be calculated, and setting out the estimates which followed from the approach they had adopted", <www.aifs.gov.au/institute/pubs/costs.html> (accessed 12 August 2005). The Child Support Agency's website also provides detailed information about the quantitative assessment of child support, <www.csa.gov.au/guide/2_4_1.htm> (accessed 12 August 2005). The Australian Council for Social Service (ACOSS) has also published work in this area: *More Help with the Cost of Caring for Babies and Toddlers*, ACOSS, Sydney, 2004.

107 See Gray and Chapman (2001) op cit. Beggs and Chapman (1988) represents an earlier study covering the same issues.

108 Dr Katherine Rake (ed), *Cabinet Office Briefing: Women's Incomes over the Lifetime* (2000, HMSO). Cited in Hale (2001) op cit, at 747–749.

109 In *Ettingshausen v Australian Consolidated Press Ltd* (1991) 23 NSWLR 443, Hunt J ruled that the matter could go before a jury. The jury awarded Ettingshausen $350,000, accepting Ettingshausen's arguments that the magazine had implied that he deliberately permitted the inclusion of the photograph and that he was held up to ridicule by its inclusion. Justice Peter Heerey comments that the "plaintiff was awarded more for people thinking he had consented to his penis being photographed than had it been chopped off in an industrial accident": Heerey, P, "Aesthetics, Culture and the Whole Damn Thing" (2003) 15 *Law & Literature* 295 at 305. On appeal in *Australian Consolidated Press Ltd v Ettingshausen* (unreported, NSWCA, Gleeson CJ, Kirby P, Clarke JA, 13 October 1993), all three judges concurred that the damages awarded were "over the top", to use Gleeson CJ's words. The court ordered a new trial limited to the question of damages. Upon retrial on 1 February 1995, the jury awarded damages in the sum of $100,000. For an account of the history of the case, see also *Ettingshausen v Australian Consolidated Press Ltd* (unreported, NSWCA, Gleeson CJ, Kirby P, Priestley JA, 17 October 1995), which deals with costs.

110 The former Deputy Prime Minister, the Hon John Anderson, expressed his views in "The *Melchior* Decision Devalues the Experience of Raising Children" *Online Opinion*, 5 August 2003, <www.onlineopinion.com.au/view.asp?article=595> (accessed 17 August 2005). As examples of the debate, see also Shanahan, A, "A Child Should Never Be Seen as Damage" *The Age*, 22 July 2003 and Bourke, V, "Romance v Reality: The Cost of Raising a Child is no Measure of a Parent's Love", *Eureka Street*, September 2003, <www.eurekastreet.com.au/articles/0309bourke.html> (accessed 12 February 2006).

South Wales and Queensland governments have placed statutory limits on recovery for these losses.[111] Deciding whether or not to compensate women for their loss, through negligence, of choice and correspondingly, their loss or impairment of reproductive autonomy, is a policy decision about the value we place on that autonomy. I have argued that court decisions (and statutes) that deny recovery do so because they do not give sufficient weight to the importance of that autonomy. That is a policy choice they have made. But it is disingenuous to argue that this is a logical application of traditional negligence doctrine. Rather, the denial of damages for the cost of raising a child who would not have been conceived and born but for a doctor's negligence is perhaps one of the clearest examples of judicial activism, made even more noteworthy by its invocation by Justice Heydon, so soon after he joined the High Court bench. To paraphrase Justice Kirby,[112] it is time we stopped resorting to judicial fairy tales and myths, and recognise and openly discuss the policy choices that courts routinely make precisely for what they are.

---

111 *Civil Liability Act 2002* (NSW) Pt 11, provides:

   71 Limitation of the award of damages for the birth of a child

   (1) In any proceedings involving a claim for the birth of a child to which this Part applies, the court cannot award damages for economic loss for:

   (a) the costs associated with rearing or maintaining the child that the claimant has incurred or will incur in the future, or

   (b) any loss of earnings by the claimant while the claimant rears or maintains the child.

   (2) Subsection (1)(a) does not preclude the recovery of any additional costs associated with rearing or maintaining a child who suffers from a disability that arise by reason of the disability.

   And see also *Civil Liability Act 2003* (Qld) Pt 5 s 49A:

   49A Failed sterilisation procedures

   (1) This section applies if, following a procedure to effect the sterilisation of an individual, the individual gives birth to, or fathers, a child because of the breach of duty of a person in advising about, or performing, the procedure.

   Examples of sterilisation procedures —

   Tubal ligation and vasectomy.

   (2) A court can not award damages for economic loss arising out of the costs ordinarily associated with rearing or maintaining a child.

   49B Failed contraceptive procedure or contraceptive advice

   (1) This section applies if, following a contraceptive procedure on an individual or the giving of contraceptive advice to an individual, the individual gives birth to, or fathers, a child because of the breach of duty of a person in advising about, or performing, the procedure or giving the advice.

   (2) A court can not award damages for economic loss arising out of the costs ordinarily associated with rearing or maintaining a child.

112 Kirby (2004), op cit.

22

Dilemmas in obstetrics and midwifery

John Seymour[1]

Introduction

This chapter examines the likely effect of the implementation of the Ipp Committee recommendations[2] on those who practise obstetrics and midwifery. Only certain aspects of these reforms will be considered: I shall focus on the way the new legislation might affect the imposition of liability on a doctor or midwife when a pregnancy does not end well.

To understand the reforms, it is necessary to appreciate the circumstances in which the committee was established. It was set up by the Commonwealth in response to concerns about the way the law of negligence imposed liability for personal injury and death. Included in the complaints were those made by the medical profession about the operation of malpractice law. The government readily – perhaps too readily – accepted that the criticisms were justified. After noting that the award of damages for personal injury "has become unaffordable and unsustainable", the committee's terms of reference requested it to develop options "to limit liability and quantum of awards for damages".[3] Specific reference was made to the need to re-formulate the standard of care applied in medical negligence matters.

The committee's recommendations and the consequent State and Territory legislation gave effect to the Commonwealth's policy. As a result, the legal context in which health care professionals work has been changed. It has been accepted that the law should impose constraints on the courts' ability to find a practitioner liable for an adverse outcome.

In addition to acknowledging this change it is necessary to recognise certain characteristics of the medical and social environment in which childbirth currently occurs in Australia. One feature of this environment is a polarisation of views, a polarisation reflecting two different assumptions. On the one hand is the belief that childbirth should be regarded as a natural, risk-free process which normally

---

1   I acknowledge the helpful comments of my Law Faculty colleagues, Joachim Dietrich and Jim Davis, and of Kathryn Dwan of the Australian National University's Research School of Social Studies.

2   Commonwealth, *Review of the Law of Negligence. Final Report*, Canberra, September 2002 (Ipp Report).

3   Ipp Report, p ix.

should be accomplished without medical intervention. This belief expresses itself in hostility to the "medicalisation" of childbirth and, in particular, in criticism of Australia's caesarean section rate. On the other hand, there is the view that there are always risks associated with childbirth and that in some situations medical expertise can make a significant contribution to the reduction or avoidance of these risks. From this perspective, decisions as to the management of a delivery should be made on a case-by-case basis without the intrusion of assumptions about the undesirability of medical intervention.

There is a number of other factors at work. The view that a pregnant woman should control the manner of her delivery is now widely held. This manifests itself in different ways. The woman may believe that she should not be pressured into accepting medical intervention. If this is the case, she may choose a birthing centre whose practitioners are committed to natural childbirth, or may arrange a home-birth. Conversely, she may seek to exercise her power of control by demanding a caesarean section. In making such a choice, she might show herself to be at odds with those opposed to the medicalisation of childbirth.

Another consideration is that, because maternal and infant mortality and morbidity are very low, expectations are high. There is widespread unwillingness to accept a less than perfect outcome. This attitude, the reduction in family size and the trend towards delaying pregnancy, result in women demanding more of those who care for them. In consequence, when an adverse outcome occurs, the temptation to blame the health care professional is increased. What would have been accepted only a few decades ago as a natural event is now more likely to be viewed as preventable and the product of negligence.

Thus a number of forces are at work. There are those who view childbirth as a natural process and who therefore disparage medical expertise. There are those who value and rely on this expertise. Whether or not they believe in natural child-birth, Australian women are likely to have high expectations. Many believe that they should be able to exercise control over the management of their deliveries. The environment in which the legislation based on the Ipp Report will be applied is therefore a difficult one. If practitioners are sued, this legislation must accommodate fundamental disagreements as to the proper management of pregnancy and childbirth and hence as to the way that allegations of negligence are assessed.

The legislative reforms

Standard of care when providing treatment

In its review of the law of medical negligence, the Ipp Committee stated that the distinction between the provision of treatment and the provision of information is very important and that the law should deal with these two activities in different ways.[4]

---

4   Ibid, para 3.1.

With regard to the standard of care governing the provision of treatment, the Ipp Report made a choice between two approaches. One was the retention of the existing law under which the court must decide whether the appropriate standard of care has been provided. The other was the adoption of the *Bolam* rule, under which conformity with practices approved by a responsible body of expert opinion would defeat an allegation of negligence.[5] For reasons that are not adequately discussed, the committee favoured the *Bolam* rule, but opted for a modified version. Its formulation of the standard of care was that:

> A medical practitioner is not negligent if the treatment provided was in accordance with an opinion widely held by a significant number of respected practitioners in the field, unless the court considers that the opinion was irrational.[6]

The committee's proposal that a court need not defer to widely held expert opinion if it considered the opinion to be "irrational" was explained by reference to *Bolitho v City and Hackney Health Authority*. There the House of Lords held that in some situations it should be open to a court to decide that the views expressed by medical witnesses are not representative of those held by a "responsible, reasonable or respectable" body of experts.[7] Why this formula was replaced by the requirement that the opinion be "irrational" before it could be rejected was not made clear. The report observed that "the chance that an opinion which was widely held by a significant number of respected practitioners in the relevant field would be held irrational is very small indeed".[8]

In the legislation enacted in most Australian jurisdictions, the Ipp Committee recommendations as to treatment standards were broadly adopted, although there are important differences in the wording employed. Section 5O(1) and (2) of the *Civil Liability Act 2002* (NSW) state:

> (1) A person practising a profession (*a professional*) does not incur a liability in negligence arising from the provision of a professional service if it is established that the professional acted in a manner that (at the time the service was provided) was widely accepted in Australia by peer professional opinion as competent professional practice.
>
> (2) However, peer professional opinion cannot be relied on for the purposes of this section if the court considers that the opinion is irrational.

In South Australia, Tasmania and Western Australia, a similar formula is employed to identify the necessary standard of care.[9] In Queensland, the Act sets the

---

5   The rule was formulated by McNair J in *Bolam v Friern Hospital Management Committee* [1957] 1 WLR 582 at 587.

6   Ipp Report, Recommendation 3.

7   [1998] 1 AC 232 at 242 per Lord Browne-Wilkinson.

8   Ipp Report, para 3.18.

9   *Civil Liability Act 1936* (SA) s 41(1) ("widely accepted in Australia by members of the same profession as competent professional practice"); *Civil Liability Act 2002* (Tas) s 22(1) ("widely accepted in Australia by peer professional opinion as competent professional practice"); *Civil Liability Act 2002* (WA) s 5PB(1) ("widely accepted by the health professional's peers as competent professional practice").

standard by reference to treatment "widely accepted by peer professional opinion by a significant number of respected practitioners in the field as competent professional practice", while in Victoria the wording used is "widely accepted in Australia by a significant number of respected practitioners in the field ... as competent professional practice in the circumstances".[10]

Two of the differences are noteworthy. The Queensland and Victorian Acts have followed the Ipp Committee's definition more closely. Whereas this definition referred to *respected* practitioners in the field, the New South Wales, South Australian, Tasmanian and Western Australian statutes set the standard by reference to peer professional opinion. This suggests that an objective standard will be employed: once an expert witness is accepted as the defendant's professional "peer", his or her evidence will normally be authoritative. It will not be open to a court to discount the evidence on the basis that, in the committee's words, it is not "soundly based".[11] The second difference is the product of the Queensland and Victorian Acts' retention of the committee's reference to *a significant number* of respected practitioners. This is clearer than the reference, in the Acts in the four other States, to practices that are "widely accepted" by peer professional opinion.

What does "widely accepted" mean? It may refer to wide geographical acceptance throughout Australia. If so, how is this acceptance to be proved by a defendant? It might be answered that such an interpretation is perverse and that an opinion that is widely accepted is one held by a significant number of the relevant group. A judge faced with such an argument, however, might well point out that if the law-makers had meant to refer to "a significant number" of practitioners they would – like the Queensland and Victorian legislatures – have done so explicitly. Further, whatever meaning is given to the expression "widely accepted", how is acceptance to be determined? One suggestion is that informal surveys might be used. Another is that the statutory changes might see an increased use of textbooks and practice guidelines. "If a practice is not approved in such standard works, an advocate may have a hard time persuading anyone that it is widely accepted as competent".[12]

Comment must also be made on the wording of the exception to the general rule. Under s 5O(2) of the New South Wales Act, a court may not rely on peer professional opinion if it considers the opinion "irrational". Similar provisions are included in the Queensland, South Australian and Tasmanian Acts.[13] "Irrational" is an emotive term and might have the effect of discouraging courts from rejecting the views of expert witnesses. "It would take a confident (some might say arrogant) non-medical decision-maker ... to decide that the widely accepted view is

---

10   *Civil Liability Act 2003* (Qld) s 22(1); *Wrongs Act 1958* (Vic) s 59(1).

11   Ipp Report, para 3.15.

12   Sant, K, "A New Bolam Test?", (2004) (September/October) 64 *Precedent* 20 at 22.

13   *Civil Liability Act 2003* (Qld) s 22(2) (the exception applies if the court considers the opinion is, "irrational or contrary to a written law"); *Civil Liability Act 1936* (SA) s 41(2); *Civil Liability Act 2002* (Tas) s 22(2).

irrational".[14] Under the Victorian statute, peer professional opinion cannot be relied on if the court determines that the opinion is "unreasonable".

The Western Australian Act provides a third formula. A health professional acting in accordance with a practice widely accepted by peers is not protected if, in the circumstances of the particular case, the practice was "so unreasonable that no reasonable health professional in the health professional's position" could have acted as the practitioner did.[15] There will be few situations in which this provision might be relied on: normally the adoption of a widely accepted practice will not be unreasonable.

Duty to provide information

The Ipp Report's conclusion that a different standard of care is needed when a failure to provide information is alleged was explained by reference to the importance of "informed consent". "People have the right to decide for themselves whether or not they will undergo medical treatment".[16] In the committee's view, the standard to be observed in the provision of information on the basis of which a patient decides to give or withhold consent to treatment should not be set by medical practitioners:

> The giving of information on which to base consent is not a matter that is appropriately treated as being one of medical expertise. Rather, it involves wider issues about the relationship between medical practitioners and patients and the right of individuals to decide their own fate. The court is the ultimate arbiter of the standard of care in regard to the giving of information by medical practitioners.[17]

The New South Wales legislation reflects an acceptance of the committee's conclusion that a court, and not the medical profession, should be the "ultimate arbiter" when the alleged negligence is a failure to provide information necessary to allow a patient to decide whether to consent to treatment. Section 5P of the *Civil Liability Act 2002* (NSW) states that s 50 "does not apply to liability arising in connection with the giving of (or the failure to give) a warning, advice or other information in respect of the risk of death of or injury to a person associated with the provision by a professional of a professional service". Similar provisions are included in the Queensland, South Australian, Tasmanian, Victorian and Western Australian Acts.[18]

In addition, the legislation deals with the problem of proving the causal link between a practitioner's omission to provide appropriate information and the harm suffered by the patient. The success of a "failure to warn" claim depends on

---

14 Sant (2004) op cit, at 22.
15 *Civil Liability Act 2002* (WA) s 5PB(4).
16 Ipp Report, para 3.35.
17 Ibid, para 3.37.
18 *Civil Liability Act 2003* (Qld) s 22(5) (the provision refers to the risk of "harm", defined in Sch 2); *Civil Liability Act 1936* (SA) s 41(5); *Civil Liability Act 2002* (Tas) s 22(5) (the provision refers to the risk of "harm", defined in s 9); *Wrongs Act 1958* (Vic) s 60; *Civil Liability Act 2002* (WA) s 5PB(2).

the plaintiff establishing that he or she would not have consented to the medical treatment if properly advised and so would have avoided the harm. The difficulties confronting a court when determining whether the causal link is established are well recognised. One is whether the question of what the plaintiff would have done should be decided objectively or subjectively. The Ipp Committee opted for the subjective test: "the question to be asked is what *that patient* would have done if the information had been given".[19] The second problem is the nature of the evidence employed in proving the causal link. On this, the committee commented: "[T]he question of what the plaintiff would have done if the defendant had not been negligent should be decided on the basis of the circumstances of the case and without regard to the plaintiff's own testimony about what they would have done".[20] The reason given was the committee's belief that "hindsight bias" would undermine the value of this testimony. Because the evidence would be self-serving, it would be unreliable.

Both recommendations were adopted by the law-makers in four States. Section 5D(3) of the *Civil Liability Act 2002* (NSW) provides:

> (3) If it is relevant to the determination of factual causation to determine what the person who suffered harm would have done if the negligent person had not been negligent:
>
>   (a) the matter is to be determined subjectively in the light of all relevant circumstances, subject to paragraph (b), and
>
>   (b) any statement made by the person after suffering the harm about what he or she would have done is inadmissible except to the extent (if any) that the statement is against his or her interest.

Similar provisions were enacted in Queensland, Tasmania and Western Australia.[21] In Victoria the legislature limited itself to providing that the issue should be determined subjectively; the statute does not impose restrictions on the type of evidence to be received.[22]

Applying the legislation to obstetricians and midwives

What are the implications of the statutory changes for those who practise obstetrics and midwifery and for their patients? In seeking to answer this question I shall initially adopt the distinction between the standard of care expected of professionals when they undertake treatment and that expected when they provide information. As will become apparent, however, the distinction is difficult to maintain when examining the obligations of those who provide antenatal care and manage childbirth.

---

19   Ipp Report, para 7.38 (original emphasis).
20   Ibid, para 7.40.
21   *Civil Liability Act 2003* (Qld) s 11(3); *Civil Liability Act 2002* (Tas) s 13(3) and *Civil Liability Act 2002* (WA) s 5C(3).
22   *Wrongs Act 1958* (Vic) s 51(3).

Standard of care expected of obstetricians and midwives

The legislation enacted following the Ipp Report must be interpreted to determine whether, when there is a difference of opinion as to the management of the delivery and there is an adverse outcome, a practitioner should be found liable in negligence. Under the New South Wales, South Australian, Tasmanian and Western Australian statutes, a health care professional does not normally incur liability in negligence if he or she acted in a manner that was widely accepted by "peer professional opinion" as competent professional practice. The Queensland and Victorian Acts set the standard by reference to practices widely accepted as competent by a significant number of respected peers.

Identifying a practitioner's "peers"

While the various provisions depart from the common law in accepting that peer opinion is normally authoritative, the common law is still relevant when considering the meaning of the sections' references to peers. The starting point is the proposition that a member of a professional group should be judged on the basis of standards accepted by that group. Thus a consultant surgeon's performance of an operation should be assessed by reference to the standards expected of a competent surgeon. A general practitioner's performance of a procedure is to be judged by reference to the standards expected of a competent general practitioner.[23] Practitioners who step outside their fields of expertise and undertake tasks that they are not qualified to perform will, except in an emergency, normally be judged by reference to standards applying to colleagues who are appropriately qualified.[24]

There are special difficulties in applying these principles in the context of childbirth. Usually the care of a woman during labour and delivery is shared. In a hospital or birthing centre, a woman's care may be provided by consultant obstetricians, general practitioners, junior doctors and midwives. Alternatively, a woman may be cared for entirely by an independent midwife and deliver either in a birthing centre or at home.

At first sight, the law can readily accommodate this diversity. If it is alleged that a consultant obstetrician has been guilty of negligence, the relevant "peer professional opinion" will be that of other consultants. Similarly, the conduct of a general practitioner or midwife will be assessed by reference to the standards set by his or her peers. This analysis, however, over-simplifies the problem, particularly when care is shared. Here the members of the three professional groups are interdependent: their fields of expertise overlap to such an extent that the borderline between them is frequently difficult to define. It may not be easy to isolate the responsibility borne by a particular member of the team. All seek the same

---

23 *Sidaway v Governors of Bethlem Hospital* [1985] AC 871 at 897 per Lord Bridge.
24 For a discussion of this principle in the context of a general practitioner's management of a pregnancy, see *Lane by Lane v Skyline Family Medical Center* 363 NW 2d 318 (Minn App, 1985).

outcome: the safe delivery of a healthy child. The ultimate question if there is an adverse outcome is whether the care fell below the expected standard.

The way this question is answered, and the extent to which separate standards can be applied, will vary. When an obstetrician closely supervises all deliveries in a hospital unit, any allegation of negligence will be judged on the basis of the standard expected of a competent specialist. In some units, however, a woman in labour may nominally be under the care of a consultant, but in fact full responsibility for the management of the delivery will be assumed by a general practitioner or midwife. In such a situation the consultant may not be aware of the woman's presence in the unit. Here it may be necessary to make distinctions on the basis of differing levels of skill and knowledge. The care provided by a general practitioner or midwife who accepts full responsibility for a delivery will be judged by reference to the standard set by his or her peers. In some instances this will mean that when an adverse outcome has occurred, any damages claim will focus not on the alleged lack of skill displayed by the practitioner but on the failure to seek advice or transfer the woman's care. For such a claim to succeed, it must be shown that a problem had arisen in the course of a woman's labour and that a competent doctor or midwife would have recognised both the problem and the fact that it was one with which he or she was not trained to deal. The negligence would consist of retaining responsibility for the patient when a competent general practitioner or midwife would not have done so.

An independent midwife who accepts full responsibility for the management of a difficult delivery is particularly vulnerable to a claim based on a failure to refer a patient to a medically qualified practitioner. The polarisation of views referred to earlier in this chapter is relevant here. The woman's decision that the midwife should manage her care may reflect a commitment to natural childbirth and hostility to any form of medical intervention. If there is an adverse outcome and the woman wishes to sue the midwife, by what standard should the midwife's management of the delivery be judged?

This question might be answered in two ways. On one view, the relevant "peer professional opinion" will be that accepted by competent midwives. In the case of a midwife's decision to continue managing a delivery in the face of a complication, it must be asked whether it was widely accepted among her peers that it was not negligent to fail to transfer to a doctor the care of a woman suffering such a complication. Alternatively, the standard could be set by regarding the midwife as having stepped outside her field of expertise and undertaken tasks that she was not qualified to perform. Such a midwife could be seen as holding herself out as competent to manage a difficult delivery. From this perspective, she should be judged by reference to standards applying to a medically trained practitioner.

An illustration

An example of a situation in which a negligence action might arise illuminates the issues. In examining this example, I shall, instead of distinguishing between the responsibilities of obstetricians, general practitioners and midwives, focus on the problems arising from the differences of opinion within the ranks of each group. While these differences sometimes reflect the polarisation of views about the medicalisation of childbirth, it would be an over-simplification to regard them solely as the product of this debate. Rather, if a court hearing a negligence action is to fulfil its function, the evidence on which the proponents of the different views rely must be scrutinised. Under the new legislation, a court must assess the standard of care by reference to "widely accepted" professional opinion.

The difficulties caused by this requirement and the variations in the way it is expressed in the statutes have been noted earlier in this chapter. These matters can be further explored by examining a case study: the delivery of a breech presentation. In this situation, there will be some practitioners who will prefer a vaginal delivery (this may or may not be because they are committed to natural childbirth). There will be others who might regard it as negligent to fail to undertake a caesarean section, on the ground that this is likely to reduce or avoid the risks faced by the woman and her foetus. If a vaginal delivery is performed, and something goes wrong, a court hearing the resulting negligence action will have to decide whether the techniques used in the management of the delivery were widely accepted as competent professional practice.

A vaginal delivery can damage a woman's pelvic floor, resulting in perineal tears that may lead to urinary and faecal incontinence. There is also an increased risk of post partum haemorrhage. Prolonged labour may cause the foetus to suffer intra-uterine asphyxia (as a result of which the child might die or suffer brain damage). Caesarean section carries risks, including severe abdominal pain, embolism (both pulmonary and amniotic fluid), infection, injury to the bladder and intra-operative haemorrhage. There is also the anaesthetic risk (although this is reduced by the use of epidural and spinal techniques).

There seems to be a high level of agreement among practitioners on the identification of these risks. Where the disagreements lie is in the differing views as to the *significance* to be attached to them in the management of a breech presentation. Those opposed to medical intervention in childbirth will tend to minimise the risks associated with a vaginal delivery. Those who adopt a different approach will believe that the benefits of a caesarean section outweigh the admitted risks of the procedure.

The Royal Australian and New Zealand College of Obstetricians and Gynaecologists' statement on the management of a breech presentation[25] leaves room for the exercise of individual clinical judgment. It indicates that, although the level of risk is in general higher in a planned vaginal breech delivery than in a planned caesarean section, it would "be wrong to surmise that planned vaginal birth is not

---

25 RANZCOG Statements, "Breech Deliveries at Term", February 2003. This statement is one of a number issued by the college; these express "a college view" on a given topic, while acknowledging that clinical management must always be responsive to the needs of individual patients; <www.ranzcog.edu.au/publications/collegestatements.shtml> (accessed 24 September 2005).

a reasonable option" in some circumstances. After noting that some fellows of the college believe that in all cases of breech presentation a caesarean section should be performed, the statement advises that obstetricians should "continue to individualise". It adds: "Within the overall cohort of breech presentation at term, there may be a sub-group that does extremely well with breech vaginal delivery". A number of factors that "may favour a planned vaginal birth" are listed. These include the woman's acceptance of continuous foetal monitoring and the rapid availability of a caesarean section, favourable foetal circumstances (such as a foetus of small or average size) and favourable maternal circumstances (such as a large pelvis). Also mentioned is a particular maternal desire to deliver vaginally rather than by caesarean section.

When this statement is tendered in evidence, how will a court applying the new legislation deal with a claim against an obstetrician when it is asserted that a failure to perform a caesarean section for a breech presentation was negligent? A statement of this kind may in time be recognised as strong (perhaps conclusive) evidence of the practices "widely accepted" as competent by consultant obstetricians. Further, if attention is focused on the variations in wording seen in the Queensland and Victorian Acts, it must be asked whether such a college statement necessarily reflects the views of a "significant number" of "respected practitioners". It is unlikely that a court would dismiss the statement on the management of a breech delivery as "irrational" or "unreasonable". This prediction, however, may prove to be wrong. Much will depend on judges' attitudes. They may feel obliged to defer to professional opinion or they may seek the opportunity to assert the courts' power to decide whether the appropriate standard of care has been provided.

What will it mean in practice if a court treats the statement as an authoritative indication of what is "widely accepted" as competent professional practice? The starting-point might be that the performance of a caesarean section is the preferred option. It might be up to the defendant doctor to justify the decision not to perform a caesarean. The college statement not only leaves room for the exercise of individual judgment, but it also lists factors favouring a vaginal delivery. The doctor might be in difficulty if he or she cannot show that a caesarean section was immediately available, that the foetus was small or average size, and that the woman had a large pelvis. Alternatively, a doctor who is able to show the presence of these factors may escape liability. Logically, this should be the outcome of the combination of the law's decision to accept reputable professional opinion as authoritative and the availability of the college's carefully formulated reflection of peer opinion. As a commentator on s 5O of the *Civil Liability Act 2002* (NSW) has remarked, the section will make it "more difficult for a judge to prefer one opinion over another. Once a defendant has produced reasonably credible evidence that a practice is widely accepted as competent, the game will be all but over".[26]

The college statement's acknowledgement of the importance of the woman's desire to deliver vaginally rather than by caesarean section is of interest. While this

---

26   Sant (2004) op cit, at 22.

reflects a recognition of the woman's wish to exercise control, the fact that she expressed a desire for a vaginal delivery may not be relevant to answering the question whether the failure to perform a caesarean was negligent.[27] Either it was widely accepted by peer professional opinion that the woman's condition and that of her foetus made a vaginal delivery a reasonable option, or it was not. A doctor who employs a procedure that peers would regard as negligent may not be able to escape liability by pleading that he or she was acceding to the patient's wishes.

The example of the management of a breech presentation can be explored in a different context: where the vaginal delivery is performed not by an obstetrician, but by a midwife. It will be recalled that there are some situations in which a midwife might accept full responsibility for the management of a delivery, either because a hospital midwife elects not to seek medical assistance when caring for a woman in hospital or when an independent midwife performs a homebirth. When a midwife acts in this manner and a vaginal delivery of a breech presentation is followed by an adverse outcome, on what basis should liability be assessed? While the Australian College of Midwives has not produced statements of the kind issued by the Royal Australian and New Zealand College of Obstetricians and Gynaecologists, it has published guidelines on consultation and referral.[28] These include a discussion of abnormalities or complications which should result either in consultation with a medical practitioner or the transfer of responsibility for a woman's care to a medical practitioner. A breech presentation is listed as a condition that should result in the transfer of care to a medical practitioner.[29]

These guidelines seem to offer a clear answer to the question of the assessment of a midwife's liability when she has retained responsibility for the management of a breech presentation. If she is sued following an adverse outcome, it might be difficult for her to deny that it was "widely accepted in Australia by peer professional opinion" that she had a duty to transfer the woman's care to a medical practitioner. She might seek to escape liability by calling evidence that a significant number of competent midwives disagreed with the directive about referral, but such an argument would be unlikely to succeed. It is probable that a court would treat the guidelines as an authoritative statement of the type of care that her peers would regard as competent.

The duty to provide information

Negligent care and failure to advise

In some circumstances there will be no difficulty applying the Ipp Report's distinction between the standard of care expected of those undertaking treatment and

---

27 Her statement would, of course, be relevant if she had made it clear that in no circumstances would she consent to a caesarean section.

28 Australian College of Midwives, *National Midwifery Guidelines for Consultation and Referral*, January 2004.

29 Ibid, p 24.

that required when information is provided to enable a patient to decide whether to consent to treatment. If an obstetrician performing an elective caesarean section inadvertently opens the bladder, the success of a negligence claim will depend on proof that the surgery did not meet the standard widely accepted by his or her peers. When there is no basis on which to question the surgeon's technique, the woman might allege that a recognised risk has eventuated and that she was not advised of this risk. In such an action, in the words of the Ipp Report, the court is the "ultimate arbiter" of the woman's claim that she was denied the opportunity to make an informed decision before giving her consent.

In the context of obstetrics and midwifery the distinction cannot always so readily be made. This suggests that the analysis on which it is based is questionable. The report distinguishes between "treatment" in a general sense (which, in the committee's words, "includes diagnosis, the prescribing of medications and the carrying out of procedures"[30]) and "treatment" to which consent must normally be given. This approach pays insufficient attention to the view expressed in *Rogers v Whitaker*[31] that a health care professional's obligation to provide a patient with information is part of "a single comprehensive duty". Talk of a patient's "right of self-determination" and of "informed consent" does not assist in determining whether there has been a breach of the duty of disclosure.[32] Indeed, it diverts attention from scrutiny of the overall standard of care.

Treatment in the broad sense includes not only procedures to which consent must normally be obtained, but also the provision of advice and information. For example, a doctor or midwife may advise a pregnant woman on exercise, diet and the avoidance of smoking. This is not advice of a kind which will assist the woman to decide whether or not to undergo "treatment". Further, it is helpful to distinguish between giving *consent* to treatment and making *a decision* about treatment. Except in an emergency, a patient must give consent to a procedure such as surgery and is entitled to information to allow her to do so in an informed manner. In some situations, however – for example, when a patient elects *not* to undergo surgery – what will be required is the making of a decision. Here the patient has a right to expect relevant information and a practitioner who fails to provide it may be found to be negligent: the provision of information is an aspect of treatment in the broad sense.

The Ipp Report did not recognise these complexities. It is not surprising, therefore, that questions can be raised about the way the various statutes distinguish between the standard of care expected of a health care professional when undertaking treatment and that applying to the obligation to advise of risks. The wording of the New South Wales Act illustrates the problem. Section 5O(1) defines the standard of care applicable to "the provision of a professional service", while s 5P indicates that this section does not apply to the obligation to provide

---

30   Ipp Report, para 3.1.
31   (1992) 175 CLR 479 (HCA).
32   Ibid, pp 489–490.

information as to specified risks "associated with the provision ... of a professional service". As the sections both refer to the provision of "a professional service", they do not make a distinction between treatment broadly defined and treatment to which consent must be given. In particular, s 5P is worded in such a way as to apply to a failure to advise of the risk of injury associated with the provision of *any* professional service.

The example of an adverse outcome following the vaginal delivery of a breech presentation can again be used to explore the issues. The risks associated with such a delivery include brain damage to the baby, fractures to the baby's long bones and a maternal perineal tear. Is a practitioner who neither explains these risks nor suggests that a caesarean section might be advisable liable to a negligence action if there is a planned vaginal delivery and one of these risks eventuates? If so, will the allegation of negligence be directed towards the failure to provide an appropriate standard of care (so that s 5O is the relevant provision) or will it take the form of a "failure to warn" claim under s 5P?

Section 5P does not refer to the obligation to provide information to enable a woman to decide whether to consent to a procedure. It refers to the obligation to advise of a risk (of injury or death) associated with the provision of a professional service. Presumably a doctor or midwife who manages a vaginal delivery is providing a professional service. If so, s 5P could apply to a claim arising from a failure to advise of the associated risks. There would be nothing to prevent its application in the situation described. The section's reference to the risk of "injury" would cover both injury to the woman (in this example, the perineal tear) and to the baby (the fractures or brain damage). The latter interpretation is the result of the fact that the New South Wales Act defines "personal injury" as including pre-natal injury.[33]

If this analysis is accepted, and s 5P applies, a claim brought following a failure to advise of the risks associated with the vaginal delivery of a breech presentation would be assessed by reference to a standard set by the court. Alternatively, such a claim could equally well be decided on the basis of the standard set by s 5O. The duty of care owed by a practitioner to a woman who is contemplating a vaginal delivery includes the provision of appropriate information. If s 5O is applied, the omission to advise of risks would be viewed as negligent only if it was widely accepted by the practitioner's peers that, in the circumstances, the information should have been provided. In the case of a consultant obstetrician, the statement of the Royal Australian and New Zealand College of Obstetricians and Gynaecologists on the management of a breech presentation does not refer to an obligation to advise of risks. Nevertheless, it would be difficult to argue that a consultant who fails to inform a woman of these

---

33   *Civil Liability Act 2002* (NSW) s 3. See also *Civil Liability Act 2003* (Qld) Sch 2; *Civil Liability Act 2002* (Tas) s 3; *Wrongs Act 1958* (Vic) s 43 and *Civil Liability Act 2002* (WA) s 5. Further, s 5PB(2) of the Western Australian Act specifically refers to the obligation to inform of a risk associated with "the treatment proposed for a patient or a foetus being carried by a pregnant patient". The definition of "injury" in s 3 of the *Civil Liability Act 1936* (SA) makes no reference to pre-natal injury.

risks is not negligent. With regard to midwives, the statement of general principles included in the Australian College of Midwives' guidelines on referral accepts that a midwife should allow a pregnant woman to make an informed choice as to her care. The principles specifically refer to the obligation "to make women aware of the scope *and limitations* of midwifery care".[34] The recognition of this obligation might suggest that a midwife who fails to provide information as to the risks associated with the vaginal delivery of a breech presentation would be regarded by her colleagues as negligent.

There are thus two ways of viewing an allegation of a failure to provide information when an adverse outcome follows a planned vaginal birth. In choosing between them, consideration must be given to more than the implications for setting the standard of care. Although s 5P is broadly drafted, courts may be inclined to interpret it as applying to situations in which a plaintiff can assert that a different choice would have been made if the information as to risks had been supplied. This would give rise to difficulties in the situation under discussion. There might be something artificial about viewing a pregnant woman as "consenting" to a vaginal delivery.[35] Further, in proceedings to which s 5P would apply it will be necessary for the plaintiff to establish that she would have made a different choice if properly advised. This might not be easy, particularly when the woman had expressed a strong desire for a vaginal delivery. To succeed in her claim, she would have to show that, although she "consented" to this mode of delivery, she would have chosen differently if better advised and would have insisted on a caesarean section. The growing recognition of the need to recognise a woman's wish to exercise control over the manner of delivery should not be overlooked. It is now common for a pregnant woman who has a strong desire to avoid medical intervention to seek out a practitioner who is committed to natural childbirth. To regard such a woman in the same way as one who approaches a surgeon for information to allow her to decide whether to consent to elective surgery is unconvincing.

It is preferable to treat an omission to provide information to a woman with a breech presentation as a failure to provide appropriate care. When undertaking antenatal and intra-partum care, doctors and midwives have, as part of their "single comprehensive duty", a responsibility to volunteer information about risks of the kind discussed. In the current climate, discharge of this responsibility may not always be easy. The temptation to cooperate with a pregnant woman committed to natural childbirth and to preserve the relationship by acceding to her wishes will be strong. This is not appropriate conduct: a doctor or midwife who fails to provide the woman with information that she may not want to hear may be liable to a negligence action if there is an adverse outcome. In some circumstances the failure will be one factor contributing to the outcome and the practitioner

---

34   Australian College of Midwives (2004) op cit, p 9 (emphasis added).

35   For a contrary view, see *Campbell v Pitt County Memorial Hospital* 352 SE 2d 902 (NC App 1987) and *Holt v Nelson* Wash App, 523 P 2d 211 (1974).

should be held accountable for it. Offering information is part of the management of a pregnancy: a practitioner who neglects this task may be liable for failing to discharge his or her duty of care.

Wrongful birth actions

There are other situations in which practitioners may be liable for failing to provide information. Of special importance is the wrongful birth action. This action takes a variety of forms.[36] It can arise, for example, when a competently performed tubal ligation is followed by the birth of a healthy child; for a negligence claim to be brought here it will have to be shown that there was a failure to advise of the risk of recanalisation. Alternatively, the action may follow the birth of a disabled child. I shall concentrate on claims of this kind. These fall into two categories. First, there are those based on a failure to diagnose variations from the norm, such as hydrocephaly, anencephaly and Down syndrome. A practitioner who does not offer diagnostic tests – for example, blood tests or an ultrasound – at the appropriate stage of a pregnancy may be regarded as negligent. Alternatively, the negligence may consist of a failure competently to interpret these tests. Second, there are claims arising from a failure to warn of the risk of a foetal abnormality. A maternal infection such as rubella can result in the birth of a seriously disabled child. A doctor who has failed to recognise the symptoms of this condition in a pregnant woman, and who has therefore failed to warn her of the risk that her child will suffer from congenital rubella syndrome, may be sued for negligence. Similarly, it may be negligent for a doctor to fail to recognise the risk (which should have been apparent from the woman's age or family history) of a hereditary or genetic condition that may affect the child. There are many such conditions. They include: Down syndrome, other trisomies, cystic fibrosis, muscular dystrophy, Huntington's disease, cleft lip and palate, thalassaemia and haemophilia.

The difficulties discussed earlier – whether a particular claim is governed by s 5O or s 5P – will not arise in a wrongful birth action. Section 5P would not apply. It refers to a failure to advise of a risk of *injury to a person* associated with the provision of a professional service. It could not be interpreted as referring to the birth of a normal child following a failed tubal ligation. It is also unlikely to be interpreted as referring to the birth of a child with a genetic abnormality: such an outcome is not an "injury". Nor is it an injury "associated with the provision of a professional service". Rather, the harm of which the woman complains is the result of a natural process.

The relevant provision would be s 5O(1). The obligation to identify the presence, or risk of, a foetal abnormality would thus be an aspect of the broad duty imposed on those who undertake antenatal care. Any allegation of a failure to diagnose an abnormality or advise of a risk would be judged by reference to the

---

36 For a discussion of the various forms of wrongful birth action, see Seymour, J *Childbirth and the Law*, Oxford University Press, Oxford, 2000, pp 86–101.

practices widely accepted by peer professional opinion. In a wrongful birth action, the questions to be asked relate to the knowledge of genetic abnormalities expected of a competent practitioner and to the practices adopted with regard to the provision of diagnostic tests.

The obligations of consultants are reasonably clear. In a series of statements on antenatal care,[37] the Royal Australian and New Zealand College of Obstetricians and Gynaecologists lists a number of tests that members and fellows are expected to offer pregnant women. In any given case, an allegation of negligence made against an obstetrician who failed to make a diagnosis, to identify a risk or to offer a relevant test, is likely to be judged by reference to these protocols: they are evidence of practices widely accepted by competent obstetricians.

When there is no consultant involvement and antenatal care is provided by a general practitioner or independent midwife, the guidelines may be less clear. A general practitioner or midwife should not normally be judged by the same standard as a consultant when there has been a failure to diagnose, or to advise of the risk of, an abnormality. They cannot be expected to be so familiar with the complexities of antenatal diagnosis. The level of skill to be expected should be assessed by reference to the opinion of their peers. In a given case (for example, a failure to advise a pregnant woman that there was a risk of her child being born with thalassaemia), the question to be asked is what level of knowledge of congenital abnormalities can be expected of a competent general practitioner or of a competent midwife.

Where a consultant's advice could be sought, it might be negligent for a general practitioner or an independent midwife to fail to advise a pregnant woman of the desirability of having an antenatal consultation with an obstetrician. A failure to give this advice would deprive her of the opportunity of obtaining information about possible congenital abnormalities. When a woman is opposed to any form of medical involvement in the management of her pregnancy, the independent midwife who cares for her might be particularly vulnerable to a wrongful birth action, should the child be born with an abnormality. If she does not offer a referral to enable appropriate diagnostic tests to be performed, the midwife might be challenged for accepting full responsibility for the woman's antenatal care.

When a child has been born with a disability, the success of a wrongful birth claim will depend on the woman establishing that, had she been properly advised, she would have terminated the pregnancy. The Ipp Committee (concerned about "hindsight bias"), made recommendations as to how a court should determine what a plaintiff would have done if the negligence had not occurred. Section 5D(3) of the *Civil Liability Act 2002* (NSW) (quoted above) is an example of legislation based on these recommendations.

---

37 RANZCOG Statements, "Joint HGSA/RANZCOG Prenatal Diagnosis Policy", March 2004; "Joint HGSA/RANZCOG Recommended 'Best Practice' Guidelines on Antenatal Screening for Down Syndrome and other Fetal Aneuploidy", March 2004; "Antenatal Screening Tests", November 2004, <www.ranzcog.edu.au/publications/collegestatements.shtml> (accessed 24 September 2005).

It is not clear how this provision could be applied in a wrongful birth action arising from the birth of a disabled child. Two examples illustrate the problem. A woman who has delivered a child with Down syndrome may rest her claim on the assertion that the condition could have been diagnosed during pregnancy and that she should have been advised of the existence of tests which would have allowed such a diagnosis. A woman who has delivered a child with congenital rubella syndrome might assert that she should have been informed of the risks associated with maternal rubella (risks that might vary depending on the stage of the pregnancy at which she contracted the disease). In each case the court hearing the action must decide whether the woman would have sought and obtained a termination of pregnancy if she had received the relevant information. Under s 5D(3), it must determine the matter subjectively in the light of all relevant circumstances, but any statement made by the woman after the birth of the child is inadmissible except to the extent that the statement is against her interest.

A court applying this provision must decide what each of the women in the two examples – not a reasonable pregnant woman – would have done if properly advised. The reference to "all relevant circumstances" would allow it to receive evidence on each woman's situation (for example, whether she already has children), but the prohibition on the reception of testimony by the woman after the birth will surely hinder the court in determining whether she would have terminated the pregnancy. It is unclear how a court could decide what the woman would have done without receiving her evidence. The need to make a decision as to termination would arise only after the unexpected birth of a disabled child. A wrongful birth action is different from the action which gave rise to *Rogers v Whitaker*.[38] There Mrs Whitaker had persistently asked about the risk of blindness and so it was possible for the trial court to conclude that she would not have consented to the procedure if she had been advised of the risk. This conclusion could be reached without her testimony after the event as to what she would have done.

A determination whether the woman in each of the situations described would have terminated the pregnancy will frequently require more than evidence of this kind. A woman's decision to have an abortion is a highly personal one. Predicting how she would have decided in the absence of evidence about her reaction to the birth would be extremely difficult. In the first illustration the court would have to speculate about the woman's attitude to giving birth to a child with Down syndrome: she might view the birth of such a child as a calamity or she might feel that it was up to her to accept the child and provide the best possible care. Perhaps the court would be assisted in its task by receiving evidence from the woman's family and friends as to her feelings about disabled children and parents who have the task of rearing them. Equally, it might rely on family and friends' evidence about her attitude to abortion. Whether such evidence would be sufficient to allow the court confidently to rule on what the woman would have done is questionable. The second example presents even greater difficulties. The court

---

38   (1992) 175 CLR 479 (HCA).

would have to determine whether she would have elected to run the risk of giving birth to a child with congenital rubella syndrome. A court required to decide how the woman would have reacted to information about the risk without allowing her to give evidence after the birth might be forced to engage in little more than guesswork.

A wrongful birth action has many unsatisfactory features.[39] The problems are likely to be increased by the new legislation's exclusion of any statement made by the woman after the birth. In recommending a statutory formula of this kind, the Ipp Committee may not have taken account of the type of evidence on which courts hearing a wrongful birth action have in the past relied. In future a woman who brings such an action in New South Wales, or in Tasmania, Queensland and Western Australia (the other States that have adopted the same formula), will be disadvantaged. It seems that, in these jurisdictions – whether by inadvertence or by stealth – this form of action has been undermined.

Conclusion

In this chapter, I have considered the way the statutes enacted as a result of the Ipp Report have re-defined the basis on which a health care professional can be liable for negligence. The changes were made with the express purpose of reducing practitioners' liability. If this aim is achieved, it may come at the cost of barring just claims. Further, application of the various statutes will pose a number of problems. The new legislation will make it necessary to determine whether a plaintiff's claim relates to the standard of treatment or to a failure to warn. Much will turn on the way an action is characterised. It will be advantageous for plaintiffs to bring themselves within the exception created by provisions such as s 5P. It will be advantageous for defendants to convince a court that their actions should be judged on the basis of the standard set by provisions like s 50(1).

The application of the legislation in the context of claims against those who practise obstetrics or midwifery will give rise to special difficulties. In some circumstances, it will not be easy to make the distinction embodied in the provisions dealing with professional negligence. There is also doubt about the future of wrongful birth actions. It is uncertain whether the relevant provisions have been drafted in such a way as to accommodate these actions.

For those working in the fields of obstetrics or midwifery, the environment in which the new laws on negligence will operate will add to the difficulties. Three factors have been identified in this chapter: the widespread belief in the desirability of natural childbirth (with the consequent rejection of the medicalisation of the process); the increasing recognition of the need to take account of the pregnant woman's wishes; and the high expectations currently prevailing in Australia. Recognition of these factors reveals that it is an over-simplification to accept that since the aim of those who care for the woman is uncontroversial – the safe

---

39   Seymour (2000) op cit, pp 247–258, 264–268, 271–277 and 315–325.

delivery of a healthy baby – they should be judged solely on the basis of how well they achieve this aim.

All three factors are likely to affect the assessment of a practitioner's liability if there is an adverse outcome. There are fundamental disagreements about the style of care that is acceptable. When there is a difference of opinion (typically as to the desirability of a vaginal delivery rather than a caesarean section) this difference involves more than disagreement as to medical technique (as, for example, when surgeons hold differing views as to the appropriateness of open abdominal surgery as opposed to laparoscopic surgery). The woman may be anxious to have a vaginal delivery and may be under the care of a practitioner who, in the words of a Senate Committee Report, assumes that it is best for her for members of the medical profession to be "removed from the scene or put at arm's length".[40] If something goes wrong, there may be disagreement about whether liability should be imposed on the practitioner. From one perspective, it might be argued that in a given situation it is justified to run the risks associated with a vaginal delivery. The alternative view is that, while a vaginal delivery is normally to be preferred, it is good practice to intervene in an attempt to reduce or avoid recognised risks.

Acknowledging the need to take account of the woman's wishes further complicates the problem. While a practitioner may understandably wish to ensure that a woman's wishes are fulfilled, acceding to them does not and should not necessarily allow the practitioner to escape liability for negligence if something goes wrong. The ultimate question is whether the management of a pregnancy or delivery is in accordance with practices approved by peer professional opinion. Answering this question may require an inquiry into whether the practitioner was at fault for failing to advise the woman of certain risks. An action framed in this way may, however, prove problematic: it is uncertain how the new legislation will accommodate a claim based on such a failure. Further, recognising a woman's wish to exercise control may require practitioners to adapt to two different views: on the one hand those of women committed to natural childbirth and, on the other, those of women who demand a caesarean section.

The significance of the high expectations currently prevailing in Australia must also be recognised. When there is an adverse outcome, there will frequently be the temptation to regard it as preventable and to hold the practitioner liable. Further, a corollary of high expectations is a decreased willingness to accept a child with a congenital disability. The rapid development of screening and diagnostic techniques is allowing the identification of more and more genetic and other abnormalities in a foetus. As a result, the pressure on those who provide antenatal care is growing: pregnant women are now more likely to expect these techniques to be used and to take legal action if a failure to do so is followed by the birth of a child with a disability.

---

40 Commonwealth, Senate Community Affairs Reference Committee, *Rocking the Cradle: A Report into Childbirth Procedures*, Canberra, 1999, p 3.

Thus a paradox emerges. While medical expertise may be denigrated by a woman who favours natural childbirth, she may succeed in a negligence action alleging that a less than perfect result was caused by a failure to intervene. Equally, as the medicalisation of childbirth increasingly becomes a target, emphasis is simultaneously placed on the contribution of medical skills to the pre-natal diagnosis of abnormalities. Rejection of the medicalisation of childbirth thus has legal ramifications requiring careful scrutiny.

23

Nurses as defendants: Emerging risks

Kim Forrester[1]

Introduction

Litigation within a health care context can arise from one or several activities that are carried out as part of the delivery and consumption of health care services. For example, legal actions against, or involving, health professionals may be based on allegations of civil assault and battery, breach of contract, criminal activity, industrial and employment law breaches or negligence, to name but a few. The ability of a patient, and or their relatives, to initiate any form of legal proceedings against health professionals, and or health care institutions, is based on a wide spectrum of obligations imposed as part of the legally recognised relationship that exists between those who provide health care services and those who consume the services.

Over the preceding decade civil litigation within the health care context has been the major focus of attention. Indeed, within Australia it could be argued that the recent "crisis" in personal injuries litigation was significantly attributable to both the perceived rise in the number of medical negligence claims, and the increasing amounts in damages awarded to successful plaintiffs. When the reported increase in the propensity of patients to sue health care professionals (and institutions) in negligence, is read in conjunction with findings that significant numbers of patients are sustaining adverse injuries within the health system, it is not unexpected that health professionals will seriously consider the possibility of being involved as defendants in a negligence action.

In circumstances in which a patient or client is injured in the course of their treatment within the health care system, there are several health professionals who may be identified as the defendant or co-defendants in any ensuing personal injuries claim. The potential defendants may include the medical practitioners, nurses, or allied health professionals carrying out or directing the treatment and

---

1   RN, BA, LLB, LLM (Advanced), PhD; Senior Lecturer, School of Medicine, Griffith University, Gold Coast Campus.

care, as well as the institution under whose auspices the treatment is given and received. In some circumstances, the manufacturer of products administered or used as part of the patient's treatment regime may also be named as defendants in a medical negligence action. Historically, members of the nursing profession in Australia and Britain have not been included as defendants in legal actions initiated by patients seeking compensation for injuries they have sustained while under the care and treatment of a health care institution. In those instances, where patients or clients have initiated a negligence action, it has predominantly been in the arena of litigation almost exclusively occupied by doctors, health care institutions, and insurance companies.[2] That is, the widely held view for many years has been that a patient who has sustained an adverse injury at the hands of health professionals will sue the doctor and/or the institution as these are the individuals and bodies that are most likely to have access to the financial resources necessary to meet the damages claimed. It is not surprising therefore that nurses, and government instrumentalities, have directed little, if any, attention to the potential liability of nurses as health professionals.[3]

However, the role of nurses within both the public and private sectors of health care delivery has changed, and will continue to change dramatically. Many nurses are now undertaking expanded and more specialised roles in increasingly diverse areas of clinical practice which require high levels of expertise and knowledge.[4]

Nurses are assuming advanced roles in the provision of health care services and expanding their professional practice to include activities that were previously considered the work of medical practitioners.[5] In addition, and primarily due to the current acute shortage of skilled registered nurses and midwives, nurses and midwives are progressively assuming more extensive supervisory roles in relation to the increasing numbers of unskilled and unregulated health workers who are undertaking patient care within the health care system. These factors cumulatively operate to increase the extent of the accountability of nurses and thereby their potential legal liability. Recognition of the increasing risk faced by nurses of being named as defendants when a patient sustains an adverse injury is evident in the relatively recent provision, by nursing professional bodies and industrial organisations, of professional indemnity insurance and the requirement by some employers in the private sector that nurses have professional indemnity insurance.[6] This chapter will examine some

---

2 Foster, C,, "Negligence", in Tingle, J and Cribb A, (eds) *Nursing Law and Ethics*, 2nd edn, Blackwell Publishing, Oxford, 2002, p 75.

3 Forrester, K and Simpson, J, "Nurses and Liability-Uncertain Times Ahead" (2003) 11(2) *Journal of Law and Medicine* 148.

4 Hughes, S, "Law and Professional Practice: Accountability and Implications" (2002) 12 *British Journal of Perioperative Nursing* 94.

5 Tingle, J, "Specialist Nurses Must Understand Clinical Negligence Litigation", (2001) 10 (11) *British Journal of Nursing* 716.

6 Foster (2002) op cit, p 76.

of the factors, including recent reforms to the civil liability laws in Australia, that influence what could be described as an emerging risk for nurses as potential defendants in medical negligence claims.

Negligence

Nurses are accountable to their patients and clients, not only through the operation of the professional regulatory legislation in each of the jurisdictions[7] but also through the operation of the civil and criminal law.[8] This fundamental prerequisite of accountability has been described as an "integral part of professional practice"[9] and has been defined in terms of the ability of nurses to explain, justify and take responsibility for their activities whether they are carried out as part of their own initiative or under the direction of other health professionals.[10] More specifically Castledine defines accountability in terms of nursing care as:

> That special phenomenon relating to nursing practice which nurses are entrusted with, answerable for, take the credit and blame for, and can be judged within legal and moral boundaries.[11]

In the civil jurisdiction a nurse is under a legal duty to act reasonably in the care and treatment of a patient or client. If the nurse fails to exercise the appropriate level of care, and thereby causes injury to their patient, the nurse may be held liable in the tort of negligence. To succeed in a negligence action the patient (plaintiff) must prove, "on the balance of probabilities" all of the elements of the claim alleged against the nurse (defendant). That is, the nurse owed the patient a duty of care, the nurse undertook some activity, or failed to undertake an activity that amounted to a breach of that duty of care, and that the breach of the duty by the nurse caused the damage now claimed by the patient. Though the elements of the tort have previously been argued on the basis of the relevant case law there have been substantial changes flowing from the recent review of personal injuries litigation in Australia.

In 2002 the Australian federal, State and Territory governments appointed a panel, known as the Ipp Committee, to review personal injuries law. The terms of reference required the committee to report on the standard of care applicable in professional negligence. The recommendations of the Ipp Committee have been incorporated into civil liability legislation in all Australian jurisdictions as a

---

7 *Nurses and Midwives Act 1991* (NSW); *Nursing Act 1992* (Qld); *Nurses Act 1999* (SA); *Nursing Act 1995* (Tas); *Nurses Act 1993* (Vic); *Nurses Act 1992* (WA); *Nurses Act 1988* (ACT); *Nursing Act 1999* (NT).

8 Hughes (2002) op cit, at 95.

9 Ibid, at 95.

10 Walsh, M, "Accountability and Institution: Justifying Nursing Practice" (1997) 11 (23) *Nursing Standard* 39.

11 Castledine, G, "Accountability in Delivering Care" (1991) 5 *Nursing Standard* 28.

means of bringing about reform to the common law of negligence. Following from, or in some circumstances replacing, the case law are the new legislative provisions which address the elements of "duty of care" and "standard of care" particularly with reference to professionals. The provisions of the civil liability legislation in most jurisdictions now underpin decisions such as, "against whom is the claim made – who owed a duty of care?" and, "what was the standard of practice required of this professional?". Under these new provisions are nurses more likely to be identifiable as potential defendants and, if so, what is the standard of care expected of them as they carry out patient and client care?

The existence of a duty of care

As a general proposition, the existence of the nurse–patient relationship will give rise to a duty of care. Lord Atkin's oft-quoted statement in *Donoghue v Stevenson* has clear application to the clinical situation in which nurses assume responsibility for the care and treatment of patients or clients. The statement reads:

> [Y]ou must not injure your neighbour. ... you must take reasonable care to avoid acts or omissions which you could reasonably foresee would be likely to injure your neighbour. Who, then in law is my neighbour? The answer seems to be persons who are so closely and directly affected by my act that I ought reasonably to have them in contemplation as being so affected when I am directing my mind to the acts and omissions which are called into question.[12]

Jones suggests that when negligence is alleged within the health care context, the existence of a duty of care between the health professionals and their patients "is usually regarded as axiomatic, and attention normally focuses on whether there has been a breach of duty or whether the breach caused the damage".[13]

In circumstances therefore, where the nurse–patient relationship establishes the existence of a duty of care, the mere fact that there are now growing demands being placed on the health care sector potentially increases the likelihood of nurses becoming involved in medical negligence litigation. This escalating risk of a nurse being identified as a defendant, may arise predominantly from two sources. First, nurses are now responsible for the care and treatment of larger numbers of patients than was previously the case and second, those patients, for whom the nurse is responsible are likely to be more acutely ill and have higher, and more complex, needs in terms of their nursing care. That is, until relatively recently, nurses delivered care in an environment in which their patient load was relatively stable and they could identify the patients for whom they assumed responsibility; those who they "ought reasonably to have in ... contemplation". It could be suggested however, that in the current health care climate, the number of patients to whom the nurse owes a duty of care has

---

12   [1932] AC 562 at 580.

13   Jones, MA, "Medical Negligence" in McHale, L and Tingle, J (eds) *Law and Nursing*, Butterworth-Heinemann, Oxford, 1992, p 28.

increased, become more fluid and not as clearly identifiable as a function of low staffing levels, high demands for service, high skill mix and high patient acuity. The combination of these factors has resulted in an increasing trend whereby many nursing care responsibilities are delegated to less skilled health workers. The numbers of patients, to whom a nurse may owe a duty, as being directly responsible for their care, or through the delegation of patient care activities and the subsequent responsibility to supervise directly, or indirectly, has expanded. Therefore, the potential risk of being named as a defendant is increasing as the numbers of patients whom the nurse "ought reasonably have in ... contemplation" increases, and the nursing care, though directed by the nurse, is more complex and may be carried out by less skilled health workers.

What then is the standard of practice required at law, in terms of the nursing care, for this increasing number of acutely ill patients and clients? What is the standard of care against which the conduct of the nurse will be considered when a patient alleges that their injuries have been caused by the nurse's breach of their duty of care to the patient?

The determination of standards of care

As the role of the nurse in the provision of health care services expands so too does the level of specialised skill and knowledge required to fulfil that role. Consistent with the overseas trends,[14] Australian nurses are more frequently assuming professional responsibility for undertaking a wide range of patient care activities.

Harris and Chaboyer[15] found that nurses in critical care and high dependency units within Australia were undertaking activities previously considered to be those of medical practitioners.

Bucknall and Thomas, in their study of 230 critical care nurses found that half of the nurses independently carried out procedures on a daily basis which, by legislation, required a physician's order.[16] In addition, this study found that non-critical care nurses also performed these activities albeit less frequently than critical care nurses. The data therefore indicates that nurses across a broad spectrum of clinical contexts, from high dependency units to community settings, are ever increasingly delivering care that was not previously considered as part of their role. At a more publicly visible level, there have been significant moves in all Australian jurisdictions to either consider, or authorise, the practice of nurse

---

14 Fletcher, J, "Some Implications for Nurses and Managers of Recent Changes to the Processing and Hearing of Medical Negligence Claims" (2000) 8 *Journal of Nursing Management* 136.

15 Harris, D and Chaboyer, W, "The Expanded Role of the Critical Care Nurse: A Review of the Current Position" (2002) 15(4) *Australian Critical Care* 133.

16 Bucknall, T and Thomas, S, "Critical Care Nurse Satisfaction with Levels of Involvement in Clinical Decisions" (1996) 23 *Journal of Advanced Nursing* 571.

practitioners[17] and expand, via amendments to the existing drugs and poisons legislation, the role of nurses in the prescribing, supply and management of patient medications. Nurses within both the private and public sectors of health care are now assuming titles such as "practitioner", "consultant" and "specialist" as a means by which of identifying themselves as having a level of expertise, knowledge and skill greater than those of other nurses and simultaneously assuming roles beyond that traditionally considered as "nursing".

Though it is outside the scope of the chapter, it can be assumed that this situation is due to the shortage of both medical practitioners and nurses within Australia, and the increasing demands being placed on the health care system. Fletcher suggests that in the United Kingdom, the sanctioning of the expansion of nursing roles has its origins in "the human resource problems resulting from the difficulty in recruiting and retaining doctors in sufficient numbers and the European Commission pressure to reduce the number of hours worked by junior hospital doctors ... [in combination with] a determined political/ professional campaign by [nursing] leaders to enhance the professional status and earning powers of nurses".[18]

Regardless of the genesis of the trend towards the expansion of nursing roles, there are significant implications in terms of increasing the exposure of nurses to claims of negligence by patients and their families. Indeed, the American experience indicates that with the expanding role of nurses and the increasing demands made on them in the care and treatment of patients came "a concomitant expansion of legal liability for malpractice ... [and] legal claims against nurses increased".[19] As Greenwald and Mondor note in relation to perinatal nurses:

> In the 4 year period of 1996–2000, the number of cases in which nurses have been named as defendant or co-defendants [rose] at least 10 percent ... It is ... likely a reflection of the fact that nurses have assumed a degree of professional accountability never seen before. Nurses today are responsible for many of the tasks once assigned to physicians. The increase in responsibility has been accompanied by an increase in expectations and ... an increase in liability.[20]

Klutz supports these observations in her examination of the impact of American tort reform on nurse practitioners. She notes that while physicians have previously been involved in cases of malpractice other health professionals, such as nurse practitioners, are "increasingly being brought [sic] into malpractice suits".[21]

---

17 *Nurse Amendment (Nurse Practitioner) Act 1998* (NSW); *Nursing Act 1992* (Qld); *Nurses Act 1993* (Vic); *Nurses Act 1992* (WA); *Nurse Practitioners Legislation Amendment Act 2004* (ACT).

18 Fletcher (2000) op cit, at 136.

19 Giordano, K, "Examining Nursing Malpractice: A Defense Attorney's Perspective" (2003) 23(2) *Critical Care Nurse* 104.

20 Greenwald, LM and Mondor, M, "Malpractice and the Perinatal Nurse" (2003) 17 (2) *Journal of Perinatal & Neonatal Nursing* 101 at 102.

21 Klutz, D, "Tort Reform: An Issue for Nurse Practitioners" (2004) 16(2) *Journal of the Academy of Nurse Practitioners* 70.

The international experience indicates that where specialist nurses expand their professional roles they increase their exposure to litigation. In discussing whether Australian nurses are risking a similar fate it is important to consider the legal standards as expressed in the legislation and the case law. It is against these standards that the conduct of the nurse will be considered in making a determination with respect to liability in negligence.

All Australian jurisdictions[22] have responded to the Ipp recommendations by passing tort law reform legislation. The statutes make specific provision for the determination of the standard of care in personal injury claims. As well, they provide that a person will not be found to be negligent when he or she fails to take precautions against a foreseeable risk; that is unless the risk would be considered as "not insignificant" and a reasonable person in the position of the defendant would have taken the precautions. The statutes also incorporate an assessment of the probability or likely seriousness of the harm, the burden of taking the precautions and the social utility of the activity. In relation to the standard of care for the provision of professional services, s 22(5) of the *Civil Liability Act 2003* (Qld), for example provides that:

1. A professional does not breach a duty arising from the provision of a professional service if it is established that the professional acted in a way that (at the time the service was provided) was widely accepted by peer professional opinion by a respected number of respected practitioners in the field as competent professional practice.

2. However, peer professional opinion can not be relied on for the purpose of this section if the court considers that the opinion is irrational or contrary to a written law.

3. The fact that there are differing peer professional opinions widely accepted by a significant number of respected practitioners in the field concerning a matter does not prevent any one or more (or all) of the opinions being relied on for the purposes of this section.

4. Peer professional opinion does not have to be universally accepted to be considered widely accepted...

Section 50 of the *Civil Liability Act 2002* (NSW) makes specific reference to the standards within an Australian context. It precludes a professional from incurring liability in negligence arising from the provision "of a professional service if it is established that the professional acted in a manner that (at the time the service was provided) was widely accepted in Australia by peer professional opinion as competent professional practice ... peer professional opinion cannot be relied on for the purposes of this section if the court considers that the opinion is irrational".

---

22 *Civil Liability Act 2002* (NSW); *Civil Liability Amendment (Personal Responsibility) Act 2002* (NSW); *Civil Liability Act 2003* (Qld); *Civil Liability Act 1936* (SA); *Civil Liability Act 2002* (Tas); *Wrongs Act 1958* (Vic); *Civil Liability Act 2002* (WA); *Civil Law (Wrongs) Act 2002* (ACT); *Personal Injuries (Liabilities and Damages) Act 2003* (NT).

In line with the Queensland legislation,[23] the New South Wales legislation expressly exempts the application of the particular section to "failure to warn" cases. The inclusion, within the respective legislation of the standard as being that which is accepted as "widely accepted by peer professional opinion by a number of respected practitioners in the field as competent professional practice" is consistent with the *Bolam* test which Kennedy and Grubb describe:

> [A]s a rule that a doctor is not negligent if he [or she] acts in accordance with a practice accepted at the time as proper by a responsible body of medical opinion even though other doctors adopt a different practice.[24]

The interpretation of legislative terms, described as the "elements" of professional negligence – such as "irrational", "practising as a professional", "the time at which the service was provided", "wide acceptance", "practice in Australia", "competent professional practice" and "peer professional opinion" – are yet to be subjected to a level of judicial interpretation that gives certainty to their application to a health care context. It has been claimed that the "real impact of the changes that have been made in some jurisdictions will not be apparent for some years. And ... subtle differences between statutory implementations in various jurisdictions ... will ... lead to inconsistencies in determining negligent medical treatment as between each Australian jurisdiction".[25]

Breach of the standard

Though the outcome of any negligence case turns on its own particular facts, it is valuable to consider generally the impact that the activities undertaken by nurses, as part of the expanding roles, may have on increasing their risk of being identified as defendants, and held liable. In circumstances in which the nurse is working as a nurse practitioner or a nurse consultant and undertaking activities that were previously those of the medical practitioner, is it reasonable for the patient to assume the nurse has the level of skill and knowledge of the medical practitioner? Will the law impose a standard of professional service commensurate with that of a nurse practitioner/consultant or a medical practitioner? Tingle suggests that where nurses are undertaking expanded roles they will be:

> [E]xpected to perform at the level of the post-holder who normally carries out the activity, in most cases a doctor. Professional practice in any sphere must accord with the law and this is particularly so with specialist nursing.[26]

---

23   *Civil Liability Act 2003* (Qld) s 22(5).

24   Kennedy, I and Grubb, A *Medical Law: Text with Materials*, 2nd edn, Butterworths, London, 1994, p 184. This test is derived from McNair J's direction to the jury in *Bolam v Friern Hospital Management Committee* [1957] 1 WLR 582.

25   Madden, B, "Changes to the Definition of Negligence" (2003) 12(1) *Australian Health Law Bulletin* 6.

26   Tingle, J, "Specialist Nurses Must Understand Clinical Negligence Litigation" (2001) 10 (11) *British Journal of Nursing* 716.

The changing roles of nurses within the present health care environment give rise to two significant issues. First, where the nursing roles are expanding, both informally (at the institutional level), and formally (through professional regulatory authorities and clinical specialty organisations), there is the real potential for a lack of clarity on behalf of both the consumers of nursing services, and the profession itself, as to what is, or is not, a reasonable expectation in terms of the standard of "competent professional practice". For example, in undertaking an activity as a nurse practitioner or clinical nurse consultant, or failing to undertake an activity, has the nurse discharged the legal duty as determined by the legislation or the case law? It has been noted in relation to nurse practitioners in the United Kingdom, where concern has been expressed in medical[27] and nursing[28] literature about the "blurring of roles", that there is a lack of consensus concerning the level of expertise and education necessary to validate professional nursing titles that may convey that the nurse possesses exceptional knowledge and skills.

Fletcher suggests that it could be assumed that:

> The courts would have to be satisfied that claims [by the nurse] to special knowledge and skills were found defensible on the grounds that the claims were responsible, reasonable and respectable. In the case of those nurses who are now, or who will in the immediate future, be assuming work formally undertaken by medical practitioners the position is particularly unclear.[29]

The second issue, which flows from the first, is that in attempting to reach a decision as to whether a nurse has breached the duty of care, by failing to meet the legal standard of "competent professional practice", how will the standard be determined? When the nursing roles are significantly changing, how is the nurse to be certain that the activities are, and are not, "widely accepted by peer professional opinion by a … number of respected practitioners in the field as competent professional practice"? The expanding roles of nurses into the many and varied areas of health service delivery therefore provides a basis for concern in relation to the potential impact of such an expansion of the practice parameters on the potential liability of nurses.

Though it is clear that nursing roles and activities, across a wide range of specialties, have been progressively expanding for decades, the most notable example lies in the recent introduction of the nurse practitioner into the suit of nursing categories eligible for registration by the individual State and Territory professional regulatory bodies. This expansion of the nursing role provides an illustration of some of the issues that may increase the risk of liability and some of the measures that may be taken into account to minimise that risk.

---

27 Dowling, S, Martin, M, Skidmore, P, Doyal, L, Cameron, A and S Lloyd,, "Nurses Taking on Junior Doctor's Work: A Confusion of Accountability" (1996) 321 *British Medical Journal* 1211.

28 Fletcher (2000) op cit, at 136.

29 Ibid, at 138.

The nurse practitioner

As noted above, professional regulatory authorities in a number of Australian jurisdictions have passed legislation authorising eligible registered nurses to practise as "nurse practitioners". The introduction of the role of nurse practitioner commenced in the early 1960s in the United States of America and has since been incorporated into the United Kingdom and Australia. The New South Wales professional regulatory body can authorise a person with sufficient qualification and experience to practise as a nurse practitioner for no longer than three years.[30] It is important to note that the legal authority to undertake activities is attached to the title of "nurse practitioner", that is, the position within the institution rather than the individual. However, for accreditation to the role of nurse practitioner, the registered nurse must have obtained qualifications, after their initial registration, that enables them to:

> Practise as an expert in their chosen specialty ... be involved in ongoing professional development ... demonstrate 5000 hours in a current advanced practice role, meet the competencies of the advanced nurse clinician and the standards of their chosen specialty ... have the skills and knowledge relevant to the privileges associated with the specific context of the practice in question ... [that is] clinical assessment and pharmacological knowledge.[31]

The criteria are broadly similar to other jurisdictions that have followed the New South Wales lead. In Queensland, the Nursing Council will authorise "eligible registered nurses" using the "Nurse Practitioner Competency Standards"[32] (developed through a project commissioned by the Australian Nursing and Midwifery Council[33]), to determine competence to practise as a nurse practitioner. The role of the nurse practitioner is described as one which functions "autonomously and collaboratively in the advanced and expanded clinical role ... [including] assessment and management of clients using nursing knowledge and skills and may include but is not limited to the direct referral of clients to other health care professionals, [the] prescribing of medications, and ordering [of] diagnostic investigations".[34]

The scope of the activities which are undertaken as part of the role of the nurse practitioner are clearly broader than those of other registered nurses. As an example, in a recent study, evaluating the extended role of nurses in one Sydney

---

30 *Nurses and Midwives Act 1991* (NSW) s 19.

31 New South Wales Department of Health, *Nurse Practitioner Services in New South Wales*, Discussion Paper, 1998, p 2.

32 Queensland Nursing Council, "Policy on the Regulation of Nurse Practitioners in Queensland", December 2004, p 1.

33 Gardner, G, Carryer, J, Dunn, SV and Gardner, A, "Report to Australian Nursing Council: Nurse Practitioner Standards Project", Australian Nursing Council, Canberra, 2004.

34 Queensland Nursing Council, "Policy on the Regulation of Nurse Practitioners in Queensland", December 2004, p 1; *Health Act 1993* (ACT) s 37B.

primary health care facility, the researchers found the nurse practitioners were undertaking clinical services which included:

> [A]ssessment of primary health care needs, sexually transmitted disease (STD) screening of sex workers, Pap smears, family planning advice, venepuncture for HIV and hepatitis A, B and C, pre and post testing counseling, methadone administration and needle and syringe exchange. Nurse practitioners also staffed the "AIDS bus", an outreach program to street sex workers, "at risk" youth and IDU.[35]

It can be assumed that these activities are but a small sample of the wide range of patient care needs that will be addressed by nurse practitioners depending on their particular area of clinical expertise. One constant however, is the authorisation of nurse practitioners to prescribe medications within the scope determined by the legislation or regulations. The legal recognition of this right, which had previously (within the health care environment) been the sole domain of medical practitioners, is a significant extension of the nursing role. Even though relatively recent amendments to the drugs and poisons legislation and regulations in a number of jurisdictions has led to the increased authority of remote or isolated practice nurses, sexual health nurses and nurses involved in community and immunisation programs in relation to possession, supply and administration of medications,[36] their authority does not include prescribing rights. The right to prescribe, by implication, brings with it the obligation to diagnose with both activities (diagnosis and prescribing) having a seemingly high correlation with patient adverse events. Based on the foregoing, it seems relatively predictable that the degree of risk to a nurse, of being sued in negligence, increases with the expansion of their role into a broader variety of high-risk activities. It is here that there is an emerging risk to nurses of being named as defendants. The success of the plaintiff in a negligence action against a nurse however, may well turn on their ability to persuade the court to the requisite standards that the nurse was in breach of the duty of care. It is in relation to this element that nurses may minimise the potential of being held liable.

Where the expanding roles of nurses are formalised and sanctioned by professional regulatory authorities and clinical specialty organisations there is a need to ensure that competency standards are validated and consistently applied at the initial stage of registration or certification. In addition these professional authorities and organisations must assume responsibility for the implementation of ongoing quality assurance measures, through continuous competency assessment strategies. At the informal or institutional level, it will be necessary for

---

35 Hooke, E, Bennett, L, Dwyer, R, Van Beek, I and Martin, C, "Nurse Practitioners: An Evaluation of the Extended Role of Nurses at the Kirketon Road Centre in Sydney, Australia" (2001) 18(3) *Australian Journal of Advanced Nursing* 21.

36 New South Wales Health Department Circular 97/10,3.1.5.5, "Non prescription" Stock Medications; *Health (Drugs and Poisons) Regulations 1996* (Qld); *Poisons and Dangerous Drugs Act 1983* (NT).

institutions, public and private providers to formalise educational requirements and assessment strategies prior to allocating nurses to roles that require levels of skill and knowledge consistent with that of an expanded nursing role. The introduction and updating of clinical risk identification protocols, nursing policies and practices that reflect both best practice and the legal standards serve in a very real way to identify to both the courts and the profession what activities, are "widely accepted by peer professional opinion ... as competent professional practice".

Conclusion

The escalating risk of nurses being sued for negligence appears to have its origins in the increasing demands being placed on nursing services, the mounting requirement to delegate care to less skilled health workers and the growing acuity of the patients and clients requiring nursing care. Simultaneously, nurses are now undertaking advanced and expanded roles which require higher levels of skill and knowledge and significantly extend their role beyond that previously considered as "nursing care". The potential in these circumstances of being involved in an adverse patient event and sued in negligence is thereby increased. While the obligation remains with the plaintiff to prove all of the elements of the negligence action it appears that it is in relation to the determination of the requisite standard of care that the nurse, as a professional may be most vulnerable. Where the case law and the legislation identify both the "duty" and the "standard of care for professionals", it is imperative that nurses, health care institutions, professional clinical specialty organisations and regulatory authorities, take all available measures to establish and maintain clearly identifiable professional standards of clinical competency.

PART IX

REGULATION

24

Regulation of health practitioners

Ian Freckelton

Regulation of health practitioners is in the midst of ideological shifts and fundamental change in terms of models and criteria for determining lack of professionalism. This arises as a result of many different factors and has expression in a variety of current developments in terms of mechanisms for accountability and debates about the ethical standards to which health professionals can be expected to comply.

Numbered among the causative factors for this dynamic situation are shifts in attitudes toward professionalism and changes in community expectations of professionals, especially health practitioners such as doctors to whom uncritical deference used often to be shown in the recent past. In addition, the availability and accessibility of information about health issues via the internet has already fundamentally reframed attitudes toward doctors and all other health practitioners. Part of this is an empowerment of patients by reason of their greater knowledge and capacity to interact with health service providers on an informed basis. It is apparent too that there is a consumer-driven demand for quality and accountability in health services, as in many other areas of service provision. Another aspect of the change in community expectations is a disillusionment with the paternalist dispensing of medicine and dentistry in particular and a concern to reduce the levels of iatrogenic and nosocomial harm. There is also an increasingly egalitarian insistence on the provision of health services as a partnership between professional and patient.

This chapter identifies pressing and dynamic issues in regulatory reform and argues that the outcome of the changes has the potential to provide improved accountability for the work of health professionals and to engender greater community confidence, provided that the models employed, and the decision-making pursuant to the models, adequately draws upon peer knowledge and values, as well as community expectations. Particular emphasis is placed on debates about the regulation of medical practitioners because discourse about health practitioners remains dominated by issues concerning medical practitioners. However, an aspiration of the chapter is that many of the issues canvassed in respect of doctors will have resonances and a relevance for the accountability of other health practitioners.

Regulation

The concept of "regulation" is subject to different interpretations. The definition of Black[1] is broad-based and helpful:

> The sustained and focused attempt to alter the behaviour of others according to defined standards or purposes with the intention of producing a broadly identified outcome or outcomes which may involve mechanisms of standard setting, information gathering and behaviour modification.[2]

Of the essence of regulation is "behaviour shaping" and "overseeing". In terms of health practitioners, this encompasses scrutiny and guidance in relation to conduct, per se, but also performance, in the sense of competency, and health conditions which may affect conduct or performance. In can also incorporate personal conduct if such behaviour has the potential to impact upon the reputation and standing of the practitioner's profession. A fundamental objective of regulation is that those who are part of the registered body of practitioners behave in such a way as to promote the values and integrity of their profession and, focusing upon the negative, in such a way as not to endanger members of the public. A principal yardstick by which regulation of health practitioners takes place is "professionalism", as understood informally amongst colleagues and as expressed in codes of ethics and practice, and guidelines issued by regulatory bodies and professional associations. Thus professionalism constitutes a mechanism by which those who are permitted to enter and remain within the professions are distinguished from others who are not. It is also an overall objective of regulation.[3]

Professionalism

While it is appropriate to expect that health practitioners behave in accordance with the tenets of professionalism, the harder issue is to identify what this means in general and also to translate it into specific scenarios, particularly those that raise ethical dilemmas confronted by health practitioners and which demand evaluation of potentially conflicting ethical values. An abiding threshold issue is what constitutes a profession, and such a definition inevitably influences analyses of professionalism. Cruess, Johnston and Cruess[4] have advanced an orthodox working definition: "its members are governed by codes of ethics and practice and profess a commitment to competence, integrity and morality, altruism, and the promotion of good within their domain".

---

1   Black, J, *Critical Reflections on Regulation*, Discussion Paper, Centre for the Analysis of Risk and Regulation, London, 2002, <www.lse.ac.uk/collections/CARR/pdf/Diss paper4.pdf> (accessed 20 March 2006).

2   See also Dixon, J, *Regulating Health Care: The Way Forward*, King's Fund, London, 2005, <www.kingsfund.org.uk/resources/publications/index.html> (accessed 20 March 2006).

3   See Freckelton, I, "Regulation at the Margins of the Health Professions" (2006) *Law in Context* (in press).

4   Cruess, SR, Johnston, S and Cruess, RL, "'Profession': A Working Definition for Medical Educators" (2004) 16(1) *Teaching & Learning in Medicine* 74.

Three recent important projects have addressed issues of professionalism in medicine. The "Medical Professionalism Project" which commenced in 1999 was a coordination of focus by the European Federation of Internal Medicine, the American College of Physicians, the American Society of Internal Medicine and the American Board of Internal Medicine.[5] It generated a charter on medical professionalism which enunciated a set of professional responsibilities, based on three principles – patients' welfare, patients' autonomy, and social justice.[6] The responsibilities were expressed as commitments to:

- competence;
- honesty;
- confidentiality;
- maintaining appropriate relationships;
- improving quality of care;
- improving access to care;
- just distribution of finite resources;
- scientific knowledge;
- maintenance of trust; and
- professional duties.

The charter argued for a need to balance rights and responsibilities within the doctor–patient partnership. It identified as unprofessional behaviour abuse of power in interactions with patients or colleagues; bias and sexual harassment; breach of confidentiality; arrogance; cheating; greed; misrepresentation of credentials and certifications of education and training; impairment; lack of conscientiousness; lying; conflicts of interest; self-referral; acceptance of gifts; over-utilisation of services; collaboration with industry; and compromising the principles of clinical investigation.

The charter has had a number of outcomes in terms of medical education[7] but it has also had its critics. Arnett,[8] for instance, maintained colourfully that the charter "places the needs of society above those of the individual patient and will increase suffering and death and destroy the patient–physician relationship".

In 2004, the King's Fund[9] reported on means to redefine medical professionalism for improved patient care. The report argued that doctors can no longer

---

5   See <www.abimfoundation.org/mpp2003/index.htm> (accessed 10 March 2006).

6   Medical Professionalism Project, "Medical Professionalism in the New Millennium: A Physician Charter" (2002) 136 *Annals of Internal Medicine* 243.

7   See, for example, <http://medschool.umaryland.edu/professionalism/FAQ.asp> (accessed 12 March 2006).

8   Arnett, JC Jr, "The Medical Professionalism Project and its Physician Charter: New Ethics for a Political Agenda", <www.aapsonline.org/jpands/hacienda/arnett3.html> (accessed 15 March 2006).

9   See Rosen, R and Dewar, S *On Being a Doctor: Redefining Medical Professionalism for Better Patient Care*, King's Fund, London, 2004.

rely upon the notion of the medical practitioner as "a selfless clinician, motivated by a strong ethos of service, equipped with unique skills and knowledge, in control of their work and practicing all hours to restore full health to 'his' or 'her' patients". It recommended that doctors need to practise in a more patient-centred ethos, defining a new "compact" between themselves and government, the public, health service managers and patient groups.

In 2005 the Royal College of Physicians generated what is likely to be an influential report entitled, *Doctors in Society: Medical Professionalism in a Changing World*.[10] Its aim was to define the nature and role of medical professionalism in modern society. Ultimately, it defined "medical professionalism" as "a set of values, behaviours, and relationships that underpin the trust the public has in doctors". It contended that:

> Medicine is a vocation in which a doctor's knowledge, clinical skills, and judgement are put in the service of protecting and restoring human well-being. This purpose is realized through a partnership between patient and doctor, one based on mutual respect, individual responsibility and appropriate accountability.[11]

The report located six themes where its definition has implications: leadership, teams, education, appraisal, careers and research. Curiously, it opted not to address regulatory or revalidation issues, preferring to confine itself to endorsing the analysis of Hilton and Slotnick[12] that professionalism must be manifested across:

- ethical practice;
- reflection and self-awareness;
- assumption of responsibility for actions;
- respect for patients;
- teamwork; and
- social responsibility.

However, the link between professionalism, or its absence, and the need for regulation has been recognised as an integral part of the debate about both the definition and operationalisation of professionalism.[13] For it is only with the provision of suitable guidance and the imposition of regulation as a mechanism for determining entry points and supervision over practitioners that professionalism can be maintained and the community protected from unacceptable practices.

---

10   Royal College of Physicians, *Doctors in Society: Medical Professionalism in a Changing World*, London, 2005, <www.rcplondon.ac.uk/pubs/books/docinsoc/docinsoc.pdf> (accessed 1 March 2006).

11   Ibid, p 14.

12   Hilton, SR and Slotnick, HB, "Proto-professionalism: How Professionalism Occurs Across the Continuum of Medical Education" (2005) 39 *Medical Education* 58.

13   See, for example, Irvine, DH, "Doctors in the UK: Their New Professionalism and its Regulatory Framework" (2001) 358 *Lancet* 1807.

The focus upon patient-centred practice as a characteristic of professionalism within medicine also forms the core of the Picker Institute Europe initiative on professionalism.[14] The Institute Director, Sir David Irvine, has argued for a new "moral contract" between the medical profession and society based on mutual respect, individual responsibility and appropriate accountability.[15] A 2006 study by Chisholm and Askham[16] for the institute has identified as common factors in medical codes: provision of technically good clinical care and keeping up-to-date; involvement of patients in their care and respect for patient autonomy; and confidentiality and consent. They have argued that a distillation of these principles may allow regulatory bodies to progress in development of codes and applying them to specific scenarios.

Other important developments

Authors[17] of an important study by the Australian Council for Safety and Quality in Health Care in 2005 argued that "regulatory thinking must transcend the polarised choice between persuasion and punishment" maintaining that rather than relying on the ancient system of medical professional autonomy, "external regulatory levers" should be used to ensure the maintenance and improvement of the quality of health care. They have maintained that the preferable regulatory approach is one that is responsive and, where possible, negotiated, as well as mediated by concepts such as restorative justice.

The Australian Productivity Commission in a 2005 report[18] introduced an important new dynamic into the debates about how the health professions should be regulated. Its report was commissioned in 2004 by the Council of Australian Governments (CoAG). It identified that there are over 450,000 health workers in Australian, more than half of whom are nurses and only 12 per cent of whom are medical practitioners. It also observed that international medical graduates (IMGs), also known as overseas trained doctors (OTDs), make up a quarter of the current medical practitioner workforce. This raises a range of issues about workforce composition, adequacy of training and experience, and the extent to which skills are being utilised.

---

14   See Chisholm, A and Askham, J *A Review of Professional Codes and Standards for Doctors in the UK, USA and* Canada, Picker Institute Europe, 2006, <www.pickereurope.org/Filestore/RapidResponse/PCP_professional_codes_FINAL.pdf> (accessed 1 April 2006); see also Irvine, DH, "New Ideas about Medical Professionalism" (2006) 184(5) *Medical Journal of Australia* 204.

15   Irvine, DH, "Time for Hard Decisions on Patient-centred Professionalism" (2004) 181 *Medical Journal of Australia* 271.

16   Chisholm and Askham (2006) op cit, pp 46–47.

17   Braithwaite, J, Healy, J and Dwan, K *The Governance of Health Safety and Quality*, Commonwealth of Australia, Canberra, 2005, <www.safetyandquality.org/governance0705.pdf> (accessed 1 April 2006).

18   Australian Productivity Commission *Australia's Health Workforce*, Canberra, 2005, <www.pc.gov.au/study/healthworkforce/finalreport/healthworkforce.pdf> (accessed 10 April 2006).

The commission regarded the existence of more than 20 bodies in accrediting health workforce education and training and more than 90 registration boards as an impediment to responsive and sustainable workforce arrangements. It also considered that regulatory arrangements continue to be obstructed by the influence of professional groups and argued in favour of a "whole of workforce perspective", which necessarily involves the performance of functions traditionally the preserve of "high status" health professionals by others, in particular nurses, a phenomenon already apparent in many areas of clinical practice. As part of its formal proposals, it also recommended the establishment of a national health workforce improvement agency to evaluate innovations with a national signifi-cance and to assess the implications for education and training, accreditation and regulation, reporting to the Australian Health Ministers Conference (AHMC).

The commission singled out for particular criticism the variation in State-based registration and regulatory arrangements for the health professions, and regarded the lack of regulatory uniformity as leading to diversity in standards, administrative duplication and impediments to health worker mobility. It identi-fied efficiency and consistency advantages in national registration boards for each profession. However, it went a step further and advocated for a single national registration board for all health workers, acknowledging advantages in profession-specific registration arrangements but reinforcing an across-profession emphasis on health workforce arrangements. It identified the potential for particular imp-rovements for rural and remote areas from fundamental systemic reform.

The commission's report is unlikely to be implemented quickly but it has identified a range of issues which must be addressed for political, commercial and service quality imperatives. The dependence of Australia upon IMGs is unsus-tainable and unacceptable for the general community – especially in the aftermath of the Patel crisis.[19] It raises a series of difficult accreditation and quality of service provision dilemmas. Already the Federal Government has announced the creation of new medical schools Australia-wide and additional places in current medical schools. Federal–State and interstate tensions, as well as constitutional impedi-ments, will delay the creation of national registration but roads toward the creation of Australia-wide registers of medical practitioners have already commenced. This is undoubtedly the direction of the future, with pressures growing to reduce the levels of duplication and variability in governance and regulation of the health professions.

---

19 See Hon Geoffrey Davies *Queensland Public Hospitals Commission of Inquiry Report*, Final Report, Brisbane, 2006, <www.qphci.qld.gov.au/> (accessed 10 April 2006); see further Harvey, K and Faunce, T, "A Critical Analysis of Overseas Trained Doctor Factors in the Bundaberg Base Hospital Surgical Inquiry" (2006) *Law in Context* (in press).

Lack of professionalism

Multiple examples can be cited of instances in which medical and other health practitioners have betrayed the core values of their professions and earned public ire and prompted community disillusionment. The phenomenon of the badly behaving health practitioner is not new but the community disenchantment that it has provoked latterly shows signs of becoming more pronounced. In part this is a function of a sensationalist absorption on the part of the media with medical malpractice and criminality but it is also influenced by changing expectations of professionals.

One of the drivers for increased regulation is often described as escalating social anxiety about the absence of professionalism amongst health practitioners. Certainly, the role of bodies such as health boards, councils and tribunals has been made controversial by controversies such as those which have engulfed the Bristol Infirmary,[20] the National Women's Hospital in New Zealand,[21] the deep sleep therapies of Chelmsford, the Royal Canberra travails,[22] the Shipman murders in England[23] and the Patel scandal in Queensland,[24] to name but a few. As Moran[25] has commented of the English experience of the regulation of medical practitioners:

> One of the most striking features of these scandalous cases is the gap they revealed between the conception of professional standards ... and what an increasingly assertive lay public thought were appropriate standards ... Here was a particularly stark instance of the encounter between the nineteenth-century club system and modern democratic society. There had consequently been increasingly legislative intervention in the regulatory affairs of the profession, including intervention to reshape the composition of the regulatory institution itself.[26]

Another aspect to the reform process has been calls for changes to the role of the coroner so as to facilitate greater potential for patterns of inappropriate conduct by medical practitioners to be identified more readily. The following part of this chapter identifies directions in which these influences are moving health practitioner regulation.

---

20 See, for example, Bristol Royal Infirmary Inquiry, 2001, <www.bristol-inquiry.org.uk/> (accessed 6 September 2005).

21 See Cartwright, S, "Revisiting the Cartwright Inquiry" (2002) 3(1) *New Zealand Bioethics Journal* 3; Coney, S, *The Unfortunate Experiment*, Penguin, Auckland, 1988.

22 See Faunce, T, Mure, K, Cox, C and Maher, B, "When Silence Threatens Safety: Lessons from the First Canberra Hospital Neurosurgical Inquiry" (2005) 12 *Journal of Law and Medicine* 112.

23 See Smith J, *Fifth Report of the Shipman Inquiry*, Command Paper CM6394, HMSO, London, 2004.

24 Queensland Public Hospitals, *Commission of Inquiry*, Queensland Government, Brisbane, 2005, <www.qphci.qld.gov.au/final_report/Final_Report.pdf> (accessed 1 April 2006).

25 Moran, M, *The British Regulatory State: High Modernism and Hyper-Innovation*, Oxford University Press, Oxford, 2003.

26 *Report of the Royal Commission into Deep Sleep Therapy*, Government Printer, Sydney, 1990.

Self-regulation and peer review

The dominant reference point for regulation of professionals has traditionally been peer review, the notion that those best able to evaluate professional conduct are colleagues of the practitioner.[27] Braithwaite et al[28] have characterised this approach as "soft", observing that it is dependent upon voluntary compliance, but observing that its advantage is that it is well accepted within the medical profession in particular.

It has been contended that peers are well-positioned to gauge propriety of conduct because of themselves being in a comparable or the same area of practice and thus able to assess whether a professional has fallen below what is to be expected of a practitioner of good repute and competency. In addition, peers should be prepared to make adverse findings so as to demarcate between ethical and unethical conduct and thereby to be seen to be ready to police high standards of behaviour within their profession – by so doing they are upholding the integrity and standing of their profession.

Critics,[29] however, have argued that a "brotherhood ethic" has led as well to a propensity on the part of peer review bodies to be unduly tolerant of unprofessional behaviour and a pattern of adopting "tap on the shoulder" strategies for regulating unprofessional conduct rather than robust adverse findings at formal inquiries: sexual transgressions have been identified as a particular example of inappropriate leniency. Also it has been asserted that the quality of decision-making by peers has lacked the hallmarks which should characterise the determination of serious allegations of misconduct against members of a profession.

Further, it has been claimed that members of the public will not have confidence in a system which consists of complaints against health practitioners being resolved by persons likely to know and to have worked with the practitioners the subject of complaint. Some disciplinary systems have incorporated investigative, prosecutorial and arbitral functions within the same body.[30] Particular concerns have been identified in relation to such forms of peer regulation on the basis of the extent to which complainants might fear that they would not receive a full and dispassionate treatment of their grievances.

The international trend appears to be away from unfettered self-regulation of health practitioners. An example of this, discussed below, is the increasing role

---

27 See Daniel, A *Medicine and the State: Professional Autonomy and Public Accountability*, Allen & Unwin, Sydney, 1990.

28 Ibid, p viii.

29 See, for example, Thomas, D, "Peer Regulation as an Outmoded Model for Health Practitioner Regulation" (2006) *Law in Context* (in press); Rogers, S, "Culling Bad Apples: Blowing Whistles and the Health Practitioners Competence Assurance Act 2003 (NZ)" (2004) 12 *Journal of Law and Medicine* 119. Thomas, D, "The Co-regulation of Medical Disciplines Challenging Medical Peer Review", (2004) *Journal of Law and Medicine* 382.

30 See Department of Human Services, *Review of the Regulation of Health Professions in Victoria*: *Options for Structural and Legislative Reform*, DHS, Melbourne, 2005, <www.dhs.vic.gov. au/pdpd/workforce/downloads/review_optionspaper_apr05.pdf> (accessed May 2006).

of non-practitioner members of regulatory bodies. Another is the fact that in a number of jurisdictions a statutory measure of unprofessional conduct is conduct of a lesser standard than is reasonably to be expected of a practitioner by members of the public.[31] This explicitly incorporates into the criteria for unsatisfactory professional behaviour an extra-professional measure, one that is reflective of contemporary community standards.

Lay participation on regulatory bodies is comparatively recent but is growing. Such a non-practitioner role reduces the extent to which decision-making fully constitutes peer review but it provides an external perspective which reduces the force of the criticism that regulatory bodies are "old boys' clubs" "looking after their own". As of 2007, in Victoria the 12 regulatory bodies for health practitioners will each have at least four non-practitioner participants out of between nine and 12 members.[32] By 2006, the United Kingdom General Medical Council has 40 per cent lay membership[33] and on performance assessments of medical practitioners there must always be a non-medical participant. In Canada there is generally significant lay participation on disciplinary hearings although lay involvement in performance assessments is not yet part of the process. The international trend is toward a greater role for non-practitioner contribution to assessment of practitioners and formal decision-making; conversely there is attrition of the extent of peer review as the major paradigm.

Forensic functions

Until comparatively recently work undertaken by health practitioners in a forensic capacity was largely exempt from evaluation by regulatory bodies. However, with a growing recognition that a substantial proportion of health practitioners are called upon to undertake some forensic work in the form of writing reports for courts and tribunals and occasionally giving evidence, regulatory bodies have confronted the criteria on the basis of which such work should be classified as unprofessional and the consequences that should attach to such a designation.

The amenability of forensic work by health practitioners to disciplinary regulation is controversial. The Australian approach is exemplified by the Western Australian Court of Appeal decision in *Mustac v Medical Board of Western Australia*[34] where it rejected an appeal by a psychiatrist against the decision of the Western Australian Medical Board to suspend his registration for six months for having engaged in improper conduct in a professional respect by reason of his methodology in writing two forensic reports. Dr Mustac was found by the Board to have

---

31 See, for example, *Medical Practice Act 1994* (Vic) s 3.

32 *Health Professions Registration Act 2005* (Vic).

33 General Medical Council *Developing Medical Regulation: A Vision for the Future*, 2005, <www.gmc-uk.org/call_for_ideas/developing_medical_regulation_200504.pdf> (accessed 7 September 2005).

34 [2004] WASCA 156.

applied a psychometric test, the Test of Memory Malingering (the TOMM) imper-missibly to questions of overall veracity in circumstances where it was not designed for that purpose. Largely on the basis of the results from the psycho-metric test, he was found to have concluded illegitimately that two patients whom he had assessed for workers' compensation purposes had exhibited an intention to deceive him.

The Court of Appeal accepted on the basis of the manual for the TOMM that the test itself only permitted a conclusion to be drawn that a subject is making a false or exaggerated claim of a memory deficit. It concluded that Dr Mustac's views about his subjects' false or exaggerated claims had not been open to him and that his conclusions about intentionality and motivation were illegitimate and unprofessional. Ultimately, it upheld the decision of the Board, holding that as the behaviour of the psychiatrist fell well short of indicating that his conduct was in accordance with a body of respectable if minority opinion, the suspension of the practitioner was justified.

However, the position in the United Kingdom is unclear[35] as a result of an appellate decision in Re Meadow.[36] The United Kingdom Fitness to Practise Panel of the General Medical Council was called upon in 2005 to evaluate the professional conduct of a well-known paediatrician who had written reports and given expert evidence in ways which it was alleged were misleading. The allegations arose from involvement as an expert by Professor Sir Roy Meadow in criminal proceedings against Sally Clark for the murder of her two children. Her conviction was later quashed by the Court of Appeal.[37]

The panel found that Sir Roy had been engaged as a consultant paediatrician by the Cheshire Constabulary of Police to assist their investigation. He was ready, willing and considered himself able to give expert evidence as to child abuse and unnatural infant deaths, Sudden Infant Death Syndrome (SIDS), the probability of occurrence and recurrence of SIDS deaths within a family, and the statistical consideration of data on such matters. It found that he owed a duty to familiarise himself with all relevant data and published (or to be published) work, sufficient to provide competent, impartial, balanced and fair expert evidence of scientific validity:

> Insofar as you chose to use statistics to support your evidence it was your respon-sibility to only use them in accordance with good statistical principles and practice in relation to matters within your expertise. You owed a duty to identify relevant matters (including assumptions) on which your statistical evidence was based.

It found that he had failed in this duty and while he should have refrained from giving expert evidence on matters beyond his competence, he had failed to do so.

---

35   See, for example, Re Patterson: Professional Conduct Committee decision, <www.gmc-uk.org/probdocs/decisions/pcc/2004/PATERSON_20040304.htm> (accessed May 2006).

36   Fitness to Practise Panel, General Medical Council, 15 July 2005, <www.gmcpressoffice.org.uk/apps/news/latest/detail.php?key-180> (accessed 1 August 2005).

37   R v Clark [2003] EWCA Crim 1020.

The panel found that Sir Roy's evidence was misleading and erroneous, although that had not been his intention, his error lying in squaring odds of matters which may have been associated and thus not amenable to the "multiplication factor", as well as failing to have regard to dependent variables which would have substantially changed the statistics which he was citing. It found that his errors had been "grave" and that his conduct had had serious implications and repercussions for many people, not least those working in the field of child protection. It concluded that his errors were so serious that in spite of his contributions to medicine and his international reputation it had no option but to strike his name from the medical register.

However the panel's decision was appealed to the Queen's Bench Division of the High Court.[38] Collins J, in the course of argument between the parties to the appeal, raised a threshold issue concerning the immunity from suit of a witness in respect of evidence given in a court of law. Such immunity has been held to apply as much to an expert as it does to evidence by any other witness[39] and extends to any civil proceedings brought against a defendant which are based on the evidence given by the witness to a court. It also extends to any statement which the witness makes for the purpose of giving evidence.

Until the decision of Collins J, the immunity had never been extended to prevent the bringing of disciplinary proceedings. He drew a distinction between oral evidence and steps along the way to the giving of such evidence:

> It is clear that to produce a report or to give information which is sufficiently flawed as properly to be regarded as serious professional misconduct will not attract immunity even though it is used as the basis for evidence given subsequently. The report must have been prepared with a view to its being used or in the knowledge that it will probably be used in evidence in court.[40]

However, he observed that immunity from civil action extends to the honest as well as the dishonest witness, being based on public policy "which requires that witnesses should not be deterred from giving evidence by the fear of litigation at the suit of those who may feel that the evidence had damaged them unjustifiably".[41] He accepted that the immunity doctrine is not untrammelled and that it does not preclude an expert being prosecuted for the criminal offence of perjury "if sufficient evidence exists". He made it clear that the reason for his extension of the immunity for witnesses was "evidence before me, and common sense points in the same direction, that the possibility of disciplinary proceedings based on a complaint by someone affected by the evidence given has a serious deterrent effect".[42]

---

38 *Meadow v General Medical Council* [2006] EWHC 146 Admin.

39 See X *(Minors) v Bedfordshire County Council* [1995] 2 AC 633, approving *Evans v London Hospital Medical College* [1981] 1 WLR 184.

40 Ibid, at [10].

41 Ibid, at [13].

42 Ibid, at [17].

Collins J accepted that there is also a public interest that practitioners should be regulated and that their standards of practice be of a high level but was content that sufficient protection existed because "[a]ny expert witness will know that he has a duty to the court and must bear in mind his obligations in that regard".[43]

The decision of Collins J has been roundly criticised for being anachronistic and unacceptably rendering health practitioners immune from disciplinary action in respect of their forensic functions.[44] It has been appealed to the Court of Appeal and may well be reversed.

Personal misconduct

Uncertainty has long existed about whether and, if so, to what extent health practitioners may be found to have engaged in professional misconduct if they have committed disreputable or illegal acts in a private capacity – not directly connected with their discharge of professional duties.

In 1999 the Privy Council grappled with this vexed issue in *Roylance v General Medical Council*[45] where it was asked to determine whether the District General Manager of the Bristol and Weston Health Authority was guilty of serious professional misconduct for having failed to take action during a time when concerns were being raised about the excessive mortality of infant patients and failing to take steps to prevent certain practitioners from undertaking cardiac operations on infants. The Privy Council held that for misconduct to be professional misconduct it must have a link with the profession of medicine but emphasised that certain behaviour may constitute professional misconduct even though it does not occur within the actual course of the carrying on of the person's professional practice, such as the abuse of a patient's confidence or the making of some dishonest private financial gain.[46] In addition, it held:

> [S]erious professional misconduct may arise where the conduct is quite removed from the practice of medicine, but is of a sufficiently immoral or outrageous or disgraceful character … One particular concern in such cases of moral turpitude is that the public reputation of the profession may suffer and public confidence in it may be prejudiced.[47]

It upheld the erasure of the District General Manager from the medical register. The *Roylance* decision constitutes an important assertion of the jurisdiction of regulatory bodies over practitioners in circumstances separate and distinct from their clinical interface with patients. The decision reaffirms that the interests of the professions in terms of their standing and their reputation and of members of the public extend beyond the direct work undertaken by health practitioners.

---

43   Ibid, at [21].
44   See, for example, Freckelton, I, "Immunity for Experts from Disciplinary Regulation" (2006) 13 *Journal of Law and Medicine* 393.
45   [1999] UKPC 16.
46   Ibid, at [41].
47   Ibid, at [42].

Complementary medicine

The fact that such a considerable percentage of health service provision is via practitioners of alternative or complementary medicine has brought with it the call for
greater regulation of therapeutic products[48] and health care practices which are
otherwise dependent upon the bringing of civil actions by aggrieved patients or
the exclusion from professional associations of poorly performing practitioners.[49]
An added fillip to extended regulatory arrangements has been the recognition that
a percentage of complementary practitioners do not function as complementary
practitioners – rather, they function separately and apart from orthodox medicine
and do not cross-refer patients and may not be adequately aware of the poten-
tiating or toxic effects of combined doses of complementary and orthodox
medications.[50] This has been of particular concern in the context of treatments for
cancer and other diseases which are potentially curable by orthodox medicine.

In Victoria a bold step was taken in relation to traditional Chinese medicine
and is mooted in relation to naturopathy.[51] The *Chinese Medicine Registration Act
2000* (Vic) provided that the practice of Chinese medicine, defined to include any
form of acupuncture or treatment with or dispensing of Chinese herbs, is illegal
save by persons duly registered by the Chinese Medicine Registration Board. This
led complex grandfathering decisions in relation to long-time practitioners with
qualifications not from Australian tertiary courses but has provided a fillip for
Chinese medicine to function in a more evidence-based way and as a genuine com-
plement to orthodox Western medicine. It has also encouraged practitioners of
Chinese medicine to become better schooled in the effects and characteristics
of orthodox pharmacotherapy as well as Chinese herbs, which also can have
lethal toxicities.

It is likely that the recognition of the potentially dangerous nature of a
number of the complementary therapies will lead to registration processes by
formal bodies, rather than simply professional associations – principally as a
mechanism for removing practitioners with inadequate qualifications and skill
levels and also as a means of inducing practitioners to function in a complementary rather than competitive capacity. It is a further example of the broadening
ambit of health practitioner regulation.

---

48   See Ellena, KR, "The Uncritical Enthusiasts Versus the Uninformed Sceptics: Regulation of
     Complementary and Alternative Medicines" (2005) 13 *Journal of Law and Medicine* 105.
49   Bensoussan, A and Myers, SP *Towards A Safer Choice: The Practice of Traditional Chinese
     Medicine in Australia*, University of Western Sydney, Sydney, 1996.
50   See, for example, *Shakoor v Situ* [2000] 4 All ER 181.
51   See Government of Victoria, Department of Human Services, *Review of Naturopathy
     and Western Herbal Medicine*, <www.health.vic.gov.au/pracreg/naturopathy.htm> (accessed
     1 April 2006).

The changing legal environment

Significant changes can be identified in the forms of disposition meted out to health practitioners found to have engaged in significantly unprofessional conduct since the 1980s. Most prominent amongst the changes have been the sanctions imposed for sexual misconduct, for conflict of interest and for lack of probity. This has been matched by a concomitant shift in decision-makers' language – both at first instance before bodies such as the General Medical Council and medical practitioner boards.

The significant change in approach by appellate courts and disciplinary tribunals has been characterised by an overt acknowledgment of the disempowerment generally existing between a patient and a health care practitioner, an imbalance prone to exploitation if the practitioner does not act ethically.[52] Robust critiques of abuse of power and predatory behaviour by health professionals published in professional literature[53] appear to have played a role in shifting the views of regulatory bodies. This has resulted in a pattern of firmer first instance decision-making by regulatory bodies and tribunals in relation to crossing of sexual boundaries, especially by psychiatrists and psychologists. Latterly the tendency has been for these decisions to have been upheld by the appellate courts.

Thus, in *Council for the Regulation of Health Care Professionals v General Medical Council*,[54] Leveson J observed that formal guidance adopted by the General Medical Council:

> [I]dentifies sexual misconduct and dishonesty, with specific reference to falsification of a curriculum vitae, as two of the most serious types of misconduct which may require erasure. It also provides that the public interest includes not only the specific risk to individual patients from doctors' misconduct, but also the maintenance of public confidence in the profession. In this regard, it is important that women are not deterred from seeking medical assistance because of a lack of confidence in doctors arising out of sexual misconduct.

The Privy Council too, in *Dare v General Medical Council*,[55] in the context of a relationship between a psychiatrist and his (medically qualified) patient observed that:

> Patients in therapy are extremely vulnerable regardless of their professional standing. Having initiated a relationship with a patient who was "functioning as a

---

52 See, for example, Freckelton, I, "The Sexually Exploitative Doctor" (1994) 1 *Journal of Law and Medicine* 203; *Re A Medical Practitioner* [1993] 2 Qd R 154 at 162.

53 See Walton, M, "Sex and the Practitioner: The Predator" (2002) 34 *Australian Journal of Forensic Sciences* 7; Gartrell, NK et al, "Physician-Patient Sexual Contact: Prevalence and Problems" (1992) 157(2) *Western Journal of Medicine* 139; Gutheil, TG and Gabbard, GO, "The Concept of Boundaries in Clinical Practice: Theoretical and Risk-Management Dimensions" (1993) 150 *American Journal of Psychiatry* 188; Lucire, Y, "Sex and the Practitioner: The Victim" (2002) 34 *Australian Journal of Forensic Science* 17; Searight, HR and Campbell, DC, "Physician-patient Sexual Contact: Ethical and legal Issues and Clinical Guidelines" (1993) 36 *Journal of Family Practice* 647.

54 [2004] EWHC 944 (Admin) at [46].

55 [2002] UKPC 54 at [17].

child" the appellant failed to stop the behaviour he displayed over a period of time. As a psychiatrist he should have known how to manage Miss A's feelings of transference without taking advantage of her in a dependent state. He should have sought advice, we have no doubt that he should have referred Miss A to another doctor at a time when he had insight into the way that the professional relationship was diminishing and his sexual feelings towards his patient were on the increase. Thus his judgment was seriously at fault in not recognising the danger signs. Their Lordships have no doubt that behaviour such as this seriously undermines the trust the public place in the profession and in particular in psychiatrists practising psycho-analysis and psycho-therapy. In their Lordships' view, the Committee having heard all the evidence were entitled to conclude that they regarded the appellant's behaviour as "abhorrent", "appalling ... a disgraceful abuse of the trust".

The issue of the incompatibility of dishonesty and ongoing registration of a health care practitioner has come before the health regulatory tribunals and the courts on a number of occasions. In the important decision of *Patel v General Medical Council*[56] a doctor appealed from a decision by the Professional Conduct Committee of the General Medical Council in England, ultimately to the Privy Council, against a decision that his name be erased from the practising register for various acts of dishonesty. The council held that "[f]or all professional persons including doctors a finding of dishonesty lies at the top end in the spectrum of gravity of misconduct".[57]

What can be discerned is a readier response by first instance regulators to pronounce decisively that a variety of forms of conduct on the part of health professionals constitute behaviour that is prima facie incompatible with registered status. This compares with the more "understanding" response of earlier generations of regulators.

Matters involving serious allegations against health practitioners have the potential to result in deregistration, suspension or the imposition of conditions upon registration. It goes without saying that such sanctions can be personally and professionally devastating for practitioners. It is apparent from the volume of appellate litigation in relation to health practitioners against whom adverse findings are made at first instance in the United Kingdom, Australia and Canada that the area of "disciplinary law" is expanding for the legal profession. There is a tendency for more technical points to be argued on behalf of practitioners, for legal principles to be explored and challenged, and for decisions adverse to practitioners to be appealed. In Australia there is no doubt that first instance hearings are becoming longer and more complex. The decisions of the Professional Conduct Committees of the General Medical Council in the United Kingdom and of the Victorian Medical Practitioners Board, the Psychologists Registration Board, the Dental Practice Board and the Chinese Medicine Registration Board and of the Civil and Administrative Tribunal on de novo review are posted on the internet, enabling transparency of reasoning with the result that the shaming and the

---

56   [2003] UKPC 16.
57   Ibid, at [10].

improprieties of practitioners are highly visible for their colleagues and even for current and potential patients.

The combination of factors has resulted in something of an impetus in the direction of adversarialism for matters that reach the formal decision-making phase in Australia, New Zealand, the United Kingdom and Canada. In practise this has meant longer and more expensive hearings, the involvement of more senior lawyers, taking of more technical points,[58] lengthier and more complex reasons for decisions, a proliferation of appellate judgments and escalating levels of attention from the media for decisions in relation to health practitioners, especially doctors.

In turn this has provided an incentive for regulatory authorities to reconfigure allegations of impropriety into matters of health, performance and competence in need of investigation, rather than conduct inquiries which are likely to lead to heavily contested and stigmatising hearings.

Awareness of broader causes for adverse outcomes

There is a growing recognition that there can be multiple causes for individual instances of unsatisfactory practitioner conduct. These include systems factors, health problems experienced by practitioners and deficiencies in skills and competence. Irvine has argued that:

> We got professional regulation the wrong way round. The emphasis was on reacting to serious events through central mechanisms, such as the GMC. Prevention, and the early recognition, diagnosis and action on problems, were not priorities. Hence, the ad hoc nature of the arrangements for supervising the quality of medical practice at the point of service delivery, and the highly variable informal systems to deal with problem doctors.[59]

Quite regularly errors and unsatisfactory outcomes for which particular practitioners are responsible can be the product of complex institutional and systems factors. Many examples can be advanced. For instance, diminished concentration on the part of a junior medical officer can be caused by his or her having worked a series of long shifts at the direction of hospital management. It accomplishes little to discipline the practitioner for an error brought about by exhaustion for which the practitioner bears little responsibility.

Likewise, hospital policy may require the discharge of certain categories of patients at an arbitrary time subsequent to surgery. The fact that a patient in the care of a surgeon or physician suffers complications which could have been

---

58   See Searles, D, "Professional Misconduct – Unprofessional Conduct. Is there a Difference?" (1992) *Queensland Law Society Journal* 239.

59   See Cruess, RL, Cruess, SL and Johnston, SE, "Professionalism: an Ideal to Be Sustained" (2000) 356 *Lancet* 156; Irvine, D, "Time for Hard Decisions on Patient-centred Professionalism" (2004) 181 *MJA* 271; Irvine, DH, "The Performance of Doctors I: Professionalism and Regulation in a Changing World" (1997) 315 *British Medical Journal* 1540; Irvine, DH, "The Performance of Doctors II: Maintaining Good Practice, Protecting Patients from Poor Performance" (1997) 314 *British Medical Journal* 1613.

identified and addressed had the patient continued to be an inpatient is technically the responsibility of the practitioner. However, resources issues which resulted in administrative decisions which in turn generated premature practitioner discharges constituted the background within which a clinical error in judgment may be identified.

Such matters are ill-addressed by disciplinary hearings and significant consequences for individual practitioners, although such results may be palatable for adversely affected patients or patients' families.

Another aetiology of unsafe practice by health practitioners can be their own state of health, ranging from cognitive impairment arising from age-related deterioration, brain injury or psychiatric illness to physical ailments, such as chronic pain or heart or other conditions to substance dependencies. A number of medical regulators in Australia, Canada and the United Kingdom have set up or facilitated health programs for doctors so as to maximise the potential for practitioners to receive the assistance they need to address their health problems and thereby render them fit once more for practise.

Australian regulatory bodies tend to take a low key approach with health issues, eschewing formal hearings as often as possible, and encouraging practitioners to have breaks from work to address their health concerns and to return to practise subject to mutually agreed restrictions on practice for a period of time until medical reports suggest that the practitioner's condition has been adequately addressed. Thus, the approach is one of working with the practitioner in order to facilitate rehabilitation and provision of education to practitioners about the risks of not having a family doctor, working too hard, becoming too stressed and yielding to substance dependence.

One of the notable features of regulation of health professionals is that cross-pollination amongst international bodies and legislatures is resulting in a reduction in the disciplinary orientation of regulation. Part of what is taking place is a redefinition of the culture of professionalism. For instance, Donald Irvine, President of the General Medical Council, argued in 1997 that such a culture should be inclusive, involving all doctors and embracing continuing medical education, personal professional development, clinical audit and quality improvement methods. He contended that it would have six core components:

1. A clear ethical framework and, where possible, the use of explicit professional and clinical standards;

2. Effective local professional regulation for maintaining good practice;

3. Regular publication by the royal colleges and others of data showing doctors' involvement in continuing medical education, audit, and other performance related activities;

4. Sound local arrangements for recognising dysfunctional doctors early and for taking appropriate action;

5. Well defined criteria and pathways for referral to the GMC when severely dysfunctional doctors cannot or should not be managed locally;

6. At all stages, practical help and support so that doctors who get into difficulties can be restored to full practice wherever possible.[60]

From a generic perspective the allegations made against health practitioners can be classified in a variety of ways, including as follows: sexual misconduct, blurring of boundaries between practitioner and client, dishonesty, breach of confidentiality, conflict of interest, unsatisfactory provision of treatment, conduct of procedures without suitable advice about options and potentially adverse consequences, and unsatisfactory communication generally. However, often particular instances of what might be classified as unprofessional conduct within these categories are indicative of deficits in skill or competence.

Starting with initiatives in Canada,[61] a new approach has been trialled in jurisdictions in North America,[62] the United Kingdom,[63] Australia[64] and New Zealand[65] whereby in appropriate cases an investigation is directed not to whether a practitioner has engaged in unprofessional conduct but into the practitioner's professional competence and skill levels. Such an assessment is generally peer-dominated and conducted by reference to professional guidelines and practices – to evaluate whether the practitioner's performance is substandard by reference to accepted norms and procedures. If it is, the orientation of regulatory bodies is to address the deficits by mandated further education, counselling or supervision, or sometimes by restrictions on practise. As with the approach in relation to health-caused deficiencies of practice, the attempt is to draw upon the skills possessed by a practitioner and enhance the potential of the practitioner to practise safely and in accordance with professional standards. Where possible, this is done collaboratively by respected colleagues of the practitioner, at the aegis of the regulatory body, identifying deficits and setting out a roadmap toward remediation.

---

60   Irvine (1997) op cit.

61   Weymouth, V, "Office Medical Practice Peer Review: the British Columbia Experience", paper presented to the Parlons Qualité Conference, Montreal, 17 June 1992, revised October 1999; Page, GG et al, "Physician-assessment and Physician-enhancement Programs in Canada" (1995) 153 Canadian Medical Association Journal 1723; Hall, W et al, "Assessment of Physician Performance in Alberta" (1999) 161 Canadian Medical Association Journal 52.

62   Norman, GR et al, "Competency Assessment of Primary Care Physicians as Part of a Peer Review Program" (1993) 270(9) Journal of the American Medical Association 1046.

63   See the work undertaken by the National Clinical Assessment Authority. However, the General Medical Council performance procedures rely upon the parameters of "good medical practice". See also McCaul, J, "The Scottish Approach to Poorly Performing Doctors", 2002, <http://careerfocus.bmjjournals.com/chi/content/full/324/7334/S51?ct> (accessed May 2006).

64   See, for example, Medical Practice Act 1994 (Vic) Pt 3, Div 3; Reid, A, "Poorly Performing Doctors" (2006) Law in Context (in press).

65   See Medical Council of New Zealand, <www.mcnz.org.nz/Default.aspx?tabid=1084> (accessed 27 September 2005).

The emerging focus on performance assessment and monitoring builds upon the trend toward mandatory continuing professional development (CPD)[66] and potential re-accreditation on the basis of demonstrated ongoing competency.[67] In the United Kingdom, which leads the world in this regard, a precondition to ongoing registration is proof of participation in CPD and accreditation. This is a major shift away from the notion that mere possession of tertiary qualifications is sufficient for a lifetime licence to practise. It provides a means whereby the general community can have a measure of confidence that health practitioners are staying abreast of current developments, are not isolated from their colleagues and remain well regarded and competent from the informed perspective of their professional peers. A corollary of this approach, though, is that fewer matters are likely to be dealt with by regulatory bodies as instances of unprofessional conduct, the focus increasingly being not upon individual acts that are unsatisfactory but upon what is giving rise to substandard performance and behaviour likely to be indicative of defective skills, technique or knowledge.

However, the days are still relatively early in relation to performance-based resolution of complaints and notifications about practitioner performance. While the application of such an approach to the skills and competence of doctors and dentists is immediately plausible – at least in some areas of practice, such as anaesthesia and endodontics – the application is less clear in relation to general practice and psychiatry amongst doctors and a number of other areas of practice by other health practitioners, such as psychology and nursing. The boundary lines between conduct and performance also have to be worked through, so that it is clear whether a conduct or performance investigation will be triggered in given circumstances. In addition, the cost and delay ramifications of performance-based investigation have to be resolved as peer assessment tends to be time-consuming and costly – who is to pay for such investigations? There is also the question of how acceptable such an approach is to aggrieved patients who may have suffered adverse consequences to what they perceive as practitioner misconduct. While many complainants cite as their reason for lodging complaints their hope that the practitioner will be prevented from behaving toward others as they have toward them, the behind-the-scenes mentoring and guidance directed toward returning the practitioner to practise may not provide a high level of satisfaction to complainants.

---

66   See Parboosingh, J, "CPD and Maintenance of Certification in the Royal College of Physicians and Surgeons of Canada" (2002) 5 *The Obstetrician & Gynaecologist* 43; Peck, CM et al, "Continuing Medical Education and Continuing Professional Development: International Comparisons" (2000) 320 *British Medical Journal* 432; World Federation for Medical Education *Continuing Professional Development of Medical Doctors WFME Global Standards for Quality Improvement: Result from Task Force Seminar*, 25–27 October 2002, WFME, 2003.

67   See Trunkey, DDT and Botney, R, "Assessing Competency: A Tale of Two Professions" (2001) 192 *Journal of the American College of Surgeons* 385.

Moves toward revalidation

A significant development, likely to be implemented internationally in varying forms[68] little by little, is the introduction of licences to practise.[69] To retain their licence, United Kingdom doctors will have to "revalidate", by demonstrating, at regular intervals to the General Medical Council, that they remain up-to-date and fit to practise. Henceforth revalidation and licensing will constitute the cornerstone of medical practitioners' accountability to United Kingdom patients and the wider public. This is not a wholly new phenomenon, clinical governance previously being regarded as based on principles of local oversight and accountability – formal procedures were introduced into the National Health System from April 1999 which included annual appraisal for doctors, based on the guidance given by the General Medical Council's *Good Medical Practice.*

Historically, doctors were admitted to the register on qualification (or on assessment, if they qualified outside the United Kingdom). No further checks were done unless the doctor's conduct or performance gave rise to concerns that led to a referral to the fitness to practise procedures.[70] The change is that revalidation will shift the emphasis of regulation away from qualifications alone towards a regular assessment of whether the doctor remains up-to-date and fit to practise.[71] It will require all doctors to establish that they reflect meaningfully on their practice, using information gathered through audit and in other ways, and to seek the views of others on their performance, throughout their medical careers.

The General Medical Council's draft guidance for doctors, current in April 2006, sets out a number of core requirements for revalidation, including:

- a description of the doctor's practice;

- evidence of participation in appraisal and completion of an agreed "personal development plan";

- a statement declaring eligibility for local certification; and

- declarations relating to health and probity.

---

68 See Dauphinee, WD, "Validation of Doctors in Canada" (1999) 319 *British Medical Journal* 1198; Rogers, S, "Culling Bad Apples: Blowing Whistles and the Health Practitioners Competence Assurance Act 2003 (NZ)" (2004) 12 *Journal of Law and Medicine* 119; Newble, D, Paget, N and McLaren, B, "Revalidation in Australia and New Zealand: Approach of Royal Australasian College of Physicians" (1999) 319 *British Medical Journal* 1185; Norcini, JJ "Recertification in the United States" (1999) 319 *British Medical Journal* 1183; Southgate, L and Dauphinee, D, "Maintaining Standards in British and Canadian Medicine: the Developing Role of the Regulatory Body" (1998) 316 *British Medical Journal* 697; Southgate, L et al, "The Assessment of Poorly Performing Doctors: the Development of the Assessment Programmes for the General Medical Council's Performance Procedures" (2001) 35 (Suppl 1) *Medical Education* 2.

69 See Cunningham, JPW et al, "Defensible Assessment of the Competency of the Practicing Physician" (1997) 72(1) *Academic Medicine* 617.

70 See Cunningham (1997) op cit.

71 See McKinley, R, Fraser, RC, and Baker, R, "Model for Directly Assessing and Improving Clinical Competence and Performance in Revalidation of Clinicians" (2001) 322 *British Medical Journal* 712.

In addition, doctors are required to submit for greater scrutiny their compliance with various topics outlined in the *Guide to Medical Practice*.

The revalidation process is intended also to ensure that doctors regularly reflect on their practice. For most doctors, the vehicle for delivering that regular reflection will be an annual appraisal but if a practitioner cannot participate in such a scheme, the General Medical Council will call for the doctor's folder. The council will also require verifiable evidence that there are no significant local concerns about a doctor's practice. Suitable evidence, for a doctor who works in a managed environment, will be confirmation by a person with formal clinical governance responsibilities that there are no unresolved concerns about the doctor's practice. In the absence of this, the results of validated questionnaires, completed by professional colleagues and, where appropriate, patients also, may provide acceptable evidence.

If a doctor cannot produce an appropriate clinical governance certificate or results from validated questionnaires, the General Medical Council will call to see the doctor's folder. Finally, doctors will be required to provide evidence as to their good health and probity. All practitioners will be required to provide a personal declaration, certified by another doctor who is registered with the council.

Dame Janet Smith has argued that within the revalidation folder, there should be information for assessment by the General Medical Council about:

- prescribing data and records of complaints or concerns;
- a record of continuing professional development activity;
- a patient satisfaction questionnaire;
- results of a clinical audit and some significant audit events;
- a copy of an appraisal form; and
- a certificate to show the successful completion of a knowledge test.

The General Medical Council has commented that for most medical practitioners in clinical settings working in council-approved environments, it expects that most of Dame Janet's suggestions will be met within the doctor's appraisal and/or clinical governance systems.[72]

What is being attempted in the United Kingdom therefore is an extensive, monitored, mandated regime for ensuring medical practitioners' fitness to practise. It is open to criticism for its bureaucratisation, its dependence upon what are likely to be pro forma processes and the burden that it will impose upon practitioners to compile relevant documentation – more time on paperwork and less on practice. However, it aims to weed out practitioners who are lacking in core competencies, who are out-of-date, who are ill thought of by peers and whose health is declining, In this objective it will be politically attractive well beyond the United Kingdom.

---

72 See General Medical Council, Good Medical Practice, <www.gmc-uk.org/med_ed/default. htm> (accessed 7 September 2005).

The future for health practitioner regulation

What can be discerned in terms of the past one-and-a-half decades of evolution in health practitioner regulation is a substantial increase in its extent and philosophical sophistication. Practitioners' conduct is now subject to assessment in their personal and professional lives wherever it has the potential to impact upon community confidence in the standing and quality of health service delivery. Future regulation is likely to be characterised by reference to more clearly enunciated values and collegiate expectations articulated in codes of ethics and practice by reference to professionalism.

The culture of regulation has become more influenced by community standards and expectations. The future model of regulation is likely to consolidate this trend. It is likely to be participatory and lay-influenced, utilising strategies borrowed from alternative dispute resolution, therapeutic jurisprudence and restorative justice where possible. However, it is likely to be more stringent than that which preceded it in relation to a variety of key aspects of professional misfeasance – most particularly, transgression of permitted boundaries, exploitation of patients, and dishonesty.

Community values about patient autonomy and the demand for treatment to be a partnership between health practitioners and their patients are likely to be enforced in the regulatory environment via demands for provision of consumer-friendly information about treatment options and the side-effects of pharmacotherapies and other interventions.

Regulation has commenced to extend into aspects of practice, such as management[73] and, at least in Australia, into forensic work.[74] The decision of Collins J in respect of Sir Roy Meadow will not succeed in turning back the clock. There is a growing awareness that health practitioners utilise their professional skills in areas outside the direct clinical interface and should be accountable for the potentially adverse effects of their decision-making and exercise of professional judgment.

Another impetus is toward more wide-scale regulatory regimes incorporating health practitioners who have previously functioned outside the establishment. The reality is that those therapeutically utilising toxic substances and intrusive procedures have the potential to do serious harm if they intersect poorly with the orthodox practice of health care, if they are inadequately trained or knowledgeable, or if their levels of performance slip below that which the public and peers would reasonably expect. This recognition is likely to lead to the broadening of the regulatory net into a number of the "alternative therapies" and to pressures for them to be regarded, at least for regulatory reasons, as complementary to traditional medicine. In turn, this will require greater levels of knowledge by orthodox and complementary practitioners about other modalities of health practice and preparedness to work cooperatively in patients' best interests.

---

73 See *Roylance v GMC* [1999] UKPC 16.
74 See, for example, *Mustac v Medical Board of Western Australia* [2004] WASCA 156.

It is apparent that a variety of new regulatory approaches will become the dominant paradigm. These will reduce the focus upon individual instances of misconduct and will construct mechanisms for measuring ongoing competence and skill levels. When specific notifications and complaints are made, the trend will be toward evaluation of the multifactorial causes of adverse outcomes. To the extent that they are identified as performance- or skill-related, intervention (where possible, by agreement) will seek to remedy deficits. To the extent that they are systemic issues, there is likely to be more preparedness by regulators, armed with additional powers, to probe indirect causes of unsatisfactory outcomes and address them with less of a punitive focus upon individuals and more of an attempt to address underlying issues which give rise to suboptimal practices and thereby risks to health and safety.

Models for health practitioner regulation will also evolve. The traditionally profession-based decision-makers within health profession boards and councils have already mostly made way for external decision-making by tribunals composed of a mixture of lawyers, health practitioners and, in some places, members of the general community. This trend is likely to be consolidated. While such a shift marks an end to the traditional forms of self-regulation, though, the opportunity remains for the health professions to formulate the yardsticks likely to guide such external decision-making bodies. It is to be hoped that the current proliferation of high level reflections upon professionalism and philosophies of regulation will produce articulations of what the various the health professions consider to be the delineation between professional and unprofessional conduct, thereby enabling external bodies to evaluate practitioner conduct in an informed way both from the perspective of peers and from contemporary members of the general community.

25

Health systems,
quality control and corporatisation:
New challenges for accountability

Beth Wilson[1]

Traditional regulation of health services

The rationale for regulating health services is to protect patients and promote public health and safety. All health services are urged to strive for best practice and to develop risk management strategies and, where mistakes have been made, to learn from them so errors are not repeated. Tools such as root cause analysis and open disclosure have more recently been utilised in the bid to improve health services, especially in hospitals. Accreditation, independent health complaints commissioners, registration boards, coroners, litigation and criminal law are all part of the heavily regulated health arena.

Since the 1980s health services have undergone significant change as large companies have purchased medical practices, pathology and related services and hospitals. Major players such as Mayne Nickless and Endeavour have, according to Alan Kohler, business journalist with the Australian Financial Review, been "conglomeratizing GP practices".[2] The companies, realising that general practitioners (GPs) are the gatekeepers of many medical services find them commercially very attractive. There have also been concerns about doctors owning pathology services to which they refer their own patients. Issues around conflicts of interest have become more pressing as corporatisation of health services continues to expand. This chapter examines whether our current regulatory regimes are sufficient and asks if corporatisation necessitates a different type of regulation.

---

1   The author is the Health Services Commissioner of Victoria.
2   Kohler, A quoted in "The Big Business of Medicine", *Health Report*, ABC Radio National, 27 August 2001. The program was a joint broadcast with the *Life Matters* program and was presented by Norman Swan and Geraldine Doogue.

The changing health scene

The provision of health services costs money. Governments in Australia and elsewhere have been finding ways of reducing the demands on their budgets by introducing market-based approaches to the provision of health care.[3] It is now not unusual to see articles in the business section of our daily newspapers with headings like: "Signs of Life in Healthcare".[4] The article continues:

> Low-risk earnings and solid growth are still available to investors through health providers with a domestic focus, despite rising concerns about the economy. Recent share price weakness in the domestic healthcare stocks has prompted Deutsche Bank to reassess the risk for reward profile of this sector to pinpoint where values can be found. Overall, the broker prefers the radiology and primary care sectors, which are both enjoying strong growth and stable funding. Across the sector, regulatory and funding risks are low, except in the case of pharmaceutical wholesalers.

The "values" referred to are not those traditionally associated with medical services. The concerns are solely about economic aspects of health care and the article is silent on matters such as good patient care, medical ethics and best practice standards. The article predicts that the Federal Government's attempts to find savings in its Pharmaceuticals Benefits Scheme (PBS) will lead to funding cuts that will have an impact on margins for at least 12 months.[5] Deutsche Bank, the broker, says the preferred services are aged care and diagnostic services as these offer reliable earnings at a reasonable price. Deutsche Bank recommends investors stay away from the private hospital sector as the risks are high.[6]

Corporatised medicine has not always been a financial success story. Mayne Nickless, Australia's largest hospital company did not initially make the huge profits expected because all the hospitals in Australia got into what they described themselves as an "arms race". They discovered their main customers are not patients but doctors – because a doctor is the person who introduces the patient to a particular hospital. The companies installed large amounts of expensive equipment and operating theatres anticipating they would be able to recover their outlay by charging higher fees and bed rates. However, the influence of the health funds meant they were unable to negotiate the services and fees as anticipated because the health funds dictated refunds. Mayne Nickless then embarked upon a public relations exercise to try to change this by purporting to be on the side of the consumer by focusing on eliminating gap payments.[7]

---

3   Hancock, L, *Health Policy in the Market State*, Allen & Unwin, Sydney, 1999.

4   *Herald Sun*, 18 April 2005, p 33.

5   The Pharmaceutical Benefits Scheme is the fastest growing sector of the Federal Government's health budget.

6   *Herald Sun*, 18 April 2005, p 33.

7   *Health Report*, ABC Radio National, 27 August 2005.

Mayne was well aware that consumers are hostile to gap payments which are often unexpected and they entered into contracts with private hospitals that agreed to send just one integrated account to consumers to avoid gap payments. These kinds of negotiations may be couched in terms of concerns for the consumer but are nonetheless all about money. The purchasing of more and more private hospitals by fewer companies has had the effect of reducing competition, and therefore consumer choice, rather than increasing it.

According to Kohler, "the doctors control the patients and the health funds control the money, and so the hospitals really are takers, of both patients and money". Kohler also said Mayne Nickless was buying hospitals to provide customers for its pathology companies. He noted that bulk billing is also becoming rarer and the advent of large corporations having very efficient low-cost operations could assist with this. He believed general practitioners were retreating from bulk billing because they simply can't afford to do it.[8] Kohler expressed concerns about the purchase and control of pharmaceutical businesses by companies like Mayne, who exercise control over pharmacy, radiology, pathology, general practice, and the largest share of the hospital system. It is now very difficult to find a radiologist or a pathologist in Australia not employed by a corporation.

Dr Ross Glasson, a former President of the Royal Australian and New Zealand College of Radiology estimated that around 45 per cent of radiology services subsidised by Medicare were, in 2001, provided by corporatised entities.[9] This figure has continued to rise. The three major players in radiology are Mayne Nickless, Sonic Health Care and Imed. These companies are also involved in other kinds of medical services. The major company involved in pathology services is Medical Imaging Australia. Glasson considered the major concern for consumers was that they could be exploited: "in a vertical chain of their pathology, radiology examinations [they] will be passed along from one hand to another, and there'll be temptation to over service".[10] He considered all regulatory parties and government needed to put into place mechanisms to ensure over-servicing did not increase.

General practices, which were once comprised of sole practitioners or partnerships operating in a "cottage industry" style, have been taken over by companies and run as businesses. Paul Fitzgerald, a general practitioner from Sydney, stated the Australian Medical Association's position as accepting corporatisation as inevitable but warned of the possibility of "ethical disassociation" where

---

8   In 2001, when the program was broadcast the actual figure was about 30 to 40 per cent, but by 2005 that had increased to 72.4 per cent according to the Health Insurance Commission figures released in February 2001 following the Federal Government's MedicarePlus incentives.

9   Ibid. The four major groups were Mayne Nickless, Radio Division, Sonic Healthcare, Medical Imaging Australia and IMED.

10   *Health Report*, ABC Radio National, 27 August 2001.

the professional standards of doctors in a corporatised environment are altered. He predicted doctors would go from being advocates for their patients to advocates for the corporations of which they are a part. Others have argued that professional standards of doctors are not compromised because responsibility for clinical and professional conduct remains with the doctors who must answer to the registration boards if they behave in an unprofessional manner.

Dr Joe Kosterich of Endeavour Healthcare, which plays a major role in the Perth marketplace, took a more optimistic view noting that practices are managed by companies but doctors working in them are not employed by the companies, they are actually contractors. They provide medical services to patients, and pay companies to provide infrastructure and management services to them on a contractual basis. The contracts, he claimed, allow the doctors to have full independence in the practice of medicine. Fitzgerald, on the other hand, noted, "the real problem comes when the corporation decides that it has problems in terms of its profitability and starts to put the pressure on. And here we see that there is a serious imbalance between the power of the corporation and the power of the individual doctor".[11]

Important issues arise in the administration of corporatised medicine such as appointment scheduling, barriers on home visits and after-hours care. The concern is that companies will be guided only by profit-making and will not be willing to provide services needed by the community but which do not make much money.

Entrepreneurial medicine

While some of the debate around corporate medicine has been couched in terms of doctors *versus* corporates many doctors have also been entrepreneurial. Merrilyn Walton has traced the history of entrepreneurial medicine in Australia from the 1980s and warns that our regulatory responses have been woefully inadequate despite numerous government inquiries, reports and committees.[12] She describes a "second wave" of commercialisation with the growth of specialised clinics that advertise aggressively. She also points to the failure of the medical profession to take seriously the challenges posed by entrepreneurs by categorising them as "bad doctors" rather than honestly facing up to the issues around conflicts of interest.[13]

A major issue for government is the potential for over-servicing by doctors and there are obvious financial benefits for those who over-service under Medicare. While there are sanctions in place are these adequate? Doctors found guilty of over-servicing may have their provider numbers cancelled, however, they may nonetheless continue practising unless found guilty of unprofessional conduct and deregistered by the relevant registration board. Walton writes:

---

11 Ibid.
12 Walton, M, *The Trouble With Medicine: Preserving the Trust Between Patients and Doctors*, Allen & Unwin, Sydney, 1998, p 37.
13 Ibid, p 38.

> In the business-orientated health-care environment today, doctors face daily chal-
> lenges to their fiduciary duties. Yet there are few barriers and guidelines to help
> doctors decide if, when and how to enter commercial agreements. How many
> doctors with investments in health services understand conflicts of interest?[14]

She also points out that entrepreneurial medicine is not just about larger clinics
employing many doctors:

> The fee-for-service arrangements under Medicare, self-referrals, ownership of
> auxiliary medical services, ownership or part-ownership of private hospitals and
> nursing homes, all increase the risk of doctors putting economic self-interest ahead
> of patients.[15]

In support of this view she cites the 1985 Commonwealth Joint Committee of
Public Accounts, which reported on medical fraud and over-servicing:

> Medical entrepreneurs usually, but not always, appear to work just within the
> bounds of the law, pay lip service to professional ethics and vigorously scrutinise
> regulatory measures for loopholes and areas of imprecise interpretation and
> specifications.[16]

Many others have also criticised entrepreneurial medical ventures for fraud
and over-servicing. These include the Health Insurance Commission, the Commonwealth Auditor-General, the Commonwealth Department of Health and
various Ministers of Health.

It is not unlawful for doctors to be involved in entrepreneurial medicine and
to own practices, hospitals and medical services. So what is the problem? Why
does it matter so much if doctors are successful at business so long as they do not
break the law? The answer lies in the nature of medical services. They are intimate,
they rely strongly on good ethical practices and the basis of the relationship
between doctors and their patients should be trust. Walton sees the involvement
of doctors in such ventures as problematic because of the obvious conflicts of
interest involved.

Similar problems arise in the context of other more recent entrepreneurial
ventures by doctors. In May 2005, the launch of a company allowing general
practitioners to set up their own cooperative pathology company was delayed
because of legal problems.[17] Diagnostic Medical Cooperative had planned to sign
up to 500 doctors who would then be able to refer their own patients to the
cooperative for testing and with related Medicare rebates paid directly to them.
To join, doctors would pay $5200 as a one-off fee and then annual fees of $1400.
Ray Moynihan has also criticised entrepreneurial medicine and conflicts of interest

---

14   Ibid, p 39.

15   Ibid, p 39.

16   Commonwealth Joint Committee of Public Accounts, *Inquiry Into Fraud and Overservicing:
     Report on Pathology*, Report No 236, 1985, p 89.

17   Limprecht, E, "Legal Concerns Hit Pathology Co-op", *Australian Doctor*, 20 May 2005 p 2.

in his book, *Selling Sickness*.[18] In May 2005, the Melbourne *Herald-Sun* ran a front-page story on doctors who sell patient data to pharmaceutical companies and this is discussed in a later section of this chapter.

Consumers

Super-clinics, or one-stop health shops run by corporations, are a relatively new phenomenon. What are the implications of these services for consumers? The corporations buy and integrate practices to include pathology, radiology, general practice and pharmacy. Obviously they want patients to be referred to their own services, which may cause concerns for competition policy advocates, however, consumers may be better served by this kind of system because of convenience and after-hours accessibility.

When they first began to appear, 24-hour clinics were criticised by some on the grounds they put profit before patient care. In some metropolitan areas the 24-hour clinics began with a fanfare but quickly disappeared when found not to be as profitable as expected. This in turn meant that patients seeking after-hours services have had to utilise emergency services at local public hospitals, placing further strain on waiting times for these services. Governments have responded by encouraging general practices to be located near or in public hospitals to take some of the load.

Long waiting lists for services like surgery make consumers more vulnerable to questionable entrepreneurial schemes such as CareCredit loans. Consumer advocates have warned people to be aware of these loans, which began in the United States and which provide finance for surgical procedures. Interest rates on CareCredit loans begin at 12.9 per cent after 12 months and jump to 18.9 per cent after three years. The credit scheme was launched in March 2005 by a United States giant financial enterprise, GE Money. Patients seeking dental, eye procedures or other cosmetic surgery, can take up the loans.

It is difficult to estimate accurately the amount of money Australian consumers spend on private elective surgery but it is thought to be about $14 million annually outside Medicare.[19] The Australian Medical Association (AMA) has warned patients and doctors not to get involved in the scheme, which it fears may bankrupt patients. It also considers such schemes to be anathema to ethical medical practice. The AMA, Catholic Health Australia and the Australian Consumers' Association have urged the Federal Government to intervene.

Stephen Leeder, Professor and Dean of Medicine at the University of Sydney, believes consumers should be very concerned about corporatised medical services:

---

18 Moynihan, R and Cassells, A, *Selling Sickness: How Drug Companies are Turning Us Into Patients*, Allen & Unwin, Sydney, 2005.

19 *Herald Sun*, 14 March 2005, p 7.

This is a very big shift in the way in which we provide health services in this country, and there is an increasing presence of big business interests in health care provision, which really challenges some of the fundamental social values like equality.[20]

Professor Leeder considered the introduction of a profit motive intruding between the provision of care by health professionals and the patient necessitates a degree of regulation not previously required. Provision of health services, he has warned, had previously been based on public values that Australia should provide equal access to equal care for equal need. Now, commercial lobby groups that represent commercial interests, rather than concerns for public health, are increasingly influencing government responses and policies.

Nicola Ballenden, Senior Policy Officer at the Australia Consumers' Association has been monitoring corporatisation and pointed out that general practice has always been about business and making money.[21] Benefits for consumers include the fact that the big clinics are more likely to bulk bill, are open longer hours, they are more convenient, services such as physiotherapy are available on site, and there are nicer toys for the kids to play with. She also identified some areas of concern for consumers in terms of choice about who they want to consult, and fear that a concentration in ownership would reduce that choice between going to a family doctor or one of the large clinics. She was concerned, however, that if all GPs within a particular region were brought under a corporate structure, with competition disappearing, then bulk-billing might disappear as well. Clearly much more consultation with consumers is needed to determine the way in which Australians want their health services to develop.

Privacy issues

Information about patients, including prescribing data, is of obvious interest to pharmaceutical companies. In May 2005, the Federal Privacy Commissioner, Karen Curtis, decided it was not unlawful for doctors to sell this information to companies so long as it is de-identified. The decision is a result of an investigation into the sale of prescribing information by GPs to CAMM Pacific via Medical Director Software. The doctors supplying the information are paid by money or department store vouchers. CAMM Pacific is paying some 200 doctors for the data. Concerns have been expressed by Dr Graeme Miller of the Health Leaders' Forum who wants the Privacy Act 1988 (Cth) to be reviewed because the decision fails to protect patients' interest.[22]

---

20 *Health Report*, ABC Radio National, 27 August 2001.
21 Ibid.
22 Limprecht, E, "Green Light to Cash In On Patient Data" *Australian Doctor*, 20 May 2005, p 3.

Sydney GP, Dr Johdi Menon, who also has plans for a scheme to assist doctors to make profits from sale of data, disagrees and sees nothing wrong with doctors making money like this so long as what they are doing is legal and ethical.[23]

The *Herald-Sun* in Victoria ran a front-page story on doctors selling patient data in this way and even though the data are de-identified responses from the public were strongly against this use of their information. The practice may not strictly speaking be unlawful but clearly the public considers it is unethical and should not be permitted. Privacy laws allow the collection of health information for the primary purpose of the organisation (in health services this is to provide patient health care) and the use or disclosure of it for the primary purpose or a closely-related secondary purpose that the person would reasonably expect. Patients would not reasonably expect their health information to be on-sold for profit. They give doctors information so their health needs can be met and do not expect it to be used in this way. The practice does not assist in maintaining trust between doctor and patient, which is vital to a good clinical relationship.

There are also some important issues around ownership of patient health information in a corporatised environment. Currently this is an issue determined by contract law and the outcome depends on the nature of the contractual arrangement between doctors and practice owners. Most consumers would have no idea of the content of those contracts and may be disadvantaged when they want to take their business elsewhere.

Following publicity about the sale of patient data the multi-million dollar general practice software market has attracted new players. In June 2005, NxtHealth, a subsidiary of IBA Health, attempted to attract doctors to its product by re-branding its software. Problems with its major competitor Medical Director, included pop-up advertisements as well as the sale of patient data.[24] IBA Health has undertaken to set up an independent ethics committee to monitor NxtHealth, however, according to *Australian Doctor*:

> IBA Health ... is pitching the idea that GPs should secure a slice of the profits gene-rated by the primary care health information technology market, pledging to offer doctors, practice managers and divisions of general practice share options in Nxt.[25]

Tony Abbott, Federal Minister of Health, has warned that existing ethical bodies are not strong enough and politicians would take on the role of "offering ethical counsel" to doctors if medical organisations failed to do so. He criticised the Australian Medical Association for failing to issue a press release on the issue.[26] Doctor's organisations responded by saying they have ethical guidelines in place.

---

23   Ibid.
24   Limprecht, E, "GP Ownership at Core of Practice Software Battle" *Australian Doctor*, 17 June 2005, p 5.
25   Ibid.
26   Ibid, p 16.

Profit and waiting lists

Health services and policies have long been influenced by profit motivations. What has changed is the size of the enterprises and the fact that in the past doctors have practised privately for profit in smaller practices. Specialists, on the other hand, tend to move between the private and the public sectors.

The Federal Government's rhetoric about its health policies is confusing. On the one hand, privatisation has been supported but in May 2005 Tony Abbott urged doctors to work in the public sector.

The Federal Government has spent millions of dollars boosting private health insurance funds arguing that privatised health care will relieve pressures on public hospital waiting lists. The 30 per cent health insurance rebate was supposed to take the burden away from the public health system.

Research conducted by Professor Stephen Duckett tested the hypothesis that increased private activity in the health system is associated with reduced waiting times using secondary analysis of hospital data for 2001–2002.[27]

He found that median waiting time is inversely related to the proportion of public patients:

> This study has confirmed the findings of previous overseas studies that increased private sector activity is associated with increased public sector waiting times, the reverse of the rhetoric supporting policies to increase support for the private sector in order to "take the burden off the public sector".[28]

Professor Duckett's findings that longer waiting times for public patients in Australia are associated with higher proportions of hospital care being provided in the private sector is consistent with other international studies.[29]

Indeed, the Federal Government's policies have probably made the waiting list situation worse as it is the specialists who move between the public and the private sector who determine what surgery will be conducted where. There are obvious financial advantages in the private hospitals for them.

There is also evidence that the Federal Government's 30 per cent private health insurance rebate is having little impact on increasing participation in private health insurance.

Research conducted by the National Centre for Social and Economic Modelling found that Federal Government initiatives such as the rebate and the lifetime

---

27   Duckett, SJ, "Private Care and Public Waiting" (2005) 29 (1) *Australian Health Review* 87.

28   Ibid, at 92.

29   Besley, T, Hall, J and Preston, I, "The Demand for Private Health Insurance: Do Waiting Lists Matter?" (1999) *Journal of Public Economics* 155; Morgan, A and Xavier, A, "Hospital Specialists' Private Practice and its Impact on the Number of NHS Patients Treated and on the Delay for Elective Surgery", Discussion Paper 01/01, Department of Economics, University of York, 2001; Iversen, T, "The Effect of a Private Sector on the Waiting Time in a National Health Service" (1997) 16 *Journal of Health Economics* 381.

health cover scheme have benefited the wealthy.[30] The rebate costs about $2.8 billion a year and is of no benefit to people who are poor.

Bare numbers do not tell the whole story about the tensions in government policy around the health funds. The Federal Government is keen to publicise increased numbers of private health care memberships. In April 2005, for example, government data indicated hospital cover membership for the over-55 age-group had risen by 24,000, however, at the same time 21,000 younger members dropped their cover. From the point of view of the funds younger members are a better risk group because they make fewer claims. Health economist John Deeble has warned that too many older members would inevitably push up premiums.[31]

John Dwyer, on behalf of the Australian Healthcare Alliance Forum, which includes 40 consumer and health care organisations, has argued that the health care systems in Australia are expensive, duplicated and dysfunctional.[32] The Forum wants the Federal Government to allow Australians a say on the kind of health system they want. At present there is increasing discrimination with health services and outcomes dictated by personal financial well-being rather than need. Moves by private health insurers to lobby government to allow them to insure members for all health care needs including GP visits rather than just hospital cover also has the potential to discriminate in favour of those who are more affluent.

Fraud and over-servicing

At the Commonwealth-level the body responsible for controlling fraud arising from health care is the Health Insurance Commission (HIC). There are also State and Territory bodies including the registration boards and the criminal law. The HIC was established by the *Health Insurance Commission Act 1973* (Cth) and commenced its work in 1975. The HIC is responsible primarily for processing payments under the Medicare and the Pharmaceutical Benefits Scheme. The HIC has a Professional Review Division (PRD), which is responsible for ensuring Commonwealth money is paid appropriately. The *Health Insurance Act 1973* and Regulations instruct the HIC to devise and implement measures intended to prevent the rendering of inappropriate services and control the cost of such services. The HIC is also responsible for detecting claims for payments that constitute offences. It also provides information to practitioners.[33]

---

30   Walker, A et al, "Public Policy and Private Health Insurance: Distributional Impact on Public and Private Hospital Usage in New South Wales", National Centre for Social and Economic Modelling, Online Conference Paper – CP2003_017, December 2003, <www.natsem.canberra.edu.au>.

31   Wroe, D, "Health Fund Dilemma as Aged Join Up", *The Age*, 17 May 2005, p 3.

32   Dwyer, J, "Let the People Decide on Health Reforms" *The Australian*, 21 June 2005, p 11.

33   Brandt, P, "Fraud control by the Health Insurance Commission: A multifaceted approach", in Smith, RG, *Health Care, Crime and Regulatory Control*, Hawkins Press, Sydney, 1998, pp 179-189.

A device used by the PRD to reduce over-servicing is feedback letters. Twice yearly the letters are posted to optometrical and medical practitioners. The letters contain a history of the number of services provided and give a comparison with peers. The HIC claims these letters have proved effective in reducing the number of services provided. The HIC also publishes information in various journals in relation to the use of item numbers, runs a fraud awareness program and provides counselling, conducts audits and investigates.

The HIC is responsible for paying doctors through Medicare for services provided to patients. Their practice with regard to corporatised medical services has been to send cheques directly to the owner of a practice in bulk. The owner then decides how to pay the doctors. Objections to this are that the HIC should be paying the doctor who performed the service rather than the practice-owner as this gives too much power to the owner.

Health complaint commissioners

Each State and Territory of Australia has a Health Complaints Commissioner to receive and resolve complaints from consumers of health services about health service providers. South Australia is the most recent State to establish a Health Complaints Commissioner with the passing of the *Health and Community Services Complaints Act 2004* (SA). The commissioners have jurisdiction to receive complaints from the private and public sectors and can deal with complaints about anyone who holds themselves out as offering health services, whether registered or not, and including organisations as well as individuals. The commissioners place a strong emphasis on conciliation and quality improvement rather than allocation of blame.[34] Conciliation is an alternative to litigation and can also deal with complaints that would not be relevant to court processes.

Complaints to the Commissioners include those concerning the practices of corporatised health services. These usually involve failure to provide informed financial consent, faulty or ineffective products such as spectacles, billing practices and communication failures. The complaints are usually resolved through negotiation, which is the same way that complaints are resolved in the more traditional practices. Where a company is responsible for numerous complaints a formal investigation can be conducted and the provider can be named publicly. In Victoria, the commissioner has expressed concerns over some "repeat offenders" and may conduct a formal investigation into their practices if their complaints procedures are not improved and complaints continue to be lodged. The Commissioners can also work in conjunction with the Australian Competition and Consumer Commission (ACCC) and State-based consumer affairs agencies.

---

34 Lapsley, H, "Quality Measures in Australian Health Care" in Bloom, A (ed), *Health Reform in Australia and New Zealand*, Oxford University Press, Melbourne, 2000. Wilson, B, Jackson, K and Punshon, T, "Conciliation" in Smith, R, *Health Care, Crime and Regulatory Control*, Hawkins Press, Sydney, 1998, pp 59-71.

Registration boards

The task of regulating registered health professionals is largely delegated to the State- and Territory-based registration boards.[35] In Victoria, for example, there are 12 registration boards regulating doctors, psychologists, nurses, Chinese medicine, optometrists, chiropractors, physiotherapists, radiologists, dentists, podiatrists and pharmacists. As well as registering practitioners, they set standards, conduct investigations and have powers to suspend, place conditions on registration, impose penalties and de-register those found guilty of unprofessional conduct. The boards, in common with the health complaint commissioners, are largely reactive in responding to complaints.

Historically, a major pre-occupation of registration boards was to eliminate "quackery" but as more and more consumers choose to use alternative or complementary medicines this has become less of a focus. Boards also had a significant role in regulating advertising and eliminating professional self-promotion. The advertising role has now been reduced to comply with the *Trade Practices Act 1974* (Cth) using the formula of false and misleading advertising. Competition policy poses a significant challenge to the registration system. Controlled federally, National Competition Policy reviews all legislation that restricts competition, licences certain activities, creates barriers to entry to an occupation or places restrictions on occupations. The registration system would be in breach of competition policy were it not for the arguments that competition policy prevails unless there is significant risk to public health and safety. Reviews of registration board legislation have been conducted and the boards have survived but there is no guarantee this will always be so or that their membership or powers may not vary.

Restricting the ownership of health "businesses" is per se anti-competitive. Dix has argued that the registration boards have had difficulties dealing with corporatised practices because they are accustomed to handling complaints about individuals rather than dealing with health professionals who shelter behind the corporate veil.[36] The health providers, it is said, are not able to influence marketing decisions of the proprietors and are under pressure to make referrals to particular related services and limit appointment times. Interference with clinical decision-making is also a concern. While the corporate health services argue that they do not do place pressure on their contracted doctors or employees and that trade practices laws are sufficient, others disagree. Many doctors have indicated dissatisfaction with working in the corporatised services and have indicated anecdotally that they will not be renewing their contracts when they expire.

---

35   Dix, A, "Disciplinary Regulation", in Smith, RG (ed), *Health Care, Crime and Regulatory Control*, Hawkins, Sydney, 1998, pp 48-58.

36   Ibid, p 56.

Some registration boards have been granted additional powers to include corporate offence provisions to regulate employers. In Victoria the legislation regulating pharmacists took a broader approach, which may well become a model provision for all other boards. It introduces the concept of an offence for directing or inciting unprofessional conduct. Section 93(1) of the *Pharmacy Practice Act 2004* (Vic) states that: "a person must not direct or incite a registered pharmacist to do any thing, in the course of providing pharmacy services, that would constitute unprofessional conduct". Section 94 of the Act empowers the Secretary of the Department of Human Services to prohibit convicted offenders from carrying on or owning pharmacy businesses.

In South Australia, a family of pharmacists can own up to 49 per cent of a pharmacy business. This option is being considered in Queensland and Tasmania. Otherwise, only pharmacists can have a proprietary interest – either solely, in partnership or in a company where the directors and shareholders are pharmacists and pharmacies have to be at least 1.5 kilometres apart. Friendly Societies are an exception. Some doctors' organisations have been campaigning against the "monopoly" enjoyed by pharmacists in trade journals like *Australian Doctor*. Ultimately dollars will prevail and Tony Abbott has insisted that under a $11.5 billion agreement negotiated with the Pharmacy Guild of Australia the location rules must be eased to ensure better access for consumers. He has also taken into account the problem for consumers in small country towns where current restrictions limit the number of pharmacies to one. Other proposals such as negative licensing are under consideration in some jurisdictions.[37]

Advertising

The corporatisation of health services has meant a much greater emphasis on advertising. Since 1975 there have been changes in laws throughout Australia to relax the previous restrictions on advertising. Such an approach is new to many health services and professionals.[38] At the federal level advertising is controlled by the *Trade Practices Act 1974* (Cth) which is administered by the ACCC.

The State and Territory fair trading laws and the registration boards also play a role. The *Trade Practices Act 1974* (Cth) is intended to prevent anti-competitive conduct to encourage competition and lead to greater choice for consumers. The Act contains a general prohibition on false and misleading or deceptive conduct, and false or misleading representations. The Act also covers advertising and promotion of medical services and products.

The ACCC has taken action against corporatised health services including the ON Clinic and Advanced Medical Institute, which provide services for

---

37   See, for example, *Review of Regulation of the Health Professions in Victoria: Options for Structural and Legislative Reform*, Department of Human Services, April 2005.

38   Advertising Medical Services – In Whose Interests? A joint conference of the ACCC and the HCCC, Thursday 14 October 1999, Sydney.

impotency. These companies have been ordered to place corrective advertise-ments and provide injunctive relief to consumers. Nonetheless such services continue to be advertised strongly and complaints to the health complaint commissioners continue to be made. In the area of impotency clinics the most common complaints are aggressive sales tactics, excessive costs and inadequacy of treatment. It would not be at all surprising if many legitimate complaints are never made formally because of the embarrassment experienced by the person who might otherwise seek to follow up a genuine grievance.

Other health services that have attracted the attention of the ACCC (and the health complaints commissioners) are hair removal, laser eye surgery, "miracle cures" and weight-loss treatments.[39] Again these services are usually corporatised, use strong advertising and are often not owned by registered health professionals. The ACCC has been opposed to the introduction of any new State-based regulation of advertising by health practitioners but recognises that the responsibility for ensuring advertising of health and medical services is honest, accurate and complete, will be a shared responsibility between practi-tioners, professional associations, State and Federal health departments and State and Federal regulators.[40]

In Victoria and New South Wales, stronger powers to regulate advertising of certain health services, including cosmetic procedures, were opposed by the ACCC. Proponents of State-based advertising regulation see the ACCC processes as being too legalistic, expensive and slow. They point to the deluge of propaganda from the advertising industry, particularly with cosmetic procedures including before and after shots of dubious integrity. In response to a recent review of registration boards in Victoria, respondents supported boards retaining their current powers to regulate advertising.[41] Some wanted breaches of advertising controls to be prima facie evidence of unprofessional conduct. There was also general support for a single set of guidelines, providing they did not undermine current controls by conforming to a "lowest common denominator".[42]

In New South Wales, s 10AB of the *Public Health Act 1991* contains powers to regulate advertising of health services regardless of whether the services are delivered by a registered practitioner. The Department of Human Services con-siders the template provisions in ss 101–103 of the *Pharmacy Practice Act 2004* (Vic) are sufficient to allow boards to regulate advertising by registered practitioners and by the corporations employing them.[43] The department also considers there is

---

39   Asher, A, "Advertising medical services – In Whose Interests?" Opening Address. Advertising Medical Services – in whose interests? A joint conference of the ACCC and the HCCC, 14 October 1999, Sydney.

40   Ibid, at 7.

41   *Review of Regulation of the Health Professions in Victoria: Options for Structural and Legislative Reform*, Department of Human Services, April 2005, p 20.

42   Ibid, at 20.

43   Ibid.

scope to revisit the need for powers to regulate advertising of health services by unregistered health providers and agencies in addition to the provisions of the *Fair Trading Act 1999* (Vic) and the *Trade Practices Act 1974* (Cth).[44] Clearly, if there is to be regulation it should be consistent across all the registration boards. The most likely form this will take is giving the boards powers to make guidelines setting minimum standards and promoting best practice.

Cosmetic procedures

In this chapter the term "cosmetic surgery" has been deliberately altered to "cosmetic procedures" to include risks associated with all cosmetic procedures whether surgical or not. The complaints commissioners continue to receive complaints from consumers who have been injured or disfigured as a result of cosmetic procedures. They are heavily advertised, the advertising is often misleading, there is no way to validate before and after shots, and advertising promises all kinds of miracle outcomes while not mentioning the substantial risks involved. There are also problems associated with failure to obtain informed consent and informed financial consent and failure to assess adequately and screen suitable patients.

Some legislative changes have resulted from the New South Wales inquiry into cosmetic surgery in 1999[45] and, in Victoria, legislation was strengthened from 2002–2003.[46] Changes include stronger powers for the Medical Practitioners Board to address sub-standard practices through performance assessment and review, and strengthened regulations for day-procedure centres including restrictions on certain procedures being carried out in unregulated clinics or premises. The Department of Human Services has indicated it considers there is scope for further reform by:

- amending legislation to ensure laser eye surgery and other risky and intrusive cosmetic procedures such as complex liposuction are included in the definition of day-procedure centres; and

- amendment of regulations to include private practitioners and hospitals who perform certain procedures even where those procedures are not a major activity to ensure health practitioner legislation includes powers to require that advertising of certain specified risky and intrusive procedures carry warning labels approved by the Minister for Health.

From 2007, the Medical Practitioners Board of Victoria will be able to issue ministerially-approved guidelines about matters such as cosmetic procedures to ensure advertising is not false or misleading and does not encourage an

44   Ibid.
45   Committee of Inquiry into Cosmetic Surgery, *Cosmetic Surgery Report*, Report to the NSW Minister for Health, Health Care Complaints Commission, 1999.
46   *Medical Practice Act 1994* (Vic).

unreasonable expectation of beneficial treatment. Other options will be to mandate that:

- consumers have a cooling-off period and counselling for specified risky and intrusive procedures;
- balanced written information be provided on risks;
- interpreters be made available, where necessary, so information can be given in the patient's preferred language; and
- an anaesthetist be available on premises for specified procedures.

The Health Services Commissioner supports these initiatives but there may be some opposition from the ACCC.

Ultimately, these kinds of entrepreneurial ventures will be driven by financial considerations. So long as consumers are prepared to seek these services and pay for them at rates that are profitable for doctors or business people they will continue to prosper. An important control is the role played by the medical indemnity funds. Increasingly they are telling their doctors that they must pay higher premiums if they want to perform these risky procedures and for those doctors against whom multiple claims are made the insurers are capping payments or refusing to cover doctors for amounts up to, for example, $10,000.

Pharmacies and prescribing rights

In the United States pharmacy advertisements are ubiquitous, particularly on television and are referred to as direct-to-consumer advertising and are claimed as a First Amendment constitutional right. There has been some pressure to have similar advertising in Australia but this has so far been resisted. Doctors have raised concerns that consumers, seeing the advertisements, may demand prescriptions for particular brands from their doctors.

A recent United States study of doctors' prescribing behaviours has revealed that the advertisements do have a strong influence on prescribing.[47] The study involved actors who were trained to pose as patients with psychological problems and the research encompassed three cities. Patients who demanded particular drugs by name were much more likely to have them prescribed. Kravitz, the researcher, concluded, "I guess our ultimate judgment is that there's enough evidence of potential harm that there's got to be a better way to get messages about prescription drugs out to consumers and we feel very strongly about that".[48]

---

47 Kravitz, R et al, "Influence of patients' requests for direct-to-consumer advertised antidepressants" (2005) 293 (16) *JAMA* 1995; Hollon, MF, "Direct-to-consumer Advertising. A Haphazard Approach to Health Promotion", Editorial (2005) 293 (16) *JAMA* 2030.
48 *Health Report*, ABC Radio National, 23 May 2005.

Currently, prescribing rights for pharmaceuticals are enjoyed only by medical practitioners, nurse practitioners, dentists, optometrists and (in Victoria) practitioners of traditional Chinese medicine. The nature and scope of prescribing rights vary amongst the States and Territories and are inconsistent. Doctors have strongly opposed any extensions to prescribing rights and stakeholders have given mixed responses to proposals to streamline processes for adding new drugs to or changes to approval processes for drugs being added to the lists of prescription drugs.[49]

These issues need to be determined taking into account public health and safety considerations. We know that the potential for medication error in contemporary health settings is significant.[50] It has been estimated to cost about $350 million per year in Australia and medication errors are usually systems based.[51]

Policies and regulation around extending prescribing rights to more professions need to be based on considerations of whether or not those professions can demonstrate adequate training and mechanisms to ensure the public are protected. In Victoria the Department of Human Services has supported the extension of prescribing rights from lists of approved drugs to suitably trained podiatrists and optometrists. This will require relevant legislative amendments to the *Podiatrists Registration Act 1997* (Vic) and the *Optometrists Registration Act 1996*.[52] The extension of prescribing rights to more professions will make ownership of these health services more attractive to the corporate sector, in particular pharmacies.

The dispensing of most prescription pharmaceuticals has long been the preserve of registered pharmacists. In recent years there has been a strong push from some doctors' associations and supermarkets to have these restrictions lifted. Woolworth's claimed in May 2005 that lifting of the restrictions would ensure consumers have access to cheaper drugs at more accessible outlets. Pharmacy groups have responded by arguing the moves are not in the interest of consumer safety because the controls and standards imposed by pharmacy registration boards will not apply to supermarkets and will lead to the demise of the local pharmacy. Tony Abbott has been lobbied strongly by the Pharmacy Guild of Australia not to allow supermarkets to dispense pharmaceuticals and so far this lobbying has been successful. Notably, pharmaceuticals are available in supermarkets in the United States, Britain, Canada, New Zealand and most of Europe.

---

49 *Review of Regulation of the Health Professions in Victoria: Options for Structural and Legislative Reform*, Department of Human Services, April 2005, p 22.

50 Health Services Commissioner, Victoria, *Inquiry Into the Royal Melbourne Hospital*, 2001, p 31.

51 Australian Council for Safety and Quality in Health Care, *Improving Medication Safety; Report of a Medication Safety Workshop*, July 2001. Australian Council for Safety and Quality in Health Care, *Second National Report on Patient Safety Improving Medication Safety*, ACT, July 2002.

52 *Review of Regulation of the Health Professions in Victoria: Options for Structural and Legislative Reform*, Department of Human Services, Melbourne, April 2005, p 22.

Conclusions

Corporatised medicine has brought with it some conveniences for doctors in the form of administrative support and shared responsibilities. It has done the same for consumers. However, we have still failed to face up to the many challenges posed by a radically different approach to health services. The profit motivation is nearly always stronger than concerns of individual consumers and the analogy of a tug-of-war with 20 strong adults on the right and 10 small children on the left is pertinent.

Current approaches have tended to be piecemeal and ad hoc with policies developing in response to media attention. Clearly there needs to be much more genuine consultation with consumers and less reliance on powerful lobby groups. There will never be one or two simple answers but a raft of solutions will need to be in place. These include consultation, clear policies, public education, some controls on advertising, powers to regulate employers of health services and some national consistency.

This story is about money and the solutions will also be financial. We will need to find ways of introducing clear policies that do not provide financial rewards for poor or unethical practices but instead, have rewards for ethical practices that are in the public interest. The complexities involved mean that there are no easy answers and the Federal Government, in consultation with the States and Territories, needs first of all to determine what Australians want from their health system. This is an approach being promoted by the Australian Health Care Forum, which is a coalition of 40 consumer and medical groups. Once there is a clear direction policies should be measured against the objectives agreed upon. Without this our health care services, providers and users will be dominated by money-making incentives and conflicts of interest will continue to escalate.

26

Vulnerability in research

George F Tomossy[1]

Human experimentation has had a troubled history. Progress in biomedicine, while laudable in terms of achievements in advancing knowledge and enhancing the quality and length of human lives, has nevertheless incurred a human cost that has all too often been borne by the most vulnerable members of society. With the exception of the more heinous examples, the exploitation of vulnerable subjects has generally occurred most often out of convenience than because of truly sinister motives. Nevertheless, even a cursory survey of the history of human experimentation reveals an extensive record of abuse.

The political response to research scandals has invariably been a call for accountability – a call for external oversight of research activities. Aspects of this response are deserving of criticism, such as the implications of increasing bureaucratisation in the process of ethics review and the corresponding impact on research practices.[2] Nevertheless, the call for accountability is an appropriate driver for the development of research governance frameworks insofar as it recognises the inherent vulnerability of human subjects to exploitation. The aim here is thus to establish why human subjects are vulnerable and in need of protection.

"Vulnerability" is developed initially by reference to the historical record of abuses of human subjects, but is then conceived more broadly to extend beyond the "classic" vulnerable populations to encompass all subjects. It is argued that vulnerability arises not only from the power imbalance inherent in the relationship between subject and investigator, irrespective of the safeguard of informed consent, but that subjects are ultimately vulnerable to the shortfalls of regulatory systems that would attempt to compensate for this power imbalance.

---

1   Lecturer, Division of Law, Macquarie University. The author is grateful to Prof Terry Carney for his feedback on earlier drafts of this chapter.

2   See, for example, Chalmers, D, and Pettit, P, "Towards a Consensual Culture in the Ethical Review of Research. Australian Health Ethics Committee" (1998) 168 *Medical Journal of Australia* 79, who raised a number of concerns about the regulatory implications of what they referred to as the "controversy machine"; Moreno, JD, "Goodbye to All That. The End of Moderate Protectionism in Human Subjects Research" (2001) 31 *Hastings Center Report* 9, who cautioned against the rise of "strong protectionism"; and Michels, R, "Are Research Ethics Bad for our Mental Health?" (1999) 340 *New England Journal of Medicine* 1427, on the disincentive of bureaucratisation for the instilment of ethical practices among researchers.

Globalisation and corporatisation are presented as significant forces that have expanded the scope of vulnerability of human subjects in the modern research endeavour.

In conclusion, I argue in this chapter that the law needs to respond to the problems posed by the commercialisation of research, and that this is the most significant current dilemma facing research ethics governance in Australia.

The classic vulnerable populations

A number of vulnerable populations – prisoners, children, the terminally ill, the poor and persons with cognitive impairments – have featured prominently as subjects in research. For example, it has been noted that criminals were used for experimental purposes by the Ptolemites in ancient times.[3] Whether or not worms could develop in human intestines after death was a question of interest to a French physician in the late 19th century, who tested his hypothesis by feeding larva-infested sausages to a woman before her execution.[4] In the early 20th century, condemned Philippine convicts were used to study beriberi in exchange for cigarettes and cigars. Some of the convicts died during the experiment.[5] Prisoners also served extensively as subjects in the United States following the Second World War,[6] with Philadelphia's Holmesburg Prison providing "acres of skin" for dermatological studies on a broad range of products by industry and the military from the early 1950s through to the mid-1970s.[7]

Classic experiments involving children include the development of the smallpox vaccine, which began with Edward Jenner's inoculation of his son in 1789 and was subsequently repeated by others in Europe and the United States.[8] Orphans have often served as subjects, including a 1911 study that involved the injection of an experimental substance into several hundred residents of an orphanage in New York to test its use as an indicator for syphilis[9] and a 1939

---

3   Katz, J, "The Education of the Physician-Investigator" (1969) 98 *Daedalus* 480 at 481; Beecher, HK *Research and the Individual: Human Studies*, Little, Brown, Boston, 1970, p 5.

4   Lederer, SE *Subjected to Science: Human Experimentation in America Before the Second World War*, Johns Hopkins University Press, Baltimore, 1995, p 12.

5   Lasagna, L, "Special Subjects in Human Experimentation", in Freund, PA (ed) *Experimentation with Human Subjects*, Allen & Unwin, London, 1969, p 262.

6   Advisory Committee on Human Radiation Experiments (ACHRE), *Final Report of the Advisory Committee on Human Radiation Experiments*, Oxford University Press, New York, 1996, pp 421–453.

7   Hornblum, AM *Acres of Skin: Human Experiments at Holmesburg Prison*, Routledge, New York, 1998.

8   Baxby, D *Jenner's Smallpox Vaccine: The Riddle of Vaccinia Virus and Its Origin*, Heinemann Educational Books, London, 1981; Rothman, DJ *Strangers at the Bedside: A History of How Law and Bioethics Transformed Medical Decision Making*, Basic Books, New York, 1991, pp 20–21.

9   Rothman, DJ, "The Nuremberg Code in Light of Previous Principles and Practices in Human Experimentation", in Tröhler, U and Reiter-Theil, S (eds) *Ethics Codes in Medicine: Foundations and Achievements of Codification Since 1947*, Ashgate, Aldershot, 1998, p 56.

experiment that induced orphans at a state facility in Iowa to stutter.[10] The Willowbrook Hepatitis Study, which involved deliberate exposure to the live hepatitis virus from 1955 to the early 1970s, and the Fernald School Radioisotope Study, which traced the effects of ingested radioisotopes from the late 1940s to early 1950s, are probably the two most publicised cases involving mentally retarded children in state facilities.[11]

The institutionalised mentally ill or disabled have also long provided a readily available source of subjects in a controlled environment. Sharav reports a number of experiments including one in 1943 that studied the use of "refrigeration therapy" on mental disease that placed "mental defectives" in refrigerated cabinets at sub-freezing temperatures for up to 120 hours.[12] And an experiment in 1963 by the Sloan-Kettering Institute for Cancer Research involving the injection of live cancer cells into patients at the Jewish Chronic Disease Hospital in New York was a highly publicised instance of exploitation of vulnerable persons in an institutional setting[13] – one which incidentally helped to spur the first stage of reforms in National Institutes of Health and Food and Drug Administration (FDA) in the late 1960s.[14] Many of the elderly patients in that study were demented, non-English speaking or very deaf.[15]

Persons in hierarchical relationships, including medical students or interns, employees and particularly military personnel, have also been susceptible to coercive recruitment.

The Advisory Committee on Human Radiation Experiments (ACHRE) thoroughly documented unethical Cold War radiation research conducted in the United States in both civilian and military contexts from 1944 to 1974.[16]

---

10 Dyer, J, "University Issues Apology for 1939 Experiment That Induced Orphans to Stutter", *San Jose Mercury News*, 14 June 2001; Reynolds, G, "The Stuttering Doctor's 'Monster Study'", *New York Times*, 16 March 2003.

11 Nelson, RM, "Children As Research Subjects", in Kahn, JP, Mastroianni, AC, and Sugarman, J (eds) *Beyond consent: Seeking justice in research*, Oxford University Press, New York, 1998, pp 49–52; Rothman, DJ and Rothman, SM, *The Willowbrook Wars*, Harper & Row, New York, 1984; ACHRE (1996) op cit, pp 342–346; Lederer, SE and Grodin, MA, "Historical Overview": Pediatric Experimentation", in Grodin, MA and Glantz, LH (eds) *Children as research subjects: Science, Ethics, and Law*, Oxford University Press, New York, 1994; West, D, "Radiation Experiments on Children at the Fernald and Wrentham Schools: Lessons for Protocols in Human Subject Research" (1998) 6 *Accountability in Research* 103.

12 Sharav, VH, "The Ethics of Conducting Psychosis-Inducing Experiments" (1999) 7 *Accountability in Research* 137.

13 This case was the 17th example in the landmark review by Beecher, HK, "Ethics and Clinical Research" (1966) 274 *New England Journal of Medicine* 1354 at 1358, referring to a study reviewed by Langer, E, "Human Experimentation: Cancer Studies at Sloan Kettering Stir Public Debate on Medical Ethics" (1964) 143 *Science* 551. See also, Katz, J, Capron, AM, and Glass, ES *Experimentation with Human Beings: The Authority of the Investigator, Subject, Professions, and State in the Human Experimentation Process*, Russell Sage Foundation, New York, 1972, pp 9–65, who presented the Sloan-Kettering experiment as a case study.

14 Rothman (1998) op cit, pp 87–94.

15 Langer (1964) op cit.

16 ACHRE (1996) op cit, pp 227–668.

International examples include chemical warfare experiments that took place in Australia during the Second World War,[17] as well as experiments involving servicemen in the United Kingdom that continued up to the 1980s at Porton Down.[18]

The poor have likewise not gone unnoticed by investigators as a source of compliant subjects. The Tuskegee Syphilis Study involved poor illiterate black men in the State of Alabama from 1932 to 1972 when it was terminated after an official in the Public Health Service revealed his concerns to the media.[19] A further example of the exploitation of "lower class people" can be found in a study conducted at the National Women's Hospital in Auckland, New Zealand, where effective treatment was withheld from a number of women with cervical carcinoma in situ that subsequently developed into invasive cancer.[20]

The examples presented above draw from an unfortunately lengthy catalogue of unethical research involving the classically vulnerable populations. The response to the litany of historical examples is likewise extensive, with ethical safeguards to protect vulnerable populations advocated by an ever-expanding body of research ethics scholarship. The bulk of these safeguards relate to facilitating decision-making ability, including through the requirement of assent where consent is unobtainable, delimiting the scope of surrogate consent and restricting the nature of permissible research, such as to conditions or illnesses affecting the population under study or to within acceptable levels of risk. Most of these concepts are solidly entrenched in official policies, both at the national and international levels.[21]

---

17   Goodwin, B, *Keen As Mustard: Britain's Horrific Chemical Warfare Experiments in Australia*, University of Queensland Press, St Lucia, Queensland, 1998.

18   Tests of chemical agents on servicemen were reported by the British Broadcasting Corporation between 1999 and 2001, including "Porton Down Probe Launched", 30 July 2001, <http://news.bbc.co.uk/1/hi/uk/1463993.stm> (accessed 6 November 2005). A second coroner's inquest, with a jury to provide greater transparency, was held. See "Porton Down Inquest Opens", 5 May 2004, <http://news.bbc.co.uk/1/hi/england/wiltshire/3686483.stm> (accessed 6 November 2005). That jury returned a verdict of unlawful killing of a young Royal Air Force engineer in 1953 in nerve gas experiments, <www.dailymail.co.uk/pages/live/articles/news/news.html?in_article_id=326246&in_page_id=1770> (accessed 4 January 2006).

19   Jones, JH and Tuskegee Institute, *Bad Blood: The Tuskegee Syphilis Experiment*, Free Press, New York, 1993.

20   New Zealand Committee *Report of the Committee of Inquiry into Allegations Concerning the Treatment of Cervical Cancer at National Women's Hospital and into Other Related Matters*, The Committee, Auckland, 1988; Coney, S *The Unfortunate Experiment*, Penguin, Auckland, 1988; McNeill, PM, "The Implications for Australia of the New Zealand Report of the Cervical Cancer Inquiry: No Cause for Complacency" (1989) 150 *Medical Journal of Australia* 264 at 271.

21   Weisstub, DN, Arboleda-Florez, J, and Tomossy, GF, "Establishing the Boundaries of Ethically Permissible Research With Vulnerable Populations", in Weisstub, DN (ed) *Research on Human Subjects: Ethics, Law, and Social Policy*, Pergamon, Oxford, United Kingdom, 1998.

Responding to the past

As Jay Katz, noted, "We have judged the past and judgments of the past become most relevant when they teach us lessons for the present and future".[22] An examination of the history of abuses in research thus yields a number of "vulnerable populations" that have provided the basis for the evolution of a range of regulatory safeguards. Invoking the past for the purpose of advocating reforms in the present, however, is not without problems. Perhaps past violations should simply be discounted as anomalies? Alternatively, is it legitimate to make retrospective judgments of wrong-doing when both the nature of research and clinical practice has changed so much over the past several decades? If these concerns are valid, then it might seem trite to offer examples of misconduct from the past in an effort to promote subjects' rights in the present. Neither reservation, however, is borne out. The litany of documented examples of misadventures in research is not a collection of random idiosyncratic events; rather, it is submitted that the examples reported to date are but a subset of a much larger collection of incidents that remain unreported or undetected. Moreover, the values against which past conduct has been judged should not be weakened by claims of ethical relativism. Even in the absence of explicit guidelines of conduct, fundamental rights of subjects have always existed.

In defence of retrospective judgment

When judgments are made in relation to events that occurred many years in the past, it raises a profound controversy relating to the universality of ethical principles. The dispute lies with the claim that ethical standards are fluid, varying with both time and place. Benedek and Erlen, for example, recently challenged the level of infamy ascribed to the Tuskegee Syphilis Study along such lines, arguing the point that the legal doctrine of informed consent was absent in medical ethics when the study was conceived.[23] On the other hand, the challenge of ethical relativism has been staunchly refuted, including notably by Macklin, a steadfast proponent of the universality of ethical principles in research.[24]

---

22 ACHRE (1996) op cit, p 856.

23 Benedek, TG, and Erlen, J, "The Scientific Environment of the Tuskegee Study of Syphilis, 1920–1960" (1999) 43 *Perspectives in Biology & Medicine* 1 at 23–24; citing: Wallace, ER, "Relevance Without Presentism: 'Mental illness and American society, 1875–1940' By Gerald Grob. Essay review" (1984) 39 *Journal of the History of Medicine & Allied Sciences* 374; and Pressman, JD, "Psychiatry and its Origins" (1997) 71 *Bulletin of the History of Medicine* 129. Benedek and Erlen cautioned against what they described as "a particularly insidious pitfall in historical interpretation, namely 'presentism', the consideration of past behaviour in terms of modern knowledge and concepts".

24 See Macklin, R, "Universality of the Nuremberg Code", in Annas, GJ and Grodin, MA (eds) *The Nazi doctors and the Nuremberg Code: Human Rights in Human Experimentation*, Oxford University Press, New York, 1992, pp 246–248, on how the doctrine of ethical relativism was invoked (unsuccessfully) in the Nuremberg Doctors' Trial, where it was claimed that purported standards in the United States should have no bearing on the determination of culpability of the Nazi physicians. See also Macklin, R, *Against Relativism: Cultural Diversity and the Search for Ethical Universals in Medicine*, Oxford University Press, New York, 1999.

A significant inquiry into the issue of retrospective judgment and support for the universality of ethical principles in research emerged from the deliberations of ACHRE.[25] Despite some reservations, the committee concluded that ethical inquiry into past conduct is both possible and appropriate. A compromise position resulted in an ethical framework that distinguished between the wrongness of actions and culpability of agents. In other words, a determination of the wrongness of a past act would not necessarily lead to the conclusion that the person who committed it is blameworthy.

Various principles (such as informed consent) were deemed to be universal and not time-bound, thus making retrospective judgment possible. However, factors such as a lack of evidence, an inability to provide a defence for one's actions, cultural variables and conflicting obligations could serve to mitigate culpability even where the underlying act was found to be "wrong".[26] While individual attribution of culpability was not forthcoming from the ACHRE report, this should not diminish its significance as it demonstrated that certain moral principles *are* universal and that retrospective judgment *is* possible.

Beauchamp steadfastly defends the value of the ACHRE report and universality of ethical principles referred to therein.[27] He praised ACHRE for being "decisive beyond what might reasonably have been anticipated in light of its broad and diverse mission".[28]

Nevertheless, he found the committee's treatment of the matters of culpability and possible exculpation to be somewhat lacking, thus compromising the essential objectives of achieving future deterrence and providing justice for wronged individuals. The committee *did* make findings of blameworthiness in a general sense, even to the level of stating that "government officials and investigators are blameworthy for not having had policies and practices in place to protect the rights and interests of human subjects";[29] but it failed to do so in the case of individuals, even where, as Beauchamp argued, the violation of basic principles could not but lead to determinations of inexcusable culpability.

The debate surrounding retrospective moral judgment has been treated extensively in research ethics scholarship and is addressed only summarily

---

25 Buchanan, A, "The Controversy Over Retrospective Moral Judgment" (1996) 6 *Kennedy Institute of Ethics Journal* 245.

26 ACHRE (1996) op cit.

27 Beauchamp, TL, "The Mettle of Moral Fundamentalism: A Reply to Robert Baker" (1998) 8 *Kennedy Institute of Ethics Journal* 389.

28 Beauchamp, TL, "Looking Back and Judging our Predecessors" (1996) 6 *Kennedy Institute of Ethics Journal* 251.

29 See ACHRE (1996) op cit, pp 788–789, finding 11c. That ACHRE ascribed general blame to government officials and investigators for their failure to prevent human rights violations in the first place is significant as it underlined the impact of *systemic* failures in human subject protection. These failures included lapses by regulatory authorities in particular, but also reflected the blind faith placed in professional elites to exercise unencumbered discretion. Both of these observations resonate with arguments in support of legal controls in research regulation insofar as it questions the reliability of self-regulation and the need for effective governmental oversight of research activities.

here.[30] Like the ACHRE, the principal aim here is not to ascribe guilt, but rather to elucidate those systemic failures that contribute to the exploitation of human subjects. Support is thus given here to proponents of the universality of ethical principles and validity of retrospective moral judgment for identifying shortfalls in regulatory frameworks and in the nature of the research exchange.

How widespread is unethical research?

One might reasonably assume that unethical conduct is characteristic of only a minority of investigators. Nevertheless, it is submitted that documented cases cannot be discounted as anomalies because, simply put, the number of ethical violations very likely exceeds those that have actually been reported. Recent experience in research ethics scholarship supports this conclusion.

For example, in relation to research in the United States between the two World Wars, McNeill expressed his surprise[31] at Rothman's comment that unethical experiments were "highly exceptional".[32] McNeill acknowledged that experiments involving human subjects were being conducted "on a relatively small scale", but reasoned that the relative absence of evidence of concern for subjects implied that many instances of unethical conduct probably transpired "without being remarked upon". As Lederer's comprehensive account of unethical research during those decades showed,[33] McNeill's intuition was correct. Indeed, citing the evidence provided by Lederer, Rothman later acknowledged that "the roster of non-therapeutic research on uninformed subjects [during that period] could be extended almost indefinitely".[34]

Turning to the post-war era, Beecher revealed an alarming number of published unethical studies, reporting only 22 of the 50 examples he had originally compiled for his watershed article in the *New England Journal of Medicine*.[35] Pappworth in the United Kingdom likewise prefaced in his own review: "It must be

---

30   For further reading, see the debate in the *Kennedy Institute of Ethics Journal* between Baker, R, "A Theory of International Bioethics: Multiculturalism, Postmodernism, and the Bankruptcy of Fundamentalism" (1998) 8 *Kennedy Institute of Ethics Journal* 201; Baker, R, "A Theory of International Bioethics: The Negotiable and the Non-Negotiable" (1998) 8 *Kennedy Institute of Ethics Journal* 233; Baker, R, "Negotiating International Bioethics: A Response to Tom Beauchamp and Ruth Macklin" (1998) 8 *Kennedy Institute of Ethics Journal* 423, who was critical of the findings of the ACHRE report and what he referred to as "moral fundamentalism", and Beauchamp (1998) op cit, and Macklin, R, "A Defense of Fundamental Principles and Human Rights: A Reply to Robert Baker" (1998) 8 *Kennedy Institute of Ethics Journal* 403, who defended the notion of universal ethical principles and the validity of the conclusions of the ACHRE Report.

31   McNeill, PM *The Ethics and Politics of Human Experimentation,* Cambridge University Press, Cambridge England, 1993, p 19.

32   Rothman, DJ, "Ethics and Human Experimentation. Henry Beecher Revisited" (1987) 317 *New England Journal of Medicine* 1195.

33   Lederer, SE *Subjected to Science: Human Experimentation in America Before the Second World War,* Johns Hopkins University Press, Baltimore, 1995.

34   Rothman, DJ *Strangers at the Bedside: A History of How Law and Bioethics Transformed Medical Decision Making,* Basic Books, New York, 1991, p 56.

35   Beecher, HK, "Ethics and Clinical Research" (1966) 274 *New England Journal of Medicine* 1354 at 1355.

emphasized that many experiments are never reported in medical journals, and I have good grounds for believing that they are often the worst of all".[36]

There is little reason to doubt that observations such as Pappworth's would continue to be valid in the modern era of research. The recent string of reported incidents of death, injury or questionable practices, including the well-known gene therapy experiment that caused the death of Jesse Gelsinger, reinforces this perception.[37] It is equally worth noting that some of these recent scandals highlight the threat of financial conflicts of interest, in respect of which Krimsky forcefully contends that "what we hear about is the proverbial tip of the iceberg".[38]

Shamoo similarly maintains that the number of adverse events – specifically deaths – in the course of research between 1990 and 2000 is grossly underreported. He noted that only eight deaths had been reported to the United States Office for Human Research Protections (OHRP) in the 10 years since 1990. Statistically, he argued, based on the number of suicides or attempted suicides expected in the general population and his estimate of at least seven million human subjects enrolled in research sponsored by the National Institutes (which does not even include privately funded research that exceeds recent NIH budgets), he would have placed this number anywhere from 5,000 to 51,000. Of course, not all of these would be attributable to unethical research – but his conclusions are suggestive of a tendency to under-report adverse events in the course of research. Interestingly, Shamoo also noted that a large percentage of protocols where deaths *were* actually reported to the OHRP and subsequently investigated had resulted in their termination or suspension.[39]

Fears of litigation or professional (and possibly criminal) sanction are understandably strong deterrents to forthright disclosure where unethical or illegal conduct has occurred. Indeed, reservations on the part of the research community might be understandable in light of the recent spate of law suits against leading research institutions in the United States, including some with stellar reputations as centres of innovation.[40] However, from the perspective of human subjects, the present environment where regulators are unable to provide any positive assurance about the frequency of unethical research rightly engenders concern.[41] But for the persistence of investigative journalists and advocates, many of the

---

36 Pappworth, MH, *Human Guinea Pigs: Experimentation on Man*, Routledge, London, 1967, p 5.

37 See below, note 50.

38 Krimsky, S *Science in the Private Interest: Has the Lure of Profits Corrupted Biomedical Research?*, Rowman & Littlefield, New York, 2003, p 9.

39 Shamoo, AE, "Adverse Events Reporting – The Tip of an Iceberg" (2001) 8 *Accountability in Research* 197.

40 Dembner, A, "Lawsuits Target Medical Research", *Boston Globe Online*, 12 August 2002; De Ville, K, "The role of Litigation in Human Research Accountability" (2002) 9 *Accountability in Research* 17.

41 To illustrate from the American context, the Office of Inspector-General observed in their review of FDA oversight of clinical investigators that in 1999 the FDA "investigated only 468 of nearly 14,000 clinical investigators potentially involved in clinical trials". It noted further, "The FDA could not provide the actual number of clinical investigators who submitted data in support of their applications". See Office of Inspector General, *FDA Oversight of Clinical Investigators*, 2000, p 1.

most recent (and past) misadventures in biomedical research might well have gone unnoticed.

In addition, one might reasonably intuit, as the practice of biomedical research grew in frequency, the potential for violations of subjects' rights to occur would likewise have increased.

First, the nature of the medical encounter changed as medicine evolved from its observational roots in the Hippocratic tradition to become increasingly reliant on experimentation. As various commentators have noted, human experimentation is "as old as medicine itself"[42] – "every time a physician administers a drug to a patient, he is in a sense performing an experiment".[43] However, the 20th century "has witnessed the amalgamation of bedside, hospital, and laboratory medicine into what is known as clinical research", with important scientific advances during the latter part of the 19th century doing much "to consolidate the relationship between medicine and research in the public mind".[44] As Rothman summarised, "with the new understanding of germ theory in the 1890s and the growing professionalization of medical training and research in the 1900s, the sheer amount of human experimentation increased".[45]

Secondly, through the rise of hospitals in the 18th century and increasing emphasis on their scientific utility in the late 19th century, the grouping of patients in numbers allowed for research to be carried out on a much larger scale.[46]

The institutionalisation of orphaned children, the mentally ill or disabled, and sick elderly presented convenient forums to conduct experiments, thereby contributing to the systematic exploitation of those groups. The demand for human subjects also increased as clinical research evolved into an organised activity through the 1930s and 1940s, with evidentiary demands for proof of drug effectiveness and safety from the 1950s onwards ushering in the modern era of the randomised clinical trial.[47]

Thirdly, the dramatic increase in available funds for scientific research in the post-war period led to a rapid proliferation of studies. This led Beecher to issue a warning about the combination of career pressures on young physicians when coupled with the increased availability of research funds:

---

42   Katz (1969) op cit, at 481.

43   Blumgart, HL, "The Medical Framework for Viewing the Problem of Human Experimentation", in Freund, PA (ed) *Experimentation with Human Subjects*, Allen & Unwin, London, 1969, p 44.

44   Bynum, W, "Reflections on the History of Human Experimentation", in Spicker, SF (ed) *The Use of Human Beings in Research: With Special Reference to Clinical Trials*, Kluwer Academic Publishers, Dordrecht, 1988, p 40.

45   Rothman (1998) p 24.

46   Bynum (1988) op cit, p 36; Lederer (1995) op cit, pp 6–7.

47   On the transformation of the clinical trial by "therapeutic reformers" in the 20th century, see Marks, HM *The Progress of Experiment: Science and Therapeutic Reform in the United States, 1900–1990*, Cambridge University Press, Cambridge England, 1997.

Medical schools and university hospitals are increasingly dominated by investigators. Every young man knows that he will never be promoted to a tenure post, to a professorship in a major medical school, unless he has proved himself as an investigator. If the ready availability of money for conducting research is added to this fact, one can see how great the pressures are on ambitious young physicians.[48]

Beecher went on to suggest that if the increasing ease with which research could be funded continued, it would eventually exhaust the availability of ethical investigators. Indeed, not only has availability of research funds from public sources increased, but the enormous profitability of drug innovation has spurred a dramatic increase in private sources of funding by industry. The latter development has in turn fuelled the demand for research subjects as well as the proliferation of financial conflicts of interest. Globalisation has also opened new avenues of access to subjects, an otherwise increasingly valuable commodity, in countries where ethics review and bureaucratic controls may be less onerous.

Thus, viewed through the lens of increased exposure and demand, the modern context of research presents not a lesser but rather a greater danger for human subjects. It is submitted, therefore, that historical examples, both recent and historical, cannot be simply discounted as idiosyncratic. One cannot help but worry that the frequency of ethical violations in research has in actuality increased, with harms occurring to subjects more often than the examples that have come to light thus far would suggest.

Vulnerability in the modern research enterprise

The pattern of abuses in the history of human experimentation reveals a number of vulnerable populations that rightly attract special safeguards in official policies governing research. Insofar as many of these safeguards draw upon historical experience with the classic vulnerable populations, one might question their continued relevance (and of the classic vulnerable populations, for that matter) in the modern context.

The research environment has changed significantly over recent decades. Institutional settings for the mentally ill, disabled, orphans and prisoners have improved, decreased in number or, as in the case of prisons, been banned as sources of subjects.[49] The likelihood of a recurrence of scandals such as at the Holmesburg Prison, Fernald State School or Jewish Chronic Disease Hospital would seem markedly reduced.

That said, recent media reports suggest a need for ongoing vigilance, legitimating continued concerns about vulnerable populations. For example, ethical

---

48 Beecher (1970) op cit, p 1355.
49 For example, after the mid-1970s, federal United States regulations significantly curtailed research involving prisoners: Maloney, DM *Protection of Human Research Subjects: A Practical Guide to Federal Laws and Regulations,* Plenum Press, New York, 1984, pp 347–360.

and safety issues in biomedical research were profiled most recently in a Bloomberg Special Report, "Big Pharma's Shameful Secret", in late 2005.[50] A primary concern in that case related to exploitation of economically disadvantaged immigrants as subjects in research in Canada and the United States. "The Body Snatchers", a multi-part exposé in the *Sydney Morning Herald* in 2001,[51] provides an Australian example that questioned the adequacy of the Australian regulatory framework to protect human subjects. It drew attention to the vulnerability of patients as subjects in clinical trials, referring specifically to emergency health research and financial conflicts of interest for physician-investigators. The controversy surrounding the former was subsequently debated in the *Medical Journal of Australia*.[52] The latter was equally contentious and resulted in an (unsuccessful) defamation action.[53] Financial conflicts of interest are part of the broader issue of commercialisation of research and constitute the most pressing concern facing research governance in Australia.[54] Moreno discusses research involving another vulnerable group, members of the military, including during the Gulf War.[55] The debate in the United States on easing restrictions on research involving prisoners has also been reopened.[56] An increase for research involving children can also be expected in the light of current calls to promote paediatric research.[57]

---

50 See <www.bloomberg.com/specialreport/bigpharma.html> (accessed 11 January 2006). On 8 August 2005, CBS Evening News discussed human subject safety and conflicts of interest, see <www.circare.org/media/cbseveningnews_20050816.pdf> (accessed 6 November 2005). Other prominent examples include: "Doing Harm: Research on the Mentally Ill", a four-part series in the *Boston Globe*, <www.boston.com/globe/nation/ packages/doing_harm/day1.htm> (accessed 11 May 2002); "The Body Hunters", a six-part series in the *Washington Post*, <www.washingtonpost.com/wp-dyn/world/issues/ bodyhunters/> (accessed 6 November 2005); "Uninformed Consent", a five-part series in the *Seattle Times*, <http://seattletimes. nwsource.com/uninformed_consent/> (accessed 6 November 2005); and "At Your Own Risk", cover story, *TIME Magazine*, <www.time. com/time/covers/1101020422/index.html> (accessed 6 November 2005).

51 See <http://old.smh.com.au/news/specials/natl/trials/index.html> (accessed 11 May 2002). These issues will be revisited: see below.

52 Rasmussen, HH et al, "Trial of a Trial by Media" (2001) 175 *Medical Journal of Australia* 625; Chapman, S, "Media Milking of Sacred Cows: A Heart-Stopping Tale" (2001) 175 *Medical Journal of Australia* 629; Komesaroff, P, "Clinical Research in the Emergency Setting: The Role of Ethics Committees" (2001) 175 *Medical Journal of Australia* 630; Kennedy, MC, "Clinical Trials Without Consent: Some Experiments Simply Cannot Be Done" (2002) 177 *Medical Journal of Australia* 40; "In Reply To: Rare Salami Trial Revisited" (2002) 177 *Medical Journal of Australia* 454; Rasmussen, HH, Hansen, PS, and Nelson, GC, "Rare Salami Trial Revisited" (2002) 177 *Medical Journal of Australia* 454.

53 *Beran v John Fairfax Publications Pty Ltd* [2004] NSWCA 107.

54 This will be argued in the conclusion of this chapter.

55 Moreno, JD *Undue Risk: Secret State Experiments on Humans*, Routledge, New York, 2001; see also: Annas, GJ, "Protecting Soldiers From Friendly Fire: The Consent Requirement for Using Investigational Drugs and Vaccines in Combat" (1998) 24 *American Journal of Law & Medicine* 245.

56 The Institute of Medicine is presently reviewing current restrictions in federal United States regulations on research involving prisoners. See: <www.iom.edu/project.asp?id=24594> (accessed 22 August 2005).

57 See the recent report by the Institute of Medicine, *Ethical Conduct of Clinical Research Involving Children*, National Academy Press, Washington, DC, 2004, which discusses the implications of the enactment by the United States Congress of the *Pediatric Research Equity Act 2003*, PL 108–146, which empowers the FDA to require paediatric studies of drugs and biological products.

In terms of litigation, a few cases have recently come before United States courts pertaining to vulnerable populations. The first example was a study conducted by the Kennedy Krieger Institute, an affiliate of Johns Hopkins University, which explored the effectiveness of different levels of lead abatement in low-income housing in Baltimore on lead uptake in young children. The case attracted a great deal of controversy.[58] Landlords participating in the study were allegedly encouraged or required to rent their properties to families with young children. An action in negligence brought by the families had been ordered back to trial in August 2001 by the Maryland Court of Appeal, overturning an earlier summary judgment in favour of the defendants. It also delivered a scathing indictment of the research protocol. The matter was subsequently settled out of court.

Internationally, a clinical trial conducted by Pfizer, a leading transnational pharmaceutical company based in the United States, of a prospective treatment for meningitis involving Nigerian children was also the subject of recent litigation. In early 1996, epidemics of bacterial meningitis and cholera broke out in northern Nigeria. Pfizer conducted a clinical trial to test the efficacy of its broad-spectrum antibiotic, Trovan,[59] as an oral treatment for meningitis in children. It was alleged by the plaintiffs that a number of child subjects died or sustained permanent disabilities, such as paralysis, deafness or blindness, as a result of participation in the trial. The trial, initiated in 2001, was finally dismissed by the United States District Court in August 2005 for lack of subject matter jurisdiction. The court also noted that the suit was subject to dismissal on forum non conveniens grounds because the plaintiffs had failed to establish either corruption or inadequate procedural safeguards in Nigeria.[60]

---

58 See: *Grimes v Kennedy Krieger Institute, Inc,* 782 A2d 807 (Md 2001). For contrasting perspectives on this case, see: Nelson, RM et al, "Ethical Issues with Genetic Testing in Pediatrics" (2001) 107 *Pediatrics* 1451; Kopelman, LM, "Pediatric Research Regulations Under Legal Scrutiny: Grimes Narrows Their Interpretation" (2002) 30 *Journal of Law & Medical Ethics* 38; Ross, LF, "In Defense of the Hopkins Lead Abatement Studies" (2002) 30 *Journal of Law & Medical Ethics* 50; Glantz, LH, "Nontherapeutic Research With Children: Grimes v Kennedy Krieger Institute" (2002) 92 *American Journal of Public Health* 1070; Mastroianni, AC, and Kahn, JP, "Risk and Responsibility: Ethics, Grimes v Kennedy Krieger, and Public Health Research Involving Children" (2002) 92 *American Journal of Public Health* 1073.

59 Trovan (trovafloxacin), an oral antibiotic also available in an intravenous formulation (alatrofloxacin or Trovan-IV), was first approved by the United States FDA in December 1997 and first became available on the market in February 1998. A public health advisory was issued on 9 June 1999, by the Center for Drug Evaluation concerning the risks of liver toxicity associated with use of the drug and its recommended use was restricted to patients fitting specific criteria. See: <www.fda.gov/ cder/news/trovan/default.htm> (accessed 2 September 2005). The drug was suspended from the European market by the European Medicines Evaluation Agency in June 1999. See <http://www.emea.eu.int/pdfs/human/press/ pus/1804699EN.pdf> (accessed 25 April 2005).

60 *Abdullahi v Pfizer Inc,* US Dist LEXIS 16126 (2005).

Lastly, in New York, regulations promulgated by the State Office of Mental Health in 1990[61] were subsequently challenged and invalidated by the courts in 1996 for not providing sufficient safeguards.[62] That action was commenced by former patient-subjects and advocacy groups. While the outcome of that litigation has been subjected to criticism,[63] it demonstrated the value of advocates and ongoing need for the protection of subjects' rights.[64] The main point at issue in that case was that the Regulations would have permitted non-therapeutic research of greater than minimal risk involving persons unable to provide consent.

In sum, recent litigation and media reports would suggest that certain populations of subjects continue to be vulnerable to exploitation or exposure to unreasonable risks. Moreover, as argued earlier, the number of ethical violations applies equally to the present as for the past, then the number of ethical violations occurring in contemporary research practice is undoubtedly much higher than has been reported or scrutinised by the courts. As the balance of this section will convey, the concept of "vulnerability" (and corresponding need for regulatory safeguards) is not restricted to the classic vulnerable populations, attracting a much broader meaning within the modern research enterprise.

The ongoing relevance of vulnerable "populations"

Policies grounded in vulnerable "populations" are open to criticism on several fronts. Safeguards for vulnerable subjects essentially have the effect of confining their involvement in research, from outright prohibition (as in the case of prisoners) to a range of restrictions delimiting the ethical permissibility of their involvement (such as in the case of children, the elderly or persons with a mental illness or disability). Proscriptions may appear paternalistic or stigmatising, reinforcing negative stereotypes that fail to acknowledge the rights of individuals to participate in or possibly benefit from research, and may impede arguably "necessary" research on a range of conditions.[65]

---

61   14 NYCRR 527.10 (1990). The contents of the regulations are reported by Delano, SJ and Zucker, JL, "Protecting Mental Health Research Subjects Without Prohibiting Progress" (1994) 45 *Hospital & Community Psychiatry* 601.

62   *TD v New York State Office of Mental Health*, 650 NYS2d 173, 65 USLW 2439 (1st Dept 1996), appeal dismissed, 91 NY2d 860 (1997).

63   Oldham, JM, Haimowitz, S, and Delano, SJ, "Regulating Research With Vulnerable Populations: Litigation Gone Awry" (1998) 1 *Journal of Health Care Law & Policy* 154.

64   Disability Advocates Inc, a non-profit consumer advocacy group, acted on behalf of the plaintiff-subjects in that case that were enrolled in trials that had been approved under the regulations Zucker, C, "Are New Laws Needed to Protect Human Subjects?" (2001) 8 *Accountability in Research* 235.

65   Such arguments are canvassed, for example, in the context of adolescents (Lind, C, Anderson, B, and Oberle, K, "Ethical Issues in Adolescent Consent for Research" (2003) 10 *Nursing Ethics* 504), persons with mental illness (Arboleda-Florez, J and Weisstub, DN, "Ethical Research With Vulnerable Populations: The Mentally Disordered", in Weisstub (1998) (ed) op cit), the elderly (Verdun-Jones, SN, Weisstub, DN, and Walker, J, "Biomedical Experimentation Involving Elderly Subjects: The Need to Balance Limited, Benevolent Protection with Recognition of a Long History of Autonomous Decision-Making" in (cont)

Neither reason provides decisive grounds for abandoning population-based safeguards. In response to the first concern, it has been rightly pointed out that drawing attention to the special needs of certain "groups", such as the elderly, may in fact be empowering.[66]

In respect of the latter, the carte blanche generally accorded to the "necessity argument" grounding the "research imperative" is also open to challenge. As Callahan advised, "[i]nstead of positioning medical research as a moral imperative we can understand it as a key part of a vision of a good society".[67]

A more significant consideration is that the classification of broad "populations" of vulnerable subjects, such as children, persons with cognitive impairment and the elderly, is intrinsically artificial. Levels of decision-making capacity can vary widely across these groups.

Decision-making abilities of children can develop at different rates,[68] and likewise, the rate of decline of mental acuity commonly expected at the other end of the human lifespan will vary greatly or never noticeably decrease at all.

Persons with mental disorders can demonstrate fluctuating periods of lucidity, while individuals with cognitive developmental disabilities may never possess the mental capacity to make life-affecting decisions or might simply require varying levels of assistance.

Owing to the functional character of mental competency, an individual may also be incapable of making some life decisions, but perfectly able to make others.[69]

It merits noting that recent revisions of official policies have tended to move away from a population-specific approach. For example, while the Australian guidelines do continue to treat children in a separate section, they do not identify "the elderly", persons with mental illness or persons with intellectual disabilities as vulnerable "populations". Instead, safeguards relate to factors such as presence of

---

(*cont*)

Weisstub (ed) (1998) op cit), and prisoners (Verdun-Jones, SN, Weisstub, DN, and Arboleda-Florez, J, "Prisoners as Subjects of Biomedical Experimentation: Examining the Arguments for and Against a Total Ban", in Weisstub (ed) (1998) op cit).

66 Verdun-Jones, Weisstub, and Walker (1998) op cit, pp 409–410.

67 Callahan, D *What Price Better Health? Hazards of the Research Imperative*, University of California Press, Berkeley, 2003, p 63.

68 For example, Sanci, LA et al, "Youth Health Research Ethics: Time for a Mature-Minor Clause?" (2004) 180 *Medical Journal of Australia* 336 recommended in the Australian context that adolescents be allowed to consent to research as "mature-minors", much as they can presently under the common law for treatment. They recommended that ethical guidelines promulgated by the NHMRC should be amended accordingly, particularly in the case of minimal-risk research.

69 Common law jurisdictions have steadfastly abandoned notions of global incapacity and recognised the functional nature of mental competency; see, for example, Weisstub *Enquiry on Mental Competency: Final Report*, Queen's Printer, Toronto, 1990. This has translated into the evolution of more flexible guardianship and substitute decision-making regimes.

an intellectual or mental impairment and dependency on medical care.[70] In the Canadian guidelines, the requirement of free and informed consent, whether direct or by proxy, provides the unifying concept that aims to protect vulnerable populations.[71] The National Bioethics Advisory Committee (NBAC) commented that a regulatory response to all possible vulnerable subjects on a population-basis would yield an "unwieldy" set of provisions. It therefore advocated an analytic approach that yielded an entirely "context-sensitive" understanding of vulnerability and identified the following types of vulnerability: cognitive or communicative, institutional, deferential, medical, economic and social.[72]

Nevertheless, any move away from population-specific ethical safeguards should not obviate their basic utility at the policy level. While acknowledging that the aforementioned groups are not homogeneous, certain general features are sufficiently prevalent or consistent – age, presence of cognitive impairment, dependent relationships – to yield a rational basis for categorisation and policy development,[73] provided some accommodation to individual circumstances is possible within those categories. If anything, as will be argued below, globalisation has created another vulnerable "population" – subjects from developing world countries – which raises unique considerations and the need for corresponding safeguards.

Expanding "vulnerability"

While not wishing to abandon population-specific safeguards entirely, it is acknowledged that the trend to describe vulnerability in terms of broader concepts is consistent with a more principled approach to the problem of human subject protection, yielding more versatile and meaningful tools for decision-making in the course of ethics review. However, if "vulnerability", as a construct, is to serve as a principal driver of regulatory policy, further distillation of the concept is warranted.

"Vulnerability" in research can be expressed most simply as "an inability to protect oneself from exploitation or exposure to unreasonable risks of harm".[74] It can

---

70 NHMRC, *National Statement on Ethical Conduct in Research Involving Humans*, NHMRC, Canberra, 1999. See also the Office for Human Research Protections, *IRB Guidebook*, United States Department of Health and Human Services, <www.hhs.gov/ohrp/irb/irb_chapter6ii.htm#g9> (accessed 16 January 2006), which explains that specific federal regulations do not exist for the elderly since an older person who happens to suffer a cognitive impairment or be in an institutional setting would benefit from the more general safeguards applicable in those situations.

71 Tri-Council, *Tri-Council Policy Statement: Ethical Conduct for Research Involving Humans*, Ministry of Supply and Services, Ottawa, 1998.

72 NBAC, *Ethical and Policy Issues in Research Involving Human Participants. Volume 1: Report and Recommendations of the National Bioethics Advisory Commission*, 2001, pp 88–91.

73 For example, Weisstub, DN, *Enquiry on Research Ethics: Final Report*, Ministry of Health, Ontario, 1995, for the Canadian province of Ontario, whose mandate was to address specifically vulnerable populations, retained a population-specific approach in framing its recommendations.

74 Weisstub, Arboleda-Florez, and Tomossy (1998) op cit, p 357.

arise in situations where a prospective subject is unable to provide informed consent as required by law, such as owing to a lack of legal or mental capacity, including age restrictions and an inability to comprehend the risks involved or competently communicate a decision not to participate. An otherwise valid consent might also be vitiated in cases where undue influence compromises its voluntary character, which can occur in potentially coercive settings, such as prisons or health care institutions. These notions are incorporated broadly into modern research ethics policies, including for example the recently revised guidelines of the Council of International Organizations of Medical Sciences, which retained its 1993 definition of "vulnerability" as:

> [A] substantial incapacity to protect one's own interests owing to such impediments as lack of capability to give informed consent, lack of alternative means of obtaining medical care or other expensive necessities, or being a junior or subordinate member of a hierarchical group.[75]

It merits reiterating that vulnerability does not relate simply to unreasonable exposure to risks but also to exploitation. The latter constitutes a more subtle harm that may seem to be more a question of ethics than law and hence more difficult to regulate. Nevertheless, both elements of vulnerability remain important drivers for regulatory policy, being particularly relevant in light of the proliferation of international research and commodification of human subjects discussed in the next section.

The notion of subject vulnerability can be expanded as follows: *all* subjects are potentially vulnerable owing to their dependence on the range of participants involved in research governance to assess, reduce and communicate risks properly, and thus to make at least some decisions on their behalf.

Subjects will not generally possess the specialised knowledge required to understand the full extent of risks they might incur through participation, at least as far as they can be reasonably predicted. Moreover, individual factors might produce an adverse interaction within otherwise sound experimental parameters. Thus, even a person who might not otherwise be considered to be "vulnerable" within the broad categories mentioned earlier could still be at risk in specific contexts. In this regard, Weijer and Fuks rightly argued that it is the duty of the investigator-clinician to screen for such factors, and that no level of ethics review or eligibility criteria can compensate for failure to carry out this responsibility.[76]

The vulnerability of subjects, however, extends beyond the scope of their immediate relationship with an investigator or investigator-clinician. Two recent cases highlight the critical role not only of investigators to preserve the welfare of their subjects, but also of the ethics review and oversight process as a whole. Thus,

---

75 CIOMS, *International Ethical Guidelines for Biomedical Research Involving Human Subjects*, CIOMS, Geneva, 2002.

76 Weijer, C, and Fuks, A, "The Duty to Exclude: EXCLUDING people at Undue Risk from Research" (1994) 17 *Clinical & Investigative Medicine* 115.

the call for accountability in response to subject vulnerability is system-wide, rather than being merely limited to an assertion of individual responsibility on the part of investigators.

One of the major reported failings in the trial that led to the death of Ellen Roche in the hexamethonium asthma study at the Johns Hopkins Asthma and Allergy Center in 2001 was the failure to conduct a proper literature review of the toxicity of the compound being tested.[77] Likewise, it appears that Jesse Gelsinger should have been excluded from the gene therapy trial that led to his death on the basis of failing to qualify under the inclusion criteria specified in the study.[78] It is worth emphasising that neither Ellen Roche nor Jesse Gelsinger was a member of a classic vulnerable population.[79] Indeed, both were undoubtedly capable of providing a valid informed consent to participate in their respective studies. The factors contributing to their deaths were completely outside their control. Savulescu is therefore justified in noting that the principal shortcomings of those experiments that led to the deaths of subjects was less a consequence of a failure to obtain an informed consent than of improper risk management, which suggests systemic problems in addition to individual failings of investigators. He added that both deaths could have been avoided, which points to the larger concern that it might be necessary to review the role and function of research ethics committees altogether, as well as to take a closer look at how financial conflicts might be impacting on decision-making.[80]

Subjects, therefore, may be vulnerable not only to exploitation or harms caused by investigators, but to shortcomings of the regulatory framework as a whole. This supports the conclusion that all subjects are potentially vulnerable within the research exchange. It is submitted further that this inherent vulnerability of subjects also provides an important vindication of the call for accountability in research.

---

77 Levine, S and Weiss, R, "Hopkins Told to Halt Trials Funded by US – Death of Medical Volunteer Prompted Federal Directive", *The Washington Post*, 20 July 2001; Argetsinger, A, "Panel Blames Hopkins in Research Death", *The Washington Post*, 30 August 2001; Savulescu, J, and Spriggs, M, "The Hexamethonium Asthma Study and the Death of a Normal Volunteer in Research" (2002) 28 *Journal of Medical Ethics* 3; Steinbrook, R, "Protecting Research Subjects – The Crisis at Johns Hopkins" (2002) 346 *New England Journal of Medicine* 716. See also: "FDA Warning Letter to Dr A Togias, Johns Hopkins Asthma & Allergy Center", 31 March 2003, <www.fda.gov/foi/warning_letters/g3936d. htm> (accessed 28 May 2003), in which the principal investigator was noted to have:

> [F]ailed to submit a summary of previous human studies with hexamethonium salts administered by oral and intravenous routes [and also failed] to summarize previous human experience with the administration of a hyperosmolar solution (such as hexamethonium bromide) to the human lung by aerosol inhalation.

78 See "Letter to Dr James Wilson", Institute of Gene Therapy, University of Pennsylvania Health System, from Dennis E Baker, Associate Commissioner for Regulatory Affairs, Food and Drug Administration, 8 February 2002, <www.fda.gov/foi/warning_letters/ m3435n.pdf> (accessed 28 May 2003).

79 One might suggest that Ellen Roche, as an employee of the centre conducting the trial, and Jesse Gelsinger, as a person suffering from a serious illness, were both potentially vulnerable to coercion. However, this consideration has not emerged in critical accounts of these cases, nor is it being suggested here that this was the case.

80 Savulescu, J, "Two Deaths and Two Lessons: Is it Time to Review the Structure and Function of Research Ethics Committees?" (2002) 28 *Journal of Medical Ethics* 1.

Implications of a global research enterprise

Traditional pressures on the research exchange that have led to the exploitation of subjects continue to be present, such as career advancement and zeal for discovery. The increasingly commodified and global character of research, while certainly affording new opportunities for humanity, has generated new pressures for investigators and consequently new threats to human subjects.[81] The forces of globalisation and corporatisation have together expanded both the range of investigators' conflicts and the scope of subjects' vulnerabilities. As a result, it is submitted that the role of external oversight over the research exchange has increased in importance. The challenge for regulatory systems is to respond to this call.

With human subjects comprising a valuable resource needed to fuel the engine of discovery, economics now feature prominently in decisions about setting research priorities as well recruiting trial participants. In the modern era of research, with the advent of significant financial demands on researchers and their institutions. Subjects cannot be expected to second-guess conflicts of interest that might influence decisions made by investigators, which further exacerbates their vulnerability.

Thus, the onus on the investigator – indeed, on all participants in the research exchange – to acknowledge, avoid and reveal such conflicts, has increased. Unfortunately, international (not to mention national) convergence of official policies on financial conflicts of interest has yet to occur. In the United States, for example, various bodies have proposed guidelines, creating confusion in their wake.[82]

The increasingly commercial nature of research has introduced conflicts of interest not only for investigators and their institutions, but may affect decision-making for other participants in research oversight. The traditional role of research ethics committees has been transformed by commercial forces, particularly when institutions themselves become investors in research. This is in addition to existing pressures of rising workloads and coping with institutional bias. The advent of commercial ethics review (contract research organisations) represents a logical trend within the transformation of the research endeavour, but nonetheless presents a host of ethical problems.[83]

---

81 Strictly speaking, globalisation and commercialisation in biomedical research are not new phenomena. It is only recently, however, that their impact on ethics committees and subjects alike have been acknowledged with regularity; for example, NBAC, *Ethical and Policy Issues in International Research: Clinical Trials in Developing Countries. Volume 1: Report and Recommendations,* 2001; United Kingdom House of Commons Health Committee, *The Influence of the Pharmaceutical Industry,* 2005.

82 Brody, BA et al, "Expanding Disclosure of Conflicts of Interest: The Views of STAKE-HOLDERS" (2003) 25 *IRB* 1.

83 Lemmens, T and Freedman, B, "Ethics Review for Sale? Conflict of Interest and Commercial Research Review Boards" (2000) 78 *Milbank Quarterly* 547.

Where commercialisation becomes particularly threatening, however, is where regulatory authorities are themselves captured by industry forces[84] or fail to capture privately funded research altogether. Regulatory frameworks that rely on public funding bodies to administer ethical guidelines are exposed to the problem that privately funded research essentially falls outside their jurisdiction.[85]

Most fundamentally, the drive for profits has obscured or at times eclipsed the traditional societal justification for research involving human subjects: the quest for a cure. It has become increasingly apparent from the number of "me-too" drugs released on the market that a growing proportion of clinical trials serve primarily commercial ends, rather than for the purpose of advancing knowledge and improving human health.[86] Added to this are concerns advanced from several fronts about the construction of diseases to promote sales of pharmaceutical products.[87]

Globalisation of the biomedical research industry has opened new doors for the recruitment of subjects while at the same time blurring lines of accountability and liability. Globalisation has made available entire populations that were previously inaccessible. Citizens of developing countries are increasingly being portrayed as "guinea pigs" in what has been described as "a global boom in overseas drug experiments".[88] The alleged motivations of corporations to conduct international research are twofold: lower cost and less interference by regulatory authorities. This powerful combination has produced an enormous class of vulnerable subjects.

Vulnerability in international research revolves primarily around the quality of subject consent: linguistic and educational barriers to properly comprehend the risks involved, cultural barriers to question authority or conceptualise individual consent, and dependency in the form of both economic and health care needs that might contribute to an environment of undue inducement.[89] "Consent" in the international context might thus be invalid because it is not understood (and thus

---

84 See, in particular, the work of Abraham and colleagues on the influence of the pharmaceutical industry on drug regulation; for example, Abraham, J *Science, Politics, and the Pharmaceutical Industry: Controversy and Bias in Drug Regulation*, ULC Press, London, 1995; Abraham, J and Sheppard, J *The Therapeutic Nightmare: The Battle Over the World's Most Controversial Sleeping Pill*, Earthscan, London, 1999.

85 This problem was acknowledged in the United States by the National Bioethics Advisory Commission (NBAC, *Ethical and Policy Issues in Research Involving Human Participants. Volume 1: Report and Recommendations of the National Bioethics Advisory Commission*, 2001) and in Medical Research Council of Canada, SCoE, *A Proposed Ethics Agenda for CIHR: Challenges and Opportunities – Recommendations of the Standing Committee on Ethics to Council As It Prepares Its Parting Advice to CIHR Governing Council*, 2000. The Australian context is discussed below.

86 Garattini, S, "Are Me-Too Drugs Justified?" (1997) 10 *Journal of Nephrology* 283.

87 Moynihan, R and Cassels, A *Selling Sickness: How Drug Companies Are Turning Us All into Patients*, Allen & Unwin, Sydney, 2005.

88 Flaherty, MP, Nelson, D, and Stephens, J, "The Body Hunters: Overwhelming the Watchdogs", 18 December 2000.

89 NBAC (2001) op cit, pp 35–54.

cannot be given), or unethical because it is obtained through what might amount to coercive means.

A more subtle problem arising from international research relates to the problem of access to justice. This can generate a form of vulnerability insofar as subjects and their families may find it difficult to obtain compensation from foreign sponsors of clinical trials. The difficulty facing Nigerian families to overcome legal hurdles in pursuing their case against United States-based Pfizer is illustrative of this problem. Moreover, the costs of litigation, evidentiary obstacles and power imbalances between the parties, can present significant hurdles to obtaining compensation.[90]

Vulnerability in international research also relates to the equitable distribution of risks and benefits in research. The ethical precept of distributive justice aims to prevent one segment of society from bearing an unfair share of risks so that another might benefit. It has thus been widely held that classic vulnerable populations should only become subjects in experiments that affect conditions or illnesses of the general group to which they belong.[91] Likewise, the principle of justice would require that populations in developing countries not become the "guinea pigs" of Western nations; that is, they should not bear the brunt of risks without having equitable access to benefits. The absence of effective regulatory oversight in most countries in Africa, Latin and South America, Eastern Europe, and Asia, coupled with international trade treaties that are highly protective of drug patents (and thus pose barriers to manufacturing inexpensive generic equivalents of new medications), combine to make this objective difficult to achieve. In short, individuals in developing countries comprise a new and rather large vulnerable population that is not adequately factored into existing domestic regulatory frameworks.[92]

Conclusion: Ethical, legal and regulatory challenges for Australia

This chapter draws heavily on the United States experience. The issues raised are nonetheless relevant for Australia, given the global nature of the research enterprise and comparable foundations in practice and training for the research professions internationally.[93] Transformative social forces that operate

---

90   The Trovan litigation is discussed more fully by Tomossy, GF and Ford, J, "Globalization and Clinical Trials: Compensating Subjects From Developing Countries", *Globalization and Health: Challenges for Health Law and Bioethics*, Springer, Amsterdam, 2006.

91   Weisstub, Arboleda-Florez and Tomossy (1998) op cit, pp 361–363.

92   Office of Inspector-General, *The Globalization of Clinical Trials: A Growing Challenge in Protecting Human Subjects*, OEI-01-00-00190, 2001; NBAC (2001) op cit.

93   One should also acknowledge the increased movement of medical practitioners between jurisdictions. See Freckelton, I, "Health Practitioner Regulation: Emerging Patterns and Challenges for the Age of Globalization" in Bennett, B and Tomossy, GF (eds) *Globalization and Health: Challenges for Health Law and Bioethics*, Springer, Amsterdam, 2006.

on a global level, such as the commercialisation of biomedical research and proliferation of clinical trials, will unavoidably affect the climate of research in Australia (as it has already done) – with corresponding implications for human subjects.

To illustrate, the lead article in the investigative series published in the *Sydney Morning Herald* mentioned earlier[94] carried the headline, "Australians used as guinea pigs for global drug market".[95] The article took exception to the use of Australians in clinical trials ultimately to satisfy regulatory requirements for the approval of new drugs for foreign markets and was critical of the perception that it was cheaper and easier to get approval to conduct clinical trials in Australia. Concerns about forum shopping in international clinical trials are not unique to Australia and present a serious dilemma in distributive justice on a global scale, particularly for developing world countries. They also present accountability challenges for national systems of research governance (where they exist). Unlike developing world countries, Australia should be in a position to respond to these challenges, having the necessary resources, expertise and regulatory infrastructure to safeguard Australian subjects in foreign- (and locally-) sponsored drug trials. Whether the current regulatory framework is up to the challenge is a separate matter.

The sustainability of the current system in Australia, with its reliance on human research ethics committees (HRECs), has been rightly questioned, with resource and workload levels being a principal concern.[96] A major reason for the increase in workload for many HRECs has been the deregulation of clinical trials, which formed a part of the rationale supporting the imposition of additional safeguards in New South Wales for research involving adults with impaired decision-making capacity.

It was an important consideration of the Standing Committee on Social Issues of the New South Wales Legislative Council in its recommendations relating to amendment of the *Guardianship Act 1987*.[97] In 1998, the approval of the Guardianship Tribunal became a requirement for clinical trials involving persons unable to provide a legal consent to participate.[98] Similar safeguards exist under the guardianship regime in Queensland,[99] which were introduced in response to recommendations by the Queensland Law Reform Commission in their report on

---

94 See above, note 50 and accompanying text.

95 Ryle, G, "The Body Snatchers", *Sydney Morning Herald,* 13 February 2001.

96 Dodds, S, "Is the Australian HREC System Sustainable?" (2002) 21 *Monash Bioethics Review* 43. The Australian Law Reform Commission (ALRC) also concluded in their recent inquiry into the protection of genetic information that "the present ethics review system could be significantly improved": ALRC *Essentially Yours: The Protection of Human Genetic Information in Australia. Volume 1,* 2003, para 17.86.

97 Standing Committee on Social Issues, *Clinical Trials and Guardianship: Maximising the Safeguards,* Report No 13, 1997.

98 *Adult Guardianship Amendment Act 1998* (NSW).

99 *Guardianship and Administration Act 2000* (Qld).

substitute decision-making.[100] A comparable structure existed in Victoria, but was recently changed.[101]

Recognition of the need for additional legal protections for one vulnerable population (adults with a legal decision-making incapacity) through guardianship regimes invites broader consideration about the adequacy of the legal framework for the regulation of research in Australia generally. If, as argued in this chapter, vulnerability is construed beyond specific categories of vulnerable "populations", then attention needs to be directed to broad transformations affecting the research endeavour. Commercialisation presents such a force, given that it affects all subjects, including those that have not traditionally been perceived to be vulnerable. Moreover, when commercial reasons provide the dominant justification for conducting research rather than other (arguably more valid) societal aims, commercialisation can invoke concerns about both elements of the definition for "vulnerability" adopted in this chapter: exposure to unreasonable risks and exploitation.

In his editorial published in the *Sydney Morning Herald* series discussed above, Tattersall acknowledged "the increasing dominance of the pharmaceutical industry in the expansion of clinical trials in Australia in the past few years". He cautioned:

> The regulations that govern the conduct of clinical trials, particularly those that lack a valid scientific intention, need to be reviewed. The current and appropriate roles of the pharmaceutical industry in the design, conduct and promotion of clinical trials need to be debated, and understood.[102]

His concerns about the influence of the pharmaceutical industry are echoed, if not amplified, in a landmark report by the United Kingdom House of Commons Health Committee.[103] The Report paints an astonishing picture, presenting evidence of industry manipulation of published research and attempts to influence the clinical judgment of physicians. The committee concluded, "[t]here is evidence that in certain areas, company influence is excessive and contrary to the public good".[104] There is no reason to doubt that an Australian inquiry, if conducted with similar vigour, would come to the same conclusion. Indeed, numerous concerns

---

100 Queensland Law Reform Commission, *Assisted and Substitute Decisions,* QLRC, Brisbane, 1996.

101 In Victoria, requirements for the approval by the Victorian Civil and Administrative Tribunal for all patients with a disability who lacked capacity to consent to participate in research came into effect on 1 January 2003. With the passage of the *Guardianship and Administration (Further Amendment) Act,* which was passed by the Legislative Assembly on 3 March 2006, approval is now delegated to a guardian (where appointed). The Act provides separately for cases of urgent necessity and non-urgent cases where a person may be expected to be able to consent in the future.

102 Tattersall, M, "Problems With Clinical Trials Need a Swift Remedy", *Sydney Morning Herald,* 15 February 2001.

103 United Kingdom House of Commons Health Committee, *The Influence of the Pharmaceutical Industry,* 2005.

104 Ibid, para 43.

have been expressed in recent years on a range of ethical issues relating to the influence of the pharmaceutical industry, including on drug advertising,[105] prescription practices,[106] access to medicines,[107] research organisations and the public research agenda,[108] medical students[109] and the medical profession generally.[110]

It is therefore timely that the Royal Australasian College of Physicians (RACP) recently revised its *Ethical Guidelines in the Relationship Between Physicians and the Pharmaceutical Industry*.[111] This is an important initiative. As the Australian Health Ethics Committee noted in their submission to the RACP,

> As one of the oldest and most respected Colleges, with a membership which can strongly influence the agenda for research into, and the prescribing of, new drugs, the RACP bears a special responsibility to show such leadership.[112]

105 Loke, TW, Koh, FC, and Ward, JE, "Pharmaceutical Advertisement Claims in Australian Medical Publications" (2002) 177 *Medical Journal of Australia* 291; Newby, DA, and Henry, DA, "Drug advertising: truths, half-truths and few statistics" (2002) 177 *Medical Journal of Australia* 285.

106 Harvey, KJ et al, "Pharmaceutical Advertisements in Prescribing Software: An Analysis" (2005) 183 *Medical Journal of Australia* 75; Ruff, TA, and Haikal-Mukhtar, H, "Doctors, Drugs, Information and Ethics: A Never-Ending Story" (2005) 183 *Medical Journal of Australia* 73.

107 Faunce, TA, and Tomossy, GF, "The UK House of Commons Report on the Influence of the Pharmaceutical Industry: Lessons for Equitable Access to Medicines in Australia" (2005) 24 *Monash Bioethics Review* 38.

108 Commens, CA, "Truth in Clinical Research Trials Involving Pharmaceutical Sponsorship" (2001) 174 *Medical Journal of Australia* 648; Van der Weyden, MB, "Confronting Conflict of Interest in Research Organisations: Time for National Action" (2001) 175 *Medical Journal of Australia* 396; Moses, H III, Perumpanani, A, and Nicholson, J, "Collaborating with Industry: Choices for Australian Medicine and Universities" (2002) 176 *Medical Journal of Australia* 543; Gotzsche, PC, "Research Integrity and Pharmaceutical Industry Sponsorship. Trial Registration, Transparency and Less Reliance on Industry Trials are Essential" (2005) 182 *Medical Journal of Australia* 549.

109 Rogers, WA et al, "The Ethics of Pharmaceutical Industry Relationships with Medical Students" (2004) 180 *Medical Journal of Australia* 411; Hutchinson, MS, "Pharmaceutical Companies and Medical Students: A Student's View" (2004) 180 *Medical Journal of Australia* 414.

110 Fitzgerald, PD, "The Ethics of Doctors and Big Business" (2001) 175 *Medical Journal of Australia* 73; Fitzgerald, PD, "General Practice Corporatisation: The Half-Time Score" (2002) 177 *Medical Journal of Australia* 90; Komesaroff, PA, and Kerridge, IH, "Ethical Issues Concerning the Relationships Between Medical Practitioners and the Pharmaceutical Industry" (2002) 176 *Medical Journal of Australia* 118; Breen, KJ, "The Medical Profession and the Pharmaceutical Industry: When Will We Open Our Eyes?" (2004) 180 *Medical Journal of Australia* 409; Graudins, LV, "The Medical Profession and the Pharmaceutical Industry: When Will We Open Our Eyes?" (2004) 181 *Medical Journal of Australia* 458; Masters, S, "The Medical Profession and the Pharmaceutical Industry: When Will We Open Our Eyes?" (2004) 181 *Medical Journal of Australia* 459; Henry, DA et al, "Medical Specialists and Pharmaceutical Industry-Sponsored Research: A Survey of the Australian Experience" (2005) 182 *Medical Journal of Australia* 557.

111 Royal Australasian College of Physicians, *Ethical Guidelines in the Relationship Between Physicians and the Pharmaceutical Industry*, RACP, Sydney, 2006.

112 Submission from the Australian Health Ethics Committee on *The Revision Of The Royal Australasian College of Physicians Document, Ethical Guidelines in the Relationship between Physicians and the Pharmaceutical Industry*, June 2004, <www.nhmrc.gov.au/ethics/human/ahec/projects/racp.htm> (accessed 11 February 2006).

The revised document represents a significant expansion in the scope of the original version.[113]

However, influencing professional conduct is by no means a straightforward exercise. As Doran and colleagues discovered in their qualitative empirical study, the relationship between medical specialists and the pharmaceutical industry in Australia is complex and defied "simplistic good/ bad dichotomizing", being complicated by considerable variance in the ethical perceptions of medical specialists.[114] Their conclusions are unsurprising and might help to explain the situation in the United States where various bodies have proposed conflict of interest guidelines but not one has achieved dominance.[115]

These difficulties should not detract, however, from the importance of generating conflict of interest guidelines. Henry and colleagues reported a high level of engagement between Australian medical specialists and the pharmaceutical industry, with a significant proportion of those with active relationships with industry reporting encounters involving potentially serious ethical breaches.[116] The question, however, is not so much the content of the revised RACP guidelines as how and to what extent the college will enforce them. Professional self-regulation, if effective, could represent a desirable option for managing certain aspects of commercialisation on research, such as scientific misconduct and financial conflicts of interest, but can only be part of the solution as medical practitioners are just one of many participants in the research exchange.[117]

It is equally timely that the Australian Law Reform Commission (ALRC) recommended in its 2003 report that the National Health and Medical Research Council (NHMRC) should "review the mechanisms for achieving compliance with the National Statement, with particular regard to human research conducted wholly within the private sector".[118] In acknowledging the need to improve compliance with research conducted "wholly within the private sector", the ALRC drew attention to a major gap in the Australian system of research governance common to other jurisdictions that have derived their regulatory framework from a public funding model.[119] By focusing on soft controls, such as the withdrawal of

---

113 See <www.racp.edu.au/public/Ethical_guide_pharm.pdf> (accessed 11 February 2006). Because the revised guidelines are currently in their draft form, this chapter will refrain from making any substantive criticism of the contents.

114 Doran, E et al, "Empirical Uncertainty and Moral Contest: A Qualitative Analysis of the Relationship Between Medical Specialists and the Pharmaceutical Industry in Australia" (2006) 62 *Social Science & Medicine* 1510.

115 Brody, BA et al, "Expanding Disclosure of Conflicts of Interest: The Views of Stakeholders" (2003) 25 *IRB* 1.

116 Henry (2005) op cit.

117 For the same reason, reliance on industry to self-regulate should also be avoided, particularly in the absence of stronger social controls to motivate meaningful self-regulation, which would require re-aligning the goals of industry to coincide better with societal aims.

118 ALRC (2003) op cit, Recommendation 14-1.

119 See above, note 85 and accompanying text.

public research funding, the NHMRC does not have jurisdiction over privately funded research. Admittedly, institutions must adhere to NHMRC requirements if they receive funding from private *and* from public sources, including for research funded entirely by private sources.[120] Certain areas of research also require approval by Human Research Ethics Committees (HRECs) constituted in accordance with NHMRC guidelines in clinical trials under the Commonwealth *Therapeutic Goods Act 1989* or State guardianship legislation noted above. Thus, in certain situations, one might argue that the NHMRC guidelines apply de facto to private institutions.[121] Chalmers nevertheless flagged certain issues:

> [I]n practice, many private institutions follow the principles of the *National Statement*. It is not clear at this early stage whether this voluntary compliance will continue. It is equally unclear whether the increasing movement toward greater private funding of research will affect this process of voluntary compliance. For example, will private funders expect ethics clearance as part of the "service" provided by the research organization? If the HREC refuses clearance will the private funder simply go to the "market" and seek approval elsewhere?[122]

Although Chalmers went on to note, "[n]o 'market' in ethics approval has arisen".[123] the inconsistency in regulatory requirements remains a significant flaw in the current system.[124] While privately funded research should not automatically imply unethical conduct, the Australian Medical Association acknowledged in their submission to the ALRC that "there is certainly more scope for unethical conduct in that sector, and this certainly means that greater scrutiny of the private sector is required".[125]

The ALRC fell short of advocating the immediate enactment of legislation to correct this deficiency. As the terms of reference for the ALRC inquiry related specifically to "genetic information and the samples from which such information was obtained",[126] this should not be taken as a weakness of the report. Indeed, the ALRC raised a number of considerations that ought to be addressed before proceeding down that path, but noted that "these problems are not insurmountable and options for further regulation should be thoroughly

---

120 NHMRC, *National Statement on Ethical Conduct in Research Involving Humans*, NHMRC, Canberra, 1999, p 3.

121 Chalmers, D, *Research Ethics in Australia. Commissioned Paper for the National Bioethics Advisory Commission Report on Ethical and Policy Issues in Research Involving Human Participants*, NBAC, Washington, DC, 2001, A-50.

122 Ibid.

123 Ibid.

124 This conclusion was also reached by the Commonwealth House of Representatives Standing Committee on Legal and Constitutional Affairs in *Human Cloning: Scientific, Ethical and Regulatory Aspects of Human Cloning and Stem Cell Research*, Commonwealth of Australia, Canberra, 2001, pp 167–168.

125 Australian Medical Association, *Submission G212*, 29 November 2002, cited in ALRC (2003) op cit, para 14.44.

126 ALRC (2003) op cit, p 33.

reviewed",[127] including the option of developing a system of accreditation for ethics committees.[128] It is notable that the National Bioethics Advisory Commission in the United States made a firm recommendation in respect of the need for federal legislation.[129] It recognised:

> A fundamental flaw in the current oversight system is the ethically indefensible difference in the protection afforded participants in federally sponsored research and those in privately sponsored research that falls outside the jurisdiction of the Food and Drug Administration ... This is wrong. *Participants should be protected from avoidable harm, whether the research is publicly or privately financed.* [emphasis in original][130]

A legislative response to make all research (whether privately or publicly financed) accountable to the same ethical and legal requirements should also occur in Australia. In the modern research enterprise, the scope of vulnerability has broadened substantially, well beyond the classically defined vulnerable populations. Where subjects are unable to protect themselves unilaterally from exploitation or exposure to risks of harm and must rely on external social controls to promote their welfare, the onus rests with legal systems to set out and enforce ethical safeguards through a regulatory framework that can operate in a uniform and publicly accountable manner.[131] If human subject protection is truly the primary objective of research governance, then to ignore or underestimate the impact of commercial forces insofar as they might contribute to the vulnerability of subjects would constitute an irresponsible, if not reprehensible, lapse in public policy. Legislatively entrenching the rights of human subjects and requirements for the review of research proposals should not automatically engender fears about further bureaucratisation of research oversight. While HRECs should not be treated merely as "as instruments of bureaucratic regulation and control",[132] they nevertheless occupy a critical role as gatekeepers in the research approval process and their role should be strengthened. Legislation should be seen as a tool to legitimate social controls that are already in place, but which presently operate in a state of legal uncertainty.

---

127 Ibid, paras 14.74–14.78.

128 Ibid, paras 17.72–17.88.

129 NBAC (2001) op cit, Recommendation 2.1.

130 Ibid, p v.

131 While not discussed in this chapter, the legitimacy of the Australian and other research governance systems also suffer from the low visibility (and therefore limited accountability) of ethics committee decision-making.

132 McNeill, PM, "Research Ethics Review and the Bureaucracy" (2002) 21 *Monash Bioethics Review* 72.

PART X

INFORMATION, PRIVACY AND CONFIDENTIALITY

27

Re-thinking confidentiality

Marilyn McMahon

Introduction

Confidentiality is frequently described as a cornerstone of good health care practice but there is evidence that the concept and associated practices need re-examination. Practitioners have called the concept "decrepit"[1] and claimed that "in medicine it is now more often absent than present".[2] Academic commentators have charted an increasing number of exceptions to the duty of confidentiality.[3] Professional bodies have also addressed change; for example, the Royal Society of Medicine convened a meeting in March 2004 entitled "Confidentiality in Medicine: Myth or Reality?"[4]

Finally, the growing body of privacy legislation governing selected information may, paradoxically, mark the demise of confidentiality by supplanting it with the related notion of privacy and establishing more accessible grievance procedures. Dissatisfaction with traditional notions of confidentiality, ossified in outmoded rituals and expectations which are inconsistent with contemporary practice, provides the springboard for re-thinking this most important concept.

---

1   Siegler, M, "Confidentiality in Medicine – A Decrepit Concept?" (1982) 307 *New England Journal of Medicine* 1518.

2   Davies, P, "Who Are We Kidding on Confidentiality?" (2004, Summer) *Hoolet: The Magazine of the RCGP Scotland*.

3   Neave, M, "AIDS – Confidentiality and the Duty to Warn" (1989) 9 *University of Tasmania Law Review* 1; Abadee, A, "The Medical Duty of Confidentiality and the Prospective Duty of Disclosure: Can They Coexist?" (1995) 3 *JLM* 7; McSherry B, "Confidentiality of Psychiatric and Psychological Communications: The Public Interest Exception" (2001) 8 *Psychiatry, Psychology and Law* 12; Sauci, LA, Sawyer, SA, Weller, PJ, Bond, LM and Patton, GC, "Youth Health Research Ethics: Time for a Mature-Minor Clause?" (2004) 180 (7) *Medical Journal of Australia* 336.

4   See <www.kcl.ac.uk/phpnews/wmview.php?ArtID=561> (accessed 19 April 2005).

Routine and ritual: Confidentiality in modern health care

> Ritual behaviour, in the sense of prescribed action repeated from time to time, in a systematic way, is a common part of human life.[5]

Information is routinely imparted by clients to health care professionals with the expectation that it will not be disseminated more widely than authorised by the client. Confidentiality is frequently held to be a defining feature of relationships between clients and medical practitioners, nurses, psychologists, physiotherapists, social workers and other health care professionals. Thus, the World Medical Association believes that confidentiality in the doctor–patient relationship is regarded by most doctors as extremely important and is taken for granted by patients.[6]

However, despite the claimed centrality of confidentiality in the relationship between health care professionals and their clients, the basis for this obligation has rarely been adequately explicated. There is considerable diversity in practice, legal remedies for breaches are often difficult to access, and there are numerous exceptions to the general duty. Interestingly, as protections for the privacy of health care information have increased there has been a concurrent circumscription of protections for the confidentiality of such information.

Nevertheless, the concept of confidentiality has a powerful impact – symbolic, professional and behavioural – on health care practitioners. For the *ritual* of confidentiality is central to modern health care practice: it provides practitioners with relatively fixed guides to behaviour, ensuring that their statements and actions are not simply individual or *ad hoc*.

Ritualistic endorsement of confidentiality is frequently contained in information brochures distributed by practitioners that guarantee clients absolute confidentiality; conversely, ritualistic setting of limits to confidentiality is common in standard consent-to-disclosure authorisations required from clients. Confidentiality is the basis of secular, professional ritual insofar as it is a customary feature of the relationship between clients and practitioners, helps to define their different roles, affirms the power of practitioners (the repositories of secret information) and is not simply immediately instrumental.[7]

In short, while the ritualistic nature of confidentiality in health care relationships demonstrates the significance of this concept, there are many limitations concerning the degree of confidentiality attached to contemporary health care relationships.

In this chapter I will analyse the concept and practice of confidentiality. The rituals of confidentiality will be located within particular historical contexts and deconstructed through an exploration of the actual behaviour (as well as the

---

5 Goring, R (ed), *Dictionary of Beliefs and Religions*, Larousse, Edinburgh, 1992, p 442.
6 World Medical Association, *Resolution on Medical Secrecy*.
7 Leach, ER, "Ritual" in Sills, DL (ed), *International Encyclopedia of the Social Sciences* Vol 13, Macmillan, United States, 1968, p 520.

rhetoric) of health care professionals. Relevant legal and ethical frameworks will also be considered, identifying the circumstances in which unauthorised disclosure may legitimately occur and, conversely, the remedies available to clients who have had confidential health care information disseminated without their consent. For the purposes of this chapter the term "health care professional" includes medical practitioners, nurses, physiotherapists, occupational therapists, dentists, psychologists and social workers.[8]

The historical landscape

> Confidentiality as a legal matter is a problem that has mainly arisen in this century. There are few references to it in the early reports of the Medical Defence Union and these usually refer to ... relatively simple "run of the mill" queries.[9]

The modern conception of confidentiality in the relationship between clients and health care professionals has evolved from ethical and legal principles developed in relation to medical practitioners and their patients. Thus, much of the discussion, including many of the legal cases regarding confidentiality, has involved medical practitioners and medical codes of ethics. Although the current chapter relies upon the similar focus and ethical commitments of other health care practitioners when treating their duties and responsibilities in relation to confidentiality as analogous to those of medical practitioners, a constant – and relatively unexplored – tension will be the degree to which different categories of health care practitioners may have dissimilar duties and responsibilities in relation to their clients.[10]

Nevertheless, in all health care relationships confidentiality concerns "the degree of secrecy" to be attached to information received by health care professionals in the course of their professional activities.[11] Confidentiality is relational: it is derived from the relationship when a client gives information to a health care practitioner, with the understanding that the recipient will not disclose it (or will disclose it only to the degree authorised by the client). In this respect confidentiality may be distinguished from privacy, for protections of privacy are often based on the *type of information* rather than the relationship in which the information is imparted.

---

8   Much of the discussion is also applicable to "natural therapists". However, uncertainty in relation to the scope of this designation and limited analogous status with the medical profession (from which much of the law and ethics relating to confidentiality is derived) suggest that consideration of these practitioners is beyond the scope of this chapter.

9   Hawkins, C, *Mishap or Malpractice?*, Blackwell, Oxford, 1985, p 219.

10   But see Jenkins, P, "Client or Patient? Contrasts Between Medical and Counselling Models of Confidentiality" (1999) 12 (2) *Counselling Psychology Quarterly* 169.

11   Fox, R, "Ethical and Legal Principles of Confidentiality for Psychologists and Social Workers", in Nixon, M (ed), *Issues in Psychological Practice*, Longman Cheshire, Sydney, 1984.

Hippocratic Oath

Although considerations of confidentiality in health care relationships routinely involve discussion of the Hippocratic Oath,[12] written five centuries BC,[13] the relevance of this oath to modern health care is complex. Followers of the Hippocratic School swore:

> Whatsoever things I see or hear concerning the life of men, in my attendance on the sick or even apart therefrom, which ought not to be noised abroad, I will keep silence thereon, counting such things to be sacred secrets ... I will respect the secrets which are confided in me, even after the patient has died.[14]

While the oath reveals an early commitment to confidentiality in the relationship between physician and patient, the historical legacy has been overstated.[15] The oath originated from an esoteric cult and, as well as protecting the interests of patients, was designed to protect trade secrets and maintain control over members.[16] The oath was never universally adopted by different schools of practice and was not generally accepted throughout English history. Interest in the oath was revived in England in the late 18th and early 19th centuries when physicians and surgeons sought increasing recognition and developed codes of conduct as part of their quest for professionalisation. Emphasising the confidential nature of the relationship between patient and practitioner enhanced the status of physicians and surgeons.

Nevertheless, the symbolic value of the oath persists and a modern adaptation is contained in the *Declaration of Geneva*, originally adopted by the World Medical Association at its first assembly in 1948.[17] Professional organisations representing health care professionals in Australia have each adopted specific provisions in relation to confidentiality in their codes of ethics (see "Professional endorsements of confidentiality" in this chapter).

While the role of confidentiality in the relationship between medical practitioner and client has a long history, disputes about confidentiality have arisen only in relatively recent times. Hawkins notes that interest in confidentiality arose mainly in the 20th century and that early discussion typically involved three types of issues:

---

12 For example, see Hawkins (1985) op cit. Also note that the Preamble to the *Code of Ethics* of the Australian Medical Association states that "This Code has grown out of other similar ethical codes stretching back into history including the Hippocratic Oath". Australian Medical Association, *Code of Ethics*, AMA, Barton, ACT, 2004.

13 Some commentators have argued that the Hippocratic Oath was actually developed by a later group of physicians who were followers of Pythagoras. See Edelstein, L, *The Hippocratic Oath: Text, Translation and Interpretation*, John Hopkins Press, Baltimore, Maryland, 1943.

14 In *The Handbook of Medical Ethics*, British Medical Association, United Kingdom, 1981.

15 For an insightful analysis of the development and function of the Hippocratic Oath, see Britton, A, "Hippocrates: Dead or Alive?" in Petersen, K, *Intersections: Women on Law, Medicine and Technology*, Ashgate, Aldershot, 1997.

16 Thompson, IE, "The Nature of Confidentiality" (1979) 5 *Journal of Medical Ethics* 57.

17 The current version of the *Declaration of Geneva* states: "I will respect the secrets which are confided in me, even after the patient has died".

- inquiries by insurance companies for information to which they were not entitled because the patient had not consented to disclosure;

- requests to doctors from solicitors in cases where the solicitor was not acting for the patient and had not obtained the necessary consent; and

- requests by the police for information about patients where consent was also absent.[18]

Confidentiality and the public interest

Historically, assessment of the appropriate scope of confidentiality in health care relationships has reflected prevailing social values. This is clearly illustrated by a case that caused controversy at the turn of the century but which would most likely be decided differently today. A general practitioner treated a railway employee for asthma. The client's attacks were sometimes so distressing that he collapsed and was incapacitated for an hour. The employee frequently was the sole operator of a signal box; at the time that he consulted his doctor he had not experienced an asthma attack while on duty. The client refused to disclose his medical condition to his employers for he feared that he would be dismissed or demoted. The editor of the *British Medical Journal* opined in 1906 that:

> The circumstances, extreme though they be, cannot be held to justify a breach of the law of professional secrecy ... the doctor ought not to write direct to the railway company without the patient's consent, and unless he fully understands the nature of the communications to be made.[19]

Commentators have argued that if this case arose today contemporary medical opinion would clearly favour disclosure,[20] reflecting the relatively recent expansion of the "public interest" exception to the duty of confidentiality.

Confidentiality and minors

Another area where discussion of confidentiality has aroused considerable controversy and reflected changing social values has been in relation to the confidentiality to be afforded to minors (persons younger than 18 years), and the age at which they should be vested with the same rights to confidentiality in their relations with health care practitioners as adults.

In earlier periods the legal position was clear: parents had a right to access information about their minor children. However, the border between childhood and adulthood has become less clearly defined, and "young persons" may assume

---

18 Hawkins (1985) op cit.

19 "Railway Signalman: Professional Secrecy" (1906) *British Medical Journal* 1753 (15 December 1906).

20 For example, Hawkins (1985) op cit.

many responsibilities: obtain employment, enter into some contracts, leave home and live independently. Significantly, young persons over 15 years of age can obtain a Medibank card in their own name (and thereby access medical services independently of their parents). Lord Denning observed in 1970 that, in relation to the legal right of a parent to the custody of their child, as a child progresses from birth to 18 years of age: "It starts with a right to control and ends with little more than advice".[21] This observation also is apposite in relation to parents' rights to access confidential information about their minor children, a right which similarly diminishes as the child matures.

Furthermore, confidentiality is necessarily entwined with other significant concepts, such as competency: it is generally conceded that minors who are competent to consent to health care should also be afforded confidentiality in relation to that care. Accordingly, a statement issued by the Medical Practitioners Board of Victoria states that "Medical practitioners have a legal and ethical duty to maintain the confidentiality of a competent young person".[22]

Contemporary discussion of this issue clearly reflects very different values: those who favour maximising parents' rights of access typically strongly endorse traditional family values[23] while those who endorse minors' rights to confidentiality usually adopt a utilitarian and "young persons' rights" approach.[24] Shifting historical views and diverse contemporary values ensure that health care practitioners dealing with minor clients frequently confront ethical and legal dilemmas. These difficulties are highlighted when issues of self-harm and suicide arise. While such matters also may cause difficulties in relation to adult clients, the extra dimension of the legal status of a young client compounds this issue.

Thus, a recent commentator on youth suicide suggested that the multiple legal and ethical provisions governing confidentiality and privacy actually may

---

21 *Hewer v Bryant* [1970] 1 QB 357 at 369.

22 Medical Practitioners Board of Victoria, *Consent for Treatment and Confidentiality in Young People*, Medical Practitioners Board of Victoria, Melbourne, 2004. Similarly, Sauci et al (2004) op cit, argue strongly for a reconsideration of young people's participation in research. Acknowledging the importance of consent and confidentiality, they favour adopting a "mature minor" approach thereby allowing minors to give informed consent (and be accorded confidentiality) when they achieve sufficient understanding and intelligence to enable them to understand fully what is proposed. These authors argue that confidentiality is a corollary of the mature-minor doctrine. Note that United Medical Protection advises that for children under 14 years of age the consent of a parent is required for the disclosure of confidential information: *Medico-Legal Handbook*, United Medical Protection, Sydney, 2003, p 50.

23 For example, when Tony Abbott (Federal Minister for Health) introduced legislation that would raise the age at which young people could obtain their own Medicare card and gave parents greater access to information held by the Health Insurance Commission about Medicare-funded consultations or tests for their children, he justified the changes by referring to the "rights of parents" and the lack of capacity of young persons to make informed decisions: "Mind Your Own Medicine" <www. theage.com.au> (accessed 19 April 2005).

24 Sauci et al (2004) op cit.

impede the delivery of adequate services. He noted that the matrix of relevant parties usually involved not only the young person but their family, school, counsellor, and health care practitioners and that "appropriate management of suicidal tendencies may be impaired by the myriad of legal provisions that dictate the levels to which the relevant parties can interact".[25]

The contemporary landscape

It is difficult to see how the doctor's duty to maintain confidentiality can be maintained in an age when records are transferred from one health care provider to another, who each adds their comment about the patient's treatment and care. Where records are computerised making them accessible via computer link-up further erosion is made in the doctor's duty to maintain patient's confidentiality.[26]

Contemporary health care professionals work within a complex framework of interrelated individual values, professional codes of ethics, employer directives,[27] organisational settings,[28] technological developments,[29] legal obligations[30]

---

25 Stewart, JG, "Taking Youth Suicide Seriously: Disclosure of Information Between School, Family and Health Professionals in New Zealand" [2001] *Victoria University of Wellington Law Review* 16.

26 *Australian Health and Medical Law Reporter* ¶48-940.

27 Health care practitioners may be compelled by the terms of their employment to disclose confidential information conveyed to them by clients. The principle is well established; 15 years ago Richard Fox, analysing the situation of psychologists, commented that:

> Whenever psychologists ... are employed in an institutional setting, whether in government or private employment, they are liable to be directed by their superiors in the hierarchy to write reports, hand over files or supply information regarding services provided to others in the course of employment.

Fox (1984) op cit, p 177.

28 Powe has commented:

> The maintenance of traditional formulations of medical confidentiality pose an impossible task for individual practitioners, given the organisational structures involved in the practice of contemporary medicine. That practice, of necessity, is fragmented as the patient and/or his record passes through an increasingly complex framework designed to ensure the delivery of proper care and treatment.

Powe, R, "Confidentiality" in Dix, A Errington, M, Nicholson K and Powe R (eds) *Law for the Medical Profession*, 2nd edn, Butterworth Heinemann, Sydney, 1996, p 78. This historical shift has been acknowledged in the *Code of Ethics* of the Royal Australian and New Zealand College of Psychiatry (RANZCP Code of Ethics), Carlton South, 1998. Annotations to the Principles 4.2: "In light of changes in information technology and organisational structures, psychiatrists have a particular accountability to protect clinical information".

29 Pargiter and Bloch reviewed the operation of the ethics committee of the RANZCP and noted that "new technology in the form of computers has complicated matters of confidentiality". Pargiter, R and Bloch, S, "The Ethics Committee of a Psychiatric College: Its Procedures and Themes" (1998) 32 *Australian & New Zealand Journal of Psychiatry* 76 at 81.

30 Increasingly salient are federal and State privacy regimes that regulate access to, and disclosure of, selected information.

and scientific developments.[31] Recent developments that may negatively impact upon confidentiality in the relationship between client and health care practitioner include: payments by third-parties (such as health insurance organisations); the demands of courts; the proliferation of huge data banks; and fear of *Tarasoff*-type litigation.[32]

Additionally, changes in the delivery of health care services have required a re-thinking of confidentiality. Traditional notions of confidentiality were based on the relationship between an individual client and single medical practitioner and must be adapted to the contemporary delivery of health care in multi-disciplinary and organisational settings. In the modern environment clients' interests in confidentiality frequently must be balanced against their interest in receiving the best possible treatment – a goal that may require the cooperation of members of different health care disciplines, necessarily involving the exchange of detailed information.[33]

The emergence of different professional specialisations within health care in the 20th century has created further dilemmas in relation to the appropriate level of exchange of client information and caused re-evaluation of the concept of confidentiality. An interesting description of the limits of confidentiality in a modern hospital setting was provided by the American physician Siegler who, after having had a patient admitted for a simple surgical procedure, noted that:

> [A]t least 25 and possibly as many as 100 health professionals and administrative personnel at our university hospital had access ... and all of them had a legitimate need, indeed a professional responsibility, to open and use [the patient's] chart. These persons included 6 attending physicians ... 12 house officers ... 20 nursing personnel ... 6 respiratory therapists; 3 nutritionists; 2 clinical pharmacists; 15 students (from medicine, nursing, respiratory therapy, and clinical pharmacy); 4 unit secretaries; 4 hospital finance officers; and 4 chart reviewers (utilisation review, quality assurance review, tissue review and insurance auditor).[34]

---

31   For example, the Human Genome Project and genetic research presents new dilemmas in relation to confidentiality. See McLean, S and Giesen, D, "Legal and Ethical Considerations of the Human Genome Project" (1994) 1 *Medical Law International* 159; Brown, IJ and Gannon, P, "Confidentiality and the Human Genome Project: A Prophecy for Conflict?" in McLean, S, (ed) *Contemporary Issues in Law, Medicine and Ethics*, Darlmouth, Brookfield, Vermont, 1995.

32   Bongar, B, "Clinicians, Microcomputers and Confidentiality" (1988) 19 *Professional Psychology* 286.

33   When a person obtains services from a practitioner at an institution or agency where a number of different groups (doctors, nurses, psychologists and so on) may be involved in their care, consent by the client for other practitioners at that institution or agency to access their health information may be implied. This is the "need-to-know" principle identified in *City of Birmingham District Council v O* [1983] 1 All ER 497. Also see Thompson (1979) op cit; Hawkins (1985) op cit. Note, however, that statutory-based privacy schemes in some States and Territories in Australia specifically regulate access to, and disclosure of, health information.

34   Siegler (1982) op cit.

Siegler concluded that the traditional medical conception of confidentiality was decrepit and needed to be revised for contemporary medical practice. Similarly, Australian health care professionals working in clinics, hospitals, community health centres, government agencies and other multidisciplinary settings are often confronted with dilemmas regarding the appropriate extent of disclosure of information to other professionals and the circumstances in which client confidentiality can be breached. Outmoded, ritualistic endorsements of confidentiality do not appear to have recognised this historical shift in the delivery of health care and the manner in which these developments have had an impact upon confidentiality in the relationship between health care professionals and their clients.

As will be discussed subsequently, the confidentiality of the client-practitioner relationship is specifically endorsed in the ethical codes of many of the health care professions and is afforded legal recognition in diverse ways. When considering the contemporary situation in Australia, interesting information regarding the practices of Australian health care professionals comes from a limited number of empirical studies which have investigated practitioners' attitudes and practices in this area. The following discussion is relevant to discussions of "common practice" in relation to confidentiality and demonstrates the diverse ways in which health care professionals perceive and enact their ethical and legal obligations of confidentiality.

Empirical information:
Attitudes and practices in relation to confidentiality

Australian data suggest that considerable variability exists in health care professionals' practices and attitudes to confidentiality, as well as in clients' beliefs and expectations about confidentiality in their relationships with such professionals.

A large-scale survey in South Australia revealed that almost four per cent of respondents believed that information had been disclosed by a health service provider without their consent. Subsequent analysis suggested that the majority of these disclosures were "legally defensible", frequently involving the release of information to other treating practitioners or disclosure mandated by legislation. Interestingly, the authors reported that nearly half the respondents appeared to be "unconcerned' about these disclosures.[35] However, further exploration of "relatively mundane" cases of disclosure of health information without client consent also revealed that routine and justified disclosure of information by health care

---

35   Mulligan, EC, "Confidentiality in Health Records: Evidence of Current Performance From a Population Survey in South Australia" (2001) 174 *Medical Journal of Australia* 637. The author identified 108 cases in which client information had been disclosed without consent; in 47 per cent (51) of these cases the respondents were reported to be "unconcerned". Of the 80 cases which could be further analysed, 60 per cent (48) were categorised as "legally defensible" disclosures.

practitioners could be "perceived as problematic" by clients,[36] suggesting a disjunction between client and practitioner attitudes.

In relation to practitioners, a survey investigating the practices and attitudes of Victorian psychologists and psychiatrists reported that most respondents believed that their clients assumed that the therapeutic relationship was absolutely confidential, although the practitioners themselves believed that confidentiality was important but could be breached in some circumstances.[37] Only a very small number of respondents believed that it was of marginal value or unimportant. Nevertheless, only a minority of practitioners routinely discussed the possibility that they might disclose confidential information although a substantial minority (approximately 20 per cent of respondents) believed that some of their clients had terminated treatment because they feared a breach of confidentiality. The results of this study indicated that, whilst confidentiality was strongly endorsed by practitioners (and assumed by clients), most of these psychiatrists and psychologists believed that some circumstances justified the unauthorised disclosure of confidential information. Further contemporary data concerning health care professionals' views on confidentiality come from studies which have investigated attitudes and practices in relation to clients infected with the human immunodeficiency virus (HIV).

Empirical data:
Confidentiality and the HIV+ client

It is commonly asserted that new diseases such as HIV and AIDS present novel confidentiality dilemmas. Hence, much discussion in recent years has occurred in relation to the unauthorised disclosure of information about clients who are HIV-positive or who have AIDS. Confidentiality in the therapeutic relationship between a health care professional and a client infected with HIV has been described as:

> [The] cornerstone of a fortress that protects people with HIV infection from the worst of society's reactions: employment discrimination, insurance problems, familial disruption and social ostracism.[38]

The need to protect infected individuals from discrimination and stigmatisation has led to the introduction of specific statutory protections federally and in some State and Territory jurisdictions to prohibit discrimination on the basis of HIV

---

36 Braunack-Mayer, AJ and Mulligan, EC, "Sharing Patient Information Between Professionals: Confidentiality and Ethics" (2003) 178 *Medical Journal of Australia* 277.

37 McMahon, M and Knowles, A, "Psychologists' and Psychiatrists' Perceptions of the Dangerous Client" (1992) 1 *Psychiatry, Psychology and Law* 207.

38 Wood, GJ, Marks, R and Dilley, JW, *AIDS Law for Mental Health Professionals*. AIDS Health Project, University of California, San Francisco, 1990, p 15; Godwin, J, Hamblin, J, Patterson, D and Buchanan, D *Australian HIV/AIDS Legal Guide*, 2nd edn, Federation Press, Sydney, 1993.

seropositivity,[39] and specific obligations to protect confidentiality have been enacted.[40] Confidentiality is also a cornerstone of current public health policy which endorses extensive voluntary testing for those who may be at risk as the principal strategy for controlling the spread of the disease.

Extensive discussion in the professional literature has also explored justifications for breaching or maintaining the confidentiality of an HIV-positive client who may be engaging in activities likely to place others at risk of infection (for example, sharing needles or engaging in unsafe sex).[41] Several professional organisations representing health care practitioners have relevant general provisions in their ethical codes. The Australian Medical Association amended its *Code of Ethics* in 1996 to permit disclosure of otherwise confidential information where a client was placing others at medical risk. The Australian Psychological Society's *Code of Ethics* specifies that a psychologist may breach client confidentiality where there is a "clear risk to the client or to others" (General Principle IIIA). Disclosure in these circumstances has been argued to be ethically justified because the patient constitutes a serious risk of harm to another and therefore the situation constitutes an exception to the general obligation of confidentiality.

Hence, many commentators have argued that practitioners have an ethical duty to warn identifiable partners of an HIV-positive client who refuses to inform a partner of his or her status and who continues to place others at risk.[42] In Tasmania, legislation empowers medical practitioners who are treating clients who have HIV/AIDS to warn third parties who may be at risk from their client.[43] Legislation in New South Wales permits, in limited circumstances, the disclosure of such information to the Director-General of the Department of Health.[44] Although other jurisdictions have legislation investing public health authorities with the power to detain or otherwise deal with persons who are placing the public at risk, the

---

39   For example, *Equal Opportunity Act 1995* (Vic) s 4. Unlawful discrimination on the basis of impairment is prohibited; the definition of "impairment" includes:

    (b)   the presence in the body of organisms that may cause disease.

Similarly, the definition of "disability" in the *Disability Discrimination Act 1992* (Cth) s 4 includes:

    (c)   the presence in the body of organisms carrying disease or illness, or
    (d)   the presence in the body of organisms capable of carrying disease or illness.

40   For example, *Public Health Act 1991* (NSW) s 17; *HIV/AIDS Preventive Measures Act 1993* (Tas) ss 17, 18, 19; *Health Act 1958* (Vic) s 128.

41   Annas, GJ and Davidson, IS, "The HIV-positive Patient Who Won't Tell the Spouse" (1987) 21 *Aspects of Human Sexuality* 16. Neave (1989) op cit; Abadee (1995) op cit; Oakley, J, "The Morality of Breaching Confidentiality to Protect Others" in Shotton, L (ed), *Health Care Law and Ethics*, Social Science Press, Katoomba, NSW, 1997.

42   Annas and Davidson (1987) op cit; Gostin L and Curran, WJ, "AIDS Screening, Confidentiality and the Duty to Warn" (1987) 77 *American Journal of Public Health* 361; Walters, L, "Ethical Issues in the Prevention and Treatment of HIV Infection and AIDS" (1988) 239 *Science* 597; Knapp, S and Vandecreek, L, "Application of the Duty to Protect to HIV-Positive Patients" (1990) 21 *Professional Psychology* 161.

43   *HIV/AIDS Preventive Measures Act 1993* (Tas) s 20(7).

44   *Public Health (General) Regulation 2002* (NSW) s 10.

provisions are cumbersome. Thus, in several jurisdictions in Australia there is no clear guidance in law or professional codes for the health care professional dealing with the HIV-positive client who may recklessly or intentionally be placing others at risk of infection.

In the general absence of clear ethical and legal guidelines regarding disclosure of this type of information in most jurisdictions in Australia, the actual practices and attitudes of health care practitioners deserve examination. Grove and Mulligan surveyed 548 general practitioners and specialist physicians in Western Australia and asked them whether they would tell a patient's sexual partner that a patient was HIV+ when the patient refused to do so.[45] The majority of practitioners indicated that they would disclose information: 41 per cent would *always* tell a partner, and 25 per cent would disclose on *some* occasions. Eleven per cent of respondents stated that they would *never* advise the partner. Interestingly, nearly one-quarter of these medical practitioners were undecided as to what they would do, causing the authors to suggest that this partly reflected uncertainty over the legal consequences of breaching confidentiality. They further noted that, when considering an appropriate response to this dilemma, respondents were concerned about the possibility of personal damage claims by patients and were also apprehensive about complaints to medical registration boards and other statutory authorities regarding inappropriate standards of professional behaviour.

Speculation exists as to the factors that influence health care practitioners to favour or oppose disclosure of confidential information. For example, it is possible that attitudes to disclosure are related to general attitudes to AIDS, particularly knowledge of a client's mode of acquiring HIV. In an earlier study I specifically investigated whether attitudes to confidentiality in counselling HIV clients was affected by knowledge of mode of infection.[46] Respondents (trainee psychologists) were asked whether they believed that a psychologist had an ethical and/or legal duty to warn the partner of an HIV-positive client who refused to disclose his seropositive status and who engaged in behaviour that placed the partner at risk of infection. Most respondents believed that the psychologist had an ethical duty to inform a client's partner of the risk; more than a third of the respondents also believed that a legal duty existed. Disquietingly, mode of infection significantly affected perceptions that the psychologist had a legal duty to act proactively and inform the client's partner. Disclosure was more favoured when the client was infected by sexual intercourse with a prostitute or homosexual activity than when the client was infected by blood transfusion or heterosexual activity.[47]

---

45 Grove, DI and Mulligan, JB, "Consent, Compulsion and Confidentiality in Relation to Testing for HIV Infection: the Views of WA Doctors" (1990) 152 *Medical Journal of Australia* 174.

46 McMahon, M, "Confidentiality in AIDS-Related Psychotherapy and Counselling", paper presented to the 26th Annual Conference of the Australian Psychological Society, Hobart, 1991.

47 Ibid.

Nevertheless, it is important to note that although the AIDS epidemic may be recent, the types of confidentiality dilemmas that have arisen are not. As Professor John Dwyer has commented:

> Informing a sexual partner of the risks involved in sexual intercourse with a HIV infected partner who has ordered confidentiality is not ethically different from staying silent while knowing that bus driver John is ... inebriated while driving.[48]

Furthermore, it should be noted that the type of "high-profile" dilemma represented in this type of research may not be representative of the circumstances in which unauthorised disclosure of confidential information typically occurs. Intentional disclosure consequent to analysis and reflection may represent an unusual act. Thus, the Medical Practitioners Board of Victoria has claimed that most breaches of confidentiality by doctors result from carelessness rather than intentional disclosure.[49]

In summary, although confidentiality is a vaunted feature of the relationship between clients and health care professionals, it is clear that there is diversity in the attitudes and practices of Australian health care practitioners and some disjunction between the expectations of clients and the behaviour of these practitioners. Examination of the ethical and legal bases of confidentiality is now appropriate.

Professional endorsements of confidentiality

> The general rule is that doctors may not, without the consent of their patients, disclose to any third party information acquired by reason of their professional relationship.[50]

The ethical and legal bases of the obligation of confidence owed by health care professionals to their clients have been acknowledged explicitly by most relevant organisations in Australia and the courts. The ethical duty of confidentiality is generally seen to be more extensive than the legal duty.[51] As previously noted, the origins of this ethical obligation have been traced to the Hippocratic Oath and its modern version in the Declaration of Geneva. More specific, local principles in relation to confidentiality are contained in the various codes of ethics of

---

48 Dwyer, JM, "The Hippocratic Irrelevance Variable (HIV)" (1990) 152 *Medical Journal of Australia* 169.

49 "Most complaints relating to breaches of confidentiality received by the Board are not flagrant. They often arise when doctors confuse their responsibilities to parties to marital or family disputes, or when doctors are careless about how they or their staff handle requests for patient information": Medical Practitioners Board of Victoria, *Annual Report*, MPBV, Melbourne, 1998, p 24.

50 Breen, K, Plueckhahn, V and Cordner, S, *Ethics, Law and Medical Practice*, Allen & Unwin, Sydney, 1997, p 39.

51 See, for example, see *Furniss v Fitchett* [1958] NZLR 396 at 404 per Barrowclough CJ.

organisations representing health care professionals in Australia. A breach of confidentiality by a member of these organisations may constitute an ethical violation and make the practitioner liable to a disciplinary hearing.

Medical practitioners

The *Code of Ethics* adopted by the Australian Medical Association (AMA), the largest national professional organisation representing medical practitioners in Australia, endorses confidentiality:

> Maintain your patient's confidentiality. Exceptions to this must be taken very seriously. They may include where there is a serious risk to the patient or another person, where required by law, where part of approved research, or where there are overwhelming societal interests.[52]

As indicated, disclosure of confidential information is permitted where required by law, for the protection of the patient or another or under the more general exception of "overwhelming societal interests".[53] The AMA Code appears to justify – but not compel – disclosure in these circumstances.

Other relevant professional organisations, such as the various medical colleges, occasionally issue guidelines to members. For example, the Royal Australian and New Zealand College of Psychiatry's (RANZCP) *Code of Ethics* endorses the principle of confidentiality but acknowledges that "[c]onfidentiality cannot always be absolute".[54] Additionally, in circumstances where a patient has an intention to seriously harm an identified person or group of persons and the psychiatrist is unable to "eliminate" this threat, the code specifies that a psychiatrist may be released from the duty to maintain confidentiality:

> In these circumstances, psychiatrists have an overriding duty to inform either the intended victim(s), the relevant authorities, or both, about the threat.[55]

Nurses

The *Code of Professional Conduct for Nurses in Australia*, adopted by the Australian Nursing and Midwifery Council, specifies that:

> 8. A nurse must treat personal information obtained in a professional capacity as confidential.[56]

---

52   Australian Medical Association, *Code of Ethics*, AMA, Canberra, 2004, Principle 1.1(l).

53   Ibid.

54   Principle 4: Psychiatrists shall hold clinical information in confidence: RANZCP Code. See further Coady, M and Bloch, S, *Codes of Ethics and the Professions*, Melbourne University Press, Melbourne, 1996.

55   RANZCP Code, Annotations to the Principles 4.6.

56   Australian Nursing and Midwifery Council, *Code of Professional Conduct for Nurses in Australia*, Australian Nursing and Midwifery Council, Canberra, 2005.

Further commentary acknowledges that clients should be informed about any limits to confidentiality. Client consent to disclosure is to be obtained "where practicable" and, in the absence of consent, a nurse is required to consider the "interests, well-being, health and safety" of the client, as well as the requirements of the law, when considering whether to disclose confidential information about a client.[57]

Psychologists

The Australian Psychological Society's (APS) *Code of Ethics* strongly endorses the principle of confidentiality in the relationship between a psychologist and client.[58] Specific provisions exist which restrict the disclosure of information obtained through consulting relationships and assessment procedures, or from other professionals. Restrictions are placed on the disclosure of information to other professionals and protections are required for the storage and disposal of records. General Principle III(a) is the clearest statement of general principle on confidentiality; it requires that psychologists respect the confidentiality of information obtained in the course of their professional work and states that disclosure may only occur with the client's consent except where "failure to disclose may result in clear risk to the client or to others".[59] Disclosure is not mandatory except where the client is imminently suicidal.[60]

Social workers

The Australian Association of Social Workers' *Code of Ethics* states that:

> Social workers will respect the rights of clients to a relationship of trust, to privacy and confidentiality of their information and to responsible use of information obtained in the course of professional service.[61]

The social worker is required to inform clients about the limits of confidentiality and the purposes for which information is obtained and how it may be used.[62] The informed consent of clients must be obtained before their activities are mechanically or electronically recorded or observed by a third party.[63]

---

57   Ibid, p 9.
58   Australian Psychological Society, *Code of Ethics*, APS, Melbourne, 2003.
59   Ibid, General Principle III(a).
60   Ibid.
61   Australian Association of Social Workers, *Code of Ethics*, AASW, Barton, ACT, 2002. Principle 4.2.5(a) (AASW Code).
62   Ibid, Principle 4.2.5(b).
63   Ibid, Principle 4.2.5(e).

Professional endorsements: Summary

A notable feature of the ethical guidelines developed by different professional organisations is that they uniformly promote confidentiality in the relationship between practitioner and client, although none endorse absolute, inviolable confidentiality: all note that some circumstances may justify the disclosure of confidential information, including the demands of the law. Thus, the *Code of Ethics* of the Australian Association of Social Workers justifies disclosure "for ethical or moral reasons" and the Australian Nursing and Midwifery Council requires that a nurse consider the "interests, well-being, health and safety" of a client when considering disclosure. Essentially, unauthorised disclosure is permitted by each of the guidelines, although the circumstances justifying disclosure vary and the individual health care practitioner is required to exercise his or her discretion in deciding whether a breach is justified in all the circumstances of a particular case. The significant exception to this general orientation is provided by the Australian Psychological Society which makes disclosure of confidential information mandatory in those circumstances where a psychologist believes that a patient is imminently suicidal, where disclosure of information is deemed essential to the well-being of the client and where the client has refused to consent to disclosure.

Health care professionals who breach the guidelines of their relevant professional organisation may have thereby breached appropriate ethical standards. An aggrieved client may complain to an ethics committee of the organisation which may, if the complaint is upheld, impose a penalty or sanction upon the practitioner. Such forms of complaint have the benefits for clients of being relatively inexpensive and usually quick. However, the efficacy of this mechanism to enforce confidentiality is severely limited as: not all practitioners belong to their relevant professional organisation; the most severe sanction that voluntary, professional organisations can impose is to expel the member; and expulsion does not by itself prevent a health care professional from continuing to practise. Finally, professional organisations usually have no power to require that a member compensate a client for any harm suffered as a result of the unauthorised disclosure.

Why confidentiality?
The ethical justification

Confidentiality pertains to the degree of secrecy to be attached to information disclosed *in a relationship*. The relationship is predicated on the authority of the practitioner.[64] Confidentiality is particularly significant in health care relationships as sensitive, intimate and secret information will be frequently conveyed by clients to their practitioners. Although infrequently explicitly addressed, the endorsement

---

64   Thompson (1979) op cit.

of confidentiality in the relationship between health care professionals and their clients has a fourfold basis:

1. Confidentiality between the practitioner and patient is good in itself for it respects the personal integrity of the person disclosing the information. Often linked to a Kantian approach, this perspective reverberates with much of the modern discussion of rights.[65]

2. Confidentiality is based upon respect for the patient's autonomy. In the relationship between health care professional and client it is the client who divulges information and, respecting that client's autonomy, it is the client who should decide what information may be disclosed (if any) and to whom. Thus, by holding secret that which a client wishes to keep secret, a health care professional is respecting the autonomy of the client.[66] This perspective also reverberates with legal reasoning, as respect for personal autonomy was identified as the basis for protecting privacy interests by several judges in a recent case decided by the High Court of Australia.[67]

3. Confidentiality has a utilitarian basis. Assurances of confidentiality are said to encourage needy individuals to enter treatment, to promote disclosure of information that may facilitate treatment and to increase trust in the thera-peutic relationship (trust being viewed as essential for effective therapeutic intervention). This basis was relied upon by Rose J in $X v Y$[68] when he granted an injunction restraining a newspaper from publishing the names of two medical practitioners who were being treated for AIDS and who were believed to be continuing to practise medicine. His Honour argued that:

    > In the long run, preservation of confidentiality is the only way of securing public health; otherwise doctors will be discredited as a source of education, for future individual patients "will not come forward if doctors are going to squeal on them".[69]

4. Confidentiality has a beneficent basis. Breaches of confidentiality are sometimes justified on this basis. Thus, breaching the confidentiality of a client who threatens serious self-harm or suicide is often justified on the basis that such disclosure is in the best interests of the client.

Organisations representing health care professionals frequently employ a mix of these principles both to justify confidentiality as well as the unauthorised disclosure of confidential information. Occasionally, ethical and legal dilemmas

---

65 Richardson, M, "Whither Breach of Confidence: A Right of Privacy for Australia?" (2002) 26 *Melbourne University Law Review* 20.

66 See the World Medical Association, *Resolution on Secrecy*; Bok, S *Lying: Moral Choice in Public and Private Life*, Random House, NY, 1978.

67 *Australian Broadcasting Commission v Lenah Game Meats Pty Ltd* (2001) 208 CLR 199.

68 [1988] 2 All ER 648.

69 Ibid, at 653.

arise when these principles conflict in a particular case. Thus, when a client threatens harm to a third party an individualist emphasis on client autonomy and integrity may clash with a utilitarian emphasis on preventing harm.

In summary, examination of the ethical codes of organisations representing health care professionals in Australia reveals a common endorsement of the principle of confidentiality with the qualification that breaches may legitimately occur – a viewpoint which is also dominant in the literature on this subject.[70] While the ethical guidelines of these organisations are not directly binding at law, they have indirect legal significance as they may be used as a benchmark of adequate practice and may become part of an implied contract, may be relevant in a legal action for negligence[71] or form the basis of a complaint to a registration board or other statutory authority. Hence, examination of the legal bases of confidentiality is now appropriate.

Legal bases of confidentiality

As a prelude to the subsequent discussion, two observations are salient:

1. The fact that both a client and health care professional may believe that information disclosed by the client to the practitioner is confidential does *not* ensure that the law will protect the confidentiality of that relationship.[72] Thus, when a client disclosed information to his psychotherapist concerning past criminal behaviour, the fact that the psychotherapist had repeatedly informed the client that the relationship was confidential did not preclude the information from subsequently being used in criminal proceedings against the client.[73]

---

70 Appelbaum, P, Kapen, G, Walters, B, Lidz, C and Roth, L, "Confidentiality: An Empirical Test of the Utilitarian Perspective" (1984) 12 *Bulletin of the American Academy of Psychiatry and Law* 109.

71 *Furniss v Fitchett* [1958] NZLR 396.

72 Note, however, that legislative reforms in New South Wales introduced privilege in relation to some confidential information disclosed in the course of a professional relationship: *Evidence Act 1995* (NSW).

73 *R v Lowe* [1997] 2 VR 465. In the particular circumstances of this case the psychotherapist had assured Lowe (the client) that the therapy sessions were confidential. After identifying Lowe as the main suspect in the investigation of a child abduction and murder, the Victorian police secretly taped his therapy sessions (originally without the knowledge of the therapist, but subsequently with her consent). At Lowe's subsequent criminal trial, information about the therapy sessions was provided via the tapes and the oral testimony of the psychotherapist. Lowe was convicted of the murder of the six-year-old girl. A key issue, at both the trial and the appeal hearings, was whether courts should be reluctant to admit evidence of a confessional nature which is obtained in trust and confidence by a psychotherapist from a client. Lowe's claim that the information should not have been admitted on the ground that it was obtained in confidence was rejected. Note that the psychotherapist at all times indicated to Lowe that their conversations were confidential: at 483.

2. The distribution of data to third parties after it has been anonymised (by removing information that would identify clients) may not necessarily breach any obligation of confidence.[74]

It has been noted that much of the case law relating to confidentiality has only imprecisely identified the nature of the interests that will be protected and the policy reasons for their protection.[75] Hence, legal commentators have tended to adopt the more pragmatic focus of examining the ways in which laws regulate confidentiality by:

- prohibiting disclosure;

- compelling disclosure; or

- offering protection from civil or criminal sanctions for health care practitioners who choose to disclose confidential information.[76]

In subsequent sections of this chapter I will adopt this pragmatic approach and explore the ways in which laws prohibit, compel or permit disclosure of confidential information by health care professionals.

Prohibitions on disclosure:
Statutory bases of confidentiality

It has sometimes been argued that, prior to the introduction of recent privacy legislation by the Commonwealth and some of the States and Territories, the law provided no general protection for the confidentiality of information disclosed to health care practitioners.[77]

However, other commentators believe that, in general, there was always a duty of confidentiality to be observed,[78] although the legal mechanisms to enforce the duty are indirect and not specific to the health care relationship. A duty of confidentiality may be specifically imposed on health care practitioners by either

---

74 See *R v Department of Health, Ex Parte Source Informatics Ltd* (unreported, Court of Appeal, England, 21 December 1999), <www.lawreports.co.uk/source.htm> (accessed 11 July 2005). Also see Gunning, P, "Anonymising Patient Data Not a Breach of Confidence: Source Informatics Ltd's Application for Judicial Review" [1999] *Privacy Law and Policy Reporter* 64.

75 Richardson, M, "Whither Breach of Confidence: A Right of Privacy for Australia?" [2002] *Melbourne University Law Review* 20. For a general discussion of the legal bases of confidentiality see Bennett, B *Law and Medicine*, LBC, Sydney, 1997, Ch 2; McFarlane, PJM *Health Law in Australia and New Zealand*, 3rd edn, Federation Press, Sydney, 2000.

76 Fox (1984) op cit.

77 "There is no general legal duty [to maintain confidentiality] but some people argue that there should be. The issue has never been tested in court in the United Kingdom and so confidentiality remains an ethical rather than legal principle – thus there is much scope for honestly held differences of view": Hawkins (1985) op cit, p 219.

78 O'Sullivan, J, *Law for Nurses*, Law Book Co, Sydney, 1983.

Commonwealth[79] and/or State legislation[80] or the common law. Legislative provisions tend to be specific to particular situations, activities (for example, research)[81] and classes of health care practitioner (most commonly medical practitioners). Examples of statutory bases of confidentiality include, but are not limited to, the following.

Federal and State privacy legislation

Elsewhere in this book Palombo discusses privacy legislation. The following brief comments are intended simply to demonstrate that analysis of confidentiality necessarily requires examination of related issues such as privacy.

In 2001, the Commonwealth government extended the application of the *Privacy Act 1988* to the private sector and introduced special provisions in relation to health information. The legislation provides that all Commonwealth employees and other defined persons in the private sector dealing with health information have obligations in relation to preserving the privacy of this information (and allowing clients to access and correct their records). Most significantly, the Act regulates the disclosure of health information to third parties. Part VIII of the Act is entitled "Obligations of Confidence" and the Act contains a number of "Privacy Principles" which regulate, inter alia, the collection, storage and dissemination of information. Additionally, this Act specifies several exceptions to the general duty of secrecy. Other relevant legislation has been passed in Victoria (*Health Records Act 2001*; *Information Privacy Act 2001*), the Australian Capital Territory (*Health Records (Privacy and Access) Act 1997*) and New South Wales (*Health Records and Information Privacy Act 2002*). The implications of these various Acts for the operation of other, common law bases of confidentiality have been little explored, however the ramifications may be profound. In jurisdictions where such legislation exists (and note that Commonwealth legislation covers the private health sector throughout Australia), it is possible that these privacy regimes may provide the primary mechanisms for regulating disclosure of information by health care professionals. For example, in Victoria the Health Services Commissioner has authority to administer the *Health Records Act 2001* and all complaints about breaches of confidentiality by health care professionals in that State are now processed within the framework of that legislation.

---

79 For example, *Privacy Act 1988* (Cth).
80 For example, *Health Services Act 1988* (Vic) s 141.
81 The *Epidemiological Studies (Confidentiality) Act 1981* (Cth) protects the confidentiality of information obtained in specified epidemiological research by making it an offence to reveal information about a study and by exempting data and records manufactured or obtained in the course of research from production in courts. The National Health and Medical Research Council (NHMRC) also has issued guidelines regulating privacy in medical research that have statutory force. Additionally, exemptions to general confidentiality provisions in other Acts permit the limited disclosure of otherwise confidential information for the purposes of research. For example, the *Privacy Act 1988* (Cth) allows health information to be accessed – without the consent of the individual client – for use in research.

Furthermore, while it is clear that health care practitioners will remain subject to specific confidentiality and disclosure provisions in other Acts (which override the general provisions of the privacy legislation), how these particular privacy statutes and common law obligations and duties interact is not clear. The overview paper accompanying the Health Records Bill in Victoria suggested that health care practitioners would continue to remain subject to the more stringent confidentiality obligations imposed by the common law.[82] While such an observation is likely to be true, in practice the less costly, more "user-friendly" complaint procedures offered under the privacy regimes may in fact mean that they increasingly "cover the field" and that the traditional, common law remedies for protecting confidentiality become archaic.

Patients of hospitals and other agencies

Employees, proprietors, hospital board members and other persons who provide services[83] in Victorian public and private hospitals, day procedure centres, multipurpose services and community health centres[84] are prohibited from disclosing information acquired in the course of their employment if the patient could be identified in any way from the information except to the extent necessary to carry out their legitimate functions and duties.[85] The duty of confidentiality is not absolute; several exceptions are specified in the legislation including: the patient consents to disclosure; the information is disclosed in the course of criminal proceedings; and the information is communicated by a medical staff member to "next of kin or a near relative of the patient in accordance with the recognised customs of medical practice".[86] Additionally, such information must be given to police who have a validly issued search warrant.[87]

Similar provisions in mental health legislation in several States impose a duty of confidentiality on persons involved in the care of the mentally ill. Employees of public and private hospitals and other specified persons are prohibited from disclosing information about psychiatric patients from which a patient could be identified.[88] An interesting amendment in 2004 to the Victorian

---

82 Health Records Bill: Overview and Key Issues, 9-10.

83 *Health Services Act 1988* (Vic) s 141(1).

84 Ibid, s 141(1).

85 Ibid, s 141.

86 The exceptions to the duty of confidentiality specified in the *Health Services Act 1988* (Vic) s 141(3) include: client consent to disclosure; the provision of client information in criminal proceedings; communications by members of medical staff to a patient's "next of kin or a near relative of the patient in accordance with the recognised customs of medical practice"; information provided to the Red Cross in relation to infected blood; information given in connection with further treatment of the patient; and information disclosed for the purposes of research.

87 *Royal Melbourne Hospital v Mathews* [1993] 1 VR 665.

88 *Mental Health Act 1990* (NSW) s 289; *Mental Health Act 2000* (Qld) ss 523–530; *Mental Health Act 1993* (SA) s 34; *Mental Health Act 1996* (Tas) s 90; *Mental Health Act 1986* (Vic) s 120A; *Mental Health Act 1996* (WA) s 206.

Mental Health Act 1986 specified that, in relation to the preparation of treatment plans for involuntary patients, members of their family, guardians and other caregivers were to be given the opportunity to participate in the treatment plan "unless the patient objects".[89] This effective reversal of the usual process of obtaining consent to disclosure was justified on the twin bases that a patient with a psychiatric disorder might have a condition that impairs their reasoning and involvement of family and other caregivers may assist clinical treatment of the patient (by facilitating the obtaining of information and so on).

HIV/AIDS

Statutory provisions in several States specifically protect information acquired confidentially by health care professionals in relation to clients who have been tested for, or have, HIV/AIDS.[90] For example, in Victoria s 128 of the *Health Act 1958* (Vic) provides that:

> A person who, in the course of providing a service, acquires information that a person has been or is required to be tested for HIV or is infected with HIV, must take all reasonable steps to develop and implement systems to protect the privacy of that person.

Generally, information about a person's HIV status can only be disclosed: with the consent of the client; if a court orders disclosure; where the disclosure is to another treating health practitioner; or to a relevant government officer if there are reasonable grounds to believe that the client is placing the health of the public at risk. Note, however, that legislation in New South Wales and Tasmania establishes, in limited circumstances, a power to breach confidentiality and warn third parties who may be harmed by an HIV-positive client.[91]

Privilege

Privilege refers to the right to withhold certain communications or information from disclosure in evidence. Historically, confidential information disclosed by clients to health care practitioners has never been protected from disclosure in courts. Thus, the common law did not provide the clients of medical practitioners with protection from having confidential information about them disclosed by their doctor in court in the course of giving testimony. However, courts had discretion in relation to such information and would not necessarily compel disclosure.[92] This remains the position in relation to criminal and coronial

---

89   *Mental Health Act 1986* (Vic) s 19A(2)(b).

90   For example, *Public Health Act 1991* (NSW) s 17(1), (2); *HIV/AIDS Preventive Measures Act 1993* (Tas) ss 17, 18, 19; *Health Act 1958* (Vic) s 128.

91   *Public Health Regulations 1991* (NSW) reg 10; *HIV/AIDS Preventive Measures Act 1993* (Tas) s 20(7). See Godwin et al, op cit.

92   *Attorney-General (UK) v Mulholland* [1963] 2 QB 477. Also see Gerber, P, "Confidentiality and the Courts" (1999) 170 *Medical Journal of Australia* 222.

proceedings in all States and Territories in Australia. However, in Victoria,[93] Tasmania[94] and the Northern Territory[95] statutory provisions have established – in relation to civil proceedings – a patient's privilege in relation to medical practitioners. New South Wales has adopted more general legislation that may privilege confidential information disclosed in the course of any professional relationship.[96]

The statutory privilege established in Victoria, Tasmania and the Northern Territory generally protects the patients of medical practitioners from having confidential information about them disclosed without their consent in civil proceedings where the information was acquired by the medical practitioner while treating the patient. In Victoria, the privilege includes communications by the patient[97] and information acquired from others in relation to the patient,[98] as well as matters revealed by medical examination. Particular limitations on the scope of the privilege apply in each jurisdiction. Thus, in Victoria, the privilege does not extend to proceedings involving the sanity or testamentary capacity of the patient, or some actions concerning the death of a patient.[99] Additionally, in most jurisdictions where the privilege has been established it is exclusive to the medical practitioner–patient relationship and does not extend to other health care professionals and their clients; only in New South Wales is it possible for the privilege to apply to other health care practitioners (and other professionals). Although the law relating to privilege and health care practitioners appeared to be well-settled, a controversial case in 1996 drew attention to the issue of privilege and victims of sexual assault who seek counselling and/or medical attention.

Sexual assault communications privilege

Without the protection of privilege, a counsellor to whom a client has disclosed confidential information may be being compelled to attend court and disclose this information. When the client has been a victim of sexual assault and the counsellor is called by defence counsel in the course of the criminal prosecution of that sexual assault there is a fundamental clash between the court's desire to have all relevant evidence and the need to protect the therapeutic relationship.[100]

---

93 *Evidence Act 1958* (Vic) s 28(2).

94 *Evidence Act 2001* (Tas).

95 *Evidence Act 1939* (NT) ss 9(6), 10, 12.

96 *Evidence Act 1995* (NSW) ss 126A–126F.

97 *National Mutual Life Association of Australia Ltd v Godrich* (1909) 10 CLR 1.

98 *Hare v Riley* [1974] VR 577 at 582 per Norris J.

99 Actions not covered by the privilege include those brought under Pt III of the *Wrongs Act 1958* (Vic), *Accident Compensation Act 1985* (Vic), *Workers Compensation Act 1958* (Vic) and civil actions in which the sanity or testamentary capacity of the client is the matter in dispute: *Evidence Act 1958* (Vic) s 28(5).

100 Cossins, A and Pilkington, R, "Balancing the Scales: the Case for the Inadmissibility of Counselling Records in Sexual Assault Trials" (1996) 19 *UNSWLJ* 222.

Although counsellors may be reluctant to divulge such information they may be obliged to do so and be held in contempt of court if they refuse. This matter arose in *Police v White*[101] where the administrator of the Canberra Rape Crisis Centre refused to comply with a subpoena requiring her to produce the counselling file of a woman who had been a victim of sexual assault and had attended the centre. The file was sought by counsel appearing for the defendant charged with the sexual assault of the victim. The refusal to deliver the counselling file resulted in the administrator being found to be in contempt of court. She was detained in the court's watch house for four hours and was only released when she produced the counselling file to the court.[102]

The parliaments of New South Wales, Victoria and Tasmania responded to this dilemma by protecting the confidentiality of information disclosed by victims of sexual assault to their counsellors and/or medical practitioners. Each State introduced specific legislation which restricts the circumstances in which counsellors can be obliged to divulge in criminal proceedings confidential information about clients who have been victims of sexual assault.[103] In general terms, in these States a victim of sexual assault who attends a medical practitioner or counsellor (broadly defined: in Tasmania this is a person who provides "psychiatric or psychological therapy to victims of sexual offences")[104] can assert privilege to protect from disclosure in criminal proceedings confidential information which has been imparted to that counsellor or medical practitioner.[105] However, the effectiveness of this protection is dubious: a court may permit such information to be adduced where it has sufficient, substantial probative value and the public interest in disclosure outweighs the public interest in maintaining confidentiality.[106]

---

101 Unreported, Queanbeyan LC, 25 January 1996. See Kingston, M, "Privacy Issue as Rape Therapist Jailed", *Sydney Morning Herald*, 15 December 1995, p 1.

102 In a compromise agreement, pending resolution of the issue of defence access to the file at a later hearing,, the counselling file was delivered in a locked briefcase to which only the administrator knew the combination: see Cossins and Pilkington (1996) op cit.

103 *Criminal Procedure Act 1986* (NSW) ss 295–306, *Evidence Act 1995* (NSW) Pt 3.10, Div 1B; *Evidence Act 2001* (Tas) s 127B; *Evidence Act 1958* (Vic) ss 32B–32G.

104 *Evidence Act 2001* (Tas) s 127B.

105 Practical advice directed to psychologists (and applicable to other health care practitioners) in relation to the operation of the new legislation in Victoria is contained in Broughton, F, "Confidentiality – New Law in Victoria" (1998, November) *In-Psych (Bulletin of the Australian Psychological Society)* 6.

106 *Evidence Act 1958* (Vic) s 32D:

> (1) A court must not grant leave to adduce protected evidence unless it is satisfied, on the balance of probabilities, that –
>
> > (a) the evidence will, either by itself or having regard to other evidence adduced or to be adduced by the party seeking to adduce it, have substantial probative value to a fact in issue; and
> >
> > (b) other evidence of similar or greater probative value concerning the matters to which the protected evidence relates is not available; and

(cont)

Actions available to clients where health care practitioners have breached the obligation of confidence

Although the Australian Consumers' Association, when reviewing health rights in Australia, claimed that "problems with confidentiality rarely arise",[107] a large-scale survey in South Australia demonstrated that a small fraction of clients perceived that unauthorised disclosure of their health information had occurred.[108] Breaches of confidentiality may lead aggrieved clients to seek redress. Unauthorised disclosure of confidential information may give rise to a number of actions. However, it has also been noted that legal rights to confidentiality are "difficult to enforce"[109] and "more academic than real",[110] suggesting that some breaches of confidence may occur without remedies being accessed by aggrieved clients.[111] Nevertheless, in this section I provide a brief overview of the remedies theoretically available to a client aggrieved by a perceived breach of confidence by a health care practitioner.

Clients who have experienced a breach of confidentiality by a health care professional may have multiple remedies available to them. Aggrieved clients who seek redress must select an appropriate remedy based on the particular facts of the case, the type of legal relationship that existed with the health care professional, the elements of the legal cause of action, the financial cost of bringing the action, the availability of statute-based remedies and the type of compensation that they seek (for example, apology, financial compensation). The principal common law bases for confidentiality in health care relationships can be found in the law of negligence, contract and equity (breach of confidence). Defamation law has also been used to obtain redress for the disclosure of (false) information, albeit rarely.

(*cont*)

  (c) the public interest in preserving the confidentiality of confidential communications and protecting a protected confider from harm is substantially outweighed by the public interest in admitting, into evidence, evidence of substantial probative value.

 (2) Without limiting the matters that the court may take into account for the purposes of subsection (1)(c), the court must take into account the likelihood, and the nature or extent, of harm that would be caused to the protected confider if the protected evidence is adduced.

The relevant provision in New South Wales is contained in the *Criminal Procedure Act 1986* s 298.

107 Australian Consumers Association, *Your Health Rights*, ACA, Sydney, 1988, p 44.

108 Mulligan, EC, "Confidentiality in Health Records: Evidence of Current Performance From a Population Survey in South Australia" (2001) 174 *Medical Journal of Australia* 637.

109 Hobart Community Legal Service, *The Tasmanian Law Handbook*, Hobart Community Legal Service, Hobart, Tasmania, 1994.

110 Thomson, CJ, "Records, Research and Access: What Interests Should Outweigh Privacy and Confidentiality? Some Australian Answers" (1993) 1 *JLM* 95.

111 Skene concluded that "a doctor's commonly assumed obligation of confidentiality is not only subject to many exceptions but is also unenforceable in most circumstances": Skene, L, *Law and Medical Practice: Rights, Duties, Claims and Defences*, Butterworths, Sydney, 1998, p 193.

Complaint to a registration board

Most health care professionals must be registered with an appropriate board or council in order that they may lawfully practise in a particular State or Territory.[112] These registration authorities are vested with the power to hear complaints about the professional conduct of registered practitioners and may discipline unethical members. A breach of confidentiality may constitute professional misconduct under relevant legislation.

Complaint to a professional organisation

Many organisations representing health care professionals have adopted codes of ethics that require their members to respect the confidentiality of information disclosed by clients. A breach of confidentiality therefore may constitute a breach of ethics for a member. Ethics committees have been established by all major organisations representing health care professionals and an aggrieved patient can lodge a complaint with such a committee. The advantages of this grievance procedure for the client are that it is typically inexpensive and quick and the process is not open to the public. However, the procedure will not be available where the practitioner is not a member of the relevant organisation. Additionally, the sanctions that can be employed are typically limited: censure, reprimand, suspension or cancellation of the practitioner's membership of the organisation.

Complaint to a health complaints office

Several Australian States and Territories have established health complaints authorities which are empowered to receive complaints against health care practitioners, including alleged breaches of confidentiality.[113] An aggrieved client may lodge a complaint with the appropriate health complaints authority.

Complaint to a privacy commissioner

Several Australian States and Territories, as well as the Commonwealth, have established privacy commissions that are empowered to receive certain complaints against, inter alia, health care practitioners, including unauthorised disclosure of information. An aggrieved client may lodge a complaint with either the federal or, where available, State or Territory privacy commissioner.[114]

---

112 For example, in Victoria relevant Acts that regulate health care professionals include the: *Medical Practice Act 1994; Nurses Act 1993; Psychologists Registration Act 2000; Physiotherapists Registration Act 1998*.

113 Breach of confidentiality is either expressly or implicitly included as a ground for complaint: *Health Services (Conciliation and Review) Act 1987* (Vic) s 16(1)(e); *Health Care Complaints Act 1993* (NSW) s 7; *Health Rights Commission Act 1991* (Qld) s 57.

114 A noteworthy case investigated under privacy provisions in New Zealand concerned a nurse who disclosed confidential details about a psychiatric patient to an opposition member of parliament. The nurse had been involved with the inpatient care of the patient before he had (inappropriately, in her view) been released into the community. (*cont*)

Breach of a duty of care

Health care practitioners who disclose confidential information about a client without authorisation may be liable to the client in negligence. Conversely, in some circumstances, the failure to counsel clients about limits on the information that may be disclosed to them about third parties (because of confidentiality requirements) may also make the practitioner liable in negligence.

1. *Negligent disclosure:* An aggrieved client must establish that the practitioner fell below the usual standard of care by disclosing the information, that he or she suffered some type of (legally recognised) harm and that the injury sustained by the client as a result of the breach was reasonably foreseeable. The disclosure must have caused some form of legally recognised harm to the client (such as psychiatric illness, financial loss and so on). These issues were illustrated in the New Zealand case *Furniss v Fitchett* where a woman successfully sued her general practitioner for negligently disclosing confidential information about her to her husband.[115]

(*cont*)

She believed that he posed a serious and imminent threat of harm to community safety. After writing letters to two government ministers and the national Director of Mental Health she wrote to a member of parliament who had expressed concern about the operation of current mental health legislation. (The last letter was the subject of investigation by the Privacy Commissioner). Although the commissioner accepted that the nurse genuinely held these views and that there were reasonable grounds on which to base them, he concluded that, under the particular terms of the relevant privacy code, the disclosure to the member of parliament was unnecessary, included unnecessary information about the patient and was not made to a "responsible authority". On this last point he noted that:

> The emphasis on disclosing to a "responsible authority" recognises that professional confidence should only be breached in the most exceptional circumstances and then only if the public interest is paramount. This is because it is the "responsible authority" which will have the powers to do something about the matter to protect the pubic interest. Disclosure to persons who do not have such power merely provides an in-road into medical confidence and privacy which does not carry any corresponding assurance of benefit to the public interest.

The Privacy Commissioner concluded that there had been an interference with the privacy of the patient but, although unable to settle the matter, did not recommend further proceedings before the Complaints Review Tribunal: "Nurse Discloses Psychiatric Patient Details to Opposition MP (Case Note 2049)" [1996] *New Zealand Privacy Commissioner* 7 .

115 *Furniss v Fitchett* [1958] NZLR 396. Both husband and wife were patients of the same medical practitioner. The doctor provided a written statement to the husband regarding his wife's mental state. The wife had not consented to the disclosure of the information in the letter and was not aware of its existence until it was produced at a later time during the course of legal proceedings for separation. As a result, she experienced considerable distress and collapsed. Subsequently, she sued the medical practitioner arguing that his negligent disclosure of confidential information had caused her psychiatric injury ("nervous shock"). The medical practitioner was found to have been negligent: (a) he owed his patient a duty of care; (b) he had breached reasonable professional standards by disclosing the information; (c)) he knew, and a reasonable doctor in his position could reasonably have foreseen, that disclosing information about his patient's mental state would cause her harm. When determining whether the doctor had breached reasonable professional standards the court considered pertinent ethical directives contained in the relevant code of ethics applicable to New Zealand doctors at the time.

2. *Negligent failure to counsel about the limits on information that may be disclosed:* In *Harvey v PD*[116] a woman (PD) sued her general practitioner and the medical director of the clinic that she attended for breach of their duty of care to her. She had jointly attended the clinic with her fiancé for testing for HIV and other sexually transmitted diseases. PD was particularly concerned about this issue because her fiancé was from Ghana and she believed that there was an increased risk that he had a sexually transmitted disease. Neither she nor her fiancé were counselled, either at the initial joint consultation or subsequently, about testing or the disclosure of results. In particular, the issue of consent to disclosing their results to one another was not discussed at the initial consultation. This issue was particularly salient as a statutory provision in New South Wales prohibited the disclosure of an individual's HIV status to another person.[117]

    PD tested negative. She requested that the clinic provide her with her fiancé's result but was told that this was not possible because the result was confidential. PD's fiancé tested positive for HIV and Hepatitis B but he subsequently presented her with a (false) negative result. Relying on this, PD later had unprotected sexual intercourse with her fiancé (later her husband). PD became infected with HIV and sued the two doctors at the clinic, alleging that they had breached their duty of care to her. Both doctors argued that to have disclosed her fiancé's HIV status to PD would have breached doctor–patient confidentiality, underpinned in New South Wales by specific statutory obligation.[118]

    The trial judge found the defendants were negligent. An appeal to the Court of Appeal was unsuccessful, the court holding that by failing (at the initial joint consultation) to advise and counsel PD and her fiancé about the disclosure of results, the doctors had breached their duty of care to PD and she had suffered a reasonably foreseeable injury (HIV infection).

    This case illustrates a complex interplay of confidentiality with torts law, further compounded by specific legislation that restricted disclosure of information about a person's HIV status. Further, if the same matter arose today, the operation of the provisions of the *Privacy Act 1988* (Cth) would also have to be considered as this Act imposes obligations on practitioners in relation to informing clients about disclosure of information. Thus, confidentiality issues may draw together ethics, common law, specific statutory provisions and privacy law.

---

116 *Harvey v PD* [2004] NSWCA 97.

117 *Public Health Act 1991* (NSW) s 17.

118 This case can be contrasted with *Tokugha v Apollo Hospital Enterprises* where a hospital in India disclosed a patient's HIV-positive status to his fiancé and the patient sued the hospital. The Supreme Court of India rejected his claim of breach of confidentiality holding that the woman that he was to marry "was saved in time by such disclosure": Kumar, S, "Medical Confidentiality Broken to Stop Marriage of Man Infected with HIV" (1998) 352 (9142) *Lancet* 1764.

Breach of confidence

Although early cases in this area involved commercial activities, later cases established that a duty to maintain confidentiality could arise in non-commercial relationships and did not require a proprietary or contractual basis. Although there is very little case law involving health care professionals being sued for breach of confidence, the possible extension of this action to professional advisers, including health care professionals, has been noted by several commentators.[119] The information imparted must be specific, have the necessary quality of confidence and not be common or public knowledge.[120] Three elements of the action identified by Megarry J in *Coco v AN Clark (Engineers) Ltd*[121] have obvious relevance to the health care relationship:

(a)   the relationship must be confidential;

(b)   the information must be imparted in circumstances importing confidentiality; and

(c)   there must be an actual or threatened misuse of that information to the detriment of the person disclosing the information.

Frequently, although not invariably, the first two criteria will be characteristic of the relationship between a patient and a health care professional. Additionally, the expansive notion of detriment adopted in relevant cases suggests that disclosure of information exposing a person's "actions to public discussion and criticism"[122] or "initial discussion and its immediate consequences"[123] may be sufficient to complete the requirements of this cause of action.

One of the few recent cases in which a health care practitioner was sued for breach of confidence arose from disclosures made by a psychiatrist after evaluating a patient detained in a secure hospital in England. In *W v Edgell* a patient (W) wished to be transferred to a less restrictive setting. A hearing was scheduled before the relevant decision-making authority. A psychiatrist was asked by W's lawyers to report on the patient's mental state for the hearing. However, after an adverse report from this psychiatrist (who had formed the opinion that W's mental state warranted his detention in a restrictive, secure setting) the patient withdrew his application for the hearing. Subsequently, the psychiatrist sent a copy of his report to the Assistant Medial Director of the secure facility where the patient was

---

119   See *Breen v Williams* (1996) 186 CLR 71 at 81 per Brennan J; Gurry, F, *Breach of Confidence*, Oxford University Press, Oxford, 1984; Fox, R, "Principles of Confidentiality for Psychologists and Social Workers" in Nixon M (ed), *Psychology and Professional Practice*, Longman Cheshire, Melbourne, 1984.

120   *Corrs, Pavey, Whiting and Byrne v Collector of Customs (Vic)* (1997) 74 ALR 428 at 437, per Gummow J.

121   [1968] FSR 415; [1969] RPC 41. See also *Commonwealth v John Fairfax and Sons Ltd* (1980) 147 CLR 39; *Attorney General v Guardian Newspapers Ltd (No 2)* [1988] 3 WLR 766.

122   *Commonwealth v John Fairfax and Sons Ltd* (1980) 147 CLR 39 at 50-51; 32 ALR 485 at 491-492.

123   *X v Y* [1988] 2 All ER 648 at 658 per Rose J.

detained and another copy to the Home Office. The patient sued the psychiatrist for breach of confidence.

The trial court dismissed the action. A subsequent appeal to the Court of Appeal was also dismissed, the latter court holding that although the psychiatrist owed a duty of confidentiality to W not to disclose the report, confidential information may be disclosed where the public interest in disclosure outweighs the public interest in confidentiality.[124]

Breach of contract

A client of a health care practitioner may sometimes be able to rely on the existence of a contract (either express or implied) to obtain redress for a breach of confidence.

Generally, the law will imply into the contract of professionals (including health care professionals) an undertaking to keep confidential information divulged by a client in the course of the professional relationship.[125] As Lord Denning MR stated:

> The law implies a term into the contract whereby a professional man is to keep his client's affairs secret and not to disclose them to anyone without just cause.[126]

Judicial comment in several cases has suggested that confidentiality will frequently be implied in the relationship between medical practitioners and their clients.[127]

By analogy, confidentiality may be regarded as an implied term of the contract between other health care practitioners and their clients.

However, in relation to the provision of health care services, a major limitation is that in many instances no contract will exist between the client and the health care professional. Thus, where treatment is provided by an employee of a hospital or other agency and/or where the fee for the service is not paid by the patient, it is unlikely that a contract will exist.[128]

Defamation

Although the action is rarely used to protect confidentiality, aggrieved clients who believe that a health care professional has disseminated *false* information about them and caused damage to their reputation may sue the practitioner for

---

124 *W v Edgell* [1990] 1 All ER 835.

125 *Parry-Jones v Law Society* [1969] 1 Ch 1; *Duncan v Medical Practitioners Disciplinary Committee* [1986] 1 NZLR 513.

126 *Parry-Jones v Law Society* [1969] 1 Ch 1 at 7.

127 Ibid, at 9 per Diplock LJ; *Argyle v Argyle* [1967] Ch 302; *Duncan v Medical Practitioners Disciplinary Committee* [1986] 1 NZLR 513 at 520 per Jeffries J; *Furniss v Fitchett* [1958] NZLR 396 at 399 per Barrowclough CJ.

128 See Hamblin J and Bell D, "Confidentiality" (Health and Guardianship) in *The Laws of Australia*, Lawbook Co, Sydney.

defamation.[129] Actions for defamation have been initiated where medical practitioners have allegedly falsely claimed that a client had a venereal disease,[130] was insane[131] or had been raped.[132] To succeed in an action for defamation against a health care professional an aggrieved client must establish four matters:

- the health care practitioner made a statement of fact or opinion or implied fact or opinion;

- the statement harmed the client's reputation;

- the statement was communicated to another person ("published"); and

- the statement referred to the client.[133]

Additionally, the client must consider whether any of the possible defences to defamation are applicable.[134] A rare example of the successful use of defamation in relation to medical information occurred in *Kitson v Playfair*[135] where a woman sued her obstetrician for defamation after he had incorrectly informed the "head of the patient's household" that she had recently had a miscarriage. Consequently, the patient was disinherited.

Exceptions to the duty to maintain confidentiality

As Dwyer observes:

There may be extraordinary conditions that would demand that a doctor not respect his or her patient's demands for silence.[136]

---

129 Defamation is covered by statute in most States and in all States by common law: *Defamation Act 1974* (NSW); *Defamation Act 1889* (Qld); *Defamation Act 2005* (SA); *Defamation Act 1957* (Tas); *Wrongs Act 1958* (Vic) Pt 1; *Criminal Code* (WA) ss 345–369.

130 *Halls v Mitchell* [1927] 1 DLR 163.

131 *Morgan v Lingan* (1863) 8 LT 800. Although the defendant (a surgeon) had written letters to relatives and others associated with the plaintiff claiming that he had no doubt that the plaintiff's mind "was affected", that she had delusions or monomania and was "fairly off her head", the plaintiff was unsuccessful in her action against him for defamation. It appears that the defendant had not treated the plaintiff as a patient but had formed these views through general social contact with her.

132 *Youssoupoff v MGM* (1934) 50 TLR 581.

133 Wallace, M, *Health Care and the Law*, Law Book Co, Sydney, 1995, pp 189–193.

134 Ibid, pp 191–193.

135 *The Times*, 23–28 March 1896. Similarly, when an American medical practitioner incorrectly interpreted a patient's medical records and the abbreviations contained therein and reported to a compensation board that the patient had a venereal disease the patient successfully sued him for defamation: *Hall v Mitchell* [1928] 2 DLR 97. Note that in Australia, courts and compensation boards possess privilege from such actions, however the general point regarding false information and the action for defamation remain valid.

136 Dwyer, JM, "The Hippocratic irrelevance variable (HIV)" (1990) 152 *Medical Journal of Australia* 169.

Neither the law nor ethical guidelines require that the obligation of confidence be absolute. As previously noted, the ethical guidelines of the various organisations representing health care professionals in Australia recognise this explicitly and in various ways. Limits to confidentiality also have been explicitly identified in legislation and the common law.

Consent by the client

Disclosure by a health care practitioner of otherwise confidential information pertaining to a client is permissible when the client consents to the disclosure. Consent may be either indicated specifically and directly (express consent) or implied from the circumstances of the relationship and/or the setting in which the meeting occurs. This exception to the obligation of confidentiality acknowledges the autonomy of the client who has consented to disclosure and is most appropriately regarded as the terminating of a duty of confidence rather than an exception to that duty.[137]

Circumstances in which consent to disclosure of confidential information may be implied to have been given by a client include: the writing of a prescription by a medical practitioner or dentist; referral to another health care practitioner; the writing of reports concerning the client to third parties (for example, the criminal courts,[138] workers compensation authorities, insurance organisations); and the keeping of common records at a clinic or other facility where access is available to other health care practitioners.[139] However, the degree to which courts will imply client consent to disclosure is unclear and health care professionals should be wary of relying on implied consent to justify disclosure of confidential information concerning clients.[140]

Disclosure: compelled by law

Disclosure compelled by the law is essentially of two types:

- statutory duties of disclosure to relevant government officials or agencies; and

- disclosure compelled during the course of judicial or similar proceedings.

Statutory duties of disclosure include (but are not limited to) the following.

---

137 Thomson, CJ, "Records, Research and Access: What Interests Should Outweigh Privacy and Confidentiality? Some Australian Answers" (1993) 1 *JLM* 95.

138 See Pargiter, R and Bloch, S, "The Ethics Committee of a Psychiatric College: Its Procedures and Themes" (1998) 32 *Australian & New Zealand Journal of Psychiatry* 76.

139 In *Duncan v Medical Practitioners Disciplinary Committee* [1986] 1 NZLR 513 at 521, Jeffries J commented that the exceptions to the duty of confidentiality included: "private discussions with colleagues in pursuance of treatment ... [that] may require full disclosure and consent ... [and] a group practice where common filing systems are used". Also see the remarks of Kelly J in *Slater v Bissett* (1986) 69 ACTR 25.

140 Skene, L, *Law and Medical Practice: Rights, Duties, Claims and Defences*, 2nd edn, Lexis–Nexis Butterworths, Sydney, 2004.

Registration of births and deaths

Relevant legislation in each State and Territory requires specified persons to notify the registrar of any birth or death at which they are present. Registered medical practitioners are usually required to notify relevant authorities of the deaths of patients for whom they provided medical care immediately before death, and to notify authorities when they examine the body of any deceased person after death.[141]

Impaired drivers

Some jurisdictions have legislation that requires medical practitioners (and sometimes other health professionals) to inform motor registration authorities when they have clients with conditions that may impair their ability to drive a car.[142] Alternatively, other jurisdictions permit any person acting in good faith to report information that suggests that another person may be unfit to drive.[143] Statutory protections available to those who make such reports may protect from civil and criminal liability health care professionals who disclose confidential client information.[144]

Drunk drivers

"Drink-driving" legislation empowers medical practitioners in some jurisdictions to report the results of blood tests on patients admitted to hospitals after a motor accident, with or without the patient's consent.[145]

Infectious diseases

Public health legislation in all States and Territories requires medical practitioners to inform specified government authorities of clients with certain infectious

---

141 For example, *Births, Deaths and Marriages Registration Act 1996* (Vic) s 37; *Registration of Births, Deaths and Marriages Act 1995* (NT) s 33. Where a birth occurs in a hospital, the Chief Executive Officer (CEO) or similar person is usually obliged to make the report. For births that occur outside hospitals, the attending doctor, nurse, or midwife often is invested with this authority. For example, in Victoria, where the birth occurs in a hospital, the CEO of the hospital must inform the relevant authorities. In other circumstances, the medical practitioner or midwife responsible for the professional care of the mother at birth has the duty to report the birth: *Births, Deaths and Marriages Registration Act 1996* (Vic) s 12. Some jurisdictions also provide for the notification of births to other agencies, such as maternal and child welfare bodies. For example, in Victoria the Director of Nursing (or similar) of the hospital in which the birth occurred, or the attendant midwife, must inform the CEO of the council of the municipal district in which the mother usually resides of the birth, in order to facilitate maternal and child care services: *Health Act 1958* (Vic) Pt I.

142 For example, *Motor Vehicles Act* (NT) s 11(4).

143 For example, *Road Safety Act 1986* (Vic) s 27(5).

144 Ibid.

145 Ibid, s 56.

diseases, typically including sexually transmitted diseases, HIV,[146] cholera, leprosy, hepatitis etcetera.[147]

Impaired health care practitioners

In some jurisdictions medical practitioners have a statutory duty to report to specified authorities (such as a registration board) a client who is a "registered health practitioner" and who has a medical condition that may seriously impair his or her ability to practise and place the public at risk.[148] The definition of registered health practitioner in the Victorian legislation includes medical practitioners, nurses, dentists, pharmacists, physiotherapists, chiropractors, osteopaths, medical imaging technologists, radiation therapy technologists and nuclear medicine technologists.[149] Doctors who report in good faith are protected from civil or criminal liability.[150]

Mandatory reporting of child abuse

The legal obligation to report maltreatment or neglect of children has been the subject of considerable comment in recent years. Mandatory reporting legislation now exists in all Australian States and Territories except Western Australia.[151] The professional groups mandated to report vary in each jurisdiction but may include medical practitioners, nurses, psychologists and other occupational groups (for example, teachers). The circumstances in which a health care practitioner is obliged to report also vary, but typically require reporting when there is a "reasonable belief" that a child requires protection. For example, in New South Wales medical practitioners (and other persons) who have "reasonable grounds to suspect" that a child is at risk of harm are required to report this to the Director-General of the Department of Community Services.[152] Health care professionals (and others) who act in good faith and report suspected abuse or neglect to the appropriate authorities have statutory protection from liability and are deemed not have breached professional ethics or accepted standards of professional conduct.[153]

---

146 For example, the *Health Act 1958* (Vic) s 130 requires that a person in charge of a prescribed place for HIV testing must send records to the Chief General Manager of the Health Department regarding testing for HIV.

147 For example, *Public Health Act 1991* (NSW) Pt 3.

148 For example, *Medical Practice Act 1994* (Vic) s 37.

149 Ibid, s 38.

150 *Health Act 1958* (Vic) s 37(3).

151 *Children and Young Persons (Care and Protection) Act 1998* (NSW) s 27; *Health Act 1937* (Qld) s 76K; *Children's Protection Act 1993* (SA) s 11; *Children, Young Persons and Their Families Act 1997* (Tas) s 14; *Children and Young Persons Act 1989* (Vic) s 64; *Children and Young People Act 1999* (ACT) s 159; *Community Welfare Act 1983* (NT) s 14.

152 *Children and Young Persons (Care and Protection) Act 1998* (NSW) s 27.

153 *Children and Young Persons (Care and Protection) Act 1998* (NSW) s 27; *Health Act 1937* (Qld) s 76K(6)(7); *Children's Protection Act 1993* (SA) s 12; *Children, Young Persons and Their Families Act 1997* (Tas) s 15; *Children and Young Persons Act 1989* (Vic) s 64(3); *Children and Young People Act 1999* (ACT) s 163; *Community Welfare Act 1983* (NT) s 14(2).

Disclosure in court

As previously noted, generally health care professionals do not have a legal right to refuse to divulge details of a client's condition and history if called upon to do so in court (more precisely, the privilege is not available to the clients of these practitioners). A refusal may constitute contempt of court. Exceptions to this situation in relation to medical practitioners have been enacted in Victoria, Tasmania and the Northern Territory. A more general exemption, potentially applicable to other health care professionals and their clients, has been enacted in New South Wales and may privilege some information disclosed by a client to a practitioner during the course of a professional relationship.

Disclosure permitted:
Discretionary breaches of confidentiality

Disclosure in the interests of the patient

Both ethical codes and the law sometimes permit disclosure of confidential information "in the interest of a client". An obvious example is when a client is, or is deemed to be, suicidal. However, the information must be divulged to relevant persons and must be limited to that information which is essential to protect the interests of the patient.

The law may permit disclosure "in the interest of the client", yet not compel such disclosure. Professional discretion, rather than legal compulsion, currently is the arbiter of such breaches of confidentiality.

Disclosure in the public interest

> There are some things which may be required to be disclosed in the public interest, in which event no confidence can be prayed in aid to keep them secret.
>
> Lord Denning[154]

Perhaps no other area relating to confidentiality has been as controversial as exceptions to the duty of confidentiality that are justified on the ground of a "public interest in disclosure". Both the law and the ethical codes of most organisations representing health care practitioners acknowledge that in some circumstances the public (or social) interest in disclosure may outweigh the duty of confidentiality to an individual client.

As previously noted, the AIDS epidemic generated considerable discussion in relation to circumstances that would justify breaching confidentiality to protect persons at risk of infection. Further areas of controversy have involved clients who have made admissions regarding past criminal behaviour, or who are perceived by a health care professional as posing a risk of future, violent behaviour.

---

154 *Fraser v Evans* [1969] 1 QB 349 at 362.

This issue is not fanciful: a survey of psychotherapists in Victoria reported that 86 per cent of the psychiatrist and 54 per cent of the psychologist respondents engaged in clinical work had treated a client whom they believed presented a risk of physical harm to another person.[155]

Reporting past criminal activity

It has occasionally been boldly asserted that health care professionals have a legal duty to report a client's admission of past criminal activity.[156] For example, Rysavy and Anderson argued that a "psychologist is legally compelled to report a crime even if this information is disclosed in a normally confidential counselling context".[157] Such a blunt assertion of a legal obligation to breach client confidentiality is misleading.

Historically, the common law established the offence of misprision of felony (that is, the offence of concealing knowledge of a felony committed by another) but this offence only applied to serious crimes and doubt has been expressed about whether a health care professional who failed to divulge information about a past crime given in confidence by a client would be prosecuted for this offence.[158] Discussion of this matter is now largely otiose, as the offence has been abolished in most jurisdictions.

There is considerable diversity in the prevailing legal obligations in the various States and Territories. In some States there is no general, positive legal obligation on health care professionals to report to the police a client who discloses past criminal offences.

For example, in Victoria health care professionals are under the same obligations as ordinary citizens and are not compelled to report a crime except in the unusual circumstances in which the crime is a serious indictable offence and the health care practitioner benefits from concealing the crime, or where the offence is treason. Conversely, in New South Wales health care practitioners (like other citizens) are required to bring information concerning the commission of a serious offence to the attention of the police or other relevant authority.[159] Queensland currently provides statutory protection for registered medical practitioners who

---

155 McMahon and Knowles (1992) op cit. Also see McSherry (2001) op cit.

156 Interestingly, in relation to *ethical* guidelines, the *Code of Ethics* of the Australian Psychological Society explicitly advises that "Members must not disclose information about criminal acts of a client unless there is an overriding legal obligation to do so or when failure to disclose may result in clear risk to themselves or others": Australian Psychological Society, *Code of Ethics*, APS, Melbourne 2003, Section B: 6.

157 Rysavy, C and Anderson, A, "Confidentiality: Implications for the Practising Psychologist" (1989) 11 *Bulletin of the Australian Psychological Society* 168.

158 See *Sykes v DPP* [1962] AC 528 at 564 per Lord Denning. Also: White, M, *Law for Youth Workers*, Allen & Unwin, Sydney, 1983; Thompson, J, *Social Workers and the Law*, Redfern Legal Centre Publishing, Sydney, 1989.

159 *Crimes Act 1900* (NSW) s 316(1).

provide information about an indictable offence to police in circumstances where the medical practitioner obtained the information in their professional capacity.[160]

A high profile case that highlighted the issue of reporting the past criminal acts of a client occurred in Victoria. In 1992, Victoria Police, in conjunction with the President of the Medical Board of Victoria and two forensic physicians, called upon medical practitioners to disclose information that might assist in the identification and apprehension of a serious, serial sexual offender known colloquially as "Mr Cruel".[161] "Mr Cruel" had abducted and sexually assaulted three adolescent girls. The severity of his offending had increased and his last victim had been murdered. A profile of the likely offender, including a description of characteristics that would be likely to make him have contact with a medical practitioner was included in a letter sent to more than 13,000 registered medical practitioners. The call for the disclosure of such information drew attention to the obligation of confidentiality in the doctor–patient relationship and to circumstances that might warrant a breach of that obligation and permit disclosure "in the public interest". The letter included the following statements:

> It is generally held that disclosure in the public interest is justified when failure to disclose exposes the public to a significant risk of death or serious harm. The Medical Board of Victoria affirms that this principle appears to apply in the present circumstances.[162]

The application of the "public interest" exception to the duty of confidentiality in the "Mr Cruel" case was unusual insofar as it requested a breach of confidentiality on the suspicion that a client might have committed serious criminal offences rather than subsequent to a client's actual admission of criminal activity.

In relation to the situation where a health care professional is informed by a client of past serious criminal activity, although in most jurisdictions there may not be a legal duty to report the information to police or other relevant authorities, it is clear that a client (or health professional) cannot rely upon the confidentiality of the relationship to prevent information from being disclosed during a police investigation and in any subsequent criminal proceedings. Thus, in *Brown v Brooks*[163] the Supreme Court of New South Wales refused to grant an injunction to prevent a nurse from disclosing to police confidential information that she had received in counselling sessions with a client (Brown). Brown had been charged with the sexual assault of his stepdaughter. He had sought assistance for depression and anxiety at a local public hospital and, during the course of counselling by the nurse, had discussed his relationship with his

---

160 *Medical Practitioners Registration Act 2001* (Qld) s 176.

161 For an extended discussion of these issues see Mendelson, D, "'Mr Cruel' and the Medical Duty of Confidentiality" (1993) 1 *JLM* 120.

162 The Spectrum Task Force and "Mr Cruel" letter. Cited in Mendelson (1993) op cit.

163 Unreported, NSWSC, 18 August 1988. See *Australian Health and Medical Law Reporter* (1991) ¶27-770.

stepdaughter. Upon learning about the counselling, police sought access to relevant medical records and wished to obtain a statement from the nurse-counsellor. Brown sought to prevent both the nurse and the hospital from disclosing the information. The New South Wales Supreme Court refused to grant an injunction restraining either the nurse or the hospital from disclosing the information, holding that it was contrary to public policy to enforce a right of confidentiality that would impede the investigation of a serious crime. Similarly, the Court of Appeal in Victoria recently noted that:

> In this State it is clear that both common law and statute law subordinate private confidence to the wider public interest; at least when it comes to disclosing information in the interests of prosecuting serious crime and/or protecting public safety.[164]

Future criminal activity: A duty to protect potential victims?

Health care professionals sometimes receive information which reveals that a client intends to do physical harm to another. As well as raising the issue of whether such statements are simply to be regarded as cathartic, or conversely, are likely to be acted upon, comes the issue of the appropriate response. These matters were the essence of a seminal American case, *Tarasoff v Regents of the University of California*,[165] that impacted upon health care practice and confidentiality in the United States and which has been extensively discussed in the professional literature in Australia.[166]

A young graduate student (Poddar) attended a university counselling service. He disclosed to the psychologist that he intended to kill another unnamed, but readily identifiable student (Tatiana Tarasoff) when she returned from a holiday in South America. The psychologist, after forming the view that Poddar

---

164 *R v Lowe* [1997] 2 VR 465 at 485. Also see *Royal Melbourne Hospital v Mathews* [1993] 1 VR 665; *Australian Health and Medical Reporter* (1991) ¶27-770.42. A person charged with knowingly infecting another person with HIV attended the outpatient department of a large hospital. Subsequently, police sought access to medical records concerning this patient. The hospital refused to deliver the records and sought an injunction to restrain police from searching the hospital and seizing the medical records. Additionally, the hospital sought clarification of its responsibilities under s 141 of the *Health Services Act 1988* (Vic) which generally prohibited the hospital from disclosing information relating to patients. The judge held that the hospital was required to deliver the records to police who had a valid search warrant for them and that this would not be a breach of patient confidentiality.

165 *Tarasoff v Regents of the University of California; Tarasoff v Regents of the University of California* 17 Cal 3d 425; 131 Cal Rptr 14; 551 P 2d 334 (1976).

166 For a general examination of legal issues pertinent to the "duty to protect" controversy under English and Australian law, see MacKay, RD, "Dangerous Patients, Third Party Safety and Psychiatrists: Walking the Tarasoff Tightrope" (1990) *Medicine, Science and the Law* 52; Mendelson D and Mendelson, G, "Tarasoff Down Under: the Psychiatrist's Duty to Warn in Australia" (1991) 19 *Journal of Psychiatry & Law* 33.

had paranoid schizophrenia and was likely to act on the threat, breached his client's confidence and requested that campus police take Poddar to a psychiatric facility for detention and evaluation. Poddar was released before he arrived at the facility. Several weeks later he killed Tatiana Tarasoff. Her parents subsequently sued the psychologist and his supervisor at the university clinic, arguing that they had been negligent in failing to warn their daughter of the threat posed to her by their client.

Although mindful of the importance of confidentiality in psychotherapy, ultimately the Supreme Court of California imposed a "duty to protect": psychotherapists have a positive duty to exercise reasonable care to protect identified victims of their clients. The "duty to protect" overrides the individual client's right to confidentiality in the relationship with his or her psychotherapist. Subsequent cases in the United States have explored the parameters of this duty and statutes have restricted it ambit in many States.

Related issues arose in the more recent Canadian case *Smith v Jones*[167] that addressed these matters within the context of lawyer–client privilege. In that case "Dr Smith" had prepared a report for a client who was due to appear in court on a charge involving the aggravated assault of a prostitute. During the preparation of the report the client made disclosures about the purpose for which he had committed the original assault and future plans involving the rape and killing of prostitutes. Dr Smith formed the view that the client was dangerous and likely to commit further offences if he did not receive adequate treatment. Subsequently, the client pleaded guilty to the charge and Dr Smith was not called to give evidence. Dr Smith then sought a declaration that he was justified in disclosing information that he had about the client in the interests of public safety.

The Supreme Court of Canada ultimately held that solicitor–client privilege may be set aside when a danger to public safety exists and death or serious bodily harm is imminent. However, there is some uncertainty in Canada as to whether a health professional in these circumstances must breach confidentiality or simply has discretion as to whether to do so.[168]

Echoing many of the discussions of professional responsibilities, legal duties and ethical liabilities that occurred in the United States following the *Tarasoff* case and the subsequent case of *Smith v Jones*, consideration in Australia has often been directed to the issue of a health care professional's responsibilities to an "endangered third party": that is, a person who may be at risk of physical harm from a client of that professional.[169]

Many commentators have stressed that a health care practitioner has an ethical duty to protect an endangered third party, even if this requires breaching the duty of confidentiality owed to a client. Similarly, the ethical codes of many

---

167 *Smith v Jones* (1999) 132 CCC (3d) 225. Also see McSherry (2001) op cit.
168 See McSherry (2001) op cit, at 20.
169 See McMahon, M, "Dangerousness, Confidentiality and the Duty to Protect" (1992) 27 *Australian Psychologist* 12 , Mendelson and Mendelson (1991) op cit, 33.

organisations permit a breach of confidentiality in such circumstances.[170] The eminent Australian psychiatrist John Ellard has stated:

> Because of my training and my concern for my patients, my first reaction is to resist any request for information, no matter from whom the request may come ... but I do not argue for absolute confidentiality. If a paranoid schizophrenic were to tell me that he intended to murder the Prime Minister ... and I believed him, I would certainly tell the police.[171]

Empirical information suggests that Australian health care practitioners will breach confidentiality if they believe that another person is at risk of serious physical harm from a client[172] and that members of the public approve of disclosure in these circumstances.[173] It is not clear whether a legal duty to protect potential victims exists in Australia. The applicability of the reasoning in *Tarasoff's* case to Australian law is uncertain, and it is not yet known whether Australian courts would impose a similar liability. Currently an Australian health care professional may be justified in disclosing confidential information to protect an endangered third party (under the umbrella of the "public interest" exception to the duty of confidentiality), but there does not yet exist a duty to do so. Although this matter was not directly before the court in *R v Lowe* (and hence the remarks of the court are *obiter dicta*), the Victorian Court of Appeal noted – without endorsing – that "there is an emerging view that a duty of disclosure exists".[174]

Conclusion

Confidentiality in the relationship between clients and health care practitioners is expected by clients, accepted by practitioners, endorsed by ethical codes and specifically protected in particular legislative initiatives. However, as the previous review has indicated, both the law and ethical codes specify that the duty of confidentiality is not absolute and numerous exceptions exist.

The landscape of confidentiality has changed. Historical changes in the delivery of health care services, technological developments facilitating the amassing of huge data banks plus difficulties in accessing legal remedies for breaches of confidentiality, as well as the expanding area of "disclosure in the public interest",

---

170　Hawkins argued that confidentiality may be breached "when the doctor believes he has an overriding duty to society": Hawkins (1985) op cit, p 220. Also see *W v Edgell* [1989] 2 WLR 689; [1990] 2 WLR 471 (CA); *Crozier* (1990) 12 Cr App R 206. The ethical codes of many health care professionals similarly permit such a breach: for example, AASW Code, Principle 5.1.2(3); RANZCP Code of Ethics, Annotations to Principles 4.6.

171　Ellard, J, "Confidentiality and the Psychiatrist in Private Practice" (1970) 4 *Australian & New Zealand Journal of Psychiatry* 191.

172　See under heading "Empirical information: attitudes and practices in relation to confidentiality".

173　Knowles A and McMahon, M, "Expectations and Preferences Regarding Confidentiality in the Psychologist-Client Relationship" (1995) 30 *Australian Psychologist* 175.

174　[1997] 2 VR 465 at 485.

contribute to the modern circumscription of the duty of confidentiality. New areas of scientific research and activity also present profound new dilemmas.[175] Most significantly – and paradoxically – it may be that modern privacy regimes mark the demise of traditional conceptions of confidentiality by supplanting them with modern, statute-based rules governing disclosure and providing "user-friendly" grievance mechanisms to enforce those rules.

I have argued in this chapter that much contemporary health care practice relating to confidentiality can be informed by conceptualising such practices as modern, secular ritual. Rituals, however outmoded, reveal our concerns about values and practices. Simply to dismiss the rituals of confidentiality is misguided. Nevertheless, "The world created by ritual is ... extremely vague. Rituals create by drama, not by exegesis".[176] Re-thinking confidentiality and recasting both under-standings and practices in a manner relevant to contemporary health care settings requires deconstruction of the ritual of confidentiality, substantial exploration of - the "drama" of ethical dilemmas and hard legal cases, and investigation of the actual behaviour of health care professionals and the expectations of their clients, as well as explication of ethical and legal standards. Somewhere between untenable promises of absolute confidentiality and unthinking disclosure of information lies the modern duty of confidentiality.

---

175 See McLean, S and Giesen, D, "Legal and Ethical Considerations of the Human Genome Project" (1994) 1 *Medical Law International* 159; Berry, RM, "The Genetic Revolution and the Physician's Duty of Confidentiality. The Role of the Old Hippocratic Virtues in the Regulation of the New Genetic Intimacy" (1997) 18 *Journal of Legal Medicine* 401; Berkendorf, JL, Reutenauer, JE, Hughes, C, Eads, N, Willison, J, Powers, M and Lermann, C, "Patients' Attitudes About Autonomy and Confidentiality in Genetic Testing for Breast-Ovarian Cancer Susceptibility" (1997) 73 *American Journal of Medical Genetics* 296.

176 Bloch, M, "Religion and Ritual" in Kuper, A and Kuper, J (eds), *The Social Sciences Encyclopedia*, 2nd edn, Routledge, London, 1996.

28

Privacy issues,
HealthConnect and beyond

*Livia Iacovino, Danuta Mendelson
and Moira Paterson*[1]

Introduction

What are the privacy implications of a national network of personal health records envisaged as a "single national resource" that captures all health encounters over a patient's lifetime? Under the Australian Health*Connect* scheme, key patient health data in the form of an event summary collected at the point of care for a given health care event, will form part of a series of event summaries pertaining to a uniquely identified patient. These summaries, which are not meant to replace providers' clinical records, will be stored in identified form, and subject to consent arrangements, made available to participating health service providers. The event summaries will also be made available in either an identified or de-identified form to authorised third parties, including researchers and health administrators.

Electronic health record initiatives such as Health*Connect* have been driven by electronic communications including the Internet, wireless technologies and data interchange standards. These systems create, capture and access patients' records across numerous organisations over their lifetimes and link or merge them with administrative health systems for billing, government reporting, and statistical analysis. A "consumer"-centred view of health and the commercialisation of the health industry underpin these developments.

Health care delivery has shifted away from the reasonably exclusive patient–doctor relationship into the environment of multiple health care providers, based on a consumer-provider business model in which consumer privacy is traded off for the perceived benefits of a cheaper health service and apparent patient autonomy. The notion of an aggregated electronic personal health record shared by many providers and also researchers strains the therapeutic relationship between patient and doctor.

Electronic health records will contain highly sensitive personal information, such as chronic health problems, sexually transmitted diseases, neurological,

---

1   The authors would like to acknowledge the invaluable comments of Barbara Reed on the draft chapter.

genetic and psychiatric conditions that affect an individual's employment and health insurance. Some of the unresolved issues of the Health*Connect* project that impact on patient and provider privacy include extensive use of the private sector, inadequate consent, underdeveloped secondary use controls, and lack of a finalised governance structure and an external auditing framework.

The possible introduction of a national health identifier that will uniquely identify a patient for Health*Connect* and other health initiatives is Australia's greatest privacy challenge since the failed Australia Card, a national ID card, proposed and opposed successfully in 1987.

Despite the fact that Health*Connect* and similar shared electronic health record systems in other countries will eventually be linked across national jurisdictions,[2] their impact on the privacy of the patient, his and her family and the treating health practitioners have not been adequately addressed in legal, ethical and technological terms.[3] Nor can the experience of other electronic health record systems be moved readily from one jurisdiction to another, as they are dependent on the health care delivery system and its legal and moral framework. For example, a relatively small single jurisdiction such as New Zealand has more easily enforced a national health identifier.

Shared electronic health record systems

Since the 1970s the term "health record" rather than medical record has been adopted by health care managers to refer to all records pertaining to an individual's health.[4] Shared electronic health records (SEHRs) differ from other forms of electronic health records in that they are specifically designed to facilitate the sharing of information rather than to store a practitioner's own patient records. As noted by Upham, an SEHR is used "to communicate with other practitioners about the delivery of care, as reference for the patient's history, to support its operations and billing, and for medical-legal purposes. It is the aggregate of the total experiences related to patient care".[5]

---

2   Health*Connect* has stated its intention to adopt health informatics standards which support interoperable systems in any jurisdiction. Health*Connect*, *Business Architecture v1.9* (Version for Comment), November 2004, Department of Health and Ageing, Canberra, 2004, p 35, <www.healthconnect.gov.au/pdf/BArc1-9.pdf> (accessed 21 April 2005).

3   *Journal of Law & Medicine*, Special Issue on Electronic Health Records, (2004) 12 (1) *Journal of Law and Medicine*, reports on research undertaken for "Electronic Health Records: Achieving an Effective and Ethical Legal and Recordkeeping Framework", Australian Research Council, Discovery Grant, 2002–2004, Chief Investigators: Associate Professor Danuta Mendelson, School of Law, Deakin University; Dr Livia Iacovino, School of Information Management and Systems, Monash University; and Associate Professor Bernadette McSherry and Moira Paterson, Faculty of Law, Monash University.

4   Benjamin, B, *Medical Records*, 2nd edn, William Heinemann Medical Books Ltd, London, 1980, p 7.

5   Upham, R, "The Electronic Health Record: Will It Become a Reality?" April 2004, <www.hipaadvisory.com/action/ehealth/EHR-reality.htm> (accessed 21 April 2005).

The proponents of the electronic sharing of patient health information claim that the quality of health care will be improved if health professionals are provided with a more complete medical history for each patient, and that sharing of health records will allow for a more holistic and integrated approach to patient treatment. However, no scientific studies have been conducted to substantiate this claim. The SEHR initiative is mainly motivated by a desire to harness technology to reduce the cost of health care budgets and provide a more convenient source of information for health care administration and medical research. Information contained in an electronic records system designed to be shared amongst a multitude of users, by definition, cannot be secure.

In Victoria, there has been a systemic abuse of the Law Enforcement Assistance Program database by police officers,[6] and in 2004 a "top secret" file with the name and address of a police informer was accessed, and may have led to the murder of an informer and his wife in their Melbourne home. These scandals demonstrate that even a "top secret" electronic record system is not secure. Thus, whatever the projected benefits of SEHRs, the fundamental civil rights issues of consent, confidentiality and health privacy are yet to be resolved. These problems are inherent in the system, because SEHRs are specifically created for the purposes of sharing information between a multiplicity of persons and organisations. In addition, shared electronic records are seen as part of a business model. This means that illness and medical treatment are conceptualised in terms of commodities to be traded between health care consumers, providers, and organisational stakeholders. Consequently, there is a risk that the use of health technologies may de-humanise personal health information by denuding it of the therapeutic context in which it is created.

Health privacy

As this chapter is concerned specifically with privacy of electronic health records, it is germane to consider what information privacy involves and why it is important. Information privacy is frequently confused with concepts such as confidentiality and secrecy. Confidentiality is an ethical principle, which has been conceptualised as a legal duty whereby those who agree to receive information on the basis that it will be kept secret, come under the obligation of confidentiality.[7] The modern

---

6   See AAP, "Ombudsman Probes Police Database Leaks", *The Age*, 7 December 2004, <www.theage.com.au/news/National/Ombudsman-probes-police-database-leaks/2004/12/07/1102182286836.html?oneclick=true> (accessed 21 April 2005). See Carbonell, R, "Fitzgerald Scathing over Leaked Police Report" *PM*, 24 February, 2005, <www.abc.net.au/pm/content/2005/s1310453.htm> (accessed 21 April 2005).

7   Sir Nicholas Browne-Wilkinson, in *Stephens v Avery* [1988] 2 All ER 477 at 482, expressed the equitable source of the duty of confidentiality in the following way:

    Although the relationship between the parties is often important in cases where it is said [sic] there is an implied as opposed to express obligation of confidence, the relationship between the parties is not the determining factor. It is the acceptance of the information on the basis that it will be kept secret that affects the conscience of the recipient of the information.

concept of a medical duty of confidentiality has its roots in the Western religious[8] and secular ethical canon embodied in the Hippocratic Oath, the penultimate clause of which states:

[W]hat I see or hear in the course of the treatment or even outside of the treatment in regard to the life of men, which on no account one must spread abroad, I will keep to myself holding such things shameful to be spoken about.[9]

Thus, unless authorised by the patient or by statute, doctors and other health care providers are under a duty to abstain from disclosing information imparted to them in the course of a professional relationship. Professional duties of confidentiality are enforceable in equity through an action for breach of confidence;[10] at common law, through the action for intentional infliction of psychiatric injury and in negligence;[11] as well as through professional codes of ethics.[12] All Australian States and Territories have numerous enactments mandating confidentiality of health information in specific circumstances.[13]

---

8   For example, negative injunctions in *Leviticus* 19.16: "Thou shalt not go ... as a tale-bearer among thy people", and in *Proverbs* 25.9: "Reveal not the secret of another". Mendelson, D, "Medical Duty of Confidentiality in the Hippocratic Tradition and Jewish Medical Ethics" (1998) 5(3) *Journal of Law and Medicine* 227.

9   Edelstein, L, *Ancient Medicine,* Johns Hopkins University Press, Baltimore, 1987, p 6.

10   *Stephens v Avery* [1988] 2 All ER 477 at 482. In *Breen v Williams* (1996) 186 CLR 71, Gaudron and McHugh JJ observed (at 107–108):

> Patients ... invariably confide intimate personal details about themselves to their doctors. In some circumstances, the dependency of the patient or the provision of confidential information may make the relationship between a doctor and patient fiduciary in nature. But that does not mean that their relationship would be fiduciary for all purposes. As Mason J pointed out in *Hospital Products Ltd v United States Surgical Corporation* (1984) 156 CLR 41 at 98, a person may stand in a fiduciary relationship to another for one purpose but not for others.

11   *Furniss v Fitchett* [1958] NZLR 396; *W v Edgell* [1989] 2 WLR 689; [1990] 2 WLR 471 at 488–489.

12   Medical boards throughout Australia have tended to interpret breach of confidentiality strictly, and regard it as serious professional misconduct.

13   For example, *Children and Young Persons (Care and Protection) Act 1998* (NSW) s 27; *Disability Services Act 1993* (NSW) Sch 1; *Health Administration Act 1982* (NSW) s 22; *Human Tissue Act 1983* (NSW) s 37; *Medical Practice Act 1992* (NSW) ss 126, 190, 190B; *Health Care Complaints Act 1993* (NSW) s 72; *Adoption of Children Act 1964* (Qld) s 59; *Health Rights Commission Act 1991* (Qld) s 141; *Mental Health Act 2000* (Qld) s 426; *Health Act 1937* (Qld) s 100I; *Workplace Health and Safety Regulation 1997* (Qld) reg 13; *Ambulance Service Act 1991* (Qld) s 49; *Transplantation and Anatomy Act 1979* (Qld) s 49; *Health Services Act 1991* (Qld) s 63; *Adoption Act 1988* (SA) s 36; *South Australian Health Commission Act 1976* (SA) s 64; *Public and Environmental Health Act 1987* (SA) s 42; *Transplantation and Anatomy Act 1983* (SA) s 39; *Guardianship and Administration Act 1995* (Tas) s 86; *Health Complaints Act 1995* (Tas) s 37; *Transplantation and Anatomy Act 1978* (Tas) s 49; *Public Health Act 1997* (Tas) s 62; *Human Tissue Act 1985* (Tas) s 31; *Mental Health Act 1986* (Vic) s 120A; *Health Act 1958* (Vic) s 162H; *Cancer Act 1958* (Vic) s 61; *Health Services Act 1988* (Vic) s 141; *Health Services (Governance) Act 2000* (Vic) s 9; *Infertility Treatment Act 1995* (Vic) ss 89, 90; *Adoption Act 1984* (Vic) s 89; *Adoption Act 1994* (WA) s 127; *Young Offenders Act 1994* (WA) s 17; *Disability Services Act 1993* (WA) s 52; *Mental Health Act 1996* (WA) s 206; *Medical Act 1894* (WA) s 9; *Royal Commission (Custody of Records) Act 1992* (WA) s 14; *Human Tissue and Transplant Act 1982* (WA) s 34; *Health Records (Privacy and Access) Act 1997* (ACT) s 17; *Health Act 1993* (ACT) s 10; *Children and Young People Act 1999* (ACT) s 404; *Adoption Act 1993* (ACT) s 60; *Health Practitioners and Allied Professionals Registration Act 1996* (NT) s 68; *Health and Community Services Complaints Act 1998* (NT) s 97; *Medical Act 1993* (NT) s 13; *Human Tissue Transplant Act 1979* (NT) s 28.

Unlike confidentiality, privacy is concerned primarily with an individual's ability to exercise control over his or her own identifiable personal data. Whereas the legal concept of confidentiality reflects notions of trust embedded in the Judeo-Christian moral and ethical heritage, the concept of privacy is grounded in the notion of a personal right to self-determination.[14] To borrow from Charles Fried, "it is not simply an absence of information about us in the minds of others; rather it is the control we have over information about ourselves".[15] That control plays a vital role in protecting individual autonomy and ensuring that every individual is treated with dignity.

Health information is uniquely sensitive because it is closely intertwined with self-perceptions and perceptions of us by others. It also has the potential to shed light on intimate aspects of our lives such as our sexual behaviour and substance abuse so its disclosure has the potential to expose individuals to a range of adverse consequences including ridicule, stigmatisation and discrimination (for example, in the context of employment). The risks of harmful exposure have been further magnified by developments in genetic technology which make it more likely that medical practitioners will include genetic data in clinical records.[16]

Privacy is also important because patients, who believe that their right to medical confidentiality has been compromised through the concept of shared health records, and who feel that they have no control over the fate of their medical information, may:

> [F]ail to disclose important medical data or even avoid seeking medical care because of concern over denial of insurance, loss of employment or housing, or stigmatisation and embarrassment. Expectation of privacy allows trust and improves communications between doctors and patients.[17]

Therefore, as noted by Applebaum, trading the privacy of health records for some other purported good, creates a "real risk of dissuading people from coming for treatment or from revealing the information that physicians need to provide adequate care".[18]

---

14 Mendelson, D, "Travels of a Medical Record and the Myth of Privacy" (2003) 11 (2) *Journal of Law and Medicine* 136.

15 Fried, C, "Privacy (a Moral Analysis)" in Schoeman, F (ed), *Philosophical Dimensions of Privacy: An Anthology*, Cambridge University Press, Cambridge, 1984, p 209.

16 Gostin, LO, "National Health Information Privacy: Regulations under the Health Insurance Portability and Accountability Act" (2001) (23) 285 *JAMA* 3015. See also Australian Law Reform Commission, *Essentially Yours: The Protection of Human Genetic Information in Australia*, Report No 96, ALRC, 2003.

17 Mandl, KD, Szolovits, P and Kohane, IS, "Public Standards and Patients' Control: How to Keep Electronic Medical Records Accessible but Private" (2001) (3 February) 322 *British Medical Journal* 283-284. See also Gostin, L, "Health care Information and the Protection of Personal Privacy: Ethical and Legal Considerations" (1997) 127 *Annals Internal Medicine* 683.

18 Appelbaum, PS, "Threats to the Confidentiality of Medical Records – No Place to Hide" (2000) (6) 283 *JAMA* 795-796.

Role of privacy-enhancing technologies

Any information system seeking to record and disseminate personal information electronically will have to employ technology-based protections. One such set of technologies of particular significance to SEHR implementation are those collectively known as privacy-enhancing technologies. "Privacy-enhancing products are those that have been designed in a way that aims at accomplishing the largest possible use of truly anonymous data".[19] Developments in technologies that operate without identifying individuals to unauthorised parties address privacy at the design level.[20]

The most significant privacy-enhancing technology (PET) has been public-key cryptography: a protocol for communication which controls access to sensitive information and guarantees the integrity and accuracy of the message.

Public key management systems act as trusted mediators between senders and recipients to certify a link between individuals and their public keys. Both the trusted mediators and the keys must themselves be controlled, thus requiring a hierarchical chain of trust.

The danger is that if the trusted authority's owner (for example, the government) has control over the decryption keys, it can build an extensive identification system and authorise who can access the data.

The cryptographic key can also be opened by a court order revealing unnecessary personal information linked to an individual's key. Even with secure key management, the design may allow law-enforcement agents, employers, or a system owner to have access to keys.[21]

Privacy-enhancing technologies can be used in shared health systems to authorise who can send, receive, and capture personal health data and who can have access.[22] In the case of shared health records, identification and authentication of the patient is required for the treating physicians; however, for statistical and other research, personal identification is generally not required.

---

19 European Commission, Data Protection Working Group, WP37, *Working Document: Privacy on the Internet – An integrated EU Approach to On-line Data Protection*, November 2000, Article 29, <http://europa.eu.int/comm/internal_market/privacy/workinggroup/wp2000/wp docs00_en.htm> (accessed 21 April 2005); Agre, P, "Beyond the Mirror World: Privacy and the Representational Practices of Computing", in Agre, P and Rotenberg, M (eds), *Technology and Privacy: the New Landscape*, MIT Press, Massachusetts, 1998, p 63.

20 National Academy of Sciences, *Authentication Technologies and Their Privacy Implications*, <www7.nationalacademies.org/cstb/project_authentication.html> (accessed 3 February 2005). Kent, ST and Millett, LI (eds), *Who Goes There?: Authentication Through the Lens of Privacy*, The National Academies Press, Washington, DC, 2003, <http://books.nap.edu/html/whogoes/> (accessed 3 February 2005).

21 Phillips, DJ, "Cryptography, Secrets, and the Structuring of Trust", in Agre and Rotenberg (1998) op cit, pp 243–276.

22 Burkett, H, "Privacy-enhancing Technologies: Typology, Critique, Vision" in Agre and Rotenberg (1998) op cit, pp 125–142.

The most developed implementation of key technology and management is public key infrastructure (PKI).[23] PKI adopts a hierarchical chain of trusted authorities that support the use of public-key based digital signatures and encryption through the issuance of digital certificates. In Australia, companies are accredited by the "gatekeeper" process.[24] In Europe and Canada doubts have been expressed as to the value of PKI.[25] The effectiveness of PKI and other PETs in protecting patient and provider privacy depends on who controls the keys and the identity information critical to distributed health systems.[26] Another solution being offered is that of formal data-sharing protocols, which specify responsibilities of the sharing partners.[27] The basic concept behind these protocols is to increase public trust in otherwise intrusive practices by openness about the extent and limits of this activity. However, while such solutions are important, what is critical for privacy is that patients should retain maximum control of the uses and disclosures of their identifiable personal information. Privacy-enhancing technologies and protocols go some way towards protecting privacy but they do not guarantee it.

Possible approaches to health data protection

Australia, Canada, the United States and Europe (the United Kingdom in particular), are significant jurisdictions in terms of the development of electronic health records (EHRs), but their privacy models for shared electronic health systems differ widely. In some national electronic health systems total control over health

---

23 "PKI is an information technology infrastructure network that enables the secure exchange of data using cryptographic key pairs, through public and private networks via a trusted authority. Therefore, PKI is a set of software tools, hardware, network services and management techniques (policy and procedures) that work together to provide a chain of 'trust'". Mynott, M, "Authentication of Electronic Medical Records", paper presented at Legal Challenges in Cybermedicine and e-Health Conference, Faculty of Law, Centre for Continuing Education, University of New South Wales, 2003.

24 Health*Connect* adopts the Health Insurance Commission's Health e-Signature Authority's PKI process which involves identity checks to issue digital certificates. The digital certificate verifies a subscriber's identity and contains his or her key pairs, thus enabling them to encrypt messages, and sign them with their unique digital signature: <www.hesa.com.au/> (accessed 21 April 2005).

25 Cornwall, A, "World Tour of e-Health Record Systems", paper presented at Legal Challenges in Cybermedicine and e-Health Conference, Faculty of Law, Centre for Continuing Education, University of New South Wales, 2003, p 20.

26 Connelly, C, "Managing Privacy in Identity Management: The Way Forward", paper presented at Australian Government, Information Management Office, *Future Challenges for E-Government*, Vol 2, Institute of Public Administration, ACT Division, May 2004, pp 18–28.

27 United Kingdom, Department for Constitutional Affairs, Public Sector Data Sharing: Guidance on the Law, November 2003, <www.dca.gov.uk/foi/sharing/toolkit/> (accessed 21 April 2005). A data-sharing protocol is a formal agreement between organisations that are sharing personal data. It explains why data is being shared and sets out the principles and commitments organisations will adopt when they collect, store and disclose personal information about members of the public.

lifestyle is intrinsic to government health policy.[28] For example, the Australian Health*Connect* system architecture includes a data element in its EHR specification for health lifestyle risk factors, which if disclosed to health insurance providers could jeopardise an individual's insurance cover.[29]

Therefore, while fundamental legal principles regarding confidentiality and privacy are the same for all EHRs, models cannot be easily transferred due to substantial differences between juridical systems, medical traditions and government policy.

In all instances of proposals for a national EHR system, government has taken the lead. Even in the United States where health services are primarily a private sector activity, the Federal Government is involved in building the national health information infrastructure. National initiatives in Canada centre on interoperable systems, with the cooperation of the provinces which are responsible for health service delivery.[30] The enforcement powers of privacy commissioners and their influence on government EHR projects are significant factors in the extent to which these projects take account of privacy.[31]

The European health insurance card introduced in May 2004 holds name, date of birth and a personal identification number but no clinical data. In Germany and France it is the patient's smartcard on which health information is stored rather than on a network or a database. The clinical data are stored in a protected area of the card and the card's access key is controlled by the patient. Health professionals also have their own smartcard that allows them to access the patient's card.[32] Conformity with European Union Directives on privacy provides an umbrella framework for individual member states.

Approaches to privacy taken in different countries to EHRs and SEHRs in particular, may be categorised as either collection-centric or disclosure-centric.[33] The former enhance privacy by imposing limitations on the collection of data thereby enhancing patient autonomy by requiring that patients must be fully

---

28 For example, the Ministry of Health in Singapore has health promotion, preventative care and screening programs that require patients to monitor their own health by completing an online interactive self-assessment tool that generates a personalised feedback report about their health, lifestyle and diet. Similar systems are being used by large corporations or government departments for their employees' health screening, which provide details of potential health problems to employers. Apostolopoulos, P and Lam, SL, "Promoting Health and Preventive Care with IT", *Proceedings, 24th Health Information Management Association of Australia Conference, Sydney, 8–10 August 2003*, HIMAA, Sydney, 2003.

29 Health*Connect, Business Architecture v1.9: Specification of HealthConnect Business Require-ments* (Version for Comment), November 2004, Department of Health and Ageing, Canberra, 2004, p 72, <http://www.healthconnect.gov.au/pdf/BAV1-9g%20 Attach.pdf> (accessed 21 April 2005).

30 Cornwall (2003) op cit, pp 4–7. Canadian provinces with EHR systems include British Columbia, Alberta and Ontario.

31 Ibid, p 21.

32 Ibid, pp 10–13.

33 Terry, NP, "Electronic Health Records: International, Structural and Legal Perspectives" (2004) 12 (1) *Journal of Law and Medicine* 26 at 36–38.

informed about the purposes of collection and that use and disclosure are consistent with those purposes. The latter emphasise confidentiality rather than privacy and seek to ensure that data are not improperly disclosed to third parties. The approach which is ultimately adopted is arguably affected by the health care context, and is best illustrated by considering the approaches taken to the development of SEHRs and to the legislative protection of health data in the United Kingdom and the United States.

United Kingdom

The health system in the United Kingdom differs substantially from that in Australia in that (apart from a very small private health sector) it is under a strong central National Health System (NHS) control. The stated objectives of the NHS's *Information for Health Strategy* include a commitment to lifelong electronic health records for every person in the United Kingdom, round-the-clock on-line access to patient records and seamless care for patients through general practitioners, hospitals and community services sharing information across the NHS information highway.[34]

In this context SEHR developments have been driven by the government as part of its health care reform and its desire to improve the efficiency of a costly NHS. To the extent that an individual's health care is largely controlled by an allocated general practitioner there is limited potential for individuals to disperse their data by attending at different practices or consulting specialists on the basis of referrals from different doctors.

The United Kingdom has laws imposing limitations and enhanced protection on the collection of health information that falls within the category of sensitive personal information.[35] Unfortunately, that protection is extensively undermined by an exception which covers the processing that is necessary for medical purposes and undertaken by a health professional or another person subject to equivalent obligations of confidentiality.[36] The expression "medical purposes" is broadly defined to include "preventative medicine, medical diagnosis, medical research, the provision of care and treatment and the management of health care services".[37] Moreover, the centralisation of records has long been the norm; this raises an issue of the extent to which other practitioners and strangers to the therapeutic relationship are able to access information that might not otherwise have been provided to them.

---

34   Schloeffel, P, "Current EHR Developments: an Australian and International Perspective – Part 1" (2004) *Health Care & Informatics Review Online*, September 2004, <www.enigma.co.nz/hcro/website/index.cfm?fuseaction=articledisplay&FeatureID=010904 > (accessed 21 April 2005).

35   See definition in *Data Protection Act 1998* (UK) s 2.

36   Ibid, Sch 3, cl 8.

37   Ibid, Sch 3, cl 8.

United States

The United States does not have a universal government-funded health care scheme; its health care is frequently provided by managed care organisations and paid for by employer-sponsored health plans. Consequently, the main impetus for SEHR developments has come from the insurers and health services managers who want to facilitate the sharing of information between different individual providers.

Models for exchange of electronic health records in the United States focus on linking existing record systems, exchanging patient data and developing systems that "pull" health data from health providers' records. Therefore, in the United States, considerable emphasis has been placed on interoperability of clinical systems that allow for the exchange of health data in a standard format.[38]

In relation to privacy legislation, the United States Federal Government has enacted the *Health Insurance Portability and Accountability Act 1996* (PL 104–191), which covers both public and private organisations that produce and use health information.

Under the *Health Insurance Portability and Accountability Act 1996*, regulations have been promulgated that apply a privacy protection regime to personal health information,[39] which sets national standards for its protection by health insurance organisations, health care clearinghouses, and health care providers. The statute came into operation on 14 April 2003 (and 14 April 2004, for small health plans), and requires the implementation of standards to protect and guard against the misuse of individually identifiable health information.

The Federal Government has become involved in building a national health information infrastructure. For example, the United States Department of Health and Human Services initiated a project in 2003 to develop a standard EHR functional specification.[40]

However, the largely private nature of health care in the United States is inimical to the setting up of a national patient database and national patient identifiers.[41] Therefore, in the United States shared health records initiatives are supported by the Federal Government but not in the form of a national set of patient health records.

---

38   Terry (2004) op cit, at 33-36.

39   Gostin, LO and Hodge, JG, Jr, "Personal Privacy and Common Goods: A Framework for Balancing Under the National Health Information Privacy Rule", (2002) 86 *Minnesota Law Review* 1439.

40   Silbert, J, "US Eyes Standardized Electronic Health Records" *NPR Morning Edition*, 22 July 2004, <www.npr.org/templates/story/story.php?storyId=3608303> (accessed 21 April 2005).

41   Quinn, J, "Observing Health care Lessons From the UK EMR: Not Exactly Apples to Apples", *HealthLeaders News*, 19 November 2004, <www.healthleaders.com/news/feature 60316.html> (accessed 21 April 2005).

Australian developments: The Health*Connect* project

In Australia, within the context of developments in national health networks, the National Electronic Health Records Taskforce published a report (HINA) in July 2000 which recommended the creation of Health*Connect*, to oversee a nationally coordinated and distributed network of SEHRs based on a common EHR architecture.[42] The HINA Report identified a number of key building blocks as being required to underpin all other activities. These included the development of legal data protection and security frameworks which were regarded as necessary to facilitate electronic transfers and storage of health information.[43] However, a number of important policy issues with regard to ownership, consent and privacy have yet to be fully debated or resolved. Despite this, in 2005 the Federal Government announced plans to implement Health*Connect* in Tasmania and South Australia, with other States to follow later.[44] Related State policy initiatives such as New South Wales's Health-e-link (formerly NSWEHR) are intended to eventually be incorporated into Health*Connect*.[45]

The Health*Connect* project is by world standards, one of the most ambitious SEHR initiatives. The model adopted is very much a product of the Australian health system which is a mix of public and private health service providers and includes three major national subsidy schemes: Medicare, the Pharmaceutical Benefits Scheme and the 30 per cent private health insurance rebate administered by the Health Insurance Commission (HIC). There are also a number of private health insurance schemes. In particular, the Commonwealth's limited constitutional power over the practice of medicine[46] may be extended by the inclusion of Medi*Connect*, which stores personal records of medications held nationally by HIC into Health*Connect*. For it is envisaged that Health*Connect* will have "national governance structures with representatives from both the public and private sectors and all main stakeholders including consumers",[47] although precise details of that structure are yet to be announced. A vital feature is that it is a voluntary "opt-in" rather than an "opt out" system for both the patient and health care provider.

---

42 The National Electronic Health Records Taskforce, *A Health Information Network for Australia*, Taskforce Report, Commonwealth Department of Health and Aged Care, Canberra, 2000.

43 National Electronic Health Records Taskforce (2000) op cit, p 19.

44 Brewin, B, "Electronic Health Records Spread" 7 December 2004, <www.fcw.com/fcw/articles/2004/1206/web-ehr-12-07-04.asp> (accessed 21 April 2005).

45 Health*Connect* (2004) *Business Architecture v1.9*: op cit, p 8.

46 Constitution s 51(xxiiiA):

> [T]he provision of maternity allowances, widows' pensions, child endowment, unemployment, pharmaceutical, sickness and hospital benefits, medical and dental services (but not so as to authorise any form of civil conscription), benefits to students and family allowances.

47 Schloeffel (2004) op cit.

Unique patient and provider identifiers

The most controversial privacy aspect of Health*Connect* is encapsulated in its central principle that: "Each consumer and their EHR information will be uniquely identified within Health*Connect* by use of a single unique identifier able to be linked to any future National Health Identifier".[48] Unique identifiers identify a person by name, number or other means in order to link his or her records across systems (data matching). The benefit of the increased accuracy of data linked by a unique identifier has to be balanced against the risk of increased privacy infringements that may occur when personal information from many sources is electronically linked to one person. It is also probable that the national health identifier will be associated with a personal identifier for all government transactions, thus linking health personal data with an ever-widening set of transactions between government (frequently via private deliverers) and the individual.

A related issue involves who controls the patient and provider identifiers. The control of the identifiers will be at the national level but the nature of the national organisation is as yet unresolved.[49] Therefore, the legal ownership and responsibilities for protecting identifiers cannot be established at present. The option of unique national health identifiers should not be introduced without educating the public about its role in linking all health information pertaining to an individual. It is imperative that the Federal Government obtains a clear social and legal mandate for this option. However, unlike the Australia Card there has been very little national discussion on the matter.

HealthConnect's electronic health record

Health*Connect* adopts the following definition of an electronic health record:

> An electronic, longitudinal collection of personal health information, usually based on the individual, entered or accepted by health care providers, which can be distributed over a number of sites or aggregated at a particular source. The information is organised primarily to support continuing, efficient and quality health care. The record is under the control of the consumer and is stored and transmitted securely.[50]

Health*Connect* is being iteratively defined, meaning that business and technical architecture models are in a constant state of development, introducing often subtle changes between document versions. For example, earlier definitions of

---

48 Health*Connect* (2004) *Business Architecture*: op cit, p 30.

49 Possibilities mooted include a departmental function without establishing an executive agency, a company, a statutory authority or an unincorporated joint venture company: ibid, pp 108 and 162.

50 Health*Connect, Systems Architecture Draft v0.9, July 2003*, Department of Health and Ageing, Canberra 2003, p 10. This definition of an electronic health record is found in the National Electronic Records Taskforce Report, 2000.

the health record also included "family" information.[51] That inclusion would have extended substantially the retention of health data beyond a person's lifetime. Although "Health*Connect* will be a repository service for consumers' lifetime health records",[52] a significant new principle is that "EHR data will be permanently recorded and preserved subject to legal constraints".[53] Control of the record by the patient/consumer has also been modified. (See below the section on patient access and amendment rights.)

The proposed system in its current form defines an EHR of a patient who has consented to join Health*Connect* as, "a series of event summaries, each containing key information about a specific health care event such as a general practitioner consultation, hospital admission or discharge, community health centre visit, pathology test or a pharmacy dispensing a prescription".[54] The event summary is sent ("pushed") by the Health*Connect* provider[55] who supplies the service, to a Health*Connect* Records System (HRS) to which the patient has been allocated. The HRS is controlled by an approved EHR manager (AEM), which may be a private or public agency.[56] The HRS forms part of a national network of EHR repositories, accessed via a nationally governed, but potentially privately supplied, directory service.

A copy of the EHR is transmitted by the responsible HRS/AEM to the national data store for archiving and long-term retention and to support all secondary use of Health*Connect* EHR data for research and planning purposes. Whilst the Health*Connect* EHR repository may be distributed across a number of federated elements, it is intended that it will be available as a single national resource from the viewpoint of access, interoperability, reporting and inquiry, while all operational interaction with a consumer's EHR will occur through the HRS.[57] Thus a national database of all Health*Connect* records will be controlled at the federal level. Access to a Health*Connect* record will be available to the patient, to health care practitioners to whom the patient has given consent via an access control list, and other authorised secondary participants subject to Health*Connect* rules.

---

51 Flinders University, *The Benefits and Difficulties of Introducing a National Approach to Electronic Health Records in Australia,* Report to the National Electronic Health Records Taskforce, Flinders University, Adelaide, April, 2000 (Appendix), in The National Electronic Health Records Taskforce Report, (2000) op cit, p 8.

52 Health*Connect* (2004) *Business Architecture* op cit, p 37.

53 Ibid, p 34.

54 Ibid, p 1.

55 A Health*Connect* provider is:

> A person practising as a health provider who is recognised for professional registration in an Australian jurisdiction will be eligible to register with Health*Connect* as an individual provider. This will require their professional registration body to have been previously recognised and registered with Health*Connect*. A registered business (including a sole trader) that delivers health services using the services of one or more individual providers will be eligible to register with HealthConnect as a 'provider organisation'.

> Ibid, p 74.

56 Ibid, pp 41–42.

57 Health*Connect* (2004) *Business Architecture* op cit, p 110.

The outsourcing to the private sector not only of operational functions such as registration, identification and access services for patients and providers, but in some instances also of the running of the HRS, are major privacy, confidentiality and ultimately legal liability issues for Health*Connect*.[58]

Specific privacy issues in HealthConnect

Like its overseas counterparts, the Australian national network of personal health records, raises profound and complex privacy issues. For patients to be able to enjoy an equivalent level of privacy protection to that which currently exists under a dispersed system requires: complex technical and administrative measures to ensure a high degree of control over what is included and capable of being accessed; strong and effective security measures; and enforceable Australia-wide health privacy laws.[59]

The Australian Federal Privacy Commissioner has noted that for Health-*Connect* to succeed it must gain the trust of the general community that personal information will be kept private.[60] It is not surprising therefore that privacy is specifically identified as a key element in the Health*Connect* system design. The documentation which outlines its business architecture states that:

> The core of Health*Connect* is a national system of sharable electronic health records, which will be established to receive, store, retrieve and deliver consumers' electronic health record (EHR) information via secure eHealth communications with strict privacy safeguards for use in the delivery of health care.[61]

It also identifies the following as major health privacy issues:

> The use of information by third parties that act against the interests of the individual concerned (eg employers and insurers); personal sensitivities or embarrassment if health information is accessed inappropriately; potential harm to an individual if information is accessed by someone who poses a threat to that person (eg domestic violence); and information being used for other purposes that are not for the health benefit of the person involved (eg unacceptable commercial use of data).[62]

Another privacy aspect of Health*Connect* that must not be overlooked is the personal data that the system will store about health practitioners in the national provider directories, and the detailed monitoring of their activities, including

---

58   Ibid, pp 110–111, 115–117 and 163.

59   Paterson, M, "Health*Connect* and Privacy: A Policy Conundrum", (2004) 12 (1) *Journal of Law and Medicine* 80.

60   Crompton, M, "The Privacy Imperative for a Successful Health*Connect*", Guest Editorial, (2004) 33(1) *HIM* 4.

61   Health*Connect* (2004) *Business Architecture* op cit, p 1.

62   Ibid, p 166. Health*Connect* has contracted with Clayton Utz to undertake the legal issues research for their project. At the time of writing Clayton Utz's final report was not available.

which EHRs they view, the procedures they perform, and their patient medication regimes.[63] Little public attention has been paid to this area to date.

The privacy measures which have been recognised as necessary to underpin Health*Connect* include legislative privacy provisions, administrative policy rules, technical and security measures and organisational practices. In addition, the system is relying on providers participating in Health*Connect* to enter into a legal agreement which includes abiding by existing privacy legislation and by specific Health*Connect* privacy protocols, covering access, contribution to and use of information from Health*Connect* records,[64] leaving individual organisations responsible for ensuring the compliance of staff of the organisation with the privacy provisions in using Health*Connect*.

Health*Connect* will operate across the private and public sectors throughout Australia with the same rules for privacy, identification, registration and consent applying everywhere. However, the existing laws which regulate privacy, do not operate uniformly across all sectors and jurisdictions, are incomplete in their coverage and to some extent overlap with each other. At present the national privacy provisions (NPPs) of the federal *Privacy Act 1988* (Cth) do not distinguish between health information and other types of personal information although they are given enhanced protection under specific NPPs as a species of "sensitive information". Private sector health records are generally protected by the private sector provisions in the *Privacy Act 1988* (Cth). Public health sector records are protected under the public sector provisions in the *Privacy Act 1988* (Cth), the *Information Act 2002* (NT) and under sui generic health records laws in Victoria, New South Wales and the Australian Capital Territory.[65] The latter also protect private records, thereby creating dual protection for private sector health records in those jurisdictions. States other than Victoria and New South Wales do not have either public sector privacy laws or sui generic health records laws.[66]

To overcome this lack of consistency, it was envisaged that the roll out of Health*Connect* would be preceded by the development of a set of National Health Privacy Principles embodied in the National Health Privacy Code (NHPC) of the Australian Health Ministers' Advisory Council National Health Privacy Working Group.[67] However, the NHPC does not specifically address the unique issues raised by shared electronic health records.[68] These are instead left to be dealt with by the

---

63   Ibid, p 93.

64   Ibid, p 5.

65   The *Health Records Act 2001* (Vic), the *Health Records and Information Privacy Act 2002* (NSW) and the *Health Records (Privacy and Access) Act 1997* (ACT).

66   Public bodies in Queensland, South Australia and Tasmania are, however, subject to the operation of administratively imposed privacy rules: see <www.justice.qld.gov.au/dept/privacy.htm>, <www.archives.sa.gov.au/privacy/index.html> and <www.justice.tas.gov.au/legpol/privacy/index.htm> (accessed 21 April 2005).

67   Australian Health Ministers' Advisory Council, *National Health Privacy Code Draft Consultation Paper*, National Health Privacy Working Group, Canberra, 2002.

68   Paterson, M and Iacovino, L, "Health Privacy: The Draft Australian National Health Privacy Code and the Shared Longitudinal Electronic Health Record" (2004) 33(1) *HIM* 5.

specific Health*Connect* rules which set out primary uses of data; authority and processes by which secondary uses of data are approved; consent processes; offences, penalties and sanctions for breaches; and complaints mechanisms. It is envisaged that the complaints process will be based on current practices, with private sector privacy complaints being directed to the Office of the Federal Privacy Commissioner and public sector privacy complaints to the State or Territory body authorised to deal with privacy and health complaints in each jurisdiction.[69] In the interim, privacy arrangements will be tailored to each jurisdiction for each implementation, with a view to making a single national system.[70]

Therefore, interim privacy rights will depend on the physical location of the HRS to which a patient's record is allocated, although it is not clear how this allocation will happen and whether one can choose, and the implications of outsourcing of the HRS. At least while the larger framework is established and promulgated, privacy arrangements will be inconsistent across jurisdictions.

Voluntary "opt-in" system

Health*Connect* has been specifically designed as a voluntary "opt-in" system for both the patient and the practitioner. Insofar as practitioners are concerned, there are health legal experts who argue that an opt-in system cannot work in practice and that fears about potential negligence claims will mean they will in effect be forced to participate.[71]

However, under the Australian federal system, only States (the constitutional position of the Territories is unclear and yet to be tested), have the power to enact legislation to control the registration of medical practitioners, and to impose conditions for the practice of medicine.[72] This means that medical practitioners could be compelled to participate in the Health*Connect* scheme by State legislatures. The Commonwealth Parliament will only have the power to regulate this aspect of medical practice if the High Court of Australia considers that participation in Health*Connect* is a financial or administrative incident of medical practice within the scope of s 51(xxiiA) of the Australian Constitution.[73]

Insofar as patients are concerned, the fact that an "opt in" facility detracts from the overall value of the system as a source of information for research and planning means that there is a danger that there will be pressure to remove this "opt in" facility once the system is in operation.[74] Projected integration of

---

69   Health*Connect* (2004) *Business Architecture* op cit, p 55.

70   Ibid, p 32.

71   Terry (2004) op cit, at 33-39.

72   *British Medical Association v Commonwealth* (1949) 79 CLR 201 at 253 per Latham CJ; compare *Kable v Director of Public Prosecutions (NSW)* (1996) 189 CLR 51.

73   *General Practitioners Society v Commonwealth* (1980) 145 CLR 532 at 560 per Gibbs J. See Mendelson, D, "Devaluation of a Constitutional Guarantee: the History of Section 51(xxiiiA) of the Commonwealth Constitution" (1999) 23 *Melbourne University Law Review* 308.

74   See Paterson (2004) op cit.

Health*Connect* with a Medicare smartcard which will store a unique identifier for patients and "flag an individual's future participation in Health*Connect*" will probably render opting-in inoperative.[75]

Consent

Privacy requires informed consent from participants for the collection, use and disclosure of personal information and explicit consent for the release of information to third parties who are not involved in the provision of health care to them. As well as being bound by Health*Connect*'s privacy rules, private health care providers are required to comply with the 10 National Privacy Principles (NPPs) of the *Privacy Act 1988* (Cth).

One of the central features of Health*Connect* is that patients have a right to choose whether or not to participate in the scheme and if they agree to do so, have the right to nominate or reject at any time the providers and provider organisations (but not individual providers in organisations) who can access their EHRs and to limit the reporting of specific events, either in full or in part.[76]

However, it is impractical to expect patients to make informed decisions about what clinical data they want included in their summary each time they consult a health practitioner.

Consent approval for secondary uses of records is not provided for, rather it is now a condition of patient consent to registration. If the consumer deregisters from Health*Connect*, his or her record will not be deleted, and will remain available for secondary uses.[77] As a consequence, patients will have some level of control over access to their records by those involved in their health care but not over access by third parties such as researchers, health administrators and health insurers. Despite significant research by Health*Connect* on consent, the implementation model offers limited flexibility in terms of the extent to which patients can control access to their identifiable health information.

Patient access and amendment rights

Another of the key privacy platforms of Health*Connect* is that patients have access to information held about them, can maintain control over how their information is used and to whom it is disclosed, and can contribute to and amend their own electronic health record.[78] Health*Connect* has postponed the ability of consumers to

---

75   Media Release, The Hon Tony Abbott MHR, Minister for Health and Ageing, 28 July 2004, ABB123/04, "Medicare Smartcard Launched", <www.health.gov.au/internet/wcms/ Publishing.nsf/Content/health-mediarel-yr2004-ta-abb123.htm> (accessed 21 April 2005). See also Health*Connect*, (2004) *Business Architecture v1.9: Specification of HealthConnect Business Requirements*, op cit, p 15.

76   Health*Connect* (2004) *Business Architecture* op cit, p 31. Access restrictions are subject to an override in the case of a request by a provider for emergency access.

77   Cancelled registrations and records can be re-activated by a consumer. Ibid, pp 34, 61.

78   Ibid, p 55.

contribute to their records until medico-legal concerns are resolved, for example there may be issues arising from an expectation by consumers that their contributions will be acted upon.[79] Although control by the patient can enhance privacy, it can also undermine the procedural controls over record creation and the accuracy of the data, and limit the usefulness of the information to the treating practitioners.[80]

Future directions: HealthConnect, EHR systems and beyond

Different cultural and legal contexts may limit the usefulness of comparing health privacy models in relation to networked health records. The diversity of SEHR systems indicates that there is not just one single answer to issues surrounding health privacy when health records are shared outside the primary zone of care. Privacy-enhancing technologies will always depend on how they are implemented and cannot fully substitute for legal and ethical controls.

Despite the fact that there are many unresolved issues regarding privacy and consent, implementation of Health*Connect* is to proceed on a State-by-State basis. The need to tailor privacy implementation for each Australian jurisdiction indicates that a full national approach to privacy is likely to be difficult, and result in an uneven legal protection for patients and provider responsibility in each State.

The merging of Medi*Connect* and Medicare with Health*Connect* provides a non-consensual means of introducing a smartcard and a unique identifier. Health*Connect* will operate on the basis of a national network of EHR repositories and a national data store for archiving and long-term retention, but much of the national level of the system is underdeveloped. There is a clear but inadequate consent model based on trials, rather than on research, with patient consent to secondary uses assumed on registration and the shelving of more sophisticated approaches that would place restrictions on those who can access highly sensitive health conditions.

Health*Connect* remains one of the most privacy-invasive projects of the Australian government. It will record not only medical conditions but lifestyle risks creating personal profiles that go beyond clinical diagnoses. The monitoring of privacy breaches is still not a fully operational model. The national data store and its secondary uses in particular by managers, will require strict research protocols that are yet to be determined. Private sector involvement, the inadequacy of the Draft National Health Privacy Code, lack of a truly voluntary system, insufficient controls on patient and provider identifiers which require the collection of further identifying data needed to verify that the record pertains to that individual, do not augur well for the privacy rights of the primary participants of Health*Connect*, that is the vast majority of Australians.

---

79   Ibid, pp 64–65.
80   Iacovino, L, "Trustworthy Shared Electronic Health Records: Recordkeeping Requirements and Health*Connect*" (2004) 12 (1) *Journal of Law and Medicine* 40.

29

Genetic privacy, discrimination and insurance

Loane Skene and Margaret Otlowski

Introduction

In the 50 years since Watson and Crick identified the double helix structure of DNA, scientists have mapped the whole human genome and started linking genes to diseases (over 1000 genes associated with disease have already been identified). As new genes have been identified and the tests have become simpler and cheaper, people have been increasingly concerned about the possible consequences if their personal information is disclosed to third parties without their knowledge or consent. Genetic information has a social, spiritual and emotional significance that other personal information does not have. It reveals details about a person's blood relatives and their community,[1] and may have long-term implications. As techniques develop, genetic information will become readily accessible. Already, it is possible to store a large amount of genetic data on a microchip. People want to know who will have access to their genetic information. Will pharmaceutical companies want to use their information and their excised tissue in research; or patent their DNA in cell lines or other biological "products"? Could it be used by the police; or by employers and insurance companies?[2] Could it be tested without their consent, for example in paternity tests? Will human tissue be commodified, undermining the significance of the human body and its parts?

---

1   The Australian Law Reform Commission and the Australian Health Ethics Committee described Aboriginal concerns about genetic technology in their joint report on genetic privacy: *Essentially Yours: The Protection of Human Genetic Information in Australia*, Report No 96, ALRC, Canberra, 2003, <www.austlii.edu.au/au/other/alrc/publications/reports/96/> (accessed 24 September 2005).

2   This is an issue especially in the United States as most health cover is offered by employers and many people do not have private health insurance. In Australia, the availability of genetic information is of less concern in relation to health insurance, due to community rating of premiums (they are not based on medical factors). However, there are concerns about life and disability insurance, as explained later in this chapter. See also: Otlowski, MFA, "Avoiding Genetic Discrimination in Insurance: An Exploration of the Legality and Ethics of Precautionary Measures in Anticipation of Unfavourable Test Outcomes" (2001) 20 (1) *Monash Bioethics Review* 24; Otlowski, MFA, "Is There Scope for Lawful Genetic Discrimination in Health Insurance in Australia?" (2001) 8 (4) *JLM* 427.

It is these concerns that are driving the move towards greater regulation of genetic testing, especially in relation to the protection of privacy. Professor David Weisbrot, Chair of the Australian Law Reform Commission (ALRC), spoke about community views when launching the Commission's issues paper on *Protection of Human Genetic Information* that was published jointly with the Australian Health Ethics Committee (AHEC), in the consultation process leading to their extensive joint report (*Essentially Yours: The Protection of Human Genetic Information in Australia* (ALRC–AHEC Report)).[3] He said that the issues paper highlighted "concerns about the use of human genetic information in medical research and practice; tissue banks and genetic data bases; health administration; employment; insurance and superannuation; access to services and entitlements; law enforcement and evidence in court".[4]

Already concerns about the privacy of medical information have led to legislation that, in our view, raises potential problems for doctors in everyday practice. A spate of recent legislation, both federal and State, places even greater emphasis on a person's right to personal privacy than the common law, although the common law has long recognised that doctors have an obligation of confidentiality.

This legislation has been passed with insufficient regard to the practical issues that arise in genetic testing in clinical practice. Doctors know that genetic discoveries give them powerful new tools in treating their patients. In the words of Dr Jim St John, who established genetic registers in Melbourne for two types of colorectal cancer that run in families: "We treat families now, not individual patients".[5]

Similarly, Professor Graham Giles, Director of the Cancer Epidemiology Centre, Cancer Council of Victoria, believes that "each member of a family owns the family history".[6] But if doctors and other health professionals reveal medical information about a patient to the patient's relatives, that will generally contravene privacy legislation and the common law, even if the doctor considers the disclosure necessary in the interests of a patient's health care.

The first part of this chapter explains the importance of genetic information in modern health care. We argue that the law should, in limited circumstances, permit disclosure of genetic information even without a person's consent, where there is a real threat of harm to a close blood relative who needs to obtain that information for his or her own health care. The same principle should apply to enable relatives, through their doctor, to gain access to stored tissue for testing or

---

3   ALRC–AHEC Report (2003) op cit.

4   The community concerns are explained in both the issues paper and the report. For ongoing discussion, see: Centre for Law and Genetics, <http://lawgenecentre.org> (accessed 24 September 2005).

5   Lecture to graduate students in Law and Human Genetics, University of Melbourne, October 2001.

6   Ibid.

re-testing for their own health care.[7] We also believe that it is justifiable in some circumstances for human tissue and the information it encodes to be used in research without consent from the person concerned, provided that the research accords with the principles of the National Health and Medical Research Council's *National Statement on Ethical Conduct in Research Involving Humans* (NHMRC Statement);[8] and the research is approved and monitored by a Human Research Ethics Committee (HREC).[9] We argue that privacy laws should treat the use of genetic information differently when it takes place in clinical care to benefit patients and their families, rather than when it is used in other contexts. This is explained in the second part of the chapter which suggests that the main focus of privacy provisions should be on the wrongful *use* of genetic information. For example, it is conceivable that employers or life or disability insurers might use genetic information as the basis for unlawful discrimination. In each part of the chapter, we look at the legal protections which exist or have been proposed to date, especially in the ALRC–AHEC Report. We note that many of the concerns that have been expressed about genetic privacy, discrimination and insurance-related issues have already been addressed in the law but there are some important recommendations in the ALRC–AHEC inquiry that are yet to be implemented.

Importance of genetic information in health care

The relatively recent knowledge that many medical conditions have a substantial genetic element has changed diagnosis, treatment and follow-up care. For example, in order to diagnose a person's genetic status for the colon cancer, familial adeno-matous polyposis (FAP), doctors have to test a relative suffering from the condition in order to find the family mutation. Once that mutation has been found, other family members should be contacted and offered testing and counselling. Information from family members is then combined in the medical records and the details concerning all family members are placed on genetic registers for each condition. In this process, the underlying value is family care, not individual privacy and each person's control of their own tissue and personal information.

---

7   The ALRC and the AHEC reached a similar conclusion: see ALRC–AHEC Report (2003) op cit, Recommendations 8-4 (first degree relatives should be permitted to gain access through a doctor to stored tissue sample for their own test if risk serious, even if not imminent); 12-1 (disclosure of genetic information to a "genetic relative" in similar circumstances); 12-3 (individuals should have a right to access genetic information about "first-degree genetic relatives").

8   NHMRC, *National Statement on Ethical Conduct in Research Involving Humans*, NHMRC, Canberra, June 1999, <www7.health.gov.au/nhmrc/publications/humans/contents.htm> (accessed 24 September 2005). The NHMRC Statement is currently under review: see *Review of the National Statement on Ethical Conduct in Research Involving Humans*, First Consultation Draft, NHMRC, Canberra, December 2004.

9   Again, the ALRC and the AHEC accepted that tissue should be allowed to be used in research without consent, subject to compliance with the NHMRC Statement and approval and monitoring by an HREC: ALRC–AHEC Report (2003) op cit, Recommendations 14–17.

Another instance of the use of family information in caring for patients is the time-hallowed "informal discussion" between doctors to obtain information about family members in order to advise a person of his or her genetic status. It has been common medical practice for doctors to tell one another on request the exact cause of death of a patient's relative, for example, or for that information to be provided to a doctor from a genetic register, without consent from the person concerned. This information is vital for checking a patient's own genetic risk, and for providing advice and prophylaxis. It is often more accessible and accurate than information coming from relatives themselves, who may be unwilling or unable to help. Families are often ill-informed, incommunicative or dysfunctional. As Professor Giles said in explaining the need to obtain information from genetic registers as well as from families: "Families have black sheep, missing sheep and dead sheep".[10]

Doctors have readily recognised the need for family information to be obtained and shared by health carers in providing genetic advice to patients. The late Professor Richard Lovell AO took this view when he chaired a working party on these issues some years ago in Melbourne.[11] More recently, Dr Kerry Breen, Chair of the AHEC, said in launching the issues paper that preceded the ALRC–AHEC Report, "doctors … have long used family medical history to provide advice or make assessments about the future health of an individual".[12] The interests of relatives in finding out information that may be important for their own health are obvious. Consider again the genetic mutation that causes FAP. Patients with FAP develop malignant polyps in the bowel which cause death if they are not detected in time to be surgically removed. People who know that this mutation exists in their family can initiate colonoscopy examinations to see if these polyps have developed and, if so, they can have surgery to remove the affected part of the bowel. Family members who are tested and who do not have the mutation can avoid the need for colonoscopies altogether – and have the reassurance of knowing that they will not pass on the mutation to their children.

For other conditions, the perceived benefits of knowing about a familial mutation are less clear. In late-onset conditions for which there is no treatment, like Huntington's disease, many people would rather not know their genetic risk, though others may welcome the chance to plan their life even if they know they will develop the symptoms later. Also, with any serious genetic condition, the risk is likely to be known in the family because others will have suffered from it. Genetic conditions that have variable "penetrance" are perhaps more problematic. With some conditions, the gene that causes a condition may have different effects in particular patients, depending on their age, general health status, environmental influences, lifestyle choice, interaction with other genes and factors that we do not

---

10 Lecture to graduate students in Law and Human Genetics, University of Melbourne, October 2001.

11 Anti-Cancer Council of Victoria, Cancer Genetics Ethics Committee, *Ethics and Familial Cancer*, 1996.

12 ALRC–AHEC, *Safeguards needed for use of genetic information*, press release, ALRC, Canberra, 14 November 2001.

yet understand. All of these variants may influence the way that a disease-causing gene is expressed. For example, two sisters may both have a gene that predisposes them to breast cancer but one may develop the condition while the other does not. Such matters are often difficult to explain to patients, many of whom do not understand the nature of probability. Some people may not want to know their risk, saying that they have a right not to know. Others may misunderstand what they are told and worry unnecessarily. There are risks that people who have the mutation (or are carriers) will have a reduced feeling of self worth, will be stigmatised or will have difficulties in forming relationships in the future.

It can be seen, therefore, that genetic information is complex as well as being especially personal or sensitive. It has immediate implications for people other than the person who first seeks a test and those people may react differently in wanting to know or not know it.[13] There will often be tension between protecting the privacy of an individual's genetic information and allowing blood relatives to have the information they need for their own health care.

Other issues arise when human tissue is used in genetic research. In future, drugs will be developed that are designed to be effective for people with particular genetic characteristics and the current practice of prescribing the same drug for everyone suffering from a particular condition will seem old-fashioned. To develop these new drugs, doctors need to undertake research on large populations over several generations, examining the interaction of their genotype (genetic make-up), phenotype (physical characteristics), lifestyle, other relevant factors and patterns of disease and symptoms.[14] Sometimes it may not be possible to obtain consent from people in the study. They may have died or be unavailable. Also, because genetic information is necessarily familial, details will be discovered about family members who are not involved in the study. But the larger the sample and the amount of information that can be collected, the more useful it will be.

It is, of course, essential that there are proper processes for protecting the confidentiality of genetic information. There are advantages for relatives in finding out matters that may affect their future health, but third parties may also want that information. Employers may be reluctant to offer jobs to people who may have to take time off due to ill health, either their own or that of a family member. Life or disability insurers (though not health insurers[15]) may refuse to insure a person with a serious genetic condition or, more commonly and problematically, a predisposition to develop such a condition. Alternatively, they may charge a higher premium and without that type of income-protection insurance, the person may not be able to borrow money for a house or business.

---

13   The special features of genetic information are discussed in Skene, L, "Patients' Rights or Family Responsibilities? Two Approaches to Genetic Testing" (1998) 6(1) *Medical Law Review* 1.

14   An example of this research is the United Kingdom Biobank, a £45 million study involving 500,000 people between the ages of 45 and 69. Its aim is to study a number of common, costly conditions, such as cardio-vascular disease, cancer and diabetes: <www.ukbiobank.ac.uk/> (accessed on 24 September 2005).

15   See above, note 2.

These are all legitimate concerns. However there are already many legal provisions to protect the confidentiality of genetic information. Although there is no legislation in Australia that deals directly with genetic testing, genetic information is covered by the same legislation and the same principles of the common (judge-made) law as other types of health information. In particular, health professionals are prohibited by recent federal and State privacy legislation from collecting or disclosing any health information about a person without lawful justification. This usually means with the consent of the patient. Parents can consent for their child so information may be lawfully provided to parents in certain circumstances. However there are other cases in which information can be collected and used without consent, such as in research approved by a Human Research Ethics Committee (HREC).

The common law has increasingly emphasised the rights of individual patients. The law on the relationship between doctor and patient is based on patient autonomy, individual rights and privacy. It is the patient's right to decide what medical procedures to have and to whom the patient's medical information will be disclosed and doctors must not disclose a patient's personal information unless the patient has consented to disclosure or disclosure is authorised by legislation. There is a limited exception to a doctor's general obligation of confidentiality where withholding the information might present a serious and imminent threat to the safety of an individual or the public, but the exception is ill-defined and there is little case law on this point.

The *Privacy Act 1988* (Cth)[16] and State legislation such as the *Health Records Act 2001* (Vic) and the *Health Records and Information Privacy Act 2002* (NSW) have emphasised similar principles of privacy and control of one's personal information. The Acts all apply to both public and private sector health agencies and the people who work in them. The Acts require that health agencies and health professionals must comply with privacy principles set out in the Acts (the principles in each of the Acts are similar but not identical). The problems that arise for doctors and genetic counsellors from this type of legislation can be seen by examining the *Health Records Act 2001* (Vic) which came into effect in June 2002. The Act deals with "personal information", which is defined specifically to include genetic information.[17] The Act applies to "organisations", both public and private, and the term "organisation" includes individuals, like doctors and counsellors.[18] The Act states that: "an organisation must not do an act, or engage in a practice, that is an interference with the privacy of an individual".[19] An act or practice is "an interference with the privacy of an individual" if it "breaches ...a Health Privacy

---

16   The *Privacy Act 1988* (Cth) is currently under review: <www.privacy.gov.au/act/review/reviewsub.html> (accessed 24 September 2005).

17   *Health Records Act 2001* (Vic) s 3(1), definition of "health information" includes "genetic information about an individual in a form which is or could be predictive of the health (at any time) of the individual or of any of his or her descendants".

18   Ibid, ss 3(1) (definition of "organisation"), 10, 11.

19   Ibid, s 21.

Principle".[20] Health Privacy Principle 1.1(a) states that: "An organisation must not collect health information about an individual unless the information is necessary for one or more of its functions or activities and ... the individual has consented".[21] Health Privacy Principle (HPP) 2.2(b) states that: "An organisation must not use or disclose health information about an individual for a purpose ... other than the primary purpose for which [it] was collected unless ... the individual has consented to the use or disclosure".[22] There is provision for disclosure to "immediate family members", but only if the person concerned is incapable of consenting.[23] There is also provision for the Health Services Commissioner to prepare guidelines allowing for the use of information, where that is necessary, to provide a health service for an individual.[24] In future, that provision may be interpreted to allow information to be used for genetic testing and treatment.[25] But that is not apparent from its current wording.

Applying these provisions to the collection of information about family members to assist in the diagnosis of a familial mutation – or the establishment and validation of a family pedigree – one can see the problems that arise for doctors and genetic counsellors. It is not lawful for them[26] to obtain information from sources other than the patient, such as the doctors of other relatives, a genetic register, or by testing stored tissue from a family member for a familial mutation, without the consent of the person concerned. Nor is it lawful to disclose information about a patient to affected relatives for use in their own health care unless that is "necessary to lessen or prevent a serious and imminent threat to [their] life, health, safety or welfare".[27] This exception may meet concerns in an

---

20   Ibid, s 18.

21   Ibid, Sch 1. Information may also be collected without consent where this is required or authorised by law; where a person cannot consent; for research; to prevent harm to a person or the public; for law enforcement; and in legal actions: ibid. The Federal Privacy Commissioner's Public Interest Determinations 9 and 9A enable health providers to collect certain information about people other than the patient when compiling a family history: <www.privacy.gov.au/health/determinations/> (accessed 5 May 2006). This may protect doctors where information is being collected but it does not authorise disclosure without consent.

22   Ibid, Sch 1. Information may be used for other purposes associated with the primary purposes and in other limited circumstances without consent, similar to those noted above, note 21: ibid.

23   Health Privacy Principle 2.4(a)(i) allows health service providers to disclose health information about an individual to an "immediate family member" of the individual if "the disclosure is necessary to provide appropriate health services to or care of the individual" but that applies only if "(c) the individual is incapable of giving consent to the disclosure": HPP2.4(c).

24   Health Privacy Principle 2.2(e).

25   Compare the Federal Privacy Commissioner's Public Interest Determinations 9 and 9A.

26   Patients may obtain and use information from family members because the Act does not apply to "the collection, holding, management, use, disclosure or transfer of health information ... only for the purposes of, or in connection with, [an individual's] personal, family or household affairs": *Health Records Act 2001* (Vic) s 13.

27   Health Privacy Principle 2.2(h)(i).

extreme case,[28] but it will not assist doctors who are seeking to collect and use information simply to establish a family pedigree.

The importance of the requirement that the risk must be "imminent" as well as serious to justify disclosure was noted in relation to the *Privacy Act 1988* (Cth) in the ALRC–AHEC Report.[29] The inquiry recommended that a health professional should be permitted:

> [T]o disclose genetic information about his or her patient to a genetic relative of that patient where the disclosure is necessary to lessen or prevent a *serious* threat to an individual's life, health or safety, even where the threat is *not imminent*".[30]

If this recommendation were adopted and the federal and State Acts were amended accordingly, that would go some way towards protecting health professionals from legal consequences if they divulge genetic information to relatives. But it would fall short of permitting the disclosure that seems to be envisaged in some of the professional guidelines that have been developed by genetic counsellors and others to assist them in treating families in which a familial mutation has been discovered.[31]

In our view, there are strong arguments in favour of the law recognising that even genetic information that does not involve a "serious" risk should be regarded as familial and that it should be shared among family members without one member having a right of veto.[32] What doctors, especially geneticists, need to explain to the law-makers is that there are two aspects of genetic information. The first is that a mutation – an allele – is present in a family. The second is the particular individual's own genetic status – whether he or she is positive for the allele. The second aspect of the information should be confidential (like any other personal information) but the first should be regarded as familial and able to be shared among the family members who are at risk of having the mutation.

It should be noted that the legal principles that have been described earlier determine when a health professional may be *justified* in disclosing information

---

28 It is difficult to imagine a genetic risk that presents a "serious and imminent threat" to life or health. Even if the medical condition in question is life-threatening and the gene is one of high penetrance so that the condition is almost certain to develop, such as FAP, the risk would rarely be regarded as "imminent". That would only be the case if there was an additional factor that increased the genetic risk. For example, if a person carries the gene for Huntington's disease and so will ultimately develop that condition, but is currently asymptomatic, the risk might be regarded as imminent if the person is engaging in an activity in which the genetic risk is greatly magnified by other factors, such as flying an aeroplane.

29 ALRC–AHEC Report (2003) op cit, para 21.54.

30 Ibid, Recommendation 21-1 (emphasis added).

31 See, for example, Human Genetics Society of Australasia, *Privacy Implications of Genetic Testing*, March 1999, <www.hgsa.com.au> under "Policies" (accessed 5 May 2006): Although the test results of an individual are confidential, the needs of blood relatives need to be assessed in each situation and there may be a duty to the family as well as the individual.

32 Skene (1998) op cit; Skene L, "Genetic Secrets and the Family: A Response to Bell and Bennett" (2001) 9(2) *Medical Law Review* 162.

without a patient's consent, so that disclosure would not then be a breach of the common law or the privacy legislation. A health professional does not have a *duty* to disclose the information to anyone, even if another person is at serious risk and could be saved by being given the information. Australian law has not recognised any "duty to warn" of this kind. The difference between the two principles may be illustrated by an example. If a health professional is justified in disclosing information about a patient, the health professional will have a defence if the patient sues or lodges a complaint with a privacy body or official. If there were a duty to warn, a close blood relative of the patient who was not warned could sue the health professional for not providing a warning if the failure to warn caused harm to the relative. Such a claim has never been permitted in Australia (though there have been some such actions in the United States).

Turning to the use of personal information in research, rather than in clinical care, such use is, in some respects, less troublesome, even when there is no consent.[33] In Victoria, information may be used without consent in research if it is "impracticable ... to seek the individual's consent"; identification is necessary in the research; and the use accords with guidelines issued by the Health Services Commissioner.[34] Similarly, under the NHMRC Statement, a HREC may waive the need for consent, both for the use of information and also bodily material, taking into account among other things "the nature of any existing consent"; whether it is "impossible or difficult or intrusive to obtain specific consent"; "proposed arrangements to protect privacy"; and "possible commercial exploitation of derivatives of the sample".[35] However, recent legislation in New South Wales prevents research without consent on tissue removed for post-mortem, unless the research is limited to tissue preserved in slide or blocks.[36]

It can be seen, therefore, that there are many principles of common law and also specific privacy legislation that protect the privacy of genetic information in a clinical context. Indeed, in this area, the law may need to be made more lenient, rather than more restrictive, to take account of issues that arise when health providers are treating patients with genetic conditions that affect families rather than individuals. There are different factors to be considered when we move to the disclosure of genetic information to third parties where there is a real possibility of wrongful use of the information.

---

33 Similarly, genetic information may be used without consent in monitoring health services: see *Health Records Act 2002* (Vic) HPP 2.2(f).

34 Health Privacy Principle 2.2(g).

35 NHMRC Statement (1999) op cit, para 15.8.

36 This follows recent amendments to the *Coroners Act 1980* (NSW) and the *Human Tissue Act 1983* (NSW) described in New South Wales Health Circulars 2003/81 *Requirements of the Human Tissue Act 1983 in relation to research utilising human tissue: Guidance for Human Research Ethics Committees*; and 2004/1 *Use and Retention of Human Tissue including Organ Donation, Post-Mortem Examination and Coronial Matters*. For all other tissue removed during post-mortem, written consent must be obtained, either from the deceased before death or next of kin after death.

Wrongful use of genetic information:
Unlawful discrimination and insurance-related issues

Discrimination

As noted in the introduction, the increased availability of genetic information, especially genetic tests, has led to concerns about the potential for unfair discrimination on the basis of genetic characteristics. A new concept of "genetic discrimination" has emerged which describes the phenomenon of discrimination against an individual on the basis of that person's genetic status or more particularly, their genetic risk stemming either from their family history and/or a genetic test result.[37] Such discrimination can be distinguished from discrimination on the grounds of a disability which has become manifest. Indeed, the very essence of genetic discrimination is that it is generally based on predictions of a condition that *may* affect a person; usually though, there is no certainty about this, as evidence of family history of a condition or even a positive genetic test is, with few exceptions, merely *predictive* information.

Instances of genetic discrimination in connection with access to insurance or employment have been documented in Australia,[38] as well as in the United States[39] and the United Kingdom;[40] and although these have largely involved anonymous and unverified cases, it would appear difficult to completely refute the occurrence of such discrimination. Much more challenging, however, is the quantification of the *incidence* of such discrimination amongst the "at risk" population. This remains unclear at the present time, although findings of a major research study into the nature and extent of genetic discrimination in Australia, due to be concluded at the end of 2005, are expected to significantly advance understanding of this issue, at least within the Australian context.[41] There has been considerable debate about the seriousness of the "problem" of genetic discrimination, with suggestions that the

37   This terminology can be attributed to the work of Billings, P et al, "Discrimination as a Consequence of Genetic Testing" (1992) 50 *American Journal of Human Genetics* 476 who were the first to highlight the potential risks of discrimination on the grounds of genetic status.

38   Barlow-Stewart, K and Keays, D, "Genetic Discrimination in Australia" (2001) 8 *JLM* 250; Taylor, S, "A Case Study of Genetic Discrimination: Social Work and Advocacy in a New Context" (1998) 51 *Australian Social Work* 51; and see the ALRC–AHEC, *Protection of Human Genetic Information*, Discussion Paper No 66, ALRC, Canberra, 2002, where individual accounts of alleged genetic discrimination are documented.

39   Billings, P et al, (1992) op cit; Lapham, E et al, "Genetic Discrimination: Perspectives of Consumers" (1996) 274 *Science* 621; Geller, L, et al, "Individual, Family, and Societal Dimensions of Genetic Discrimination: A Case Study Analysis" (1996) 2 *Science & Engineering Ethics* 71; and Wertz, D, "'Genetic Discrimination': Results of a Survey of Genetics Professionals, Primary Care Physicians, Patients and Public" (1998) 7 *Health Law Review* 7.

40   Low, L, King, S and Wilkie, T, "Genetic Discrimination in Life Insurance: Empirical Evidence from a Cross Sectional Survey of Genetic Support Groups in the United Kingdom" (1998) 317 *British Medical Journal* 1632.

41   The Chief Investigators are Professor Margaret Otlowski, Dr Sandra Taylor and Dr Kris-Barlow-Stewart (Partner Investigator). For information about the project, including reference to published papers, see <www.gdproject.org> (accessed 24 September 2005).

concerns have been overstated.[42] Regardless of the actual extent of genetic discrimination, it seems that awareness of the *potential* of such discrimination is already having some impact on genetic counselling practices and uptake of genetic testing and participation in genetic research.[43] The significance of this issue cannot, therefore, be underestimated as a potential barrier to full community engagement with the new genetic technologies.

A key issue is whether the Australian legal system is equipped to respond to this emerging development; in particular, what redress, if any, is available to individuals who allege that they have been wrongfully discriminated against on the basis of their genetic status? Although not specifically referred to, as a matter of interpretation, "genetic discrimination" comes within the scope of existing anti-discrimination legislation, in particular, the protection from "disability" discrimination. Such legislation exists in all Australian States and Territories, and, at the federal level, takes the form of the *Disability Discrimination Act 1992* (Cth). Through its broad approach to disability, including *future* disabilities, and disabilities which are *imputed* to a person, it arguably encompasses discrimination on the basis of genetic status,[44] provided that in other respects, the case can be brought within the legislative framework (discrimination occurring within a specified sphere of activity, for example, insurance or employment), and no relevant exemption applies. There has, however, been no case law to date to test this interpretation.

The view of the ALRC–AHEC Inquiry was that the matter should be put beyond doubt and the report recommended amendment of the definition of "disability" in the *Disability Discrimination Act 1992* (Cth) to make clear that the legislation applies to discrimination based on genetic status. It was also recommended that the objects clause of the Act be amended to clarify that it applies to discrimination in relation to past, present, possible future or imputed disability, including discrimination on the ground of genetic status[45] in order to raise awareness about the applicability of the legislation to genetic discrimination. Significantly, however, the ALRC–AHEC Report strongly recommended that discrimination on the basis of genetic status continue to be dealt with under *existing* anti-discrimination laws rather than by creating stand alone legislation.[46]

There are a number of further aspects of the ALRC–AHEC Report that warrant attention in the context of the present discussion about wrongful use of genetic information and resulting unlawful discrimination. These relate to the

---

42   See, for example, Nowlan, W, "A Scarlet Letter or a Red Herring?" (2003) 241 *Nature* 313; Rothenberg, K and Terry, S, "Before It's Too Late – Addressing Fear of Genetic Information" (2002) 297 *Science* 196.

43   Hadley, D et al, "Genetic Counselling and Testing in Families with Hereditary Nonpolyposis Colorectal Cancer" (2003) 163 *Archives of Internal Medicine* 573; Geer, K, Ropka, ME, Cohn, WF, Jones, SM and Miesfeldt, S, "Factors Influencing Patients' Decisions to Decline Cancer Genetic Counselling Services" (2001) 10 *Journal of Genetic Counselling* 25.

44   *Disability Discrimination Act 1992* (Cth) s 4.

45   ALRC–AHEC Report (2003) op cit, p 304, Recommendation 9-2.

46   Ibid, p 301, Recommendation 9-1.

proposals to extend privacy protection to genetic *samples* and to prohibit non-consensual testing of samples. The first of these proposals has met with considerable resistance from some quarters and it is unclear, at this stage, whether it will be implemented into law. However, viewed objectively, the logic behind this recommendation to extend the existing federal privacy protection which applies to genetic information[47] to genetic samples is compelling.[48] It is also consistent with the ALRC–AHEC Inquiry's preferred approach of using *existing* legislative frameworks rather than enacting new legislation aimed specifically at the protection of genetic privacy. Under present laws, genetic samples do not come within the protection of the privacy principles contained in the *Privacy Act 1988* (Cth) because they are not in themselves, "information". This clearly has implications in relation to the collection of genetic samples, their transfer and use, as well as issues of access to those samples, particularly as the law, under current interpretation, does not recognise an individual as having a property right in their genetic samples. This leaves the person from whom the sample was taken with little or no control over the sample or the use to which it is put. Indeed, it seems rather anomalous that greater protection is presently given to the *information* that is derived from a genetic sample than the sample itself which is a rich repository of genetic information about that individual. It is noteworthy, particularly in light of the objections raised in relation to this proposal, that in New South Wales, genetic samples have been brought within the scope of privacy information protection pursuant to the *Privacy and Personal Information Protection Act 1998* (NSW).[49] This lends support to the practicability of this proposal, although opponents to the idea have questioned the appropriateness of extending legislation aimed at the protection of privacy of information to the protection of genetic samples.[50] Others have sought to highlight the regulatory burden that this would create for organisations that hold tissue samples, suggesting that compliance with the requirements of privacy regulation would be impracticable. Our view is that those who are in the business of collecting samples should be required to take steps to protect their privacy, and we believe the ALRC–AHEC proposal for the protection of genetic samples would be an easily achievable and convenient solution to the problem that the current lack of protection of samples creates.[51]

The other recommendation noted above which also seeks to protect the privacy of genetic samples, through guarding against illegitimate use, is the proposed prohibition on unauthorised testing. There is significant potential for unauthorised

47   Through the broad definition of health information *Privacy Act 1988* (Cth) s 6.

48   Through redefining "personal information" and "health information" to include bodily samples from an identifiable individual and redefining a "record" to include a bodily sample.

49   See the definition of personal information in s 4(2) which is defined as including "body samples".

50   See the submission to the ALRC–AHEC Inquiry from the Privacy Commissioner referred to in ALRC–AHEC Report (2003) op cit, Ch 8.

51   We also support the proposed creation of a limited exception to enable relatives to gain access to stored genetic material for their own tests: see Recommendation 8-4.

testing of genetic samples, particularly as the sample can be in the form of hair, or saliva, for example left on a glass. Nor is this a completely far-fetched scenario, as media accounts involving a number of high profile identities including Steve Bing, attest.[52] In addressing this issue, the ALRC–AHEC Inquiry recognised that non-consensual testing of samples could give rise to a wide range of possible harms, including interference with human dignity and autonomy, breach of information privacy, emotional harm, and harms arising from misuse of the information derived from that testing. Such misuse might, for example, comprise use of genetic information by third parties for discriminatory purposes, or inflicting on an individual information about their genetic status in breach of that individual's right not to know.[53] The inquiry found existing protection under Australian laws for non-consensual genetic testing to be inadequate to meet the potential harms arising. The ALRC–AHEC Report accordingly recommended that a new criminal offence be created to prohibit someone submitting another person's sample for genetic testing, knowing that this is done without consent or other lawful authority such as a court order.[54] This is, in our view, a sensible proposal and is consistent with developments in other jurisdictions, including the United Kingdom, aimed at strengthening the protection of genetic samples.[55]

Insurance

As mentioned earlier, a key site for concern in the debates about genetic discrimination has been insurance. For reasons outlined above, in Australia, the focus of attention has been on the life insurance sector where underwriting of applications routinely involves assessing the applicant's family history and health status.[56] It is interesting to note that although family history has long been in use in individual risk assessment, this has generally not been problematic. What appears to have generated particular angst is the use by insurers of *genetic test* information. The significance of a positive genetic test result will depend on the nature of the condition being tested for; typically, it will indicate that the person is predisposed to developing the condition (such as for the BRAC test for breast cancer or genetic testing for FAP). For some rare, late onset conditions, of which Huntington's disease is the best-known example, testing will indicate almost certain future onset of the condition. Importantly, however, this situation is very much the exception, and genetic test information is usually only predictive in nature. In this sense, this kind of information has a lot in common with family history information although clearly, the status of an individual's risk is much clearer if it is known whether or not they have inherited the relevant mutation.

---

52   See the ALRC–AHEC Report op cit, p 360, where reference is made to a claim that dental floss had been removed from Bing's garbage for use in a paternity dispute.
53   Ibid, pp 361–362.
54   Ibid, p 374, Recommendation 12-1.
55   *Human Tissue Act 2004* (UK).
56   This refers to the method used by insurers to classify people according to risk.

The earlier discussion in this chapter has drawn attention to problems in relation to the protection of genetic samples and the potential for unauthorised testing of such samples, and associated risks of unauthorised disclosure of information to third parties resulting in illegitimate use. Whilst these are, without question, valid concerns, it must be made clear that debates about insurers gaining access to and making use of genetic information have occurred in quite a different context. Insurance contracts are contracts of the "utmost good faith".[57] Individuals are under an obligation to make full disclosure to the insurer of all relevant information before the contract is entered into, and failure to do so can result in the contract being invalidated.[58] Thus, insurers' access to family history and/or genetic test information is obtained openly, as a result of the individual's obligation of disclosure. Whilst it is difficult to question insurers' entitlement to this information under prevailing laws, there has been vigorous debate about whether insurers *ought* to be entitled to have access to *genetic test results* and to use this information in the underwriting of applications. Community opinion is decisively against such access being allowed.[59] Given the close relationship between family history and genetic test information, one might question why the concerns have focussed on genetic test results: the explanation probably lies in the fact that genetic testing yields apparently more specific and accurate information, linked with concerns about the human tendency to accept "scientific information" as "correct".

In order to evaluate this issue, it is important to understand the nature of underwriting for life insurance products and the legitimacy that is given to this process by virtue of the exemption from liability under disability discrimination legislation. In Australia, life insurance is different from health insurance, where insurers are legislatively mandated to offer cover on the basis of "community rating" rather than individual risk assessment. For life insurance and other related products such as sickness or permanent disablement cover, applications are usually underwritten having regard to the specific risk status of the applicant.[60] This involves assessment of the applicant's current state of health and future health prognosis, and may result in the application being declined or accepted on non-standard conditions, for example, with loaded premiums and/or subject to exclusions or for limited duration of cover. Information about the applicant's family health history and any results from genetic tests undertaken would clearly be of relevance in this assessment.

Life insurance is characterised as voluntary, "mutually rated" insurance for which individual risk assessment is undertaken. In practice, approximately one-

---

57 This is a long-standing principle at common law, and has more recently also been enshrined in legislation.

58 *Insurance Contracts Act 1984* (Cth) s 13.

59 See, for example, Human Genetics Commission, *Public Attitudes to Human Genetic Information*, People's Panel Quantitative Study, HGC, London, December 2000, pp 33–34.

60 As noted earlier (see above, note 2) this differs from health insurance in Australia: insurers are legislatively mandated under the *National Health Act 1953* (Cth) to offer cover on the basis of community rating rather than individual risk assessment: s 73(2A).

third of the Australian population has such cover. Recognising the voluntary nature of the market and its commercial underpinnings, disability discrimination legislation confers on insurers an exemption in certain circumstances. Specifically, insurers are permitted to discriminate in granting cover and setting premiums but they must be able to substantiate their decision-making on actuarial or statistical grounds or, in the event such data is not available and cannot reasonably be obtained, "the discrimination must be reasonable having regard to any other relevant factors".[61]

Understandably, the life insurance sector has sought to defend its use of genetic information on the grounds that full disclosure of all health risks is an established practice, and excluding genetic test information could expose insurers to "adverse selection".[62] The peak life insurance body in Australia, the Investment and Financial Services Association (IFSA) has developed a policy on genetic testing which is now an industry standard,[63] and binding on member companies. This policy states that insurers will not initiate genetic testing, nor create inducements for individuals to undergo testing through offering reduced premiums to those with a "good" genetic profile.[64] It does, however, uphold the right of insurers to have access to existing genetic test results and to take these into account for underwriting purposes.

Whilst a number of concerns have been raised about insurers using genetic test information,[65] the main objection centres on the current state of genetic test information and whether it is at present sufficiently reliable to allow insurers to exclude people from insurance, or impose non-standard conditions within the terms of the exemption. In particular, it is suggested that insurers currently lack relevant actuarial, statistical or other data on which it is reasonable for them to rely. Cases which have challenged insurance underwriting under this exemption suggest that insurers will be kept accountable,[66] but there have been no cases specifically testing the applicability of the exemption to genetic test information. Notably, however, in many overseas jurisdictions, insurers' access to and use of genetic test information has been prohibited or severely limited pursuant to legislation or moratoria. In the United Kingdom, a moratorium on the use of genetic test information by insurers has been in place since 1997 as a result of an agreement between the British Government and the Association of British Insurers, and has recently been extended to 2011. A ceiling approach has been taken under

---

61 *Disability Discrimination Act 1992* (Cth) s 46.

62 This refers to the potential for individuals armed with knowledge about their risk which the insurer does not have, to take out large amounts of insurance.

63 Investment and Financial Services Association, *Genetic Testing Policy*, IFSA Standard No 11.00, January 2002.

64 Ibid.

65 These concerns are more fully canvassed in Otlowski, M, *Implications of Genetic Testing for Australian Insurance Law and Practice*, Centre for Law and Genetics, Occasional Paper No 1, 2001.

66 *QBE Travel Insurance v Bassanelli* [2004] FCA 396.

the terms of the current moratorium: applicants can secure policies for up to £500,000 of life insurance and £300,000 of critical illness, income protection and long-term care insurance, without having to disclose any genetic test results. The advantage of such an approach is that for the majority of applicants, genetic test information will not be part of their risk assessment. For policies in *excess* of the specified ceiling, to mitigate potential losses to insurers from adverse selection, relevant genetic test results must be disclosed, but insurers are only entitled to use those tests which have been authorised by a special committee established for this purpose – the Genetics and Insurance Committee (GAIC). To date, only the test for Huntington's disease has been approved by this committee.

The use by Australian insurers of genetic test information in underwriting was one of the key issues before the ALRC–AHEC Inquiry. Notwithstanding the more interventionist approach in other jurisdictions, the ALRC–AHEC Inquiry was clearly reluctant to make too substantial inroads on established insurance principles which require the applicant to make full disclosure of relevant information. However, in response to the concerns raised about the reliability of genetic test information, and to ensure consumers can have confidence in the use that is made of this information, the ALRC–AHEC Report recommends that insurers should only be permitted to use the results of those genetic tests for underwriting which have been approved for this purpose. Drawing to some extent on the United Kingdom model involving the GAIC, the recommendations proposed that a new body, the Human Genetics Commission of Australia (HGCA), would carry out this role of assessing the scientific reliability and actuarial relevance of genetic tests.[67] Although this falls short of the stricter protections which exist in the United Kingdom and other European jurisdictions, this would represent an objective check on insurers' use of genetic test information and would significantly enhance consumer protection. Assuming that the vetting of tests for insurance underwriting is vigilantly undertaken, this recommendation, together with a package of other proposed reforms,[68] would have the potential of largely addressing the concerns that have been raised about the use of genetic test information in insurance.

Conclusion

Throughout this chapter, we have argued that there are already many legal safeguards to protect the privacy of genetic information. In a clinical context, the law is too restrictive. The federal and State privacy legislation should be modified so that health providers are legally justified in telling a patient's close blood

---

67 This recommendation is in the process of being implemented. In the federal Budget announced on 10 May 2005, the government allocated new funding of $7.6 million over four years from 2005–2006 to establish an independent expert advisory body on human genetics as a principal committee of the NHMRC.

68 These include recommendations for expansion of appeal options for aggrieved individuals and for ensuring that applicants are given clear and understandable reasons for adverse decisions: see ALRC–AHEC Report (2003) op cit, Chs 26–28.

relatives if there is a genetic mutation in the family that affects them as well as the patient. Relatives should also be entitled to test stored tissue when that is necessary for their own health care but should be given only information concerning the familial mutation that affects them. The fact that the mutation exists in the family should be regarded as familial, as distinct from a particular person's status for the mutation, which should be regarded as personal, like other medical information. We do not believe that health providers should have a legal duty to warn relatives; it should remain at their discretion. With regard to the use of genetic information and stored human tissue in research, we support such uses without consent in limited circumstances, subject to compliance with the NHMRC Statement and approval and monitoring by a HREC.

On the other hand, the law on anti-discrimination and other potential wrongful use of genetic information should be closely monitored and, if necessary, tightened. Protecting the privacy of genetic information in the hands of third parties is justified and this requires protection also to be extended to genetic samples. Further, genetic testing of samples should only be permitted with the consent of the person or other legal process (for example, forensic purposes) or to enable close family members to test for their own health care, as mentioned above. In the insurance sector, it is recognised that competing interests have to be balanced: those of consumers and the interests of the insurance sector seeking to protect the ongoing viability of the life insurance industry. Whilst the Australian life insurance sector through its peak body IFSA has sought to be progressive and transparent in its approach to the use of genetic testing, it is in our view important that the industry is kept accountable and that genetic test results are only used in underwriting when there are clear grounds to substantiate this; that is, insurers should not be permitted to rely on genetic tests as a basis for granting cover and setting premiums unless they can prove a clear correlation between a particular test result and a particular outcome. At present there is little information of that kind available.

The ALRC–AHEC Report has made a wide range of recommendations that suggest the type of legal changes that may be adopted in the future. We are in broad agreement with the proposals in the report and support the implementation of the recommendations to which we have referred in this chapter.

30

Record creation and access:
The impact of legislative changes

Angela Palombo

Introduction

Federal privacy legislation covering the private sector began operating in 2001, followed by various State and Territory privacy legislation. In the health care context this was the first time health information collection was regulated by statute. The manner of creating health information had previously been guided by standards of practice. The privacy legislation also gave people a right of access to health information held in the private sector for the first time. Previously, it was only individuals who had issued court proceedings against private health professionals who were able to obtain a copy of their health records. This chapter explores the impact of the privacy legislation on record creation. It also examines the access provisions and the policy considerations in giving access in the private sector compared to the public sector.

Quality of health records

It has long been accepted that good record-keeping in health care is essential for the proper treatment of patients. Properly kept records also provide protection to health professionals in the event of a complaint or litigation. Records should be contemporaneous, complete, up-to-date and accurate. They should enable another health provider to continue the care of the patient. As stated in the Royal Australian College of General Practitioners' *Handbook for the Management of Health Information in Private Medical Practice*, although medical practitioners may have differing styles of record-keeping and may adopt their own abbreviations, the record should nonetheless be comprehensible to others. The medical record is also a tool for facilitating better patient care through the use of health summaries and a recall system.[1] Health records increasingly exist only in electronic form. The only way to ensure that electronic records were made contemporaneously and have not been altered is for the computer program to record when the entry and any

---

1   Royal Australian College of General Practitioners, *Handbook for the Management of Health Information in Private Medical Practice*, RACGP, 2002, p 1.

alterations were made. Most programs have provision for this. It is important that health professionals who treat families maintain separate files for each family member and do not have a composite clinical record of attendances upon all members of the family. By maintaining separate files, confidentiality is less likely to be inadvertently breached.[2]

My focus will be on the situation in Victoria, which is the jurisdiction covered by the Office of the Health Services Commissioner, Victoria. The *Privacy Act 1988* (Cth) together with State and Territory privacy legislation regulates the handling of health information in their jurisdictions. The legislation deals with the collection and management of health information and provides a right of access for people to their own health information.

After the High Court of Australia's decision of *Rogers v Whitaker*,[3] it was recognised that health records are critical in determining whether a patient has been warned of the material risks of a procedure. The duty to warn as set out in *Rogers v Whitaker* has survived the tort law reforms enacted in all States and the Australian Capital Territory that defined the standard of care for professionals.[4] If a plaintiff claims he or she did not receive enough information to make an informed choice about treatment, the absence of supporting documentation about health practitioner–patient communications may be seen to lend weight to a plaintiff's claim.

A decision that illustrates the value of good records in successfully defending claims of medical negligence is that of the New South Wales Court of Appeal in *Deeb v Guirguis*.[5]

The defendant orthopaedic surgeon successfully defended a claim where the plaintiff alleged he had not been properly advised of the risks of surgery performed on him. The plaintiff had a total hip reconstruction to treat his congenital hip displacement, but the surgery was not successful. The surgeon's clinical records were tendered at trial. They supported his claim that he had properly warned the plaintiff. The trial judge at first instance and then the Court of Appeal accepted that they were accurate contemporaneous records. The trial judge had relied on a letter the surgeon had sent to the referring general practitioner shortly after the consultation which substantially reproduced the material that was in the clinical notes. The letter comprehensively set out the patient's health concerns, the surgeon's examination and the possible reconstructive procedures that had been discussed between him and his patient. His letter stated that he indicated to the patient that the operation was not a magic cure and that he had advised the patient about possible difficulties and complications. The trial judge

---

2   Medical Defence Association, *Medical Defence Outlook*, Issue 3, December 2004, Medical Defence Association of Victoria Ltd, <www.mdav.org/files/documents/Outlook-3-FINAL.pdf> (accessed 22 September 2005).

3   (1992) 175 CLR 479.

4   *Civil Liability Act 2002* (NSW); *Civil Liability Act 2003* (Qld); *Civil Liability Act 2002* (Tas); *Wrongs Act 1958* (Vic); *Civil Liability Act 2002* (WA); *Civil Law (Wrongs) Act 2002* (ACT).

5   [2000] NSWCA 149.

therefore found that in the light of the medical evidence, a total hip replacement was an appropriate option and the advice and warnings that were given had been appropriate.

Unprofessional conduct

Failure to keep adequate records by a registered health provider can amount to unprofessional conduct under State legislation regulating professional practice. The Medical Practitioners Board of Victoria (MPBV) has stated in a number of its decisions that medical records can be brief, provided they enable continuity of care. In the case of *Dr LMN*[6] the MPBV found that the doctor's management of the patient's conditions, including the lack of reassessment and the excessive prescribing of Panadeine Forte, fell below the standard that might reasonably be expected from a doctor by the public and her peers. The MPBV found that the doctor engaged in unprofessional conduct in this regard. However, it extended some latitude in respect of the practitioner's record-keeping. The MPBV found that while the doctor's records were not optimal, they did not fall below the standard that might reasonably be expected at that time. The records were brief and abbreviated but it found that they did contain sufficient information to allow continuity of care by other practitioners.

Negligent professional practice and poor record-keeping are often connected. This is best illustrated in the case of *PD v Harvey and Chen*.[7] The plaintiff successfully sued two medical practitioners for negligence in failing to protect her from HIV infection, and was awarded damages. She contracted HIV from her husband, who was also a patient of the same practice. The Supreme Court of New South Wales found this was a foreseeable danger. The plaintiff had been a patient of the medical centre operated by Dr Chen and which employed Dr Harvey. In November 1998 the plaintiff and her future husband (FH) attended Dr Harvey together for blood tests to ensure that neither carried HIV nor any other sexually transmitted disease because they were proposing to get married. Dr Harvey was told that FH came from Ghana and the plaintiff was concerned there was a higher risk that a person from Ghana would be HIV-positive than a person from Australia. Dr Harvey made brief notes of the consultation on both of their medical records but did not include any reference on either of their records to a joint consultation having taken place. As well, the plaintiff's record did not indicate that she was about to enter a new relationship with FH or why she was requesting the HIV test. Dr Harvey failed to inform either patient that in the absence of consent he could not disclose any information about HIV to the other partner. He also failed to discuss the question of the possibility of discordant results. Cripps AJ found these to be significant omissions.

---

6   [2003] MPBV 17.
7   [2003] NSWSC 487.

A week later, the plaintiff attended the medical centre, and obtained a copy of her pathology report from the receptionist, which showed she was HIV-negative. The plaintiff asked for a copy of FH's results but was told she could not have them as they were confidential. There had been no discussion at the joint consultation as to whether the plaintiff could receive her future husband's results. The results for FH showed he was HIV-positive. Dr Harvey telephoned FH, advised him of the results and referred him to a specialist clinic. He did not raise with him any issue arising out of the joint consultation and in particular, asked no questions about whether he was proposing to tell the plaintiff of the test results. The next day, FH attended the medical centre and spoke to Dr Chen. He gave the future husband a letter of appointment at the specialist clinic. Dr Chen made no notes of the consultation and only a short note was made by a nurse at the medical centre.

Cripps AJ found the advice given by Dr Chen fell far short of what was expected of a general practitioner. Dr Chen did not discuss disclosing FH's HIV status to his sexual partner. He did not know who that partner was, as FH's file did not record the joint consultation and there was no cross-referencing. He was not aware that the patient's HIV-negative future wife was also the patient of the practice. Cripps AJ also found that had FH been properly counselled, the plaintiff would probably have become aware of his HIV status. If the doctors had been aware that FH did not intend to tell his future wife that he was HIV-positive, the doctors could have informed the Director-General of the Department of Health who would have been able to contact her. FH did not attend the appointment with the specialist clinic and when asked by the plaintiff for a copy of his test results, gave her a forged pathology result which showed he was HIV-negative. She later married him and they had unprotected sex. She became pregnant and found a copy of her husband's genuine pathology report amongst his papers. It showed he was HIV-positive. She asked Dr Chen why she had not been told of her husband's HIV status. She did not know she was HIV-positive at the time. Dr Chen's brief notes recorded that he told her that confidentiality prevented him from giving her a copy of her husband's records. He advised her to attend with her husband to resolve the issue. She made an almost contemporaneous and detailed note of her conversation with Dr Chen. Dr Chen's evidence on what was said during the consultation differed from her recollections and to the extent that there was inconsistency Cripps AJ accepted her version. Cripps AJ criticised the doctors for their poor record-keeping and for the absence of appropriate administrative systems such as cross-referencing.

The appeal was unsuccessful.[8] The New South Wales Court of Appeal focused less on the poor record-keeping and relied on Dr Harvey having breached

---

8   *Harvey v PD* [2004] NSWCA 97. The NSW Court of Appeal found that the trial judge was correct in concluding that Dr Harvey owed both his patients a duty to address, in the course of the initial consultation, the need for consent to mutual disclosure of their results, the manner of disclosure and the possibility of discordant results. Had Dr Harvey raised these issues, the parties would probably have consented to their results being *(cont)*

his duty at the first consultation. It found that if the practitioners had generated proper records, Dr Chen would have realised that FH was in a relationship with a patient of the practice who was HIV-negative. He should have discussed with the patient his obligation to tell his future wife.

The events in *PD v Harvey and Chen* occurred before the *Privacy Act 1988* (Cth) became relevant as the private sector amendments took effect in December 2001. This legislation requires organisations to make individuals aware of certain matters at the time they collect health information. It is a requirement that patients are informed of the purpose for which their health information is collected and to whom it is usually disclosed.[9] This is discussed further below.

In the context of a joint consultation concerning mutual HIV-testing, this would necessitate discussion of whether there was consent to mutual disclosure, which would have prevented the breach of duty that took place by Dr Harvey. In these circumstances, the privacy legislation enshrines a proper standard of medical care in relation to collection of information and joint consultations.

Collection of health information

The Federal Privacy Commissioner's *Guidelines on Privacy in the Private Health Sector* state that clear and open communication between the health service provider and health consumer is integral to privacy protection. When such communication occurs, many of the privacy obligations of health service providers will be met which means there are likely to be fewer complaints.[10]

The National Privacy Principles contained in the *Privacy Act 1988* (Cth) regulate the handling of personal information by private health service providers in Australia and by other private sector organisations that are large businesses (having turnover of more than $3 million annually). Personal information is any information or opinion about an identifiable person. Health information is a sub-set of personal information. Health information is one form of "sensitive information" and a higher privacy standard applies.

Two States, Victorian and New South Wales, as well as the Australian Capital Territory,[11] have comprehensive legislation dealing with health records in the private and public sectors. The legislation provides that an individual can make a complaint to the relevant commissioner if they believe their privacy has been breached.

(*cont*)

  made available to each other. If FH had refused, then the plaintiff would have terminated their relationship. In either case, the plaintiff would not have become infected with HIV because FH would not have been in a position to deceive her.

9   See National Privacy Principle 1.3.

10 Federal Privacy Commissioner, *Guidelines on Privacy in the Private Health Sector*, Office of the Privacy Commissioner, 8 November 2001, Foreword.

11 *Health Records and Information Privacy Act 2002* (NSW); *Health Records Act 2001* (Vic); *Health Records (Privacy and Access) Act 1997* (ACT).

While the common law recognises actions for breach of confidence committed by medical practitioners and others who owe a duty of confidentiality, privacy legislation goes further and regulates, amongst other things, the collection of health information. The general requirement of privacy legislation is that information should only be collected if it is necessary to the organisation's functions or activities, and in most cases should only be collected with the consent of the individual. Privacy legislation does not deal with how records are to be maintained, but requires that organisations take reasonable steps to ensure that the personal health information they keep is accurate, complete and up-to-date.[12]

Australian health privacy legislation requires that personal health information must be collected by lawful and fair means and not in an unreasonably intrusive way. Wherever it is reasonable and practicable to do so, personal health information must be collected directly from the individual rather than from third parties. The individual must consent to the collection of health information unless an exemption applies. At the time of collecting personal health information, organisations must take reasonable steps to ensure the individual is aware of:

- the identity of the organisation and how to contact it;
- the fact that he or she is able to gain access to the information;
- the purposes for which the information is collected;
- the types of organisations to which the organisation usually discloses information of that kind;
- any law that requires the particular information to be collected; and
- the main consequences (if any) for the individual if all or part of the information is not provided.

The decision in *KJ v Wentworth Area Health Service*[13] shows how one jurisdiction has dealt with the collection of health information in a particular health care setting. The case was decided by the New South Wales Administrative Decisions Tribunal under the *Privacy and Personal Information Protection Act 1998* (NSW) which previously covered health information held in the public sector.

A patient had been treated for cancer by a public hospital. She also saw a psychologist and psychiatrist at the same hospital for temporary help with the distress caused by her diagnosis and treatment but not for treatment of a mental illness. She had a high degree of sensitivity about her information and was not aware that the hospital kept a combined file, which included both her general medical records and her psychological records. KJ claimed that it did not occur to her that the psychiatrist and the psychologist would make her psychological information available to doctors, nurses, the dietician and the physiotherapist,

---

12   See National Privacy Principle 6.5.
13   [2004] NSWADT 84.

who were treating her physical illness – most of whom did not know her very well.

KJ said that had she been asked, she would not have given her consent to the wider sharing of the information. When she discovered that the hospital kept a combined file, she made a complaint to the New South Wales Privacy Commissioner claiming that the *Privacy and Personal Information Protection Act 1998* (NSW) had been breached. She complained that she was not informed about what records were being created about her, how they were to be used and to whom they were to be disclosed. Her complaint was upheld by the tribunal which found that if a patient is notified that personal information disclosed during a consultation with a practitioner employed by an agency will be shared with her treating team, the patient then can choose whether to disclose any information, or only certain information, to the practitioner. The ability to exercise such choice is contemplated by s 10(d) of the Act, which requires an agency to notify an individual whether the provision of information is mandatory or voluntary. It may be appropriate for an agency to advise an individual about the potential benefits and adverse effects of a decision to provide or withhold particular information. However, an individual's choice to provide or withhold personal information is not dependent on an agency's opinion.

The health service was ordered to refrain from collecting personal information without informing people as to why the information is being collected and who will share the information. The decision may not apply to other jurisdictions because of different wording in comparable provisions. However, much of its underlying reasoning is likely to be regarded as persuasive.

The decision in *KJ v Wentworth Area Health Service* initially caused concern in New South Wales hospitals where it was considered that combining general medical files with psychiatric files, was a breach of privacy laws. What is important is that the hospital must demonstrate why a combined file is necessary and that patients are made aware of this. If the patient does not agree, they can discuss their objections with the organisation and if their concerns are accepted, a different file management system may be appropriate. When deciding which records are to be released to other sections of the same health organisation, privacy laws tend to focus on "who needs to know".

In *KJ v Wentworth Area Health Service*, the tribunal decided that it was not necessary for the general medical unit to know about the complainant's psychological treatment, as it was not relevant to the care she was receiving. This will not always be so.

Right of access

Privacy legislation operating in Australia gives individuals a right of access to their personal information (including health information) held by relevant private sector organisations in the various jurisdictions. The relevant privacy principles oblige those who hold health information about a person to give them access on request, subject to certain exceptions and the payment of charges. Sharing information with patients is fundamental to good doctor–patient communication and to high quality care; it provides an opportunity for health promotion and for building trust.[14] In privacy legislation, the giving of information to third parties is referred to as "disclosure".

Freedom of Information Acts continue to apply to individuals seeking access to their health information in the public sector.[15] An organisation "holds" health information if it is in its possession or control. The organisation does not need to be a health service provider. If a private sector organisation has received reports or other health information from another organisation, such as a medical specialist, they are required to provide access to the individual in the same manner as for the records they create. If the specialist has written "not to be disclosed to a third party" on their report, this has no legal effect in relation to an access request. This has involved a shift in thinking by medical practitioners in particular, some of whom continue to assert that they own the copyright in the reports they write and can control how they are used and disclosed. However, the situation in New South Wales remains to be finally determined as s 28(3) of the *Health Records and Information Privacy Act 2002* (NSW) permits access to be refused if it would involve an infringement of copyright subsisting in the information.

The general advice given by the Office of the Health Services Commissioner, Victoria to health service providers is to assume that what is recorded in files can be read by the individual, subject to certain exceptions. The exceptions mirror those in the freedom of information legislation and are based on public interest grounds for withholding certain information from the individual.

In *Breen v Williams*,[16] the High Court of Australia held that patients had no legally enforceable right at common law to have access to their medical records held by a medical practitioner in the private sector. The doctor in that case was willing to provide a medical report, but the patient sought a copy of the doctor's records to facilitate her participation in overseas litigation in relation to silicone implants. The court held that the records were owned by the doctor and observed that it was up to governments to legislate if a different outcome was desired.

Amendments made to the *Privacy Act 1988* (Cth) gave individuals a right of access to health information held by private health service providers and large private businesses. The changes apply to information created after 21 December 2001. If the information pre-dates 21 December 2001, individuals have a right of access if the information was used after 21 December 2001. It is likely that

---

14   Note 1 at p 6.

15   *Freedom of Information Act 1982* (Cth); *Freedom of Information Act 1989* (NSW); *Freedom of Information Act 1992* (Qld); *Freedom of Information Act 1991* (SA); *Freedom of Information Act 1991* (Tas); *Freedom of Information Act 1982* (Vic); *Freedom of Information Act 1992* (WA); *Freedom of Information Act 1989* (ACT).

16   (1996) 70 ALJR 772.

providing a medico-legal opinion on pre-21 December 2001 health information is a sufficient use of that health information to give a person the right of access.

Overlapping State privacy legislation means that private health service providers and relevant private sector organisations are bound by two separate pieces of privacy legislation. While this can potentially lead to confusion, privacy legislation throughout Australia is largely consistent.

The Health Services Commissioner Victoria advises Victorian organisations that compliance with the more specific *Health Records Act 2001* (Vic) will generally ensure compliance with the Commonwealth *Privacy Act*. The advantage of State legislation is that health service providers in both the public sector and in the private sector are governed, by and large, by the same privacy laws.

The *Health Records Act 2001* (Vic) provides for limited retrospectivity prior to 1 July 2002 when it became operational. For records created before 1 July 2002, individuals have a right to receive an accurate summary. The retrospective provisions are therefore differently drafted to the Federal Act. The position taken in Victoria is that this reflects the fact that providers have compiled records on the understanding they would not be available to be viewed as of right by the individual. However, the provider can agree to provide access in full if they choose. The Office of the Health Services Commissioner encourages health service providers to give access in full if appropriate; many providers have no objection providing access in full to "old information".

On some occasions, full access is needed because of proposed litigation. If, for example, a person is considering suing a doctor or hospital and there is a dispute about whether he or she was advised of the risks of a certain procedure, a copy of the records is required to see if the information was recorded by the doctor. An accurate summary is not sufficient for this purpose. Obtaining a copy of the records prior to issuing proceedings enables plaintiffs to be better placed to decide whether to initiate legal action, rather than relying on obtaining the records in the course of discovery.

As Professor Loane Skene notes, patients can obtain a court order for preliminary discovery for forensic purposes, but that is likely to be less important now that patients can gain access to their records.[17]

The privacy laws create provisions similar to the Freedom of Information Acts for private health service providers in dealing with requests for access. The State and Commonwealth freedom of information laws require access requests to be processed within a specific time frame. Government departments and hospitals employ freedom of information officers to process requests for access, who are familiar with the applicable time limits and the exemptions that apply. Reasons for the decision must be given when access to documentation is declined and applicants must be advised of their appeal rights.

---

17   Skene L, *Law and Medical Practice: Rights, Duties, Claims & Defences*, 2nd edn LexisNexis Butterworths, 2004, p 251.

Private health service providers can range from a sole practitioner to a multi-site medical practice or a large rehabilitation provider employing various health professionals. There may be no central coordination of procedures and policies in relation to access as there is for agencies who are subject to the *Freedom of Information Act*. The various offices which administer privacy legislation have statute-imposed responsibilities to educate consumers and providers about their respective legislation.

Inquiries received by the Office of the Health Services Commissioner Victoria from consumers about a denial of access can sometimes be resolved on an informal basis by a preliminary contact with the provider, advising them of their legal obligations. Providers are sometimes unaware of their access obligations, the applicable time limits and the applicable fees, despite continuing education.

Refusing access to health information

In some cases, an organisation can refuse a person access to his or her health information in full or in part but it must give written reasons for doing so. The person can challenge such a decision by making a complaint to the Federal Privacy Commissioner.

In Victoria, the complaint can be lodged with the Health Services Commissioner under the *Health Records Act 2001*. In New South Wales, a complaint can be lodged with the State Privacy Commissioner under the *Health Records and Information Privacy Act 2002*.

The privacy laws enable organisations to refuse access in certain circumstances, such as when providing access would pose a serious threat to the individual's life or health or the life or health of any other person.[18] In this situation, it is suggested that before providing access the organisation should delete or remove from any copy to be given or viewed the information that is to be refused and the identity of any person they are seeking to protect. This is similar to how a *Freedom of Information Act* request is processed. The principle of "therapeutic privilege" (where information is to be withheld in the best interests of the patient) is not a basis for refusing access under the legislative provisions, unless a threat to life or health can be made out.[19]

Skene refers to the concerns of many doctors about showing patients their medical records. The records may contain conclusions, commentary or "musings" which the doctor might not record if the patient were to see the records, but which may be valuable for the patient's later care, especially if the patient sees another doctor.

---

18 National Privacy Principle 6.1(b) *Privacy Act 1998* (Cth); Health Privacy Principle 6.1(a) *Health Records Act 2001* (Vic); s 29(a) *Health Records and Information Privacy Act 2002* (NSW).

19 See, Mulheron, R, "The Defence of Therapeutic Privilege in Australia" (2003) 11 *Journal of Law and Medicine* 201.

The records may cause confusion, unnecessary worry and stress to patients.[20] Understandably, where compensation for an injury is claimed, a comment in the medical records that a patient's symptoms are in excess of the pathology could be interpreted by the patient to mean the doctor believes the patient is malingering. This is not necessarily the case; good communication between doctor and patient can clarify misunderstandings in many instances.

If an organisation refuses access on the ground that giving the information would pose a serious threat to the patient's life or health, the respondent is required to consider whether the use of mutually agreed intermediaries would allow sufficient access to meet the needs of both parties.[21] In Victoria, the individual is entitled to a second opinion from a nominated health service provider. This is not available if the serious threat is to another person. In New South Wales, the individual may request the organisation to give access to a registered medical practitioner nominated by them.

National Privacy Principle 6.1 lists other situations where an organisation may choose not to give the individual access to health information, namely where providing access would:

- have an unreasonable impact on the privacy of other people;
- reveal the intentions of the organisation in relation to negotiations with the individual (other than about the provision of a health service), in such a way as to expose the organisation unreasonably to disadvantage;
- be unlawful;
- be likely to prejudice an investigation of possible unlawful activity;

or

- the request for access is frivolous or vexatious;
- the information relates to existing or anticipated legal proceedings between the organisation and the individual and the information would not be accessible by the process of discovery in those proceedings;
- denying access is required or authorised by or under law.

There are also law enforcement exceptions.

The *Health Records Act 2001* (Vic) contains an additional ground to refuse access if the health information has been provided in confidence by a person other than the individual or another health service provider (such as a relative, friend or employer) with a request that the information not be revealed to the person.[22] Although the federal *Privacy Act* and the *Health Records and Information Privacy Act 2002* (NSW) do not have this provision, such "information given in confidence"

---

20   Skene (2004) op cit, p 238.
21   National Privacy Principle 6.3.
22   *Health Records Act 2001* (Vic) s 27 and Health Privacy Principle 6.1 (e).

can be exempted on the ground that it would have an unreasonable impact of the privacy of another person.[23]

Reports commissioned by third parties

Many of the inquiries received by the Office of the Health Services Commissioner Victoria relate to medical reports commissioned by an insurer or an employer. Under the *Health Records Act 2001* (Vic), a person has a right of access to the report unless one of the exemptions applies or there is another law (such as the *Accident Compensation Act 1985* (Vic)) which authorises the organisation to refuse access.[24] If the report is subject to legal professional privilege, a person is not able to obtain access to it.

If, for example, a psychiatrist has been requested by an employer (through a solicitor) to assess a person's continuing fitness to work, it would not appear to be subject to legal professional privilege, as the dominant purpose of obtaining the report is not for the purpose of anticipated legal proceedings. The relationship between the doctor providing the medico–legal report and the individual has become a more complex one. Doctors in these situations generally perceive their responsibility to be the preparation of the report to the organisation that commissioned it, and leave to the organisation the responsibility of whether the individual is to be given a copy.

Since the *Health Records Act 2001* (Vic) came into force a person can request a copy of the report either from the doctor or from the organisation that com-missioned it. It is the responsibility of the doctor to process the request and decide whether any of the exemptions apply. If legal proceedings have been issued (either against the health service provider or another party) and the defendant commissions a medico–legal report, the person does not have a right of access to the report if the report is not accessible through discovery or if it is subject to legal professional privilege.[25] Any such report would need to be provided to the plaintiff pursuant to the rules of the court governing such litigation.

An interesting decision was made by the Supreme Court of Victoria's Court of Appeal on 21 April 2006.[26] In that case the Royal Women's Hospital (the hos-pital) lost an appeal to the Court of Appeal, relating to the medical records of Ms X, who underwent a late term abortion at the hospital in 2000. The effect of the Court of Appeal decision is that an order of a Magistrate releasing Ms X's medical file to the Medical Practitioners Board of Victoria will take effect.

The facts of the case began in 2000 when a woman presented at the hospital, 32-weeks pregnant. She was seeking a termination after the foetus was diagnosed

---

23 *Privacy Act 1988* (Cth), National Privacy Principle 6.1(c); *Health Records and Information Privacy Act 2002* (NSW) s 29(b).

24 See Health Privacy Principle 6.2(g).

25 See National Privacy Principle 6.1(e) and Health Privacy Principle 6.1(c).

26 *Royal Women's Hospital v Medical Practitioners Board of Victoria* [2006] VSCA 85.

with skeletal dysplasia. She was examined by relevant doctors including a psychiatrist who found her to be severely distressed and suicidal. The termination was carried out. Subsequently Senator Julian McGauran, who is an anti-abortion campaigner, obtained a copy of the woman's medical file from the State Coroner. Senator McGauran lodged a complaint with the Medical Practitioners Board of Victoria seeking an investigation into the professional conduct of the doctors involved. The hospital opposed a search warrant from the Medical Practitioners' Board seeking production of the patient's medical records, on several grounds including that of public statutory immunity and the patient's privacy. The matter went before a Magistrate, who on 1 October 2004, ordered the file to be released to the board. The hospital appealed this decision to the Supreme Court of Victoria and, on 29 June 2005, Gillard J also found in favour of the board in dismissing the appeal. The Royal Women's Hospital then appealed to the Court of Appeal. On 21 April 2006 the Court of Appeal unanimously dismissed the hospital's appeal against the earlier Supreme Court ruling.

A major question of the appeal was whether the hospital could refuse production to the board of the medical records on the ground of public interest immunity. The board sought the records as part of its investigation of a complaint about the patient's treatment. The patient had not lodged any complaint with the board. The complaint came from a politician who was an anti-abortion campaigner. The hospital claimed that the public interest required that all medical records of women patients in public hospitals seeking advice and treatment concerning reproductive matters including obstetrics and gynaecological care should be immune from compulsory production.

The Court of Appeal held that public interest immunity is a form of immunity from compulsory production of documents. It protects documents (and the information they contain) from production to a court and statutory bodies carrying out investigations in the public interest. The Court of Appeal decided that public interest immunity is restricted to what must be kept secret for the protection of government at the highest level and in sensitive areas of executive responsibility. It decided the information in Ms X's documents was not of that kind. It was personal health information relating to her.

The court acknowledged the concerns of the hospital in relation to doctor-patient confidentiality which, it said, must be maintained *via* the statutory regime for ensuring health privacy in Victoria, that is the *Health Records Act 2001* and the *Medical Practice Act 1994* (which governs the Medical Practitioners Board of Victoria). The decision that public interest immunity does not apply to the patient records means that the documents would have to be delivered to the board for use in its investigation (and for no other purpose). The board gave an assurance to the court that whatever the outcome of the appeal, confidential patient information in the documents will not be made public.

Understandably the case received wide media attention and has caused concern among health providers who may have search warrants served on them for the production of patient records. The Royal Women's Hospital has announced it is not seeking special leave to appeal to the High Court.

Conclusion

Although there is a duplication of Commonwealth privacy laws with State and Territory laws, the laws are largely consistent. State and Territory privacy regimes have the advantage of providing individuals with an accessible complaint mechanism that is familiar with the local health care setting. Both consumers and providers can obtain advice on their privacy rights and obligations from State- and Territory-based regulators that are responsive to their needs. Individuals often deal with both the public and private sectors when obtaining health services. Therefore it is appropriate that the same privacy laws cover both health sectors. This can only be done by State and Territory privacy laws. In the case of individuals seeking to have their disputes resolved, there is a significant advantage in having the same complaint body deal with both public and private sector agencies.

While the access provisions in the privacy legislation operating throughout Australia may appear to be complex for small private organisations to administer, they reflect the access that has been available in the public sector since the 1980s. Ultimately statutory rights of access will create certainty for both individuals using the privacy laws to gain access to their records, and for health professionals providing access. Rights of access result in improved communication between individuals and health professionals, which enhances the provision of health care.

SELECT BIBLIOGRAPHY

Abadee, A, "The Medical Duty of Confidentiality and the Prospective Duty of Disclosure: Can They Coexist?" (1995) 3 *Journal of Law and Medicine* 7

Abbott, FM, "The TRIPS-legality of Measures Taken to Address Public Health Crises: Responding to USTR-State-industry Positions that Undermine the WTO" in Kennedy, DL and Southwick, JD (eds), *The Political Economy of International Trade Law*, Cambridge University Press, Cambridge, 2002

Abraham, J and Reed, T, "Progress, Innovation and Regulatory Science in Drug Development. The Politics of International Standard Setting" (2002) 32(3) *Social Studies of Science* 337

Abraham, J and Sheppard, J, *The Therapeutic Nightmare: The Battle Over the World's Most Controversial Sleeping Pill,* Earthscan, London, 1999

Abraham, J *Science, Politics, and the Pharmaceutical Industry: Controversy and Bias in Drug Regulation,* ULC Press, London, 1995

ACOSS, *More Help with the Cost of Caring for Babies and Toddlers,* ACOSS, Sydney, 2004

Addison, T, "Negligent Failure to Inform: Developments in the Law Since Rogers v Whitaker" (2003) 11 *Torts Law Journal* 165

Advisory Committee on Human Radiation Experiments (ACHRE), *Final Report of the Advisory Committee on Human Radiation Experiments,* Oxford University Press, New York, 1996

Agre, P, "Beyond the Mirror World: Privacy and the Representational Practices of Computing", in Agre, P and Rotenberg, M (eds), *Technology and Privacy: the New Landscape,* MIT Press, Massachusetts, 1998

Agreement on Trade-Related Aspects of Intellectual Property Rights, Annex 1C of the *Marrakech Agreement Establishing the World Trade Organization,* [1995], 278

Ahronheim, JC and Gasner, MR, "The Sloganism of Starvation" (1990) 335 *Lancet* 278

Alfred, A, "The Past, Present and Future of Mental Health Law: A Therapeutic Jurisprudence Analysis" (2003) 20 *Law in Context* 2

Allars, M, *Inquiry into the Use of Pituitary Derived Hormones in Australia and Creutzfeldt-Jakob Disease,* tabled in the House of Representatives, 28 June 1994

Almond, J and Pattison, J, "Human BSE" (1997) 389 *Nature* 437

ALRC, *Essentially Yours: The Protection of Human Genetic Information in Australia. Volume 1,* ALRC, 2003

Anaya, S, "The United States Supreme Court and Indigenous Peoples: Still a Long Way to Go Toward a Therapeutic Role" (2000) 24 *Seattle University Law Review* 229

ANCJDR Semi-Annual Report, December 2004

Andrews, K, *National Strategy for an Ageing Australia,* Department of Health and Ageing, Canberra, 2002

Angell, M, *The Truth About Drug Companies: How They Deceive Us and What to Do About it?* Random House, New York, 2005

Annandale, E, *The Sociology of Health and Medicine,* Polity Press, Cambridge, 1998

Annas, G, "Unspeakably Cruel – Torture, Medical Ethics and the Law" (2005) 352 *New England Journal of Medicine* 20

Annas, G, "Why We Should Ban Human Cloning" (1998) 339 (2) *New England Journal of Medicine* 122

Annas, GJ and Davidson, IS, "The HIV-positive Patient Who Won't Tell the Spouse" (1987) 21 *Aspects of Human Sexuality* 16

Annas, GJ Andrews, LB and Isasi, RM, "Protecting the Endangered Human: Toward an International Treaty Prohibiting Cloning and Inheritable Alterations" (2002) 28(2–3) *American Journal of Law and Medicine* 151

Annas, GJ, "Protecting Soldiers from Friendly Fire: The Consent Requirement for Using Investigational Drugs and Vaccines in Combat" (1998) 24 *American Journal of Law and Medicine* 245

Anti-Cancer Council of Victoria, Cancer Genetics Ethics Committee, *Ethics and Familial Cancer,* 1996

Aponte, T and Roberto, P, "Sanity in International Relations: An Experience in Therapeutic Jurisprudence" (2000) 30 *University of Miami Inter-American Law Review* 659

Apostolopoulos, P and Lam, SL, "Promoting Health and Preventive Care with IT", *Proceedings, 24th Health Information Management Association of Australia Conference, Sydney, 8–10 August 2003*, HIMAA, Sydney, 2003

Appelbaum, P, *Almost a Revolution: Mental Health Law and the Limits of Change*, Oxford University Press, New York, 1994

Appelbaum, P, Kapen, G, Walters, B, Lidz, C and Roth, L, "Confidentiality: An Empirical Test of the Utilitarian Perspective" (1984) 12 *Bulletin of the American Academy of Psychiatry and Law* 109

Appelbaum, PS, "Threats to the Confidentiality of Medical Records – No Place to Hide" (2000) (6) 283 *Journal of the American Medical Association* 795

Arboleda-Florez, J and Weisstub, DN, "Ethical Research With Vulnerable Populations: The Mentally Disordered", in Weisstub, DN (ed) *Research on Human Subjects: Ethics, Law, and Social Policy*, Pergamon, Oxford, United Kingdom, 1998

Argetsinger, A, "Panel Blames Hopkins in Research Death", *The Washington Post*, 30 August 2001

Armstrong, M, "Therapeutic Justice: An Interdisciplinary Approach to Family Law Cases" (1999) 3 *Maricopa Lawyer* 1 (July)

Arrigo, B, "The Ethics of Therapeutic Jurisprudence: A Critical and Theoretical Inquiry of Law, Psychology and Crime" (2004) 11 *Psychiatry, Psychology and Law* 23

Ashby, M and Mendelson D, "Natural Death in 2003: Are We Slipping Backwards?" (2003) 10 *Journal of Law and Medicine* 260

Ashby, M, "Natural causes? Palliative Care and Death Causation in Public Policy and the Law", unpublished MD Thesis, University of Adelaide, 2001

Ashby, M, Kellehear, A and Stoffell, B, "Resolving Conflict in End-of-Life Care" (2005) 183 *Medical Journal of Australia* 230

Atherton, R and Vines P, *Succession – Families, Property and Death; Text and Cases*, 2nd edn, Butterworths, Sydney, 2003

Atherton, R, "Book Symposia – Commentary on Davies and Naffine, *Are Persons Property? Legal Debates About Property and Personality*, Ashgate 2001" (2003) 28 *Australian Journal of Law and Philosophy* 206

Atherton, R, "Claims on the Deceased: The Corpse as Property" (2000) 7(4) *Journal of Legal Medicine* 361

Atherton, R, "Who Owns Your Body?" (2003) 77 *Australian Law Journal* 178

Atkinson, R, Beachy, RN, Conway, G, Cordara, FA, Fox, MA, Holbrook, KA, Klessig, DF, McCormick, RL, McPherson, PM, Rawlings III, HR, Rapson R, Vanderhoef, LN, Wiley, JK and Young CE, "Public Sector Collaboration for Agricultural IP Management" (2003) 301 *Science* 174

Austin, AD, "Jury Perceptions on Advocacy: A Case Study" (1982) 8 *Litigation* 15

Austin, M, "In Need of Physical Protection", in Hogan, R, Brown, D and Hogg, R (eds) *Death in the Hands of the State*, Redfern Legal Centre Publishing, Sydney, 1988

Australia and New Zealand Organ Donation Registry, *1997 Report*, Vol 1

Australian Academy of Science Symposium on *Therapeutic Cloning for Tissue Repair*, Canberra, 16 September 1999

Australian and New Zealand Intensive Care Society, *Statement and Guidelines on Brain Death and Organ Donation – 1993*, a report of the ANZICS Working Party on Brain Death and Organ Donation, May 1993

Australian and New Zealand Intensive Care Society, *Statement and Guidelines on Brain Death and Organ Donation – 1993*, report of the ANZICS Working Party on Brain Death and Organ Donation, May 1993

Australian Consumers Association, *Your Health Rights*, ACA, Sydney, 1988

Australian Consumers' Association, *Your Health Rights*, Random House, Sydney, 1992

Australian Council for Safety and Quality in Health Care, *Improving Medication Safety; Report of a Medication Safety Workshop*, July 2001

Australian Council for Safety and Quality in Health Care, *Second National Report on Patient Safety Improving Medication Safety*, ACT, July 2002

Australian Health Ethics Committee, *Scientific, Ethical and Regulatory Considerations Relevant to Cloning of Human Beings*, NHMRC, December 1998

Australian Health Ministers' Advisory Council, *National Health Privacy Code Draft Consultation Paper*, National Health Privacy Working Group, Canberra, 2002

Australian Law Reform Commission and Australian Health Ethics Committee, *Essentially Yours: The Protection of Human Genetic Information in Australia*, Report No 96, ALRC, Canberra, 2003

Australian Law Reform Commission, *Essentially Yours: The Protection of Human Genetic Information in Australia,* Report No 96, ALRC, 2003

Australian Law Reform Commission, *Genes and Ingenuity: Gene Patenting and Human Health,* Report No 99, ALRC, Canberra, 2004

Australian Law Reform Commission, *Human Tissue Transplants,* AGPS, Canberra, 1977

Australian Law Reform Commission, New South Wales Law Reform Commission and Victorian Law Reform Commission, *Uniform Evidence Law,* 2005

Australian Productivity Commission, *International Pharmaceutical Price Differences Research Report,* AusInfo, Canberra, 2001

Babb, B and Moran, J, "Substance Abuse, Families and Unified Family Courts: The Creation of a Caring Justice System" (1999) 3 *Journal of Health Care Law and Policy* 1

Baier, A, "Trust and Antitrust" (1986) 96 *Ethics* 248

Baker, R, "A Theory of International Bioethics: Multiculturalism, Postmodernism, and the Bankruptcy of Fundamentalism" (1998) 8 *Kennedy Institute of Ethics Journal* 201

Baker, R, "A Theory of International Bioethics: the Negotiable and the Non-Negotiable" (1998) 8 *Kennedy Institute of Ethics Journal* 233

Baker, R, "Negotiating International Bioethics: A Response to Tom Beauchamp and Ruth Macklin" (1998) 8 *Kennedy Institute of Ethics Journal* 423

Baldry, E, *The Development of the Health Consumer Movement and its Effect on Value Changes and Health Policy in Australia,* University of New South Wales Press, Sydney, 1992

Balkin, R and Davis, J, *Law of Torts,* 2nd edn, Butterworths, Sydney, 1996;

Ballard, J, "Australia: Participation and Innovation in a Federal System" in Kirp, D and Bayer, R (eds), *AIDS in the Industrialized Democracies: Passions, Politics, and* Policies, Rutgers University Press, New Brunswick, 1992

Barlow-Stewart, K and Keays, D, "Genetic Discrimination in Australia" (2001) 8 *Journal of Law and Medicine* 250

Barraclough, BH, "Safety and Quality in Australian Healthcare: Making Progress" (2001) 174 *Medical Journal of Australia* 616

Bates, P, Blackwood J, Boersig J, Mackie K, McPhee J. *The Australian Social Worker and the Law,* 4th edn, Lawbook Co, Sydney, 1996

Baxby, D *Jenner's Smallpox Vaccine: The Riddle of Vaccinia Virus and Its Origin,* Heinemann Educational Books, London, 1981

Beauchamp, TL and Childress, JF, *Principles of Biomedical Ethics,* 5th edn, Oxford University Press, New York, 2001

Beauchamp, TL, "Looking Back and Judging Our Predecessors" (1996) 6 *Kennedy Institute of Ethics Journal* 251

Beauchamp, TL, "The mettle of moral fundamentalism: A reply to Robert Baker" (1998) 8 *Kennedy Institute of Ethics Journal* 389

Becker, E and Pear, R, "Trade Pact May Undercut Inexpensive Drug Imports", *New York Times,* 12 July 2004

Beecher, HK, "Ethics and Clinical Research" (1966) 274 *New England Journal of Medicine* 1354

Benaroyo, L and Widdershoven, G, "Competence in Mental Health Care: A Hermeneutic Perspective" (2004) 12 *Health Care Analysis* 295

Benedek, TG, and Erlen, J, "The scientific environment of the Tuskegee Study of Syphilis, 1920–1960" (1999) 43 *Perspectives in Biology and Medicine* 1

Benjamin, B, *Medical Records,* 2nd edn, William Heinemann Medical Books Ltd, London, 1980,

Bennett B (ed), *Health Rights and Globalisation,* Ashgate, Aldershot, 2006

Bennett B, "Prenatal Diagnosis, Genetics and Reproductive Decision-making" (2001) 9 *Journal of Law and Medicine* 28

Bennett, B and Tomossy, GF (ed), *Globalization and Health: Challenges for Health Law and Bioethics,* Springer, Dordrecht, 2006

Bennett, B, "Prenatal Diagnosis, Genetics and Reproductive Decision-making" (2001) 9 *Journal of Law and Medicine* 28

Bennett, B, *Law and Medicine,* Lawbook Co, Sydney, 1997

Bennett, RC, "The Changing Role of the Coroner" (1978) 118 *Canadian Medical Association Journal* 1133

Bensoussan, A and Myers, SP, *Towards A Safer Choice: The Practice of Traditional Chinese Medicine in Australia,* University of Western Sydney, Sydney, 1996

Berghmans, R, Dickenson, D and Ter Meulen, R, "Mental Capacity: In Search of Alternative Perspectives" (2004) 12(4) *Health Care Analysis* 251

Berkendorf, JL, Reutenauer, JE, Hughes, C, Eads, N, Willison, J, Powers, M and Lermann, C, "Patients' Attitudes About Autonomy and Confidentiality in Genetic Testing for Breast-Ovarian Cancer Susceptibility" (1997) 73 *American Journal of Medical Genetics* 296

Bernstein, D, "Junk Science in the United States and the Commonwealth" (1996) 21 *Yale Journal of International Law* 123

Berry, RM, "The Genetic Revolution and the Physician's Duty of Confidentiality. The Role of the Old Hippocratic Virtues in the Regulation of the New Genetic Intimacy" (1997) 18 *Journal of Legal Medicine* 401

Besley, T, Hall, J and Preston, I, "The Demand for Private Health Insurance: Do Waiting Lists Matter?" (1999) *Journal of Public Economics* 155

Best, WM, *A Treatise on the Law of Evidence*, Sweet, London, 1849

Beyleveld D, Townend, D, Rouillé-Mirza, S and Wright, J, *The Data Protection Directive and Medical Research Across Europe*, Ashgate, Aldershot, 2004

Bickenbach, JE, "Damages for Wrongful Conception: Doiron v Orr" (1980) 18 *University of Western Ontario Law Review* 493

Billings, P, Kohn, MA, de Ceuvas, M, Beckwith, J, Alper, JS and Natowicz, MR, "Discrimination as a Consequence of Genetic Testing" (1992) 50 *American Journal of Human Genetics* 476

Bird, S, "Attributable Testing for Abnormal Prion Protein, Database Linkage, and Blood-Borne vCJD Risks" (2004) 364 *Lancet* 1362

Black, J, "Regulation as Facilitation: Negotiating the Genetic Revolution, (1998) 61 *Modern Law Review* 621

Blendon RJ, Schoen C, DesRoches CM, Osborn R, Scoles KL and Zapert K, "Inequities In Health Care: A Five-Country Survey' (2002) 21 *Health Affairs* 182

Bloch, M, "Religion and Ritual" in Kuper, A and Kuper, J (eds), *The Social Sciences Encyclopedia*, 2nd edn, Routledge, London, 1996

Blumgart, HL, "The Medical Framework for Viewing the Problem of Human Experimentation", in Freund, PA (ed) *Experimentation with Human Subjects,* Allen & Unwin, London, 1969

Bonduelle, M, Camus M, De Vos A, Staessen C, Tournaye H, Van Assche E, Verheyen G, Devroey P, Liebaers I, Van Steirteghem A, "Seven Years of Intracytoplasmic Sperm Injection and Follow-up of 1987 Subsequent Children" (1999) 14(Suppl 1) *Human Reproduction* 2339

Bongar, B, "Clinicians, Microcomputers and Confidentiality" (1988) 19 *Professional Psychology* 286

Bonnicksen, A, "Human Embryonic Stem Cell Research: the Role of Private Policy" in Healy, DL, Kovacs, GT, McLachlan, R, Rodriguez-Armas, O (eds) *Reproductive Medicine in the Twenty-first Century*, Parthenon, New York, 2002

Boston Women's Health Collective, *Our Bodies, Our Selves – A Book by and for Women*, Simon & Schuster, New York, 1976

Bourke, J, "Misapplied Science: Unreliability in Scientific Test Evidence (Pt 1)" (1993) 10 *Australian Bar Review* 123

Bowden, B, *Black Hawk Down: A Story of Modern War*, Atlantic Monthly Press, 1999

Brady, LS and Kirschner, KL, "Ethical Issues for Persons with Aphasia and their Families" (1995) 2 (3) *Topics in Stroke Rehabilitation* 76

Bramble, M and Ironside J, "Creutzfeldt-Jakob Disease: Implications for Gastroenterology" (2002) 50 *Gut* 888

Brandt, P, "Fraud control by the Health Insurance Commission: A multifaceted approach", in Smith, RG, *Health Care, Crime and Regulatory Control*, Hawkins Press, Sydney, 1998

Braude, PR, de Wert, G, Evers-Kiebooms, G, Pettigrew, RA and Geredts, J, "Non-disclosure Preimplantation Genetic Diagnosis for Huntington's Disease: Practical and Ethical Dilemmas" (1998) 18(13) *Prenatal Diagnosis* 1422

Braunack-Mayer, AJ and Mulligan, EC, "Sharing Patient Information Between Professionals: Confidentiality and Ethics" (2003) 178 *Medical Journal of Australia* 277

Breden, TM and Vollmann, J, "The Cognitive Based Approach of Capacity Assessment in Psychiatry: A Philosophical Critique of the MacCAT-T" (2004) 12 *Health Care Analysis* 273

Breen, K, Plueckhahn, V and Cordner, S, *Ethics, Law and Medical Practice*, Allen & Unwin, Sydney, 1997

Breen, KJ, "The Medical Profession and the Pharmaceutical Industry: When Will We Open Our Eyes?" (2004) 180 *Medical Journal of Australia* 409

Brekke, N and Borgida, E, "Expert Psychological Testimony in Rape Trials: A Social-Cognitive Analysis" (1988) 55 *Journal of Personality and Social Psychology* 372

Brekke, NJ, Enko, PJ, Clavet, G and Seelau, E, "Of Juries and Court-Appointed Experts" (1991) 15 *Law and Human Behavior* 451

Brend, W, "Bills of Mortality" (1907) 5 *Transactions of the Medico-Legal Society* 140

Brennan, TA, Leape LL, Laird, NM et al, "The Nature of Adverse Events in Hospitalized Patients: Results of the Harvard Medical Practice Study II" (1991) 324(6) *New England Journal of Medicine* 377

Brennan, TA, Leape, LL and Laird, NM, "Incidence of Adverse Events and Negligence in Hospitalized Patients: Results of the Harvard Medical Practice Study I" (1991) 324 *New England Journal of Medicine* 370

British Medical Association, *The Handbook of Medical Ethics*, British Medical Association, UK, 1981

Britton, A, "Hippocrates: Dead or Alive?" in Petersen, K, *Intersections: Women on Law, Medicine and Technology*, Ashgate, Aldershot, 1997

Brock, DW, "Decision-Making Competence and Risk" (1991) 5 *Bioethics* 105

Brody, BA, Anderson, C, McCleary, SU, McCullough, L, Mogan, R, Wray, N, "Expanding Disclosure of Conflicts of Interest: The Views of Stakeholders" (2003) 25 *Institutional Review Board* 1, 551

Brookbanks, W, "Narrative Medical Competence and Therapeutic Jurisprudence: Moving Towards a Synthesis" (2003) 20 *Law in Context* 2

Brooke, F, Boyd, A, Klug, G, et al, "Lyodura Use and the Risk of Iatrogenic Creutzfeldt-Jakob Disease in Australia" (2004) 180 *Medical Journal of Australia* 177

Broom, D, *Damned if We Do: Contradictions in Women's Health Care*, Allen & Unwin Sydney, 1991

Brophy, E, "Does a Doctor Have a Duty to Provide Information and Advice About Complementary and Alternative Medicine?" (2003) 10(3) *Journal of Law and Medicine* 271

Broughton, F, "Confidentiality – New Law in Victoria" (1998, November) *In-Psych (Bulletin of the Australian Psychological Society)* 6

Brown, A, "Drug Courts Help Keep Families Together" (15 September 2001) 1 *Florida Bar News*

Brown, IJ and Gannon, P, "Confidentiality and the Human Genome Project: A Prophecy for Conflict?" in McLean, S (ed) *Contemporary Issues in Law, Medicine and Ethics*, Dartmouth, Brookfield, Vermont, 1995

Brownsword, R, "Regulating Human Genetics: New Dilemmas for a New Millennium" (2004) 12 *Medical Law Review* 14

Bruce, M, Will, R, Ironside, J, et al, "Transmissions to Mice Indicate that 'New Variant' CJD is Caused by the BSE Agent" (1997) 389 *Nature* 498

Bryson, J, *Evil Angels*, Penguin Books, Melbourne, 1985

Buchanan, A, "The Controversy Over Retrospective Moral Judgment" (1996) 6 *Kennedy Institute of Ethics Journal* 245

Buchanan, AE and Brock, DW, *Deciding for Others: The Ethics of Surrogate Decision-Making*, Cambridge University Press, Cambridge, 1989

Bucknall, T and Thomas, S, "Critical Care Nurse Satisfaction with Levels of Involvement in Clinical Decisions" (1996) 23 *Journal of Advanced Nursing* 571

Bugeja, L and Ranson, D, "Coroners' Recommendations: a Lost Opportunity" (2005) 13 *Journal of Law and Medicine* 173

Burley, J and Harris, J, *A Companion to Genethics*, Blackwell Publishing, London, 2004

Burns, K, "The Way the World is: Social Facts in High Court Negligence Cases" (2004) 12 *Torts Law Journal* 215

Burris, S, "Governance, Microgovernance and Health", Conference on SARS and the Global Governance of Public Health, Temple University Beasley School of Law, 2004

Burris, S, Lazzarini, Z and Gostin, L, "Taking Rights Seriously in Health", (2002) 30 *Journal of Law, Medicine and Ethics* 490

Bynum, W, "Reflections on the History of Human Experimentation", in Spicker, SF (ed) *The Use of Human Beings in Research: With Special Reference to Clinical Trials*, Kluwer Academic Publishers, Dordrecht, 1988

Cain, JM and Hammes, BJ, "Ethics and Pain Management: Respecting Patient Wishes" (1994) 9(3) *Journal of Pain and Symptom Management* 160

Cale, G, "Continuing the Debate Over Risk-Related Standards of Competence" (1999) 13 *Bioethics* 131

Callahan, D *What Price Better Health? Hazards of the Research Imperative*, University of California Press, Berkeley, 2003

Callahan, D, "Cloning: The Work Not Done" (1997) 27 *Hastings Centre Report* 18

Callinan, I *The Coroner's Conscience*, Central Queensland University Press, 1999

Cameron, A, Welborn, T, Zimmet, P, Dunstan, D, Owen, N, Salmon, J, Dalton, M, Jolley, D and Shaw, J, "Overweight and Obesity in Australia: The 1999–2000 Australian Diabetes, Obesity and Lifestyle Study (AusDiab)" (2003) 178 *Medical Journal of Australia* 427

Cane, P (ed), *Centenary Essays for the High Court of Australia*, LexisNexis Butterworths, Australia, 2004

Cane, P, "Another Failed Sterilisation" (2004) 120 *Law Quarterly Review* 189

Cane, P, "The Doctor, the Stork and the Court: A Modern Morality Play" (2004) 120 *Law Quarterly Review* 23, 443

Cantor, NL, "Twenty-Five Years after Quinlan: A Review of the Jurisprudence of Death and Dying" (2001) 29 *Journal of Law, Medicine and Ethics* 182

Carpenter, B et al, "Issues Surrounding the Reduction in the Internal Autopsy in the Coronial System" (2006) 14 *Journal of Law and Medicine* (in press), 313

Cartwright, AM, Williams, GM, Steinberg, MA and Najman, GM, *Community and Heath/Allied Health Professionals' Attitudes to Euthanasia: What are the Driving Forces?* Report to the NHMRC, 2002

Cartwright, S, "Revisiting the Cartwright Inquiry" (2002) 3(1) *New Zealand Bioethics Journal* 3; Coney, S, *The Unfortunate Experiment*, Penguin, Auckland, 1988

Cassell, EJ, "The Sorcerer's Broom – Medicine's Rampant Technology" (1993) 23(6) *Hastings Center Report* 32

Castledine, G, "Accountability in Delivering Care" (1991) 5 *Nursing Standard* 28

Caulfield, T, Knowles, L, and Meslin, EM, "Law and Policy in an Era of Reproductive Genetics" (2004) 30 *Journal of Medical Ethics* 414

Cecil, JS and Willging, TE *Court-Appointed Experts: Defining the Role of Experts Appointed Under Federal Rule of Evidence*, Federal Judicial Center, Washington DC, 1993, 420

Chalmers, D and Nicol, D, "Embryonic Stem Cell Research: Can the Law Balance Ethical, Scientific and Economic Values?" Parts 1 and 2 (2003) 18 *Law and the Human Genome Review* 43 and 91

Chalmers, D, "Professional Self-regulation and Guidelines in Assisted Reproduction" (2002) 9 *Journal of Law and Medicine* 414

Chalmers, D, and Pettit, P, "Towards a Consensual Culture in the Ethical Review of Research. Australian Health Ethics Committee" (1998) 168 *Medical Journal of Australia* 79

Chalmers, D, Nicol, D and Gogarty, B, "Regulating Biomedical Advances: Embryonic Stem Cell Research" (2002) 2 *Macquarie Law Journal* 31

Champagne, A, Shuman, D and Whitaker, E, "An Empirical Examination of the Use of Expert Witnesses in American Courts" (1991) 31 *Jurimetrics Journal* 375

Champagne, A, Shuman, DW and Whitaker, E, "The Problem with Empirical Examination of the Use of Court-Appointed Experts: A Report of Non-findings" (1996) 14 *Behavioral Sciences and the Law* 361

Charland, LC, "Appreciation and Emotion: Theoretical Reflections on the MacArthur Treatment Competence Study" (1998) 8 *Kennedy Institute of Ethics Journal* 359

Charlesworth, M, *Bioethics in a Liberal Society*, Cambridge University Press, 1993, Cambridge

Checkland, D, "On Risk and Decisional Capacity" (2001) 26 *Journal of Medicine and Philosophy* 35

Chernichovsky D, "Health System Reforms in Industrialised Democracies: An Emerging Paradigm" (1995) 73(3) *Milbank Quarterly* 339

Childress, J, "The Challenges of Public Ethics: Reflections on NBAC's Report" (1997) 27 *Hastings Centre Report* 9

Childress, JF, "Organ and Tissue Procurement: Ethical and Legal Issues Regarding Cadavers" in Reich, WT (ed), *Encyclopedia of Bioethics*, rev edn, Simon & Schuster Macmillan, New York, 1995

CIOMS, *International Ethical Guidelines for Biomedical Research Involving Human Subjects*, CIOMS, Geneva, 2002

Clark, CM, Sheppard, L, Fillenbaum, GG, Galasko, D Morris, JC, Koss, E, Mohs, R, Heyman, A, "Variability in Annual Mini-mental State Examination Score in Patients with Probable Alzheimer Disease: a Clinical Perspective of Data from the Consortium to Establish a Registry for Alzheimer Disease" (1999) 56 *Archives of Neurology* 857

Clarke, C and Magnusson, R, "Data Registers in Respiratory Medicine" (2002) 10 *Journal of Law and Medicine* 69

Clouser, KD and Gert, B, "A Critique of Principlism" (1990) 15 *Journal of Medicine and Philosophy* 219

Coady, M and Bloch, S, *Codes of Ethics and the Professions*, Melbourne University Press, Melbourne, 1996

Cock, K, Mbori-Bgacha D, and Marum E, "Shadow on the Continent: Public Health and HIV/AIDS in Africa in the 21st Century" (2002) 360 *Lancet* 67

Cohen, JR, "In God's Garden Creation and Cloning in Jewish Thought" (1999) 29 *Hastings Center Report* 7

Collier, B, Coyne, C and Sullivan, K (eds), *Mental Capacity: Powers of Attorney and Advance Health Directives*, Federation Press, Sydney, 2005

Collins, S, Lawson, V and Masters, C, "Transmissible Spongiform Encephalopathies" (2004) 363 *Lancet* 51

Collins, S, Lewis, V, Brazier, M et al, "Extended Period of Asymptomatic Prion Disease After Low Dose Inoculation: Assessment of Detection Methods and Implications for Infection Control" (2005) 20(2) *Neurobiology of Disease* 336-346

Collins, S, Lewis, V, Brazier, M et al, "Extended Period of Asymptomatic Prion Disease After Low Dose Inoculation: Assessment of Detection Methods and Implications for Infection Control" (2005) 20(2) *Neurobiology of Disease* 336

Commens, CA, "Truth in Clinical Research Trials Involving Pharmaceutical Sponsorship" (2001) 174 *Medical Journal of Australia* 648

Committee of Inquiry into Cosmetic Surgery, *Cosmetic Surgery Report*, Report to the NSW Minister for Health, Health Care Complaints Commission, 1999

Commonwealth Department of Health and Ageing, *Infection Control Guidelines for the Prevention of Transmission of Infectious Diseases in the Health Care Setting* (January 2004), §31.9.2

Commonwealth House of Representatives Standing Committee on Legal and Constitutional Affairs in *Human Cloning: Scientific, Ethical and Regulatory Aspects of Human Cloning and Stem Cell Research*, Commonwealth of Australia, Canberra, 2001

Commonwealth Joint Committee of Public Accounts, *Inquiry Into Fraud and Overservicing: Report on Pathology*, Report No 236, 1985

Commonwealth, Senate Community Affairs Reference Committee, *Rocking the Cradle: A Report into Childbirth Procedures*, Canberra, 1999

Conaghan, J, "Tort Litigation in the Context of Intra-Familial Abuse" (1998) 61 *Modern Law Review* 132

Coney, S *The Unfortunate Experiment*, Penguin, Auckland, 1988

Conway, H, "Dead, But Not Buried: Bodies, Burial and Family Conflicts" (2003) 23(3) *Legal Studies* 423

Cornish, W, Llewelyn, M and Adcock, M, *Intellectual Property Rights (IPRs) and Genetics*, Public Health Genetics Unit University of Cambridge, 2003

Correll, P, Law, M, Seed, C et al, "Variant Creutzfeldt-Jakob Disease in Australian Blood Donors: Estimation of Risk and the Impact of Deferral Strategies" (2001) 81 *Vox Sanguinis* 6

Cossins, A and Pilkington, R, "Balancing the Scales: the Case for the Inadmissibility of Counselling Records in Sexual Assault Trials" (1996) 19 *University of NSW Law Journal* 222

Crawford, C, "Legalizing Medicine: Early Modern Legal Systems and the Growth of Medico-Legal Knowledge" in Clarke, M and Crawford, C *Legal Medicine in History*, Cambridge University Press, Cambridge, 1994

Crespi, R, "Patenting and Ethics: A Dubious Connection" (2001/2002) 5 *Bio-Science Law Review* 71

Critser, G, *Fat Land: How Americans became the Fattest People in the World*, Penguin, London, 2003

Crompton, M, "The Privacy Imperative for a Successful Health*Connect*", Guest Editorial, (2004) 33(1) *Health Information Management Journal* 4

Cruess, RL, Cruess, SL and Johnston, SE, "Professionalism: an Ideal to Be Sustained" (2000) 356 Lancet 156

Cruess, SR, Johnston, S and Cruess, RL, "'Profession': A Working Definition for Medical Educators" (2004) 16(1) *Teaching and Learning in Medicine* 74

Cunningham, JPW et al, "Defensible Assessment of the Competency of the Practicing Physician" (1997) 72(1) *Academic Medicine* 617

Dahl, E, Beutel, M, Brosig, B and Hinsch, KD, "Preconception Sex Selection for Non-medical Reasons: a Representative Survey from Germany" (2003) 18 (7) *Human Reproduction* 1368

Daniel, A *Medicine and the State: Professional Autonomy and Public Accountability*, Allen & Unwin, Sydney, 1990

Darvall, LW, *Medicine, Law and Social Change: The Impact of Bioethics, Feminism and Rights Movement on Medical Decision-making*, Dartmouth, Aldershot, 1993

Dauphinee, WD, "Validation of Doctors in Canada" (1999) 319 *British Medical Journal* 1198

Daver, EA, "A Therapeutic Jurisprudence Perspective on Legal Responses to Medical Error" (2003) 24 *Journal of Legal Medicine* 37

Davies, M and Naffine, N, *Are Persons Property? Legal Debates About Property and Personality*, Ashgate, Aldershot, 2001

Davies, P, "Who Are We Kidding on Confidentiality?" (2004, Summer) *Hoolet: The Magazine of the RCGP Scotland*

Davis, OK, "Elective Single-Embryo Transfer – Has its Time Arrived?" (2004) 351(23) *New England Journal of Medicine* 2440

Delaney, S, "An Optimally Rights Recognising Mental Health Tribunal" (2003) 10 *Psychiatry, Psychology and Law* 71

Delano, SJ and Zucker, JL, "Protecting Mental Health Research Subjects Without Prohibiting Progress" (1994) 45 *Hospital and Community Psychiatry* 601

Demaine, L and Fellmeth, A, "Reinventing the Double Helix: A Novel and Nonobvious Reconceptualization of the Biotechnology Patent" (2002) 55 *Stanford Law Review* 303

Dembner, A, "Lawsuits Target Medical Research", *Boston Globe Online*, 12 August 2002; De Ville, K, "The role of litigation in human research accountability" (2002) 9 *Accountability in Research* 17

Department of Community Services and Health, *National HIV/AIDS Strategy*, AGPS, Canberra, 1989

Dickens, B, "Can Sex Selection be Ethically Tolerated? (2002) 28 *Journal of Medical Ethics* 335, 225

Dickey, A, "More on Parental Rights to Bury a Child" (1993) 67 *Australian Law Journal* 149

Dickey, A, "Parental Rights and Duties upon the Death of a Child" (1992) 66 *Australian Law Journal* 35

Diesfeld, K and Freckelton, I (eds) *Involuntary Detention and Therapeutic Jurisprudence: International Perspectives on Civil Commitment*, Ashgate, Aldershot, 2003

Diesfeld, K and McKenna, B, "The Therapeutic Intent of the New Zealand Mental Health Review Tribunal" (2006) 13(1) *Psychiatry, Psychology and Law* (in press)

Diesfeld, K and McKenna, B, *Insight and Other Puzzles in the Decisions of New Zealand Mental Health Review Tribunal*, Mental Health Commission of New Zealand, Wellington, 2005

Diesfeld, K and Sjostrom, S, "Interpretive Flexibility: Why Doesn't Insight Incite Controversy in Mental Health Law?" (2006) 24 *Behavioral Sciences and Law* 1

Dimopoulos, P and Bagaric, M, "Why Wrongful Birth Actions are Right" (2003) 11 *Journal of Law and Medicine* 230

Dix, A, "Disciplinary Regulation", in Smith, RG (ed), *Health Care, Crime and Regulatory Control*, Hawkins Press, Sydney, 1998

Dix, A, Errington, M, Nicholson, K and Powe, R, *Law for the Medical Profession*, 2nd edn, Butterworth Heinemann, Australia, 1996

Dodds, S, "Is the Australian HREC System Sustainable?" (2002) 21 *Monash Bioethics Review* 43

Donnelly, C, Ferguson, N, Ghani, A, et al, "Implications of BSE Infection Screening Data for the Scale of the British BSE Epidemic and Current European Infection Levels" (2002) 269 *Proceedings of the Royal Society of London: Biological Sciences* 2179

Dooley, LG, "Sounds of Silence on the Civil Jury" (1991) 26 *Valparaiso University Law Review* 405

Doran, E et al, "Empirical Uncertainty and Moral Contest: A Qualitative Analysis of the Relationship between Medical Specialists and the Pharmaceutical Industry in Australia" (2006) 62 *Social Science and Medicine* 1510

Dowling, S, Martin, M, Skidmore, P, Doyal, L, Cameron, A and Lloyd, S, "Nurses Taking on Junior Doctor's Work: A Confusion of Accountability" (1996) 321 *British Medical Journal* 1211

Drahos, P and Braithwaite, J, *Information Feudalism. Who Owns the Knowledge Economy?*, New Press, New York, 2003

Drahos, P, "BITS and BIPS: Bilateralism in Intellectual Property" (2001) 4 *Journal of Intellectual Property* 791

Drahos, P, "The TNC Bias in TRIPS" in Drahos, P (ed), *Intellectual Property*, Ashgate, Dartmouth, 1999

Duckett, SJ, "Private Care and Public Waiting" (2005) 29 (1) *Australian Health Review* 87

Dwyer, JM, "The Hippocratic Irrelevance Variable (HIV)" (1990) 152 *Medical Journal of Australia* 169

Dyer, O, "Judges Support Doctors' Decision to Stop Treating a Dying Man" (2005) 331 *British Medical Journal* 536

Eastman, N and Peay, J (eds) *Law Without Enforcement: Integrating Mental Health and Justice*, Hart Publishing, Oxford, 1999

Edelstein, L, *Ancient Medicine*, Johns Hopkins University Press, Baltimore, 1987

Edelstein, L, *The Hippocratic Oath: Text, Translation and Interpretation*, John Hopkins Press, Baltimore, Maryland, 1943

Edmond, G and Mercer, D, "Keeping 'Junk' History, Philosophy and Sociology of Science Out of the Courtroom: Problems with the Reception of *Daubert v Merrell Dow Pharmaceuticals Inc*" (1997) 20 *University of NSW Law Journal* 48

Edmond, G and Mercer, D, "The Politics of Jury Competence" in Martin, B (ed), *Technology and Public Participation*, University of Wollongong, Wollongong, 1999

Edmond, G and Mercer, D, "The Secret Life of (Mass) Torts: The 'Bendectin Litigation' and the Construction of Law-Science Knowledges" (1997) 20(3) *University of NSW Law Journal* 666

Edwards, R and Steptoe, P *A Matter of Life: The Story of a Medical Breakthrough,* Sphere, London, 1980

Ehrenreich, B and English, D, *For Her Own Good: 150 Years of the Experts' Advice to Women*, Anchor, New York, 1978;

Eisenberg, R, "Patents and the Progress of Science: Exclusive Rights and Experimental Use" (1989) 56 *University of Chicago Law Review* 1017

Ellard, J, "Confidentiality and the Psychiatrist in Private Practice" (1970) 4 *Australian and New Zealand Journal of Psychiatry* 191

Ellena, KR, "The Uncritical Enthusiasts Versus the Uninformed Sceptics: Regulation of Complementary and Alternative Medicines" (2005) 13 *Journal of Law and Medicine* 105

Evans, M, Kaufman, M, "Establishment and Culture of Pluripotential Cells from Mouse Embryos" (1981) 292 *Nature* 154

Faigman, DL and Baglioni, AJ, "Bayes' Theorem in the Trial Process: Instructing Jurors on the Value of Statistical Evidence" (1988) 12 *Law and Human Behavior* 1

Families USA Foundation, *Profiting from Pain: Where Prescription Drug Dollars Go*, Publication No 02-10, Families USA, 2002

Farmer, P, *Pathologies of Power: Health, Human Rights and the New War on the Poor*, University of California Press, Berkeley, 2003

Farrell, MM and Levin, DL, "Brain Death in the Paediatric Patient: Historical, Sociological, Medical, Religious, Cultural, Legal, and Ethical Considerations" (1993) 21(12) *Critical Care Medicine* 1951

Faunce T, Doran E, Henry D, Drahos P, Searles P, Pekarsky B, Neville, W, "Assessing the impact of the Australia-United States Free Trade Agreement of Australian and Global Medicines Policy" (2005) 1 *Globalisation and Health* 1

Faunce TA and Gatenby P, "Flexner's Ethical Oversight Reprised? Contemporary Medical Education and the Health Impacts of Corporate Globalization" (2005) 39(10) *Medical Education* 1066-74

Faunce TA and Johnston K, "Impact of the AUSFTA on Medicines Policy in Australia, New Zealand and their Region" *Wellington University Law Review* (in press)

Faunce TA, (2005), "Global Intellectual Property Protection for Innovative iPharmaceuticals: Challenges for Bioethics and Health Law" in B Bennett and Tomossy, GF (eds), *Globalisation and Health: Challenges for Health Law and Bioethics*, Springer, Dordrecht

Faunce TA, "Health Legislation: Interpretation Coherent with Conscience and International Human Rights" in S Corcoran and S Bottomley (eds) *Interpreting Statutes*, Federation Press, Sydney, 2005

Faunce TA, "Nurturing Personal and Professional Conscience in an Age of Corporate Globalisation: Bill Viola's The Passions" (2005) 183(11/12) *Medical Journal of Australia* 599-601

Faunce, T, Mure, K, Cox, C and Maher, B, "When Silence Threatens Safety: Lessons from the First Canberra Hospital Neurosurgical Inquiry" (2005) 12 *Journal of Law and Medicine* 112

Faunce, TA, and Tomossy, GF, "The UK House of Commons Report on the Influence of the Pharmaceutical Industry: Lessons for Equitable Access to Medicines in Australia" (2005) 24 *Monash Bioethics Review* 38

Feichtinger, W, "Preimplantation Genetic Diagnosis (PGD) – A European Clinician's Point of View" (2004) 21(1) *Journal of Assisted Reproduction and Genetics* 15

Ferner RE, "The Influence of Big Pharma" (2005) 330 *British Medical Journal* 855

Fichet, G, Comoy, E and Duval, C, "Novel Methods for Disinfection of Prion-Contaminated Medical Devices" (2004) 364 *Lancet* 521

Firestone, S, *The Dialectic of Sex*, Jonathan Cape, London, 1971

Fitzgerald, PD, "General Practice Corporatisation: The Half-Time Score" (2002) 177 *Medical Journal of Australia* 90

Fitzgerald, PD, "The Ethics of Doctors and Big Business" (2001) 175 *Medical Journal of Australia* 73

Flaherty, MP, Nelson, D, and Stephens, J, "The Body Hunters: Overwhelming the Watchdogs", 18 December 2000

Fleming, J, *The Law of Torts*, 9th edn, Lawbook Co, Sydney, 1998

Fletcher, J, "Some Implications for Nurses and Managers of Recent Changes to the Processing and Hearing of Medical Negligence Claims" (2000) 8 *Journal of Nursing Management* 136

Flinders University, *The Benefits and Difficulties of Introducing a National Approach to Electronic Health Records in Australia*, Report to the National Electronic Health Records Taskforce, Flinders University, Adelaide, April, 2000 (Appendix), in The National Electronic Health Records Taskforce Report, (2000)

Folstein, MF, Folstein, SE and McHugh, PR, "Mini-Mental State. A Practical Method for Grading the Cognitive State of Patients for the Clinician" (1975) 12 *Journal of Psychiatric Research* 189

Forrester, K and Simpson, J, "Nurses and Liability-Uncertain Times Ahead" (2003) 11(2) *Journal of Law and Medicine* 148

Foster, C, "Negligence", in Tingle, J and Cribb A, (eds) *Nursing Law and Ethics*, 2nd edn, Blackwell Publishing, Oxford, 2002

Foster, WL, "Expert Testimony – Prevalent Complaints and Proposed Remedies" (1897–1898) 11 *Harvard Law Review* 169

Fox, R, "Ethical and Legal Principles of Confidentiality for Psychologists and Social Workers", in Nixon, M (ed), *Issues in Psychological Practice*, Longman Cheshire, Sydney, 1984

Fraser, H, *The Federation House*, New Holland Publishers, Sydney, 2002

Freckelton I and List, D, "The Transformation of Regulation of Psychologists by Therapeutic Jurisprudence" (2004) 11(2) *Psychiatry, Psychology and Law* 296

Freckelton, I and Flynn, J, "Paths Toward Reclamation: Therapeutic Jurisprudence and the Regulation of Medical Practitioners" (2004) 12 *Journal of Law and Medicine* 91

Freckelton, I and Henning, T, "Speculation, Uncorroborated Opinions and Forensic Expertise in Child Sex Prosecutions" (1999) 6(1) *Psychiatry, Psychology and Law* 105

Freckelton, I and Loff, B, "Health Law and Human Rights" in Kinley, D, *Human Rights in Australian Law: Principles, Practice and Potential*, Federation Press, Sydney, 1998

Freckelton, I and Petersen, K (ed) *Controversies in Health Law*, Federation Press, Sydney, 1999

Freckelton, I and Ranson, D, *Death Investigation and the Coroner's Inquest*, Oxford University Press, Melbourne, 2006

Freckelton, I and Selby, H *Expert Evidence: Law, Practice, Procedure and Advocacy*, LBC, Sydney, 2005

Freckelton, I *The Trial of the Expert*, Oxford University Press, Melbourne, 1987

Freckelton, I, "Bipolar Disorders and the Law" (2005) 13 *Journal of Law and Medicine* 153

Freckelton, I, "Civil Commitment: Due Process, Procedural Fairness and the Quality of Decision-making" (2001) 8(1) *Psychiatry, Psychology and Law* 105

Freckelton, I, "Decision-Making About Involuntary Psychiatric Treatment: An Analysis of the Principles Behind Victorian Practice" (1998) 5 *Psychiatry, Psychology and Law* 249

Freckelton, I, "Distractors and Distressors in Involuntary Status Decision-making" (2005) 12(1) *Psychiatry, Psychology and Law* 88;

Freckelton, I, "Exemplary Damages in Medico-legal Litigation" (1996) 4 *Journal of Law and Medicine* 103

Freckelton, I, "Expert Evidence and the Role of the Juries" (1994) 12(1) *Australian Bar Review* 73

Freckelton, I, "Expert Evidence in the Family Court: the New Regime" (2005) 12 *Psychiatry, Psychology and Law* 234

Freckelton, I, "Health Practitioner Regulation: Emerging Patterns and Challenges for the Age of Globalization" in Bennett, B and Tomossy, GF (eds) *Globalization and Health: Challenges for Health Law and Bioethics*, Springer, Amsterdam, 2006

Freckelton, I, "Human rights and Health Law: New Statutory Developments" (2006) 14(1) *Journal of Law and Medicine* 5

Freckelton, I, "Human Rights and Health Law" (2006) 14 *Journal of Law and Medicine* 5

Freckelton, I, "Ideological Divarication and Civil Commitment Decision-making" (2003) 10(2) *Psychiatry, Psychology and Law* 390

Freckelton, I, "Immunity for Experts from Disciplinary Regulation" (2006) 13 *Journal of Law and Medicine* 393

Freckelton, I, "Judicial Attitudes Toward Scientific Evidence: An Antipodean Perspective" (1997) *University of California Davis Law Review* 1137

Freckelton, I, "Materiality of Risk and Proficiency Assessment: The Onset of Health Care Report Cards?" (1999) 6 *Journal of Law and Medicine* 313

Freckelton, I, "Novel Scientific Evidence: the Challenge of Tomorrow" (1987) 3 *Australian Bar Review* 243

Freckelton, I, "Regulation at the Margins of the Health Professions" (2006) *Law in Context* (in press)

Freckelton, I, "Science and the Legal Culture" (1993) 2 *Expert Evidence* 107

Freckelton, I, "The Area of Expertise Rule" in Freckelton, I and Selby, H *Expert Evidence*, Lawbook Co, Sydney, 1993

Freckelton, I, "The Sexually Exploitative Doctor" (1994) 1 *Journal of Law and Medicine* 203; *Re A Medical Practitioner* [1993] 2 Qd R 154 at 162

Freckelton, I, "Untimely Death, Law and Suicidality" (2005) 12(2) *Psychiatry, Psychology and Law* 265

Freckelton, I, "Withdrawal of Life Support" (2004) 11 *Journal of Law and Medicine* 265

Freckelton, I, Reddy, P and Selby, H, *Australian Judicial Perspectives on Expert Evidence: An Empirical Study*, AIJA, Melbourne, 1999

Freckelton, I, Reddy, P and Selby, H, *Magistrates' Perspectives on Expert Evidence: An Empirical Study*, AIJA, Melbourne, 2001

Freestone, R, *Model Communities: The Garden City Movement in Australia*, Nelson, Melbourne, 1989

Fried, C, "Privacy (a Moral Analysis)" in Schoeman, F (ed), *Philosophical Dimensions of Privacy: An Anthology*, Cambridge University Press, Cambridge, 1984

Fukuyama, F, *Our Posthuman Future: Consequences of the Biotechnology Revolution*, Farrar, Straus & Giroux, New York, 2002

Furrow, BR, Greaney, TL, Johnson, SH, Jost, TS and Schwartz, RL, *Health Law*, West Publishing, St Paul, Minnesota, 1995

Gantz, J, "State Statutory Preclusion of Wrongful Birth Relief: A Troubling Rewriting of a Woman's Right to Choose and the Doctor-Patient Relationship" (1997) 4 *Virginia Journal of Social Policy and the Law* 795

Garattini, S, "Are Me-Too Drugs Justified?" (1997) 10 *Journal of Nephrology* 283

Gardner, G, Carryer, J, Dunn, SV and Gardner, A, "Report to Australian Nursing Council: Nurse Practitioner Standards Project", Australian Nursing Council, Canberra, 2004

Gartrell, NK et al, "Physician-Patient Sexual Contact: Prevalence and Problems" (1992) 157(2) *Western Journal of Medicine* 139

Gathii, JT, "The Legal Status of the Doha Declaration on TRIPS and Public Health Under the Vienna Convention on the Law of Treaties" (2002) 15(2) *Harvard J Law and Technology* 291

Geer, K, Ropka, ME, Cohn, WF, Jones, SM and Miesfeldt, S, "Factors Influencing Patients' Decisions to Decline Cancer Genetic Counselling Services" (2001) 10 *Journal of Genetic Counselling* 25

Geller, L, Alper, JS, Billings, PR, Barash, CI, Beckwith, J and Natowicz, MR, "Individual, Family, and Societal Dimensions of Genetic Discrimination: A Case Study Analysis" (1996) 2 *Science and Engineering Ethics* 71

Gerber, P, "Playing Dice with Expert Evidence: The Lessons to Emerge from *R v Chamberlain*" (1987) 147 *Medical Journal of Australia* 243

Gervais, D, *The TRIPS Agreement: Drafting History and Analysis*, 2nd edn, Sweet & Maxwell, London, 2003

Gibbs, A, Dawson, J, Ansley, C and Mullen, R, "How Patients in New Zealand View Community Treatment Orders" (2005) 14 *Journal of Mental Health* 357

Gillam, L, "Resource Allocation: the Unavoidable Debate" (1992) 11(3) *Bioethics News* 49

Gilligan, C, *In a Different Voice: Psychological Theory and Women's Development*, Harvard University Press, Cambridge MA, 1982

Gillon, R, "Defending the 'Four Principles' Approach to Biomedical Ethics" (1995) 21 *Journal of Medical Ethics* 323

Giordano, K, "Examining Nursing Malpractice: A Defense Attorney's Perspective" (2003) 23(2) *Critical Care Nurse* 104

Giugni, P, "*Runjanjic v R*" (1992) 14 *Sydney University Law Review* 511

Glantz, LH, "Nontherapeutic research with children: Grimes v Kennedy Krieger Institute" (2002) 92 *American Journal of Public Health* 1070

Glatzel, M, Stoeck, K Seeger, H et al, "Human Prion Diseases: Molecular and Clinical Aspects" (2005) 62 *Archives of Neurology* 545

Godwin, J, Hamblin, J, Patterson, D and Buchanan, D *Australian HIV/AIDS Legal Guide*, 2nd edn, Federation Press, Sydney, 1993

Gold, AG *Expert Evidence in Criminal Law: The Scientific Approach*, Irwin Law, Ontario, 2003

Gold, R, "Gene Patents and Medical Access" (2000) 49 *Intellectual Property Forum* 20

Gold, S, "An Equality Approach to Wrongful Birth Statutes" (1996) 65 *Fordham Law Review* 1005

Goldberg MA and White, J, "The Relation between Universal Health Insurance and Cost Control' I(1995) 332 (11) *New England Journal of Medicine* 742

Golder, B, "From McFarlane to Melchior and Beyond: Love, Sex, Money and Commodification in the Anglo-Australian Law of Torts" (2004) 12 *Torts Law Journal* 128

Goldwater, P, "Bovine Spongiform Encephalopathy and Variant Creutzfeldt-Jakob Disease: Implications for Australia" (2001) 175 *Medical Journal of Australia* 154

Goodwin, B, *Keen As Mustard: Britain's Horrific Chemical Warfare Experiments in Australia,* University of Queensland Press, St Lucia, Queensland, 1998

Goring, R (ed), *Dictionary of Beliefs and Religions*, Larousse, Edinburgh, 1992

Gosden, R, *Designer Babies: The Brave New World of Reproductive Technology*, Phoenix, London, 2000

Gostin L and Curran, WJ, "AIDS Screening, Confidentiality and the Duty to Warn" (1987) 77 *American Journal of Public Health* 361

Gostin, L, "Health Care Information and the Protection of Personal Privacy: Ethical and Legal Considerations" (1997) 127 *Annals Internal Medicine* 683

Gostin, L, *Public Health Law and Ethics: A Reader*, University of California Press and the Milbank Memorial Fund, 2002

Gostin, L, *Public Health Law: Power, Duty, Restraint*, University of California Press and the Milbank Memorial Fund, 2000

Gostin, LO and Hodge, JG, Jr, "Personal Privacy and Common Goods: A Framework for Balancing Under the National Health Information Privacy Rule", (2002) 86 *Minnesota Law Review* 1439

Gostin, LO, "National Health Information Privacy: Regulations under the Health Insurance Portability and Accountability Act" (2001) (23) 285 *Journal of the Americal Medical Association* 3015

Gostin, LO, Bayer, R, and Fairchild A, "Ethical and Legal Challenges Posed by Severe Acute Respiratory Syndrome: Implications for the Control of Severe Infectious Disease Threats" (2003) 290 *Journal of the Americal Medical Association* 24

Gostin, LO, *The AIDS Pandemic: Complacency, Injustice, and Unfulfilled Expectations*, University of North Carolina Press, Chapel Hill, 2003

Gotzsche, PC, "Research Integrity and Pharmaceutical Industry Sponsorship. Trial Registration, Transparency and Less Reliance on Industry Trials are Essential" (2005) 182 *Medical Journal of Australia* 549

Graudins, LV, "The Medical Profession and the Pharmaceutical Industry: When will we open our eyes?" (2004) 181 *Medical Journal of Australia* 458

Gray, M and Chapman, B, "Foregone Earnings from Child Rearing" (2001) 58 *Family Matters* 4

Graycar, R and Morgan, J, "Unnatural Rejection of Womanhood and Motherhood: Pregnancy, Damages and the Law" (1996) 18 *Sydney Law Review* 323

Graycar, R, "Sex, Golf and Stereotypes: Measuring, Valuing and Imagining the Body in Law" (2002) 10 *Torts Law Journal* 205

Graycar, R, and Morgan, J, *The Hidden Gender of Law,* 2nd edn, Federation Press, Sydney, 2002

Green, R, "Benefiting from Evil: an Incipient Moral Problem in Stem Cell Research" (2002) 16 *Bioethics* 544, 255

Greenwald, LM and Mondor, M, "Malpractice and the Perinatal Nurse" (2003) 17 (2) *Journal of Perinatal and Neonatal Nursing* 101

Gregori, L, McCombie, N, Palmer, D et al, "Effectiveness of Leucoreduction for Removal of Infectivity of Transmissible Spongiform Encephalopathies From Blood" (2004) 364 *Lancet* 529

Griggs, L, "The Ownership of Excised Body Parts: Does an Individual Have the Right to Sell?" (1994) 1 *Journal of Law and Medicine* 223

Grove, DI and Mulligan, JB, "Consent, Compulsion and Confidentiality in Relation to Testing for HIV Infection: the Views of WA Doctors" (1990) 152 *Medical Journal of Australia* 174

Gruskin, S and Loff, B, "Do Human Rights Have a Role in Public Health Work?" (2002) 360 *Lancet* 1880

Gutheil, TG and Gabbard, GO, "The Concept of Boundaries in Clinical Practice: Theoretical and Risk-Management Dimensions" (1993) 150 *American Journal of Psychiatry* 188

Hadley, D, Jenkins, J, Dimond, E, Nakahara, K, Grogan, L, Liewehr, KJ, Steinberg, SM and Kirsch, I, "Genetic Counselling and Testing in Families with Hereditary Nonpolyposis Colorectal Cancer" (2003) 163 *Archives of Internal Medicine* 573

Hale, Baroness, "The Value of Life and the Cost of Living – Damages for Wrongful Birth" (2001) 7 *British Actuarial Journal* 747

Halevy, A and Brody, B, "Brain Death: Reconciling Definitions, Criteria, and Tests" (1993) 119(6) *Annals of Internal Medicine* 519

Hall, W et al, "Assessment of Physician Performance in Alberta" (1999) 161 *Canadian Medical Association Journal* 52

Halliday, S, "A Comparative Approach to the Regulation of Human Embryonic Stem Cell Research in Europe" (2004) 12 *Medical Law Review* 40

Hammond, C, "Property Rights in Human Corpses and Human Tissue: The Position in Western Australia" (2002) 4 *University of Notre Dame Australia Law Review* 97 at 105

Hampton, T, "Panel Reviews Health Effects Data for Assisted Reproductive Technologies" (2004) 292(24) *Journal of the Americal Medical Association* 2961

Hancock, L, *Health Policy in the Market State*, Allen & Unwin, Sydney, 1999

Hand, L, "Historical and Practical Considerations Regarding Expert Testimony" (1901–1902) 15 *Harvard Law Review* 40

Handford, P, *Mullany and Handfords' Tort Liability for Psychiatric Injury*, 2nd edn, Thomson, Sydney, 2006

Harding, A, "The Politics of Science" (2005) 19(2) *Scientist* 37

Hare, RM, *The Language of Morals*, Oxford University Press, Oxford, 1964

Harris, D and Chaboyer, W, "The Expanded Role of the Critical Care Nurse: A Review of the Current Position" (2002) 15(4) *Australian Critical Care* 133

Harris, J, "Cloning and Human Dignity" (1998) 7 *Cambridge Quarterly of Health Care Ethics* 163

Harris, J, "Goodbye Dolly? The Ethics of Human Cloning" (1997) 23 *Journal of Medical Ethics* 353

Harvey, K and Faunce, T, "A Critical Analysis of Overseas Trained Doctor Factors in the Bundaberg Base Hospital Inquiry" (2006) *Law in Context* (in press)

Harvey, K and Murray, M, "Medicinal Drug Policy", in Gardner, H (ed), *The Politics of Health: The Australian Experience*, 2nd edn, Churchill Livingstone, Melbourne, 1995

Harvey, KJ et al, "Pharmaceutical Advertisements in Prescribing Software: An Analysis" (2005) 183 *Medical Journal of Australia* 75

Hastie, R, Penrod, SD and Pennington, N, *Inside the Jury*, Harvard University Press, Cambridge, 1983, 427

Hawkins, C, *Mishap or Malpractice?*, Blackwell, Oxford, 1985

Hayder, M, *Tokyo*, Bantam Press Ltd, New York, 2004

Heinemann, T and Honnefelder, L, "Principles in Ethical Decision-Making" (2002) 16 *Bioethics* 530

Henry, DA et al, "Medical Specialists and Pharmaceutical Industry-Sponsored Research: A Survey of the Australian Experience" (2005) 182 *Medical Journal of Australia* 557, 556

Heydon, D, "Judicial Activism and the Death of the Rule of Law" (2003) 47 *Quadrant* 9

Hilary, J, *The Wrong Model: GATS, Trade Liberalization and Children's Right to Health*, Save the Children, London, 2001

Hilton, D, Ghani, A Conyers, L et al, "Prevalence of Lymphoreticular Prion Protein Accumulation in UK Tissue Samples" (2004) 203 *Journal of Pathology* 733

Hilton, SR and Slotnick, HB, "Proto-Professionalism: How Professionalism Occurs Across the Continuum of Medical Education" (2005) 39 *Medical Education* 58

Hobart Community Legal Service, *The Tasmanian Law Handbook*, Hobart Community Legal Service, Hobart, Tasmania, 1994

Hogan, M, "Let Sleeping Watchdogs Lie: The NSW Coronial System and Deaths Involving State Agencies'", in Hogan, R, Brown, D and Hogg, R (eds) *Death in the Hands of the State*, Redfern Legal Centre Publishing, Sydney, 1988

Hogan, R, Brown, D and Hogg, R (eds) *Death in the Hands of the State*, Redfern Legal Centre Publishing, Sydney, 1988

Hogffenberg, R, Lock, M, Tilney, N, Casabona, C, Daar, AS, Guttmann, RD, Kennedy, I, Mundy, S, Radcliffe-Richards, J, Sells, RA, "Should Organs from Patients in Permanent Vegetative State be Used for Transplantation?" (1997) 350 *Lancet* 1320

Holdenson, OP, "The Admission of Expert Evidence of Opinion as to the Potential Unreliability of Evidence of Visual Identification" (1988) 16 *Melbourne University Law Review* 521

Holdsworth, W, *A History of English Law*, vol 1, 7th edn, Methuen & Co, London, 1956

Hollon, MF, "Direct-to-consumer Advertising. A Haphazard Approach to Health Promotion", Editorial (2005) 293 (16) *Journal of the Americal Medical Association* 2030

Hooke, E, Bennett, L, Dwyer, R, Van Beek, I and Martin, C, "Nurse Practitioners: An Evaluation of the Extended Role of Nurses at the Kirketon Road Centre in Sydney, Australia" (2001) 18(3) *Australian Journal of Advanced Nursing* 21

Hora, P, "A Dozen Years of Drug Treatment Courts: Uncovering Our Theoretical Foundations and the Construction of the Mainstream Paradigm" in Harrison, L, Scarpitti, F, Amir, F and Einstein, S (eds), *Drug Courts: Current Issues and Future Perspectives*, Office of International Criminal Justice Publishers, 2002

Hora, P, Schma, W, and Rosenthal, J, "Therapeutic Jurisprudence and the Drug Treatment Court Movement: Revolutionizing the Criminal Justice System's Response to Drug Abuse and Crime in America" (1999) 74 *Notre Dame Law Review* 439

Hornblum, AM *Acres of Skin: Human Experiments at Holmesburg Prison*, Routledge, New York, 1998

Howard, D and Westmore, B *Crime and Mental Health Law in New South Wales*, LexisNexis Butterworths, Sydney, 2005

Hoyano, L, "Misconceptions about Wrongful Conception" (2002) 65 *Modern Law Review* 883

Hughes, S, "Law and Professional Practice: Accountability and Implications" (2002) 12 *British Journal of Perioperative Nursing* 94

Hume, SG, "Dead Bodies" (1956) 2 *Sydney Law Review* 109

Hunnisett, RF *The Medieval Coroner*, Cambridge University Press, Cambridge, 1961

Hunter, N, Foster, J, Chong, A et al, "Transmission of Diseases by Blood Transfusion" (2002) 83 *Journal of General Virology* 2897

Hurlbut, W, "Stanford Bioethicist Closes Gap Between Ethics and Science of Embryo Stem Cells" (2004) 143 *Bioedge* 3

Hurley, A, "Prospects of Recovery in Negligence and Under Statute for Creutzfeld[t]-Jakob Disease Resulting from Human Pituitary Gland Derived Hormone Products" (1996) 4 *Torts Law Journal* 60

Hutchinson, MS, "Pharmaceutical Companies and Medical Students: A Student's View" (2004) 180 *Medical Journal of Australia* 414

Iacovino, L, "Trustworthy Shared Electronic Health Records: Recordkeeping Requirements and Health*Connect*" (2004) 12 (1) *Journal of Law and Medicine* 40

Institut Curie and Assistance Publique Hôpitaux de Paris and Institut Gustave-Roussy, *Against Myriad Genetics's Monopoly on Tests for Predisposition to Breast and Ovarian Cancer Associated with the BRCA1 Gene*, 2002

Institute of Medicine, *Ethical Conduct of Clinical Research Involving Children*, National Academy Press, Washington, DC, 2004

Intellectual Property and Competition Review Committee, *Review of Intellectual Property Legislation under the Competition Principles Agreement*, IP Australia, Canberra, 2000

Intergovernmental Committee on AIDS Legal Working Party, *Civil Liability for Transmission of HIV/AIDS*, Department of Health, Housing and Community Services, Canberra, 1992

Intromassi, C, "Reproductive Self-Determination in the Third Circuit: The Statutory Proscription of Wrongful Birth and Wrongful Life Claims as an Unconstitutional Violation of Planned Parenthood v Casey's Undue Burden Principle" (2003) 24 *Women's Rights Law Reporter* 101

Irvine, D, "Time for Hard Decisions on Patient-centred Professionalism" (2004) 181 *MJA* 271

Irvine, DH, "Doctors in the UK: Their New Professionalism and its Regulatory Framework" (2001) 358 *Lancet* 1807

Irvine, DH, "New Ideas about Medical Professionalism" (2006) 184(5) *Medical Journal of Australia* 204

Irvine, DH, "The Performance of Doctors I: Professionalism and Regulation in a Changing World" (1997) 315 *British Medical Journal* 1540

Irvine, DH, "The Performance of Doctors II: Maintaining Good Practice, Protecting Patients from Poor Performance" (1997) 314 *British Medical Journal* 1613

Irvine, DH, "Time for Hard Decisions on Patient-centred Professionalism" (2004) 181 *Medical Journal of Australia* 271

Isasi, R et al, "Legal and Ethical Approaches to Stem Cell and Cloning Research: A Comparative Analysis of Policies in Latin America, Asia and Africa" 32 (2004) *Journal of Law &Medical Ethics* 626

Isasi, R Knoppers, B, Singer, P and Daar, A, "Legal and Ethical Approaches to Stem Cell and Cloning Research: A Comparative Analysis of Policies in Latin America, Asia and Africa" (2004) 32 *Journal of Law and Medical Ethics* 626

Iserson, KV, "Voluntary Organ Donation: Autonomy ... Tragedy" Letter (1993) 270(16) *Journal of the American Medical Association* 1930

Iversen, T, "The Effect of a Private Sector on the Waiting Time in a National Health Service" (1997) 16 *Journal of Health Economics* 381

Jackson PE, *The Law of Cadavers*, 2nd edn, Prentice-Hall, New York, 1950

Jackson, G, McKintosh, E and Flechsig, E, "An Enzyme-Detergent Method for Effective Prion Decontamination of Surgical Steel" (2005) 86 *Journal of General Virology* 869

Jaenisch, R, "Human cloning: The Science and Ethics of Nuclear Transplantation" (2004) 351 *New England Journal of Medicine* 27: 2787-2791

Jenkins, P, "Client or Patient? Contrasts Between Medical and Counselling Models of Confidentiality" (1999) 12 (2) *Counselling Psychology Quarterly* 169

Johnson, L, "Particular Issues of Public Health: Infectious Diseases" in Martin, R and Johnson, L, *Law and the Public Dimension of Health*, Cavendish Publishing, London, 2001

Johnson, M, "A Biomedical Perspective on Parenthood" in Bainham, A Sclater, SD and M Richards *What is a Parent? A Socio-Legal Analysis*, Hart Publishing, Oxford, 1999

Johnstone, G, "Coroners' Recommendations" in Selby, H (ed), *The Aftermath of Death*, Federation Press, Sydney, 1999

Jones, CAG, *Expert Witnesses*, Clarendon Press, Oxford, 1994; Golan, T, *Laws of Men and Laws of Nature*, Harvard University Press, Cambridge, MA, 2004

Jones, JH and Tuskegee Institute, *Bad Blood: The Tuskegee Syphilis Experiment*, Free Press, New York, 1993

Jones, MA, "Medical Negligence" in McHale, L and Tingle, J (eds) *Law and Nursing*, Butterworth-Heinemann, Oxford, 1992

Justice (Chair: E Stone QC), *Coroners' Courts in England and Wales*, Justice, London, 1986 (Justice Report)

Kackelman, TJ, "Violation of an Individual's Right to Die: The Need for a Wrongful Living Cause of Action" (1996) 64 *University of Cincinnati Law Review* 1355

Kadri, S *The Trial: A History from Socrates to OJ Simpson*, Harper Collins, London, 2005

Kapardis, A, *Psychology and Law*, Cambridge University Press, Cambridge, 2004

Kass, L, "Patenting Life" (1981) 63 *Journal of the Patent Office Society* 570

Kassirer, JP, *On the Take: How Medicine's Complicity with Big Business can Endanger Your Health*, Oxford University Press, New York, 2004

Katayama, AC, "US ART Practitioners Soon to Begin Their Forced March into a Regulated Future" (2003) 20(7) *Journal of Assisted Reproduction and Genetics* 265

Katz, J, "The education of the physician-investigator" (1969) 98 *Daedalus* 480 at 481; Beecher, HK *Research and the Individual: Human Studies*, Little, Brown, Boston, 1970

Katz, J, Capron, AM, and Glass, ES *Experimentation with Human Beings: The Authority of the Investigator, Subject, Professions, and State in the Human Experimentation Process*, Russell Sage Foundation, New York, 1972

Keays, D, "Patenting DNA and Amino Acid Sequences: An Australian Perspective" (1999) 7 *Health Law Journal* 69

Kennedy, I and Grubb, A *Medical Law: Text with Materials*, 2nd edn, Butterworths, London, 1994,

Kennedy, I *Treat Me Right: Essays in Medical Law and Ethics*, Clarendon Press, Oxford, 1991

Kennedy, MC, "Clinical trials without consent: Some experiments simply cannot be done" (2002) 177 *Medical Journal of Australia* 40

Kennedy, SE, Shen, Y, Charlesworth, JA, Mackie, JD, Mahony, JD, Kelly, JJP and Pussell, BA, "Outcome of Overseas Commercial Kidney Transplantation: an Australian Perspective" (2005) 182(5) *Medical Journal of Australia* 224

Kerridge, I, Lowe, M and McPhee, J, *Ethics and Law for the Professions*, 2nd edn, Federation Press, Sydney, 2005

Kerridge, I, Saul, P and Batey, R, "The Clinical and Ethical Implications of Hepatitis C for Organ Transplantation in Australia" (1996) 165 *Medical Journal of Australia* 282

Kirby, M, "Beyond the Judicial Fairy Tales" (2004) 48 *Quadrant* 26

Kissane, D, Clarke, D and Street, A, "Demoralization Syndrome – a Relevant Psychiatric Diagnosis for Palliative Care" (2000) 17 *Journal of Palliative Care* 12

Kitcher, P, "Creating Perfect People" in Burley, J, and Harris, J, *A Companion to Genethics*, Blackwell Publishing, London, 2004

Kjervik, D, "TJ and Nursing" (2000) 8 *Journal of Nursing Law* 4

Klutz, D, "Tort Reform: An Issue for Nurse Practitioners" (2004) 16(2) *Journal of the Academy of Nurse Practitioners* 70

Kmietowicz, Z, "Patients Informed of Increased Risk of vCJD Contact" (2004) 329 *British Medical Journal* 702

Knapp, S and Vandecreek, L, "Application of the Duty to Protect to HIV-Positive Patients" (1990) 21 *Professional Psychology* 161

Knapp, W and Hamilton, F, "Wrongful Living: Resuscitation as Tortious Interference with a Patient's Right to Give Informed Refusal" (1992) 19 *Northern Kentucky Law Review* 253

Knight, R, "Background and Epidemiology of vCJD" in Blajchman, M, Goldman, M, Webert, K et al, "Proceedings of a Consensus Conference: the Screening of Blood Donors for Variant CJD" (2004) 18(2) *Transfusion Medicine Reviews* 73

Knott, DH (ed), *The Trial of William Palmer*, rev ER Watson, Notable British Trials Series, Hodges & Co, London, 1856

Knowles A and McMahon, M, "Expectations and Preferences Regarding Confidentiality in the Psychologist-Client Relationship" (1995) 30 *Australian Psychologist* 175

Komesaroff, P, "Clinical Research in the Emergency Setting: The Role of Ethics Committees" (2001) 175 *Medical Journal of Australia* 630

Komesaroff, PA, and Kerridge, IH, "Ethical Issues Concerning the Relationships Between Medical Practitioners and the Pharmaceutical Industry" (2002) 176 *Medical Journal of Australia* 118

Kondo, L, "Advocacy of the Establishment of Mental Health Speciality Courts in the Provision of Therapeutic Justice for Mentally Ill Offenders" (2000) 24 *Seattle University Law Review* 373

Kopelman, LM, "Pediatric research regulations under legal scrutiny: Grimes narrows their interpretation" (2002) 30 *Journal of Law and Medical Ethics* 38

Kowitz, JF, "Not Your Garden Variety Tort Reform: Statutes Barring Claims for Wrongful Life and Wrongful Birth are Unconstitutional Under the Purpose Prong of Planned Parenthood v Casey" (1995) 61 *Brooklyn Law Review* 235

Kramer, MR and Sprung, CL, "Living Related Donation in Lung Transplantation" (1995) 155 *Archives of Internal Medicine* 1734

Kravitz, R et al, "Influence of Patients' Requests for Direct-to-Consumer Advertised Antidepressants" (2005) 293 (16) *Journal of the American Medical Association* 1995

Krimsky, S, *Science in the Private Interest: Has the Lure of Profits Corrupted Biomedical Research?*, Rowman & Littlefield, New York, 2003

Kuehn, B, "Researchers Coax Human Stem Cells to Become Motor Neurons" (2005) 293 *Journal of the Americal Medical Association* 1047

Langer, E, "Human Experimentation: Cancer Studies at Sloan Kettering Stir Public Debate on Medical Ethics" (1964) 143 *Science* 551

Lapham, E, Kozma, C and Weiss, JO, "Genetic Discrimination: Perspectives of Consumers" (1996) 274 *Science* 621

Lapsley, H, "Quality Measures in Australian Health Care" in Bloom, A (ed), *Health Reform in Australia and New Zealand*, Oxford University Press, Melbourne, 2000

Larcher, V, "Consent, Competence and Confidentiality" (2005) *British Medical Journal* 353

Lasagna, L, "Special Subjects in Human Experimentation", in Freund, PA (ed) *Experimentation with Human Subjects*, Allen & Unwin, London, 1969

Leach, ER, "Ritual" in Sills, DL (ed), *International Encyclopedia of the Social Sciences* Vol 13, Macmillan, United States, 1968

Leape LL et al, "The Nature of Adverse Events in Hospitalised Patients: Results of the Harvard Medical Practice Study II" (1991) 324 *New England Journal of Medicine* 377

Lederer, SE and Grodin, MA, "Historical Overview: Pediatric Experimentation", in Grodin, MA and Glantz, LH (eds), *Children as research subjects: Science, Ethics, and Law*, Oxford University Press, New York, 1994

Lederer, SE, *Subjected to Science: Human Experimentation in America Before the Second World War*, Johns Hopkins University Press, Baltimore, 1995

Lee, RG, and Morgan, D, *Human Fertilisation and Embryology. Regulating the Reproductive Revolution*, Blackstone, London, 2001

Legname, G, Baskakov, I, Nguyen H-O et al, "Synthetic Mammalian Prions" (2004) 305 *Science* 673

Lemmens, T and Freedman, B, "Ethics Review for Sale? Conflict of Interest and Commercial Research Review Boards" (2000) 78 *Milbank Quarterly* 547

Levine, M and Pyke, J, *Levine on Coroners' Courts*, Sweet & Maxwell, London, 1999

Levine, S and Weiss, R, "Hopkins Told to Halt Trials Funded by US – Death of Medical Volunteer Prompted Federal Directive", *The Washington Post*, 20 July 2001

Ligertwood, A, *Australian Evidence*, 3rd edn, Butterworths, Sydney, 1998

Limprecht, E, "GP Ownership at Core of Practice Software Battle" *Australian Doctor*, 17 June 2005

Limprecht, E, "Green Light to Cash In On Patient Data" *Australian Doctor*, 20 May 2005

Limprecht, E, "Legal Concerns Hit Pathology Co-op", *Australian Doctor*, 20 May 2005

Lind, C, Anderson, B, and Oberle, K, "Ethical Issues in Adolescent Consent for Research" (2003) 10 *Nursing Ethics* 504

Lippel, K, "Therapeutic and Anti-therapeutic Consequences of Workers' Compensation" (1999) 22 *International Journal of Law and Psychiatry* 521

Llewelyn, C, Hewitt, P, Knight, R et al, "Possible Transmission of Variant Creutzfeldt-Jakob Disease by Blood Transfusion" (2004) 363 *Lancet* 417

Loke, TW, Koh, FC, and Ward, JE, "Pharmaceutical Advertisement Claims in Australian Medical Publications" (2002) 177 *Medical Journal of Australia* 291

Lovell, RRH, "Ethics Law and Resources at the Growing Edge of Medicine" (1990) 10(3) *Bioethics News* 7

Low, L, King, S and Wilkie, T, "Genetic Discrimination in Life Insurance: Empirical Evidence from a Cross Sectional Survey of Genetic Support Groups in the United Kingdom" (1998) 317 *British Medical Journal* 1632

Lucire, Y, "Sex and the Practitioner: The Victim" (2002) 34 *Australian Journal of Forensic Science* 17

Luntz H, *Assessment of Damages for Personal Injury and Death*, 4th edn, Butterworths, Sydney, 2002

Luntz, H and Hambly, D, *Torts: Cases and Commentary*, 5th edn, LexisNexis Butterworths, Sydney, 2002

Luntz, H, "Damages in Medical Litigation in New South Wales" (2005) 12 *Journal of Law and Medicine* 280

MacKay, RD, "Dangerous Patients, Third Party Safety and Psychiatrists: Walking the Tarasoff Tightrope" (1990) *Medicine, Science and the Law* 52

Macklin, R, "A defense of fundamental principles and human rights: A reply to Robert Baker" (1998) 8 *Kennedy Institute of Ethics Journal* 403

Macklin, R, "Cloning and Public Policy" in Burley, J and Harris, J (eds), *A Companion to Genetics*, Blackwell Publishing, London, 2004

Macklin, R, "Universality of the Nuremberg Code", in Annas, GJ and Grodin, MA (eds) *The Nazi doctors and the Nuremberg Code: Human Rights in Human Experimentation*, Oxford University Press, New York, 1992

Macklin, R, *Against Relativism: Cultural Diversity and the Search for Ethical Universals in Medicine*, Oxford University Press, New York, 1999

Macpherson, S *Stephen Lawrence Inquiry Report*, Cmnd 4262, HMSO, London, 1999

Madden, B, "Changes to the Definition of Negligence" (2003) 12(1) *Australian Health Law Bulletin* 6

Magnusson, R, "Data Linkage, Health Research and Privacy: Regulating Data Flows in Australia's Health Information System" (2002) 24 *Sydney Law Review* 5

Magnusson, R, "Proprietary Rights in Human Tissue" in Palmer, N and McKendrick, E (eds), *Interests in Goods*, 2nd edn, Lloyds of London Press, London, 1998

Magnusson, R, "Public Interest Immunity and the Confidentiality of Blood Donor Identity in AIDS Litigation" (1992) 8(3) *Australian Bar Review* 226

Magnusson, R, *Angels of Death: Exploring the Euthanasia Underground*, Melbourne University Press, Melbourne, 2002

Malloy, SEW, "Beyond Misguided Paternalism: Resuscitating the Right to Refuse Medical Treatment" (1998) 33 *Wake Forest Law Review* 1035

Maloney, DM *Protection of Human Research Subjects: A Practical Guide to Federal Laws and Regulations*, Plenum Press, New York, 1984

Mandel, TE, "Future Directions in Transplantation" (1993) 158 *Medical Journal of Australia* 269

Mandl, KD, Szolovits, P and Kohane, IS, "Public Standards and Patients' Control: How to Keep Electronic Medical Records Accessible but Private" (2001) 322 *British Medical Journal* 283

Mann, J, Gostin, LO, Gruskin S, Brennan T, Lazzarini Z, and Fineberg, H, "Health and Human Rights" (1994) 1 *Health and Human Rights* 1 at 12

Mann, J, Gruskin, S, Grodin, M and Annas, G (eds), *Health and Human Rights: A Reader*, Routledge, New York, 2001, 79

Marks, HM *The Progress of Experiment: Science and Therapeutic Reform in the United States, 1900–1990,* Cambridge University Press, Cambridge England, 1997

Martin, G, "Isolation of a Pluripotent Cell Line from Early Mouse Embryos Cultured in Medium Condition by Teratocarcinoma Stem Cells" (1981) 78 *Proceedings of the National Academy of Science* 7634

Mason, JK, "Wrongful Pregnancy, Wrongful Birth and Wrongful Terminology" (2002) 6 *Edinburgh Law Review* 46

Masters, C, "The Emerging European Epidemic of Variant Creutzfeldt-Jakob Disease and Bovine Spongiform Encephalopathy: Lessons for Australia" (2001) 174 *Medical Journal of Australia* 160

Masters, S, "The medical profession and the pharmaceutical industry: when will we open our eyes?" (2004) 181 *Medical Journal of Australia* 459

Mastroianni, AC, and Kahn, JP, "Risk and responsibility: ethics, Grimes v Kennedy Krieger, and public health research involving children" (2002) 92 *American Journal of Public Health* 1073

Matei, L, "Quarantine Revision and the Model State Emergency Health Powers Act: "Laws for the Common Good'" (2002) 18 *Santa Clara Computer and High Tech Law Journal* 433

Mathers, CD, Vos, ET, Stevenson, CE and Begg, SJ, "The Australian Burden of Disease Study: measuring the loss of health from diseases, injuries and risk factors" (2000) 172 *Medical Journal of Australia* 592

Mathew T, Faull R and Snelling P, "The Shortage of Kidneys for Transplantation in Australia" (2005) 182(5) *Medical Journal of Australia* 204

Matthews, *Jervis on the Office and Duties of Coroners,* 12th edn, 2002

Mayor, S, "Claim of Human Reproductive Cloning Provokes Calls for International Ban" (2004) 328 *British Medical Journal* 185

Mayor, S, "Only a Few More Deaths from vCJD Likely in UK" (2005) 330 *British Medical Journal* 164

Mayor, S, "UN Committee Approves Declaration on Human Cloning" (2005) 330 *British Medical Journal* 496

McClelland, B and Contreras, M, "Appropriateness and Safety of Blood Transfusion" (2005) 330 *British Medical Journal* 104

McDermott, FT, Cordner, SM and Tremayne, AB, "Evaluation of the Medical Management and Preventability of Death in 137 Road Traffic Fatalities in Victoria, Australia: An Overview" (1996) 40(4) *Journal of Trauma: Injury, Infection and Critical Care* 520

McEwen, J *Evidence and the Adversarial Process – The Modern Law,* 2nd edn, Hart Publishing, Oxford, 1998

McFarlane, PJM, *Health Law in Australia and New Zealand,* 3rd edn, Federation Press, Sydney, 2000

McGuire, J, "Can the Criminal Law Ever be Therapeutic?" (2000) 18(4) *Behavioral Sciences and the Law* 413

McHugh, PR, "Zygote and 'Clonote' – The Ethical Use of Embryonic Stem-Cells" (2004) 351(3) *New England Journal of Medicine* 209

McKenna, B Simpson, AIF, Coverdale, J and Laidlaw, T, "An Analysis of Procedural Justice During Psychiatric Hospital Admission" (2001) 24 *International Journal of Law and Psychiatry* 573

McKenna, BG, Simpson, AIF and Coverdale, JH, "Outpatient Commitment and Coercion in New Zealand: A Matched Comparison Study" (2006) 29 *International Journal of Psychiatry and Law* 145

McKeough, J, "The Origins of the Coronial Jurisdiction" (1983) 6 *University of NSW Law Journal* 191

McKinley, R, Fraser, RC, and Baker, R, "Model for Directly Assessing and Improving Clinical Competence and Performance in Revalidation of Clinicians" (2001) 322 *British Medical Journal* 712.

McLean, S and Giesen, D, "Legal and Ethical Considerations of the Human Genome Project" (1994) 1 *Medical Law International* 159, 570

McLean, S, *Contemporary Issues in Law, Medicine and Ethics,* Dartmouth Publishing, Aldershot, England, 1996

McMahon, M and Knowles, A, "Psychologists' and Psychiatrists' Perceptions of the Dangerous Client" (1992) 1 *Psychiatry, Psychology and Law* 207

McMahon, M, "Dangerousness, Confidentiality and the Duty to Protect" (1992) 27 *Australian Psychologist* 12

McNeill, PM *The Ethics and Politics of Human Experimentation,* Cambridge University Press, Cambridge England, 1993

McNeill, PM, "Research Ethics Review and the Bureaucracy" (2002) 21 *Monash Bioethics Review* 72

McNeill, PM, "The Implications for Australia of the New Zealand Report of the Cervical Cancer Inquiry: No Cause for Complacency" (1989) 150 *Medical Journal of Australia* 264 at 271

McSherry B, "Confidentiality of Psychiatric and Psychological Communications: The Public Interest Exception" (2001) 8 *Psychiatry, Psychology and Law* 12

McSherry, B, "Amici Curiae and the Public Interest in Medical Law Cases" (2003) 11 *Journal of Law and Medicine* 5

Meade, CE and Bowden, SC, "Diagnosing Dementia: Mental Status Testing and Beyond" (2005) 28 *Australian Prescriber* 11

Medical Professionalism Project, "Medical Professionalism in the New Millennium: A Physician Charter" (2002) 136 *Annals of Internal Medicine* 243

Medical Research Council of Canada, SCoE, *A Proposed Ethics Agenda for CIHR: Challenges and Opportunities – Recommendations of the Standing Committee on Ethics to Council As It Prepares Its Parting Advice to CIHR Governing Council*, 2000

Medico-Legal Handbook, United Medical Protection, Sydney, 2003

Meiser, B, "Psychological Effect of Genetic Testing for Huntington's Disease: An Update of the Literature" (2000) 69 *Journal of Neurology, Neurosurgery and Psychiatry* 574

Melton, D, Daley, G and Jennings, C, "Altered Nuclear Transfer in Stem Cells: A Flawed Proposal" (2004) 351 *New England Journal of Medicine* 27

Mendelson D and Mendelson, G, "Tarasoff Down Under: the Psychiatrist's Duty to Warn in Australia" (1991) 19 *Journal of Psychiatry and Law* 33

Mendelson D, "Historical Evolution and Modern Implications of the Concepts of Consent to, and Refusal of, Medical Treatment in the Context of the Law of Trespass" (1996) 17 *Journal of Legal Medicine* 1

Mendelson, D and Ashby, M, "The Medical Provision of Hydration and Nutrition: Two Very Different Outcomes in Victoria and Florida" (2004) 11 *Journal of Law and Medicine* 282

Mendelson, D and Jost, TS, "A Comparative Study of the Law of Palliative Care and End-of-Life Treatment" (2003) 31(1) (Spring) *Journal of Law, Medicine and Ethics* 130, 363

Mendelson, D, "'Mr Cruel' and the Medical Duty of Confidentiality" (1993) 1 *Journal of Law and Medicine* 120

Mendelson, D, "Australian Tort Law Reform: Statutory Principles of Causation and the Common Law" (2004) 11 *Journal of Law and Medicine* 492

Mendelson, D, "Devaluation of a Constitutional Guarantee: the History of Section 51(xxiiiA) of the Commonwealth Constitution" (1999) 23 *Melbourne University Law Review* 308

Mendelson, D, "Medical Duty of Confidentiality in the Hippocratic Tradition and Jewish Medical Ethics" (1998) 5(3) *Journal of Law and Medicine* 227

Mendelson, D, "The Case of Backwell v AAA: Negligence – A Compensatory Remedy or an Instrument of Vengeance?" (1996) 4 *Journal of Law and Medicine* 114

Mendelson, D, "The Modern Australian Law of Mental Harm: Parochialism Triumphant" (2005) 13 *Journal of Law and Medicine* 164

Mendelson, D, "The Northern Territory's Euthanasia Legislation in Historical Perspective" (1995) 3 *Journal of Law and Medicine* 136

Mendelson, D, "Travels of a Medical Record and the Myth of Privacy" (2003) 11 (2) *Journal of Law and Medicine* 136

Mendelson, D, Jost, TS and Ashby, M, "Comparative Legal and Ethical Aspects of End of Life Treatment in Australia, Canada, the United Kingdom, France, Poland, Germany, the Netherlands, and Japan", in Dostrovsky, JO, Carr, DB and Koltzenburg, M (ed), *Proceedings of the 10th World Congress on Pain, Progress in Pain Research and Management*, IASP Press, Seattle, 2003

Merry, A and McCall-Smith, A, Errors, *Medicine and the Law*, Cambridge University Press, Cambridge, 2001

Merz, J, "Disease Gene Patents: Overcoming Unethical Constraints on Clinical Laboratory Medicine" (1999) 45 *Clinical Chemistry* 324

Michels, R, "Are research ethics bad for our mental health?" (1999) 340 *New England Journal of Medicine* 1427

Milani, A, "Better off Dead than Disabled? Should Courts Recognize a 'Wrongful Living' Cause of Action When Doctors Fail to Honor Patients" Advance Directives?" (1997) 54 *Washington and Lee Law Review* 149

Minkowitz, T, *No Force Advocacy by Users and Survivors of Psychiatry*, Mental Health Commission of New Zealand, Wellington, 2006

Mitchell, SV, Smallwood, RA, Angus, PW and Lapsley, HM, "Can we afford to transplant?" (1993) 158 *Medical Journal of Australia* 190

Moore, FD, "Three Ethical Revolutions: Ancient Assumptions Remodelled under Pressure of Transplantation" (1988) 38(1) *Transplantation Proceedings* 1061

Moran, M *The British Regulatory State: High Modernism and Hyper-Innovation*, Oxford University Press, Oxford, 2003

Moreno, JD *Undue Risk: Secret State Experiments on Humans*, Routledge, New York, 2001

Moreno, JD, "Goodbye to All That. The enD of Moderate Protectionism in Human Subjects Research" (2001) 31 *Hastings Center Report* 9

Morgan, A and Xavier, A, "Hospital Specialists' Private Practice and its Impact on the Number of NHS Patients Treated and on the Delay for Elective Surgery", Discussion Paper 01/01, Department of Economics, University of York, 2001

Morris, A and Saintier, S, "To Be or Not to Be: Is that the Question? Wrongful Life and Misconceptions" (2003) 11 *Medical Law Review* 167

Moses, H, III, Perumpanani, A, and Nicholson, J, "Collaborating with industry: choices for Australian medicine and universities" (2002) 176 *Medical Journal of Australia* 543

Moynihan, R and Cassells, A, *Selling Sickness: How Drug Companies are Turning Us Into Patients*, Allen & Unwin, Sydney, 2005

Mueller, J, "No 'Dilettante Affair': Rethinking the Experimental Use Exception to Patent Infringement for Biomedical Research Tools" (2001) 76 *Washington Law Review*

Mulheron, L, "The Defence of Therapeutic Privilege in Australia" (2003) 11 *Journal of Law and Medicine* 201

Mullany, NJ, "Tort Reform and the Damages Dilemma" (2002) 25(3) *University of NSW Law Journal* 876

Mulligan, EC, "Confidentiality in Health Records: Evidence of Current Performance From a Population Survey in South Australia" (2001) 174 *Medical Journal of Australia* 637, 571

Multi-Society Task Force on PVS, "Medical Aspects of the Persistent Vegetative State" (First of Two Parts) (1994) 330(21) *New England Journal of Medicine* 1499

Nair, B, Kerridge, I, Dobson, A, McPhee, J and Saul, P, "Advance Care Planning in Residential Care" (2000) 30 *Australian and New Zealand Journal of Medicine* 339

National Academies Committee on the Biological and Biomedical Application of Stem Cell Research, *Stem Cells and the Future of Regenerative Medicine*, National Academies Press, Washington DC, 2001

National Electronic Health Records Taskforce, *A Health Information Network for Australia*, Taskforce Report, Commonwealth Department of Health and Aged Care, Canberra, 2000

National Health and Medical Research Council, "NHMRC Licensing Committee Issues Seventh Licence" (2004) 1(2) *NHMRC Licensing Committee Bulletin* 1

National Health and Medical Research Council, *Ethical Guidelines on the Use of Assisted Reproductive Technology in Clinical Practice and Research*, NHMRC, Canberra, 2004

National Health and Medical Research Council, *Ethical Issues Raised by Allocation of Transplant Resources, Ethical Issues in Organ Donation*, Discussion Paper No 3, AGPS, Canberra, 1997

National Health and Medical Research Council, *National Statement on Ethical Conduct in Research Involving Humans*, NHMRC, Canberra, 1999

National Science Foundation, *Research and Development in Industry 2000*, NSF, Division of Science Resources Statistics, 2003

Neave, M, "AIDS – Confidentiality and the Duty to Warn" (1989) 9 *University of Tasmania Law Review* 1

Nelson, RM, "Children As Research Subjects", in Kahn, JP, Mastroianni, AC, and Sugarman, J (eds) *Beyond consent: Seeking justice in research*, Oxford University Press, New York, 1998

Nestle, M, *Food Politics: How the Industry Influences Nutrition and Health*, University of California Press, Berkeley, 2002, Ch 9

New South Wales Department of Health, *Nurse Practitioner Services in New South Wales*, Discussion Paper, 1998

New South Wales Law Reform Commission, *Expert Witnesses*, NSWLRC, Sydney, 2005

New South Wales Law Reform Commission, *Minor's Consent to Medical Treatment*, Issues Paper No 24, NSWLRC, 2004

New Zealand Committee *Report of the Committee of Inquiry into Allegations Concerning the Treatment of Cervical Cancer at National Women's Hospital and into Other Related Matters*, The Committee, Auckland, 1988

Newble, D, Paget, N and McLaren, B, "Revalidation in Australia and New Zealand: Approach of Royal Australasian College of Physicians" (1999) 319 *British Medical Journal* 1185

Newby, DA, and Henry, DA, "Drug Advertising: Truths, Half-Truths and Few Statistics" (2002) 177 *Medical Journal of Australia* 285

Nichols Hill, A, "One Man's Trash is Another Man's Treasure, Bioprospecting: Protecting the Rights and Interests of Human Donors of Genetic Material" (2002) 5 *Journal of Health Care Law and Policy* 259

Nicholson, RH, "This Little Pig Went to Market" (1996) 26(4) *Hastings Center Report* 3

Nisselle, P, "Shifting Medicolegal Sands" (1995) 163 *Medical Journal of Australia* 229

Nolan, J *Justifying Government at Century's End*, New York University Press, New York, 1998

Norcini, JJ, "Recertification in the United States" (1999) 319 *British Medical Journal* 1183

Norman, GR et al, "Competency Assessment of Primary Care Physicians as Part of a Peer Review Program" (1993) 270(9) *Journal of the American Medical Association* 1046

Northern Territory Law Reform Committee, *Report on Privilege Against Self-Incrimination*, Report No 23, 2001

Nottenbaum, C, Pardey, PG and Wright, BD, "Accessing Other People's Technology for Non-Profit Research" (2002) 43 *Australian Journal of Agricultural and Resource Economics* 3.

Nowlan, W, "A Scarlet Letter or a Red Herring?" (2003) 241 *Nature* 313

Nuffield Council on Bioethics, *Stem Cell Therapy: the Ethical Issues*, Discussion Paper, 2000 (updated July 2004)

Nuffield Council on Bioethics, *The Ethics of Patenting DNA*, NCB, London, 2002

Nys, H, Welie, S, Garanis-Papadatos, T and Ploumpidis, D, "Patient Capacity in Mental Health Care: Legal Overview" (2004) 12 *Health Care Analysis* 329

O'Dea, J, "Differences in Overweight and Obesity Among Australian Schoolchildren of Low and Middle/high Socioeconomic Status" (2003) 179(1) *Medical Journal of Australia* 63

O'Donovan K and Gilbar R, "The Loved Ones: Families, Intimates and Patient Autonomy" (2003) 23 (2) *Legal Studies* 332

O'Hara, DA and Carson, NJ, "Reporting of Adverse Events in Hospitals in Victoria 1994–1995" (1997) 166 *Medical Journal of Australia* 460

O'Sullivan, J, *Law for Nurses*, Law Book Co, Sydney, 1983

Oakley, J, "The Morality of Breaching Confidentiality to Protect Others" in Shotton, L (ed), *Health Care Law and Ethics*, Social Science Press, Katoomba, NSW, 1997

Oddi, S, "The Tort of Interference with the Right to Die: the Wrongful Living Cause of Action" (1986) 75 *Georgetown Law Journal* 625

Odgers, SJ and Richardson, J, "Keeping Bad Science out of the Courtroom – Changes in American and Australian Expert Evidence Law" (1995) 18 *UNSWLR* 108

Office of Inspector General, *FDA Oversight of Clinical Investigators*, 2000

Oldham, JM, Haimowitz, S, and Delano, SJ, "Regulating Research with Vulnerable Populations: Litigation Gone Awry" (1998) 1 *Journal of Health Care Law and Policy* 154

Olick, RS, "Brain Death, Religious Freedom, and Public Policy: New Jersey's Landmark Legislative Initiative" (1991) 1(4) *Kennedy Institute of Ethics Journal* 285

Ontario Ministry of Health and Long-Term Care, *Genetics, Testing and Gene Patenting: Charting New Territory in Healthcare: Report to the Provinces and Territories*, 2002, 284

Organisation for Economic Cooperation and Development, *Genetic Inventions, Intellectual Property Rights and Licensing Practices: Evidence and Policies*, 2002

Otlowski, M *Voluntary Euthanasia and the Common Law*, Oxford University Press, Oxford, 2000

Otlowski, M, "Avoiding Genetic Discrimination in Insurance: An Exploration of the Legality and Ethics of Precautionary Measures in Anticipation of Unfavourable Test Outcomes" (2001) 20 (1) *Monash Bioethics Review* 24

Otlowski, M, "Is There Scope for Lawful Genetic Discrimination in Health Insurance in Australia?" (2001) 8 (4) *Journal of Law and Medicine* 427

Otlowski, M, *Implications of Genetic Testing for Australian Insurance Law and Practice*, Centre for Law and Genetics, Occasional Paper No 1, 2001

Overall, C, *Ethics and human reproduction*, Allen & Unwin, London, 1983

Page, GG et al, "Physician-assessment and Physician-Enhancement Programs in Canada" (1995) 153 *Canadian Medical Association Journal* 1723

Pallis, C, "Further Thoughts on Brainstem Death" (1995) 23(1) A*naesthesia and Intensive Care* 20

Pappworth, MH, *Human Guinea Pigs: Experimentation on Man*, Routledge, London, 1967

Parboosingh, J, "CPD and Maintenance of Certification in the Royal College of Physicians and Surgeons of Canada" (2002) 5 *The Obstetrician and Gynaecologist* 43

Pargiter, R and Bloch, S, "The Ethics Committee of a Psychiatric College: Its Procedures and Themes" (1998) 32 *Australian and New Zealand Journal of Psychiatry* 76

Parker, M, "Changes to Confidentiality for Young People" (2004) *Doctor Q* 30

Parker, M, "Judging Capacity: Paternalism and the Risk-Related Standard" (2004) 11 *Journal of Law and Medicine* 482

Parker, M, "Medicine, Psychiatry and Euthanasia: an Argument Against Mandatory Psychiatric Review" (2000) 34 *Australian and New Zealand Journal of Psychiatry* 318

Paterson, M and Iacovino, L, "Health Privacy: The Draft Australian National Health Privacy Code and the Shared Longitudinal Electronic Health Record" (2004) 33(1) *Health Information Management Journal* 5

Paterson, M, "Health*Connect* and Privacy: A Policy Conundrum", (2004) 12 (1) *Journal of Law and Medicine* 80

Pattinson, S, "Current Legislation in Europe" in Gunning, J and Szoke, H (eds), *The Regulation of Assisted Reproductive Technology*, Ashgate, Aldershot, 2003

Pearson, IY and Zurynski, Y, "A Survey of Personal and Professional Attitudes of Intensivists to Organ Donation and Transplantation" (1995) 23(1) *Anaesthesia and Intensive Care* 68

Peck, CM et al, "Continuing Medical Education and Continuing Professional Development: International Comparisons" (2000) 320 *British Medical Journal* 432

Peden, A, Head, M, Ritchie, D, et al, "Preclinical vCJD After Blood Transfusion in a PRNP Codon 129 Heterozygous Patient" (2004) 364 *Lancet* 527

Pennings, G, Schots, R, and Liebaers, I, "Ethical Considerations on Preimplantation Genetic Diagnosis for HLA Typing to Match a Future Child as a Donor of Haematopoietic Stem Cells to a Sibling" (2002) 17 (3) *Human Reproduction* 534 at 536

Percival, T *Medical Jurisprudence; or a Code of Ethics and Institutes, Adapted to the Professions of Physic and Surgery*, Manchester, 1794

Perkins, E *Decision-making in Mental Health Review Tribunals*, Central Books, London, 2002

Perkins, E, Arthur, S and Nazroo, I *Decision-making in Mental Health Review Tribunals*, University of Liverpool Health and Community Care Research Unit, 2000

Perlin, M, *Mental Disability Law: Civil and Criminal*, 2nd edn, Michie Publishing, Charlottesville, 1998

Petersen, K, Pitts, M, Baker, HW and Thorpe, R, "Assisted Reproductive Technologies: Professional and Legal Restrictions in Australian Clinics" (2005) 12 *Journal of Law and Medicine* 366

Peterson, K, "The Regulation of Assisted Reproductive Technology: A Comparative Study of Permissive and Prescriptive Laws and Policies" (2002) 9 *Journal of Law and Medicine* 483, 232.

Pincock, S, "Patient's Death from vCJD May be Linked to Blood Transfusion" (2004) 363 *Lancet* 43

Podewils, LA, "Traditional Tort Principles and Wrongful Conception Child-Rearing Damages" (1993) 73 *Boston University Law Review* 407

Pollard, D, "Wrongful Analysis in Wrongful Life Jurisprudence" (2004) 55 *Alabama Law Review* 327

Pollock, AM, Shaoul, J, and Vickers, J, "Private Finance and 'Value for Money' in NHS Hospitals: A Policy in Search of a Rationale?" (2002) 324 *British Medical Journal* 1205

Poulin, AB, "The Jury: the Criminal Justice System's Different Voice" (1994) 62 *University of Cincinnati Law Review* 1377

Powe, R, "Confidentiality" in Dix, A Errington, M, Nicholson K and Powe R (eds) *Law for the Medical Profession*, 2nd edn, Butterworth Heinemann, Sydney, 1996

Powner, DJ, Ackerman, BM and Grenvik, A, "Medical Diagnosis of Death in Adults: Historical Contributions to Current Controversies" (1996) 348 *Lancet* 1219

Pressman, JD, "Psychiatry and its origins" (1997) 71 *Bulletin of the History of Medicine* 129

Priaulx, N, "Joy to the World! A (Healthy) Child is Born! Reconceptualizing 'Harm' in Wrongful Conception" (2004) 13 *Social and Legal Studies* 5

Priaulx, N, "That's One Heck of an 'Unruly Horse"! Riding Roughshod Over Autonomy in Wrongful Conception" (2004) 12 *Feminist Legal Studies* 317

Price, DPT, "Organ Transplant Initiatives: the Twilight Zone" (1997) 23 *Journal of Medical Ethics* 170

Queensland Law Reform Commission, *Consent to Medical Treatment of Young People*, Report No 51, QLRC, 1996

Queensland Nursing Council, "Policy on the Regulation of Nurse Practitioners in Queensland", December 2004

Quill, TE and Battin, MP (eds), *Physician-Assisted Dying. The Case for Palliative Care and Choice,* The Johns Hopkins Press, Baltimore, 2004

Rai, A, "Genome Patents: A Case Study in Patenting Research Tools" (2002) 77 *Academic Medicine* 1368

Ranson, DL, "How Effective? How Efficient? The Coroner's Role in Medical Treatment Related Deaths" (1998) 23 *Alternative Law Journal* 284

Rasmussen, HH et al, "Trial of a trial by media" (2001) 175 *Medical Journal of Australia* 5

Raymont, V, Bingley, W, Buchanan, A, David, AS, Hayward, P, Wessely, S and Hotopf, M, "Prevalence of Mental Incapacity in Medical Inpatients and Associated Risk-factors: Cross-sectional Study" (2004) 364 *Lancet* 1421

Rechitsky, S, Verlinsky O, and Chistokhina A, "Preimplantation Genetic Diagnosis for Cancer Predisposition" (2002) 5(2) *Reprod Biomed Online* 148

Rees, G, Fry, A and Cull, A, "A Family History of Breast Cancer: Women's Experiences from a Theoretical Perspective" (2001) 52 *Social Science and Medicine* 1433

Reichman, A, "Damages in Tort for Wrongful Conception – Who Bears the Cost of Raising the Child?" (1985) 10 *Sydney Law Review* 568

Reid, A, "Poorly Performing Doctors" (2006) *Law in Context* (in press)

Report of the Royal Commission into Deep Sleep Therapy, Government Printer, Sydney, 1990

Retained Organ Commission, *Report of the Independent Investigation into Organ Retention at Central Manchester and Manchester Children's Hospital Trust,* London, July 2002

Reynolds, C, *Plagues and Prejudice: Boundaries Outsiders and Public Health,* unpublished doctoral thesis, University of Adelaide, 1992

Reynolds, C, *Public Health Law and Regulation,* Federation Press, Sydney, 2004

Rhodes, R, "Ethical Issues in Selecting Embryos" (2001) *Annals of the New York Academy of Sciences* 360

Riad, H and Nicholls, A, "An Ethical Debate: Elective Ventilation of Potential Organ Donors" (1995) 310 *British Medical Journal* 714

Rich, B, *Strange Bedfellows: How Medical Jurisprudence Has Influenced Medical Ethics and Medical Practice,* Kluwer Academic, New York, 2001

Richardson, M, "Whither Breach of Confidence: A Right of Privacy for Australia?" (2002) 26 *Melbourne University Law Review* 20, 579

Rimmer, M, "Myriad Genetics: Patent Law and Genetic Testing" (2003) 25 *European Intellectual Property Review* 20

Rimmer, M, "The Freedom to Tinker: Patent Law and Experimental Use" (2005) 15 *Expert Opinion* 167

Robertson, J, "Extending Preimplantation Genetic Diagnosis: Medical and Non-Medical Uses" (2003) 29 *Journal of Medical Ethics* 213

Robertson, J, "Human Cloning and the Challenge of Regulation" (1998) 339 *New England Journal of Medicine* 119

Rogers, S, "Culling Bad Apples: Blowing Whistles and the Health Practitioners Competence Assurance Act 2003 (NZ)" (2004) 12 *Journal of Law and Medicine* 119, 500

Rogers, WA et al, "The Ethics of Pharmaceutical Industry Relationships with Medical Students" (2004) 180 *Medical Journal of Australia* 411

Romeo-Casabona, C, "Embryonic Stem Cell Research and Therapy: The Need for a Common European Framework" (2002) 16 *Bioethics* 557

Rosen, R and Dewar, S *On Being a Doctor: Redefining Medical Professionalism for Better Patient Care,* King's Fund, London, 2004

Rosenthal, P, "Nature of Jury Response to the Expert Witness" (1983) 28 *Journal of Forensic Science* 528

Ross, LF, "In defense of the Hopkins Lead Abatement Studies" (2002) 30 *Journal of Law and Medical Ethics* 50

Roth, L, Meisel, A and Lidz, C, "Tests of Competency to Consent to Treatment" (1977) 134 *American Journal of Psychiatry* 279

Rothenberg, K and Terry, S, "Before It's Too Late – Addressing Fear of Genetic Information" (2002) 297 *Science* 196

Rothman, BK *The Tentative Pregnancy: Amniocentesis and the Sexual Politics of Motherhood,* Pandora, London, 1988

Rothman, DJ and Rothman, SM, *The Willowbrook Wars,* Harper & Row, New York, 1984

Rothman, DJ *Strangers at the Bedside: A History of How Law and Bioethics Transformed Medical Decision Making,* Basic Books, New York, 1991

Rothman, DJ, "Ethics and Human Experimentation. Henry Beecher Revisited" (1987) 317 *New England Journal of Medicine* 1195

Rothman, DJ, "The Nuremberg Code in Light of Previous Principles and Practices in Human Experimentation", in Tröhler, U and Reiter-Theil, S (eds) *Ethics Codes in Medicine: Foundations and Achievements of Codification Since 1947,* Ashgate, Aldershot, 1998

Rothschild, A, "Gardner; Re BWV: Resolved and Unresolved Issues at End of Life" (2004) 11 *Journal of Law and Medicine* 292

Rottman, D, "Does Effective Therapeutic Jurisprudence Require Specialized Courts (and Do Specialized Courts Imply Specialized Judges?)" (2000) 37 *Court Review* 22

Royal Australasian College of Physicians, *Ethical Guidelines in the Relationship Between Physicians and the Pharmaceutical Industry,* RACP, Sydney, 1994

Royal Australian College of General Practitioners, *Handbook for the Management of Health Information in Private Medical Practice,* RACGP, 2002

Royal College of Pathologists of Australasia, Position Statement, "Autopsy and the Use of Tissues Removed at Autopsy" (1994)

RTAC, *Code of Practice for Assisted Reproductive Technology Units,* February 2005

Ruff, TA, and Haikal-Mukhtar, H, "Doctors, Drugs, Information and Ethics: A Never-Ending Story" (2005) 183 *Medical Journal of Australia* 73

Russo, E, "Follow the Money – the Politics of Embryonic Stem Cell Research" (2005) 3(7) *PLoS Biology* 234

Ryan, S, "Competence and the Elderly Patient with Cognitive Impairments" (1996) 30 *Australian and New Zealand Journal of Psychiatry* 769

Rysavy, C and Anderson, A, "Confidentiality: Implications for the Practising Psychologist" (1989) 11 *Bulletin of the Australian Psychological Society* 168

Saks, MJ and Wisler, RL, "Legal and Psychological Bases of Expert Testimony: Surveys of the Law and Jurors" (1984) 2 *Behavioral Sciences and the Law* 361

Samuels, G, "Is This the Best We Can Do?" (1993) 25 *Australian Journal of Forensic Sciences* 3

Sanci, LA et al, "Youth Health Research Ethics: Time for a Mature-Minor Clause?" (2004) 180 *Medical Journal of Australia* 336

Sandel, MJ, "Embryo Ethics – The Moral Logic of Stem-Cell Research" (2004) 351(3) *New England Journal of Medicine* 207

Sant, K, "A New Bolam Test?", (2004) (September/October) 64 *Precedent* 20, 461

Sauci, LA, Sawyer, SA, Weller, PJ, Bond, LM and Patton, GC, "Youth Health Research Ethics: Time for a Mature-Minor Clause?" (2004) 180 (7) *Medical Journal of Australia* 336

Savulescu, J and Dahl, E 'Sex Selection and Preimplantation Diagnosis (2000) (15) 9 *Human Reproduction* 1879

Savulescu, J, "Sex Selection: The Case For" (1999) 171 *Medical Journal of Australia* 373

Savulescu, J, "Two Deaths and Two Lessons: Is it Time to Review the Structure and Function of Research Ethics Committees?" (2002) 28 *Journal of Medical Ethics* 1

Savulescu, J, and Spriggs, M, "The Hexamethonium Asthma Study and the Death of a Normal Volunteer in Research" (2002) 28 *Journal of Medical Ethics* 3

Say, K, "Wrongful Birth: Preserving Justice for Women and their Families" (2003) 28 *Oklahoma City University Law Review* 251

Schlosser, E, *Fast Food Nation,* Penguin, London, 2002

Schopp, RF *Competence, Condemnation and Commitment,* American Psychological Association, Washington DC, 2001

Searight, HR and Campbell, DC, "Physician-Patient Sexual Contact: Ethical and legal Issues and Clinical Guidelines" (1993) 36 *Journal of Family Practice* 647

Searles, D, "Professional Misconduct – Unprofessional Conduct. Is there a Difference?" (1992) *Queensland Law Society Journal* 239

Secretariat of the Pacific Community, *Public Health Programme, Tobacco and Alcohol in the Pacific Island Countries Trade Agreement,* Noumea, New Caledonia, 2005

Sell, SK, *Private Power, Public Law. The Globalisation of Intellectual Property Rights,* Cambridge University Press, Cambridge, 2003

Seymour, J *Childbirth and the Law,* Oxford University Press, Oxford, 2000

Seymour, J, "*Cattanach v Melchior*: Legal Principles and Public Policy" (2003) 11 *Torts Law Journal* 208

Seymour, J, Case Note:, "Cattanach v Melchior: Legal Principles and Public Policy" (2003) 11 *Torts Law Journal* 208

Shackford, SR, Hollingsworth-Fridlund, P, McArdle, M. Eastman, AB, "Assuring Quality in a Trauma System – The Medical Audit Committee: Composition, Cost and Results" (1986) 27(8) *Journal of Trauma* 866

Shafer, T, Schkade, LL, Warner, HE, Eakin, M, O'Connor, K, Springer J, Jankiewicz T, Reitsma W, Steele J, Keen-Denton K, "Impact of Medical Examiner/Coroner Practices on Organ Recovery in the United States" (1994) 272(20) *Journal of the American Medical Association* 1607

Shafer, TJ, Schkade, LL, Evans, RW, O'Connor KJ and Reitsma, W, "Vital Role of Medical Examiners and Coroners in Organ Transplantation" (2004) 4(2) *Am J Transplant* 160

Shaffer, E, Waitzkin, H, Brenner, J and Jasso-Aguilar, R, "Global Trade and Public Health" (2005) 95(1) *American Journal of Public Health* 23

Shaffer, ER and Brenner, JE, "International Trade Agreements: Hazards to Health?" (2004) 34(3) *International Journal of Health Services* 467

Shamoo, AE, "Adverse events reporting – the tip of an iceberg" (2001) 8 *Accountability in Research* 197

Sharav, VH, "The ethics of conducting psychosis-inducing experiments" (1999) 7 *Accountability in Research* 137

Sherwin, S, *No Longer Patient: Feminist Ethics and Health Care*, Temple University Press, Philadelphia, 1992

Shimmel, EM, "The Hazards of Hospitalization" (1964) 60 *Annals of Internal Medicine* 100

Shuman, DW, Champagne, A and Whitaker, E, "An Empirical Examination of the Use of Expert Witnesses in the Courts – Part II: A Three City Study" (1994) 34 *Jurimetrics Journal* 193

Shuman, DW, Champagne, A and Whitaker, E, "Juror Assessments of the Believability of Expert Witnesses: A Literature Review" (1996) 36 *Jurimetrics Journal* 371

Siegler, M, "Confidentiality in Medicine – A Decrepit Concept?" (1982) 307 *New England Journal of Medicine* 1518

Silver, L, *Re-making Eden*, Weidenfeld & Nicholson, London, 1998

Singer P and D Wells, *The Reproductive Revolution*, Oxford University Press, Oxford, 1984

Singer, P, *Practical Ethics*, Cambridge University Press, Cambridge, 1979

Sink, JM, "The Unused Power of a Federal Judge to Call His Own Expert Witness" (1956) 29 *Southern California Law Review* 195

Skene L, "Genetic Secrets and the Family: A Response to Bell and Bennett" (2001) 9(2) *Medical Law Review* 162

Skene, L, "Arguments Against People Legally 'Owning' their Own Bodies, Body Parts and Tissue" (2002) 2 *Macquarie Law Journal* 165

Skene, L, "Patients' Rights or Family Responsibilities? Two Approaches to Genetic Testing" (1998) 6(1) *Medical Law Review* 1

Skene, L, "Proprietary Rights in Human Bodies, Body Parts and Tissue: Regulatory Contexts and Proposals for New Laws" (2002) 22 *Legal Studies* 102

Skene, L, "Risk-Related Standard Inevitable in Assessing Competence" (1991) 5 *Bioethics* 113

Skene, L, *Law and Medical Practice: Rights, Duties, Claims and Defences*, 2nd edn, LexisNexis Butterworths, 2004

Skene, L, *You, Your Doctor and the Law*, Oxford University Press, Melbourne, 1990;

Slate, R, "From the Jailhouse to Capitol Hill: Impacting Mental Health Court Legislation and Defining What Constitutes a Mental Health Court" (2003) 49 *Crime and Delinquency* 6

Sloan, CA, *History of the Pharmaceutical Benefits Scheme 1947–1992*, Department of Human Services and Health, Canberra, 1995

Slobogin, S *Minding Justice: Laws that Deprive People with Mental Disability of Life and Liberty*, Harvard University Press, Cambridge, Massachusetts, 2006

Smith 0, *Fifth Report of the Shipman Inquiry*, Command Paper CM6394, HMSO, London, 2004

Smith, A, Dickson, J, Aitken, J et al, "Contaminated Dental Instruments" (2002) 51 *Journal of Hospital Infection* 233

Smith, Dame Janet, *Third Report: Death Certification and the Investigation of Death by Coroners*, Cmnd 5834, 2003

Smith, P, "The Epidemics of Bovine Spongiform Encephalopathy and Variant Creutzfeldt-Jakob Disease: Current Status and Future Prospects" (2003) 81(2) *Bulletin of the World Health Organization* 123

Smith, R, "Medical Journals are an Extension of the Marketing Arm of Pharmaceutical Companies" (2005) 2(5) *PLoS Medicine* 100

Sobel, S and Dowan, D, "Impact of Genetic Testing for Huntington Disease on the Family System" (2000) 90 *American Journal of Medical Genetics* 49

Somerville, M, *The Ethical Canary: Science, Society and the Human Spirit*, Viking, Victoria, 2000

South Australian Council on Reproductive Technology, "Donor Conception in South Australia" (2000) (15) *SACRT Quarterly Bulletin* 5

Southgate, L and Dauphinee, D, "Maintaining Standards in British and Canadian Medicine: the Developing Role of the Regulatory Body" (1998) 316 *British Medical Journal* 697

Southgate, L et al, "The Assessment of Poorly Performing Doctors: the Development of the Assessment Programmes for the General Medical Council's Performance Procedures" (2001) 35 (Suppl 1) *Medical Education* 2

Spencer, M, Knight R, Will, R, "First Hundred Cases of Variant Creutzfeldt-Jakob Disease: Retrospective Case Note Review of Early Psychiatric and Neurological Features" (2002) 324 *British Medical Journal* 1479

Spriggs, M and Savulescu, J, "Saviour Siblings" (2002) 28 *Journal Medical Ethics* 289

Starzl, T, "Organ Transplantation: A Practical Triumph and Epistemologic Collapse", (2003) 147(3) *Proc An Philos Soc* 226

Steadman, H, Redlich, A, Griffin, P, Petrila, J and Monahan, J, "From Referral to Disposition: Case Processing in Seven Mental Health Courts" (2005) 23 *Behavioral Sciences and the Law* 215

Steinbrook, R, "Protecting research subjects – the crisis at Johns Hopkins" (2002) 346 *New England Journal of Medicine* 716

Stephenson, GM, *The Psychology of Criminal Justice*, Blackwell, Oxford, 1992

Stewart, C and Biegler, P, "A Primer on the Law of Competence to Refuse Medical Treatment" (2004) 78 *Australian Law Journal* 325

Stewart, C and Lynch, A, "Undue Influence, Consent and Medical Treatment" (2003) 96 Journal of the Royal Society of Medicine 598

Stewart, C, "Advance Directives, the Right to Die and the Common Law: Recent Problems with Blood Transfusions" (1999) 23 *Melbourne University Law Review* 161

Stewart, C, "Qumsieh's case, Civil Liabilities and the Right to Refuse Medical Treatment" (2000) 8 *Journal of Law and Medicine* 56

Stewart, C, *Public Interests and the Right to Die: Compelling Reasons for Overriding the Right to Self-determination*, Issues Paper 14, Australian Institute of Health Law and Ethics, 2001

Stewart, JG, "Taking Youth Suicide Seriously: Disclosure of Information Between School, Family and Health Professionals in New Zealand" (2001) *Victoria University of Wellington Law Review* 16

Stolle, D, "Advance Directives, AIDS and Mental Health: TJ Preventive Law for the HIV-positive Client" (1998) 4 *Psychology, Public Policy and Law* 854

Stolle, D, "Professional Responsibility in Elder Law: A Synthesis of Preventive Law and Therapeutic Jurisprudence" (1996) 14 *Behavioral Sciences and the Law* 459

Strandburg, K, "What Does the Public Get? Experimental Use and the Patent Bargain" (2004) *Wisconsin Law Review* 81

Strang, D, Molloy, DW and Harrison, C, "Capacity to Choose Place of Residence: Autonomy vs Beneficence?" (1998) 14 *Journal of Palliative Care* 25

Strasser, M, "Misconceptions and Wrongful Births: A Call for a Principled Jurisprudence" (1999) 31 *Arizona State Law Journal* 161

Strasser, M, "Yes, Virginia, There Can Be Wrongful Life: On Consistency, Public Policy, and the Birth-Related Torts" (2003) 4 *Georgetown Journal of Gender and the Law* 821

Sullivan, D, "How Can Valid Informed Consent be Obtained from a Psychotic Patient for Research into Psychosis? Three Perspectives (III)" (2003) 22(4) *Monash Bioethics Review* 69

Sun, FZ and Moor, RM, "Nuclear Transplantation in Mammalian Eggs and Embryos" (1995) 10 *Current Topics in Developmental Biology* 147

SUPPORT Principle Investigators, "A controlled trial to improve care for seriously ill hospitalized patients – The Study to Understand Prognoses and Preferences for Outcomes and Risks of Treatment (SUPPORT)" (1995) 274 *Journal of the American Medical Association* 1591

Szoke, H, "Regulation of Assisted Reproductive Technology: The State of Play in Australia" in Freckelton, I and Petersen, K (eds), *Controversies in Health Law*, Federation Press, Sydney, 1999

Szoke, H, "Social Regulation, Reproductive Technology and the Public Interest: Policy and Process in Pioneering Jurisdictions", unpublished doctoral dissertation, University of Melbourne, 2004

t'Hoen, E, "TRIPS, Pharmaceutical Patents and Access to Essential Medicines: A Long Way from Seattle to Doha" (2002) 3 *Chi J Int'l L* 27

Tanton, RL, "Jury Preconceptions and their Effect on Expert Scientific Testimony" (1979) 24 *Journal of Forensic Science* 681

Tauer, C, "International Policy Failures: Cloning and Stem-cell Research" (2004) 364 (9429) *Lancet* 209

Taylor, A, Chaloupka, FJ, Guindon, E and Corbett, M, "The Impact of Trade Liberalization on Tobacco Consumption" in Jha, P and Chaloupka, FJ (eds), *Tobacco Control in Developing Countries*, Oxford University Press, Oxford, 2000

Taylor, C and Myers, R, "Long-Term Impact of Huntington Disease Linkage Testing" (1997) 70 *American Journal of Medical Genetics* 365

Taylor, D, McD, Ugoni, AM, Cameron, PA and McNeill, JJ, "Advance Directives and Emergency Department Patients: Ownership Rates and Perceptions of Use" (2003) 33 *Internal Medicine Journal* 586

Taylor, S, "A Case Study of Genetic Discrimination: Social Work and Advocacy in a New Context" (1998) 51 *Australian Social Work* 51

Telford, P, "Assessing the Cost of Our Children: Case Note: Cattanach v Melchior" (2003) 19 *Australian Insurance Law Bulletin* 1

Terry, NP, "Electronic Health Records: International, Structural and Legal Perspectives" (2004) 12 (1) *Journal of Law and Medicine* 26

The Choice Handbook of Your Health Rights: The Essential Guide for Every Australian, Australasian Publishing, Sydney, 1998;

Thomas, C, "Claims for Wrongful Pregnancy and Damages for the Upbringing of the Child" (2003) 26 *University of NSW Law Journal* 125

Thomas, D, "Peer Regulation as an Outmoded Model for Health Practitioner Regulation" (2006) *Law in Context* (in press)

Thomas, EJ, Studdert, DM et al, "Incidence and Type of Adverse Events and Negligent Care in Utah and Colorado" (2000) 38(3) *Medical Care* 261

Thomas, L, Friedman, F and Christian, L *Inquests – A Practitioner's Guide*, Legal Action Group, London, 2002

Thompson, IE, "The Nature of Confidentiality" (1979) 5 *Journal of Medical Ethics* 57

Thomson, J, "Legal and Ethical Problems of Human Cloning" (2000) 8 *Journal of Law and Medicine* 31

Thomson, CJ, "Records, Research and Access: What Interests Should Outweigh Privacy and Confidentiality? Some Australian Answers" (1993) 1 *Journal of Law and Medicine* 95, 587

Thurin, A, Hausken J, Hillensjo T, Jablonowska B, Pinborg A, Strandell A, Bergh C, "Elective Single-Embryo Transfer versus Double-Embryo Transfer in In Vitro Fertilization" (2004) 351(23) *New England Journal of Medicine* 2392

Tingle, J, "Specialist Nurses Must Understand Clinical Negligence Litigation" (2001) 10 (11) *British Journal of Nursing* 716

Tingle, J, "Specialist Nurses Must Understand Clinical Negligence Litigation", (2001) 10 (11) *British Journal of Nursing* 716

Todd, A, "Outrageous Negligence" (2004) 12 *Tort Law Review* 8

Torrey, EF and Zdanowicz, M, "Outpatient Commitment: What, Why, and for Whom?" (2001) 52 *Psychiatric Services* 337–341

Trachtman, JP, "The Domain of WTO Dispute Resolution" (1999) 40 *Harvard International Law Journal* 333

Tri-Council, *Tri-Council Policy Statement: Ethical Conduct for Research Involving Humans*, Ministry of Supply and Services, Ottawa, 1998

Trouson, A and Gillam, L, "What Does Cloning Offer Human Medicine?" (1999) 11 (2) *Today's Life Science* 12

Trunkey, DDT and Botney, R, "Assessing Competency: A Tale of Two Professions" (2001) 192 *Journal of the American College of Surgeons* 385

Truog, RD, "Is It Time to Abandon Brain Death?" (1997) 27(1) *Hastings Center Report* 29

Trupin, E and Richards, H, "Seattle's Mental Health Courts: Early Indicators of Effectiveness" (2003) 26 *International Journal of Law and Psychiatry* 1

Tulskey, JA, Fischer, GS, Rose, MR and Arnold, RM, "Opening the Black Box: How do Physicians Communicate about Advance Directives?" (1998) 129 *Annals of Internal Medicine* 441

Tyler, TR, "The Psychological Consequences of Judicial Procedures: Implications for Civil Commitment Hearings" (1992) 46 *Southern Methodist University Law Review* 433

United Kingdom Law Reform Commission, *Mental Incapacity*, Report No 231, 1995

Van der Broek, K, "A Critical Look at the Ethics of Care" in Shotton L (ed) *Health Care Law and Ethics*, Social Science Press, New South Wales, 1997

Van der Weyden, MB, "Confronting Conflict of Interest in Research orgAnisations: Time for National Action" (2001) 175 *Medical Journal of Australia* 396

Van Dyck, J, *Manufacturing Babies and Public Consent*, Macmillan, Basingstoke, 1995

Van Leeuwen, E and Vellinga, A, "Knowing Well Or Living Well: Is Competence Relevant to Moral Experience and Capacity in Clinical Decision-Making?" in Thomasma, D and Weisstub, D (eds), *The Variables of Moral Capacity*, Kluwer, Dordrecht, 2004

Verdun-Jones, SN, Weisstub, DN (ed) *Research on Human Subjects: Ethics, Law, and Social Policy*, Pergamon, Oxford, United Kingdom, 1998

Verlinsky, Y, Cohen, J, Munne, S, Gianaroli, L, Simpson, JL, Ferraretti, A and KulievA, "Over a Decade of Experience with Preimplantation Genetic Diagnosis: A Multicenter Report" (2004) 82(2) *Fertility and Sterility* 292

Verlinsky, Y, Rechitsky, S, Sharapova, T, Morris, R, Taranissi, M and Kuliev, A, "Preimplantation HLA testing" (2004) 291(17) *Journal of the Americal Medical Association* 2079

Vickers, RH *The Powers and Duties of Police Officers and Coroners*, TH Flood, Chicago, 1889

Victorian Department of Human Services, *Background Paper for the Consensus Workshop: Creutzfeldt-Jakob Disease: Preventing Transmission in the Health Care Setting*, December 2004

Victorian Department of Human Services, Clinical Governance Unit, *Report of the Consensus Workshop: Creutzfeldt-Jakob Disease: Preventing Transmission in the Health Care Setting* (draft), March 2005

Vincent, C, Neale, G and Woloshynowych, M, "Adverse Events in British Hospitals: Preliminary Retrospective Record Review" (2001) 322 *British Medical Journal* 517

Vines, P and Atherton, R, "Religion and Death in the Common Law" in Radan, P, Meyerson, D and Croucher, R *Law and Religion – God, the State and the Common Law*, Routledge, London, 2005

Vines, P, "Apologising to Avoid Liability: Cynical Civility or Practical Morality?" (2005) 27 *Sydney Law Review* 483

Vranken, M, "Damages for 'Wrongful Birth': Where to After *Cattanach*?" (2003) 24 *Adelaide Law Review* 243

Waldo, FJ, "The Ancient Office of Coroner" (1910) 8 *Transactions of the Medico-Legal Society* 101

Wallace, ER, "Relevance without presentism: 'Mental illness and American society, 1875–1940' By Gerald Grob. Essay review" (1984) 39 *Journal of the History of Medicine and Allied Sciences* 374

Wallace, M, *Health Care and the Law*, Law Book Co, Sydney, 1995

Wallach, L and Sforza, M, *The WTO: Five Years of Reasons to Resist Corporate Globalization*, Seven Stories Press, New York, 1999

Walsh, M, "Accountability and Institution: Justifying Nursing Practice" (1997) 11 (23) *Nursing Standard* 39

Walters, L, "Ethical Issues in the Prevention and Treatment of HIV Infection and AIDS" (1988) 239 *Science* 597

Walters, L, "The United Nations and Human Cloning: a Debate on Hold" (2004) 34 *The Hastings Center Report* 5

Walton, M, "Sex and the Practitioner: The Predator" (2002) 34 *Australian Journal of Forensic Sciences* 7

Walton, M, *The Trouble With Medicine: Preserving the Trust Between Patients and Doctors*, Allen & Unwin, Sydney, 1998

Waters, E and Baur, L, "Childhood Obesity: Modernity's Scourge" (2003) 178(9) *Medical Journal of Australia* 422

Wear, S, " Informed Consent" in Khushf, G (ed), *Handbook of Bioethics: Taking Stock of the Field from a Philosophical Perspective*, Kluwer Academic Publishers, Dordrecht, 2004

Weijer, C, and Fuks, A, "The duty to exclude: excluding people at undue risk from research" (1994) 17 *Clinical and Investigative Medicine* 115

Weir, M, "Obligation to Advise of Options for Treatment: Medical Doctors and Complementary and Alternative Medicine Practitioners" (2003) 10(3) *Journal of Law and Medicine* 296

Weir, RF, *Abating Treatment with Critically Ill Patients. Ethical and Legal Limits to the Prolongation of Life*, Oxford University Press, New York, 1989

Weisstub, DN, Arboleda-Florez, J, and Tomossy, GF, "Establishing the Boundaries of Ethically Permissible Research With Vulnerable Populations", in Weisstub, DN (ed) *Research on Human Subjects: Ethics, Law, and Social Policy*, Pergamon, Oxford, United Kingdom, 1998

Weisstub, DN, *Enquiry on Research Ethics: Final Report*, Ministry of Health, Ontario, 1995

Weisz, V, "A Teen Court Evaluation with a Therapeutic Jurisprudence Perspective" (2002) 20 *Behavioral Sciences and the Law* 381

Wendel, B, "Legal Ethics and the Separation of Law and Morals", *Cornell Law School Legal Studies Research Paper Series*, Cornell Law School, New York, 2004.

Werth, JL, "Requests for Physician-Assisted Death: Guidelines for Assessing Mental Capacity and Impaired Judgment" (2000) 6 *Psychology, Public Policy and Law* 348

Wertz, D, "'Genetic Discrimination': Results of a Survey of Genetics Professionals, Primary Care Physicians, Patients and Public" (1998) 7 *Health Law Review* 7, 631

West, D, "Radiation experiments on children at the Fernald and Wrentham schools: lessons for protocols in human subject research" (1998) 6 *Accountability in Research* 103

Wexler, D and Winick, B (eds) *Law in a Therapeutic Key*, Carolina Academic Press, Durham, 1996

White, B, "Cattanach v Melchior: Babies, Blessings and Burdens" (2004) 24 *Queensland Lawyer* 296

White, BC, *Competence to Consent*, Georgetown University Press, Washington, 1994

White, S, "A Burial Ahead of its Time? The Crookenden burial case and the sanctioning of cremation in England and Wales" (2002) 7(2) *Mortality* 171

White, S, "The Law Relating to Dealing with Dead Bodies" (2000) 4 *Medical Law International* 145

Wicclair, M, "Patient Decision-Making Capacity and Risk" (1991) 5 *Bioethics* 91

Wiersma, S, et al, "Probable Variant Creutzfeldt-Jakob Disease in a U.S. Residence – Florida, 2002" (2002) 51(41) *MMWR* 927

Wilkinson, W, "Therapeutic Jurisprudence and Workers' Compensation" (1994) 30 *Arizona Attorney* 28

Will, R, "Acquired Prion Disease: Iatrogenic CJD, Variant CJD, Kuru" (2003) 66 *British Medical Bulletin* 255

Will, R, Ironside, J, Zeidler, M et al, "A New Variant of Creutzfeldt-Jakob Disease in the United Kingdom" (1996) 347 *Lancet* 921

Williams, CR, "Evidence and the Expert Witness" (1994) 26 *Australian Journal of Forensic Sciences* 3

Williamson, S, "Sex (ist) Selection" (2004) *Medical Law International* 185

Wilson R et al, "The Quality in Australian Health Care Study" (1995) 163 *Medical Journal of Australia* 458

Wilson, B, Jackson, K and Punshon, T, "Conciliation" in Smith, R, *Health Care, Crime and Regulatory Control*, Hawkins Press, Sydney, 1998

Wilson, R, Harrison, BT, Gibberd, R and Hamilton, J, "An Analysis of the Cause of Adverse Events from the Quality in Australian Health Care Study" (1999) 170 *Medical Journal of Australia* 411

Wilson, R, Runciman, WB, Gibberd, R et al, "The Quality in Australian Health Care Study" (1995) 163 *Medical Journal of Australia* 458

Winick, B *Civil Commitment: A Therapeutic Jurisprudence Model*, Carolina Academic Press, Durham, 2005

Winick, BJ, "Coercion and Mental Health Treatment" (1997) 74 *Denver Law Journal* 1145

Wolf, S, "Shifting Paradigms in Bioethics and Health Law: The Rise of a New Pragmatism" (1994) 20 *American Journal of Law and Medicine* 395

Wolf, SM (ed), *Feminism and Bioethics: Beyond Reproduction*, Oxford University Press, New York, 1996, 26

Wolf, SM, Kahn, JP and Wagner, JE, "Using Preimplantation Genetic Diagnosis to Create a Stem Cell Donor: Issues, Guidelines and Limits" (2003) 31(3) *Journal of Law, Medicine and Ethics* 327

Wolff, A, "Limited Adverse Occurrence Screening: Using Medical Record Review to Reduce Hospital Adverse Patient Events" (1996) 164 *Medical Journal of Australia* 458

Wong, JG, Clare, ICH, Gunn, MG and Holland, AJ, "Capacity to Make Health Care Decisions: its Importance in Clinical Practice" (1999) 29 *Psychological Medicine* 437

Wood, GJ, Marks, R and Dilley, JW, *AIDS Law for Mental Health Professionals*. AIDS Health Project, University of California, San Francisco, 1990

Woolf MR, Lord, *Access to Justice*, Final Report to the Lord Chancellor on the Civil Justice System in England and Wales, HMSO, London, 1996

World Medical Association, *Resolution on Secrecy*; Bok, S, *Lying: Moral Choice in Public and Private Life*, Random House, NY, 1978

World Trade Organisation, Doha Declaration on the TRIPS Agreement and Public Health, WT/MIN/(01)/Dec/W/2, 2001

Yang, X, "An Embryonic Nation" (2004) 428 *Nature* 210

Young, G, Kane, AW and Nicholson, K (ed) *Psychological Knowledge in Court*, Springer, Dordrecht, 2006

Youngner, S, "Bureaucratizing Suicide" (2000) 6 *Psychology, Public Policy and Law* 402

Zander, M and Henderson, P, "The Crown Court Study. Royal Commission on Criminal Justice", Study No 19, Research Bulletin No 35, Home Office, Research and Statistics Department, 1994

Zucker, C, "Are new laws needed to protect human subjects?" (2001) 8 *Accountability in Research* 235

INDEX